MW01600120

JOEL WHITBURN'S
TOP
COUNTRY
SINGLES 1944-1988

Compiled from **Billboard's** *Country charts*, 1944-1988

Record Research Inc.
P.O. Box 200
Menomonee Falls, Wisconsin 53051

ISBN 0-89820-070-9

Published independently by Record Research Inc.
P.O. Box 200, Menomonee Falls, Wisconsin 53051

The author wishes to extend a special note of thanks to:

Betty Grendysa for her diligent and enthusiastic research of the chart data;

Peter Grendysa for his devotion and energy in compiling much of the biographical information;

Otto Kitsinger of Nashville for digging up novel facts about the artists and their songs;

And the entire Record Research staff: Bill Hathaway, Kim Whitburn, Brent Olynick, Kim Gaarder, Joanne Wagner, Janet Ko, Brian Niese, Phil Summers, Oscar Vidotto, Fran Whitburn, Joyce Riehl and Ruth Whitburn.

A special thank you to Terry Horn for supplying us with many of the charted Country records missing from our library. Most of them were on small independent labels and proved to be invaluable in helping us validate the pertinent data for each title.

If you are interested in buying Country or pop records, Terry has a huge inventory and can be reached at:

Music Mood Enterprise
P.O. Box 79
Homer, IN 46146
(317) 663-2757

CONTENTS

THE ARTIST SECTION

An alphabetical listing, by artist, of every record
to hit Billboard's Country Singles charts from 1942 through 1988.

THE SONG TITLE SECTION

An alphabetical listing, by song title, of every record
to hit Billboard's Country Singles charts from 1942 through 1988.

THE RECORD HOLDERS

AUTHOR'S NOTE

The world of country music has mushroomed since the release of our first country book in 1972. Nearly 10,000 more titles, 1250 new artists and 17 years later, I am proud to introduce the second edition of the *Top Country Singles* book. Since the first edition, the number of country radio stations on the air increased by 4100. Even the *Hot Country Singles* chart was enlarged by 25 positions. The boundaries of country music have stretched, yet the trendy nature of the entertainment industry has not swayed this art form far from its roots.

Look at the life of *Billboard's* country charts and loyalty appears to be a 45-year trend. The longevity and consistent success of hit country artists are a testimony to their fans' devotion. Eddy Arnold, Hank Snow and Hank Thompson are among the five artists who have had country hits *in all five decades!* In the same company, Patti Page's 20 hits span 34 years. And, modern technology has allowed the late Hank Williams to spread his chart success over five decades with the recent duet with his son Hank Williams, Jr.

In comparison to other music genres, the artist turnover rate in country is remarkably low. Close to 1900 artists have charted country hits since 1944. The last 35 years of the *Billboard* pop charts claim twice as many artists. The same is true of the Rhythm & Blues charts which have been in existence only two years longer than the country charts.

With fewer acts sharing chart space, there is a greater chance for a new artist's follow-up singles to hit the country charts. 49 artists have charted 50 or more singles on the country charts. Only 20 pop artists and 16 R&B artists have matched that number on their respective rankings.

Once an artist cracks the upper reaches of the country charts, they are initiated into the fraternity of hit country acts. Rarely are they shunned by their fans. One-hit-wonder artists, common to the pop and R&B charts, are seldom occurrences on the country charts. It is unlikely that new country artists will fade fast. They may repeat Alabama's string of 21 chart-toppping hits, or follow Bobby Bare's example and chart a whopping 70 singles with only one of those peaking at #1.

The faithfulness of country artists themselves is evident in recording contracts. Two artists charted an astonishing number of hits on one record label. Every one of Hank Snow's 85 charted singles were on RCA, as were Elvis Presley's 84 country hits.

Fidelity is but one characteristic of country music revealed in 45 years of chart research. We would like to adopt this running theme into our revision schedule of the *Top Country Singles*. Our loyal readers can look forward to shorter intervals between future editions. In the meantime, we'll keep researching the charts.

JOEL WHITBURN

COUNTRY MUSIC — *An Introduction*

It's been a lot of years since country music was confined to the "country." If the term still evokes images of red-dirt farms, beautiful mountain vistas, cowboys and rodeo riders, and honest and true plain folks, that's because the songs have remained honest and true to the dreams and desires of the people.

Ethnomusicologists have spent entire careers tracing and dissecting the origins of country music, and some of them even agree on a few points with their colleagues. It seems that the early Anglo-Saxon settlers in the United States brought their own music along with them; a music that soon became tempered and blended with that of the peoples they lived among: Afro-Americans and Acadians in the deep South, Mexicans and Native Americans in the West.

Despite this broad base of input and support, the one thing that country music lacked in its early years was respect. Suffering from similar prejudices to those that kept black music in its "place" for many years, country music was unglamorously tagged "hillbilly" and "corn," and almost always presented as a comic exercise performed by gap-toothed hayseeds in bib overalls flaying away at homemade instruments.

In those early years, country music was, perhaps even more so than rhythm & blues, a child of the radio. It was radio that spread the sound of old and dear folk songs, played and sung by plain folks, far outside of the rural south. As early as 1922, radio station WSB in Atlanta was broadcasting a Barn Dance program, and local talent was heard on WBAP in Fort Worth around the same time.

Almost simultaneously, WLS, the Prairie Farmer Station in Chicago, began carrying the songs and storytelling of Bradley Kincaid, "The Original Authentic Folksong Singer." Then, on April 19, 1924, the station began broadcasting the Chicago Barn Dance, produced by George Hay. Later called the National Barn Dance, the WLS program introduced such stellar names as Gene Autry, Homer & Jethro, and Red Foley to a wide and truly national audience.

Carried on the NBC network, the Barn Dance regularly achieved high Crossley ratings (an early forerunner of the Nielsen system), and those ratings were only taken in large cities. "Country" music had found a place in the urban centers.

After a year with the WLS program, George Hay moved to Nashville and started a rival Barn Dance show on WSM. At first strictly a local broadcast, the WSM Barn Dance usually followed a network program of grand opera and classics. One evening, after hearing the conductor of the National Symphony Orchestra declare: "While we do not believe there is a place in the classics for realism, this work so depicts the onrush of the locomotive that I have decided to include it in the program of grand opera," Hay replied on his own show: "From here on out, folks, it will be nothing but realism of the realest kind. You've been up in the clouds with grand opera; now get down to earth with us in a shindig of grand ole opry!" From then on it was The Grand Ole Opry, and it became the most popular and longest-lived of all the country shows.

Also very important in bringing the music to the people and the musicians out of the woods and fields were Cincinnati's Midwestern Hayride, which started as the Boone Country Jamboree in 1938, and Shreveport's Louisiana Hayride, first aired on April 3, 1948. Throughout the biographies in this book, you will see mention of one or more of these programs as launching points for the careers of many famous country stars.

When live music on the radio was augmented by that marvelous invention, the disc jockey, the doors to national fame and sometimes fortune were opened to a much larger number of country talents. Probably the first nationally-known country singer was Fiddlin' John Carson, whose recorded renditions of old folk songs such as "The Little Log Cabin In The Lane," "Old Joe Clark" and "Arkansas Traveler" sold very well in 1924-1925.

Substantial sales of records would not be ignored, even in the "good ole days," and all major labels of the time soon turned their attention to this "new" form of music. They began combing the backwoods for artists to put on their special "hillbilly" or "folk and western" record lines.

In this way, the Victor Talking Machine Company found Jimmie Rodgers, a sickly ex-railroad brakeman who became known as "The Father Of Country Music" with his immensely popular "Blue Yodel (T For Texas)" and his innovative combining of traditional hillbilly with southern blues. At the same time, August, 1927, Victor also recorded the Carter Family, starting a family tradition that has survived for over 60 years.

A new ingredient in the country music stew was added in the 1930's with the rise of the singing cowboy. Gene Autry, Tex Ritter, Roy Rogers, and dozens of others followed the lead of Ken Maynard (first singing cowboy, "The Wagon Master," 1930) in pausing from their labors of chasing bad guys and Indians across the movie screen to strum guitars and sing about horses, sunsets, or school-marms.

The popularity of big-band swing music, beginning in the mid-1930's, brought about a hybrid with country and western that survives today as Western Swing. Thankfully, no one thought to call it Swingabilly.

In 1944, after the unprecedented success of "Pistol Packin' Mama" by Al Dexter the year before, Billboard began taking the music seriously enough to start its first tabulation of best-selling "folk" music. The magazine wasn't too certain about what, exactly, constituted "folk" music, and frequently included black hot string combos such as the Four Clefs in that category. It became apparent very soon that this "folk" music was going to have to include a wide variety of singing cowboys, hot string bands, honky-tonkers, and ballad crooners so, in 1949, the name of the chart was changed to Country & Western.

The war years were good for country musicians, as they were for black artists. While the blacks were busily creating rhythm & blues, the country singers came up with honky-tonk, a high-volume, gritty music with a beat, designed to overwhelm the noisy atmosphere and uncertain acoustics of the bars, county fairs, and roller rinks where country was played. If Hank Williams is the King Of Country Music, his throne was built on honky-tonk.

Along about the early 1950's, country joined with rhythm & blues to create rock 'n' roll, and has had an uneasy relationship with its child ever since. The term "crossover" first meant a country singer going over to rock 'n' roll. In later years the flow reversed, a lot of former rockers decided they felt more at home in the country.

Country music has not escaped the evolutionary forces that have changed the face and sound of American music over the past four decades. But it has weathered and adapted to those changes with one foot planted firmly in the past, leading to such delightful contradictions as "new traditionalism," exemplified by Randy Travis, Dwight Yoakam, George Strait, Patty Loveless, Becky Hobbs, and many other exciting new artists of the 1980's. That these artists with strong affections for the roots of country music can coexist with daring newcomers such as K. T. Oslin, Lyle Lovett, Rosanne Cash, and Shenandoah is a further indicator of the broad sweep of the music.

And, from a music that was once the sole province of rural Southerners, country has grown to the point where it has a capitol city known the world over (Nashville, with branch offices in Memphis, Bakersfield, Austin, and New York City), two satellite TV networks (TNN and CMT), a museum and research center second to none (Country Music Foundation and Hall Of Fame), several competing awards societies, and Fan Fair, an extraordinary annual event where fans can rub shoulders with their favorite artists and recording stars.

Acknowledging and encompassing all of the accomplishments of the past, tolerant of all peripheral forms (bluegrass, western swing, rockabilly, gospel), the music lives on. Its fans are the most devoted followers of any type of music, providing longevity for country artists unmatched in the pop music world.

From the Carter Family to the McCarters, from Bob Wills to Dan Seals, from the Kendalls to the Girls Next Door, from Kitty Wells to Kathy Mattea, country music brings its message to a growing number of people every day and, while the messengers may change from time to time, the message remains the same: realism of the realest kind.

PETER GRENDYSA

DATE	POSITIONS	CHART TITLE

JUKE BOX

1/8/44	2-8	Most Played Juke Box Folk Records
		(9/6/47-11/1/47 shown as Most-Played Juke Box Hillbilly Records)
1/31/48	9-15	Most Played Juke Box Folk Records
6/25/49	7-15	Most Played Juke Box (Country & Western) Records
11/4/50	6-10	Most Played Juke Box Folk (Country & Western) Records
11/15/52	8-10	Most Played in Juke Boxes
6/30/56	9-10	Most Played C&W in Juke Boxes
6/17/57 final chart		

BEST SELLERS

5/15/48	10-15	Best Selling Retail Folk Records
6/25/49	5-15	Best Selling Retail Folk (Country & Western) Records
11/15/52	8-10	National Best Sellers
2/20/54	9-15	Best Sellers in Stores
6/30/56	13-20	C&W Best Sellers in Stores
10/13/58 final chart		

JOCKEYS

12/10/49	8-10	Country & Western Records Most Played By Folk Disk Jockeys
11/15/52	9-15	Most Played by Jockeys
6/30/56	12-15	Most Played C&W by Jockeys
10/13/58 final chart		

HOT COUNTRY SINGLES

10/20/58	30	Hot C&W Sides
11/3/62	30	Hot Country Singles
1/11/64	50	Hot Country Singles
10/15/66	75	Hot Country Singles
7/14/73	100	Hot Country Singles

JANUARY 8, 1944 — DECEMBER 31, 1988

The research for this book begins with *Billboard Magazine's* first country chart, the *Juke Box Folk Records* chart, initially published on January 8, 1944. It ends 44 years later, with the December 31, 1988 *Hot Country Singles* chart. See the *Billboard Country Chart History* on the preceding page for a synopsis of the chart changes.

JUKE BOX / BEST SELLERS / JOCKEY CHARTS

In 1948, a second country chart was introduced, the *Best Selling* chart. The *Jockeys* chart began its run in late 1949. During the years in which *Billboard* published multiple country charts, 1948 to 1958, many records hit on more than one of these charts. The chart data shown for the records that made multiple charts is as follows:

Debut Date = the earliest of the dates charted.
Peak Position = the highest ranking achieved on any of the charts.
Weeks Charted = the most weeks charted on any of the charts.
Weeks at #1 or #2 = the highest total achieved on any of the charts.

A chart-by-chart breakdown of the highest position a record attained on any of the multiple charts is listed below the title. Remember that prior to 1948, there was only one country chart, the *Juke Box Folk Records*.

With the end of the multiple charts, *Billboard* introduced an all-encompassing *Hot C&W Sides* chart on October 20, 1958.

DUETS

Songs by duos are listed under both artists if each artist had at least one solo hit. For example, duets by Bill Anderson and Jan Howard are listed under both Anderson and Howard.

Due to the exceptional number of duos on the country charts, we have revised our policy regarding duets:

If an artist and his duo partner had only one or two hits together, these are mixed in chronologically with the artist's solo hits. The precise duo name, as it appeared on the record, is shown in bold type below the song title.

If an artist charted more than three titles with one duo partner, these titles are grouped together and shown at the end of the artist's solo hits.

If an artist had five or more duo partners, their duets are not mixed in chronologically with their solo hits but are grouped together and shown at the end of the artist's solo hits. For example, Waylon Jennings' last charted solo hit is followed by the extra large bold heading: ***WAYLON JENNINGS DUOS with:***. Below this heading, his duos are listed in alphabetical order according to the last name of each partner. Each partner's name appears in bold italicized type.

CHART DATES

A record's Debut Date is *Billboard's* actual issue date from the chart it first appeared on. It is not the "week ending" date shown on the country charts from 1944-1962. The issue and week ending dates were different until January 13, 1962, when *Billboard* began using one date system for both the issue and the charts inside.

ACCURACY FACTOR

Approximately 85% of the titles within this book were checked for accuracy of title, artist name, and label and number against the records within our library. Discrepancies between the published *Billboard* title, artist name, record label and number, and the actual records were corrected whenever possible. Please let us know of any corrections to title, artist, or label listing of the remaining 15% of the records. Suggestions for improvement are always welcome.

BIOGRAPHICAL NOTES

Biographical information was gathered from a wide variety of published materials, private correspondence, and personal interviews, with factual conflicts resolved by all available means.

The artist section lists each artist's charted hits in chronological order. Each of an artist's song titles is sequentially numbered. All Top 10 hits are highlighted in dark type.

EXPLANATION OF COLUMNAR HEADINGS:

DEBUT DATE: Date record first charted

PEAK POS: Record's highest charted position (highlighted in bold type)

WKS CHR: Total weeks charted

POP POS: Peak position achieved on *Billboard*'s early pop charts, *Hot 100* chart or *Bubbling Under the Hot 100* chart

LABEL & NUMBER: Original record label and number

OTHER DATA AND SYMBOLS

(★★42★★)   Number indicates the artist's ranking among the All-Time Top 200 Country artists

(¹)   A superior number next to a record that peaked at No. 1 or No. 2 indicates the total weeks the record held that position

(+)   Indicates record peaked in the year after it first charted

(●)   RIAA certified gold record (million seller)
(▲)   RIAA certified platinum record (two million seller)

The Record Industry Association of America began certifying gold records in 1958 and platinum records in 1976. Prior to these dates, there are most certainly some hits that would have qualified for these certifications. Also, some record labels have never requested RIAA certification for their hits. As of January 1, 1989, RIAA lowered the certification for gold singles to sales of 500,000 units and platinum to one million units.

(*Flp*)   The letters *Flp* in the pop position column indicates that the title made *Billboard*'s pop charts as a flip side and did not have its own peak position.

Letter(s) in brackets after titles indicate:

[I]   Instrumental recording
[N]   Novelty recording
[S]   Spoken recording
[F]   Foreign language recording
[X]   Christmas recording
[R]   Reissue or remake of a previous recording

(/)   This symbol is shown when dividing a two-sided hit. Complete chart data (debut date, peak position, etc.) is shown for both sides if each side achieved its own peak position. If a title was shown only as the B-side, then only the weeks it was shown as a "tag along" are listed.

See *Researching the Billboard Country Charts* for an explanation of chart names listed under record titles from 1948-1958.

THE ARTIST SECTION

Lists, alphabetically by artist name, every record that made **Billboard's** country charts from January 8, 1944 through December 31, 1988.

A

JERRY ABBOTT
Singer/songwriter from Dallas.

DEBUT DATE	PEAK POS	WKS CHR		ARTIST — Record Title	POP POS	Label & Number
4/29/78	63	7	1	I Want A Little Cowboy		Churchill 7712
9/09/78	80	6	2	I Owe It All To You		Churchill 7715
1/09/82	82	4	3	One Night Stanley		Dallas S. 102581

MACK ABERNATHY

11/12/88	98	2	1	Slippin' Around		CMI 81

ROY ACUFF
Born Roy Claxton Acuff on 9/15/03 in Maynardsville, Tennessee. Moved to Knoxville in 1919. An attack of sunstroke kept him from pursuing a career in baseball. Worked with a medicine show from 1932-33, then had own band, the Tennessee Crackerjacks, on WROL-Knoxville. New band, the Crazy Tennesseans, appeared on KNOX-Knoxville in 1935. First recorded for ARC (later merged with Columbia) in 1936, and this session included "Great Speckle Bird" and "Wabash Cannonball". Began appearing on the Grand Ole Opry in 1937, then changed band name to Smoky Mountain Boys. Formed Acuff-Rose music publishing company with composer Fred Rose (d: 12/1/54) in 1942. They also formed the Hickory label in the late 50s. First living artist elected to the Country Music Hall Of Fame in 1962. Fondly known as "The King Of Country Music".

DEBUT DATE	PEAK POS	WKS CHR		ARTIST — Record Title	POP POS	Label & Number
2/12/44	4	2	1	The Prodigal Son	19	Okeh 6716
11/04/44	3	8	2	I'll Forgive You, But I Can't Forget/	26	
11/11/44	6	4	3	Write Me, Sweetheart		Okeh 6723
4/19/47	4	6	4	Jole Blon		Columbia 37287
2/07/48	8	5	5	Waltz Of The Wind		Columbia 38042
				Juke Box #8 / Best Seller #13		
6/19/48	14	2	6	Unloved And Unclaimed/		
				Best Seller #14		
8/07/48	12	1	7	This World Can't Stand Long		Columbia 20454
				Best Seller #12		
11/06/48	12	1	8	The Tennessee Waltz		Columbia 20551
				Juke Box #12		
				huge #1 pop hit for Patti Page in 1950		
12/18/48	14	1	9	A Sinner's Death		Columbia 20475
				Best Seller #14		
3/31/58	8	7	10	Once More		Hickory 1073
				Jockey #8		
12/28/58+	16	11	11	So Many Times		Hickory 1090
6/15/59	20	3	12	Come And Knock		Hickory 1097
5/15/65	45	5	13	Freight Train Blues		Hickory 1291
11/27/71	56	6	14	I Saw The Light		United Art. 50849
				NITTY GRITTY DIRT BAND with ROY ACUFF		
2/16/74	51	11	15	Back In The Country		Hickory 314
6/22/74	97	3	16	Old Time Sunshine Song		Hickory 319

DON ADAMS
Born on 1/4/41 in Ross County, Ohio. Worked with George Jones. Don's brother Dime (real name: Gary) played lead guitar for Faron Young.

DEBUT DATE	PEAK POS	WKS CHR		ARTIST — Record Title	POP POS	Label & Number
4/01/67	64	4	1	Two Of The Usual		Jack O'Dia. 1002
7/14/73	91	5	2	I'll Be Satisfied		Atlantic 4002
				#20 pop hit for Jackie Wilson in 1959		
11/24/73+	34	12	3	I've Already Stayed Too Long		Atlantic 4009
4/27/74	80	4	4	Baby Let Your Long Hair Down		Atlantic 4017
				with The Greenfield Express		
8/17/74	52	9	5	That's Love		Atlantic 4027

KAY ADAMS
Born Princetta Kay Adams on 4/9/41 in Knox City, Texas.

DEBUT DATE	PEAK POS	WKS CHR		ARTIST — Record Title	POP POS	Label & Number
10/15/66	30	7	1	Little Pink Mack		Tower 269
				with The Cliffie Stone Group		

KAYLEE ADAMS
Session and jingle singer from Navarre, Ohio.

DEBUT DATE	PEAK POS	WKS CHR		ARTIST — Record Title	POP POS	Label & Number
10/18/86	68	4	1	I Can't Help The Way I Don't Feel		Warner 28567

PEGGY JO ADAMS - see O.B. McCLINTON

DEBUT DATE	PEAK POS	WKS CHR	ARTIST — Record Title	POP POS	Label & Number
			TERRY ADEN		
			Born on 8/11/52 in Poplar Bluff, Missouri.		
10/31/81	81	3	1 What's So Good About Goodbye		B&B 21
4/03/82	73	5	2 She Doesn't Belong To You		AMI 1303
			WENDEL ADKINS		
			Born in Kentucky. Discovered by Willie Nelson. Long-time favorite at Gilley's club.		
2/19/77	80	4	1 I Will		Hitsville 6050
4/30/77	91	3	2 Laid Back Country Picker		Hitsville 6055
11/26/77	98	2	3 Julieanne (Where Are You Tonight)		MC 5007
			ALABAMA ★★63★★		
			Group formed in Fort Payne, Alabama, in 1969 as Wildcountry. Consisted of Randy Owen (b: 12/13/49; guitar), Jeff Cook (b: 8/27/49; keyboards, fiddle), Teddy Gentry (b: 1/22/52; bass) and John Vartanian (drums). Owen, Cook and Gentry are cousins. Worked local clubs in Myrtle Beach, South Carolina beginning in 1973. Mark Herndon replaced Vartanian as drummer in 1976. Produced and promoted their first records. Adopted the name Alabama in 1977. CMA award: Entertainer of the Year - 1982, 1983 and 1984. Also see Lionel Richie.		
7/23/77	78	8	1 I Wanna Be With You Tonight		GRT 129
9/29/79	33	12	2 I Wanna' Come Over		MDJ 7906
2/02/80	17	13	3 My Home's In Alabama		MDJ 1002
			later released on RCA 12008		
5/31/80	1¹	17	4 Tennessee River		RCA 12018
9/20/80	1¹	19	5 Why Lady Why		RCA 12091
2/14/81	1¹	14	6 Old Flame	103	RCA 12169
5/23/81	1²	13	7 Feels So Right	20	RCA 12236
10/24/81	1²	16	8 Love In The First Degree	15	RCA 12288
3/06/82	1¹	18	9 Mountain Music	101	RCA 13019
5/29/82	1¹	17	10 Take Me Down	18	RCA 13210
8/28/82	1¹	17	11 Close Enough To Perfect	65	RCA 13294
12/11/82+	35	7	12 Christmas In Dixie [X]		RCA 13358
			flip side of the Louise Mandrell/RC Bannon Christmas single		
2/12/83	1¹	16	13 Dixieland Delight		RCA 13446
5/14/83	1¹	17	14 The Closer You Get	38	RCA 13524
8/20/83	1¹	20	15 Lady Down On Love	76	RCA 13590
1/21/84	1¹	17	16 Roll On (Eighteen Wheeler)		RCA 13716
4/21/84	1¹	19	17 When We Make Love	72	RCA 13763
8/04/84	1¹	19	18 If You're Gonna Play In Texas (You Gotta Have A Fiddle In The Band)/		
		2	19 I'm Not That Way Anymore		RCA 13840
11/10/84+	1¹	19	20 (There's A) Fire In The Night		RCA 13926
2/09/85	1¹	21	21 There's No Way		RCA 13992
5/18/85	1¹	19	22 Forty Hour Week (For A Livin')		RCA 14085
8/24/85	1¹	22	23 Can't Keep A Good Man Down		RCA 14165
1/25/86	1¹	21	24 She And I		RCA 14281
9/20/86	1¹	20	25 Touch Me When We're Dancing		RCA 5003
1/24/87	1¹	22	26 "You've Got" The Touch		RCA 5081
8/22/87	7	17	27 Tar Top		RCA 5222
			title refers to Randy Owen's nickname		
12/05/87+	1¹	22	28 Face To Face		RCA 5328
			guest vocal: K.T. Oslin		
4/23/88	1¹	17	29 Fallin' Again		RCA 6902
11/26/88+	1¹	19	30 Song Of The South		RCA 8744
			BUDDY ALAN		
			Born Alvis Alan Owens on 5/22/48 in Tempe, Arizona. The son of Buck & Bonnie Owens.		
7/27/68	7	15	1 Let The World Keep On A Turnin'		Capitol 2237
			BUCK OWENS & BUDDY ALAN & THE BUCKAROOS		
11/23/68	54	6	2 When I Turn Twenty-One		Capitol 2305
			written by Merle Haggard		
10/25/69	23	10	3 Lodi		Capitol 2653
			#52 pop hit for Creedence Clearwater Revival in 1969		
2/07/70	23	8	4 Big Mama's Medicine Show		Capitol 2715
5/02/70	38	9	5 Down In New Orleans		Capitol 2784
8/08/70	57	7	6 Santo Domingo		Capitol 2852

DEBUT DATE	PEAK POS	WKS CHR	ARTIST — Record Title	POP POS	Label & Number
			BUDDY ALAN — Continued		
11/07/70	19	12	7 Cowboy Convention .... BUDDY ALAN & DON RICH		Capitol 2928
1/16/71	37	9	8 Lookin' Out My Back Door .... #2 pop hit for Creedence Clearwater Revival in 1970		Capitol 3010
3/06/71	54	5	9 I'm On The Road To Memphis....................... BUDDY ALAN & DON RICH		Capitol 3040
6/05/71	48	9	10 Fishin' On The Mississippi		Capitol 3110
8/21/71	46	9	11 I Will Drink Your Wine.................................		Capitol 3146
12/04/71+	29	10	12 Too Old To Cut The Mustard .... BUCK (Owens) & BUDDY		Capitol 3215
3/04/72	68	4	13 White Line Fever		Capitol 3266
6/24/72	47	10	14 I'm In Love		Capitol 3346
9/23/72	49	7	15 Things .... #3 pop hit for Bobby Darin in 1962		Capitol 3427
12/30/72+	60	6	16 Move It On Over..		Capitol 3482
4/07/73	64	4	17 Why, Because I Love You		Capitol 3555
5/19/73	67	4	18 Caribbean... #27 pop hit for Mitchell Torok in 1959		Capitol 3598
8/11/73	68	6	19 Summer Afternoons		Capitol 3680
11/24/73+	67	8	20 All Around Cowboy Of 1964		Capitol 3749
5/04/74	70	8	21 I Never Had It So Good		Capitol 3861
2/15/75	35	11	22 Chains .... #17 pop hit for The Cookies in 1962		Capitol 4019
6/07/75	88	5	23 Another Saturday Night .... #10 pop hit for Sam Cooke in 1963		Capitol 4075
			UREL ALBERT Noted for his impersonations of Country superstars.		
10/13/73	97	2	1 Country And Pop Music............................. [N]		Toast 311
			WYVON ALEXANDER Born in Weaverville, California.		
2/14/81	90	2	1 Frustration		Gervasi 633
4/18/81	86	2	2 Old Familiar Feeling		Gervasi 644
8/15/81	74	4	3 Women..		Gervasi 659
1/16/82	83	3	4 Don't Lead Me On..		Gervasi 671
8/28/82	69	6	5 Alice In Dallas (Sweet Texas)........................ written by Merle Haggard		Gervasi 660
11/27/82	76	4	6 Midnight Cabaret		Gervasi 661
12/10/83+	68	8	7 The Look Of A Lovin' Lady		Gervasi 663
			ALIBI Canadian 6-man band.		
10/03/87	84	2	1 Roller Coaster		Comstock 1856
5/21/88	61	6	2 Do You Have Any Doubts		Comstock 1884
			SUSIE ALLANSON Born on 3/17/52 in Minneapolis. Performed in the musicals "Hair" and "Jesus Christ Superstar". Also appeared in the film "Jesus Christ Superstar".		
7/09/77	23	14	1 Baby, Don't Keep Me Hangin' On....................		Oak 1001
11/05/77+	20	14	2 Baby, Last Night Made My Day		Warner 8473
3/04/78	7	13	3 **Maybe Baby** .... #17 pop hit for Buddy Holly & The Crickets in 1958		Warner 8534
6/24/78	2²	13	4 **We Belong Together**		Warner 8597
10/28/78	17	11	5 Back To The Love		Warner 8686
2/03/79	8	11	6 **Words**... #15 pop hit for the Bee Gees in 1968		Elektra 46009
4/28/79	6	12	7 **Two Steps Forward And Three Steps Back**.....		Elektra 46036
8/18/79	79	4	8 Without You.. #1 pop hit for Nilsson in 1972		Elektra 46503
12/01/79+	38	10	9 I Must Be Crazy		Elektra 46565
8/02/80	31	12	10 While I Was Makin' Love To You.....................		United Art. 1365
11/08/80+	23	14	11 Dance The Two Step		Liberty 1383
5/30/81	53	7	12 Run To Her .... Bobby Vee's "Run To Him" was a #2 pop hit in 1961		Liberty 1408
9/05/81	44	8	13 Love Is Knockin' At My Door (Here Comes Forever Again)		Liberty 1425

DEBUT DATE	PEAK POS	WKS CHR	ARTIST — Record Title	POP POS	Label & Number
			SUSIE ALLANSON — Continued		
12/05/81	**60**	7	14 Hearts (Our Hearts)..		Liberty 1422
4/24/82	**62**	6	15 Wasn't That Love..		Liberty 1460
12/27/86+	**67**	7	16 Where's The Fire...		TNP 75001
6/20/87	**70**	5	17 She Don't Love You		TNP 75005
			DEBORAH ALLEN		
			Born Deborah Lynn Thurmond on 9/30/53 in Memphis. Successful songwriter; wrote "Don't Worry 'Bout Me, Baby" for Janie Fricke, "You Do It" for Sheena Easton, "Can I See You Tonight" for Tanya Tucker, and many others in country and soul. Married to songwriter Rafe Van Hoy. On soundtrack of film "The River Rat".		
11/22/80+	**24**	15	1 Nobody's Fool..		Capitol 4945
8/15/81	**20**	11	2 You (Make Me Wonder Why)..........................		Capitol 5014
1/09/82	**33**	10	3 You Look Like The One I Love		Capitol 5080
5/29/82	**82**	3	4 After Tonight		Capitol 5110
8/20/83	**4**	24	5 Baby I Lied	26	RCA 13600
1/28/84	**2**²	24	6 I've Been Wrong Before		RCA 13694
5/26/84	**10**	20	7 I Hurt For You		RCA 13776
10/20/84	**23**	17	8 Heartache And A Half.................................		RCA 13921
			JIM REEVES/DEBORAH ALLEN:		
6/23/79	**10**	14	9 Don't Let Me Cross Over............................		RCA 11564
11/03/79+	**6**	15	10 Oh, How I Miss You Tonight		RCA 11737
4/12/80	**10**	16	11 Take Me In Your Arms And Hold Me		RCA 11946
			JOE ALLEN		
			Popular session musician in Nashville. Recorded with Doc & Merle Watson. Wrote "Manhattan Kansas" for Glen Campbell and "The Midnight Oil" for Barbara Mandrell.		
1/25/75	**83**	5	1 Should I Come Home (Or Should I Go Crazy).......		Warner 8052
7/05/75	**88**	8	2 Carolyn At The Broken Wheel Inn...................		Warner 8098
			JUDY ALLEN		
1/28/78	**94**	4	1 Sweet Little Devil...		Polydor 14440
			MELODY ALLEN		
2/01/75	**91**	6	1 Once Again I Go To Sleep With Lovin' On My Mind..		Mercury 73638
5/10/75	**68**	8	2 May You Rest In Peace.................................		Mercury 73674
			RED ALLEN - see OSBORNE BROTHERS		
			REX ALLEN		
			Born on 12/31/20 in Wilcox, Arizona. Singer/guitarist/actor. Professional rodeo rider as a teenager. Had own radio show on WTTM-Trenton, New Jersey in 1944. With the Sleepy Hollow Gang in Allentown, Pennsylvania in 1944. On the National Barn Dance, WLS-Chicago, from 1945 to 1949; CBS network radio from Hollywood in 1949. Signed to Republic Pictures, made 32 westerns from 1950-57. His first film was "The Arizona Cowboy" in 1950. Own TV series, "Frontier Doctor", in 1954. Narrator for over 80 Walt Disney films. Elected to the Cowboy Hall Of Fame in 1968.		
9/03/49	**14**	1	1 Afraid .... Juke Box #14		Mercury 6192
4/21/51	**10**	1	2 **Sparrow In The Tree Top** .... Juke Box #10	28	Mercury 5597
8/08/53	**4**	13	3 **Crying In The Chapel**................................ Best Seller #4 / Juke Box #4 / Jockey #6 #3 pop hit for Elvis Presley in 1965	8	Decca 28758
8/14/61	**21**	4	4 Marines Let's Go		Mercury 71844
9/29/62	**4**	13	5 **Don't Go Near The Indians**	17	Mercury 71997
1/11/64	**44**	3	6 Tear After Tear		Mercury 72205
6/22/68	**71**	5	7 Tiny Bubbles... #57 pop hit for Don Ho in 1967		Decca 32322
			REX ALLEN, JR. ★★**112**★★		
			Born on 8/23/47 in Chicago; son of Rex Allen. Traveled with father from age 6; played the rhythm guitar and worked as a rodeo clown. Moved to Nashville in the late 60s.		
12/29/73+	**63**	10	1 The Great Mail Robbery		Warner 7753
4/20/74	**19**	14	2 Goodbye..		Warner 7788
8/24/74	**31**	14	3 Another Goodbye Song...............................		Warner 8000
12/07/74+	**36**	11	4 Never Coming Back Again		Warner 8046
5/31/75	**70**	7	5 Lying In My Arms		Warner 8095

DEBUT DATE	PEAK POS	WKS CHR	ARTIST — Record Title	POP POS	Label & Number
			REX ALLEN, JR. — Continued		
1/24/76	34	9	6 Play Me No Sad Songs		Warner 8171
5/01/76	17	12	7 Can You Hear Those Pioneers		Warner 8204
			backing vocals by Rex Allen, Sr. & The Sons of The Pioneers		
8/07/76	18	13	8 Teardrops In My Heart		Warner 8236
12/11/76+	8	16	9 **Two Less Lonely People**.....................		Warner 8297
4/09/77	10	12	10 **I'm Getting Good At Missing You (Solitaire)** ...		Warner 8354
8/06/77	15	11	11 Don't Say Goodbye		Warner 8418
11/12/77+	8	15	12 **Lonely Street**		Warner 8482
			#5 pop hit for Andy Williams in 1959		
3/25/78	8	15	13 **No, No, No (I'd Rather Be Free)**.....................		Warner 8541
7/29/78	10	12	14 **With Love**		Warner 8608
11/25/78+	12	14	15 It's Time We Talk Things Over.....................		Warner 8697
4/14/79	9	12	16 **Me And My Broken Heart**.....................		Warner 8786
8/04/79	18	12	17 If I Fell In Love With You.....................		Warner 49020
2/16/80	25	10	18 Yippy Cry Yi.....................		Warner 49168
5/24/80	14	13	19 It's Over.....................		Warner 49128
9/27/80	25	12	20 Drink It Down, Lady		Warner 49562
12/20/80+	12	14	21 Cup Of Tea.....................		Warner 49626
			REX ALLEN, JR. & MARGO SMITH		
3/14/81	35	9	22 Just A Country Boy.....................		Warner 49682
6/13/81	26	12	23 While The Feeling's Good		Warner 49738
			REX ALLEN, JR. & MARGO SMITH		
3/27/82	43	10	24 Last Of The Silver Screen Cowboys		Warner 50035
			with Roy Rogers & Rex Allen, Sr.		
7/10/82	44	10	25 Cowboy In A Three Piece Business Suit............		Warner 29968
11/27/82	85	3	26 Ride Cowboy Ride		Warner 29890
10/22/83	37	15	27 The Air That I Breathe.....................		Moon Shine 3017
			#6 pop hit for The Hollies in 1974		
3/10/84	44	9	28 Sweet Rosanna		Moon Shine 3022
7/14/84	18	16	29 Dream On Texas Ladies.....................		Moon Shine 3030
11/10/84+	24	19	30 Running Down Memory Lane.....................		Moon Shine 3034
4/20/85	62	7	31 When You Held Me In Your Arms.....................		Moon Shine 3036
11/14/87	59	8	32 We're Staying Together		TNP 75010

ROSALIE ALLEN

Born Julie Marlene Bedra on 6/27/24 in Old Forge, Pennsylvania. Moved to New York in the late 30s and worked with Denver Darling's Swing Billies radio show. Teamed with Elton Britt on Zeke Manner's radio shows. Had own TV show in New York in the early 50s and later worked as a disc jockey on WOV-New York. One of the first female country stars; known as "The Prairie Star" and "Queen Of The Yodelers".

DEBUT DATE	PEAK POS	WKS CHR	ARTIST — Record Title	POP POS	Label & Number
8/10/46	5	1	1 **I Want To Be A Cowboy's Sweetheart**/		
8/17/46	3	4	2 **Guitar Polka**		RCA 1924
2/04/50	7	4	3 **Beyond The Sunset**		RCA 3105
			THE THREE SUNS with ELTON BRITT & ROSALIE ALLEN Jockey #7		
2/25/50	3	10	4 **Quicksilver**		RCA 0168
			ELTON BRITT & ROSALIE ALLEN Jockey #3 / Juke Box #6 / Best Seller #9		

JIM ALLEY

Vocalist/guitarist from Hemphill, West Virginia.

DEBUT DATE	PEAK POS	WKS CHR	ARTIST — Record Title	POP POS	Label & Number
1/20/68	73	2	1 Only Daddy That'll Walk The Line		Dot 17051
3/15/75	96	2	2 Her Memory's Gonna Kill Me.........................		Avco 606

THE ALMOST BROTHERS

New York City duo: guitarist/pianist Steve Mosto (b: 12/21/61, Paramonga, Peru) and guitarist/songwriter/arranger Mike Ragogna (b: 1/30/58, New York City). Worked as Mickey & The Mostones with Steve's sister Joanne. Duo first called the Bird Dogs.

DEBUT DATE	PEAK POS	WKS CHR	ARTIST — Record Title	POP POS	Label & Number
8/17/85	55	7	1 Don't Tell Me Love Is Kind...........................		MTM 72053
2/22/86	63	6	2 Birds Of A Feather		MTM 72062
8/09/86	72	6	3 What's Your Name		MTM 72072
			#7 pop hit for Don & Juan in 1962		
11/22/86	52	8	4 I Don't Love Her Anymore		MTM 72079

AMARILLO

Amarillo is actually Breakfast Barry (Barry Grant).

DEBUT DATE	PEAK POS	WKS CHR	ARTIST — Record Title	POP POS	Label & Number
12/27/80+	82	4	1 That's The Way My Woman Loves...................		NSD 72

DEBUT DATE	PEAK POS	WKS CHR	ARTIST — Record Title	POP POS	Label & Number
			AMARILLO — Continued		
3/21/81	**87**	3	2 How Long Has This Been Going On/		
6/13/81	**70**	5	3 Somehow, Someway And Someday		NSD 81
10/10/81	**86**	4	4 A Little Bit Crazy................................		NSD 104
			THE AMAZING RHYTHM ACES		
			Memphis group consisting of Russell Smith (lead vocals, guitar), Barry "Byrd" Burton (guitar, dobro), Billy Earhart III (keyboards), Jeff Davis (bass) and Butch McDade (drums). Davis and McDade had been with Jesse Winchester. Disbanded in 1980. Smith went on to a solo career. Earhart joined the Bama Band in 1986.		
7/05/75	**11**	14	1 Third Rate Romance................................	*14*	ABC 12078
11/29/75+	**9**	14	2 Amazing Grace (Used To Be Her Favorite Song)	*72*	ABC 12142
8/07/76	**12**	14	3 The End Is Not In Sight (The Cowboy Tune)........	*42*	ABC 12202
7/15/78	**100**	1	4 Ashes Of Love		ABC 12369
3/24/79	**88**	4	5 Lipstick Traces (On A Cigarette)	*104*	ABC 12454
11/29/80	**77**	6	6 I Musta Died And Gone To Texas		Warner 49600
			DURELLE AMES		
			Maiden name: Durelle Upchurch. Born on 5/4/65 in Gaffney, South Carolina.		
8/15/87	**72**	5	1 Dancin' In The Moonlight		Advantage 175
1/16/88	**75**	4	2 Break Down The Walls......................		Advantage 185
			shown as: **DE DE AMES**		
			AMY		
2/03/79	**76**	4	1 Please Be Gentle................................		Scorpion 0570
			written by Mac Davis		
			BILL ANDERSON ★★**24**★★		
			Born James William Anderson, III on 11/1/37 in Columbia, South Carolina. Worked as a sportswriter and disc jockey in Commerce, Georgia in 1957. Wrote "City Lights" hit for Ray Price and "Once A Day" for Connie Smith. Co-wrote "Saginaw, Michigan" for Lefty Frizzell. Currently hosts Nashville Network's TV game show "Fandango". Appeared in the films "Las Vegas Hillbillies", "Forty Acre Farm", "Road To Nashville" and several others. Member of the Grand Ole Opry since 1961. Known as "Whispering Bill".		
12/28/58+	**12**	17	1 That's What It's Like To Be Lonesome		Decca 30773
7/06/59	**13**	19	2 Ninety-Nine Years		Decca 30914
12/28/59+	**19**	8	3 Dead Or Alive		Decca 30993
6/20/60	**7**	18	4 Tip Of My Fingers.......................		Decca 31092
12/26/60+	**9**	14	5 Walk Out Backwards		Decca 31168
7/10/61	**9**	19	6 Po' Folks		Decca 31262
4/21/62	**14**	10	7 Get A Little Dirt On Your Hands		Decca 31358
7/28/62	**1** [7]	27	8 Mama Sang A Song	89	Decca 31404
2/23/63	**1** [7]	27	9 Still	8	Decca 31458
8/24/63	**2** [2]	23	10 8 X 10	53	Decca 31521
1/25/64	**5**	18	11 Five Little Fingers/	*118*	
2/15/64	**14**	20	12 Easy Come-Easy Go		Decca 31577
7/25/64	**8**	16	13 Me........................		Decca 31630
11/07/64	**38**	5	14 In Case You Ever Change Your Mind/		
11/14/64+	**8**	18	15 Three A.M..........................		Decca 31681
4/03/65	**12**	17	16 Certain......................		Decca 31743
9/04/65	**11**	16	17 Bright Lights And Country Music		Decca 31825
1/22/66	**11**	13	18 Golden Guitar/		
2/12/66	**4**	24	19 I Love You Drops		Decca 31890
8/27/66	**1** [1]	20	20 I Get The Fever		Decca 31999
1/14/67	**5**	19	21 Get While The Gettin's Good......................		Decca 32077
7/01/67	**10**	19	22 No One's Gonna Hurt You Anymore/		
7/15/67	**64**	5	23 Papa.......................		Decca 32146
11/11/67	**42**	9	24 Stranger On The Run		Decca 32215
3/16/68	**2** [1]	18	25 Wild Week-End		Decca 32276
8/17/68	**2** [2]	16	26 Happy State Of Mind......................		Decca 32360
3/01/69	**1** [2]	19	27 My Life (Throw It Away If I Want To).............		Decca 32445
7/12/69	**2** [3]	15	28 But You Know I Love You		Decca 32514
			#19 pop hit for Kenny Rogers & The First Edition in 1969		
3/14/70	**5**	15	29 Love Is A Sometimes Thing......................		Decca 32643
10/24/70	**6**	14	30 Where Have All Our Heroes Gone .... [S]	93	Decca 32744

DEBUT DATE	PEAK POS	WKS CHR		ARTIST — Record Title	POP POS	Label & Number
				BILL ANDERSON — Continued		
3/13/71	**6**	15	31	**Always Remember**.....................................	*111*	Decca 32793
7/24/71	**3**	17	32	**Quits**..		Decca 32850
3/18/72	**5**	15	33	**All The Lonely Women In The World**..............		Decca 32930
9/09/72	**2²**	16	34	**Don't She Look Good**................................		Decca 33002
2/24/73	**2¹**	14	35	**If You Can Live With It (I Can Live Without It)**..		MCA 40004
7/07/73	**2³**	15	36	**The Corner Of My Life**............................ `.		MCA 40070
12/15/73+	**1¹**	14	37	**World Of Make Believe**		MCA 40164
6/01/74	**24**	14	38	Can I Come Home To You		MCA 40243
10/05/74	**7**	13	39	**Every Time I Turn The Radio On**...................		MCA 40304
2/08/75	**14**	11	40	I Still Feel The Same About You		MCA 40351
5/10/75	**36**	11	41	**Country D.J.**		MCA 40404
8/23/75	**24**	11	42	**Thanks**		MCA 40443
8/14/76	**10**	14	43	**Peanuts And Diamonds**		MCA 40595
12/04/76+	**6**	14	44	**Liars One, Believers Zero**		MCA 40661
5/07/77	**7**	13	45	**Head To Toe**		MCA 40713
10/01/77	**11**	12	46	Still The One		MCA 40794
				#5 pop hit for Orleans in 1976		
4/29/78	**4**	14	47	**I Can't Wait Any Longer**	*80*	MCA 40893
11/11/78	**30**	9	48	Double S..		MCA 40964
2/17/79	**20**	13	49	This Is A Love Song.....................................		MCA 40992
7/21/79	**40**	9	50	The Dream Never Dies		MCA 41060
				#48 pop hit for The Cooper Brothers in 1978		
12/08/79+	**51**	8	51	More Than A Bedroom Thing...........................		MCA 41150
4/12/80	**35**	9	52	Make Mine Night Time		MCA 41212
6/21/80	**46**	7	53	Get A Little Dirt On Your Hands .... [R]		Columbia 11277
				DAVID ALLAN COE & BILL ANDERSON new version of Bill's solo hit in 1962		
8/23/80	**58**	7	54	Rock 'N' Roll To Rock Of Ages........................		MCA 41297
11/22/80	**83**	3	55	I Want That Feelin' Again..............................		MCA 51017
2/21/81	**44**	8	56	Mister Peepers..		MCA 51052
8/15/81	**74**	4	57	Homebody		MCA 51150
12/26/81+	**76**	4	58	Whiskey Made Me Stumble (The Devil Made Me Fall)		MCA 51204
8/21/82	**42**	10	59	Southern Fried		So. Tracks 1007
12/25/82+	**82**	5	60	Laid Off...		So. Tracks 1011
3/12/83	**70**	6	61	Thank You Darling		So. Tracks 1014
7/09/83	**71**	6	62	Son Of The South/		
		6	63	20th Century Fox..		So. Tracks 1021
5/12/84	**76**	7	64	Your Eyes		So. Tracks 1026
2/09/85	**58**	7	65	Wino The Clown...		Swanee 4013
4/27/85	**62**	6	66	Pity Party		Swanee 5015
8/17/85	**75**	5	67	When You Leave That Way, You Can Never Go Back		Swanee 5018
12/27/86+	**80**	5	68	Sheet Music		So. Tracks 1067
5/09/87	**78**	5	69	No Ordinary Memory.....................................		So. Tracks 1077
				BILL ANDERSON & JAN HOWARD:		
2/19/66	**29**	8	70	I Know You're Married (But I Love You Still)/		
3/12/66	**44**	1	71	Time Out		Decca 31884
10/28/67	**1⁴**	20	72	**For Loving You**		Decca 32197
11/15/69+	**2¹**	15	73	**If It's All The Same To You**		Decca 32511
6/20/70	**4**	15	74	**Someday We'll Be Together**.........................		Decca 32689
				#1 pop hit for Diana Ross & The Supremes in 1969		
10/09/71	**4**	15	75	**Dis-Satisfied**		Decca 32877
				BILL ANDERSON & MARY LOU TURNER:		
11/29/75+	**1¹**	16	76	**Sometimes**		MCA 40488
3/27/76	**7**	12	77	**That's What Made Me Love You**		MCA 40533
7/16/77	**18**	12	78	Where Are You Going, Billy Boy		MCA 40753
1/28/78	**25**	10	79	I'm Way Ahead Of You		MCA 40852

DEBUT DATE	PEAK POS	WKS CHR	ARTIST — Record Title	POP POS	Label & Number
			IVIE ANDERSON		
			Duke Ellington's featured vocalist from 1931-42. Died on 12/28/49 (45).		
4/08/44	**4**	2	1 **Mexico Joe**	*16*	Exclusive 3113
			accompanied by Ceele Burke's Orchestra		
			JOHN ANDERSON ★★86★★		
			Born on 12/13/54 in Apopka, Florida. Played guitar from age 7. Had own band, Living End, while still a teenager. Sang with sister Donna in the early 70s. Moved to Nashville in 1972, became staff writer for Gallico Music. First recorded for Ace of Hearts label in 1974.		
12/10/77+	**62**	8	1 I've Got A Feelin' (Somebody's Stealin')............		Warner 8480
6/24/78	**69**	5	2 Whine, Whistle, Whine		Warner 8585
11/25/78	**40**	9	3 The Girl At The End Of The Bar.....................		Warner 8705
3/24/79	**41**	8	4 My Pledge Of Love.....................................		Warner 8770
			#14 pop hit for The Joe Jeffrey Group in 1969		
7/14/79	**31**	11	5 Low Dog Blues		Warner 8863
10/27/79+	**15**	16	6 Your Lying Blue Eyes		Warner 49089
3/15/80	**13**	15	7 She Just Started Liking Cheatin' Songs		Warner 49191
7/26/80	**21**	14	8 If There Were No Memories		Warner 49275
11/22/80+	**7**	17	9 1959..		Warner 49582
3/28/81	**4**	16	10 I'm Just An Old Chunk Of Coal (But I'm Gonna Be A Diamond Someday)...............		Warner 49699
8/01/81	**8**	15	11 **Chicken Truck/**		
8/01/81	**54**	15	12 I Love You A Thousand Ways....................		Warner 49772
11/21/81+	**7**	18	13 **I Just Came Home To Count The Memories**.....		Warner 49860
4/17/82	**6**	19	14 **Would You Catch A Falling Star**		Warner 50043
9/25/82	**1**²	20	15 **Wild And Blue**		Warner 29917
1/15/83	**1**¹	22	16● **Swingin'**..	*43*	Warner 29788
6/25/83	**5**	17	17 **Goin' Down Hill**		Warner 29585
9/24/83	**1**¹	21	18 **Black Sheep**		Warner 29497
1/14/84	**10**	16	19 **Let Somebody Else Drive**		Warner 29385
5/12/84	**14**	17	20 I Wish I Could Write You A Song....................		Warner 29276
8/18/84	**3**	25	21 **She Sure Got Away With My Heart**		Warner 29207
12/08/84+	**20**	17	22 Eye Of A Hurricane		Warner 29127
5/04/85	**15**	17	23 It's All Over Now.....................................		Warner 29002
			#26 pop hit for The Rolling Stones in 1964		
8/24/85	**30**	14	24 Toyko, Oklahoma......................................		Warner 28916
11/16/85+	**12**	22	25 Down In Tennessee...................................		Warner 28855
3/22/86	**31**	11	26 You Can't Keep A Good Memory Down.............		Warner 28748
8/16/86	**10**	22	27 **Honky Tonk Crowd**		Warner 28639
12/06/86+	**44**	12	28 Countrified		Warner 28502
3/07/87	**55**	8	29 What's So Different About You		Warner 28433
9/05/87	**48**	8	30 When Your Yellow Brick Road Turns Blue		MCA 53155
12/05/87+	**23**	15	31 Somewhere Between Ragged And Right.............		MCA 53226
			guest vocal: Waylon Jennings		
4/23/88	**65**	4	32 It's Hard To Keep This Ship Together		MCA 53307
7/09/88	**35**	12	33 If It Ain't Broke Don't Fix It		MCA 53366
11/05/88	**68**	4	34 Down In The Orange Grove		MCA 53441
			LIZ ANDERSON		
			Born Elizabeth Jane Haaby on 3/13/30 in Roseau, Minnesota; raised in Grand Forks, North Dakota. Wrote "(My Friends Are Gonna Be) Strangers" and "The Fugitive" for Merle Haggard, and many others. Mother of Lynn Anderson.		
4/02/66	**23**	10	1 Go Now Pay Later		RCA 8778
7/30/66	**45**	4	2 So Much For Me, So Much For You		RCA 8861
10/15/66	**5**	17	3 **The Game Of Triangles**		RCA 8963
			BOBBY BARE, NORMA JEAN, LIZ ANDERSON		
12/03/66+	**22**	12	4 The Wife Of The Party.................................		RCA 8999
4/22/67	**5**	17	5 **Mama Spank**		RCA 9163
9/02/67	**24**	13	6 Tiny Tears		RCA 9271
12/23/67+	**40**	12	7 Thanks A Lot For Tryin' Anyway....................		RCA 9378
2/24/68	**21**	12	8 Mother, May I		RCA 9445
			LIZ ANDERSON & LYNN ANDERSON		
5/11/68	**43**	9	9 Like A Merry-Go-Round...............................		RCA 9508

DEBUT DATE	PEAK POS	WKS CHR		ARTIST — Record Title	POP POS	Label & Number
				LIZ ANDERSON — Continued		
8/24/68	**65**	7	10	Me, Me, Me, Me, Me/		
8/31/68	**58**	4	11	Cry, Cry Again.................................		RCA 9586
11/23/68	**51**	5	12	Love Is Ending		RCA 9650
2/14/70	**26**	8	13	Husband Hunting		RCA 9796
8/15/70	**64**	6	14	All Day Sucker		RCA 9876
12/19/70	**75**	2	15	When I'm Not Lookin'		RCA 9924
10/23/71	**69**	3	16	It Don't Do No Good To Be A Good Girl		Epic 10782
4/08/72	**56**	7	17	I'll Never Fall In Love Again......................		Epic 10840
				#6 pop hit for Dionne Warwick in 1979		
8/12/72	**67**	4	18	Astrology		Epic 10896
3/17/73	**72**	2	19	Time To Love Again		Epic 10952

LYNN ANDERSON   ★★41★★

Born on 9/26/47 in Grand Forks, North Dakota; raised in Sacramento. Daughter of Liz Anderson. An accomplished equestrian, she was the California Horse Show Queen in 1966. On American Swingaround in Chicago from 1967-68. Regular on TV's "Lawrence Welk Show" from 1968. Appeared on three Bob Hope specials, acted in "Starsky & Hutch" TV show and in the film "Country Gold".

DEBUT DATE	PEAK POS	WKS CHR		ARTIST — Record Title	POP POS	Label & Number
10/29/66+	**36**	17	1	Ride, Ride, Ride		Chart 1375
3/18/67	**5**	19	2	If I Kiss You (Will You Go Away)..................		Chart 1430
7/01/67	**49**	6	3	Keeping Up Appearances......................		Chart 1425
				LYNN ANDERSON & JERRY LANE		
8/12/67	**28**	13	4	Too Much Of You		Chart 1475
12/02/67+	**4**	18	5	Promises, Promises		Chart 1010
2/24/68	**21**	12	6	Mother, May I		RCA 9445
				LIZ ANDERSON & LYNN ANDERSON		
3/30/68	**8**	14	7	No Another Time		Chart 1026
8/03/68	**12**	14	8	Big Girls Don't Cry		Chart 1042
11/30/68+	**11**	14	9	Flattery Will Get You Everywhere		Chart 1059
3/08/69	**18**	12	10	Our House Is Not A Home (If It's Never Been Loved In)..............................		Chart 5001
8/02/69	**2**²	15	11	That's A No No		Chart 5021
11/22/69+	**15**	12	12	He'd Still Love Me		Chart 5040
2/14/70	**16**	10	13	I've Been Everywhere		Chart 5053
3/21/70	**7**	16	14	Stay There 'Til I Get There		Columbia 45101
6/06/70	**17**	10	15	Rocky Top		Chart 5068
8/01/70	**15**	12	16	No Love At All/		
				#16 pop hit for B.J. Thomas in 1971		
		12	17	I Found You Just In Time............................		Columbia 45190
10/31/70	**20**	11	18	I'm Alright	*112*	Chart 5098
11/07/70	**1**⁵	20	19●	Rose Garden...................................	*3*	Columbia 45252
2/06/71	**20**	13	20	It Wasn't God Who Made Honky Tonk Angels.....		Chart 5113
5/08/71	**1**²	15	21	You're My Man	*63*	Columbia 45356
5/15/71	**74**	3	22	Jim Dandy		Chart 5125
				#17 pop hit for LaVern Baker in 1957		
7/24/71	**54**	5	23	He Even Woke Me Up To Say Goodbye		Chart 5136
8/21/71	**1**³	16	24	How Can I Unlove You	*63*	Columbia 45429
1/29/72	**3**	16	25	Cry	*71*	Columbia 45529
				#1 pop hit for Johnnie Ray in 1951		
6/10/72	**4**	13	26	Listen To A Country Song	*107*	Columbia 45615
10/14/72	**4**	14	27	Fool Me..	*101*	Columbia 45692
				#78 pop hit for Joe South in 1971		
1/13/73	**1**¹	16	28	Keep Me In Mind.................................	*104*	Columbia 45768
6/02/73	**2**¹	15	29	Top Of The World	*74*	Columbia 45857
				#1 pop hit for the Carpenters in 1973		
9/15/73	**3**	17	30	Sing About Love		Columbia 45918
3/09/74	**15**	13	31	Smile For Me		Columbia 46009
6/29/74	**7**	14	32	Talkin' To The Wall		Columbia 46056
10/26/74	**1**¹	13	33	What A Man, My Man Is	*93*	Columbia 10041
3/08/75	**13**	12	34	He Turns It Into Love Again....................		Columbia 10100
6/28/75	**14**	14	35	I've Never Loved Anyone More		Columbia 10160
11/22/75+	**26**	11	36	Paradise		Columbia 10240
2/07/76	**20**	14	37	All The King's Horses		Columbia 10280

DEBUT DATE	PEAK POS	WKS CHR		ARTIST — Record Title	POP POS	Label & Number
				LYNN ANDERSON — Continued		
6/05/76	44	9	38	Rodeo Cowboy/		
		3	39	Dixieland, You Will Never Die........................		Columbia 10337
9/25/76	23	11	40	Sweet Talkin' Man		Columbia 10401
1/22/77	12	14	41	Wrap Your Love All Around Your Man		Columbia 10467
5/28/77	22	10	42	I Love What Love Is Doing To Me		Columbia 10545
9/03/77	19	12	43	He Ain't You		Columbia 10597
12/03/77+	26	13	44	We Got Love		Columbia 10650
4/29/78	44	9	45	Rising Above It All		Columbia 10721
9/02/78	43	8	46	Last Love Of My Life..................................		Columbia 10809
3/10/79	10	13	47	**Isn't It Always Love**		Columbia 10909
6/23/79	18	12	48	I Love How You Love Me		Columbia 11006
				#5 pop hit for The Paris Sisters in 1961		
10/13/79	33	9	49	Sea Of Heartbreak		Columbia 11104
7/05/80	26	13	50	Even Cowgirls Get The Blues........................		Columbia 11296
10/25/80	27	13	51	Blue Baby Blue..		Columbia 11374
4/09/83	42	11	52	You Can't Lose What You Never Had		Permian 82000
7/16/83	18	16	53	What I Learned From Loving You...................		Permian 82001
12/17/83+	9	23	54	**You're Welcome To Tonight**		Permian 82003
				LYNN ANDERSON & GARY MORRIS		
9/13/86	49	9	55	Fools For Each Other		RCA 5005
				ED BRUCE with LYNN ANDERSON		
12/20/86+	45	9	56	Didn't We Shine		Mercury 888209
9/19/87	38	12	57	Read Between The Lines		Mercury 888839
7/30/88	24	17	58	Under The Boardwalk		Mercury 870528
				#4 pop hit for The Drifters in 1964		
12/03/88+	50	10	59	What He Does Best		Mercury 872220

ANDREWS SISTERS - see BING CROSBY and ERNEST TUBB

SHEILA ANDREWS
Alabama-born, Ohio-raised singer.

DEBUT DATE	PEAK POS	WKS CHR		ARTIST — Record Title	POP POS	Label & Number
12/16/78+	88	4	1	Too Fast For Rapid City		Ovation 1116
9/22/79	88	3	2	I Gotta Get Back The Feeling........................		Ovation 1128
1/26/80	48	7	3	What I Had With You		Ovation 1138
				SHEILA ANDREWS with JOE SUN		
7/26/80	42	10	4	It Don't Get Better Than This........................		Ovation 1146
11/29/80	58	8	5	Where Could You Take Me		Ovation 1160

ANDY & THE BROWN SISTERS
Trio from Albany, Oregon. Andi Brown and her sister Robin, with Darby Huffman.

DEBUT DATE	PEAK POS	WKS CHR		ARTIST — Record Title	POP POS	Label & Number
10/08/88	94	2	1	I'd Do Anything For You, Baby		Killer 1013

LISA ANGELLE
Born near New Orleans. Staff writer for Tom Collins Music.

DEBUT DATE	PEAK POS	WKS CHR		ARTIST — Record Title	POP POS	Label & Number
4/06/85	78	4	1	Love, It's The Pits		EMI America 8258
11/16/85	96	3	2	Bring Back Love		EMI America 8294

RAYBURN ANTHONY
Bass player born in Jackson, Tennessee. Worked with Billy Walker; wrote Billy's hit "Sing Me A Love Song To Baby". Backed up Bobby Bare for two years.

DEBUT DATE	PEAK POS	WKS CHR		ARTIST — Record Title	POP POS	Label & Number
10/09/76	84	5	1	Crazy Again		Polydor 14346
3/26/77	39	9	2	Lonely Eyes		Polydor 14380
6/25/77	57	8	3	Hold Me..		Polydor 14398
10/15/77	75	5	4	She Keeps Hangin' On		Polydor 14423
3/25/78	31	9	5	Maybe I Should've Been Listenin'...................		Polydor 14457
10/21/78	75	5	6	I Thought You Were Easy		Mercury 55042
2/03/79	28	11	7	Shadows Of Love......................................		Mercury 55053
6/23/79	79	3	8	It Won't Go Away		Mercury 55063
10/06/79	60	6	9	The Wild Side Of Life		Mercury 57006
				RAYBURN ANTHONY with KITTY WELLS		

VINCE ANTHONY
Singer from Berwick, Louisiana.

DEBUT DATE	PEAK POS	WKS CHR		ARTIST — Record Title	POP POS	Label & Number
3/06/82	82	3	1	Call Me Friend		Midnight G. 160

SUSAN ANTON - see FRED KNOBLOCK

DEBUT DATE	PEAK POS	WKS CHR		ARTIST — Record Title	POP POS	Label & Number
				TONY ARATA		
				Born in Savannah, Georgia on 10/10/57. Wrote "The Man In The Mirror" for Jim Glaser.		
9/22/84	**76**	4	1	Come On Home		Noble Vision 106
2/09/85	**65**	7	2	Sure Thing		Noble Vision 108
				JUDY ARGO		
4/07/79	**83**	6	1	Night Time Music Man..................................		ASI 1019
8/11/79	**95**	3	2	He's A Good Man		MDJ 51379
9/29/79	**55**	7	3	Hide Me (In The Shadow Of Your Love).............		MDJ 4633
				WAYNE ARMSTRONG		
				Acted in a TV "soap" in 1980.		
8/09/80	**59**	8	1	Hot Sunday Morning		NSD 57
				EDDY ARNOLD ★★1★★		
				Born Richard Edward Arnold on 5/15/18 near Henderson, Tennessee. Became popular on Nashville's Grand Ole Opry as a singer with Pee Wee King (1940-43). Nicknamed "The Tennessee Plowboy" on all RCA recordings through 1954. Country music's most prolific recording artist fom 1945-55. Elected to the Country Music Hall Of Fame in 1966. CMA award: Entertainer of the Year - 1967.		
6/30/45	**5**	2	1	**Each Minute Seems A Million Years**..............		Bluebird 0527
7/13/46	**7**	1	2	**All Alone In This World Without You**............		RCA 1855
10/12/46	**2**⁴	17	3	**That's How Much I Love You/**		
10/12/46	**3**	2	4	**Chained To A Memory**		RCA 1948
3/01/47	**1**¹	22	5	**What Is Life Without Love?**		RCA 2058
5/31/47	**1**⁵	38	6	**It's A Sin/**		
6/21/47	**4**	2	7	**I Couldn't Believe It Was True**		RCA 2241
8/23/47	**1**²¹	46	8●	**I'll Hold You In My Heart (Till I Can Hold You In My Arms)** .... Juke Box #1 / Best Seller #7	*22*	RCA 2332
11/08/47	**2**²	15	9	**To My Sorrow**.. Juke Box #2		RCA 2481
2/07/48	**10**	2	10	**Molly Darling** .... Juke Box #10 / Best Seller #14		RCA 2489
3/20/48	**1**⁹	39	11●	**Anytime/** Juke Box #1(9) / Best Seller #1(3) #2 pop hit for Eddie Fisher in 1952	*17*	
3/27/48	**2**⁵	21	12	**What A Fool I Was** .... Juke Box #2 / Best Seller #7	*29*	RCA 2700
5/15/48	**1**¹⁹	54	13●	**Bouquet Of Roses/** Best Seller #1(19) / Juke Box #1(18)	*13*	
5/15/48	**1**³	26	14	**Texarkana Baby**... Juke Box #1 (3) / Best Seller #1(1)	*18*	RCA 2806
8/28/48	**1**⁸	32	15●	**Just A Little Lovin' (Will Go A Long, Long Way)/** Juke Box #1(8) / Best Seller #1(4)	*13*	
8/28/48	**5**	19	16	**My Daddy Is Only A Picture**....................... Best Seller #5 / Juke Box #6		RCA 3013
11/20/48	**1**¹	21	17	**A Heart Full Of Love (For A Handful Of Kisses)/** Best Seller #1 / Juke Box #3	*23*	
11/20/48+	**2**¹	17	18	**Then I Turned And Walked Slowly Away**...... Juke Box #2 / Best Seller #4	*30*	RCA 3174
2/05/49	**10**	1	19	**Many Tears Ago** .... [R] Juke Box #10 originally released in 1946; all of above label nos. are 78 rpm		RCA 1871
2/19/49	**1**¹²	31	20	**Don't Rob Another Man's Castle/** Juke Box #1(12) / Best Seller #1(6)	*23*	
2/12/49	**3**	10	21	**There's Not A Thing (I Wouldn't Do For You)** Juke Box #3 / Best Seller #7 - 78 rpm: 21-0002		RCA 0042
5/14/49	**1**³	22	22	**One Kiss Too Many** .... Juke Box #1 / Best Seller #2	*23*	RCA 0051
5/21/49	**2**³	19	23	**The Echo Of Your Footsteps** .... Best Seller #2 / Juke Box #3 - 78 rpm: 21-0051		RCA 0083
7/02/49	**1**⁴	22	24	**I'm Throwing Rice (At The Girl I Love)/** Best Seller #1(4) / Juke Box #1(3)	*18*	
7/16/49	**7**	4	25	**Show Me The Way Back To Your Heart** .... Best Seller #7 / Juke Box #11 - 78 rpm: 21-0083		RCA 0080

DEBUT DATE	PEAK POS	WKS CHR		ARTIST — Record Title	POP POS	Label & Number
				EDDY ARNOLD — Continued		
11/19/49	**7**	8	26	**C-H-R-I-S-T-M-A-S/** [X]		
				Best Seller #7 / Jockey #7 / Juke Box #9		
12/10/49	**5**	4	27	**Will Santy Come To Shanty Town** .... [X]		RCA 0127
				Jockey #5 / Juke Box #6 / Best Seller #8 - 78 rpm: 21-0124		
12/17/49+	**6**	2	28	**There's No Wings On My Angel**		RCA 0137
				Juke Box #6 / Best Seller #11 - 78 rpm: 21-0134		
				from the film "Feudin' Rhythm"		
12/31/49+	**1**[1]	17	29	**Take Me In Your Arms And Hold Me/**		
				Juke Box #1 / Jockey #4 / Best Seller #5		
1/14/50	**6**	7	30	**Mama And Daddy Broke My Heart**...............		RCA 0150
				Best Seller #6 / Juke Box #8 - 78 rpm: 21-0146		
4/15/50	**3**	12	31	**Little Angel With The Dirty Face/**		
				Best Seller #3 / Juke Box #7 / Jockey #10		
4/22/50	**3**	13	32	**Why Should I Cry?**....................................		RCA 0300
				Juke Box #3 / Best Seller #5 / Jockey #5		
7/01/50	**2**[2]	17	33	**Cuddle Buggin' Baby/**		
				Best Seller #2 / Juke Box #3 / Jockey #4		
7/01/50	**6**	12	34	**Enclosed, One Broken Heart**		RCA 0342
				Juke Box #6 / Best Seller #7 / Jockey #7		
9/30/50	**2**[8]	16	35	**Lovebug Itch/**		
				Best Seller #2 / Jockey #2 / Juke Box #2		
12/09/50	**10**	1	36	**Prison Without Walls**		RCA 0382
				Juke Box #10		
1/13/51	**1**[11]	23	37	**There's Been A Change In Me**......................		RCA 0412
				Jockey #1(11) / Best Seller #1(4) / Juke Box #2		
2/24/51	**8**	5	38	**May The Good Lord Bless And Keep You**		RCA 0425
				Best Seller #8 / Jockey #10		
4/14/51	**1**[3]	17	39	**Kentucky Waltz**.......................................		RCA 0444
				Best Seller #1(3) / Juke Box #1(3) / Jockey #4		
6/23/51	**1**[11]	24	40	**I Wanna Play House With You/**		RCA 0476
				Juke Box #1(11) / Best Seller #1(6) / Jockey #2		
7/07/51	**4**	9	41	**Something Old, Something New**...................		
				Juke Box #4 / Best Seller #7		
10/27/51	**2**[1]	16	42	**Somebody's Been Beating My Time/**		
				Juke Box #2 / Jockey #3 / Best Seller #5		
10/27/51	**5**	12	43	**Heart Strings**..		RCA 4273
				Best Seller #5 / Juke Box #8		
1/26/52	**4**	12	44	**Bundle Of Southern Sunshine/**		
				Best Seller #4 / Juke Box #4 / Jockey #5		
2/23/52	**9**	1	45	**Call Her Your Sweetheart**..........................		RCA 4413
				Jockey #9		
4/05/52	**1**[1]	14	46	**Easy On The Eyes**		RCA 4569
				Best Seller #1 / Jockey #4 / Juke Box #6		
7/19/52	**1**[4]	18	47	**A Full Time Job**.......................................		RCA 4787
				Jockey #1 / Best Seller #3 / Juke Box #3		
10/25/52	**3**	11	48	**Older And Bolder/**		
				Best Seller #3 / Juke Box #4 / Jockey #7		
12/06/52	**9**	1	49	**I'd Trade All Of My Tomorrows (For Just One Yesterday)**		RCA 4954
				Juke Box #9		
1/24/53	**1**[3]	13	50	**Eddy's Song**..		RCA 5108
				Best Seller #1 / Juke Box #2 / Jockey #5		
				tune includes titles of all of Eddy's past hits		
6/20/53	**4**	9	51	**Free Home Demonstration/**		
				Best Seller #4 / Jockey #5 / Juke Box #5		
7/18/53	**4**	10	52	**How's The World Treating You?**..................		RCA 5305
				Jockey #4 / Juke Box #7		
10/03/53	**4**	10	53	**Mama, Come Get Your Baby Boy**..................		RCA 5415
				Jockey #4 / Best Seller #9 / Juke Box #9		
1/09/54	**1**[1]	37	54	**I Really Don't Want To Know**		RCA 5525
				Juke Box #1 / Best Seller #2 / Jockey #2		
				there have been 6 charted pop versions from 1954-71		
4/10/54	**7**	9	55	**My Everything**...		RCA 5634
				Best Seller #7 / Jockey #7		
8/28/54	**3**	23	56	**This Is The Thanks I Get (For Loving You)/**		
				Best Seller #3 / Jockey #3 / Juke Box #3		
8/21/54	**7**	14	57	**Hep Cat Baby**..		RCA 5805
				Best Seller #7 / Juke Box #9 / Jockey #14		
12/18/54+	**12**	3	58	**Christmas Can't Be Far Away**.................... [X]		RCA 5905
				Jockey #12		

DEBUT DATE	PEAK POS	WKS CHR		ARTIST — Record Title	POP POS	Label & Number
				EDDY ARNOLD — Continued		
1/29/55	**2**⁴	25	59	**I've Been Thinking/** Juke Box #2 / Best Seller #3 / Jockey #4		
2/05/55	**12**	7	60	Don't Forget........................ Best Seller #12		RCA 6000
4/23/55	**6**	9	61	**In Time/** Jockey #6 / Best Seller #7		
4/23/55	**9**	8	62	**Two Kinds Of Love**...................... Best Seller #9 / Juke Box #9		RCA 6069
6/25/55	**1**²	26	63	**The Cattle Call/** Best Seller #1 / Juke Box #2 / Jockey #4	42	
7/09/55	**8**	7	64	**The Kentuckian Song**.................... Juke Box #8 from the Burt Lancaster film "The Kentuckian"		RCA 6139
8/20/55	**1**²	15	65	**That Do Make It Nice/** Juke Box #1 / Jockey #4 / Best Seller #11		
8/20/55	**2**⁷	31	66	**Just Call Me Lonesome**................... Juke Box #2 / Best Seller #2 / Jockey #2		RCA 6198
11/12/55	**10**	10	67	**The Richest Man (In The World)/** Best Seller #10 / Jockey #14	99	
11/26/55	**6**	8	68	**I Walked Alone Last Night**.................... Best Seller #6		RCA 6290
1/28/56	**7**	3	69	**Trouble In Mind** .... Best Seller #7		RCA 6365
8/25/56	**15**	1	70	Casey Jones (The Brave Engineer)................... Jockey #15 written in 1909 about the engineer of the "Cannonball Express"		RCA 6601
9/01/56	**10**	8	71	**You Don't Know Me**........................ Best Seller #10 / Jockey #15		RCA 6502
5/27/57	**12**	3	72	Gonna Find Me A Bluebird .... Jockey #12 / Best Seller #15	51	RCA 6905
3/16/59	**12**	9	73	Chip Off The Old Block	97	RCA 7435
6/22/59	**5**	19	74	Tennessee Stud	48	RCA 7542
1/09/61	**23**	3	75	Before This Day Ends		RCA 7794
5/29/61	**27**	1	76	(Jim) I Wore A Tie Today		RCA 7861
10/16/61	**17**	10	77	One Grain Of Sand	107	RCA 7926
3/17/62	**7**	10	78	Tears Broke Out On Me	102	RCA 7984
6/30/62	**3**	19	79	**A Little Heartache/**	103	
8/04/62	**7**	19	80	After Loving You	112	RCA 8048
12/08/62+	**5**	15	81	**Does He Mean That Much To You?**...............	98	RCA 8102
4/27/63	**11**	10	82	Yesterday's Memories		RCA 8160
8/10/63	**13**	12	83	A Million Years Or So		RCA 8207
12/07/63+	**12**	12	84	Jealous Hearted Me...............................		RCA 8253
2/01/64	**5**	20	85	Molly...................................... with The Needmore Creek Singers		RCA 8296
7/18/64	**26**	13	86	Sweet Adorable You		RCA 8363
11/07/64+	**8**	19	87	**I Thank My Lucky Stars**............................		RCA 8445
3/27/65	**1**²	25	88	**What's He Doing In My World**	60	RCA 8516
9/18/65	**15**	9	89	I'm Letting You Go	135	RCA 8632
10/09/65	**1**³	25	90	**Make The World Go Away**........................	6	RCA 8679
2/12/66	**1**⁶	19	91	**I Want To Go With You**............................	36	RCA 8749
5/14/66	**2**¹	16	92	**The Last Word In Lonesome Is Me**	40	RCA 8818
7/23/66	**3**	15	93	**The Tip Of My Fingers**	43	RCA 8869
10/15/66	**1**⁴	19	94	**Somebody Like Me**	53	RCA 8965
12/24/66+	**51**	8	95	The First Word		RCA 9027
2/18/67	**1**²	16	96	**Lonely Again**	87	RCA 9080
5/06/67	**3**	16	97	**Misty Blue**	57	RCA 9182
8/26/67	**1**¹	16	98	**Turn The World Around**	66	RCA 9265
12/02/67+	**2**²	15	99	**Here Comes Heaven**...............................	91	RCA 9368
2/17/68	**4**	14	100	**Here Comes The Rain, Baby**	74	RCA 9437
6/01/68	**4**	12	101	**It's Over**	74	RCA 9525
8/31/68	**1**²	14	102	**Then You Can Tell Me Goodbye** .... #6 pop hit for The Casinos in 1967	84	RCA 9606
11/23/68+	**10**	14	103	**They Don't Make Love Like They Used To**	99	RCA 9667
3/29/69	**10**	13	104	**Please Don't Go**	129	RCA 0120

DEBUT DATE	PEAK POS	WKS CHR	ARTIST — Record Title	POP POS	Label & Number
			EDDY ARNOLD — Continued		
6/28/69	**19**	12	105 But For Love	*125*	RCA 0175
9/27/69	**69**	2	106 You Fool		RCA 0226
12/27/69+	**73**	2	107 Since December		RCA 0282
2/28/70	**22**	11	108 Soul Deep		RCA 9801
			#18 pop hit in 1969 for The Box Tops		
6/13/70	**28**	11	109 A Man's Kind Of Woman/		
		10	110 Living Under Pressure		RCA 9848
9/12/70	**22**	9	111 From Heaven To Heartache		RCA 9889
1/02/71	**26**	12	112 Portrait Of My Woman		RCA 9935
5/01/71	**49**	8	113 A Part Of America Died .... [S]		RCA 9968
			backing tune: "The Old Rugged Cross"		
7/03/71	**34**	9	114 Welcome To My World		RCA 9993
11/13/71	**55**	7	115 I Love You Dear		RCA 0559
2/26/72	**38**	9	116 Lonely People		RCA 0641
8/05/72	**62**	4	117 Lucy		RCA 0747
1/20/73	**28**	12	118 So Many Ways		MGM 14478
			#6 pop hit for Brook Benton in 1959		
5/19/73	**56**	9	119 If The Whole World Stopped Lovin'...................		MGM 14535
8/18/73	**29**	11	120 Oh, Oh, I'm Falling In Love Again....................		MGM 14600
			#7 pop hit for Jimmie Rodgers in 1958		
12/08/73+	**24**	13	121 She's Got Everything I Need		MGM 14672
3/30/74	**56**	9	122 Just For Old Times Sake		MGM 14711
			#20 pop hit for The McGuire Sisters in 1961		
8/03/74	**19**	12	123 I Wish That I Had Loved You Better		MGM 14734
12/28/74+	**47**	9	124 Butterfly		MGM 14769
			#78 pop hit for Danyel Gerard in 1972		
6/07/75	**60**	12	125 Red Roses For A Blue Lady............................		MGM 14780
			#10 pop hit for Vic Dana in 1965		
10/11/75	**86**	6	126 Middle Of A Memory		MGM 14827
6/19/76	**13**	13	127 Cowboy		RCA 10701
10/23/76	**43**	9	128 Put Me Back Into Your World		RCA 10794
3/05/77	**22**	13	129 (I Need You) All The Time		RCA 10899
7/23/77	**53**	7	130 Freedom Ain't The Same As Being Free		RCA 11031
11/12/77	**83**	3	131 Where Lonely People Go.................................		RCA 11133
4/22/78	**23**	12	132 Country Lovin'		RCA 11257
8/05/78	**91**	2	133 I'm The South...		RCA 11319
12/09/78+	**13**	14	134 If Everyone Had Someone Like You		RCA 11422
4/14/79	**21**	11	135 What In Her World Did I Do...........................		RCA 11537
8/04/79	**22**	11	136 Goodbye..		RCA 11668
11/17/79+	**28**	13	137 If I Ever Had To Say Goodbye To You		RCA 11752
3/08/80	**6**	13	138 **Let's Get It While The Gettin's Good**		RCA 11918
6/28/80	**10**	15	139 **That's What I Get For Loving You**...............		RCA 12039
12/06/80+	**11**	16	140 Don't Look Now (But We Just Fell In Love)		RCA 12136
5/16/81	**32**	10	141 Bally-Hoo Days/		
		5	142 Two Hearts Beat Better Than One..................		RCA 12226
12/12/81+	**30**	11	143 All I'm Missing Is You		RCA 13000
4/24/82	**73**	5	144 Don't Give Up On Me.....................................		RCA 13094
3/19/83	**76**	6	145 The Blues Don't Care Who's Got 'Em		RCA 13452
			LEON ASHLEY		
			Born near Covington, Georgia. Emcee of his own country music radio show at age 11. Married Margie Singleton in 1965. Formed own label, Ashley, in 1967.		
7/29/67	**1**[1]	18	1 **Laura (What's He Got That I Ain't Got)**.........	*120*	Ashley 2003
11/11/67	**54**	7	2 Hangin' On..		Ashley 2015
			LEON ASHLEY & MARGIE SINGLETON		
12/02/67+	**28**	12	3 Anna, I'm Taking You Home		Ashley 2025
3/30/68	**14**	14	4 Mental Journey		Ashley 2075
5/11/68	**55**	6	5 You'll Never Be Lonely Again		Ashley 3000
			LEON ASHLEY & MARGIE SINGLETON		
7/27/68	**8**	15	6 **Flower Of Love**		Ashley 4000
1/11/69	**25**	9	7 While Your Lover Sleeps		Ashley 7000
4/19/69	**23**	10	8 Walkin' Back To Birmingham...........................		Ashley 9000
8/16/69	**55**	7	9 Ain't Gonna Worry		Ashley 22

14

DEBUT DATE	PEAK POS	WKS CHR	ARTIST — Record Title	POP POS	Label & Number
			ERNEST ASHWORTH ★★158★★		
			Born on 12/15/28 in Huntsville, Alabama. Worked on local radio stations, then WSIX-Nashville. Recorded for MGM as "Billy Worth" in 1955. Out of music until 1960. A regular on the Grand Ole Opry since 1964. In film "The Farmer's Other Daughter".		
5/30/60	4	16	1 Each Moment (Spent With You)		Decca 31085
10/24/60	8	20	2 You Can't Pick A Rose In December...............		Decca 31156
5/15/61	15	2	3 Forever Gone		Decca 31237
6/30/62	3	20	4 Everybody But Me..		Hickory 1170
12/29/62+	7	15	5 I Take The Chance..		Hickory 1189
6/22/63	1¹	36	6 Talk Back Trembling Lips	101	Hickory 1214
2/01/64	10	20	7 A Week In The Country		Hickory 1237
6/20/64	4	23	8 I Love To Dance With Annie........................		Hickory 1265
11/07/64+	11	21	9 Pushed In A Corner		Hickory 1281
5/15/65	18	13	10 Because I Cared...		Hickory 1304
8/07/65	8	20	11 The DJ Cried..		Hickory 1325
			ERNIE ASHWORTH:		
1/29/66	29	11	12 I Wish		Hickory 1358
7/16/66	13	17	13 At Ease Heart...		Hickory 1400
12/03/66+	31	9	14 Sad Face		Hickory 1428
4/01/67	63	4	15 Just An Empty Place		Hickory 1445
8/05/67	48	10	16 My Love For You (Is Like A Mountain Range)		Hickory 1466
11/25/67	48	7	17 Tender And True		Hickory 1484
5/25/68	39	8	18 A New Heart..		Hickory 1503
3/29/69	69	4	19 Where Do You Go (When You Don't Go With Me).		Hickory 1528
7/12/69	72	3	20 Love, I Finally Found It		Hickory 1538
7/18/70	72	3	21 That Look Of Goodbye		Hickory 1570
			ASLEEP AT THE WHEEL		
			Group formed in Paw Paw, West Virginia in 1970. Consisted of Ray Benson (vocals, guitar), Reuben "Lucky Oceans" Gosfield (steel guitar), Danny Levin (fiddle, mandolin) and Chris O'Connell (vocals, guitar). Worked local clubs in West Virginia and Washington, DC, then moved to San Francisco in 1973, where they were joined by Floyd Domino (keyboards). Relocated to Austin in 1974. Personnel in 1987 included Benson, Larry Franklin (fiddle), Michael Francis (sax), John Ely (steel guitar), Tim Alexander (keyboards), Dave Dawson (bass) and David Sanger (drums).		
12/21/74+	69	8	1 Choo Choo Ch'Boogie..................................		Epic 50045
			#1 R&B hit for Louis Jordan in 1946		
8/09/75	10	18	2 The Letter That Johnny Walker Read...........		Capitol 4115
12/13/75+	31	11	3 Bump Bounce Boogie		Capitol 4187
4/03/76	35	11	4 Nothin' Takes The Place Of You.....................		Capitol 4238
8/28/76	48	8	5 Route 66		Capitol 4319
			#11 pop hit for Nat King Cole in 1946		
11/20/76+	38	10	6 Miles And Miles Of Texas.............................		Capitol 4357
3/19/77	42	9	7 The Trouble With Lovin' Today		Capitol 4393
12/02/78	75	6	8 Texas Me & You..		Capitol 4659
2/28/87	39	17	9 Way Down Texas Way...................................		Epic 06671
5/30/87	17	18	10 House Of Blue Lights		Epic 07125
			#9 pop hit for Chuck Miller in 1955		
10/17/87	53	7	11 Boogie Back To Texas...................................		Epic 07610
1/09/88	59	9	12 Blowin' Like A Bandit		Epic 07659
7/23/88	55	6	13 Walk On By		Epic 07966
10/29/88	65	11	14 Hot Rod Lincoln..		Epic 08087
			pop hit for Johnny Bond and Charlie Ryan in 1960		
			BOB ATCHER		
			Born James Robert Atcher on 5/11/14 in Hardin County, Kentucky; raised in North Dakota. Worked on WHAS-Louisville in the mid-30s and Chicago radio from 1931-48. First recorded for Columbia in 1937. With the WLS National Barn Dance from 1948-70 and had own TV show. Mayor of Schaumburg, Illinois for 20 years.		
7/13/46	7	1	1 I Must Have Been Wrong		Columbia 36983
1/31/48	6	11	2 Signed, Sealed And Delivered		Columbia 37991
5/07/49	12	1	3 Tennessee Border		Columbia 20557
			Juke Box #12		
10/08/49	9	2	4 Why Don't You Haul Off And Love Me?		Columbia 20611
			Juke Box #9		

DEBUT DATE	PEAK POS	WKS CHR	ARTIST — Record Title	POP POS	Label & Number
			THE ATKINS STRING COMPANY		
			A Chet Atkins studio production.		
9/20/75	77	5	1 The Night Atlanta Burned......................... [I]		RCA 10346
			BIG BEN ATKINS		
			Born in 1943 in Vernon, Alabama. Appeared at the Southernaire Club in Columbus, Mississippi from 1963-71. Toured with B.J. Thomas and The Buckinghams.		
5/13/78	72	4	1 We Don't Live Here, We Just Love Here		GRT 161
			CHET ATKINS		
			Born Chester Burton Atkins on 6/20/24 in Luttrell, Tennessee. First worked on WNOX in Knoxville from 1942-44, and toured with Archie Campbell and Bill Carlisle. On WLW-Cincinnati from 1944-46; Red Foley's radio show in Chicago in 1946. Recorded with Wally Fowler's Georgia Clodhoppers for Capitol in 1946. Recorded solo for Bullet in 1946. Began recording for RCA in 1947. Moved to Nashville in 1950 and became prolific studio musician and producer. RCA's A&R manager in Nashville from 1960-68; RCA vice-president from 1968 to 1982. Revered as an exceptional guitarist in all fields of music. Entered the Country Music Hall Of Fame in 1973 as the youngest inductee (49).		
1/15/55	13	2	1 Mr. Sandman.................................... [I]		RCA 5956
			Jockey #13 / Best Seller #15		
			#1 pop hit for The Chordettes in 1954		
4/02/55	15	1	2 Silver Bell..................................... [I]		RCA 5995
			HANK SNOW & CHET ATKINS		
			Best Seller #15		
6/26/65	4	19	3 Yakety Axe .... [I]	98	RCA 8590
			same tune as Boots Randolph's pop hit "Yakety Sax"		
10/15/66	30	10	4 Prissy .... [I]		RCA 8927
12/01/73	75	6	5 Fiddlin' Around .... [I-N]		RCA 0146
			featuring Johnny Gimble on fiddle		
6/12/76	40	12	6 Frog Kissin' .... [I]		RCA 10614
3/01/80	83	3	7 Blind Willie		RCA 11892
8/23/80	83	4	8 I Can Hear Kentucky Calling Me		RCA 12064
			ATLANTA		
			Group formed in Atlanta in 1983. Consisted of Brad Griffis, Dick Stevens, Bill Packard, Allen Collay, Jeff Baker, Darrell "Boo Boo" McAfee and Jody Warrell. Griffis, Stevens, Packard and Davidson had been in the Vogues in the late 70s. Ingram had been in Spurrz, and Collay had worked with Pete Fountain.		
5/21/83	9	17	1 **Atlanta Burned Again Last Night**................		MDJ 4831
9/10/83	11	19	2 Dixie Dreaming.................................		MDJ 4832
2/18/84	5	23	3 **Sweet Country Music**		MCA 52336
6/16/84	35	12	4 Pictures.......................................		MCA 52391
9/15/84	22	16	5 Wishful Drinkin'		MCA 52452
			from the film "Ellie"		
4/06/85	57	10	6 My Sweet-Eyed Georgia Girl		MCA 52552
6/22/85	58	7	7 Why Not Tonight...............................		MCA 52603
1/31/87	75	6	8 We Always Agree On Love		So. Tracks 1074
1/23/88	70	5	9 Sad Cliches		So. Tracks 1091
			ATLANTA POPS - see ALBERT COLEMAN		
			ATLANTA RHYTHM SECTION		
			Group of session musicians from Studio One, Doraville, Georgia; formed in 1971.		
7/07/79	92	3	1 Do It Or Die...................................	19	Polydor 14568
12/06/80	75	7	2 Silver Eagle...................................	101	Polydor 2142
			BOBBY AUSTIN		
			Born on 5/5/33 in Wenatchee, Washington. Session fiddler. Had own band in Vancouver, Washington. Member of Wynn Stewart's band in Las Vegas.		
10/08/66	21	14	1 Apartment #9		Tally 500
4/08/67	59	6	2 Cupid's Last Arrow.............................		Capitol 5867
12/30/67+	68	5	3 This Song Is Just For You......................		Capitol 2039
12/27/69+	65	4	4 For Your Love		Capitol 2681
			#13 pop hit for Ed Townsend in 1958		
11/11/72	39	8	5 Knoxville Station		Atlantic 2913
			CHRIS AUSTIN		
7/30/88	62	5	1 Lonesome For You		Warner 27815
12/10/88	89	6	2 I Know There's A Heart In There Somewhere		Warner 27661

DEBUT DATE	PEAK POS	WKS CHR	ARTIST — Record Title	POP POS	Label & Number
			DARLENE AUSTIN		
			Born in Salina, Kansas. Sang with family group from age 4.		
6/26/82	**68**	6	1 Sunday Go To Cheatin' Clothes		Myrtle 1002
10/09/82	**75**	5	2 Take Me Tonight............................		Myrtle 1003
3/12/83	**79**	4	3 I'm On The Outside Looking In		Myrtle 1004
			#15 pop hit for Little Anthony & The Imperials in 1964		
7/05/86	**81**	4	4 Guilty Eyes		CBT 4146
9/12/87	**63**	6	5 I Had A Heart		Magi 4444
			KAY AUSTIN		
			Born in Long Beach, California. Frequent appearances on the Grand Ole Opry.		
5/31/80	**86**	3	1 The Rest Of Your Life		e.i.o. 1122
9/13/80	**75**	4	2 Two Hearts Beat (Better Than One)		e.i.o. 1127
			GENE AUTRY ★★**101**★★		
			Born Orvon Gene Autry on 9/29/07 in Tioga Springs, Texas. Worked as a cowboy and telegrapher for the Frisco Railroad after attending Ravia High School in Oklahoma. Played saxophone with the Fields Brothers Medicine Show, then switched to guitar so he could sing along. Sang on KVOO-Tulsa from 1929-30, recorded for ARC and Victor. Worked the WLS-Chicago "National Barn Dance" and vaudeville from 1930-34. First film appearance "Old Santa Fe" in 1934. Made over 90 other starring films beginning with "Tumbling Tumbleweeds". Very popular "Melody Ranch" radio series began on CBS on 1/7/40. Enlisted in the Army Air Corps; returned to radio from September, 1945 until 1956. Owner of several record companies and the California Angels baseball team. Wrote "That Silver-Haired Daddy Of Mine", "Back In The Saddle Again", "Here Comes Santa Claus", and many others. Elected to the Country Music Hall Of Fame in 1969.		
1/29/44	**3**	9	1 I'm Thinking Tonight Of My Blue Eyes		Okeh 06648
4/29/44	**4**	1	2 I Hang My Head And Cry		Okeh 06627
2/10/45	**2**[1]	8	3 Gonna Build A Big Fence Around Texas/		
2/17/45	**4**	3	4 Don't Fence Me In		Okeh 6728
4/28/45	**1**[8]	22	5 At Mail Call Today/		
4/28/45	**7**	2	6 I'll Be Back..................................		Okeh 6737
10/27/45	**4**	2	7 Don't Hang Around Me Anymore		Columbia 36840
12/29/45	**4**	1	8 Don't Live A Lie/		
12/29/45	**4**	1	9 I Want To Be Sure		Columbia 36880
2/23/46	**4**	5	10 Silver Spurs (On The Golden Stairs)		Columbia 36904
5/25/46	**3**	7	11 I Wish I Had Never Met Sunshine/		
7/06/46	**7**	1	12 You Only Want Me When You're Lonely........		Columbia 36970
6/15/46	**4**	8	13 Wave To Me, My Lady............................		Columbia 36984
10/19/46	**3**	12	14 Have I Told You Lately That I Love You/		
10/26/46	**4**	3	15 Someday		Columbia 37079
3/08/47	**3**	2	16 You're Not My Darling Anymore...................		Columbia 37201
1/03/48	**5**	1	17●Here Comes Santa Claus........................[X]	9	Columbia 37942
10/09/48	**6**	12	18 Buttons And Bows	17	Columbia 20469
			Best Seller #6 / Juke Box #6 from the film "Paleface"		
11/27/48	**4**	7	19 Here Comes Santa Claus....................[X-R]	8	Columbia 20377
			Best Seller #4 / Juke Box #7		
12/10/49+	**1**[1]	5	20●Rudolph, The Red-Nosed Reindeer............ [X]	1	Columbia 38610
			Jockey #1 / Best Seller #4 / Juke Box #7 with the Pinafores; eventually sold over 8 million copies, second in the pre-1955 era to "White Christmas"		
12/10/49+	**8**	3	21 Here Comes Santa Claus.......................[X-R]	24	Columbia 20377
			Jockey #8 / Best Seller #13		
4/08/50	**3**	4	22 Peter Cottontail	5	Columbia 38750
			Best Seller #3 / Jockey #5 / Juke Box #7		
12/09/50+	**4**	4	23●Frosty The Snow Man .... [X]	7	Columbia 38907
			Best Seller #4 with the Cass County Boys		
12/16/50	**5**	3	24 Rudolph, The Red-Nosed Reindeer.......... [X-R]	3	Columbia 38610
			Best Seller #5 / Jockey #5 / Juke Box #5		
6/09/51	**9**	1	25 Old Soldiers Never Die		Columbia 39405
			Jockey #9		

HOYT AXTON

Born on 3/25/38 in Comanche, Oklahoma. Son of songwriter Mae Axton ("Heartbreak Hotel"). First worked as a folk singer on the West Coast in the late 50s. Wrote hits "Greenback Dollar" for The Kingston Trio, "The Pusher" for Steppenwolf, and "Joy To The World" for Three Dog Night. Started own label, Jeremiah, in 1978. Appeared in films "The Black Stallion" and "Gremlins".

DEBUT DATE	PEAK POS	WKS CHR	#	ARTIST — Record Title	POP POS	Label & Number
3/30/74	10	15	1	When The Morning Comes .... *guest vocal: Linda Ronstadt (also #4 below)*	54	A&M 1497
8/24/74	8	16	2	Boney Fingers .... *female vocal: Renee Armand*		A&M 1607
2/08/75	61	9	3	Nashville	105	A&M 1657
5/10/75	57	7	4	Lion In The Winter		A&M 1683
5/15/76	18	14	5	Flash Of Fire		A&M 1811
4/16/77	57	7	6	You're The Hangnail In My Life		MCA 40711
6/18/77	65	6	7	Little White Moon		MCA 40731
5/12/79	17	15	8	Della And The Dealer		Jeremiah 1000
10/06/79	14	14	9	A Rusty Old Halo		Jeremiah 1001
1/12/80	21	12	10	Wild Bull Rider		Jeremiah 1003
4/12/80	37	12	11	Evangelina		Jeremiah 1005
10/11/80	80	3	12	Where Did The Money Go		Jeremiah 1008
5/09/81	78	3	13	Flo's Yellow Rose		Elektra 47133
7/25/81	86	4	14	The Devil		Jeremiah 1011

B

BACKROADS

2/19/83	72	5	1	So Close		Soundwaves 4698

BACKTRACK featuring JOHN HUNT

4/06/85	94	3	1	Mexico		Goldmine 11

ANDY BADALE Orch.

Born Angelo Daniel Badalamenti on 3/22/37 in Brooklyn. Writer of TV and film scores.

1/26/80	93	4	1	Nashville Beer Garden .... [I]		GP 577

EDDIE BAILES

2/21/76	93	3	1	Love Isn't Love (Till You Give It Away)		Cin Kay 101

GLEN BAILEY

Born in Thunder Bay, Ontario in 1952.

3/06/82	87	3	1	Stomping On My Heart		Yatahey 1221
6/26/82	85	3	2	Designer Jeans		Yatahey 3024

JOHNNY BAILEY

2/05/83	86	2	1	What's She Doing To My Mind/		
		2	2	This Country Music's Driving Me Crazy		Soundwaves 4695

JUDY BAILEY

Born on 1/6/55 in Winchester, Kentucky; 11th of 12 children.

11/29/80+	10	14	1	Following The Feeling .... *MOE BANDY featuring JUDY BAILEY*		Columbia 11395
5/09/81	56	7	2	Slow Country Dancin'		Columbia 02045
10/03/81	54	7	3	The Best Bedroom In Town		Columbia 02505
2/12/83	72	4	4	Tender Lovin' Lies		Warner 29799
2/09/85	96	3	5	There's A Lot Of Good About Goodbye		White G. 22249

LYNN BAILEY

Born on 4/18/42 in Indianapolis. First recorded for Fraternity in 1975.

4/05/80	94	2	1	Cheater Fever		Wartrace 613

MARY BAILEY

Born in Toronto in 1945. First recorded for RCA in 1977. E & R was her own label.

8/15/81	84	3	1	Too Much, Too Little, Too Late		E & R 8101

DEBUT DATE	PEAK POS	WKS CHR	ARTIST — Record Title	POP POS	Label & Number
			RAZZY BAILEY ★★114★★		
			Born Rasie Michael Bailey on 2/14/39 in Five Points, Alabama. Own band while a teenager, then left music for nearly 10 years. Own pop group, Daily Bread, in 1958; recorded with the Aquarians for MGM in 1972. Also recorded only as Razzy on MGM in 1974. Wrote "9,999,999 Tears" hit for Dickey Lee.		
10/30/76	99	2	1 Keepin' Rosie Proud Of Me		Erastus 526
8/12/78	9	15	2 What Time Do You Have To Be Back To Heaven		RCA 11338
12/23/78+	6	14	3 Tonight She's Gonna Love Me (Like There Was No Tomorrow)		RCA 11446
4/21/79	6	13	4 If Love Had A Face		RCA 11536
8/18/79	10	14	5 I Ain't Got No Business Doin' Business Today		RCA 11682
12/22/79+	5	14	6 I Can't Get Enough Of You		RCA 11885
4/19/80	13	14	7 Too Old To Play Cowboy............................		RCA 11954
8/02/80	1¹	15	8 Loving Up A Storm		RCA 12062
11/22/80+	1¹	17	9 I Keep Coming Back/		
		17	10 True Life Country Music............................		RCA 12120
3/28/81	1¹	16	11 Friends/		
		16	12 Anywhere There's A Jukebox		RCA 12199
7/11/81	1¹	18	13 Midnight Hauler/		
7/11/81	8	18	14 Scratch My Back (And Whisper in My Ear) ...		RCA 12268
12/19/81+	1¹	20	15 She Left Love All Over Me		RCA 13007
4/10/82	10	15	16 Everytime You Cross My Mind (You Break My Heart)		RCA 13084
8/21/82	8	17	17 Love's Gonna Fall Here Tonight		RCA 13290
12/04/82+	30	14	18 Poor Boy		RCA 13383
4/30/83	19	13	19 After The Great Depression.........................		RCA 13512
10/29/83	62	10	20 This Is Just The First Day		RCA 13630
2/25/84	14	17	21 In The Midnight Hour..............................		RCA 13718
			#21 pop hit for Wilson Pickett in 1965		
8/04/84	29	14	22 Knock On Wood...................................		MCA 52421
			#1 pop hit for Amii Stewart in 1979		
12/08/84+	43	13	23 Touchy Situation		MCA 52500
3/23/85	51	10	24 Modern Day Marriages		MCA 52547
7/27/85	78	4	25 Fightin' Fire With Fire		MCA 52628
12/14/85+	48	9	26 Old Blue Yodeler..................................		MCA 52701
			tribute to Jimmie Rodgers (the Father of Country Music)		
6/28/86	63	7	27 Rockin' In The Parkin' Lot........................		MCA 52851
10/31/87	69	5	28 If Love Ever Made A Fool.........................		SOA 001
1/23/88	58	6	29 Unattended Fire....................................		SOA 002
12/24/88+	73	6	30 Starting All Over Again		SOA 003
			BAILLIE & THE BOYS		
			East Coast trio of songwriters, session vocalists: Kathy Baillie, Michael Bonagura (husband & wife), & Alan LeBoeuf. LeBoeuf starred in Broadway show "Beatlemania". Trio became duo when LeBoeuf left in early 1989.		
4/18/87	9	21	1 Oh Heart		RCA 5130
8/08/87	18	16	2 He's Letting Go......................................		RCA 5227
12/19/87+	9	18	3 Wilder Days		RCA 5327
10/01/88+	5	27	4 Long Shot		RCA 8631
			ADAM BAKER		
			Born in 1965 in Oklahoma City; raised in Edmond, Oklahoma.		
3/09/85	97	3	1 I Can See Him In Her Eyes		Signature 2484
2/08/86	48	10	2 In Love With Her....................................		Avista 8610
10/18/86	46	9	3 Weren't You Listening		Avista 8602
2/07/87	54	7	4 You've Got A Right.................................		Avista 8703
10/31/87	63	4	5 Standing Invitation		Avista 8704
			BUTCH BAKER		
			Born in Sweetwater, Tennessee in 1960. Attended the University of Tennessee, Knoxville, at age 16. Moved to Nashville in 1979. In the film "Country Gold".		
8/04/84	80	3	1 Burn Georgia Burn (There's A Fire In Your Soul).		Mercury 880020
10/27/84	56	7	2 Thinking 'Bout Leaving		Mercury 880256
8/09/86	41	14	3 That's What Her Memory Is For		Mercury 884857
11/15/86	53	9	4 Your Loving Side		Mercury 888133

DEBUT DATE	PEAK POS	WKS CHR	ARTIST — Record Title	POP POS	Label & Number
			BUTCH BAKER — Continued		
5/16/87	**51**	10	5 Don't It Make You Wanta Go Home..................		Mercury 888543
			#41 pop hit in 1969 for Joe South		
11/28/87	**60**	10	6 I'll Fall In Love Again		Mercury 888926
7/02/88	**69**	5	7 Party People..		Mercury 870486
			CARROLL BAKER		
			Born in Bridgewater, Nova Scotia. First recorded for Gaiety in 1970. Voted Top Female Country Singer in Canada in 1975; own CBC-TV show, "Sounds Good Country".		
7/04/81	**82**	3	1 Mama What Does Cheatin' Mean		Excelsior 1013
7/06/85	**95**	1	2 It Always Hurts Like The First Time.................		Tembo 8520
			GEORGE BAKER SELECTION		
			Dutch pop group led by Johannes (George Baker) Bouwens (b: 12/9/44).		
1/10/76	**33**	15	1 Paloma Blanca	*26*	Warner 8115
			DAVID BALL		
			Singer/songwriter from Rock Hill, South Carolina.		
5/07/88	**46**	10	1 Steppin' Out..		RCA 6899
8/20/88	**55**	7	2 You Go, You're Gone		RCA 8636
			MARCIA BALL		
			Born Marcia Mouton in Orange, Texas in 1950. Worked as "Freida" with Austin, Texas group, Freida & The Firedogs.		
11/18/78	**91**	2	1 I'm A Fool To Care		Capitol 4633
			#24 pop hit for Joe Barry in 1961		
			MICHAEL BALLEW		
11/07/81	**67**	6	1 Your Daddy Don't Live In Heaven (He's In Houston)		Liberty 1437
2/13/82	**71**	5	2 Pretending Fool		Liberty 1447
			THE BAMA BAND		
			Backing group for Hank Williams, Jr. Consisted of Lamar Morris (lead vocals, guitar), Wayne "Animal" Turner (vocals, guitar), Jerry McKinney, Jr. (saxophone), Eddie "Cowboy" Long and Vernon Derrick (pedal steel, fiddle), Paul Eugene "Dixie" Hatfield (keyboards), Ray Barrickman (bass) and Bill Marshall (drums). Billy Earhart (co-founder/leader of the Amazing Rhythm Aces) replaced Hatfield in 1986.		
12/18/82+	**54**	9	1 Dallas		Oasis 1
5/07/83	**56**	9	2 Tijuana Sunrise		Soundwaves 4707
			first released on Oasis 2		
7/20/85	**60**	8	3 What Used To Be Crazy		Compleat 144
3/29/86	**70**	4	4 I've Changed My Mind		Compleat 152
1/31/87	**64**	7	5 Suddenly Single		Compleat 163
8/27/88	**71**	5	6 Southern Accent		Mercury 870603
12/24/88+	**69**	6	7 Real Old-Fashioned Broken Heart		Mercury 872150
			BANDANA		
			Formed in Nashville in 1981 by lead vocalist Lonnie Wilson and bassist Jerry Fox. Originally included Tim Menzies (guitar), Joe Van Dyke (keyboards) and Jerry Ray Johnston (drums). In 1986 group consisted of Wilson, Fox, Michael Black and Billy Kemp (guitars) and Bob Mummert (drums).		
1/09/82	**37**	12	1 Guilty Eyes		Warner 49872
5/01/82	**61**	7	2 Cheatin' State Of Mind		Warner 50045
8/21/82	**17**	18	3 The Killin' Kind		Warner 29936
12/11/82+	**29**	15	4 I Can't Get Over You (Getting Over Me).............		Warner 29831
9/03/83	**18**	18	5 Outside Lookin' In......................................		Warner 29524
4/14/84	**26**	13	6 Better Our Hearts Should Bend (Than Break)		Warner 29315
8/18/84	**52**	12	7 All I Wanna Do (Is Make Love To You)		Warner 29226
5/04/85	**46**	13	8 It's Just Another Heartache...........................		Warner 29029
9/14/85	**37**	12	9 Lovin' Up A Storm		Warner 28939
5/17/86	**54**	9	10 Touch Me		Warner 28721
			THE BANDIT BAND		
			5-man band from Lexington, Kentucky.		
4/04/87	**73**	4	1 Do You Wanna Fall In Love...........................		Pegasus 108
			CHARLIE BANDY		
			Born in 1954 in Grundy, Virginia. Arrested for selling cocaine in March of 1985.		
7/28/84	**95**	2	1 Tenamock Georgia		RCI 2386

DEBUT DATE	PEAK POS	WKS CHR		ARTIST — Record Title	POP POS	Label & Number
				MOE BANDY ★★49★★		
				Born Marion Bandy on 2/12/44 in Meridian, Mississippi; raised in San Antonio. Played with father's band, the Mission City Playboys, in San Antonio; also worked as a rodeo rider. Own TV show with The Mavericks in the early 70s; went solo in 1973.		
3/30/74	17	15	1	I Just Started Hatin' Cheatin' Songs Today........		GRC 2006
				originally issued on Footprint 1006		
8/03/74	24	11	2	Honky Tonk Amnesia		GRC 2024
11/23/74+	7	14	3	**It Was Always So Easy (To Find An Unhappy Woman)**		GRC 2036
3/22/75	13	11	4	Don't Anyone Make Love At Home Anymore......		GRC 2055
6/28/75	7	16	5	**Bandy The Rodeo Clown**		GRC 2070
12/20/75+	2²	15	6	**Hank Williams, You Wrote My Life**		Columbia 10265
4/17/76	27	10	7	The Biggest Airport In The World....................		Columbia 10313
7/04/76	11	14	8	Here I Am Drunk Again............................		Columbia 10361
10/30/76+	11	15	9	She Took More Than Her Share		Columbia 10428
3/05/77	9	14	10	**I'm Sorry For You, My Friend**		Columbia 10487
				written in 1952 by Hank Williams		
6/18/77	13	12	11	Cowboys Ain't Supposed To Cry		Columbia 10558
10/08/77	11	14	12	She Just Loved The Cheatin' Out Of Me		Columbia 10619
1/28/78	13	14	13	Soft Lights And Hard Country Music...............		Columbia 10671
5/20/78	11	14	14	That's What Makes The Juke Box Play		Columbia 10735
9/16/78	7	13	15	**Two Lonely People**		Columbia 10820
1/27/79	2²	15	16	**It's A Cheating Situation**		Columbia 10889
				backing vocal: Janie Fricke		
6/16/79	9	14	17	**Barstool Mountain**		Columbia 10974
10/06/79	1¹	14	18	I Cheated Me Right Out Of You		Columbia 11090
2/02/80	13	12	19	One Of A Kind		Columbia 11184
4/26/80	22	12	20	The Champ		Columbia 11255
8/02/80	10	15	21	**Yesterday Once More**		Columbia 11305
11/29/80+	10	14	22	**Following The Feeling**		Columbia 11395
				MOE BANDY featuring JUDY BAILEY		
4/18/81	15	14	23	My Woman Loves The Devil Out Of Me		Columbia 02039
10/17/81+	10	17	24	Rodeo Romeo...................................		Columbia 02532
2/27/82	21	16	25	Someday Soon		Columbia 02735
6/19/82	4	18	26	**She's Not Really Cheatin' (She's Just Gettin' Even)**		Columbia 02966
10/23/82+	12	19	27	Only If There Is Another You		Columbia 03309
3/05/83	19	15	28	I Still Love You In The Same Ol' Way...............		Columbia 03625
6/25/83	10	18	29	**Let's Get Over Them Together**		Columbia 03970
				MOE BANDY featuring BECKY HOBBS		
11/05/83	34	16	30	You're Gonna Lose Her Like That		Columbia 04204
2/18/84	31	13	31	It Took A Lot Of Drinkin' (To Get That Woman Over Me)..		Columbia 04353
8/04/84	12	22	32	Woman Your Love..		Columbia 04466
8/10/85	45	14	33	Barroom Roses		Columbia 05438
11/15/86	42	14	34	One Man Band		MCA/Curb 52950
2/28/87	6	27	35	**Till I'm Too Old To Die Young**......................		MCA/Curb 53033
8/01/87	11	27	36	You Haven't Heard The Last Of Me..................		MCA/Curb 53132
1/30/88	8	21	37	**Americana**		Curb 10504
6/25/88	47	10	38	Ashes In The Wind		Curb 10510
9/10/88	21	19	39	I Just Can't Say No To You		Curb 10513
				MOE BANDY & JOE STAMPLEY:		
7/14/79	1¹	16	40	**Just Good Ol' Boys**		Columbia 11027
11/17/79+	7	14	41	**Holding The Bag**..................................		Columbia 11147
4/12/80	11	15	42	Tell Ole I Ain't Here, He Better Get On Home		Columbia 11244
3/14/81	10	15	43	**Hey Joe (Hey Moe)**..................................		Columbia 60508
8/01/81	12	14	44	Honky Tonk Queen...............................		Columbia 02198
6/02/84	8	16	45	**Where's The Dress**.................................. [N]		Columbia 04477
				parody about pop singer Boy George		
10/13/84	36	10	46	The Boy's Night Out		Columbia 04601
1/26/85	48	10	47	Daddy's Honky Tonk		Columbia 04756
4/20/85	58	8	48	Still On A Roll		Columbia 04843

DEBUT DATE	PEAK POS	WKS CHR	ARTIST — Record Title	POP POS	Label & Number
			R.C. BANNON		
			Born Dan Shipley on 5/2/45 in Dallas. Worked with rock and soul bands and as a disc jockey in Seattle. Toured with Marty Robbins in 1973. Moved to Nashville in 1976, worked as a staff writer for Warner Records. Married Louise Mandrell in February of 1976. Music director for the Barbara Mandrell TV show.		
7/30/77	99	1	1 Southbound		Columbia 10570
10/01/77	90	4	2 Rainbows And Horseshoes		Columbia 10612
12/24/77+	33	12	3 It Doesn't Matter Anymore...........................		Columbia 10655
			written by Paul Anka; #13 pop hit for Buddy Holly in 1959		
4/22/78	64	7	4 (The Truth Is) We're Livin' A Lie.....................		Columbia 10714
11/11/78	64	5	5 Somebody's Gonna Do It Tonight		Columbia 10847
9/22/79	26	11	6 Winners And Losers		Columbia 11081
3/01/80	65	5	7 Lovely Lonely Lady		Columbia 11210
5/24/80	61	7	8 If You're Serious About Cheatin'....................		Columbia 11267
9/13/80	36	10	9 Never Be Anyone Else................................		Columbia 11346
			#6 pop hit for Ricky Nelson in 1959		
1/23/82	46	11	10 Til Something Better Comes Along		RCA 13029
			LOUISE MANDRELL & R.C. BANNON:		
3/10/79	46	8	11 I Thought You'd Never Ask		Epic 50668
6/02/79	13	12	12 Reunited		Epic 50717
			#1 pop hit for Peaches & Herb in 1979		
11/17/79	48	8	13 We Love Each Other		Epic 50789
11/28/81+	35	11	14 Where There's Smoke There's Fire		RCA 12359
6/05/82	56	7	15 Our Wedding Band/		
		7	16 Just Married		RCA 13095
12/11/82+	35	7	17 Christmas Is Just A Song For Us This Year.... [X]		RCA 13358
			flip side of Alabama's Christmas single		
			AVA BARBER		
			Born on 6/28/54 in Knoxville. Singing professionally since age 10. Regular on the Lawrence Welk TV series from 1974-82. Worked on the Grand Ole Opry.		
2/12/77	70	8	1 Waitin' At The End Of Your Run		Ranwood 1071
6/18/77	92	2	2 Your Love Is My Refuge..............................		Ranwood 1077
8/13/77	69	8	3 Don't Take My Sunshine Away		Ranwood 1080
2/04/78	14	14	4 Bucket To The South		Ranwood 1083
6/17/78	44	7	5 You're Gonna Love Love		Ranwood 1085
10/28/78	75	6	6 Healin'		Ranwood 1087
2/28/81	70	5	7 I Think I Could Love You Better Than She Did ...		Oak 1029
			DEBRA BARBER		
			Born on 11/3/53 in Tupelo, Mississippi. Has unique baritone voice.		
3/22/75	98	1	1 You Can't Follow Where He's Been/		
3/29/75	97	1	2 Help Yourself To Me		RCA 10190
			GLENN BARBER		
			Born on 2/2/35 in Hollis, Oklahoma. Raised in Pasadena, Texas.		
1/25/64	48	2	1 How Can I Forget You		Sims 148
8/22/64	42	7	2 If Anyone Can Show Cause/		
8/29/64	27	9	3 Stronger Than Dirt....................................		Starday 676
11/09/68	41	8	4 Don't Worry 'Bout The Mule (Just Load The Wagon)		Hickory 1517
9/20/69	24	11	5 Kissed By The Rain, Warmed By The Sun..........		Hickory 1545
1/10/70	28	11	6 She Cheats On Me		Hickory 1557
6/20/70	72	2	7 Poison Red Berries		Hickory 1568
1/16/71	75	2	8 Yes, Dear, There Is A Virginia		Hickory 1585
3/25/72	28	12	9 I'm The Man On Susie's Mind		Hickory 1626
8/05/72	23	12	10 Unexpected Goodbye		Hickory 1645
1/06/73	67	4	11 Yes Ma'm (I Found Her In A Honky Tonk)		Hickory 1653
9/08/73	61	8	12 Country Girl (I Love You Still)		Hickory 302
12/29/73+	45	11	13 Daddy Number Two		Hickory 311
4/13/74	65	7	14 You Only Live Once (In Awhile).....................		Hickory 316
11/26/77	79	6	15 (You Better Be) One Hell Of A Woman		Groovy 102
1/14/78	67	6	16 Cry, Cry Darling		Groovy 103
9/30/78	30	10	17 What's The Name Of That Song?.....................		Century 21 100
1/06/79	27	10	18 Love Songs Just For You.............................		Century 21 101

DEBUT DATE	PEAK POS	WKS CHR	ARTIST — Record Title	POP POS	Label & Number
			GLENN BARBER — Continued		
4/14/79	**76**	2	19 Everybody Wants To Disco		MMI 1029
6/23/79	**70**	4	20 Woman's Touch		MMI 1031
8/16/80	**74**	5	21 First Love Feelings		Sunbird 7551
			BOBBY BARE ★★**35**★★		
			Born Robert Joseph Bare on 4/7/35 in Ironton, Ohio. Worked with local bands in the early 50s; worked in California and Hawaii in 1953. First recorded for Capitol in 1956. Drafted in 1958; left a demo tape of "The All American Boy" with Fraternity Records. The song was released as by Bill Parsons, and became a smash pop hit (POS 2-1959). Wrote songs for the film "Teenage Millionaire" and acted in the film "A Distant Trumpet" in 1964. His daughter Cari, heard on the "Singin' In The Kitchen" LP, died of heart failure in 1976 at the age of 15. Own TV series in the mid-80s.		
9/15/62	**18**	8	1 Shame On Me	*23*	RCA 8032
7/06/63	**6**	18	2 **Detroit City**	*16*	RCA 8183
10/26/63+	**5**	16	3 **500 Miles Away From Home**......................	*10*	RCA 8238
2/08/64	**4**	17	4 **Miller's Cave**	*33*	RCA 8294
6/06/64	**47**	3	5 Have I Stayed Away Too Long	*94*	RCA 8358
11/14/64+	**3**	19	6 **Four Strong Winds**	*60*	RCA 8443
3/27/65	**30**	8	7 Times Are Gettin' Hard		RCA 8509
6/05/65	**7**	16	8 It's Alright	*122*	RCA 8571
10/02/65	**31**	6	9 Just To Satisfy You		RCA 8654
11/20/65+	**26**	12	10 Talk Me Some Sense		RCA 8699
3/12/66	**34**	6	11 In The Same Old Way	*131*	RCA 8758
6/25/66	**5**	20	12 **The Streets Of Baltimore**........................	*124*	RCA 8851
11/05/66	**38**	11	13 Homesick		RCA 8988
3/04/67	**16**	13	14 Charleston Railroad Tavern		RCA 9098
5/20/67	**14**	16	15 Come Kiss Me Love		RCA 9191
10/07/67	**15**	13	16 The Piney Wood Hills		RCA 9314
3/02/68	**15**	11	17 Find Out What's Happening.........................		RCA 9450
7/27/68	**14**	13	18 A Little Bit Later On Down The Line		RCA 9568
10/26/68	**16**	12	19 The Town That Broke My Heart		RCA 9643
3/15/69	**4**	17	20 **(Margie's At) The Lincoln Park Inn**...............		RCA 0110
8/02/69	**19**	11	21 Which One Will It Be		RCA 0202
11/15/69	**16**	12	22 God Bless America Again		RCA 0264
8/08/70	**3**	16	23 **How I Got To Memphis**		Mercury 73097
12/26/70+	**7**	17	24 **Come Sundown**	*122*	Mercury 73148
5/15/71	**8**	15	25 **Please Don't Tell Me How The Story Ends**		Mercury 73203
9/25/71	**57**	9	26 Short And Sweet		Mercury 73236
4/01/72	**13**	14	27 What Am I Gonna Do		Mercury 73279
8/26/72	**12**	14	28 Sylvia's Mother		Mercury 73317
			#5 pop hit for Dr. Hook in 1972		
1/06/73	**25**	11	29 I Hate Goodbyes....................................		RCA 0866
4/14/73	**11**	15	30 Ride Me Down Easy		RCA 0918
9/08/73	**30**	13	31 You Know Who		RCA 0063
12/22/73+	**2²**	16	32 **Daddy What If**....................................	*41*	RCA 0197
			with 5-year-old son, Bobby, Jr.		
5/04/74	**1¹**	18	33 **Marie Laveau**		RCA 0261
9/07/74	**41**	8	34 Where'd I Come From .... [N]		RCA 10037
			BOBBY BARE, JR. & MAMA (Bobby's son and wife, Jeannie)		
11/16/74+	**29**	13	35 Singin' In The Kitchen .... [N]		RCA 10096
			BOBBY BARE & THE FAMILY		
3/15/75	**23**	11	36 Back In Huntsville Again............................		RCA 10223
7/19/75	**18**	12	37 Alimony		RCA 10318
10/25/75	**29**	11	38 Cowboys And Daddys		RCA 10409
3/13/76	**13**	14	39 The Winner		RCA 10556
7/10/76	**23**	11	40 Put A Little Lovin' On Me		RCA 10718
10/09/76	**17**	11	41 Dropkick Me, Jesus		RCA 10790
3/12/77	**21**	14	42 Look Who I'm Cheating On Tonight/		
		14	43 If You Think I'm Crazy Now (You Should Have Seen Me When I Was A Kid)....................		RCA 10902
7/30/77	**85**	3	44 Red-Neck Hippie Romance		RCA 11037
4/15/78	**29**	11	45 Too Many Nights Alone		Columbia 10690
10/14/78	**11**	11	46 Sleep Tight, Good Night Man		Columbia 10831

DEBUT DATE	PEAK POS	WKS CHR	ARTIST — Record Title	POP POS	Label & Number
			BOBBY BARE — Continued		
1/27/79	**23**	11	47 Healin'..		Columbia 10891
6/09/79	**42**	8	48 Till I Gain Control Again		Columbia 10998
1/05/80	**11**	14	49 Numbers...		Columbia 11170
4/26/80	**31**	12	50 Tequila Sheila		Columbia 11259
10/04/80	**41**	8	51 Food Blues...		Columbia 11365
12/20/80+	**19**	12	52 Willie Jones..		Columbia 11408
			backing vocal and fiddle: Charlie Daniels		
4/25/81	**28**	13	53 Learning To Live Again................................		Columbia 02038
8/08/81	**28**	11	54 Take Me As I Am (Or Let Me Go)		Columbia 02414
11/07/81	**35**	11	55 Dropping Out Of Sight		Columbia 02577
1/30/82	**18**	16	56 New Cut Road...		Columbia 02690
5/29/82	**31**	11	57 If You Ain't Got Nothin' (You Ain't Got Nothin' To Lose)...		Columbia 02895
8/21/82	**37**	11	58 (I'm Not) A Candle In The Wind......................		Columbia 03149
11/20/82	**83**	3	59 Praise The Lord And Send Me The Money.........		Columbia 03334
5/28/83	**29**	15	60 The Jogger..		Columbia 03809
10/01/83	**69**	7	61 Diet Song..		Columbia 04092
8/10/85	**53**	9	62 When I Get Home		EMI America 8279
11/23/85	**76**	4	63 Reno And Me...		EMI America 8296
8/02/86	**67**	6	64 Real Good...		EMI America 8333
			BOBBY BARE DUOS with:		
			JEANNIE BARE:		
1/08/77	**30**	9	65 Vegas..		RCA 10852
			ROSANNE CASH:		
9/08/79	**17**	12	66 No Memories Hangin' Round		Columbia 11045
			LACY J. DALTON:		
3/12/83	**30**	14	67 It's A Dirty Job...		Columbia 03628
			SKEETER DAVIS:		
3/13/65	**11**	12	68 A Dear John Letter	*114*	RCA 8496
1/24/70	**22**	7	69 Your Husband, My Wife................................		RCA 9789
			NORMA JEAN, LIZ ANDERSON:		
10/15/66	**5**	17	70 **The Game Of Triangles**		RCA 8963

BAREFOOT JERRY - see CHARLIE McCOY

JACK BARLOW
Born Jack Butcher in Muscatine, Iowa. Worked as a deejay on WQUA-Moline; WIRE-Indianapolis. Staff writer for Tree Music. Also see Zoot Fenster.

DEBUT DATE	PEAK POS	WKS CHR	ARTIST — Record Title	POP POS	Label & Number
10/26/68	**40**	4	1 Baby, Ain't That Love		Dot 17139
5/03/69	**55**	6	2 Birmingham Blues..		Dot 17212
12/13/69+	**68**	5	3 Nobody Wants To Hear It Like It Is..................		Dot 17317
1/23/71	**59**	4	4 Dayton, Ohio		Dot 17366
11/06/71+	**26**	13	5 Catch The Wind		Dot 17396
5/13/72	**58**	7	6 They Call The Wind Maria		Dot 17414
			from the film "Paint Your Wagon"		
8/04/73	**55**	9	7 Oh Woman		Dot 17468

RANDY BARLOW ★★192★★
Singer from Detroit. Worked as emcee with Dick Clark's Caravan Of Stars. Settled in Los Angeles in 1965, worked local clubs.

DEBUT DATE	PEAK POS	WKS CHR	ARTIST — Record Title	POP POS	Label & Number
7/20/74	**80**	6	1 Throw Away The Pages		Capitol 3883
2/14/76	**74**	6	2 Johnny Orphan...		Gazelle 153
5/15/76	**53**	9	3 Goodnight My Love.......................................		Gazelle 217
			there have been 5 pop hit versions from 1957-69		
8/21/76	**46**	9	4 Lonely Eyes		Gazelle 280
11/27/76+	**18**	14	5 Twenty-Four Hours From Tulsa		Gazelle 330
			#10 pop hit for Gene Pitney in 1963		
3/26/77	**26**	11	6 Kentucky Woman..		Gazelle 381
			#22 pop hit for Neil Diamond in 1967		
6/25/77	**31**	9	7 California Lady		Gazelle 413
10/01/77	**48**	8	8 Walk Away With Me		Gazelle 427
4/01/78	**10**	17	9 **Slow And Easy**		Republic 017
8/12/78	**10**	13	10 **No Sleep Tonight**		Republic 024
12/09/78+	**10**	14	11 **Fall In Love With Me Tonight**		Republic 034

DEBUT DATE	PEAK POS	WKS CHR	ARTIST — Record Title	POP POS	Label & Number
			RANDY BARLOW — Continued		
4/07/79	**10**	12	12 **Sweet Melinda**		Republic 039
8/11/79	**25**	10	13 Another Easy Lovin' Night		Republic 044
11/03/79+	**13**	14	14 Lay Back In The Arms Of Someone		Republic 049
10/25/80	**46**	8	15 Willow Run		Paid 110
1/24/81	**25**	10	16 Dixie Man		Paid 116
4/18/81	**13**	13	17 Love Dies Hard		Paid 133
9/12/81	**32**	10	18 Try Me		Paid 144
12/19/81+	**30**	13	19 Love Was Born		Jamex 002
10/29/83	**67**	6	20 Don't Leave Me Lonely Loving You		Gazelle 001
			BENNY BARNES		
			Born Ben M. Barnes, Jr. in Beaumont, Texas.		
9/29/56	**2**[1]	17	1 **Poor Man's Riches**		Starday 262
			Juke Box #2 / Jockey #8 / Best Seller #15		
6/12/61	**22**	4	2 Yearning		Mercury 71806
7/30/77	**94**	2	3 I've Got Some Gettin' Over You To Do		Playboy 5808
			KATHY BARNES		
			Born in Henderson, Kentucky; singing since age 7. Sang in duo with brother Larry, and later worked with Gene Autry. Went solo in 1975. In 1978, she had 2 R&B-styled records that made the Soul Singles charts.		
4/26/75	**64**	9	1 I'm Available (For You To Hold Me Tight)		MGM 14797
			#9 pop hit for Margie Rayburn in 1957		
8/30/75	**94**	3	2 Shhh		MGM 14822
12/06/75	**92**	5	3 Be Honest With Me		MGM 14836
			written in 1946 by Gene Autry (also #9 below)		
5/15/76	**73**	6	4 Sleeping With A Memory		Republic 223
9/11/76	**39**	11	5 Someday Soon		Republic 293
1/08/77	**37**	9	6 Good 'N' Country		Republic 338
3/26/77	**92**	3	7 If We Can't Do It Right		Republic 369
			KATHY & LARRY BARNES		
4/02/77	**50**	8	8 Catch The Wind		Republic 376
			#23 pop hit for Donovan in 1965		
7/09/77	**88**	3	9 Tweedle-O-Twill		Republic 389
10/08/77	**62**	7	10 The Sun In Dixie		Republic 005
12/24/77+	**81**	5	11 Something's Burning		Republic 012
			#11 pop hit for Kenny Rogers & The First Edition in 1970		
			MAX D. BARNES		
			Born on 7/24/36 in Hardscratch, Iowa. Began playing guitar at age 11. Moved to Nashville in 1971. Songwriter of hits for many top country artists.		
10/22/77	**97**	1	1 Allegheny Lady		Polydor 14419
1/05/80	**88**	5	2 Dear Mr. President [S]		Ovation 1139
			backing song: "Battle Hymn Of The Republic"		
3/08/80	**79**	4	3 Mean Woman Blues		Ovation 1142
6/28/80	**68**	6	4 Cowboys Are Common As Sin		Ovation 1149
11/22/80	**88**	3	5 Heaven On A Freight Train		Ovation 1158
3/07/81	**84**	2	6 Don't Ever Leave Me Again		Ovation 1164
			BOBBY BARNETT		
			Born on 2/15/36 in Cushing, Oklahoma.		
10/10/60	**24**	1	1 This Old Heart		Razorback 306
2/22/64	**47**	2	2 Worst Of Luck		Sims 159
5/20/67	**52**	12	3 Down, Down, Came My World		K-Ark 741
10/14/67	**74**	2	4 The Losing Kind		K-Ark 766
8/10/68	**14**	14	5 Love Me, Love Me		Columbia 44589
1/04/69	**44**	10	6 Your Sweet Love Lifted Me		Columbia 44716
6/21/69	**59**	8	7 Drink Canada Dry		Columbia 44861
3/18/78	**97**	3	8 Burn Atlanta Down		Cin Kay 128
			LESLEE BARNHILL		
2/25/78	**92**	2	1 Let's Call It A Day (And Get On With The Night)		Republic 014
5/19/79	**62**	6	2 Bad Day For A Breakup		Republic 040

DEBUT DATE	PEAK POS	WKS CHR	ARTIST — Record Title	POP POS	Label & Number
			SAM D. BASS Born in Oklahoma. Joined the backing band for Tommy Duncan, Tex Ritter, T. Texas Tyler and Moon Mullican. Later, lead vocalist for Leon McAuliffe.		
7/05/80	92	2	1 How Could I Do This To Me		3J 1003
			KATHY BAUER Born in League City, Texas. Performing in Gilley's Club when discovered by Sylvia.		
4/23/83	82	4	1 Hold Me Till The Last Waltz Is Over		NSD 164
			PHIL BAUGH Born in Olivehurst, California. Session guitarist; moved to Nashville in 1975. Worked in the Nashville Superpickers. Former owner of Soundwaves Records.		
6/12/65	16	15	1 Country Guitar .... [N]		Longhorn 559
11/06/65	27	7	2 One Man Band .... [N]		Longhorn 563
			BAXTER, BAXTER & BAXTER Brothers Rick, Mark and Duncan Baxter.		
2/28/81	76	4	1 Take Me Back To The Country		Sun 1160
			JIM BEAN		
9/17/88	96	1	1 Lay, Lady Lay .... #7 pop hit for Bob Dylan in 1969		Hub 47
			BEAR CREEK BAND		
10/22/88	99	1	1 Falling In Love Right And Left........................		Bear Creek 103
			THE BEARDS Brothers Randy (guitar, vocals) and Ronnie (drums, vocals) Beard from Indiana.		
5/14/88	75	4	1 Stone Cold Love...		Beardo 001
11/26/88	71	6	2 Fearless Heart		Beardo 002
			CLYDE BEAVERS Born on 6/8/32 in Tennega, Georgia. Worked as a disc jockey in Atlanta during the mid-50s. With the Grand Ole Opry from 1961.		
10/24/60	13	15	1 Here I Am Drunk Again.................................		Decca 31173
3/16/63	27	2	2 Still Loving You		Tempwood 1039
8/03/63	21	1	3 Sukiyaki (I Look Up When I Walk) .... #1 pop hit for Kyu Sakamoto in 1963		Tempwood 1044
3/12/66	47	3	4 That's You...		Hickory 1346
			BOB BECKHAM Singer from Stratford, Oklahoma. Moved to Nashville in 1959. Formed Combine Music Company with Fred Foster in 1966.		
9/02/67	73	2	1 Cherokee Strip		Monument 1018
			CHARLIE BECKHAM		
6/18/88	84	3	1 Think I'll Go Home		Oak 1048
			BEE GEES Pop trio of brothers from Manchester, England: Barry (b: 9/1/47) and twins Robin and Maurice Gibb (b: 12/22/49). First performed in December of 1955.		
11/25/78+	39	12	1 Rest Your Love On Me.................................... flip side of their #1 pop hit "Too Much Heaven"		RSO 913
			KATHY BEE		
10/08/88	100	1	1 Let's Go Party		Lilac 1213
			MOLLY BEE Born Molly Beachboard on 8/18/39 in Oklahoma City. As a child, appeared on Rex Allen radio shows in Tucson. Moved to Los Angeles in 1950 and appeared on Cliffie Stone's "Hometown Jamboree" TV shows. Also appeared on Pinky Lee, Tennessee Ernie Ford shows. Worked in musicals "The Boy Friend", "Paint Your Wagon" and "Finian's Rainbow". In films "The Chartreuse Caboose" and "The Young Swingers".		
9/21/74	55	8	1 She Kept On Talkin'		Granite 509
2/22/75	83	7	2 Right Or Left On Oak Street		Granite 515
			CARL BELEW Born on 3/21/31 in Salina, Oklahoma. Worked on Louisiana Hayride in the early 50s. Wrote hits "Lonely Street" for Andy Williams, "Stop The World" for Johnnie And Jack, and "What's He Doing In My World" for Eddy Arnold.		
4/06/59	9	20	1 **Am I That Easy To Forget** .... #25 pop hit for Debbie Reynolds in 1960		Decca 30842
6/13/60	19	15	2 Too Much To Lose		Decca 31086
9/29/62	8	12	3 **Hello Out There**................................... *120*		RCA 8058

DEBUT DATE	PEAK POS	WKS CHR	ARTIST — Record Title	POP POS	Label & Number
			CARL BELEW — Continued		
9/26/64	**23**	13	4 In The Middle Of A Memory..........................		RCA 8406
8/07/65	**12**	18	5 Crystal Chandelier		RCA 8633
2/05/66	**43**	4	6 Boston Jail		RCA 8744
11/26/66	**64**	3	7 Walking Shadow, Talking Memory..................		RCA 8996
9/09/67	**65**	2	8 Girl Crazy		RCA 9272
3/16/68	**68**	2	9 Mary's Little Lamb		RCA 9446
4/24/71	**51**	10	10 All I Need Is You		Decca 32802
			CARL BELEW & BETTY JEAN ROBINSON		
9/14/74	**56**	11	11 Welcome Back To My World..........................		MCA 40276
			DELIA BELL		
			Born in Bonham, Texas; raised in Hugo, Oklahoma. Discovered by Emmylou Harris.		
5/07/83	**45**	11	1 Flame In My Heart...............................		Warner 29653
8/13/83	**82**	3	2 Coyote Song..................................		Warner 29550
			JAMES BELL		
5/04/68	**51**	7	1 He Ain't Country.........................		Bell 710
			TOMMY BELL		
			Born in 1950 in Lansing, Michigan. Started as a drummer. Moved to Las Vegas in 1977; with comic David Frye. Discovered by Tommy DeVito, formerly with The Four Seasons.		
10/02/82	**83**	3	1 Georgiana		Gold Sound 8013
9/24/83	**97**	2	2 Honky Tonk Crazy		Gold Sound 8016
			VIVIAN BELL		
3/19/77	**71**	7	1 The Angel In Your Arms............................		GRT 118
			#6 pop hit for Hot in 1977		
			THE BELLAMY BROTHERS ★★69★★		
			Duo from Darby, Florida: brothers Howard (b: 2/2/46; guitar) and David Bellamy (b: 9/16/50; guitar, keyboards). Made their professional debut in 1958. David played with the Accidents and wrote "Spiders And Snakes" for Jim Stafford. Both worked in the band Jericho from 1968-71.		
3/13/76	**21**	12	1 Let Your Love Flow	1	Warner 8169
2/18/78	**86**	4	2 Bird Dog		Warner 8521
			#1 pop hit for The Everly Brothers in 1958		
4/29/78	**19**	12	3 Slippin' Away		Warner 8558
9/16/78	**99**	2	4 Wild Honey		Warner 8627
11/18/78+	**16**	14	5 Lovin' On..................................		Warner 8692
3/24/79	**1³**	15	6 **If I Said You Have A Beautiful Body Would You Hold It Against Me**........................	39	Warner 8790
8/18/79	**5**	13	7 **You Ain't Just Whistlin' Dixie**		Warner 49032
2/02/80	**1¹**	14	8 **Sugar Daddy**		Warner 49160
5/24/80	**1¹**	17	9 **Dancin' Cowboys**		Warner 49241
10/11/80	**3**	15	10 **Lovers Live Longer**		Warner 49573
1/17/81	**1¹**	13	11 **Do You Love As Good As You Look**		Warner 49639
6/06/81	**12**	13	12 They Could Put Me In Jail		Warner 49729
10/10/81	**7**	17	13 **You're My Favorite Star**		Warner 49815
12/19/81+	**62**	7	14 It's So Close To Christmas (And I'm So Far From Home).................................... [X]		Warner 49875
3/27/82	**1¹**	18	15 **For All The Wrong Reasons**		Elektra 47431
7/17/82	**21**	13	16 Get Into Reggae Cowboy		Elektra 69999
9/25/82	**1¹**	18	17 **Redneck Girl**		Warner 29923
1/15/83	**1¹**	18	18 **When I'm Away From You**........................		Elektra 69850
5/21/83	**4**	17	19 **I Love Her Mind**		Warner 29645
9/10/83	**15**	15	20 Strong Weakness		Warner 29514
6/02/84	**5**	18	21 **Forget About Me**		Curb 52380
9/22/84	**6**	21	22 **World's Greatest Lover**		Curb 52446
1/19/85	**1¹**	20	23 **I Need More Of You**		Curb 52518
5/04/85	**2²**	20	24 **Old Hippie**		Curb 52579
9/14/85	**2¹**	22	25 **Lie To You For Your Love**......................		Curb 52668
2/08/86	**2¹**	20	26 **Feelin' The Feelin'**...........................		Curb 52747
9/27/86	**1¹**	20	27 **Too Much Is Not Enough**......................		Curb 52917
			THE BELLAMY BROTHERS with THE FORESTER SISTERS		
1/24/87	**1¹**	22	28 **Kids Of The Baby Boom**		Curb 53018

DEBUT DATE	PEAK POS	WKS CHR	ARTIST — Record Title	POP POS	Label & Number
			THE BELLAMY BROTHERS — Continued		
5/09/87	**31**	10	29 Country Rap..		Curb 52834
8/15/87	**3**	24	30 **Crazy From The Heart**		MCA 53154
1/09/88	**5**	21	31 **Santa Fe**..		MCA/Curb 53222
5/07/88	**6**	21	32 **I'll Give You All My Love Tonight**.................		MCA/Curb 53310
9/03/88	**9**	19	33 **Rebels Without A Clue**		MCA/Curb 53399
			ERNIE BENEDICT		
10/08/49	**15**	1	1 Over Three Hills..		RCA 3389
			Juke Box #15		
			BARBI BENTON		
			Ex-Playboy model from Sacramento, California.		
3/15/75	**5**	14	1 **Brass Buckles**		Playboy 6032
8/16/75	**61**	8	2 Movie Magazine, Stars In Her Eyes		Playboy 6043
10/18/75	**32**	9	3 Roll You Like A Wheel...............................		Playboy 6045
			MICKEY GILLEY & BARBI BENTON		
12/27/75+	**74**	5	4 The Reverend Bob......................................		Playboy 6056
			CRAIG BICKHARDT		
			Singer/songwriter; worked clubs in Philadelphia with own band, Wire And Wood. Joined Schuyler, Knobloch & Bickhardt in 1987.		
5/26/84	**86**	4	1 You Are What Love Means To Me.....................		Liberty 1518
			from the film "Tender Mercies"		
			BILLY the KID		
6/16/79	**50**	7	1 What I Feel Is You......................................		Cyclone 103
			VICKI BIRD		
			From Bird's Hollow, West Virginia; first recorded for Avco.		
10/24/87	**64**	6	1 I've Got Ways Of Making You Talk		16th Ave. 70405
4/23/88	**61**	6	2 A Little Bit Of Lovin' (Goes A Long Long Way) ...		16th Ave. 70413
			BOB BISHOP		
			Born Bishop M. Sykes on 8/6/28. Guitarist with Marty Robbins. Recorded as Johnny Freedom on Robbins label. Currently with Hank Snow's Rainbow Ranch Boys.		
11/09/68	**42**	6	1 Roses To Reno...		ABC 11132
			JONI BISHOP		
8/01/87	**71**	4	1 Heart Out Of Control....................................		Columbia 07225
			TERRI BISHOP		
7/22/78	**97**	3	1 One More Kiss		United Art. 1194
			BILL BLACK'S COMBO		
			Bill was born on 9/17/26 in Memphis; died of a brain tumor on 10/21/65. Bass guitarist. Backed Elvis Presley (with Scotty Moore, guitar; D.J. Fontana, drums) on most of his early records. Formed own band in 1959.		
4/05/75	**29**	13	1 Boilin' Cabbage.. [I]		Hi 2283
9/20/75	**84**	5	2 Back Up And Push .... [I]		Hi 2291
1/24/76	**57**	8	3 Fire On The Bayou .... [I]		Hi 2301
7/24/76	**100**	2	4 Jump Back Joe Joe.................................... [I]		Hi 2311
11/20/76	**89**	7	5 Redneck Rock .... [I]		Hi 2317
4/08/78	**96**	4	6 Cashin' In.. [I]		Hi 78508
			JEANNE BLACK		
			Born Gloria Jeanne Black on 10/25/37 in Pomona, California.		
5/02/60	**6**	12	1 **He'll Have To Stay**.......................................	*4*	Capitol 4368
			answer song to "He'll Have To Go" by Jim Reeves		
			KARON BLACKWELL		
			Spells her name "Karon" (pronounced "Kay'Ron"). Born in Ellisville, Mississippi. On local radio at age 9. Moved to Chicago at age 18, made 7-Up commercials.		
1/22/77	**93**	3	1 Blue Skies And Roses		Blackland 254
			R.W. BLACKWOOD		
			Born in Memphis. Member of the Blackwood Boys gospel group.		
8/07/76	**32**	10	1 Sunday Afternoon Boatride In The Park On The Lake..		Capitol 4302
11/13/76	**91**	4	2 Memory Go Round.....................................		Capitol 4346
			above 2: with The Blackwood Singers		

DEBUT DATE	PEAK POS	WKS CHR	ARTIST — Record Title	POP POS	Label & Number
			R.W. BLACKWOOD — Continued		
10/28/78	57	6	3 Dolly..		Scorpion 0561
			a tribute to Dolly Parton		
			KENNY BLAIR		
7/02/88	84	2	1 Lost In Austin		Awesome 119
			CLAY BLAKER		
			San Antonio-based singer.		
5/16/87	91	2	1 South Of The Border...		Texas 6153
2/27/88	75	5	2 A Honky Tonk Heart..		Rain F. 120187
			ARTHUR BLANCH		
			Vocalist from Australia; father of Jewel Blanch.		
9/16/78	73	4	1 The Little Man's Got The Biggest Smile In Town .		MC 5015
9/01/79	82	7	2 Maybe I'll Cry Over You..		Ridgetop 00479
			JEWEL BLANCH		
			Born Jewel Evelyn Blanch. Singer/actress from Australia; daughter of Arthur and Bernice Blanch. Sang in family group, The Blanches, in Australia until 1969.		
9/30/78	68	6	1 So Good...		RCA 11329
2/10/79	33	12	2 Can I See You Tonight		RCA 11464
			JACK BLANCHARD & MISTY MORGAN		
			Husband-and-wife team, both born in Buffalo. Jack, born on 5/8/42, plays saxophone and keyboards; Misty, born on 5/23/45, plays keyboards. Met and married while working in Florida.		
3/01/69	59	4	1 Big Black Bird (Spirit Of Our Love)		Wayside 1028
2/07/70	1²	19	2 **Tennessee Bird Walk** .... [N]	23	Wayside 010
6/20/70	5	13	3 **Humphrey The Camel**............................ [N]	78	Wayside 013
9/26/70	27	11	4 You've Got Your Troubles (I've Got Mine)		Wayside 015
			#7 pop hit for The Fortunes in 1965		
7/24/71	25	13	5 There Must Be More To Life (Than Growing Old)/		
7/24/71	46	13	6 Fire Hydrant #79...		Mega 0031
11/06/71+	15	14	7 Somewhere In Virginia In The Rain		Mega 0046
3/25/72	38	11	8 The Legendary Chicken Fairy...................... [N]		Mega 0063
9/30/72	60	7	9 Second Tuesday In December		Mega 0089
3/10/73	65	4	10 A Handfull Of Dimes		Mega 0101
12/01/73+	23	13	11 Just One More Song...		Epic 11058
5/11/74	53	10	12 Something On Your Mind................................		Epic 11097
9/28/74	41	12	13 Down To The End Of The Wine		Epic 50023
7/26/75	74	7	14 Because We Love		Epic 50122
12/27/75+	68	6	15 I'm High On You		Epic 50181
			LOY BLANTON		
			Male singer born in Victoria, Texas.		
6/15/85	77	4	1 California Sleeping		Soundwaves 4750
9/07/85	63	11	2 Sailing Home To Me		Soundwaves 4760
			TIM BLIXSETH with KATHY WALKER		
5/04/85	91	2	1 It Can't Be Done		Compleat 141
			DOUG BLOCK		
12/22/84	73	4	1 Have Another Drink		Revolver 005
			THE BLUE BOYS		
			Jim Reeves' former backing group: Bud Logan, Leo Jackson, Jimmy Orr and Bunky Keels.		
7/15/67	63	3	1 My Cup Runneth Over		RCA 9201
			#8 pop hit in 1967 for Ed Ames (from Broadway's "I Do! I Do!")		
2/03/68	58	6	2 I'm Not Ready Yet		RCA 9418
			THE BLUE RIDGE RANGERS - see JOHN FOGERTY		
			BLUESTONE		
			Ray Pennington and Jerry McBee.		
2/09/80	84	3	1 Haven't I Loved You Somewhere Before		Dimension 1002
			BOBBY BLUE		
			Born in Los Angeles; professional singer since age 15.		
2/01/86	80	3	1 Once Upon A Time		Nite 108

DEBUT DATE	PEAK POS	WKS CHR	ARTIST — Record Title	POP POS	Label & Number
			LIZ BOARDO		
			Born on 10/22/62 in Dorchester, Massachusetts.		
2/07/87	58	6	1 There's Still Enough Of Us		Master 02
6/27/87	65	5	2 I Need To Be Loved Again............................		Master 03
			SUZY BOGGUSS		
			Born on 12/30/56 in Aledo, Illinois.		
3/14/87	68	6	1 I Don't Want To Set The World On Fire		Capitol 5669
			#1 pop hit for Horace Hiedt & His Orchestra in 1941		
8/15/87	69	6	2 Love Will Never Slip Away		Capitol 44045
8/13/88	77	2	3 I Want To Be A Cowboy's Sweetheart		Capitol 44187
			AL BOLT		
			Born Almos Bolt in 1940 in Atlanta, Texas. Began performing on radio at age 11.		
2/28/76	85	6	1 I'm In Love With My Pet Rock .... [N]		Cin Kay 102
6/12/76	92	3	2 Family Man..		Cin Kay 103
			BOBBY BOND		
			From Grand Rapids, Michigan. Played in rock bands while a teenager.		
9/30/72	66	7	1 You Don't Mess Around With Jim		Hickory 1649
			#8 pop hit for Jim Croce in 1972		
			JOHNNY BOND		
			Born Cyrus Whitfield Bond on 6/1/15 in Enville, Oklahoma. Died of a heart attack on 6/12/78 (63). Singer/songwriter/actor; worked on radio from age 19. Appeared with Jimmy Wakely in 1937 and joined Gene Autry's Melody Ranch in 1940. Appeared in many films, including "Wilson", "Gallant Bess" and "Duel In The Sun". Worked "Town Hall Party" TV shows from Compton, California. Wrote the books "Reflections" (his autobiography) and "The Tex Ritter Story". Famous for his novelty recordings about drunkeness.		
2/22/47	4	1	1 **Divorce Me C.O.D.**..............................		Columbia 37217
3/08/47	3	5	2 **So Round, So Firm, So Fully Packed**.............		Columbia 37255
8/16/47	4	3	3 **The Daughter Of Jole Blon**		Columbia 37566
6/12/48	9	6	4 **Oklahoma Waltz**		Columbia 38160
			Juke Box #9		
4/09/49	12	2	5 Till The End Of The World		Columbia 20549
			Juke Box #12		
7/23/49	11	1	6 Tennessee Saturday Night		Columbia 20545
			Juke Box #11		
4/15/50	8	2	7 **Love Song In 32 Bars**............................		Columbia 20671
			Juke Box #8		
8/04/51	7	3	8 **Sick, Sober And Sorry**............................		Columbia 20808
			Juke Box #7		
11/02/63	30	1	9 Three Sheets In The Wind............................		Starday 649
2/06/65	2⁴	21	10 **10 Little Bottles**............................ [N-R]	43	Starday 704
			originally released by Bond on Columbia in the 40s		
2/20/71	59	6	11 Here Come The Elephants............................		Starday 916
			THE BONNERS		
			Black family led by Jim Bonner and wife Edith.		
9/10/88	99	1	1 Way Beyond The Blue.................................		OL 126
			BONNIE & BUDDY - see BONNIE GUITAR		
			BONNIE LOU		
			Born Bonnie Lou Kath on 10/27/24 in Bloomington, Illinois. Worked on radio KMBC-Kansas City and WLW-Cincinnati. On Midwestern Hayride for over 20 years.		
5/16/53	7	5	1 **Seven Lonely Days**		King 1192
			Jockey #7 / Best Seller #8 / Juke Box #9 #5 pop hit for Georgia Gibbs in 1953		
10/31/53	6	9	2 **Tennessee Wig Walk**		King 1237
			Best Seller #6 / Juke Box #6		
			JAY BOOKER		
			Singer/songwriter/guitarist born in Pensacola, Florida.		
5/02/87	61	8	1 Hot Red Sweater		EMI America 8379
			DEBBY BOONE		
			Born Deborah Anne Boone on 9/22/56 in Hackensack, New Jersey. Third daughter of Pat and Shirley Boone, granddaughter of Red Foley. Worked with the Boone Family from 1969, sang with sisters in the Boones gospel quartet. Went solo in 1977. Married to Gabriel Ferrer, the son of Rosemary Clooney and Jose Ferrer.		
10/22/77	4	14	1▲**You Light Up My Life**	1	Warner 8455
			originally released on Warner 8446		

DEBUT DATE	PEAK POS	WKS CHR	ARTIST — Record Title	POP POS	Label & Number
			DEBBY BOONE — Continued		
5/20/78	22	8	2 God Knows/		
4/29/78	33	11	3 Baby, I'm Yours	74	Warner 8554
11/18/78	61	4	4 In Memory Of Your Love		Warner 8700
1/13/79	11	13	5 My Heart Has A Mind Of Its Own		Warner 8739
			#1 pop hit for Connie Francis in 1960		
5/26/79	25	10	6 Breakin' In A Brand New Broken Heart		Warner 8814
			#7 pop hit for Connie Francis in 1961		
9/01/79	41	7	7 See You In September		Warner 49042
			#3 pop hit for The Happenings in 1966		
11/10/79	48	6	8 Everybody's Somebody's Fool		Warner 49107
			#1 pop hit for Connie Francis in 1960		
2/16/80	1¹	15	9 **Are You On The Road To Lovin' Me Again**		Warner 49176
7/26/80	14	13	10 Free To Be Lonely Again		Warner 49281
11/08/80	44	10	11 Take It Like A Woman		Warner 49585
2/07/81	23	12	12 Perfect Fool		Warner 49652
6/27/81	46	7	13 It'll Be Him		Warner 49720
			LARRY BOONE		
			Singer/songwriter from Cooper City, Florida. Former substitute teacher.		
7/26/86	64	9	1 Stranger Things Have Happened		Mercury 884858
10/25/86	52	9	2 She's The Trip That I've Been On		Mercury 888044
3/21/87	48	10	3 Back In The Swing Of Things Again		Mercury 888427
6/06/87	52	8	4 I Talked A Lot About Leaving		Mercury 888598
12/19/87+	44	19	5 Roses In December		Mercury 870086
4/09/88	48	10	6 Stop Me (If You've Heard This One Before)		Mercury 870267
6/18/88	10	19	7 **Don't Give Candy To A Stranger**		Mercury 870454
11/19/88+	16	21	8 I Just Called To Say Goodbye Again		Mercury 872046
			PAT BOONE		
			Born Charles Eugene Boone on 6/1/34 in Jacksonville, Florida. Married Red Foley's daughter, Shirley, in 1954. His pop chart success during the 50s was eclipsed only by Elvis Presley.		
4/05/75	72	7	1 Indiana Girl		Melodyland 6005
9/27/75	84	6	2 I'd Do It With You		Melodyland 6018
			PAT BOONE with SHIRLEY BOONE		
7/17/76	34	10	3 Texas Woman		Hitsville 6037
10/16/76	86	4	4 Oklahoma Sunshine		Hitsville 6042
11/15/80	60	6	5 Colorado Country Morning		Warner 49596
			LARRY BOOTH		
			Bass player with Gene Watson's Farewell Party band.		
5/27/78	99	2	1 I See Love In Your Eyes		Cream 7823
			TONY BOOTH		
			Born on 2/7/43 in Tampa, Florida. Former member of Buck Owens' Buckaroos.		
3/28/70	67	3	1 Irma Jackson		MGM 14112
12/04/71+	45	12	2 Cinderella		Capitol 3214
3/25/72	15	15	3 The Key's In The Mailbox		Capitol 3269
7/08/72	18	12	4 A Whole Lot Of Somethin'		Capitol 3356
9/30/72	16	13	5 Lonesome 7-7203		Capitol 3441
1/27/73	32	10	6 When A Man Loves A Woman (The Way That I Love You)		Capitol 3515
4/28/73	41	8	7 Loving You		Capitol 3528
7/07/73	49	6	8 Old Faithful		Capitol 3639
10/06/73	47	11	9 Secret Love		Capitol 3723
			#1 pop hit for Doris Day in 1954		
12/29/73+	49	11	10 Happy Hour		Capitol 3795
4/20/74	84	6	11 Lonely Street		Capitol 3853
			#5 pop hit for Andy Williams in 1959		
8/31/74	27	13	12 Workin' At The Car Wash Blues		Capitol 3943
			#32 pop hit for Jim Croce in 1976		
12/28/74+	72	8	13 Watch Out For Lucy		Capitol 3994
5/21/77	95	2	14 Letting Go		United Art. 962

DEBUT DATE	PEAK POS	WKS CHR		ARTIST — Record Title	POP POS	Label & Number
				BOBBY BORCHERS		
				Singer/songwriter born in Cincinnati; raised in Kentucky. Currently living in Santa Barbara, California.		
3/06/76	29	10	1	Someone's With Your Wife Tonight, Mister		Playboy 6065
8/21/76	32	9	2	They Don't Make 'Em Like That Anymore		Playboy 6083
12/04/76+	12	15	3	Whispers		Playboy 6092
5/14/77	7	14	4	**Cheap Perfume And Candlelight**..................		Playboy 5803
9/03/77	18	11	5	What A Way To Go...................................		Playboy 5816
12/10/77+	18	13	6	I Promised Her A Rainbow		Playboy 5823
4/08/78	23	10	7	I Like Ladies In Long Black Dresses		Playboy 5827
8/12/78	20	11	8	Sweet Fantasy		Epic 50585
1/13/79	32	8	9	Wishing I Had Listened To Your Song		Epic 50650
5/05/79	43	8	10	I Just Wanna Feel The Magic		Epic 50687
2/21/87	80	3	11	It Was Love What It Was		Longhorn 3002
5/02/87	86	2	12	(I Remember When I Thought) Whiskey Was A River		Longhorn 3003
				DENNIS BOTTOMS		
				Born in 1955 in Springfield, Illinois. Won Illinois 5-String Banjo contest in 1970.		
4/27/85	74	7	1	Did I Stay Too Long.....................................		Warner 29035
8/03/85	80	5	2	Bring On The Sunshine		Warner 28944
				JESSICA BOUCHER - see JOE STAMPLEY		
				MARGIE BOWES		
				Born on 3/18/41 in Roxboro, North Carolina. Appeared on local radio beginning at age 13. Worked on the Virginia Barn Dance. With the Grand Ole Opry from 1958. Appeared on Jubilee USA TV series on ABC. In the film "Gold Guitar". Married for a time to Doyle Wilburn (Wilburn Brothers).		
3/23/59	10	16	1	**Poor Old Heartsick Me**		Hickory 1094
8/31/59	15	14	2	My Love And Little Me		Hickory 1102
7/24/61	21	6	3	Little Miss Belong To No One		Mercury 71845
1/11/64	33	4	4	Our Things...		Decca 31557
5/23/64	26	7	5	Understand Your Gal .... answer song to "Understand Your Man" by Johnny Cash		Decca 31606
				ROGER BOWLING		
				Wrote "Lucille" for Kenny Rogers and "Blanket On The Ground" for Billie Jo Spears.		
6/10/78	96	5	1	Dance With Me Molly		Louis. Hay. 783
9/16/78	90	5	2	A Loser's Just A Learner (On His Way To Better Things)		Louis. Hay. 784
2/23/80	55	7	3	Friday Night Fool		NSD 37
5/31/80	78	3	4	The Diplomat		NSD 46
8/23/80	52	8	5	Long Arm Of The Law...............................		NSD 58
11/29/80+	30	15	6	Yellow Pages		NSD 71
4/11/81	50	8	7	Little Bit Of Heaven		Mercury 57049
				BILLY BOB BOWMAN		
				Pseudonym for record producer and disc jockey Biff Collie.		
11/04/72	55	5	1	Miss Pauline...................................... with the Beaumont Bag & Burlap Company		United Art. 50957
				DON BOWMAN		
				Comedian born on 8/26/37 in Lubbock, Texas. Worked as a disc jockey, then with Waylon Jennings in local clubs. Discovered by Chet Atkins.		
7/25/64	14	16	1	Chit Atkins, Make Me A Star .... [N]		RCA 8384
6/18/66	49	2	2	Giddyup Do-Nut .... [N]		RCA 8811
12/03/66	73	2	3	Surely Not .... [N]		RCA 8990
2/24/68	72	2	4	For Loving You.. [N]		RCA 9415
				SKEETER DAVIS & DON BOWMAN		
10/05/68	74	2	5	Folsom Prison Blues #2 .... [N]		RCA 9617
5/17/69	70	5	6	Poor Old Ugly Gladys Jones .... [N] guest vocals: Waylon Jennings, Willie Nelson and Bobby Bare		RCA 0133

DEBUT DATE	PEAK POS	WKS CHR	ARTIST — Record Title	POP POS	Label & Number
			BOXCAR WILLIE Born Lecil Travis Martin on 9/1/31 in Sterratt, Texas. Sang on local radio beginning at age 10, then worked as a disc jockey. Re-entered music in 1975 and scored a big success at the Wembly Festival Of Country Music in England in 1979. Joined the Grand Ole Opry in 1981.		
4/26/80	95	3	1 Train Medley... Fireball Mail/Train Of Love/Walking Cane/Wreck Of The Old '97/Orange Blossom Special/Wabash Cannonball/Night Train To Memphis		Column One 1012
3/13/82	36	12	2 Bad News..		Main St. 951
7/10/82	77	5	3 We Made Memories...................................... **BOXCAR WILLIE & PENNY DeHAVEN**		Main St. 952
9/11/82	80	4	4 Last Train To Heaven/		
11/13/82	70	6	5 Keep On Rollin' Down The Line		Main St. 953
2/05/83	76	6	6 Country Music Nightmare/ [N]		
4/16/83	61	8	7 Train Medley .... [R]		Main St. 954
12/24/83+	44	12	8 The Man I Used To Be		Main St. 93017
5/05/84	87	3	9 Not On The Bottom Yet		Main St. 93020
7/14/84	69	6	10 Luther		Main St. 93021
			BILL BOYD & his Cowboy Ramblers Born on 9/29/10 in Fannin County, Texas; died on 12/7/77 (67). Singer/actor. Own band with his brother Jim in the 20s. The band became the Cowboy Ramblers and recorded for Bluebird in 1934. Own radio show on WRR-Dallas from 1932 into the 60s. Not to be confused with William "Hopalong Cassidy" Boyd.		
9/08/45	4	2	1 Shame On You..		Bluebird 0530
8/24/46	5	1	2 New Steel Guitar Rag..................................		Victor 1907
			JIMMY BOYD Born on 1/9/40 in McComb, Mississippi. "I Saw Mommy Kissing Santa Claus", which sold 250,000 copies in one day, was written by Tommie Connor, a British writer who also did the English lyrics to "Lili Marlene".		
12/20/52	7	3	1 I Saw Mommy Kissing Santa Claus .... [X-N] *1* Jockey #7 / Juke Box #7		Columbia 39871
			MIKE BOYD		
5/22/76	98	2	1 The Leaving Was Easy		Claridge 417
8/20/77	93	6	2 Stop And Think It Over .... #8 pop hit for Dale & Grace in 1964		MBI 4816
2/11/78	80	5	3 Love And Hate...		Inergi 305
			THE BOYER TWINS Gene and Dean Boyer.		
2/09/80	91	4	1 Three Little Words		Sabre 4516
			BOBBY BRADDOCK Songwriter born on 8/5/40 in Lakeland, Florida. Marty Robbins' pianist from 1965-66. Wrote Tammy Wynette's hits "D-I-V-O-R-C-E" and "Womanhood" and George Jones' hits "Golden Ring", "Her Name Is", "He Stopped Loving Her Today" and many others.		
7/29/67	74	4	1 I Know How To Do It.................................		MGM 13737
1/11/69	62	6	2 The Girls In Country Music		MGM 14017
6/02/79	58	5	3 Between The Lines.....................................		Elektra 46038
2/09/80	87	3	4 Nag, Nag, Nag .... [N]		Elektra 46585
			KEITH BRADFORD Born Arthur Guilbeault in Burrillville, Rhode Island. Discovered by Dick Curless.		
6/17/78	83	4	1 Lonely People..		Mu-Sound 421
3/17/79	86	2	2 Lonely Coming Down .... written & produced by Porter Wagoner		Scorpion 0572
			SUSIE BRADING Born Susan Storment in Lincoln, Illinois. With twin sister Chris in a country duo.		
2/04/84	94	3	1 Dream Lover		Riddle 1010
			OWEN BRADLEY Quintet Owen was born on 10/21/15 in Westmoreland, Tennessee. Music director at WSM-Nashville from 1940-58. Leader of popular dance band; Nashville producer for Decca from 1947. Country A&R director for Decca from 1958-68, vice president of MCA from 1968. Elected to the Country Music Hall Of Fame in 1974.		
12/03/49+	7	4	1 Blues Stay Away From Me .... *11* Jockey #7 / Juke Box #8 / Best Seller #9 vocals: Jack Shook & Dottie Dillard		Coral 60107

DEBUT DATE	PEAK POS	WKS CHR	ARTIST — Record Title	POP POS	Label & Number
			CAROLYN BRADSHAW		
8/22/53	**10**	1	1 **Marriage Of Mexican Joe**		Abbott 141
			Juke Box #10		
			follow-up song to Jim Reeves' "Mexican Joe"		
			TERRY BRADSHAW		
			Former Pittsburgh Steelers' quarterback. In the films "Hooper", "Smokey & The Bandit 2" and "Cannonball Run".		
1/31/76	**17**	13	1 I'm So Lonesome I Could Cry	*91*	Mercury 73760
			written in 1949 by Hank Williams		
7/10/76	**90**	4	2 The Last Word In Lonesome Is Me..................		Mercury 73808
4/26/80	**73**	5	3 Until You...		Benson 2001
			SHERRY BRANE		
12/09/78+	**56**	7	1 It's My Party		Oak 1013
			#1 pop hit for Lesley Gore in 1963		
5/17/80	**83**	2	2 Little Girls Need Daddies		Tejas 1015
10/11/80	**86**	2	3 Falling In Trouble Again.............................		e.i.o. 1129
			KIPPI BRANNON		
			Female singer from Nashville; 15 years old in 1981.		
9/26/81	**37**	11	1 Slowly..		MCA 51166
4/03/82	**55**	7	2 If I Could See You Tonight		MCA 52023
9/11/82	**87**	4	3 He Don't Make Me Cry.................................		MCA 52096
			BREAKFAST BARRY		
			Barry Grant. Also see Amarillo.		
9/29/79	**95**	2	1 We're In For Hard Times		Countrystk. 1602
			WALTER BRENNAN		
			Beloved character actor born on 7/25/1894 in Swampscott, Massachusetts. Died on 9/21/74. First film role in 1924. Played "Grandpa" on "The Real McCoys" TV series.		
5/05/62	**3**	13	1 **Old Rivers** .... [S]	5	Liberty 55436
			BRENTWOOD		
			Trio from Nashville: Jay Kencke, Kenny Wrinn and Ron Freeman.		
10/01/83	**96**	1	1 Love The One You're With		Hot Schatz 0051
			#14 pop hit for Stephen Stills in 1971		
3/17/84	**80**	3	2 Anything For Your Love		Hot Schatz 0052
			TOM BRESH		
			Singer and actor born in Hollywood. Began playing guitar at age 7, and plays many other instruments. Worked as a stuntman as a child. Performed with Hank Penny in the early 60s. Appeared on the TV shows "Gunsmoke" and "Cheyenne"; stage shows "Finian's Rainbow", "Harvey" and "The Music Man". Had own TV series, "Nashville Swing", in Canada. Moved to Nashville in 1983.		
4/24/76	**6**	16	1 **Home Made Love**		Farr 004
8/14/76	**17**	11	2 Sad Country Love Song		Farr 009
11/20/76+	**33**	11	3 Hey Daisy (Where Have All The Good Times Gone)......................................		Farr 012
6/11/77	**57**	7	4 Until I Met You		ABC/Dot 17703
9/24/77	**48**	7	5 That Old Cold Shoulder		ABC/Dot 17720
1/28/78	**78**	4	6 Smoke! Smoke! Smoke! (That Cigarette)		ABC/Dot 17738
4/29/78	**74**	6	7 Ways Of A Woman In Love............................		ABC 12352
8/12/78	**84**	4	8 First Encounter Of A Close Kind		ABC 12389
12/11/82	**77**	5	9 When It Comes To Love...............................		Liberty 1487
			THOM BRESH & LANE BRODY		
			JEBRY LEE BRILEY		
			Band singer with Harry James as "Judy Branch", singing since 1968. Formed a country band in 1981; worked the World's Fair, Knoxville, in 1982.		
10/13/79	**89**	3	1 I Just Wonder Where He Could Be Tonight		IBC 0004
			HILKA & JEBRY		
2/13/82	**80**	4	2 Let Your Fingers Do The Walkin'		Paid 141
			ELTON BRITT		
			Born James Britt Baker on 6/27/13 in Marshall, Arkansas; died on 6/23/72 (58). Raised in Oklahoma, he moved to Los Angeles in 1932 and began a radio series. Recorded with The Beverly Hillbillies. Appeared in films "Laramie", "The Last Doggie" and "The Prodigal Son". His 1942 hit "There's A Star-Spangled Banner Waving Somewhere" was one of the biggest-selling country records up to that time.		
1/27/45	**7**	1	1 **I'm A Convict With Old Glory In My Heart**		Bluebird 0517

DEBUT DATE	PEAK POS	WKS CHR	ARTIST — Record Title	POP POS	Label & Number
			ELTON BRITT — Continued		
1/26/46	**2**⁵	18	2 **Someday (You'll Want Me To Want You)**		Bluebird 0521
3/16/46	**3**	9	3 **Wave To Me, My Lady/**	*19*	
3/16/46	**4**	1	4 **Blueberry Lane**		Victor 1789
5/11/46	**5**	1	5 **Detour**...		Victor 1817
7/27/46	**6**	1	6 **Blue Texas Moonlight**............................		Victor 1873
8/24/46	**4**	1	7 **Gotta Get Together With My Gal**		Victor 1927
10/30/48	**6**	6	8 **Chime Bells**		Victor 3090
			Best Seller #6 / Juke Box #12		
3/19/49	**4**	12	9 **Candy Kisses**		RCA 0006
			ELTON BRITT & THE SKYTOPPERS		
			Best Seller #4 / Juke Box #12		
2/04/50	**7**	4	10 **Beyond The Sunset**		RCA 3105
			THE THREE SUNS with ELTON BRITT & ROSALIE ALLEN		
			Jockey #7		
2/25/50	**3**	10	11 **Quicksilver**		RCA 0168
			ELTON BRITT & ROSALIE ALLEN		
			Jockey #3 / Juke Box #6 / Best Seller #9		
5/04/68	**26**	10	12 The Jimmie Rodgers Blues............................		RCA 9503
1/04/69	**71**	4	13 The Bitter Taste		RCA 9658
			JOE BROCK		
			From Lake Placid, Florida. Worked for the Florida Highway Patrol from 1963-75.		
5/29/76	**98**	3	1 Everything You'd Never Want To Be		Ronnie 7601
			LANE BRODY		
			Born Eleni Connie Voorlas in Oak Park, Illinois; raised in Racine, Wisconsin. Played guitar from age 12, worked in local bands while a teenager. Had her own band, Sargasso, while attending the University of Wisconsin. Moved to Los Angeles in 1977. Appeared on "Taxi" TV series in 1979. Moved to Nashville in 1983. Acted in "Heart Of The City" TV series.		
4/24/82	**60**	6	1 He's Taken		Liberty 1457
·7/17/82	**61**	7	2 More Nights.....................................		Liberty 1470
12/11/82	**77**	5	3 When It Comes To Love..........................		Liberty 1487
			THOM BRESH & LANE BRODY		
5/21/83	**15**	19	4 Over You		Liberty 1498
			from the film "Tender Mercies"		
11/19/83	**60**	7	5 It's Another Silent Night.........................		Liberty 1509
2/04/84	**1**¹	22	6 **The Yellow Rose**		Warner 29375
			JOHNNY LEE with LANE BRODY		
			theme song of the short-lived TV series of the same title		
5/12/84	**59**	7	7 Hanging On.....................................		Liberty 1519
8/25/84	**81**	5	8 Alibis...		EMI America 8218
5/18/85	**29**	14	9 He Burns Me Up...............................		EMI America 8266
9/07/85	**51**	10	10 Baby's Eyes		EMI America 8283
4/05/86	**50**	8	11 I Could Get Used To This........................		Warner 28747
			JOHNNY LEE & LANE BRODY		
			BROOKS BROTHERS BAND		
			Group formed in Dallas in 1978. Led by brothers Bill and Randy Brooks.		
1/12/85	**81**	6	1 Hurry On Home..............................		Buckboard 115
			KAREN BROOKS		
			Born on 4/29/54 in Dallas. Sang in clubs in Austin, then joined Rodney Crowell as back-up vocalist. Wrote hits "Couldn't Do Nothin' Right" for Rosanne Cash, "Tennessee Rose" for Emmylou Harris and "Girls Like Me" for Tanya Tucker.		
7/31/82	**17**	19	1 New Way Out..................................		Warner 29958
11/20/82+	**1**¹	20	2 **Faking Love**.................................		Warner 29854
			T.G. SHEPPARD & KAREN BROOKS		
2/05/83	**21**	14	3 If That's What You're Thinking..................		Warner 29789
6/18/83	**30**	12	4 Walk On		Warner 29644
4/28/84	**40**	11	5 Born To Love You		Warner 29302
7/21/84	**19**	16	6 Tonight I'm Here With Someone Else		Warner 29225
1/05/85	**63**	8	7 A Simple I Love You		Warner 29154
7/13/85	**45**	9	8 I Will Dance With You..........................		Warner 28979
			KAREN BROOKS with JOHNNY CASH		
			KIX BROOKS		
			Louisiana native.		
9/10/83	**73**	4	1 Baby, When Your Heart Breaks Down		Avion 103

DEBUT DATE	PEAK POS	WKS CHR	ARTIST — Record Title	POP POS	Label & Number
			BILLY BROWN		
			Born in 1956 in Port Orange, Florida.		
12/15/79	95	3	1 What It Means To Be An American............... [S]		Bernes 101
			backing tune: "America"		
			FLOYD BROWN		
			Born in Baton Rouge, Louisiana. Winner on the "You Can Be A Star" TV talent show. Own TV series, "Play It Again", in Nashville.		
6/18/77	100	1	1 Let's Get Acquainted Again.............................		ABC/Dot 17702
7/09/83	79	6	2 Kiss Me Just One More Time...........................		Magnum 1002
			JIM ED BROWN ★★62★★		
			Born on 4/1/34 in Sparkman, Arkansas. Appeared with older sister Maxine on KCLA-Pine Bluff in the late 40s and KLRA-Little Rock's Barnyard Frolics in the early 50s. Recorded in duo with Maxine in 1953, joined by younger sister Bonnie in 1955. Began solo recording in 1965. Host of Nashville Network's "You Can Be A Star!" TV show. Reunited with Helen Cornelius in February of 1988. Member of the Grand Ole Opry since 1963.		
			JIM EDWARD BROWN:		
7/10/65	33	8	1 I Heard From A Memory Last Night		RCA 8566
10/16/65	37	5	2 I'm Just A Country Boy.................................		RCA 8644
4/09/66	41	4	3 Regular On My Mind		RCA 8766
7/30/66	23	10	4 A Taste Of Heaven		RCA 8867
11/19/66	57	7	5 The Last Laugh		RCA 8997
2/04/67	18	11	6 You Can Have Her.......................................		RCA 9077
			#12 pop hit for Roy Hamilton in 1961		
			JIM ED BROWN:		
5/20/67	3	20	7 **Pop A Top**		RCA 9192
10/14/67	13	13	8 Bottle, Bottle..		RCA 9329
2/10/68	23	11	9 The Cajun Stripper		RCA 9434
5/25/68	13	12	10 The Enemy		RCA 9518
9/28/68	49	8	11 Jack And Jill		RCA 9616
12/14/68+	35	12	12 Longest Beer Of The Night		RCA 9677
3/22/69	17	11	13 Man And Wife Time		RCA 0144
7/19/69	29	10	14 The Three Bells		RCA 0190
			new version of Jim's #1 hit with The Browns in 1959		
12/13/69+	35	9	15 Ginger Is Gentle And Waiting For Me/		
		7	16 Drink Boys Drink		RCA 0279
4/04/70	71	4	17 Lift Ring, Pull Open		RCA 9810
7/11/70	31	9	18 Baby, I Tried		RCA 9858
10/24/70	4	18	19 **Morning**..	47	RCA 9909
3/27/71	13	15	20 Angel's Sunday..		RCA 9965
9/18/71	37	13	21 She's Leavin' (Bonnie, Please Don't Go).............		RCA 0509
3/04/72	55	7	22 Evening		RCA 0642
6/10/72	57	8	23 How I Love Them Old Songs		RCA 0712
9/30/72	67	6	24 All I Had To Do		RCA 0785
12/16/72+	29	12	25 Unbelievable Love		RCA 0846
4/28/73	6	15	26 **Southern Loving**		RCA 0928
9/01/73	15	14	27 Broad-Minded Man		RCA 0059
12/08/73+	10	15	28 **Sometime Sunshine**		RCA 0180
5/04/74	10	17	29 **It's That Time Of Night**.............................		RCA 0267
9/21/74	47	8	30 Get Up I Think I Love You		RCA 10047
1/11/75	63	7	31 Don Junior		RCA 10131
3/29/75	41	9	32 Barroom Pal, Goodtime Gals		RCA 10233
9/20/75	52	10	33 Fine Time To Get The Blues..........................		RCA 10370
1/03/76	24	12	34 Another Morning..		RCA 10531
4/17/76	69	6	35 Let Me Love You Where It Hurts		RCA 10619
10/16/76	65	7	36 I've Rode With The Best		RCA 10786
11/12/77	66	8	37 When I Touch Her There		RCA 11134
10/27/79	38	11	38 You're The Part Of Me................................		RCA 11742
			JIM ED BROWN/HELEN CORNELIUS:		
7/04/76	1²	16	39 **I Don't Want To Have To Marry You**		RCA 10711
11/20/76+	2¹	17	40 **Saying Hello, Saying I Love You, Saying Goodbye**		RCA 10822
5/07/77	12	12	41 Born Believer		RCA 10967

DEBUT DATE	PEAK POS	WKS CHR	ARTIST — Record Title	POP POS	Label & Number
			JIM ED BROWN — Continued		
8/20/77	12	12	42 If It Ain't Love By Now.............................		RCA 11044
12/24/77+	91	3	43 Fall Softly Snow.................................. [X]		RCA 11162
3/11/78	11	13	44 I'll Never Be Free		RCA 11220
7/29/78	6	15	45 **If The World Ran Out Of Love Tonight**..........		RCA 11304
11/25/78+	10	14	46 **You Don't Bring Me Flowers**		RCA 11435
			#1 pop hit for Barbra Streisand & Neil Diamond in 1978		
3/31/79	2²	13	47 **Lying In Love With You**............................		RCA 11532
8/04/79	3	13	48 **Fools**		RCA 11672
3/08/80	5	14	49 **Morning Comes Too Early**		RCA 11927
7/19/80	24	12	50 The Bedroom.....................................		RCA 12037
5/09/81	13	14	51 Don't Bother To Knock		RCA 12220
			JOSIE BROWN		
			Born Linda Brown in Corning, New York. Vocalist with father's band, then worked with Lee Caron in Cocoa Beach, Florida, and the Pete Drake Show.		
9/15/73	44	13	1 Precious Memories Follow Me..........................		RCA 0042
2/02/74	58	8	2 Both Sides Of The Line.............................		RCA 0209
5/18/74	83	7	3 Satisfy Me And I'll Satisfy You		RCA 0266
			MARTI BROWN		
			Female singer from Chattanooga. Toured with Jack Greene.		
7/21/73	78	5	1 Let My Love Shine...................................		Atlantic 4003
			MAX BROWN		
5/19/79	91	5	1 Take Time To Smell The Flowers		Door Knob 095
8/18/79	73	8	2 Take Good Care Of My Love		Door Knob 105
			MAXINE BROWN		
			Eldest member of The Browns.		
12/14/68+	64	11	1 Sugar Cane County.................................		Chart 1061
			ROY BROWN		
			R&B vocalist/pianist, born on 9/10/25 in New Orleans. One of the originators of the New Orleans R&B sound. Wrote "Good Rocking Tonight". Died on 5/25/81 in Los Angeles.		
12/25/48	12	1	1 'Fore Day In The Morning		DeLuxe 3198
			Juke Box #12		
			T. GRAHAM BROWN		
			Born Anthony Graham Brown in Arabi, Georgia in 1954. Played baseball for the University of Georgia. Worked local clubs, toured with Dirk Howell as "Dirk & Tony". Formed own country band, REO Diamond. Had soul band, Rack Of Spam, in 1979. Worked as staff writer for CBS Songs. In the films "Greased Lightning" and "The Farm". Former jingle singer for McDonald's, Miller and Budweiser beer.		
7/27/85	39	10	1 Drowning In Memories		Capitol 5499
10/19/85+	7	27	2 **I Tell It Like It Used To Be**		Capitol 5524
4/26/86	3	19	3 **I Wish That I Could Hurt That Way Again**		Capitol 5571
9/06/86	1¹	23	4 **Hell And High Water**		Capitol 5621
1/31/87	1¹	21	5 **Don't Go To Strangers**		Capitol 5664
5/30/87	9	20	6 **Brilliant Conversationalist**		Capitol 44008
9/12/87	4	22	7 **She Couldn't Love Me Anymore**		Capitol 44061
1/23/88	4	20	8 **The Last Resort**		Capitol 44125
7/30/88	1¹	21	9 **Darlene**		Capitol 44205
12/10/88+	7	20	10 **Come As You Were**		Capitol 44273
			FAMILY BROWN - see FAMILY		
			THE BROWNS ★★157★★		
			Brother and sisters trio consisting of Jim Edward (b: 4/1/34, Sparkman, AR), Ella Maxine (b: 4/27/32, Samti, LA) and Bonnie (b: 7/31/37, Sparkman, AR). Maxine and Jim Ed had worked as a duo from the late 40s and Bonnie joined them in 1955. The trio worked Red Foley's Arkansas Jamboree radio shows. Sister Norma subbed for Jim Ed while he was in the service. Joined the Grand Ole Opry in 1963. The Trio disbanded in 1967, with Jim Ed and Maxine continuing as solo artists.		
			JIM EDWARD & MAXINE BROWN:		
6/26/54	8	15	1 **Looking Back To See**................................		Fabor 107
			Jockey #8		
			JIM EDWARD, MAXINE & BONNIE BROWN:		
11/12/55	7	7	2 **Here Today And Gone Tomorrow**		Fabor 126
			Jockey #7		

DEBUT DATE	PEAK POS	WKS CHR	ARTIST — Record Title	POP POS	Label & Number
			THE BROWNS — Continued		
4/28/56	2 [1]	24	3 I Take The Chance.................................... Jockey #2 / Best Seller #6 / Juke Box #9		RCA 6480
9/22/56	11	2	4 Just As Long As You Love Me .... Jockey #11		RCA 6631
3/23/57	15	1	5 Money.................................... Jockey #15		RCA 6823
9/02/57	4	17	6 I Heard The Bluebirds Sing .... Jockey #4 / Best Seller #15		RCA 6995
10/20/58	13	2	7 Would You Care?		RCA 7311
			THE BROWNS:		
2/23/59	11	12	8 Beyond The Shadow		RCA 7427
8/03/59	1 [10]	19	9 **The Three Bells**	*1*	RCA 7555
11/09/59+	7	16	10 Scarlet Ribbons (For Her Hair)	*13*	RCA 7614
			THE BROWNS featuring Jim Edward Brown:		
4/11/60	20	7	11 The Old Lamplighter	*5*	RCA 7700
12/31/60	23	3	12 Send Me The Pillow You Dream On...................	*56*	RCA 7804
1/18/64	42	1	13 Oh No!.........................		RCA 8242
5/16/64	12	26	14 Then I'll Stop Loving You		RCA 8348
11/07/64	40	6	15 Everybody's Darlin', Plus Mine	*135*	RCA 8423
2/05/66	46	4	16 Meadowgreen		RCA 8714
			THE BROWNS:		
7/02/66	16	13	17 I'd Just Be Fool Enough		RCA 8838
10/08/66	19	10	18 Coming Back To You		RCA 8942
5/06/67	54	7	19 I Hear It Now.........................		RCA 9153
12/16/67+	52	7	20 Big Daddy/		
12/30/67+	64	4	21 I Will Bring You Water		RCA 9364
			ED BRUCE ★★105★★ Born William Edwin Bruce, Jr. on 12/29/40 in Keiser, Arkansas; raised in Memphis. Recorded for Sun in 1957. Moved to Nashville in 1964 and worked with the Marijohn Wilkins Singers. Did TV commercials as "The Tennessean"; appeared in the TV series "Maverick". Wrote "Mamas, Don't Let Your Babies Grow Up To Be Cowboys", "The Man That Turned My Mama On", "Working Man's Prayer", and many others.		
1/14/67	57	9	1 Walker's Woods		RCA 9044
4/15/67	69	5	2 Last Train To Clarksville......................... #1 pop hit for The Monkees in 1966		RCA 9155
7/13/68	52	5	3 Painted Girls And Wine		RCA 9553
1/04/69	53	10	4 Song For Jenny		Monument 1118
5/24/69	52	7	5 Everybody Wants To Get To Heaven		Monument 1138
12/15/73+	77	8	6 July, You're A Woman		United Art. 353
11/15/75+	15	14	7 Mammas Don't Let Your Babies Grow Up To Be Cowboys		United Art. 732
3/20/76	32	10	8 The Littlest Cowboy Rides Again		United Art. 774
6/19/76	57	7	9 Sleep All Mornin'		United Art. 811
9/25/76	36	10	10 For Love's Own Sake		United Art. 862
8/13/77	52	10	11 When I Die, Just Let Me Go To Texas		Epic 50424
11/19/77	54	10	12 Star-Studded Nights.........................		Epic 50475
2/11/78	57	7	13 Love Somebody To Death		Epic 50503
5/20/78	94	3	14 Man Made Of Glass		Epic 50544
10/07/78	70	6	15 The Man That Turned My Mama On...................		Epic 50613
12/16/78+	60	9	16 Angeline.........................		Epic 50645
3/08/80	21	15	17 Diane.........................		MCA 41201
7/05/80	12	15	18 The Last Cowboy Song .... guest vocal: Willie Nelson		MCA 41273
11/08/80+	14	16	19 Girls, Women And Ladies		MCA 51018
3/28/81	24	14	20 Evil Angel.........................		MCA 51076
7/25/81	14	15	21 (When You Fall In Love) Everything's A Waltz....		MCA 51139
11/28/81+	1 [1]	21	22 **You're The Best Break This Old Heart Ever Had**		MCA 51210
4/24/82	13	16	23 Love's Found You And Me		MCA 52036
8/28/82	4	19	24 **Ever, Never Lovin' You**.........................		MCA 52109
1/22/83	6	18	25 **My First Taste Of Texas**.........................		MCA 52156
5/14/83	21	15	26 You're Not Leavin' Here Tonight		MCA 52210

DEBUT DATE	PEAK POS	WKS CHR	ARTIST — Record Title	POP POS	Label & Number
			ED BRUCE — Continued		
8/06/83	19	17	27 If It Was Easy		MCA 52251
11/12/83+	4	21	28 **After All**		MCA 52295
8/18/84	45	12	29 Tell 'Em I've Gone Crazy		MCA 52433
11/03/84+	3	22	30 **You Turn Me On (Like a Radio)**		RCA 13937
3/23/85	17	16	31 When Givin' Up Was Easy.............................		RCA 14037
8/03/85	20	16	32 If It Ain't Love...		RCA 14150
4/12/86	4	19	33 **Nights**		RCA 14305
9/13/86	49	9	34 Fools For Each Other		RCA 5005
			ED BRUCE with LYNN ANDERSON		
12/06/86+	36	14	35 Quietly Crazy		RCA 5077
			BRUSH ARBOR		
			San Diego-based group, formed in 1972, featuring lead singer, Jim Rice.		
11/25/72+	56	10	1 Proud Mary..		Capitol 3468
			#2 pop hit for Creedence Clearwater Revival in 1969		
3/10/73	41	7	2 Brush Arbor Meeting		Capitol 3538
			includes portions of "I'll Fly Away" and "Old Time Religion"		
8/04/73	72	4	3 Alone Again (Naturally)		Capitol 3672
			#1 pop hit for Gilbert O'Sullivan in 1972		
11/17/73	98	2	4 Now That It's Over		Capitol 3733
12/08/73+	73	8	5 Trucker And The U.F.O.		Capitol 3774
7/31/76	90	3	6 Emmylou...		Monument 8702
11/12/77	56	11	7 Get Down Country Music		Monument 230
			SHERRY BRYCE		
			Born in Duncanville, Alabama. Worked as a songwriter for Mel Tillis in 1969.		
8/11/73	64	10	1 Leaving's Heavy On My Mind...........................		MGM 14548
2/09/74	45	11	2 Don't Stop Now		MGM 14695
6/29/74	62	9	3 Treat Me Like A Lady		MGM 14726
10/05/74	70	6	4 Oh, How Happy		MGM 14747
			#12 pop hit for Shades Of Blue in 1966		
4/26/75	96	3	5 Love Song..		MGM 14793
2/28/76	97	2	6 Hang On Feelin'		MGM 14842
11/13/76	93	3	7 Everything's Coming Up Love		MCA 40630
10/01/77	79	5	8 The Lady Ain't For Sale		Pilot 45100
			MEL TILLIS & SHERRY BRYCE:		
6/05/71	8	15	9 **Take My Hand**..	*110*	MGM 14255
10/30/71	9	14	10 **Living And Learning**		MGM 14303
4/08/72	38	10	11 Anything's Better Than Nothing		MGM 14365
11/17/73+	26	13	12 Let's Go All The Way Tonight		MGM 14660
4/13/74	11	14	13 Don't Let Go		MGM 14714
			#13 pop hit for Roy Hamilton in 1958		
1/04/75	14	13	14 You Are The One		MGM 14776
5/17/75	32	13	15 Mr. Right And Mrs. Wrong		MGM 14803
			BUCHANAN BROTHERS		
			Chester and Lester Buchanan from Trenton, Georgia.		
6/29/46	6	3	1 **Atomic Power**		Victor 1850
			WES BUCHANAN		
			Born in Vallejo, California. Worked as a TV actor. Own "Hollywood Jamboree" TV series in 1967. Discovered by Marty Robbins. In the film "From Nashville With Love".		
12/07/68	72	3	1 Warm Red Wine		Columbia 44686
			GARY BUCK		
			Born on 3/21/40 in Sault Sainte Marie, Canada. Had own band, the Rock-A-Billies, while a teenager. First recorded for Chateau in 1962.		
6/29/63	11	17	1 Happy To Be Unhappy....................................		Petal 1011
4/11/64	37	3	2 The Wheel Song		Petal 1500
2/13/82	93	2	3 Midnight Magic		Dimension 1029

39

DEBUT DATE	PEAK POS	WKS CHR	ARTIST — Record Title	POP POS	Label & Number
			THE BUCKAROOS		
			Backing band for Buck Owens. Included Don Rich (lead guitar, vocals), Tom Brumley (steel guitar), Doyle Holly (bass) and Willie Cantu (drums). Don Rich (real name: Don Ulrich) was killed in a motorcycle accident on 7/17/74. Also see Buddy Alan and Buck Owens.		
			BUCK OWENS & THE BUCKAROOS:		
10/30/65	1 ²	17	1 **Buckaroo** .... [I]	60	Capitol 5517
			THE BUCKAROOS:		
11/25/67	69	4	2 Chicken Pickin' .... [I]		Capitol 2010
			BUCK OWENS' BUCKAROOS Featuring DON RICH:		
6/08/68	38	9	3 I'm Coming Back Home To Stay......................		Capitol 2173
9/21/68	50	8	4 I'm Goin' Back Home Where I Belong...............		Capitol 2264
			THE BUCKAROOS Featuring DON RICH:		
4/19/69	63	2	5 Anywhere USA		Capitol 2420
10/25/69	43	6	6 Nobody But You...		Capitol 2629
4/04/70	71	3	7 The Night They Drove Old Dixie Down		Capitol 2750
			#3 pop hit for Joan Baez in 1971		
			RUSTY BUDDE		
			Native of Houston.		
12/27/86	77	4	1 Misty Mississippi...		BPC 1002
			BEVERLY BUFF		
			Born in Washington, Georgia.		
11/24/62+	22	3	1 I'll Sign		Bethlehem 3027
3/30/63	23	5	2 Forgive Me..		Bethlehem 3065
			JIMMY BUFFETT		
			Born on 12/25/46 in Mobile, Alabama. Has BS degree in history and journalism from the University of Southern Mississippi. After working in New Orleans, moved to Nashville in 1969. Settled in Key West in 1971. Owns a store called Margaritaville and own line of tropical clothing.		
5/12/73	58	10	1 The Great Filling Station Holdup.....................		Dunhill 4348
6/15/74	58	7	2 Come Monday	30	Dunhill 4385
8/23/75	88	5	3 Door Number Three	102	ABC 12113
4/30/77	13	17	4 Margaritaville..	8	ABC 12254
10/01/77	24	10	5 Changes In Latitudes, Changes In Attitudes.......	37	ABC 12305
8/19/78	91	3	6 Livingston Saturday Night	52	ABC 12391
9/08/84	42	13	7 When The Wild Life Betrays Me		MCA 52438
12/08/84+	58	13	8 Bigger Than The Both Of Us...........................		MCA 52499
3/23/85	37	15	9 Who's The Blonde Stranger?		MCA 52550
6/29/85	56	9	10 Gypsies In The Palace		MCA 52607
9/07/85	16	19	11 If The Phone Doesn't Ring, It's Me..................		MCA 52664
2/08/86	50	9	12 Please Bypass This Heart		MCA 52752
			BURBANK STATION		
			Fargo, North Carolina group, featuring Bunny Davis, lead vocals.		
8/06/88	77	3	1 Divided		Prairie D. 8841
			GARY BURBANK with Band McNally		
			Gary is a disc jockey at WLW in Cincinnati.		
7/26/80	91	2	1 Who Shot J.R.?.. [N]	67	Ovation 1150
			inspired by the J.R. shooting episode on TV's "Dallas"		
			THE BURCH SISTERS		
			Sisters Cathy, Charlene and Cindy Burch from Screven, Georgia.		
5/21/88	23	18	1 Everytime You Go Outside I Hope It Rains		Mercury 870362
10/15/88	61	5	2 What Do Lonely People Do.............................		Mercury 870687
12/17/88+	45	11	3 I Don't Want To Mention Any Names		Mercury 872324
			KATHY BURDICK - see DICKEY LEE		
			FRANK BURGESS		
11/26/88	88	3	1 American Man		True 94
			WILMA BURGESS		
			Born on 6/11/39 in Orlando, Florida. Attended Stetson University, majoring in physical education. Started work as a demo singer in Nashville in 1960.		
12/11/65+	7	18	1 **Baby**		Decca 31862
5/07/66	12	17	2 Don't Touch Me		Decca 31941

DEBUT DATE	PEAK POS	WKS CHR	ARTIST — Record Title	POP POS	Label & Number
			WILMA BURGESS — Continued		
10/29/66	4	18	3 Misty Blue		Decca 32027
			#3 pop hit for Dorothy Moore in 1976		
3/25/67	24	15	4 Fifteen Days................................		Decca 32105
8/26/67	16	15	5 Tear Time...................................		Decca 32178
8/17/68	59	9	6 Look At The Laughter......................		Decca 32359
3/22/69	68	3	7 Parting (Is Such Sweet Sorrow)		Decca 32437
8/09/69	48	10	8 The Woman In Your Life		Decca 32522
12/27/69+	48	9	9 The Sun's Gotta' Shine....................		Decca 32593
7/11/70	63	6	10 Lonely For You............................		Decca 32684
9/22/73	61	11	11 I'll Be Your Bridge (Just Lay Me Down)		Shannon 813
12/22/73+	14	17	12 Wake Me Into Love........................		Shannon 816
			BUD LOGAN & WILMA BURGESS		
7/06/74	53	10	13 The Best Day Of The Rest Of Our Love..............		Shannon 820
			BUD LOGAN & WILMA BURGESS		
9/14/74	46	11	14 Love Is Here/		
2/08/75	86	6	15 Sweet Lovin' Baby........................		Shannon 821
			FIDDLIN' FRENCHIE BURKE		
			Born Frenchie Bourque in Kaplan, Louisiana. Cajun fiddler from age 11; worked with Johnny Bush, Jimmy Dickens and Ray Price. Formed own band, the Song Masters.		
			FIDDLIN' FRENCHIE BOURQUE & THE OUTLAWS:		
11/23/74+	39	15	1 Big Mamou................................		20th Century 2152
			FIDDLIN' FRENCHIE BURKE & THE OUTLAWS:		
4/19/75	30	9	2 Colinda		20th Century 2182
10/11/75	73	5	3 The Fiddlin' Of Jacques Pierre Bordeaux		20th Century 2225
			FRENCHIE BURKE:		
7/01/78	94	5	4 Knock Knock Knock.......................		Cherry 644
			FIDDLIN' FRENCHIE BURKE:		
3/28/81	93	3	5 Fire On The Mountain .... [I]		Delta 11332
			BILLY BURNETTE		
			Born William Burnette III on 5/8/53 in Memphis. Son of Dorsey Burnette, nephew of Johnny Burnette. First recorded at age 11 for A&M. Played guitar since age 16. Led band behind his father in the 70s.		
11/03/79	76	5	1 What's A Little Love Between Friends		Polydor 2024
8/10/85	51	8	2 Ain't It Just Like Love...................		Curb 52626
12/28/85+	68	9	3 Try Me		Curb 52749
7/12/86	54	7	4 Soldier Of Love............................		Curb 52852
			DORSEY BURNETTE		
			Born on 12/28/32 in Memphis; died of a heart attack on 8/19/79 in Canoga Park, California. Older brother of Johnny Burnette, father of Billy Burnette. Was a Golden Gloves contender in 1949. Worked on KWEM-Memphis "West Memphis Jamboree" with Johnny and Paul Burlison as the Johnny Burnette Rock 'N Roll Trio. Recorded for Von in 1954. Winner on Ted Mack's Amateur Hour and appeared at Madison Square Garden with trio in September of 1956. Went solo in 1958.		
5/13/72	21	12	1 In The Spring (The Roses Always Turn Red).......		Capitol 3307
9/02/72	40	8	2 I Just Couldn't Let Her Walk Away		Capitol 3404
2/17/73	42	9	3 I Let Another Good One Get Away..................		Capitol 3529
5/12/73	53	5	4 Keep Out Of My Dreams		Capitol 3588
8/11/73	26	14	5 Darlin' (Don't Come Back)...............		Capitol 3678
1/12/74	85	7	6 It Happens Every Time		Capitol 3796
3/09/74	69	8	7 Bob, All The Playboys And Me..........		Capitol 3829
			above 3: with Sound Company		
6/15/74	62	8	8 Daddy Loves You Honey.................		Capitol 3887
11/23/74	71	5	9 What Ladies Can Do (When They Want To)		Capitol 3963
5/31/75	28	12	10 Molly (I Ain't Gettin' Any Younger)...................		Melodyland 6007
10/18/75	97	3	11 Lyin' In Her Arms Again.................		Melodyland 6019
4/24/76	74	5	12 Ain't No Heartbreak		Melodyland 6031
6/11/77	31	15	13 Things I Treasure........................		Calliope 8004
11/05/77	53	7	14 Soon As I Touched Her..................		Calliope 8012
9/01/79	77	4	15 Here I Go Again		Elektra 46513
			BRENT BURNS		
			Writer and producer from Phoenix.		
5/06/78	91	4	1 I Hear You Coming Back................		Pan. Des. 79

DEBUT DATE	PEAK POS	WKS CHR	ARTIST — Record Title	POP POS	Label & Number
			GEORGE BURNS		
			Born Nathan Birnbaum on 1/20/1896 in New York City. Top radio, film and TV comedian. In film "The Sunshine Boys" in 1976, "Oh God", and many others since then.		
1/05/80	15	14	1 I Wish I Was Eighteen Again	*49*	Mercury 57011
5/24/80	85	4	2 The Arizona Whiz		Mercury 57021
2/14/81	66	5	3 Willie, Won't You Sing A Song With Me		Mercury 57045
			an ode to Willie Nelson		
			HUGHIE BURNS		
3/08/80	95	2	1 The Family Inn		C-S-I 002
			JACKIE BURNS		
			Female vocalist from Long Beach, California. Discovered by Gordon Terry.		
10/11/69	60	5	1 Something's Missing (It's You)		Honor Brigade 5
10/21/72	71	2	2 (If Loving You Is Wrong) I Don't Want To Be Right		JMI 8
			#3 pop hit for Luther Ingram in 1972		
			BURRITO BROTHERS		
			In 1981, group consisted of Gib Guilbeau (fiddle), John Beland (guitar), "Sneaky" Pete Kleinow (steel guitar), and Skip Battin (bass). From their 4th hit on, consisted of Guilbeau and Beland as a duo.		
1/24/81	67	5	1 She's A Friend Of A Friend		Curb 5402
4/18/81	20	13	2 Does She Wish She Was Single Again		Curb 01011
8/08/81	16	14	3 She Belongs To Everyone But Me		Curb 02243
12/26/81+	27	14	4 If Something Should Come Between Us (Let It Be Love)		Curb 02641
4/17/82	40	10	5 Closer To You..		Curb 02835
7/24/82	39	10	6 I'm Drinkin' Canada Dry		Curb 03023
11/13/82	48	10	7 Blue And Broken Hearted Me		Curb 03314
1/28/84	49	9	8 Almost Saturday Night.................................		Curb 52329
			#78 pop hit for John Fogerty in 1975		
5/26/84	53	8	9 My Kind Of Lady		Curb 52379
			from the film "Dream Chaser"		
			JOHNNY BUSH		
			Born John Bush Shin III on 2/17/35 in Houston. Guitarist and drummer. Worked local clubs in San Antonio from 1952. Worked with Willie Nelson and Ray Price in the early 60s. Joined Willie Nelson's band in the mid-60s. Went solo in 1967. Known as "The Country Caruso".		
11/25/67	69	3	1 You Oughta Hear Me Cry		Stop 126
3/16/68	29	13	2 What A Way To Live.....................................		Stop 160
8/03/68	10	16	3 **Undo The Right**		Stop 193
12/28/68+	16	13	4 Each Time		Stop 232
			written by Ray Price		
3/22/69	7	15	5 **You Gave Me A Mountain**............................		Stop 257
			#24 pop hit for Frankie Laine in 1969		
8/16/69	26	10	6 My Cup Runneth Over		Stop 310
			#8 pop hit for Ed Ames in 1967		
1/03/70	56	8	7 Jim, Jack, And Rose/		
		5	8 I'll Go To A Stranger		Stop 354
5/16/70	25	11	9 Warmth Of The Wine		Stop 371
11/07/70	44	11	10 My Joy...		Stop 380
4/10/71	53	6	11 City Lights..		Stop 392
4/22/72	17	12	12 I'll Be There		Million 1
7/22/72	14	15	13 Whiskey River		RCA 0745
			Willie Nelson's theme song		
12/30/72+	34	9	14 There Stands The Glass		RCA 0867
5/05/73	38	11	15 Here Comes The World Again		RCA 0931
9/01/73	53	8	16 Green Snakes On The Ceiling		RCA 0041
12/01/73+	37	10	17 We're Back In Love Again..............................		RCA 0164
3/23/74	48	10	18 Toy Telephone/		
		4	19 From Tennessee To Texas		RCA 0240
10/15/77	78	7	20 You'll Never Leave Me Completely/		
4/29/78	99	2	21 Put Me Out Of My Memory		Gusto 165
9/02/78	89	3	22 She Just Made Me Love You More		Gusto 9006
5/19/79	83	5	23 When My Conscience Hurts The Most		Whiskey R. 791

DEBUT DATE	PEAK POS	WKS CHR	ARTIST — Record Title	POP POS	Label & Number
			JOHNNY BUSH — Continued		
2/28/81	92	2	24 Whiskey River .... [R]		Delta 10041
			new version of his 1972 hit on RCA		
			BOBBY "Sofine" BUTLER		
			Disc jockey born in El Paso. Worked stations in Tucson, El Paso and Phoenix.		
12/04/76	98	2	1 Teddy Toad..		Pan. Des. 77
5/26/79	46	6	2 Cheaper Crude Or No More Food .... [N]		IBC 0001
			CARL BUTLER		
			Born on 6/2/27 in Knoxville, Tennessee. Singing since age 12. Joined by wife Pearl (b: Pearl Dee Jones; d: 3/1/80) as a duo in 1962. Appeared in the film "Second Fiddle To A Steel Guitar" in 1967.		
8/07/61	25	2	1 Honky Tonkitis		Columbia 41997
			CARL BUTLER & PEARL:		
12/08/62	1 11	24	2 **Don't Let Me Cross Over**...........................	88	Columbia 42593
7/06/63	14	14	3 Loving Arms		Columbia 42778
1/11/64	9	8	4 **Too Late To Try Again/**		
1/11/64	36	1	5 My Tears Don't Show		Columbia 42892
6/06/64	14	16	6 I'm Hanging Up The Phone.........................		Columbia 43030
9/26/64	23	10	7 Forbidden Street		Columbia 43102
2/27/65	38	10	8 We'd Destroy Each Other/		
3/27/65	22	13	9 Just Thought I'd Let You Know		Columbia 43210
12/11/65	42	2	10 Our Ship Of Love....................................		Columbia 43433
8/06/66	31	7	11 Little Pedro		Columbia 43685
8/17/68	28	12	12 Punish Me Tomorrow		Columbia 44587
1/04/69	46	8	13 I Never Got Over You		Columbia 44694
7/05/69	63	6	14 We'll Sweep Out The Ashes In The Morning		Columbia 44862
			RUTH BUZZI		
			Born in Wequetequock, Connecticut. Comedienne featured on "Laugh-In" TV series.		
4/02/77	90	4	1 You Oughta Hear The Song		United Art. 951
			BRENDA BYERS		
			Banjo player from Canterbury, Connecticut. Worked with Arthur Godfrey in 1970.		
10/26/68	51	9	1 The Auctioneer...		MTA 160
			#19 pop hit for Leroy Van Dyke in 1957		
10/11/69	65	6	2 Thank You For Loving Me.............................		MTA 176
1/24/70	66	4	3 Homeward Bound...................................		MTA 177
			#5 pop hit for Simon & Garfunkel in 1966		
			JUDY BYRAM		
12/05/87	71	5	1 No More One More Time		F&L 554
6/04/88	74	5	2 One Fire Between Us....................................		Regal 001

C

DEBUT DATE	PEAK POS	WKS CHR	ARTIST — Record Title	POP POS	Label & Number
			BUDDY CAGLE		
			Born on 2/8/36 in Concord, North Carolina. Raised in the Children's Home in Winston-Salem. Worked with Hank Thompson's Brazos Valley Boys.		
5/18/63	29	3	1 Your Mother's Prayer...................................		Capitol 4923
11/16/63	26	2	2 Sing A Sad Song		Capitol 5043
9/25/65	37	8	3 Honky Tonkin' Again		Mercury 72452
4/23/66	31	10	4 Tonight I'm Coming Home		Imperial 66161
1/14/67	57	7	5 Apologize		Imperial 66218
8/12/67	75	2	6 Longtime Traveling		Imperial 66245
			from the Broadway musical "A Joyful Noise"		
			HUNTER CAIN		
7/16/88	82	2	1 Hollywood Heroes		Discovery 4587
			CALAMITY JANE		
			Female vocal quartet includes Pam Rose and songwriters Mary Ann Kennedy, Mary Fielder and Linda Moore.		
10/17/81	61	7	1 Send Me Somebody To Love...........................		Columbia 02503
2/27/82	44	9	2 I've Just Seen A Face		Columbia 02715
			written by John Lennon/Paul McCartney		

DEBUT DATE	PEAK POS	WKS CHR	ARTIST — Record Title	POP POS	Label & Number
			CALAMITY JANE — Continued		
6/19/82	**60**	7	3 Walkin' After Midnight...............................		Columbia 02958
10/16/82	**87**	3	4 Love Wheel..		Columbia 03229
			LINDA CALHOUN		
4/28/79	**85**	4	1 I Can Feel Love......................................		Grape 2004
			BART CAMERON		
11/01/86	**76**	4	1 Dark Eyed Lady......................................		Revolver 013
5/30/87	**77**	3	2 Do It For The Love Of It		Revolver 015
			COLLEEN CAMP		
			TV and movie actress.		
1/23/82	**72**	4	1 One Day Since Yesterday..............................		Moon Pic. 0001
			ARCHIE CAMPBELL		
			Born on 11/7/14 in Bulls Gap, Tennessee. Died on 8/29/87 in Knoxville. From the late 30s to early 40s, worked on the "Mid-Day Merry-Go-Round" radio show, KNOX-Knoxville. Served in the US Navy in World War II. Returned to radio, then own TV show on WATE-Knoxville from 1952-58. Joined the Grand Ole Opry in 1968. Chief writer and a star of the TV series "Hee Haw". Hosted the Nashville Network's interview TV show, "Yesteryear in Nashville".		
3/14/60	**24**	4	1 Trouble In The Amen Corner........................		RCA 7660
1/22/66	**16**	8	2 The Men In My Little Girl's Life		RCA 8741
			#6 pop hit for Mike Douglas in 1960		
3/11/67	**44**	10	3 The Cockfight............................. [N]		RCA 9081
12/08/73	**87**	4	4 Freedom Ain't The Same As Bein' Free		RCA 0155
			ARCHIE CAMPBELL & LORENE MANN:		
1/06/68	**24**	15	5 The Dark End Of The Street		RCA 9401
6/29/68	**31**	10	6 Tell It Like It Is		RCA 9549
			#2 pop hit for Aaron Neville in 1967		
9/28/68	**57**	8	7 Warm And Tender Love		RCA 9615
			#17 pop hit for Percy Sledge in 1966		
1/04/69	**36**	9	8 My Special Prayer		RCA 9691
			CECIL CAMPBELL		
			Born on 3/22/11 in Danbury, North Carolina; raised in Belews Creek, North Carolina. In the films "My Darling Clementine" and "Swing Your Partner".		
5/21/49	**9**	1	1 **Steel Guitar Ramble**		RCA 0014
			Juke Box #9		
			GLEN CAMPBELL ★★33★★		
			Born on 4/22/36 in Billstown, Arkansas. Vocalist/guitarist/composer. With his uncle Dick Bills' band, 1954-58. To Los Angeles; recorded with The Champs in 1960; became prolific studio musician; with The Beach Boys, 1965. Own TV show, "The Glen Campbell Goodtime Hour", 1968-72. In films "True Grit", "Norwood" and "Strange Homecoming". CMA award: Entertainer of the Year - 1968.		
12/29/62	**20**	5	1 Kentucky Means Paradise	*114*	Capitol 4867
			THE GREEN RIVER BOYS featuring GLEN CAMPBELL		
12/10/66+	**18**	13	2 Burning Bridges..................................		Capitol 5773
			#3 pop hit for Jack Scott in 1960		
4/29/67	**73**	2	3 I Gotta Have My Baby Back.........................		Capitol 5854
7/29/67	**30**	12	4 Gentle On My Mind	39	Capitol 5939
10/28/67+	**2²**	18	5 **By The Time I Get To Phoenix**......................	*26*	Capitol 2015
2/03/68	**13**	12	6 Hey Little One	*54*	Capitol 2076
4/13/68	**1³**	16	7 **I Wanna Live**	*36*	Capitol 2146
7/06/68	**3**	15	8 **Dreams Of The Everyday Housewife**..............	*32*	Capitol 2224
10/19/68	**44**	3	9 Gentle On My Mind .... [R]		Capitol 5939
11/02/68	**1²**	19	10●Wichita Lineman	*3*	Capitol 2302
3/15/69	**1³**	14	11●Galveston	*4*	Capitol 2428
5/10/69	**28**	10	12 Where's The Playground Susie	*26*	Capitol 2494
7/26/69	**9**	12	13 **True Grit**....................................	*35*	Capitol 2573
			from the film of the same title starring John Wayne and Campbell		
10/25/69	**2¹**	13	14 **Try A Little Kindness**	*23*	Capitol 2659
1/24/70	**2³**	13	15 **Honey Come Back**	*19*	Capitol 2718
4/25/70	**25**	9	16 Oh Happy Day	*40*	Capitol 2787
7/18/70	**5**	12	17 Everything A Man Could Ever Need	*52*	Capitol 2843
9/19/70	**3**	15	18 It's Only Make Believe.........................	*10*	Capitol 2905
			#1 pop hit for Conway Twitty in 1958		
3/13/71	**7**	14	19 Dream Baby (How Long Must I Dream)	*31*	Capitol 3062

DEBUT DATE	PEAK POS	WKS CHR	ARTIST — Record Title	POP POS	Label & Number
			GLEN CAMPBELL — Continued		
7/03/71	**21**	14	20 The Last Time I Saw Her	*61*	Capitol 3123
1/08/72	**15**	12	21 Oklahoma Sunday Morning	*104*	Capitol 3254
4/01/72	**6**	13	22 **Manhattan Kansas**	*114*	Capitol 3305
8/26/72	**45**	10	23 I Will Never Pass This Way Again	*61*	Capitol 3411
12/16/72+	**33**	10	24 One Last Time	*78*	Capitol 3483
3/24/73	**48**	8	25 I Knew Jesus (Before He Was A Star)	*45*	Capitol 3548
7/28/73	**49**	9	26 Bring Back My Yesterday		Capitol 3669
10/20/73	**20**	12	27 Wherefore And Why	*111*	Capitol 3735
2/02/74	**20**	10	28 Houston (I'm Comin' To See You)	*68*	Capitol 3808
8/03/74	**3**	18	29 **Bonaparte's Retreat** written in 1950 by Pee Wee King		Capitol 3926
12/14/74+	**16**	13	30 It's A Sin When You Love Somebody		Capitol 3988
6/07/75	**1** ³	21	31 ● **Rhinestone Cowboy**	*1*	Capitol 4095
11/01/75	**3**	15	32 **Country Boy (You Got Your Feet In L.A.)**	*11*	Capitol 4155
4/10/76	**4**	12	33 **Don't Pull Your Love/Then You Can Tell Me Goodbye**	*27*	Capitol 4245
7/10/76	**18**	11	34 See You On Sunday		Capitol 4288
1/29/77	**1** ²	17	35 ● **Southern Nights**	*1*	Capitol 4376
7/02/77	**4**	15	36 **Sunflower**	*39*	Capitol 4445
12/03/77+	**39**	10	37 God Must Have Blessed America		Capitol 4515
6/10/78	**21**	12	38 Another Fine Mess/		
9/23/78	**16**	16	39 Can You Fool	*38*	Capitol 4584
2/17/79	**13**	11	40 I'm Gonna Love You		Capitol 4682
5/26/79	**45**	7	41 California		Capitol 4715
9/01/79	**25**	10	42 Hound Dog Man #58 pop hit for Lenny LeBlanc in 1977		Capitol 4769
11/24/79	**66**	6	43 My Prayer		Capitol 4799
8/30/80	**80**	4	44 Hollywood Smiles		Capitol 4909
11/22/80+	**10**	17	45 **Any Which Way You Can** from the Clint Eastwood film of the same title		Warner 49609
2/07/81	**54**	7	46 I Don't Want To Know Your Name	*65*	Capitol 4959
8/08/81	**15**	12	47 I Love My Truck	*94*	Mirage 3845
10/30/82	**44**	8	48 Old Home Town		Atln. Am. 99967
1/15/83	**17**	17	49 I Love How You Love Me #5 pop hit for The Paris Sisters in 1961		Atln. Am. 99930
6/11/83	**85**	3	50 On The Wings Of My Victory		Atln. Am. 99893
6/23/84	**10**	22	51 **Faithless Love**		Atln. Am. 99768
12/01/84+	**4**	20	52 **A Lady Like You**		Atln. Am. 99691
5/18/85	**14**	21	53 (Love Always) Letter To Home		Atln. Am. 99647
11/16/85+	**7**	21	54 **It's Just A Matter Of Time** #3 pop hit for Brook Benton in 1959		Atln. Am. 99600
4/26/86	**38**	11	55 Cowpoke		Atln. Am. 99559
7/26/86	**52**	8	56 Call Home		Atln. Am. 99525
10/03/87+	**5**	23	57 **Still Within The Sound Of My Voice**		MCA 53172
2/20/88	**32**	12	58 I Remember You #5 pop hit for Frank Ifield in 1962		MCA 53245
5/28/88	**7**	23	59 **I Have You**		MCA 53218
10/01/88	**35**	10	60 Light Years		MCA 53426
			GLEN CAMPBELL DUOS with:		
			RITA COOLIDGE:		
5/24/80	**60**	6	61 Somethin' 'Bout You Baby I Like	*42*	Capitol 4865
			BOBBIE GENTRY:		
11/23/68	**44**	7	62 Less Of Me flip side "Mornin' Glory" made the pop charts (POS 74)		Capitol 2314
2/08/69	**14**	14	63 Let It Be Me	*36*	Capitol 2387
2/21/70	**6**	13	64 **All I Have To Do Is Dream**	*27*	Capitol 2745
			ANNE MURRAY:		
10/30/71	**40**	8	65 I Say A Little Prayer/By The Time I Get To Phoenix	*81*	Capitol 3200
			MEL TILLIS:		
10/27/84	**47**	12	66 Slow Nights		MCA 52474

DEBUT DATE	PEAK POS	WKS CHR	ARTIST — Record Title	POP POS	Label & Number
			GLEN CAMPBELL — Continued		
			TANYA TUCKER:		
9/27/80	**59**	6	67 Dream Lover		MCA 41323
			#2 pop hit for Bobby Darin in 1959		
4/11/81	**85**	4	68 Why Don't We Just Sleep On It Tonight		Capitol 4986
			STEVE WARINER:		
5/30/87	**6**	28	69 **The Hand That Rocks The Cradle**.................		MCA 53108
			JO ANN CAMPBELL		
			Born on 7/20/38 in Jacksonville, Florida. First recorded for El Dorado in 1957. In the films "Johnny Melody", "Go Johnny Go" and "Hey, Let's Twist". Married Troy Seals in the early 60s; recorded together as Jo Ann & Troy in 1964.		
9/22/62	**24**	3	1 (I'm The Girl On) Wolverton Mountain	*38*	Cameo 223
			MIKE CAMPBELL		
12/26/81+	**65**	6	1 Barroom Games		Columbia 02622
10/02/82	**57**	8	2 No Room To Cry		Columbia 03154
5/14/83	**76**	5	3 Don't Say You Love Me (Just Love Me Again)		Columbia 03838
12/17/83+	**57**	9	4 Sweet And Easy To Love		Columbia 04225
3/17/84	**52**	10	5 One Sided Love Affair		Columbia 04387
7/14/84	**77**	3	6 You're The Only Star (In My Blue Heaven)		Columbia 04488
			written & recorded in 1946 by Gene Autry		
			THE CANADIAN SWEETHEARTS		
			Canadian husband and wife duo: Bob Regan and Lucille Star.		
2/01/64	**45**	1	1 Hootenanny Express................................		A&M 727
2/10/68	**51**	5	2 Let's Wait A Little Longer		Epic 10258
			ACE CANNON		
			Born on 5/5/34 in Grenada, Mississippi. Saxophonist since age 10. Worked with Bill Black's Combo (Hi Records' studio band).		
2/19/77	**73**	4	1 Blue Eyes Crying In The Rain..................... [I]		Hi 2313
			JIMMI CANNON		
			Female vocalist from Sylacauga, Alabama. Performed with Dean Martin's Golddiggers from 1971-73. Worked clubs in Hollywood during the mid-70s.		
10/24/81	**63**	5	1 Whole Lot Of Cheatin' Goin' On		Warner 49806
3/20/82	**78**	5	2 Even If It's Wrong		Warner 50024
8/28/82	**81**	4	3 Fool's Gold		Warner 29949
			THE CANNONS		
			Family trio from Oklahoma. Consisted of twins Karla (piano, trumpet, fiddle) and Darla (guitar, saxophone), and brother Larry (guitar, trumpet, banjo).		
12/03/83	**90**	2	1 One Step Closer		Compleat 116
11/08/86	**72**	7	2 Do You Mind If I Step Into Your Dreams		Mercury 888048
8/01/87	**73**	4	3 Love'll Come Lookin' For You		Mercury 888648
			CANYON		
			Texas group featuring Steve "Coop" Cooper, lead vocals.		
2/06/88	**59**	6	1 Overdue		16th Ave. 70410
5/28/88	**54**	9	2 In The Middle Of The Night		16th Ave. 70415
9/10/88	**55**	9	3 I Guess I Just Missed You......................		16th Ave. 70419
11/26/88+	**47**	10	4 Love Is On The Line		16th Ave. 70423
			THE CAPITALS		
			Columbus, Ohio quartet: Arti Portilla, lead singer.		
1/05/80	**91**	4	1 Me Touchin' You................................		Ridgetop 00779
9/27/80	**29**	11	2 A Little Ground In Texas.......................		Ridgetop 01080
3/07/81	**45**	8	3 Bridge Over Broadway		Ridgetop 01281
			HANK CAPPS		
9/16/72	**33**	13	1 Bowling Green		Capitol 3416
			CAPTAIN & TENNILLE		
			Captain: Daryl Dragon (b: 8/27/42, Los Angeles); and Toni Tennille (b: 5/8/43, Montgomery, AL). Husband and wife. Own TV show on ABC from 1976-77.		
5/06/78	**97**	3	1 I'm On My Way	*74*	A&M 2027

DEBUT DATE	PEAK POS	WKS CHR		ARTIST — Record Title	POP POS	Label & Number
				CAPTAIN STUBBY & THE BUCCANEERS Band led by Tom C. "Captain Stubby" Fouts (b: 11/24/18, Carroll County, IN). Worked on WLW-Cincinnati, own band from 1937. On WLS National Barn Dance for 10 years; made appearances on Don McNeil's Breakfast Club. Own Polka-Go-Round TV series on ABC from 1965-68. Later worked as a disc jockey on WLS-Chicago.		
7/16/49	**12**	1	1	Money, Marbles & Chalk/ Juke Box #12		
7/23/49	**14**	1	2	Come Wet Your Mustache With Me Juke Box #14		Decca 46149
				JACK CARDWELL Born in Chapman, Alabama; raised in Mobile. Own band while a teenager; worked as singing deejay with Tom Jackson as "Tom & Jack", on WKAB-Mobile, in the late 40s.		
2/14/53	**3**	9	1	**The Death Of Hank Williams** Best Seller #3 / Jockey #4 / Juke Box #5		King 1172
9/26/53	**7**	2	2	**Dear Joan** Best Seller #7		King 1269
				HENSON CARGILL Born on 2/5/41 in Oklahoma City. Studied animal husbandry at Colorado State; worked as a deputy sheriff in Oklahoma County. Performed with The Kimberleys in the mid-60s. Appeared on the TV series "Country Hayride" in Cincinnati. Operates a large cattle ranch in Stillwater, Oklahoma.		
12/09/67+	**1**[5]	19	1	**Skip A Rope**	25	Monument 1041
4/27/68	**11**	12	2	Row Row Row		Monument 1065
8/10/68	**39**	8	3	She Thinks I'm On That Train		Monument 1084
1/25/69	**8**	14	4	**None Of My Business**		Monument 1122
5/31/69	**40**	8	5	This Generation Shall Not Pass		Monument 1142
9/20/69	**32**	9	6	Then The Baby Came		Monument 1158
5/16/70	**18**	11	7	The Most Uncomplicated Goodbye I've Ever Heard		Monument 1198
7/17/71	**44**	9	8	Pencil Marks On The Wall		Mega 0030
11/27/71	**65**	3	9	Naked And Crying		Mega 0043
3/04/72	**64**	4	10	I Can't Face The Bed Alone		Mega 0060
10/14/72	**62**	7	11	Red Skies Over Georgia		Mega 0090
10/13/73	**28**	13	12	Some Old California Memory		Atlantic 4007
3/02/74	**78**	7	13	She Still Comes To Me (To Pour The Wine)		Atlantic 4016
5/25/74	**29**	13	14	Stop And Smell The Roses #9 pop hit for Mac Davis in 1974		Atlantic 4021
12/22/79+	**29**	13	15	Silence On The Line		Copper Mt. 201
5/03/80	**67**	5	16	Have A Good Day		Copper Mt. 589
				CARLETTE		
2/09/85	**60**	5	1	Anyway That You Want Me		Oak 1079
4/06/85	**71**	5	2	Showdown		Luv 106
6/08/85	**52**	9	3	You Can't Measure My Love		Luv 107
8/17/85	**65**	7	4	Tonight's The Night		Luv 109
2/22/86	**72**	5	5	Two Steps From The Blues		Luv 116
4/12/86	**61**	6	6	Sugar Shack #1 pop hit for Jimmy Gilmer & The Fireballs in 1963		Luv 118
10/18/86	**52**	7	7	We Belong Together		Luv 125
5/02/87	**63**	4	8	Waltzin' With Daddy		Luv 137
5/30/87	**57**	4	9	You've Lost That Loving Feeling #1 pop hit for The Righteous Brothers in 1965		Luv 142
				TOM CARLILE Singer/songwriter from Florida.		
6/20/81	**93**	2	1	Gold Cadillac		Door Knob 157
8/29/81	**73**	6	2	Get It While You Can		Door Knob 162
10/17/81	**49**	12	3	Catch Me If You Can		Door Knob 167
1/30/82	**84**	3	4	Feel		Door Knob 172
2/20/82	**70**	5	5	Lover (Right Where I Want You)		Door Knob 170
5/08/82	**59**	9	6	Hurtin' For Your Love		Door Knob 176
7/17/82	**39**	11	7	Back In Debbie's Arms		Door Knob 180
10/23/82	**37**	12	8	Green Eyes		Door Knob 187
1/08/83	**55**	7	9	Rainin' Down In Nashville		Door Knob 191

DEBUT DATE	PEAK POS	WKS CHR	ARTIST — Record Title	POP POS	Label & Number
			BILL CARLISLE		
			Born on 12/19/08 in Wakefield, Kentucky. Brother of Cliff Carlisle; performed as a team from 1930-47. On WLAP-Lexington from 1931, with own show starting in 1937. Cliff retired in 1947, and Bill formed and led The Carlisles who were noted for their humorous recordings. Member of the Grand Ole Opry since 1953.		
10/26/46	5	1	1 **Rainbow At Midnight** .... [N]		King 535
6/19/48	14	2	2 **Tramp On The Street** .... [N]		King 697
			Best Seller #14 / Juke Box #14		
12/11/65+	4	17	3 **What Kinda Deal Is This** .... [N]		Hickory 1348
			THE CARLISLES		
			See Bill Carlisle for bio.		
12/15/51+	6	8	1 **Too Old To Cut The Mustard**		Mercury 6348
			Jockey #6		
1/10/53	1⁴	24	2 **No Help Wanted**		Mercury 70028
			Jockey #1(4) / Juke Box #1(4) / Best Seller #2		
4/11/53	3	13	3 **Knothole** .... [N]		Mercury 70109
			Jockey #3 / Best Seller #8		
7/25/53	2¹	8	4 **Is Zat You, Myrtle** .... [N]		Mercury 70174
			Jockey #2 / Best Seller #9		
11/07/53+	5	6	5 **Tain't Nice**		Mercury 70232
			Jockey #5 / Juke Box #6		
7/03/54	15	1	6 **Shake-A-Leg**		Mercury 70351
			Jockey #15		
10/09/54	12	5	7 **Honey Love**		Mercury 70434
			Jockey #12		
			KATHY CARLLILE		
			Born Mary Katherine Carllile, daughter of Kenneth Ray "Thumbs" Carllile (guitarist with Jimmy Dickens and Roger Miller).		
4/05/80	61	8	1 Stay Until The Rain Stops.............................		Frontline 705
			PAULETTE CARLSON		
			Born in Northfield, Minnesota. Sang back-up with Gail Davies. Formed own band, Highway 101, in 1986.		
6/25/83	65	7	1 You Gotta Get To My Heart (Before You Lay A Hand On Me)		RCA 13546
12/03/83	67	8	2 I'd Say Yes..		RCA 13599
3/10/84	72	4	3 Can You Fool		RCA 13745
			ERIC CARMEN - see LOUISE MANDRELL		
			KIM CARNES		
			Born on 7/20/45 in Los Angeles. Vocalist/pianist/composer. Member of The New Christy Minstrels with husband/co-writer Dave Ellingson and Kenny Rogers, late 1960s.		
7/29/78	99	2	1 You're A Part Of Me.....................................		Ariola 7704
			GENE COTTON with KIM CARNES		
4/05/80	3	14	2 **Don't Fall In Love With A Dreamer**...............	4	United Art. 1345
			KENNY ROGERS with KIM CARNES		
11/10/84	70	10	3 What About Me?	15	RCA 13899
			KENNY ROGERS with KIM CARNES & JAMES INGRAM		
8/20/88	70	7	4 Speed Of The Sound Of Loneliness		MCA 53387
			backing vocal: Lyle Lovett		
10/29/88	68	5	5 Crazy In Love...		MCA 53433
			RICK & JANIS CARNES		
			Husband and wife team: Rick (b: Memphis, TN; guitar) and Janis (b: Shelbyville, TN; keyboards). Married in 1973; moved to Nashville in 1978.		
12/18/82+	67	6	1 Have You Heard		Elektra 69928
7/30/83	51	8	2 Poor Girl		Warner 29656
11/26/83+	32	16	3 Does He Ever Mention My Name......................		Warner 29448
8/18/84	74	4	4 Long Lost Causes		MCA 52414
			KRIS CARPENTER		
2/21/81	76	4	1 My Song Don't Sing The Same		Door Knob 146
			CARPENTERS		
			Brother and sister duo from New Haven, Connecticut: Richard (b: 10/15/46) and Karen Carpenter (b: 3/2/50). Karen died of heart failure due to anorexia on 2/4/83.		
2/18/78	8	14	1 **Sweet, Sweet Smile**	44	A&M 2008

JOE "FINGERS" CARR - see TENNESSEE ERNIE FORD

DEBUT DATE	PEAK POS	WKS CHR	ARTIST — Record Title	POP POS	Label & Number
			KENNY CARR		
9/10/88	96	1	1 The Writing On The Wall		Kottage 0090
			JOE CARSON		
			Singer from Brownwood, Texas. Died in an automobile accident in March of 1964.		
8/03/63	27	2	1 I Gotta Get Drunk (And I Shore Do Dread It).......		Liberty 55578
			· written by Willie Nelson		
11/09/63+	19	10	2 Helpless		Liberty 55614
3/07/64	34	11	3 Double Life		Liberty 55664
			WAYNE CARSON		
			Born Wayne Carson Thompson in Denver. Wrote hits "Always On My Mind" for Elvis Presley and Willie Nelson; "No Love At All" for Lynn Anderson; and "Somebody Like Me" for Eddy Arnold.		
9/29/73	77	7	1 You're Gonna Love Yourself In The Morning		Monument 8581
12/25/76+	82	5	2 Barstool Mountain...............................		Elektra 45358
6/25/77	99	2	3 Bugle Ann		Elektra 45407
4/02/83	61	7	4 1 Yr 2 Mo 11 Days................................		EMH 0017
			ALAN CARTEE		
10/08/77	98	1	1 Let My Fingers Do The Walking (I'm Your Telephone Man).............................. [N]		Groovy 101
			THE CARTER FAMILY		
			Group from Virginia, first recorded in August of 1927. Founded by Alvin Pleasant "A.P." Carter (b: 4/15/1891, Maces Spring, VA; d: 11/7/60); with wife Sara Dougherty (b: 7/21/1898) and sister-in-law Maybelle Addington (b: 5/10/09; d: 10/23/78). Joined during 1936-39 by Maybelle's daughters Anita, June and Helen, and A.P.'s children Janette and Joe. This group disbanded in 1943 and was re-formed by Maybelle and her daughters as the Carter Sisters and Mother Maybelle. Worked on the Tennessee Barn Dance, WRVA-Richmond from 1943-48. Joined the Grand Ole Opry in 1948. Joined Johnny Cash's road show in 1961. Original group entered the Country Music Hall Of Fame in 1970. Chart hits feature Maybelle and her daughters.		
9/04/71	37	11	1 A Song To Mama		Columbia 45428
			narration and vocal backing: Johnny Cash		
4/29/72	42	7	2 Travelin' Minstrel Band................................		Columbia 45581
9/30/72	35	8	3 The World Needs A Melody		Columbia 45679
			THE CARTER FAMILY with JOHNNY CASH		
8/04/73	57	7	4 Praise The Lord And Pass The Soup		Columbia 45890
			JOHNNY CASH with THE CARTER FAMILY & THE OAK RIDGE BOYS		
			ANITA CARTER		
			Born in Maces Spring, Virginia on 3/31/34. Member of the famous Carter Family group. Daughter of Maybelle and Ezra Carter; sister of June and Helen. Member of "Nita, Rita & Ruby" trio (see Ruby Wright).		
4/21/51	4	11	1 **Bluebird Island/**		
			Best Seller #4 / Juke Box #7		
5/19/51	2¹	14	2 **Down The Trail Of Achin' Hearts**		RCA 0441
			Juke Box #2 / Best Seller 37 / Jockey #7		
			above 2: HANK SNOW with ANITA CARTER		
9/03/66	44	3	3 I'm Gonna Leave You..................................		RCA 8923
10/21/67	61	3	4 Love Me Now		RCA 9307
3/30/68	4	15	5 **I Got You**		RCA 9480
			WAYLON JENNINGS & ANITA CARTER		
11/09/68	65	5	6 To Be A Child Again		United Art. 50444
4/12/69	50	7	7 The Coming Of The Roads.............................		United Art. 50503
			JOHNNY DARRELL & ANITA CARTER		
1/16/71	41	8	8 Tulsa County		Capitol 2994
10/23/71	61	8	9 A Whole Lotta Lovin'................................		Capitol 3194
			BENNY CARTER & HIS ORCHESTRA		
			Born Bennett Lester Carter on 8/8/07 in New York City. Alto saxophonist/trumpeter/clarinetist/pianist. "America's Amazing Man Of Music". Played in several bands, including Duke Ellington, until 1935. Own band to 1946. Moved to Los Angeles and did movie soundtrack work. Appeared in the film "The Snows Of Kilimanjaro" in 1952.		
2/19/44	2¹	5	1 **Hurry, Hurry!**..	*27*	Capitol 144
			vocal: Savannah Churchill		
			BRENDA CARTER - see GEORGE JONES		

DEBUT DATE	PEAK POS	WKS CHR	ARTIST — Record Title	POP POS	Label & Number
			CARLENE CARTER Born on 9/26/55, the daughter of June Carter and Carl Smith. Worked with the Carter Family from the late 60s into the early 70s. Went solo thereafter. Appeared in the London production of "Pump Boys And Dinettes". Married for a time to rocker Nick Lowe.		
10/27/79	42	8	1 Do It In A Heartbeat	*108*	Warner 49083
10/25/80	76	5	2 Baby Ride Easy.. CARLENE CARTER with DAVE EDMUNDS		Warner 49572
			FRED CARTER, JR. Born on 12/31/33 in Winnsboro, Louisiana. Guitarist with Conway Twitty in the late 50s. Prominent session musician in Nashville; country A&R director for ABC Records from 1967. President of Nugget Records.		
10/14/67	70	3	1 And You Wonder Why................................		Monument 1022
			JUNE CARTER Born on 6/23/29 in Maces Spring, Virginia. Member of famous Carter Family group. Daughter of Maybelle and Ezra Carter, sister of Anita and Helen. Worked with Elvis Presley, then joined the Johnny Cash road show in 1961. Married Cash in 1968. Also see Johnny Cash.		
8/27/49	9	1	1 **Baby It's Cold Outside** .... HOMER & JETHRO & JUNE CARTER		RCA 0075
4/03/71	27	11	2 A Good Man .... JUNE CARTER CASH		Columbia 45338
			WILF CARTER Wilf "Montana Slim" Carter, born on 12/18/04 in Guysboro, Nova Scotia. Rodeo performer from 1924. Worked on radio in Calgary and Vancouver from 1933. First recorded for Bluebird in 1935. Member of the Horsemen's Hall of Fame.		
9/17/49	14	1	1 Sittin' On The Doorstep.............................. Juke Box #14		Macy's Rec. 100
			LIONEL CARTWRIGHT Singer/actor from West Virginia. Starred on The Nashville Network's TV series "Pickin' At The Paradise"; also a songwriter/musical director/arranger of that show.		
11/19/88+	45	13	1 You're Gonna Make Her Mine		MCA 53444
			JOHNNY CARVER ★★**160**★★ Born John David Carver on 11/24/40 in Jackson, Mississippi. Sang with family gospel group from age 5, had own band in high school. Lived in Milwaukee from 1961-65, then worked in Los Angeles as singer with the house band at The Palomino in Hollywood.		
12/23/67+	21	13	1 Your Lily White Hands.................................		Imperial 66268
6/01/68	48	8	2 I Still Didn't Have The Sense To Go		Imperial 66297
12/07/68+	32	11	3 Hold Me Tight... #5 pop hit for Johnny Nash in 1968		Imperial 66341
4/05/69	26	9	4 Sweet Wine		Imperial 66361
8/02/69	41	10	5 That's Your Hang Up		Imperial 66389
12/13/69+	43	9	6 Willie And The Hand Jive .... #9 pop hit for the Johnny Otis Show in 1958		Imperial 66423
6/20/70	68	4	7 Harvey Harrington IV..................................		Imperial 66442
12/12/70	73	2	8 If You See My Baby		United Art. 50713
8/14/71	34	15	9 If You Think That It's All Right		Epic 10760
12/25/71+	27	11	10 I Start Thinking About You...........................		Epic 10813
6/24/72	35	9	11 I Want You		Epic 10872
4/07/73	5	17	12 **Yellow Ribbon** .... #1 pop hit for Tony Orlando & Dawn in 1973		ABC 11357
7/28/73	6	13	13 **You Really Haven't Changed**........................		ABC 11374
12/08/73+	12	16	14 Tonight Someone's Falling In Love		ABC 11403
4/13/74	27	12	15 Country Lullabye		ABC 11425
8/24/74	10	16	16 **Don't Tell (That Sweet Ole Lady Of Mine)**.......		ABC 12017
1/18/75	39	11	17 January Jones		ABC 12052
6/07/75	64	7	18 Strings		ABC 12097
10/04/75	74	7	19 Start All Over Again		ABC/Dot 17576
3/06/76	77	5	20 Snap, Crackle And Pop................................		ABC/Dot 17614
7/04/76	9	14	21 **Afternoon Delight** .... #1 pop hit for the Starland Vocal Band in 1976		ABC/Dot 17640
11/06/76	47	9	22 Love Is Only Love (When Shared By Two)		ABC/Dot 17661
2/12/77	48	6	23 Sweet City Woman .... #8 pop hit for The Stampeders in 1971		ABC/Dot 17675
3/12/77	29	10	24 Living Next Door To Alice............................ #25 pop hit for Smokie in 1977		ABC/Dot 17685

DEBUT DATE	PEAK POS	WKS CHR	ARTIST — Record Title	POP POS	Label & Number
			JOHNNY CARVER — Continued		
6/18/77	**36**	9	25 Down At The Pool		ABC/Dot 17707
11/26/77	**72**	6	26 Apartment		ABC/Dot 17729
6/14/80	**90**	3	27 Fingertips		Equity 1902
1/24/81	**73**	5	28 S.O.S.		Tanglewood 1905
			KAREN CASEY		
2/23/80	**92**	2	1 Leavin' on Your Mind		Western Pr. 112
			JOHNNY CASH ★★3★★		
			Born on 2/26/32 in Kingsland, Arkansas. To Dyess, Arkansas at age 3. Brother Roy had the Dixie Rhythm Ramblers band in late 40s. In US Air Force, 1950-54. Formed trio with Luther Perkins (guitar) and Marshall Grant (bass) in 1955. First recorded for Sun in 1955. On Louisiana Hayride and Grand Ole Opry in 1957. Own TV show for ABC from 1969-71. Worked with June Carter from 1961, married her in March of 1968. Daughter Rosanne Cash and stepdaughter Carlene Carter currently enjoying successful singing careers. CMA award: Entertainer of the Year - 1969. Elected to the Country Music Hall Of Fame in 1980.		
11/26/55	**14**	1	1 Cry! Cry! Cry! .... Best Seller #14		Sun 221
2/04/56	**4**	23	2 **So Doggone Lonesome/** Juke Box #4 / Best Seller #6 / Jockey #6		
2/11/56	**4**	19	3 **Folsom Prison Blues** .... Jockey #4 / Juke Box #5 / Best Seller #5		Sun 232
6/09/56	**1**⁶	43	4 **I Walk The Line/** Juke Box #1(6) / Jockey #1(1) / Best Seller #2	*17*	
		9	5 Get Rhythm .... Juke Box flip / Best Seller flip		Sun 241
12/22/56+	**1**⁵	28	6 **There You Go/** Juke Box #1 / Best Seller #2 / Jockey #2		
1/12/57	**7**	12	7 **Train Of Love** .... Jockey #7 / Best Seller #13		Sun 258
5/27/57	**9**	15	8 **Next In Line/** Best Seller #9 / Jockey #9	*99*	
		9	9 Don't Make Me Go .... Best Seller flip		Sun 266
9/16/57	**3**	23	10 **Home Of The Blues/** Jockey #3 / Best Seller #5	*88*	
10/07/57	**13**	2	11 Give My Love To Rose .... Jockey #13		Sun 279
1/20/58	**1**¹⁰	23	12 **Ballad Of A Teenage Queen/** Jockey #1(10) / Best Seller #1(8)	*14*	
2/10/58	**4**	14	13 **Big River** .... Jockey #4		Sun 283
5/26/58	**1**⁸	24	14 **Guess Things Happen That Way/** Best Seller #1(8) / Jockey #1(3)	*11*	
6/02/58	**6**	13	15 **Come In Stranger** .... Jockey #6	*66*	Sun 295
8/25/58	**2**⁴	16	16 **The Ways Of A Woman In Love/** Best Seller #2 / Jockey #2	*24*	
9/01/58	**5**	16	17 **You're The Nearest Thing To Heaven**		Sun 302
10/13/58	**4**	19	18 **All Over Again/**	*38*	
10/13/58	**7**	15	19 **What Do I Care**	*52*	Columbia 41251
1/19/59	**1**⁶	20	20 **Don't Take Your Guns To Town**	*32*	Columbia 41313
1/19/59	**30**	1	21 It's Just About Time	*47*	Sun 309
3/30/59	**8**	13	22 **Luther Played The Boogie/**		
3/30/59	**12**	9	23 Thanks A Lot		Sun 316
5/04/59	**9**	11	24 **Frankie's Man, Johnny/** new version of tune written in 1870: "Frankie & Johnny"	*57*	
5/11/59	**13**	11	25 You Dreamer You		Columbia 41371
7/20/59	**11**	11	26 Katy Too	*66*	Sun 321
8/10/59	**4**	20	27 **I Got Stripes/**	*43*	
8/24/59	**14**	9	28 Five Feet High And Rising	*76*	Columbia 41427
11/09/59	**22**	5	29 Goodby Little Darlin' .... written in 1946 by Gene Autry		Sun 331
1/04/60	**24**	1	30 The Little Drummer Boy .... [X]	*63*	Columbia 41481
2/15/60	**16**	10	31 Straight A's In Love/	*84*	
3/07/60	**20**	2	32 I Love You Because .... vocal backing: The Gene Lowery Singers (also #37 below)		Sun 334

DEBUT DATE	PEAK POS	WKS CHR		ARTIST — Record Title	POP POS	Label & Number
				JOHNNY CASH — Continued		
4/25/60	**10**	15	33	**Seasons Of My Heart/**		
5/09/60	**13**	8	34	Smiling Bill McCall	110	Columbia 41618
8/22/60	**15**	7	35	Second Honeymoon	79	Columbia 41707
12/26/60	**30**	1	36	Mean Eyed Cat		Sun 347
2/06/61	**13**	9	37	Oh Lonesome Me..	93	Sun 355
				all of above Sun's with The Tennessee Two		
6/12/61	**24**	2	38	The Rebel - Johnny Yuma..............................	108	Columbia 41995
				original theme from the TV western series "The Rebel"		
12/18/61+	**11**	14	39	Tennessee Flat-Top Box	84	Columbia 42147
				daughter Rosanne Cash's version hit POS 1 in 1988		
3/31/62	**24**	3	40	The Big Battle		Columbia 42301
7/14/62	**8**	10	41	**In The Jailhouse Now**		Columbia 42425
				Jimmie Rodgers' original hit made the charts in 1928		
4/06/63	**13**	3	42	Busted		Columbia 42665
				#4 pop hit for Ray Charles in 1963		
6/08/63	**1** [7]	26	43	**Ring Of Fire**..	17	Columbia 42788
11/09/63	**2** [3]	16	44	**The Matador**	44	Columbia 42880
2/22/64	**1** [6]	22	45	**Understand Your Man/**	35	
3/07/64	**49**	1	46	Dark As A Dungeon....................................	119	Columbia 42964
7/11/64	**3**	20	47	**The Ballad Of Ira Hayes/**		
				Hayes: Indian who helped raise the flag at Iwo Jima in WWII		
7/25/64	**8**	15	48	**Bad News**..		Columbia 43058
2/20/65	**3**	16	49	**Orange Blossom Special**	80	Columbia 43206
7/10/65	**15**	13	50	Mister Garfield..		Columbia 43313
				ballad about President Garfield's assassination		
9/04/65	**10**	9	51	**The Sons Of Katie Elder**........................	119	Columbia 43342
				from the film of the same title		
11/20/65+	**9**	14	52	**Happy To Be With You**		Columbia 43420
2/12/66	**2** [2]	18	53	**The One On The Right Is On The Left**	46	Columbia 43496
7/02/66	**17**	9	54	Everybody Loves A Nut.................................	96	Columbia 43673
9/10/66	**39**	5	55	Boa Constrictor .... [N]	107	Columbia 43763
12/24/66+	**20**	13	56	You Beat All I Ever Saw		Columbia 43921
10/28/67	**60**	6	57	The Wind Changes		Columbia 44288
12/23/67+	**2** [2]	15	58	**Rosanna's Going Wild**	91	Columbia 44373
6/01/68	**1** [4]	18	59	**Folsom Prison Blues** .... [R]	32	Columbia 44513
				new live version of Johnny's 1956 Sun hit		
12/07/68+	**1** [6]	20	60	**Daddy Sang Bass**	42	Columbia 44689
7/26/69	**1** [5]	14	61●	**A Boy Named Sue** .... [N]	2	Columbia 44944
				recorded live at San Quentin prison		
10/11/69	**23**	12	62	Get Rhythm .... [R]	60	Sun 1103
				reissue of Johnny's Sun 241 hit (live effects dubbed in)		
11/22/69	**4**	13	63	**Blistered/**	50	
		12	64	See Ruby Fall..		Columbia 45020
2/28/70	**35**	7	65	Rock Island Line...	93	Sun 1111
				#8 pop hit for Lonnie Donegan in 1956		
4/18/70	**3**	14	66	**What Is Truth**	19	Columbia 45134
9/05/70	**1** [2]	15	67	**Sunday Morning Coming Down**......................	46	Columbia 45211
12/05/70	**41**	8	68	Big River .... [R]		Sun 1121
				reissue of Johnny's Sun 283 hit		
12/19/70+	**1** [1]	13	69	**Flesh And Blood**	54	Columbia 45269
				from the film "I Walk The Line"		
3/27/71	**3**	13	70	**Man In Black**..	58	Columbia 45339
6/26/71	**18**	10	71	Singing In Viet Nam Talking Blues	124	Columbia 45393
10/16/71	**16**	11	72	Papa Was A Good Man	104	Columbia 45460
1/29/72	**2** [1]	16	73	**A Thing Called Love**	103	Columbia 45534
				above 2: with The Evangel Temple Choir		
5/06/72	**2** [3]	12	74	**Kate**..	75	Columbia 45590
				written by Marty Robbins; with The Tennessee Three		
8/26/72	**2** [2]	15	75	**Oney**	101	Columbia 45660
12/23/72+	**3**	15	76	**Any Old Wind That Blows**........................		Columbia 45740
4/21/73	**30**	9	77	Children		Columbia 45786
				from the film "The Gospel Road"		
2/23/74	**52**	8	78	Orleans Parish Prison		Columbia 45997
4/27/74	**31**	13	79	Ragged Old Flag..		Columbia 46028

DEBUT DATE	PEAK POS	WKS CHR		ARTIST — Record Title	POP POS	Label & Number
				JOHNNY CASH — Continued		
12/14/74+	14	12	80	Lady Came From Baltimore		Columbia 10066
4/12/75	42	9	81	My Old Kentucky Home (Turpentine And Dandelion Wine)		Columbia 10116
7/26/75	17	12	82	Look At Them Beans		Columbia 10177
11/15/75+	35	12	83	Texas - 1947		Columbia 10237
2/07/76	54	7	84	Strawberry Cake		Columbia 10279
4/10/76	1²	15	85	**One Piece At A Time**	29	Columbia 10321
7/24/76	29	8	86	Sold Out Of Flagpoles............................		Columbia 10381
10/23/76	41	8	87	It's All Over		Columbia 10424
				above 3: with The Tennessee Three		
2/26/77	38	9	88	The Last Gunfighter Ballad		Columbia 10483
8/06/77	46	9	89	Lady............................		Columbia 10587
10/22/77	32	12	90	After The Ball		Columbia 10623
2/11/78	12	13	91	I Would Like To See You Again............................		Columbia 10681
9/09/78	44	8	92	Gone Girl............................		Columbia 10817
12/09/78	89	2	93	It'll Be Her............................		Columbia 10855
1/13/79	21	13	94	I Will Rock And Roll With You............................		Columbia 10888
5/19/79	2¹	16	95	(Ghost) Riders In The Sky............................		Columbia 10961
				#1 pop hit for Vaughn Monroe in 1949		
10/20/79	42	7	96	I'll Say It's True............................		Columbia 11103
				guest vocal: George Jones		
4/19/80	66	5	97	Bull Rider............................		Columbia 11237
6/07/80	54	8	98	Song Of The Patriot............................		Columbia 11283
				vocal harmony: Marty Robbins		
8/23/80	53	8	99	Cold Lonesome Morning		Columbia 11340
11/29/80	85	4	100	The Last Time		Columbia 11399
1/24/81	78	5	101	Without Love		Columbia 11424
3/21/81	10	15	102	**The Baron**............................		Columbia 60516
7/25/81	60	5	103	Mobile Bay............................		Columbia 02189
1/23/82	71	5	104	The Reverend Mr. Black/		
				#8 pop hit for The Kingston Trio in 1963		
		5	105	Chattanooga City Limit Sign		Columbia 02669
4/17/82	26	12	106	The General Lee		Scotti Br. 02803
				title refers to TV's "Dukes Of Hazzard" car		
8/07/82	55	8	107	Georgia On A Fast Train............................		Columbia 03058
2/26/83	84	2	108	We Must Believe In Magic		Columbia 03524
9/24/83	75	4	109	I'm Ragged But I'm Right............................		Columbia 04060
5/12/84	84	5	110	That's The Truth		Columbia 04428
7/14/84	45	11	111	The Chicken In Black .... [N]		Columbia 04513
3/28/87	43	11	112	The Night Hank Williams Came To Town..........		Mercury 888459
				features brief guest vocals by Waylon Jennings		
12/12/87	72	5	113	W. Lee O'Daniel (And The Light Crust Dough Boys)............................		Mercury 870010
				JOHNNY CASH DUOS with:		
				KAREN BROOKS:		
7/13/85	45	9	114	I Will Dance With You............................		Warner 28979
				JUNE CARTER:		
11/07/64+	4	22	115	It Ain't Me, Babe............................	58	Columbia 43145
				#8 pop hit for The Turtles in 1965		
3/04/67	2¹	17	116	**Jackson**............................		Columbia 44011
				#14 pop hit for Nancy Sinatra & Lee Hazlewood in 1967		
6/24/67	6	17	117	**Long-Legged Guitar Pickin' Man**..................		Columbia 44158
1/24/70	2¹	15	118	**If I Were A Carpenter**............................	36	Columbia 45064
				#8 pop hit for Bobby Darin in 1966		
9/11/71	15	13	119	No Need To Worry		Columbia 45431
7/15/72	29	7	120	If I Had A Hammer		Columbia 45631
				#10 pop hit for Peter, Paul & Mary in 1962		
1/20/73	27	10	121	The Loving Gift............................		Columbia 45758
9/29/73	69	10	122	Allegheny............................		Columbia 45929
11/20/76+	26	11	123	Old Time Feeling............................		Columbia 10436
				MOTHER MAYBELLE CARTER:		
11/17/73+	34	10	124	Pick The Wildwood Flower............................		Columbia 45938

DEBUT DATE	PEAK POS	WKS CHR	ARTIST — Record Title	POP POS	Label & Number
			JOHNNY CASH — Continued		
			CARTER FAMILY:		
9/30/72	35	8	125 The World Needs A Melody		Columbia 45679
			CARTER FAMILY & OAK RIDGE BOYS:		
8/04/73	57	7	126 Praise The Lord And Pass The Soup		Columbia 45890
			WAYLON JENNINGS:		
5/20/78	2²	13	127 **There Ain't No Good Chain Gang/**		
11/17/79+	22	12	128 I Wish I Was Crazy Again		Columbia 10742
5/17/86	35	11	129 Even Cowgirls Get The Blues........................		Columbia 05896
			WAYLON JENNINGS, WILLIE NELSON, KRIS KRISTOFFERSON:		
5/18/85	1¹	20	130 **Highwayman**		Columbia 04881
9/14/85	15	18	131 Desperados Waiting For A Train		Columbia 05594
			HANK WILLIAMS, JR.:		
9/24/88	21	20	132 That Old Wheel..		Mercury 870688
			ROSANNE CASH ★★118★★		
			Born on 5/24/55 in Memphis, daughter of Johnny Cash and Vivian Liberto. Raised by her mother in California, then moved to Nashville after high school graduation. Worked in the Johnny Cash Road Show. Married Rodney Crowell in 1979.		
9/08/79	17	12	1 No Memories Hangin' Round		Columbia 11045
			ROSANNE CASH with BOBBY BARE		
2/02/80	15	13	2 Couldn't Do Nothin' Right............................		Columbia 11188
5/31/80	25	12	3 Take Me, Take Me		Columbia 11268
2/21/81	1¹	19	4 **Seven Year Ache**....................................	22	Columbia 11426
8/29/81	1¹	16	5 **My Baby Thinks He's A Train**		Columbia 02463
12/19/81+	1¹	18	6 **Blue Moon With Heartache**	104	Columbia 02659
5/29/82	4	18	7 Ain't No Money.......................................		Columbia 02937
10/09/82+	8	20	8 I Wonder		Columbia 03283
3/12/83	14	15	9 It Hasn't Happened Yet		Columbia 03705
6/01/85	1¹	24	10 **I Don't Know Why You Don't Want Me**		Columbia 04809
10/05/85+	1¹	24	11 **Never Be You**		Columbia 05621
2/15/86	5	22	12 **Hold On**		Columbia 05794
7/19/86	5	20	13 **Second To No One**		Columbia 06159
6/27/87	1¹	23	14 **The Way We Make A Broken Heart**		Columbia 07200
11/14/87+	1¹	22	15 **Tennessee Flat Top Box**		Columbia 07624
			#11 hit in 1962 for her dad, Johnny Cash		
1/23/88	1¹	23	16 **It's Such A Small World**		Columbia 07693
			RODNEY CROWELL & ROSANNE CASH		
4/02/88	1¹	22	17 **If You Change Your Mind**		Columbia 07746
8/13/88	1¹	23	18 **Runaway Train**....................................		Columbia 07988
			all of above (except #12): produced by Rodney Crowell		
			TOMMY CASH		
			Born on 4/5/40 in Dyess, Arkansas; younger brother of Johnny Cash. Own band at Treadwell High School in 1957. Disc jockey for the US Army in Frankfurt, Germany in 1958. Worked with Hank Williams Jr. in the mid-60s.		
8/31/68	41	9	1 The Sounds Of Goodbye		United Art. 50337
6/21/69	43	11	2 Your Lovin' Takes The Leavin' Out Of Me..........		Epic 10469
11/22/69+	4	16	3 **Six White Horses**	79	Epic 10540
			tribute to John F. Kennedy, Robert Kennedy and Martin Luther King		
3/28/70	9	14	4 **Rise And Shine**....................................		Epic 10590
7/18/70	9	13	5 **One Song Away**		Epic 10630
11/21/70	36	9	6 The Tears On Lincoln's Face		Epic 10673
3/13/71	20	11	7 So This Is Love.......................................		Epic 10700
7/10/71	28	10	8 I'm Gonna Write A Song		Epic 10756
12/04/71	67	2	9 Roll Truck Roll		Epic 10795
3/25/72	32	11	10 You're Everything		Epic 10838
7/15/72	22	11	11 That Certain One		Epic 10885
10/28/72	24	11	12 Listen		Epic 10915
3/24/73	37	10	13 Workin' On A Feelin'		Epic 10964
7/28/73	16	13	14 I Recall A Gypsy Woman		Epic 11026
11/24/73+	21	13	15 She Met A Stranger, I Met A Train.................		Epic 11057
3/22/75	58	9	16 The One I Sing My Love Songs To		Elektra 45241
1/10/76	94	4	17 Broken Bones		20th Century 2263
			from the film "Death Riders"		

DEBUT DATE	PEAK POS	WKS CHR	ARTIST — Record Title	POP POS	Label & Number
			TOMMY CASH — Continued		
7/16/77	63	6	18 The Cowboy And The Lady		Monument 222
2/11/78	98	3	19 Take My Love To Rita		Monument 238
			CASHMAN & WEST		
			Duo of record producers Dennis "Terry Cashman" Minogue (b: 7/5/41) and Thomas "Tommy West" Picardo, Jr. (b: 8/17/42).		
2/10/73	69	2	1 Songman	*59*	Dunhill 4333
			LINDA CASSADY		
5/22/76	83	8	1 C.B. Widow		Cin Kay 107
9/11/76	91	4	2 If It's Your Song You Sing It		Cin Kay 111
1/29/77	79	6	3 Little Things Mean A Lot		Cin Kay 115
			#1 pop hit for Kitty Kallen in 1954		
4/09/77	92	4	4 I Don't Hurt Anymore		Cin Kay 116
2/04/78	91	3	5 Little Teardrops (Are Smarter Than You Think)..		Cin Kay 127
4/29/78	87	4	6 There's Nothing Like The Love Between A Woman And A Man		Cin Kay 036
			LINDA CASSADY/BOBBY SPEARS		
8/05/78	76	6	7 The Lonely Side Of The Bed		Cin Kay 131
			THE CATES SISTERS		
			Duo of fiddlers Margie and Marcy Cates. Worked as back-up act for Jim Ed Brown.		
9/11/76	82	5	1 Mr. Guitar		Caprice 2024
1/29/77	50	8	2 Out Of My Mind		Caprice 2030
5/21/77	74	6	3 Can't Help It		Caprice 2032
8/13/77	87	5	4 Throw Out Your Lifetime		Caprice 2038
10/01/77	30	11	5 I'll Always Love You		Caprice 2036
12/24/77+	29	11	6 I've Been Loved		Caprice 2041
3/18/78	61	7	7 Long Gone Blues		Caprice 2047
9/02/78	39	8	8 Lovin' You Off My Mind		Caprice 2051
			THE CATES:		
2/17/79	78	5	9 Going Down Slow		Ovation 1123
6/30/79	57	8	10 Make Love To Me		Ovation 1126
12/22/79+	68	7	11 Let's Go Through The Motions		Ovation 1134
5/24/80	72	5	12 Gonna Get Along Without You Now		Ovation 1144
			#11 pop hit for Patience & Prudence in 1956		
10/25/80	75	4	13 Lightnin' Strikin'		Ovation 1155
			CONNIE CATO		
			Born on 3/30/55 in Bethalte, Illinois.		
2/02/74	33	16	1 Superskirt		Capitol 3788
7/13/74	73	7	2 Super Kitten		Capitol 3908
10/19/74	92	6	3 Lincoln Autry		Capitol 3958
3/08/75	14	14	4 Hurt		Capitol 4035
			#4 pop hit for Timi Yuro in 1961		
7/26/75	83	6	5 Yes...		Capitol 4113
11/22/75+	53	10	6 Who Wants A Slightly Used Woman..................		Capitol 4169
4/24/76	91	4	7 I Love A Beautiful Guy................................		Capitol 4243
8/07/76	80	5	8 Here Comes That Rainy Day Feeling Again		Capitol 4303
			#15 pop hit for The Fortunes in 1971		
11/06/76	76	6	9 I'm Sorry		Capitol 4345
			#1 pop hit for Brenda Lee in 1960		
2/19/77	92	3	10 Don't You Ever Get Tired (Of Hurting Me)		Capitol 4379
8/16/80	49	7	11 You Better Hurry Home (Somethin's Burnin')		MCA 41287
			LANE CAUDELL		
			Born in Asheboro, North Carolina. Recorded with the duo, Shady Lane, and with the group, Skyband. Portrayed Woody King on TV's "Days Of Our Lives".		
9/19/87	66	5	1 Souvenirs		16th Ave. 70403
4/16/88	77	5	2 I Need A Good Woman Bad		16th Ave. 70411
			C COMPANY Featuring TERRY NELSON		
5/01/71	49	3	1● Battle Hymn Of Lt. Calley .... [S]	*37*	Plantation 73
			Calley: U.S. Army officer court-martialled for the massacre of civilians at My Lai, Vietnam		

DEBUT DATE	PEAK POS	WKS CHR	ARTIST — Record Title	POP POS	Label & Number
			CEDAR CREEK		
11/14/81	80	4	1 Looks Like A Set-Up To Me		Moon Shine 3001
2/06/82	42	10	2 Took It Like A Man, Cried Like A Baby		Moon Shine 3003
1/22/83	83	3	3 Take A Ride On A Riverboat		Moon Shine 3008
8/06/83	81	3	4 Lonely Heart		Moon Shine 3013
			DAVID CHAMBERLAIN Born in Ft. Worth, Texas in 1944.		
1/30/88	72	4	1 I Owe, I Owe (It's Off To Work I Go).................		Country I. 214
			CARL CHAMBERS		
2/28/81	91	2	1 Take Me Home With You		Prairie D. 8001
			CHANCE Quintet, originally called Texas Pride. Consisted of Jeff Barosh (vocals, steel guitar, fiddle, sax), Mick Barosh (vocals, drums), Jon Mulligan (keyboards), John Buckley (vocals, guitar), and Billy Hafer (bass). Jeff began solo recording career as "Jeff Chance" in 1988.		
4/20/85	35	13	1 To Be Lovers...		Mercury 880555
7/27/85	45	11	2 You Could Be The One Woman		Mercury 880959
10/26/85	30	15	3 She Told Me Yes		Mercury 884178
3/29/86	53	7	4 I Need Some Good News Bad		Mercury 884545
8/30/86	60	10	5 What Did You Do With My Heart		Mercury 884918
			JEFF CHANCE Vocalist/guitarist/fiddler born Jeff Barosh, from El Campo, Texas. Led the band, Chance, with brother Mick Barosh, in 1985. Began solo career in 1988.		
3/19/88	64	7	1 So Far Not So Good/		
6/18/88	52	7	2 Hopelessly Falling		Curb 10506
11/26/88+	57	9	3 Let It Burn...		Curb 10516
			HANK CHANEY		
8/16/86	98	1	1 Be-Bop-A-Lula "86"		CMI 04
			#7 pop hit for Gene Vincent in 1956		
			CHANTILLY Group features Kim Williams (lead singer) and Debbie Pierce (daughter of Webb).		
5/01/82	81	4	1 Whatever Turns You On		Jaroco 31082
6/26/82	43	10	2 Stumblin' In..		Jaroco 51282
			#4 pop hit for Suzi Quatro & Chris Norman in 1979		
10/09/82	65	6	3 Right Back Loving You Again.........................		F&L 519
12/25/82+	75	6	4 Better Off Blue		F&L 520
2/12/83	60	7	5 Storm Of Love		F&L 523
9/17/83	60	7	6 Have I Got A Heart For You		F&L 527
2/11/84	72	4	7 Baby's Walkin'		F&L 534
			CHAPARRAL BROTHERS Vocal duo of John and Paul Chaparral.		
5/11/68	65	4	1 Standing In The Rain		Capitol 2153
2/14/70	70	2	2 Running From A Memory..............................		Capitol 2708
			TAMMY CHAPARRO Born in Billings, Montana in 1967. Sang at parent's night club from age 9.		
5/07/83	89	3	1 Stay With Me..		Compass 60
			CEE CEE CHAPMAN & SANTA FE Female singer Chapman was born in Portsmouth and raised in Norfolk, Virginia.		
11/26/88	60	8	1 Gone But Not Forgotten		Curb 10518
			GARY CHAPMAN Singer/songwriter from Texas. Married to Amy Grant since 1982.		
1/09/88	60	6	1 When We're Together		RCA 5285
4/16/88	76	4	2 Everyday Man		RCA 7601
			MARSHALL CHAPMAN Born on 1/7/49 in Spartanburg, South Carolina. Moved to Nashville in 1973.		
3/05/77	100	2	1 Somewhere South Of Macon..........................		Epic 50307

DEBUT DATE	PEAK POS	WKS CHR	ARTIST — Record Title	POP POS	Label & Number
			CHARLENE Born Charlene D'Angelo on 6/1/50 in Hollywood.		
4/10/82	60	8	1 I've Never Been To Me.................................... originally released on Prodigal in 1977	*3*	Motown 1611
			KIM CHARLES Male singer.		
2/10/79	35	9	1 Want To Thank You		MCA 40987
			RAY CHARLES Born Ray Charles Robinson on 9/23/30 in Albany, Georgia. To Greenville, Florida while still an infant. Partially blind at age 5, completely blind at 7 (glaucoma). Studied classical piano and clarinet at State School for Deaf and Blind Children, St. Augustine, Florida, 1937-45. With local Florida bands, moved to Seattle in 1948. Formed the McSon Trio (also known as the Maxim Trio and the Maxine Trio) with G.D. McGhee (guitar) and Milton Garred (bass). First recordings were very much in the King Cole Trio style. Formed own band in 1954. Inducted into the Rock 'N' Roll Hall Of Fame in 1986. Extremely popular performer with many TV and film appearances.		
12/18/82+	20	18	1 Born To Love Me...		Columbia 03429
4/23/83	37	11	2 3/4 Time		Columbia 03810
9/24/83	82	3	3 Ain't Your Memory Got No Pride At All		Columbia 04083
4/14/84	50	10	4 Do I Ever Cross Your Mind		Columbia 04420
7/19/86	34	13	5 The Pages Of My Mind.................................		Columbia 06172
11/01/86	66	4	6 Dixie Moon/		
1/31/87	76	3	7 A Little Bit Of Heaven.................................		Columbia 06370
			RAY CHARLES DUOS with: *CLINT EASTWOOD:*		
11/22/80	55	10	8 Beers To You.. from the film "Any Which Way You Can" starring Eastwood		Warner 49608
			MICKEY GILLEY:		
5/04/85	12	17	9 It Ain't Gonna Worry My Mind........................		Columbia 04860
			GEORGE JONES:		
12/17/83+	6	18	10 **We Didn't See A Thing** .... featuring Chet Atkins, guitar		Columbia 04297
			WILLIE NELSON:		
12/15/84+	1¹	27	11 **Seven Spanish Angels**		Columbia 04715
			B.J. THOMAS:		
8/04/84	14	18	12 Rock And Roll Shoes		Columbia 04531
			HANK WILLIAMS, JR.:		
8/31/85	14	17	13 Two Old Cats Like Us..................................		Columbia 05575
			CHARLESTON EXPRESS with Jesse Wales		
12/15/84+	69	7	1 Sweet Love, Don't Cry..................................		Soundwaves 4743
5/18/85	82	4	2 Leaving..		Soundwaves 4749
			CHARNISSA - see JOHNNY PAYCHECK		
			BECKY CHASE		
1/12/85	77	6	1 Until The Music Is Gone		Spirit Horse 102
			CAROL CHASE Born in Minot, North Dakota. Wrote "We Belong Together" for Susie Allanson.		
11/10/79+	32	13	1 This Must Be My Ship		Casabl. W. 4501
2/23/80	48	7	2 Sexy Song..		Casabl. W. 4502
10/18/80	87	3	3 Regrets		Casablanca 2301
			DAWN CHASTAIN Former fashion model for the Neiman-Marcus stores. Member of the Illinois Country Opry in Springfield, Illinois.		
4/15/78	83	4	1 Never Knew (How Much I Loved You 'Til I Lost You)		Prairie D. 7623
1/06/79	72	4	2 Me Plus You Equals Love..............................		Oak 1018
5/05/79	91	2	3 Love Talks...		SCR 164
9/08/79	74	4	4 That's You, That's Me		SCR 178
			CHER Pop singer/Oscar-winning actress (for "Moonstruck"). Born Cherilyn LaPierre in El Centro, California on 5/20/46. In successful recording duo with husband Sonny Bono from 1963 until their divorce in 1974.		
7/14/79	87	2	1 It's Too Late To Love Me Now		Casablanca 987

57

DEBUT DATE	PEAK POS	WKS CHR	ARTIST — Record Title	POP POS	Label & Number
			DON CHERRY Born on 1/11/24 in Wichita Falls, Texas. Vocalist with Jan Garber band in the late 40s. Accomplished professional golfer.		
10/05/68	71	2	1 Take A Message To Mary .... #16 pop hit for The Everly Brothers in 1959		Monument 1088
			JIM CHESNUT Born on 12/1/44 in Midland, Texas. Former DJ and TV weatherman. One-time member of The Dan Blocker Singers.		
7/23/77	99	1	1 Let Me Love You Now		ABC/Hick. 54013
12/10/77+	76	8	2 The Wrong Side Of The Rainbow		ABC/Hick. 54021
4/15/78	76	6	3 The Ninth Of September		ABC/Hick. 54027
8/05/78	56	9	4 Show Me A Sign		ABC/Hick. 54033
11/18/78	57	7	5 Get Back To Loving Me		ABC/Hick. 54038
6/02/79	80	3	6 Just Let Me Make Believe		MCA 41015
9/15/79	27	11	7 Let's Take The Time To Fall In Love Again........		MCA 41106
9/13/80	46	9	8 Out Run The Sun		United Art. 1372
6/06/81	36	10	9 Bedtime Stories		Liberty 1405
10/24/81	70	4	10 The Rose Is For Today		Liberty 1434
			JAY CHEVALIER & SHELLEY FORD		
3/17/79	90	2	1 Disco Blues.....................		Creole G. 1114
			CHICK & HIS HOT RODS Act is actually Don Reno and Red Smiley.		
9/18/61	27	2	1 Jimmy Caught The Dickens (Pushing Ernest In The Tub) .... [N]		King 5537
			LISA CHILDRESS Born in Springfield, Missouri. Sang with the Childress family band.		
4/26/86	51	8	1 This Time It's You.....................		AMI 1941
1/17/87	55	6	2 It's Goodbye And So-Long To You		AMI 1947
5/07/88	63	6	3 (I Wanna Hear You) Say You Love Me Again.......		True 89
8/20/88	73	3	4 You Didn't Have To Jump The Fence		True 91
			BILLY CHINNOCK Son-in-law of Dick Curless. Appeared in "Search For Tomorrow" TV soap.		
1/19/85	91	3	1 The Way She Makes Love		Paradise 630
			HARRY CHOATES Cajun fiddler, died in jail on 7/17/51 in Austin, at the age of 25. "Jole Blon", a traditional Cajun song, was first recorded by Amade Breaux in the late 20s.		
1/04/47	4	2	1 Jole Blon		Modern Mt. 511
			ANNE CHRISTINE Born Anne Christine Poux on 12/17/33 in Meadville, Pennsylvania.		
7/17/71	69	5	1 Summer Man.....................		CME 4634
			DARRELL CLANTON Born in Indianapolis. Guitarist, bassist and banjo player. Played in father's band from age 9. Worked in Florida trio, Just Us Brothers, from age 17-22.		
10/15/83+	24	19	1 Lonesome 7-7203		Audiograph 474
3/31/84	75	6	2 I'll Take As Much Of You As I Can Get		Audiograph 479
1/19/85	56	9	3 I Forgot That I Don't Live Here Anymore...........		Warner 29185
			ERIC CLAPTON Prolific rock-blues guitarist/vocalist; born on 3/30/45 in Ripley, England. A member of The Roosters, The Yardbirds and John Mayall's Bluesbreakers. Founder of Cream and Blind Faith.		
3/18/78	26	9	1 ● Lay Down Sally.....................	3	RSO 886
10/21/78	82	7	2 Promises	9	RSO 910
			GUY CLARK Born on 11/6/41 in Rockport, Texas; raised in Monahans, Texas. Moved to Nashville in 1971. Wrote "Desperados Waiting For A Train", "The Last Gunfighter Ballad", "L.A. Freeway", "Texas-1947" and "New Cut Road".		
1/06/79	96	2	1 Fools For Each Other		Warner 8714
7/11/81	38	11	2 The Partner Nobody Chose		Warner 49740
7/02/83	42	13	3 Homegrown Tomatoes.....................		Warner 29595

DEBUT DATE	PEAK POS	WKS CHR	ARTIST — Record Title	POP POS	Label & Number
			JAY CLARK		
			Born in 1958 in Missouri; raised in Round Rock, Texas. Sang with family gospel group, did solo gospel work during the mid-70s. Turned to Country music in 1983.		
12/21/85	**73**	5	1 Love Gone Bad		Concorde 301
4/12/86	**75**	4	2 Modern Day Cowboy		Concorde 302
			LUCKY CLARK		
6/04/77	**99**	1	1 Everytime Two Fools Collide		Polydor 14393
			MICKEY CLARK		
			Born Bruce Clark on 11/2/47 in Bloomington, Illinois. Led own band, the Adventures, while in high school. Worked with Ferlin Husky and Marty Robbins.		
3/12/83	**74**	6	1 She's Gone To L.A. Again		Monument 03519
2/14/87	**54**	9	2 When I'm Over You (What You Gonna Do).........		Evergreen 1051
9/26/87	**76**	4	3 You Take The Leavin' Out Of Me....................		Evergreen 1058
			PETULA CLARK		
			Pop singer/actress born on 11/15/32 in Epsom, England.		
2/06/82	**20**	14	1 Natural Love	*66*	Scotti Br. 02676
			ROY CLARK ★★85★★		
			Born on 4/15/33 in Meherrin, Virginia. Won National Country Music Banjo Competition twice in the late 40s. Moved to Washington, DC and worked with the Clark family group, appearing on the Hayloft Conservatory Of Musical Interpretation TV series in 1948. Worked on the Jimmy Dean and George Hamilton IV TV shows. Acted in TV series "The Beverly Hillbillies", appearing as both "Cousin Roy" and his mother "Big Mama Halsey". With the TV series "Hee-Haw" from the first show in 1969. Plays several instruments; lives in Tulsa. Joined the Grand Ole Opry in 1987. CMA award: Entertainer of the Year - 1973.		
7/06/63	**10**	16	1 **Tips Of My Fingers**	*45*	Capitol 4956
2/08/64	**31**	3	2 Through The Eyes Of A Fool	*128*	Capitol 5099
3/20/65	**37**	10	3 When The Wind Blows In Chicago		Capitol 5350
			written by actor Audie Murphy		
8/03/68	**53**	8	4 Do You Believe This Town		Dot 17117
1/18/69	**57**	6	5 Love Is Just A State Of Mind..........................		Dot 17187
6/07/69	**9**	16	6 **Yesterday, When I Was Young**......................	*19*	Dot 17246
9/27/69	**40**	7	7 September Song...	*103*	Dot 17299
			first popularized by actor Walter Huston in 1939		
12/06/69+	**21**	9	8 Right Or Left At Oak Street............................	*123*	Dot 17324
1/24/70	**31**	9	9 Then She's A Lover	*94*	Dot 17335
6/06/70	**5**	15	10 **I Never Picked Cotton**	*122*	Dot 17349
9/26/70	**6**	14	11 **Thank God And Greyhound**	*90*	Dot 17355
3/27/71	**74**	2	12 Love Story		Dot 17360
			from the film of the same title		
4/24/71	**45**	9	13 A Simple Thing As Love		Dot 17368
8/14/71	**63**	4	14 She Cried..		Dot 17386
10/30/71	**39**	9	15 Magnificent Sanctuary Band		Dot 17395
			written by Dorsey Burnette		
8/19/72	**9**	14	16 **The Lawrence Welk - Hee Haw Counter-Revolution Polka** .... [N]		Dot 17426
2/17/73	**1**[1]	16	17 **Come Live With Me**	*89*	Dot 17449
7/07/73	**27**	11	18 Riders In The Sky .... [I]		Dot 17458
			#1 pop hit for Vaughn Monroe in 1948		
10/27/73+	**2**[1]	16	19 **Somewhere Between Love And Tomorrow**	*81*	Dot 17480
3/16/74	**4**	16	20 **Honeymoon Feelin'**		Dot 17498
8/17/74	**12**	17	21 The Great Divide		Dot 17518
12/21/74+	**64**	6	22 Dear God		ABC/Dot 17530
3/29/75	**35**	10	23 You're Gonna Love Yourself In The Morning		ABC/Dot 17545
8/09/75	**16**	14	24 Heart To Heart		ABC/Dot 17565
1/24/76	**2**[2]	16	25 **If I Had It To Do All Over Again**...................		ABC/Dot 17605
6/05/76	**21**	11	26 Think Summer...		ABC/Dot 17626
12/25/76+	**26**	11	27 I Have A Dream, I Have A Dream/		
4/09/77	**80**	4	28 Half A Love		ABC/Dot 17667
8/13/77	**40**	10	29 We Can't Build A Fire In The Rain		ABC/Dot 17712
2/11/78	**60**	6	30 Must You Throw Dirt In My Face....................		ABC 12328
6/03/78	**65**	6	31 Where Have You Been All Of My Life		ABC 12365

DEBUT DATE	PEAK POS	WKS CHR	ARTIST — Record Title	POP POS	Label & Number
			ROY CLARK — Continued		
9/23/78	89	2	32 The Happy Days/		
2/17/79	34	10	33 Shoulder To Shoulder (Arm and Arm)		ABC 12402
12/15/79+	21	13	34 Chain Gang Of Love..		MCA 41153
4/12/80	48	7	35 If There Were Only Time For Love....................		MCA 41208
8/16/80	73	5	36 For Love's Own Sake		MCA 41288
12/20/80+	60	8	37 I Ain't Got Nobody....................................		MCA 51031
4/04/81	86	2	38 She Can't Give It Away		MCA 51079
5/23/81	63	6	39 Love Takes Two...		MCA 51111
9/26/81	73	4	40 The Last Word In Jesus Is Us		Songbird 51167
5/15/82	54	9	41 Paradise Knife And Gun Club........................		Churchill 94002
9/11/82	85	3	42 Tennessee Saturday Night		Churchill 94007
10/30/82	65	7	43 Here We Go Again		Churchill 94011
			#15 pop hit for Ray Charles in 1967		
2/19/83	74	5	44 I'm A Booger/		
		5	45 A Way Without Words		Churchill 94017
8/27/83	55	9	46 Wildwood Flower .... [I]		Churchill 94025
10/27/84	48	11	47 Another Lonely Night With You......................		Churchill 52469
4/12/86	56	7	48 Tobacco Road..		Silver D. 70001
			#14 pop hit for the Nashville Teens in 1964		
8/30/86	61	7	49 Jukebox Saturday Night/		
			#7 pop hit for Glenn Miller in 1942		
		7	50 Night Life		Silver D. 7004
			SANFORD CLARK		
			Born in 1935 in Tulsa, Oklahoma. Moved to Phoenix in his teens.		
10/06/56	14	1	1 The Fool...	7	Dot 15481
			Jockey #14		
			STEVE CLARK		
			Singer/songwriter from Big Hill, Kentucky.		
3/10/84	68	5	1 That It's All Over Feeling (All Over Again)		Mercury 818058
			JACK CLEMENT		
			Born on 4/5/31 in Memphis. Moved to Washington, DC in 1952 and worked with the Stoneman Family, Roy Clark and Buzz Busby & the Banjo Boys. Returned to Memphis in 1955 and worked with the Dixie Ramblers. Own record labels, Fernwood and JMI. Producer for Sun Records from 1956-59. Wrote "Guess Things Happen That Way" and "Ballad Of A Teenage Queen". Produced dozens of hits, including Charley Pride's first, "Ring Of Fire" for Johnny Cash, and records for Louis Armstrong and Waylon Jennings. Producer of the film "Dear Dead Delilah". Married to Jessi Colter's sister, Sharon.		
6/24/78	86	4	1 We Must Believe In Magic/		
		4	2 When I Dream		Elektra 45474
9/16/78	84	4	3 All I Want To Do In Life		Elektra 45518
			BOOTS CLEMENTS		
			Born in Tifflin, Ohio; raised in San Diego. Worked as a disc jockey.		
4/19/86	96	1	1 Sukiyaki "My First Lonely Night"		West 719
			#1 pop hit for Kyu Sakamoto in 1963		
			VASSAR CLEMENTS		
			Born on 4/25/28 in Kinard, South Carolina. Fiddler with Jim & Jesse's Virginia Boys, Faron Young and Earl Scruggs. With Bill Monroe on the Grand Ole Opry in 1949. Popular session man, has worked with the Nitty Gritty Dirt Band, Grateful Dead, Hot Tuna and Marshall Tucker Band. Had own band since 1973.		
7/12/80	70	5	1 There'll Be No Teardrops Tonight		Fly. Fish 4004
			written in 1949 by Hank Williams		
4/09/88	83	2	2 I Hear The South...		Shikata 10102
			BUZZ CLIFFORD		
			Born Reese Francis Clifford III on 10/8/42 in Berwyn, Illinois.		
3/20/61	28	1	1 Baby Sittin' Boogie................................... [N]	6	Columbia 41876
			babies' voices are by the children (boy & girl) of the producer		

DEBUT DATE	PEAK POS	WKS CHR	ARTIST — Record Title	POP POS	Label & Number
			PATSY CLINE ★★166★★		
			Born Virginia Hensley on 9/8/32 in Winchester, Virginia. Died in a plane crash on 3/5/63 near Patterson, Tennessee. Worked local clubs as a singer, and briefly in Nashville in 1948. On "Arthur Godfrey's Talent Scouts" TV show in January of 1957. With the Grand Ole Opry from 1961. Plane crash also claimed the lives of Hawkshaw Hawkins and Cowboy Copas. Elected to the Country Music Hall Of Fame in 1973. Film based on her life, "Sweet Dreams", was produced in 1985.		
3/02/57	2²	19	1 **Walkin' After Midnight**/ Juke Box #2 / Best Seller #3 / Jockey #3	*12*	
6/10/57	14	1	2 A Poor Man's Roses (Or A Rich Man's Gold) ..... Jockey #14		Decca 30221
4/03/61	1²	39	3 **I Fall To Pieces**	*12*	Decca 31205
11/13/61+	2²	21	4 **Crazy** .... written by Willie Nelson	*9*	Decca 31317
3/03/62	1⁵	19	5 **She's Got You**	*14*	Decca 31354
6/02/62	10	12	6 **When I Get Thru With You (You'll Love Me Too)**/	*53*	
6/30/62	21	3	7 Imagine That........................	*90*	Decca 31377
8/25/62	14	10	8 So Wrong........................	*85*	Decca 31406
2/16/63	8	17	9 Leavin' On Your Mind	*83*	Decca 31455
5/11/63	5	16	10 Sweet Dreams (Of You)	*44*	Decca 31483
9/14/63	7	13	11 Faded Love	*96*	Decca 31522
1/11/64	47	3	12 When You Need A Laugh		Decca 31552
10/31/64	23	12	13 He Called Me Baby		Decca 31671
1/25/69	73	2	14 Anytime		Decca 25744
4/08/78	98	1	15 Life's Railway To Heaven		4 Star 1033
8/30/80	18	12	16 Always................. there have been 10 pop charted versions of this Irving Berlin tune		MCA 41303
12/20/80+	61	7	17 I Fall To Pieces................. [R] newly mixed version (with orchestra and chorus added)		MCA 51038
11/07/81+	5	17	18 **Have You Ever Been Lonely (Have You Ever Been Blue)** .... **JIM REEVES & PATSY CLINE**		RCA 12346
6/05/82	54	8	19 I Fall To Pieces................. [R] **PATSY CLINE/JIM REEVES** Patsy and Jim never recorded together; their voices were spliced together electronically		MCA 52052
			CLIFF COCHRAN		
			Born in Pascagoula, Mississippi; raised in Greenville, Mississippi. Cousin of Hank Cochran. In duo with brother Bob in the mid-60s. Moved to Nashville in 1967.		
8/10/74	54	10	1 The Way I'm Needing You		Enterprise 9103
1/11/75	73	7	2 All The Love You'll Ever Need		Enterprise 9109
5/26/79	24	13	3 Love Me Like A Stranger		RCA 11562
9/22/79	29	9	4 First Thing Each Morning (Last Thing at Night)...		RCA 11711
			HANK COCHRAN		
			Born Garland Perry on 8/2/35 in Isola, Mississippi. Worked in oil fields in New Mexico until moving to Los Angeles in the early 50s. Worked local clubs and teamed with Eddie Cochran (no relation) as the Cochran Brothers. Recorded for Ekko. Duo disbanded, Hank worked on the California Hayride. Moved to Nashville in 1959. Wrote "I Fall To Pieces", "She's Got You", "Funny Way Of Laughin'", "Make The World Go Away", and many others. Married to Jeannie Seely.		
9/01/62	20	5	1 Sally Was A Good Old Girl		Liberty 55461
11/10/62	23	2	2 I'd Fight The World		Liberty 55498
10/05/63	25	1	3 A Good Country Song		Gaylord 6431
4/15/67	70	2	4 All Of Me Belongs To You		Monument 994
7/08/78	91	4	5 Willie................. guest vocal: Merle Haggard		Capitol 4585
10/14/78	77	5	6 Ain't Life Hell................. **HANK COCHRAN & WILLIE NELSON**		Capitol 4635
11/08/80	57	9	7 A Little Bitty Tear................. harmony vocal: Willie Nelson		Elektra 47062
			BETTY CODY		
			Born Rita M. Cote in Auburn, Maine. Worked on SCOU-Lewiston, Maine at age 15. Featured vocalist on the WWVA Jamboree. Married to Harold "Lone Pine" Breau.		
12/26/53	10	1	1 **I Found Out More Than You Ever Knew** .... Juke Box #10 answer song to "I Forgot More Than You'll Ever Know"		RCA 5462

DEBUT DATE	PEAK POS	WKS CHR	ARTIST — Record Title	POP POS	Label & Number
			DAVID ALLAN COE ★★178★★		
			Born on 9/6/39 in Akron, Ohio. Billed as "The Mysterious Rhinestone Cowboy" until 1978. Wrote hit "Would You Lay With Me (In A Field Of Stone)" for Tanya Tucker. In films "Take This Job And Shove It" (also wrote the title tune for Johnny Paycheck) and "Last Days Of Frank And Jesse James". Acted in and co-wrote the music for the film "Stagecoach".		
11/30/74	80	6	1 (If I Could Climb) The Walls Of The Bottle..........		Columbia 10024
5/10/75	91	4	2 Would You Be My Lady..................................		Columbia 10093
7/05/75	8	17	3 **You Never Even Called Me By My Name**..........		Columbia 10159
12/27/75+	17	11	4 Longhaired Redneck.....................................		Columbia 10254
4/24/76	60	6	5 When She's Got Me (Where She Wants Me)........		Columbia 10323
9/25/76	25	11	6 Willie, Waylon And Me................................ [N]		Columbia 10395
2/26/77	49	8	7 Lately I've Been Thinking Too Much Lately		Columbia 10475
8/06/77	82	5	8 Just To Prove My Love For You......................		Columbia 10583
10/29/77	92	3	9 Face To Face		Columbia 10621
3/25/78	86	3	10 Divers Do It Deeper		Columbia 10701
7/22/78	85	4	11 You Can Count On Me...............................		Columbia 10753
9/09/78	45	8	12 If This Is Just A Game		Columbia 10816
3/17/79	72	5	13 Jack Daniel's, If You Please		Columbia 10911
6/21/80	46	7	14 Get A Little Dirt On Your Hands		Columbia 11277
			DAVID ALLAN COE & BILL ANDERSON		
3/14/81	88	3	15 Stand By Your Man		Columbia 60501
7/04/81	77	5	16 Tennessee Whiskey.................................		Columbia 02118
			with Billy Sherrill		
1/23/82	62	5	17 Now I Lay Me Down To Cheat		Columbia 02678
4/10/82	58	8	18 Take Time To Know Her.............................		Columbia 02815
			#11 pop hit for Percy Sledge in 1968		
3/19/83	4	19	19 **The Ride**...		Columbia 03778
7/23/83	45	10	20 Cheap Thrills		Columbia 03997
10/22/83	85	5	21 Crazy Old Soldier		Columbia 04136
12/24/83+	48	13	22 Ride 'Em Cowboy		Kat Fam. 04258
3/17/84	2¹	22	23 **Mona Lisa Lost Her Smile**		Columbia 04396
8/25/84	44	11	24 It's Great To Be Single Again		Columbia 04553
12/08/84+	11	19	25 She Used To Love Me A Lot		Columbia 04688
4/13/85	29	12	26 Don't Cry Darlin'....................................		Columbia 04846
			recitation: George Jones		
11/02/85	52	8	27 I'm Gonna Hurt Her On The Radio..................		Columbia 05631
5/10/86	44	10	28 A Country Boy (Who Rolled The Rock Away)......		Columbia 05876
8/02/86	56	8	29 I've Already Cheated On You........................		Columbia 06227
			DAVID ALLAN COE & WILLIE NELSON		
2/14/87	34	16	30 Need A Little Time Off For Bad Behavior		Columbia 06661
6/06/87	62	5	31 Tanya Montana.......................................		Columbia 07129
			title is the name of Coe's daughter		
			R.C. COIN		
10/17/87	76	3	1 Bed Of Roses.................................		BGM 82087
			BEN COLDER		
			Ben is actually Sheb Wooley doing humorous versions of pop/country hits.		
12/29/62	18	1	1 Don't Go Near The Eskimos .... [N]	62	MGM 13104
3/02/63	30	2	2 Hello Wall No. 2...................................... [N]	131	MGM 13122
9/24/66	6	15	3 **Almost Persuaded No. 2** .... [N]	58	MGM 13590
10/26/68	24	6	4 Harper Valley P.T.A. (Later That Same Day)... [N]	67	MGM 13997
1/04/69	65	3	5 Little Green Apples No. 2 .... [N]		MGM 14015
2/13/71	50	6	6 Fifteen Beers Ago................................... [N]		MGM 14209
			BRENDA COLE		
			Singer/actress. First recorded for Epic at age 8.		
6/27/87	83	3	1 But I Never Do..		Melody D. 77701
12/19/87	86	3	2 Gone, Gone, Gone.....................................		Melody D. 77702
4/16/88	84	2	3 Boots		Melody D. 77703

DEBUT DATE	PEAK POS	WKS CHR	ARTIST — Record Title	POP POS	Label & Number
			THE KING COLE TRIO First recorded in 1939 in Hollywood for Davis & Schwegler Records. Consisted of Nat "King" Cole, piano, vocals; Oscar Moore (brother of Johnny Moore), guitar; and Wesley Prince, bass.		
5/13/44	1⁶	15	1 Straighten Up And Fly Right/	9	
5/20/44	2¹	5	2 I Can't See For Lookin'	28	Capitol 154
			SAMI JO COLE Female vocalist from Batesville, Arkansas. Sang gospel on the radio from age 3. Sang with the Lassies vocal group while attending Arkansas College. SAMI JO:		
2/09/74	52	12	1 Tell Me A Lie	21	MGM South 7029
7/06/74	61	9	2 It Could Have Been Me	46	MGM South 7034
1/04/75	62	9	3 I'll Believe Anything You Say		MGM 14773
5/15/76	91	4	4 God Loves Us (When We All Sing Together)		Polydor 14315
9/04/76	67	6	5 Take Me To Heaven		Polydor 14341
			SAMI JO COLE:		
5/02/81	76	4	6 One Love Over Easy		Elektra 47127
10/31/81	82	3	7 I Can't Help Myself (Here Comes The Feeling)		Elektra 47211
			ALBERT COLEMAN'S ATLANTA POPS Studio discofied versions of many Country classics.		
5/29/82	42	15	1 Just Hooked On Country (Parts I & II) [I]		Epic 02938
9/25/82	77	4	2 Just Hooked On Country (Part III) [I]		Epic 03215
			BIFF COLLIE - see BILLY BOB BOWMAN		
			SHIRLEY COLLIE Born Shirley Caddell on 3/16/31 in Chillicothe, Missouri. Worked on the Brush Creek Follies, KMBC-Kansas City. Formerly married to deejay Biff Collie and Willie Nelson.		
6/12/61	25	5	1 Dime A Dozen		Liberty 55324
9/11/61	23	3	2 Why, Baby, Why		Liberty 55361
			WARREN SMITH & SHIRLEY COLLIE		
3/17/62	10	13	3 **Willingly**		Liberty 55403
			WILLIE NELSON & SHIRLEY COLLIE		
			BRIAN COLLINS From Texas City, Texas. Played in local bands from age 11. Had own band, The Nomads, while in junior high school. Discovered by Dolly Parton in 1969.		
10/16/71	67	3	1 All I Want To Do Is Say I Love You		Mega 0038
2/21/72	47	8	2 There's A Kind Of Hush (All Over the World) #4 pop hit for Herman's Hermits in 1967		Mega 0058
7/01/72	61	6	3 Spread It Around		Mega 0078
7/14/73	24	14	4 I Wish (You Had Stayed)		Dot 17466
12/08/73+	43	12	5 I Don't Plan On Losing You		Dot 17483
5/18/74	10	15	6 **Statue Of A Fool**		Dot 17499
11/09/74+	23	14	7 That's The Way Love Should Be		ABC/Dot 17527
4/26/75	84	5	8 I'd Still Be In Love With You		ABC/Dot 17546
12/06/75	83	5	9 Queen Of Temptation		ABC/Dot 17593
3/06/76	65	8	10 To Show You That I Love You		ABC/Dot 17613
5/07/77	83	6	11 If You Love Me (Let Me Know)		ABC/Dot 17694
6/24/78	86	3	12 Old Flames (Can't Hold A Candle To You)		RCA 11277
3/10/79	94	3	13 Hello Texas		RCA 11478
4/17/82	80	4	14 Before I Got To Know Her		Primero 1001
7/02/83	80	4	15 Nickel's Worth Of Heaven		Primero 1018
			DUGG COLLINS		
5/21/77	92	4	1 I'm The Man		SCR 143
9/17/77	99	2	2 How Do You Talk To A Baby		SCR 147
			GWEN & JERRY COLLINS Husband and wife duo from Miami.		
1/17/70	34	9	1 Get Together #5 pop hit for The Youngbloods in 1969		Capitol 2710
			JIM COLLINS Born in Nacogdoches, Texas in 1959. Moved to Houston in 1975. Worked as a session musician and leader of the house band at Moe & Joe's.		
6/08/85	78	3	1 You Can Always Say Good-Bye In The Morning...		White G. 22250

DEBUT DATE	PEAK POS	WKS CHR	ARTIST — Record Title	POP POS	Label & Number
			JIM COLLINS — Continued		
8/24/85	59	6	2 I Wanna Be A Cowboy 'Til I Die		White G. 22252
12/14/85	75	6	3 What A Memory You'd Make		White G. 22251
6/21/86	65	5	4 The Things I've Done To Me		TKM 111216
11/01/86	59	5	5 Romance		TKM 111217
			JUDY COLLINS - see T.G. SHEPPARD		
			TOMMY COLLINS		
			Born Leonard Raymond Sipes on 9/28/30 in Oklahoma City. Worked local radio stations, first with KLPR-Oklahoma City. Served in US Marines, then moved to Los Angeles after discharge. Worked on Town Hall Party radio series in the early 50s. First recorded for Capitol in 1953. Married Wanda Shahan in 1955 and sang duets with her. Had own band with Buck Owens as lead guitarist. Minister from 1961-64; joined Buck Owens' show in 1964. The song "Leonard" by Merle Haggard in 1981 was about Collins. Wrote several of Haggard's hits.		
2/20/54	2⁷	21	1 **You Better Not Do That**..............................		Capitol 2701
			Jockey #2 / Juke Box #2 / Best Seller #2		
9/04/54	4	15	2 **Whatcha Gonna Do Now**		Capitol 2891
			Jockey #4 / Best Seller #7		
2/05/55	10	1	3 **Untied**		Capitol 3017
			Juke Box #10 / Best Seller #15		
4/30/55	5	9	4 **It Tickles**...		Capitol 3082
			Juke Box #5 / Jockey #9 / Best Seller #10		
10/01/55	13	2	5 I Guess I'm Crazy/		
			Best Seller #13		
10/01/55	15	2	6 You Oughta See Pickles Now		Capitol 3190
			Best Seller #15		
1/11/64	47	1	7 I Can Do That..		Capitol 5051
			TOMMY & WANDA COLLINS		
2/05/66	7	13	8 **If You Can't Bite, Don't Growl**		Columbia 43489
7/16/66	47	2	9 Shindig In The Barn		Columbia 43628
2/11/67	62	4	10 Don't Wipe The Tears That You Cry For Him/		
3/04/67	60	5	11 Birmingham...		Columbia 43972
9/23/67	52	6	12 Big Dummy		Columbia 44260
1/13/68	64	6	13 I Made The Prison Band		Columbia 44386
			JESSI COLTER		
			Born Miriam Johnson on 5/25/47 in Phoenix. Played piano in church from age 11. Worked with Duane Eddy from 1961, married to him from 1962-68. With Waylon Jennings from 1969, married him in October, 1969.		
2/15/75	1¹	18	1 **I'm Not Lisa**	4	Capitol 4009
8/23/75	5	17	2 **What's Happened To Blue Eyes**	57	Capitol 4087
1/03/76	11	13	3 It's Morning (And I Still Love You)...................		Capitol 4200
4/17/76	50	7	4 Without You..		Capitol 4252
9/04/76	29	12	5 I Thought I Heard You Calling My Name		Capitol 4325
11/04/78	45	10	6 Maybe You Should've Been Listening...............		Capitol 4641
4/14/79	91	4	7 Love Me Back To Sleep		Capitol 4696
2/13/82	70	4	8 Holdin' On		Capitol 5073
			WAYLON JENNINGS & JESSI COLTER:		
11/14/70	25	10	9 Suspicious Minds		RCA 9920
			#1 pop hit for Elvis Presley in 1969		
6/19/71	39	8	10 Under Your Spell Again...............................		RCA 9992
5/01/76	2¹	14	11 **Suspicious Minds**................................. [R]		RCA 10653
2/21/81	17	12	12 Storms Never Last.......................................		RCA 12176
6/06/81	10	13	13 **Wild Side Of Life/It Wasn't God Who Made Honky Tonk Angels**		RCA 12245
			COMMANDER CODY & HIS LOST PLANET AIRMEN		
			Group formed in California in 1967, and led by George "Commander Cody" Frayne.		
5/06/72	51	9	1 Hot Rod Lincoln.. [N]	9	Paramount 0146
7/28/73	97	2	2 Smoke! Smoke! Smoke! (That Cigarette) .... [N]	94	Paramount 0216
			PERRY COMO		
			Born on 5/18/12 in Canonsburg, Pennsylvania. One of America's most enduring and beloved singers.		
1/17/76	100	1	1 Just Out Of Reach.......................................		RCA 10402
			#24 pop hit for Solomon Burke in 1961		

DEBUT DATE	PEAK POS	WKS CHR	ARTIST — Record Title	POP POS	Label & Number
			THE COMPTON BROTHERS		
			Harry and Bill Compton from St. Louis, Missouri. Won a Columbia Records talent contest in 1965. Operate their own publishing company, Wepedol Music.		
12/31/66+	61	5	1 Pickin' Up The Mail		Dot 16948
3/23/68	64	5	2 Honey..		Dot 17070
8/03/68	75	2	3 Two Little Hearts		Dot 17110
11/23/68	62	5	4 Everybody Needs Somebody		Dot 17167
9/20/69	11	12	5 Haunted House		Dot 17294
			#11 pop hit for Gene Simmons in 1964		
1/24/70	16	11	6 Charlie Brown		Dot 17336
			#2 pop hit for The Coasters in 1959		
8/22/70	61	3	7 That Ain't No Stuff................................		Dot 17352
6/12/71	65	6	8 Pine Grove		Dot 17378
9/04/71	62	6	9 May Old Acquaintance Be Forgot		Dot 17391
2/26/72	49	10	10 Yellow River.....................................		Dot 17408
			#23 pop hit for Christie in 1970		
8/26/72	41	9	11 Claudette...		Dot 17427
			#30 pop hit for The Everly Brothers in 1958		
10/06/73	65	12	12 California Blues (Blue Yodel No. 4)		Dot 17477
			written and recorded in 1929 by Jimmie Rodgers		
3/15/75	97	2	13 Cat's In The Cradle.................................		ABC/Dot 17538
			#1 pop hit for Harry Chapin in 1974		
			CONCRETE COWBOY BAND		
			Nashville session musicians led by Buddy Skipper.		
7/11/81	87	2	1 Country Is The Closest Thing To Heaven		Excelsior 1011
			JOHN CONLEE ★★79★★		
			Born on 8/11/46 in Versailles, Kentucky. Worked as a mortician for 6 years, then a newsreader in Fort Knox. Moved to WLAC-Nashville in 1971; worked as a disc jockey and music director. Wrote "Rose Colored Glasses" with Glenn Barber. Joined the Grand Ole Opry in 1981. Chairman of the Family Farm Defense Fund.		
5/27/78	5	20	1 **Rose Colored Glasses**		ABC 12356
11/04/78+	1¹	16	2 **Lady Lay Down**...............................		ABC 12420
3/03/79	1¹	15	3 **Backside Of Thirty**		ABC 12455
8/11/79	2²	15	4 **Before My Time**		MCA 41072
12/15/79+	7	14	5 **Baby, You're Something**		MCA 41163
5/03/80	2²	16	6 **Friday Night Blues**		MCA 41233
9/13/80	2²	17	7 **She Can't Say That Anymore**.....................		MCA 41321
1/24/81	12	14	8 What I Had With You		MCA 51044
5/30/81	26	12	9 Could You Love Me (One More Time).................		MCA 51112
8/29/81	2²	20	10 **Miss Emily's Picture**		MCA 51164
2/20/82	6	18	11 **Busted**...		MCA 52008
			#4 pop hit for Ray Charles in 1963		
7/03/82	26	12	12 Nothing Behind You, Nothing In Sight		MCA 52070
10/02/82+	10	22	13 **I Don't Remember Loving You**...................		MCA 52116
3/05/83	1¹	19	14 **Common Man**		MCA 52178
6/25/83	1¹	20	15 **I'm Only In It For The Love**		MCA 52231
10/15/83+	1¹	23	16 **In My Eyes**		MCA 52282
3/10/84	1¹	19	17 **As Long As I'm Rockin' With You**...............		MCA 52351
6/23/84	4	19	18 **Way Back**		MCA 52403
10/20/84+	2²	21	19 **Years After You**..................................		MCA 52470
3/02/85	7	20	20 **Working Man**		MCA 52543
7/06/85	15	17	21 Blue Highway		MCA 52625
10/26/85+	5	21	22 **Old School**		MCA 52695
2/22/86	10	20	23 Harmony..		Columbia 05778
6/14/86	1¹	22	24 **Got My Heart Set On You**		Columbia 06104
10/25/86+	6	19	25 **The Carpenter**.................................		Columbia 06311
2/28/87	4	24	26 **Domestic Life**..................................		Columbia 06707
7/18/87	11	21	27 Mama's Rockin' Chair		Columbia 07203
11/28/87	55	7	28 Living Like There's No Tomorrow (Finally Got To Me Tonight)......................................		Columbia 07643

DEBUT DATE	PEAK POS	WKS CHR		ARTIST — Record Title	POP POS	Label & Number

EARL THOMAS CONLEY ★★71★★

Born on 10/17/41 in Portsmouth, Ohio. Worked clubs in Huntsville, Alabama in the early 70s, wrote songs for Billy Larkin and Bobby G. Rice. Wrote hits "Smokey Mountain Memories" for Mel Street, and "This Time I've Hurt Her More Than She Loves Me" for Conway Twitty. Also recorded as "The ETC Band".

DEBUT DATE	PEAK POS	WKS CHR	#	ARTIST — Record Title	Label & Number
				EARL CONLEY:	
7/26/75	87	4	1	I Have Loved You Girl (But Not Like This Before)	GRT 027
11/22/75	87	5	2	It's The Bible Against The Bottle (In The Battle For Daddy's Soul)	GRT 032
3/27/76	67	6	3	High And Wild	GRT 041
8/14/76	77	5	4	Queen Of New Orleans	GRT 064
1/06/79	32	12	5	Dreamin's All I Do	Warner 8717
				EARL THOMAS CONLEY:	
6/23/79	41	8	6	Middle-Age Madness	Warner 8798
10/06/79	26	11	7	Stranded On A Dead End Street	Warner 49072
				THE ETC BAND	
11/15/80+	7	20	8	Silent Treatment	Sunbird 7556
4/04/81	1¹	19	9	Fire & Smoke	Sunbird 7561
10/17/81+	10	18	10	Tell Me Why	RCA 12344
2/06/82	16	13	11	After The Love Slips Away/	RCA 13053
		13	12	Smokey Mountain Memories	RCA 13053
6/12/82	8	18	13	Heavenly Bodies	RCA 13246
10/02/82	1¹	18	14	Somewhere Between Right And Wrong	RCA 13320
1/15/83	2²	21	15	I Have Loved You, Girl (But Not Like This Before) [R]	RCA 13414
				new version of Earl's first hit	
5/14/83	1¹	19	16	Your Love's On The Line	RCA 13525
9/10/83	1¹	25	17	Holding Her And Loving You	RCA 13596
1/14/84	1¹	18	18	Don't Make It Easy For Me	RCA 13702
5/05/84	1¹	21	19	Angel In Disguise	RCA 13758
9/08/84	1¹	22	20	Chance Of Lovin' You	RCA 13877
11/10/84+	8	21	21	All Tangled Up In Love	RCA 13938
				GUS HARDIN with EARL THOMAS CONLEY	
1/05/85	1¹	22	22	Honor Bound	RCA 13960
5/04/85	1¹	19	23	Love Don't Care (Whose Heart It Breaks)	RCA 14060
9/14/85	1¹	21	24	Nobody Falls Like A Fool	RCA 14172
2/01/86	1¹	22	25	Once In A Blue Moon	RCA 14282
8/02/86	2¹	20	26	Too Many Times	RCA 14380
				EARL THOMAS CONLEY & ANITA POINTER	
11/29/86+	1¹	23	27	I Can't Win For Losin' You	RCA 5064
4/04/87	1¹	21	28	That Was A Close One	RCA 5129
8/01/87	1¹	23	29	Right From The Start	RCA 5226
3/12/88	1¹	23	30	What She Is (Is A Woman In Love)	RCA 6894
7/02/88	1¹	21	31	We Believe In Happy Endings	RCA 8632
				EARL THOMAS CONLEY with EMMYLOU HARRIS	
11/12/88+	1¹	24	32	What I'd Say	RCA 8717

DAVE CONWAY

DEBUT DATE	PEAK POS	WKS CHR	#	ARTIST — Record Title	Label & Number
8/06/77	68	6	1	If You're Gonna Love (You Gotta Hurt)	True 105

STEVEN LEE COOK

Born in Shelbyville, Kentucky. Worked as a salesman for WHAS radio.

DEBUT DATE	PEAK POS	WKS CHR	#	ARTIST — Record Title	Label & Number
12/22/79+	92	5	1	Please Play More Kenny Rogers [N]	Grind. Sw. 1709
				with The Jordanaires	

SPADE COOLEY

Born Donnell Clyde Cooley on 2/22/10 in Grand, Oklahoma. Died of a heart attack on 11/23/69 (59). Played fiddle at square dances from age 8. Moved to Hollywood in the mid-30s and worked as an actor in Roy Rogers films. Worked with Cal Shrum, sang with the Riders Of The Purple Sage. From 1941, led big band at the Venice Ballroom, including Tex Williams. Appeared in many films including own short subjects "King Of Western Swing" and "Spade Cooley & His Orchestra" in 1949. Own TV shows from the late 40s to 1958. Married Ella Mae Evans in 1945, convicted of her murder in April of 1961. Sentenced to life imprisonment at Vacaville, California. Died performing at the Oakland Deputy Sheriff's Show two months before he was to be paroled.

DEBUT DATE	PEAK POS	WKS CHR	#	ARTIST — Record Title	Label & Number
3/03/45	1⁹	31	1	Shame On You!	
4/28/45	8	1	2	A Pair Of Broken Hearts	Okeh 6731
10/06/45	4	1	3	I've Taken All I'm Gonna Take From You	Okeh 6746

DEBUT DATE	PEAK POS	WKS CHR	ARTIST — Record Title	POP POS	Label & Number
			SPADE COOLEY — Continued		
3/16/46	**2**[1]	11	4 **Detour/**		
4/20/46	**3**	11	5 **You Can't Break My Heart**........................		Columbia 36935
3/08/47	**4**	1	6 **Crazy 'Cause I Love You**.............................		Columbia 37058
			vocal by Tex Williams		
			RITA COOLIDGE		
			Born on 5/1/44 in Nashville. Had her own group, R.C. And The Moonpies, at Florida State University. Moved to Los Angeles in the late 60s. Did back-up work for Delaney & Bonnie, Leon Russell, Joe Cocker and Eric Clapton. With Kris Kristofferson from 1971, married to him from 1973-80. Known as "The Delta Lady", for whom Leon Russell wrote the song of the same name.		
8/31/74	**94**	5	1 Mama Lou...............................		A&M 1545
10/15/77	**82**	8	2 ● We're All Alone	7	A&M 1965
11/25/78	**63**	9	3 The Jealous Kind/		
11/25/78	**83**	9	4 Love Me Again.............................	68	A&M 2090
12/22/79+	**32**	10	5 I'd Rather Leave While I'm In Love................	38	A&M 2199
5/24/80	**60**	6	6 Somethin' 'Bout You Baby I Like	42	Capitol 4865
			GLEN CAMPBELL & RITA COOLIDGE		
1/31/81	**72**	4	7 Fool That I Am	46	A&M 2281
			KRIS KRISTOFFERSON & RITA COOLIDGE:		
12/22/73+	**92**	5	8 A Song I'd Like To Sing...................	49	A&M 1475
3/23/74	**98**	2	9 Loving Arms	86	A&M 1498
12/28/74+	**87**	4	10 Rain		Monument 8630
			JERRY COOPER		
			Born in Arlington, Virginia. Prior to his musical career, founded highly successful construction company.		
10/03/87	**88**	2	1 I'll Forget You		Bear 178
1/09/88	**83**	3	2 As Long As There's Women Like You		Bear 187
			WILMA LEE & STONEY COOPER		
			Husband-and-wife duo: Wilma Lee Leary (b: 2/7/21, Valley Head, WV), vocals, guitar, banjo, piano; and Dale T. "Stoney" Cooper (b: 10/16/18, Harman, WV; d: 3/22/77 [heart attack]), vocals, fiddle. Wilma was with the Leary Family gospel group when Stoney joined the group as a fiddler. With the Leary Family until the mid-40s. On the WWVA Wheeling Jamboree from 1947-57. Joined the Grand Ole Opry in 1957. Own band, the Clinch Mountain Clan.		
9/29/56	**14**	1	1 Cheated Too.....................................		Hickory 1051
			Jockey #14		
12/15/58+	**4**	26	2 **Come Walk With Me**		Hickory 1085
5/25/59	**4**	23	3 **Big Midnight Special**		Hickory 1098
			Paul Evans' "Midnite Special" was a #16 pop hit in 1960		
10/19/59	**3**	24	4 **There's A Big Wheel**......................		Hickory 1107
			written by Don Gibson		
5/16/60	**17**	8	5 Johnny, My Love (Grandma's Diary)		Hickory 1118
9/12/60	**16**	14	6 This Ole House		Hickory 1126
			#1 pop hit for Rosemary Clooney in 1954		
6/12/61	**8**	7	7 **Wreck On The Highway**		Hickory 1147
			COWBOY COPAS ★★179★★		
			Born Lloyd Estel Copas on 7/15/13 in Muskogee, Oklahoma. Died in a plane crash on 3/5/63 in Camden, Tennessee. Fiddler and guitarist from age 10. Moved to Cincinnati in 1929 and formed duo with Indian fiddler Natchee. Went solo in 1940, performed on Midwest Hayride radio show, Cincinnati, in the early 40s. With Pee Wee King on the Grand Ole Opry in the late 40s. Career waned in the 50s, but recovered with hit "Alabam" in 1960. Plane crash also killed Patsy Cline, Hawkshaw Hawkins, and Copas's son-in-law, pilot Randy Hughes.		
8/31/46	**4**	1	1 **Filipino Baby**		King 505
1/03/48	**2**[3]	20	2 **Signed Sealed And Delivered**		King 658
5/01/48	**3**	17	3 **Tennessee Waltz**..............................		King 696
			Best Seller #3 / Juke Box #4		
7/03/48	**7**	9	4 **Tennessee Moon**		King 714
			Best Seller #7 / Juke Box #7		
9/18/48	**12**	1	5 Breeze		King 618
			Juke Box #12		
2/12/49	**12**	1	6 I'm Waltzing With Tears In My Eyes		King 775
2/19/49	**5**	13	7 **Candy Kisses**		King 777
			Juke Box #5 / Best Seller #7		
11/12/49	**14**	2	8 Hangman's Boogie........................		King 811
			Best Seller #14 / Juke Box #14		

DEBUT DATE	PEAK POS	WKS CHR	ARTIST — Record Title	POP POS	Label & Number
			COWBOY COPAS — Continued		
4/28/51	**5**	11	9 **The Strange Little Girl**		King 951
			Jockey #5 / Best Seller #7 / Juke Box #10		
1/19/52	**8**	3	10 **'Tis Sweet To Be Remembered**......................		King 1000
			Jockey #8		
7/04/60	**1**¹²	34	11 **Alabam**...	63	Starday 501
4/24/61	**9**	8	12 **Flat Top**		Starday 542
7/31/61	**12**	10	13 Sunny Tennessee		Starday 552
9/11/61	**10**	8	14 **Signed Sealed And Delivered** .... [R]		Starday 559
4/27/63	**12**	14	15 Goodbye Kisses		Starday 621
			RAY CORBIN		
			Born in Duncan, Oklahoma; now deceased. Co-writer of "You're The One" for Buddy Holly. Co-owner of KLLL-Lubbock, Texas. Also known as "Slim Corbin".		
1/11/69	**67**	2	1 Passin' Through....................................		Monument 1102
			THE CORBIN/HANNER BAND		
			Bob Corbin and Dave Hanner from Ford City, Pennsylvania; met while in high school. Originally known as the Gravel Band, worked Pittsburgh clubs. Band included Al Snyder (keyboards), Kip Paxton (bass) and Dave Freeland (drums).		
1/20/79	**85**	4	1 America's Sweetheart		Lifesong 1783
			shown only as: **CORBIN & HANNER**		
5/30/81	**64**	6	2 Time Has Treated You Well.........................		Alfa 7001
8/08/81	**46**	9	3 Livin' The Good Life		Alfa 7007
11/28/81+	**49**	10	4 Oklahoma Crude		Alfa 7010
4/10/82	**46**	9	5 Everyone Knows I'm Yours		Alfa 7022
12/04/82	**75**	7	6 One Fine Morning...................................		Lifesong 45120
			HELEN CORNELIUS ★★**188**★★		
			Born on 12/6/41 in Hannibal, Missouri. Performed in vocal group with sisters Judy and Sharon while in high school. Went solo and won on the Ted Mack Amateur Hour. Staff writer with Screen Gems in 1970. Teamed with Jim Ed Brown and appeared in the "Nashville On The Road" TV series from 1976-80, when she again went solo. Reunited with Brown in February of 1988.		
10/30/76	**91**	3	1 There's Always A Goodbye		RCA 10795
9/30/78	**30**	8	2 What Cha Doin' After Midnight, Baby		RCA 11375
12/01/79	**68**	5	3 It Started With A Smile		RCA 11753
12/05/81+	**42**	10	4 Love Never Comes Easy		Elektra 47237
11/26/83	**70**	6	5 If Your Heart's A Rollin' Stone		Ameri-Can 1011
			JIM ED BROWN/HELEN CORNELIUS:		
7/04/76	**1**²	16	6 **I Don't Want To Have To Marry You**		RCA 10711
11/20/76+	**2**¹	17	7 **Saying Hello, Saying I Love You, Saying Goodbye**		RCA 10822
5/07/77	**12**	12	8 **Born Believer**		RCA 10967
8/20/77	**12**	12	9 If It Ain't Love By Now		RCA 11044
12/24/77+	**91**	3	10 Fall Softly Snow.................................. [X]		RCA 11162
3/11/78	**11**	13	11 I'll Never Be Free		RCA 11220
7/29/78	**6**	15	12 **If The World Ran Out Of Love Tonight**..........		RCA 11304
11/25/78+	**10**	14	13 **You Don't Bring Me Flowers**		RCA 11435
			#1 pop hit for Barbra Streisand & Neil Diamond in 1978		
3/31/79	**2**²	13	14 **Lying In Love With You**..........................		RCA 11532
8/04/79	**3**	13	15 **Fools**		RCA 11672
3/08/80	**5**	14	16 **Morning Comes Too Early**		RCA 11927
7/19/80	**24**	12	17 The Bedroom..		RCA 12037
5/09/81	**13**	14	18 Don't Bother To Knock		RCA 12220
			RANDY CORNOR		
			Born in 1954 in Houston. Played guitar with Gene Watson at age 13. With Frenchie Burke for 3 years. Top session guitarist in Houston.		
11/01/75+	**9**	15	1 **Sometimes I Talk In My Sleep**		ABC/Dot 17592
5/15/76	**33**	11	2 Heart Don't Fail Me Now............................		ABC/Dot 17625
10/02/76	**72**	6	3 I Guess You Never Loved Me Anyway		ABC/Dot 17655
3/05/77	**86**	3	4 Love Doesn't Live Here Anymore		ABC/Dot 17676
7/01/78	**95**	3	5 Ring Telephone Ring (Damn Telephone)		Cherry 643
12/23/78	**100**	2	6 Hurt As Big As Texas................................		Cherry 783

DEBUT DATE	PEAK POS	WKS CHR	ARTIST — Record Title	POP POS	Label & Number
			GENE COTTON		
			Born in Columbus, Ohio. Attended Ohio State University. Recording since 1972.		
12/11/76+	92	7	1 You've Got Me Runnin'..	*33*	ABC 12227
7/29/78	99	2	2 You're A Part Of Me....................	*36*	Ariola 7704
			GENE COTTON with KIM CARNES		
5/22/82	78	4	3 If I Could Get You (Into My Life)......................	*76*	Knoll 5002
			ORVILLE COUCH		
			Born in Ferris, Texas. First recorded for Derby in 1954.		
11/24/62+	**5**	21	1 **Hello Trouble**		Vee Jay 470
9/28/63	**25**	1	2 Did I Miss You?..		Vee Jay 528
			THE COULTERS		
			Trio from Durham, North Carolina.		
2/26/83	70	5	1 Caroline's Still In Georgia...........................		Dolphin 45003
			THE COUNTRY CAVALEERS		
			Musical comedy duo of James Marvell (b: Tampa, FL) and Buddy Good (b: Buffalo, NY). Duo formed in Tampa in 1965. Marvell and Good were members of the vocal group Mercy (hit in 1969 with "Love Can Make You Happy"). Moved to Nashville in 1970.		
10/20/73	99	2	1 Humming Bird		MGM 14606
8/28/76	97	2	2 Te' Quiero (I Love You In Many Ways)...............		C'ntry Show. 171
			THE COUNTRY GENTLEMEN		
			Bluegrass group formed in Washington, DC in 1957, featuring Charles Waller. Ricky Skaggs played fiddle in the group in 1972.		
10/30/65	43	4	1 Bringing Mary Home		Rebel 250
			DON COX		
12/01/79	94	3	1 Smooth Southern Highway............................		ARC 5902
			BILLY "CRASH" CRADDOCK ★★70★★		
			Born on 6/16/39 in Greensboro, North Carolina. With his brother Ronald in rock band the Four Rebels, in the mid-50s. First recorded for Colonial in 1957. Semi-retired from recording and worked outside of music in Greensboro from 1960-69. Known as "Mr. Country Rock".		
2/13/71	**3**	17	1 **Knock Three Times**...............................	*113*	Cartwheel 193
			#1 pop hit for Dawn in 1971		
6/19/71	**5**	14	2 **Dream Lover**		Cartwheel 196
			#2 pop hit for Bobby Darin in 1959		
11/06/71	**10**	14	3 **You Better Move On**		Cartwheel 201
			#24 pop hit for Arthur Alexander in 1962		
3/04/72	**10**	16	4 **Ain't Nothin' Shakin' (But the Leaves on the Trees)**		Cartwheel 210
7/01/72	**5**	16	5 **I'm Gonna Knock On Your Door**		Cartwheel 216
			#12 pop hit for Eddie Hodges in 1961		
11/18/72+	**22**	12	6 Afraid I'll Want To Love Her One More Time		ABC 11342
			originally released on Cartwheel 222		
2/24/73	**33**	9	7 Don't Be Angry		ABC 11349
5/26/73	**14**	11	8 Slippin' And Slidin'....................................		ABC 11364
			#33 pop hit for Little Richard in 1956		
9/01/73	**8**	15	9 'Till The Water Stops Runnin'		ABC 11379
1/05/74	**3**	16	10 **Sweet Magnolia Blossom**...........................		ABC 11412
6/01/74	**1**²	16	11 **Rub It In**..	*16*	ABC 12013
11/09/74+	**1**¹	14	12 **Ruby, Baby**...	*33*	ABC 12036
			#2 pop hit for Dion in 1963		
2/22/75	**4**	14	13 **Still Thinkin' 'Bout You**		ABC 12068
6/21/75	**10**	14	14 **I Love The Blues And The Boogie Woogie**		ABC 12104
10/18/75	**2**³	17	15 **Easy As Pie**	*54*	ABC/Dot 17584
4/03/76	**7**	13	16 **Walk Softly**		ABC/Dot 17619
7/04/76	**4**	13	17 **You Rubbed It In All Wrong**........................		ABC/Dot 17635
10/23/76+	**1**¹	16	18 **Broken Down In Tiny Pieces**		ABC/Dot 17659
3/12/77	**28**	10	19 Just A Little Thing......................................		ABC/Dot 17682
6/04/77	**7**	15	20 **A Tear Fell**...		ABC/Dot 17701
			#5 pop hit for Teresa Brewer in 1956		
11/12/77+	**10**	15	21 **The First Time**		ABC/Dot 17725
2/04/78	**4**	15	22 **I Cheated On A Good Woman's Love**..............		Capitol 4545
2/18/78	92	2	23 Another Woman.......................................		ABC 12335

DEBUT DATE	PEAK POS	WKS CHR	ARTIST — Record Title	POP POS	Label & Number
			BILLY "CRASH" CRADDOCK — Continued		
5/06/78	**50**	9	24 Think I'll Go Somewhere (And Cry Myself To Sleep)		ABC 12357
5/20/78	**28**	10	25 I've Been Too Long Lonely Baby		Capitol 4575
7/29/78	**57**	6	26 Don Juan		ABC 12384
9/16/78	**14**	12	27 Hubba Hubba		Capitol 4624
1/06/79	**4**	14	28 **If I Could Write A Song As Beautiful As You ..**		Capitol 4672
4/28/79	**28**	10	29 My Mama Never Heard Me Sing		Capitol 4707
8/04/79	**16**	13	30 Robinhood		Capitol 4753
11/10/79+	**24**	14	31 Till I Stop Shaking		Capitol 4792
3/15/80	**22**	11	32 I Just Had You On My Mind...........................		Capitol 4838
6/14/80	**50**	8	33 Sea Cruise		Capitol 4875
			#14 pop hit for Frankie Ford in 1959		
10/18/80	**20**	13	34 A Real Cowboy (You Say You're)		Capitol 4935
2/14/81	**37**	10	35 It Was You		Capitol 4972
6/20/81	**11**	16	36 I Just Need You For Tonight		Capitol 5011
10/17/81	**38**	10	37 Now That The Feeling's Gone		Capitol 5051
7/17/82	**28**	12	38 Love Busted...		Capitol 5139
11/20/82	**62**	5	39 The New Will Never Wear Off Of You................		Capitol 5170
10/22/83	**86**	2	40 Tell Me When I'm Hot		Cee Cee 5400
			PAUL CRAFT		
			Singer/songwriter/publisher. Wrote "Drop Kick Me Jesus (Through The Goal Posts Of Life)" hit for Bobby Bare and "Hank Williams, You Wrote My Life" for Moe Bandy.		
10/12/74	**55**	10	1 It's Me Again, Margaret .... [N]		Truth 3205
6/11/77	**98**	2	2 We Know Better...		RCA 10971
10/01/77	**55**	7	3 Lean On Jesus "Before He Leans On You"		RCA 11078
3/04/78	**84**	6	4 Teardrops In My Tequila..............................		RCA 11211
			FLOYD CRAMER		
			Born on 10/27/33 in Samti, Louisiana; raised in Huttig, Arkansas. Played piano from age 5. Joined KWKH-Shreveport Louisiana Hayride in 1951. Staff musician for Abbott Records, toured with Elvis Presley. Moved to Nashville in 1955. Top session pianist.		
11/07/60+	**11**	18	1 Last Date .... [I]	*2*	RCA 7775
6/19/61	**8**	10	2 **San Antonio Rose** .... [I]	*8*	RCA 7893
2/18/67	**53**	7	3 Stood Up .... [I]		RCA 9065
4/16/77	**67**	7	4 Rhythm Of The Rain.............................. [I]		RCA 10908
			#3 pop hit for The Cascades in 1963		
3/15/80	**32**	10	5 Dallas .... [I]	*104*	RCA 11916
			theme from the TV series of the same title		
			CALVIN CRAWFORD - see DAVID HOUSTON		
			ALICE CREECH		
			Vocalist from Panther Branch, North Carolina.		
5/29/71	**73**	2	1 The Hunter		Target 00313
11/13/71	**33**	11	2 The Night They Drove Old Dixie Down		Target 0138
			#3 pop hit for Joan Baez in 1971		
2/12/72	**34**	11	3 We'll Sing In The Sunshine		Target 0144
			#4 pop hit for Gale Garnett in 1964		
			CREEDENCE CLEARWATER REVIVAL		
			Rock group formed in El Cerrito, California by John Fogerty.		
12/05/81+	**50**	8	1 Cotton Fields..		Fantasy 920
			#13 pop hit for The Highwaymen in 1962		
			JIM CROCE		
			Born on 1/10/43 in Philadelphia. Killed in a plane crash on 9/20/73.		
4/13/74	**68**	7	1 I'll Have To Say I Love You In A Song	*9*	ABC 11424
			HOWARD CROCKETT		
			Born Howard Hausey in Minden, Louisiana. Wrote "Honky Tonk Man", "Whispering Pines", and "Ole Slew-Foot" for Johnny Horton.		
5/19/73	**52**	10	1 Last Will And Testimony (Of A Drinking Man)		Dot 17457
			SANDY CROFT		
			Born in 1969 in Chattanooga, Tennessee. Winner of the 10-12 year old age group at the International Miss Cinderella Pageant in 1980. In the 8th grade at Brainerd Baptist junior high at the time of her first hit record.		
1/22/83	**61**	8	1 Easier		Angelsong 1821

DEBUT DATE	PEAK POS	WKS CHR	ARTIST — Record Title	POP POS	Label & Number
			SANDY CROFT — Continued		
8/04/84	**91**	2	2 Easier .... [R]		Capitol 5363
6/15/85	**68**	6	3 Piece Of My Heart		Capitol 5471
			#12 pop hit for Janis Joplin (Big Brother...) in 1968		
			BING CROSBY		
			The most popular entertainer of the 20th century's first 50 years. Harry Lillis Crosby was born on 5/2/01 (or 04) in Tacoma, Washington. Bing died of a heart attack on a golf course near Madrid, Spain on 10/14/77.		
1/08/44	**1**⁵	11	1 Pistol Packin' Mama	2	Decca 23277
			BING CROSBY & the ANDREWS SISTERS		
8/30/52	**10**	1	2 Till The End Of The World.......................	16	Decca 28265
			BING CROSBY & GRADY MARTIN & His Slew Foot Five Juke Box #10		
			EDDIE CROSBY		
12/10/49	**7**	2	1 Blues, Stay Away From Me		Decca 46180
			Jockey #7 / Juke Box #10		
			CROSBY, STILLS & NASH		
			David Crosby (guitar; from The Byrds); Stephen Stills (guitar, bass; from Buffalo Springfield) and Graham Nash (guitar; from The Hollies).		
8/14/82	**87**	4	1 Wasted On The Way	9	Atlantic 4058
			ALVIN CROW		
			Born on 9/29/50 in Oklahoma City. Leader of the western swing band, The Pleasant Valley Boys, based in Austin, Texas.		
6/11/77	**83**	4	1 Yes She Do, No She Don't (I'm Satisfied With My Gal)...		Polydor 14387
9/10/77	**97**	2	2 Crazy Little Mama (At My Front Door)...............		Polydor 14410
			#7 pop hit for Pat Boone in 1955		
12/17/77	**94**	4	3 Nyquil Blues..		Polydor 14437
			RODNEY CROWELL		
			Born on 8/7/50 in Houston. Had own band, the Arbitrators, in 1965. Moved to Nashville in 1972 and worked as staff writer for Jerry Reed. Worked with Emmylou Harris from 1975-77. Wrote "Till I Gain Control Again" hit for Harris, "Leavin' Louisiana In The Broad Daylight" for the Oak Ridge Boys, "I Ain't Livin' Long Like This" for Waylon Jennings, and "An American Dream" for the Dirt Band. Married vocalist Rosanne Cash, daughter of Johnny Cash, in 1979.		
9/09/78	**95**	3	1 Elvira		Warner 8637
5/19/79	**90**	3	2 (Now And Then, There's) A Fool Such As I........		Warner 8794
			#2 pop hit for Elvis Presley in 1959		
5/31/80	**78**	6	3 Ashes By Now	37	Warner 49224
10/10/81	**30**	11	4 Stars On The Water	105	Warner 49810
2/13/82	**34**	11	5 Victim Or A Fool		Warner 50008
11/15/86+	**38**	12	6 When I'm Free Again		Columbia 06415
3/21/87	**71**	7	7 She Loves The Jerk		Columbia 06584
6/20/87	**59**	8	8 Looking For You		Columbia 07137
1/23/88	**1**¹	23	9 It's Such A Small World		Columbia 07693
			RODNEY CROWELL & ROSANNE CASH		
6/11/88	**1**¹	21	10 I Couldn't Leave You If I Tried.....................		Columbia 07918
10/15/88+	**1**¹	19	11 She's Crazy For Leavin'		Columbia 08080
			J. C. CROWLEY		
			Songwriter/guitarist/singer from Galveston Bay, Texas. During the late 1970's, was a member of the pop group Player; co-wrote their #1 pop hit "Baby Come Back".		
9/03/88	**49**	7	1 Boxcar 109		RCA 8634
10/29/88+	**13**	19	2 Paint The Town And Hang The Moon Tonight.....		RCA 8747
			SIMON CRUM		
			Simon is actually Ferlin Husky portraying a comic philosopher.		
4/16/55	**5**	15	1 Cuzz You're So Sweet .... [N]		Capitol 3063
			Jockey #5		
11/03/58+	**2**³	24	2 Country Music Is Here To Stay .... [N]		Capitol 4073
			BARBARA CUMMINGS		
12/24/66+	**69**	8	1 She's The Woman		London 104
			BURTON CUMMINGS		
			Born on 12/31/47 in Winnipeg, Canada. Lead singer of The Guess Who.		
3/03/79	**33**	12	1 Takes A Fool To Love A Fool		Portrait 70024

DEBUT DATE	PEAK POS	WKS CHR	ARTIST — Record Title	POP POS	Label & Number
			RICK CUNHA		
			Los Angeles session guitarist/vocalist.		
5/18/74	49	10	1 (I'm A) YoYo Man	*61*	GRC 2016
			J.C. CUNNINGHAM		
			Born John Collins Cunningham on 11/13/50 in Brownsville, Texas. Appeared in the film "Day Of The Wolves".		
7/05/80	85	2	1 The Pyramid Song .... [N]	*104*	Scotti Br. 601
4/21/84	70	6	2 Light Up		Viva 29311
			DICK CURLESS ★★**200**★★		
			Born on 3/17/32 in Fort Fairfield, Maine. With the Trail Blazers band in the early 40s. Had his own radio show as the "Tumbleweed Kid" in Ware, Massachusetts, in 1948. On Armed Forces Radio Network as "The Rice-Paddy Ranger" from 1951-54. Worked in Las Vegas and Hollywood clubs in the late 50s, toured with Buck Owens' All-American Show. Heard on soundtrack for the film "Killer's Three" in 1968.		
3/13/65	5	17	1 **A Tombstone Every Mile**..........................		Tower 124
6/19/65	12	13	2 Six Times A Day (The Trains Came Down)		Tower 135
11/06/65	42	3	3 'Tater Raisin' Man...................................		Tower 161
1/15/66	44	3	4 Travelin' Man.......................................		Tower 193
10/15/66	63	3	5 The Baron		Tower 255
2/04/67	28	11	6 All Of Me Belongs To You		Tower 306
7/29/67	72	1	7 House Of Memories...................................		Tower 335
11/04/67	70	2	8 Big Foot		Tower 362
3/23/68	55	7	9 Bury The Bottle With Me		Tower 399
6/15/68	34	9	10 I Ain't Got Nobody...................................		Tower 415
5/02/70	27	11	11 Big Wheel Cannonball..............................		Capitol 2780
			new version of Vaughn Horton's "Wabash Cannonball"		
8/08/70	31	10	12 Hard, Hard Traveling Man.............................		Capitol 2848
11/21/70	29	9	13 Drag 'Em Off The Interstate, Sock It To 'Em, J.P. Blues...		Capitol 2949
2/20/71	41	9	14 Juke Box Man		Capitol 3034
7/31/71	36	9	15 Loser's Cocktail.....................................		Capitol 3105
10/02/71	40	10	16 Snap Your Fingers...................................		Capitol 3182
			#8 pop hit for Joe Henderson in 1962		
2/26/72	34	11	17 January, April And Me................................		Capitol 3267
7/01/72	31	9	18 Stonin' Around		Capitol 3354
11/25/72	55	7	19 She Called Me Baby		Capitol 3470
3/24/73	54	7	20 Chick Inspector (That's Where My Money Goes)..		Capitol 3541
7/14/73	80	3	21 China Nights (Shina No Yoru)		Capitol 3630
			#58 pop hit for Kyu Sakamoto in 1963		
9/15/73	65	7	22 The Last Blues Song		Capitol 3698
			LARRY CURTIS		
6/10/78	88	5	1 It Feels Like Love For The First Time		ScrimShaw 1315
			MAC CURTIS		
			Born Wesley Erwin Curtis on 1/16/39 in Fort Worth, Texas; raised in Olney, Texas. Moved to Weatherford, Texas in 1954 and formed his own band. On KNOK radio in 1955. Had rockabilly hits starting in 1956 and worked Alan Freed shows in New York. Toured with Little Richard and George Hamilton IV. In the service from 1957-60, worked as Armed Forces radio and TV broadcaster. Worked as a disc jockey in Dallas and on WPLO-Atlanta into the late 60s. Moved to Los Angeles in 1971.		
6/15/68	64	5	1 The Quiet Kind		Epic 10324
10/19/68	54	7	2 The Sunshine Man....................................		Epic 10385
5/24/69	63	7	3 Happiness Lives In This House		Epic 10468
11/08/69	60	5	4 Don't Make Love		Epic 10530
2/28/70	43	9	5 Honey, Don't		Epic 10574
			written by Carl Perkins (on the "Beatles '65" LP)		
10/17/70	35	10	6 Early In The Morning		GRT 26
			recorded by Bobby Darin (Rinky-Dinks) and Buddy Holly in 1958		
			SONNY CURTIS		
			Born in Meadow, Texas. Original fiddler/guitarist in 1956 with Buddy Holly & The Three Tunes. Wrote "I Fought The Law" hit for Bobby Fuller and the theme for TV's "Mary Tyler Moore" show.		
10/08/66	49	2	1 My Way Of Life	*134*	Viva 602
9/23/67	50	11	2 I Wanna Go Bummin' Around.........................		Viva 617
2/24/68	36	11	3 Atlanta Georgia Stray	*120*	Viva 626

DEBUT DATE	PEAK POS	WKS CHR	ARTIST — Record Title	POP POS	Label & Number
			SONNY CURTIS — Continued		
7/20/68	**45**	9	4 The Straight Life............................		Viva 630
			#36 pop hit for Bobby Goldsboro in 1968		
11/29/75	**78**	5	5 Lovesick Blues		Capitol 4158
9/15/79	**77**	6	6 The Cowboy Singer..........................		Elektra 46526
1/19/80	**86**	3	7 Do You Remember Roll Over Beethoven		Elektra 46568
3/29/80	**38**	9	8 The Real Buddy Holly Story		Elektra 46616
			Sonny recalls Buddy's rise to fame		
7/19/80	**29**	10	9 Love Is All Around		Elektra 46663
11/08/80	**70**	3	10 Fifty Ways To Leave Your Lover		Elektra 47048
			#1 pop hit for Paul Simon in 1976		
4/25/81	**15**	16	11 Good Ol' Girls..............................		Elektra 47129
8/22/81	**33**	10	12 Married Women		Elektra 47176
1/25/86	**69**	5	13 Now I've Got A Heart Of Gold		'Steem 110185

D

TED DAFFAN'S TEXANS

Born Theron Eugene Daffan on 9/21/12 in Beauregard Parish, Louisiana; raised in Houston. Played with the Blue Islanders and Blue Ridge Playboys from 1934-36, 1936-40. Had own band, the Texans, from 1940 to late 50s. Wrote "Truck Driver's Blues", "A Worried Mind", "Born To Lose", and "No Letter Today", all between 1939 and 1942. Worked Venice Pier until 1946, then formed new band in Houston. Had publishing company with Hank Snow in Nashville in 1958, and own company in Houston from 1961.

DEBUT DATE	PEAK POS	WKS CHR	ARTIST — Record Title	POP POS	Label & Number
1/08/44	**2**³	8	1 **No Letter Today/**	*9*	
			vocals by Chuck Keeshan & Leon Seago		
1/15/44	**3**	21	2 **Born To Lose**..............................	*19*	Okeh 6706
			vocal: Leon Seago; #41 pop hit for Ray Charles in 1962		
6/03/44	**4**	2	3 **Look Who's Talkin'**.......................................		Okeh 6719
2/24/45	**6**	2	4 **Time Won't Heal My Broken Heart/**		
3/03/45	**5**	3	5 **You're Breaking My Heart**........................		Okeh 6729
8/25/45	**5**	3	6 **Shadow Of My Heart/**		
9/01/45	**2**³	13	7 **Headin' Down The Wrong Highway**		Okeh 6744
10/26/46	**5**	3	8 **Shut That Gate**		Columbia 37087
			vocal: George Strange		

PAT DAISY

Born Patricia Key Deasy on 10/10/44 in Gallatin, Tennessee. In girl trio while in high school. Moved to Huntsville, Alabama in 1966, worked in a folk group.

DEBUT DATE	PEAK POS	WKS CHR	ARTIST — Record Title	POP POS	Label & Number
2/19/72	**20**	13	1 Everybody's Reaching Out For Someone...........	*112*	RCA 0637
7/29/72	**48**	7	2 Beautiful People		RCA 0743
			pop hits for Bobby Vee and Kenny O'Dell in 1967		
5/05/73	**49**	7	3 The Lonesomest Lonesome		RCA 0932
10/13/73	**53**	9	4 My Love Is Deep, My Love Is Wide...................		RCA 0087

KENNY DALE

Singer from Artesia, New Mexico. Worked clubs in Houston; first recorded in 1976.

DEBUT DATE	PEAK POS	WKS CHR	ARTIST — Record Title	POP POS	Label & Number
3/05/77	**11**	17	1 Bluest Heartache Of The Year		Capitol 4389
			originally released on Earthrider label in 1976		
7/30/77	**11**	14	2 Shame, Shame On Me (I Had Planned To Be Your Man)..		Capitol 4457
1/21/78	**17**	14	3 Red Hot Memory		Capitol 4528
5/06/78	**28**	11	4 The Loser		Capitol 4570
9/02/78	**18**	13	5 Two Hearts Tangled In Love...................		Capitol 4619
4/21/79	**16**	11	6 Down To Earth Woman		Capitol 4704
7/21/79	**7**	15	7 **Only Love Can Break A Heart**		Capitol 4746
			#2 pop hit for Gene Pitney in 1962		
11/03/79	**15**	13	8 Sharing		Capitol 4788
2/23/80	**23**	10	9 Let Me In		Capitol 4829
6/28/80	**33**	11	10 Thank You, Ever-Lovin'.......................		Capitol 4882
11/22/80+	**31**	13	11 When It's Just You And Me....................		Capitol 4943
3/06/82	**65**	6	12 Moanin The Blues		Funderburg 5001
1/28/84	**85**	6	13 Two Will Be One		Republic 8301
9/01/84	**86**	3	14 Take It Slow................................		Republic 8403
4/13/85	**83**	3	15 Look What Love Did To Me		Saba 9214

DEBUT DATE	PEAK POS	WKS CHR	ARTIST — Record Title	POP POS	Label & Number
			KENNY DALE — Continued		
5/31/86	63	7	16 I'm Going Crazy		BGM 30186
			TERRY DALE		
1/09/82	93	2	1 Intimate Strangers		Lanedale 1001
3/27/82	73	4	2 Loving You Is Always On My Mind...................		Lanedale 711
			JOHNNY DALLAS		
12/24/66+	62	7	1 A Heart Full Of Love...............................		Little Dar. 0013
			BOB DALTON		
			Singer from Itman, West Virginia.		
10/17/70	73	3	1 Mama Call Me Home		Mega 0003
			LACY J. DALTON ★★151★★		
			Born Jill Byrem on 10/13/48 in Bloomsburg, Pennsylvania. Began career as a folk singer. Moved to Santa Cruz, California in the late 60s. Sang with the rock group Office in the early 70s. First recorded for Harbor in 1978, as Jill Croston.		
10/06/79	17	13	1 Crazy Blue Eyes..		Columbia 11107
2/02/80	18	12	2 Tennessee Waltz.......................................		Columbia 11190
			#1 pop hit for Patti Page in 1950		
4/26/80	14	14	3 Losing Kind Of Love		Columbia 11253
8/30/80	7	14	4 **Hard Times**		Columbia 11343
12/13/80+	8	15	5 **Hillbilly Girl With The Blues**		Columbia 11410
4/04/81	10	13	6 Whisper..		Coiumbia 01036
7/18/81	2²	18	7 **Takin' It Easy**......................................		Columbia 02188
12/05/81+	5	17	8 **Everybody Makes Mistakes**/		
		16	9 Wild Turkey..		Columbia 02637
5/01/82	13	15	10 Slow Down	106	Columbia 02847
9/11/82	7	19	11 **16th Avenue**		Columbia 03184
3/12/83	30	14	12 It's A Dirty Job.....................................		Columbia 03628
			BOBBY BARE & LACY J. DALTON		
6/11/83	9	20	13 **Dream Baby (How Long Must I Dream)**		Columbia 03926
			#4 pop hit for Roy Orbison in 1962		
10/15/83	54	8	14 Windin' Down		Columbia 04133
11/24/84+	15	20	15 If That Ain't Love...............................		Columbia 04696
4/27/85	19	18	16 Size Seven Round (Made Of Gold)		Epic 04876
			GEORGE JONES & LACY J. DALTON		
6/08/85	20	17	17 You Can't Run Away From Your Heart..............		Columbia 04884
10/19/85	58	8	18 The Night Has A Heart Of It's Own		Columbia 05644
1/18/86	43	16	19 Don't Fall In Love With Me		Columbia 05759
6/14/86	16	19	20 Working Class Man....................................		Columbia 06098
12/06/86+	33	14	21 This Ol' Town		Columbia 06360
			LARRY DALTON & THE DALTON GANG		
			Larry was born on 4/24/46 in Big Stone Gap, Virginia. Organist with Oral Roberts Crusades in the mid-60s. Founder of Living Sound International in 1969. Musical director for Oral Roberts TV shows from 1973-75.		
9/05/81	82	3	1 Cowboy		Soundwaves 4645
			DANDY		
4/14/79	57	6	1 Stay With Me...		Warner 8771
7/28/79	67	5	2 I Don't Want To Love You Anymore		Warner 8880
12/01/79	71	6	3 I'm Just Your Yesterday...............................		Warner 49111
10/18/80	54	7	4 Who Were You Thinkin' Of............................	49	Columbia 11355
			DANDY & THE DOOLITTLE BAND (later as The Doolittle Band)		
			DANIEL		
			Born Daniel Willis on 11/23/53 in Washington, DC.		
6/25/77	91	3	1 But Tonight I'm Gonna Love You		LS 122
12/03/77	100	1	2 Stolen Moments		LS 136
7/29/78	78	5	3 I Bow My Head (When They Say Grace)		LS 166
			COOTER DANIEL		
			Born in 1956 in Knoxville, Tennessee. Worked as a staff writer for Twitty Music.		
3/22/80	89	2	1 Where Are We Going From Here		Connection 1
			PEBBLE DANIEL		
6/21/80	86	3	1 Goodbye Eyes...		Elektra 46643

DEBUT DATE	PEAK POS	WKS CHR	ARTIST — Record Title	POP POS	Label & Number
			TINA DANIELLE Singer from Jena, Louisiana.		
11/15/86	75	4	1 Standing Too Close To The Moon		Charta 202
2/14/87	71	5	2 Burned Out		Charta 204
5/09/87	73	4	3 Warmed Over Romance		Charta 206
			THE CHARLIE DANIELS BAND Formed in Nashville in 1971. Consisted of Charlie Daniels (b: 10/28/36, Wilmington, NC; vocals, guitar, fiddle), Tom Crain (guitar), Joe "Taz" DiGregorio (keyboards), Charles Hayward (bass) and James W. Marshall (drums). Daniels led the Jaguars from 1958-67. Went solo in 1968 and worked as a session musician in Nashville. Played on Bob Dylan's "Nashville Skyline" hit LP. In the film "Urban Cowboy".		
8/04/73	67	6	1 Uneasy Rider..	9	Kama Sutra 576
1/31/76	36	11	2 Texas..	91	Kama Sutra 607
6/26/76	22	11	3 Wichita Jail		Epic 50243
1/22/77	75	4	4 Billy The Kid		Epic 50322
10/22/77	85	5	5 Heaven Can Be Anywhere (Twin Pines Theme) ...		Epic 50456
6/30/79	1¹	14	6● **The Devil Went Down To Georgia**	3	Epic 50700
10/06/79	19	11	7 Mississippi		Epic 50768
1/12/80	87	4	8 Behind Your Eyes		Epic 50806
2/23/80	27	10	9 Long Haired Country Boy		Epic 50845
6/07/80	13	11	10 In America..	11	Epic 50888
9/06/80	80	4	11 The Legend Of Wooley Swamp.........................	31	Epic 50921
12/27/80+	44	10	12 Carolina (I Remember You)		Epic 50955
7/25/81	94	2	13 Sweet Home Alabama	110	Epic 02185
			#8 pop hit for Lynyrd Skynyrd in 1974		
7/17/82	76	4	14 Ragin' Cajun	109	Epic 02995
10/16/82	69	5	15 We Had It All One Time................................		Epic 03251
8/13/83	65	6	16 Stroker's Theme		Epic 03918
			based on the Burt Reynolds film "Stroker Ace"		
10/05/85	54	10	17 American Farmer..		Epic 05638
12/07/85+	33	17	18 Still Hurtin' Me		Epic 05699
3/22/86	8	22	19 **Drinkin' My Baby Goodbye**		Epic 05835
8/20/88	10	17	20 **Boogie Woogie Fiddle Country Blues**.............		Epic 08002
			BOBBY DARIN Born Walden Robert Cassotto on 5/14/36 in the Bronx, New York. Died of heart failure on 12/20/73 (37) in Los Angeles.		
8/04/58	14	3	1 Splish Splash	3	Atco 6117
			Best Seller #14		
			JOHNNY DARRELL Born on 7/23/40 in Hopewell, Alabama.		
12/25/65+	30	7	1 As Long As The Wind Blows		United Art. 943
6/04/66	44	3	2 Johnny Lose It All		United Art. 50008
11/12/66	72	4	3 She's Mighty Gone		United Art. 50047
			written by Johnny Cash & June Carter		
4/01/67	9	15	4 **Ruby, Don't Take Your Love To Town**...........		United Art. 50126
			#6 pop hit for Kenny Rogers & The First Edition in 1969		
7/22/67	73	3	5 My Elusive Dreams		United Art. 50183
10/07/67	37	10	6 Come See What's Left Of Your Man		United Art. 50207
12/23/67+	22	14	7 The Son Of Hickory Holler's Tramp		United Art. 50235
			#40 pop hit for O.C. Smith in 1968		
4/27/68	3	18	8 **With Pen In Hand**	126	United Art. 50292
			written by Bobby Goldsboro; Billy Vera & Vikki Carr had pop hits		
9/21/68	27	10	9 I Ain't Buying..		United Art. 50442
11/30/68+	20	13	10 Woman Without Love		United Art. 50481
4/12/69	50	7	11 The Coming Of The Roads.............................		United Art. 50503
			JOHNNY DARRELL & ANITA CARTER		
4/26/69	17	13	12 Why You Been Gone So Long		United Art. 50518
9/13/69	23	10	13 River Bottom..		United Art. 50572
2/14/70	68	7	14 Mama Come'n Get Your Baby Boy		United Art. 50629
7/11/70	75	2	15 Brother River		United Art. 50675
11/14/70	74	2	16 They'll Never Take Her Love From Me		United Art. 50716
7/28/73	66	10	17 Dakota The Dancing Bear		Monument 8579
10/12/74	63	9	18 Orange Blossom Special		Capricorn 0207

DEBUT DATE	PEAK POS	WKS CHR	ARTIST — Record Title	POP POS	Label & Number
			JAMES DARREN		
			Born James Ercolani on 10/3/36 in Philadelphia. In films from 1956-64.		
7/29/78	53	9	1 Let Me Take You In My Arms Again		RCA 11316
			written by Neil Diamond		
			DAVE & SUGAR ★★**164**★★		
			Trio consisting of David Rowland (b: 1/26/42, Los Angeles), Vicki Hackman and Jackie Frantz. Rowland had been with the Stamps Quartet. Trio worked as back-up singers for Charley Pride. Hackman married Ron Baker, guitarist in Pride's band, replaced by Sue Powell. Powell was replaced by Jamie Jaye in 1980 and Rowland went solo in 1982.		
11/15/75+	25	17	1 Queen Of The Silver Dollar		RCA 10425
4/17/76	1¹	19	2 The Door Is Always Open............................		RCA 10625
9/11/76	3	17	3 I'm Gonna Love You...................................		RCA 10768
2/12/77	5	13	4 Don't Throw It All Away.............................		RCA 10876
7/16/77	7	14	5 That's The Way Love Should Be		RCA 11034
10/29/77	2⁴	16	6 I'm Knee Deep In Loving You		RCA 11141
4/08/78	4	14	7 Gotta' Quit Lookin' At You Baby.................		RCA 11251
8/12/78	1¹	16	8 Tear Time...................................		RCA 11322
1/20/79	1³	14	9 Golden Tears............................		RCA 11427
6/30/79	6	13	10 Stay With Me		RCA 11654
10/20/79	4	14	11 My World Begins And Ends With You/		
		14	12 Why Did You Have To Be So Good..................		RCA 11749
4/05/80	18	12	13 New York Wine And Tennessee Shine		RCA 11947
8/16/80	40	8	14 A Love Song....................................		RCA 12063
2/07/81	32	9	15 It's A Heartache......................		RCA 12168
			#3 pop hit for Bonnie Tyler in 1978		
5/09/81	6	15	16 Fool By Your Side		Elektra 47135
8/29/81	32	8	17 The Pleasure's All Mine..................................		Elektra 47177
			14, 16 & 17: **DAVE ROWLAND & SUGAR**		
			GAIL DAVIES ★★**155**★★		
			Born in Broken Bow, Oklahoma on 4/4/48. Moved to Seattle, worked as jazz vocalist. In a duo with brother Ron in the early 70s. Did session work in Los Angeles and worked as staff writer for Vogue Music. Moved to Nashville in the mid-70s. Wrote "Bucket To The South" hit for Ava Barber. Lead singer with the Wild Choir in 1986.		
7/08/78	26	12	1 No Love Have I		Lifesong 1771
10/21/78	27	12	2 Poison Love		Lifesong 1777
2/10/79	11	16	3 Someone Is Looking For Someone Like You		Lifesong 1784
11/17/79+	7	16	4 Blue Heartache...................................		Warner 49108
3/22/80	21	11	5 Like Strangers...		Warner 49199
			#22 pop hit for The Everly Brothers in 1960		
6/28/80	21	12	6 Good Lovin' Man..		Warner 49263
11/29/80+	4	16	7 I'll Be There (If You Ever Want Me)...............		Warner 49592
4/04/81	5	18	8 It's A Lovely, Lovely World.........................		Warner 49694
8/15/81	9	15	9 Grandma's Song		Warner 49790
2/13/82	9	18	10 'Round The Clock Lovin'		Warner 50004
6/26/82	17	15	11 You Turn Me On I'm A Radio.......................		Warner 29972
			#25 pop hit for Joni Mitchell in 1973		
10/30/82+	24	15	12 Hold On..		Warner 29892
3/26/83	17	15	13 Singing The Blues		Warner 29726
			#1 pop hit for Guy Mitchell in 1956		
10/15/83	18	19	14 You're A Hard Dog (To Keep Under The Porch) ...		Warner 29472
2/25/84	19	17	15 Boys Like You..		Warner 29374
8/04/84	55	12	16 It's You Alone		Warner 29219
10/06/84	20	25	17 Jagged Edge Of A Broken Heart......................		RCA 13912
2/23/85	37	12	18 Nothing Can Hurt Me Now...........................		RCA 14017
6/22/85	56	8	19 Unwed Fathers		RCA 14095
9/21/85	15	25	20 Break Away		RCA 14184
			THE DAVIS SISTERS		
			Duo from Lexington, Kentucky, formed in 1949. Consisted of Mary Frances "Skeeter Davis" Penick and Betty Jack Davis (killed in an auto accident on 8/2/53). The two were not related. Worked on WLEX-Lexington, WWVA-Wheeling Jamboree. First recorded for Fortune in 1952. Skeeter was seriously injured in the wreck that killed Betty. Betty was replaced by her sister Georgia.		
8/15/53	1⁸	26	1 I Forgot More Than You'll Ever Know...........	18	RCA 5345
			Jockey #1(8) / Best Seller #1(6) / Juke Box #1(2)		

DEBUT DATE	PEAK POS	WKS CHR	ARTIST — Record Title	POP POS	Label & Number
			DANNY DAVIS & THE NASHVILLE BRASS		
			Danny's real name: George Nowlan. Born on 4/29/25 in Dorchester, Massachusetts. Trumpet player/leader educated at the New England Conservatory of Music. Played and sang in swing bands including Gene Krupa, Bob Crosby, Freddy Martin, Blue Barron, and Sammy Kaye. Producer for Joy and MGM Records in the late 50s. Production assistant to Chet Atkins in 1965. Formed The Nashville Brass in 1968.		
1/03/70	68	3	1 Please Help Me, I'm Falling		RCA 0287
			HANK LOCKLIN & DANNY DAVIS & THE NASHVILLE BRASS		
2/14/70	63	3	2 Wabash Cannon Ball .... [I]	131	RCA 9785
6/27/70	56	6	3 Flying South		RCA 9849
			HANK LOCKLIN & DANNY DAVIS & THE NASHVILLE BRASS		
7/04/70	70	2	4 Columbus Stockade Blues .... [I]		RCA 9847
10/15/77	91	6	5 How I Love Them Old Songs........................		RCA 11073
2/02/80	20	12	6 Night Life		RCA 11893
			DANNY DAVIS & WILLIE NELSON with THE NASHVILLE BRASS		
5/17/80	41	8	7 Funny How Time Slips Away..........................		RCA 11999
			DANNY DAVIS & WILLIE NELSON with THE NASHVILLE BRASS		
3/23/85	82	3	8 I Dropped Your Name..................................		Wartrace 730
10/10/87	62	5	9 Green Eyes (Cryin' Those Blue Tears)		Jaroco 8742
			DANNY DAVIS & THE NASHVILLE BRASS & DONA MASON		
			GENE DAVIS		
			Wrote the hit "I Won't Come In While He's There" for Jim Reeves.		
11/27/76	97	4	1 Oh Those Texas Women		Maverick 301
			JIMMIE DAVIS		
			Born on 9/11/02 in Beech Grove, Louisiana. Sang in college group, the Tiger Four, and appeared on KWKH-Shreveport. Taught history at Dodd College in the late 20s. Recorded for Victor from 1929-34, then switched to Decca. Wrote "You Are My Sunshine" with Charles Mitchell in 1940. Also wrote "Nobody's Darlin' But Mine". In films "Strictly In The Groove", "Frontier Fury", "Louisiana" and "Square Dance Katy". Governor of Louisiana from 1944-48 and 1960-64. Elected to the Country Music Hall Of Fame in 1972.		
9/02/44	3	2	1 Is It Too Late Now/		
9/30/44	4	2	2 **There's A Chill On The Hill Tonight**		Decca 6100
2/24/45	1¹	18	3 **There's A New Moon Over My Shoulder**		Decca 6105
3/02/46	4	1	4 **Grievin' My Heart Out For You**		Decca 18756
1/18/47	4	2	5 **Bang Bang**		Decca 46016
6/16/62	15	9	6 Where The Old Red River Flows......................		Decca 31368
			JOEY DAVIS		
8/12/78	99	1	1 Why Don't You Leave Me Alone.......................		MRC 1017
12/16/78	94	3	2 Takin' It Easy..		MRC 1023
			LINDA DAVIS		
			Singer from Gary, Texas. Recorded in duet, Skip & Linda, with Skip Eaton. Sang Dr. Pepper and Kentucky Fried Chicken jingles. Also see Skip & Linda.		
10/29/88	50	10	1 All The Good One's Are Taken		Epic 08057
			MAC DAVIS ★★139★★		
			Born on 1/21/42 in Lubbock, Texas. Vocalist/guitarist/composer. Worked as a regional rep for Vee-Jay and Liberty Records. Wrote "In The Ghetto", "Don't Cry Daddy", hits for Elvis Presley. Host of his own musical variety TV series from 1974-76. Appearances in several films, including "North Dallas Forty" in 1979.		
4/25/70	43	13	1 Whoever Finds This, I Love You......................	53	Columbia 45117
8/29/70	68	4	2 I'll Paint You A Song	110	Columbia 45192
			from the film "Norwood"		
8/26/72	26	11	3●Baby Don't Get Hooked On Me........................	1	Columbia 45618
2/24/73	47	8	4 Dream Me Home...	73	Columbia 45773
5/12/73	36	11	5 Your Side Of The Bed...................................	88	Columbia 45839
9/01/73	29	15	6 Kiss It And Make It Better	105	Columbia 45911
9/07/74	40	12	7 Stop And Smell The Roses	9	Columbia 10018
1/04/75	29	11	8 Rock N' Roll (I Gave You The Best Years Of My Life)	15	Columbia 10070
4/12/75	69	6	9 (If You Add) All The Love In The World	54	Columbia 10111
6/07/75	31	12	10 Burnin' Thing	53	Columbia 10148
9/27/75	81	5	11 I Still Love You (You Still Love Me)..................		Columbia 10187
3/27/76	17	13	12 Forever Lovers	76	Columbia 10304
10/09/76	34	10	13 Every Now And Then		Columbia 10418
5/21/77	42	9	14 Picking Up The Pieces Of My Life		Columbia 10535

DEBUT DATE	PEAK POS	WKS CHR	ARTIST — Record Title	POP POS	Label & Number
			MAC DAVIS — Continued		
6/10/78	92	5	15 Music In My Life		Columbia 10745
3/22/80	10	12	16 **It's Hard To Be Humble**.......................... [N]	43	Casablanca 2244
7/12/80	10	15	17 **Let's Keep It That Way**		Casablanca 2286
10/11/80	9	17	18 **Texas In My Rear View Mirror**	51	Casablanca 2305
2/21/81	2²	15	19 **Hooked On Music**.................................	102	Casablanca 2327
7/18/81	47	10	20 Secrets..	76	Casablanca 2336
10/24/81+	5	18	21 **You're My Bestest Friend**	106	Casablanca 2341
5/29/82	37	10	22 Rodeo Clown		Casablanca 2350
9/25/82	58	8	23 The Beer Drinkin' Song		Casablanca 2355
12/18/82+	62	7	24 Lying Here Lying		Casablanca 2363
2/11/84	41	14	25 Most Of All.......................................		Casa. 818168
5/19/84	76	5	26 Caroline's Still In Georgia		Casa. 818929
5/25/85	10	24	27 **I Never Made Love (Till I Made Love With You)**..		MCA 52573
10/05/85	34	16	28 I Feel The Country Callin' Me		MCA 52669
2/01/86	46	,9	29 Sexy Young Girl...................................		MCA 52765
6/07/86	65	5	30 Somewhere In America		MCA 52826
			PAUL DAVIS		
			Born on 4/21/48 in Meridian, Mississippi. Singer/songwriter/producer.		
1/11/75	47	8	1 Ride 'Em Cowboy	23	Bang 712
12/16/78+	85	4	2 Sweet Life.......................................	17	Bang 738
8/30/86	1¹	21	3 **You're Still New To Me**............................		Capitol 5613
			MARIE OSMOND with PAUL DAVIS		
11/21/87+	1¹	24	4 **I Won't Take Less Than Your Love**		Capitol 44100
			TANYA TUCKER with PAUL DAVIS & PAUL OVERSTREET		
8/20/88	47	8	5 Sweet Life....................................... [R]		Capitol 44215
			MARIE OSMOND with PAUL DAVIS		
			PAUL DAVIS		
7/18/60	28	5	1 One Of Her Fools...............................		Doke 107
			SAMMY DAVIS, JR.		
			Born on 12/8/25 in New York City. Vocalist/dancer/actor.		
12/11/82	89	2	1 Smoke, Smoke, Smoke (That Cigarette)		Applause 100
			SKEETER DAVIS ★★82★★		
			Born Mary Frances Penick on 12/30/31 in Dry Ridge, Kentucky. Worked in duo with close friend Betty Jack Davis, and later with Georgia Davis. Went solo in 1956. Toured with Eddy Arnold and Elvis Presley. Joined the Grand Ole Opry in 1959. Married to TV's "Nashville Now" host, Ralph Emery, 1960-64.		
2/24/58	15	1	1 Lost To A Geisha Girl		RCA 7084
			Jockey #15		
			answer song to Hank Locklin's "Geisha Girl"		
3/30/59	5	17	2 **Set Him Free**.....................................		RCA 7471
9/21/59	15	13	3 Homebreaker.......................................		RCA 7570
3/07/60	11	12	4 Am I That Easy To Forget?		RCA 7671
8/29/60	2³	16	5 **(I Can't Help You) I'm Falling Too**	39	RCA 7767
			answer song to Hank Locklin's "Please Help Me, I'm Falling"		
12/31/60+	5	13	6 **My Last Date (With You)**..........................	26	RCA 7825
			vocal version of Floyd Cramer's "Last Date"		
4/24/61	11	11	7 The Hand You're Holding Now		RCA 7863
10/16/61	10	11	8 **Optimistic**.......................................		RCA 7928
3/10/62	9	9	9 **Where I Ought To Be/**		
6/02/62	23	3	10 Something Precious..............................		RCA 7979
9/08/62	22	1	11 The Little Music Box..............................		RCA 8055
12/15/62+	2³	24	12 **The End Of The World**...........................	2	RCA 8098
5/25/63	9	14	13 **I'm Saving My Love**...............................	41	RCA 8176
10/12/63	14	10	14 I Can't Stay Mad At You	7	RCA 8219
1/25/64	17	15	15 He Says The Same Things To Me...................	47	RCA 8288
5/16/64	8	14	16 **Gonna Get Along Without You Now**..............	48	RCA 8347
9/26/64	45	4	17 Let Me Get Close To You	106	RCA 8397
11/14/64	38	5	18 What Am I Gonna Do With You......................	123	RCA 8450
3/13/65	11	12	19 A Dear John Letter	114	RCA 8496
			SKEETER DAVIS & BOBBY BARE		

DEBUT DATE	PEAK POS	WKS CHR	ARTIST — Record Title	POP POS	Label & Number
			SKEETER DAVIS — Continued		
9/11/65	30	7	20 Sun Glasses	*120*	RCA 8642
10/15/66	36	9	21 Goin' Down The Road (Feelin' Bad)..................		RCA 8932
1/28/67	11	16	22 Fuel To The Flame		RCA 9058
7/22/67	5	18	23 **What Does It Take (To Keep A Man Like You Satisfied)**...	*121*	RCA 9242
12/16/67+	52	7	24 Set Him Free .... [R] new version of Skeeter's second hit		RCA 9371
2/24/68	72	2	25 For Loving You.............................. [N]		RCA 9415
			SKEETER DAVIS & DON BOWMAN		
3/23/68	54	7	26 Instinct For Survival................................		RCA 0459
6/22/68	16	10	27 There's A Fool Born Every Minute..................		RCA 9543
1/11/69	66	7	28 The Closest Thing To Love (I've Ever Seen)........		RCA 9695
12/13/69+	9	15	29 **I'm A Lover (Not a Fighter)**........................		RCA 0292
1/24/70	22	7	30 Your Husband, My Wife.............................		RCA 9789
			BOBBY BARE & SKEETER DAVIS		
5/09/70	65	5	31 It's Hard To Be A Woman		RCA 9818
8/08/70	69	3	32 We Need A Lot More Of Jesus.......................		RCA 9871
9/26/70	65	2	33 Let's Get Together		RCA 9893
			SKEETER DAVIS & GEORGE HAMILTON IV #5 pop hit for The Youngbloods in 1969		
3/06/71	21	13	34 Bus Fare To Kentucky		RCA 9961
7/17/71	58	8	35 Love Takes A Lot Of My Time		RCA 9997
1/08/72	54	7	36 One Tin Soldier .... Coven and The Original Caste had pop hits; from the film "Billy Jack"		RCA 0608
5/20/72	46	8	37 Sad Situation		RCA 0681
6/16/73	12	17	38 I Can't Believe That It's All Over....................	*101*	RCA 0968
12/15/73+	44	10	39 Don't Forget To Remember .... written and popularized by The Bee Gees in 1969		RCA 0188
5/25/74	65	8	40 One More Time		RCA 0277
9/18/76	60	7	41 I Love Us...		Mercury 73818
			DON DEAL		
6/16/79	90	2	1 Second Best		Don-Jim 1008
			EDDIE DEAN Born Edgar Dean Glosup on 7/9/07 in Posey, Texas. Teamed with older brother Jimmy and worked the WLS-Chicago National Barn Dance. Moved to Los Angeles in 1937; made films with Gene Autry and did his own film series from 1946-48. Featured on the Judy Canova network radio show.		
9/25/48	11	1	1 One Has My Name, The Other Has My Heart....... Best Seller #11		Crystal 132
1/22/55	10	3	2 **I Dreamed Of A Hill-Billy Heaven** .... Juke Box #10 / Jockey #10 / Best Seller #15 with The Frontiersmen; #20 pop hit for Tex Ritter in 1961		Sage & Sand 180
			JIMMY DEAN ★★**140**★★ Born Seth Ward on 8/10/28 in Plainview, Texas. With the Tennessee Haymakers in Washington, DC in 1948. Own Texas Wildcats in 1952. Recorded for 4 Star in 1952. Own CBS-TV series from 1957-58; ABC-TV series from 1963-66.		
3/07/53	5	7	1 Bumming Around .... Jockey #5 / Best Seller #9 / Juke Box #10		4 Star 1613
10/16/61	1²	22	2●**Big Bad John**	*1*	Columbia 42175
2/03/62	9	10	3 **Dear Ivan** .... [S]	*24*	Columbia 42259
2/10/62	16	10	4 The Cajun Queen/ .... [S]	*22*	
3/10/62	15	6	5 To A Sleeping Beauty .... [S] background tune: "Memories"	*26*	Columbia 42282
4/21/62	3	13	6 P.T. 109	*8*	Columbia 42338
9/29/62	10	11	7 Little Black Book....................................	*29*	Columbia 42529
2/01/64	35	6	8 Mind Your Own Business .... written and popularized in 1949 by Hank Williams		Columbia 42934
6/05/65	1²	17	9 **The First Thing Ev'ry Morning (And The Last Thing Ev'ry Night)**	*91*	Columbia 43263
10/30/65	35	6	10 Harvest Of Sunshine		Columbia 43382
10/22/66	10	18	11 **Stand Beside Me**		RCA 8971
2/18/67	16	14	12 Sweet Misery		RCA 9091
7/22/67	41	9	13 Ninety Days		RCA 9241

DEBUT DATE	PEAK POS	WKS CHR	ARTIST — Record Title	POP POS	Label & Number
			JIMMY DEAN — Continued		
11/18/67+	30	10	14 I'm A Swinger		RCA 9350
3/09/68	21	14	15 A Thing Called Love		RCA 9454
8/10/68	52	8	16 Born To Be By Your Side		RCA 9567
11/09/68	22	11	17 A Hammer And Nails		RCA 9652
4/05/69	52	7	18 A Rose Is A Rose Is A Rose		RCA 0122
1/30/71	29	11	19 Slowly...		RCA 9947
			JIMMY DEAN & DOTTIE WEST		
4/17/71	54	7	20 Everybody Knows		RCA 9966
1/01/72	38	12	21 The One You Say Good Mornin' To		RCA 0600
10/06/73	90	6	22 Your Sweet Love (Keeps Me Homeward Bound)...		Columbia 45922
5/15/76	9	6	23● I.O.U. .... [S]	35	Casino 052
			Jimmy Dean's ode of thanks to his mother		
9/25/76	85	3	24 To A Sleeping Beauty ....[S-R]		Casino 074
			new version of Jimmy's 1962 hit		
5/14/77	90	2	25 I.O.U. ....[S-R]		Casino 052
5/14/83	77	4	26 I.O.U. ....[S-R]		Churchill 94024
			DEBONAIRES		
4/13/85	79	6	1 I'm On Fire		MTM 72051
			DUANE DEE		
			Born Duane DeRosia in Hartford, Wisconsin. Discovered by dee-jay Bill Ericksen. Worked in Milwaukee clubs. Appeared on Bobby Lord's TV show, Midwestern Hayride.		
11/11/67+	44	12	1 Before The Next Teardrop Falls		Capitol 5986
12/21/68+	58	7	2 True Love Travels On A Gravel Road		Capitol 2332
2/06/71	71	2	3 I've Got To Sing		Cartwheel 192
10/16/71	36	13	4 How Can You Mend A Broken Heart		Cartwheel 200
			#1 pop hit for The Bee Gees in 1971		
3/04/72	64	6	5 Sweet Apple Wine		Cartwheel 207
4/20/74	88	3	6 Morning Girl..		ABC 11417
			#17 pop hit for Neon Philharmonic in 1969		
			GORDON DEE		
			Born Gordon Dillingham in New Bridge, North Carolina. Worked in a carnival band from age 19. Leader of the house band at Mama's Country Showcase in Atlanta.		
12/15/84	87	5	1 (Nothing Left Between Us) But Alabama		So. Tracks 1029
			KATHY DEE		
			Born Kathleen Dearth in Moundsville, West Virginia. Own group, Kathy's Clowns, from 1963-68. Died on 11/3/68.		
9/21/63	18	3	1 Unkind Words		United Art. 627
2/15/64	44	4	2 Don't Leave Me Lonely Too Long		United Art. 687
			PENNY DeHAVEN		
			Born on 5/17/48 in Winchester, Virginia. In the films "Valley Of Blood", "Traveling Light" and "Country Music Story". Also recorded as Penny Starr.		
1/07/67	69	3	1 Grain Of Salt		Band Box 372
			PENNY STARR		
8/09/69	34	11	2 Mama Lou..		Imperial 66388
11/15/69	37	10	3 Down In The Boondocks		Imperial 66421
			#9 pop hit for Billy Joe Royal in 1965		
3/21/70	59	5	4 I Feel Fine		Imperial 66437
			#1 pop hit for The Beatles in 1964		
5/30/70	20	12	5 Land Mark Tavern.......................................		United Art. 50669
			DEL REEVES & PENNY DeHAVEN		
9/19/70	69	2	6 Awful Lotta Lovin'		United Art. 50703
1/30/71	46	9	7 The First Love		United Art. 50742
6/19/71	42	9	8 Don't Change On Me		United Art. 50787
12/25/71+	61	9	9 Another Day Of Loving...............................		United Art. 50854
6/24/72	54	6	10 Crying In The Rain		United Art. 50829
			DEL REEVES & PENNY DeHAVEN		
7/14/73	96	2	11 The Lovin' Of Your Life..............................		Mercury 73384
12/01/73+	67	8	12 I'll Be Doggone		Mercury 73434
			#8 pop hit for Marvin Gaye in 1965		
5/04/74	93	5	13 Play With Me		Mercury 73468
8/07/76	83	4	14 (The Great American) Classic Cowboy		Starcrest 066
7/10/82	77	5	15 We Made Memories....................................		Main St. 952
			BOXCAR WILLIE & PENNY DeHAVEN		

DEBUT DATE	PEAK POS	WKS CHR	ARTIST — Record Title	POP POS	Label & Number
			PENNY DeHAVEN — Continued		
11/05/83	74	5	16 Only The Names Have Been Changed		Main St. 93015
4/14/84	78	4	17 Friendly Game Of Hearts		Main St. 93019
			MIKE DEKLE		
			Insurance agent from Athens, Georgia. Singing since 1963. Staff writer for Kenny Rogers; wrote "Scarlet Fever" hit for Kenny.		
6/30/84	93	2	1 Hanky Panky		NSD 188
11/03/84	79	4	2 The Minstrel.....................................		NSD 195
			PAUL DELICATO		
9/13/75	91	5	1 Lean On Me......................................		Art. Of Am. 101
			#1 pop hit for Bill Withers in 1972		
			DELMORE BROTHERS		
			Duo from Elkmont, Alabama, formed in the 20s. Consisted of brothers Alton (b: 12/25/08; d: 6/8/64, Huntsville, AL) and Rabon (b: 12/3/16; d: 12/4/52, Athens, AL). Both played guitars and fiddles. On the Grand Ole Opry from 1932-38. Moved to Houston in the late 40s. After Rabon's death, Alton moved to Huntsville, Alabama and taught music. Duo elected to the Songwriter's Hall Of Fame in 1971.		
12/14/46	2¹	4	1 **Freight Train Boogie**		King 570
9/17/49+	1¹	23	2 **Blues Stay Away From Me**		King 803
			Juke Box #1 / Best Seller #2 / Jockey #3		
2/18/50	7	1	3 **Pan American Boogie**		King 826
			Juke Box #7		
			JOHN DENVER ★★153★★		
			Born John Henry Deutschendorf on 12/31/43 in Roswell, New Mexico. To Los Angeles in 1964. With the Chad Mitchell Trio from 1965-68. Wrote "Leaving On A Jet Plane". Starred in the film "Oh, God" in 1978. CMA award: Entertainer of the Year - 1975.		
6/26/71	50	12	1●Take Me Home, Country Roads	2	RCA 0445
			backing vocals by Fat City (Bill Danoff & Taffy Nivert)		
12/15/73+	69	7	2 Please, Daddy...............................	69	RCA 0182
2/16/74	42	12	3●Sunshine On My Shoulders	1	RCA 0213
6/08/74	9	14	4● **Annie's Song**	1	RCA 0295
			written by Denver for his wife Ann Martell (married 1967-83)		
9/28/74	1¹	14	5● **Back Home Again**	5	RCA 10065
1/04/75	7	12	6 **Sweet Surrender**	13	RCA 10148
3/29/75	1¹	14	7● **Thank God I'm A Country Boy**	1	RCA 10239
			above 2: recorded live at Universal City Amphitheater, California		
8/16/75	1¹	18	8● **I'm Sorry**	1	RCA 10353
12/13/75+	12	11	9 Fly Away	13	RCA 10517
			backing vocal: Olivia Newton-John		
3/13/76	30	10	10 Looking For Space	29	RCA 10586
5/29/76	70	5	11 It Makes Me Giggle	60	RCA 10687
9/18/76	34	9	12 Like A Sad Song	36	RCA 10774
12/18/76+	22	11	13 Baby, You Look Good To Me Tonight	65	RCA 10854
3/12/77	62	7	14 My Sweet Lady	32	RCA 10911
			also the flip side of "Thank God I'm A Country Boy"		
11/26/77+	22	13	15 How Can I Leave You Again	44	RCA 11036
2/25/78	72	6	16 It Amazes Me	59	RCA 11214
2/17/79	64	5	17 Downhill Stuff	106	RCA 11479
4/07/79	47	7	18 What's On Your Mind/	107	
		7	19 Sweet Melinda		RCA 11535
3/01/80	84	5	20 Autograph	52	RCA 11915
6/13/81	10	18	21 **Some Days Are Diamonds (Some Days Are Stone)**	36	RCA 12246
11/14/81	50	9	22 The Cowboy And The Lady	66	RCA 12345
7/09/83	14	19	23 Wild Montana Skies		RCA 13562
			JOHN DENVER & EMMYLOU HARRIS		
12/14/85+	9	21	24 **Dreamland Express**.........................		RCA 14227
8/30/86	57	9	25 Along For The Ride ('56 T-Bird)		RCA 14406
10/29/88	96	2	26 Country Girl In Paris		Windstar 75720
			THE DESERT ROSE BAND		
			Features Chris Hillman, John Jorgenson and Herb Pedersen. Hillman was a founding member of The Byrds and the Flying Burrito Brothers.		
3/21/87	26	18	1 Ashes Of Love		MCA/Curb 53048
7/11/87	6	21	2 **Love Reunited**		MCA/Curb 53142

DEBUT DATE	PEAK POS	WKS CHR	ARTIST — Record Title	POP POS	Label & Number
			THE DESERT ROSE BAND — Continued		
10/31/87+	**2** ¹	25	3 One Step Forward.................................		MCA/Curb 53201
3/26/88	**1** ¹	19	4 He's Back And I'm Blue...........................		MCA/Curb 53274
7/30/88	**2** ¹	20	5 Summer Wind......................................		MCA/Curb 53354
11/26/88+	**1** ¹	20	6 I Still Believe In You............................		MCA/Curb 53454
			THE DESERT WIND BAND - see RON SHAW		
			BUDDY DeVAL - see MYRNA LORRIE		
			LEW DeWITT		
			Born Lewis Calvin DeWitt on 3/12/38 in Roanoke, Virginia. Founding member of the Statler Brothers; with that group from 1955. Wrote "Flowers On The Wall". Semi-retired from music, 1981-83, then resumed career as a soloist.		
11/30/85	**77**	7	1 You'll Never Know................... #1 pop hit for Dick Haymes in 1943		Compleat 147
			AL DEXTER ★★136★★		
			Born Clarence Albert Poindexter on 5/4/02 in Troup, Texas. Died on 1/28/84. Vocalist/guitarist/violinist/composer.		
1/08/44	**1** ³	10	1 Pistol Packin' Mama/	*1*	
1/08/44	**1** ¹	25	2 Rosalita...	*29*	Okeh 6708
3/11/44	**1** ¹³	30	3 So Long, Pal/		
3/11/44	**1** ²	30	4 Too Late To Worry, Too Blue To Cry............	*23*	Okeh 6718
1/20/45	**1** ⁷	21	5 I'm Losing My Mind Over You/		
1/27/45	**2** ¹	10	6 I'll Wait For You, Dear............................		Okeh 6727
7/07/45	**2** ⁵	11	7 Triflin' Gal/		
8/25/45	**5**	3	8 I'm Lost Without You..............................		Okeh 6740
2/02/46	**1** ¹⁶	29	9 Guitar Polka/	[I] *16*	
2/09/46	**2** ¹	8	10 Honey Do You Think It's Wrong..................		Columbia 36898
8/31/46	**1** ⁵	13	11 Wine, Women And Song/		
9/14/46	**3**	5	12 It's Up To You..................................		Columbia 37062
1/25/47	**4**	1	13 Kokomo Island		Columbia 37200
5/10/47	**4**	7	14 Down At The Roadside Inn		Columbia 37303
7/03/48	**14**	1	15 Rock And Rye Rag .... Juke Box #14		Columbia 20422
9/18/48	**11**	2	16 Calico Rag .... Juke Box #11		Columbia 20438
			NEIL DIAMOND		
			Born on 1/24/41 in Brooklyn. Pop vocalist/guitarist/prolific composer.		
11/25/78	**70**	8	1 ●You Don't Bring Me Flowers........................... **BARBRA STREISAND & NEIL DIAMOND**	*1*	Columbia 10840
2/17/79	**73**	7	2 Forever In Blue Jeans.................................	*20*	Columbia 10897
			THE DIAMONDS		
			Re-formed pop group from Canada that had a long string of hits from 1956-61.		
2/14/87	**63**	8	1 Just A Little Bit.................................		Churchill 94101
7/11/87	**83**	3	2 Two Kinds Of Women..............................		Churchill 94102
			DIANA		
			Born Diana Murrell on 5/26/55 in Cincinnati. Sister of Jimmy Murrell, leader of Tom T. Hall's band.		
6/23/79	**40**	8	1 Just When I Needed You Most .... #4 pop hit for Randy Vanwarmer in 1979		Elektra 46061
10/06/79	**41**	9	2 Lonely Together		Elektra 46539
8/01/81	**29**	12	3 He's The Fire....................................		Sunbird 7564
12/18/82	**88**	3	4 Who's Been Sleeping In My Bed		Adamas 103
			"LITTLE" JIMMY DICKENS ★★190★★		
			Born James Cecil Dickens on 12/19/20 in Bolt, West Virginia. First worked as "Jimmy The Kid" with Johnny Bailes & His Happy Valley Boys in 1942. Worked radio stations in Indianapolis, Cincinnati and Saginaw. With the Grand Ole Opry since 1948. Nicknamed "Tater". Elected to the Country Music Hall Of Fame in 1982.		
4/16/49	**7**	7	1 Take An Old Cold 'Tater (And Wait)/ [N] Best Seller #7 / Juke Box #11		
9/03/49	**12**	1	2 Pennies For Papa .... Best Seller #12		Columbia 20548
6/25/49	**7**	10	3 Country Boy.................................... Best Seller #7 / Juke Box #8		Columbia 20585

DEBUT DATE	PEAK POS	WKS CHR	ARTIST — Record Title	POP POS	Label & Number
			"LITTLE" JIMMY DICKENS — Continued		
9/24/49	**10**	1	4 **My Heart's Bouquet** .... Juke Box #10		Columbia 20598
1/14/50	**6**	3	5 **A-Sleeping At The Foot Of The Bed** .... Best Seller #6 / Jockey #7		Columbia 20644
4/22/50	**3**	10	6 **Hillbilly Fever** .... Jockey #3 / Best Seller #5 / Juke Box #9		Columbia 20677
8/07/54	**9**	7	7 **Out Behind The Barn** .... Jockey #9		Columbia 21247
11/03/62	**10**	8	8 **The Violet And A Rose**		Columbia 42485
12/14/63	**28**	2	9 Another Bridge To Burn		Columbia 42845
4/10/65	**21**	18	10 He Stands Real Tall		Columbia 43243
10/09/65	**1**²	19	11 **May The Bird Of Paradise Fly Up Your Nose** .... [N]	15	Columbia 43388
2/26/66	**27**	8	12 When The Ship Hit The Sand..................... [N]	103	Columbia 43514
7/09/66	**41**	5	13 Who Licked The Red Off Your Candy .... [N]		Columbia 43701
3/11/67	**23**	14	14 Country Music Lover .... [N]		Columbia 44025
			JIMMY DICKENS:		
7/06/68	**69**	5	15 How To Catch An African Skeeter Alive .... [N]		Decca 32326
1/25/69	**55**	8	16 When You're Seventeen.............................		Decca 32426
5/09/70	**75**	2	17 Raggedy Ann		Decca 32644
2/13/71	**70**	3	18 Everyday Family Man		United Art. 50730
4/15/72	**61**	6	19 Try It, You'll Like It................................		United Art. 50889
			DAN DICKEY Born on 6/22/49 in Houston. Worked in local clubs from 1977.		
6/09/79	**96**	2	1 Hot Mama		Chartwheel 123
10/06/79	**96**	2	2 Bye, Bye, Baby		Chartwheel 126
			HAL DICKINSON		
10/29/66	**73**	2	1 You're Cheatin' On Me Again.........................		Grass 3301
			CRAIG DILLINGHAM Born in Brownwood, Texas. Sang in a group with his sisters from age 8. Worked with Ray Price. Appeared on the Louisiana Hayride from 1976.		
12/03/83+	**32**	14	1 Have You Loved Your Woman Today		MCA/Curb 52301
3/31/84	**47**	9	2 Honky Tonk Women Make Honky Tonk Men		MCA/Curb 52352
7/21/84	**58**	6	3 1984		MCA/Curb 52406
8/31/85	**78**	5	4 Next To You		MCA/Curb 52647
6/14/86	**80**	3	5 I'll Pull You Through .... **TISH HINOJOSA/CRAIG DILLINGHAM**		MCA/Curb 52823
			DEAN DILLON Born on 3/26/55 in Lake City, Tennessee. Wrote "Lying In Love With You" hit for Jim Ed Brown and Helen Cornelius. Also wrote many hits for George Strait.		
12/15/79+	**30**	12	1 I'm Into The Bottle (To Get You Out of My Mind).		RCA 11881
5/31/80	**28**	12	2 What Good Is A Heart		RCA 12003
11/01/80+	**25**	15	3 Nobody In His Right Mind (Would've Left Her)		RCA 12109
5/30/81	**57**	6	4 They'll Never Take Me Alive.........................		RCA 12234
10/17/81	**77**	5	5 Jesus Let Me Slide		RCA 12319
6/19/82	**74**	4	6 Play This Old Working Day Away....................		RCA 13208
9/18/82	**65**	6	7 You To Come Home To..............................		RCA 13295
11/12/83	**67**	6	8 Famous Last Words Of A Fool		RCA 13628
7/02/88	**51**	9	9 The New Never Wore Off My Sweet Baby		Capitol 44179
9/17/88	**39**	12	10 I Go To Pieces .... #9 pop hit for Peter & Gordon in 1965		Capitol 44239
12/24/88+	**58**	9	11 Hey Heart .... **GARY STEWART & DEAN DILLON:**		Capitol 44294
4/10/82	**41**	11	12 Brotherly Love		RCA 13049
1/08/83	**47**	12	13 Those Were The Days		RCA 13401
4/16/83	**71**	4	14 Smokin' In The Rockies..............................		RCA 13472
			LOLA JEAN DILLON - see L.E. WHITE		

DEBUT DATE	PEAK POS	WKS CHR	ARTIST — Record Title	POP POS	Label & Number
			SENATOR EVERETT McKINLEY DIRKSEN		
			U.S. senator from Illinois, 1950-69. Born in Pekin, Illinois in 1896; died on 9/7/69 (73).		
1/07/67	58	7	1 Gallant Men .... [S]	29	Capitol 5805
			DR. HOOK		
			Group formed in New Jersey in 1968. Fronted by Ray Sawyer (Dr. Hook - because of eye patch) and Dennis Locorriere.		
3/06/76	55	8	1● Only Sixteen	6	Capitol 4171
6/19/76	51	12	2 A Couple More Years		Capitol 4280
			flip side "A Little Bit More" made the pop charts (POS 11)		
12/04/76+	26	13	3 If Not You..	55	Capitol 4364
6/25/77	92	3	4 Walk Right In	46	Capitol 4423
10/07/78	50	11	5● Sharing The Night Together	6	Capitol 4621
2/10/79	82	4	6 All The Time In The World...........................	54	Capitol 4677
5/19/79	68	9	7● When You're In Love With A Beautiful Woman...	6	Capitol 4705
11/03/79	91	4	8 Better Love Next Time	12	Capitol 4785
			DARRELL DODSON		
4/16/77	99	2	1 Love Song Sing Along		SCR 139
			JIMMIE DOLAN		
			Born in Missouri in 1924. First worked on KWK-St. Louis. In the US Navy from 1941-45. Formed own band in 1946. Known as "America's Country Troubador".		
2/03/51	7	4	1 **Hot Rod Race**		Capitol 1322
			Best Seller #7		
			MADONNA DOLAN		
			Singer/multi-instrumentalist born in McLeansboro, Illinois.		
9/24/88	82	3	1 The Home Team.......................................		True 92
			JOHNNY DOLLAR		
			Born John Washington Dollar, Jr. on 3/8/33 in Kilgore, Texas; died on 4/13/86. Leader of the Texas Sons, worked on radio in Dallas and Shreveport from 1953-54.		
2/12/66	49	2	1 Tear-Talk		Columbia 43343
3/19/66	15	15	2 Stop The Start (Of Tears In My Heart)		Columbia 43537
2/25/67	65	5	3 Your Hands		Dot 16990
9/16/67	47	12	4 The Wheels Fell Off The Wagon Again..............		Date 1566
1/13/68	42	12	5 Everbody's Got To Be Somewhere		Date 1585
11/16/68	48	7	6 Big Rig Rollin' Man..................................		Chart 1057
3/15/69	65	4	7 Big Wheels Sing For Me		Chart 1070
			above 3 shown as: **JOHNNY $ DOLLAR**		
2/14/70	71	3	8 Truck Driver's Lament		Chart 5049
			FATS DOMINO		
			Born Antoine Domino on 2/26/28 in New Orleans. One of the most influential and popular R&B stars.		
12/20/80+	51	9	1 Whiskey Heaven		Warner 49610
			from the film "Any Which Way You Can"		
			DON JUAN		
			Trio of Stu Stuart (lead vocals), Ed Allen and Toby Strause, formed in Rock Island, Illinois. Hosted own cable TV show "Music Seen" in Iowa for 18 months.		
3/12/88	75	4	1 We're Gonna Love Tonight............................		Maxx 821
8/20/88	78	2	2 Let It Go..		Maxx 827
			CRAIG DONALDSON		
9/25/76	99	2	1 I Believe He's Gonna Drive That Rig To Glory.....		Great Amer. 281
			THE DOOLITTLE BAND - see DANDY		
			DOTTSY		
			Born Dottsy Brodt on 4/6/54 in Seguin, Texas. Won talent contest on KBER-San Antonio in 1966. Own TV show, "San Antonio", in 1968.		
5/31/75	17	17	1 Storms Never Last...................................		RCA 10280
11/22/75+	12	14	2 I'll Be Your San Antone Rose		RCA 10423
5/29/76	86	4	3 The Sweetest Thing (I've Ever Known)..............		RCA 10666
			#7 pop hit for Juice Newton in 1982		
9/25/76	68	6	4 Love Is A Two-Way Street............................		RCA 10766
6/04/77	10	16	5 (After Sweet Memories) Play Born To Lose Again..		RCA 10982

DEBUT DATE	PEAK POS	WKS CHR	ARTIST — Record Title	POP POS	Label & Number
			DOTTSY — Continued		
10/29/77	**22**	13	6 It Should Have Been Easy		RCA 11138
2/11/78	**20**	12	7 Here In Love		RCA 11203
7/08/78	**21**	11	8 I Just Had You On My Mind............................		RCA 11293
1/20/79	**12**	14	9 Tryin' To Satisfy You....................................		RCA 11448
			written by Waylon Jennings (also on backing vocals)		
6/16/79	**22**	10	10 Slip Away		RCA 11610
11/10/79	**34**	10	11 When I'm Gone		RCA 11743
6/27/81	**32**	12	12 Somebody's Darling, Somebody's Wife		Tanglewood 1908
9/19/81	**58**	8	13 Let The Little Bird Fly		Tanglewood 1910
			DOUGLAS		
			Douglas Block from New York. Reportedly deceased.		
1/31/81	**82**	3	1 Have Another Drink		Door Knob 80143
			JOE DOUGLAS		
1/20/79	**84**	5	1 You're Still On My Mind		D 1315
1/26/80	**88**	2	2 Back Street Affair		Foxy Cajun 1001
6/20/81	**75**	4	3 Leavin You Is Easier (Than Wishing You Were Gone)/		
		4	4 Louisiana Joe		Foxy Cajun 1005
			STEVE DOUGLAS		
			Born on 2/17/51 in Greenville, Mississippi. Moved to Silsbee, Texas in 1964.		
6/07/80	**67**	7	1 This Is True		Demon 1954
			TONY DOUGLAS		
			Born in Martins Mill, Texas on 4/12/29. Member of Louisiana Hayride for 3 years.		
3/30/63	**23**	1	1 His And Hers..		Vee Jay 481
12/30/72+	**35**	15	2 Thank You For Touching My Life		Dot 17443
6/30/73	**37**	9	3 My Last Day...		Dot 17464
12/13/75+	**72**	7	4 If I Can Make It (Through The Mornin')..............		20th Century 2257
2/20/82	**87**	3	5 His 'N Hers .... [R]		Cochise 118
			new version of Tony's first hit		
			RONNIE DOVE		
			Born on 9/7/40 in Herndon, Virginia; raised in Baltimore. Sang in rock vocal group while in high school. Served in US Coast Guard. Worked clubs in Baltimore.		
1/29/72	**61**	8	1 Kiss The Hurt Away		Decca 32919
2/03/73	**69**	5	2 Lilacs In Winter		Decca 33038
4/12/75	**75**	7	3 Please Come To Nashville		Melodyland 6004
6/14/75	**25**	12	4 Things		Melodyland 6011
			#3 pop hit for Bobby Darin in 1962		
4/25/87	**77**	4	5 Heart		Diamond 378
11/07/87	**73**	7	6 Rise And Shine		Diamond 379
			SEAN MORTON DOWNEY		
			TV talk show host, Morton Downey, Jr.		
3/14/81	**95**	2	1 Green Eyed Girl		ESO 932
			AL DOWNING		
			Black country singer/songwriter/pianist, born on 1/9/40 in Lenapah, Oklahoma. Session work with Wanda Jackson. First recorded for White Rock in 1958.		
12/02/78+	**20**	13	1 Mr. Jones		Warner 8716
4/21/79	**18**	13	2 Touch Me (I'll Be Your Fool Once More).............		Warner 8787
9/08/79	**59**	5	3 Midnight Lace...		Warner 49034
11/17/79	**73**	4	4 I Ain't No Fool		Warner 49141
2/09/80	**33**	8	5 The Story Behind The Story		Warner 49161
7/12/80	**20**	11	6 Bring It On Home		Warner 49270
7/03/82	**48**	9	7 I'll Be Loving You		Team 1001
10/23/82	**67**	7	8 Darlene		Team 1002
2/12/83	**38**	11	9 It Takes Love		Team 1004
10/01/83	**64**	5	10 Let's Sing About Love.................................		Team 1003
1/07/84	**45**	11	11 The Best Of Families..................................		Team 1007
4/28/84	**76**	4	12 There'll Never Be A Better Night For Bein' Wrong..		Team 1008
1/17/87	**69**	5	13 How Beautiful You Are (To Me)		Vine St. 103

DEBUT DATE	PEAK POS	WKS CHR	ARTIST — Record Title	POP POS	Label & Number
			AL DOWNING — Continued		
9/12/87	**67**	5	14 Just One Night Won't Do		Vine St. 105
			LAVERNE DOWNS		
7/04/60	**16**	7	1 But You Use To		Peach 735
			GUY DRAKE		
			Humorist from Weir, Kentucky. Worked as a high school band director in Central City, Kentucky in 1947. Own western swing band in the late 40s.		
1/10/70	**6**	14	1 **Welfare Cadilac** .... [N]	63	Royal Amer. 1
			RUSTY DRAPER		
			Born Farrell Draper in Kirksville, Missouri. In show business from age 12; worked radio stations in Tulsa, Des Moines, and Quincy, Illinois. Singing emcee at the Mel Hertz Club in San Francisco for 7 years.		
8/29/53	**6**	5	1 **Gambler's Guitar**....................................	6	Mercury 70167
			Best Seller #6 / Juke Box #6		
7/08/67	**70**	3	2 My Elusive Dreams		Monument 1019
3/02/68	**70**	4	3 California Sunshine		Monument 1044
8/03/68	**58**	3	4 Buffalo Nickel..		Monument 1074
4/25/70	**73**	2	5 Two Little Boys		Monument 1188
1/19/80	**87**	3	6 Harbor Lights		KL 001
			there's been 10 pop charted versions from 1937-60		
			LEE DRESSER		
			Born on 5/22/41 in Washington, DC; raised in Moberly, Missouri. Own band, The Krazy Kats, from 1957-65. Moved to Los Angeles in 1968 and worked clubs and TV shows. On the soundtrack of film "The Wilderness Family" in 1975.		
2/11/78	**78**	5	1 You're All The Woman I'll Ever Need		Capitol 4535
12/02/78	**86**	5	2 A Beautiful Song (For A Beautiful Lady)...........		Capitol 4613
4/02/83	**77**	4	3 The Hero		Air Int'l. 10021
9/03/83	**96**	1	4 Feeling's Feelin' Right..............................		Air Int'l. 10022
			THE DRIFTING COWBOYS		
			Backing band for Hank Williams. Originally consisted of Jerry Rivers (b: 8/25/28; fiddle), Bob McNett (b: 10/16/25; guitar), Don Helms (b: 2/28/27; steel guitar) and Hillous B. Butrum (b: 4/21/28; bass).		
1/28/78	**97**	2	1 Lovesick Blues		Epic 50498
			featuring Jim Owen, lead singer		
5/06/78	**90**	4	2 Rag Mop		Epic 50543
			there were 7 pop charted versions in 1950		
			JIMMY DRIFTWOOD		
			Born James Corbett Morris on 6/20/18 in Mountain View, Arkansas. Added his own lyrics to dance tune "The Eighth Of January" to create song "The Battle Of New Orleans", a giant #1 hit for Johnny Horton in 1959.		
6/01/59	**24**	3	1 The Battle Of New Orleans		RCA 7534
			DON DRUMM		
			Pianist/guitarist/singer from Springfield, Massachusetts.		
11/30/74+	**86**	7	1 In At Eight And Out At Ten		Chart 5223
1/07/78	**18**	14	2 Bedroom Eyes		Churchill 7704
5/27/78	**35**	8	3 Just Another Rhinestone.........................		Churchill 7710
10/07/78	**81**	3	4 Something To Believe In		Churchill 7717
			ROY DRUSKY ★★**73**★★		
			Born on 6/22/30 in Atlanta. Learned to play guitar while in the US Navy in the late 40s. Attended Emory College School of Veterinary Medicine in 1950, and formed band, The Southern Ranch Boys, to earn money for his education. Worked as a disc jockey on WEAS-Decatur, Georgia. First recorded for Starday in 1953. Moved to Minneapolis and worked as a disc jockey while singing in local clubs. With the Grand Ole Opry since 1958. Wrote "Alone With You" hit for Faron Young. In films "The Golden Guitar" and "Forty-Acre Feud".		
1/18/60	**2**³	24	1 **Another**......................................		Decca 31024
7/11/60	**3**	20	2 **Anymore**		Decca 31109
12/19/60	**26**	3	3 I Can't Tell My Heart That		Decca 31164
			KITTY WELLS & ROY DRUSKY		
2/20/61	**10**	12	4 I'd Rather Loan You Out/		
3/13/61	**2**⁴	27	5 **Three Hearts In A Tangle**........................	35	Decca 31193
9/11/61	**9**	20	6 I Went Out Of My Way (To Make You Happy)...		Decca 31297
4/21/62	**17**	2	7 There's Always One (Who Loves A Lot)		Decca 31366
12/22/62+	**3**	21	8 **Second Hand Rose**		Decca 31443

DEBUT DATE	PEAK POS	WKS CHR		ARTIST — Record Title	POP POS	Label & Number
				ROY DRUSKY — Continued		
12/07/63+	8	19	9	Peel Me A Nanner		Mercury 72204
5/09/64	13	16	10	Pick Of The Week................................		Mercury 72265
12/26/64+	41	3	11	Summer, Winter, Spring And Fall..............		Decca 31717
1/16/65	6	21	12	(From Now On All My Friends Are Gonna Be) Strangers		Mercury 72376
10/23/65	21	15	13	White Lightnin' Express		Mercury 72471
2/26/66	20	14	14	Rainbows And Roses		Mercury 72532
6/25/66	10	16	15	The World Is Round		Mercury 72586
11/19/66+	12	14	16	If The Whole World Stopped Lovin'..............		Mercury 72627
6/24/67	25	11	17	New Lips		Mercury 72689
11/11/67+	18	16	18	Weakness In A Man		Mercury 72742
3/30/68	28	10	19	You Better Sit Down Kids		Mercury 72784
				#9 pop hit for Cher in 1967		
7/20/68	24	11	20	Jody And The Kid		Mercury 72823
1/25/69	10	15	21	Where The Blue And Lonely Go		Mercury 72886
6/07/69	14	11	22	My Grass Is Green		Mercury 72928
10/04/69	7	11	23	Such A Fool		Mercury 72964
1/17/70	11	11	24	I'll Make Amends		Mercury 73007
5/09/70	5	16	25	Long Long Texas Road		Mercury 73056
9/19/70	9	12	26	All My Hard Times		Mercury 73111
3/06/71	15	12	27	I Love The Way That You've Been Lovin' Me......		Mercury 73178
7/03/71	37	10	28	I Can't Go On Loving You		Mercury 73212
12/11/71+	17	13	29	Red Red Wine......................................		Mercury 73252
				written and popularized by Neil Diamond (& UB40)		
5/20/72	58	9	30	Sunshine And Rainbows/		
		2	31	The Night's Not Over Yet		Mercury 73293
8/12/72	25	12	32	The Last Time I Called Somebody Darlin'		Mercury 73314
1/13/73	32	10	33	I Must Be Doin' Something Right.................		Mercury 73356
5/12/73	50	7	34	That Rain Makin' Baby Of Mine		Mercury 73376
8/04/73	25	11	35	Satisfied Mind		Mercury 73405
4/20/74	81	6	36	Close To Home		Capitol 3859
9/21/74	45	11	37	Dixie Lily..		Capitol 3942
				written by Elton John		
1/15/77	81	5	38	Night Flying		Scorpion 0521
8/13/77	91	4	39	Betty's Song......................................		Scorpion 0540
				ROY DRUSKY & PRISCILLA MITCHELL:		
5/29/65	1²	23	40	Yes, Mr. Peters...................................		Mercury 72416
12/04/65	45	2	41	Slippin' Around		Mercury 72497
3/25/67	61	5	42	I'll Never Tell On You............................		Mercury 72650
				DAVE DUDLEY ★★72★★		
				Born David Pedruska on 5/3/28 in Spencer, Wisconsin. Played baseball for semi-pro team in Wausau, Wisconsin and with the Gainesville Texas Owls. After injury to his arm, he worked as a disc jockey and singer at WTWT-Wausau in 1950. Formed his own trio and worked throughout the Midwest. He has a gold card from the Nashville truck driver's union in recognition of his trucking songs.		
10/16/61	28	2	1	Maybe I Do.......................................		Vee 7003
9/15/62	18	9	2	Under Cover Of The Night		Jubilee 5436
6/01/63	2²	21	3	Six Days On The Road...........................	32	Golden Wing 3020
10/05/63	3	20	4	Cowboy Boots	95	Golden Ring 3030
12/14/63+	7	16	5	Last Day In The Mines	125	Mercury 72212
10/10/64	6	17	6	Mad..		Mercury 72308
3/13/65	15	17	7	Two Six Packs Away		Mercury 72384
7/10/65	3	21	8	Truck Drivin' Son-Of-A-Gun	125	Mercury 72442
11/20/65+	4	16	9	What We're Fighting For		Mercury 72500
3/12/66	12	12	10	Viet Nam Blues..................................	127	Mercury 72550
7/02/66	13	14	11	Lonelyville......................................		Mercury 72585
10/08/66	15	12	12	Long Time Gone.................................		Mercury 72618
2/25/67	12	15	13	My Kind Of Love		Mercury 72655
7/15/67	23	14	14	Trucker's Prayer		Mercury 72697
11/04/67+	12	16	15	Anything Leaving Town Today		Mercury 72741
3/02/68	10	13	16	There Ain't No Easy Run		Mercury 72779

DEBUT DATE	PEAK POS	WKS CHR		ARTIST — Record Title	POP POS	Label & Number
				DAVE DUDLEY — Continued		
7/13/68	**14**	11	17	I Keep Coming Back For More		Mercury 72818
11/16/68+	**10**	16	18	**Please Let Me Prove (My Love For You)**		Mercury 72856
3/29/69	**12**	15	19	One More Mile		Mercury 72902
8/30/69	**10**	13	20	**George (And The North Woods)**		Mercury 72952
3/14/70	**1**[1]	16	21	**The Pool Shark**		Mercury 73029
8/01/70	**20**	12	22	This Night (Ain't Fit For Nothing But Drinking)...		Mercury 73089
11/14/70	**23**	13	23	Day Drinkin'		Mercury 73139
				DAVE DUDLEY & TOM T. HALL		
12/26/70+	**15**	13	24	Listen Betty (I'm Singing Your Song)..............		Mercury 73138
4/17/71	**8**	14	25	**Comin' Down**		Mercury 73193
8/21/71	**8**	15	26	**Fly Away Again**		Mercury 73225
3/18/72	**14**	14	27	If It Feels Good Do It...............................		Mercury 73274
7/22/72	**12**	16	28	You've Gotta Cry Girl...............................		Mercury 73309
12/09/72+	**40**	10	29	We Know It's Over...................................		Mercury 73345
				DAVE DUDLEY & KAREN O'DONNAL		
3/03/73	**19**	12	30	Keep On Truckin'...................................		Mercury 73367
8/04/73	**37**	9	31	It Takes Time		Mercury 73404
11/03/73	**47**	12	32	Rollin' Rig		Rice 5064
4/06/74	**67**	7	33	Have It Your Way....................................		Rice 5067
8/31/74	**61**	9	34	Counterfeit Cowboy		Rice 5069
2/08/75	**74**	10	35	How Come It Took So Long (To Say Goodbye).....		United Art. 585
5/03/75	**21**	12	36	Fireball Rolled A Seven.............................		United Art. 630
10/25/75+	**12**	15	37	Me And Ole C.B......................................		United Art. 722
2/28/76	**47**	8	38	Sentimental Journey		United Art. 766
				#1 pop hit for Doris Day (Les Brown Orch.) in 1945		
8/21/76	**83**	5	39	38 And Lonely.......................................		United Art. 836
3/04/78	**95**	3	40	One A.M. Alone......................................		Rice 5077
9/06/80	**77**	5	41	Rolaids, Doan's Pills And Preparation H...........		Sun 1154
				ARLIE DUFF		
				Born Arleigh Elton Duff on 3/28/24 in Jack's Branch, near Warren, Texas. Longtime disc jockey in Colorado and Texas.		
12/05/53+	**7**	10	1	**You All Come**		Starday 104
				Best Seller #7 / Jockey #7 / Juke Box #8		
				JEFF DUGAN		
8/15/87	**68**	12	1	Once A Fool, Always A Fool..........................		Warner 28376
5/28/88	**52**	8	2	I Wish It Was That Easy Going Home................		Warner 27995
				JOHNNY DUNCAN ★★87★★		
				Born on 10/5/38 in Dublin, Texas. Attended Texas Christian University and lived in Clovis, New Mexico from 1959-64. Moved to Nashville in 1964 and worked as a disc jockey on WAGG-Franklin, Tennessee. Appeared on WSM-TV shows with Ralph Emery. Cousin of Jimmy Seals and England Dan Seals.		
8/12/67	**54**	7	1	Hard Luck Joe.......................................		Columbia 44196
1/13/68	**67**	3	2	Baby Me Baby		Columbia 44383
8/17/68	**47**	9	3	To My Sorrow		Columbia 44580
10/19/68	**21**	8	4	Jackson Ain't A Very Big Town		Columbia 44656
				JOHNNY DUNCAN & JUNE STEARNS		
2/08/69	**70**	4	5	I Live To Love You		Columbia 44693
3/15/69	**74**	3	6	Back To Back (We're Strangers)....................		Columbia 44752
				JOHNNY DUNCAN & JUNE STEARNS		
6/21/69	**30**	12	7	When She Touches Me		Columbia 44864
12/13/69+	**65**	6	8	Window Number Five		Columbia 45006
5/09/70	**39**	10	9	You're Gonna Need A Man		Columbia 45124
9/19/70	**68**	3	10	My Woman's Love		Columbia 45201
10/31/70	**27**	13	11	Let Me Go (Set Me Free)............................		Columbia 45227
3/13/71	**19**	13	12	There's Something About A Lady....................		Columbia 45319
7/24/71	**39**	9	13	One Night Of Love		Columbia 45418
11/27/71+	**12**	13	14	Baby's Smile, Woman's Kiss.........................		Columbia 45479
3/18/72	**19**	12	15	Fools		Columbia 45556
9/30/72	**66**	5	16	Here We Go Again		Columbia 45674
3/31/73	**6**	16	17	**Sweet Country Woman**		Columbia 45818
9/08/73	**18**	14	18	Talkin' With My Lady		Columbia 45917

DEBUT DATE	PEAK POS	WKS CHR	ARTIST — Record Title	POP POS	Label & Number
			JOHNNY DUNCAN — Continued		
4/06/74	**47**	9	19 The Pillow		Columbia 46018
9/21/74	**66**	9	20 Scarlet Water		Columbia 10007
3/08/75	**57**	8	21 Charley Is My Name..................................		Columbia 10085
8/23/75	**26**	14	22 Jo And The Cowboy		Columbia 10182
			the part of Jo is sung by Janie Fricke		
12/20/75+	**86**	7	23 Gentle Fire..		Columbia 10262
3/27/76	**4**	20	24 **Stranger**..		Columbia 10302
10/02/76	**1²**	17	25 **Thinkin' Of A Rendezvous**		Columbia 10417
2/05/77	**1¹**	15	26 **It Couldn't Have Been Any Better**		Columbia 10474
			above 3 feature harmony vocals by Janie Fricke		
6/04/77	**5**	16	27 **A Song In The Night**		Columbia 10554
10/29/77+	**4**	16	28 **Come A Little Bit Closer**..........................		Columbia 10634
			JOHNNY DUNCAN with JANIE FRICKE		
			#3 pop hit for Jay & The Americans in 1964		
3/11/78	**1¹**	17	29 **She Can Put Her Shoes Under My Bed (Anytime)**...		Columbia 10694
7/15/78	**4**	14	30 **Hello Mexico (And Adios Baby To You)**		Columbia 10783
2/24/79	**6**	14	31 **Slow Dancing**		Columbia 10915
			#10 pop hit for Johnny Rivers in 1977		
9/29/79	**9**	12	32 **The Lady In The Blue Mercedes**		Columbia 11097
1/05/80	**17**	14	33 Play Another Slow Song		Columbia 11185
6/07/80	**17**	14	34 I'm Gonna Love You Tonight (In My Dreams)......		Columbia 11280
7/12/80	**17**	14	35 He's Out Of My Life		Columbia 11312
			JOHNNY DUNCAN & JANIE FRICKE		
			#10 pop hit for Michael Jackson ("She's Out...") in 1980		
11/08/80+	**16**	14	36 Acapulco		Columbia 11385
11/07/81	**40**	10	37 All Night Long		Columbia 02570
4/12/86	**69**	6	38 The Look Of A Lady In Love		Pharoah 2502
8/16/86	**81**	2	39 Texas Moon...		Pharoah 2503
			TOMMY DUNCAN		
			Born on 1/11/11 in Hillsboro, Texas. Died of a heart attack on 7/24/67 (56). Sang with Bob Wills in the Light Crust Doughboys from 1932-33. With Bob Wills' Texas Playboys from 1933-48. Own band, the Western All-Stars, from 1948-49.		
8/13/49	**8**	3	1 **Gamblin' Polka Dot Blues**...........................		Capitol 40178
			Best Seller #8 / Juke Box #8		
			HOLLY DUNN		
			Born on 8/22/57 in San Antonio, Texas. Sister of composer Chris Waters. Guitarist/ drummer; lead vocalist with the Freedom Folk Singers from 1975-76. Formed songwriting team with brother Chris. Former staff writer at CBS and MTM Records.		
6/08/85	**62**	6	1 Playing For Keeps		MTM 72052
10/05/85	**64**	8	2 My Heart Holds On		MTM 72057
5/17/86	**39**	12	3 Two Too Many		MTM 72064
8/23/86	**7**	25	4 **Daddy's Hands**		MTM 72075
2/07/87	**4**	21	5 **A Face In The Crowd**.............................		Warner 28471
			MICHAEL MARTIN MURPHEY & HOLLY DUNN		
5/02/87	**2²**	25	6 **Love Someone Like Me**		MTM 72082
8/29/87	**4**	25	7 **Only When I Love**.................................		MTM 72091
1/16/88	**7**	24	8 **Strangers Again**		MTM 72093
6/25/88	**5**	20	9 **That's What Your Love Does To Me**		MTM 72108
11/05/88+	**11**	19	10 (It's Always Gonna Be) Someday		MTM 72116
			RONNIE DUNN		
			Born in Texas; attended Abilene Christian College. Moved to Tulsa, formed the house band at Duke's Nightclub.		
3/05/83	**59**	7	1 It's Written All Over Your Face....................		Churchill 94018
6/23/84	**59**	8	2 She Put The Sad In All His Songs....................		Churchill 52383
			BOBBY DURHAM		
			Singer from Bakersfield, California.		
5/21/88	**92**	2	1 Let's Start A Rumor Today		Hightone 502
			SAM DURRENCE		
9/15/73	**98**	3	1 Last Days Of Childhood..............................		River 3875

DEBUT DATE	PEAK POS	WKS CHR	ARTIST — Record Title	POP POS	Label & Number
			JERRY DYCKE		
			Born in Topeka, Kansas. Two-time winner of the Kansas State Fair talent contest while a teenager. Settled in Coral Gables, Florida, in 1975.		
5/03/80	93	3	1 Daddy Played Harmonica.............................		Churchill 7757
2/28/81	94	2	2 Beethoven Was Before My Time......................		Churchill 7766

E

			EAGLES		
			Formed in Los Angeles in 1971. Consisted of Glenn Frey (vocals, guitar), Bernie Leadon (guitar), Randy Meisner (bass) and Don Henley (drums). Meisner had founded Poco; Leadon had been in the Flying Burrito Brothers; and Frey and Henley were with Linda Ronstadt. Debut album recorded in England in 1972. Don Felder (guitar) added in 1975. Leadon replaced by Joe Walsh in 1975; and Meisner replaced by Timothy B. Schmit in 1977. Disbanded in 1982.		
10/11/75	8	13	1 **Lyin' Eyes**..	2	Asylum 45279
1/08/77	43	12	2●New Kid In Town.................................	1	Asylum 45373
1/24/81	55	7	3 Seven Bridges Road	21	Asylum 47100
			KENNY EARLE		
			Also see The Wolfpack.		
5/09/81	84	3	1 We Have To Start Meeting Like This................		Kik 904
9/19/81	73	4	2 Wasn't It Supposed To Be Me		Kari 124
			STEVE EARLE		
			Born in San Antonio. Moved to Nashville in 1974. Had bit part in the film "Nashville". Worked local clubs. Lived in Mexico from 1980-81. Worked as the manager of a music publishing company in Nashville, sang on demos.		
10/01/83	70	4	1 Nothin' But You.......................................		Epic 04070
12/08/84	76	6	2 What'll You Do About Me?...........................		Epic 04666
3/22/86	37	13	3 Hillbilly Highway....................................		MCA 52785
6/21/86	7	22	4 **Guitar Town**		MCA 52856
10/25/86	28	15	5 Someday		MCA 52920
2/14/87	8	19	6 **Goodbyes All We've Got Left**		MCA 53011
6/13/87	20	16	7 Nowhere Road		MCA 53103
			STEVE EARLE & THE DUKES:		
10/17/87	37	13	8 Sweet Little '66		MCA 53182
1/09/88	29	13	9 Six Days On The Road.................................		Hughes 53249
			from the film "Planes, Trains & Automobiles"		
			MUNDO EARWOOD		
			Born Raymond Earwood on 10/13/52 in Del Rio, Texas. Mundo is pronounced "moon-doe". Own band, Tumbling Tumbleweeds, in 9th grade. Attended San Jacinto College; majored in business administration.		
10/21/72	57	10	1 Behind Blue Eyes..		Royal Amer. 65
6/29/74	59	10	2 Let's Hear It For Loneliness		GRT 003
10/25/75	91	4	3 She Brings Her Lovin' Home To Me..................		Epic 50141
			MUNDO RAY		
2/07/76	86	7	4 I Can't Quit Cheatin' On You		Epic 50185
6/26/76	70	7	5 Lonesome Is A Cowboy		Epic 50232
3/19/77	86	4	6 I Can Give You Love		True 101
7/09/77	32	11	7 Behind Blue Eyes................................. [R]		True 104
12/17/77+	69	8	8 Angelene		True 111
5/20/78	36	11	9 When I Get You Alone...............................		GMC 102
9/02/78	18	13	10 Things I'd Do For You		GMC 104
12/02/78+	25	13	11 Fooled Around And Fell In Love		GMC 105
4/28/79	38	10	12 My Heart Is Not My Own		GMC 106
8/04/79	34	9	13 We Got Love		GMC 107
10/13/79	73	3	14 Philodendron/		
11/24/79	67	6	15 Sometimes Love		GMC 108
4/05/80	27	13	16 You're In Love With The Wrong Man		GMC 109
			harmony vocal: Mel Tillis		
9/27/80	26	12	17 Can't Keep My Mind Off Of Her		GMC 111
2/14/81	40	9	18 Blue Collar Blues		Excelsior 1005
5/16/81	32	12	19 Angela		Excelsior 1010

DEBUT DATE	PEAK POS	WKS CHR	ARTIST — Record Title	POP POS	Label & Number
			MUNDO EARWOOD — Continued		
10/17/81	**45**	8	20 I'll Still Be Loving You		Excelsior 1019
4/17/82	**58**	8	21 All My Lovin		Primero 1002
			#45 pop hit for The Beatles in 1964		
9/04/82	**68**	5	22 Pyramid Of Cans		Primero 1009
			LYNDEL EAST		
			Singer from Oklahoma City.		
7/29/78	**97**	2	1 Why Do You Come Around...........................		NSD 2
			SHEENA EASTON		
			Born on 4/27/59 in Glasgow, Scotland. Vocalist/actress. Portrayed singer in the 1980 BBC-TV documentary "The Big Time". Sang the opening credits for the James Bond film "For Your Eyes Only". Won the 1981 Best New Artist Grammy Award. Appeared Born on 4/27/59 in Glasgow, Scotland. Pop vocalist/actress.		
1/29/83	**1**¹	17	1 **We've Got Tonight**	6	Liberty 1492
			KENNY ROGERS & SHEENA EASTON		
3/24/84	**86**	7	2 Almost Over You..	25	EMI America 8186
			CLINT EASTWOOD - see RAY CHARLES and MERLE HAGGARD		
			CONNIE EATON		
			Born on 3/1/50 in Nashville. Performing since age 14. Appeared on "Arthur Godfrey", "Lawrence Welk" and "Hee-Haw" TV shows in the late 60s.		
2/07/70	**34**	7	1 Angel Of The Morning		Chart 5048
			Merrilee Rush and Juice Newton had top 10 pop versions		
5/23/70	**44**	9	2 Hit The Road Jack		Chart 5066
			CONNIE EATON & DAVE PEEL		
			#1 pop hit for Ray Charles in 1961		
11/07/70	**56**	7	3 It Takes Two		Chart 5099
			CONNIE EATON & DAVE PEEL		
			#14 pop hit for Marvin Gaye & Kim Weston in 1967		
2/06/71	**74**	2	4 Sing A Happy Song		Chart 5110
9/11/71	**56**	10	5 Don't Hang No Halos On Me		Chart 5138
1/25/75	**23**	13	6 Lonely Men, Lonely Women		Dunhill 15022
6/14/75	**93**	4	7 If I Knew Enough To Come Out Of The Rain		ABC 12098
			SKIP EATON - see SKIP & LINDA		
			BOB EBERLY & THE SUNSHINE SERENADERS		
			Born Robert Eberle on 7/24/16 in Mechanicsville, New York; died on 12/17/81. Vocalist with Jimmy Dorsey from 1935-43. Made popular duets with Helen O'Connell.		
1/01/49	**8**	1	1 **One Has My Name (The Other Has My Heart)** ..		Decca 24492
			Juke Box #8 / Best Seller #15		
			DUANE EDDY		
			Born on 4/26/38 in Corning, New York. Duane originated the "twangy" guitar sound and is the all-time #1 rock and roll instrumentalist.		
8/04/58	**17**	5	1 Rebel-'Rouser .... [I]	6	Jamie 1104
			Best Seller #17		
5/07/77	**69**	6	2 You Are My Sunshine		Elektra 45359
			vocals: Waylon Jennings, Willie Nelson, Deed (Duane's wife, 1979-present) and Kin Vassy (First Edition)		
			KATHY EDGE		
			Singer born in Huntsville, Alabama and raised in Memphis.		
3/21/87	**89**	5	1 I Take The Chance		NSD 228
			DAVE EDMUNDS - see CARLENE CARTER		
			BOBBY EDWARDS		
			Born Robert Moncrief in Anniston, Alabama. Own band, the Four Young Men.		
9/04/61	**4**	24	1 You're The Reason.....................................	11	Crest 1075
9/14/63	**23**	2	2 Don't Pretend		Capitol 5006
			JIMMY EDWARDS		
			Born in Cardwell, Missouri.		
11/11/57+	**12**	6	1 Love Bug Crawl	78	Mercury 71209
			Jockey #12		
			JONATHAN EDWARDS		
			Born on 7/28/46 in Minnesota. Formed bluegrass band, Sugar Creek, in 1965.		
9/17/88	**64**	6	1 We Need To Be Locked Away		MCA/Curb 53390

DEBUT DATE	PEAK POS	WKS CHR	ARTIST — Record Title	POP POS	Label & Number
			JONATHAN EDWARDS — Continued		
12/10/88+	56	14	2 Look What We Made (When We Made Love).......		MCA/Curb 53467
			STONEY EDWARDS		
			Born Frenchy Edwards on 12/24/29 in Seminole, Oklahoma. Played guitar from age 15. Moved to California in 1950, worked outside of music. First recorded for Capitol in 1970. Moved to San Antonio in the late 70s. One of the few successful black Country singers.		
1/23/71	68	3	1 A Two Dollar Toy....................		Capitol 3005
4/03/71	61	7	2 Poor Folks Stick Together		Capitol 3061
8/28/71	73	2	3 The Cute Little Waitress...................		Capitol 3131
11/11/72+	20	14	4 She's My Rock...............		Capitol 3462
3/17/73	54	6	5 You're A Believer...................		Capitol 3550
8/11/73	39	10	6 Hank And Lefty Raised My Country Soul..........		Capitol 3671
12/22/73+	85	7	7 Daddy Bluegrass....................		Capitol 3766
2/08/75	77	8	8 Clean Your Own Tables....................		Capitol 4015
4/19/75	20	12	9 Mississippi You're On My Mind		Capitol 4051
11/29/75+	41	11	10 Blackbird (Hold Your Head High)...................		Capitol 4188
4/10/76	51	8	11 Love Still Makes The World Go 'Round		Capitol 4246
10/23/76	90	4	12 Don't Give Up On Me....................		Capitol 4337
11/04/78	60	7	13 If I Had It To Do All Over Again		JMI 47
5/24/80	53	10	14 No Way To Drown A Memory......................		Music Amer. 107
9/20/80	85	3	15 One Bar At A Time....................		Music Amer. 109
			JIMMY ELLEDGE		
			Born on 1/8/43 in Nashville. Discovered by Chet Atkins.		
5/17/75	95	4	1 One By One....................		4 Star 1003
			MIKE ELLIS		
7/29/78	89	3	1 I Never Meant To Harm You		Cin Kay 130
			ELMO 'N PATSY		
			Husband and wife team of Elmo and Patsy Shropshire, originally known as The Homestead Act. First performed "Grandma Got Run Over By A Reindeer" in 1979, recorded in San Francisco. In film "The Right Stuff".		
1/07/84	92	2	1 Grandma Got Run Over By A Reindeer....... [N-X]		Soundwaves 4658
			JOE ELY		
			Born on 2/9/47 in Amarillo, Texas; raised in Lubbock. Moved to Fort Worth in the early 60s. Worked with the Flatlanders in the mid-70s; own band since 1977.		
2/12/77	89	3	1 All My Love		MCA 40666
			EME		
2/21/81	86	2	1 Every Breath I Take		EPI 1541
			RALPH EMERY		
			Born on 3/10/33 in McEwen, Tennessee. Popular host of Nashville Network's TV show "Nashville Now". Married to Skeeter Davis from 1960-64.		
8/28/61	4	15	1 Hello Fool .... [S]		Liberty 55352
			answer song to Faron Young's "Hello Walls"		
			ESMERELDY		
			Married to opera singer Harry Boersma. Daughter is pop singer Amy Holland.		
3/20/48	10	1	1 Slap 'Er Down Again, Paw....................... [N]		Musicraft 524
			THE ETC BAND - see EARL THOMAS CONLEY		
			ETHEL & THE SHAMELESS HUSSIES		
			Female trio formed in 1986 in Huntsville, Alabama. "Ethel" (Gayle Zeiler), "Blanche" (Valerie Hunt), and "Bunny" (Beki Fogle). Band name taken from a line in Ray Stevens' song "The Streak".		
5/21/88	71	5	1 One Nite Stan... [N]		MCA 53323
			PAUL EVANS		
			Born on 3/5/38 in New York City. Singer/songwriter. Wrote "When" (Kalin Twins) and "Roses Are Red" (Bobby Vinton). Currently a pop jingle singer in New York.		
5/20/78	57	10	1 Hello, This Is Joannie (The Telephone Answering Machine Song)........................		Spring 183
5/05/79	81	4	2 Disneyland Daddy		Spring 193
8/16/80	80	4	3 One Night Led To Two....................		Cinnamon 604

DEBUT DATE	PEAK POS	WKS CHR	ARTIST — Record Title	POP POS	Label & Number
			PAULA KAY EVANS		
4/23/77	100	2	1 Runnin' Out Again		Autumn 368
			LEON EVERETTE ★★150★★		
			Born Leon Everette Baughman on 6/21/48 in Aiken, South Carolina; raised in New York City. First recorded for Doral Records.		
12/03/77	84	5	1 I Love That Woman (Like The Devil Loves Sin) ...		True 110
1/20/79	89	3	2 We Let Love Fade Away		Orlando 100
4/07/79	81	4	3 Giving Up Easy		Orlando 102
6/09/79	33	10	4 Don't Feel Like The Lone Ranger		Orlando 103
9/15/79	42	7	5 The Sun Went Down In My World Tonight		Orlando 104
12/08/79+	28	12	6 I Love That Woman (Like The Devil Loves Sin) ... . [R] new version of Leon's first hit		Orlando 105
3/01/80	30	12	7 I Don't Want To Lose		Orlando 106
5/31/80	10	17	8 **Over**		Orlando 107
10/25/80+	5	18	9 **Giving Up Easy** .... [R] reissue (same version) of Leon's 3rd hit		RCA 12111
3/07/81	11	13	10 If I Keep On Going Crazy		RCA 12177
7/18/81	4	16	11 **Hurricane**		RCA 12270
11/14/81+	9	17	12 **Midnight Rodeo**		RCA 12355
3/27/82	7	18	13 **Just Give Me What You Think Is Fair**		RCA 13079
8/07/82	10	17	14 **Soul Searchin'**		RCA 13282
11/27/82+	15	18	15 Shadows Of My Mind		RCA 13391
3/19/83	9	18	16 **My Lady Loves Me (Just As I Am)**		RCA 13466
8/13/83	31	13	17 The Lady, She's Right .... harmony vocal by Rex Gosdin		RCA 13584
2/04/84	6	20	18 **I Could'a Had You**		RCA 13717
7/07/84	30	14	19 Shot In The Dark		RCA 13834
3/30/85	47	10	20 Too Good To Say No To..............................		Mercury 880611
6/15/85	53	9	21 A Good Love Died Tonight		Mercury 880829
10/05/85	44	9	22 'Til A Tear Becomes A Rose.........................		Mercury 884040
5/24/86	46	9	23 Danger List (Give Me Someone I Can Love)		Orlando 112
8/02/86	59	5	24 Sad State Of Affairs.................................		Orlando 114
11/15/86	56	6	25 Still In The Picture		Orlando 115
			THE EVERLY BROTHERS ★★181★★		
			Donald (real name: Isaac Donald) was born on 2/1/37 in Brownie, Kentucky; Philip on 1/19/39 in Chicago. Vocal duo/guitarists/songwriters. Parents were Folk and Country singers. Don (beginning at age 8) and Phil (age 6) sang with parents through high school. Invited to Nashville by Chet Atkins and first recorded there for Columbia in 1955. Signed to Archie Bleyer's Cadence Records in 1957. Phil married for a time to the daughter of Archie and Janet (Chordettes) Bleyer. Duo split up in July of 1973 and reunited in September of 1983. Inducted into the Rock And Roll Hall Of Fame in 1986.		
5/13/57	1⁷	26	1 **Bye Bye Love**.. Best Seller #1(7) / Jockey #1(7)	2	Cadence 1315
9/30/57	1⁸	22	2 **Wake Up Little Susie** .... Jockey #1(8) / Best Seller #1(7)	1	Cadence 1337
2/10/58	4	13	3 **This Little Girl Of Mine/** Best Seller #4 / Jockey #5	26	
3/24/58	10	1	4 **Should We Tell Him** .... Jockey #10		Cadence 1342
4/28/58	1³	20	5 **All I Have To Do Is Dream/** Best Seller #1(3) / Jockey #1(1)	1	
6/16/58	15	1	6 Claudette .... Jockey #15; written by Roy Orbison	30	Cadence 1348
8/18/58	1⁶	13	7 **Bird Dog/** Best Seller #1 / Jockey #3	1	
9/01/58	7	5	8 **Devoted To You** .... Jockey #7	10	Cadence 1350
12/01/58+	17	7	9 Problems	2	Cadence 1355
8/31/59	8	12	10 **('Til) I Kissed You**	4	Cadence 1369
3/06/61	25	3	11 Ebony Eyes	8	Warner 5199
9/29/84	49	12	12 On The Wings Of A Nightingale..................... written by Paul McCartney; produced by Dave Edmunds	50	Mercury 880213
1/05/85	44	11	13 The First In Line		Mercury 880423
3/01/86	17	18	14 Born Yesterday..		Mercury 884428

DEBUT DATE	PEAK POS	WKS CHR	ARTIST — Record Title	POP POS	Label & Number
			THE EVERLY BROTHERS — Continued		
7/05/86	56	6	15 I Know Love/		
9/13/86	57	8	16 These Shoes..		Mercury 884694
			DON EVERLY		
			Eldest of The Everly Brothers duo.		
4/10/76	50	8	1 Yesterday Just Passed My Way Again..............		Hickory 368
2/05/77	84	4	2 Since You Broke My Heart		ABC/Hick. 54005
5/07/77	96	4	3 Brother Juke-Box..		ABC/Hick. 54012
			PHIL EVERLY		
			Youngest of The Everly Brothers duo.		
12/27/80+	63	7	1 Dare To Dream Again		Curb 5401
6/13/81	52	8	2 Sweet Southern Love		Curb 02116
2/19/83	37	12	3 Who's Gonna Keep Me Warm........................		Capitol 5197
			E.W.B.		
			Jerrel Elliott, Richard Wesley, Gerald Bennett.		
9/12/81	96	2	1 We Could Go On Forever		Paid 142
			SKIP EWING		
			Singer/songwriter born in Redlands, California. To Nashville in 1984, at age 19.		
3/05/88	17	18	1 Your Memory Wins Again		MCA 53271
6/25/88	8	24	2 **I Don't Have Far To Fall**		MCA 53353
10/29/88+	3	22	3 **Burnin' A Hole In My Heart**		MCA 53435
			EXILE ★★**144**★★		
			Band formed in Lexington, Kentucky in 1963 as The Exiles. Toured with Dick Clark in 1965. Changed name to Exile in 1973. Had several pop hits in the late 70s. In 1983, the group consisted of J.P. Pennington (lead guitar), Les Taylor (rhythm guitar), Marlon Hargis (keyboards), Sonny Lemaire (bass) and Steve Goetzman (drums). Hargis was replaced by Lee Carroll in 1985. Carroll was in the Hatfield Clan and worked as music director for the Judds. Pennington wrote "Take Me Down" and "The Closer You Get" for Alabama; left band in early 1989.		
8/20/83	27	16	1 High Cost Of Leaving		Epic 04041
12/03/83+	1¹	22	2 Woke Up In Love..		Epic 04247
4/07/84	1¹	24	3 I Don't Want To Be A Memory......................		Epic 04421
8/11/84	1¹	26	4 Give Me One More Chance............................		Epic 04567
12/08/84+	1¹	23	5 Crazy For Your Love		Epic 04722
3/30/85	86	4	6 Stay With Me.. [R]		MCA/Curb 52551
			reissue of a recording from 1978		
4/06/85	1¹	22	7 **She's A Miracle**		Epic 04864
8/17/85	1¹	24	8 **Hang On To Your Heart**............................		Epic 05580
12/07/85+	1¹	22	9 **I Could Get Used To You**............................		Epic 05723
4/05/86	14	16	10 Super Love		Epic 05860
7/26/86	1¹	22	11 **It'll Be Me**		Epic 06229
6/06/87	1¹	23	12 **She's Too Good To Be True**		Epic 07135
10/10/87+	1¹	22	13 **I Can't Get Close Enough**		Epic 07597
2/20/88	60	4	14 Feel Like Foolin' Around		Epic 07710
4/23/88	9	18	15 **Just One Kiss**...		Epic 07775
9/03/88	21	18	16 It's You Again		Epic 08020

F

DEBUT DATE	PEAK POS	WKS CHR	ARTIST — Record Title	POP POS	Label & Number
			BARBARA FAIRCHILD ★★**162**★★		
			Born on 11/12/50 in Knobel, Arkansas. Moved to St. Louis in 1963, worked on TV from 1965. First recorded for Norman Records in 1965. Moved to Nashville in 1968 and worked as a songwriter. Lived in Texas from 1980-85, then returned to Nashville and made appearances on Ralph Emery's TV show and the Grand Ole Opry.		
5/31/69	69	5	1 Love Is A Gentle Thing.................................		Columbia 44797
8/09/69	66	6	2 A Woman's Hand		Columbia 44925
2/14/70	26	11	3 A Girl Who'll Satisfy Her Man.......................		Columbia 45063
8/01/70	52	6	4 Find Out What's Happenin'		Columbia 45173
1/02/71	33	10	5 (Loving You Is) Sunshine		Columbia 45272
4/10/71	62	8	6 What Do You Do		Columbia 45344
8/07/71	28	11	7 Love's Old Song		Columbia 45422

DEBUT DATE	PEAK POS	WKS CHR	ARTIST — Record Title	POP POS	Label & Number
			BARBARA FAIRCHILD — Continued		
1/15/72	**38**	8	8 Color My World		Columbia 45522
			#16 pop hit for Petula Clark in 1967		
5/27/72	**29**	10	9 Thanks For The Mem'ries		Columbia 45589
10/14/72	**53**	9	10 A Sweeter Love (I'll Never Know)		Columbia 45690
12/30/72+	**1²**	19	11 **Teddy Bear Song**	32	Columbia 45743
7/28/73	**2²**	16	12 **Kid Stuff**	95	Columbia 45903
1/26/74	**6**	14	13 **Baby Doll**		Columbia 45988
6/29/74	**17**	13	14 Standing In Your Line		Columbia 46053
11/02/74	**31**	10	15 Little Girl Feeling		Columbia 10047
5/10/75	**52**	10	16 Let's Love While We Can		Columbia 10128
9/06/75	**41**	11	17 You've Lost That Lovin' Feelin'		Columbia 10195
			#1 pop hit for The Righteous Brothers in 1965		
12/20/75+	**63**	8	18 I Just Love Being A Woman		Columbia 10261
4/10/76	**65**	7	19 Under Your Spell Again................................		Columbia 10314
			top 10 versions for Ray Price and Buck Owens in 1959		
7/24/76	**31**	11	20 Mississippi		Columbia 10378
10/30/76	**15**	13	21 Cheatin' Is		Columbia 10423
3/12/77	**22**	14	22 Let Me Love You Once Before You Go		Columbia 10485
10/01/77	**49**	8	23 For All The Right Reasons		Columbia 10607
3/04/78	**96**	3	24 She Can't Give It Away		Columbia 10686
5/27/78	**72**	6	25 The Other Side Of The Morning......................		Columbia 10607
10/14/78	**91**	5	26 It's Sad To Go To The Funeral (Of A Good Love That Has Died)		Columbia 10825
5/17/86	**84**	4	27 Just Out Riding Around ....:...		Capitol 5582
			BILLY WALKER & BARBARA FAIRCHILD:		
7/12/80	**74**	5	28 Let Me Be The One		Paid 102
10/11/80	**79**	3	29 Love's Slipping Through Our Fingers (Leaving Time On Our Hands)/		
12/20/80+	**70**	7	30 Bye Bye Love		Paid 107
			#2 pop hit for The Everly Brothers in 1957		
			RUBY FALLS		
			Born in Jackson, Tennessee. Moved to Milwaukee, sang with local country bands. Appeared on many TV music programs. One of the very few black female country singers. Died on 6/15/86.		
3/15/75	**86**	7	1 Sweet Country Music		50 States 31
7/12/75	**77**	8	2 He Loves Me All To Pieces		50 States 33
2/07/76	**81**	9	3 Show Me Where		50 States 39
7/17/76	**81**	7	4 Beware Of The Woman (Before She Gets To Your Man)......................		50 States 43
3/12/77	**88**	4	5 Do The Buck Dance		50 States 50
9/24/77	**40**	8	6 You've Got To Mend This Heartache		50 States 56
4/15/78	**81**	5	7 Three Nights A Week		50 States 60
			#15 pop hit for Fats Domino in 1960		
9/30/78	**86**	3	8 If That's Not Loving You (You Can't Say I Didn't Try)		50 States 63
6/09/79	**56**	7	9 I'm Gettin' Into Your Love		50 States 70
			FAMILY BROWN		
			Canadian group featuring Tracey and Barry Brown.		
7/18/81	**57**	8	1 It's Really Love This Time		Ovation 1174
1/23/82	**30**	11	2 But It's Cheating		RCA 13015
8/21/82	**61**	7	3 Some Never Stand A Chance		RCA 13285
10/22/83	**67**	5	4 We Really Got A Hold On Love		RCA 13565
3/03/84	**56**	10	5 Repeat After Me		RCA 13734
11/30/85	**66**	7	6 Feel The Fire		RCA 50837
4/05/86	**80**	3	7 What If It's Right		RCA 50851
			DONNA FARGO ★★80★★		
			Born Yvonne Vaughan on 11/10/49 in Mount Airy, North Carolina. Taught high school in Covina, California while working local clubs as Donna Fargo. Recorded for Ramco in 1969. Quit teaching in June of 1972. Stricken with multiple sclerosis in 1978. Has own music publishing company.		
3/25/72	**1³**	23	1●**The Happiest Girl In The Whole U.S.A.**	11	Dot 17409
9/02/72	**1³**	16	2●**Funny Face**...	5	Dot 17429

DEBUT DATE	PEAK POS	WKS CHR	ARTIST — Record Title	POP POS	Label & Number
			DONNA FARGO — Continued		
2/17/73	**1**¹	14	3 Superman	*41*	Dot 17444
5/26/73	**1**¹	14	4 You Were Always There	*93*	Dot 17460
9/29/73	**2**¹	14	5 Little Girl Gone	*57*	Dot 17476
2/23/74	**6**	12	6 I'll Try A Little Bit Harder		Dot 17491
6/08/74	**1**¹	15	7 You Can't Be A Beacon (If Your Light Don't Shine)	*57*	Dot 17506
10/12/74+	**9**	15	8 U.S. of A	*86*	ABC/Dot 17523
2/15/75	**7**	11	9 It Do Feel Good	*98*	ABC/Dot 17541
6/07/75	**14**	14	10 Hello Little Bluebird		ABC/Dot 17557
10/04/75	**38**	11	11 Whatever I Say		ABC/Dot 17579
12/20/75+	**58**	7	12 What Will The New Year Bring?		ABC/Dot 17586
2/28/76	**60**	6	13 You're Not Charlie Brown (And I'm Not Raggedy Ann)		ABC/Dot 17609
4/03/76	**20**	10	14 Mr. Doodles		Warner 8186
7/17/76	**15**	13	15 I've Loved You All The Way		Warner 8227
10/23/76+	**3**	19	16 **Don't Be Angry**		ABC/Dot 17660
2/12/77	**9**	13	17 **Mockingbird Hill**		Warner 8305
			Patti Page and Les Paul & Mary Ford had hit versions in 1951		
4/30/77	**1**¹	14	18 **That Was Yesterday**		Warner 8375
9/10/77	**8**	15	19 **Shame On Me**		Warner 8431
			#23 pop hit for Bobby Bare in 1962		
1/07/78	**2**²	15	20 **Do I Love You (Yes In Every Way)**		Warner 8509
5/27/78	**19**	11	21 Ragamuffin Man		Warner 8578
8/26/78	**10**	13	22 **Another Goodbye**		Warner 8643
1/13/79	**6**	15	23 **Somebody Special**		Warner 8722
7/21/79	**14**	13	24 Daddy		Warner 8867
11/17/79	**45**	7	25 Preacher Berry		Warner 49093
3/08/80	**43**	7	26 Walk On By		Warner 49183
			#5 pop hit for Leroy Van Dyke in 1961		
8/09/80	**63**	7	27 Land Of Cotton		Warner 49514
11/01/80	**55**	6	28 Seeing Is Believing		Warner 49575
8/01/81	**73**	6	29 Lonestar Cowboy		Warner 49757
11/21/81	**72**	4	30 Jacamo		Warner 49852
7/10/82	**40**	9	31 It's Hard To Be The Dreamer (When I Used to be the Dream)		RCA 13264
10/09/82	**80**	3	32 Did We Have To Go This Far (To Say Goodbye)		RCA 13329
10/01/83	**72**	4	33 The Sign Of The Times		Columbia 04097
7/07/84	**80**	4	34 My Heart Will Always Belong To You		Clev. Int. 1
7/19/86	**58**	8	35 Woman Of The 80's		Mercury 884712
11/08/86+	**29**	17	36 Me And You		Mercury 888093
6/27/87	**23**	15	37 Members Only		Mercury 888680
			DONNA FARGO & BILLY JOE ROYAL		

JIMMY LEE FAUTHEREE - see JIMMY & JOHNNY

JOSE FELICIANO
Born on 9/8/45 in Puerto Rico; raised in New York City. Blind since birth. Virtuoso acoustic guitarist. Won the 1968 Best New Artist Grammy Award.

9/03/83	**64**	7	1 Let's Find Each Other Tonight		Motown 1674

TERRY FELL
Wrote the pop/country hit "You're The Reason" for Bobby Edwards.

8/07/54	**4**	11	1 **Don't Drop It**		"X" 0010
			Juke Box #4 / Best Seller #11 / Jockey #12		

DICK FELLER
Born on 1/2/43 in Bronaugh, Missouri. Moved to Nashville in 1966, worked sessions with Mel Tillis, Warner Mack, Skeeter Davis and Stu Phillips. Staff writer for Johnny Cash in the early 70s. Staff writer for Jerry Reed in 1974.

11/17/73+	**22**	11	1 Biff, The Friendly Purple Bear [S]	*101*	United Art. 316
6/08/74	**11**	14	2 Makin' The Best Of A Bad Situation [N]	*85*	Asylum 11037
9/21/74	**10**	15	3 **The Credit Card Song** [N]	*105*	United Art. 535
12/06/75+	**49**	9	4 Uncle Hiram And The Homemade Beer [N]		Asylum 45290

DEBUT DATE	PEAK POS	WKS CHR		ARTIST — Record Title	POP POS	Label & Number
				NARVEL FELTS ★★107★★		
				Born on 11/1/38 near Bernie, Missouri. Rockabilly-country singer/songwriter/guitarist. Also see The Wolfpack.		
6/16/73	**8**	16	1	**Drift Away**..		Cinnamon 763
				#5 pop hit for Dobie Gray in 1973		
10/13/73	**13**	13	2	All In The Name Of Love		Cinnamon 771
1/19/74	**14**	14	3	When Your Good Love Was Mine.....................		Cinnamon 779
4/27/74	**39**	11	4	Until The End Of Time		Cinnamon 793
				NARVEL FELTS & SHARON VAUGHN		
5/11/74	**26**	13	5	I Want To Stay		Cinnamon 798
9/14/74	**33**	13	6	Raindrops...		Cinnamon 809
				#2 pop hit for Dee Clark in 1961		
4/05/75	**2**¹	21	7	**Reconsider Me**	67	ABC/Dot 17549
8/23/75	**12**	15	8	Funny How Time Slips Away		ABC/Dot 17569
				written by Willie Nelson (5 pop hit versions from 1962-83)		
12/06/75+	**10**	16	9	**Somebody Hold Me (Until She Passes By)**........		ABC/Dot 17598
4/03/76	**5**	16	10	**Lonely Teardrops**	62	ABC/Dot 17620
				#7 pop hit for Jackie Wilson in 1959		
8/07/76	**14**	11	11	My Prayer		ABC/Dot 17643
				#1 pop hit for The Platters in 1956		
11/13/76+	**20**	12	12	My Good Thing's Gone		ABC/Dot 17664
2/26/77	**19**	11	13	The Feeling's Right..		ABC/Dot 17680
5/28/77	**37**	10	14	I Don't Hurt Anymore		ABC/Dot 17700
8/20/77	**22**	11	15	To Love Somebody		ABC/Dot 17715
				#17 pop hit for The Bee Gees in 1967		
12/03/77+	**34**	11	16	Please/		
		6	17	Blue Darlin'		ABC/Dot 17731
3/18/78	**30**	10	18	Runaway		ABC 12338
				#1 pop hit for Del Shannon in 1961		
7/01/78	**31**	9	19	Just Keep It Up		ABC 12374
				#18 pop hit for Dee Clark in 1959		
10/21/78	**26**	10	20	One Run For The Roses.................................		ABC 12414
1/06/79	**14**	11	21	Everlasting Love		ABC 12441
				Robert Knight and Carl Carlton had pop hit versions		
4/21/79	**43**	8	22	Moment By Moment.......................................		MCA 41011
7/07/79	**33**	9	23	Tower Of Strength		MCA 41055
				#5 pop hit for Gene McDaniels in 1961		
10/20/79	**73**	4	24	Because Of Losing You.................................		Collage 101
8/22/81	**67**	5	25	Louisiana Lonely		GMC 114
12/12/81	**84**	4	26	Fire In The Night..		GMC 115
2/13/82	**58**	8	27	I'd Love You To Want Me...............................		Lobo III
				#2 pop hit for Lobo in 1972		
6/05/82	**84**	3	28	Sweet Southern Moonlight		Lobo VIII
7/17/82	**64**	6	29	Roll Over Beethoven		Lobo XI
				#29 pop hit for Chuck Berry in 1956		
11/13/82	**84**	3	30	Smoke Gets In Your Eyes/		
				#1 pop hit for The Platters in 1959		
12/11/82	**82**	4	31	You're The Reason		Compleat 101
4/02/83	**52**	9	32	Cry Baby		Compleat 104
9/17/83	**79**	4	33	Anytime You're Ready		Evergreen 1011
12/10/83+	**52**	10	34	Fool..		Evergreen 1014
3/10/84	**70**	6	35	You Lay So Easy On My Mind		Evergreen 1017
6/30/84	**53**	8	36	Let's Live This Dream Together		Evergreen 1022
10/06/84	**63**	5	37	I'm Glad You Couldn't Sleep Last Night............		Evergreen 1025
1/05/85	**51**	10	38	Hey Lady		Evergreen 1027
6/01/85	**68**	4	39	If It Was Any Better (I Couldn't Stand It)		Evergreen 1030
9/07/85	**71**	5	40	Out Of Sight Out Of Mind		Evergreen 1034
				#23 pop hit for The Five Keys in 1956		
6/07/86	**70**	5	41	Rockin' My Angel...		Evergreen 1041
5/16/87	**60**	7	42	When A Man Loves A Woman.........................		Evergreen 1054
				#1 pop hit for Percy Sledge in 1966		

DEBUT DATE	PEAK POS	WKS CHR	ARTIST — Record Title	POP POS	Label & Number
			FREDDY FENDER ★★**156**★★		
			Born Baldemar G. Huerta on 6/4/37 in San Benito, Texas. First recorded in Spanish under his real name for Falcon in 1956. In Angola State Prison for marijuana possession from 1960-63. Did session work in New Orleans after parole. Out of music from 1969-74. In the film "The Milagro Beanfield War".		
1/11/75	**1**²	17	1● Before The Next Teardrop Falls	1	ABC/Dot 17540
6/21/75	**1**²	16	2● Wasted Days And Wasted Nights	8	ABC/Dot 17558
			originally recorded by Fender on the Duncan label in 1959		
10/04/75	**10**	14	3 Since I Met You Baby	45	GRT 031
			#12 pop hit for Ivory Joe Hunter in 1956		
10/11/75	**1**¹	16	4 Secret Love	20	ABC/Dot 17585
			#1 pop hit for Doris Day in 1954		
1/10/76	**13**	12	5 Wild Side Of Life		GRT 039
2/07/76	**1**¹	15	6 You'll Lose A Good Thing	32	ABC/Dot 17607
			#8 pop hit for Barbara Lynn in 1962		
5/22/76	**7**	13	7 Vaya Con Dios	59	ABC/Dot 17627
			#1 pop hit for Les Paul & Mary Ford in 1953		
9/18/76	**2**²	14	8 Living It Down	72	ABC/Dot 17652
3/19/77	**4**	15	9 The Rains Came/		
			#31 pop hit for Sir Douglas Quintet in 1966		
		15	10 Sugar Coated Love		ABC/Dot 17686
7/30/77	**11**	12	11 If You Don't Love Me (Why Don't You Just Leave Me Alone)		ABC/Dot 17713
11/26/77+	**18**	11	12 Think About Me		ABC/Dot 17730
3/11/78	**34**	9	13 If You're Looking For A Fool		ABC 12339
6/17/78	**13**	12	14 Talk To Me	103	ABC 12370
			pop versions by Little Willie John and Sunny & The Sunglows		
10/14/78	**26**	9	15 I'm Leaving It All Up To You		ABC 12415
			#1 pop hit for Dale & Grace in 1963		
2/17/79	**22**	12	16 Walking Piece Of Heaven		ABC 12453
6/23/79	**22**	11	17 Yours..		Starflite 4900
10/13/79	**61**	5	18 Squeeze Box		Starflite 4904
			#16 pop hit for The Who in 1976		
1/12/80	**83**	3	19 My Special Prayer		Starflite 4906
4/05/80	**82**	3	20 Please Talk To My Heart		Starflite 4908
2/19/83	**87**	3	21 Chokin' Kind..		Warner 29794
			sung in Spanish and English; #13 pop hit for Joe Simon in 1969		
			THE FENDERMEN		
			Duo of Jim Sundquist and Phil Humphrey, both born on 11/26/37; both play guitars; Sundquist was born in Niagara, Wisconsin and Humphrey was born in Madison, Wisconsin. Teamed up in Madison in 1959. John Howard (drums), added in 1960.		
7/11/60	**16**	8	1 Mule Skinner Blues	5	Soma 1137
			originally recorded in 1959 on the Cuca label; tune written and recorded by Jimmie Rodgers in 1930 (Victor 23503)		
			ZOOT FENSTER		
			Zoot is actually Jack Barlow.		
11/08/75	**30**	10	1 The Man On Page 602 .... [N]		Antique 106
			title refers to a revealing photo in a Sear's catalog		
			C. W. FERRARI		
3/19/88	**76**	4	1 Country Highway		Southern S. 1001
			MAURY FINNEY		
			Saxophonist and popular session musician.		
1/03/76	**84**	9	1 Maiden's Prayer/	[F]	
		9	2 San Antonio Stroll .... [I]		Soundwaves 4525
4/24/76	**76**	7	3 Rollin' In My Sweet Baby's Arms/	[I]	
4/24/76	**78**	7	4 Wild Side Of Life.................................... [I]		Soundwaves 4531
9/04/76	**81**	7	5 Waltz Across Texas/	[I]	
		7	6 Off And Running...................................... [I]		Soundwaves 4536
1/29/77	**85**	6	7 Everybody's Had The Blues........................ [I]		Soundwaves 4541
6/25/77	**72**	10	8 Coconut Grove..		Soundwaves 4548
11/19/77	**85**	5	9 Poor People of Paris/	[I]	
			#1 pop hit for Les Baxter in 1956		
		5	10 Almost Persuaded................................... [I]		Soundwaves 4557
4/15/78	**88**	6	11 I Don't Wanna Cry.................................... [I]		Soundwaves 4566

DEBUT DATE	PEAK POS	WKS CHR	ARTIST — Record Title	POP POS	Label & Number
			MAURY FINNEY — Continued		
8/12/78	**84**	7	12 Whispering .... [I]		Soundwaves 4572
			#1 pop hit for Paul Whiteman in 1920		
2/03/79	**92**	2	13 Happy Sax .... [I]		Soundwaves 4578
6/16/79	**93**	2	14 Your Love Takes Me So High/	[I]	
		2	15 I Want To Play My Horn On The Grand Ole' Opry		Soundwaves 4585
9/20/80	**75**	5	16 Lonely Wine .... [I]		Soundwaves 4613
			THE FIRST EDITION - see KENNY ROGERS		
			GEORGE FISCHOFF		
			Born on 8/3/38 in South Bend, Indiana. Pianist/songwriter.		
3/31/79	**74**	7	1 The Piano Picker .... [I]		Drive 6273
			ELLA FITZGERALD		
			The most honored jazz singer of all-time. Born on 4/25/18 in Newport News, Virginia.		
3/18/44	**2**¹	1	1 **When My Sugar Walks Down The Street**	27	Decca 18587
			THE FIVE RED CAPS		
			Formed as the Toppers in Los Angeles in 1938. Consisted of Steve Gibson, Emmett Matthews, Dave Patillo, Jimmy Springs and Romaine Brown. Also known as Steve Gibson's Red Caps.		
4/29/44	**2**¹	8	1 **I Learned A Lesson I'll Never Forget**	14	Beacon 7120
			LESTER FLATT & EARL SCRUGGS ★★171★★		
			Bluegrass duo of Lester Raymond Flatt (b: 6/19/14, Overton County, TN; d: 5/11/79); guitar, mandolin; and Earl Eugene Scruggs (b: 1/6/24, Flintville, NC), banjo. Flatt had been in the Harmonizers and Charlie Monroe's Band and joined Bill Monroe in 1944. Scruggs had been in the Carolina Wildcats and the Morris Brothers, and had broadcast with Lost John Miller on WSM-Nashville in 1945. He joined Bill Monroe in 1945. The duo left Monroe in 1948 and formed their own Foggy Mountain Boys, which included Mac Wiseman. Worked on WCYB-Bristol, Tennessee until 1949. Toured with Ernest Tubb and Lefty Frizzell in the early 50s. Own radio series, "Martha White Biscuit Time" on WSM from 1953. Own TV show for a time, and joined the Grand Ole Opry in 1955. Disbanded in 1969; Flatt formed Nashville Grass and Scruggs started his Earl Scruggs Revue. Elected to the Country Music Hall Of Fame in 1985.		
2/02/52	**9**	1	1 'Tis Sweet To Be Remembered		Columbia 20886
			Jockey #9		
6/08/59	**9**	30	2 **Cabin On The Hill**		Columbia 41389
2/01/60	**21**	6	3 Crying My Heart Out Over You		Columbia 41518
12/05/60+	**12**	14	4 Polka On A Banjo		Columbia 41786
10/09/61	**10**	16	5 **Go Home**		Columbia 42141
4/07/62	**16**	8	6 Just Ain't		Columbia 42280
6/23/62	**27**	1	7 The Legend Of The Johnson Boys		Columbia 42413
12/08/62+	**1**³	20	8 **The Ballad Of Jed Clampett**	44	Columbia 42606
			theme song for the TV series "The Beverly Hillbillies"		
5/11/63	**8**	11	9 **Pearl Pearl Pearl**	113	Columbia 42755
			featured on the TV series "The Beverly Hillbillies"		
9/28/63	**26**	3	10 New York Town		Columbia 42840
2/15/64	**12**	18	11 You Are My Flower/		
2/22/64	**40**	2	12 My Saro Jane		Columbia 42954
3/14/64	**14**	11	13 Petticoat Junction		Columbia 42982
			theme from the TV series of the same title		
8/15/64	**21**	15	14 Workin' It Out		Columbia 43080
3/13/65	**43**	10	15 I Still Miss Someone		Columbia 43204
4/15/67	**54**	5	16 Nashville Cats		Columbia 44040
			#8 pop hit for The Lovin' Spoonful in 1967		
7/29/67	**20**	14	17 California Up Tight Band		Columbia 44194
1/13/68	**45**	8	18 Down In The Flood		
4/06/68	**58**	6	19 Foggy Mountain Breakdown .... [I]	55	Columbia 44380
			different version of tune recorded in 1949 and released in 1968 on Mercury 72739 as "Theme From Bonnie & Clyde"		
9/14/68	**58**	8	20 Like A Rolling Stone/	125	Columbia 44623
			#2 pop hit for Bob Dylan in 1965		
			VICKY FLETCHER		
			Long-time popular country entertainer in Las Vegas.		
7/20/74	**92**	3	1 Touching Me, Touching You		Columbia 46043
6/12/76	**97**	2	2 Ain't It Good To Be In Love Again		Music Row 213

DEBUT DATE	PEAK POS	WKS CHR	ARTIST — Record Title	POP POS	Label & Number
			ROSIE FLORES		
			Singer/songwriter born in San Antonio. Moved to San Diego at age 12.		
9/12/87	**51**	10	1 Crying Over You		Reprise 28250
12/26/87+	**67**	6	2 Somebody Loses, Somebody Wins		Reprise 28134
7/09/88	**74**	3	3 He Cares..		Reprise 27980
			FLYING BURRITO BROTHERS		
			Group formed by ex-Byrds Gram Parsons and Chris Hillman.		
3/01/80	**95**	2	1 White Line Fever		Regency 45001
			live recording; written by Merle Haggard		
			DAN FOGELBERG		
			Born on 8/13/51 in Peoria, Illinois. Vocalist/composer. Worked as a folk singer in Los Angeles. With Van Morrison in the early 70s. Session work in Nashville.		
2/16/80	**85**	8	1 Longer	*2*	Full Moon 50824
4/20/85	**56**	16	2 Go Down Easy		Full Moon 04835
8/24/85	**33**	13	3 Down The Road Mountain Pass......................		Full Moon 05446
			JOHN FOGERTY		
			Born on 5/28/45 in Berkeley, California. Leader of Creedence Clearwater Revival. Although listed as a group, John recorded entirely solo as The Blue Ridge Rangers.		
2/10/73	**66**	6	1 Jambalaya (On The Bayou)	*16*	Fantasy 689
			THE BLUE RIDGE RANGERS		
2/02/85	**38**	11	2 Big Train (From Memphis)...........................		Warner 29100
			flip side of the pop hit "The Old Man Down The Road"		
			BETTY FOLEY		
			Born on 2/3/33 in Chicago; raised in Berea, Kentucky. Daughter of Red and Pauline Foley. Worked on Renfro Valley Barn Dance from 1950-54, Midwestern Hayride, WCKY, Cincinnati, Grand Ole Opry from 1956-57, Tennessee Barn Dance, Louisiana Hayride in 1958. With her father on the TV series "Jubilee USA". Also see Red Foley.		
8/31/59	**7**	12	1 **Old Moon**		Bandera 1304
			RED FOLEY ★★27★★		
			Born Clyde Julian Foley on 6/17/10 in Blue Lick, Kentucky. Died of a heart attack on 9/19/68 in Fort Wayne, Indiana. On the WLS National Barn Dance from 1930-37 and the Renfro Valley Show from 1937-39. On Avalon Time radio shows with Red Skelton in 1939. Member of the Grand Ole Opry from 1946-54. Hosted the Ozark Jubilee Show series on ABC-TV from 1954-60. Co-starred with Fess Parker in the TV series "Mr. Smith Goes To Washington" in the early 60s. Elected to the Country Music Hall Of Fame in 1967. Signed off on radio and TV broadcasts with his famous "Goodnight mama, goodnight papa".		
8/26/44	**1**¹³	27	1 **Smoke On The Water/**	*7*	
9/30/44	**5**	1	2 **There's A Blue Star Shining Bright**............		Decca 6102
6/23/45	**4**	2	3 **Hang Your Head In Shame/**		
6/23/45	**5**	1	4 **I'll Never Let You Worry My Mind**		Decca 6108
3/15/47	**4**	1	5 **That's How Much I Love You**........................		Decca 46028
4/05/47	**1**²	16	6 **New Jole Blonde**		Decca 46034
6/21/47	**5**	1	7 **Freight Train Boogie**		Decca 46035
11/22/47	**2**¹	13	8 **Never Trust A Woman**		Decca 46074
10/02/48+	**1**¹	40	9 **Tennessee Saturday Night**........................		Decca 46136
			Juke Box #1 / Best Seller #3		
3/26/49	**4**	15	10 **Candy Kisses/**		
			Juke Box #4 / Best Seller #6		
4/02/49	**3**	21	11 **Tennessee Border**		Decca 46151
			Juke Box #3 / Best Seller #4		
5/14/49	**15**	1	12 Blues In My Heart		Decca 46136
			Best Seller #15		
6/25/49	**4**	13	13 **Tennessee Polka/**		
			Juke Box #4 / Best Seller #6		
7/23/49	**11**	2	14 I'm Throwing Rice (At The Girl I Love)		Decca 46170
			Best Seller #11 / Juke Box #14		
8/06/49	**8**	4	15 Two Cents, Three Eggs And A Postcard		Decca 46165
			Juke Box #8		
12/17/49+	**3**	6	16 **Sunday Down In Tennessee**........................		Decca 46197
			Jockey #3 / Juke Box #3 / Best Seller #10		
1/07/50	**10**	1	17 **I Gotta Have My Baby Back/**		
			Juke Box #10 / Best Seller #13		
1/14/50	**8**	1	18 **Careless Kisses**		Decca 46201
			Juke Box #8 / Best Seller #14		

DEBUT DATE	PEAK POS	WKS CHR		ARTIST — Record Title	POP POS	Label & Number
				RED FOLEY — Continued		
1/21/50	**1** 13	20	19	**Chattanoogie Shoe Shine Boy/**	*1*	
				Jockey #1(13) / Juke Box #1(13) / Best Seller #1(12)		
2/18/50	**4**	11	20	**Sugarfoot Rag**	*24*	Decca 46205
				Juke Box #4 / Jockey #8		
				guitar solo: Hank "Sugarfoot" Garland		
5/06/50	**9**	1	21	**Steal Away/**		
				Best Seller #9		
7/22/50	**9**	5	22	**Just A Closer Walk With Thee**		Decca 14505
				Best Seller #9		
5/13/50	**1** 4	15	23	**Birmingham Bounce**	*14*	Decca 46234
				Best Seller #1(4) / Juke Box #1(3) / Jockey #4		
6/03/50	**1** 1	14	24	**M-I-S-S-I-S-S-I-P-P-I**	*22*	Decca 46241
				Juke Box #1 / Best Seller #2 / Jockey #3		
6/03/50	**5**	4	25	**Choc'late Ice Cream Cone**		Decca 46234
				Jockey #5 / Juke Box #8 / Best Seller #10		
9/09/50	**2** 1	12	26	**Cincinnati Dancing Pig**	*7*	Decca 46261
				Best Seller #2 / Juke Box #3 / Jockey #6		
11/04/50	**8**	4	27	**Our Lady Of Fatima**	*16*	Decca 14526
				Best Seller #8		
				with the Anita Kerr Singers		
2/17/51	**7**	3	28	**Hot Rod Race**		Decca 46286
				Best Seller #7 / Juke Box #8 / Jockey #10		
5/12/51	**8**	3	29	**Hobo Boogie**		Decca 46304
				Juke Box #8		
7/07/51	**5**	11	30	**(There'll Be) Peace In The Valley (For Me)**.......		Decca 46319
				Jockey #5 / Juke Box #5 / Best Seller #7		
				with The Sunshine Boys Quartet; first million-selling gospel song		
11/24/51	**3**	16	31	**Alabama Jubilee**	*28*	Decca 27810
				Juke Box #3 / Best Seller #5 / Jockey #6		
				with the Nashville Dixielanders, including Francis Craig on bones		
3/08/52	**8**	3	32	**Milk Bucket Boogie/**		
				Juke Box #8		
3/29/52	**8**	2	33	**Salty Dog Rag**		Decca 27981
				Juke Box #8		
11/15/52+	**1** 1	11	34	**Midnight**..		Decca 28420
				Best Seller #1 / Juke Box #2 / Jockey #5		
				written by Chet Atkins		
1/10/53	**8**	2	35	**Don't Let The Stars Get In Your Eyes**............	*25*	Decca 28460
				Best Seller #8		
3/21/53	**6**	4	36	**Hot Toddy**..		Decca 28587
				Juke Box #6 / Best Seller #10		
5/02/53	**8**	1	37	**Slaves Of A Hopeless Love Affair**..................		Decca 28567
				Juke Box #8		
10/10/53	**6**	4	38	**Shake A Hand**		Decca 28839
				Best Seller #6 / Juke Box #7 / Jockey #10		
5/08/54	**7**	4	39	**Jilted**		Decca 29100
				Juke Box #7 / Best Seller #9		
				above 2: with the Anita Kerr Singers		
1/08/55	**4**	15	40	**Hearts Of Stone**		Decca 29375
				Jockey #4 / Juke Box #4 / Best Seller #6		
				#1 pop hit for The Fontane Sisters in 1955		
6/29/59	**29**	1	41	Travelin' Man		Decca 30882
				RED FOLEY DUOS with:		
				BETTY FOLEY:		
3/06/54	**8**	10	42	**As Far As I'm Concerned**		Decca 29000
				Juke Box #8 / Jockey #8 / Best Seller #11		
6/25/55	**3**	23	43	**Satisfied Mind**		Decca 29526
				Juke Box #3 / Best Seller #4 / Jockey #6		
				EVELYN KNIGHT:		
2/17/51	**6**	1	44	**My Heart Cries For You**.............................	*28*	Decca 27378
				Jockey #6		
				ROY ROSS & HIS RAMBLERS:		
5/04/46	**4**	1	45	**Harriet**		Decca 9003
11/30/46	**5**	1	46	**Have I Told You Lately That I Love You?**		Decca 46014
				ERNEST TUBB:		
12/31/49+	**2** 2	10	47	**Tennessee Border No. 2/**		
				Best Seller #2 / Juke Box #2		
1/21/50	**7**	2	48	**Don't Be Ashamed Of Your Age**...................		Decca 46200
				Juke Box #7 / Jockey #9		

DEBUT DATE	PEAK POS	WKS CHR	ARTIST — Record Title	POP POS	Label & Number
			RED FOLEY — Continued		
8/19/50	**1³**	15	49 **Goodnight, Irene**/ Juke Box #1(3) / Best Seller #1(2) / Jockey #2	*10*	
9/02/50	**9**	2	50 **Hillbilly Fever No. 2** .... Juke Box #9		Decca 46255
5/19/51	**9**	1	51 **Strange Little Girl**................................. Juke Box #9		Decca 46311
2/02/52	**5**	9	52 **Too Old To Cut The Mustard** .... Best Seller #5 / Juke Box #8 / Jockey #10		Decca 46387
4/18/53	**7**	2	53 **No Help Wanted #2** .... Best Seller #7 / Juke Box #9		Decca 28634
			LAWRENCE WELK & HIS ORCHESTRA:		
9/08/45	**1¹**	14	54 **Shame On You**/	*13*	
11/10/45	**3**	2	55 **At Mail Call Today**		Decca 18698
			KITTY WELLS:		
5/22/54	**1¹**	41	56 **One By One**/ Juke Box #1 / Best Seller #2 / Jockey #2		
7/10/54	**12**	1	57 **I'm A Stranger In My Home**....................... Jockey #12 / Best Seller #15		Decca 29065
2/26/55	**3**	17	58 **Make Believe ('Til We Can Make It Come True)**/ Juke Box #3 / Best Seller #7 / Jockey #14		
2/26/55	**7**	16	59 **As Long As I Live** .... Best Seller #7 / Jockey #8		Decca 29390
1/28/56	**3**	31	60 **You And Me**/ Best Seller #3 / Jockey #3 / Juke Box #6		
		6	61 **No One But You** .... Best Seller flip / Juke Box flip		Decca 29740
5/06/67	**43**	11	62 Happiness Means You/		
6/03/67	**60**	5	63 Hello Number One		Decca 32126
12/30/67+	**63**	4	64 Living As Strangers		Decca 32223
1/18/69	**74**	2	65 Have I Told You Lately That I Love You?		Decca 32427

JOY FORD
Born on 3/10/46 in Brilliant, Alabama; raised in Chicago and Poplar Bluff, Missouri. Toured with the Nashville Magic Band in 1979. Raises appaloosa horses.

DEBUT DATE	PEAK POS	WKS CHR	ARTIST — Record Title	POP POS	Label & Number
12/16/78+	**87**	4	1 Love Isn't Love (Till You Give It Away).............		Country I. 416
10/13/79	**97**	4	2 Take My Love		Country I. 142
3/26/83	**97**	1	3 You Are The Music In Time With My Heart		Country I. 190
8/10/85	**96**	2	4 Melted Down Memories		Country I. 206
8/20/88	**99**	1	5 Yesterday's Rain.................................		Country I. 216

SHELLEY FORD - see JAY CHEVALIER

TENNESSEE ERNIE FORD ★★113★★
Born Ernest Jennings Ford on 2/13/19 in Bristol, Tennessee. Worked as staff announcer on WOAI-Bristol in 1937. Worked as a disc jockey in Atlanta and Knoxville in the early 40s. Served as an Air Corps bombardier during the war. Worked as a disc jockey in San Bernadino and Pasadena, California. Sang with Cliffie Stone's quartet on Hometown Jamboree radio shows. First recorded for Capitol in 1948. Own TV series from 1955-65. Later turned to inspirational music.

DEBUT DATE	PEAK POS	WKS CHR	ARTIST — Record Title	POP POS	Label & Number
			TENNESSEE ERNIE:		
4/30/49	**8**	1	1 **Tennessee Border** .... Juke Box #8 / Best Seller #15		Capitol 15400
5/28/49	**14**	1	2 **Country Junction**................................. Juke Box #14		Capitol 15430
9/10/49	**8**	4	3 **Smokey Mountain Boogie**............................. Best Seller #8 / Juke Box #13		Capitol 40212
11/26/49	**1⁴**	10	4 **Mule Train**/ Jockey #1 / Juke Box #3 / Best Seller #4	*9*	
12/10/49	**3**	11	5 **Anticipation Blues** .... Jockey #3 / Best Seller #5 / Juke Box #8		Capitol 40258
2/11/50	**2²**	10	6 **The Cry Of The Wild Goose** .... Best Seller #2 / Jockey #3 / Juke Box #5	*15*	Capitol 40280
8/26/50	**5**	6	7 **Ain't Nobody's Business But My Own**/ *KAY STARR & TENNESSEE ERNIE* Jockey #5 / Juke Box #10	*22*	
9/16/50	**2¹**	16	8 **I'll Never Be Free** .... *KAY STARR & TENNESSEE ERNIE* Jockey #2 / Juke Box #2 / Best Seller #4	*3*	Capitol 1124

DEBUT DATE	PEAK POS	WKS CHR	ARTIST — Record Title	POP POS	Label & Number
			TENNESSEE ERNIE FORD — Continued		
12/16/50+	**1** ^{14}	25	9 **The Shot Gun Boogie** .... Juke Box #1(14) / Best Seller #1(3) / Jockey #1(1)	*14*	Capitol 1295
3/03/51	**8**	2	10 **Tailor Made Woman** .... TENNESSEE ERNIE & JOE "FINGERS" CARR Juke Box #8		Capitol 1349
6/16/51	**2** ^{1}	7	11 **Mister And Mississippi** .... Jockey #2 / Best Seller #4 / Juke Box #6	*18*	Capitol 1521
6/16/51	**9**	1	12 **The Strange Little Girl** .... Best Seller #9		Capitol 1470
9/20/52	**6**	7	13 **Blackberry Boogie** .... Juke Box #6 / Best Seller #9 / Jockey #9		Capitol 2170
6/06/53	**8**	3	14 **Hey, Mr. Cotton Picker** .... Juke Box #8		Capitol 2443
			TENNESSEE ERNIE FORD:		
8/14/54	**9**	9	15 **River Of No Return** .... Best Seller #9 from the film of the same title		Capitol 2810
3/26/55	**4**	16	16 **Ballad Of Davy Crockett** .... Best Seller #4 / Juke Box #5 / Jockey #6 from the Walt Disney film "Davy Crockett"	*5*	Capitol 3058
7/09/55	**13**	2	17 His Hands .... Best Seller #13		Capitol 3135
11/12/55	**1** ^{10}	21	18 **Sixteen Tons** .... Best Seller #1(10) / Juke Box #1(7) / Jockey #1(3)	*1*	Capitol 3262
3/17/56	**12**	5	19 That's All .... Best Seller #12	*17*	Capitol 3343
6/26/65	**9**	16	20 **Hicktown**		Capitol 5425
7/26/69	**54**	3	21 Honey-Eyed Girl (That's You That's You)		Capitol 2522
4/24/71	**58**	9	22 Happy Songs Of Love		Capitol 3079
3/31/73	**66**	4	23 Printers Alley Stars		Capitol 3556
7/14/73	**73**	5	24 Farther Down The River		Capitol 3631
9/22/73	**70**	7	25 Colorado Country Morning		Capitol 3704
1/04/75	**52**	8	26 Come On Down		Capitol 3916
4/19/75	**63**	9	27 Baby .... TENNESSEE ERNIE FORD & ANDRA WILLIS		Capitol 4044
11/22/75	**96**	4	28 The Devil Ain't A Lonely Woman's Friend		Capitol 4160
7/31/76	**95**	3	29 I Been To Georgia On A Fast Train		Capitol 4285
			THE FORESTER SISTERS ★★**193**★★ Family group from Lookout Mountain, Georgia. Consists of Kathy (b: 1955, lead), Kim (b: 1960, second lead), June (b: 1956), and Christy (b: 1962). The three oldest sisters had sung with small bands since leaving college. Worked as opening act for the Gatlin Brothers. Christy joined them in 1982. First recorded in 1983.		
1/26/85	**10**	22	1 (That's What You Do) When You're In Love.....		Warner 29114
6/29/85	**1** ^{1}	22	2 **I Fell In Love Again Last Night**		Warner 28988
11/02/85+	**1** ^{1}	20	3 **Just In Case**		Warner 28875
3/15/86	**1** ^{1}	22	4 **Mama's Never Seen Those Eyes**		Warner 28795
7/05/86	**2** ^{2}	24	5 **Lonely Alone**		Warner 28687
9/27/86	**1** ^{1}	20	6 **Too Much Is Not Enough** .... THE BELLAMY BROTHERS with THE FORESTER SISTERS		Curb 52917
3/07/87	**5**	23	7 **Too Many Rivers** .... #13 pop hit for Brenda Lee in 1965		Warner 28442
6/27/87	**1** ^{1}	24	8 **You Again**		Warner 28368
10/31/87+	**5**	25	9 **Lyin' In His Arms Again**		Warner 28208
6/25/88	**9**	24	10 **Letter Home**		Warner 27839
11/05/88+	**8**	22	11 **Sincerely** .... #1 pop hit for The McGuire Sisters in 1955		Warner 27686
			PEGGY FORMAN Born in Centerville, Louisiana. Wrote hit "Out Of My Head (And Back In My Bed)" for Loretta Lynn.		
8/20/77	**98**	4	1 The Danger Zone..................................		MCA 40757
5/24/80	**89**	4	2 There Ain't Nothing Like A Rainy Night		Dimension 1006
8/02/80	**78**	5	3 Burning Up Your Memory		Dimension 1008
7/04/81	**70**	6	4 You're More To Me (Than He's Ever Been).........		Dimension 1020
10/24/81	**54**	6	5 I Wish You Could Have Turned My Head (And Left My Heart Alone)		Dimension 1023
2/27/82	**71**	6	6 That's What Your Lovin' Does To Me		Dimension 1027

103

DEBUT DATE	PEAK POS	WKS CHR	ARTIST — Record Title	POP POS	Label & Number
			FOSTER & LLOYD		
			Vocal duo of songwriters Radney Foster and Bill Lloyd. Wrote hit "Love Someone Like Me" for Holly Dunn.		
7/04/87	**4**	21	1 **Crazy Over You**		RCA 5210
11/07/87+	**8**	21	2 **Sure Thing**		RCA 5281
4/09/88	**18**	17	3 Texas In 1880..		RCA 6900
8/06/88	**6**	23	4 **What Do You Want From Me This Time**.........		RCA 8633
			JERRY FOSTER		
			Born Jerry Gaylon Foster on 11/19/35 in Tallapoosa, Missouri. First recorded for Backbeat in 1958. Gifted songwriter with partner Bill Rice, holder of over 60 ASCAP awards, including 10 in 1972 and 11 in 1977. Wrote "Song And Dance Man" hit for Johnny Paycheck, "Here Comes The Hurt Again" hit for Mickey Gilley, and "39 And Holding" hit for Jerry Lee Lewis.		
8/18/73	**98**	3	1 Copperhead		Cinnamon 764
12/08/73+	**51**	13	2 Looking Back		Cinnamon 774
			#5 pop hit for Nat King Cole in 1958		
11/27/76	**86**	6	3 I Knew You When..		Hitsville 6043
7/15/78	**84**	3	4 I Want To Love You.......................................		Monument 256
			JERRY FOSTER & TENNESSEE TORNADO		
			LLOYD DAVID FOSTER		
			Born in 1952 in Wills Point, Texas. Played guitar since his teens. Drove a beer truck in Dallas, worked clubs on weekends. First recorded for Autumn Leaves in 1981.		
6/19/82	**32**	13	1 Blue Rendezvous		MCA 52061
10/23/82	**65**	7	2 Honky Tonk Magic		MCA 52123
2/26/83	**32**	12	3 Unfinished Business		MCA 52173
9/03/83	**60**	6	4 You've Got That Touch		MCA 52248
11/24/84+	**44**	15	5 I'm Gonna Love You Right Out Of The Blues		Columbia 04670
4/13/85	**55**	9	6 I Can Feel The Fire Goin' Out		Columbia 04836
10/12/85	**68**	6	7 I'm As Over You As I'm Ever Gonna Get...........		Columbia 05601
			THE FOUR GUYS		
			Group has had frequent personnel changes. Worked WWVA-Wheeling Jamboree USA before joining the Grand Ole Opry in 1967.		
10/19/74	**88**	3	1 Too Late To Turn Back Now...........................		RCA 10055
12/08/79	**93**	4	2 Mama Rocked Us To Sleep (With Country Music).		Collage 102
3/13/82	**85**	4	3 Made In The U.S.A..		JNB 1001
			KEN FOWLER		
2/08/86	**96**	2	1 You're A Heartache To Follow........................		Deja Vu 111
			DOLLY FOX		
12/09/78	**93**	2	1 I've Got A Reason For Living...........................		Artic 1025
			KENT FOX		
			Born Walter Kent Fox on 10/16/47 in Lexington, Kentucky. Operates his own studio and production company.		
6/02/73	**73**	4	1 New York Callin' Miami		MCA 40038
			FOXFIRE		
			Nashville-based trio: Dave Hall, Russ Allison and Don Miller.		
6/09/79	**30**	10	1 Fell Into Love		NSD 24
4/26/80	**38**	9	2 I Can See Forever Loving You.........................		Elektra 46625
11/15/80	**55**	8	3 Whatever Happened To Those Drinking Songs....		Elektra 47070
			KELLY FOXTON - see HANK SNOW		
			GARLAND FRADY		
			Born in Lexington, North Carolina. Moved to Los Angeles in 1962; worked with the house band at the Palomino Club. Band leader for Bob Luman and Dorsey Burnette.		
8/18/73	**89**	7	1 The Barrooms Have Found You		Countrysd. 45104
			CONNIE FRANCIS		
			Born Concetta Rosa Maria Franconero on 12/12/38 in Newark, New Jersey. The #1 pop singer of the past 30 years.		
7/25/60	**24**	3	1 Everybody's Somebody's Fool........................	*1*	MGM 12899
3/01/69	**33**	10	2 The Wedding Cake	*91*	MGM 14034
3/12/83	**84**	3	3 There's Still A Few Good Love Songs Left In Me .		Polydor 810087

DEBUT DATE	PEAK POS	WKS CHR	ARTIST — Record Title	POP POS	Label & Number
			BILL FRANKLIN & BUD MESSNER		
6/03/50	**7**	6	1 **Slippin' Around With Jole Blon**		Abbey 15004
			Juke Box #7 / Best Seller #9		
			TILLMAN FRANKS		
			Singer/guitarist. Debuted on Louisiana Hayride in 1947. Became artist manager, including Slim Whitman, Johnny Horton, Webb Pierce and David Houston. Wrote "Sink The Bismarck". With Horton in the car crash that killed the singer in 1960.		
12/21/63	**30**	4	1 Tadpole		Starday 651
5/02/64	**30**	11	2 When The World's On Fire		Starday 670
			BRENDA FRAZIER		
12/06/80	**92**	2	1 I've Given Up Giving In To The Blues		Tyro 1004
			DALLAS FRAZIER		
			Born on 10/27/39 in Spiro, Oklahoma; raised in Bakersfield, California. Toured with Ferlin Husky at age 12. Appeared on "Cliffie Stone's Hometown Jamboree" TV series. Wrote "Alley Oop", "There Goes My Everything", "Son Of Hickory Holler's Tramp", "Elvira", and many others.		
11/11/67+	**28**	11	1 Everybody Oughta Sing A Song		Capitol 2011
4/13/68	**43**	8	2 The Sunshine Of My World		Capitol 2133
9/21/68	**59**	5	3 I Hope I Like Mexico Blues		Capitol 2257
3/08/69	**63**	9	4 The Conspiracy Of Homer Jones		Capitol 2402
11/08/69	**45**	10	5 California Cotton Fields		RCA 0259
8/29/70	**45**	7	6 The Birthmark Henry Thompson Talks About		RCA 9881
2/27/71	**43**	8	7 Big Mable Murphy		RCA 9950
7/29/72	**42**	11	8 North Carolina		RCA 0748
			JOHNNY FREE		
4/28/79	**100**	1	1 Borrowed Time		Sabre 4509
			ERNIE FREEMAN		
			Born on 8/16/22 in Cleveland; died of a heart attack on 5/16/81 in North Hollywood. Pianist/composer/conductor for many top artists, including Frank Sinatra.		
1/13/58	**11**	2	1 Raunchy .... [I]	**4**	Imperial 5474
			Best Seller #11		
			JANIE FRICKIE ★★**66**★★		
			Born on 12/19/47 in South Whitney, Indiana. Worked as a back-up singer in Dallas, Memphis and Los Angeles in the early 70s. With Judy Rodman and Karen Taylor-Good in Phase II in Memphis, in the late 70s. Moved to Nashville and sang back-up for Dolly Parton, Elvis Presley, Billy Swan, Ronnie Milsap, Crystal Gayle, Johnny Duncan, and others. Made numerous commercial jingles. Own TV special in 1983, frequent other appearances on TV. Originally spelled her name "Fricke".		
			JANIE FRICKE:		
9/17/77	**21**	13	1 What're You Doing Tonight		Columbia 10605
10/29/77+	**4**	16	2 **Come A Little Bit Closer**		Columbia 10634
			JOHNNY DUNCAN with JANIE FRICKE		
			#3 pop hit for Jay & The Americans in 1964		
3/04/78	**21**	12	3 Baby It's You		Columbia 10695
5/27/78	**12**	13	4 Please Help Me, I'm Falling (In Love With You) ...		Columbia 10743
			giant #1 hit for Hank Locklin in 1960		
10/07/78	**1**¹	14	5 **On My Knees**		Epic 50616
			CHARLIE RICH with JANIE FRICKE		
11/11/78+	**22**	12	6 Playin' Hard To Get		Columbia 10849
3/03/79	**14**	12	7 I'll Love Away Your Troubles For Awhile		Columbia 10910
7/07/79	**28**	10	8 Let's Try Again		Columbia 11029
11/17/79+	**26**	13	9 But Love Me		Columbia 11139
3/22/80	**22**	12	10 Pass Me By (If You're Only Passing Through)		Columbia 11224
7/12/80	**17**	14	11 He's Out Of My Life		Columbia 11312
			JOHNNY DUNCAN & JANIE FRICKE		
			#10 pop hit for Michael Jackson ("She's Out...") in 1980		
11/01/80+	**2**¹	18	12 **Down To My Last Broken Heart**		Columbia 11384
3/14/81	**12**	14	13 Pride		Columbia 60509
7/25/81	**4**	18	14 **I'll Need Someone To Hold Me (When I Cry)**		Columbia 02197
12/12/81+	**4**	19	15 **Do Me With Love**		Columbia 02644
5/08/82	**1**¹	18	16 **Don't Worry 'Bout Me Baby**		Columbia 02859
9/18/82	**1**¹	19	17 **It Ain't Easy Bein' Easy**		Columbia 03214
1/15/83	**4**	19	18 **You Don't Know Love**		Columbia 03498
			backing vocal: Bill Warren		

DEBUT DATE	PEAK POS	WKS CHR	ARTIST — Record Title	POP POS	Label & Number
			JANIE FRICKIE — Continued		
5/21/83	**1**¹	20	19 **He's A Heartache (Looking For A Place To Happen)**..		Columbia 03899
9/17/83	**1**¹	20	20 **Tell Me A Lie**..		Columbia 04091
1/14/84	**1**¹	18	21 **Let's Stop Talkin' About It**.......................		Columbia 04317
5/12/84	**8**	17	22 **If The Fall Don't Get You**		Columbia 04454
9/01/84	**1**¹	23	23 **Your Heart's Not In It**		Columbia 04578
10/27/84+	**1**¹	22	24 **A Place To Fall Apart**		Epic 04663
			MERLE HAGGARD with JANIE FRICKE		
1/05/85	**7**	19	25 **The First Word In Memory Is Me**		Columbia 04731
5/18/85	**2**¹	22	26 **She's Single Again**...................................		Columbia 04896
9/21/85	**4**	23	27 **Somebody Else's Fire**		Columbia 05617
2/01/86	**5**	22	28 **Easy To Please**		Columbia 05781
			JANIE FRICKIE:		
6/28/86	**1**¹	22	29 **Always Have Always Will**...........................		Columbia 06144
11/08/86+	**20**	16	30 When A Woman Cries		Columbia 06417
3/14/87	**32**	11	31 Are You Satisfied		Columbia 06985
			#11 pop hit for Rusty Draper in 1956		
5/09/87	**21**	12	32 From Time To Time (It Feels Like Love Again)....		Columbia 07088
			LARRY GATLIN & JANIE FRICKIE (with THE GATLIN BROTHERS)		
8/29/87	**63**	4	33 Baby You're Gone		Columbia 07353
4/16/88	**54**	8	34 Where Does Love Go (When It's Gone)..............		Columbia 07770
6/25/88	**50**	8	35 I'll Walk Before I'll Crawl............................		Columbia 07927
9/24/88	**64**	4	36 Heart		Columbia 08031

KINKY FRIEDMAN

Born Richard Friedman on 10/31/44 in Rio Duckworth, Texas. First recorded with his own band, King Arthur & The Carrots, in 1966. Moved to Los Angeles with his band, The Texas Jewboys, in 1971. Band members used names Little Jewford, Big Nig, Panama Red, Rainbow Colors, and Snakebite Jacobs.

DEBUT DATE	PEAK POS	WKS CHR	ARTIST — Record Title	POP POS	Label & Number
7/14/73	**69**	8	1 Sold American..		Vanguard 35173

ALLEN FRIZZELL

Younger brother of Lefty and David Frizzell. Dottie West's guitarist and front man. Teamed with brother David and Shelly West in 1977. Married to Shelly until 1985.

DEBUT DATE	PEAK POS	WKS CHR	ARTIST — Record Title	POP POS	Label & Number
5/16/81	**86**	4	1 Beer Joint Fever		Snd. Factory 429
8/29/81	**81**	3	2 She's Livin' It Up (And I'm Drinkin' 'em Down) ...		Snd. Factory 447
6/08/85	**73**	3	3 It'll Be Love By Morning		Epic 04870

DAVID FRIZZELL ★★148★★

Born on 9/26/41 in Texas; younger brother of Lefty Frizzell. Toured with Lefty while a teenager. Worked with Buck Owens in the early 70s. Made a series of successful duets with Shelly West, daughter of Dottie West.

DEBUT DATE	PEAK POS	WKS CHR	ARTIST — Record Title	POP POS	Label & Number
6/20/70	**67**	3	1 L.A. International Airport...............................		Columbia 45139
10/31/70	**36**	10	2 I Just Can't Help Believing...........................		Columbia 45238
			#9 pop hit for B.J. Thomas in 1970		
12/18/71	**73**	2	3 Goodbye...		Cartwheel 202
5/19/73	**63**	5	4 Words Don't Come Easy		Capitol 3589
8/25/73	**94**	4	5 Take Me One More Ride...............................		Capitol 3684
10/02/76	**100**	1	6 A Case Of You		RSO 856
9/05/81	**45**	9	7 Lefty		Warner 49778
			guest vocal: Merle Haggard		
5/29/82	**1**¹	23	8 **I'm Gonna Hire A Wino To Decorate Our Home**		Warner 50063
10/09/82+	**5**	20	9 **Lost My Baby Blues**		Warner 29901
5/28/83	**10**	16	10 **Where Are You Spending Your Nights These Days**		Viva 29617
10/08/83	**39**	13	11 A Million Light Beers Ago		Viva 29498
1/14/84	**64**	6	12 Black And White		Viva 29388
4/28/84	**60**	6	13 Who Dat		Viva 29332
7/28/84	**49**	9	14 When We Get Back To The Farm (That's When We Really Go To Town)...............................		Viva 29232
12/01/84+	**49**	13	15 No Way Jose		Viva 29158
3/02/85	**63**	7	16 Country Music Love Affair		Viva 29066
3/29/86	**71**	5	17 Celebrity		Nash. Am. 1002
5/09/87	**74**	7	18 Beautiful Body...		Compleat 168

DEBUT DATE	PEAK POS	WKS CHR		ARTIST — Record Title	POP POS	Label & Number
				DAVID FRIZZELL — Continued		
				DAVID FRIZZELL & SHELLY WEST:		
1/17/81	**1**¹	17	19	**You're The Reason God Made Oklahoma**.........		Warner 49650
				from the Clint Eastwood film "Any Which Way You Can"		
6/20/81	**9**	15	20	**A Texas State Of Mind**		Warner 49745
10/10/81	**16**	16	21	**Husbands And Wives**		Warner 49825
				#26 pop hit for Roger Miller in 1966		
2/06/82	**8**	18	22	**Another Honky-Tonk Night On Broadway**.......		Warner 50007
7/17/82	**4**	18	23	**I Just Came Here To Dance**.......................		Warner 29980
12/04/82+	**43**	11	24	**Please Surrender**.......................		Warner 29850
				from the Clint Eastwood film "Honkytonk Man"		
3/26/83	**52**	10	25	**Cajun Invitation**.......................		Warner 29756
9/03/83	**71**	4	26	**Pleasure Island**		Viva 29544
2/04/84	**20**	17	27	**Silent Partners**		Viva 29404
9/15/84	**13**	20	28	**It's A Be Together Night**		Viva 29187
4/13/85	**60**	8	29	**Do Me Right**		Viva 29048
				above 5 shown only as: **FRIZZELL & WEST**		
				LEFTY FRIZZELL ★★76★★		
				Born William Orville Frizzell on 3/31/28 in Corsicana, Texas. Died of a stroke on 7/19/75 in Nashville. Nicknamed Lefty during amateur boxing career. Worked local clubs in Waco and Dallas. Appeared on Town Hall Party and Country America TV shows. Moved to Nashville in 1962. Recorded with June Stearns as Agnes & Orville on Columbia in 1968. Elected to the Country Music Hall Of Fame in 1982.		
10/28/50	**1**³	22	1	**If You've Got The Money I've Got The Time/**		
				Juke Box #1 / Best Seller #2 / Jockey #2		
11/04/50+	**1**³	32	2	**I Love You A Thousand Ways**.......................		Columbia 20739
				Jockey #1 / Juke Box #3 / Best Seller #5		
3/03/51	**4**	12	3	**Look What Thoughts Will Do/**		
				Jockey #4 / Best Seller #9 / Juke Box #9		
3/10/51	**7**	2	4	**Shine, Shave, Shower**...............................		Columbia 20772
				Juke Box #7		
4/14/51	**1**¹¹	27	5	**I Want To Be With You Always**.....................	29	Columbia 20799
				Jockey #1(11) / Best Seller #1(5) / Juke Box #1(5)		
8/04/51	**1**¹²	28	6	**Always Late (With Your Kisses)/**		
				Best Seller #1(12) / Jockey #1(6) / Juke Box #1(6)		
8/18/51	**2**⁸	29	7	**Mom And Dad's Waltz**...............................		Columbia 20837
				Best Seller #2 / Jockey #2 / Juke Box #3		
10/13/51	**6**	9	8	**Travellin' Blues**.......................		Columbia 20842
				Best Seller #6 / Juke Box #7 / Jockey #8		
12/22/51+	**1**³	21	9	**Give Me More, More, More (Of Your Kisses)/**		
				Jockey #1(3) / Juke Box #1(3) / Best Seller #3		
1/12/52	**7**	5	10	**How Long Will It Take (To Stop Loving You).**		Columbia 20885
				Jockey #7		
4/12/52	**2**¹	12	11	**Don't Stay Away (Till Love Grows Cold)**		Columbia 20911
				Best Seller #2 / Juke Box #2 / Jockey #4		
9/27/52	**6**	5	12	**Forever**...............................		Columbia 20997
				Best Seller #6		
12/06/52+	**3**	9	13	**I'm An Old, Old Man (Tryin' To Live While I Can)**.........		Columbia 21034
				Best Seller #3 / Juke Box #4		
5/23/53	**8**	1	14	**(Honey, Baby, Hurry!) Bring Your Sweet Self Back To Me**.........		Columbia 21084
				Jockey #8		
2/20/54	**8**	2	15	**Run 'Em Off**		Columbia 21194
				Juke Box #8		
1/15/55	**11**	4	16	**I Love You Mostly**		Columbia 21328
				Best Seller #11 / Jockey #13		
11/24/58+	**13**	11	17	Cigarettes And Coffee Blues...........................		Columbia 41268
				written by Marty Robbins		
6/08/59	**6**	15	18	**The Long Black Veil**...............................		Columbia 41384
4/27/63	**23**	2	19	Forbidden Lovers		Columbia 42676
11/09/63	**30**	1	20	Don't Let Her See Me Cry		Columbia 42839
1/11/64	**1**⁴	26	21	**Saginaw, Michigan**	85	Columbia 42924
8/08/64	**28**	11	22	The Nester		Columbia 43051
1/16/65	**50**	2	23	'Gator Hollow		Columbia 43169
5/01/65	**12**	15	24	She's Gone Gone Gone		Columbia 43256
10/16/65	**36**	5	25	A Little Unfair/		
11/13/65	**41**	4	26	Love Looks Good On You		Columbia 43364

DEBUT DATE	PEAK POS	WKS CHR	ARTIST — Record Title	POP POS	Label & Number
			LEFTY FRIZZELL — Continued		
10/15/66	**51**	6	27 I Just Couldn't See The Forest		Columbia 43734
3/25/67	**49**	10	28 You Gotta Be Puttin' Me On		Columbia 44023
9/02/67	**63**	4	29 Get This Stranger Out Of Me		Columbia 44205
8/10/68	**59**	3	30 The Marriage Bit....................................		Columbia 44563
3/22/69	**64**	4	31 An Article From Life................................		Columbia 44738
8/22/70	**49**	10	32 Watermelon Time In Georgia..........................		Columbia 45197
8/12/72	**59**	10	33 You, Babe..		Columbia 45652
9/22/73	**43**	13	34 I Can't Get Over You To Save My Life		ABC 16462
2/16/74	**25**	12	35 I Never Go Around Mirrors..........................		ABC 11416
6/15/74	**52**	9	36 Railroad Lady.....................................		ABC 11442
9/21/74	**21**	14	37 Lucky Arms.......................................		ABC 12023
2/22/75	**67**	7	38 Life's Like Poetry.................................		ABC 12061
7/05/75	**50**	11	39 Falling		ABC 12103
			RAY FRUSHAY		
			Born Raymond Frusha on 3/1/49 in Austin, Texas. Discovered by Rocky Marciano.		
9/08/79	**93**	2	1 I Got Western Pride		Western Pr. 105
3/22/80	**90**	2	2 Pickin' Up Love		Western Pr. 113
			MICKI FUHRMAN		
			Female vocalist/songwriter from Coushatta, Louisiana. Regular on the Louisiana Hayride for over 6 years. Song "Look Again" won 1st prize in the Music City Song Festival. Very popular in gospel music.		
11/11/78	**93**	4	1 Leave While I'm Sleeping..........................		Louis. Hay. 785
7/28/79	**86**	3	2 Blue River Of Tears		MCA 41057
11/22/80	**60**	7	3 Hold Me, Thrill Me, Kiss Me.......................		MCA 51005
			#8 pop hit for Mel Carter in 1965		
2/18/84	**48**	10	4 I Bet You Never Thought I'd Go This Far		MCA 52321
			JERRY FULLER		
			Full name: Jerrell Lee Fuller. Singer/songwriter/producer from Fort Worth, Texas.		
1/13/79	**98**	1	1 Salt On The Wound		ABC 12436
6/02/79	**90**	4	2 Lines		MCA 41022

G

			GABRIEL		
			Born Gabriel Ernest Miklos Farago in Hungary; at 4 months old, fled with family to Innsbruch, Austria. Emmigrated to Buffalo, New York at age 4.		
1/24/81	**85**	3	1 I Think I Could Love You (Better Than He Did) ...		NSD 70
4/18/81	**93**	2	2 Friends Before Lovers		Ridgetop 01381
			BYRON GALLIMORE		
			His song "No Ordinary Woman" won 1st prize in the Music City Song Festival in 1979.		
6/14/80	**93**	2	1 No Ordinary Woman		Little Giant 025
			BOB GALLION		
			Born on 4/22/31 in Ashland, Kentucky. Own band, the Country Boys; worked on the Louisiana Hayride and WWVA Jamboree from 1952-55. Performed with Stoney Cooper's Clinch Mountain Clan.		
11/03/58	**28**	1	1 That's What I Tell My Heart		MGM 12700
5/18/59	**18**	9	2 You Take The Table (And I'll Take The Chairs)...		MGM 12777
11/28/60+	**7**	22	3 **Loving You (Was Worth This Broken Heart)**....		Hickory 1130
6/19/61	**20**	4	4 One Way Street....................................		Hickory 1145
12/04/61	**20**	2	5 Sweethearts Again		Hickory 1154
11/10/62	**5**	15	6 **Wall To Wall Love**................................		Hickory 1181
8/31/63	**23**	2	7 Ain't Got Time For Nothin'		Hickory 1220
7/20/68	**71**	2	8 Pick A Little Happy Song..........................		United Art. 50309
9/08/73	**99**	2	9 Love By Appointment		Metro. Cnt. 0037
			PATI POWELL & BOB GALLION		

JAMES GALWAY - see SYLVIA

DEBUT DATE	PEAK POS	WKS CHR	ARTIST — Record Title	POP POS	Label & Number
			GALE GARNETT		
			Born on 7/17/42 in Auckland, New Zealand. Came to the United States in 1951. Worked as an actress from age 15. Appeared on many TV shows.		
12/05/64	43	3	1 We'll Sing In The Sunshine	4	RCA 8388
			PAT GARRETT		
			Born in Lebanon, Pennsylvania. Worked local clubs as lead singer/bassist for the Triumphs, recorded for Diamond. Toured with Shorty Long & The Santa Fe Rangers. Own record company, Gold Dust.		
11/12/77	98	1	1 A Little Something On The Side		Kansa 3000
8/02/80	80	5	2 Sexy Ole Lady		Gold Dust 101
10/18/80	89	3	3 Your Magic Touch		Gold Dust 102
11/07/81	73	5	4 Everlovin' Woman		Gold Dust 104
9/13/86	74	6	5 Rockin' My Country Heart		Compleat 157
10/03/87	82	3	6 Suck It In		MDJ 73087
			AL GARRISON		
9/26/87	87	2	1 Where Do I Go From Here		Motown 1032
			GLEN GARRISON		
			Born on 6/13/41 in Slarcy, Arkansas.		
11/04/67	72	2	1 Goodbye Swingers		Imperial 66257
6/22/68	48	6	2 I'll Be Your Baby Tonight		Imperial 66300
			written by Bob Dylan		
			JESS GARRON		
3/31/79	30	11	1 Lo Que Sea (What Ever May The Future Be)		Charta 131
8/04/79	65	6	2 It's Summer Time....................................		Charta 136
			LARRY GATLIN & THE GATLIN BROTHERS ★★67★★		
			Trio of brothers reared in several West Texas towns: Larry (b: 5/2/48, Seminole, TX), Steve (b: 4/4/51) and Rudy (b: 8/20/52). Steve and Rudy both born in Olney, Texas. Worked as a gospel trio and had their own TV series in Abilene. Joined by younger sister LaDonna. Larry was a staff writer for Dottie West. He moved to Nashville in 1972. Also wrote for Elvis Presley, Tom Jones, Kris Kristofferson and Glen Campbell. His songs were used in the Johnny Cash film "The Glory Road". Steve, Rudy, LaDonna and her husband, Tim Johnson, worked as "Young Country", did back-up for for Tammy Wynette. The brothers rejoined Larry after finishing college. Own ABC-TV special in 1981. Members of the Grand Ole Opry since 1976.		
			LARRY GATLIN:		
10/20/73	40	13	1 Sweet Becky Walker		Monument 8584
3/16/74	45	12	2 Bitter They Are Harder They Fall...................		Monument 8602
9/07/74	14	15	3 Delta Dirt	84	Monument 8622
8/23/75	71	7	4 Let's Turn The Lights On		Monument 8657
			LARRY GATLIN with Family & Friends:		
12/27/75+	5	19	5 **Broken Lady**		Monument 8680
6/12/76	43	9	6 Warm And Tender		Monument 8696
10/30/76+	5	16	7 **Statues Without Hearts**............................		Monument 201
2/26/77	12	11	8 Anything But Leavin'...............................		Monument 212
5/28/77	3	16	9 **I Don't Wanna Cry**.................................		Monument 221
9/10/77	3	14	10 **Love Is Just A Game**		Monument 226
			LARRY GATLIN with Brothers & Friends:		
12/10/77+	1¹	16	11 **I Just Wish You Were Someone I Love**...........		Monument 234
			LARRY GATLIN:		
4/15/78	2²	14	12 **Night Time Magic**		Monument 249
8/12/78	13	11	13 Do It Again Tonight		Monument 259
11/11/78+	7	14	14 **I've Done Enough Dyin' Today**		Monument 270
			LARRY GATLIN & THE GATLIN BROTHERS BAND:		
8/25/79	1²	15	15 **All The Gold In California**		Columbia 11066
1/05/80	43	8	16 The Midnight Choir................................		Columbia 11169
3/08/80	12	12	17 Taking Somebody With Me When I Fall	108	Columbia 11219
6/14/80	18	13	18 We're Number One		Columbia 11282
10/04/80	5	17	19 **Take Me To Your Lovin' Place**......................		Columbia 11369
2/21/81	25	11	20 It Don't Get No Better Than This...................		Columbia 11438
6/06/81	20	12	21 Wind Is Bound To Change		Columbia 02123
10/03/81	4	17	22 **What Are We Doin' Lonesome**......................		Columbia 02522
2/06/82	15	13	23 In Like With Each Other		Columbia 02698
5/29/82	19	12	24 She Used To Sing On Sunday........................		Columbia 02910

DEBUT DATE	PEAK POS	WKS CHR	ARTIST — Record Title	POP POS	Label & Number
			LARRY GATLIN & THE GATLIN BROTHERS — Continued		
9/11/82	5	19	25 **Sure Feels Like Love**.....................................		Columbia 03159
1/29/83	20	15	26 Almost Called Her Baby By Mistake		Columbia 03517
5/21/83	32	11	27 Easy On The Eye..		Columbia 03885
9/24/83	1²	22	28 **Houston (Means I'm One Day Closer To You)**...		Columbia 04105
3/24/84	7	18	29 **Denver**..		Columbia 04395
			LARRY GATLIN & THE GATLIN BROTHERS:		
7/21/84	3	24	30 **The Lady Takes The Cowboy Everytime**		Columbia 04533
10/12/85	43	13	31 Runaway Go Home		Columbia 05632
1/18/86	12	19	32 Nothing But Your Love Matters		Columbia 05764
			LARRY, STEVE, RUDY: THE GATLIN BROTHERS:		
8/23/86	2¹	22	33 **She Used To Be Somebody's Baby**.................		Columbia 06252
12/27/86+	4	21	34 **Talkin' To The Moon**.................................		Columbia 06592
5/09/87	21	12	35 From Time To Time (It Feels Like Love Again)....		Columbia 07088
			LARRY GATLIN & JANIE FRICKIE (with The Gatlin Brothers)		
8/15/87	16	15	36 Changin' Partners		Columbia 07320
3/26/88	4	21	37 **Love Of A Lifetime**		Columbia 07747
8/13/88	34	13	38 Alive And Well		Columbia 07998
			LENNY GAULT		
9/30/78	87	3	1 Turn On The Bright Lights.............................		MRC 1020
1/06/79	78	4	2 I Just Need A Coke (To Get The Whiskey Down) .		MRC 1024
4/07/79	89	3	3 The Honky-Tonks Are Calling Me Again		King Coal 03
			CRYSTAL GAYLE ★★37★★		
			Born Brenda Gail Webb on 1/9/51 in Paintsville, Kentucky; raised in Wabash, Indiana. Youngest sister of Loretta Lynn. Worked with the Loretta Lynn Road Show from age 16. First country artist to tour China (1979). On soundtrack of the film "One From The Heart".		
9/19/70	23	13	1 I've Cried (The Blues Right Out Of My Eyes)		Decca 32721
3/11/72	70	2	2 Everybody Oughta Cry		Decca 32925
7/01/72	49	5	3 I Hope You're Havin' Better Luck Than Me		Decca 32969
5/25/74	39	12	4 Restless		United Art. 428
10/26/74+	6	21	5 **Wrong Road Again**		United Art. 555
3/29/75	27	11	6 Beyond You		United Art. 600
7/26/75	21	15	7 This Is My Year For Mexico...........................		United Art. 680
11/29/75+	8	16	8 **Somebody Loves You**................................		United Art. 740
4/03/76	1¹	18	9 **I'll Get Over You**	71	United Art. 781
8/21/76	31	9	10 One More Time (Karneval)		United Art. 838
11/06/76+	1¹	16	11 **You Never Miss A Real Good Thing (Till He Says Goodbye)**.................................		United Art. 883
3/26/77	2²	15	12 **I'll Do It All Over Again**		United Art. 948
7/09/77	1⁴	18	13●**Don't It Make My Brown Eyes Blue**	2	United Art. 1016
12/10/77+	40	11	14 I've Cried (The Blues Right Out Of My Eyes) ... [R]		MCA 40837
2/11/78	1¹	14	15 **Ready For The Times To Get Better**..............	52	United Art. 1136
6/17/78	1²	16	16 **Talking In Your Sleep**	18	United Art. 1214
12/02/78+	1²	14	17 **Why Have You Left The One You Left Me For** .		United Art. 1259
4/14/79	3	13	18 **When I Dream**	84	United Art. 1288
7/21/79	7	13	19 **Your Kisses Will**		United Art. 1306
9/01/79	2³	15	20 **Half The Way**	15	Columbia 11087
12/08/79+	5	14	21 **Your Old Cold Shoulder**............................		United Art. 1329
2/09/80	1¹	14	22 **It's Like We Never Said Goodbye**..................	63	Columbia 11198
5/03/80	64	6	23 River Road..		United Art. 1347
5/10/80	8	15	24 **The Blue Side**..	81	Columbia 11270
7/26/80	58	7	25 Heart Mender		United Art. 1362
9/13/80	1¹	18	26 **If You Ever Change Your Mind**		Columbia 11359
2/07/81	17	14	27 Take It Easy..		Columbia 11436
5/23/81	1¹	17	28 **Too Many Lovers**		Columbia 02078
10/10/81	3	18	29 **The Woman In Me**	76	Columbia 02523
2/20/82	5	19	30 **You Never Gave Up On Me**		Columbia 02718
8/07/82	9	15	31 **Livin' In These Troubled Times**...................		Columbia 03048
10/09/82	1¹	19	32 **You And I**...	7	Elektra 69936
			EDDIE RABBITT with CRYSTAL GAYLE		

DEBUT DATE	PEAK POS	WKS CHR		ARTIST — Record Title	POP POS	Label & Number
				CRYSTAL GAYLE — Continued		
11/20/82+	1^1	22	33	'Til I Gain Control Again		Elektra 69893
4/02/83	1^1	16	34	Our Love Is On The Faultline		Warner 29719
7/16/83	1^1	19	35	Baby, What About You	83	Warner 29582
9/24/83	49	9	36	Keepin' Power		Columbia 04093
10/29/83+	1^1	21	37	The Sound Of Goodbye	84	Warner 29452
2/25/84	2^2	19	38	I Don't Wanna Lose Your Love		Warner 29356
7/07/84	1^1	20	39	Turning Away		Warner 29254
10/27/84+	4	23	40	Me Against The Night		Warner 29151
3/23/85	3	21	41	Nobody Wants To Be Alone		Warner 29050
8/10/85	5	18	42	A Long And Lasting Love		Warner 28963
7/26/86	1^1	19	43	Cry		Warner 28689
				#1 pop hit for Johnnie Ray in 1951		
11/22/86+	1^1	22	44	Straight To The Heart		Warner 28518
7/18/87	26	15	45	Nobody Should Have To Love This Way		Warner 28409
10/24/87+	11	18	46	Only Love Can Save Me Now		Warner 28209
8/27/88	22	15	47	Nobody's Angel		Warner 27811
				CRYSTAL GAYLE & GARY MORRIS:		
11/23/85+	1^1	19	48	Makin' Up For Lost Time (The Dallas Lovers' Song)		Warner 28856
				theme from the TV series "Dallas"		
4/25/87	4	18	49	Another World		Warner 28373
				theme from the daytime TV series of the same title		
2/13/88	26	15	50	All Of This & More		Warner 28106
				THE GEEZINSLAW BROTHERS		
				Austin, Texas-based comedy duo of Sam Alldred and DeWayne "Son" Smith.		
10/15/66	66	3	1	You Wouldn't Put The Shuck On Me ...... [N]		Capitol 5722
7/15/67	57	6	2	Change Of Wife ...... [N]		Capitol 5918
10/21/67	48	8	3	Chubby (Please Take Your Love To Town ...... [N]		Capitol 2002
				answer song to Kenny Rogers' "Ruby, Don't Take Your Love To Town"		
				BOBBIE GENTRY		
				Born Roberta Streeter on 7/27/44 in Chickasaw County, Mississippi; raised in Greenwood, MS. Guitarist/pianist/bassist/banjo player. Moved to Palm Springs, California while still in high school. Own TV series in England in the late 60s. Own production company in Los Angeles. Married singer Jim Stafford in 1978.		
9/09/67	17	8	1●	Ode To Billie Joe	*1*	Capitol 5950
6/01/68	72	4	2	Louisiana Man	*100*	Capitol 2147
12/13/69+	26	12	3	Fancy	*31*	Capitol 2674
				BOBBIE GENTRY & GLEN CAMPBELL:		
11/23/68	44	7	4	Less Of Me		Capitol 2314
				flip side "Mornin' Glory" made the pop charts		
2/08/69	14	14	5	Let It Be Me	*36*	Capitol 2387
2/21/70	6	13	6	All I Have To Do Is Dream	*27*	Capitol 2745
				GARY GENTRY		
				Singer/songwriter from Athens, Texas.		
4/25/81	84	2	1	I Sold All Of Tom T's Songs Last Nigh ...... [N]		Elektra 47122
12/19/81	83	4	2	(s.o.b.) Same Old Boy		Elektra 47238
				GEORGE & GENE - see GEORGE JONES		
				TERRI GIBBS		
				Born on 6/15/54 in Augusta, Georgia. Blind vocalist/pianist. Sang gospel as a child and had own band, Sound Dimension, from 1974. Worked at the Steak & Ale in Augusta from 1975-80.		
10/11/80+	8	20	1	Somebody's Knockin'	*13*	MCA 41309
6/06/81	19	12	2	Rich Man	*89*	MCA 51119
9/26/81	38	10	3	I Wanna Be Around		MCA 51180
				#14 pop hit for Tony Bennett in 1963		
12/26/81+	12	17	4	Mis'ry River		MCA 51225
5/01/82	19	13	5	Ashes To Ashes		MCA 52040
8/14/82	45	8	6	Some Days It Rains All Night Long		MCA 52088
11/13/82+	33	14	7	Baby I'm Gone		MCA 52134
8/13/83	17	17	8	Anybody Else's Heart But Mine		MCA 52252
12/03/83	65	8	9	Tell Mama		MCA 52308
				#23 pop hit for Etta James in 1968		

DEBUT DATE	PEAK POS	WKS CHR	ARTIST — Record Title	POP POS	Label & Number
			TERRI GIBBS — Continued		
3/30/85	**43**	12	10 A Few Good Men		Warner 29056
7/06/85	**70**	5	11 Rockin' In A Brand New Cradle........................		Warner 28993
11/02/85	**70**	5	12 Someone Must Be Missing You Tonight		Warner 28895
10/24/87	**87**	3	13 Turn Around		Horizon 2963
			DON GIBSON ★★**28**★★		
			Born Donald Eugene Gibson on 4/3/28 in Shelby, North Carolina. Worked local clubs and radio while still in high school. Moved to Knoxville in 1953 and worked on WNOX Barn Dance radio series. Wrote "Sweet Dreams", "I Can't Stop Loving You", "Oh Lonesome Me", and many of his other hits. Joined the Grand Ole Opry in 1958.		
8/11/56	**9**	1	1 **Sweet Dreams**		MGM 12194
			Jockey #9		
2/17/58	**1** 8	34	2 **Oh Lonesome Me/**	7	
			Best Seller #1(8) / Jockey #1(8)		
3/17/58	**7**	14	3 **I Can't Stop Lovin' You**............................	81	RCA 7133
			Jockey #7		
6/09/58	**1** 2	24	4 **Blue Blue Day**	20	RCA 7010
			Best Seller #1 / Jockey #2		
9/29/58	**5**	19	5 **Give Myself A Party/**	46	
10/06/58	**8**	9	6 **Look Who's Blue**	58	RCA 7330
			Jockey #8		
2/02/59	**3**	16	7 **Who Cares/**	43	
2/23/59	**27**	2	8 A Stranger To Me.......................................		RCA 7437
5/11/59	**11**	13	9 Lonesome Old House	71	RCA 7505
8/17/59	**5**	16	10 **Don't Tell Me Your Troubles**	85	RCA 7566
12/07/59+	**14**	9	11 I'm Movin' On/		
1/04/60	**29**	1	12 Big Hearted Me		RCA 7629
3/07/60	**2** 1	21	13 **Just One Time**	29	RCA 7690
8/08/60	**11**	11	14 Far, Far Away	72	RCA 7762
11/28/60+	**6**	16	15 **Sweet Dreams** .... [R]	93	RCA 7805
			new version of Don's first hit		
3/13/61	**22**	6	16 What About Me..................................	100	RCA 7841
6/19/61	**2** 1	26	17 **Sea Of Heartbreak**	21	RCA 7890
12/18/61+	**2** 1	21	18 **Lonesome Number One**	59	RCA 7959
5/19/62	**5**	14	19 **I Can Mend Your Broken Heart**	105	RCA 8017
11/17/62	**22**	4	20 So How Come (No One Loves Me).....................		RCA 8085
4/06/63	**12**	10	21 Head Over Heels In Love With You		RCA 8144
8/31/63	**22**	5	22 Anything New Gets Old (Except My Love For You)......................................		RCA 8192
11/28/64+	**23**	16	23 Cause I Believe In You		RCA 8456
7/03/65	**19**	13	24 Again..................................		RCA 8589
10/09/65	**10**	13	25 **Watch Where You're Going**		RCA 8678
1/22/66	**12**	12	26 A Born Loser..................................		RCA 8732
5/07/66	**6**	17	27 **(Yes) I'm Hurting**		RCA 8812
11/05/66+	**8**	17	28 **Funny, Familiar, Forgotten, Feelings**		RCA 8975
6/03/67	**51**	4	29 Lost Highway		RCA 9177
8/26/67	**23**	12	30 All My Love		RCA 9266
3/23/68	**37**	7	31 Ashes Of Love/		
6/01/68	**71**	3	32 Good Morning, Dear..................................		RCA 9460
7/13/68	**12**	14	33 It's A Long, Long Way To Georgia		RCA 9563
11/23/68+	**30**	9	34 Ever Changing Mind..................................		RCA 9663
5/03/69	**28**	9	35 Solitary.................................		RCA 0143
9/06/69	**21**	8	36 I Will Always		RCA 0219
3/14/70	**17**	12	37 Don't Take All Your Loving		Hickory 1559
6/27/70	**16**	13	38 A Perfect Mountain		Hickory 1571
10/10/70	**37**	12	39 Someway		Hickory 1579
1/23/71	**19**	13	40 Guess Away The Blues..................................		Hickory 1588
5/22/71	**29**	11	41 (I Heard That) Lonesome Whistle		Hickory 1598
10/23/71	**5**	17	42 **Country Green**.................................		Hickory 1614
2/19/72	**12**	13	43 Far Far Away .... [R]		Hickory 1623
			new version of Don's 14th hit		
6/10/72	**1** 1	18	44 **Woman (Sensuous Woman)**		Hickory 1638
10/21/72	**11**	13	45 Is This The Best I'm Gonna Feel		Hickory 1651

DEBUT DATE	PEAK POS	WKS CHR	ARTIST — Record Title	POP POS	Label & Number
			DON GIBSON — Continued		
2/17/73	**26**	11	46 If You're Goin' Girl		Hickory 1661
5/26/73	**6**	14	47 **Touch The Morning**....................		Hickory 1671
10/06/73	**30**	11	48 That's What I'll Do		Hickory 306
12/29/73+	**12**	13	49 Snap Your Fingers....................		Hickory 312
5/04/74	**8**	15	50 **One Day At A Time**		Hickory 318
8/31/74	**9**	17	51 **Bring Back Your Love To Me**....................		Hickory 327
1/18/75	**27**	12	52 I'll Sing For You....................		Hickory 338
4/19/75	**24**	11	53 (There She Goes) I Wish Her Well		Hickory 345
8/16/75	**43**	11	54 Don't Stop Loving Me....................		Hickory 353
12/06/75+	**76**	8	55 I Don't Think I'll Ever (Get Over You)....................		Hickory 361
3/13/76	**79**	5	56 You've Got To Stop Hurting Me Darling		Hickory 365
5/29/76	**39**	10	57 Doing My Time		Hickory 372
11/06/76	**23**	12	58 I'm All Wrapped Up In You		ABC/Hick. 54001
3/12/77	**30**	10	59 Fan The Flame, Feed The Fire		ABC/Hick. 54010
7/02/77	**16**	13	60 If You Ever Get To Houston (Look Me Down)		ABC/Hick. 54014
10/22/77	**67**	5	61 When Do We Stop Starting Over....................		ABC/Hick. 54019
2/11/78	**16**	14	62 Starting All Over Again		ABC/Hick. 54024
			#19 pop hit for Mel & Tim in 1972		
6/03/78	**22**	10	63 The Fool....................		ABC/Hick. 54029
			#7 pop hit for Sanford Clark in 1956		
10/07/78	**61**	7	64 Oh, Such A Stranger/		
		7	65 I Love You Because		ABC/Hick. 54036
			#3 pop hit for Al Martino in 1963		
12/23/78+	**26**	12	66 Any Day Now		ABC/Hick. 54039
			#23 pop hit for Chuck Jackson in 1962		
6/09/79	**37**	10	67 Forever One Day At A Time		MCA 41031
3/29/80	**42**	7	68 Sweet Sensuous Sensations		Warner 49193
12/13/80+	**80**	6	69 Love Fires		Warner 49602
			DON GIBSON & SUE THOMPSON:		
8/28/71	**50**	8	70 The Two Of Us Together		Hickory 1607
4/22/72	**71**	3	71 Did You Ever Think		Hickory 1629
8/12/72	**37**	11	72 I Think They Call It Love....................		Hickory 1646
12/23/72	**64**	5	73 Cause I Love You....................		Hickory 1654
3/17/73	**52**	6	74 Go With Me		Hickory 1665
9/15/73	**53**	9	75 Warm Love		Hickory 303
8/10/74	**31**	12	76 Good Old Fashioned Country Love		Hickory 324
7/19/75	**36**	11	77 Oh, How Love Changes....................		Hickory 350
4/03/76	**98**	2	78 Get Ready-Here I Come		Hickory 367
			DOTTIE WEST & DON GIBSON:		
2/22/69	**2**[1]	17	79 **Rings Of Gold**		RCA 9715
7/12/69	**32**	10	80 Sweet Memories....................		RCA 0178
12/13/69+	**7**	13	81 **There's A Story (Goin' 'Round)**....................		RCA 0291
7/18/70	**46**	10	82 Til I Can't Take It Anymore		RCA 9867

TERRY GILKYSON - see THE WEAVERS

VINCE GILL
    Born Vincent Grant Gill on 4/5/57 in Norman, Oklahoma. Guitarist from age 10; vocalist/lead guitarist for his own band at age 15. Worked with Mountain Smoke while still in high school. Moved to Louisville in 1975, played with Bluegrass Alliance. With Pure Prairie League from 1979. With Rodney Crowell and Rosanne Cash in the Cherry Bombs. Session work in Nashville; solo since 1983.

DEBUT DATE	PEAK POS	WKS CHR	ARTIST — Record Title	POP POS	Label & Number
2/11/84	**40**	13	1 Victim Of Life's Circumstances....................		RCA 13731
5/19/84	**38**	11	2 Oh Carolina....................		RCA 13809
9/22/84	**39**	15	3 Turn Me Loose		RCA 13860
3/16/85	**32**	17	4 True Love		RCA 14020
7/13/85	**10**	18	5 **If It Weren't For Him**		RCA 14140
11/23/85+	**9**	25	6 **Oklahoma Borderline**		RCA 14216
6/07/86	**33**	15	7 With You		RCA 14371
5/02/87	**5**	21	8 **Cinderella**		RCA 5131
9/19/87	**16**	16	9 Let's Do Something		RCA 5257
1/30/88	**11**	17	10 Everybody's Sweetheart		RCA 5331
6/04/88	**39**	10	11 The Radio....................		RCA 8301

DEBUT DATE	PEAK POS	WKS CHR		ARTIST — Record Title	POP POS	Label & Number
				STEVE GILLETTE		
				Born in Southern California. Worked as a folk singer/songwriter from the late 60s. First recorded for Vanguard in 1968. Wrote TV and film scores.		
2/23/80	**76**	5	1	Lost The Good Thing		Regency 45002
				MICKEY GILLEY ★★**42**★★		
				Born on 3/9/36 in Ferriday, Louisiana. Worked local clubs, moved to Houston in the early 50s. Recorded for Minor in 1953. Worked in construction for a time. Had own record label, Astro, in 1964. Played at the Nesadel Club in Houston throughout the 60s. Co-owner with Sherwood Cryer of "Gilley's" nightclub since 1971. Club closed in 1989. Gilley and the club were featured in the film "Urban Cowboy". Cousin of Jerry Lee Lewis and Reverend Jimmy Swaggert.		
10/19/68	**68**	6	1	Now I Can Live Again................................		Paula 1200
4/20/74	**1**[1]	16	2	**Room Full Of Roses**	*50*	Playboy 50056
8/10/74	**1**[1]	18	3	**I Overlooked An Orchid**		Playboy 6004
12/07/74+	**1**[1]	12	4	**City Lights**		Playboy 6015
3/15/75	**1**[1]	15	5	**Window Up Above**		Playboy 6031
7/05/75	**11**	13	6	Bouquet Of Roses		Playboy 6041
10/18/75	**32**	9	7	Roll You Like A Wheel		Playboy 6045
				MICKEY GILLEY & BARBI BENTON		
11/22/75+	**7**	13	8	**Overnight Sensation**		Playboy 6055
2/21/76	**1**[1]	16	9	**Don't The Girls All Get Prettier At Closing Time**		Playboy 6063
6/26/76	**1**[1]	14	10	**Bring It On Home To Me**	*101*	Playboy 6075
				#13 pop hit for Sam Cooke in 1962		
10/16/76	**3**	14	11	**Lawdy Miss Clawdy**...............................		Playboy 6089
				rock classic, written by Lloyd Price		
2/19/77	**1**[1]	17	12	**She's Pulling Me Back Again**		Playboy 6100
6/11/77	**4**	14	13	**Honky Tonk Memories**............................		Playboy 5807
11/05/77	**9**	14	14	**Chains Of Love**....................................		Playboy 5818
				#1 R&B hit for Joe Turner in 1951		
3/18/78	**8**	13	15	**The Power Of Positive Drinkin'**		Playboy 5826
7/29/78	**9**	14	16	**Here Comes The Hurt Again**		Epic 50580
11/18/78+	**13**	15	17	The Song We Made Love To		Epic 50631
3/17/79	**10**	14	18	**Just Long Enough To Say Goodbye**..............		Epic 50672
7/21/79	**8**	14	19	**My Silver Lining**		Epic 50740
11/17/79+	**17**	14	20	A Little Getting Used To............................		Epic 50801
5/10/80	**1**[1]	16	21	**True Love Ways**	*66*	Epic 50876
5/31/80	**1**[1]	17	22	**Stand By Me**	*22*	Full Moon 46640
				featured in the film "Urban Cowboy"		
10/18/80	**1**[1]	16	23	**That's All That Matters**	*101*	Epic 50940
2/14/81	**1**[1]	15	24	**A Headache Tomorrow (Or A Heartache Tonight)**		Epic 50973
7/04/81	**1**[1]	16	25	**You Don't Know Me**...............................	*55*	Epic 02172
				#2 pop hit for Ray Charles in 1962		
11/07/81+	**1**[1]	18	26	**Lonely Nights**.....................................		Epic 02578
3/20/82	**3**	18	27	**Tears Of The Lonely**		Epic 02774
7/31/82	**1**[1]	16	28	**Put Your Dreams Away**		Epic 03055
11/13/82+	**1**[1]	18	29	**Talk To Me**	*106*	Epic 03326
				#20 pop hit for Little Willie John in 1958		
4/02/83	**1**[1]	18	30	**Fool For Your Love**		Epic 03783
9/03/83	**5**	21	31	**Your Love Shines Through**		Epic 04018
1/07/84	**2**[1]	20	32	**You've Really Got A Hold On Me**.................		Epic 04269
				#8 pop hit for The Miracles in 1963		
9/01/84	**4**	22	33	**Too Good To Stop Now**		Epic 04563
2/02/85	**10**	17	34	**I'm The One Mama Warned You About**		Epic 04746
5/04/85	**12**	17	35	It Ain't Gonna Worry My Mind......................		Columbia 04860
				RAY CHARLES with MICKEY GILLEY		
8/24/85	**10**	22	36	**You've Got Something On Your Mind**		Epic 05460
12/21/85+	**5**	21	37	**Your Memory Ain't What It Used To Be**.........		Epic 05744
7/26/86	**6**	19	38	**Doo-Wah Days**		Epic 06184
4/04/87	**16**	14	39	Full Grown Fool		Epic 07009
7/16/88	**49**	8	40	I'm Your Puppet		Airborne 10002
				#6 pop hit for James & Bobby Purify in 1966		
10/29/88+	**23**	19	41	She Reminded Me Of You............................		Airborne 10008

DEBUT DATE	PEAK POS	WKS CHR		ARTIST — Record Title	POP POS	Label & Number
				MICKEY GILLEY — Continued		
				CHARLY McCLAIN & MICKEY GILLEY:		
7/16/83	1¹	22	42	**Paradise Tonight**		Epic 04007
2/18/84	5	18	43	**Candy Man**		Epic 04368
				#25 pop hit for Roy Orbison in 1961		
6/16/84	14	17	44	The Right Stuff		Epic 04489
				JIMMIE DALE GILMORE		
				From Austin, Texas.		
8/27/88	72	5	1	White Freight Liner Blues		Hightone 504
				GIRLS NEXT DOOR		
				Group formed as Belle in 1982. Consisted of Doris King (b: 2/13/57, Nashville), first alto; Diane Williams (b: 8/9/59, Hahn AFB, Germany), first soprano; Cindy Nixon (b: 8/3/58, Nashville), second alto; and Tammy Stephens (b: 4/13/61, Arlington, TX), second soprano. Stephens had sung with family gospel group, the Wills Family, from age 6. Married to Jeff Smith of the Hee-Haw TV series. All had worked in different shows at Opryland and as backup vocalists.		
2/01/86	14	21	1	Love Will Get You Through Times With No Money		MTM 72059
6/14/86	8	21	2	**Slow Boat To China**		MTM 72068
11/01/86	26	14	3	Baby I Want It		MTM 72078
2/07/87	28	13	4	Walk Me In The Rain		MTM 72084
7/04/87	43	9	5	What A Girl Next Door Could Do		MTM 72088
10/17/87	57	6	6	Easy To Find		MTM 72095
9/10/88	73	4	7	Love And Other Fairy Tales		MTM 72106
				CHUCK GLASER		
				Born on 2/27/36 in Spalding, Nebraska. Baritone and second oldest of The Glaser Brothers. Suffered a stroke in 1975, but recovered by 1977. Reunited with brothers in 1979.		
1/05/74	81	7	1	Gypsy Queen		MGM 14663
				JIM GLASER ★★195★★		
				Born on 12/16/37 in Spalding, Nebraska. Tenor and youngest of The Glaser Brothers. Co-wrote "Woman, Woman" hit for Gary Puckett & The Union Gap.		
8/31/68	32	8	1	God Help You Woman		RCA 9587
1/04/69	40	10	2	Please Take Me Back		RCA 9696
5/10/69	52	7	3	I'm Not Through Loving You		RCA 0142
10/11/69	53	5	4	Molly		RCA 0231
9/01/73	67	12	5	I See His Love All Over You		MGM 14590
6/15/74	68	8	6	Fool Passin' Through		MGM 14713
12/21/74+	51	12	7	Forgettin' 'Bout You		MGM 14758
5/31/75	88	5	8	One, Two, Three (Never Gonna Fall In Love Again)		MGM 14798
11/15/75	43	10	9	Woman, Woman		MGM 14834
11/06/76	66	10	10	She's Free But She's Not Easy		MCA 40636
7/23/77	88	4	11	Chasin' My Tail		MCA 40742
11/26/77	86	4	12	Don't Let My Love Stand In Your Way		MCA 40813
11/20/82+	16	22	13	When You're Not A Lady		Noble Vision 101
4/02/83	28	13	14	You Got Me Running		Noble Vision 102
8/27/83	17	21	15	The Man In The Mirror		Noble Vision 103
1/28/84	10	24	16	**If I Could Only Dance With You**		Noble Vision 104
6/09/84	1¹	24	17	**You're Gettin' To Me Again**		Noble Vision 105
11/17/84+	16	19	18	Let Me Down Easy		Noble Vision 107
6/29/85	54	8	19	I'll Be Your Fool Tonight		MCA 52619
9/14/85	27	18	20	In Another Minute		MCA 52672
12/28/85+	53	9	21	If I Don't Love You		MCA 52748
4/26/86	40	11	22	The Lights Of Albuquerque		MCA 52808
				TOMPALL GLASER		
				Born on 9/3/33 in Spalding, Nebraska. Lead singer and oldest of The Glaser Brothers. Formed own Outlaw Band, toured with Waylon Jennings and Willie Nelson.		
10/06/73	77	7	1	Bad, Bad, Bad Cowboy		MGM 14622
3/23/74	96	5	2	Texas Law Sez		MGM 14701
9/14/74	63	8	3	Musical Chairs		MGM 14740

115

DEBUT DATE	PEAK POS	WKS CHR	ARTIST — Record Title	POP POS	Label & Number
			TOMPALL GLASER — Continued		
5/24/75	**21**	19	4 Put Another Log On The Fire (Male Chauvinist National Anthem)	*103*	MGM 14800
			shown only as: **TOMPALL**		
4/24/76	**36**	9	5 T For Texas		Polydor 14314
			TOMPALL & His Outlaw Band		
			originally recorded in 1927 as "Blue Yodel" by Jimmie Rodgers		
4/09/77	**45**	9	6 It'll Be Her		ABC 12261
12/03/77	**91**	3	7 It Never Crossed My Mind		ABC 12309
2/25/78	**79**	6	8 Drinking Them Beers		ABC 12329
			TOMPALL & THE GLASER BROTHERS ★★**167**★★		
			Brothers Tompall, Chuck and Jim (see individual bios) performed at local fairs and festivals in their home state of Nebraska. Signed by Marty Robbins to his Robbins label in 1957. Signed with Decca in 1959 as Tompall & The Glaser Brothers; then hooked up with producer Jack Clement and MGM in 1965. Opened own recording studio in Nashville in 1969 which was a hangout for the budding "outlaw" music movement. Trio split-up in 1973 to follow separate careers. Reunited in 1979 and then split-up once again in 1982.		
12/31/66+	**24**	15	1 Gone On The Other Hand.............................		MGM 13611
7/22/67	**27**	16	2 Through The Eyes Of Love..........................		MGM 13754
2/24/68	**42**	9	3 Moods Of Mary		MGM 13880
7/27/68	**36**	10	4 One Of These Days		MGM 13954
3/22/69	**11**	16	5 California Girl (And The Tennessee Square)	*92*	MGM 14036
7/19/69	**24**	11	6 Wicked California.......................................		MGM 14064
12/27/69+	**30**	9	7 Walk Unashamed		MGM 14096
4/11/70	**33**	11	8 All That Keeps Ya Goin'		MGM 14113
10/24/70	**23**	11	9 Gone Girl..		MGM 14169
6/12/71	**22**	9	10 Faded Love		MGM 14249
8/28/71	**7**	15	11 **Rings**		MGM 14291
			#17 pop hit for Cymarron in 1971		
1/15/72	**23**	13	12 Sweet, Love Me Good Woman		MGM 14339
6/17/72	**15**	15	13 Ain't It All Worth Living For		MGM 14390
			with The London Symphony		
1/20/73	**46**	9	14 A Girl Like That		MGM 14462
5/12/73	**47**	8	15 Charlie...		MGM 14516
4/19/80	**43**	8	16 Weight Of My Chains		Elektra 46595
11/08/80	**34**	11	17 Sweet City Woman		Elektra 47056
			#8 pop hit for the Stampeders in 1971		
5/02/81	**2²**	16	18 **Lovin' Her Was Easier (Than Anything I'll Ever Do Again)**............................		Elektra 47134
			#26 pop hit for Kris Kristofferson in 1971		
9/19/81	**17**	14	19 Just One Time		Elektra 47193
			#29 pop hit for Don Gibson in 1960		
2/13/82	**19**	13	20 It'll Be Her		Elektra 47405
6/12/82	**28**	10	21 I Still Love You (After All These Years)		Elektra 47461
11/06/82	**88**	3	22 Maria Consuela..		Elektra 69947
			DARRELL GLENN		
			Born in Waco, Texas. Singing since age 6. Son of Artie Glenn, the writer of "Crying In The Chapel". Darrell's version of this song on Valley Records, recorded when he was 16, was the first. Became a recording engineer and producer. Started IRC, Inc. in 1981, producing gospel artists.		
7/25/53	**4**	13	1 **Crying In The Chapel**.................................	*6*	Valley 105
			Jockey #4 / Juke Box #4 / Best Seller #7		
			HOWDY GLENN		
9/17/77	**62**	6	1 Touch Me		Warner 8447
			written by Willie Nelson		
7/29/78	**72**	5	2 You Mean The World To Me		Warner 8616
			ROY GODFREY		
6/27/60	**8**	15	1 **The Picture**..		J&J 001
12/29/62+	**20**	6	2 Better Times A Comin'		Sims 130
			JEFF GOLDEN		
9/10/88	**91**	2	1 Southern And Proud Of It		MGA 30274
11/26/88	**91**	2	2 This Old World Ain't The Same......................		MGA 3027

DEBUT DATE	PEAK POS	WKS CHR	ARTIST — Record Title	POP POS	Label & Number
			WILLIAM LEE GOLDEN		
			Born on 1/12/35 in Browton, Alabama. Baritone with the Oak Ridge Boys from 1965-87.		
6/21/86	53	7	1 Love Is The Only Way Out		MCA 52819
11/01/86	72	4	2 You Can't Take It With You		MCA 52944
			THE GOLDENS		
			Sons of William Lee Golden: Chris (b: 10/17/62) and Rusty (b: 1/3/59). Chris formerly with Cedar Creek, and both were in the Boys Band (had pop hit in 1982).		
3/05/88	55	6	1 Put Us Together Again		Epic 07716
7/02/88	63	6	2 Sorry Girls..		Epic 07928
			BOBBY GOLDSBORO ★★**186**★★		
			Born on 1/18/41 in Marianna, Florida. Singer/songwriter/guitarist. To Dothan, Alabama in 1956. Toured with Roy Orbison, 1962-64.		
3/09/68	56	5	1 I Just Wasted The Rest		United Art. 50243
			DEL REEVES & BOBBY GOLDSBORO		
3/30/68	1³	15	2●Honey..	1	United Art. 50283
7/13/68	15	11	3 Autumn Of My Life	19	United Art. 50318
10/26/68	37	10	4 The Straight Life..	36	United Art. 50461
3/15/69	49	5	5 Glad She's A Woman	61	United Art. 50497
5/03/69	22	11	6 I'm A Drifter	46	United Art. 50525
8/30/69	15	10	7 Muddy Mississippi Line	53	United Art. 50565
11/01/69	31	10	8 Take A Little Good Will Home		United Art. 50591
			BOBBY GOLDSBORO & DEL REEVES		
12/20/69+	56	7	9 Mornin Mornin..	78	United Art. 50614
5/16/70	71	2	10 Can You Feel It	75	United Art. 50650
1/02/71	7	15	11 **Watching Scotty Grow**	11	United Art. 50727
5/29/71	48	7	12 And I Love You So	83	United Art. 50776
8/04/73	100	2	13 Summer (The First Time)	21	United Art. 251
1/19/74	52	10	14 Marlena..		United Art. 371
5/11/74	62	6	15 I Believe The South Is Gonna Rise Again		United Art. 422
			backing vocals: TSU Chorus		
9/07/74	79	5	16 Hello Summertime......................................		United Art. 529
5/15/76	22	14	17 A Butterfly For Bucky................................	101	United Art. 793
3/19/77	82	5	18 Me And The Elephants	104	Epic 50342
7/09/77	85	4	19 The Cowboy And The Lady		Epic 50413
10/25/80+	17	15	20 Goodbye Marie...		Curb 5400
3/07/81	20	12	21 Alice Doesn't Love Here Anymore....................		Curb 70052
7/04/81	19	14	22 Love Ain't Never Hurt Nobody		Curb 02117
11/14/81	31	11	23 The Round-Up Saloon		Curb 02583
2/20/82	49	9	24 Lucy And The Stranger		Curb 02726
			GARY GOODNIGHT		
			(His real name.) Born in 1954 in Immokalee, Florida.		
11/08/80	90	3	1 I Have To Break The Chains That Bind Me.........		Door Knob 138
1/24/81	91	2	2 Make Me Believe		Door Knob 141
3/21/81	90	3	3 Get Me High, Off This Low		Door Knob 149
5/16/81	75	5	4 Tell Me So...		Door Knob 155
8/08/81	72	5	5 Let Me Fill For You A Fantasy		Door Knob 159
11/28/81	90	3	6 Losin' Myself In You		Door Knob 166
1/16/82	67	7	7 Lady, Lay Down (Lay Down On My Pillow)		Door Knob 169
7/17/82	64	7	8 Bringing Out The Fool In Me		Soundwaves 4675
			C.L. GOODSON		
9/13/75	93	4	1 18 Yellow Roses..		Island 030
			#10 pop hit for Bobby Darin in 1963		
			LLOYD GOODSON		
12/11/76	80	6	1 Jesus Is The Same In California......................		United Art. 891
			MITCH GOODSON		
			Born in Dothan, Alabama. Worked at the Ozark Holiday Inn.		
2/09/80	95	3	1 Draggin' Leather		Partridge 002
4/12/80	70	6	2 Do You Wanna Spend The Night		Partridge 011

DEBUT DATE	PEAK POS	WKS CHR	ARTIST — Record Title	POP POS	Label & Number
			BILL GOODWIN		
			Born on 6/2/30 in Cumberland City, Tennessee. First recorded for Chart.		
5/11/63	17	8	1 Shoes Of A Fool		Vee Jay 501
			LUKE GORDON		
			Born on 4/15/32 in Quincy, Kentucky. Worked on WPAY-Portsmouth, Ohio. Toured with Jimmy Dean in 1953. First recorded for Starday in 1953.		
12/22/58+	13	7	1 Dark Hollow		Island 0640
			ROBERT GORDON		
			Born in Washington, DC in 1947. Own bands, Confidentials and Newports; worked local clubs in the mid-60s. Moved to New York City in the early 70s and recorded with own band, the Tuff Darts. Went solo in 1976.		
3/31/79	99	1	1 It's Only Make Believe.................................		RCA 11471
			#1 pop hit for Conway Twitty in 1958		
6/23/79	98	1	2 Walk On By..		RCA 11608
			#5 pop hit for Leroy Van Dyke in 1961		
			EYDIE GORME		
			Born on 8/16/31 in New York City. Vocalist with big bands of Tommy Tucker and Tex Beneke in the late 40s. Featured on Steve Allen's Tonight Show from 1953. Married Steve Lawrence in December, 1957.		
8/11/73	94	5	1 Take One Step		MGM 14563
			THE GOSDIN BROS.		
			Duo from Woodland, Alabama: Vern and Rex Gosdin.		
10/07/67	37	11	1 Hangin' On..		Bakers. I. 1002
			REX GOSDIN		
			Brother of Vern Gosdin. Died on 5/23/83 at the age of 45.		
7/14/79	94	3	1 We're Making Up For Lost Time.....................		MRC 10589
5/31/80	51	10	2 Just Give Me What You Think Is Fair		Sabre 4520
			REX GOSDIN with TOMMY JENNINGS		
11/08/80	92	2	3 Lovin' You Is Music To My Mind		Grape Vn. 120461
6/11/83	90	3	4 That Old Time Feelin'		Sun 1178
			VERN GOSDIN ★★94★★		
			Born on 8/5/34 in Woodland, Alabama. Joined the Gosdin Family Gospel radio show from Birmingham in the early 50s. Moved to California in 1960 and formed The Golden State Boys with his brother Rex. Out of music from 1962-76.		
10/30/76+	16	15	1 Hangin' On/		
			new version of his hit with The Gosdin Bros.		
3/05/77	9	15	2 **Yesterday's Gone**....................................		Elektra 45353
			harmony vocal on above 2: Emmylou Harris		
6/25/77	7	15	3 **Till The End**		Elektra 45411
10/22/77	17	13	4 Mother Country Music.................................		Elektra 45436
1/21/78	23	11	5 It Started All Over Again		Elektra 45411
5/20/78	9	12	6 **Never My Love**		Elektra 45483
			#2 pop hit for The Association in 1967; harmony vocal: Janie Fricke (also on #4 above)		
10/07/78	13	11	7 Break My Mind		Elektra 45532
3/17/79	16	13	8 You've Got Somebody, I've Got Somebody		Elektra 46021
7/07/79	21	14	9 All I Want And Need Forever.........................		Elektra 46052
11/03/79	57	6	10 Sarah's Eyes		Elektra 46550
1/24/81	28	11	11 Too Long Gone		Ovation 1163
5/16/81	7	17	12 **Dream Of Me**		Ovation 1171
1/16/82	28	15	13 Don't Ever Leave Me Again		AMI 1302
7/10/82	22	13	14 Your Bedroom Eyes....................................		AMI 1307
10/23/82+	10	19	15 **Today My World Slipped Away**		AMI 1310
2/12/83	5	21	16 **If You're Gonna Do Me Wrong (Do It Right)**.....		Compleat 102
2/12/83	49	7	17 Friday Night Feelin'...................................		AMI 1312
6/04/83	5	22	18 **Way Down Deep**		Compleat 108
10/01/83	10	21	19 I Wonder Where We'd Be Tonight		Compleat 115
3/31/84	1¹	25	20 **I Can Tell By The Way You Dance (You're Gonna Love Me Tonight)**........................		Compleat 122
7/21/84	10	20	21 **What Would Your Memories Do**		Compleat 126
12/01/84+	10	20	22 **Slow Burning Memory**		Compleat 135
5/04/85	20	17	23 Dim Lights, Thick Smoke (And Loud, Loud Music)..		Compleat 142
			harmony vocal: Lou Reid		

DEBUT DATE	PEAK POS	WKS CHR	ARTIST — Record Title	POP POS	Label & Number
			VERN GOSDIN — Continued		
8/31/85	**35**	13	24 I Know The Way To You By Heart		Compleat 145
3/22/86	**68**	8	25 It's Only Love Again		Compleat 153
6/07/86	**61**	10	26 Was It Just The Wine...............................		Compleat 155
9/13/86	**51**	8	27 Time Stood Still		Compleat 158
11/07/87+	**4**	23	28 **Do You Believe Me Now**...........................		Columbia 07627
4/09/88	**1**¹	22	29 **Set 'Em Up Joe**.................................		Columbia 07762
8/27/88	**6**	23	30 **Chiseled In Stone**..............................		Columbia 08003
			BILLY GRAMMER		
			Born on 8/28/25 in Benton, Illinois. Worked on WRAL-Arlington, VA in 1947. First recorded for Plaza in 1949. Toured with T. Texas Tyler and Hawkshaw Hawkins in the early 50s. On the Jimmy Dean TV show from 1955; on the Grand Ole Opry since 1959. Designed the Grammer Flat-Top guitar, the first model of which was added to the Country Music Hall Of Fame in 1969. Prominent session musician in Nashville.		
1/05/59	**5**	13	1 **Gotta Travel On** *4*		Monument 400
			based on 19th century tune that originated in the British Isles		
1/19/63	**18**	5	2 I Wanna Go Home		Decca 31449
			Bobby Bare recorded this tune as "Detroit City" in 1963		
1/11/64	**43**	2	3 I'll Leave The Porch Lights A-Burning		Decca 31562
8/27/66	**35**	3	4 Bottles		Epic 10052
12/31/66+	**30**	12	5 The Real Thing		Epic 10103
9/23/67	**48**	11	6 Mabel (You Have Been A Friend To Me)		Rice 5025
8/31/68	**70**	4	7 The Ballad Of John Dillinger		Mercury 72836
10/18/69	**66**	5	8 Jesus Is A Soul Man		Stop 321
			BARRY GRANT		
12/15/79	**91**	5	1 Out With The Boys/		
4/26/80	**89**	3	2 Pretty Poison		CSI 001
			TOM GRANT		
			Born on 8/28/50 in Milwaukee. Sang in trio with his brothers from age 8. Own Country band at age 16. Moved to Nashville in 1977, worked on WSM Waking Crew, The Noon Show, and the Ralph Emery Show. Also see Trinity Lane.		
1/27/79	**40**	8	1 If You Could See You Through My Eyes.............		Republic 036
6/30/79	**63**	5	2 We've Gotta Get Away From It All..................		Republic 043
9/08/79	**16**	11	3 Sail On		Republic 045
			#4 pop hit for the Commodores in 1979		
10/16/82	**76**	4	4 I'm Gonna Love You Right Out Of This World.....		Elektra 69961
8/10/85	**63**	8	5 Everyday People		Bermuda D. 110
			MARGO SMITH & TOM GRANT		
			BILLY GRAY - see WANDA JACKSON		
			CLAUDE GRAY ★★174★★		
			Born on 1/26/32 in Henderson, Texas. Worked as a disc jockey on WDAL-Meridian, Mississippi in the late 50s. Known as "The Tall Texan"; he's 6'5".		
3/21/60	**10**	13	1 **Family Bible**		D 1118
1/09/61	**4**	23	2 **I'll Just Have A Cup Of Coffee (Then I'll Go)** ... *84*		Mercury 71732
6/26/61	**3**	19	3 **My Ears Should Burn (When Fools Are Talked About)**................................		Mercury 71826
1/13/62	**26**	1	4 Let's End It Before It Begins........................		Mercury 71898
10/20/62	**20**	5	5 Daddy Stopped In		Mercury 72001
2/09/63	**18**	6	6 Knock Again, True Love............................		Mercury 72063
3/21/64	**43**	12	7 Eight Years (And Two Children Later)...............		Mercury 72236
7/30/66	**22**	10	8 Mean Old Woman		Columbia 43614
11/26/66+	**9**	18	9 **I Never Had The One I Wanted**		Decca 32039
6/03/67	**45**	9	10 Because Of Him/		
6/24/67	**67**	3	11 If I Ever Need A Lady (I'll Call You)		Decca 32122
9/23/67	**12**	14	12 How Fast Them Trucks Can Go......................		Decca 32180
5/18/68	**31**	12	13 Night Life		Decca 32312
11/09/68	**68**	2	14 The Love Of A Woman		Decca 32393
5/03/69	**41**	11	15 Don't Give Me A Chance		Decca 32456
10/25/69	**34**	10	16 Take Off Time		Decca 32566
4/11/70	**54**	6	17 The Cleanest Man In Cincinnati		Decca 32648
7/18/70	**40**	8	18 Everything Will Be Alright		Decca 32697
3/27/71	**41**	9	19 Angel..		Decca 32786

DEBUT DATE	PEAK POS	WKS CHR	ARTIST — Record Title	POP POS	Label & Number
			CLAUDE GRAY — Continued		
9/02/72	66	7	20 What Every Woman Wants To Hear		Million 18
1/20/73	58	8	21 Woman Ease My Mind		Million 31
10/16/76	88	5	22 Rockin' My Memories		Granny 10001
1/22/77	92	4	23 We Fell In Love That Way		Granny 10002
6/03/78	68	7	24 If I Ever Need A Lady .... [R]		Granny 10006
1/13/79	78	6	25 I Never Had The One I Wanted .... [R]		Granny 10007
2/06/82	68	6	26 Let's Go All The Way		Granny 1009
			CLAUDE GRAY & NORMA JEAN		
2/22/86	77	4	27 Sweet Caroline		Country I. 208
			#4 pop hit for Neil Diamond in 1969		
			DOBIE GRAY		
			Born Leonard Victor Ainsworth on 7/26/42 in Brookshire, Texas. Moved to Los Angeles in 1960. Worked as an actor on Broadway, and in the L.A. production of "Hair". Lead singer of Pollution in 1971.		
3/22/86	35	13	1 That's One To Grow On		Capitol 5562
7/12/86	42	9	2 The Dark Side Of Town		Capitol 5596
11/15/86	67	9	3 From Where I Stand		Capitol 5647
11/21/87	82	2	4 Take It Real Easy		Capitol 44087
			JAN GRAY		
			Born in Oneida, Kentucky. Worked on WPFB-Middletown, Ohio at age 4.		
11/15/80	80	3	1 No Love At All		Paid 106
			#16 pop hit for B.J. Thomas in 1971		
8/21/82	85	3	2 There I Go Dreamin' Again		Jamex 006
11/06/82	89	3	3 Closer To Crazy		Jamex 008
6/18/83	49	11	4 No Fair Fallin' In Love		Jamex 010
10/15/83	55	7	5 Before We Knew It		Jamex 011
1/21/84	51	9	6 Bad Night For Good Girls		Jamex 012
5/10/86	64	6	7 Cross My Heart		Cypress 8510
			MARK GRAY		
			Singer/songwriter born in Mississippi. Played piano from age 12. Own gospel group at age 19. Worked in the office for the Oak Ridge Boys. Worked as a writer for Troy Seals. One-time member of Exile.		
5/28/83	25	20	1 It Ain't Real (If It Ain't You)		Columbia 03893
10/15/83+	18	18	2 Wounded Hearts		Columbia 04137
1/28/84	10	22	3 **Left Side Of The Bed**		Columbia 04324
5/26/84	9	23	4 **If All The Magic Is Gone**		Columbia 04464
9/29/84	9	21	5 **Diamond In The Dust**		Columbia 04610
2/23/85	6	22	6 **Sometimes When We Touch**		Columbia 04782
			MARK GRAY & TAMMY WYNETTE		
			#3 pop hit for Dan Hill in 1978		
7/27/85	43	13	7 Smooth Sailing (Rock In The Road)		Columbia 05403
11/23/85+	7	21	8 **Please Be Love**		Columbia 05695
4/12/86	14	17	9 Back When Love Was Enough		Columbia 05857
5/28/88	69	5	10 Song In My Heart		615 1014
			MARK GRAY & BOBBI LACE		
12/17/88+	70	5	11 It's Gonna Be Love		615 1016
			MARK GRAY & BOBBI LACE		
			JACK GRAYSON		
4/14/79	92	3	1 I Ain't Never Been To Heaven (But I've Spent The Night With You)		Churchill 7729
12/22/79+	65	8	2 Tonight I'm Feelin' You (All Over Again)		Hitbound 4501
6/14/80	70	6	3 The Stores Are Full Of Roses		Hitbound 4503
8/30/80	59	7	4 The Devil Stands Only Five Foot Five		Hitbound 4504
12/13/80+	37	14	5 A Loser's Night Out		Koala 328
4/04/81	56	6	6 Magic Eyes		Koala 331
7/25/81	45	9	7 My Beginning Was You		Koala 334
12/19/81+	18	17	8 When A Man Loves A Woman		Koala 340
			above 4: JACK GRAYSON & BLACKJACK		
			#1 pop hit for Percy Sledge in 1966		
5/22/82	38	11	9 Tonight I'm Feeling You (All Over Again) .... [R]		Joe-Wes 81000
8/14/82+	68	6	10 I Ain't Giving Up On Her Yet		Joe-Wes 81006

DEBUT DATE	PEAK POS	WKS CHR	ARTIST — Record Title	POP POS	Label & Number
			JACK GRAYSON — Continued		
1/14/84	**77**	4	11 Lean On Me...		AMI 1318
			#1 pop hit for Bill Withers in 1972		
			KIM GRAYSON		
			Singer/actress born in Dallas; raised in Plano, Texas. Appeared in the 1985 film "Target", the TV show "Dallas", and other CBS-TV movies.		
8/01/87	**74**	3	1 Love's Slippin' Up On Me		Soundwaves 4787
12/05/87	**62**	7	2 If You Only Knew		Soundwaves 4795
4/16/88	**65**	6	3 Missin' Texas		Soundwaves 4800
			THE GREEN RIVER BOYS - see GLEN CAMPBELL		
			BILL GREEN		
			Born in Athens, Alabama. Started performing at age 43, worked with local bands. First recorded for Silver Stirrups in 1975.		
9/18/76	**94**	3	1 Texas On A Saturday Night...........................		Phono 2629
12/09/78	**98**	1	2 Fool Such As I		NSD 11
			#2 pop hit for Elvis Presley in 1959		
			JERRY GREEN		
10/15/77	**96**	1	1 I Know The Feeling		Concorde 152
12/10/77	**96**	4	2 Genuine Texas Good Guy.............................		Concorde 154
			LLOYD GREEN		
			Born on 10/4/37 in Mobile, Alabama. Leading session steel guitarist. Attended the University of Mississippi from 1954-56. Moved to Nashville in 1956 and worked as a session musician. Toured with Faron Young from 1956-58 and recorded with George Jones. Featured on "Sweetheart Of The Rodeo" LP by the Byrds.		
2/10/73	**36**	10	1 I Can See Clearly Now................................ [I]		Monument 8562
			#1 pop hit for Johnny Nash in 1972		
6/30/73	**73**	3	2 Here Comes The Sun .... [I]		Monument 8574
			#16 pop hit for Richie Havens in 1971		
12/25/76+	**92**	6	3 You And Me		October 1002
			JACK GREENE ★★**98**★★		
			Born on 1/7/30 in Maryville, Tennessee. Worked with the Cherokee Trio in Atlanta in the 40s. On radio with Clyde Grubbs in Maryville and worked as a drummer with the Rhythm Ranch Boys in the early 50s. Played with the Peachtree Cowboys in the mid-50s. Joined Ernest Tubb in 1962. Own band, the Jolly Green Giants, later named the Renegades, since 1965. Joined the Grand Ole Opry in 1967. Known as the "Jolly Green Giant".		
12/25/65+	**37**	7	1 Ever Since My Baby Went Away......................		Decca 31856
10/22/66	**1** 7	23	2 **There Goes My Everything**...........................	65	Decca 32023
4/22/67	**1** 5	20	3 **All The Time/**	103	
5/13/67	**63**	5	4 Wanting You But Never Having You		Decca 32123
9/30/67	**2** 4	20	5 **What Locks The Door**................................		Decca 32190
2/17/68	**1** 1	15	6 **You Are My Treasure**		Decca 32261
7/20/68	**4**	16	7 **Love Takes Care Of Me**..............................		Decca 32352
12/14/68+	**1** 2	17	8 **Until My Dreams Come True**		Decca 32423
5/10/69	**1** 2	18	9 **Statue Of A Fool**......................................		Decca 32490
10/04/69	**4**	14	10 **Back In The Arms Of Love/**		
10/25/69	**66**	2	11 The Key That Fits Her Door		Decca 32558
3/14/70	**16**	11	12 Lord Is That Me		Decca 32631
7/18/70	**14**	14	13 The Whole World Comes To Me/		
		14	14 If This Is Love		Decca 32699
11/14/70	**15**	12	15 Something Unseen/		
11/14/70	**45**	12	16 What's The Use		Decca 32755
4/10/71	**13**	14	17 There's A Whole Lot About A Woman (A Man Don't Know)/		
		13	18 Makin' Up His Mind		Decca 32823
9/04/71	**26**	12	19 Hanging Over Me		Decca 32863
3/25/72	**31**	11	20 If You Ever Need My Love		Decca 32939
12/09/72+	**17**	12	21 Satisfaction..		Decca 33008
4/14/73	**40**	12	22 The Fool I've Been Today		MCA 40035
8/18/73	**11**	16	23 I Need Somebody Bad		MCA 40108
2/09/74	**13**	13	24 It's Time To Cross That Bridge		MCA 40179
7/27/74	**66**	9	25 Sing For The Good Times............................		MCA 40263
11/22/75	**88**	5	26 He Little Thing'd Her Out Of My Arms..............		MCA 40481

DEBUT DATE	PEAK POS	WKS CHR		ARTIST — Record Title	POP POS	Label & Number
				JACK GREENE — Continued		
1/05/80	**28**	11	27	Yours For The Taking		Frontline 704
5/17/80	**48**	7	28	The Rock I'm Leaning On		Frontline 706
11/01/80	**63**	6	29	Devil's Den		Firstline 709
3/05/83	**98**	2	30	The Jukebox Never Plays Home Sweet Home		EMH 0016
6/11/83	**92**	3	31	From Cotton To Satin		EMH 0019
7/14/84	**93**	3	32	Dying To Believe..		EMH 0031
11/17/84	**81**	5	33	If It's Love (Then Bet It All)........................		EMH 0035
				JACK GREENE & JEANNIE SEELY:		
11/15/69+	**2**²	16	34	**Wish I Didn't Have To Miss You**		Decca 32580
12/11/71+	**15**	13	35	**Much Oblige**		Decca 32898
8/12/72	**19**	12	36	What In The World Has Gone Wrong With Our Love...		Decca 32991

LORNE GREENE
Born on 2/12/14 in Ottawa, Canada. Died on 9/11/87 of cardiac arrest. Studied acting, appeared in films "The Silver Chalice" and "Tight Spot"; starred in the TV series "Bonanza" and "Battlestar Galactica".

DEBUT DATE	PEAK POS	WKS CHR		ARTIST — Record Title	POP POS	Label & Number
12/05/64	**21**	10	1	Ringo .... [S]	*1*	RCA 8444
8/13/66	**50**	2	2	Waco .... [S]		RCA 8901
				from the film of the same title		

LEE GREENWOOD　★★**96**★★
Born on 10/27/42 in Los Angeles; raised in Sacramento. Multi-instrumentalist. Own band, the Moonbeams, while in high school. Toured with Del Reeves and own band, the Apollos, in the early 60s. Worked in Las Vegas as a sax and piano player. With Felix Cavaliere (later of the Young Rascals) in the Scotties. Worked as a dealer in Vegas casinos until 1981. Has own band, Trick.

DEBUT DATE	PEAK POS	WKS CHR		ARTIST — Record Title	POP POS	Label & Number
9/19/81+	**17**	22	1	It Turns Me Inside Out		MCA 51159
3/27/82	**5**	18	2	Ring On Her Finger, Time On Her Hands		MCA 52026
8/07/82	**7**	17	3	She's Lying		MCA 52087
12/11/82+	**7**	21	4	Ain't No Trick (It Takes Magic).....................		MCA 52150
4/09/83	**6**	20	5	I.O.U.	53	MCA 52199
8/20/83	**1**¹	22	6	Somebody's Gonna Love You.........................	96	MCA 52257
12/17/83+	**1**¹	19	7	Going, Going, Gone		MCA 52322
5/26/84	**7**	17	8	God Bless The USA		MCA 52386
7/21/84	**3**	20	9	To Me		MCA 52415
				BARBARA MANDRELL/LEE GREENWOOD		
8/18/84	**3**	25	10	Fool's Gold..		MCA 52426
12/22/84+	**9**	19	11	You've Got A Good Love Comin'		MCA 52509
2/02/85	**19**	15	12	It Should Have Been Love By Now..................		MCA 52525
				BARBARA MANDRELL/LEE GREENWOOD		
4/20/85	**1**¹	20	13	Dixie Road..		MCA 52564
8/31/85	**1**¹	23	14	I Don't Mind The Thorns (If You're The Rose) .		MCA 52656
12/28/85+	**1**¹	20	15	Don't Underestimate My Love For You		MCA 52741
4/19/86	**1**¹	22	16	Hearts Aren't Made To Break (They're Made To Love)		MCA 52807
8/09/86	**10**	18	17	Didn't We		MCA 52896
11/29/86+	**1**¹	24	18	Mornin' Ride...		MCA 52984
5/09/87	**5**	17	19	Someone		MCA 53096
8/29/87	**9**	19	20	If There's Any Justice.................................		MCA 53156
12/26/87+	**5**	22	21	Touch And Go Crazy		MCA 53234
4/30/88	**12**	18	22	I Still Believe..		MCA 53312
8/20/88	**20**	17	23	You Can't Fall In Love When You're Cryin'		MCA 53386

TERRY GREGORY
Born Teresa Gregory Burdine in Takoma Park, Maryland. Moved to Berkeley Springs, West Virginia at age 16. Made professional debut at age 18. Toured with the rock band Fire And Ice. Moved to Hollywood in the late 70s.

DEBUT DATE	PEAK POS	WKS CHR		ARTIST — Record Title	POP POS	Label & Number
5/02/81	**16**	15	1	Just Like Me		Handshake 70071
9/05/81	**59**	6	2	Cinderella..		Handshake 02442
11/14/81+	**30**	13	3	I Can't Say Goodbye To You..........................		Handshake 02563
3/13/82	**44**	11	4	I Never Knew The Devil's Eyes Were Blue..........		Handshake 02736
6/26/82	**48**	7	5	I'm Takin' A Heart Break		Handshake 02959
4/21/84	**75**	5	6	Cowgirl In A Coupe deVille		Scotti Br. 04410
2/02/85	**66**	7	7	Pardon Me, But This Heart's Taken		Scotti Br. 04735

DEBUT DATE	PEAK POS	WKS CHR		ARTIST — Record Title	POP POS	Label & Number
				RAY GRIFF		
				Born John Ray Griff on 4/22/40 in Vancouver; raised in Winfield, Alberta. Guitarist/ pianist/drummer. Played drums in the Winfield Amateurs from age 6. Appeared on Calgary TV with own band, the Blue Echoes. Wrote "Mr. Moonlight" for Johnny Horton; "Where Do I Go" for Jim Reeves. Moved to Nashville in 1964. Own TV series on CBC.		
12/23/67+	49	9	1	Your Lily White Hands		MGM 13855
4/27/68	50	7	2	The Sugar From My Candy		Dot 17082
10/03/70	26	9	3	Patches		Royal Amer. 19
				#4 pop hit for Clarence Carter in 1970		
11/20/71+	14	15	4	The Mornin' After Baby Let Me Down		Royal Amer. 46
12/02/72	62	6	5	It Rains Just The Same In Missouri		Dot 17440
4/28/73	66	3	6	A Song For Everyone		Dot 17456
8/25/73	46	10	7	What Got To You/		
11/24/73+	42	11	8	Darlin'		Dot 17471
5/11/74	65	7	9	That Doesn't Mean (I Don't Love My God)		Dot 17501
10/12/74	91	2	10	The Hill		Dot 17519
3/08/75	65	9	11	If That's What It Takes		ABC/Dot 17542
9/06/75	16	16	12	You Ring My Bell		Capitol 4126
1/24/76	11	15	13	If I Let Her Come In		Capitol 4208
5/22/76	40	10	14	I Love The Way That You Love Me		Capitol 4266
8/28/76	24	12	15	That's What I Get (For Doin' My Own Thinkin')		Capitol 4320
12/18/76+	27	11	16	The Last Of The Winfield Amateurs/		
		6	17	You Put The Bounce Back Into My Step		Capitol 4368
4/23/77	28	10	18	A Passing Thing		Capitol 4415
7/30/77	69	5	19	A Cold Day In July		Capitol 4446
10/22/77	52	9	20	Raymond's Place		Capitol 4492
11/07/81	87	3	21	Draw Me A Line		Vision 440
7/03/82	95	2	22	Things That Songs Are Made Of		Vision 442
5/07/83	86	3	23	If Tomorrow Never Comes		RCA 50722
4/19/86	71	5	24	What My Woman Does To Me		RCA 50846
				GLENDA GRIFFITH		
1/07/78	96	4	1	Don't Worry ('Bout Me)		Ariola Am. 7680
				#3 pop hit for Marty Robbins in 1961		
				NANCI GRIFFITH		
				Folk singer born in Austin, Texas. First recorded in 1977 for B.F. Deal Records. Wrote "Love At The Five And Dime", hit for Kathy Mattea.		
6/21/86	85	3	1	Once In A Very Blue Moon		Philo 1096
1/17/87	36	14	2	Lone Star State Of Mind		MCA 53008
4/25/87	57	7	3	Trouble In The Fields		MCA 53082
8/01/87	64	6	4	Cold Hearts/Closed Minds		MCA 53147
12/05/87	58	7	5	Never Mind		MCA 53184
4/09/88	37	13	6	I Knew Love		MCA 53306
7/23/88	64	5	7	Anyone Can Be Somebody's Fool		MCA 53374
				LARRY GROCE		
				Born on 4/22/48 in Dallas. Pop-folk singer/songwriter. Wrote children's songs for Walt Disney Records.		
1/31/76	61	8	1	Junk Food Junkie [N]	9	Warner 8165
				SHERRY GROOMS		
				Born in Caruthersville, Missouri; raised in West Memphis.		
10/15/77	97	1	1	The King Of Country Music Meets The Queen Of Rock & Roll		Elektra 45430
				EVEN STEVENS & SHERRY GROOMS		
9/09/78	87	4	2	Me		Parachute 514
				EDGEL GROVES		
5/09/81	42	9	1	Footprints In The Sand [S]		Silver Star 20
				backed by a chorus, Edgel recites a religious message		
				BONNIE GUITAR		
				Born Bonnie Buckingham on 3/25/24 in Seattle. Own group in the early 50s. Worked as session guitarist in Los Angeles in the mid-50s. Owner of Dolphin/Dolton Records in Seattle in 1958. Director of Country music A&R for Dot and ABC-Paramount.		
6/10/57	14	1	1	Dark Moon	6	Dot 15550
				Jockey #14		

DEBUT DATE	PEAK POS	WKS CHR	ARTIST — Record Title	POP POS	Label & Number
			BONNIE GUITAR — Continued		
11/11/57	**15**	1	2 Mister Fire Eyes................................	*71*	Dot 15612
			Jockey #15		
3/05/66	**9**	16	3 **I'm Living In Two Worlds**	*99*	Dot 16811
7/23/66	**14**	9	4 Get Your Lie The Way You Want It..............		Dot 16872
10/15/66	**24**	10	5 The Tallest Tree		Dot 16919
2/25/67	**64**	5	6 The Kickin' Tree		Dot 16987
4/29/67	**33**	11	7 You Can Steal Me		Dot 17007
8/12/67	**4**	16	8 **A Woman In Love**...........................		Dot 17029
12/23/67+	**13**	16	9 Stop The Sun		Dot 17057
6/08/68	**10**	14	10 **I Believe In Love**		Dot 17097
9/28/68	**41**	10	11 Leaves Are The Tears Of Autumn		Dot 17150
7/05/69	**55**	5	12 A Truer Love You'll Never Find (Than Mine).......		Paramount 0004
			BONNIE & BUDDY (Killen)		
8/23/69	**36**	7	13 That See Me Later Look		Dot 17276
10/24/70	**70**	3	14 Allegheny		Paramount 0045
8/05/72	**54**	7	15 Happy Everything		Columbia 45643
12/14/74+	**95**	6	16 From This Moment On		MCA 40306
4/19/80	**92**	3	17 Honey On The Moon		4 Star 1003
			J.W. GUNN		
11/27/82	**87**	3	1 Love Me Today, Love Me Forever		Primero 1013
			RANDY GURLEY		
			Born Eleanor Rand Gurley on 11/29/53 in Salem, Massachusetts; raised in Burbank, California. Sang with a bluegrass band at age 14, later joined "Up With People" troupe. Worked in group, Country Heritage, in Nashville.		
9/02/78	**77**	5	1 True Love Ways...............................		ABC 12392
			written by Buddy Holly		
7/14/79	**97**	2	2 Don't Treat Me Like A Stranger		RCA 11611
10/27/79	**92**	3	3 If I Ever...................................		RCA 11726
			JACK GUTHRIE		
			Born Leon Guthrie on 11/13/15 in Olive, Oklahoma; died on 1/15/48. Moved to California in 1932 and worked on radio stations in Marysville and Chico. He was in the service in the South Pacific when "Oklahoma Hills" became a hit. Cousin of Woody Guthrie.		
7/07/45	**1** [6]	19	1 **Oklahoma Hills/**		
7/21/45	**5**	2	2 **I'm A Brandin' My Darlin' With My Heart**		Capitol 201
3/01/47	**3**	3	3 **Oakie Boogie**		Capitol 341
			JACK GUTHRIE & HIS OKLAHOMANS		
			GUY & RALNA		
			Guy Hovis and Ralna English. Regulars on TV's "Lawrence Welk Show" from 1970-82.		
7/26/75	**95**	3	1 We've Got It All Together Now........................		Ranwood 1029

H

DEBUT DATE	PEAK POS	WKS CHR	ARTIST — Record Title	POP POS	Label & Number
			DURWOOD HADDOCK		
			Born on 8/16/34 in Lamesco, Texas. Master fiddler/singer/songwriter. Former disc jockey at KERB-Kermit, Texas.		
11/23/74+	**67**	8	1 Angel In An Apron		Caprice 2004
3/12/77	**98**	1	2 Low Down Time		Eagle Int. 1137
6/17/78	**75**	9	3 The Perfect Love Song		Country I. 132
11/04/78	**87**	4	4 Everynight Sensation......................		Eagle Int. 1148
5/12/79	**96**	2	5 Low Down Time .... [R]		Country I. 140
10/25/80	**89**	3	6 It Sure Looks Good On You.................		Eagle Int. 1161
			THE HAGERS		
			Twin brothers Jim and John, born in Chicago. Long time favorites on TV's "Hee-Haw".		
11/08/69	**41**	8	1 Gotta Get To Oklahoma ('Cause California's Gettin' To Me)		Capitol 2647
4/04/70	**74**	2	2 Loneliness Without You		Capitol 2740
5/23/70	**50**	6	3 Goin' Home To Your Mother		Capitol 2803
9/12/70	**59**	8	4 Silver Wings...............................		Capitol 2887
			written by Merle Haggard		

DEBUT DATE	PEAK POS	WKS CHR	ARTIST — Record Title	POP POS	Label & Number
			THE HAGERS — Continued		
1/23/71	**47**	6	5 I'm Miles Away		Capitol 3012
			MARTY HAGGARD		
			Son of Merle Haggard, born on 6/18/58; named after Marty Robbins. Toured with Merle in the early 70s. Worked with sister Dana and The Driftwood Band. Worked outside of music for a time, then joined the Strangers.		
3/07/81	**85**	3	1 Charleston Cotton Mill		Dimension 1016
9/13/86	**62**	7	2 Talkin' Blue Eyes..		MTM 72073
3/21/87	**75**	6	3 Weekend Cowboys...		MTM 72085
3/26/88	**57**	8	4 Trains Make Me Lonesome		MTM 72103
6/25/88	**70**	5	5 Now You See 'Em, Now You Don't		MTM 72107
			MERLE HAGGARD ★★**4**★★		
			Born on 4/6/37 in Bakersfield, California. Served nearly three years in San Quentin prison for burglary, from 1957-60. Granted full pardon by Governor Ronald Reagan on 3/14/72. Worked in local clubs from 1960. First recorded for Tally in 1962. Signed to Capitol Records in 1965 and formed his backing band, The Strangers. In the films "Bronco Billy", "Huckleberry Finn", "Killers Three" and "Doc Elliot". Appeared on "The Waltons" and "Centennial" TV series. Formerly married to country singers Bonnie Owens and Leona Williams. Wrote the majority of his hits. CMA award: Entertainer of the Year - 1970.		
12/28/63+	**19**	3	1 Sing A Sad Song		Tally 155
6/06/64	**45**	5	2 Sam Hill		Tally 178
1/02/65	**10**	22	3 **(My Friends Are Gonna Be) Strangers**		Tally 179
			MERLE HAGGARD & THE STRANGERS:		
9/18/65	**42**	4	4 I'm Gonna Break Every Heart I Can.................		Capitol 5460
4/09/66	**5**	27	5 **Swinging Doors**		Capitol 5600
8/27/66	**3**	20	6 **The Bottle Let Me Down**		Capitol 5704
12/17/66+	**1**¹	18	7 **The Fugitive**/		
			later titled as "I'm A Lonesome Fugitive"		
12/31/66+	**32**	11	8 Someone Told My Story		Capitol 5803
3/18/67	**2**²	18	9 **I Threw Away The Rose**.............................		Capitol 5844
7/08/67	**1**¹	16	10 **Branded Man**		Capitol 5931
11/18/67+	**1**²	20	11 **Sing Me Back Home**		Capitol 2017
3/09/68	**1**²	15	12 **The Legend Of Bonnie And Clyde**		Capitol 2123
			flip side is the classic "I Started Loving You Again"		
7/27/68	**1**⁴	15	13 **Mama Tried**		Capitol 2219
			ballad from the film "Killers Three"		
11/09/68+	**3**	16	14 **I Take A Lot Of Pride In What I Am**..............		Capitol 2289
2/22/69	**1**¹	17	15 **Hungry Eyes**		Capitol 2383
7/05/69	**1**¹	15	16 **Workin' Man Blues**.....................................		Capitol 2503
10/11/69	**1**⁴	16	17 **Okie From Muskogee**...................................	41	Capitol 2626
2/07/70	**1**³	14	18 **The Fightin' Side Of Me**	92	Capitol 2719
4/18/70	**9**	13	19 **Street Singer** ....[I]	124	Capitol 2778
6/13/70	**3**	14	20 **Jesus, Take A Hold**....................................	107	Capitol 2838
10/10/70	**3**	17	21 **I Can't Be Myself**/	106	
		16	22 Sidewalks Of Chicago....................................		Capitol 2891
2/20/71	**3**	13	23 **Soldier's Last Letter**................................	90	Capitol 3024
7/03/71	**2**²	15	24 **Someday We'll Look Back**	119	Capitol 3112
10/16/71	**1**²	14	25 **Daddy Frank (The Guitar Man)**		Capitol 3198
12/04/71+	**1**³	16	26 **Carolyn**	58	Capitol 3222
3/25/72	**1**²	15	27 **Grandma Harp**/		
		10	28 Turnin' Off A Memory.......................................		Capitol 3294
9/02/72	**1**¹	14	29 **It's Not Love (But It's Not Bad)**		Capitol 3419
12/09/72+	**1**¹	14	30 **I Wonder If They Ever Think Of Me**		Capitol 3488
3/10/73	**3**	14	31 **The Emptiest Arms In The World**		Capitol 3552
6/30/73	**1**²	16	32 **Everybody's Had The Blues**	62	Capitol 3641
10/27/73	**1**⁴	17	33 **If We Make It Through December**	28	Capitol 3746
3/02/74	**1**¹	15	34 **Things Aren't Funny Anymore**....................		Capitol 3830
6/29/74	**1**¹	14	35 **Old Man From The Mountain**		Capitol 3900
11/09/74+	**1**¹	15	36 **Kentucky Gambler**.....................................		Capitol 3974
			written by Dolly Parton		
2/15/75	**1**²	14	37 **Always Wanting You**		Capitol 4027
5/24/75	**1**¹	15	38 **Movin' On**		Capitol 4085
			theme from the NBC-TV series of the same title		

DEBUT DATE	PEAK POS	WKS CHR		ARTIST — Record Title	POP POS	Label & Number
				MERLE HAGGARD — Continued		
10/04/75	**1**¹	15	39	It's All In The Movies................................		Capitol 4141
1/17/76	**1**¹	14	40	**The Roots Of My Raising**		Capitol 4204
5/22/76	**10**	11	41	**Here Comes The Freedom Train**		Capitol 4267
9/11/76	**1**¹	13	42	**Cherokee Maiden/**		
				tune originally written and recorded in 1941 by Bob Wills		
		13	43	What Have You Got Planned Tonight Diana		Capitol 4326
				MERLE HAGGARD:		
4/02/77	**2**²	14	44	**If We're Not Back In Love By Monday**		MCA 40700
7/02/77	**2**²	14	45	**Ramblin' Fever/**		
		12	46	When My Blue Moon Turns To Gold Again.......		MCA 40743
				#19 pop hit for Elvis Presley in 1956		
9/03/77	**16**	13	47	A Working Man Can't Get Nowhere Today		Capitol 4477
10/08/77	**4**	15	48	**From Graceland To The Promised Land**	58	MCA 40804
				an Elvis Presley tribute; vocal backing: Jordanaires		
1/14/78	**12**	12	49	Running Kind/		
		9	50	Making Believe		Capitol 4525
3/18/78	**2**²	16	51	**I'm Always On A Mountain When I Fall**.........		MCA 40869
8/12/78	**2**³	13	52	**It's Been A Great Afternoon/**		
		7	53	Love Me When You Can		MCA 40936
10/28/78	**82**	4	54	The Way It Was In '51..................................		Capitol 4636
				originally released as the flip side of #40 above		
4/14/79	**4**	13	55	**Red Bandana/**		
		13	56	I Must Have Done Something Bad...................		MCA 41007
9/15/79	**4**	13	57	**My Own Kind Of Hat/**		
		13	58	Heaven Was A Drink Of Wine.......................		MCA 41112
3/15/80	**2**²	14	59	**The Way I Am**		MCA 41200
7/05/80	**3**	15	60	**Misery And Gin**		MCA 41255
				above 2: from the Clint Eastwood film "Bronco Billy"		
10/25/80+	**1**¹	17	61	**I Think I'll Just Stay Here And Drink**		MCA 51014
2/14/81	**9**	14	62	**Leonard**...		MCA 51048
				an ode of thanks to songwriter Leonard "Tommy Collins" Sipes		
6/06/81	**4**	16	63	**Rainbow Stew**......................................		MCA 51120
9/19/81	**1**¹	17	64	**My Favorite Memory**		Epic 02504
1/16/82	**1**¹	19	65	**Big City**..		Epic 02686
				harmony vocal: Leona Williams		
4/17/82	**49**	10	66	Dealing With The Devil		MCA 52020
5/15/82	**2**²	18	67	**Are The Good Times Really Over (I Wish A Buck Was Still Silver)**		Epic 02894
10/23/82+	**1**¹	21	68	**Going Where The Lonely Go**		Epic 03315
3/12/83	**1**¹	18	69	**You Take Me For Granted**		Epic 03723
7/16/83	**3**	20	70	**What Am I Gonna Do (With The Rest Of My Life)**...		Epic 04006
10/08/83	**54**	10	71	It's All In The Game		MCA 52276
				#1 pop hit for Tommy Edwards in 1958		
11/19/83+	**1**¹	21	72	**That's The Way Love Goes**........................		Epic 04226
3/24/84	**1**¹	21	73	**Someday When Things Are Good**		Epic 04402
7/14/84	**1**¹	18	74	**Let's Chase Each Other Around The Room**		Epic 04512
3/16/85	**1**¹	19	75	**Natural High**.......................................		Epic 04830
6/15/85	**55**	10	76	Make-Up And Faded Blue Jeans....................		MCA 52595
7/06/85	**10**	17	77	**Kern River**..		Epic 05426
10/05/85	**36**	15	78	Amber Waves Of Grain...............................		Epic 05659
12/14/85	**60**	11	79	American Waltz.......................................		Epic 05734
1/25/86	**5**	20	80	**I Had A Beautiful Time**		Epic 05782
5/31/86	**9**	23	81	**A Friend In California**.............................		Epic 06097
10/18/86	**21**	15	82	Out Among The Stars		Epic 06344
4/18/87	**58**	8	83	Almost Persuaded		Epic 07036
11/21/87+	**1**¹	22	84	**Twinkle, Twinkle Lucky Star**.......................		Epic 07631
3/19/88	**9**	19	85	**Chill Factor**		Epic 07754
7/09/88	**22**	18	86	We Never Touch At All................................		Epic 07944
11/19/88+	**23**	17	87	You Babe..		Epic 08111

DEBUT DATE	PEAK POS	WKS CHR		ARTIST — Record Title	POP POS	Label & Number
				MERLE HAGGARD — Continued		
				MERLE HAGGARD DUOS with:		
				CLINT EASTWOOD:		
5/17/80	**1**¹	16	88	**Bar Room Buddies**		Elektra 46634
				JANIE FRICKE:		
10/27/84+	**1**¹	22	89	**A Place To Fall Apart**		Epic 04663
				GEORGE JONES:		
8/07/82	**1**¹	15	90	**Yesterday's Wine**....................................		Epic 03072
12/04/82+	**10**	19	91	**C.C. Waterback**		Epic 03405
				WILLIE NELSON:		
1/15/83	**6**	18	92	**Reasons To Quit**		Epic 03494
4/30/83	**1**¹	21	93	**Pancho And Lefty**		Epic 03842
9/19/87	**58**	5	94	**If I Could Only Fly**		Epic 07400
				BONNIE OWENS:		
9/12/64	**28**	26	95	**Just Between The Two Of Us**........................		Tally 181
				JOHNNY PAYCHECK:		
3/28/81	**41**	8	96	I Can't Hold Myself In Line.............................		Epic 51012
				LEONA WILLIAMS:		
10/28/78	**8**	12	97	**The Bull And The Beaver**............................		MCA 40962
5/28/83	**42**	14	98	We're Strangers Again		Mercury 812214
				CONNIE HALL		
				Born on 6/24/29 in Walden, Kentucky; raised in Cincinnati. Worked on WZIP-Covington, Kentucky. With the Jimmie Skinner Show, WNOP-Newport, Kentucky, in 1954.		
2/15/60	**21**	4	1	The Bottle Or Me..		Mercury 71540
10/10/60	**25**	2	2	Poison In Your Hand....................................		Decca 31130
10/17/60	**17**	2	3	It's Not Wrong		Decca 31190
4/24/61	**20**	5	4	Sleep, Baby, Sleep		Decca 31208
1/20/62	**23**	5	5	What A Pleasure		Decca 31310
1/05/63	**14**	3	6	Fool Me Once		Decca 31438
				REBECCA HALL		
				Born in Rustburg, Virginia. Had own 8-piece band in Savannah, Georgia. Winner of "You Can Be A Star" talent competition, leading to a recording contract.		
8/03/85	**83**	3	1	Heartbeat		Capitol 5486
				SAMMY HALL		
				Gosepl singer from North Carolina. Sang with rock band, The Birdwatchers, in Florida. Turned to gospel music in 1982.		
4/28/84	**88**	3	1	Anything For Your Love................................		Dream 300
				TOM T. HALL ★★48★★		
				Born Thomas Hall on 5/25/36 in Olive Hill, Kentucky. Played guitar from age 8; own band, the Kentucky Travelers, at age 16. Worked as a disc jockey on WMOR-Morehead, Kentucky. Worked on Armed Forces Radio in Germany while in service from 1957-61. Moved to Nashville in 1964. Wrote "Harper Valley P.T.A." hit for Jeannie C. Riley. Host of "Pop Goes The Country" TV series. Joined the Grand Ole Opry in 1980. Added "T" to his name when he began his singing career. Famous for his story-telling style of writing and singing.		
8/05/67	**30**	10	1	I Washed My Face In The Morning Dew		Mercury 72700
5/11/68	**66**	3	2	The World The Way I Want It		Mercury 72786
9/14/68	**68**	4	3	Ain't Got The Time.....................................		Mercury 72835
11/16/68+	**4**	18	4	**Ballad Of Forty Dollars**		Mercury 72863
5/10/69	**40**	8	5	Strawberry Farms		Mercury 72913
8/23/69	**5**	15	6	**Homecoming**..		Mercury 72951
12/20/69+	**1**²	15	7	**A Week In A Country Jail**		Mercury 72998
4/04/70	**8**	14	8	**Shoeshine Man**		Mercury 73039
7/11/70	**8**	13	9	**Salute To A Switchblade**		Mercury 73078
11/14/70	**23**	13	10	Day Drinkin'		Mercury 73139
				DAVE DUDLEY & TOM T. HALL		
12/26/70+	**14**	12	11	One Hundred Children		Mercury 73140
4/03/71	**21**	11	12	Ode To A Half A Pound Of Ground Round		Mercury 73189
7/10/71	**1**²	20	13	**The Year That Clayton Delaney Died**	42	Mercury 73221
3/18/72	**8**	15	14	**Me And Jesus**	98	Mercury 73278
				vocal accompaniment: the Mt. Pisgah United Methodist Church Choir		
7/08/72	**11**	12	15	The Monkey That Became President.................		Mercury 73297
10/07/72	**26**	9	16	More About John Henry		Mercury 73327

DEBUT DATE	PEAK POS	WKS CHR	ARTIST — Record Title	POP POS	Label & Number
			TOM T. HALL — Continued		
12/02/72+	**1**¹	15	17 **(Old Dogs-Children And) Watermelon Wine**		Mercury 73346
12/16/72+	**14**	12	18 Hello We're Lonely		Mercury 73347
			PATTI PAGE & TOM T. HALL		
5/05/73	**3**	13	19 **Ravishing Ruby**		Mercury 73377
6/30/73	**16**	11	20 Watergate Blues/	*101*	
		11	21 Spokane Motel Blues		Mercury 73394
11/10/73+	**1**²	18	22 **I Love**	*12*	Mercury 73436
6/01/74	**2**²	15	23 **That Song Is Driving Me Crazy**	*63*	Mercury 73488
9/14/74	**1**¹	16	24 **Country Is**		Mercury 73617
12/28/74+	**1**¹	15	25 **I Care/**		
12/21/74	**69**	16	26 Sneaky Snake	*55*	Mercury 73641
5/31/75	**8**	15	27 **Deal**		Mercury 73686
9/06/75	**4**	16	28 **I Like Beer**		Mercury 73704
1/10/76	**1**¹	16	29 **Faster Horses (The Cowboy And The Poet)**......		Mercury 73755
5/15/76	**24**	12	30 Negatory Romance		Mercury 73795
10/16/76	**9**	14	31 **Fox On The Run**		Mercury 73850
4/09/77	**4**	16	32 **Your Man Loves You, Honey**...................		Mercury 73899
8/06/77	**12**	12	33 It's All In The Game		Mercury 55001
			#1 pop hit for Tommy Edwards in 1958		
12/03/77+	**13**	14	34 May The Force Be With You Always		RCA 11158
4/08/78	**13**	13	35 I Wish I Loved Somebody Else		RCA 11253
			above 2: backing vocals by Maxine & Bonnie Brown		
9/16/78	**9**	13	36 **What Have You Got To Lose**.........................		RCA 11376
1/20/79	**14**	12	37 Son Of Clayton Delaney.........................		RCA 11453
5/12/79	**20**	10	38 There Is A Miracle In You		RCA 11568
9/29/79	**11**	14	39 You Show Me Your Heart (And I'll Show You Mine)		RCA 11713
1/05/80	**9**	13	40 **The Old Side Of Town/**		
		13	41 Jesus On The Radio (Daddy on the Phone).......		RCA 11888
5/24/80	**51**	7	42 Soldier Of Fortune		RCA 12005
8/16/80	**36**	10	43 Back When Gas Was Thirty Cents A Gallon		RCA 12066
5/02/81	**41**	8	44 The All New Me		RCA 12219
5/22/82	**77**	4	45 There Ain't No Country Music On This Jukebox .		Columbia 02858
			TOM T. HALL & EARL SCRUGGS		
7/31/82	**72**	5	46 Song Of The South		Columbia 03033
			TOM T. HALL & EARL SCRUGGS		
7/30/83	**42**	10	47 Everything From Jesus To Jack Daniels...........		Mercury 812835
7/14/84	**81**	3	48 Famous In Missouri		Mercury 880030
9/08/84	**8**	21	49 **P.S. I Love You**.................................		Mercury 880216
			#12 pop hit for Rudy Vallee in 1934		
5/25/85	**40**	9	50 A Bar With No Beer		Mercury 880690
8/31/85	**42**	11	51 Down In The Florida Keys		Mercury 884017
7/19/86	**52**	8	52 Susie's Beauty Shop/		
10/04/86	**79**	3	53 Love Letters In The Sand		Mercury 884850
			#1 pop hit for Pat Boone in 1957		
12/06/86	**65**	7	54 Down At The Mall		Mercury 888155

VICTORIA HALLMAN

DEBUT DATE	PEAK POS	WKS CHR	ARTIST — Record Title	POP POS	Label & Number
8/22/87	**92**	2	1 Next Time I Marry		Evergreen 1055

ROGER HALLMARK & THE THRASHER BROTHERS

Roger was born in Cullman, Alabama. Worked in local bands from age 15. Worked as guitarist with the Thrasher Brothers.

DEBUT DATE	PEAK POS	WKS CHR	ARTIST — Record Title	POP POS	Label & Number
12/15/79+	**72**	5	1 A Message To Khomeini .... [N]		Vulcan 10004

STUART HAMBLEN

Born Carl Stuart Hamblen on 10/20/08 in Kellerville, Texas. Died on 3/8/89, after surgery on a brain tumor. Singer/actor, on radio from age 17. Moved to Hollywood in the early 30s and appeared in many western films and on radio with own band. Wrote "It Is No Secret (What God Can Do)", "This Ole House", "Open Up Your Heart (And Let The Sun Shine In)", and many others. Ran for President on Prohibition Party ticket in 1952. Producer with wife Suzy of films and radio programs, including "The Cowboy Church" and "Stuart's Scrapbook".

DEBUT DATE	PEAK POS	WKS CHR	ARTIST — Record Title	POP POS	Label & Number
11/12/49+	**3**	7	1 **But I'll Go Chasin' Women**		Columbia 20625
			Juke Box #3 / Best Seller #9		

DEBUT DATE	PEAK POS	WKS CHR	ARTIST — Record Title	POP POS	Label & Number
			STUART HAMBLEN — Continued		
8/05/50	**2**⁹	26	2 **(Remember Me) I'm The One Who Loves You** ...		Columbia 20714
			Jockey #2 / Best Seller #3 / Juke Box #4		
			#32 pop hit for Dean Martin in 1965		
1/06/51	**8**	2	3 **It's No Secret**		Columbia 0390
			Jockey #8		
8/21/54	**2**¹	30	4 **This Ole House**	26	RCA 5739
			Jockey #2 / Best Seller #3 / Juke Box #5		
			GEORGE HAMILTON IV ★★81★★		
			Born on 7/19/37 in Winston-Salem, North Carolina. Recorded "A Rose And A Baby Ruth" for Colonial in 1956. Toured with Buddy Holly, Gene Vincent and The Everly Brothers. Moved to Nashville in 1959 and joined the Grand Ole Opry in 1960. Own TV series on ABC in 1959, and in Canada in the late 70s.		
10/10/60	**4**	17	1 **Before This Day Ends**...................		ABC-Para. 10125
6/12/61	**9**	13	2 **Three Steps To The Phone (Millions of Miles)** ..		RCA 7881
11/13/61	**13**	8	3 To You And Yours...................		RCA 7934
6/16/62	**22**	2	4 China Doll		RCA 8001
			#38 pop hit for The Ames Brothers in 1960		
8/25/62	**6**	14	5 **If You Don't Know I Ain't Gonna Tell You**		RCA 8062
1/19/63	**21**	5	6 In This Very Same Room		RCA 8118
6/15/63	**1**⁴	24	7 Abilene...........................	15	RCA 8181
1/18/64	**21**	8	8 There's More Pretty Girls Than One	116	RCA 8250
3/28/64	**25**	8	9 Linda With The Lonely Eyes/		
4/18/64	**28**	6	10 Fair And Tender Ladies		RCA 8304
8/29/64	**9**	14	11 **Fort Worth, Dallas Or Houston**		RCA 8392
12/05/64+	**11**	18	12 Truck Driving Man		RCA 8462
7/10/65	**18**	16	13 Walking The Floor Over You		RCA 8608
			Ernest Tubb's classic hit of the early 40s		
12/04/65+	**16**	12	14 Write Me A Picture		RCA 8690
4/23/66	**15**	17	15 Steel Rail Blues		RCA 8797
9/03/66	**9**	16	16 **Early Morning Rain**		RCA 8924
			written by Gordon Lightfoot		
1/21/67	**7**	21	17 **Urge For Going**...................		RCA 9059
7/01/67	**6**	17	18 **Break My Mind**		RCA 9239
12/23/67+	**18**	13	19 Little World Girl		RCA 9385
6/01/68	**50**	8	20 It's My Time		RCA 9519
10/19/68	**38**	10	21 Take My Hand For Awhile		RCA 9637
3/15/69	**26**	10	22 Back to Denver.....................		RCA 0100
6/21/69	**25**	13	23 Canadian Pacific...................		RCA 0171
11/08/69	**29**	9	24 Carolina On My Mind		RCA 0256
5/02/70	**3**	16	25 **She's A Little Bit Country**.............		RCA 9829
8/29/70	**16**	12	26 Back Where It's At		RCA 9886
9/26/70	**65**	2	27 Let's Get Together		RCA 9893
			SKEETER DAVIS & GEORGE HAMILTON IV		
			#5 pop hit for The Youngbloods in 1969		
1/30/71	**13**	12	28 Anyway............................		RCA 9945
5/22/71	**35**	11	29 Countryfied.......................		RCA 0469
9/18/71	**23**	12	30 West Texas Highway................		RCA 0531
2/05/72	**33**	10	31 10 Degrees & Getting Colder		RCA 0622
5/13/72	**63**	8	32 Country Music In My Soul............		RCA 0697
9/09/72	**52**	9	33 Travelin' Light.....................		RCA 0776
12/23/72+	**22**	13	34 Blue Train (Of The Heartbreak Line)................		RCA 0854
5/19/73	**38**	10	35 Dirty Old Man		RCA 0948
9/22/73	**50**	7	36 Second Cup Of Coffee		RCA 0084
1/26/74	**59**	9	37 Claim On Me.......................		RCA 0203
4/09/77	**81**	5	38 I Wonder Who's Kissing Her Now		ABC/Dot 17687
			#1 pop hit for Henry Burr in 1909		
10/15/77	**93**	2	39 Everlasting (Everlasting Love)		ABC/Dot 17723
4/01/78	**81**	4	40 Only The Best.......................		ABC 12342
			GEORGE HAMILTON V		
			Son of George Hamilton IV.		
2/20/88	**75**	3	1 She Says		MTM 72101

DEBUT DATE	PEAK POS	WKS CHR	ARTIST — Record Title	POP POS	Label & Number
			PENNY HAMILTON		
8/04/79	94	4	1 You Lit The Fire, Now Fan The Flame		Door Knob 096
			CHERYL HANDY		
			Born in 1969 in Virginia; raised in Goodlettsville, Tennessee. Recorded at age 10, played Las Vegas at age 12.		
4/14/84	83	4	1 Here I Go Again		Audiograph 475
1/24/87	67	5	2 One Of The Boys		RCM 00105
8/08/87	56	6	3 Will You Still Love Me Tomorrow?		Compleat 176
			#1 pop hit for The Shirelles in 1961		
			CONNIE HANSON & Friend		
			Born in Houston; regular appearances on local TV at age 9. In the films "Urban Cowboy" and "Hot Wire". "Friend" is Darrell McCall.		
12/25/82+	64	9	1 There's Still A Lot Of Love In San Antone		Soundwaves 4692
			THE HARDEN TRIO		
			Family trio from England, Arkansas: Bobby and sisters Robbie and Arleen. On Barnyard Frolics in Little Rock while still teenagers. Worked on Ozark Mountain Jubilee, Louisiana Hayride, and Grand Ole Opry. Disbanded in 1968.		
2/12/66	2¹	21	1 **Tippy Toeing**	*44*	Columbia 43463
11/05/66	28	11	2 Seven Days Of Crying (Makes One Weak)		Columbia 43844
4/22/67	16	14	3 Sneaking 'Cross The Border		Columbia 44059
2/10/68	56	4	4 He Looks A Lot Like You		Columbia 44420
6/29/68	47	7	5 Everybody Wants To Be Somebody Else		Columbia 44552
			ARLENE HARDEN		
			Born on 3/1/45. Part of The Harden Trio with brother Bobby and sister Robbie. Appeared on the Grand Ole Opry from 1966, went solo in 1967. Made appearances on the Porter Wagoner and Wilburn Brothers TV shows, and Midwestern Hayride.		
7/15/67	48	9	1 Fair Weather Love		Columbia 44133
12/09/67+	49	7	2 You're Easy To Love		Columbia 44310
4/06/68	32	11	3 He's A Good Ole Boy		Columbia 44461
8/17/68	41	9	4 What Can I Say		Columbia 44581
12/07/68+	64	6	5 Who Loves Who		Columbia 44675
			ARLENE & BOBBY HARDEN		
5/03/69	45	9	6 Too Much Of A Man (To Be Tied Down)..............		Columbia 44783
12/20/69+	63	4	7 My Friend		Columbia 45016
4/25/70	13	14	8 Lovin' Man (Oh Pretty Woman)		Columbia 45120
			female version of Roy Orbison's #1 hit in 1964		
8/29/70	28	11	9 Crying		Columbia 45203
			#2 pop hit for Roy Orbison in 1961		
1/09/71	22	11	10 True Love Is Greater Than Friendship		Columbia 45287
			from the film "Little Fauss And Big Halsy"		
5/01/71	25	11	11 Married To A Memory		Columbia 45365
7/31/71	49	9	12 Congratulations (You Sure Made A Man Out Of Him)		Columbia 45420
12/18/71+	46	9	13 Ruby Gentry's Daughter		Columbia 45489
4/15/72	29	12	14 A Special Day		Columbia 45577
11/04/72	45	8	15 It Takes A Lot Of Tenderness		Columbia 45708
6/30/73	21	13	16 Would You Walk With Me Jimmy		Columbia 45845
			ARLEEN HARDEN:		
7/20/74	72	8	17 Leave Me Alone (Ruby Red Dress)		Capitol 3911
			#3 pop hit for Helen Reddy in 1973		
10/29/77	100	2	18 A Place Where Love Has Been		Elektra 45434
4/01/78	74	4	19 You're Not Free And I'm Not Easy		Elektra 45463
			BOBBY HARDEN		
			Born in England, Arkansas. Part of The Harden Trio with sisters Robbie and Arlene.		
3/15/75	48	8	1 One Step...		United Art. 597
			GUS HARDIN		
			Born Carolyn Ann Blankenship on 4/9/45 in Tulsa. Long time favorite in Tulsa clubs.		
2/19/83	10	16	1 **After The Last Goodbye**		RCA 13445
5/28/83	26	14	2 If I Didn't Love You		RCA 13532
9/24/83	32	12	3 Loving You Hurts		RCA 13597
12/24/83+	41	12	4 Fallen Angel (Flyin' High Tonight)		RCA 13704
3/24/84	43	11	5 I Pass..		RCA 13751

DEBUT DATE	PEAK POS	WKS CHR	ARTIST — Record Title	POP POS	Label & Number
			GUS HARDIN — Continued		
6/23/84	52	8	6 How Are You Spending My Nights		RCA 13814
11/10/84+	8	21	7 **All Tangled Up In Love**.................................		RCA 13938
			GUS HARDIN with EARL THOMAS CONLEY		
4/20/85	79	4	8 My Mind Is On You		RCA 14040
8/17/85	72	7	9 Just As Long As I Have You..........................		RCA 14159
			GUS HARDIN & DAVE LOGGINS		
1/11/86	73	7	10 What We Gonna Do		RCA 14255
			GAYLE HARDING		
11/11/78	92	2	1 Sexy Eyes..		Robchris 1008
1/27/79	84	3	2 I'm Lovin' The Lovin' Out Of You		Robchris 1009
			JOHNNY HARDY		
			Born in Rockmont, Georgia.		
2/13/61	17	10	1 In Memory Of Johnny Horton		J&J 003
			DANNY HARGROVE		
			Born in Detroit; first recorded rock 'n' roll for Chess in 1959. Moved to St. Paul, Minnesota in 1965. Formed his first country band in 1970.		
5/13/78	73	7	1 Sweet Mary		50 States 61
9/23/78	98	2	2 I Wanna Be Her #1		50 States 64
			LINDA HARGROVE		
			Born on 2/3/51 in Tallahasee. Moved to Nashville in 1970 and worked as a songwriter and session musician. Turned to gospel music in 1978.		
10/19/74	98	2	1 Blue Jean Country Queen..............................		Elektra 45204
12/28/74+	82	4	2 I've Never Loved Anyone More		Elektra 45215
11/08/75+	39	13	3 Love Was (Once Around The Dance Floor)		Capitol 4153
3/06/76	86	5	4 Love, You're The Teacher		Capitol 4228
7/24/76	86	4	5 Fire At First Sight		Capitol 4283
4/02/77	91	3	6 Down To My Pride		Capitol 4390
9/24/77	61	9	7 Mexican Love Songs		Capitol 4447
10/14/78	93	4	8 You Are Still The One		RCA 11378
			OGDEN HARLESS		
			Born William Harless in Hattiesburg, Mississippi in 1949.		
9/19/87	84	2	1 Somebody Ought To Tell Him That She's Gone ...		Door Knob 283
11/28/87	74	3	2 Walk On Boy		Door Knob 287
1/16/88	64	5	3 I Wish We Were Strangers		Door Knob 293
4/23/88	82	3	4 Down On The Bayou		Door Knob 297
8/27/88	92	2	5 Together Alone...		MSC 188
			CARLY HARRINGTON		
8/06/88	64	6	1 Badland Preacher..		Oak 1055
			DONNA HARRIS		
10/01/66	45	18	1 He Was Almost Persuaded		ABC 10839
			answer song to David Houston's "Almost Persuaded"		
			EMMYLOU HARRIS ★★50★★		
			Born on 4/2/47 in Birmingham, Alabama. Worked as a folk singer in Washington, DC in the late 60s. First recorded for Jubilee in 1969. Toured with the Flying Burrito Brothers and Gram Parsons until 1973. Own band from 1975. Married to British songwriter Paul Kennerley in 1985. Also see Southern Pacific.		
4/19/75	73	8	1 Too Far Gone		Reprise 1326
7/05/75	4	17	2 **If I Could Only Win Your Love**.....................	58	Reprise 1332
			harmony vocal: Herb Pedersen (also #8 below)		
12/27/75	99	1	3 Light Of The Stable .... [X]		Reprise 1341
			backing vocals: Dolly Parton, Linda Ronstadt, Neil Young		
3/06/76	1¹	14	4 **Together Again**		Reprise 1346
			flip side "Here, There And Everywhere" made the pop charts		
6/05/76	3	16	5 **One Of These Days**...................................		Reprise 1353
10/23/76	1²	14	6 **Sweet Dreams**		Reprise 1371
2/26/77	6	13	7 **(You Never Can Tell) C'est La Vie**		Warner 8329
			#14 pop hit for Chuck Berry in 1964		
5/28/77	8	14	8 **Making Believe**		Warner 8388
12/03/77+	3	15	9 **To Daddy**	102	Warner 8498
			written by Dolly Parton		

DEBUT DATE	PEAK POS	WKS CHR		ARTIST — Record Title	POP POS	Label & Number
				EMMYLOU HARRIS — Continued		
4/15/78	**1**¹	14	10	**Two More Bottles Of Wine**...............................		Warner 8553
8/05/78	**12**	11	11	Easy From Now On..		Warner 8623
2/03/79	**13**	13	12	Too Far Gone ....[R]		Warner 8732
6/02/79	**4**	14	13	**Save The Last Dance For Me**........................		Warner 8815
				#1 pop hit for The Drifters in 1960		
9/22/79	**6**	12	14	**Blue Kentucky Girl**....................................		Warner 49056
3/01/80	**1**¹	14	15	**Beneath Still Waters**................................		Warner 49164
5/31/80	**7**	15	16	**Wayfaring Stranger**		Warner 49239
9/13/80	**13**	11	17	The Boxer		Warner 49551
				#7 pop hit for Simon & Garfunkel in 1969		
3/07/81	**10**	12	18	**Mister Sandman**	37	Warner 49684
				#1 pop hit for The Chordettes in 1954		
6/13/81	**44**	8	19	I Don't Have To Crawl................................	106	Warner 49739
1/16/82	**9**	16	20	**Tennessee Rose**		Warner 49892
				backing vocals: Sharon & Cheryl White		
5/29/82	**3**	17	21	**Born To Run**		Warner 29993
10/16/82+	**1**¹	20	22	**(Lost His Love) On Our Last Date**		Warner 29898
				vocal version of Floyd Cramer's "Last Date"		
3/19/83	**5**	17	23	**I'm Movin' On**......................................		Warner 29729
7/02/83	**28**	13	24	So Sad (To Watch Good Love Go Bad)		Warner 29583
				#7 pop hit for The Everly Brothers in 1960		
11/19/83+	**26**	13	25	Drivin' Wheel		Warner 29443
3/24/84	**9**	21	26	**In My Dreams**		Warner 29329
8/11/84	**9**	22	27	**Pledging My Love**		Warner 29218
				#17 pop hit for Johnny Ace in 1955		
11/24/84+	**26**	18	28	Someone Like You		Warner 29138
3/30/85	**14**	17	29	White Line		Warner 29041
7/20/85	**44**	11	30	Rhythm Guitar		Warner 28952
11/30/85	**55**	9	31	Timberline		Warner 28852
3/01/86	**60**	6	32	I Had My Heart Set On You		Warner 28770
5/03/86	**43**	13	33	Today I Started Loving You Again..................		Warner 28714
				written by Merle Haggard & Bonnie Owens		
7/11/87	**60**	7	34	Someday My Ship Will Sail........................		Warner 28302
12/12/87+	**53**	13	35	Back In Baby's Arms		Hughes 53236
				from the film "Planes, Trains & Automobiles"		
12/17/88+	**8**	22	36	**Heartbreak Hill**		Reprise 27635
				EMMYLOU HARRIS DUOS with:		
				EARL THOMAS CONLEY:		
7/02/88	**1**¹	21	37	**We Believe In Happy Endings**....................		RCA 8632
				JOHN DENVER:		
7/09/83	**14**	19	38	Wild Montana Skies................................		RCA 13562
				CHARLIE LOUVIN:		
9/08/79	**91**	6	39	Love Don't Care....................................		Little Dar. 7922
				ROY ORBISON:		
6/28/80	**6**	15	40	**That Lovin' You Feelin' Again**	55	Warner 49262
				from the film "Roadie"		
				BUCK OWENS:		
5/12/79	**11**	13	41	Play Together Again Again		Warner 8830
				DOLLY PARTON, LINDA RONSTADT:		
2/21/87	**1**¹	19	42	**To Know Him Is To Love Him**		Warner 28492
				#1 pop hit for The Teddy Bears in 1958		
5/30/87	**3**	18	43	**Telling Me Lies**..................................		Warner 28371
9/26/87	**5**	22	44	**Those Memories Of You**		Warner 28248
3/26/88	**6**	18	45	**Wildflowers**......................................		Warner 27970
				LINDA RONSTADT:		
1/03/76	**11**	12	46	The Sweetest Gift		Asylum 45295
				DON WILLIAMS:		
9/19/81	**3**	17	47	**If I Needed You**		Warner 49809
				B.J. HARRISON		
5/24/80	**93**	2	1	I Need A Little More Time........................		TeleSonic 801

DEBUT DATE	PEAK POS	WKS CHR	ARTIST — Record Title	POP POS	Label & Number
			DIXIE HARRISON		
			Born in Hammond, Indiana. Part Native American. Played accordion and guitar, sang gospel as a youngster. Contestant in the Miss Indiana beauty pageant in 1970.		
10/23/82	98	2	1 Yes Ma'am, He Found Me In A Honky Tonk........		Air Int'l. 10078
			CLAY HART		
			Born in Providence, Rhode Island. Attended Amherst College. Worked as an engineer in studios in Tampa, Florida. On Lawrence Welk TV series from 1968-73. Wife Sally Flynn was on Welk shows in duo with Sandy Jensen.		
5/31/69	30	11	1 Spring....................		Metromedia 119
9/20/69	25	9	2 Another Day, Another Mile, Another Highway		Metromedia 140
1/31/70	73	3	3 Face Of A Dear Friend..................................		Metromedia 158
5/02/70	62	7	4 If I'd Only Come And Gone..........................		Metromedia 172
			FREDDIE HART ★★57★★		
			Born Fred Segrest on 12/21/26 in Lochapoka, Alabama. Served in US Marines during World War II. Moved to Phoenix in 1950 and worked with Lefty Frizzell from 1951-52. Appeared on Home Town Jamboree TV series. Operates a trucking company and school for handicapped children in Burbank, California.		
4/20/59	24	4	1 The Wall.....................................		Columbia 41345
11/16/59	17	4	2 Chain Gang		Columbia 41456
5/02/60	18	11	3 The Key's In The Mailbox		Columbia 41597
1/09/61	27	2	4 Lying Again		Columbia 41805
11/06/61	23	2	5 What A Laugh!		Columbia 42146
10/30/65	23	12	6 Hank Williams' Guitar......................		Kapp 694
5/07/66	45	4	7 Why Should I Cry Over You......................		Kapp 743
7/08/67	63	5	8 I'll Hold You In My Heart		Kapp 820
12/30/67+	24	15	9 Togetherness		Kapp 879
6/08/68	21	15	10 Born A Fool		Kapp 910
11/23/68	70	2	11 Don't Cry Baby		Kapp 944
1/03/70	27	10	12 The Whole World Holding Hands.................		Capitol 2692
4/11/70	48	9	13 One More Mountain To Climb		Capitol 2768
7/04/70	41	11	14 Fingerprints		Capitol 2839
11/21/70	68	4	15 California Grapevine..........................		Capitol 2933
7/10/71	1³	24	16●**Easy Loving**	17	Capitol 3115
			CMA Song of the Year for both 1971 and 1972		
1/29/72	1⁶	19	17 **My Hang-Up Is You**		Capitol 3261
6/24/72	1²	14	18 **Bless Your Heart**		Capitol 3353
10/14/72	1³	17	19 **Got The All Overs For You (All Over Me)**		Capitol 3453
2/03/73	1¹	14	20 **Super Kind Of Woman**.................		Capitol 3524
5/19/73	41	10	21 Born A Fool ....[R]		MCA 40011
6/02/73	1¹	16	22 **Trip To Heaven**		Capitol 3612
10/06/73	3	16	23 **If You Can't Feel It (It Ain't There)**		Capitol 3730
2/23/74	2¹	12	24 **Hang In There Girl**		Capitol 3827
6/22/74	3	14	25 **The Want-To's**.......................		Capitol 3898
11/02/74+	3	16	26 **My Woman's Man**		Capitol 3970
3/01/75	5	15	27 **I'd Like To Sleep Til I Get Over You**		Capitol 4031
6/28/75	2²	16	28 **The First Time**		Capitol 4099
10/18/75	6	15	29 **Warm Side Of You**		Capitol 4152
1/31/76	11	11	30 You Are The Song (Inside Of Me)		Capitol 4210
4/10/76	12	14	31 She'll Throw Stones At You		Capitol 4251
8/21/76	11	14	32 That Look In Her Eyes		Capitol 4313
12/04/76+	8	14	33 **Why Lovers Turn To Strangers**...................		Capitol 4363
			18-33 shown as: **FREDDIE HART & THE HEARTBEATS**		
4/16/77	11	11	34 Thank God She's Mine		Capitol 4409
7/16/77	13	12	35 The Pleasure's Been All Mine/		
		10	36 It's Heaven Loving You		Capitol 4448
11/05/77	43	10	37 The Search		Capitol 4498
			written by Sheb Wooley		
1/21/78	27	11	38 So Good, So Rare, So Fine..........................		Capitol 4530
4/22/78	34	10	39 Only You		Capitol 4561
			#1 pop hit for The Platters in 1955		
8/19/78	21	12	40 Toe To Toe		Capitol 4609
2/24/79	40	8	41 My Lady		Capitol 4684
5/26/79	28	12	42 Wasn't It Easy Baby		Capitol 4720

133

DEBUT DATE	PEAK POS	WKS CHR	ARTIST — Record Title	POP POS	Label & Number
			FREDDIE HART — Continued		
6/07/80	15	12	43 Sure Thing..		Sunbird 7550
9/13/80	33	10	44 Rose's Are Red		Sunbird 7553
4/18/81	31	10	45 You're Crazy Man..................................		Sunbird 7560
9/12/81	38	9	46 You Were There		Sunbird 7565
6/29/85	81	4	47 I Don't Want To Lose You.....................		El Dorado 101
9/05/87	77	4	48 Best Love I Never Had............................		Fifth St. 1091
			ROD HART Born in Beulah, Michigan. Appeared in the Steve McQueen film "Junior Bonner".		
11/27/76+	23	11	1 C.B. Savage............................... [N]	67	Plantation 144
			SALLY JUNE HART		
9/20/75	91	3	1 Takin' What I Can Get		Buddah 479
			CHAPIN HARTFORD Born Paula Hartford Foster on 5/15/44 in Boston. First recorded for Pic in 1977.		
8/26/78	91	3	1 I Knew The Mason..................................		LS 165
			JOHN HARTFORD Born on 12/30/37 in New York City; raised in St. Louis. Plays guitar, banjo and fiddle. Moved to Nashville and worked as a session musician. Wrote "Gentle On My Mind" hit for Glen Campbell. Regular on the Smothers Brothers TV series.		
5/27/67	60	7	1 Gentle On My Mind		RCA 9175
8/18/84	81	3	2 Piece Of My Heart		Fly. Fish 4013
			JIMMY HARTSOOK Born on 8/10/59 in Lenoir City, Tennessee. Own band, the Hart Throbs, on Jim Clayton's Startime TV series. Own TV series in Knoxville, Tennessee.		
1/26/74	94	5	1 Anything To Prove My Love		RCA 0202
			DOLLY HARTT		
2/13/88	85	3	1 Here Comes The Night..............................		Kass 1015
			NATE HARVELL Singer/songwriter from Alabama.		
7/15/78	23	13	1 Three Times A Lady		Republic 025
			#1 pop hit for the Commodores in 1978		
12/02/78	73	5	2 One In A Million......................................		Republic 033
			VINCE & DIANNE HATFIELD		
8/01/81	83	4	1 I Won't Last A Day Without You		Soundwaves 4638
			#11 pop hit for the Carpenters in 1974		
5/01/82	81	3	2 Back In My Baby's Arms		Soundwaves 4668
7/02/83	90	2	3 Love Has Made A Woman Out Of You...............		Soundwaves 4704
			BRUCE HAUSER & THE SAWMILL CREEK BAND Bruce was born and raised in Kansas.		
10/24/81	90	3	1 Barely Gettin' By .... SAWMILL CREEK		Cowboy 1045
12/21/85	77	6	2 I Just Came Back.....................................		Cowboy 200
7/19/86	81	3	3 Bidding America Goodbye............................		Cowboy 202
			BOBBY HAVENS		
12/09/78	100	2	1 Hey You		Cin Kay 043
			DEBI HAWKINS Bakersfield-based singer, Deborah Kaye Hawkins.		
3/22/75	61	9	1 Making Believe		Warner 8076
7/26/75	80	5	2 What I Keep Sayin', Is A Lie........................		Warner 8104
11/08/75	88	3	3 When I Stop Dreaming		Warner 8140
3/27/76	97	2	4 Walnut Street Wrangler.............................		Warner 8188
6/18/77	57	8	5 Love Letters..		Warner 8394
			#5 pop hit for Ketty Lester in 1962		
			ERSKINE HAWKINS & HIS ORCHESTRA Born on 7/26/14 in Birmingham, Alabama. Trumpeter/bandleader/composer.		
2/05/44	6	1	1 **Don't Cry, Baby**..	11	Bluebird 30-0813

DEBUT DATE	PEAK POS	WKS CHR	ARTIST — Record Title	POP POS	Label & Number
			HAWKSHAW HAWKINS		
			Born Harold Franklin Hawkins on 12/22/21 in Huntington, West Virginia. Died in a plane crash on 3/5/63 near Camden, Tennessee. Worked on local radio from age 15. In service during World War II. Worked on WWVA-Wheeling Jamboree from 1946. With the Grand Ole Opry from 1955. Married to Jean Shepard. Plane crash also killed Patsy Cline, Cowboy Copas, and pilot Randy Hughes.		
5/01/48	9	4	1 **Pan American**		King 689
			Juke Box #9		
8/21/48	6	15	2 **Dog House Boogie**		King 720
			Juke Box #6 / Best Seller #12		
12/24/49	15	1	3 I Wasted A Nickel..............................		King 821
			Best Seller #15		
3/17/51	8	1	4 **I Love You A Thousand Ways**		King 918
			Jockey #8		
10/13/51	8	2	5 **I'm Waiting Just For You**		King 969
			Jockey #8		
12/08/51+	7	4	6 **Slow Poke**	26	King 998
			Juke Box #7 / Best Seller #8		
8/10/59	15	7	7 Soldier's Joy	87	Columbia 41419
3/02/63	1⁴	25	8 **Lonesome 7-7203**	108	King 5712
			HAZARD		
4/02/83	69	5	1 Love Letters................................		Warner 29755
			#5 pop hit for Ketty Lester in 1962		
			DONNA HAZARD		
1/17/81	45	9	1 My Turn		Excelsior 1004
5/02/81	55	7	2 Go Home and Go To Pieces		Excelsior 1009
7/11/81	54	8	3 Love Never Hurt So Good.....................		Excelsior 1016
12/26/81+	76	5	4 Slow Texas Dancing.........................		Excelsior 1020
			ROY HEAD		
			Born on 1/9/43 in Three Rivers, Texas. Had pop hit "Treat Her Right" (POS 2) with own band, the Traits, in 1965.		
10/19/74	66	9	1 Baby's Not Home............................		Mega 1219
4/05/75	19	14	2 The Most Wanted Woman In Town		Shannon 829
8/16/75	47	10	3 Help Yourself To Me		Shannon 833
11/22/75+	55	8	4 I'll Take It		Shannon 838
2/07/76	28	11	5 The Door I Used To Close		ABC/Dot 17608
6/05/76	50	8	6 Bridge For Crawling Back		ABC/Dot 17629
9/04/76	51	8	7 One Night		ABC/Dot 17650
			#4 pop hit for Elvis Presley in 1958		
12/25/76+	57	8	8 Angel With A Broken Wing		ABC/Dot 17669
7/02/77	79	6	9 Julianne...................................		ABC/Dot 17706
10/08/77+	16	20	10 Come To Me		ABC/Dot 17722
4/01/78	19	13	11 Now You See 'Em, Now You Don't		ABC 12346
7/22/78	28	10	12 Tonight's The Night (Its Gonna Be Alright)........		ABC 12383
			#1 pop hit for Rod Stewart in 1976		
11/04/78	45	7	13 Love Survived		ABC 12418
3/24/79	74	5	14 Kiss You And Make It Better		ABC 12462
11/10/79	79	4	15 In Our Room		Elektra 46549
2/02/80	65	4	16 The Fire Of Two Old Flames		Elektra 46582
7/05/80	59	6	17 Long Drop................................		Elektra 46653
9/27/80	70	5	18 Drinkin' Them Long Necks....................		Elektra 47029
10/24/81	75	5	19 After Texas		Churchill 7778
5/29/82	89	3	20 Play Another Gettin' Drunk And Take Somebody Home Song...........................		NSD 129
9/11/82	64	7	21 The Trouble With Hearts		NSD 146
1/08/83	85	4	22 Your Mama Don't Dance.....................		NSD 156
			#4 pop hit for Loggins & Messina in 1973		
12/10/83	79	5	23 Where Did He Go Right		Avion 105
9/07/85	93	2	24 Break Out The Good Stuff....................		Texas Crude 614

DEBUT DATE	PEAK POS	WKS CHR	ARTIST — Record Title	POP POS	Label & Number
			JIMMY HEAP with PERK WILLIAMS		
			Jimmy was born on 3/3/22 in Taylor, Texas; died on 12/4/77. Worked on KTAE-Taylor from 1948-58. Worked on Big D Jamboree, KRLD-Dallas. Had own band, The Melody Masters, featuring lead singer Perk Williams.		
1/09/54	**5**	13	1 **Release Me**		Capitol 2518
			Best Seller #5 / Juke Box #8 / Jockey #10		
			Esther Phillips and Engelbert Humperdinck had pop hit versions		
			HEART OF NASHVILLE		
			Assemblage of Country stars - similar to USA for Africa. Included George Jones, Eddy Arnold, Roy Acuff, Lynn Anderson, Faron Young, Webb Pierce, Bobby Bare, Porter Wagoner, Sonny James, Tanya Tucker, Jerry Reed and many others.		
6/08/85	**61**	9	1 One Big Family		Compleat 679001
			written and produced by Ronnie McDowell		
			HEARTLAND		
			Quartet of former gospel singers.		
9/24/88	**79**	3	1 New River		Tra-Star 1221
12/17/88	**82**	3	2 Making Love To Dixie		Tra-Star 1222
			BOYD HEATH		
5/05/45	**7**	1	1 **Smoke On The Water**		Bluebird 33-0522
			DAVID HEAVENER		
			Born on 12/22/53 in Louisville, Kentucky. Attended Jefferson Community College, Kentucky. Worked as a record promoter. Wrote "Tip Toe To The Gas Pumps".		
11/28/81	**73**	4	1 Cheat On Him Tonight		Brent 1017
2/20/82	**70**	4	2 Honky Tonk Tonight...............................		Brent 1019
7/31/82	**86**	3	3 I Am The Fire		Brent 1020
			BEVERLY HECKEL		
			Born in Elkins, West Virginia. In trio at age 9 with sister Susie and father Pee Wee. After father left the group, worked as duo on WWVA Jamboree in 1972.		
6/11/77	**88**	5	1 Don't Hand Me No Hand Me Down Love		RCA 10981
9/16/78	**56**	7	2 Bluer Than Blue		RCA 11360
			THE HECKELS		
			Trio consisting of sisters Beverly and Susie Heckel, and Susie's husband Denny Franks. Trio disbanded in 1976; Beverly continued as a soloist.		
6/26/76	**91**	5	1 A Cowboy Like You		RCA 10685
			JOANNE HEEL		
4/22/72	**44**	10	1 One More Time		Decca 32950
			BOBBY HELMS		
			Born on 8/15/33 in Bloomington, Indiana. Singer/guitarist. Appeared on father's local TV show for 6 years.		
3/30/57	**1⁴**	52	1 **Fraulein**	*36*	Decca 30194
			Jockey #1(4) / Best Seller #1(3) / Juke Box #9		
10/14/57	**1⁴**	26	2 **My Special Angel**.................................	*7*	Decca 30423
			Best Seller #1(4) / Jockey #1(1)		
12/23/57	**13**	1	3 Jingle Bell Rock .... [X]	*6*	Decca 30513
			Jockey #13		
3/03/58	**10**	9	4 **Just A Little Lonesome**		Decca 30557
			Best Seller #10 / Jockey #12		
5/12/58	**5**	12	5 **Jacqueline**	*63*	Decca 30619
			Best Seller #5		
			from the film "The Case Against Brooklyn"		
3/30/59	**26**	3	6 New River Train.....................................		Decca 30831
10/24/60	**16**	4	7 Lonely River Rhine.................................		Decca 31148
6/24/67	**46**	7	8 He Thought He'd Die Laughing		Little Dar. 0030
12/30/67+	**60**	6	9 The Day You Stop Loving Me....................		Little Dar. 0034
4/20/68	**53**	9	10 I Feel You, I Love You............................		Little Dar. 0041
8/02/69	**43**	9	11 So Long..		Little Dar. 0062
6/27/70	**41**	9	12 Mary Goes 'Round		Certron 10002
			BRICE HENDERSON		
			Born on 1/4/54 in Frederick, Maryland. Recorded a gospel album in 1986.		
1/22/83	**61**	7	1 Lonely Eyes		Union Sta. 1000
4/30/83	**55**	8	2 Lovers Again		Union Sta. 1001
9/17/83	**64**	5	3 Flames		Union Sta. 1003

DEBUT DATE	PEAK POS	WKS CHR	ARTIST — Record Title	POP POS	Label & Number
			HENHOUSE FIVE PLUS TOO		
			A Ray Stevens creation.		
1/08/77	**39**	7	1 In The Mood.......................................[N]	*40*	Warner 8301
			novelty version of Glenn Miller's 1940 #1 classic		
			AUDIE HENRY		
			Born in Brazil; raised in Canada. Twice-nominated as Canada's Top Female Artist.		
1/19/85	**97**	3	1 You'll Never Find A Good Man (Playin' In A Country Band)......................................		Canyon Cr. 2025
4/27/85	**91**	2	2 Being A Fool Again...............................		Canyon Cr. 2008
7/27/85	**73**	5	3 Heaven Knows....................................		Canyon Cr. 5020
10/19/85	**71**	5	4 Sweet Salvation		Canyon Cr. 8019
			TARI HENSLEY		
			Born Tari Dean Hodges on 3/6/53 in Independence, Missouri. Name is pronounced "Terry". Married to Dan Hensley in 1972, toured with his band for 10 years.		
4/09/83	**86**	3	1 Falling In Love		Mercury 76197
9/08/84	**69**	4	2 Love Isn't Love ('Til You Give It Away).............		Mercury 880054
2/09/85	**61**	6	3 I'm The One Who's Breaking Up....................		Mercury 880424
7/27/85	**64**	6	4 Hard Baby To Rock		Mercury 880801
4/05/86	**57**	7	5 Oh Yes I Can		Mercury 884484
7/26/86	**52**	10	6 I've Cried A Mile		Mercury 884852
			WOODY HERMAN - see MAC WISEMAN		
			RED HERRING		
7/04/60	**27**	2	1 Wasted Love		Country Jub. 533
			HOOT HESTER		
			Real name: Hubert Hester. Prolific session musician.		
4/21/79	**95**	3	1 I Still Love Her Memory..........................		Little Dar. 7911
			DOLPH HEWITT		
			Born Dolph Edward Hewitt on 7/15/14 in West Finley, Pennsylvania. Regular on the WLS Barn Dance from 1946-60.		
12/17/49	**8**	1	1 I Wish I Knew		RCA 0107
			Jockey #8		
			SARA "HONEYBEAR" HICKEY		
6/25/83	**82**	2	1 This Ain't Tennessee And He Ain't You		PCM 203
			JEANETTE HICKS - see GEORGE JONES		
			LANEY HICKS - see CHARLIE McCOY		
			BERTIE HIGGINS		
			Singer/songwriter, born in 1946 in Tarpon Springs, Florida. First recorded for ABC in 1964. Worked as a drummer with the Roemans from 1964-66.		
3/13/82	**50**	10	1 Key Largo..	*8*	Kat Fam. 02524
			inspired by Humphrey Bogart/Lauren Bacall film of the same title		
6/19/82	**90**	3	2 Just Another Day In Paradise	*46*	Kat Fam. 02839
9/03/88	**72**	5	3 You Blossom Me		So. Tracks 2000
			GEORGE HIGHFILL		
			Singer/songwriter born in Ft. Smith, Arkansas and raised in Stigler, Oklahoma.		
7/18/87	**69**	4	1 Waitin' Up		Warner 28312
10/31/87	**72**	4	2 Mad Money		Warner 28177
			HIGHWAY 101		
			Quartet consisting of Paulette Carlson (lead vocals, guitar), Scott "Cactus" Moser (vocals, drums), Curtis Stone (vocals, bass) and Jack Daniels (vocals, guitar). Stone is the son of Cliffie Stone.		
1/10/87	**4**	24	1 The Bed You Made For Me		Warner 28483
5/23/87	**2** [1]	23	2 Whiskey, If You Were A Woman...................		Warner 28372
9/26/87	**1** [2]	23	3 Somewhere Tonight		Warner 28223
2/13/88	**1** [1]	19	4 Cry, Cry, Cry		Warner 28105
6/18/88	**1** [1]	20	5 (Do You Love Me) Just Say Yes....................		Warner 27867
10/22/88+	**5**	19	6 All The Reasons Why		Warner 27735

DEBUT DATE	PEAK POS	WKS CHR	ARTIST — Record Title	POP POS	Label & Number
			HILKA		
			Born Hilka Maria Cornelius in Germany. Moved to Salt Lake City, Utah at age 13. Sings in four different languages.		
10/13/79	**89**	3	1 I Just Wonder Where He Could Be Tonight		IBC 0004
			HILKA & JEBRY (Jebry Lee Briley)		
2/09/80	**96**	2	2 (I'm Just The) Cuddle Up Kind.........................		IBC 0006
			HILL CITY		
8/10/85	**86**	3	1 I'd Do It In A Heartbeat.................................		Moon Shine 3040
			GOLDIE HILL		
			Born on 1/11/33 in Karnes City, Texas. Appeared on the Louisiana Hayride radio shows starting in the early 50s. Married Carl Smith in 1957. Billed as "The Golden Hillbilly".		
1/10/53	**1**³	9	1 I Let The Stars Get In My Eyes		Decca 28473
			Juke Box #1 / Best Seller #4		
			answer song to Slim Willet's "Don't Let The Stars..."		
7/03/54	**4**	21	2 Looking Back To See.............................		Decca 29145
			GOLDIE HILL - JUSTIN TUBB		
			Juke Box #4 / Best Seller #5 / Jockey #5		
1/08/55	**11**	1	3 Sure Fire Kisses.................................		Decca 29349
			JUSTIN TUBB - GOLDIE HILL		
			Jockey #11 / Best Seller #13		
3/26/55	**14**	2	4 Are You Mine?.....................................		Decca 29411
			RED SOVINE & GOLDIE HILL		
			Best Seller #14		
2/23/59	**17**	4	5 Yankee, Go Home................................		Decca 30826
			narration by Red Sovine		
4/06/68	**73**	2	6 Lovable Fool		Epic 10296
			GOLDIE HILL SMITH		
			TINY HILL		
			Born Harry Hill in Sullivan Township, Illinois. Worked as a truck driver. Formed his own trio in 1931, later had The Five Jacks. Own big band in 1933. Worked as drummer with Byron Dunbar in the mid-30s.		
1/26/46	**3**	4	1 Sioux City Sue		Mercury 2024
1/10/48	**5**	1	2 Never Trust A Woman		Mercury 6062
2/03/51	**7**	2	3 Hot Rod Race	29	Mercury 5547
			Best Seller #7		
3/24/51	**10**	1	4 I'll Sail My Ship Alone		Mercury 5508
			Juke Box #10		
			CHRIS HILLMAN		
			Born on 12/4/44 in San Diego County, California. Member of The Byrds from 1964-68. Formed the Flying Burrito Brothers with Gram Parsons in 1968. Went solo in 1972. Formed the country group the Desert Rose Band in 1986.		
9/29/84	**81**	6	1 Somebody's Back In Town		Sugar Hill 4105
4/27/85	**77**	5	2 Running The Road Blocks............................		Sugar Hill 4106
			DENNY HILTON		
			Star and producer of the Country Shindig Opry Show in the Ozarks since 1969.		
3/28/81	**84**	2	1 Layin' Low.....................................		Oak 1027
2/13/82	**92**	2	2 How Did You Get So Good.........................		Rosebridge 0014
2/05/83	**88**	2	3 Sharing The Night Together		Rosebridge 010
			TISH HINOJOSA - see CRAIG DILLINGHAM		
			STAN HITCHCOCK		
			Born on 3/21/37 in Pleasant Hope, Missouri. Worked as a deejay on KWTO and KTTS in Springfield, Missouri. Moved to Nashville in 1962. Own TV series in the mid-60s. Program director for Country Music Television.		
9/16/67	**54**	6	1 She's Looking Good		Epic 10182
12/09/67	**66**	2	2 Rings		Epic 10246
5/18/68	**57**	8	3 I'm Easy To Love		Epic 10307
10/19/68	**60**	4	4 The Phoenix Flash..............................		Epic 10388
10/11/69	**17**	11	5 Honey, I'm Home................................		Epic 10525
4/18/70	**46**	6	6 Call Me Gone		Epic 10586
10/17/70	**54**	7	7 Dixie Belle		GRT 23
3/13/71	**59**	7	8 At Least Part Of The Way		GRT 39
7/14/73	**65**	7	9 The Same Old Way		Cinnamon 759
12/08/73	**91**	4	10 Half-Empty Bed...............................		Cinnamon 770
3/09/74	**80**	7	11 I'm Free		Cinnamon 782

DEBUT DATE	PEAK POS	WKS CHR	ARTIST — Record Title	POP POS	Label & Number
			STAN HITCHCOCK — Continued		
6/03/78	**100**	2	12 Falling		MMI 1024
3/10/79	**85**	3	13 Finders Keepers Losers Weepers....................		MMI 1028
			STAN HITCHCOCK with SUE RICHARDS		
4/11/81	**81**	4	14 She Sings Amazing Grace		Ramblin' 1711
			BECKY HOBBS		
			Born Rebecca A. Hobbs on 1/24/50 in Bartlesville, Oklahoma. In an all-girl band, Surprise Package, while attending Tulsa University. Moved to Baton Rouge, performed with Swamp Fox from 1971-73. Moved to Los Angeles in 1973 and wrote songs for Helen Reddy, Shirley Bassey, Jane Olivor, and others. Moved to Nashville in 1982.		
12/23/78+	**95**	5	1 The More I Get The More I Want		Mercury 55049
6/30/79	**44**	11	2 I Can't Say Goodbye To You..........................		Mercury 55062
12/08/79+	**52**	9	3 Just What The Doctor Ordered		Mercury 57010
5/03/80	**79**	6	4 I'm Gonna Love You Tonight (Like There's No Tomorrow)..........................		Mercury 57020
10/11/80	**87**	2	5 I Learned All About Cheatin' From You		Mercury 57033
2/07/81	**84**	4	6 Honky-Tonk Saturday Night.........................		Mercury 57041
6/25/83	**10**	18	7 **Let's Get Over Them Together**		Columbia 03970
			MOE BANDY featuring BECKY HOBBS		
6/02/84	**46**	10	8 Oklahoma Heart............................		Liberty 1520
9/08/84	**64**	6	9 Pardon Me (Haven't We Loved Somewhere Before)..........................		EMI America 8224
12/08/84	**77**	6	10 Wheels In Emotion		EMI America 8247
6/22/85	**37**	12	11 Hottest "Ex" In Texas		EMI America 8273
3/05/88	**31**	19	12 Jones On The Jukebox........................		MTM 72104
7/09/88	**43**	10	13 They Always Look Better When They're Leavin'.		MTM 72109
10/08/88	**53**	9	14 Are There Any More Like You (Where You Came From)		MTM 72114
			BUD HOBBS		
			Vocalist/guitarist. Own radio show in San Francisco during the mid-40s.		
9/25/48	**13**	1	1 Lazy Mary		MGM 10206
			Juke Box #13		
1/29/49	**12**	4	2 I Heard About You		MGM 10305
			Juke Box #12 / Best Seller #13		
5/21/49	**12**	1	3 Candy Kisses		MGM 10366
			Juke Box #12 / Best Seller #15		
			LOU HOBBS		
			Born in Cape Girardeau, Louisiana. First recorded in 1962. Worked in Southern Illinois from the late 60s to the early 70s. Worked in Narvel Felts' band.		
3/07/81	**79**	3	1 Loving You Was All I Ever Needed....................		Kik 902
9/05/81	**93**	2	2 We're Building Our Love On A Rock		Kik 911
			PAM HOBBS		
2/07/81	**85**	4	1 Have You Ever Seen The Rain		50 States 79
			#8 pop hit for Creedence Clearwater Revival in 1971		
5/02/81	**88**	2	2 I Thought I Heard You Calling My Name		50 States 81
9/26/81	**93**	2	3 You're The Only Dancer		50 States 85
			ROY HOGSED		
8/21/48	**15**	1	1 Cocaine Blues................................		Capitol A. 40120
			Juke Box #15		
			SUZI JANE HOKUM		
9/09/67	**51**	7	1 Here We Go Again		LHI 17018
2/24/68	**65**	4	2 Storybook Children		LHI 1204
			above 2: **VIRGIL WARNER & SUZI JANE HOKUM**		
8/30/69	**75**	2	3 Reason To Believe........................		LHI 14
			DAVE HOLLADAY		
12/13/86	**83**	4	1 Now She's In Paris..........................		Step One 365
			JILL HOLLIER		
			Singer/songwrtier from Port Arthur, Texas.		
11/15/86	**79**	2	1 Sweet Time		Warner 28559

DEBUT DATE	PEAK POS	WKS CHR	ARTIST — Record Title	POP POS	Label & Number
			TERRI HOLLOWELL		
			Female vocalist. Born on 7/2/56 in Jeffersonville, Indiana.		
6/17/78	81	4	1 Happy Go Lucky Morning		Con Brio 134
9/23/78	76	4	2 Strawberry Fields Forever		Con Brio 139
			#8 pop hit for The Beatles in 1967		
12/23/78+	76	6	3 Just Stay With Me..		Con Brio 144
3/24/79	35	11	4 May I		Con Brio 150
7/21/79	56	8	5 It's Too Soon To Say Goodbye		Con Brio 156
			DOYLE HOLLY		
			Born on 6/30/36 in Perkins, Oklahoma. Worked oilfields in Oklahoma, Kansas and California. Played for a time with the Johnny Burnette band. Worked with Buck Owens' Buckaroos from 1963-70. Own band, the Vanishing Breed, from 1970.		
11/18/72	63	6	1 My Heart Cries For You		Barnaby 5004
			there were 9 top 40 pop versions in 1951		
6/16/73	29	14	2 Queen Of The Silver Dollar		Barnaby 5018
10/06/73	17	13	3 Lila		Barnaby 5027
3/02/74	58	9	4 Lord How Long Has This Been Going On		Barnaby 5030
6/15/74	75	8	5 A Rainbow In My Hand................................		Barnaby 602
9/07/74	69	6	6 Just Another Cowboy Song...........................		Barnaby 605
11/16/74+	53	11	7 Richard And The Cadillac Kings		Barnaby 608
			JOHNNY HOLM		
			Born in Fargo, North Dakota.		
10/01/77	100	2	1 Lightnin' Bar Blues		ASI 1012
			DARRELL HOLT		
12/12/87+	57	10	1 Catch 22..		Anoka 222
3/26/88	58	9	2 I Can't Take Her Anywhere...........................		Anoka 221
10/01/88	66	6	3 I'd Throw It All Away..................................		Anoka 224
			HOMER & JETHRO		
			Comedy duo of Henry D. "Homer" Haynes (b: 7/29/17, Knoxville; d: 8/7/71), guitar; and Kenneth C. "Jethro" Burns (b: 3/10/23, Knoxville; d: 2/4/89), mandolin. Duo formed in 1932 and worked local radio shows and fairs. Appeared on WLS-Chicago National Barn Dance beginning in 1950. Worked with Chet Atkins as the "Nashville String Band".		
3/26/49	14	1	1 I Feel That Old Age Coming On.................... [N]		King 749
			Juke Box #14		
8/27/49	9	1	2 **Baby It's Cold Outside** .... [N]		RCA 0075
			HOMER & JETHRO & JUNE CARTER		
			Best Seller #9		
11/05/49	14	1	3 Tennessee Border No. 2............................ [N]		King 0113
			Juke Box #14		
5/23/53	2²	9	4 **(How Much Is) That Hound Dog In The Window** .... [N]		RCA 5280
			Best Seller #2 / Juke Box #3 / Jockey #10		
8/14/54	14	1	5 Hernando's Hideaway .... [N]		RCA 5788
			Best Seller #14		
10/19/59	26	3	6 The Battle Of Kookamonga .... [N]	14	RCA 7585
4/18/64	49	1	7 I Want To Hold Your Hand........................ [N]		RCA 8345
			THE HOMESTEADERS		
10/15/66	44	7	1 Show Me The Way To The Circus		Little Dar. 0010
8/03/68	67	2	2 Gonna Miss Me		Little Dar. 0045
			BOBBY HOOD		
			Gospel singer from Alabama.		
4/01/78	91	3	1 Come On In		Plantation 169
8/05/78	60	7	2 I've Got An Angel (That Loves Me Like The Devil)..		Chute 101
10/14/78	87	3	3 Come To Me		Chute 102
2/24/79	85	3	4 Slow Tunes And Promises............................		Chute 0004
8/11/79	45	8	5 Easy		Chute 0008
12/08/79	72	5	6 It Takes One To Know One		Chute 0009
3/22/80	75	4	7 When She Falls..		Chute 0010
9/13/80	85	3	8 Mexico Winter		Chute 015
11/29/80	89	3	9 Pick Up The Pieces, Joanne		Chute 016
9/26/81	74	4	10 Woman In My Heart...................................		Chute 018

DEBUT DATE	PEAK POS	WKS CHR	ARTIST — Record Title	POP POS	Label & Number
			HOOSIER HOT SHOTS		
			Novelty group from Fort Wayne, Indiana. Consisted of Paul "Hezzie" Trietsch (song whistle, washboard, drums, alto horn), Kenneth "Rudy" Trietsch (banjo, guitar, bass horn), Charles Otto "Gabe" Ward (clarinet, saxophone, fife) and Frank Kettering (banjo, guitar, flute, piano, bass fiddle). Regulars on WLS-Chicago National Barn Dance from 1933-42. Also appeared in several western movies. Group disbanded in the mid-50s.		
6/17/44	**3**	2	1 **She Broke My Heart In Three Places** .... [N]		Decca 4442
1/26/46	**3**	10	2 **Someday (You'll Want Me To Want You)** ..... [N]	*12*	Decca 18738
			vocal: Sally Foster		
2/09/46	**2**[1]	16	3 **Sioux City Sue** .... [N]		Decca 18745
			DeANNE HORN		
2/18/78	**97**	2	1 I Just Want To Love You		Chartwheel 102
7/08/78	**100**	1	2 I Know		Chartwheel 108
			BRUCE HORNSBY & THE RANGE		
			Piano-based, jazz influenced pop quintet led by singer/songwriter/pianist Hornsby, who was raised in Williamsburg, Virginia and moved to Los Angeles in 1980. The Range includes George Marinelli, Jr., Peter Harris, Joe Puerta and John Molo.		
3/14/87	**38**	10	1 Mandolin Rain	*4*	RCA 5087
			BILLIE JEAN HORTON		
			Widow of Hank Williams and Johnny Horton.		
8/28/61	**29**	3	1 Ocean Of Tears		Fox 266
			JOHNNY HORTON ★★**184**★★		
			Born on 4/3/29 in Los Angeles; died in an automobile accident on 11/5/60. Raised in Tyler, Texas. Attended Baylor University and University of Seattle on athletic scholarships. Worked in the fishing industry in Alaska. Appeared on Hometown Jamboree, KLAC-Los Angeles, and KXLA-Pasadena. Billed as "The Singing Fisherman". Joined the Louisiana Hayride in 1951. First recorded for Cormac in 1951. On KLTV-Tyler radio in the mid-50s. Married to Billie Jean Jones, widow of Hank Williams.		
5/05/56	**9**	12	1 **Honky-Tonk Man**		Columbia 21504
			Jockey #9 / Best Seller #14		
9/08/56	**7**	13	2 **I'm A One Woman Man**		Columbia 21538
			Jockey #7 / Best Seller #9 / Juke Box #9		
2/23/57	**11**	5	3 I'm Coming Home...		Columbia 40813
			Jockey #11 / Best Seller #15		
5/27/57	**9**	1	4 Woman I Need		Columbia 40919
			Juke Box #9		
9/29/58	**8**	8	5 **All Grown Up**		Columbia 41210
			Jockey #8		
1/12/59	**1**[1]	23	6 **When It's Springtime In Alaska (It's Forty Below)**		Columbia 41308
4/27/59	**1**[10]	21	7●**The Battle Of New Orleans**	*1*	Columbia 41339
			original melody written in celebration of the final battle of the War of 1812		
9/07/59	**10**	9	8 **Johnny Reb/**	*54*	
9/07/59	**19**	7	9 Sal's Got A Sugar Lip	*81*	Columbia 41437
3/28/60	**6**	15	10 **Sink The Bismarck**	*3*	Columbia 41568
			inspired by the film of the same title		
11/14/60+	**1**[5]	22	11 **North To Alaska**.......................................	*4*	Columbia 41782
			from the John Wayne film of the same title		
4/24/61	**9**	8	12 Sleepy-Eyed John	*54*	Columbia 41963
4/14/62	**11**	12	13 Honky-Tonk Man .... [R]	*96*	Columbia 42302
2/09/63	**26**	5	14 All Grown Up .... [R]		Columbia 42653
			LARRY HOSFORD		
			Born in 1943 in Alisal, California. First played in folk groups in Monterey.		
12/07/74+	**62**	8	1 Long Distance Kisses..................................		Shelter 40312
4/26/75	**78**	6	2 Everything's Broken Down..............................		Shelter 40381
			DAVID HOUSE		
			Founder of the West Texas Saturday Night Opry in Lubbock, Texas. Also appeared on the Hayloft Opry Show in Lubbock.		
6/26/82	**96**	2	1 Everything's All Right.................................		Door Knob 177
10/09/82	**88**	2	2 Little White Lies		Door Knob 183

DEBUT DATE	PEAK POS	WKS CHR		ARTIST — Record Title	POP POS	Label & Number
				DAVID HOUSTON ★★**40**★★		
				Born on 12/9/38 in Bossier City, Louisiana. Godson of 1920s pop star Gene Austin, and descended from Sam Houston and Robert E. Lee. Worked on Louisiana Hayride radio show from age 12. In the film "Cottonpickin' Chicken-Pluckers" in 1967. With the Grand Ole Opry since 1972.		
10/19/63	2¹	18	1	**Mountain Of Love**	*132*	Epic 9625
3/07/64	37	6	2	Passing Through/		
3/28/64	17	15	3	Chickashay................................		Epic 9658
7/11/64	11	17	4	One If For Him, Two If For Me....................		Epic 9690
10/10/64	17	14	5	Love Looks Good On You		Epic 9720
1/30/65	18	17	6	Sweet, Sweet Judy		Epic 9746
9/11/65	3	18	7	**Livin' In A House Full Of Love**	*117*	Epic 9831
3/05/66	47	2	8	Sammy..		Epic 9884
6/25/66	1⁹	25	9	**Almost Persuaded**	*24*	Epic 10025
12/10/66+	14	12	10	Where Could I Go? (But To Her)/	*133*	
12/24/66+	3	16	11	**A Loser's Cathedral**.................................	*135*	Epic 10102
4/29/67	1¹	18	12	**With One Exception**		Epic 10154
7/15/67	1²	18	13	**My Elusive Dreams**	*89*	Epic 10194
				DAVID HOUSTON & TAMMY WYNETTE		
9/23/67	1²	17	14	**You Mean The World To Me**	*75*	Epic 10224
1/20/68	11	14	15	It's All Over		Epic 10274
				DAVID HOUSTON & TAMMY WYNETTE		
3/09/68	1¹	14	16	**Have A Little Faith**.................................	*98*	Epic 10291
6/15/68	1¹	16	17	**Already It's Heaven**		Epic 10338
10/19/68	2²	14	18	**Where Love Used To Live**........................		Epic 10394
1/18/69	4	17	19	**My Woman's Good To Me**		Epic 10430
6/28/69	3	16	20	**I'm Down To My Last "I Love You"**..............		Epic 10488
11/08/69+	1⁴	17	21	**Baby, Baby (I Know You're A Lady)**		Epic 10539
4/04/70	3	17	22	**I Do My Swinging At Home**		Epic 10596
8/08/70	6	15	23	**Wonders Of The Wine**		Epic 10643
1/09/71	2⁴	16	24	**A Woman Always Knows**		Epic 10696
6/12/71	9	13	25	**Nashville**		Epic 10748
10/09/71	10	14	26	**A Maiden's Prayer/**		
9/25/71	32	16	27	Home Sweet Home		Epic 10778
2/19/72	18	13	28	The Day That Love Walked In		Epic 10830
6/10/72	8	12	29	**Soft, Sweet And Warm**		Epic 10870
10/14/72	41	9	30	I Wonder How John Felt (When He Baptized Jesus)..		Epic 10911
12/30/72+	2²	16	31	**Good Things**..		Epic 10939
6/02/73	3	14	32	**She's All Woman**.....................................		Epic 10995
11/03/73	22	11	33	The Lady Of The Night		Epic 11048
3/30/74	33	12	34	That Same Ol' Look Of Love........................		Epic 11096
9/14/74	9	15	35	**Can't You Feel It**		Epic 50009
3/01/75	36	10	36	A Man Needs Love....................................		Epic 50066
6/14/75	40	10	37	I'll Be Your Steppin' Stone		Epic 50113
9/27/75	69	6	38	Sweet Molly		Epic 50134
				DAVID HOUSTON & CALVIN CRAWFORD		
11/01/75	35	10	39	The Woman On My Mind.............................		Epic 50156
2/07/76	51	9	40	What A Night		Epic 50186
9/25/76	24	12	41	Come On Down (To Our Favorite Forget-About-Her Place)...		Epic 50275
4/30/77	33	9	42	So Many Ways		Gusto/Star. 156
				#6 pop hit for Brook Benton in 1959		
8/06/77	68	6	43	Ain't That Lovin' You Baby..........................		Gusto/Star. 162
				top 10 R&B hit for Jimmy Reed in 1956		
11/19/77	98	1	44	The Twelfth Of Never		Gusto/Star. 168
				#9 pop hit for Johnny Mathis in 1957		
12/24/77+	56	9	45	It Started All Over Again		Gusto/Star. 172
4/08/78	72	5	46	No Tell Motel		Gusto 184
6/24/78	51	9	47	Waltz Of The Angels		Colonial 101
12/09/78+	46	10	48	Best Friends Make The Worst Enemies..............		Elektra 45552
4/21/79	33	10	49	Faded Love And Winter Roses		Elektra 46028
8/18/79	57	8	50	Let Your Love Fall Back On Me		Derrick 126

DEBUT DATE	PEAK POS	WKS CHR	ARTIST — Record Title	POP POS	Label & Number
			DAVID HOUSTON — Continued		
11/10/79	60	8	51 Here's To All The Too Hard Working Husbands (In The World)		Derrick 127
5/31/80	64	7	52 You're The Perfect Reason...........................		Country I. 145
9/13/80	78	4	53 Sad Love Song Lady		Country I. 148
5/09/81	69	6	54 Texas Ida Red...		Excelsior 1012
			DAVID HOUSTON & BARBARA MANDRELL:		
10/03/70	6	14	55 After Closing Time		Epic 10656
10/02/71	20	12	56 We've Got Everything But Love		Epic 10779
9/16/72	24	13	57 A Perfect Match		Epic 10908
12/22/73+	6	16	58 **I Love You, I Love You**		Epic 11068
5/25/74	40	12	59 Lovin' You Is Worth It...............................		Epic 11120
8/10/74	14	16	60 Ten Commandments Of Love......................		Epic 20005
			#22 pop hit for Harvey & The Moonglows in 1958		
			CHUCK HOWARD		
			From Flat Fork, Kentucky. Producer of the pop hit "Surfin' Bird" by The Trashmen. Wrote "Happy Birthday Darlin'" for Conway Twitty. Died on 8/15/83.		
8/23/80	66	7	1 I've Come Back (To Say I Love You One More Time).....................................		Warner 49509
			EDDY HOWARD		
			Born on 9/12/14 in Woodland, California; died on 5/23/63 (48). One of the top popular singers of the 40s and early 50s.		
8/09/47	5	1	1 **Ragtime Cowboy Joe**	*16*	Majestic 1155
			HARLAN HOWARD		
			Born on 9/8/27 in Lexington, Kentucky; raised in Detroit. Moved to Los Angeles in the mid-50s. Hit songwriter, won 10 BMI awards in 1961. Married for a time to Jan Howard.		
4/10/71	38	15	1 Sunday Morning Christian		Nugget 1058
			JAN HOWARD ★★126★★		
			Born Lula Grace Johnson on 3/13/30 in West Plains, Missouri. Moved to Los Angeles in 1953. Married songwriter Harlan Howard. Moved to Nashville in the mid-60s, did tours and TV shows with Bill Anderson for 7 years. Worked with the Johnny Cash and Tammy Wynette shows. Two of her three sons from a previous marriage have died, one in Vietnam shortly after the release of her song "My Son". Joined the Grand Ole Opry in 1971.		
1/11/60	13	12	1 The One You Slip Around With		Challenge 59059
5/30/60	26	2	2 Wrong Company		Challenge 59071
			WYNN STEWART & JAN HOWARD		
11/16/63	27	3	3 I Wish I Was A Single Girl Again		Capitol 5035
1/16/65	25	13	4 What Makes A Man Wander?.......................		Decca 31701
4/23/66	5	20	5 **Evil On Your Mind**		Decca 31933
10/08/66	10	13	6 **Bad Seed**		Decca 32016
3/11/67	32	11	7 Any Old Way You Do		Decca 32096
7/22/67	26	10	8 Roll Over And Play Dead		Decca 32154
3/09/68	16	13	9 Count Your Blessings, Woman......................		Decca 32269
8/10/68	27	11	10 I Still Believe In Love		Decca 32357
11/23/68+	15	14	11 My Son......................................		Decca 32407
3/08/69	24	11	12 When We Tried		Decca 32447
9/20/69	20	9	13 We Had All The Good Things Going		Decca 32543
3/21/70	26	10	14 Rock Me Back To Little Rock		Decca 32636
11/14/70	64	5	15 The Soul You Never Had......................		Decca 32743
2/13/71	56	10	16 Baby Without You/		
		2	17 Marriage Has Ruined More Good Love Affairs...		Decca 32778
12/25/71+	36	14	18 Love Is Like A Spinning Wheel		Decca 32905
5/06/72	43	10	19 Let Him Have It		Decca 32955
3/31/73	74	2	20 Too Many Ties That Bind.......................		MCA 40020
11/09/74	96	4	21 Seein' Is Believin'...............................		GRT 010
4/30/77	70	6	22 I'll Hold You In My Heart (Till I Can Hold You In My Arms)		Con Brio 118
10/01/77	65	7	23 Better Off Alone...........................		Con Brio 125
4/22/78	93	3	24 To Love A Rolling Stone...........................		Con Brio 132

DEBUT DATE	PEAK POS	WKS CHR	ARTIST — Record Title	POP POS	Label & Number
			JAN HOWARD — Continued		
			BILL ANDERSON & JAN HOWARD:		
2/19/66	**29**	8	25 I Know You're Married (But I Love You Still)/		
3/12/66	**44**	1	26 Time Out		Decca 31884
10/28/67	**1**[4]	20	27 **For Loving You**		Decca 32197
11/15/69+	**2**[1]	15	28 **If It's All The Same To You**		Decca 32511
6/20/70	**4**	15	29 **Someday We'll Be Together**		Decca 32689
			#1 pop hit for Diana Ross & The Supremes in 1969		
10/09/71	**4**	15	30 **Dis-Satisfied**		Decca 32877
			JIM HOWARD		
7/18/64	**38**	9	1 Meet Me Tonight Outside Of Town		Del-Mar 1013
			RANDY HOWARD		
			Born Randall Lamar Howard on 5/9/50 in Macon, Georgia. Worked at local clubs, appeared on the Buddy Knox TV series. Had own TV shows. Wrote "God Don't Live In Nashville Tennessee", "She's A Lover" and "All-American Redneck".		
4/09/83	**84**	4	1 All-American Redneck		Warner 29781
1/09/88	**66**	5	2 Ring Of Fire		Atln. Am. 99387
			#1 hit for Johnny Cash in 1963		
			HAL HUBBLE		
			Born in 1940 in Indianapolis.		
11/25/78	**76**	6	1 My Pulse Pumps Passions		50 States 66
			HELEN HUDSON		
			Born on 1/19/53 in Sydney, Australia. Professional model in New York City by age 12. Graduated cum laude from Stanford in 1973. Taught high school English.		
5/26/79	**91**	5	1 Nothing But Time		Cyclone 102
			LARRY G. HUDSON		
			Born in 1949 in Hawkinsville, Georgia; raised in Unadilla, Georgia. Guitarist at age 11 in Future Farmer's Of America String Band. Replaced Razzy Bailey at the Nashville South Club, in Macon, Georgia in 1974.		
6/12/76	**89**	4	1 Singing A Happy Song		Aquarian 605
10/14/78	**37**	10	2 Just Out Of Reach Of My Two Open Arms		Lone Star 702
			#24 pop hit for Solomon Burke in 1961		
1/27/79	**31**	10	3 Loving You Is A Natural High		Lone Star 706
3/15/80	**34**	10	4 I Can't Cheat		Mercury 57015
8/16/80	**39**	9	5 I'm Still In Love With You		Mercury 57029
			HOLLIE HUGHES		
			Singer from Carrollton, Texas.		
2/14/87	**75**	3	1 67 Miles To Cow Town		Luv 130
			JOEL HUGHES		
			Born on 10/2/55 in Jenkins, Kentucky. Performing since age 8.		
3/13/82	**75**	4	1 Handy Man		Sunbird 7569
			#2 pop hit for Jimmy Jones in 1960		
			THE HUMMERS		
7/21/73	**38**	7	1 Old Betsy Goes Boing, Boing, Boing		Capitol 3646
6/01/74	**91**	4	2 Julianna		Capitol 3870
			ENGELBERT HUMPERDINCK		
			Born Arnold George Dorsey on 5/2/36 in Madras, India. To Leicester, England in 1947. First recorded for Decca in 1958. Met Tom Jones' manager, Gordon Mills, in 1965, who suggested his name change to Engelbert Humperdinck (a famous German opera composer). Starred in his own musical variety TV series in 1970.		
1/08/77	**40**	12	1● After The Lovin'	8	Epic 50270
7/02/77	**93**	3	2 Goodbye My Friend	97	Epic 50365
1/27/79	**93**	4	3 This Moment In Time	58	Epic 50632
5/14/83	**39**	14	4 Til You And Your Lover Are Lovers Again	77	Epic 03817
			CON HUNLEY ★★**172**★★		
			Born Conrad Logan Hunley on 4/9/45 in Luttrell, Tennessee. Worked local clubs in Knoxville and formed his own band in 1976. Moved to Nashville in 1978 and worked at George Jones' Possum Holler Club.		
1/29/77	**96**	4	1 Pick Up The Pieces		Prairie D. 7608
4/16/77	**75**	6	2 I'll Always Remember That Song		Prairie D. 7614
7/23/77	**67**	7	3 Breaking Up Is Hard To Do		Prairie D. 7618
2/04/78	**34**	10	4 Cry Cry Darling		Warner 8520

DEBUT DATE	PEAK POS	WKS CHR		ARTIST — Record Title	POP POS	Label & Number
				CON HUNLEY — Continued		
5/13/78	**13**	12	5	Week-End Friend..........................		Warner 8572
10/07/78	**14**	13	6	You've Still Got A Place In My Heart................		Warner 8671
1/27/79	**14**	14	7	I've Been Waiting For You All Of My Life...........		Warner 8723
				#48 pop hit for Paul Anka in 1981		
5/26/79	**20**	12	8	Since I Fell For You.....................		Warner 8812
				#4 pop hit for Lenny Welch in 1963		
11/03/79+	**20**	14	9	I Don't Want To Lose You.................		Warner 49090
3/08/80	**19**	12	10	You Lay A Whole Lot Of Love On Me		Warner 49187
8/16/80	**19**	13	11	They Never Lost You		Warner 49528
12/20/80+	**11**	16	12	What's New With You		Warner 49613
8/29/81	**17**	15	13	She's Steppin' Out.......................		Warner 49800
1/09/82	**20**	14	14	No Relief In Sight		Warner 49887
5/22/82	**12**	15	15	Oh Girl.....................		Warner 50058
				#1 pop hit for The Chi-Lites in 1972; backing vocals: The Oak Ridge Boys		
10/09/82	**43**	9	16	Confidential		Warner 29902
4/30/83	**42**	10	17	Once You Get The Feel Of It................		MCA 52208
9/03/83	**84**	4	18	Satisfied Mind		MCA 52259
				guest vocal: Porter Wagoner (#2 hit for him in 1955)		
3/17/84	**75**	7	19	Deep In The Arms Of Texas........................		Prairie D. 84110
12/15/84+	**57**	11	20	All American Country Boy........................		Capitol 5428
3/16/85	**54**	8	21	I'd Rather Be Crazy		Capitol 5457
7/13/85	**49**	9	22	Nobody Ever Gets Enough Love		Capitol 5485
11/30/85+	**48**	15	23	What Am I Gonna Do About You...................		Capitol 5525
5/31/86	**49**	13	24	Blue Suede Blues		Capitol 5586
9/27/86	**55**	9	25	Quittin' Time........................		Capitol 5631
				ED HUNNICUTT		
				Born on 7/29/51 in Troy, New York; raised in Columbia, South Carolina.		
5/21/83	**69**	6	1	Fade To Blue.....................		MCA 52207
10/08/83	**59**	7	2	My Angel's Got The Devil In Her Eyes.............		MCA 52262
3/17/84	**41**	9	3	In Real Life		MCA 52353
				TOMMY HUNTER		
				Born in 1937 in London, Ontario. Singing in Vancouver, British Columbia at age 16. Featured on Country Hoedown CBC-TV series from 1956-65. Host of the Tommy Hunter TV Show since 1965. Known as "Canada's Country Gentleman".		
9/09/67	**66**	3	1	Mary In The Morning		Columbia 44234
				#27 pop hit for Al Martino in 1967		
				LIBBY HURLEY		
10/03/87	**60**	6	1	Don't Get Me Started		Epic 07366
1/16/88	**43**	10	2	You Just Watch Me		Epic 07650
4/23/88	**59**	8	3	Don't Talk To Me		Epic 07771
				CHARLOTTE HURT		
9/16/78	**85**	5	1	The Price Of Borrowed Love Is Just Too High.....		Compass 0020
				CINDY HURT		
				Born in 1956 in Mundelein, Illinois. Studied music, drama and voice at Butler University in Indianapolis. Did commercials in Chicago, worked with all-girl quartet, Magic. Toured with the musical "Sophisticated Ladies" in 1980.		
3/21/81	**74**	5	1	Single Girl		Churchill 7767
				#12 pop hit for Sandy Posey in 1966		
6/06/81	**56**	8	2	Headin For A Heartache		Churchill 7772
9/05/81	**46**	10	3	Dreams Can Come In Handy........................		Churchill 7777
1/30/82	**28**	13	4	Don't Come Knockin.....................		Churchill 94000
6/12/82	**35**	10	5	Talk To Me Loneliness		Churchill 94004
11/20/82	**67**	8	6	What's Good About Goodbye........................		Churchill 94010
7/02/83	**65**	6	7	I'm In Love All Over Again........................		Churchill 94013
				KENNI HUSKEY		
				Female vocalist, born Nora Carolyn Huskey in 1954 in Newport, Arkansas. Toured with Buck Owens for 4 years.		
10/23/71	**71**	6	1	A Living Tornado		Capitol 3184
1/29/72	**74**	2	2	Within My Loving Arms........................		Capitol 3229

DEBUT DATE	PEAK POS	WKS CHR		ARTIST — Record Title	POP POS	Label & Number
				FERLIN HUSKY ★★60★★		
				Born on 12/3/25 near Flat River, Missouri. Spent five years in the US Merchant Marines during World War II. After discharge, worked clubs in Bakersfield. Recorded as "Terry Preston" in the early 50s; also did humorous recordings as "Simon Crum". Worked with Tennessee Ernie Ford in the early 50s. Appeared as a dramatic actor on Kraft TV theater. In the films "Mr. Rock & Roll" (1957) and "Country Music Holiday" (1958). Married 6 times; he has 7 children. Had a heart operation in 1977. Backing group called The Hushpuppies. Also see Simon Crum.		
				JEAN SHEPARD & FERLIN HUSKEY:		
7/25/53	**1** 6	23	1	**A Dear John Letter**	**4**	Capitol 2502
				Best Seller #1(6) / Juke Box #1(4) / Jockey #2		
10/10/53	**4**	7	2	**Forgive Me John**	24	Capitol 2586
				Best Seller #4 / Juke Box #6 / Jockey #8		
				FERLIN HUSKEY:		
1/15/55	**6**	10	3	**I Feel Better All Over (More Than Anywhere's Else)/**		
				Jockey #6 / Best Seller #15		
1/15/55	**7**	8	4	**Little Tom**		Capitol 3001
				Jockey #7		
5/28/55	**14**	1	5	I'll Baby Sit With You		Capitol 3097
				Best Seller #14		
				FERLIN HUSKY:		
2/23/57	**1** 10	27	6	**Gone**	**4**	Capitol 3628
				Best Seller #1(10) / Jockey #1(9) / Juke Box #1(5) originally recorded by Husky in 1952 as by Terry Preston		
7/01/57	**8**	13	7	**A Fallen Star/**	47	
				Best Seller #8 / Jockey #8		
7/15/57	**12**	1	8	Prize Possession		Capitol 3742
				Jockey #12		
10/27/58	**23**	1	9	I Will		Capitol 4046
2/16/59	**14**	12	10	My Reason For Living		Capitol 4123
6/01/59	**11**	10	11	Draggin' The River		Capitol 4186
11/16/59	**21**	8	12	Black Sheep		Capitol 4278
9/05/60	**1** 10	36	13	**Wings Of A Dove**	12	Capitol 4406
10/09/61	**23**	1	14	Willow Tree		Capitol 4594
1/27/62	**13**	10	15	The Waltz You Saved For Me	94	Capitol 4650
				Wayne King's familiar theme song - written by King in 1930		
5/26/62	**16**	11	16	Somebody Save Me		Capitol 4721
9/22/62	**28**	1	17	Stand Up		Capitol 4779
12/01/62	**21**	2	18	It Was You		Capitol 4853
2/22/64	**13**	21	19	Timber I'm Falling		Capitol 5111
4/10/65	**46**	7	20	True, True Lovin'		Capitol 5355
12/11/65	**48**	2	21	Money Greases The Wheels		Capitol 5522
6/04/66	**27**	5	22	I Could Sing All Night		Capitol 5615
7/09/66	**17**	12	23	I Hear Little Rock Calling		Capitol 5679
12/03/66+	**4**	17	24	**Once**		Capitol 5775
4/01/67	**37**	11	25	What Am I Gonna Do Now		Capitol 5852
7/15/67	**14**	15	26	You Pushed Me Too Far		Capitol 5938
12/23/67+	**4**	18	27	**Just For You**		Capitol 2048
5/25/68	**26**	10	28	I Promised You The World		Capitol 2154
10/19/68	**25**	10	29	White Fences And Evergreen Trees		Capitol 2288
3/15/69	**33**	10	30	Flat River, Mo.		Capitol 2411
6/21/69	**16**	14	31	That's Why I Love You So Much		Capitol 2512
11/22/69	**21**	10	32	Every Step Of The Way		Capitol 2666
5/16/70	**11**	13	33	Heavenly Sunshine		Capitol 2793
9/12/70	**45**	9	34	Your Sweet Love Lifted Me		Capitol 2882
12/26/70+	**14**	11	35	Sweet Misery		Capitol 2999
3/27/71	**28**	11	36	One More Time		Capitol 3069
9/11/71	**45**	9	37	Open Up The Book (And Take A Look)		Capitol 3165
4/22/72	**39**	10	38	Just Plain Lonely		Capitol 3308
9/09/72	**53**	8	39	How Could You Be Anything But Love		Capitol 3415
1/13/73	**35**	10	40	True True Lovin' ....[R]		ABC 11345
4/28/73	**46**	9	41	Between Me And Blue		ABC 11364
8/11/73	**75**	4	42	Baby's Blue		ABC 11381
11/03/73+	**17**	13	43	Rosie Cries A Lot		ABC 11395

DEBUT DATE	PEAK POS	WKS CHR	ARTIST — Record Title	POP POS	Label & Number
			FERLIN HUSKY — Continued		
5/04/74	**26**	15	44 Freckles And Polliwog Days		ABC 11432
9/21/74	**60**	7	45 A Room For A Boy...Never Used......................		ABC 12021
12/28/74+	**34**	11	46 Champagne Ladies And Blue Ribbon Babies.......		ABC 12048
4/19/75	**37**	11	47 Burning...		ABC 12085
10/04/75	**74**	5	48 She's Not Yours Anymore/		
9/27/75	**90**	6	49 An Old Memory (Got In My Eye)		ABC/Dot 17574
			LONEY HUTCHINS Born on 11/7/46 in rural Sullivan County, Tennessee. Developed a new music therapy program.		
7/04/87	**92**	2	1 Still Dancing		ARC 0005

I

DEBUT DATE	PEAK POS	WKS CHR	ARTIST — Record Title	POP POS	Label & Number
			FRANK IFIELD Born on 11/30/37 in Coventry, England. Began career as a teenager in Australia with his own radio and TV shows. Signed to Columbia Records in England in 1959.		
8/27/66	**42**	6	1 No One Will Ever Know		Hickory 1397
10/22/66	**28**	14	2 Call Her Your Sweetheart		Hickory 1411
12/23/67+	**68**	4	3 Oh, Such A Stranger................................. written by Don Gibson		Hickory 1486
10/05/68	**67**	3	4 Good Morning, Dear.......................................		Hickory 1514
			JULIO IGLESIAS Born on 9/23/43 in Madrid, Spain. Immensely popular Spanish singer, worldwide. Soccer goalie for the pro Real Madrid team until temporary paralysis from car crash.		
3/10/84	**1**^{2}	20	1 ● **To All The Girls I've Loved Before**................ JULIO IGLESIAS & WILLIE NELSON	*5*	Columbia 04217
9/17/88	**8**	19	2 **Spanish Eyes** .... WILLIE NELSON with JULIO IGLESIAS		Columbia 08066
			INDIANA		
4/18/87	**85**	2	1 Midnite Rock...		Killer 1005
			RED INGLE & THE NATURAL SEVEN Red's real name is Ernest I. Ingle. Comic singer, also played clarinet, saxophone and violin. Active into the 50s, now reportedly deceased.		
6/21/47	**2**^{11}	18	1 **Temptation (Tim-Tayshun)** .... [N] vocal: Jo Stafford as "Cinderella G. Stump"	*1*	Capitol 412
			DAVID INGLES Country/gospel singer; program director at KTOW-Tulsa. Regular on Mack Daniels' TV show "Proud Country".		
11/29/69	**72**	2	1 Johnny Let The Sunshine In		Capitol 2648
			JAMES INGRAM - see KENNY ROGERS		
			AUTRY INMAN Born Robert Autry Inman on 1/6/29 in Florence, Alabama. Died on 9/6/88. Worked on WLAY-Muscle Shoals and WWVA Jamboree. With Cowboy Copas' Oklahoma Cowboys from 1949-50. Played bass for George Morgan's Candy Kids from 1950-52.		
7/11/53	**4**	4	1 **That's All Right** .... Juke Box #4		Decca 28629
4/13/63	**22**	3	2 The Volunteer		Sims 131
11/02/68	**14**	15	3 Ballad Of Two Brothers .... patriotic-styled narrative, featuring strains of "The Battle Hymn Of The Republic"	*48*	Epic 10389
			JERRY INMAN Lead singer with the house band at the Palomino Club in North Hollywood.		
12/28/74+	**95**	2	1 You're The One...		Chelsea 3006
8/26/78	**95**	2	2 Why, Baby, Why		Elektra 45508
2/17/79	**94**	2	3 Why Don't We Lie Down And Talk It Over		Elektra 46006
			JERRY IRBY & HIS TEXAS RANCHERS		
6/19/48	**11**	2	1 Crying In My Beer .... Juke Box #11		MGM 10151
7/03/48	**10**	1	2 **Great Long Pistol** .... Juke Box #10		MGM 10188

DEBUT DATE	PEAK POS	WKS CHR	ARTIST — Record Title	POP POS	Label & Number
			LONNIE IRVING Born on 6/11/32 in Stoneville, North Carolina. Died of leukemia.		
3/14/60	**13**	15	1 Pinball Machine		Starday 486
			PETER ISAACSON From rural Vermont. First recorded on Philo label.		
7/23/83	**76**	5	1 Froze In Her Line Of Fire.............................		Union Sta. 1002
11/26/83	**61**	6	2 Don't Take Much..		Union Sta. 1004
3/24/84	**93**	2	3 No Survivors		Union Sta. 1005
5/12/84	**71**	5	4 It's A Cover Up		Union Sta. 1006
			BURL IVES Born on 6/14/09 in Huntington Township, Illinois. Actor/author/singer. Played semi-pro football. Began Broadway career in the late 30s. Worked in "This Is The Army" service show during World War II. Own CBS network radio show "The Wayfaring Stranger" in 1944. Appeared in many films, including "Our Man In Havana", "East Of Eden", "Smokey", "Cat On A Hot Tin Roof" and "The Big Country". Worked on TV series "The Bold Ones" in the early 70s.		
2/12/49	**13**	1	1 Lavender Blue (Dilly Dilly) .... Best Seller #13 with "Captain Stubby & The Buccaneers"	*16*	Decca 24547
5/21/49	**8**	5	2 **Riders In The Sky**................................... Juke Box #8 / Best Seller #15	*21*	Columbia 38445
7/26/52	**6**	4	3 **Wild Side Of Life** .... Juke Box #6 / Best Seller #10 with Grady Martin & His Slew Foot Five		Decca 28055
2/03/62	**2²**	17	4 **A Little Bitty Tear**	*9*	Decca 31330
4/28/62	**9**	13	5 **Funny Way Of Laughin'**.............................	*10*	Decca 31371
8/11/62	**3**	11	6 **Call Me Mr. In-Between**	*19*	Decca 31405
12/01/62+	**12**	7	7 Mary Ann Regrets	*39*	Decca 31433
9/17/66	**47**	6	8 Evil Off My Mind		Decca 31997
2/04/67	**72**	2	9 Lonesome 7-7203		Decca 32078
			ROGER IVIE & SILVERCREEK		
9/12/81	**94**	2	1 You And Me And Tennessee..........................		Cardinal 8102
			IVORY JACK Played piano and harmonica for Vassar Clements.		
2/09/80	**78**	4	1 Made In The USA		NSD 36
5/09/81	**81**	4	2 Love Signs		Country I. 154

J

DEBUT DATE	PEAK POS	WKS CHR	ARTIST — Record Title	POP POS	Label & Number
			JACK & TRINK Jack and Trink Ruthven.		
9/09/78	**93**	4	1 I'm Tired Of Being Me		NSD 4
			CARL JACKSON Born in Louisville, Mississippi in 1953. Played banjo and guitar from age 5. Worked in family bluegrass group at age 13. Toured with Jim and Jesse. First recorded for Prize in the late 60s. Worked with the Sullivan Family gospel group.		
11/03/84	**44**	15	1 She's Gone, Gone, Gone		Columbia 04647
3/02/85	**70**	7	2 All That's Left For Me................................		Columbia 04786
6/01/85	**45**	9	3 Dixie Train...		Columbia 04926
1/25/86	**85**	7	4 You Are The Rock (And I'm A Rolling Stone)......		Columbia 05645
			NISHA JACKSON Winner on TV's "You Can Be A Star" show.		
10/24/87	**81**	3	1 Alive And Well		Capitol 44064
			STONEWALL JACKSON ★★**68**★★ His real name. Born on 11/6/32 in Tabor City, North Carolina. In the US Army in 1948; joined the US Navy and served from 1949-54. Moved to Nashville in 1956; with the Grand Ole Opry since that time. Descended from General "Stonewall" Jackson.		
11/03/58+	**2¹**	23	1 **Life To Go**... written by George Jones		Columbia 41257
6/08/59	**1⁵**	19	2 **Waterloo/**	*4*	
6/29/59	**24**	5	3 Smoke Along The Track...............................		Columbia 41393
11/23/59	**29**	1	4 Igmoo (The Pride Of South Central High)	*95*	Columbia 41488

DEBUT DATE	PEAK POS	WKS CHR		ARTIST — Record Title	POP POS	Label & Number
				STONEWALL JACKSON — Continued		
1/18/60	**12**	12	5	Mary Don't You Weep	*41*	Columbia 41533
4/04/60	**6**	17	6	**Why I'm Walkin'/**	*83*	
4/25/60	**15**	5	7	Life Of A Poor Boy		Columbia 41591
11/07/60	**13**	15	8	A Little Guy Called Joe		Columbia 41785
3/13/61	**26**	6	9	Greener Pastures		Columbia 41932
8/07/61	**27**	2	10	Hungry For Love		Columbia 42028
1/20/62	**3**	22	11	**A Wound Time Can't Erase/**		
2/03/62	**18**	3	12	Second Choice..		Columbia 42229
6/30/62	**11**	10	13	One Look At Heaven/		
7/21/62	**9**	7	14	**Leona**..		Columbia 42426
1/26/63	**11**	10	15	Can't Hang Up The Phone		Columbia 42628
5/18/63	**8**	14	16	**Old Showboat**...		Columbia 42765
11/09/63	**15**	8	17	Wild Wild Wind...		Columbia 42846
12/07/63+	**1**[1]	22	18	**B.J. The D.J.**..		Columbia 42889
4/25/64	**24**	13	19	Not My Kind Of People		Columbia 43011
8/22/64	**4**	25	20	**Don't Be Angry**		Columbia 43076
2/27/65	**8**	19	21	**I Washed My Hands In Muddy Water**.............		Columbia 43197
				#19 pop hit for Johnny Rivers in 1966		
7/17/65	**30**	9	22	Trouble And Me/		
8/14/65	**22**	7	23	Lost In The Shuffle....................................		Columbia 43304
11/06/65	**44**	3	24	Poor Red Georgia Dirt/		
11/27/65+	**24**	12	25	If This House Could Talk		Columbia 43411
4/30/66	**24**	8	26	The Minute Men (Are Turning In Their Graves) ...		Columbia 43552
8/06/66	**12**	15	27	Blues Plus Booze (Means I Lose)		Columbia 43718
2/04/67	**5**	17	28	**Stamp Out Loneliness**		Columbia 43966
6/10/67	**15**	15	29	Promises And Hearts (Were Made To Break).......		Columbia 44121
10/07/67	**27**	12	30	This World Holds Nothing (Since You're Gone)....		Columbia 44283
2/17/68	**39**	10	31	Nothing Takes The Place Of Loving You		Columbia 44416
6/08/68	**31**	9	32	I Believe In Love		Columbia 44501
9/28/68	**16**	15	33	Angry Words		Columbia 44625
3/01/69	**52**	7	34	Somebody's Always Leaving		Columbia 44726
6/14/69	**25**	9	35	"Never More" Quote The Raven.......................		Columbia 44863
10/04/69	**19**	10	36	Ship In The Bottle		Columbia 44976
3/07/70	**72**	2	37	Better Days For Mama		Columbia 45075
7/04/70	**72**	2	38	Born That Way		Columbia 45151
10/10/70	**63**	4	39	Oh, Lonesome Me.......................................		Columbia 45217
				#1 hit for Don Gibson in 1958		
5/22/71	**7**	13	40	**Me And You And A Dog Named Boo**		Columbia 45381
				#5 pop hit for Lobo in 1971		
3/11/72	**51**	9	41	That's All This Old World Needs		Columbia 45546
				with The Brentwood Children's Choir		
7/29/72	**71**	5	42	Torn From The Pages Of Life..........................		Columbia 45632
1/27/73	**70**	3	43	I'm Not Strong Enough (To Build Another Dream)...		Columbia 45738
7/28/73	**41**	9	44	Herman Schwartz.......................................		MGM 14569
				WANDA JACKSON ★★**130**★★		
				Born on 10/20/37 in Maud, Oklahoma. Moved to Bakersfield, California in 1941. Guitarist/pianist from age 9. Moved to Oklahoma City in 1949. Own radio show on KLPR-Oklahoma City in 1950. Recorded with Hank Thompson in 1954. Had 3 solo records released while still in high school. Worked with Red Foley's Ozark Jubilee from 1955-62; toured with Elvis Presley in 1955 and 1956.		
7/24/54	**8**	8	1	**You Can't Have My Love**.............................		Decca 29140
				WANDA JACKSON & BILLY GRAY Best Seller #8 / Jockey #8 / Juke Box #10		
10/20/56	**15**	1	2	I Gotta Know..		Capitol 3485
				Jockey #15		
7/31/61	**9**	14	3	**Right Or Wrong**	*29*	Capitol 4553
11/20/61+	**6**	15	4	**In The Middle Of A Heartache**.....................	*27*	Capitol 4635
6/09/62	**28**	1	5	If I Cried Every Time You Hurt Me....................	*58*	Capitol 4723
1/25/64	**46**	1	6	Slippin'		Capitol 5072
3/28/64	**36**	11	7	The Violet And A Rose.................................		Capitol 5142
2/26/66	**18**	11	8	The Box It Came In.....................................		Capitol 5559

DEBUT DATE	PEAK POS	WKS CHR	ARTIST — Record Title	POP POS	Label & Number
			WANDA JACKSON — Continued		
6/25/66	**28**	7	9 Because It's You		Capitol 5645
9/03/66	**46**	10	10 This Gun Don't Care		Capitol 5712
12/17/66+	**11**	18	11 Tears Will Be The Chaser For Your Wine..........		Capitol 5789
4/22/67	**21**	12	12 Both Sides Of The Line...................................		Capitol 5863
8/19/67	**51**	7	13 My Heart Gets All The Breaks/		
8/19/67	**64**	2	14 You'll Always Have My Love		Capitol 5960
11/25/67+	**22**	12	15 A Girl Don't Have To Drink To Have Fun..........		Capitol 2021
1/27/68	**46**	6	16 By The Time You Get To Phoenix......................		Capitol 2085
			answer song to Glen Campbell's "By The Time I Get To Phoenix"		
5/04/68	**34**	10	17 My Baby Walked Right Out On Me....................		Capitol 2151
9/07/68	**46**	6	18 Little Boy Soldier		Capitol 2245
11/16/68+	**51**	9	19 I Wish I Was Your Friend..............................		Capitol 2315
			above 8: **WANDA JACKSON & THE PARTY TIMERS**		
2/08/69	**41**	10	20 If I Had A Hammer		Capitol 2379
			#10 pop hit for Peter, Paul & Mary in 1962		
7/12/69	**48**	7	21 Everything's Leaving		Capitol 2524
9/27/69	**20**	11	22 My Big Iron Skillet		Capitol 2614
1/03/70	**35**	10	23 Two Separate Bar Stools		Capitol 2693
4/04/70	**17**	11	24 A Woman Lives For Love...............................		Capitol 2761
9/12/70	**50**	7	25 Who Shot John..		Capitol 2872
12/12/70+	**13**	11	26 Fancy Satin Pillows		Capitol 2986
8/07/71	**25**	12	27 Back Then		Capitol 3143
11/27/71+	**35**	11	28 I Already Know (What I'm Getting For My Birthday)...		Capitol 3218
4/08/72	**57**	7	29 I'll Be Whatever You Say		Capitol 3293
1/26/74	**98**	4	30 Come On Home (To This Lonely Heart).............		Myrrh 125
			LORI JACOBS		
3/15/80	**94**	2	1 Tugboat Annie..		Neostat 102
			RICK JACQUES		
5/06/78	**89**	2	1 Song Man		Caprice 2046
			ATLANTA JAMES		
			Pseudonym for songwriter Mack Vickery.		
6/08/74	**95**	3	1 That Kind Of Fool		MCA 40233
			DUSTY JAMES		
7/14/79	**76**	4	1 You're All The Woman I'll Ever Need		SCR 172
			GEORGE JAMES		
			Born in 1958 in Rockford, Illinois. Own band, Mood Express, from 1975.		
5/12/79	**94**	3	1 It's Gonna Be Magic......................................		Janc 10417
10/20/79	**95**	2	2 When Our Love Began...................................		Janc 103
			JESSECA JAMES - see KATHY TWITTY		
			MARY KAY JAMES		
			Born Mary Kay Mulkey in Atlanta, Georgia. Vocalist and guitarist with family gospel group. Went solo in 1970.		
5/04/74	**78**	6	1 Please Help Me Say No		JMI 38
9/14/74	**48**	13	2 It Amazes Me (Sweet Lovin' Time)		JMI 46
1/25/75	**57**	8	3 The Crossroad		Avco 605
5/03/75	**76**	7	4 I Think I'll Say Goodbye		Avco 610
			SONNY JAMES ★★**19**★★		
			Born James Loden on 5/1/29 in Hackleburg, Arkansas. Singer/songwriter/guitarist. Sang with his four sisters in the Loden Family group from age 4. Own radio show in Birmingham, Alabama while still a teenager. Performed while in the service in the early 50s. In the films "Second Fiddle To A Steel Guitar", "Nashville Rebel", "Las Vegas Hillbillies" and "Hillbilly In A Haunted House". Known as "The Southern Gentleman".		
2/07/53	**9**	1	1 **That's Me Without You**		Capitol 2259
			Jockey #9		
11/20/54	**14**	1	2 She Done Give Her Heart To Me......................		Capitol 2906
			Jockey #14		
3/24/56	**7**	11	3 **For Rent**		Capitol 3357
			Jockey #7 / Juke Box #8 / Best Seller #12		

DEBUT DATE	PEAK POS	WKS CHR		ARTIST — Record Title	POP POS	Label & Number
				SONNY JAMES — Continued		
6/30/56	**11**	6	4	Twenty Feet Of Muddy Water		Capitol 3441
				Jockey #11		
11/10/56	**12**	1	5	The Cat Came Back		Capitol 3542
				Jockey #12		
12/22/56+	**1**⁹	24	6	**Young Love/**	*1*	
				Jockey #1(9) / Best Seller #1(7) / Juke Box #1(3)		
1/26/57	**6**	12	7	**You're The Reason I'm In Love**...................		Capitol 3602
				Jockey #6		
4/13/57	**9**	9	8	**First Date, First Kiss, First Love**..............	25	Capitol 3674
				Best Seller #9 / Jockey #9		
8/12/57	**15**	1	9	Lovesick Blues		Capitol 3734
				Jockey #15		
1/06/58	**8**	5	10	**Uh-Huh--mm**	92	Capitol 3840
				Jockey #8 / Best Seller #14		
5/09/60	**22**	6	11	Jenny Lou	67	NRC 050
7/20/63	**9**	15	12	**The Minute You're Gone**........................	95	Capitol 4969
12/21/63	**17**	9	13	Going Through The Motions (Of Living)		Capitol 5057
3/28/64	**6**	17	14	**Baltimore**................................	*134*	Capitol 5129
7/18/64	**27**	6	15	Sugar Lump/		
8/08/64	**19**	13	16	Ask Marie		Capitol 5197
11/14/64+	**1**⁴	25	17	**You're The Only World I Know**	91	Capitol 5280
4/03/65	**2**¹	20	18	**I'll Keep Holding On (Just To Your Love)**	*116*	Capitol 5375
8/14/65	**1**³	22	19	**Behind The Tear**................................	*113*	Capitol 5454
12/11/65+	**3**	18	20	**True Love's A Blessing**........................		Capitol 5536
4/09/66	**1**²	20	21	**Take Good Care Of Her**		Capitol 5612
				#7 pop hit for Adam Wade in 1961		
8/13/66	**2**²	20	22	**Room In Your Heart**		Capitol 5690
2/25/67	**1**²	18	23	**Need You**		Capitol 5833
6/10/67	**1**⁴	17	24	**I'll Never Find Another You**	97	Capitol 5914
				#4 pop hit for The Seekers in 1965		
9/23/67	**1**⁵	18	25	**It's The Little Things**		Capitol 5987
1/20/68	**1**³	17	26	**A World Of Our Own**	*118*	Capitol 2067
				#19 pop hit for The Seekers in 1965		
6/01/68	**1**¹	17	27	**Heaven Says Hello**		Capitol 2155
10/12/68	**1**¹	16	28	**Born To Be With You**	81	Capitol 2271
				#5 pop hit for The Chordettes in 1956		
1/18/69	**1**³	16	29	**Only The Lonely**	92	Capitol 2370
				#2 pop hit for Roy Orbison in 1960		
5/10/69	**1**³	15	30	**Running Bear**................................	94	Capitol 2486
				#1 pop hit for Johnny Preston in 1960		
9/06/69	**1**³	15	31	**Since I Met You, Baby**	65	Capitol 2595
				#12 pop hit for Ivory Joe Hunter in 1956		
1/17/70	**1**⁴	14	32	**It's Just A Matter Of Time**	87	Capitol 2700
				#3 pop hit for Brook Benton in 1959		
4/11/70	**1**³	15	33	**My Love**................................	*125*	Capitol 2782
				#1 pop hit for Petula Clark in 1966		
7/04/70	**1**⁴	15	34	**Don't Keep Me Hangin' On**		Capitol 2834
10/17/70	**1**³	16	35	**Endlessly**................................	*108*	Capitol 2914
				#12 pop hit for Brook Benton in 1959		
2/27/71	**1**⁴	16	36	**Empty Arms**................................	93	Capitol 3015
				#13 pop hit for Teresa Brewer in 1957		
6/19/71	**1**¹	13	37	**Bright Lights, Big City**	91	Capitol 3114
				#58 pop hit for Jimmy Reed in 1961		
10/02/71	**1**¹	15	38	**Here Comes Honey Again**		Capitol 3174
1/15/72	**2**²	16	39	**Only Love Can Break A Heart**		Capitol 3232
				#2 pop hit for Gene Pitney in 1962		
5/13/72	**1**¹	11	40	**That's Why I Love You Like I Do**		Capitol 3322
7/22/72	**1**¹	15	41	**When The Snow Is On The Roses**	*103*	Columbia 45644
9/02/72	**30**	9	42	Traces..................................		Capitol 3398
				#2 pop hit for the Classics IV in 1969		
10/21/72	**5**	14	43	**White Silver Sands**		Columbia 45706
				#7 pop hit for Don Rondo in 1957		
12/02/72+	**32**	10	44	Downfall Of Me		Capitol 3475
2/10/73	**4**	14	45	**I Love You More And More Everyday**............		Columbia 45770
				#9 pop hit for Al Martino in 1964		
4/14/73	**61**	4	46	Reach Out Your Hand And Touch Me...............		Capitol 3564

DEBUT DATE	PEAK POS	WKS CHR	ARTIST — Record Title	POP POS	Label & Number
			SONNY JAMES — Continued		
6/09/73	**15**	11	47 If She Just Helps Me Get Over You		Columbia 45871
7/21/73	**66**	5	48 Heaven On Earth..		Capitol 3653
12/15/73+	**49**	9	49 Surprise, Surprise		Capitol 3779
3/02/74	**1**¹	15	50 **Is It Wrong (For Loving You)**........................		Columbia 46003
7/27/74	**4**	17	51 **A Mi Esposa Con Amor (To My Wife With Love)**.........................		Columbia 10001
1/25/75	**6**	12	52 **A Little Bit South Of Saskatoon**....................		Columbia 10072
4/26/75	**5**	15	53 **Little Band Of Gold**		Columbia 10121
			#21 pop hit for James Gilreath in 1963		
8/09/75	**10**	15	54 **What In The World's Come Over You**		Columbia 10184
			#5 pop hit for Jack Scott in 1960		
12/13/75+	**67**	8	55 Eres Tu (Touch The Wind)		Columbia 10249
			#9 pop hit for Mocedades in 1974		
1/31/76	**14**	13	56 The Prisoner's Song/		
			million-selling song for Vernon Dalhart in 1925		
		12	57 Back In The Saddle Again...........................		Columbia 10276
			Gene Autry's theme song		
5/15/76	**6**	15	58 **When Something Is Wrong With My Baby**		Columbia 10335
			#42 pop hit for Sam & Dave in 1967		
8/28/76	**8**	14	59 **Come On In**		Columbia 10392
1/29/77	**9**	13	60 **You're Free To Go**....................................		Columbia 10466
6/18/77	**15**	11	61 In The Jailhouse Now		Columbia 10551
			a 1928 Jimmie Rodgers' tune		
10/22/77	**24**	13	62 Abilene		Columbia 10628
			#15 pop hit for George Hamilton IV in 1963; above 2: live recordings at the Tennessee State Prison		
3/18/78	**16**	12	63 This Is The Love		Columbia 10703
7/22/78	**18**	12	64 Caribbean...		Columbia 10764
			#26 pop hit for Mitchell Torok in 1953		
12/02/78+	**30**	12	65 Building Memories......................................		Columbia 10852
3/31/79	**36**	9	66 Hold What You've Got..................................		Monument 280
			#5 pop hit for Joe Tex in 1965		
7/21/79	**62**	6	67 Lorelei		Monument 288
12/26/81+	**19**	16	68 Innocent Lies		Dimension 1026
5/15/82	**60**	7	69 A Place In The Sun......................................		Dimension 1033
			SONNY JAMES & SILVER:		
10/09/82	**66**	7	70 I'm Looking Over The Rainbow		Dimension 1036
12/25/82+	**33**	13	71 The Fool In Me		Dimension 1040
8/13/83	**58**	9	72 A Free Roamin' Mind		Dimension 1045
			TOMMY JAMES Born Thomas Jackson on 4/29/47 in Dayton, Ohio. To Niles, Michigan at age 11. Formed group, The Shondells, at age 12.		
3/15/80	**93**	2	1 Three Times In Love.................................	*19*	Millennium 11785
			CODY JAMESON Songstress from New York City.		
4/16/77	**64**	7	1 Brooklyn	*74*	Atco 7073
			JAN & MALCOLM		
3/12/77	**99**	2	1 Rainbow In Your Eyes (Loves Got A Hold On Me)		Paula 421
			JANO Jano Bourland.		
10/20/79	**94**	2	1 Sundown Sideshow.....................................		SCR 180
			CLIFTON JANSKY Born in 1956 in Pleasanton, Texas. Worked San Antonio clubs in the late 70s.		
4/13/85	**97**	2	1 Will You Love Me In The Morning...................		Axbar 6033
			JERRY JAYE Born Jerald Jaye Hatley on 10/19/37 in Manila, Arkansas.		
8/09/75	**53**	8	1 It's All In The Game		Columbia 10170
			#1 pop hit for Tommy Edwards in 1958		
6/12/76	**32**	13	2 Honky Tonk Women Love Red Neck Men..........		Hi 2310
11/20/76	**78**	9	3 Hot And Still Heatin'		Hi 2318
			JEAN - see NORMA JEAN		

DEBUT DATE	PEAK POS	WKS CHR	ARTIST — Record Title	POP POS	Label & Number
			BOB JENKINS		
2/06/82	**76**	3	1 The Cube.. [N]		Liberty 1448
			with 3-year-old daughter Mandy		
2/19/83	**86**	3	2 Workin' In A Coalmine..................................		Picap 009
			BOBBY JENKINS		
			Born in 1942 in Corpus Christi, Texas.		
6/16/84	**69**	5	1 Blackjack Whiskey		Zone 7 40984
8/25/84	**82**	3	2 Louisiana Heatwave		Zone 7 61884
5/11/85	**85**	3	3 Me And Margarita		Zone 7 30185
			LARRY JENKINS		
			Singer/songwriter from West Helena, Arkansas; nephew of Conway Twitty.		
10/30/82	**76**	6	1 I'm So Tired Of Going Home Drunk..................		Capitol 5167
7/28/84	**87**	3	2 You're The Best I Never Had		MCA 52396
			BOB JENNINGS		
			Born on 9/26/24 in Liberty, Tennessee. Own bands, the Eagle Rangers, from 1947-49; the Radio Playboys from 1949-52; and the Farm Hands from 1952-55.		
5/09/64	**32**	13	1 The First Step Down (Is The Longest)...............		Sims 161
11/14/64	**34**	8	2 Leave A Little Play (In The Chain Of Love)........		Sims 202
			TOMMY JENNINGS		
			Born on 8/8/38 in Littlefield, Texas. Younger brother of Waylon Jennings.		
8/02/75	**96**	4	1 Make It Easy On Yourself		Paragon 102
4/15/78	**71**	7	2 Don't You Think It's Time		Monument 248
5/31/80	**51**	10	3 Just Give Me What You Think Is Fair		Sabre 4520
			REX GOSDIN with TOMMY JENNINGS		
			WAYLON JENNINGS ★★11★★		
			Born on 6/15/37 in Littlefield, Texas. On local radio from age 12. Moved to Lubbock, Texas in 1954 and worked as a disc jockey. Toured with Buddy Holly as his bass player from 1958-59. Moved to Phoenix and formed his own band, the Waylors, in 1960. Recorded for Trend in 1961. Moved to Nashville in 1965. Established himself in the mid-70s as a leader of the "Outlaw" movement in Country music. Married to Jesse Colter since 1969. In the films "Nashville Rebel", "MacKintosh And T.J." and "Urban Cowboy".		
8/21/65	**49**	2	1 That's The Chance I'll Have To Take		RCA 8572
9/25/65	**16**	13	2 Stop The World (And Let Me Off).....................		RCA 8652
1/15/66	**17**	15	3 Anita, You're Dreaming.................................		RCA 8729
6/04/66	**17**	13	4 Time To Bum Again.....................................		RCA 8822
9/03/66	**9**	18	5 (That's What You Get) For Lovin' Me		RCA 8917
			#30 pop hit for Peter, Paul & Mary in 1965		
12/17/66+	**11**	15	6 Green River		RCA 9025
			from the film "Nashville Rebel"		
4/01/67	**12**	16	7 Mental Revenge		RCA 9146
8/19/67	**8**	17	8 The Chokin' Kind/		
			#13 pop hit for Joe Simon in 1969		
9/09/67	**67**	5	9 Love Of The Common People.........................		RCA 9259
1/27/68	**5**	16	10 Walk On Out Of My Mind		RCA 9414
7/13/68	**2⁵**	18	11 Only Daddy That'll Walk The Line		RCA 9561
11/16/68+	**5**	17	12 Yours Love..		RCA 9642
3/08/69	**19**	12	13 Something's Wrong In California.....................		RCA 0105
5/24/69	**20**	12	14 The Days Of Sand And Shovels/		
			#34 pop hit for Bobby Vinton in 1969		
5/31/69	**37**	6	15 Delia's Gone...	124	RCA 0157
8/23/69	**23**	11	16 MacArthur Park...	93	RCA 0210
			with The Kimberlys		
11/29/69+	**3**	15	17 Brown Eyed Handsome Man		RCA 0281
			written and recorded by Chuck Berry in 1956		
4/18/70	**12**	14	18 Singer Of Sad Songs..................................		RCA 9819
8/29/70	**5**	15	19 The Taker..	94	RCA 9885
12/05/70+	**16**	12	20 (Don't Let the Sun Set on You) Tulsa		RCA 9925
4/03/71	**14**	14	21 Mississippi Woman		RCA 9967
8/07/71	**12**	15	22 Cedartown, Georgia		RCA 1003
1/08/72	**3**	18	23 Good Hearted Woman................................		RCA 0615
			also see version by Waylon & Willie below		
6/10/72	**7**	13	24 Sweet Dream Woman.................................		RCA 0716
10/21/72	**6**	15	25 Pretend I Never Happened		RCA 0808

DEBUT DATE	PEAK POS	WKS CHR		ARTIST — Record Title	POP POS	Label & Number
				WAYLON JENNINGS — Continued		
2/17/73	**7**	14	26	**You Can Have Her**	*114*	RCA 0886
				#12 pop hit for Roy Hamilton in 1961		
5/26/73	**28**	10	27	We Had It All...........................		RCA 0961
10/06/73	**8**	15	28	**You Ask Me To**		RCA 0086
4/27/74	**1**¹	13	29	**This Time**		RCA 0251
8/10/74	**1**¹	13	30	**I'm A Ramblin' Man**	75	RCA 10020
12/21/74+	**2**¹	15	31	**Rainy Day Woman/**		
		12	32	Let's All Help The Cowboys (Sing The Blues)....		RCA 10142
5/03/75	**10**	14	33	**Dreaming My Dreams With You**.....................		RCA 10270
				flip side "Waymore's Blues" hit POS 110 on the pop charts		
9/06/75	**1**¹	16	34	**Are You Sure Hank Done It This Way/**	60	
		15	35	Bob Wills Is Still The King...........................		RCA 10379
				above 2: tributes to the legendary Hank Williams and Bob Wills		
7/31/76	**4**	14	36	**Can't You See/**	97	
		8	37	I'll Go Back To Her..........................		RCA 10721
11/20/76+	**7**	14	38	**Are You Ready For The Country/**		
		13	39	So Good Woman		RCA 10842
4/16/77	**1**⁶	18	40	**Luckenbach, Texas (Back to the Basics of Love)**..............	25	RCA 10924
				ending vocal: Willie Nelson		
10/08/77	**1**²	16	41	**The Wurlitzer Prize (I Don't Want To Get Over You)/**		
		16	42	Lookin' For A Feeling		RCA 11118
7/29/78	**1**³	13	43	**I've Always Been Crazy**		RCA 11344
10/28/78	**5**	13	44	**Don't You Think This Outlaw Bit's Done Got Out Of Hand/**		
		11	45	Girl I Can Tell (You're Trying To Work It Out) ..		RCA 11390
5/19/79	**1**³	14	46	**Amanda**..........................	54	RCA 11596
9/22/79	**1**²	13	47	**Come With Me**		RCA 11723
1/05/80	**1**¹	15	48	**I Ain't Living Long Like This**		RCA 11898
5/31/80	**7**	13	49	**Clyde**..........................	103	RCA 12007
8/23/80	**1**¹	17	50●	**Theme From The Dukes Of Hazzard (Good Ol' Boys)**..........	21	RCA 12067
				original song used on the "Dukes Of Hazzard" TV series		
11/21/81+	**5**	19	51	**Shine**		RCA 12367
6/26/82	**4**	16	52	**Women Do Know How To Carry On**		RCA 13257
3/19/83	**1**¹	16	53	**Lucille (You Won't Do Your Daddy's Will)**.......		RCA 13465
				#21 pop hit for Little Richard in 1957		
				above 10 shown only as: **WAYLON**		
7/02/83	**10**	18	54	**Breakin' Down**..........................		RCA 13543
3/03/84	**4**	20	55	**I May Be Used (But Baby I Ain't Used Up)**.......		RCA 13729
6/16/84	**6**	18	56	**Never Could Toe The Mark**		RCA 13827
9/29/84	**6**	21	57	**America**..........................		RCA 13908
1/19/85	**10**	19	58	**Waltz Me To Heaven**		RCA 13984
6/22/85	**2**²	21	59	**Drinkin' And Dreamin'**..........................		RCA 14094
11/16/85+	**13**	18	60	The Devil's On The Loose		RCA 14215
2/15/86	**7**	19	61	**Working Without A Net**		MCA 52776
5/17/86	**5**	19	62	**Will The Wolf Survive**		MCA 52830
9/20/86	**8**	21	63	**What You'll Do When I'm Gone**....................		MCA 52915
1/31/87	**1**¹	19	64	**Rose In Paradise**		MCA 53009
5/16/87	**8**	19	65	**Fallin' Out**..........................		MCA 53088
9/12/87	**6**	22	66	**My Rough And Rowdy Days**..........................		MCA 53158
1/23/88	**16**	16	67	If Ole Hank Could Only See Us Now (Chapter Five...Nashville)..........................		MCA 53243
9/24/88	**38**	9	68	How Much Is It Worth To Live In L.A.		MCA 53314
				WAYLON JENNINGS DUOS with:		
				ANITA CARTER:		
3/30/68	**4**	15	69	**I Got You**		RCA 9480
				JOHNNY CASH:		
5/20/78	**2**²	13	70	**There Ain't No Good Chain Gang/**		
11/17/79+	**22**	12	71	I Wish I Was Crazy Again		Columbia 10742
5/17/86	**35**	11	72	Even Cowgirls Get The Blues..........................		Columbia 05896

DEBUT DATE	PEAK POS	WKS CHR		ARTIST — Record Title	POP POS	Label & Number
				WAYLON JENNINGS — Continued		
				JESSI COLTER:		
11/14/70	**25**	10	73	Suspicious Minds		RCA 9920
				#1 pop hit for Elvis Presley in 1969		
6/19/71	**39**	8	74	Under Your Spell Again		RCA 9992
5/01/76	**2**¹	14	75	**Suspicious Minds**................................ [R]		RCA 10653
2/21/81	**17**	12	76	Storms Never Last................................		RCA 12176
6/06/81	**10**	13	77	**Wild Side Of Life/It Wasn't God Who Made Honky Tonk Angels**		RCA 12245
				WILLIE NELSON (WAYLON & WILLIE):		
12/27/75+	**1**³	17	78	**Good Hearted Woman**........................... [R]	25	RCA 10529
				Willie's vocal overdubbed on a cut from the "Waylon Live" LP		
1/21/78	**1**⁴	16	79	**Mammas Don't Let Your Babies Grow Up To Be Cowboys/**	42	
		15	80	I Can Get Off On You		RCA 11198
3/13/82	**1**²	18	81	**Just To Satisfy You**	52	RCA 13073
10/23/82	**13**	15	82	(Sittin' On) The Dock Of The Bay..............		RCA 13319
10/08/83	**8**	19	83	**Take It To The Limit**	102	Columbia 04131
				WILLIE NELSON, JOHNNY CASH, KRIS KRISTOFFERSON:		
5/18/85	**1**¹	20	84	**Highwayman**		Columbia 04881
9/14/85	**15**	18	85	Desperados Waiting For A Train		Columbia 05594
				JERRY REED:		
8/06/83	**20**	14	86	Hold On, I'm Comin'		RCA 13580
				#21 pop hit for Sam & Dave in 1966		
				HANK WILLIAMS, JR.:		
10/22/83	**15**	16	87	The Conversation..................................		RCA 13631
				originally released on a Hank Williams, Jr. album in 1979		
				JEREMIAH		
10/08/88	**96**	1	1	To Be Loved....................................		Chariot 1921
				SHERRI JERRICO		
10/08/77	**95**	2	1	Thanks For Leaving, Lucille..........................		Gusto/Star. 164
				answer song to Kenny Rogers' 1977 hit "Lucille"		
				JIM & JESSE		
				Duo of brothers from Coeburn, Virginia: Jim (b: 2/13/27, guitar) and Jesse McReynolds (b: 7/9/29, mandolin). Worked on radio in Norton, Virginia, then on WNOX-Knoxville Tennessee Barn Dance. Regulars on the Grand Ole Opry since 1964.		
7/18/64	**43**	2	1	Cotton Mill Man		Epic 9676
12/19/64+	**39**	6	2	Better Times A-Coming		Epic 9729
4/01/67	**18**	16	3	Diesel On My Tail...............................		Epic 10138
9/23/67	**44**	4	4	Ballad Of Thunder Road		Epic 10213
				#62 pop hit for Robert Mitchum in 1958		
1/27/68	**49**	6	5	Greenwich Village Folk Song Salesman		Epic 10263
9/07/68	**56**	6	6	Yonder Comes A Freight Train		Epic 10370
1/10/70	**38**	9	7	The Golden Rocket................................		Epic 10563
2/13/71	**41**	9	8	Freight Train		Capitol 3026
				#6 pop hit for Rusty Draper in 1957		
6/05/82	**56**	9	9	North Wind		Soundwaves 4671
				JIM & JESSE and CHARLIE LOUVIN:		
9/27/86	**78**	3	10	Oh Louisiana....................................		MSR 198310
				JIMMY & JOHNNY		
				Duo of Jimmy Lee Fautheree and "Country" Johnny Mathis.		
9/25/54	**3**	18	1	**If You Don't Someone Else Will**		Chess 4859
				Juke Box #3 / Jockey #5 / Best Seller #6		
				SAMI JO - see SAMI JO COLE		
				JOE BOB'S NASHVILLE SOUND COMPANY		
				Studio group led by Joe Bob Barnhill (b: 10/14/33, Tuhey, Texas).		
5/17/75	**84**	6	1	In The Mood .... [I]		Capitol 4059
				#1 pop hit for Glenn Miller & His Orchestra in 1940		
				THE JOHN DEER COMPANY		
10/10/70	**57**	7	1	Waxahachie Woman		Royal Amer. 21

DEBUT DATE	PEAK POS	WKS CHR	ARTIST — Record Title	POP POS	Label & Number
			JOHNNIE & JACK ★★189★★		
			Duo of Johnnie Wright (b: 5/13/14, Mount Juliet, TN) and Jack Anglin (b: 5/13/16, Columbia, TN; d: 3/8/63 [auto crash]). The team was formed in 1938 and worked WSIX-Nashville. Wright married Kitty Wells in 1938. First recorded for Apollo in 1947. Worked as a team with Wells from 1948. On the Louisiana Hayride from 1948-52, switched to the Grand Ole Opry in 1952. Anglin was killed enroute to Patsy Cline's memorial service. Wright continued as a solo.		
1/20/51	**4**	17	1 **Poison Love** .... Jockey #4 / Best Seller #5 / Juke Box #9		RCA 0377
8/04/51	**5**	11	2 **Crying Heart Blues** .... Juke Box #5 / Jockey #6 / Best Seller #10		RCA 0478
5/10/52	**7**	5	3 **Three Ways Of Knowing** .... Juke Box #7		RCA 4555
4/10/54	**1** ²	18	4 **Oh, Baby Mine (I Get So Lonely)** .... Jockey #1 / Best Seller #5		RCA 5681
7/17/54	**3**	17	5 **Goodnight, Sweetheart, Goodnight/** Jockey #3 / Best Seller #4 / Juke Box #4		
8/07/54	**15**	1	6 Honey, I Need You.............................. Jockey #15		RCA 5775
11/13/54	**9**	10	7 **Beware Of It/** Best Seller #9 / Juke Box #9 / Jockey #10		
11/27/54+	**7**	4	8 Kiss Crazy Baby.............................. Juke Box #7 / Best Seller #13		RCA 5880
5/21/55	**14**	3	9 No One Dear But You......................... Jockey #14		RCA 6094
12/17/55	**15**	1	10 S.O.S. .... Jockey #15		RCA 6296
3/03/56	**13**	3	11 I Want To Be Loved .... Jockey #13		RCA 6395
2/24/58	**7**	18	12 **Stop The World (And Let Me Off)** .... Best Seller #7 / Jockey #9		RCA 7137
10/20/58	**18**	3	13 Lonely Island Pearl		RCA 7324
8/10/59	**16**	12	14 Sailor Man		RCA 7545
8/11/62	**17**	4	15 Slow Poison .... shown as: **JOHNNY & JACK**		Decca 31397
			SAMMY JOHNS		
			Born on 2/7/46 in Charlotte, North Carolina. Played guitar from age 10. Own band, the Devilles, from 1963-73.		
11/30/74+	**79**	7	1 Early Morning Love	68	GRC 2021
9/19/81	**50**	7	2 Common Man		Elektra 47189
9/03/88	**80**	6	3 Chevy Van .... [R] new version of his 1975 pop hit (Pos 5)		MCA 53398
			SARAH JOHNS		
8/30/75	**75**	3	1 I'm Ready To Love You Now........................		RCA 10333
1/10/76	**97**	4	2 Feelings .... #6 pop hit for Morris Albert in 1975		RCA 10465
3/27/76	**86**	3	3 Let The Big Wheels Roll		RCA 10590
			TRICIA JOHNS		
			Born in Austin, Texas. Sang R&B and rock in the 60s. Moved to Los Angeles in 1971.		
5/14/77	**100**	1	1 The Heat Is On		Warner 8357
12/27/80+	**90**	3	2 Did We Fall Out Of Love		Elektra 47057
8/08/81	**57**	8	3 Cathy's Clown .... #1 pop hit for The Everly Brothers in 1960		Elektra 47172
			BUDDY JOHNSON		
			Born Woodrow Wilson Johnson on 1/10/15 in Darlington, South Carolina. Died on 2/9/77 of a brain tumor. R&B bandleader from 1940s to 60s whose vocalists included Arthur Prysock and Buddy's sister, Ella Johnson. Composer of "Since I Fell For You".		
3/11/44	**2** ²	7	1 **When My Man Comes Home** .... vocal by Ella Johnson	23	Decca 8655
			LOIS JOHNSON		
			Born in Knoxville, Tennessee. Worked on local radio from age 11. Regular appearances on WWVA Jamboree. Toured for 4 years with Hank Williams, Jr.		
1/25/69	**74**	3	1 Softly And Tenderly		Columbia 44725
12/05/70+	**48**	9	2 When He Touches Me (Nothing Else Matters)		MGM 14186
2/27/71	**65**	2	3 From Warm To Cool To Cold		MGM 14217
7/15/72	**63**	8	4 Rain-Rain		MGM 14401
11/17/73	**97**	2	5 Love Will Stand		MGM 14638

DEBUT DATE	PEAK POS	WKS CHR	ARTIST — Record Title	POP POS	Label & Number
			LOIS JOHNSON — Continued		
7/20/74	**19**	19	6 Come On In And Let Me Love You		20th Century 2106
12/28/74+	**6**	15	7 **Loving You Will Never Grow Old**		20th Century 2151
5/17/75	**48**	8	8 You Know Just What I'd Do		20th Century 2187
9/13/75	**95**	4	9 Hope For The Flowers		20th Century 2223
10/11/75	**70**	8	10 The Door's Always Open		20th Century 2242
7/24/76	**87**	2	11 Weep No More My Baby		Polydor 14328
1/15/77	**20**	13	12 Your Pretty Roses Came Too Late		Polydor 14371
5/14/77	**40**	8	13 I Hate Goodbyes		Polydor 14392
11/19/77	**97**	3	14 All The Love We Threw Away		Polydor 14435
			LOIS JOHNSON & BILL RICE		
5/20/78	**63**	7	15 When I Need You		Polydor 14476
			#1 pop hit for Leo Sayer in 1977		
6/02/84	**89**	3	16 It Won't Be Easy		EMH 0030
			HANK WILLIAMS, JR. & LOIS JOHNSON:		
7/04/70	**23**	12	17 Removing The Shadow		MGM 14136
10/03/70	**12**	13	18 So Sad (To Watch Good Love Go Bad)		MGM 14164
4/01/72	**14**	14	19 Send Me Some Lovin'		MGM 14356
11/18/72+	**22**	11	20 Whole Lotta Loving		MGM 14443
			#6 pop hit for Fats Domino in 1959		
			MICHAEL JOHNSON		
			Born in 1945 in Alamosa, Colorado; raised in Denver. Studied classical guitar in 1966 in Spain. In the Chad Mitchell Trio with John Denver in 1968.		
11/16/85+	**9**	25	1 **I Love You By Heart**		RCA 14217
			SYLVIA & MICHAEL JOHNSON		
4/26/86	**12**	20	2 Gotta Learn To Love Without You		RCA 14294
9/27/86+	**1**¹	23	3 **Give Me Wings**		RCA 14412
1/31/87	**1**¹	26	4 **The Moon Is Still Over Her Shoulder**		RCA 5091
6/13/87	**26**	13	5 Ponies		RCA 5171
10/17/87+	**4**	20	6 **Crying Shame**		RCA 5279
4/02/88	**7**	22	7 **I Will Whisper Your Name**		RCA 6833
8/27/88	**9**	20	8 **That's That**		RCA 8650
12/17/88+	**52**	8	9 Roller Coaster Run (Up Too Slow, Down Too Fast)		RCA 8748
			ROLAND JOHNSON		
3/02/59	**25**	3	1 I Traded Her Love (For Deep Purple Wine)		Brunswick 55110
			TIM JOHNSON		
9/19/87	**78**	3	1 Hard Headed Heart		Sundial 135
			DAY JOHNSTON		
			Female singer; New Mexico native. Appeared on TV's "You Can Be A Star" in 1988.		
9/03/88	**82**	3	1 What Cha' Doin' To Me		Roadrunner 4639
			THE JOHNSTONS		
2/28/87	**82**	5	1 Two-Name Girl		Hidden Val. 1286
			JON & LYNN		
			Jon Hargis with wife Lynn		
12/19/81+	**59**	7	1 Let The Good Times Roll		Soundwaves 4656
			#20 pop hit for Shirley & Lee in 1956		
8/21/82	**86**	3	2 (What A Day For A) Day Dream		Soundwaves 4677
			#2 pop hit for The Lovin' Spoonful in 1966		
			ANN JONES		
			Born in Kansas; raised in Enid, Oklahoma. On WCRL-Enid radio shows at age 14.		
10/15/49	**15**	1	1 Give Me A Hundred Reasons		Capitol 15414
			Juke Box #15		
			ANTHONY ARMSTRONG JONES		
			Born Ronnie Jones in 1950 in Ada, Oklahoma. Professional golfer. Discovered by Conway Twitty in 1962; worked with Twitty's band. Stage name came from English photographer who married Princess Margaret.		
6/28/69	**22**	13	1 Proud Mary		Chart 5017
			#2 pop hit for Creedence Clearwater Revival in 1969		
10/18/69	**28**	8	2 New Orleans		Chart 5033
			#6 pop hit for U.S. Bonds in 1960		

DEBUT DATE	PEAK POS	WKS CHR	ARTIST — Record Title	POP POS	Label & Number
			ANTHONY ARMSTRONG JONES — Continued		
1/10/70	8	11	3 Take A Letter Maria .... #2 pop hit for R.B. Greaves in 1969		Chart 5045
5/23/70	56	5	4 Lead Me Not Into Temptation		Chart 5064
7/25/70	38	11	5 Sugar In The Flowers.................................		Chart 5083
11/21/70	40	9	6 Sweet Caroline .... #4 pop hit for Neil Diamond in 1969		Chart 5100
4/14/73	70	3	7 I'm Right Where I Belong............................		Epic 10970
7/07/73	33	10	8 Bad, Bad Leroy Brown .... #1 pop hit for Jim Croce in 1973		Epic 11002
11/17/73	69	8	9 I've Got Mine...		Epic 11042
5/03/86	74	5	10 Those Eyes		AIR 103
			DAVID LYNN JONES Singer/songwriter from Bexar, Arkansas.		
8/22/87	10	20	1 **Bonnie Jean (Little Sister)**.........................		Mercury 888733
3/26/88	14	19	2 High Ridin' Heroes .... special guest appearance by Waylon Jennings		Mercury 870128
7/30/88	36	10	3 The Rogue		Mercury 870525
11/12/88	66	6	4 Tonight In America		Mercury 872054
			GEORGE JONES ★★2★★ Born George Glenn Jones on 9/12/31 in Saratoga, Texas. Worked on KTXJ-Jasper, Texas. Worked with Eddie & Pearl on KRIC-Beaumont, Texas in 1947. Served in US Marines from 1950-52. First recorded for Starday in 1953. Appeared on KNUZ-Houston Jamboree and worked as a disc jockey on KTRM-Beaumont in the early 50s. Appearances on Louisiana Hayride in 1956. Also recorded rockabilly as "Thumper Jones" and "Hank Smith". Married to Tammy Wynette from 1969-75. Joined the Grand Ole Opry in 1969. Fondly known as the "Rolls Royce of Country Singers".		
10/29/55	4	18	1 **Why, Baby, Why** .... Juke Box #4 / Best Seller #4 / Jockey #4		Starday 202
1/28/56	7	7	2 **What Am I Worth**.................................... Juke Box #7 / Jockey #10 / Best Seller #14		Starday 216
7/14/56	7	8	3 **You Gotta Be My Baby** .... Juke Box #7 / Jockey #10		Starday 247
10/20/56	3	11	4 **Just One More/** Juke Box #3		
		5	5 Gonna Come Get You................................. Juke Box flip		Starday 264
3/09/57	10	2	6 **Don't Stop The Music/** Juke Box #10 / Best Seller #15 / Jockey #15		
		1	7 Uh, Uh, No .... Juke Box flip		Mercury 71029
6/10/57	13	6	8 Too Much Water .... Best Seller #13		Mercury 71096
4/14/58	7	10	9 **Color Of The Blues**................................. Jockey #7 / Best Seller #18		Mercury 71257
11/17/58	6	16	10 **Treasure Of Love/**		
12/08/58	29	1	11 If I Don't Love You		Mercury 71373
3/09/59	1^5	22	12 **White Lightning** .... written by the Big Bopper, J.P. Richardson	73	Mercury 71406
7/20/59	7	13	13 **Who Shot Sam/**	93	Mercury 71464
11/23/59+	15	12	14 Money To Burn/		
11/23/59	19	12	15 Big Harlan Taylor		Mercury 71514
4/04/60	16	12	16 Accidently On Purpose/		
4/25/60	30	1	17 Sparkling Brown Eyes................................		Mercury 71583
8/22/60	25	2	18 Out Of Control		Mercury 71641
11/07/60+	2^1	34	19 **The Window Up Above**		Mercury 71700
5/29/61	16	2	20 Family Bible...		Mercury 71721
6/19/61	1^7	32	21 **Tender Years**	76	Mercury 71804
2/24/62	5	12	22 **Aching, Breaking Heart**		Mercury 71910
4/14/62	1^6	23	23 **She Thinks I Still Care/**		
4/28/62	17	5	24 Sometimes You Just Can't Win......................		United Art. 424
7/21/62	13	11	25 Open Pit Mine.......................................		United Art. 462
8/25/62	28	1	26 You're Still On My Mind		Mercury 72010
10/06/62	3	18	27 **A Girl I Used To Know/**		
10/13/62	13	9	28 Big Fool Of The Year		United Art. 500

DEBUT DATE	PEAK POS	WKS CHR		ARTIST — Record Title	POP POS	Label & Number
				GEORGE JONES — Continued		
2/09/63	7	18	29	**Not What I Had In Mind/**		
4/06/63	29	1	30	I Saw Me....................................		United Art. 528
7/13/63	5	22	31	**You Comb Her Hair**.............................		United Art. 578
				flip "Ain't It Funny What A Fool Will Do" hit #124 on pop charts		
2/01/64	5	18	32	**Your Heart Turned Left (And I Was On The Right)/**		
2/08/64	15	9	33	My Tears Are Overdue		United Art. 683
3/28/64	39	3	34	The Last Town I Painted		Mercury 72233
6/06/64	31	7	35	Something I Dreamed/		
6/20/64	10	16	36	**Where Does A Little Tear Come From**		United Art. 724
9/26/64	3	28	37	**The Race Is On**	96	United Art. 751
1/30/65	15	15	38	Least Of All		United Art. 804
3/13/65	9	21	39	**Things Have Gone To Pieces**		Musicor 1067
6/05/65	14	12	40	Wrong Number		United Art. 858
8/28/65	6	18	41	**Love Bug**		Musicor 1098
10/09/65	40	3	42	What's Money................................		United Art. 901
11/06/65+	8	18	43	**Take Me**....................................		Musicor 1117
3/12/66	6	17	44	**I'm A People**...............................		Musicor 1143
3/12/66	46	3	45	World's Worse Loser..........................		United Art. 965
6/25/66	30	7	46	Old Brush Arbors		Musicor 1174
7/30/66	5	16	47	**Four-O-Thirty Three**........................		Musicor 1181
1/21/67	1²	22	48	**Walk Through This World With Me**..............		Musicor 1226
5/20/67	5	17	49	**I Can't Get There From Here**		Musicor 1243
10/07/67	7	18	50	**If My Heart Had Windows**		Musicor 1267
2/03/68	8	14	51	**Say It's Not You**		Musicor 1289
4/13/68	35	11	52	Small Time Laboring Man......................		Musicor 1297
7/06/68	3	13	53	**As Long As I Live**		Musicor 1298
11/23/68+	2²	17	54	**When The Grass Grows Over Me**................		Musicor 1333
3/29/69	2²	18	55	**I'll Share My World With You**...................	124	Musicor 1351
7/19/69	6	14	56	**If Not For You**		Musicor 1366
11/15/69+	6	14	57	**She's Mine/**		
11/22/69	72	13	58	No Blues Is Good News.........................		Musicor 1381
3/14/70	28	10	59	Where Grass Won't Grow		Musicor 1392
7/04/70	13	14	60	Tell Me My Lying Eyes Are Wrong..................		Musicor 1408
11/21/70+	2¹	15	61	**A Good Year For The Roses**	112	Musicor 1425
3/20/71	10	13	62	**Sometimes You Just Can't Win** .... [R]		Musicor 1432
				new version of George's 1962 hit		
6/12/71	7	14	63	**Right Won't Touch A Hand**		Musicor 1440
10/02/71	13	12	64	I'll Follow You (Up To Our Cloud)		Musicor 1446
2/12/72	6	14	65	**We Can Make It**		Epic 10831
2/12/72	30	8	66	A Day In The Life Of A Fool		RCA 0625
5/20/72	2¹	14	67	**Loving You Could Never Be Better**...............		Epic 10858
10/14/72	46	7	68	Wrapped Around Her Finger....................		RCA 0792
10/28/72	5	16	69	**A Picture Of Me (Without You)**		Epic 10917
3/03/73	6	14	70	**What My Woman Can't Do**		Epic 10959
6/23/73	7	13	71	**Nothing Ever Hurt Me (Half As Bad)**		Epic 11006
11/24/73+	3	16	72	**Once You've Had The Best**		Epic 11053
6/08/74	1¹	17	73	**The Grand Tour**		Epic 11122
10/26/74+	1¹	13	74	**The Door**		Epic 50038
3/22/75	10	14	75	**These Days (I Barely Get By)**..................		Epic 50088
7/26/75	21	11	76	Memories Of Us/		
11/01/75	92	4	77	I Just Don't Give A Damn...........................		Epic 50127
2/07/76	16	12	78	The Battle		Epic 50187
5/22/76	37	9	79	You Always Look Your Best (Here In My Arms) ..		Epic 50227
9/04/76	3	16	80	**Her Name Is...**		Epic 50271
5/21/77	34	8	81	Old King Kong		Epic 50385
8/13/77	24	10	82	If I Could Put Them All Together (I'd Have You)..		Epic 50423
1/07/78	6	14	83	**Bartender's Blues**..........................		Epic 50495
				vocal accompaniment: James Taylor		
7/01/78	11	13	84	I'll Just Take It Out In Love......................		Epic 50564

DEBUT DATE	PEAK POS	WKS CHR		ARTIST — Record Title	POP POS	Label & Number
				GEORGE JONES — Continued		
6/30/79	**22**	11	85	Someday My Day Will Come............................		Epic 50684
4/12/80	**1**[1]	18	86	**He Stopped Loving Her Today**......................		Epic 50867
8/23/80	**2**[1]	17	87	**I'm Not Ready Yet**.....................................		Epic 50922
1/17/81	**8**	15	88	**If Drinkin' Don't Kill Me (Her Memory Will)**		Epic 50968
10/03/81	**1**[1]	17	89	**Still Doin' Time**.......................................		Epic 02526
2/06/82	**5**	19	90	**Same Ole Me**		Epic 02696
				background vocals: The Oak Ridge Boys		
1/15/83	**3**	19	91	**Shine On (Shine All Your Sweet Love On Me)** ..		Epic 03489
5/07/83	**1**[1]	18	92	**I Always Get Lucky With You**		Epic 03883
9/10/83	**2**[1]	22	93	**Tennessee Whiskey**		Epic 04082
4/07/84	**3**	19	94	**You've Still Got A Place In My Heart**		Epic 04413
9/22/84	**2**[3]	23	95	**She's My Rock**		Epic 04609
8/03/85	**3**	20	96	**Who's Gonna Fill Their Shoes**		Epic 05439
11/23/85+	**3**	22	97	**The One I Loved Back Then (The Corvette Song)**.....................		Epic 05698
4/19/86	**9**	21	98	**Somebody Wants Me Out Of The Way**............		Epic 05862
9/13/86	**10**	23	99	**Wine Colored Roses**.................................		Epic 06296
1/17/87	**8**	23	100	**The Right Left Hand**		Epic 06593
5/16/87	**26**	18	101	I Turn To You..		Epic 07107
12/19/87+	**26**	14	102	The Bird		Epic 07655
3/26/88	**52**	10	103	I'm A Survivor		Epic 07748
6/04/88	**63**	6	104	The Old Man No One Loves		Epic 07913
12/17/88+	**5**	20	105	**I'm A One Woman Man**		Epic 08509
				GEORGE JONES DUOS with:		
				BRENDA CARTER:		
9/28/68	**12**	12	106	Milwaukee, Here I Come		Musicor 1325
				RAY CHARLES:		
12/17/83+	**6**	18	107	**We Didn't See A Thing**		Columbia 04297
				featuring Chet Atkins, guitar		
				LACY J. DALTON:		
4/27/85	**19**	18	108	Size Seven Round (Made Of Gold)		Epic 04876
				MERLE HAGGARD:		
8/07/82	**1**[1]	15	109	**Yesterday's Wine**....................................		Epic 03072
12/04/82+	**10**	19	110	**C.C. Waterback**		Epic 03405
				JEANETTE HICKS:		
1/26/57	**10**	1	111	**Yearning**		Starday 279
				Juke Box #10		
				BRENDA LEE:		
12/22/84+	**15**	16	112	Hallelujah, I Love You So............................		Epic 04723
				#5 R&B hit for Ray Charles in 1956		
				SHELBY LYNNE:		
9/03/88	**43**	10	113	If I Could Bottle This Up		Epic 08011
				MELBA MONTGOMERY:		
5/04/63	**3**	28	114	**We Must Have Been Out Of Our Minds**		United Art. 575
11/30/63	**20**	5	115	What's In Our Heart/		
12/07/63	**17**	7	116	Let's Invite Them Over...............................		United Art. 635
9/05/64	**31**	5	117	Please Be My Love		United Art. 732
12/12/64+	**25**	15	118	Multiply The Heartaches		United Art. 784
11/19/66	**70**	3	119	Close Together (As You and Me)......................		Musicor 1204
9/09/67	**24**	10	120	Party Pickin'		Musicor 1238
				JOHNNY PAYCHECK:		
12/09/78+	**7**	13	121	**Mabellene**		Epic 50647
				#5 pop hit for Chuck Berry in 1955		
5/26/79	**14**	11	122	You Can Have Her		Epic 50708
				#12 pop hit for Roy Hamilton in 1961		
6/21/80	**31**	9	123	When You're Ugly Like Us (You Just Naturally Got To Be Cool)		Epic 50891
12/13/80+	**18**	12	124	You Better Move On.....................................		Epic 50949
				#24 pop hit for Arthur Alexander in 1962		
				GENE PITNEY (GEORGE & GENE):		
4/24/65	**16**	10	125	I've Got Five Dollars And It's Saturday Night	99	Musicor 1066
7/03/65	**25**	7	126	Louisiana Man...		Musicor 1097
				flip side "I'm A Fool To Care" hit #115 on the pop charts		

DEBUT DATE	PEAK POS	WKS CHR		ARTIST — Record Title	POP POS	Label & Number
				GEORGE JONES — Continued		
11/20/65	**50**	2	127	Big Job		Musicor 1115
6/04/66	**47**	3	128	That's All It Took..............................		Musicor 1165
				MARGIE SINGLETON:		
9/18/61	**15**	3	129	Did I Ever Tell You		Mercury 71856
6/16/62	**11**	10	130	Waltz Of The Angels		Mercury 71955
				TINA & DADDY (George & his stepdaughter):		
4/06/74	**25**	12	131	The Telephone Call		Epic 11099
				TAMMY WYNETTE:		
12/25/71+	**9**	13	132	**Take Me**.....................................		Epic 10815
7/08/72	**6**	15	133	**The Ceremony**		Epic 10881
11/25/72+	**38**	9	134	Old Fashioned Singing		Epic 10923
4/07/73	**32**	9	135	Let's Build A World Together		Epic 10963
9/01/73	**1**²	17	136	**We're Gonna Hold On**		Epic 11031
2/09/74	**15**	13	137	(We're Not) The Jet Set		Epic 11083
7/27/74	**8**	12	138	**We Loved It Away**		Epic 11151
5/17/75	**25**	13	139	God's Gonna Get'cha (For That)		Epic 50099
6/05/76	**1**¹	15	140	**Golden Ring**		Epic 50235
12/11/76+	**1**²	16	141	**Near You**		Epic 50314
				#1 pop hit (17 weeks) for Francis Craig in 1947		
7/16/77	**5**	13	142	**Southern California**		Epic 50418
3/01/80	**2**¹	14	143	**Two Story House**		Epic 50849
9/06/80	**19**	11	144	A Pair Of Old Sneakers........................		Epic 50930

GRANDPA JONES
Born Louis Marshall Jones on 10/20/13 in Niagra, Kentucky. Raised in Akron, Ohio, where he had his own radio show in the early 30s. Worked with Bradley Kincaid in 1935 and began appearing as "Grandpa" Jones. Own band, the Granchildren, in 1937. Served in US Army from 1944-46. With the Grand Ole Opry since 1946. Regular on the "Hee-Haw" TV series since 1969. Elected to the Country Music Hall of Fame in 1978.

DEBUT DATE	PEAK POS	WKS CHR		ARTIST — Record Title	POP POS	Label & Number
2/23/59	**21**	2	1	The All-American Boy................................		Decca 30823
				#2 pop hit for Bobby Bare (Bill Parsons) in 1959		
12/15/62+	**5**	16	2	**T For Texas**		Monument 801
				#2 pop hit (entitled "Blue Yodel") for Jimmie Rodgers in 1928		

HARRISON JONES
Born on 2/13/47 in Corbin, Kentucky. Performing since age 8.

DEBUT DATE	PEAK POS	WKS CHR		ARTIST — Record Title	POP POS	Label & Number
6/22/74	**72**	7	1	But Tonight I'm Gonna Love You		GRT 004

MICKEY JONES

DEBUT DATE	PEAK POS	WKS CHR		ARTIST — Record Title	POP POS	Label & Number
3/03/79	**94**	5	1	She Loves My Troubles Away		Bayshore 100

TOM JONES
Born Thomas Jones Woodward on 6/7/40 in Pontypridd, South Wales. Worked local clubs as Tommy Scott; formed own trio, The Senators, in 1963. Began solo career in London in 1964. Won the 1965 Best New Artist Grammy Award. Host of own TV musical variety series from 1969-71.

DEBUT DATE	PEAK POS	WKS CHR		ARTIST — Record Title	POP POS	Label & Number
12/25/76+	**1**¹	17	1	**Say You'll Stay Until Tomorrow**	*15*	Epic 50308
6/04/77	**87**	3	2	Take Me Tonight..	*101*	Epic 50382
11/19/77	**71**	8	3	What A Night		Epic 50468
4/18/81	**19**	14	4	Darlin'	*103*	Mercury 76100
8/08/81	**25**	11	5	What In The World's Come Over You	*109*	Mercury 76115
				#5 pop hit for Jack Scott in 1960		
11/28/81+	**26**	14	6	Lady Lay Down...		Mercury 76125
9/18/82	**16**	18	7	A Woman's Touch		Mercury 76172
2/26/83	**4**	18	8	**Touch Me (I'll Be Your Fool Once More)**.........		Mercury 810445
7/02/83	**34**	12	9	It'll Be Me		Mercury 812631
12/10/83+	**13**	22	10	I've Been Rained On Too		Mercury 814820
4/28/84	**30**	14	11	This Time		Mercury 818801
9/01/84	**53**	9	12	All The Love Is On The Radio...........................		Mercury 880173
12/08/84+	**67**	9	13	I'm An Old Rock And Roller (Dancin' To a Different Beat)...............................		Mercury 880402
3/02/85	**48**	9	14	Give Her All The Roses (Don't Wait Until Tomorrow)...		Mercury 880569
9/14/85	**76**	6	15	Not Another Heart Song		Mercury 884039
11/23/85+	**36**	13	16	It's Four In The Morning................................		Mercury 884252

DEBUT DATE	PEAK POS	WKS CHR	ARTIST — Record Title	POP POS	Label & Number
			JILL JORDAN Born in Wooster, Ohio; granddaughter of Denny Galehouse Sr, a World Series pitcher for the former St. Louis Browns baseball team.		
2/20/88	68	5	1 Calendar Blues		Maxx 822
6/11/88	72	4	2 I Did It For Love		Maxx 823
			LOUIS JORDAN Born on 7/8/08 in Brinkley, Arkansas. Died of a heart attack on 2/4/75 (66). R&B vocalist/saxophonist. First recorded for Brunswick in 1929, with the Jungle Band. Innovative, extremely popular vocal style paved the way for later R&B styles. Inducted into the Rock And Roll Hall Of Fame in 1987.		
2/26/44	1³	13	1 Ration Blues/	11	
1/29/44	7	1	2 Deacon Jones		Decca 8654
7/01/44	1⁵	9	3 Is You Is Or Is You Ain't (Ma' Baby) .... from the film "Follow The Boys"	2	Decca 8659
			HOMER JOY		
3/23/74	80	5	1 John Law		Capitol 3834
			BRENDA JOYCE Born in 1955 in Indianapolis. Confined to a wheelchair since 1972.		
9/15/79	96	1	1 Don't Touch Me		Western Pac. 107
			DON JUAN - see DON		
			THE JUDDS ★★128★★ Family duo from Ashland, Kentucky consisting of Naomi (born Diana Ellen Judd on 1/11/46) and daughter Wynonna (born Christina Ciminella in 1964). Moved to Hollywood in 1968. Both appeared in the film "More American Graffiti". Moved to Nashville in May of 1979. Added guitarist Don Potter and made stage debut in Omaha, Nebraska in mid-1984.		
12/17/83+	17	18	1 Had A Dream (For The Heart) .... pop hit for Elvis Presley in 1976 ("For The Heart")		RCA 13673
4/28/84	1¹	23	2 Mama He's Crazy..		RCA 13772
10/06/84	1²	22	3 Why Not Me...		RCA 13923
2/02/85	1¹	22	4 Girls Night Out		RCA 13991
6/08/85	1¹	21	5 Love Is Alive		RCA 14093
10/05/85	1²	22	6 Have Mercy		RCA 14193
2/15/86	1¹	20	7 Grandpa (Tell Me 'Bout The Good Old Days) ...		RCA 14290
5/24/86	1¹	18	8 Rockin' With The Rhythm Of The Rain		RCA 14362
10/18/86+	1¹	20	9 Cry Myself To Sleep		RCA 5000
2/14/87	10	13	10 Don't Be Cruel .... #1 pop/country/R&B hit for Elvis Presley in 1956		RCA 5094
5/09/87	1¹	19	11 I Know Where I'm Going		RCA 5164
8/22/87	1¹	22	12 Maybe Your Baby's Got The Blues		RCA 5255
1/16/88	1¹	17	13 Turn It Loose		RCA 5329
6/11/88	2²	17	14 Give A Little Love... all of above shown as: **THE JUDDS** (Wynonna & Naomi)		RCA 8300
10/22/88+	1¹	20	15 Change Of Heart..		RCA 8715
			DICK JURGENS & HIS ORCHESTRA Born on 1/9/10 in Sacramento. Own big band from 1928. Wrote "Elmer's Tune", "Careless", "One Dozen Roses", "If I Knew Then", and many others.		
3/08/47	4	2	1 (Oh Why, Oh Why, Did I Ever Leave) Wyoming vocals: Jimmy Castle and Al Galante	14	Columbia 37210
			BILL JUSTIS Born on 10/14/26 in Birmingham, Alabama. Died on 7/15/82 in Nashville. Session saxophonist/arranger/producer. Led house band for Sun Records.		
11/25/57+	6	16	1 Raunchy .... [I] Best Seller #6 / Jockey #14 guitar: Sid Manker; sax: Bill Justis	2	Phillips 3519

K

			KALIN TWINS Herbert and Harold Kalin, born on 2/16/39 in Port Jervis, New York.		
8/04/58	13	7	1 When... Best Seller #13	5	Decca 30642

DEBUT DATE	PEAK POS	WKS CHR	ARTIST — Record Title	POP POS	Label & Number
			JIM KANDY		
9/04/65	**29**	6	1 I'm The Man..		K-Ark 647
			KIERAN KANE		
			Songwriter from Queens, New York. Drummer in rock band from age 9. Moved to Los Angeles in the early 70s, worked as a session musician. Moved to Nashville in 1979, teamed with songwriter Jamie O'Hara. Wrote "Grandpa (Tell Me 'Bout The Good Old Days)" for The Judds. Kane and O'Hara formed singing duo, The O'Kanes, in 1986.		
3/21/81	**80**	4	1 The Baby..		Elektra 47111
6/20/81	**14**	16	2 You're The Best.....................................		Elektra 47148
11/07/81+	**16**	18	3 It's Who You Love..................................		Elektra 47228
3/06/82	**26**	14	4 I Feel It With You..................................		Elektra 47415
7/10/82	**26**	12	5 I'll Be Your Man Around The House.............		Elektra 47478
10/30/82	**45**	8	6 Gonna Have A Party...............................		Elektra 69943
4/30/83	**30**	12	7 It's You...		Warner 29711
3/17/84	**28**	14	8 Dedicate..		Warner 29336
			HILLARY KANTER		
			Female vocalist/songwriter/pianist from Miami. Staff writer for Tree Music. Moved to Los Angeles, worked as back-up singer for Julio Iglesias.		
8/18/84	**51**	9	1 Good Night For Falling In Love		RCA 13835
12/01/84+	**54**	18	2 Hey		RCA 13935
5/04/85	**50**	9	3 We Work		RCA 14053
			MELISSA KAY		
			Singer from Winter Garden, Florida.		
2/06/88	**75**	3	1 Don't Forget Your Way Home		Reed 1115
			produced by Porter Wagoner		
8/06/88	**79**	3	2 After Lovin' You		Reed 1119
			ANGELA KAYE		
			15-year-old singer in 1981.		
10/10/81	**81**	5	1 Catching Fire		Yatahey 804
			BARRY KAYE		
			Born on 4/24/46 in Los Angeles.		
3/11/78	**89**	5	1 Easy		MCA 40868
			#4 pop hit for the Commodores in 1977		
			DEBBIE LORI KAYE		
			Born on 5/6/50 in New York. Moved to Fort Williams, Canada in 1965.		
6/22/68	**68**	3	1 Come On Home		Columbia 44538
			LOIS KAYE		
			Born Lois Kaye Edmiston on 12/8/50 in Knox, Indiana; raised in Beecher, Indiana.		
11/03/79	**96**	2	1 Drown In The Flood		Ovation 1130
			SANDRA KAYE		
			Born Sandra Kaye Van Auken in Longview, Washington.		
7/29/78	**52**	7	1 This Magic Moment		Door Knob 068
			The Drifters and Jay & The Americans had pop versions		
10/21/78	**80**	5	2 One More Time		Door Knob 075
12/23/78+	**84**	5	3 I'll Still Love You In My Dreams................		Door Knob 088
3/03/79	**83**	5	4 I've Seen It All.....................................		Door Knob 093
8/18/79	**95**	4	5 You Broke My Heart So Gently (It Almost Didn't Break)		Door Knob 097
			RAMSEY KEARNEY		
			Born William Ramsey Kearney on 10/30/33 in Bolivar, Tennessee.		
8/24/85	**96**	1	1 King Of Oak Street		Safari 114
9/10/88	**97**	1	2 One Time Thing		Safari 117
			JOHN KELLEY		
			Singer born in Little Rock, Arkansas, and raised in Indiana.		
7/24/82	**81**	4	1 This Morning I Woke Up In New York City		Comstar 8201
			MURRY KELLUM		
			Born in Jackson, Tennessee; raised in Plain, Texas.		
6/19/71	**26**	10	1 Joy To The World		Epic 10741
			#1 pop hit for Three Dog Night in 1971		
11/20/71	**74**	2	2 Train Train (Carry Me Away).....................		Epic 10784

DEBUT DATE	PEAK POS	WKS CHR	ARTIST — Record Title	POP POS	Label & Number
			MURRY KELLUM — Continued		
2/02/74	55	9	3 Lovely Lady		Cinnamon 777
5/25/74	98	2	4 Girl Of My Life		Cinnamon 794
			JERRI KELLY		
			Female singer born on 10/11/47 in Phoenix; raised in Stephenville, Texas.		
1/18/75	65	10	1 I Can't Help Myself (Sugar Pie, Honey Bunch) ..... PRICE MITCHELL & JERRI KELLY #1 pop hit for the Four Tops in 1965		GRT 016
1/26/80	90	2	2 For A Slow Dance With You		Little Giant 021
8/02/80	66	9	3 Fallin' For You		Little Giant 026
11/08/80	85	3	4 Forsaking All The Rest		Little Giant 030
1/31/81	85	3	5 Be My Lover, Be My Friend .... MICK LLOYD & JERRI KELLY		Little Giant 040
8/08/81	85	4	6 Sweet Natural Love .... MICK LLOYD & JERRI KELLY		Little Giant 046
8/14/82	56	8	7 Walk Me 'Cross The River............................		Carrere 03017
			KAREN KELLY		
9/19/70	75	2	1 Let Me Go, Lover............................. #1 pop hit for Joan Weber in 1955		Capitol 2883
			DAVE KEMP		
5/28/83	75	4	1 Ain't That The Way It Goes...........................		Soundwaves 4702
			WAYNE KEMP		
			Born on 6/1/41 in Greenwood, Arkansas. Auto racer while a teenager. Own band in the early 60s. Wrote hit "Love Bug" for George Jones, "The Image Of Me", and other hits for Conway Twitty and Ricky Van Shelton.		
2/01/69	61	6	1 Won't You Come Home (And Talk To A Stranger)		Decca 32422
9/27/69	73	2	2 Bar Room Habits....................................		Decca 32534
1/09/71	57	8	3 Who'll Turn Out The Lights		Decca 32767
5/29/71	52	9	4 Award To An Angel		Decca 32824
12/18/71	72	2	5 Did We Have To Come This Far......................		Decca 32891
6/03/72	53	5	6 Darlin'		Decca 32946
3/17/73	17	14	7 Honky Tonk Wine		MCA 40019
9/01/73	53	10	8 Kentucky Sunshine		MCA 40112
2/02/74	32	11	9 Listen		MCA 40176
7/06/74	57	11	10 Harlan County		MCA 40249
6/12/76	72	7	11 Waiting For The Tables To Turn		United Art. 805
8/28/76	71	5	12 I Should Have Watched That First Step		United Art. 850
5/21/77	91	3	13 Leona Don't Live Here Anymore		United Art. 980
8/27/77	76	6	14 I Love It (When You Love All Over Me)		United Art. 1031
7/12/80	62	6	15 Love Goes To Hell When It Dies		Mercury 57023
11/15/80	47	10	16 I'll Leave This World Loving You		Mercury 57035
4/04/81	35	12	17 Your Wife Is Cheatin' On Us Again		Mercury 57047
7/25/81	46	7	18 Just Got Back From No Man's Land		Mercury 57053
11/14/81	75	5	19 Why Am I Doing Without		Mercury 57060
4/10/82	78	4	20 Sloe Gin And Fast Women		Mercury 76139
9/04/82	64	6	21 She Only Meant To Use Him........................		Mercury 76165
7/16/83	55	10	22 Don't Send Me No Angels..........................		Door Knob 200
6/30/84	75	4	23 I've Always Wanted To.............................		Door Knob 211
3/08/86	70	4	24 Red Neck And Over Thirty .... WAYNE KEMP & BOBBY G. RICE		Door Knob 243
			THE KENDALLS ★★92★★		
			Father-and-daughter duo from St. Louis, consisting of Royce (b: 9/25/34) and Jeannie Kendall (b: 11/30/54). Royce and his brother Floyce had worked together as the Austin Brothers in the late 50s.		
7/25/70	52	6	1 Leavin' On A Jet Plane .... #1 pop hit for Peter, Paul & Mary in 1969		Stop 373
2/12/72	53	9	2 Two Divided By Love .... #16 pop hit for The Grass Roots in 1971		Dot 17405
7/01/72	66	4	3 Everything I Own .... #5 pop hit for Bread in 1972		Dot 17422
4/02/77	80	7	4 Makin' Believe....................................		Ovation 1101
8/06/77	1⁴	20	5 **Heaven's Just A Sin Away**	69	Ovation 1103

DEBUT DATE	PEAK POS	WKS CHR		ARTIST — Record Title	POP POS	Label & Number
				THE KENDALLS — Continued		
2/11/78	**2**²	15	6	**It Don't Feel Like Sinnin' To Me**		Ovation 1106
5/27/78	**6**	14	7	**Pittsburgh Stealers**		Ovation 1109
9/23/78	**1**¹	15	8	**Sweet Desire/**		
		15	9	**Old Fashioned Love**		Ovation 1112
1/13/79	**5**	14	10	**I Had A Lovely Time**		Ovation 1119
5/05/79	**11**	11	11	Just Like Real People		Ovation 1125
8/18/79	**16**	11	12	I Don't Do Like That No More/		
		11	13	Never My Love....................................		Ovation 1129
11/17/79+	**5**	15	14	**You'd Make An Angel Wanna Cheat**..............		Ovation 1136
4/05/80	**5**	13	15	**I'm Already Blue**		Ovation 1143
8/02/80	**9**	15	16	**Put It Off Until Tomorrow**		Ovation 1154
				written by Dolly Parton		
3/28/81	**26**	11	17	Heart Of The Matter...............................		Ovation 1169
8/22/81	**7**	16	18	**Teach Me To Cheat**		Mercury 57055
12/12/81+	**10**	19	19	**If You're Waiting On Me (You're Backing Up)**..		Mercury 76131
6/05/82	**30**	12	20	Cheater's Prayer		Mercury 76155
9/18/82	**35**	10	21	That's What I Get For Thinking		Mercury 76178
5/28/83	**19**	14	22	Precious Love......................................		Mercury 812300
				harmony vocal: Emmylou Harris		
8/27/83	**20**	19	23	Movin' Train		Mercury 814195
1/14/84	**1**¹	23	24	**Thank God For The Radio**		Mercury 818056
6/02/84	**15**	17	25	My Baby's Gone		Mercury 822203
10/27/84+	**20**	17	26	I'd Dance Every Dance With You..................		Mercury 880306
3/02/85	**27**	14	27	Four Wheel Drive		Mercury 880588
6/01/85	**26**	14	28	If You Break My Heart		Mercury 880828
10/12/85	**45**	8	29	Two Heart Harmony		Mercury 884140
6/28/86	**42**	9	30	Too Late...		MCA/Curb 52850
9/27/86	**60**	7	31	Fire At First Sight		MCA/Curb 52933
12/06/86+	**46**	9	32	Little Doll		MCA/Curb 52983
5/02/87	**54**	8	33	Routine		Step One 371
7/11/87	**51**	8	34	Dancin' With Myself Tonight		Step One 374
12/12/87+	**62**	7	35	Still Pickin' Up After You		Step One 379
4/16/88	**57**	7	36	The Rhythm Of Romance...........................		Step One 384
				GENE KENNEDY & KAREN JEGLUM		
				Husband and wife duo. Gene is from Florence, South Carolina (b: 10/3/33). First recorded for Old Town in 1960. Karen is from Blanchardville, Wisconsin and did back-up work for Cristy Lane. Co-owners of Door Knob Records in Nashville.		
2/28/81	**80**	4	1	I Want To See Me In Your Eyes......................		Door Knob 145
4/25/81	**84**	4	2	I'd Rather Be The Stranger In Your Eyes		Door Knob 151
7/18/81	**87**	2	3	Easier To Go		Door Knob 158
3/20/82	**49**	9	4	A Thing Or Two On My Mind		Door Knob 173
7/24/82	**80**	4	5	What About Tonight (We Might Find Something Beautiful Tonight).................................		Door Knob 179
4/23/83	**86**	3	6	Be Happy For Me....................................		Door Knob 192
8/02/86	**78**	4	7	My Wife's House		Society 110
				GENE KENNEDY		
				LARRY WAYNE KENNEDY		
11/30/85	**83**	3	1	She Almost Makes Me Forget About You		Jere 1001
				KENNY O.		
				Kenny O. Smith.		
8/22/81	**83**	3	1	Old Fangled Country Songs		Rhinestone 1002
				GEORGE KENT		
				Born on 6/12/35 in Dallas. Moved to Metaire, Louisiana, worked on WARB-Covington, Louisiana. Owner of the Cow Palace in Ft. Collins, Colorado.		
12/13/69+	**26**	15	1	Hello, I'm A Jukebox		Mercury 72985
				female vocal: Diana Duke		
7/04/70	**70**	3	2	Doogie Ray		Mercury 73066
12/05/70+	**62**	7	3	Mama Bake A Pie (Daddy Kill A Chicken)		Mercury 73127
5/18/74	**48**	9	4	Take My Life And Shape It With Your Love.......		Shannon 818
12/28/74+	**65**	6	5	Whole Lotta Difference In Love.....................		Shannon 824

165

DEBUT DATE	PEAK POS	WKS CHR	ARTIST — Record Title	POP POS	Label & Number
			GEORGE KENT — Continued		
11/22/75	97	3	6 She'll Wear It Out Leaving Town......................		Shannon 834
3/13/76	75	6	7 Shake 'Em Up and Let 'Em Roll		Shannon 840
2/26/77	89	5	8 Low Class Reunion		Soundwaves 4542
			JOE KENYON		
			Pseudonym for producer/guitarist Jerry Kennedy and pianist David Briggs.		
6/27/87	33	15	1 Hymne .... [I]		Mercury 888642
			tune written by Vangelis and featured in Gallo Wine commercials		
			DOUG KERSHAW		
			Born on 1/24/36 in Tiel Ridge, Louisiana. Sang with his mother from age 8. At 12 years old, had own band, the Continental Playboys, with brothers Russell "Rusty" and Nelson "Pee Wee". Teamed with Rusty in a duo, recorded for Feature in 1953. Went solo in 1964. In the films "Zachariah", "Medicine Ball Caravan" and "Days Of Heaven". Also see Rusty & Doug.		
10/11/69	70	3	1 Diggy Liggy Lo .... [R]		Warner 7329
			first charted in 1961 by Rusty & Doug		
2/02/74	77	9	2 Mama's Got The Know How...........................		Warner 7763
5/01/76	76	6	3 It Takes All Day To Get Over Night		Warner 8195
5/21/77	96	3	4 I'm Walkin'		Warner 8374
			#4 pop hit for Fats Domino in 1957		
6/27/81	29	13	5 Hello Woman..		Scotti Br. 02137
8/27/88	52	7	6 Cajun Baby		BGM 81588
			DOUG KERSHAW with HANK WILLIAMS JR.		
			MERLE KILGORE		
			Born Wyatt Merle Kilgore on 9/8/34 in Chickasha, Oklahoma; raised in Shreveport, Louisiana. Worked as a disc jockey at KENT-Shreveport in 1950. Appeared on the Louisiana Hayride and the Grand Ole Opry in the early 50s. Wrote many hits for other artists, including "More And More" for Webb Pierce, "Wolverton Mountain" for Claude King, "Johnny Reb" for Johnny Horton, and "Ring Of Fire" for Johnny Cash. In the films "Nevada Smith" and "Five Card Stud". Long-time opening act for Hank Williams, Jr., whom he now manages.		
2/01/60	12	13	1 Dear Mama		Starday 469
7/04/60	10	11	2 **Love Has Made You Beautiful/**		
7/18/60	29	1	3 Gettin' Old Before My Time..........................		Starday 497
10/21/67	71	3	4 Fast Talkin' Louisiana Man........................		Columbia 44279
8/24/74	95	4	5 Montgomery Mable		Warner 7831
1/16/82	54	7	6 Mister Garfield		Elektra 47252
			with Friends: Hank Williams, Jr. and Johnny Cash		
7/14/84	74	4	7 Just Out Of Reach...........................		Warner 29267
			#24 pop hit for Solomon Burke in 1961		
5/11/85	92	4	8 Guilty		Warner 29062
			BUDDY KILLEN - see BONNIE GUITAR		
			KIMBERLY SPRINGS		
			Four sisters and brothers, and a cousin (children of The Kimberlys).		
6/23/84	49	10	1 Slow Dancin'		Capitol 5366
10/20/84	74	5	2 Old Memories Are Hard To Lose......................		Capitol 5404
			KING EDWARD IV & THE KNIGHTS		
			King Edward Smith IV is a member of the Country Music Disc Jockey's Hall Of Fame. Died on 3/24/81. Group featured male vocalist Cary Len.		
9/03/77	90	5	1 Greenback Shuffle		Soundwaves 4550
3/11/78	87	5	2 Wipe You From My Eyes (Gettin' Over You).......		Soundwaves 4563
7/22/78	68	8	3 Baby Blue.....................................		Soundwaves 4573
5/26/79	89	3	4 A Couple More Years		Soundwaves 4583
4/26/80	91	2	5 A Song For Noel		Soundwaves 4597
1/31/81	48	9	6 Dixie Road		Soundwaves 4626
5/30/81	49	8	7 Keep On Movin'		Soundwaves 4635
			THE KING SISTERS		
			Family vocal group from Salt Lake City. Consisted of sisters Alyce, Yvonne, Donna and Louise Driggs. Own TV series, "The King Family", in the 60s.		
12/28/46	5	1	1 **Divorce Me C.O.D.**............................		Victor 20-2018
			with the Buddy Cole Orchestra		

DEBUT DATE	PEAK POS	WKS CHR	ARTIST — Record Title	POP POS	Label & Number
			CLAUDE KING ★★119★★		
			Born on 2/5/33 in Shreveport, Louisiana. Guitarist from age 12. Attended University of Idaho on a baseball scholarship. Worked on the Louisiana Hayride from 1952. First recorded for Gotham in 1952. In the films "Swamp Girl" and "Year Of The Wahoo". August 7, 1981 was declared "Wolverton Mountain Day" by Arkansas Governor Frank White. Acted in the TV mini-series "The Blue And The Gray" in 1982.		
7/03/61	7	16	1 **Big River, Big Man**	82	Columbia 42043
11/13/61+	7	15	2 **The Comancheros**	71	Columbia 42196
			inspired by the John Wayne film of the same title		
5/05/62	1⁹	26	3 **Wolverton Mountain**	6	Columbia 42352
			title is an actual place in Arkansas where Clifton Clowers lives		
10/20/62	10	7	4 **The Burning Of Atlanta**	53	Columbia 42581
12/22/62+	11	9	5 I've Got The World By The Tail	111	Columbia 42630
3/09/63	12	9	6 Sheepskin Valley		Columbia 42688
6/29/63	12	5	7 Building A Bridge		Columbia 42782
8/17/63	13	5	8 Hey Lucille!		Columbia 42833
2/29/64	33	7	9 That's What Makes The World Go Around		Columbia 42959
8/15/64	11	18	10 Sam Hill		Columbia 43083
12/26/64+	47	3	11 Whirlpool (Of Your Love)		Columbia 43157
6/26/65	6	18	12 **Tiger Woman**	110	Columbia 43298
11/27/65+	17	11	13 Little Buddy		Columbia 43416
3/12/66	13	15	14 Catch A Little Raindrop		Columbia 43510
11/26/66+	50	12	15 Little Things That Every Girl Should Know		Columbia 43867
4/29/67	32	10	16 The Watchman		Columbia 44035
8/26/67	50	10	17 Laura (What's He Got That I Ain't Got)		Columbia 44237
12/09/67	59	2	18 Yellow Haired Woman		Columbia 44340
6/08/68	67	3	19 Parchman Farm Blues		Columbia 44504
10/19/68	48	6	20 The Power Of Your Sweet Love		Columbia 44642
3/01/69	52	7	21 Sweet Love On My Mind		Columbia 44749
5/17/69	9	15	22 **All For The Love Of A Girl**		Columbia 44833
			tune is the "B" side of Johnny Horton's "Battle Of New Orleans"		
11/08/69	18	10	23 Friend, Lover, Woman, Wife		Columbia 45015
5/30/70	33	10	24 I'll Be Your Baby Tonight		Columbia 45142
			written by Bob Dylan		
11/07/70+	17	15	25 Mary's Vineyard		Columbia 45248
4/10/71	23	13	26 Chip 'N' Dale's Place		Columbia 45340
9/18/71	54	5	27 When You're Twenty-One		Columbia 45441
2/05/72	57	6	28 Darlin' Raise The Shade (Let The Sun Shine In)		Columbia 45515
11/04/72	48	8	29 He Ain't Country		Columbia 45704
5/28/77	94	3	30 Cotton Dan		True 103
			DON KING		
			Born on 5/1/54 in Omaha, Nebraska. Singer/songwriter/guitarist. To Nashville in 1974. Own Don King Music Group publishing company in Nashville.		
9/11/76	78	5	1 Cabin High (In the Blue Ridge Mountains)		Con Brio 112
2/19/77	16	13	2 I've Got You (To Come Home To)		Con Brio 116
6/04/77	17	13	3 She's The Girl Of My Dreams		Con Brio 120
10/08/77	41	9	4 I Must Be Dreaming		Con Brio 126
1/28/78	29	9	5 Music Is My Woman		Con Brio 129
5/13/78	29	10	6 Don't Make No Promises (You Can't Keep)		Con Brio 133
8/05/78	26	11	7 The Feelings So Right Tonight		Con Brio 137
11/25/78+	28	13	8 You Were Worth Waiting For		Con Brio 142
3/10/79	39	8	9 Live Entertainment		Con Brio 149
6/23/79	73	3	10 I've Got Country Music In My Soul		Con Brio 153
2/16/80	40	9	11 Lonely Hotel		Epic 50840
5/24/80	32	12	12 Here Comes That Feeling Again		Epic 50877
9/27/80	44	8	13 Take This Heart		Epic 50928
5/09/81	38	11	14 I Still Miss Someone		Epic 02046
			written by Johnny Cash - flip of "Don't Take Your Guns To Town"		
9/19/81	27	12	15 The Closer You Get		Epic 02468
			#1 hit for Alabama in 1983		
1/16/82	40	9	16 Running On Love		Epic 02674
10/02/82	64	6	17 Maximum Security (To Minimum Wage)		Epic 03155
3/15/86	71	6	18 All We Had Was One Another		Bench Mark 8601

DEBUT DATE	PEAK POS	WKS CHR	ARTIST — Record Title	POP POS	Label & Number
			DON KING — Continued		
10/15/88	86	2	19 Can't Stop The Music		615 1014
			DONNY KING		
			Singer from Texas.		
3/01/75	20	11	1 Mathilda		Warner 8074
			#47 pop hit for Cookie & His Cupcakes in 1959		
11/08/75	72	6	2 I'm A Fool To Care		Warner 8145
			#24 pop hit for Joe Barry in 1961		
7/31/76	91	4	3 Stop The World (And Let Me Off)		Warner 8229
			PEE WEE KING		
			Born Julius Frank Kuczynski on 2/18/14 in Abrams, Wisconsin; raised in Milwaukee. Played fiddle and accordion. With the Log Cabin Boys in Louisville, from 1935-36. Led own band, the Golden West Cowboys, from 1936. On the Grand Ole Opry from 1937-47. Own radio and TV series on WAVE-Louisville from 1947-57. Wrote "Slow Poke", "Tennessee Waltz", "Bonaparte's Retreat", "You Belong To Me", "Bimbo" and "Change Partners". Worked with Minnie Pearl from 1959-63; continued touring until 1968. Elected to the Country Music Hall Of Fame in 1974. Redd Stewart was lead singer on all of King's hits.		
			PEE WEE KING & his Golden West Cowboys:		
4/03/48	3	35	1 **Tennessee Waltz**	*30*	RCA 2680
			Best Seller #3 / Juke Box #4		
6/18/49	12	2	2 Tennessee Tears		RCA 0037
			Best Seller #12		
9/10/49	3	3	3 **Tennessee Polka**		RCA 0085
			Juke Box #3		
1/21/50	10	1	4 **Bonaparte's Retreat**		RCA 0114
			Jockey #10		
2/17/51	6	4	5 **Tennessee Waltz** .... [R]		RCA 0407
			Jockey #6 / Juke Box #7		
9/29/51	1 [15]	31	6● **Slow Poke**	*1*	RCA 0489
			Juke Box #1(15) / Best Seller #1(14) / Jockey #1(9)		
			PEE WEE KING & his Band:		
2/16/52	5	14	7 **Silver And Gold**	*18*	RCA 4458
			Juke Box #5 / Best Seller #5 / Jockey #7		
5/17/52	8	3	8 **Busybody**	*27*	RCA 4655
			Juke Box #8 / Jockey #9		
1/02/54	4	10	9 **Changing Partners/**		
			Jockey #4		
1/23/54	9	2	10 **Bimbo**		RCA 5537
			Juke Box #9 / Best Seller #10 / Jockey #10		
7/10/54	15	1	11 Backward, Turn Backward		RCA 5694
			Jockey #15		
			SHERRI KING		
10/02/76	95	2	1 Almost Persuaded		United Art. 855
			LARRY KINGSTON		
			Wrote hits "Biloxi" for Kenny Price and "The Lovin' Machine" for Johnny Paycheck.		
4/06/74	61	10	1 Good Morning Loving		JMI 37
12/13/75	91	4	2 Good Morning Lovin' .... [R]		Warner 8139
			DAVE KIRBY		
			Wrote "Is Anybody Goin' To San Antone" for Charley Pride, and many more. Married singer Leona Williams.		
11/08/69	67	4	1 Her And The Car And The Mobile Home		Monument 1168
5/16/81	37	11	2 North Alabama		Dimension 1019
9/12/81	64	5	3 Moccasin Man.............................		Dimension 1022
			EDDIE KIRK & THE STRING BAND		
			Born on 3/21/19 in Greeley, Colorado. With the Beverly Hillbillies in the early 30s. National Yodeling Champion in 1935 and 1936. On the Gene Autry radio shows and Town Hall Party, Compton, California, in the late 40s. Appeared in western films.		
10/02/48	9	6	1 **The Gods Were Angry With Me**		Capitol 15176
			Juke Box #9 / Best Seller #10		
3/12/49	9	3	2 **Candy Kisses**		Capitol 15391
			Best Seller #9 / Juke Box #10		
			RED KIRK		
			Worked on WNOX-Knoxville with Archie "Grandpappy" Campbell in 1947. Worked on WIMA-Lima, Ohio in 1951. Known as "The Voice Of The Country".		
6/25/49	14	1	1 Lovesick Blues		Mercury 6189
			Juke Box #14		

DEBUT DATE	PEAK POS	WKS CHR	ARTIST — Record Title	POP POS	Label & Number
			RED KIRK — Continued		
7/22/50	**7**	7	2 Lose Your Blues		Mercury 6257
			Jockey #7		
			EVELYN KNIGHT - see RED FOLEY		
			FRED KNOBLOCK		
			Born in Jackson, Mississippi. Performed with the rock band, Let's Eat, in the late 70s. Member of the singing songwriter trio of Schuyler, Knobloch & Overstreet (SKO) and Schuyler, Knobloch & Bickhardt.		
8/02/80	**30**	11	1 Why Not Me	*18*	Scotti Br. 518
10/18/80	**53**	6	2 Let Me Love You.......................................		Scotti Br. 607
11/29/80+	**10**	18	3 Killin' Time	*28*	Scotti Br. 609
			FRED KNOBLOCK & SUSAN ANTON		
8/22/81	**10**	14	4 **Memphis**..	*102*	Scotti Br. 02434
			written by Chuck Berry; Lonnie Mack and Johnny Rivers had pop hits		
3/20/82	**33**	10	5 I Had It All..		Scotti Br. 02752
			BUDDY KNOX		
			Born Buddy Wayne Knox on 7/20/33 in Happy, Texas. Formed The Rhythm Orchids at West Texas State University: Knox (guitar), Jimmy Bowen (bass), Don Lanier (guitar) and Dave "Dicky Doo" Alldred (drums). Formed own record label, Triple-D, named after KDDD radio in Dumas, Texas. Buddy currently lives near Winnipeg, Canada.		
6/22/68	**64**	6	1 Gypsy Man..		United Art. 50301
			REX KRAMER		
			Born in Smackover, Arkansas; raised in Baytown, Texas. Had own surf/rock band, The Coastliners, in the early 60s. Played banjo with the New Christy Minstrels, 1965-69.		
3/06/76	**100**	2	1 You Oughta Be Against The Law......................		Columbia 10286
			KRIS KRISTOFFERSON		
			Born on 6/22/36 in Brownsville, Texas. Attended Pomona College and earned Rhodes Scholarship to Oxford University in England; attended from 1958-59. Wrote "Me And Bobby McGee", "For The Good Times" and "Help Me Make It Through The Night". Moved to Nashville in 1965. Married to Rita Coolidge from 1973-80. Has starred in many films since 1972.		
4/22/72	**70**	2	1 Josie	*63*	Monument 8536
4/07/73	**1**[1]	20	2● Why Me..	*16*	Monument 8571
			backing vocals: Rita Coolidge and Larry Gatlin		
1/05/80	**91**	5	3 Prove It To You One More Time Again		Columbia 11160
4/18/81	**68**	7	4 Nobody Loves Anybody Anymore.....................		Columbia 60507
11/03/84	**46**	11	5 How Do You Feel About Foolin' Around		Columbia 04652
			WILLIE NELSON & KRIS KRISTOFFERSON		
5/18/85	**1**[1]	20	6 **Highwayman**		Columbia 04881
			WAYLON JENNINGS, WILLIE NELSON, JOHNNY CASH, KRIS KRISTOFFERSON		
9/14/85	**15**	18	7 Desperados Waiting For A Train		Columbia 05594
			WAYLON JENNINGS, WILLIE NELSON, JOHNNY CASH, KRIS KRISTOFFERSON		
2/28/87	**67**	6	8 They Killed Him..		Mercury 888345
			tribute to Jesus Christ, Gandhi and Martin Luther King		
			KRIS KRISTOFFERSON & RITA COOLIDGE:		
12/22/73+	**92**	5	9 A Song I'd Like To Sing................................	*49*	A&M 1475
3/23/74	**98**	2	10 Loving Arms	*86*	A&M 1498
12/28/74+	**87**	4	11 Rain		Monument 8630
			LEAH KUNKEL - see LIVINGSTON TAYLOR		

L

DEBUT DATE	PEAK POS	WKS CHR	ARTIST — Record Title	POP POS	Label & Number
			SLEEPY LaBEEF		
			Born Thomas Paulsley LaBeff (LaBouef) on 7/20/35 in Smackover, Arkansas. Guitarist from age 15. Recorded for Starday in 1956. Also recorded under various names, including "Tommy LaBeff", for several other labels. Moved to Nashville in 1964.		
4/13/68	**73**	3	1 Every Day..		Columbia 44455
6/19/71	**67**	5	2 Blackland Farmer		Plantation 74
			BOBBI LACE		
			Model/actress/singer. Appeared in the film "Scarface".		
3/29/86	**94**	2	1 You've Been My Rock For Ages		GBS 730
6/13/87	**79**	4	2 Skin Deep...		615 1008

DEBUT DATE	PEAK POS	WKS CHR	ARTIST — Record Title	POP POS	Label & Number
			BOBBI LACE — Continued		
12/19/87	88	3	3 There's A Real Woman In Me		615 1010
3/05/88	89	2	4 Another Woman's Man..............................		615 1011
5/28/88	69	5	5 Song In My Heart		615 1014
			MARK GRAY & BOBBI LACE		
8/20/88	77	3	6 If Hearts Could Talk		615 1012
12/17/88+	70	5	7 It's Gonna Be Love		615 1016
			MARK GRAY & BOBBI LACE		
			LA COSTA		
			Born LaCosta Tucker on 4/6/51 in Seminole, Texas. Elder sister of Tanya Tucker. With Tanya in the Country Westerners in Phoenix in the 60s. Left music for a career in medicine, returned to show business in 1972.		
4/20/74	25	15	1 I Wanta Get To You		Capitol 3856
9/14/74	3	17	2 Get On My Love Train		Capitol 3945
2/15/75	10	13	3 He Took Me For A Ride		Capitol 4022
6/07/75	19	12	4 This House Runs On Sunshine.......................		Capitol 4082
9/27/75	11	14	5 Western Man		Capitol 4139
1/31/76	28	9	6 I Just Got A Feeling		Capitol 4209
5/15/76	23	12	7 Lovin' Somebody On A Rainy Night		Capitol 4264
9/11/76	37	10	8 What'll I Do.....................................		Capitol 4327
5/07/77	75	7	9 We're All Alone		Capitol 4414
			#7 pop hit for Rita Coolidge in 1977		
11/26/77	100	1	10 Jessi And The Light		Capitol 4495
2/25/78	79	7	11 Even Cowgirls Get The Blues......................		Capitol 4541
6/03/78	94	3	12 #1 With A Heartache		Capitol 4577
5/17/80	68	6	13 Changing All The Time...........................		Capitol 4830
2/27/82	48	9	14 Love Take It Easy On Me		Elektra 47414
			LaCOSTA TUCKER		
			DON LaFLEUR		
10/08/88	97	2	1 Beggars Can't Be Choosers		Worth 102
			LANA RAE - see RAE		
			LYNDA K. LANCE		
			Born in 1949 in Smithfield, Pennsylvania. Toured Vietnam with Jimmy Case in 1968.		
11/01/69	59	5	1 A Woman's Side Of Love		Royal Amer. 290
1/30/71	46	6	2 My Guy		Royal Amer. 24
			#1 pop hit for Mary Wells in 1964		
8/21/71	74	2	3 Will You Love Me Tomorrow		Royal Amer. 35
			#1 pop hit for The Shirelles in 1961		
8/11/73	77	5	4 You, You, You		Triune 7207
			#1 pop hit for The Ames Brothers in 1953		
10/23/76	93	5	5 Say You Love Me		Gar-Pax 081
			#11 pop hit for Fleetwood Mac in 1976		
1/13/79	78	4	6 I Hate The Way Our Love Is		Vista 101
			JIMMY PETERS & LYNDA K. LANCE		
4/28/79	98	3	7 First Class Fool		Vista 106
			JIMMIE PETERS/LYNDA K. LANCE		
			DAVE LANDERS		
7/09/49	10	7	1 Before You Call		MGM 10427
			Best Seller #10 / Juke Box #12		
			RICH LANDERS		
			Born in St. Louis. Played piano and guitar from age 8, worked professionally from age 16. Nephew of Dave Landers.		
3/28/81	41	10	1 Friday Night Feelin'		Ovation 1166
7/11/81	40	9	2 Hold On		Ovation 1173
12/19/81+	52	9	3 Lay Back Down And Love Me		AMI 1301
6/12/82	74	5	4 Pull My String		AMI 1305
1/29/83	40	10	5 Take It All		AMI 1311
9/10/83	68	5	6 Every Breath You Take		AMI 1316
			#1 pop hit for the Police in 1983		
			THE LANE BROTHERS		
			New York-based vocal trio.		
3/28/81	83	4	1 Marianne..		FXL 0026
			new version of their 1957 pop hit (POS 64)		

DEBUT DATE	PEAK POS	WKS CHR	ARTIST — Record Title	POP POS	Label & Number
			CRISTY LANE ★★175★★		
			Born Eleanor Johnston on 1/8/40 in Peoria, Illinois. Owned a nightclub in Peoria. Moved to Nashville in 1972. Her husband, Lee Stoller, formed LS Records in 1976.		
2/12/77	52	10	1 Tryin' To Forget About You		LS 110
6/04/77	53	7	2 Sweet Deceiver		LS 121
8/20/77	7	16	3 **Let Me Down Easy**		LS 131
12/17/77+	16	13	4 Shake Me I Rattle............................		LS 148
			#42 pop hit for Marion Worth in 1963		
4/01/78	10	14	5 **I'm Gonna Love You Anyway**.......................		LS 156
7/22/78	7	14	6 **Penny Arcade**............................		LS 167
12/02/78+	5	16	7 **I Just Can't Stay Married To You**.................		LS 169
5/05/79	10	14	8 **Simple Little Words**		United Art. 1304
			also released on LS 172		
8/25/79	17	11	9 Slippin' Up, Slippin' Around		United Art. 1314
12/15/79+	16	13	10 Come To My Love.........................		United Art. 1328
3/29/80	1¹	18	11 **One Day At A Time**		United Art. 1342
8/16/80	8	14	12 **Sweet Sexy Eyes**		United Art. 1369
1/17/81	17	14	13 I Have A Dream		Liberty 1396
			first recorded by Abba on their "Voulez-Vous" LP in 1979		
5/02/81	21	13	14 Love To Love You		Liberty 1406
10/10/81	38	10	15 Cheatin' Is Still On My Mind.........................		Liberty 1432
1/09/82	22	14	16 Lies On Your Lips		Liberty 1443
5/08/82	52	8	17 Fragile-Handle With Care.........................		Liberty 1461
11/13/82	81	3	18 The Good Old Days		Liberty 1483
7/23/83	63	7	19 I've Come Back (To Say I Love You One More Time).........................		Liberty 1501
10/29/83	80	4	20 Footprints In The Sand		Liberty 1508
5/09/87	88	2	21 I Wanna Wake Up With You/		
		2	22 He's Got The Whole World In His Hands.........		LS 1987
			#1 pop hit for Laurie London in 1958		
			JERRY "MAX" LANE		
			Leader of house band at Billy Bob's club in Fort Worth, Texas.		
7/01/67	49	6	1 Keeping Up Appearances		Chart 1425
			LYNN ANDERSON & JERRY LANE		
11/16/74	63	8	2 Right Out Of This World		ABC 12031
6/14/75	81	5	3 I've Got A Lotta Missin' You To Do.................		ABC 12091
4/23/83	87	2	4 When The Music Stops		Stockyard 1000
12/17/83	96	3	5 I've Got A Lot Of Missin' You To Do .... [R]		Stockyard 003
			RED LANE		
			Real name: Hollis R. DeLaughter. Born on 2/9/39 in Bogalusa, Louisiana; raised in Michigan. Singer/songwriter. Did session work in Nashville from the early 60s.		
4/24/71	32	11	1 The World Needs A Melody		RCA 9970
10/30/71	68	2	2 Set The World On Fire (With Love)		RCA 0534
1/22/72	66	5	3 Throw A Rope Around The Wind.....................		RCA 0616
7/08/72	65	3	4 It Was Love While It Lasted		RCA 0721
			TERRI LANE		
			Born in Joelton, Tennessee. Vocalist with studio band on WSM-Nashville. Made numerous radio and TV commercials.		
3/24/73	37	11	1 Daisy May (And Daisy May Not)		Monument 8565
10/20/73	98	2	2 Be Certain		Monument 8582
5/25/74	94	3	3 Mockingbird		Monument 8610
			TERRI LANE & JIMMY NALL		
			Inez Foxx and Carly Simon & James Taylor had top 10 pop hits		
			TRINITY LANE - see TRINITY		
			K.D. LANG		
			Singer/songwriter Kathy Dawn Lang from Consort, Alberta, Canada.		
12/05/87+	42	13	1 Crying..		Virgin 99388
			ROY ORBISON/K.D. LANG		
			from the film "Hiding Out"; remake of Roy's 1961 pop hit (POS 2)		
5/14/88	21	17	2 I'm Down To My Last Cigarette......................		Sire 27919
9/17/88	53	8	3 Lock, Stock And Teardrops...........................		Sire 27813
			written by Roger Miller		

171

DEBUT DATE	PEAK POS	WKS CHR	ARTIST — Record Title	POP POS	Label & Number
			KELLY LANG Born on 1/10/67 in Oklahoma City; raised in Hendersonville, Tennessee. Her father is road manager for Conway Twitty.		
9/25/82	88	2	1 Lady, Lady		Soundwaves 4681
			PERRY LaPOINTE Born in Orange, Texas. Long-time featured artist on the Louisiana Hayride.		
6/21/86	64	5	1 New Shade Of Blue		Door Knob 249
10/18/86	92	2	2 You're A Better Man Than I		Door Knob 252
12/27/86+	73	5	3 Chosen...		Door Knob 260
4/11/87	73	4	4 Walk On By..		Door Knob 270
8/01/87	72	4	5 The Power Of A Woman................................		Door Knob 281
9/17/88	76	4	6 Clean Livin' Folk .... BOBBY G. RICE & PERRY LaPOINTE		Door Knob 307
			BILLY LARGE		
10/15/66	62	6	1 The Goodie Wagon		Columbia 43741
			BILLY LARKIN Born in Huntland, Tennessee. Attended Middle Tennessee State University.		
1/11/75	22	13	1 Leave It Up To Me		Bryan 1010
5/03/75	23	12	2 The Devil In Mrs. Jones................................		Bryan 1018
9/06/75	34	10	3 Indian Giver		Bryan 1026
6/05/76	66	7	4 #1 With A Heartache		Casino 053
8/28/76	36	9	5 Kiss And Say Goodbye .... #1 pop hit for the Manhattans in 1976		Casino 076
12/18/76+	88	4	6 Here's To The Next Time		Casino 097
10/07/78	67	4	7 My Side Of Town..		Mercury 55040
4/19/80	72	4	8 I Can't Stop Now		Sunbird 107
1/10/81	35	13	9 20/20 Hindsight		Sunbird 7557
5/30/81	24	13	10 Longing For The High		Sunbird 7562
			IRIS LARRATT Born in Lloydminster, Saskatchewan; raised in Prince George, British Columbia.		
7/21/79	100	1	1 You Can't Make Love To A Memory.................		Infinity 50015
			NICOLETTE LARSON Born on 7/17/52 in Helena, Montana; raised in Kansas City. Attended the University of Missouri. Moved to California in 1974, worked with the Nocturnes. Worked as back-up singer for Hoyt Axton, Neil Young, Linda Ronstadt, Emmylou Harris, the Doobie Brothers, Van Halen, Graham Nash, and many others.		
2/09/85	42	12	1 Only Love Will Make It Right.........................		MCA 52528
5/04/85	46	11	2 When You Get A Little Lonely		MCA 52571
9/21/85	72	8	3 Building Bridges		MCA 52653
3/22/86	63	5	4 Let Me Be The First		MCA 52797
6/07/86	9	23	5 **That's How You Know When Love's Right** ...... guest vocal: Steve Wariner		MCA 52839
10/11/86	49	8	6 That's More About Love (Than I Wanted To Know)...		MCA 52937
			BUDDY LATHAM Born in Cookville, Tennessee. As a teen, was a drummer for several groups; backed Conway Twitty, Del Reeves, Trini Lopez and The Beach Boys.		
9/03/88	97	2	1 (She Likes) Warm Summer Days		Prairie D. 8853
			JIM LAUDERDALE		
12/17/88	86	3	1 Stay Out Of My Arms...................................		Epic 08113
			VICKI LAWRENCE Born on 5/26/49 in Los Angeles. Sang folk music and performed in college. With the Young Americans from 1964-67. Uncanny resemblance to Carol Burnett earned her a spot on that network show. Later became a regular on the series. Married to songwriter Bobby Russell in 1972. Own successful TV series, "Mama's Family".		
4/28/73	36	8	1●The Night The Lights Went Out In Georgia........	*1*	Bell 45303
			JANET LAWSON		
7/25/70	74	2	1 Two Little Rooms.....................................		United Art. 50671

DEBUT DATE	PEAK POS	WKS CHR		ARTIST — Record Title	POP POS	Label & Number
				RODNEY LAY		
				Born in Coffeyville, Kansas. Worked as deejay on KGGF-Coffeyville. Toured with Wanda Jackson from 1964-66. In the film "Pat Garrett And Billy The Kid".		
5/30/81	85	4	1	Seven Days Come Sunday.............................		Sun 1164
4/24/82	72	5	2	Happy Country Birthday Darling......................		Churchill 94001
8/14/82	45	11	3	I Wish I Had A Job To Shove..........................		Churchill 94005
1/08/83	53	8	4	You Could've Heard A Heart Break...................		Churchill 94012
5/14/83	64	5	5	Mary Lee		Churchill 94020
				above 4: **RODNEY LAY & The Wild West**		
11/29/86	79	3	6	Walk Softly On The Bridges		Evergreen 1046
				LEAPY LEE		
				Born Lee Graham on 7/2/42 in Eastbourne, England. Acted on stage and TV in England. Nicknamed "Leapy" in school because "I was always a leaper!".		
10/19/68	11	15	1	Little Arrows..	*16*	Decca 32380
3/21/70	55	4	2	Good Morning		Decca 32625
11/08/75	82	5	3	Every Road Leads Back To You		MCA 40470
				BILL LEATHERWOOD		
7/11/60	11	13	1	The Long Walk		Country Jub. 539
				PATTI LEATHERWOOD		
				Born Patti DiAngelo, in 1950, in Cleveland. Moved to Nashville in 1969. Staff writer at Combine Music.		
12/18/76+	79	7	1	It Should Have Been Easy		Epic 50303
7/30/77	98	1	2	Feels So Much Better		Epic 50409
				TIM LeBEAU		
10/22/88	98	1	1	Playing With Matches		Rose Hill 001
				JACK LEBSOCK		
8/11/73	94	3	1	For Lovers Only		Capitol 3665
1/05/74	76	6	2	Lovin' Comes Easy		Capitol 3751
				CHRIS LeDOUX		
				Born on 10/2/48 in Biloxi, Mississippi. Moved to Austin in 1960. Inter-Collegiate National Champion Bareback Rider; World Bareback Champion in 1976.		
4/14/79	99	1	1	Lean, Mean And Hungry		Lucky Man 10270
11/17/79	98	3	2	Cabello Diablo (Devil Horse)		Lucky Man 6520
8/23/80	96	2	3	Ten Seconds In The Saddle		Lucky Man 6834
				BILLY LEE - see EARL NUNN		
				BRENDA LEE ★★116★★		
				Born Brenda Mae Tarpley on 12/11/44 in Lithonia, Georgia. Professional singer since age six. Signed to Decca Records in 1956. Became known as "Little Miss Dynamite".		
4/06/57	15	1	1	One Step At A Time......................................	*43*	Decca 30198
				Best Seller #15		
2/15/69	50	11	2	Johnny One Time...	*41*	Decca 32428
8/07/71	30	13	3	If This Is Our Last Time		Decca 32848
1/29/72	37	12	4	Misty Memories...		Decca 32918
7/08/72	45	10	5	Always On My Mind		Decca 32975
2/17/73	5	15	6	**Nobody Wins**	*70*	MCA 40003
8/18/73	6	15	7	**Sunday Sunrise**.......................................		MCA 40107
1/12/74	6	15	8	**Wrong Ideas**...		MCA 40171
7/13/74	4	14	9	**Big Four Poster Bed**.................................		MCA 40262
11/02/74+	6	14	10	**Rock On Baby**		MCA 40318
4/12/75	8	13	11	**He's My Rock**		MCA 40385
				vocal accompaniment: The Holladays		
8/09/75	23	12	12	Bringing It Back...		MCA 40442
2/07/76	38	9	13	Find Yourself Another Puppet		MCA 40511
7/17/76	77	5	14	Brother Shelton		MCA 40584
11/13/76	41	9	15	Takin' What I Can Get		MCA 40640
3/19/77	78	5	16	Ruby's Lounge...		MCA 40683
6/17/78	62	6	17	Left-Over Love		Elektra 45492
10/20/79	8	15	18	**Tell Me What It's Like**		MCA 41130
2/16/80	10	12	19	**The Cowgirl And The Dandy**		MCA 41187
7/12/80	49	7	20	Don't Promise Me Anything (Do It)..................		MCA 41270

DEBUT DATE	PEAK POS	WKS CHR	ARTIST — Record Title	POP POS	Label & Number
			BRENDA LEE — Continued		
9/20/80	**9**	14	21 **Broken Trust**		MCA 41322
			vocal accompaniment: The Oak Ridge Boys		
1/31/81	**26**	10	22 Every Now And Then		MCA 51047
6/06/81	**67**	5	23 Fool, Fool		MCA 51113
8/15/81	**75**	5	24 Enough For You..		MCA 51154
10/24/81	**32**	13	25 Only When I Laugh..		MCA 51195
			from the film of the same title		
1/30/82	**33**	11	26 From Levis To Calvin Klein Jeans....................		MCA 51230
6/19/82	**70**	6	27 Keeping Me Warm For You..............................		MCA 52060
11/06/82	**78**	4	28 Just For The Moment......................................		MCA 52124
			vocal accompaniment: The Oak Ridge Boys		
4/09/83	**43**	9	29 You're Gonna Love Yourself (In The Morning).....		Monument 03781
			WILLIE NELSON/BRENDA LEE		
9/24/83	**75**	4	30 Didn't We Do It Good		MCA 52268
8/11/84	**22**	16	31 A Sweeter Love (I'll Never Know)		MCA 52394
12/22/84+	**15**	16	32 Hallelujah, I Love You So...............................		Epic 04723
			GEORGE JONES with BRENDA LEE		
			#5 R&B hit for Ray Charles in 1956		
8/24/85	**54**	9	33 I'm Takin' My Time		MCA 52654
12/21/85+	**50**	12	34 Why You Been Gone So Long		MCA 52720
			CHANDY LEE		
7/07/79	**100**	2	1 She's Still Around		ODC 548
			DICKEY LEE ★★**137**★★		
			Born Dickey Lipscomb on 9/21/41 in Memphis. First recorded for Sun Records in 1957.		
6/19/71	**55**	8	1 The Mahogany Pulpit		RCA 9988
9/18/71	**8**	14	2 **Never Ending Song Of Love**		RCA 1013
			#13 pop hit for Delaney & Bonnie in 1971		
1/22/72	**25**	13	3 I Saw My Lady		RCA 0623
6/17/72	**15**	13	4 Ashes Of Love		RCA 0710
10/07/72	**31**	11	5 Baby, Bye Bye		RCA 0781
3/10/73	**43**	11	6 Crying Over You		RCA 0892
6/30/73	**30**	7	7 Put Me Down Softly		RCA 0980
9/22/73	**49**	9	8 Sparklin' Brown Eyes....................................		RCA 0082
2/23/74	**46**	11	9 I Use The Soap		RCA 0227
8/17/74	**90**	4	10 Give Me One Good Reason		RCA 10014
11/30/74+	**22**	13	11 The Busiest Memory In Town		RCA 10091
8/23/75	**1**¹	18	12 **Rocky**..		RCA 10361
			#9 pop hit for Austin Roberts in 1975		
1/31/76	**9**	14	13 **Angels, Roses, And Rain**.............................		RCA 10543
6/05/76	**35**	10	14 Makin' Love Don't Always Make Love Grow		RCA 10684
9/11/76	**3**	18	15 **9,999,999 Tears**	52	RCA 10764
			written by Razzy Bailey		
3/19/77	**20**	13	16 If You Gotta Make A Fool Of Somebody.............		RCA 10914
			#22 pop hit for James Ray in 1962		
7/02/77	**22**	11	17 Virginia, How Far Will You Go		RCA 11009
10/15/77	**21**	14	18 Peanut Butter..		RCA 11125
2/04/78	**27**	11	19 Love Is A Word		RCA 11191
7/15/78	**49**	6	20 My Heart Won't Cry Anymore..........................		RCA 11294
10/21/78	**58**	6	21 It's Not Easy		RCA 11389
7/28/79	**58**	9	22 I'm Just A Heartache Away		Mercury 55068
11/10/79	**94**	3	23 He's An Old Rock 'N' Roller		Mercury 57005
3/29/80	**61**	5	24 Don't Look Back		Mercury 57017
7/26/80	**30**	12	25 Workin' My Way To Your Heart		Mercury 57027
11/08/80+	**30**	12	26 Lost In Love..		Mercury 57036
			DICKEY LEE with KATHY BURDICK		
			#3 pop hit for Air Supply in 1980		
6/27/81	**37**	10	27 Honky Tonk Hearts		Mercury 57052
10/03/81	**53**	7	28 I Wonder If I Care As Much		Mercury 57056
			tune was flip side of The Everly Brothers' "Bye Bye Love"		
1/30/82	**56**	6	29 Everybody Loves A Winner		Mercury 76129

DEBUT DATE	PEAK POS	WKS CHR	ARTIST — Record Title	POP POS	Label & Number
			DON LEE Prominent lead guitarist. Wrote hits "Is This All There Is To A Honky Tonk?" for Jerry Naylor and "Beartrap" for Tex Williams.		
9/11/82	**86**	3	1 16 Lovin' Ounces To The Pound		Crescent 103
			HAROLD LEE		
4/06/68	**56**	6	1 The Two Sides Of Me		Columbia 44458
9/25/71	**74**	3	2 Mountain Woman		Cartwheel 198
			JOHNNY LEE ★★**111**★★ Born John Lee Ham on 7/3/46 in Texas City; raised in Alta Loma, Texas. Played in rock bands in the early 60s. Own band, the Road Runners, in high school. Served in US Navy during Vietnam conflict. Worked at Gilley's nightclub, later opened his own club a few miles away. Married to actress Charlene Tilton from 1982-84.		
12/27/75+	**59**	9	1 Sometimes		ABC/Dot 17603
7/31/76	**22**	12	2 Red Sails In The Sunset .... #1 pop hit for both Bing Crosby and Guy Lombardo in 1935		GRT 065
12/04/76+	**37**	10	3 Ramblin' Rose .... #2 pop hit for Nat King Cole in 1962		GRT 096
5/21/77	**15**	13	4 Country Party .... country version of Rick Nelson's "Garden Party"		GRT 125
10/29/77	**58**	7	5 Dear Alice		GRT 137
3/04/78	**43**	8	6 This Time .... #6 pop hit for Troy Shondell in 1961		GRT 144
7/19/80	**1**³	14	7●Lookin' For Love .... from the film "Urban Cowboy" (also #10 below)	5	Full Moon 47004
10/25/80	**1**²	16	8 **One In A Million**	102	Asylum 47076
2/14/81	**3**	14	9 **Pickin' Up Strangers**		Full Moon 47105
4/25/81	**52**	6	10 Rode Hard And Put Up Wet		Full Moon 02012
5/30/81	**3**	16	11 **Prisoner Of Hope**		Full Moon 47138
10/03/81	**1**¹	15	12 **Bet Your Heart On Me**	54	Full Moon 47215
1/23/82	**10**	15	13 **Be There For Me Baby**		Full Moon 47301
5/15/82	**14**	13	14 When You Fall In Love		Full Moon 47444
10/09/82	**10**	18	15 **Cherokee Fiddle** .... with friends Michael Martin Murphey and Charlie Daniels		Full Moon 69945
2/05/83	**6**	18	16 **Sounds Like Love**		Full Moon 69848
6/11/83	**2**²	22	17 **Hey Bartender**		Full Moon 29605
10/08/83	**23**	16	18 My Baby Don't Slow Dance		Full Moon 29486
2/04/84	**1**¹	22	19 **The Yellow Rose/** **JOHNNY LEE with LANE BRODY** theme song of the short-lived TV series of the same title		
		3	20 Say When		Warner 29375
5/26/84	**42**	12	21 One More Shot		Warner 29270
8/25/84	**1**¹	24	22 **You Could've Heard A Heart Break**		Warner 29206
1/05/85	**9**	20	23 **Rollin' Lonely**		Warner 29110
5/11/85	**12**	18	24 Save The Last Chance		Warner 29021
10/05/85	**19**	18	25 They Never Had To Get Over You		Warner 28901
1/25/86	**56**	9	26 The Loneliness In Lucy's Eyes (The life Sue Ellen is living) .... written by David Allan Coe		Warner 28839
4/05/86	**50**	8	27 I Could Get Used To This .... **JOHNNY LEE & LANE BRODY**		Warner 28747
			JONI LEE Born Joni Lee Jenkins in 1957 in Arkansas; raised in Oklahoma City. Eldest daughter of Conway Twitty. Singing since age 4. Also see Conway Twitty.		
12/13/75+	**16**	12	1 I'm Sorry Charlie		MCA 40501
5/15/76	**42**	9	2 Angel On My Shoulder .... #22 pop hit for Shelby Flint in 1961		MCA 40553
7/31/76	**62**	6	3 Baby Love .... #1 pop hit for The Supremes in 1964		MCA 40592
4/23/77	**97**	2	4 The Reason Why I'm Here		MCA 40687
1/07/78	**94**	4	5 I Love How You Love Me .... #5 pop hit for The Paris Sisters in 1961		MCA 40826
			ROBIN LEE Female vocalist; born Robin Irwin in Nashville. Graduate of Overton High School.		
2/26/83	**87**	3	1 Turning Back The Covers		Evergreen 1003
6/11/83	**81**	3	2 Heart For A Heart		Evergreen 1006

DEBUT DATE	PEAK POS	WKS CHR	ARTIST — Record Title	POP POS	Label & Number
			ROBIN LEE — Continued		
1/07/84	54	10	3 Angel In Your Arms		Evergreen 1016
			#6 pop hit for Hot in 1977		
4/28/84	63	7	4 Want Ads		Evergreen 1018
			#1 pop hit for Honey Cone in 1971		
8/11/84	62	5	5 Cold In July		Evergreen 1023
12/01/84	71	7	6 I Heard It On The Radio.....................		Evergreen 1026
6/29/85	49	7	7 Paint The Town Blue		Evergreen 1033
			ROBIN LEE & LOBO		
11/16/85	44	10	8 Safe In The Arms Of Love		Evergreen 1037
3/29/86	37	12	9 I'll Take Your Love Anytime		Evergreen 1039
8/02/86	48	8	10 If You're Anything Like Your Eyes		Evergreen 1043
4/23/88	52	8	11 This Old Flame		Atln. Am. 99353
8/20/88	56	7	12 Shine A Light On A Lie		Atln. Am. 99307
11/26/88	51	8	13 Before You Cheat On Me Once (You Better Think Twice)................................		Atln. Am. 99264
			T L LEE with KATHY WALKER		
2/21/87	78	4	1 A Silent Understanding		Compleat 164
			VICKI LEE		
			Vocalist from Pensacola, Florida. Worked with George Jones and Tammy Wynette.		
11/01/86	93	2	1 Bluemonia		Sunshine 1400
			WILMA LEE - see STONEY COOPER		
			THE LeGARDES		
			Duo of twin brothers Ted and Tom LeGarde (b: 3/15/31), from MacKay, Australia. Moved to the U.S.A. in 1957. Worked on Doye O'Dell's Western Varieties shows in Hollywood. Own TV series on KTLA-Los Angeles.		
6/03/78	88	3	1 True Love.......................................		Raindrop 012
			#3 pop hit for Bing Crosby & Grace Kelly in 1956		
3/24/79	82	4	2 I Can Almost Touch The Feelin'...........		4 Star 1037
			THE LeGARDE TWINS:		
10/18/80	92	3	3 Daddy's Making Records In Nashville............		Invitation 101
8/27/88	92	1	4 Crocodile Man From Walk-About Creek............		Bear 194
			ZELLA LEHR		
			Born in 1951 in Burbank, California. Worked in family vaudeville team, the Crazy Lehrs, from age 6. Act later re-named the Young Lehrs. Regular on TV's "Hee-Haw".		
12/17/77+	7	18	1 **Two Doors Down**.............................		RCA 11174
5/27/78	31	10	2 When The Fire Gets Hot		RCA 11265
8/26/78	20	12	3 Danger, Heartbreak Ahead..................		RCA 11359
1/06/79	24	10	4 Play Me A Memory		RCA 11433
5/05/79	59	5	5 Only Diamonds Are Forever		RCA 11543
7/14/79	34	10	6 Once In A Blue Moon		RCA 11648
12/15/79+	26	12	7 Love Has Taken Its' Time		RCA 11754
4/12/80	25	12	8 Rodeo Eyes		RCA 11953
10/11/80	34	10	9 Love Crazy Love		RCA 12073
8/15/81	16	15	10 Feedin' The Fire.............................		Columbia 02431
1/23/82	56	6	11 Blue Eyes Don't Make An Angel..........		Columbia 02677
9/25/82	85	2	12 What A Way To Spend The Night		Columbia 03164
3/19/83	86	4	13 Haven't We Loved Somewhere Before		Columbia 03593
9/29/84	72	5	14 All Heaven Is About To Break Loose		Compleat 129
2/09/85	66	6	15 You Bring Out The Lover In Me............		Compleat 136
			BONNIE LEIGH		
12/06/86	76	3	1 Runaway		R.C.P. 010
			#1 pop hit for Del Shannon in 1961		
7/25/87	80	3	2 That's When (You Can Call Me Your Own).........		R.C.P. 016
12/19/87	77	3	3 Moon Walking		R.C.P. 020
			RICHARD LEIGH		
			Born on 5/26/51 in McLean, Virginia. Actor at the Barter Theater in Abingdon.		
8/13/83	65	5	1 Ain't Gonna Worry My Mind..............		Capitol 5247
			SHANNON LEIGH		
10/02/82	90	2	1 Rock 'N' Roll Stories........................		AMI 1308

DEBUT DATE	PEAK POS	WKS CHR	ARTIST — Record Title	POP POS	Label & Number
			DAVE LEMMON		
			Born in Preston, Idaho. Worked as a cowboy and professional hunter.		
1/29/83	89	2	1 Too Good To Be Through.............................		SCP 9781
			CHESTER LESTER		
			Born Chester Arthur Lester in Charleston, West Virginia.		
2/10/79	86	4	1 Mama, Make Up My Room.........................		Con Brio 148
			BOBBY LEWIS ★★185★★		
			Guitarist, lute player born in Hodgerville, Kentucky. On radio and TV shows from age 13. Worked on "High Varieties", "Old Kentucky Barn Dance", "Saturday Night Country Style" and "Hayloft Hoedown" TV series.		
10/15/66	6	18	1 **How Long Has It Been**		United Art. 50067
3/25/67	49	7	2 Two Of The Usual.................................		United Art. 50133
6/17/67	12	14	3 Love Me And Make It All Better		United Art. 50161
10/21/67	26	12	4 I Doubt It.......................................		United Art. 50208
3/23/68	29	10	5 Ordinary Miracle		United Art. 50263
7/27/68	10	16	6 **From Heaven To Heartache**......................		United Art. 50327
12/28/68+	27	13	7 Each And Every Part Of Me........................		United Art. 50476
5/31/69	41	8	8 Til Something Better Comes Along		United Art. 50528
9/13/69	25	10	9 Things For You And I.............................		United Art. 50573
1/17/70	41	10	10 I'm Going Home		United Art. 50620
5/30/70	14	16	11 Hello Mary Lou.................................		United Art. 50668
			#9 pop hit for Ricky Nelson in 1961		
11/14/70	67	3	12 Simple Days & Simple Ways.........................		United Art. 50719
7/31/71	51	7	13 If I Had You....................................		United Art. 50791
11/27/71	45	9	14 Today's Teardrops		United Art. 50850
			#54 pop hit for Rick Nelson in 1964		
7/14/73	95	4	15 Here With You..................................		Ace of H. 0466
10/06/73	21	15	16 Too Many Memories.............................		Ace of H. 0472
2/16/74	32	10	17 I Never Get Through Missing You		Ace of H. 0480
4/27/74	47	12	18 Ladylover		GRT 007
10/12/74	78	8	19 I See Love......................................		GRT 008
6/21/75	71	8	20 Let Me Take Care Of You.........................		Ace of H. 7502
11/22/75	79	5	21 It's So Nice To Be With You		Ace of H. 7503
			#4 pop hit for Gallery in 1972		
9/11/76	52	7	22 For Your Love		RPA 7603
			#13 pop hit for Ed Townsend in 1958		
1/08/77	74	5	23 I'm Getting High Remembering		RPA 7613
5/07/77	81	6	24 What A Diff'rence A Day Makes		RPA 7622
			#8 pop hit for Dinah Washington in 1959		
4/21/79	39	10	25 She's Been Keepin' Me Up Nights		Capricorn 0318
7/06/85	91	3	26 Love Is An Overload		HME 04853
			HUGH X. LEWIS		
			Born Hubert Brad Lewis on 12/7/32 in Yeaddiss, Kentucky. Worked on Tennessee Barn Dance, CBC-TV, in 1963; Grand Ole Opry in 1964; American Swingaround, on ABC-TV, in 1967. Appeared in the films "40-Acre Feud", "Gold Guitar" and "Cottonpickin' Chicken- Pluckers". Wrote "B.J. The D.J." for Stonewall Jackson.		
12/26/64+	21	16	1 What I Need Most		Kapp 622
9/04/65	32	6	2 Out Where The Ocean Meets The Sky		Kapp 673
12/18/65+	30	10	3 I'd Better Call The Law On Me		Kapp 717
6/25/66	45	2	4 I'm Losing You (I Can Tell)........................		Kapp 757
10/15/66	61	2	5 Wish Me A Rainbow		Kapp 771
7/01/67	38	11	6 You're So Cold (I'm Turning Blue)		Kapp 830
12/09/67+	49	9	7 Wrong Side Of The World.........................		Kapp 868
3/23/68	36	10	8 Evolution And The Bible		Kapp 895
1/04/69	69	5	9 Tonight We're Calling It A Day		Kapp 955
3/29/69	72	6	10 All Heaven Broke Loose		Kapp 978
7/26/69	74	2	11 Restless Melissa.................................		Kapp 2020
1/17/70	56	6	12 Everything I Love................................		Columbia 45047
11/28/70	68	4	13 Blues Sells A Lot Of Booze........................		GRT 28
7/22/78	93	4	14 Love Don't Hide From Me		Little Dar. 7803
4/21/79	92	5	15 What Can I Do (To Make You Love Me).............		Little Dar. 7913

DEBUT DATE	PEAK POS	WKS CHR		ARTIST — Record Title	POP POS	Label & Number
				JERRY LEE LEWIS ★★36★★		
				Born on 9/29/35 in Ferriday, Louisiana. Played piano since age 9, professionally since age 15. First recorded for Sun in 1956. Appeared in the film "Disc Jockey Jamboree" in 1957. Career waned in 1958 after marriage to 13-year-old cousin, Myra Gale Brown, daughter of his bass player. Made comeback in country music beginning in 1968. "The Killer", surrounded by personal tragedies in the past 2 decades, survived several serious illnesses in the past 6 years. Cousin to country singer Mickey Gilley and TV evangelist Jimmy Swaggart. Had several duets with his sister, Linda Gail Lewis. Inducted into the Rock And Roll Hall Of Fame in 1986. Jerry's career documented in the 1989 film "Great Balls Of Fire" starring Dennis Quaid.		
6/17/57	**1** ²	23	1	**Whole Lot Of Shakin' Going On**................... Best Seller #1 / Jockey #6	**3**	Sun 267
12/02/57+	**1** ²	19	2	**Great Balls Of Fire/** Best Seller #1 / Jockey #4	**2**	
12/23/57+	**2** ²	10	3	**You Win Again** .... Best Seller #2 / Jockey #4	**95**	Sun 281
3/17/58	**4**	13	4	**Breathless** .... Best Seller #4 / Jockey #12	**7**	Sun 288
6/09/58	**9**	10	5	**High School Confidential**.......................... Best Seller #9	**21**	Sun 296
10/13/58	**19**	1	6	**I'll Make It All Up To You** .... Best Seller #19	**85**	Sun 303
5/08/61	**27**	1	7	What'd I Say	**30**	Sun 356
8/07/61	**22**	5	8	Cold Cold Heart .... 3 & 8: written by Hank Williams		Sun 364
2/01/64	**36**	2	9	Pen And Paper .... flip side "Hit The Road Jack" hit #103 on the pop charts		Smash 1857
3/09/68	**4**	17	10	**Another Place Another Time**.......................	**97**	Smash 2146
6/08/68	**2** ²	16	11	**What's Made Milwaukee Famous (Has Made A Loser Out Of Me)**	**94**	Smash 2164
9/28/68	**2** ²	12	12	**She Still Comes Around (To Love What's Left Of Me)**		Smash 2186
12/28/68+	**1** ¹	15	13	**To Make Love Sweeter For You**		Smash 2202
5/24/69	**9**	11	14	**Don't Let Me Cross Over**......................... JERRY LEE LEWIS & LINDA GAIL LEWIS		Smash 2220
5/31/69	**3**	15	15	**One Has My Name (The Other Has My Heart)** ..		Smash 2224
8/16/69	**6**	12	16	**Invitation To Your Party**........................		Sun 1101
10/04/69	**2** ²	13	17	**She Even Woke Me Up To Say Goodbye**		Smash 2244
11/29/69+	**2** ²	16	18	**One Minute Past Eternity**........................		Sun 1107
1/10/70	**71**	2	19	Roll Over Beethoven .... LINDA GAIL LEWIS & JERRY LEE LEWIS #29 pop hit for Chuck Berry in 1956		Smash 2254
2/21/70	**2** ²	14	20	**Once More With Feeling**		Smash 2257
4/25/70	**7**	15	21	**I Can't Seem To Say Goodbye**....................		Sun 1115
8/22/70	**1** ²	15	22	**There Must Be More To Love Than This**		Mercury 73099
11/21/70+	**11**	12	23	Waiting For A Train (All Around The Watertank) #14 pop hit for Jimmie Rodgers in 1929		Sun 1119
1/30/71	**48**	8	24	In Loving Memories		Mercury 73155
3/27/71	**3**	16	25	**Touching Home**	**110**	Mercury 73192
6/26/71	**31**	9	26	Love On Broadway		Sun 1125
7/24/71	**11**	13	27	When He Walks On You (Like You Have Walked On Me)		Mercury 73227
11/06/71+	**1** ¹	17	28	**Would You Take Another Chance On Me/**		
		15	29	Me And Bobby McGee	**40**	Mercury 73248
3/11/72	**1** ³	15	30	**Chantilly Lace/** #6 pop hit for the Big Bopper in 1958	**43**	
		15	31	Think About It Darlin'		Mercury 73273
6/17/72	**11**	11	32	Lonely Weekends............................... flip side "Turn On Your Love Light" hit #95 on the pop charts		Mercury 73296
10/07/72	**14**	13	33	Who's Gonna Play This Old Piano		Mercury 73328
2/17/73	**19**	10	34	No More Hanging On		Mercury 73361
4/21/73	**20**	11	35	Drinking Wine Spo-Dee O'Dee .... #2 R&B hit for Stick McGhee in 1949	**41**	Mercury 73374
8/04/73	**60**	6	36	No Headstone On My Grave.......................	**104**	Mercury 73402
9/29/73	**6**	14	37	**Sometimes A Memory Ain't Enough**		Mercury 73423
2/09/74	**21**	12	38	I'm Left, You're Right, She's Gone.................. recorded by Elvis Presley on the Sun label in 1955		Mercury 73452
6/22/74	**18**	12	39	Tell Tale Signs.................................		Mercury 73491

DEBUT DATE	PEAK POS	WKS CHR	ARTIST — Record Title	POP POS	Label & Number
			JERRY LEE LEWIS — Continued		
10/19/74	**8**	12	40 He Can't Fill My Shoes		Mercury 73618
2/22/75	**13**	12	41 I Can Still Hear The Music In The Restroom		Mercury 73661
6/28/75	**24**	13	42 Boogie Woogie Country Man..........................		Mercury 73685
12/06/75	**68**	5	43 A Damn Good Country Song..........................		Mercury 73729
2/14/76	**58**	6	44 Don't Boogie Woogie		Mercury 73763
8/07/76	**6**	15	45 **Let's Put It Back Together Again**.................		Mercury 73822
12/18/76+	**27**	11	46 The Closest Thing To You............................		Mercury 73872
10/29/77+	**4**	18	47 **Middle Age Crazy**		Mercury 55011
			title of 1980 film, based on this song		
3/11/78	**10**	12	48 **Come On In**		Mercury 55021
6/24/78	**10**	12	49 **I'll Find It Where I Can**		Mercury 55028
12/16/78+	**26**	13	50 Save The Last Dance For Me		Sun 1139
4/07/79	**84**	3	51 Cold, Cold Heart .... [R]		Sun 1141
			above 2 feature dubbed in vocals by Elvis impersonator, Orion		
4/07/79	**18**	11	52 Rockin' My Life Away/	*101*	
		11	53 I Wish I Was Eighteen Again		Elektra 46030
7/21/79	**20**	11	54 Who Will The Next Fool Be		Elektra 46067
2/09/80	**11**	12	55 When Two Worlds Collide		Elektra 46591
5/24/80	**28**	12	56 Honky Tonk Stuff....................................		Elektra 46642
9/06/80	**10**	12	57 **Over The Rainbow**		Elektra 47026
			Judy Garland, Glenn Miller and Bob Crosby had hit versions in 1939		
1/17/81	**4**	15	58 **Thirty Nine And Holding**		Elektra 47095
4/24/82	**43**	11	59 I'm So Lonesome I Could Cry		Mercury 76148
9/25/82	**52**	7	60 I'd Do It All Again		Elektra 69962
12/18/82+	**44**	10	61 My Fingers Do The Talkin'............................		MCA 52151
3/19/83	**66**	6	62 Come As You Were		MCA 52188
7/09/83	**69**	5	63 Why You Been Gone So Long		MCA 52233
8/23/86	**61**	6	64 Sixteen Candles		Amer. S. 884934
			#2 pop hit for The Crests in 1959		
			LINDA GAIL LEWIS		
			Born on 7/18/47 in Ferriday, Louisiana. Youngest sister of Jerry Lee Lewis. Appeared on Shindig TV shows with Jerry Lee. Retired from music in 1977.		
5/24/69	**9**	11	1 **Don't Let Me Cross Over**		Smash 2220
			JERRY LEE LEWIS & LINDA GAIL LEWIS		
1/10/70	**71**	2	2 Roll Over Beethoven		Smash 2254
			LINDA GAIL LEWIS & JERRY LEE LEWIS		
			#29 pop hit for Chuck Berry in 1956		
8/19/72	**39**	8	3 Smile, Somebody Loves You...........................		Mercury 73316
			MARGARET LEWIS		
			Songwriter for Shelby Singleton's publishing companies.		
6/29/68	**74**	3	1 Honey (I Miss You Too)................................		SSS 289
			answer song to Bobby Goldsboro's "Honey"		
			MELISSA LEWIS		
			Born on 10/16/64 in Exeter, New Hampshire; raised in New Hope, North Carolina.		
3/01/80	**75**	5	1 The First Time.............................		Door Knob 122
5/17/80	**71**	6	2 One Good Reason		Door Knob 129
			ROSS LEWIS		
12/17/88	**89**	4	1 Hold Your Fire.............................		Wolf Dog 21
			TEXAS JIM LEWIS		
			Born on 10/15/09 in Meigs, Georgia. Moved to Bedias, Texas in 1928. Worked in New York City with the Lone Star Cowboys, 1935. Made first films in 1937; first recorded for Vocalion in 1937. Own Kiddie TV series, "Safety Junction", from 1950-57 in Seattle. Appeared in 42 films.		
9/02/44	**3**	6	1 **Too Late To Worry, Too Blue To Cry**............		Decca 6099
			BRENDA LIBBY		
11/26/83	**97**	1	1 Give It Back		Comstock 1726
			GORDON LIGHTFOOT		
			Born on 11/17/38 in Orilla, Ontario. Worked on "Country Hoedown", CBC-TV series. Teamed with Jim Whalen as the Two Tones in the mid-60s. Wrote hits "Early Morning Rain" for Peter, Paul & Mary, "Ribbon Of Darkness" for Marty Robbins, and many others. First recorded for Chateau in 1965.		
6/01/74	**13**	15	1● Sundown	*1*	Reprise 1194

DEBUT DATE	PEAK POS	WKS CHR	ARTIST — Record Title	POP POS	Label & Number
			GORDON LIGHTFOOT — Continued		
10/19/74	**81**	6	2 Carefree Highway	*10*	Reprise 1309
4/05/75	**47**	7	3 Rainy Day People	*26*	Reprise 1328
10/09/76	**50**	11	4 The Wreck Of The Edmund Fitzgerald	*2*	Reprise 1369
			true story of an ore vessel that sank in Lake Superior on 11/10/75		
2/25/78	**92**	4	5 The Circle Is Small (I Can See It In Your Eyes)	*33*	Warner 8518
9/02/78	**100**	2	6 Dreamland		Warner 8644
5/24/80	**80**	5	7 Dream Street Rose		Warner 49230
8/30/86	**71**	9	8 Anything For Love		Warner 28655
			LINCOLN COUNTY		
			Trio from Lincoln County, Mississippi.		
4/11/81	**84**	4	1 Making The Night The Best Part Of My Day		Soundwaves 4629
			BENNIE LINDSEY		
11/13/76	**100**	2	1 Save The Last Dance		Phono 2633
			LaWANDA LINDSEY		
			Born on 1/12/53 in Tampa, Florida; raised in Savannah, Georgia. Debuted with father's band, the Dixie Showboys, in 1962. First recorded at age 14.		
12/20/69	**48**	10	1 Partly Bill		Chart 5042
7/25/70	**63**	6	2 We'll Sing In The Sunshine		Chart 5076
			#4 pop hit for Gale Garnett in 1964		
2/26/72	**60**	7	3 Wish I Was A Little Boy Again		Chart 5153
7/14/73	**38**	10	4 Today Will Be The First Day Of The Rest Of My Life		Capitol 3652
11/17/73	**87**	5	5 Sunshine Feeling		Capitol 3739
2/23/74	**62**	8	6 Hello Trouble		Capitol 3819
6/01/74	**28**	14	7 Hello Out There		Capitol 3875
9/28/74	**67**	7	8 I Ain't Hangin' 'Round		Capitol 3950
4/02/77	**76**	5	9 Walk Right Back		Mercury 73889
			#7 pop hit for The Everly Brothers in 1961		
10/07/78	**85**	4	10 I'm A Woman In Love		Mercury 55041
			LaWANDA LINDSEY & KENNY VERNON:		
1/04/69	**58**	9	11 Eye To Eye		Chart 1063
3/21/70	**27**	14	12 Pickin' Wild Mountain Berries		Chart 5055
			#27 pop hit for Peggy Scott & Jo Jo Benson in 1968		
9/19/70	**51**	9	13 Let's Think About Where We're Going		Chart 5090
2/27/71	**42**	9	14 Crawdad Song		Chart 5114
			SHERWIN LINTON		
			Born in Volga, South Dakota. Played piano from age 7. Worked as a deejay in Watertown, South Dakota. Worked in band, the Fenderbenders.		
10/22/77	**88**	3	1 Jesse I Wanted That Award		Soundwaves 4556
			PEGGY LITTLE		
			Born in Waco, Texas. On radio at age 10. Appeared on Shindig TV series. Married at age 16. Regular on the Mike Douglas TV series.		
3/15/69	**40**	10	1 Son Of A Preacher Man		Dot 17199
			#10 pop hit for Dusty Springfield in 1969		
6/21/69	**43**	10	2 Sweet Baby Girl		Dot 17259
10/18/69	**44**	9	3 Put Your Lovin' Where Your Mouth Is		Dot 17308
2/21/70	**37**	11	4 Mama, I Won't Be Wearing A Ring		Dot 17338
8/08/70	**59**	3	5 I Knew You'd Be Leaving		Dot 17353
5/01/71	**75**	2	6 I've Got To Have You		Dot 17371
4/14/73	**70**	2	7 Listen, Spot		Epic 10968
8/18/73	**37**	10	8 Sugarman		Epic 11028
			MICK LLOYD & JERRI KELLY		
			Songwriter/producer Mick Lloyd was born in Hollywood. Wrote "I Was Made For Dancing" hit for Leif Garrett.		
1/31/81	**85**	3	1 Be My Lover, Be My Friend		Little Giant 040
8/08/81	**85**	4	2 Sweet Natural Love		Little Giant 046
			LOBO		
			Born Roland Kent Lavoie on 7/31/43 in Tallahassee, Florida. Played with Legends in Tampa in 1961. This group included Jim Stafford, Gerald Chambers and Gram Parsons. Own publishing company, Boo Publishing, since 1974. Also see The Wolfpack.		
12/05/81+	**40**	12	1 I Don't Want To Want You		Lobo I

DEBUT DATE	PEAK POS	WKS CHR	ARTIST — Record Title	POP POS	Label & Number
			LOBO — Continued		
3/27/82	63	7	2 Come Looking For Me		Lobo IV
9/04/82	88	3	3 Living My Life Without You		Lobo X
3/09/85	57	5	4 Am I Going Crazy (Or Just Out Of Her Mind).......		Evergreen 1028
6/29/85	49	7	5 Paint The Town Blue .... ROBIN LEE & LOBO		Evergreen 1033
			HANK LOCKLIN ★★**110**★★ Born Lawrence Hankins Locklin on 2/15/18 in McLellan, Florida. Worked on WCOA-Pensacola in 1942. Joined the Louisiana Hayride in the late 40s. With the Grand Ole Opry since 1960. Toured Europe in 1957. Elected mayor of McLellan in the early 60s. Own TV series in Houston and Dallas in the 70s.		
6/25/49	8	5	1 **The Same Sweet Girl**............................... Juke Box #8 / Best Seller #15		Four Star 1313
9/05/53	1 3	32	2 **Let Me Be The One**............................... Jockey #1(3) / Juke Box #1(2) / Best Seller #2		Four Star 1641
3/24/56	9	1	3 **Why, Baby, Why** .... Jockey #9		RCA 6247
8/19/57	4	39	4 **Geisha Girl** .... Best Seller #4 / Jockey #6	66	RCA 6984
3/31/58	5	35	5 **Send Me The Pillow You Dream On** .... Jockey #5 / Best Seller #5	77	RCA 7127
		6	6 Livin' Alone .... Best Seller flip		RCA 6984
4/28/58	3	23	7 **It's A Little More Like Heaven/** Jockey #3 / Best Seller #8		
		7	8 Blue Glass Skirt.. Best Seller flip		RCA 7203
3/07/60	1 14	36	9 **Please Help Me, I'm Falling**	8	RCA 7692
12/31/60+	14	12	10 One Step Ahead Of My Past...........................		RCA 7813
6/05/61	12	7	11 From Here To There To You............................		RCA 7871
9/11/61	14	12	12 You're The Reason/	107	
10/02/61	7	14	13 **Happy Birthday To Me**		RCA 7921
1/13/62	10	14	14 **Happy Journey**.......................................		RCA 7965
6/23/62	14	11	15 We're Gonna Go Fishin'...............................		RCA 8034
4/20/63	23	4	16 Flyin' South		RCA 8156
1/18/64	41	4	17 Wooden Soldier..		RCA 8248
3/21/64	15	17	18 Followed Closely By My Teardrops		RCA 8318
5/15/65	32	9	19 Forty Nine, Fifty One		RCA 8560
12/25/65+	35	9	20 The Girls Get Prettier (Every Day)		RCA 8695
4/09/66	48	2	21 Insurance		RCA 8783
10/15/66	69	2	22 The Best Part Of Loving You		RCA 8928
3/04/67	41	10	23 Hasta Luego (See You Later)		RCA 9092
7/01/67	73	4	24 Nashville Women		RCA 9218
10/21/67+	8	20	25 **The Country Hall Of Fame**		RCA 9323
3/30/68	40	8	26 Love Song For You		RCA 9476
8/24/68	57	5	27 Everlasting Love		RCA 9582
11/02/68	62	6	28 Lovin' You (The Way I Do)		RCA 9646
2/01/69	34	10	29 Where The Blue Of The Night Meets The Gold Of The Day		RCA 9710
1/03/70	68	3	30 Please Help Me, I'm Falling .... [R] HANK LOCKLIN & DANNY DAVIS & THE NASHVILLE BRASS		RCA 0287
6/27/70	56	6	31 Flying South .... [R] HANK LOCKLIN & DANNY DAVIS & THE NASHVILLE BRASS		RCA 9849
10/10/70	68	4	32 Bless Her Heart...I Love Her		RCA 9894
3/13/71	61	4	33 She's As Close As I Can Get To Loving You		RCA 9955
			BOBBY WAYNE LOFTIS Keyboard player from Battle Creek, Michigan.		
8/14/76	85	6	1 See The Big Man Cry....................................		Charta 100
12/25/76+	54	11	2 Poor Side Of Town....................................... #1 pop hit for Johnny Rivers in 1966		Charta 104
6/11/77	75	6	3 You're So Good For Me (And That's Bad)		Charta 108
3/04/78	87	5	4 Can't Shake You Off My Mind		Charta 118
4/21/79	89	2	5 Small Time Picker		Charta 132

DEBUT DATE	PEAK POS	WKS CHR	ARTIST — Record Title	POP POS	Label & Number
			BUD LOGAN & WILMA BURGESS		
			Bud is former lead singer of The Blue Boys (vocal backing group for Jim Reeves).		
12/22/73+	**14**	17	1 Wake Me Into Love.....................................		Shannon 816
7/06/74	**53**	10	2 The Best Day Of The Rest Of Our Love..............		Shannon 820
			JOSH LOGAN		
			Kentucky native; former auto yard worker.		
12/10/88+	**58**	9	1 Everytime I Get To Dreamin'.........................		Curb 10519
			LOGGINS & MESSINA		
			Kenny Loggins (b: 1/7/47) and ex-Buffalo Springfield/Poco member, Jim Messina (b: 12/5/47). Messina was originally hired as producer for Loggins, however, they formed a partnership that lasted for 4 years.		
12/20/75+	**92**	6	1 Oh, Lonesome Me....................................		Columbia 10222
			flip side "A Lover's Question" made the pop charts (POS 89)		
			DAVE LOGGINS - see GUS HARDIN and ANNE MURRAY		
			SHORTY LONG & THE SANTA FE RANGERS		
			Shorty was born on 10/11/23 in Reading, Pennsylvania. Worked on the WLS-Chicago Barn Dance, and the Hayloft Hoedown in Philadelphia.		
10/30/48	**12**	1	1 Sweeter Than The Flowers............................		Decca 46139
			Best Seller #12		
			LONZO & OSCAR		
			Originally a comedy duo consisting of Rollin Sullivan (b: 1/19/19, Edmonton, KY) and Ken Marvin. Marvin was replaced in 1945 by Rollin's brother John (b: 7/7/17; d: 6/5/67). Joined the Grand Ole Opry in 1947. After John's death, Rollin teamed with David Hooten.		
1/31/48	**5**	7	1 I'm My Own Grandpaw .... [N]		Victor 20-2563
			Juke Box #5		
6/05/61	**26**	1	2 Country Music Time		Starday 543
1/12/74	**29**	12	3 Traces Of Life...................................		GRC 1006
			BOBBY LORD		
			Born on 1/6/34 in Sanford, Florida. Featured on Paul Whiteman's TV shows in the early 50s. Worked on Red Foley's Jubilee USA TV series in the late 50s. Own Bobby Lord Show in the mid-60s.		
9/08/56	**10**	2	1 Without Your Love.................................		Columbia 21539
			Juke Box #10 / Jockey #15		
1/11/64	**21**	10	2 Life Can Have Meaning.............................		Hickory 1232
4/06/68	**44**	11	3 Live Your Life Out Loud		Decca 32277
9/14/68	**49**	5	4 The True And Lasting Kind.........................		Decca 32373
2/15/69	**40**	9	5 Yesterday's Letters................................		Decca 32431
11/22/69+	**28**	11	6 Rainbow Girl......................................		Decca 32578
5/02/70	**15**	13	7 You And Me Against The World		Decca 32657
8/22/70	**21**	14	8 Wake Me Up Early In The Morning		Decca 32718
3/27/71	**75**	2	9 Goodbye Jukebox..................................		Decca 32797
			MIKE LORD		
			San Antonio-based drummer/singer.		
6/27/87	**94**	2	1 Just Try Texas		NSD 230
			LORIE ANN		
9/03/88	**81**	3	1 Down On Market Street		Sing Me 34
			MYRNA LORRIE & BUDDY DeVAL		
			Myrna was born in Thunder Bay, Ontario. Vocalist from age 9. Wrote "Are You Mine" at age 13. Own TV series at age 15.		
1/01/55	**6**	14	1 Are You Mine		Abbott 172
			Jockey #6 / Juke Box #7 / Best Seller #12		
			LOS LOBOS		
			Hispanic-American rock quintet based in Los Angeles. Includes: David Hidalgo (lead vocals), Cesar Rosas, Conrad Lozano, Louie Perez and Steve Berlin.		
8/22/87	**57**	8	1 La Bamba.................................... [F]	1	Slash 28336
			from the film of the same title about Ritchie Valens' life		
3/19/88	**55**	10	2 One Time One Night................................		Slash 28464
			BONNIE LOU - see BONNIE		

DEBUT DATE	PEAK POS	WKS CHR	ARTIST — Record Title	POP POS	Label & Number
			JOHN D. LOUDERMILK		
			Born on 3/31/34 in Durham, North Carolina. First cousin of The Louvin Brothers. Recorded as "Johnny Dee" and "Ebe Sneezer" on Colonial in 1956. Very gifted songwriter, wrote "A Rose And A Baby Ruth", "Sittin' In The Balcony", "Tobacco Road", "Then You Can Tell Me Goodbye", "Waterloo", "Abilene", "Talk Back Trembling Lips", "Ebony Eyes", "Sad Movies", "Norman", and countless others.		
6/29/63	23	4	1 Bad News..		RCA 8154
3/07/64	44	7	2 Blue Train (Of The Heartbreak Line).................	132	RCA 8308
9/26/64	45	5	3 Th' Wife .... [N]		RCA 8389
7/03/65	20	11	4 That Ain't All..		RCA 8579
6/17/67	51	5	5 It's My Time..		RCA 9189
			THE LOUVIN BROTHERS		
			Duo of brothers (real name: Loudermilk) Lonnie Ira (b: 4/21/24, d: 6/28/65 in an auto crash), and Charlie Elzer (b: 7/7/27). Worked with the Foggy Mountain Boys in Chattanooga in 1943, then had own radio show. Ira was in Charlie Monroe's Kentucky Partners in the mid-40s. First known as The Louvin Brothers in 1947 when they worked on WROL-Knoxville. First recorded for Decca in 1949. On the Grand Ole Opry from 1955-57 and returned in 1959. Disbanded in 1963. Charlie was in the films "Music City USA" and "The Golden Guitar".		
9/10/55	8	13	1 **When I Stop Dreaming** .... Jockey #8 / Best Seller #13		Capitol 3177
1/14/56	1²	24	2 **I Don't Believe You've Met My Baby**.............. Jockey #1 / Best Seller #5 / Juke Box #5		Capitol 3300
5/26/56	7	10	3 **Hoping That You're Hoping** .... Jockey #7 / Best Seller #8		Capitol 3413
10/06/56	7	12	4 **You're Running Wild/** Best Seller #7 / Jockey #11		
10/20/56	10	3	5 **Cash On The Barrel Head** .... Jockey #10		Capitol 3523
3/09/57	11	4	6 Don't Laugh................................. Jockey #11		Capitol 3630
7/15/57	14	1	7 Plenty Of Everything But You........................ Jockey #14		Capitol 3715
10/20/58+	9	22	8 **My Baby's Gone**..................................		Capitol 4055
2/16/59	19	7	9 Knoxville Girl		Capitol 4117
3/13/61	12	14	10 I Love You Best Of All.............................		Capitol 4506
9/25/61	26	1	11 How's The World Treating You		Capitol 4628
11/17/62	21	6	12 Must You Throw Dirt In My Face....................		Capitol 4822
			CHARLIE LOUVIN ★★147★★		
			Younger of The Louvin Brothers.		
6/20/64	4	27	1 **I Don't Love You Anymore**		Capitol 5173
12/12/64+	27	15	2 Less And Less		Capitol 5296
3/27/65	7	17	3 **See The Big Man Cry**...............................		Capitol 5369
10/23/65	26	8	4 Think I'll Go Somewhere And Cry Myself To Sleep		Capitol 5475
12/18/65+	15	12	5 You Finally Said Something Good (When You Said Goodbye)		Capitol 5550
10/15/66	58	5	6 The Proof Is In The Kissing...........................		Capitol 5729
12/24/66+	38	11	7 Off And On..		Capitol 5791
4/22/67	44	10	8 On The Other Hand		Capitol 5872
8/05/67	46	9	9 I Forgot To Cry		Capitol 5948
11/04/67+	36	12	10 The Only Way Out (Is To Walk Over Me)		Capitol 2007
3/09/68	20	14	11 Will You Visit Me On Sundays?.....................		Capitol 2106
8/17/68	15	12	12 Hey Daddy		Capitol 2231
12/21/68+	19	13	13 What Are Those Things (With Big Black Wings) ..		Capitol 2350
4/19/69	27	11	14 Let's Put Our World Back Together		Capitol 2448
9/27/69	29	9	15 Little Reasons		Capitol 2612
1/17/70	42	9	16 Here's A Toast To Mama		Capitol 2703
7/04/70	47	8	17 Come And Get It Mama		Capitol 2824
11/28/70+	54	7	18 Sittin' Bull..		Capitol 2972
5/20/72	70	2	19 Just In Time (To Watch Love Die)		Capitol 3319
1/05/74	36	13	20 You're My Wife, She's My Woman		United Art. 368
6/15/74	76	8	21 It Almost Felt Like Love.............................		United Art. 430
9/08/79	91	6	22 Love Don't Care.. **CHARLIE LOUVIN with EMMYLOU HARRIS**		Little Dar. 7922

DEBUT DATE	PEAK POS	WKS CHR	ARTIST — Record Title	POP POS	Label & Number
			CHARLIE LOUVIN — Continued		
6/05/82	**56**	9	23 North Wind		Soundwaves 4671
			JIM & JESSE and CHARLIE LOUVIN		
			CHARLIE LOUVIN & MELBA MONTGOMERY:		
10/24/70	**18**	14	24 Something To Brag About............................		Capitol 2915
2/13/71	**26**	12	25 Did You Ever		Capitol 3029
6/12/71	**30**	10	26 Baby, You've Got What It Takes		Capitol 3111
			#5 pop hit for Dinah Washington & Brook Benton in 1960		
11/27/71	**60**	5	27 I'm Gonna Leave You.................................		Capitol 3208
8/19/72	**66**	4	28 Baby, What's Wrong With Us.........................		Capitol 3388
1/20/73	**59**	6	29 A Man Likes Things Like That.......................		Capitol 3508
			IRA LOUVIN		
			Elder of The Louvin Brothers. Killed in an automobile accident on 6/28/65.		
8/14/65	**44**	4	1 Yodel, Sweet Molly		Capitol 5428
			PATTY LOVELESS		
			Born Patricia Ramey on 1/4/57 in Pikesville, Kentucky. Worked in duo with brother Roger from age 14. Toured with the Wilburn Brothers while still in high school. Worked clubs in North Carolina from 1973-85. Staff writer for Acuff-Rose. Joined the Grand Ole Opry in 1988.		
12/07/85+	**46**	10	1 Lonely Days, Lonely Nights.........................		MCA 52694
11/29/86+	**49**	10	2 Wicked Ways..		MCA 52969
3/14/87	**56**	8	3 I Did		MCA 53040
6/20/87	**43**	10	4 After All..		MCA 53097
10/31/87	**43**	11	5 You Saved Me		MCA 53179
2/06/88	**10**	20	6 **If My Heart Had Windows**		MCA 53270
6/04/88	**2**[1]	20	7 **A Little Bit In Love**...........................		MCA 53333
10/08/88+	**4**	20	8 **Blue Side Of Town**		MCA 53418
			LYLE LOVETT		
			Singer/songwriter born on 11/1/57 in Klein, Texas. Made professional debut in 1979. Appeared in the CBS-TV film "Bill On His Own" in 1983.		
7/12/86	**21**	19	1 Farther Down The Line		MCA/Curb 52818
11/01/86+	**10**	19	2 **Cowboy Man**.....................................		MCA/Curb 52951
2/21/87	**18**	14	3 God Will		MCA/Curb 53030
6/06/87	**15**	14	4 Why I Don't Know		MCA/Curb 53102
10/03/87	**13**	18	5 Give Back My Heart.................................		MCA/Curb 53157
1/30/88	**17**	16	6 She's No Lady		MCA/Curb 53246
5/21/88	**24**	14	7 I Loved You Yesterday		MCA/Curb 53316
9/17/88	**66**	4	8 If I Had A Boat....................................		MCA/Curb 53401
12/10/88+	**45**	9	9 I Married Her Just Because She Looks Like You .		MCA/Curb 53471
			JIM LOWE		
			Born on 5/7/27 in Springfield, Missouri. Vocalist/pianist/composer. Disc jockey in New York City when he recorded "Green Door" in 1956.		
5/20/57	**8**	3	1 **Talkin' To The Blues/**	20	
			Best Seller #8		
7/08/57	**15**	1	2 Four Walls..	15	Dot 15569
			Best Seller #15		
			THE LOWES		
7/19/86	**61**	5	1 Good And Lonesome.................................		Soundwaves 4775
11/08/86	**84**	4	2 Cry Baby		API 1001
1/17/87	**70**	5	3 I Ain't Never		API 1002
			RON LOWRY		
2/28/70	**39**	11	1 Marry Me		Republic 1409
8/22/70	**65**	6	2 Oh How I Waited		Republic 1415
			BOB LUMAN ★★108★★		
			Born on 4/15/37 in Nacogdoches, Texas. Died on 12/27/78 in Nashville. Country-rockabilly singer/songwriter/guitarist.		
10/10/60	**9**	10	1 **Let's Think About Living**	7	Warner 5172
2/22/64	**24**	14	2 The File...		Hickory 1238
1/29/66	**39**	5	3 Five Miles From Home (Soon I'll See Mary)........		Hickory 1355
6/04/66	**39**	5	4 Poor Boy Blues		Hickory 1382
			written by Carl Perkins		

DEBUT DATE	PEAK POS	WKS CHR	ARTIST — Record Title	POP POS	Label & Number
			BOB LUMAN — Continued		
9/24/66	**42**	11	5 Come On And Sing		Hickory 1410
2/18/67	**59**	6	6 Hardly Anymore		Hickory 1430
7/22/67	**61**	2	7 If You Don't Love Me (Then Why Don't You Leave Me Alone)		Hickory 1460
5/11/68	**19**	14	8 Ain't Got Time To Be Unhappy		Epic 10312
9/28/68	**50**	7	9 I Like Trains		Epic 10381
2/22/69	**24**	12	10 Come On Home And Sing The Blues To Daddy....		Epic 10439
6/07/69	**65**	5	11 It's All Over (But The Shouting)		Hickory 1536
6/28/69	**23**	13	12 Every Day I Have To Cry Some		Epic 10480
11/29/69+	**60**	9	13 The Gun		Epic 10535
3/28/70	**56**	5	14 Gettin' Back To Norma...............................		Epic 10581
5/09/70	**56**	8	15 Still Loving You..		Hickory 1564
7/11/70	**22**	14	16 Honky Tonk Man		Epic 10631
11/28/70+	**44**	10	17 What About The Hurt		Epic 10667
3/27/71	**60**	5	18 Is It Any Wonder That I Love You		Epic 10699
7/17/71	**40**	9	19 I Got A Woman		Epic 10755
11/06/71	**30**	10	20 A Chain Don't Take To Me		Epic 10786
1/29/72	**6**	17	21 **When You Say Love**..................................		Epic 10823
			#32 pop hit for Sonny & Cher in 1972		
6/03/72	**21**	10	22 It Takes You		Epic 10869
9/02/72	**4**	19	23 **Lonely Women Make Good Lovers**		Epic 10905
1/27/73	**7**	14	24 **Neither One Of Us**....................................		Epic 10943
			#2 pop hit for Gladys Knight & The Pips in 1973		
6/09/73	**23**	11	25 A Good Love Is Like A Good Song		Epic 10994
10/20/73+	**7**	15	26 **Still Loving You** .... [R]		Epic 11039
3/09/74	**23**	11	27 Just Enough To Make Me Stay........................		Epic 11087
7/13/74	**25**	11	28 Let Me Make The Bright Lights Shine For You....		Epic 11138
2/08/75	**22**	13	29 Proud Of You Baby		Epic 50065
9/13/75	**48**	12	30 Shame On Me		Epic 50136
2/07/76	**41**	9	31 A Satisfied Mind		Epic 50183
5/08/76	**82**	4	32 The Man From Bowling Green		Epic 50216
8/07/76	**89**	4	33 How Do You Start Over		Epic 50247
11/27/76	**94**	4	34 Labor Of Love...		Epic 50297
1/22/77	**63**	8	35 He's Got A Way With Women		Epic 50323
			above 2: produced by Johnny Cash		
8/06/77	**33**	9	36 I'm A Honky-Tonk Woman's Man		Polydor 14408
10/08/77	**13**	16	37 The Pay Phone		Polydor 14431
12/24/77+	**92**	3	38 A Christmas Tribute .... [X]		Polydor 14444
2/11/78	**47**	8	39 Proud Lady		Polydor 14454
			MIKE LUNSFORD		
			Born on 6/30/50 in Guyman, Oklahoma. Graduated from Panhandle State University in 1973, then moved to Nashville and worked at local clubs.		
3/01/75	**56**	12	1 While The Feelings Good		Gusto 124
11/08/75	**87**	5	2 Sugar Sugar		Starday 133
			#1 pop hit for The Archies in 1969		
7/31/76	**16**	12	3 Honey Hungry		Starday 143
11/20/76+	**28**	11	4 Stealin' Feelin'		Starday 146
2/26/77	**61**	7	5 If There Ever Comes A Day		Starday 149
7/16/77	**71**	5	6 I Can't Stop Now		Starday 160
5/27/78	**85**	4	7 The Reason Why I'm Here..............................		Starday 187
11/18/78	**91**	5	8 I Wish I'd Never Borrowed Anybody's Angel.......		Gusto 9013
5/26/79	**82**	4	9 I Still Believe In You....................................		Gusto 9018
2/23/80	**93**	3	10 Is It Wrong..		Gusto 9024
4/23/88	**89**	2	11 Tonight She Went Crazy Without Me		Evergreen 1068
			BILL LYERLY		
6/20/81	**53**	7	1 My Baby's Coming Home Again Today		RCA 12255

DEBUT DATE	PEAK POS	WKS CHR		ARTIST — Record Title	POP POS	Label & Number
				LIZ LYNDELL		
				Born Elizabeth Jones Tidwell from Fairview, Tennessee. Singer/songwriter. In the Miss Tennessee Beauty Pageant. Winner of the American Song Festival, Hollywood, in 1976. In the film "That's Country" in 1977.		
10/11/80	88	2	1	Undercover Man		Koala 326
3/07/81	78	4	2	I'm Gonna Let Go (And Love Somebody)		Koala 330
7/11/81	85	3	3	Right In The Wrong Direction		Koala 332
				TRACY LYNDEN		
5/25/85	80	5	1	Straight Laced Lady		RCA 14059
				JENNY LYNN		
9/23/78	86	3	1	Taste Of Love		Colonial 102
				JUDY LYNN		
				Born Judy Voiten on 4/12/36 in Boise, Idaho. For 21 years a featured artist in Nevada Casinos. Retired in 1980 to become an ordained minister.		
8/18/62	7	16	1	**Footsteps Of A Fool**		United Art. 472
1/26/63	29	1	2	My Secret		United Art. 519
4/06/63	16	15	3	My Father's Voice		United Art. 571
5/15/71	74	2	4	Married To A Memory	104	Amaret 131
1/18/75	92	5	5	Padre		Warner 8059
				#13 pop hit for Toni Arden in 1958		
				LORETTA LYNN ★★15★★		
				Born Loretta Webb on 4/14/35 in Butcher's Hollow, Kentucky. Married to Oliver "Moonshine" Lynn in 1949. Moved to Custer, Washington and worked in a band with her brother Jay Lee Webb. Joined the Grand Ole Opry in 1962. Toured with the Wilburn Brothers Show from 1960-68. Her autobiography and film version called "Coal Miner's Daughter". Elected to the Country Music Hall Of Fame in 1988. CMA award: Entertainer of the Year - 1972.		
6/13/60	14	9	1	Honky Tonk Girl		Zero 1011
7/07/62	6	16	2	**Success**		Decca 31384
6/08/63	13	11	3	The Other Woman		Decca 31471
11/16/63+	4	25	4	**Before I'm Over You**		Decca 31541
5/02/64	3	24	5	**Wine Women And Song**		Decca 31608
12/05/64+	3	23	6	**Happy Birthday**		Decca 31707
5/22/65	7	18	7	**Blue Kentucky Girl**		Decca 31769
9/18/65	10	16	8	**The Home You're Tearin' Down**		Decca 31836
2/05/66	4	14	9	**Dear Uncle Sam**		Decca 31893
6/04/66	2²	23	10	**You Ain't Woman Enough**		Decca 31966
11/12/66+	1¹	19	11	**Don't Come Home A'Drinkin' (With Lovin' On Your Mind)**		Decca 32045
5/13/67	7	17	12	**If You're Not Gone Too Long/**		
6/10/67	72	2	13	A Man I Hardly Know		Decca 32127
9/23/67	5	17	14	**What Kind Of A Girl (Do You Think I Am?)**		Decca 32184
2/24/68	1¹	17	15	**Fist City**		Decca 32264
6/15/68	2¹	16	16	**You've Just Stepped In (From Stepping Out On Me)**		Decca 32332
10/26/68	3	16	17	**Your Squaw Is On The Warpath**		Decca 32392
2/22/69	1¹	16	18	**Woman Of The World (Leave My World Alone)**		Decca 32439
7/19/69	3	15	19	**To Make A Man (Feel Like A Man)**		Decca 32513
11/29/69+	11	16	20	Wings Upon Your Horns		Decca 32586
3/07/70	4	14	21	**I Know How**		Decca 32637
6/27/70	6	15	22	**You Wanna Give Me A Lift**		Decca 32693
10/31/70	1¹	15	23	**Coal Miner's Daughter**	83	Decca 32749
				also see Sissy Spacek's soundtrack version in 1980		
3/27/71	3	15	24	**I Wanna Be Free**	94	Decca 32796
7/31/71	5	16	25	**You're Lookin' At Country**		Decca 32851
12/11/71+	1²	16	26	**One's On The Way**		Decca 32900
7/08/72	3	15	27	**Here I Am Again**		Decca 32974
12/09/72+	1¹	16	28	**Rated "X"**		Decca 33039
5/19/73	1²	15	29	**Love Is The Foundation**	102	MCA 40058
11/17/73+	3	16	30	**Hey Loretta**		MCA 40150
4/27/74	4	15	31	**They Don't Make 'Em Like My Daddy**		MCA 40223
9/07/74	1¹	17	32	**Trouble In Paradise**		MCA 40283

186

DEBUT DATE	PEAK POS	WKS CHR		ARTIST — Record Title	POP POS	Label & Number
				LORETTA LYNN — Continued		
2/15/75	**5**	12	33	**The Pill**	70	MCA 40358
8/02/75	**10**	14	34	**Home**		MCA 40438
11/15/75+	**2**¹	14	35	**When The Tingle Becomes A Chill**		MCA 40484
4/10/76	**20**	10	36	Red, White And Blue		MCA 40541
9/11/76	**1**²	17	37	**Somebody Somewhere (Don't Know What He's Missin' Tonight)**		MCA 40607
2/26/77	**1**¹	17	38	**She's Got You**		MCA 40679
8/06/77	**7**	13	39	**Why Can't He Be You**		MCA 40747
12/03/77+	**1**²	15	40	**Out Of My Head And Back In My Bed**		MCA 40832
5/27/78	**12**	11	41	Spring Fever		MCA 40910
11/04/78	**10**	13	42	**We've Come A Long Way, Baby**		MCA 40954
5/05/79	**3**	14	43	**I Can't Feel You Anymore**		MCA 41021
10/13/79	**5**	14	44	**I've Got A Picture Of Us On My Mind**		MCA 41129
3/01/80	**35**	8	45	Pregnant Again		MCA 41185
6/07/80	**30**	11	46	Naked In The Rain		MCA 41250
10/25/80	**20**	13	47	Cheatin' On A Cheater		MCA 51015
2/28/81	**20**	12	48	Somebody Led Me Away		MCA 51058
1/23/82	**9**	19	49	**I Lie**		MCA 52005
8/14/82	**19**	16	50	Making Love From Memory		MCA 52092
1/22/83	**39**	12	51	Breakin' It/		
		12	52	There's All Kinds Of Smoke (In The Barroom) ..		MCA 52158
5/28/83	**53**	10	53	Lyin', Cheatin', Woman Chasin', Honky Tonkin', Whiskey Drinkin' You...............................		MCA 52219
11/26/83	**59**	9	54	Walking With My Memories		MCA 52289
7/20/85	**19**	18	55	Heart Don't Do This To Me		MCA 52621
11/09/85	**72**	5	56	Wouldn't It Be Great		MCA 52706
2/08/86	**81**	5	57	Just A Woman		MCA 52766
4/16/88	**57**	12	58	Who Was That Stranger		MCA 53320
				ERNEST TUBB & LORETTA LYNN:		
7/25/64	**11**	23	59	Mr. And Mrs. Used To Be		Decca 31643
7/24/65	**24**	11	60	Our Hearts Are Holding Hands......................		Decca 31793
2/25/67	**45**	9	61	Sweet Thang		Decca 32091
6/14/69	**18**	10	62	Who's Gonna Take The Garbage Out		Decca 32496
				LORETTA LYNN/CONWAY TWITTY:		
2/06/71	**1**²	14	63	**After The Fire Is Gone**	56	Decca 32776
10/02/71	**1**¹	17	64	**Lead Me On**		Decca 32873
6/23/73	**1**¹	14	65	**Louisiana Woman, Mississippi Man**................		MCA 40079
6/15/74	**1**¹	15	66	**As Soon As I Hang Up The Phone**		MCA 40251
6/21/75	**1**¹	16	67	**Feelins'**		MCA 40420
6/19/76	**3**	12	68	**The Letter**		MCA 40572
6/04/77	**2**³	14	69	**I Can't Love You Enough**		MCA 40728
6/24/78	**6**	11	70	**From Seven Till Ten/**		
		9	71	You're The Reason Our Kids Are Ugly		MCA 40920
11/10/79+	**9**	14	72	**You Know Just What I'd Do/**		
		14	73	The Sadness Of It All................................		MCA 41141
5/10/80	**5**	15	74	**It's True Love**		MCA 41232
1/31/81	**7**	15	75	**Lovin' What Your Lovin' Does To Me**		MCA 51050
5/30/81	**2**²	18	76	**I Still Believe In Waltzes**		MCA 51114
				MARCIA LYNN		
				Born on 11/19/63 in North Adams, Massachusetts.		
3/14/87	**77**	5	1	You've Got That Leaving Look In Your Eye........		Soundwaves 4784
12/26/87+	**62**	8	2	Don't Start The Fire		Evergreen 1063
				REBECCA LYNN		
7/08/78	**39**	8	1	Music, Music, Music..................................		Scorpion 0550
				#1 pop hit for Teresa Brewer in 1950		
10/14/78	**69**	5	2	Minstrel Man		Scorpion 0559
2/24/79	**83**	5	3	Goody Goody...		Scorpion 0573
				#1 pop hit for Benny Goodman's Orchestra in 1936		

DEBUT DATE	PEAK POS	WKS CHR	ARTIST — Record Title	POP POS	Label & Number
			REBECCA LYNN — Continued		
6/02/79	82	3	4 Disco Girl Go Away/		
7/21/79	69	6	5 Make Believe You Love Me		Scorpion 0581
3/01/80	87	3	6 Fairytale		Sunbird 106
			TRISHA LYNN		
7/02/88	76	2	1 I Go To Pieces		Oak 1053
			#9 pop hit for Peter & Gordon in 1965		
			SHELBY LYNNE - see GEORGE JONES		

M

			JIMMY MAC		
6/23/84	93	1	1 You Really Know How To Break A Heart		AV 924
			BYRON MacGREGOR		
			25 year-old news director at CKLW-Detroit when he did the narration for "Americans". The narration was originally written and delivered as an editorial by Gordon Sinclair for CFRB-Toronto on 6/5/73.		
1/26/74	59	5	1● Americans .... [S]	4	Westbound 222
			backed by instrumental version of "America The Beautiful"		
			MARY MacGREGOR		
			Born on 5/6/48 in St. Paul, Minnesota.		
1/08/77	3	16	1● Torn Between Two Lovers	1	Ariola Am. 7638
4/23/77	36	10	2 This Girl (Has Turned Into A Woman)	46	Ariola Am. 7662
8/06/77	86	3	3 For A While	90	Ariola Am. 7667
			BOBBY MACK		
8/18/73	79	6	1 Love Will Come Again (Just Like The Roses)......		Ace of H. 0467
			GARY MACK		
			Born in Odessa, Texas. Sang in family gospel group in West Texas.		
3/20/76	94	2	1 To Be With You Again....................................		Soundwaves 4528
6/26/76	95	2	2 One Love Down...		Soundwaves 4532
4/02/83	90	2	3 I've Been Out Of Love Too Long......................		Grand Prize 5205
			WARNER MACK ★★135★★		
			Born Warner McPherson on 4/2/38 in Nashville; raised in Vicksburg, Mississippi. Began playing while in high school and worked in local clubs. Appeared on the Louisiana Hayride and Ozark Jubilee in the mid-50s.		
8/12/57+	9	36	1 Is It Wrong (For Loving You)........................	61	Decca 30301
			Best Seller #9 / Jockey #11		
1/11/64	34	7	2 Surely..		Decca 31559
11/28/64+	4	24	3 Sittin' In An All Nite Cafe		Decca 31684
5/29/65	1¹	23	4 The Bridge Washed Out................................		Decca 31774
11/06/65+	3	19	5 Sittin' On A Rock (Crying In A Creek)...........		Decca 31853
3/26/66	3	20	6 Talkin' To The Wall.....................................		Decca 31911
9/03/66	4	17	7 It Takes A Lot Of Money...............................		Decca 32004
2/11/67	8	17	8 Drifting Apart...		Decca 32082
6/24/67	4	17	9 How Long Will It Take		Decca 32142
11/11/67+	11	16	10 I'd Give The World (To Be Back Loving You)		Decca 32211
5/18/68	7	16	11 I'm Gonna Move On.....................................		Decca 32308
11/23/68+	23	19	12 Don't Wake Me I'm Dreaming		Decca 32394
5/03/69	6	15	13 Leave My Dream Alone		Decca 32473
9/27/69	8	13	14 I'll Still Be Missing You		Decca 32547
4/04/70	19	12	15 Love Hungry		Decca 32646
9/12/70	16	13	16 Live For The Good Times.............................		Decca 32725
2/20/71	34	11	17 You Made Me Feel Like A Man.......................		Decca 32781
8/28/71	53	9	18 I Wanna Be Loved Completely		Decca 32858
2/26/72	45	9	19 Draggin' The River		Decca 32926
8/05/72	59	6	20 You're Burnin' My House Down		Decca 32982
1/27/73	54	7	21 Some Roads Have No Ending.........................		Decca 33045
11/10/73+	91	7	22 Goodbyes Don't Come Easy...........................		MCA 40137

DEBUT DATE	PEAK POS	WKS CHR	ARTIST — Record Title	POP POS	Label & Number
			WARNER MACK — Continued		
11/19/77	**87**	5	23 These Crazy Thoughts		Pageboy 31
			BOBBY MACKEY		
			Born on 3/25/48 in Concord, Kentucky. With Red Jenkins from 1971-78. Own night club in Wilder, Kentucky, opened in 1978. Own radio series since 1980.		
6/12/82	**57**	8	1 Pepsi Man..		Moon Shine 3007
			ROSE MADDOX		
			Born Roseea Arbana Brogdon on 12/15/26 near Boaz, Alabama; raised in Bakersfield. Worked with family band on KTRB-Modesto in the mid-40s. First recorded with brothers Cal, Henry, Fred, and Don, as the Maddox Brothers and Sister Rose for Four Star in 1947. Appeared on the Louisiana Hayride and Grand Ole Opry before the group disbanded in 1959. Went solo in 1959.		
5/18/59	**22**	3	1 Gambler's Love...................................		Capitol 4177
1/30/61	**14**	13	2 Kissing My Pillow/		
2/13/61	**15**	7	3 I Want To Live Again		Capitol 4487
8/14/61	**14**	6	4 Conscience, I'm Guilty		Capitol 4598
11/10/62+	**3**	18	5 **Sing A Little Song Of Heartache**		Capitol 4845
3/16/63	**18**	8	6 Lonely Teardrops...............................		Capitol 4905
6/15/63	**18**	13	7 Down To The River.............................		Capitol 4975
11/23/63	**18**	6	8 Somebody Told Somebody		Capitol 5038
3/07/64	**44**	6	9 Alone With You		Capitol 5110
8/01/64	**30**	8	10 Blue Bird Let Me Tag Along		Capitol 5186
			BUCK OWENS & ROSE MADDOX:		
5/15/61	**8**	12	11 **Mental Cruelty/**		
5/22/61	**4**	14	12 **Loose Talk**..................................		Capitol 4550
8/03/63	**15**	6	13 We're The Talk Of The Town/		
8/10/63	**19**	6	14 Sweethearts In Heaven.............................		Capitol 4992
			CLEDUS MAGGARD & The Citizen's Band		
			Cledus' real name: Jay Huguely; born in Quick Sand, Kentucky.		
12/20/75+	**1**[1]	14	1 **The White Knight** .... [N]	19	Mercury 73751
4/17/76	**42**	7	2 Kentucky Moonrunner .... [N]	85	Mercury 73789
			above 2: with The Citizen's Band		
8/14/76	**73**	4	3 Virgil And The $300 Vacation .... [N]		Mercury 73823
7/15/78	**82**	4	4 The Farmer.................................... [N]		Mercury 55033
			THE MAINES BROTHERS BAND		
			Family band with Kenny (guitar, harmonica), Steve (guitar), Lloyd (steel guitar) and Donnie (drums). With Richard Bowden (fiddle), Gary Banks (keyboards) and Jerry Brownlow (bass).		
12/03/83	**72**	6	1 Louisiana Anna		Mercury 814561
3/24/84	**85**	3	2 You Are A Miracle..............................		Mercury 818346
2/09/85	**24**	16	3 Everybody Needs Love On Saturday Night		Mercury 880536
8/10/85	**84**	4	4 When My Blue Moon Turns To Gold Again		Mercury 880995
			#19 pop hit for Elvis Presley in 1956		
11/23/85	**72**	8	5 Some Of Shelly's Blues................................		Mercury 884228
3/15/86	**59**	7	6 Danger Zone....................................		Mercury 884483
			TIM MALCHAK		
			Born in Binghamton, New York. Worked as a folksinger in California and New York City. Teamed with Dwight Rucker in 1980.		
11/22/86	**68**	7	1 Easy Does It....................................		Alpine 004
3/07/87	**37**	13	2 Colorado Moon		Alpine 006
8/01/87	**39**	11	3 Restless Angel..................................		Alpine 007
1/30/88	**35**	14	4 It Goes Without Saying		Alpine 008
10/01/88	**43**	11	5 Not A Night Goes By		Alpine 009
			MALCHAK & RUCKER		
			Tim Malchak and Dwight Rucker. The only charted Country white/black duo.		
11/10/84	**92**	2	1 Just Like That..................................		Revolver 004
3/23/85	**67**	5	2 Why Didn't I Think Of That............................		Revolver 007
11/02/85	**69**	6	3 I Could Love You In A Heartbeat....................		Alpine 001
5/03/86	**67**	5	4 Let Me Down Easy		Alpine 002
8/02/86	**64**	6	5 Slow Motion		Alpine 003

DEBUT DATE	PEAK POS	WKS CHR		ARTIST — Record Title	POP POS	Label & Number
				DON MALENA		
				Born and raised in Bakersfield, California.		
1/10/87	72	4	1	Ready Or Not..		Maxima 1256
6/27/87	76	4	2	Moonwalkin'...		Maxima 1277
1/23/88	75	4	3	Dance For Me		Maxima 1311
				DOUG MALLORY - see ANNE MURRAY		
				HENRY MANCINI - see CHARLEY PRIDE		
				BARBARA MANDRELL ★★39★★		
				Born on 12/25/48 in Houston; raised in Oceanside, California. Plays steel guitar, bass, banjo and saxophone. Worked in the family band and appeared on Town Hall Party, Johnny Cash Show, Red Foley Show TV series in the early 60s. First recorded for Mosrite in 1963. Moved to Nashville in 1971. Own TV series from 1980-82 with sisters Louise, Irlene and other family members. Suffered severe injuries in an auto accident in 1984, from which she fully recovered. Joined the Grand Ole Opry in 1972. CMA award: Entertainer of the Year - 1980 and 1981.		
9/13/69	55	7	1	I've Been Loving You Too Long.......................		Columbia 44955
				#21 pop hit for Otis Redding in 1965		
5/23/70	18	12	2	Playin' Around With Love...............................		Columbia 45143
1/30/71	17	12	3	Do Right Woman - Do Right Man	128	Columbia 45307
6/26/71	12	12	4	Treat Him Right..		Columbia 45391
				#2 pop hit for Roy Head ("Treat Her Right") in 1965		
12/11/71+	10	13	5	**Tonight My Baby's Coming Home**		Columbia 45505
4/15/72	11	13	6	Show Me...		Columbia 45580
11/04/72	27	12	7	Holdin' On (To The Love I Got)........................		Columbia 45702
4/21/73	24	11	8	Give A Little, Take A Little.............................		Columbia 45819
8/18/73	7	17	9	**Burning The Midnight Oil**		Columbia 45904
6/15/74	12	16	10	This Time I Almost Made It		Columbia 46054
2/22/75	39	9	11	Wonder When My Baby's Comin' Home		Columbia 10082
12/20/75+	5	17	12	**Standing Room Only**		ABC/Dot 17601
5/08/76	16	13	13	That's What Friends Are For		ABC/Dot 17623
8/14/76	24	12	14	Love Is Thin Ice		ABC/Dot 17644
12/18/76+	16	12	15	Midnight Angel		ABC/Dot 17668
4/02/77	3	17	16	**Married But Not To Each Other**		ABC/Dot 17688
9/03/77	12	14	17	Hold Me...		ABC/Dot 17716
12/24/77+	4	16	18	**Woman To Woman**.....................................	92	ABC/Dot 17736
5/20/78	5	13	19	**Tonight**	103	ABC 12362
9/09/78	1³	15	20	**Sleeping Single In A Double Bed**	102	ABC 12403
2/17/79	1¹	14	21	**(If Loving You Is Wrong) I Don't Want To Be Right**	31	ABC 12451
8/11/79	4	14	22	**Fooled By A Feeling**	89	MCA 41077
12/15/79+	1¹	15	23	**Years**	102	MCA 41162
6/21/80	3	16	24	**Crackers**...	105	MCA 41263
10/11/80	6	17	25	**The Best Of Strangers**..............................		MCA 51001
2/07/81	13	13	26	Love Is Fair/		
		13	27	Sometime, Somewhere, Somehow...................		MCA 51062
5/09/81	1¹	13	28	**I Was Country When Country Wasn't Cool**......		MCA 51107
				guest vocalist: George Jones		
9/05/81	2²	16	29	**Wish You Were Here**.................................		MCA 51171
5/01/82	1¹	19	30	**'Till You're Gone**		MCA 52038
9/04/82	9	15	31	**Operator, Long Distance Please**		MCA 52111
4/23/83	4	19	32	**In Times Like These**..................................		MCA 52206
8/27/83	1¹	21	33	**One Of A Kind Pair Of Fools**		MCA 52258
2/18/84	3	21	34	**Happy Birthday Dear Heartache**		MCA 52340
6/09/84	2¹	21	35	**Only A Lonely Heart Knows**		MCA 52397
7/21/84	3	20	36	**To Me**..		MCA 52415
				BARBARA MANDRELL/LEE GREENWOOD		
10/06/84	11	20	37	Crossword Puzzle.......................................		MCA 52465
2/02/85	19	15	38	It Should Have Been Love By Now...................		MCA 52525
				BARBARA MANDRELL/LEE GREENWOOD		
3/09/85	7	20	39	**There's No Love In Tennessee**		MCA 52537
8/24/85	8	18	40	**Angel In Your Arms**		MCA 52645
				#6 pop hit for the group Hot in 1977		
12/07/85+	4	19	41	**Fast Lanes And Country Roads**		MCA 52737

DEBUT DATE	PEAK POS	WKS CHR		ARTIST — Record Title	POP POS	Label & Number
				BARBARA MANDRELL — Continued		
3/29/86	20	14	42	When You Get To The Heart............................		MCA 52802
				BARBARA MANDRELL with the OAK RIDGE BOYS		
8/16/86	6	22	43	**No One Mends A Broken Heart Like You**		MCA 52900
7/04/87	13	17	44	Child Support		EMI Amer. 43032
12/05/87	48	11	45	Sure Feels Good..		EMI Amer. 50102
3/12/88	49	11	46	Angels Love Bad Men......................................		EMI Amer. 43042
				guest vocalist: Waylon Jennings		
8/20/88	5	22	47	**I Wish That I Could Fall In Love Today**.........		Capitol 44220
				DAVID HOUSTON & BARBARA MANDRELL:		
10/03/70	6	14	48	**After Closing Time**		Epic 10656
10/02/71	20	12	49	We've Got Everything But Love		Epic 10779
9/16/72	24	13	50	A Perfect Match		Epic 10908
12/22/73+	6	16	51	**I Love You, I Love You**		Epic 11068
5/25/74	40	12	52	Lovin' You Is Worth It....................................		Epic 11120
8/10/74	14	16	53	Ten Commandments Of Love............................		Epic 20005
				#22 pop hit for Harvey & The Moonglows in 1958		
				LOUISE MANDRELL ★★**146**★★		
				Born on 7/13/54 in Corpus Christi, Texas. Younger sister of Barbara Mandrell. Guitarist/bassist, worked with Barbara's band, the Do-Rights, at age 15. Toured with Merle Haggard in the early 70s. Married to R.C. Bannon in 1979.		
8/26/78	77	5	1	Put It On Me..		Epic 50565
1/06/79	69	5	2	Everlasting Love		Epic 50651
				#6 pop hit for Carl Carlton in 1974		
9/01/79	72	5	3	I Never Loved Anyone Like I Love You.............		Epic 50752
3/29/80	63	5	4	Wake Me Up		Epic 50856
7/19/80	82	4	5	Beggin' For Mercy		Epic 50896
9/27/80	61	6	6	Love Insurance..		Epic 50935
2/13/82	35	12	7	(You Sure Know Your Way) Around My Heart.....		RCA 13039
7/24/82	20	15	8	Some Of My Best Friends Are Old Songs............		RCA 13278
11/06/82+	22	16	9	Romance		RCA 13373
2/26/83	6	17	10	**Save Me**		RCA 13450
7/16/83	10	19	11	**Too Hot To Sleep**		RCA 13567
11/05/83+	13	17	12	Runaway Heart..		RCA 13649
3/24/84	7	20	13	**I'm Not Through Loving You Yet**		RCA 13752
8/18/84	24	15	14	Goodbye Heartache		RCA 13850
12/08/84+	52	12	15	This Bed's Not Big Enough............................		RCA 13954
3/30/85	8	19	16	**Maybe My Baby**		RCA 14039
8/17/85	5	21	17	**I Wanna Say Yes**..		RCA 14151
12/14/85+	22	17	18	Some Girls Have All The Luck		RCA 14251
				#10 pop hit for Rod Stewart ("Some Guys Have...") in 1984		
6/28/86	35	11	19	I Wanna Hear It From Your Lips		RCA 14364
2/28/87	28	13	20	Do I Have To Say Goodbye..............................		RCA 5115
11/21/87	74	3	21	Tender Time		RCA 5208
4/09/88	51	9	22	As Long As We Got Each Other		RCA 20288
				LOUISE MANDRELL with ERIC CARMEN only available as a promo single for radio airplay		
				LOUISE MANDRELL & R.C. BANNON:		
3/10/79	46	8	23	I Thought You'd Never Ask		Epic 50668
6/02/79	13	12	24	Reunited		Epic 50717
				#1 pop hit for Peaches & Herb in 1979		
11/17/79	48	8	25	We Love Each Other		Epic 50789
11/28/81+	35	11	26	Where There's Smoke There's Fire....................		RCA 12359
6/05/82	56	7	27	Our Wedding Band/		
		7	28	Just Married		RCA 13095
12/11/82+	35	7	29	Christmas Is Just A Song For Us This Year.... [X]		RCA 13358
				flip side of Alabama's Christmas single		
				CARL MANN		
				Born on 8/24/42 in Huntingdon, Tennessee. Own band at age 12. First recorded for Jaxon in 1957. With Carl Perkins band from 1962-64. Left music from 1967-74.		
5/15/76	100	1	1	Twilight Time		ABC/Dot 17621
				#1 pop hit for The Platters in 1958		

DEBUT DATE	PEAK POS	WKS CHR	ARTIST — Record Title	POP POS	Label & Number
			LORENE MANN		
			Born on 1/4/37 in Huntland, Tennessee. Singer/songwriter. Wrote "Don't Go Near The Indians" for Rex Allen and "Left To Right" for Kitty Wells.		
10/02/65	23	9	1 Hurry, Mr. Peters		RCA 8659
			JUSTIN TUBB & LORENE MANN answer to Roy Drusky & Priscilla Mitchell's "Yes, Mr. Peters"		
7/30/66	44	2	2 We've Gone Too Far Again...........................		RCA 8834
			JUSTIN TUBB & LORENE MANN		
1/07/67	47	11	3 Don't Put Your Hands On Me...........................		RCA 9045
5/20/67	50	8	4 Have You Ever Wanted To?...........................		RCA 9183
9/23/67	63	6	5 You Love Me Too Little		RCA 9288
			ARCHIE CAMPBELL & LORENE MANN:		
1/06/68	24	15	6 The Dark End Of The Street		RCA 9401
6/29/68	31	10	7 Tell It Like It Is		RCA 9549
			#2 pop hit for Aaron Neville in 1967		
9/28/68	57	8	8 Warm And Tender Love		RCA 9615
			#17 pop hit for Percy Sledge in 1966		
1/04/69	36	9	9 My Special Prayer		RCA 9691
			ZEKE MANNERS		
			Pianist/accordionist born on 10/10/11 in San Francisco. Founder of the Beverly Hillbillies band with brother Tom in 1928. Worked on KELK-Beverly Hills. Moved to New York City, worked with Elton Britt in 1935.		
2/16/46	2⁸	19	1 **Sioux City Sue/**		
12/14/46	5	2	2 **Inflation**		Victor 20-2013
			LINDA MANNING		
			Born in Cullman, Arkansas. Own TV series on WKUL-Cullman.		
12/28/68+	54	8	1 Since They Fired The Band Director (At Murphy High)		Mercury 72875
			RHONDA MANNING		
			Born in Nashville. Daughter of country singer/disc jockey Ron Manning.		
12/19/87	87	3	1 Out With The Boys		Soundwaves 4792
6/11/88	73	3	2 You Really Know How To Break A Heart		RAM/Sound. 4799
			STEVE MANTELLI		
10/09/82	94	2	1 I'll Baby You		Picap 008
1/08/83	84	4	2 You're A Keep Me Wondering Kind Of Woman....		Picap 0005
			THE MARCY BROS.		
			Kevin, Kris and Kendal Marcy - from Oroville, California.		
5/07/88	68	5	1 The Things I Didn't Say		Warner 27938
			MARGO & NORRO - see MARGO SMITH and/or NORRO WILSON		
			THE MARLIN SISTERS - see FRANKIE YANKOVIC		
			BEN MARNEY		
			Born in Jackson, Mississippi. Leader of the Homecookin' Band.		
7/18/81	92	2	1 Where Cheaters Go..		Soul Bisquit 107
			LEAH MARR		
10/01/88	83	3	1 Sealed With A Kiss.................................		Oak 1060
			THE MARSHALL TUCKER BAND		
			Southern rock band formed in South Carolina in 1971: Doug Gray (lead singer), Toy Caldwell (lead guitarist), George McCorkle (rhythm guitar), Paul Riddle (drums), Jerry Eubanks (sax) and Tommy Caldwell (bass; d: 4/28/80).		
3/13/76	82	3	1 Searchin' For A Rainbow	104	Capricorn 0251
9/04/76	63	7	2 Long Hard Ride		Capricorn 0258
4/16/77	51	10	3 Heard It In A Love Song	14	Capricorn 0270
6/25/83	62	7	4 A Place I've Never Been		Warner 29619
9/05/87	44	11	5 Hangin' Out In Smokey Places........................		Mercury 888775
1/16/88	79	3	6 Once You Get The Feel Of It		Mercury 870050
			ROGER MARSHALL		
7/16/88	73	4	1 Hocus Pocus		AVM 17
11/19/88	99	1	2 Take A Letter Maria		Master 05

DEBUT DATE	PEAK POS	WKS CHR	ARTIST — Record Title	POP POS	Label & Number
			MARTY MARTEL		
			Born Don Robert Martel on 3/9/39 in Ogdensburg, New York. Worked on WCHI-Chillicothe, Ohio in 1961. With the Grand Ole Opry since 1961.		
11/17/79	96	2	1 First Step		Ridgetop 00679
			LINDA MARTELL		
			Born in Leesville, South Carolina. Worked R&B clubs in Columbia, South Carolina. First black female country singer on the Grand Ole Opry, 1969.		
8/02/69	22	10	1 Color Him Father		Plantation 24
			#7 pop hit for The Winstons in 1969		
12/13/69+	33	8	2 Before The Next Teardrop Falls		Plantation 35
			#1 pop hit for Freddy Fender in 1975		
3/28/70	58	6	3 Bad Case Of The Blues		Plantation 46
			BENNY MARTIN		
			Born on 5/8/28 in Sparta, Tennessee. Worked on WNOX-Knoxville Mid-Day Merry-Go-Round. Moved to WLAC-Nashville in 1944.		
5/25/63	28	1	1 Rosebuds And You		Starday 623
1/08/66	46	3	2 Soldier's Prayer In Viet Nam		Monument 912
			DON RENO & BENNY MARTIN		
			BETTY MARTIN		
			Singer/songwriter from Powhatan, Virginia.		
10/07/78	77	4	1 Don't You Feel It Now		Door Knob 071
			BOBBI MARTIN		
			Born Barbara Anne Martin on 11/29/43 in Brooklyn; raised in Baltimore. Toured the Far East with Bob Hope's Christmas Shows.		
10/15/66	64	3	1 Oh, Lonesome Me *134*		Coral 62488
			DEAN MARTIN		
			Born Dino Crocetti on 6/7/17 in Steubenville, Ohio. Vocalist/actor. To California in 1937, worked local clubs. Teamed with comedian Jerry Lewis in Atlantic City in 1946.		
7/09/83	35	12	1 My First Country Song		Warner 29584
			written by Conway Twitty, who also does a guest vocal		
			GRADY MARTIN - see BING CROSBY and BURL IVES		
			GYPSY MARTIN		
10/10/81	93	2	1 This Ain't Tennessee And He Ain't You		Omni 61581
			J.D. MARTIN		
			Nashville songwriter, born James Dean Martin in Harrisonburg, Virginia.		
5/10/86	72	6	1 Running Out Of Reasons To Run		Capitol 5573
9/06/86	77	5	2 Wrap Me Up In Your Love		Capitol 5606
			JIMMY MARTIN		
			Born on 8/10/27 in Sneedville, Tennessee. Played with Bill Monroe's Bluegrass Boys from 1949-54. Worked with the Osborne Brothers in the mid-50s. Own band, the Sunny Mountain Boys, and worked the WJR-Detroit Barn Dance, and Louisiana Hayride.		
12/08/58	14	6	1 Rock Hearts		Decca 30703
5/25/59	26	3	2 Night		Decca 30877
2/08/64	19	15	3 Widow Maker		Decca 31558
5/07/66	49	2	4 I Can't Quit Cigarettes		Decca 31931
5/18/68	72	2	5 Tennessee		Decca 32300
			JOEY MARTIN		
			Singer/actor born in North Georgia. Appeared on the "Daniel Boone" TV series.		
10/14/78	92	1	1 I've Been A Long Time Leavin' (But I'll Be A Long Time Gone)		Nickelodeon 102
			MIKE MARTIN		
			Born in Texarkana, Arkansas. Wrote "Old Fashioned Love" hit for The Kendalls.		
3/23/85	76	3	1 Temptation		Compleat 139
			WINK MARTINDALE		
			Born Winston Martindale in Jackson, Tennessee in 1933. Disc jockey since 1950. Own TV shows starting with "Teenage Dance Party". Host of "Tic Tac Dough" and other game shows.		
10/19/59	11	10	1 Deck Of Cards .... [S]	7	Dot 15968
			LAYNG MARTINE, JR.		
			Wrote hits "Way Down" for Elvis Presley and "Rub It In" for Crash Craddock.		
8/28/76	93	2	1 Summertime Lovin'		Playboy 6081

DEBUT DATE	PEAK POS	WKS CHR	ARTIST — Record Title	POP POS	Label & Number
			AL MARTINO		
			Born Alfred Cini on 10/7/27 in Philadelphia. Acted in "The Godfather", 1972.		
12/20/69+	69	3	1 I Started Loving You Again	86	Capitol 2674
			JAMES MARVELL		
			Born in Tampa, Florida. Formerly in the pop group Mercy and the Country Cavaleers.		
3/14/81	94	2	1 Urban Cowboys, Outlaws, Cavaliers		Cavalier 117
5/30/81	90	3	2 Love (Can Make You Happy)		Cavalier 118
			#2 pop hit for Marvell's group, Mercy, in 1969		
			MASON DIXON		
			Trio from Lamar University, Beaumont, Texas. Consisted of Frank Gilligan (b: 11/2/55, Queens, NY), lead vocals; Jerry Dengler (b: 5/29/55, Colorado Springs), guitar, banjo; and Rick Henderson (b: 5/29/53, Beaumont, TX), vocalist.		
10/22/83	69	7	1 Every Breath You Take		Texas 5502
			#1 pop hit for the Police in 1983		
4/21/84	51	11	2 I Never Had A Chance With You		Texas 5556
9/22/84	49	15	3 Gettin' Over You		Texas 5557
2/23/85	47	10	4 Only A Dream Away		Texas 5558
8/31/85	76	9	5 Houston Heartache		Texas 5508
1/11/86	72	10	6 Got My Heart Set On You		Texas 5510
8/02/86	53	10	7 Home Grown		Premier One 101
4/18/87	39	14	8 3935 West End Avenue		Premier One 112
10/10/87	51	8	9 Don't Say No Tonight		Premier One 115
8/06/88	62	5	10 Dangerous Road		Capitol 44189
11/05/88	49	13	11 When Karen Comes Around		Capitol 44249
			DONA MASON - see DANNY DAVIS & THE NASHVILLE BRASS		
			SANDY MASON		
			Born Sandy Theoret in Birdville, Pennsylvania. Worked as a ventriloquist from age 11. Own TV series, Popeye & Friends.		
5/13/67	64	5	1 There You Go		Hickory 1442
			WAYNE MASSEY		
			Singer/actor from Glendale, California. Played "Johnny Drummond" on TV's daytime soap opera "One Life To Live". Married to Charly McClain.		
1/17/81	82	3	1 Diamonds And Teardrops		Polydor 2147
5/21/83	71	6	2 Lover In Disguise		MCA 52211
8/06/83	57	7	3 Say You'll Stay		MCA 52246
			CHARLY McCLAIN & WAYNE MASSEY:		
7/06/85	5	22	4 With Just One Look In Your Eyes		Epic 05398
11/16/85+	10	20	5 You Are My Music, You Are My Song		Epic 05693
3/29/86	17	15	6 When It's Down To Me And You		Epic 05842
12/06/86	74	6	7 When Love Is Right		Epic 06433
			A.J. MASTERS		
			Born Arthur John Masters in Walden, New York. Played bass in his own band at age 14. Moved to Nashville in 1985.		
11/16/85	98	1	1 Lonely Together		Bermuda D. 111
3/08/86	48	9	2 Back Home		Bermuda D. 112
7/26/86	54	9	3 Love Keep Your Distance		Bermuda D. 114
11/08/86	65	5	4 I Don't Mean Maybe		Bermuda D. 115
1/17/87	58	6	5 Take A Little Bit Of It Home.....................		Bermuda D. 104
4/18/87	70	4	6 In It Again		Bermuda D. 116
8/15/87	67	7	7 255 Harbor Drive/		
11/21/87	77	3	8 Our Love Is Like The South		Bermuda D. 117
			BILLY MATA		
			Singer/hat-maker from San Antonio, Texas.		
1/30/88	82	3	1 Macon Georgia Love		BGM 92087
			"COUNTRY" JOHNNY MATHIS		
			Born on 9/28/33 in Maud, Texas. Worked on the Big D Jamboree, Louisiana Hayride and Grand Ole Opry. Recorded with Jimmy Lee Fautheree as "Jimmy & Johnny".		
9/25/54	3	18	1 **If You Don't Someone Else Will**		Chess 4859
			JIMMY & JOHNNY		
			Juke Box #3 / Jockey #5 / Best Seller #6		

DEBUT DATE	PEAK POS	WKS CHR	ARTIST — Record Title	POP POS	Label & Number
			"COUNTRY" JOHNNY MATHIS — Continued		
3/09/63	**14**	13	2 Please Talk To My Heart		United Art. 536
			JOEL MATHIS		
			Singer from Valdosta, Georgia.		
6/08/74	**89**	3	1 Ann...............................		Chart 5217
1/28/78	**89**	2	2 The Farmer's Song (We Ain't Gonna Work For Peanuts)/		
		2	3 Dirt Farming Man........................		Soundwaves 4562
			KATHY MATTEA ★★**187**★★		
			Born on 6/21/59 in Cross Lane, West Virginia. Guitarist since high school. Attended West Virginia University, played in the bluegrass group, Pennsboro. Moved to Nashville and worked as a tour guide at the Country Music Hall Of Fame. Toured with Bobby Goldsboro, Don Williams, Oak Ridge Boys, and Gary Morris.		
10/08/83	**25**	18	1 Street Talk		Mercury 814375
2/25/84	**26**	16	2 Someone Is Falling In Love		Mercury 818289
6/16/84	**44**	10	3 You've Got A Soft Place To Fall		Mercury 822218
9/15/84	**50**	11	4 That's Easy For You To Say		Mercury 880192
3/16/85	**34**	14	5 It's Your Reputation Talkin'........................		Mercury 880595
7/06/85	**22**	19	6 He Won't Give In........................		Mercury 880867
11/02/85	**46**	11	7 Heart Of The Country		Mercury 884177
4/12/86	**3**	22	8 **Love At The Five & Dime**		Mercury 884573
9/13/86	**10**	24	9 **Walk The Way The Wind Blows**		Mercury 884978
2/07/87	**5**	25	10 **You're The Power**		Mercury 888319
5/23/87	**6**	20	11 **Train Of Memories**		Mercury 888574
10/17/87+	**1**[1]	24	12 **Goin' Gone**		Mercury 888874
3/12/88	**1**[2]	20	13 **Eighteen Wheels And A Dozen Roses**		Mercury 870148
7/09/88	**4**	19	14 **Untold Stories**		Mercury 870476
11/12/88+	**4**	22	15 **Life As We Knew It**		Mercury 872082
			RALPH MAY		
5/02/81	**93**	2	1 Cajun Lady		Soundwaves 4630
2/20/82	**83**	3	2 In A Strangers Eyes........................		AMI 1901
8/28/82	**88**	3	3 Here Comes That Feelin' Again........................		Primero 1006
2/19/83	**57**	8	4 Angels Get Lonely Too........................		Primero 1021
1/17/87	**73**	4	5 Memory Attack........................		Evergreen 1048
			RALPH MAY & THE OHIO RIVER BAND		
			LEON McAULIFF		
			Born William Leon McAuliff on 1/3/17 in Houston. Worked with Texas Jim Lewis, The Light Crust Doughboys, and recorded for Brunswick in 1933. With Bob Wills' Texas Playboys from 1935-42. In the service from 1942-46. Own band, the Cimarron Boys, from 1946. Appeared in 10 western films. Wrote "Steel Guitar Rag", "Blue Bonnet Rag", "Pan Handle Rag" and "San Antonio Rose". One of the first to play electric steel guitar. Died on 8/20/88 in Tulsa.		
6/04/49	**6**	5	1 **Pan Handle Rag**........................		Columbia 20546
			Best Seller #6 / Juke Box #10		
8/21/61	**16**	15	2 Cozy Inn........................		Cimarron 4050
12/22/62+	**22**	11	3 Faded Love		Cimarron 4057
			LEON McAULIFFE:		
1/11/64	**35**	1	4 Shape Up Or Ship Out/		
2/08/64	**47**	1	5 I Don't Love Nobody		Capitol 5066
			JERRY McBEE		
			Also see Bluestone.		
4/12/80	**86**	4	1 That's The Chance We'll Have To Take		Dimension 1004
			DALE McBRIDE		
			Born in Bell County, Texas; raised in Lampasas, Texas. Played guitar since age 13. Original member of the Downbeats; worked with Jimmy Heap.		
3/27/71	**70**	2	1 Corpus Christi Wind		Thunderbird 539
5/22/76+	**90**	6	2 Getting Over You Again........................		Con Brio 109
11/20/76+	**26**	13	3 Ordinary Man		Con Brio 114
3/12/77	**60**	8	4 I'm Savin' Up Sunshine		Con Brio 117
7/09/77	**53**	7	5 Love I Need You		Con Brio 121
9/24/77	**73**	6	6 My Girl		Con Brio 124
12/10/77+	**37**	10	7 Always Lovin Her Man		Con Brio 127

DEBUT DATE	PEAK POS	WKS CHR	ARTIST — Record Title	POP POS	Label & Number
			DALE McBRIDE — Continued		
3/18/78	56	8	8 A Sweet Love Song The World Can Sing		Con Brio 131
7/15/78	45	7	9 I Don't Like Cheatin' Songs............................		Con Brio 135
10/21/78	72	5	10 Lets Be Lonely Together		Con Brio 140
2/03/79	66	5	11 It's Hell To Know She's Heaven		Con Brio 145
5/12/79	67	7	12 Getting Over You Again........................... [R]		Con Brio 151
9/22/79	61	7	13 Get Your Hands On Me Baby		Con Brio 158
			C.W. McCALL		
			Born William Fries on 11/15/28 in Audubon, Iowa. The character "C.W. McCall" was created for the Metz Bread Company. Fries was their advertising man. Elected Mayor of Ouray, Colorado in the early 80s.		
7/13/74	19	11	1 Old Home Filler-Up An' Keep On-A-Truckin' Cafe .... [N]	54	MGM 14738
12/07/74+	12	16	2 Wolf Creek Pass.............................. [N]	40	MGM 14764
5/10/75	13	12	3 Classified .... [N]	101	MGM 14801
9/20/75	24	11	4 Black Bear Road............................... [N]		MGM 14825
11/29/75	1⁶	15	5 ● Convoy .... [N]	1	MGM 14839
3/27/76	19	10	6 There Won't Be No Country Music (There Won't Be No Rock 'N' Roll) .... [S]	73	Polydor 14310
7/04/76	32	9	7 Crispy Critters .... [N]		Polydor 14331
10/16/76	88	4	8 Four Wheel Cowboy............................ [N]		Polydor 14352
12/18/76+	40	8	9 'Round The World With The Rubber Duck ..... [N]	101	Polydor 14365
2/26/77	56	7	10 Audubon .... [N]		Polydor 14377
9/17/77	2²	15	11 **Roses For Mama** .... [S]		Polydor 14420
1/20/79	81	4	12 Outlaws And Lone Star Beer		Polydor 14527
			DARRELL McCALL		
			Born in Hillsboro, Ohio. Lead tenor with the Little Dippers. Toured with Faron Young and Ray Price. Co-writer of the hit "Eleven Roses" for Hank Williams, Jr.		
1/12/63	17	8	1 A Stranger Was Here		Philips 40079
4/27/68	67	5	2 I'd Love To Live With You Again....................		Wayside 1011
8/17/68	60	8	3 Wall Of Pictures...................................		Wayside 1021
7/12/69	53	9	4 Hurry Up		Wayside 003
2/07/70	62	4	5 The Arms Of My Weakness		Wayside 008
4/27/74	48	9	6 There's Still A Lot Of Love In San Antone		Atlantic 4019
3/20/76	52	8	7 Pins And Needles (In My Heart)...................		Columbia 10296
3/12/77	32	13	8 Lily Dale		Columbia 10480
			DARRELL McCALL & WILLIE NELSON		
7/16/77	35	10	9 Dreams Of A Dreamer		Columbia 10576
1/07/78	59	9	10 Down The Roads Of Daddy's Dreams		Columbia 10653
5/13/78	91	5	11 The Weeds Outlived The Roses		Columbia 10723
3/01/80	89	5	12 San Antonio Medley		Hillside 01
			CURTIS POTTER/DARRELL McCALL		
8/09/80	43	9	13 Long Line Of Empties..............................		RCA 12033
6/09/84	79	4	14 Memphis In May.................................		Indigo 304
			THE McCARTERS		
			Trio of sisters from Sevierville, Tennessee: Jennifer and twins Lisa and Teresa.		
1/16/88	5	20	1 **Timeless And True Love**..............................		Warner 28125
6/11/88	4	20	2 **The Gift**..		Warner 27868
10/08/88	28	15	3 I Give You Music		Warner 27721
			PAUL McCARTNEY		
			Born on 6/18/42 in Liverpool, England. Writer of over 50 Top 10 singles. Founding member/bass guitarist of The Beatles. Married Linda Eastman on 3/12/69.		
12/21/74+	51	10	1 Sally G...	39	Apple 1875
			shown as: **WINGS**		
			flip side "Junior's Farm" hit #3 on pop charts		
			CHARLY McCLAIN ★★78★★		
			Born Charlotte Denise McClain on 3/26/56 in Jackson, Tennessee. Sang in band with brother at age 9. Worked on the Mid-South Jamboree from 1973-75. Toured with O.B. McClinton. Appeared on "Hart To Hart", "CHIPS", "Austin City Limits" and "Solid Gold" TV shows. Married to actor Wayne Massey in July of 1984.		
10/23/76	67	11	1 Lay Down		Epic 50285
3/05/77	82	5	2 Lay Something On My Bed Besides A Blanket		Epic 50338
5/14/77	87	4	3 It's Too Late To Love Me Now		Epic 50378

DEBUT DATE	PEAK POS	WKS CHR	ARTIST — Record Title	POP POS	Label & Number
			CHARLY McCLAIN — Continued		
10/01/77	**73**	5	4 Make The World Go Away...................................		Epic 50436
			#6 pop hit in 1965 for Eddy Arnold		
4/08/78	**13**	16	5 Let Me Be Your Baby		Epic 50525
9/16/78	**8**	14	6 **That's What You Do To Me**		Epic 50598
1/27/79	**24**	11	7 Take Me Back...		Epic 50653
5/19/79	**11**	14	8 When A Love Ain't Right..................................		Epic 50706
9/15/79	**20**	12	9 You're A Part Of Me..		Epic 50759
10/20/79	**16**	14	10 I Hate The Way I Love It..............................		Epic 50791
			JOHNNY RODRIGUEZ & CHARLY McCLAIN		
1/12/80	**7**	15	11 **Men**..		Epic 50825
5/03/80	**23**	13	12 Let's Put Our Love In Motion.......................		Epic 50873
8/09/80	**18**	13	13 Women Get Lonely		Epic 50916
11/29/80+	**1**¹	17	14 **Who's Cheatin' Who**		Epic 50948
4/11/81	**5**	18	15 **Surround Me With Love**		Epic 01045
8/22/81	**4**	16	16 **Sleepin' With The Radio On**		Epic 02421
12/26/81+	**5**	18	17 **The Very Best Is You**		Epic 02656
6/26/82	**3**	20	18 **Dancing Your Memory Away**		Epic 02975
10/23/82+	**7**	21	19 **With You**		Epic 03308
4/09/83	**20**	15	20 Fly Into Love...		Epic 03808
11/05/83+	**3**	21	21 **Sentimental Ol' You**................................		Epic 04172
4/07/84	**22**	15	22 **Band Of Gold**..		Epic 04423
			#3 pop hit for Freda Payne in 1970		
9/22/84	**25**	18	23 Some Hearts Get All The Breaks		Epic 04586
2/16/85	**1**¹	23	24 **Radio Heart**		Epic 04777
8/16/86	**41**	11	25 So This Is Love		Epic 06167
3/07/87	**20**	24	26 Don't Touch Me There..................................		Epic 06980
8/22/87	**51**	9	27 And Then Some		Epic 07244
2/06/88	**60**	5	28 Still I Stay		Epic 07670
8/20/88	**55**	7	29 Sometimes She Feels Like A Man		Mercury 870508
11/12/88	**58**	6	30 Down The Road		Mercury 872036
			CHARLY McCLAIN & MICKEY GILLEY:		
7/16/83	**1**¹	22	31 **Paradise Tonight**		Epic 04007
2/18/84	**5**	18	32 **Candy Man**..		Epic 04368
			#25 pop hit for Roy Orbison in 1961		
6/16/84	**14**	17	33 The Right Stuff		Epic 04489
			CHARLY McCLAIN with WAYNE MASSEY:		
7/06/85	**5**	22	34 With Just One Look In Your Eyes.................		Epic 05398
11/16/85+	**10**	20	35 You Are My Music, You Are My Song		Epic 05693
3/29/86	**17**	15	36 When It's Down To Me And You......................		Epic 05842
12/06/86	**74**	6	37 When Love Is Right		Epic 06433
			O.B. McCLINTON		
			Born Obie Burnett McClinton on 4/25/40 in Senatobia, Mississippi. Died of abdominal cancer on 9/23/87. Worked on WDIA-Memphis and as staff writer for Stax/Volt Records. First recorded for Stax in 1971. One of the few black country stars.		
7/01/72	**70**	6	1 Six Pack Of Trouble......................................		Enterprise 9051
11/04/72+	**37**	13	2 Don't Let The Green Grass Fool You...............		Enterprise 9059
			#17 pop hit for Wilson Pickett in 1971		
3/10/73	**36**	8	3 My Whole World Is Falling Down.....................		Enterprise 9062
6/30/73	**67**	6	4 I Wish It Would Rain....................................		Enterprise 9070
			#4 pop hit for the Temptations in 1968		
3/16/74	**62**	9	5 Something Better		Enterprise 9091
6/29/74	**86**	6	6 If You Loved Her That Way		Enterprise 9100
1/04/75	**77**	6	7 Yours And Mine		Enterprise 9108
5/01/76	**100**	1	8 It's So Good Lovin' You		Mercury 73777
7/08/78	**90**	4	9 Hello, This Is Anna.......................................		Epic 50563
			featuring Peggy Jo Adams		
12/02/78	**82**	5	10 Natural Love		Epic 50620
5/19/79	**79**	5	11 The Real Thing		Epic 50698
8/25/79	**58**	8	12 Soap		Epic 50749
10/04/80	**62**	5	13 Not Exactly Free		Sunbird 7554
6/09/84	**69**	5	14 Honky Tonk Tan		Moon Shine 3024
3/14/87	**61**	6	15 Turn The Music On......................................		Epic 6682

DEBUT DATE	PEAK POS	WKS CHR	ARTIST — Record Title	POP POS	Label & Number
			CALI McCORD		
12/12/87+	46	10	1 Bad Day For A Break Up		Gazelle 011
4/16/88	60	6	2 All In My Mind...		Gazelle 012
			DAN McCORISON		
			Born in Denver; raised in Detroit.		
6/25/77	96	3	1 That's The Why My Woman Loves Me		MCA 40729
			CHARLIE McCOY		
			Born on 3/28/41 in Oak Hill, West Virginia. Toured with Stonewall Jackson in the early 60s. Worked with the band Area Code 615 in 1969. Top Nashville harmonica player and session musician.		
2/05/72	16	15	1 I Started Loving You Again .... [I]		Monument 8529
7/08/72	23	12	2 I'm So Lonesome I Could Cry .... [I]		Monument 8546
11/04/72	19	11	3 I Really Don't Want To Know .... [I]		Monument 8554
3/10/73	26	10	4 Orange Blossom Special .... [I]	101	Monument 8566
7/14/73	33	9	5 Shenandoah.. [I]		Monument 8576
10/20/73	33	13	6 Release Me .... [I]		Monument 8589
3/02/74	68	6	7 Silver Threads And Golden Needles.............. [I]		Monument 8600
6/01/74	22	13	8 Boogie Woogie (a/k/a T.D.'s Boogie Woogie) .... [I]		Monument 8611
			CHARLIE McCOY & BAREFOOT JERRY		
8/14/76	97	2	9 Wabash Cannonball.................................... [I]		Monument 8703
2/05/77	98	3	10 Summit Ridge Drive.................................. [I]		Monument 210
8/12/78	30	10	11 Fair And Tender Ladies		Monument 258
12/16/78	96	3	12 Drifting Lovers		Monument 272
4/28/79	94	3	13 Midnight Flyer		Monument 282
9/08/79	94	2	14 Ramblin' Music Man		Monument 289
12/19/81	92	3	15 Until The Nights		Monument 21001
			CHARLIE McCOY & LANEY SMALLWOOD written by Billy Joel		
4/16/83	74	4	16 The State Of Our Union		Monument 03518
			CHARLIE McCOY & LANEY HICKS		
			PAULA McCULLA		
2/06/88	69	5	1 Thanks For Leavin' Him (For Me)		Rivermark 1001
			GARY McCULLOUGH		
5/23/87	80	2	1 I'd Know A Lie		Soundwaves 4786
			MEL McDANIEL ★★88★★		
			Born on 9/6/42 in Checotah, Oklahoma. Performing since age 14. Worked clubs in Oklahoma, Arkansas and Kansas. Worked in Anchorage, Alaska from 1970-72. Moved to Nashville in 1973 and worked as staff writer and demo singer for Combine Music. Joined the Grand Ole Opry in 1986.		
5/08/76	51	10	1 Have A Dream On Me		Capitol 4249
9/18/76	70	7	2 I Thank God She Isn't Mine		Capitol 4324
			above 2 shown as: **MEL McDANIELS**		
1/22/77	39	11	3 All The Sweet		Capitol 4373
6/04/77	18	14	4 Gentle To Your Senses		Capitol 4430
9/17/77	27	11	5 Soul Of A Honky Tonk Woman		Capitol 4481
12/17/77+	11	16	6 God Made Love		Capitol 4520
5/20/78	80	5	7 The Farm..		Capitol 4569
8/19/78	26	11	8 Bordertown Woman		Capitol 4597
3/17/79	33	10	9 Love Lies		Capitol 4691
6/30/79	24	13	10 Play Her Back To Yesterday........................		Capitol 4740
10/20/79	27	11	11 Lovin' Starts Where Friendship Ends..............		Capitol 4784
7/05/80	39	9	12 Hello Daddy, Good Morning Darling		Capitol 4886
11/29/80+	23	14	13 Countryfied		Capitol 4949
3/28/81	7	14	14 **Louisiana Saturday Night**		Capitol 4983
7/18/81	10	16	15 **Right In The Palm Of Your Hand**..............		Capitol 5022
11/14/81+	19	16	16 Preaching Up A Storm................................		Capitol 5059
3/20/82	10	16	17 **Take Me To The Country**		Capitol 5095
7/03/82	4	18	18 **Big Ole Brew**		Capitol 5138
11/06/82+	20	16	19 I Wish I Was In Nashville		Capitol 5169
4/09/83	22	15	20 Old Man River (I've Come To Talk Again)..........		Capitol 5218
7/30/83	39	12	21 Hot Time In Old Town Tonight.....................		Capitol 5259

DEBUT DATE	PEAK POS	WKS CHR		ARTIST — Record Title	POP POS	Label & Number
				MEL McDANIEL — Continued		
11/05/83+	**9**	20	22	**I Call It Love**		Capitol 5298
3/10/84	**49**	9	23	Where'd That Woman Go		Capitol 5333
5/19/84	**59**	8	24	Most Of All I Remember You		Capitol 5349
7/28/84	**64**	6	25	All Around The Water Tank		Capitol 5371
				above 3: with Oklahoma Wind		
11/10/84+	**1**[1]	28	26	**Baby's Got Her Blue Jeans On**		Capitol 5418
3/16/85	**6**	21	27	**Let It Roll (Let It Rock)**		Capitol 5458
				#64 pop hit for Chuck Berry in 1960		
9/14/85	**5**	21	28	**Stand Up**		Capitol 5513
1/25/86	**22**	16	29	Shoe String		Capitol 5544
5/31/86	**53**	9	30	Doctor's Orders		Capitol 5587
9/27/86	**12**	19	31	Stand On It		Capitol 5620
				written by Bruce Springsteen		
2/07/87	**56**	7	32	Oh What A Night		Capitol 5682
5/16/87	**49**	17	33	Anger & Tears		Capitol 5705
8/15/87	**60**	8	34	Love Is Everywhere		Capitol 44052
11/21/87	**64**	8	35	Now You're Talkin'		Capitol 44106
2/13/88	**58**	7	36	Ride This Train		Capitol 44127
5/14/88	**9**	21	37	**Real Good Feel Good Song**		Capitol 44158
10/22/88	**62**	6	38	Henrietta		Capitol 44244
				SKEETS McDONALD		
				Born Enos William McDonald on 10/1/15 in Greenway, Arkansas; died of a heart attack on 3/31/68. Worked clubs in Michigan in the early 40s. Moved to California in 1946 and appeared on the Town Hall Party series in Compton.		
10/25/52	**1**[3]	18	1	**Don't Let The Stars Get In Your Eyes**		Capitol 2216
				Juke Box #1 / Best Seller #2 / Jockey #3		
				#1 pop hit for Perry Como in 1953		
10/24/60	**21**	6	2	This Old Heart		Columbia 41773
9/28/63	**9**	18	3	**Call Me Mr. Brown**		Columbia 42807
12/25/65+	**29**	5	4	Big Chief Buffalo Nickel		Columbia 43425
1/07/67	**28**	11	5	Mabel		Columbia 43946
				RONNIE McDOWELL ★★**90**★★		
				Born in Fountain Head, Tennessee; raised in Portland, Tennessee. Began singing while in the service. Worked as a commercial sign painter. Appeared on "Solid Gold", "American Bandstand" and "Nashville Now" TV series. Sang on the soundtrack for the film "Elvis" in 1979.		
9/10/77	**13**	9	1●	The King Is Gone	13	Scorpion 135
				a tribute to Elvis Presley		
12/24/77+	**5**	17	2	**I Love You, I Love You, I Love You**	81	Scorpion 149
4/29/78	**15**	12	3	Here Comes The Reason I Live		Scorpion 159
7/29/78	**59**	5	4	I Just Wanted You To Know/		
7/29/78	**68**	5	5	Animal		Scorpion 0553
10/07/78	**39**	8	6	This Is A Holdup		Scorpion 0560
1/13/79	**68**	4	7	He's A Cowboy From Texas		Scorpion 0569
4/28/79	**18**	14	8	World's Most Perfect Woman		Epic 50696
8/25/79	**26**	11	9	Love Me Now/		
1/05/80	**29**	10	10	Never Seen A Mountain So High ...		Epic 50753
3/29/80	**37**	8	11	Lovin' A Livin' Dream		Epic 50857
7/05/80	**80**	4	12	How Far Do You Want To Go		Epic 50895
8/23/80	**36**	11	13	Gone		Epic 50925
12/27/80+	**2**[1]	17	14	**Wandering Eyes**		Epic 50962
6/27/81	**1**[1]	16	15	**Older Women**		Epic 02129
11/14/81+	**4**	18	16	**Watchin' Girls Go By**		Epic 02614
5/08/82	**11**	19	17	I Just Cut Myself		Epic 02884
9/11/82	**7**	17	18	**Step Back**		Epic 03203
1/29/83	**10**	19	19	**Personally**		Epic 03526
6/11/83	**1**[1]	22	20	**You're Gonna Ruin My Bad Reputation**		Epic 03946
10/15/83+	**3**	23	21	**You Made A Wanted Man Of Me**		Epic 04167
2/25/84	**7**	19	22	**I Dream Of Women Like You**		Epic 04367
6/23/84	**8**	21	23	**I Got A Million Of 'Em**		Epic 04499
2/23/85	**5**	23	24	**In A New York Minute**		Epic 04816
7/20/85	**9**	20	25	**Love Talks**		Epic 05404

DEBUT DATE	PEAK POS	WKS CHR	ARTIST — Record Title	POP POS	Label & Number
			RONNIE McDOWELL — Continued		
5/03/86	6	18	26 All Tied Up		MCA/Curb 52816
9/06/86	37	14	27 When You Hurt, I Hurt		MCA/Curb 52907
12/13/86+	30	14	28 Lovin' That Crazy Feelin'		MCA/Curb 52994
6/20/87	55	8	29 Make Me Late For Work Today		MCA 53126
12/26/87+	8	23	30 It's Only Make Believe............................		Curb 10501
			guest vocal: Conway Twitty		
5/28/88	36	12	31 I'm Still Missing You/		
7/16/88	27	14	32 Suspicion		Curb 10508
			#3 pop hit for Terry Stafford in 1964		
			PAKE McENTIRE		
			Born Dale Stanley McEntire in 1953 in Chockie, Oklahoma. Older brother of Reba and Susie, sang with them as the Singing McEntires at rodeos until 1975. Member of the Professional Rodeo Cowboys Association from 1971. Continues to compete in Roping events. Recorded for own Old Cross Records. Sang back-up harmony for Reba.		
1/18/86	20	16	1 Every Night		RCA 14220
5/10/86	3	22	2 Savin' My Love For You		RCA 14336
10/11/86	12	19	3 Bad Love		RCA 5004
2/21/87	25	12	4 Heart Vs. Heart..		RCA 5092
			harmony vocal: Reba McEntire		
6/06/87	46	11	5 Too Old To Grow Up Now...........................		RCA 5207
9/26/87	29	21	6 Good God, I Had It Good		RCA 5256
2/27/88	62	6	7 Life In The City		RCA 5332
			REBA McENTIRE ★★65★★		
			Born on 3/28/54 on a ranch in Chockie, Oklahoma. Sang with older brother Pake and younger sister Susie at rodeos as the Singing McEntires while still a teenager. Competed in rodeos as a horseback barrel rider. Family trio recorded for Boss in 1972. Discovered by Red Steagall when she sang the National Anthem at the National Rodeo Finals in Oklahoma City in 1974. Married rodeo champion Charlie Battles on 6/21/76; separated in 1987. First worked on the Grand Ole Opry in 1977, became a member in 1985. CMA award: Entertainer of the Year - 1986.		
5/08/76	88	5	1 I Don't Want To Be A One Night Stand..............		Mercury 73788
2/12/77	86	4	2 (There's Nothing Like The Love) Between A Woman And A Man		Mercury 73879
8/06/77	88	4	3 Glad I Waited Just For You.........................		Mercury 73929
9/02/78	28	12	4 Last Night, Ev'ry Night................................		Mercury 55036
4/21/79	36	10	5 Runaway Heart..		Mercury 55058
9/22/79	19	12	6 Sweet Dreams..		Mercury 57003
1/05/80	40	8	7 (I Still Long To Hold You) Now And Then..........		Mercury 57014
6/14/80	8	15	8 (You Lift Me) Up To Heaven.........................		Mercury 57025
10/18/80	18	14	9 I Can See Forever In Your Eyes		Mercury 57034
3/14/81	13	16	10 I Don't Think Love Ought To Be That Way........		Mercury 57046
7/04/81	5	19	11 Today All Over Again.................................		Mercury 57054
11/21/81+	13	18	12 Only You (And You Alone)		Mercury 57062
			#5 pop hit for the Platters in 1955		
6/05/82	3	19	13 I'm Not That Lonely Yet		Mercury 76157
10/02/82+	1¹	22	14 Can't Even Get The Blues...........................		Mercury 76180
2/05/83	1¹	21	15 You're The First Time I've Thought About Leaving...		Mercury 810338
7/30/83	7	18	16 Why Do We Want (What We Know We Can't Have)..		Mercury 812632
12/03/83+	12	22	17 There Ain't No Future In This		Mercury 814629
3/17/84	5	19	18 Just A Little Love		MCA 52349
6/23/84	15	20	19 He Broke Your Mem'ry Last Night		MCA 52404
10/13/84+	1¹	23	20 How Blue		MCA 52468
2/16/85	1¹	22	21 Somebody Should Leave		MCA 52527
6/15/85	6	19	22 Have I Got A Deal For You..........................		MCA 52604
10/05/85	5	24	23 Only In My Mind		MCA 52691
2/22/86	1¹	23	24 Whoever's In New England..........................		MCA 52767
6/28/86	1¹	19	25 Little Rock..		MCA 52848
10/11/86+	1¹	22	26 What Am I Gonna Do About You...................		MCA 52922
2/07/87	4	17	27 Let The Music Lift You Up		MCA 52990
5/23/87	1¹	21	28 One Promise Too Late		MCA 53092
9/19/87	1¹	22	29 The Last One To Know		MCA 53159

DEBUT DATE	PEAK POS	WKS CHR	ARTIST — Record Title	POP POS	Label & Number
			REBA McENTIRE — Continued		
1/23/88	**1**¹	20	30 Love Will Find Its Way To You		MCA 53244
5/14/88	**5**	16	31 Sunday Kind Of Love		MCA 53315
			#15 pop hit for Jo Stafford in 1947		
9/10/88	**1**¹	22	32 I Know How He Feels.................................		MCA 53402
12/24/88+	**1**¹	21	33 New Fool At An Old Game..........................		MCA 53473
			JACKY WARD & REBA McENTIRE:		
5/20/78	**20**	12	34 Three Sheets In The Wind/		
		11	35 I'd Really Love To See You Tonight...............		Mercury 55026
			#2 pop hit for England Dan & John Ford Coley in 1976		
7/07/79	**26**	11	36 That Makes Two Of Us		Mercury 55054
			JOHN McEUEN		
			Banjo player, original member of the Nitty Gritty Dirt Band.		
4/06/85	**81**	4	1 Blue Days Black Nights		Warner 29047
			TONY McGILL		
1/17/87	**76**	4	1 Like An Oklahoma Morning		Killer 1004
6/27/87	**82**	3	2 Taming My Mind		Killer 1006
1/09/88	**78**	4	3 For Your Love		Killer 1008
			#13 pop hit for Ed Townsend in 1958		
			MAUREEN McGOVERN		
			Born on 7/27/49 in Youngstown, Ohio. Pop singer.		
3/03/79	**93**	3	1 Can You Read My Mind	*52*	Warner 8750
			love theme from the film "Superman"		
			NEAL McGOY		
			Singer born and raised in Jacksonville, Florida.		
8/27/88	**85**	2	1 That's How Much I Love You..........................		16th Ave. 70417
			McGUFFEY LANE		
			Country/rock sextet from Columbus, Ohio. Lead singer Bob McNelley committed		
			suicide on 1/7/87 (36).		
11/20/82+	**44**	13	1 Making A Living's Been Killing Me		Atco 99959
3/26/83	**62**	6	2 Doing It Right..		Atco 99908
5/12/84	**44**	12	3 Day By Day...		Atln. Am. 99778
9/01/84	**63**	8	4 The First Time..		Atln. Am. 99717
			DOUG McGUIRE		
7/26/80	**64**	6	1 Stranger, I'm Married...................................		Multi-Media 7
			LANIER McKUHEN		
			Singer from Macon, Georgia.		
4/25/87	**75**	4	1 Searching (For Someone Like You)		Soundwaves 4785
			DON McLEAN		
			Born on 10/02/45 in New Rochelle, New York. Singer/songwriter/poet. The hit "Killing		
			Me Softly With His Song" was written about Don.		
1/31/81	**6**	14	1 Crying..	*5*	Millennium 11799
5/09/81	**68**	6	2 Since I Don't Have You................................	*23*	Millennium 11804
4/18/87	**73**	4	3 He's Got You		EMI America 8375
			male version of Patsy Cline's "She's Got You"		
11/14/87	**49**	8	4 You Can't Blame The Train...........................		Capitol 44098
7/30/88	**65**	4	5 Love In The Heart		Capitol 44186
			JIMMY McMILLAN		
12/20/80	**92**	3	1 Footsteps...		Blum 001
3/14/81	**96**	2	2 Her Empty Pillow (Lying Next To Mine)		Blum 767
			TERRY McMILLAN		
			Leading Nashville studio harmonica player, born in High Point, North Carolina.		
12/11/82	**85**	4	1 Love Is A Full Time Thing		RCA 13360
			WYLEY McPHERSON		
			Stage name for Paul Richey. Brother George Richey is married to Tammy Wynette.		
8/07/82	**89**	2	1 Jedediah Jones		i.e. 007
10/09/82	**81**	3	2 The Devil Inside..		i.e. 009

DEBUT DATE	PEAK POS	WKS CHR	ARTIST — Record Title	POP POS	Label & Number
			DANA McVICKER		
			Singer/songwriter born in Baltimore and raised in Phillipe, West Virginia.		
3/14/87	64	6	1 I'd Rather Be Crazy		EMI America 8371
6/27/87	64	5	2 Call Me A Fool...		EMI Amer. 43017
5/28/88	65	5	3 Rock-A-Bye Heart..		Capitol 44155
10/22/88	88	2	4 I'm Loving The Wrong Man Again		Capitol 44223
			DONNA MEADE		
			Born in 1953 in Chase City, Virginia. Nashville club singer (at Buddy Killen's Bullpen Lounge).		
1/09/88	63	8	1 Be Serious		Mercury 888993
5/07/88	50	9	2 Love's Last Stand		Mercury 870283
7/30/88	69	4	3 Congratulations		Mercury 870527
10/29/88	78	3	4 Leavin' On Your Mind		Mercury 872010
			BILL MEDLEY		
			Born on 9/19/40 in Santa Ana, California. Baritone of the Righteous Brothers duo.		
1/06/79	91	3	1 Statue Of A Fool		United Art. 1270
12/10/83+	28	18	2 Till Your Memory's Gone		RCA 13692
4/14/84	17	18	3 I Still Do		RCA 13753
8/04/84	26	14	4 I've Always Got The Heart To Sing The Blues.....		RCA 13851
3/02/85	47	9	5 Is There Anything I Can Do.............................		RCA 14021
5/11/85	55	7	6 Women In Love..		RCA 14081
			TERRI MELTON - see JIM MUNDY		
			MEMPHIS		
			Quartet formed in 1980, featuring Woody Wright (lead vocals, guitar).		
8/25/84	85	4	1 We've Got To Start Meeting Like This		MPI 1691
			BUDDY MEREDITH		
			Born William G. Meredith on 4/13/26 in Beaver Falls, Pennsylvania.		
5/12/62	27	2	1 I May Fall Again		Nashville 5042
			MERRILL & JESSICA		
			Merrill is one of the Osmond Brothers. Jessica Boucher, prominent backing vocalist, is married to Paul Worley, producer of Marie Osmond and Highway 101.		
5/09/87	62	6	1 You're Here To Remember (I'm Here To Forget) ..		EMI America 8388
			BUD MESSNER - see BILL FRANKLIN		
			AUGIE MEYERS		
			Keyboardist/vocalist/accordionist from San Antonio, Texas. Co-founded the San Francisco "Tex-Mex" rock group, Sir Douglas Quintet in the mid-60's.		
2/20/88	86	3	1 Kep Pa So...		Atln. Am. 99382
			MICHAEL MEYERS		
1/16/82	94	2	1 I'm Just The Leavin' Kind		MBP 1980
			JILL MICHAELS - see JOHN SCHNEIDER		
			EDDIE MIDDLETON		
			Born in Albany, Georgia. In R.C. & The Moonpies with Mickey Thomas.		
6/11/77	87	6	1 Midnight Train To Georgia		Epic 50388
			#1 pop hit for Gladys Knight & The Pips in 1973		
9/10/77	38	10	2 Endlessly..		Epic 50431
			#12 pop hit for Brook Benton in 1959		
12/10/77+	44	10	3 What Kind Of Fool (Do You Think I Am)		Epic 50481
			#9 pop hit for The Tams in 1964		
			DICK MILES		
3/16/68	17	10	1 The Last Goodbye	*114*	Capitol 2113
			CARL MILLER		
6/18/83	84	3	1 Life Of The Party		Country B. 0004
			FRANKIE MILLER		
			Born on 12/17/32 in Victoria, Texas. Singer/songwriter. Worked on KNAL-Victoria and appeared on Jubilee USA on ABC-TV. Regular on Cowtown Hoedown, Fort Worth, in 1959.		
4/13/59	5	19	1 **Black Land Farmer**....................................		Starday 424
10/05/59	7	21	2 **Family Man**		Starday 457
5/23/60	15	14	3 Baby Rocked Her Dolly		Starday 496

DEBUT DATE	PEAK POS	WKS CHR	ARTIST — Record Title	POP POS	Label & Number
			FRANKIE MILLER — Continued		
7/17/61	16	5	4 Black Land Farmer .... [R]	82	Starday 424
2/15/64	34	6	5 A Little South Of Memphis...........................		Starday 655
			JODY MILLER ★★161★★		
			Born on 11/29/41 in Phoenix; raised in Blanchard, Oklahoma. In vocal trio, the Melodies, while still in high school. Worked local clubs. Appeared on the Tom Paxton TV show in the early 60s. Moved to Los Angeles in 1963. Owns an 1100 acre ranch in Blanchard and raises quarter horses.		
5/29/65	5	11	1 **Queen Of The House**.................................. answer to Roger Miller's "King Of The Road"	12	Capitol 5402
11/09/68	73	2	2 Long Black Limousine		Capitol 2290
8/15/70	21	13	3 Look At Mine		Epic 10641
1/02/71	19	13	4 If You Think I Love You Now (I've Just Started)..		Epic 10692
6/12/71	5	15	5 **He's So Fine**...	53	Epic 10734
10/09/71	5	14	6 **Baby I'm Yours**.....................................	91	Epic 10785
3/25/72	15	13	7 Be My Baby... #2 pop hit for The Ronettes in 1963		Epic 10835
5/27/72	13	11	8 Let's All Go Down To The River..................... **JODY MILLER & JOHNNY PAYCHECK**		Epic 10863
6/17/72	4	14	9 **There's A Party Goin' On**	115	Epic 10878
11/04/72	18	11	10 To Know Him Is To Love Him .... #1 pop hit for The Teddy Bears in 1958		Epic 10916
3/17/73	9	12	11 **Good News**		Epic 10960
7/14/73	5	13	12 **Darling, You Can Always Come Back Home**		Epic 11016
11/24/73+	29	13	13 The House Of The Rising Sun .... #1 pop hit for The Animals in 1964		Epic 11056
3/16/74	55	9	14 Reflections..		Epic 11094
6/22/74	46	11	15 Natural Woman .... #8 pop hit for Aretha Franklin in 1967		Epic 11134
11/16/74+	41	10	16 Country Girl..		Epic 50042
3/15/75	78	9	17 The Best In Me		Epic 50079
7/12/75	67	9	18 Don't Take It Away		Epic 50117
11/08/75	69	8	19 Will You Love Me Tomorrow?........................ #1 pop hit for The Shirelles in 1961		Epic 50158
3/27/76	48	9	20 Ashes Of Love		Epic 50203
12/04/76+	25	12	21 When The New Wears Off Our Love		Epic 50304
4/09/77	71	7	22 Spread A Little Love Around.........................		Epic 50360
9/17/77	76	5	23 Another Lonely Night		Epic 50432
4/15/78	97	2	24 Soft Lights And Slow Sexy Music		Epic 50512
7/15/78	67	6	25 (I Wanna) Love My Life Away .... #39 pop hit for Gene Pitney in 1961		Epic 50568
10/07/78	65	4	26 Kiss Away .... #25 pop hit for Ronnie Dove in 1965		Epic 50612
7/07/79	97	2	27 Lay A Little Lovin' On Me............................ #11 pop hit for Robin McNamara in 1970		Epic 50734
			MARY K. MILLER Born in Houston. First recordecd at age 14 for Reprise.		
7/30/77	89	5	1 I Fall To Pieces .... shown only as: **MARY MILLER**		Inergi 300
10/08/77	54	8	2 You Just Don't Know.................................. written by Bobby Darin		Inergi 302
12/24/77+	33	10	3 The Longest Walk .... #6 pop hit for Jaye P. Morgan in 1955		Inergi 304
3/04/78	41	9	4 Right Or Wrong		Inergi 306
6/03/78	28	8	5 I Can't Stop Loving You.............................. #1 pop hit for Ray Charles in 1962		Inergi 307
9/16/78	19	11	6 Handcuffed To A Heartache		Inergi 310
12/09/78+	45	9	7 Going, Going, Gone		Inergi 311
3/10/79	17	14	8 Next Best Feeling		Inergi 312
7/28/79	47	7	9 Guess Who Loves You		RCA 11665
4/05/80	85	3	10 Say A Long Goodbye..................................		Inergi 315
			NED MILLER Born Henry Ned Miller on 4/12/25 in Raines, Utah. Singer/songwriter.		
12/15/62+	2⁴	19	1 From A Jack To A King...............................	6	Fabor 114
5/25/63	27	3	2 One Among The Many................................		Fabor 116

DEBUT DATE	PEAK POS	WKS CHR	ARTIST — Record Title	POP POS	Label & Number
			NED MILLER — Continued		
9/14/63	**28**	1	3 Another Fool Like Me		Fabor 121
4/25/64	**13**	22	4 Invisible Tears...	*131*	Fabor 128
1/16/65	**7**	20	5 **Do What You Do Do Well**...........................	*52*	Fabor 137
8/14/65	**28**	8	6 Whistle Walkin'		Capitol 5431
6/18/66	**39**	8	7 Summer Roses...		Capitol 5661
10/15/66	**44**	9	8 Teardrop Lane...		Capitol 5742
5/13/67	**53**	6	9 Hobo...		Capitol 5868
2/17/68	**61**	5	10 Only A Fool..		Capitol 2074
4/25/70	**39**	9	11 The Lover's Song		Republic 1411
			ROGER MILLER ★★**77**★★		
			Born on 1/2/36 in Fort Worth, Texas; raised in Erick, Oklahoma. Vocalist/humorist/ guitarist/composer. To Nashville in the mid-50s, began songwriting career. With Faron Young as writer/drummer in 1962. Won 6 Grammies in 1965. Own TV show in 1966. Songwriter of 1985's Tony Award-winning Broadway musical "Big River".		
10/31/60+	**14**	16	1 You Don't Want My Love		RCA 7776
6/05/61	**6**	18	2 **When Two Worlds Collide**		RCA 7878
6/01/63	**26**	1	3 Lock, Stock And Teardrops...........................		RCA 8175
6/06/64	**1**[6]	25	4 **Dang Me**	*7*	Smash 1881
9/19/64	**3**	17	5 **Chug-A-Lug**	*9*	Smash 1926
12/12/64+	**15**	11	6 Do-Wacka-Do..	*31*	Smash 1947
2/13/65	**1**[5]	20	7 ●**King Of The Road**	*4*	Smash 1965
5/22/65	**2**[2]	18	8 **Engine Engine #9**	*7*	Smash 1983
7/24/65	**10**	12	9 **One Dyin' And A Buryin'**	*34*	Smash 1994
10/02/65	**7**	13	10 **Kansas City Star**	*31*	Smash 1998
11/20/65+	**3**	16	11 **England Swings**......................................	*8*	Smash 2010
2/26/66	**5**	14	12 **Husbands And Wives/**	*26*	
2/26/66	**13**	10	13 I've Been A Long Time Leavin' (But I'll Be A Long Time Gone)	*103*	Smash 2024
7/09/66	**35**	5	14 You Can't Roller Skate In A Buffalo Herd	*40*	Smash 2043
9/24/66	**39**	9	15 My Uncle Used To Love Me But She Died..........	*58*	Smash 2055
11/19/66	**55**	3	16 Heartbreak Hotel	*84*	Smash 2066
4/01/67	**7**	17	17 **Walkin' In The Sunshine**	*37*	Smash 2081
10/28/67	**27**	11	18 The Ballad Of Waterhole #3 (Code Of The West) .. from the film "Waterhole #3"	*102*	Smash 2121
3/09/68	**6**	13	19 **Little Green Apples**	*39*	Smash 2148
12/14/68+	**15**	12	20 Vance	*80*	Smash 2197
7/05/69	**12**	16	21 Me And Bobby McGee .... #1 pop hit for Janis Joplin in 1971	*122*	Smash 2230
10/18/69	**14**	10	22 Where Have All The Average People Gone		Smash 2246
3/14/70	**36**	7	23 The Tom Green County Fair..........................		Smash 2258
8/29/70	**15**	12	24 South/		
		12	25 Don't We All Have The Right......................		Mercury 73102
4/17/71	**11**	14	26 Tomorrow Night In Baltimore		Mercury 73190
8/07/71	**28**	11	27 Loving Her Was Easier (Than Anything I'll Ever Do Again)		Mercury 73230
3/25/72	**34**	11	28 We Found It In Each Other's Arms/		
3/25/72	**63**	11	29 Sunny Side Of My Life.............................		Mercury 73268
9/09/72	**41**	11	30 Rings For Sale		Mercury 73321
12/30/72+	**42**	8	31 Hoppy's Gone		Mercury 73354
7/14/73	**14**	14	32 Open Up Your Heart	*105*	Columbia 45873
11/17/73+	**24**	11	33 I Believe In The Sunshine		Columbia 45948
3/09/74	**86**	3	34 Whistle Stop.. from the Walt Disney film "Robin Hood"		Columbia 46000
12/07/74+	**44**	10	35 Our Love		Columbia 10052
4/12/75	**57**	10	36 I Love A Rodeo		Columbia 10107
9/10/77	**68**	6	37 Baby Me Baby		Windsong 11072
10/27/79	**98**	2	38 The Hat		20th Century 2421
10/10/81	**36**	10	39 Everyone Gets Crazy Now And Then..................		Elektra 47192
6/05/82	**19**	16	40 Old Friends		Columbia 02681
			ROGER MILLER & WILLIE NELSON (with RAY PRICE)		
10/05/85	**36**	12	41 River In The Rain....................................... from the Broadway musical "Big River"		MCA 52663

DEBUT DATE	PEAK POS	WKS CHR	ARTIST — Record Title	POP POS	Label & Number
			ROGER MILLER — Continued		
8/02/86	**81**	8	42 Some Hearts Get All The Breaks		MCA 52855
			LUCKY MILLINDER		
			Born Lucius Millinder on 8/8/1900 in Anniston, Alabama. Died on 9/28/66 in New York City. R&B vocalist/bandleader.		
1/15/44	**4**	5	1 **Sweet Slumber** .... [I]		Decca 18569
7/29/44	**4**	2	2 **Hurry, Hurry**		Decca 18609
			vocal: Wynonie Harris		
			THE MILLS BROTHERS		
			Smooth R&B/pop family vocal group from Piqua, Ohio. Consisted of Herbert (b: 1912; d: 4/12/89 [77]), Harry (b: 1913; d: 6/28/82) and Donald (b: 1915).		
3/21/70	**64**	3	1 It Ain't No Big Thing....................................		Dot 17321
			FRANK MILLS		
			Pianist/composer/producer/arranger.		
2/24/79	**44**	14	1●Music Box Dancer .... [I]	3	Polydor 14517
			RONNIE MILSAP ★★30★★		
			Born on 1/16/46 in Robbinsville, North Carolina. Singer/pianist/guitarist. Blind since birth; multi-instrumentalist by age 12. With J.J. Cale band, own band from 1965. Joined the Grand Ole Opry in 1976. CMA award: Entertainer of the Year - 1977.		
6/30/73	**10**	14	1 I Hate You/		
		14	2 (All Together Now) Let's Fall Apart		RCA 0969
11/03/73+	**11**	18	3 That Girl Who Waits On Tables........................		RCA 0097
3/30/74	**1**¹	15	4 **Pure Love**		RCA 0237
			written by Eddie Rabbitt		
7/20/74	**1**²	14	5 **Please Don't Tell Me How The Story Ends**	95	RCA 0313
11/30/74+	**1**¹	13	6 **(I'd Be) A Legend In My Time**		RCA 10112
3/15/75	**6**	14	7 **Too Late To Worry, Too Blue To Cry**..............	101	RCA 10228
7/19/75	**1**²	16	8 **Daydreams About Night Things**		RCA 10335
9/20/75	**15**	13	9 She Even Woke Me Up To Say Goodbye.............		Warner 8127
10/25/75+	**4**	16	10 **Just In Case**		RCA 10420
12/27/75+	**77**	6	11 A Rose By Any Other Name		Warner 8160
3/20/76	**1**¹	14	12 **What Goes On When The Sun Goes Down**........		RCA 10593
6/19/76	**79**	5	13 Crying..		Warner 8218
			#2 pop hit for Roy Orbison in 1961		
7/10/76	**1**²	14	14 **(I'm A) Stand By My Woman Man**		RCA 10724
11/27/76+	**1**¹	15	15 **Let My Love Be Your Pillow**		RCA 10843
5/28/77	**1**³	18	16 **It Was Almost Like A Song**	16	RCA 10976
11/19/77+	**1**¹	16	17 **What A Difference You've Made In My Life**	80	RCA 11146
6/03/78	**1**³	13	18 **Only One Love In My Life**	63	RCA 11270
9/02/78	**1**¹	12	19 **Let's Take The Long Way Around The World**..		RCA 11369
12/16/78+	**2**³	15	20 **Back On My Mind Again/**		
		15	21 Santa Barbara		RCA 11421
4/28/79	**1**¹	15	22 **Nobody Likes Sad Songs**............................		RCA 11553
8/18/79	**6**	13	23 **In No Time At All/**		
		13	24 Get It Up	43	RCA 11695
1/12/80	**1**¹	15	25 **Why Don't You Spend The Night**		RCA 11909
4/12/80	**1**³	15	26 **My Heart/**		
		15	27 Silent Night (After The Fight)		RCA 11952
6/21/80	**1**¹	16	28 **Cowboys And Clowns/**	103	
		16	29 Misery Loves Company		RCA 12006
10/11/80	**1**¹	14	30 **Smoky Mountain Rain**	24	RCA 12084
3/21/81	**1**¹	14	31 **Am I Losing You**		RCA 12194
7/04/81	**1**²	15	32 **(There's) No Gettin' Over Me**	5	RCA 12264
10/31/81+	**1**¹	16	33 **I Wouldn't Have Missed It For The World**	20	RCA 12342
5/01/82	**1**¹	17	34 **Any Day Now**..	14	RCA 13216
8/07/82	**1**¹	18	35 **He Got You**	59	RCA 13286
11/20/82+	**1**¹	19	36 **Inside/**		
		18	37 Carolina Dreams....................................		RCA 13362
4/02/83	**5**	18	38 **Stranger In My House**	23	RCA 13470
7/23/83	**1**¹	19	39 **Don't You Know How Much I Love You**	58	RCA 13564
11/12/83+	**1**¹	19	40 **Show Her**..	103	RCA 13658

DEBUT DATE	PEAK POS	WKS CHR	ARTIST — Record Title	POP POS	Label & Number
			RONNIE MILSAP — Continued		
5/19/84	**1**¹	19	41 **Still Losing You**		RCA 13805
9/01/84	**6**	19	42 **Prisoner Of The Highway**...........................		RCA 13847
			flip side "She Loves My Car" made the pop charts (POS 84)		
4/06/85	**1**¹	20	43 **She Keeps The Home Fires Burning**		RCA 14034
7/13/85	**1**²	23	44 **Lost In The Fifties Tonight (In the Still of the Night)**		RCA 14135
3/08/86	**1**¹	20	45 **Happy, Happy Birthday Baby**......................		RCA 14286
			#5 pop hit for The Tune Weavers in 1957		
7/05/86	**1**¹	20	46 **In Love**		RCA 14365
11/22/86+	**1**¹	21	47 **How Do I Turn You On**		RCA 5033
5/23/87	**1**¹	19	48 **Snap Your Fingers**...........................		RCA 5169
			#8 pop hit for Joe Henderson in 1962		
6/27/87	**1**¹	17	49 **Make No Mistake, She's Mine**		RCA 5209
			RONNIE MILSAP & KENNY ROGERS		
10/24/87+	**1**¹	20	50 **Where Do The Nights Go**....................		RCA 5259
3/05/88	**2**¹	21	51 **Old Folks**		RCA 6896
			RONNIE MILSAP & MIKE REID		
7/23/88	**4**	18	52 **Button Off My Shirt**		RCA 8389
12/24/88+	**1**¹	20	53 **Don't You Ever Get Tired (Of Hurting Me)**		RCA 8746
			MINNIE PEARL Born Sarah Ophelia Colley on 10/25/12 in Centerville, Tennessee. Comedienne and actress, taught drama in Atlanta, Georgia in 1934. With the Grand Ole Opry since 1940. Elected to the Country Music Hall Of Fame in 1975.		
3/05/66	**10**	12	1 **Giddyup Go - Answer** .... [S]		Starday 754
			CHARLES MITCHELL Steel guitarist with Jimmie Davis, co-writer of "You Are My Sunshine". Worked for the State of Louisiana while Davis was Governor.		
4/29/44	**4**	1	1 **If It's Wrong To Love You**...........................		Bluebird 33-0508
			CHARLIE MITCHELL		
11/12/88	**81**	4	1 **I'm Goin' Nowhere**		Soundwaves 4810
			GUY MITCHELL Born Al Cernik on 2/27/27 in Detroit. Worked at Warner Brothers movie studio as a singer while still a child. On radio programs in San Francisco in the early 40s. Worked with Carmen Cavallaro from 1947-48. In the films "Those Red Heads From Seattle" (1953) and "Red Garters" (1954).		
11/04/67	**51**	8	1 **Traveling Shoes**		Starday 819
2/24/68	**61**	5	2 **Alabam**		Starday 828
12/14/68	**71**	3	3 **Frisco Line**		Starday 846
			MARTY MITCHELL From Birmingham, Alabama. Recorded for Atlantic at age 17.		
6/15/74	**64**	7	1 **Midnight Man**		Atlantic 4023
12/11/76	**87**	4	2 **My Eyes Adored You**....................................		Hitsville 6044
			#1 pop hit for Frankie Valli in 1975		
2/18/78	**34**	10	3 **You Are The Sunshine Of My Life**		MC 5005
			#1 pop hit for Stevie Wonder in 1973		
			PRICE MITCHELL		
1/18/75	**65**	10	1 **I Can't Help Myself (Sugar Pie, Honey Bunch)**		GRT 016
			PRICE MITCHELL & JERRI KELLY #1 pop hit for the Four Tops in 1965		
4/19/75	**29**	11	2 **Personality**		GRT 020
			#2 pop hit for Lloyd Price in 1959		
2/07/76	**83**	5	3 **Seems Like I Can't Live With You, But I Can't Live Without You**.................................		GRT 037
5/29/76	**75**	5	4 **Tra-La-La-La Suzy**.......................................		GRT 050
			#35 pop hit for Dean & Jean in 1964		
9/04/76	**75**	4	5 **You're The Reason I'm Living**........................		GRT 067
			#3 pop hit for Bobby Darin in 1963		
1/05/80	**45**	9	6 **Mr. & Mrs. Untrue**		Sunbird 101
			PRICE MITCHELL/RENE SLOANE		
			PRISCILLA MITCHELL Born on 9/18/41 in Marietta, Georgia. Sang on WFOM-Marietta at age 4. First recorded as a rock & roll singer under the name "Sadina" in the late 50s. Married to Jerry Reed; worked as back-up singer.		
6/17/67	**53**	4	1 **He's Not For Real**		Mercury 72681

DEBUT DATE	PEAK POS	WKS CHR	ARTIST — Record Title	POP POS	Label & Number
			PRISCILLA MITCHELL — Continued		
2/03/68	**73**	3	2 Your Old Handy Man..........................		Mercury 72757
			written by Dolly Parton		
			ROY DRUSKY & PRISCILLA MITCHELL:		
5/29/65	**1** ²	23	**3 Yes, Mr. Peters**........................		Mercury 72416
12/04/65	**45**	2	4 Slippin' Around		Mercury 72497
3/25/67	**61**	5	5 I'll Never Tell On You..................		Mercury 72650
			ROBERT MITCHUM		
			Born on 8/6/17 in Bridgeport, Connecticut. Leading man in films since 1943.		
5/13/67	**9**	17	**1 Little Old Wine Drinker Me**........................	*96*	Monument 1006
10/21/67	**55**	7	2 You Deserve Each Other.................................		Monument 1025
			BILLY MIZE		
			Born on 4/29/29 in Kansas City, Kansas; raised in California. Steel guitarist. Worked as a disc jockey on KPMC. On KERO-TV Trading Post Show from 1953-66. Host of Gene Autry's Melody Ranch shows from 1966-67. A TV producer with his own production company.		
10/15/66	**57**	5	1 You Can't Stop Me....................		Columbia 43770
			BILLY MIZE with The Jordanaires		
9/28/68	**58**	7	2 Walking Through The Memories Of My Mind		Columbia 44621
4/26/69	**40**	9	3 Make It Rain		Imperial 66365
9/13/69	**43**	9	4 While I'm Thinkin' About It		Imperial 66403
6/20/70	**71**	2	5 If This Was The Last Song		Imperial 66447
11/14/70	**49**	7	6 Beer Drinking, Honky Tonkin' Blues..............		United Art. 50717
9/02/72	**66**	5	7 Take It Easy.......................		United Art. 50945
7/28/73	**99**	2	8 California Is Just Mississippi................		United Art. 265
2/16/74	**79**	5	9 Thank You For The Feeling............		United Art. 372
9/25/76	**31**	13	10 It Hurts To Know The Feeling's Gone..............		Zodiac 1011
2/12/77	**68**	5	11 Livin' Her Life In A Song		Zodiac 1014
			DICK MOEBAKKEN		
9/30/78	**98**	3	1 Heaven Is Being Good To Me		ASI 1016
			HUGH MOFFATT		
			Born in Fort Worth, Texas. Worked as a folksinger in Austin.		
5/06/78	**95**	2	1 The Gambler		Mercury 55024
			KATY MOFFATT		
			Born in Fort Worth, Texas; sister of songwriter Hugh Moffatt. Had singing role in the film "Billy Jack".		
1/17/76	**83**	5	1 I Can Almost See Houston From Here		Columbia 10271
7/04/81	**83**	3	2 Take It As It Comes................................		Epic 02075
			MICHAEL MURPHEY with KATY MOFFATT		
11/05/83	**66**	6	3 Under Loved And Over Lonely........................		Permian 82002
2/11/84	**82**	4	4 Reynosa		Permian 82004
5/05/84	**66**	6	5 This Ain't Tennessee & He Ain't You...............		Permian 82005
			CARLA MONDAY		
10/24/87	**79**	3	1 No One Can Touch Me.................................		MCM 001
			BILL MONROE		
			Born on 9/13/11 in Rosine, Kentucky. Moved to Indiana in 1929. In band with brothers Birch and Charlie in East Chicago from 1929-34. Worked on WLS Barn Dance. Toured with Charlie as the Monroe Brothers and recorded for Victor in 1936. Duo split up in 1938. Formed own band, the Kentuckians, later named the Blue Grass Boys. On the Grand Ole Opry since 1939. Wrote "Blue Moon Of Kentucky", "Gotta Travel On", "Kentucky Waltz". Elected to the Country Music Hall Of Fame in 1970. Known as "The Father Of Bluegrass".		
3/23/46	**3**	6	**1 Kentucky Waltz**........................		Columbia 36907
12/07/46	**5**	4	**2 Footprints In The Snow**.......................		Columbia 37151
6/19/48	**11**	1	3 Sweetheart, You Done Me Wrong		Columbia 38172
			Juke Box #11		
11/06/48	**13**	1	4 Wicked Path Of Sin..........................		Columbia 20503
			Best Seller #13		
11/27/48	**11**	5	5 Little Community Church		Columbia 20488
			Best Seller #11 / Juke Box #12		
4/16/49	**12**	2	6 Toy Heart		Columbia 20552
			Best Seller #12		

DEBUT DATE	PEAK POS	WKS CHR	ARTIST — Record Title	POP POS	Label & Number
			BILL MONROE — Continued		
8/06/49	12	1	7 When You Are Lonely		Columbia 20526
			Juke Box #12		
11/03/58	27	1	8 Scotland.. [I]		Decca 30739
3/02/59	15	6	9 Gotta Travel On		Decca 30809
			BILL MONROE & His Blue Grass Boys		
			VAUGHN MONROE		
			Born on 10/7/11 in Akron, Ohio; died on 5/21/73. Trumpet playing bandleader/singer.		
5/14/49	2¹	5	1 ● Riders In The Sky.......................................	1	RCA Victor 2902
			Best Seller #2 / Juke Box #10; 78 rpm: 78-3411		
			MONTANA		
			Montana-based band, formerly known as "The Mission Mountain Wood Band" until 1980. Longtime Reno area favorites.		
11/14/81	83	3	1 The Shoe's On The Other Foot.........................		Waterhs. 15005
			BILLY MONTANA & THE LONG SHOTS		
			Quintet from Voorheesville, New York: Billy and Kyle Montana, Dave Flint, Bobby Kendall and Doug Bernhard.		
3/21/87	46	9	1 Crazy Blue		Warner 28426
8/22/87	40	11	2 Baby I Was Leaving Anyhow		Warner 28256
8/20/88	48	9	3 Oh Jenny...		Warner 27809
			MONTANA SKYLINE		
12/26/81+	87	4	1 Full Moon Empty Pockets		Snow 2022
			MELBA MONTGOMERY ★★149★★		
			Born on 10/14/38 in Iron City, Tennessee; raised in Florence, Alabama. Guitarist and fiddle player. Won Pet Milk Amateur contest in Nashville, 1958. Toured with Roy Acuff's Smokey Mountain Boys from 1958-62. Solo work since 1962.		
8/24/63	26	6	1 Hall Of Shame		United Art. 576
12/07/63+	22	9	2 The Greatest One Of All		United Art. 652
1/15/66	15	12	3 Baby, Ain't That Fine		Musicor 1135
			GENE PITNEY & MELBA MONTGOMERY		
7/08/67	61	3	4 What Can I Tell The Folks Back Home		Musicor 1241
6/19/71	61	4	5 He's My Man		Capitol 3091
10/06/73	38	11	6 Wrap Your Love Around Me		Elektra 45866
1/12/74	58	9	7 He'll Come Home...		Elektra 45875
3/16/74	1¹	16	8 **No Charge**..	39	Elektra 45883
7/20/74	67	8	9 Your Pretty Roses Came Too Late		Elektra 45894
10/19/74	59	10	10 If You Want The Rainbow		Elektra 45211
2/01/75	15	12	11 Don't Let The Good Times Fool You		Elektra 45229
5/24/75	45	9	12 Searchin' (For Someone Like You)....................		Elektra 45247
1/10/76	67	7	13 Love Was The Wind		Elektra 45296
7/16/77	83	4	14 Never Ending Love Affair.............................		United Art. 1008
12/10/77+	22	14	15 Angel Of The Morning		United Art. 1115
			Merrilee Rush and Juice Newton had top 10 pop versions		
10/25/80	92	2	16 The Star		Kari 111
8/30/86	79	4	17 Straight Talkin		Compass 45-7
			GEORGE JONES & MELBA MONTGOMERY:		
5/04/63	3	28	18 **We Must Have Been Out Of Our Minds**		United Art. 575
11/30/63	20	5	19 What's In Our Heart/		United Art. 635
12/07/63	17	7	20 Let's Invite Them Over.............................		
9/05/64	31	5	21 Please Be My Love		United Art. 732
12/12/64+	25	15	22 Multiply The Heartaches		United Art. 784
11/19/66	70	3	23 Close Together (As You and Me)......................		Musicor 1204
9/09/67	24	10	24 Party Pickin'		Musicor 1238
			CHARLIE LOUVIN & MELBA MONTGOMERY:		
10/24/70	18	14	25 Something To Brag About............................		Capitol 2915
2/13/71	26	12	26 Did You Ever		Capitol 3029
6/12/71	30	10	27 Baby, You've Got What It Takes		Capitol 3111
			#5 pop hit for Dinah Washington & Brook Benton in 1960		
11/27/71	60	5	28 I'm Gonna Leave You..................................		Capitol 3208
8/19/72	66	4	29 Baby, What's Wrong With Us.......................		Capitol 3388
1/20/73	59	6	30 A Man Likes Things Like That......................		Capitol 3508

DEBUT DATE	PEAK POS	WKS CHR	ARTIST — Record Title	POP POS	Label & Number
			NANCY MONTGOMERY		
7/04/81	85	2	1 All I Have To Do Is Dream		Ovation 1172
			#1 pop hit for The Everly Brothers in 1958		
			CLYDE MOODY		
			Born on 9/19/15 on a Cherokee Reservation in North Carolina; raised in Marion, North Carolina. Died on 4/7/89. Guitarist from age 8. With J. Hugh Hall as "Bill & Joe" on WSPA-Spartanburg in 1929. First recorded for ARC in 1935. Worked with Mainer's Sons Of The Mountaineers, Bill Monroe and Roy Acuff to the mid-40s. Own TV shows in Washington, DC and North Carolina. Known as "The Hillbilly Waltz King".		
6/19/48	15	1	1 Carolina Waltz/		
			Best Seller #15		
8/14/48	8	1	2 **Red Roses Tied In Blue**		King 706
			Best Seller #8		
3/11/50	8	2	3 **I Love You Because**.................................		King 837
			Jockey #8		
			BETH MOORE		
			Born Bethany Ann Moore on 11/27/44 in Michigan. Toured with Paul Harper's Band.		
1/23/71	61	8	1 Put Your Hand In The Hand		Capitol 3013
			#2 pop hit for Ocean in 1971		
			JIM MOORE & SIDEWINDER		
9/03/88	88	2	1 Ain't She Shinin' Tonight		Willow Wind 0511
			LATTIE MOORE		
			Born on 10/17/24 in Scotsville, Kentucky. Toured with Lash LaRue in the late 40s. Own radio show, Midwest Jamboree, in Indianapolis in 1951. First recorded for Speed in 1952. Considered by many to be the original rockabilly artist.		
1/30/61	25	3	1 Drunk Again		King 5413
			AL MORGAN		
			Pianist from Chicago. Own Dumont TV series in 1947. Known as "Mr. Flying Fingers".		
9/17/49	8	1	1 **Jealous Heart**..	4	London 500
			Best Seller #8; first released on Universal 148		
			BILLY MORGAN		
			Born on 12/13/22 in Nashville. Worked on KAMD-Camden, Arkansas from 1945-46.		
3/23/59	22	3	1 Life To Live		Starday 420
			GEORGE MORGAN ★★104★★		
			Born on 6/28/25 in Waverly, Tennessee; died of a heart attack in July, 1975. Raised in Barberton, Ohio. Worked on WWVA Wheeling Jamboree in the late 40s. Wrote "Candy Kisses". On the Grand Ole Opry from 1948-56 and again from 1959. Own show on WLAC-TV, Nashville from 1956-59. Father of Lorrie Morgan.		
2/26/49	1³	23	1 **Candy Kisses/**		
			Best Seller #1 / Juke Box #2		
3/19/49	4	14	2 **Please Don't Let Me Love You**		Columbia 20547
			Best Seller #4 / Juke Box #4		
4/30/49	8	6	3 **Rainbow In My Heart/**		
			Best Seller #8 / Juke Box #10		
5/07/49	11	1	4 All I Need Is Some More Lovin'		Columbia 20563
			Best Seller #11		
7/23/49	4	12	5 **Room Full Of Roses**....................................	25	Columbia 20594
			Best Seller #4 / Juke Box #10		
10/29/49	5	9	6 **Cry-Baby Heart/**		
			Best Seller #5 / Juke Box #6 / Jockey #7		
12/10/49	4	4	7 **I Love Everything About You**......................		Columbia 20627
			Jockey #4 / Best Seller #14		
4/19/52	2⁶	23	8 **Almost**..		Columbia 20906
			Best Seller #2 / Jockey #2 / Juke Box #2		
3/07/53	10	1	9 (I Just Had A Date) A Lover's Quarrel		Columbia 21070
			Juke Box #10		
1/26/57	15	1	10 There Goes My Love		Columbia 40792
			Jockey #15		
2/16/59	3	23	11 **I'm In Love Again**		Columbia 41318
8/17/59	20	9	12 Little Dutch Girl/		
8/24/59	26	1	13 The Last Thing I Want To Know		Columbia 41420
1/11/60	4	20	14 **You're The Only Good Thing (That's Happened To Me)**.................................		Columbia 41523
1/18/64	23	7	15 One Dozen Roses (And Our Love)/		
3/07/64	45	2	16 All Right (I'll Sign The Papers).....................		Columbia 42882

DEBUT DATE	PEAK POS	WKS CHR	ARTIST — Record Title	POP POS	Label & Number
			GEORGE MORGAN — Continued		
5/09/64	23	17	17 Slipping Around............................		Columbia 43020
			MARION WORTH & GEORGE MORGAN		
9/26/64	37	9	18 Tears And Roses............................		Columbia 43098
12/11/65+	27	10	19 A Picture That's New		Columbia 43393
4/15/67	40	12	20 I Couldn't See.............................		Starday 804
8/19/67	58	5	21 Shiny Red Automobile		Starday 814
1/13/68	55	6	22 Barbara...................................		Starday 825
4/27/68	56	7	23 Living		Starday 834
8/31/68	31	10	24 Sounds Of Goodbye		Starday 850
4/19/69	30	9	25 Like A Bird		Stop 252
4/18/70	17	13	26 Lilacs And Fire...........................		Stop 365
12/11/71	68	3	27 Gentle Rains Of Home....................		Decca 32886
1/20/73	62	7	28 Makin' Heartaches		Decca 33037
6/30/73	56	9	29 Mr. Ting-A-Ling (Steel Guitar Man)		MCA 40069
12/15/73+	21	14	30 Red Rose From The Blue Side Of Town ...		MCA 40159
6/01/74	66	6	31 Somewhere Around Midnight		MCA 40227
11/02/74	82	6	32 A Candy Mountain Melody		MCA 40298
2/22/75	65	9	33 In The Misty Moonlight		4 Star 1001
			#19 pop hit for Jerry Wallace in 1964		
7/05/75	62	11	34 From This Moment On		4 Star 1009
			above 7: featuring "Little" Roy Wiggins		
11/24/79	93	3	35 I'm Completely Satisfied With You		4 Star 1040
			LORRIE & GEORGE MORGAN		
			JANE MORGAN		
			Born Jane Currier in Boston; raised in Florida. Popular singer in France before achieving U.S. fame via TV and night club entertaining.		
5/30/70	61	5	1 A Girl Named Johnny Cash..............		RCA 9839
			answer song to Johnny Cash's "A Boy Named Sue"		
11/07/70	70	2	2 The First Day		RCA 9901
			LORRIE MORGAN		
			Born Loretta Lynn Morgan on 6/27/60. Youngest daughter of George Morgan. Worked on the Grand Ole Opry since 1984. Married Keith Whitley in November of 1986.		
3/10/79	75	5	1 Two People In Love		ABC/Hick. 54041
7/28/79	88	3	2 Tell Me I'm Only Dreaming..............		MCA 41052
11/24/79	93	3	3 I'm Completely Satisfied With You		4 Star 1040
			LORRIE & GEORGE MORGAN		
3/17/84	69	5	4 Don't Go Changing		MCA 52331
12/10/88+	20	19	5 Trainwreck Of Emotion		RCA 8638
			MISTY MORGAN - see JACK BLANCHARD		
			MIKI MORI		
			Female vocalist from Nephi, Utah. Worked on radio since age 13.		
6/30/79	91	1	1 Tell All Your Troubles To Me		Red Feather 2280
10/20/79	79	4	2 The Part Of Me That Needs You Most...............		Oak 002
2/02/80	48	7	3 Driftin Away		Oak 1010
7/19/80	51	8	4 The Last Farewell		NSD 49
1/10/81	59	6	5 Rainin' In My Eyes		Starcom 1001
			BOB MORRIS		
			Died on 12/12/81.		
2/25/67	62	5	1 Fishin' On The Mississippi		Tower 307
			GARY MORRIS ★★106★★		
			Born on 12/7/48 in Fort Worth, Texas. Sang in duo with twin sister Carrie while in the 3rd grade. Appeared on the Ted Mack Amateur Hour while in high school. Own band, Breakaway, in Colorado. Moved to Nashville in 1979. Had lead part with Linda Ronstadt in "La Boheme", New York City, in 1984; and in "Les Miserables" in 1988. Appeared as "Wayne Masterson", a blind country singer, on The Colby's, ABC-TV.		
10/18/80	40	13	1 Sweet Red Wine		Warner 49564
3/07/81	40	10	2 Fire In Your Eyes		Warner 49668
10/17/81	8	17	3 Headed For A Heartache		Warner 49829
2/27/82	12	17	4 Don't Look Back.........................		Warner 50017
7/10/82	15	15	5 Dreams Die Hard.........................		Warner 29967
11/27/82+	9	19	6 Velvet Chains.............................		Warner 29853

DEBUT DATE	PEAK POS	WKS CHR		ARTIST — Record Title	POP POS	Label & Number
				GARY MORRIS — Continued		
4/16/83	5	20	7	The Love She Found In Me............................		Warner 29683
8/06/83	4	25	8	The Wind Beneath My Wings....................		Warner 29532
11/26/83+	4	19	9	Why Lady Why		Warner 29450
12/17/83+	9	23	10	You're Welcome To Tonight		Permian 82003
				LYNN ANDERSON & GARY MORRIS		
4/07/84	7	18	11	Between Two Fires....................................		Warner 29321
7/28/84	7	19	12	Second Hand Heart...................................		Warner 29230
11/24/84+	1¹	20	13	Baby Bye Bye		Warner 29131
5/04/85	9	20	14	Lasso The Moon		Warner 29028
8/24/85	1¹	23	15	I'll Never Stop Loving You.......................		Warner 28947
1/11/86	1¹	20	16	100% Chance Of Rain................................		Warner 28823
5/17/86	28	12	17	Anything Goes...		Warner 28713
7/12/86	27	13	18	Honeycomb		Warner 28654
				#1 pop hit for Jimmie Rodgers in 1957		
11/01/86+	1¹	21	19	Leave Me Lonely		Warner 28542
2/28/87	9	20	20	Plain Brown Wrapper		Warner 28468
10/10/87	64	5	21	Finishing Touches		Warner 28218
				CRYSTAL GAYLE & GARY MORRIS:		
11/23/85+	1¹	19	22	Makin' Up For Lost Time (The Dallas Lovers' Song)		Warner 28856
4/25/87	4	18	23	Another World...		Warner 28373
				theme from the daytime TV series of the same title		
2/13/88	26	15	24	All Of This & More......................................		Warner 28106

LAMAR MORRIS
Born in Andalusia, Alabama. With Hank Williams, Jr. since 1964. Leader of the Bama Band since 1976. Formerly married to Hank's stepsister, Lucretia.

DEBUT DATE	PEAK POS	WKS CHR		ARTIST — Record Title	POP POS	Label & Number
11/12/66	69	2	1	Send Me A Box Of Kleenex............................		MGM 13586
1/13/68	46	10	2	The Great Pretender		MGM 13866
				#1 pop hit for The Platters in 1956		
6/13/70	74	3	3	She Came To Me		MGM 14114
1/02/71	59	6	4	You're The Reason I'm Living.......................		MGM 14187
				#3 pop hit for Bobby Darin in 1963		
4/17/71	27	12	5	If You Love Me (Really Love Me)		MGM 14236
				#4 pop hit for Kay Starr in 1954		
11/27/71	74	3	6	Near You		MGM 14289
				#1 pop hit for Francis Craig in 1947		
2/17/73	71	3	7	You Call Everybody Darlin'		MGM 14487
				tune had 9 hit versions in 1948		

KATHY MORRISON - see BILL WILBOURN

ANN J. MORTON
Born Anna Jane White on 4/4/43 in Muldrow, Oklahoma. Sister of Jim Mundy and Bill White of Greyghost (formerly Razorback).

DEBUT DATE	PEAK POS	WKS CHR		ARTIST — Record Title	POP POS	Label & Number
11/06/76	82	7	1	Poor Wilted Rose		Prairie D. 7606
3/26/77	63	10	2	You Don't Have To Be A Baby To Cry		Prairie D. 7613
				#3 pop hit for The Caravelles in 1963		
7/16/77	86	4	3	Don't Want To Take A Chance (On Loving You) ..		Prairie D. 7617
10/01/77	72	6	4	Blueberry Hill...		Prairie D. 7619
				#2 pop hit for Fats Domino in 1957		
2/18/78	83	3	5	Black And Blue Heart		Prairie D. 7621
9/30/78	83	4	6	Share Your Love Tonight.............................		Prairie D. 7627
1/27/79	59	6	7	I'm Not In The Mood (For Love).......................		Prairie D. 7629
6/16/79	86	3	8	Don't Stay On Your Side Of The Bed Tonight......		Prairie D. 7631
8/18/79	42	10	9	My Empty Arms		Prairie D. 7632
1/26/80	63	5	10	(We Used To Kiss Each Other On The Lips But It's) All Over Now/		
		5	11	I Like Being Lonely		Prairie D. 7633
2/14/81	89	3	12	You've Got The Devil In Your Eyes..................		Prairie D. 8004

JOHNNY & JONIE MOSBY
Husband and wife team of Johnny (b: Fort Smith, AR) and wife Jonie (real name: Janice Irene Shields; b: 8/10/40 in Van Nuys, CA).

DEBUT DATE	PEAK POS	WKS CHR		ARTIST — Record Title	POP POS	Label & Number
5/18/63	13	9	1	Don't Call Me From A Honky Tonk		Columbia 42668

DEBUT DATE	PEAK POS	WKS CHR	ARTIST — Record Title	POP POS	Label & Number
			JOHNNY & JONIE MOSBY — Continued		
10/12/63+	12	16	2 Trouble In My Arms/		
11/02/63	27	1	3 Who's Been Cheatin' Who............................		Columbia 42841
4/18/64	16	13	4 Keep Those Cards And Letters Coming In..........		Columbia 43005
10/10/64	21	11	5 How The Other Half Lives.............................		Columbia 43100
10/07/67	36	12	6 Make A Left And Then A Right.......................		Capitol 5980
2/17/68	53	6	7 Mr. & Mrs. John Smith		Capitol 2087
6/22/68	58	5	8 Our Golden Wedding Day.............................		Capitol 2179
2/15/69	12	15	9 Just Hold My Hand.....................................		Capitol 2384
6/21/69	38	12	10 Hold Me, Thrill Me, Kiss Me.......................		Capitol 2505
			#8 pop hit for Mel Carter in 1965		
10/25/69	26	9	11 I'll Never Be Free		Capitol 2608
2/28/70	34	8	12 Third World		Capitol 2730
5/09/70	18	13	13 I'm Leavin' It Up To You............................		Capitol 2796
			#1 pop hit for Dale & Grace in 1963		
9/05/70	47	7	14 My Happiness		Capitol 2865
			#2 pop hit for Connie Francis in 1959		
3/06/71	41	9	15 Oh, Love Of Mine...................................		Capitol 3039
12/18/71+	70	3	16 Just One More Time		Capitol 3219
1/06/73	72	2	17 I've Been There		Capitol 3454
			JONIE MOSBY		
			BRUCE MULLEN		
5/25/74	88	3	1 Auctioneer Love		Chart 5215
			MOON MULLICAN		
			Born Aubrey Mullican on 3/27/09 near Corrigan, Texas; died of a heart attack on 1/1/67. Toured Texas and Louisiana with own band in the mid-30s. Worked with the Blue Ridge Playboys and the Texas Wanderers in the early 40s. Went solo in 1946. Worked on the Grand Ole Opry from 1949-55. Toured with Jimmie Davis from 1960-63. His distinctive two finger, right-hand style won him fame as the "King of The Hillbilly Piano Players".		
2/08/47	2¹	15	1 **New Pretty Blonde (Jole Blon)**		King 578
7/26/47	4	1	2 **Jole Blon's Sister**		King 632
5/15/48	3	26	3 **Sweeter Than The Flowers**		King 673
			Best Seller #3 / Juke Box #3		
3/18/50	1⁴	36	4 **I'll Sail My Ship Alone**		King 830
			Juke Box #1(4) / Best Seller #1(1) / Jockey #2		
8/26/50	4	11	5 **Mona Lisa/**		
			Juke Box #4 / Jockey #7 / Best Seller #8		
8/26/50	5	7	6 **Goodnight Irene**		King 886
			Juke Box #5 / Best Seller #10 / Jockey #10		
8/04/51	7	2	7 **Cherokee Boogie (Eh-Oh-Aleena)**..................		King 965
			Best Seller #7 / Juke Box #10		
5/29/61	15	4	8 Ragged But Right		Starday 545
			DEE MULLINS		
			Male vocalist from Ft. Worth. Sang in duo with his sister while in high school.		
2/10/68	64	3	1 I Am The Grass................................		SSS Int'l. 728
7/13/68	51	7	2 Texas Tea................................		SSS Int'l. 745
4/26/69	53	6	3 The Big Man................................		Plantation 17
1/09/71	71	2	4 Remember Bethlehem.......................... [X]		Plantation 68
4/14/73	61	9	5 Circle Me		Triune 7205
			JIM MUNDY		
			Born James L. White on 2/8/34 in Muldrow, Oklahoma. Professional singer since 1950. Wrote commercials for Miller Beer, Kentucky Fried Chicken and Pizza Hut. Brother of Ann J. Morton and Bill White.		
12/01/73+	13	15	1 The River's Too Wide................................		ABC 11400
4/13/74	49	11	2 Come Home................................		ABC 11428
9/07/74	71	5	3 She's No Ordinary Woman (Ordinarily)...............		ABC 12001
4/19/75	37	9	4 She's Already Gone		ABC 12074
8/30/75	81	8	5 Blue Eyes And Waltzes		ABC 12120
4/17/76	86	4	6 I'm Knee Deep In Loving You		ABC/Dot 17617
8/07/76	94	4	7 I Never Met A Girl I Didn't Like		ABC/Dot 17638
7/30/77	70	6	8 Summertime Blues................................		Hill Country 778
			#8 pop hit for Eddie Cochran in 1958		

DEBUT DATE	PEAK POS	WKS CHR	ARTIST — Record Title	POP POS	Label & Number
			JIM MUNDY — Continued		
			JIM MUNDY & TERRI MELTON:		
9/09/78	76	4	9 If You Think I Love You Now............................		MCM 100
1/06/79	87	2	10 Kiss You All Over...		MCM 101
			#1 pop hit for Exile in 1978		
			MICHAEL MARTIN MURPHEY ★★125★★		
			Born in Dallas, Texas. Sang in the Texas Twosome while still in high school. Toured as Travis Lewis of The Lewis & Clarke Expedition in 1967. Worked as a staff writer for Screen Gems. Lived in Austin from 1971-74; Colorado from 1974-79. Based in Taos, New Mexico since 1979. In the films "Take This Job And Shove It" and "Hard Country".		
			MICHAEL MURPHEY:		
2/21/76	36	10	1 A Mansion On The Hill.....................................		Epic 50184
1/22/77	58	8	2 Cherokee Fiddle...		Epic 50319
4/28/79	93	3	3 Chain Gang..		Epic 50686
			#2 pop hit for Sam Cooke in 1960		
8/18/79	92	3	4 Backslider's Wine		Epic 50739
7/04/81	83	3	5 Take It As It Comes..		Epic 02075
			MICHAEL MURPHEY with KATY MOFFATT		
3/27/82	44	10	6 The Two-Step Is Easy......................................		Liberty 1455
6/19/82	1¹	24	7 **What's Forever For**.......................................	19	Liberty 1466
11/13/82+	3	20	8 **Still Taking Chances**	76	Liberty 1486
3/26/83	11	17	9 Love Affairs		Liberty 1494
9/10/83	9	21	10 **Don't Count The Rainy Days**.......................		Liberty 1505
1/28/84	7	18	11 **Will It Be Love By Morning**		Liberty 1514
			MICHAEL MARTIN MURPHEY:		
5/12/84	12	17	12 Disenchanted		Liberty 1517
8/25/84	19	16	13 Radio Land		Liberty 1523
12/01/84+	8	23	14 **What She Wants**		EMI America 8243
5/25/85	9	20	15 **Carolina In The Pines**		EMI America 8265
2/08/86	26	14	16 Tonight We Ride		Warner 28797
5/24/86	15	16	17 Rollin' Nowhere		Warner 28694
8/30/86	40	14	18 Fiddlin' Man		Warner 28598
2/07/87	4	21	19 **A Face In The Crowd**...................................		Warner 28471
			MICHAEL MARTIN MURPHEY & HOLLY DUNN		
5/23/87	1¹	23	20 **A Long Line Of Love**		Warner 28370
11/21/87+	3	17	21 I'm Gonna Miss You, Girl...............................		Warner 28168
4/16/88	4	20	22 **Talkin' To The Wrong Man**...........................		Warner 27947
			MICHAEL MARTIN MURPHEY with RYAN MURPHEY (Michael's son)		
9/10/88	29	13	23 Pilgrims On The Way (Matthew's Song).............		Warner 27810
12/17/88+	3	25	24 **From The Word Go**......................................		Warner 27668
			JIMMY MURPHY		
10/25/86	74	4	1 Two Sides...		Encore 10033
1/31/87	51	9	2 Keep The Faith..		Encore 10036
			VERN MURPHY		
7/28/73	96	2	1 Blue And Lonely		Sunset 0021
			ANNE MURRAY ★★47★★		
			Born Morna Anne Murray on 6/20/45 in Springhill, Nova Scotia. With CBC-TV show "Sing Along Jubilee". First recorded for ARC in 1969. Regular on Glen Campbell's "Goodtime Hour" TV series. Currently resides in Toronto.		
7/25/70	10	19	1 ●Snowbird...	8	Capitol 2738
1/16/71	53	5	2 Sing High - Sing Low..	83	Capitol 2988
3/20/71+	27	12	3 A Stranger In My Place	122	Capitol 3059
5/22/71	67	2	4 Put Your Hand In The Hand		Capitol 3082
			#2 pop hit for Ocean in 1971		
10/30/71	40	8	5 I Say A Little Prayer/By The Time I Get To Phoenix	81	Capitol 3200
			GLEN CAMPBELL/ANNE MURRAY		
1/22/72	11	15	6 Cotton Jenny	71	Capitol 3260
12/23/72+	10	17	7 **Danny's Song**	7	Capitol 3481
			written by Kenny Loggins for his nephew		
6/02/73	20	10	8 What About Me..	64	Capitol 3600

DEBUT DATE	PEAK POS	WKS CHR	ARTIST — Record Title	POP POS	Label & Number
			ANNE MURRAY — Continued		
8/25/73	**79**	7	9 Send A Little Love My Way	*72*	Capitol 3648
			from the film "Oklahoma Crude"		
12/22/73+	**5**	15	10 **Love Song**	*12*	Capitol 3776
4/27/74	**1**²	17	11 **He Thinks I Still Care**		Capitol 3867
			flip side "You Won't See Me" made the pop charts (POS 8)		
9/28/74	**5**	16	12 **Son Of A Rotten Gambler**		Capitol 3955
			flip side "Just One Look" made the pop charts (POS 86)		
2/15/75	**28**	10	13 Uproar		Capitol 4025
6/07/75	**79**	6	14 A Stranger In My Place .... [R]		Capitol 4072
10/25/75	**49**	9	15 Sunday Sunrise	*98*	Capitol 4142
2/07/76	**19**	14	16 The Call	*91*	Capitol 4207
5/29/76	**41**	8	17 Golden Oldie		Capitol 4265
9/11/76+	**22**	12	18 Things	*89*	Capitol 4329
2/05/77	**57**	8	19 Sunday School To Broadway		Capitol 4375
1/21/78	**4**	16	20 **Walk Right Back**	*103*	Capitol 4527
			#7 pop hit for The Everly Brothers in 1961		
5/13/78	**4**	18	21● **You Needed Me**	*1*	Capitol 4574
1/27/79	**1**³	15	22 **I Just Fall In Love Again**	*12*	Capitol 4675
5/19/79	**1**¹	15	23 **Shadows In The Moonlight**	*25*	Capitol 4716
9/29/79	**1**¹	14	24 **Broken Hearted Me**	*12*	Capitol 4773
1/05/80	**3**	14	25 **Daydream Believer**	*12*	Capitol 4813
			#1 pop hit for The Monkees in 1967		
4/05/80	**9**	14	26 **Lucky Me**	*42*	Capitol 4848
6/28/80	**23**	11	27 I'm Happy Just To Dance With You	*64*	Capitol 4878
			#95 pop hit for The Beatles in 1964		
9/06/80	**1**¹	16	28 **Could I Have This Dance**	*33*	Capitol 4920
			from the film "Urban Cowboy"		
4/04/81	**1**¹	14	29 **Blessed Are The Believers**	*34*	Capitol 4987
7/04/81	**16**	13	30 We Don't Have To Hold Out....................		Capitol 5013
9/12/81	**9**	15	31 **It's All I Can Do**	*53*	Capitol 5023
1/16/82	**4**	18	32 **Another Sleepless Night**	*44*	Capitol 5083
7/31/82	**7**	16	33 **Hey! Baby!**		Capitol 5145
			#1 pop hit for Bruce Channel in 1962		
11/20/82+	**7**	19	34 **Somebody's Always Saying Goodbye**		Capitol 5183
9/17/83	**1**¹	20	35 **A Little Good News**	*74*	Capitol 5264
2/04/84	**46**	12	36 That's Not The Way (It's S'posed To Be)	*106*	Capitol 5305
4/28/84	**1**¹	20	37 **Just Another Woman In Love**		Capitol 5344
9/08/84	**1**¹	22	38 **Nobody Loves Me Like You Do**..................	*103*	Capitol 5401
			ANNE MURRAY with DAVE LOGGINS		
1/19/85	**2**¹	22	39 **Time Don't Run Out On Me**		Capitol 5436
5/18/85	**7**	20	40 **I Don't Think I'm Ready For You**..................		Capitol 5472
			from the film "Stick"		
1/25/86	**1**¹	19	41 **Now And Forever (You And Me)**	*92*	Capitol 5547
5/24/86	**62**	9	42 Who's Leaving Who		Capitol 5576
8/23/86	**26**	15	43 My Life's A Dance		Capitol 5610
12/27/86+	**23**	14	44 On And On		Capitol 5655
5/09/87	**20**	23	45 Are You Still In Love With Me		Capitol 44005
8/29/87	**27**	13	46 Anyone Can Do The Heartbreak.................		Capitol 44053
2/20/88	**52**	8	47 Perfect Strangers		Capitol 44134
			ANNE MURRAY with DOUG MALLORY		
9/03/88	**52**	7	48 Flying On Your Own		Capitol 44219
11/26/88+	**36**	12	49 Slow Passin' Time		Capitol 44272
			MUSIC ROW		
3/07/81	**86**	4	1 There Ain't A Song............................		Debut 8013
5/16/81	**92**	2	2 Lady's Man		Debut 8115
6/27/81	**88**	3	3 It's Not The Rain................................		Debut 8116
			FRANK MYERS		
			Singer/songwriter from Snowdoun, Alabama; raised in Montgomery.		
8/03/74	**82**	7	1 Hangin' On To What I've Got		Caprice 1999

N

LINDA NAIL
Born Linda Louise Naile on 1/19/54 in Wabash, Arkansas. Performer at Opryland, USA from 1974-80. Worked on Opryland tours and guested on the Grand Ole Opry.

12/09/78+	58	9	1 Me Touchin' You		Ridgetop 00178
3/10/79	67	5	2 There Hangs His Hat		Ridgetop 00279
2/05/83	85	2	3 You're A Part Of Me		Grand Prix 2
			DANNY WHITE & LINDA NAIL		
5/14/83	80	4	4 Reminiscing		Grand Prix 3

JERRY NAILL

2/02/80	92	4	1 Her Cheatin Heart (Made A Drunken Fool Of Me).		El Dorado 156

JIMMY NALL - see TERRI LANE

BILL NASH
Born in Pharr, Texas. Worked in Nash Family Trio from age 11.

7/04/81	79	4	1 Burning Bridges		Liberty 1410
			#3 pop hit for Jack Scott in 1960		
10/17/81	61	6	2 Slippin' Out, Slippin' In		Liberty 1433
5/22/82	65	6	3 Survivor		Liberty 1463

LINDA NASH

10/27/73	83	10	1 Country Boogie Woogie		Ace of H. 0473

NASHVILLE BRASS - see DANNY DAVIS

NASHVILLE NIGHTSHIFT

8/31/85	89	2	1 Nightshift		NCA 133737
			a tribute to Marty Robbins (same tune as the Commodores pop hit)		

NASHVILLE SUPERPICKERS
Top session musicians including Johnny Gimble (fiddle), Phil Baugh (guitar), Charlie McCoy (harmonica), Buddy Emmons (steel guitar), Hargus 'Pig' Robbins (piano), Russ Hicks (guitar), Henry Strzelecki (bass) and Buddy Harman (drums).

2/07/81	83	2	1 New York Cowboy		Snd. Factory 426

JERRY NAYLOR
Born on 3/6/39 in Stephenville, Texas. Own band at age 14, worked on the Louisiana Hayride. Worked as a disc jockey in San Angelo, Texas. Replaced Joe B. Mauldin in The Crickets in 1961. Suffered a heart attack in 1964, but fully recovered. Had award-winning radio series, "Continental Country", in the early 70s.

1/25/75	27	12	1 Is This All There Is To A Honky Tonk?		Melodyland 6003
10/02/76	94	2	2 The Bad Part Of Me		Hitsville 6041
12/04/76+	50	9	3 The Last Time You Love Me		Hitsville 6046
2/04/78	37	9	4 If You Don't Want To Love Her		MC 5004
5/27/78	80	4	5 Rave On/		
			#37 pop hit for Buddy Holly in 1958		
		2	6 Lady, Would You Like To Dance		MC 5010
3/24/79	54	5	7 But For Love .... [R]		Warner 8767
			originally made pop charts in 1970 on Columbia 45106 (POS 69)		
7/07/79	72	4	8 She Wears It Well		Warner 8881
11/17/79	69	4	9 Don't Touch Me		Jeremiah 1002
			JERRY NAYLOR/KELLI WARREN		
3/08/80	61	5	10 Cheating Eyes		Oak 1014
11/29/86	75	4	11 For Old Time Sake		West 723

JOANNA NEEL
One of the very few black female country singers.

11/13/71	68	5	1 Daddy Was A Preacher But Mama Was A Go-Go Girl		Decca 32865

SAM NEELY
Born on 8/22/48 in Cuero, Texas. Performing since age 11. Worked with local rock groups. Played clubs in Corpus Christi, especially at The Rogue, in the late 60s. Long residency at the Electric Eel in Corpus Christi, in the late 70s.

9/14/74	49	12	1 You Can Have Her	34	A&M 1612
2/01/75	61	8	2 I Fought The Law	54	A&M 1651

DEBUT DATE	PEAK POS	WKS CHR	ARTIST — Record Title	POP POS	Label & Number
			SAM NEELY — Continued		
9/10/77	**98**	3	3 Sail Away	*84*	Elektra 45419
3/12/83	**78**	4	4 The Party's Over (Everybody's Gone)		MCA 52194
6/18/83	**77**	5	5 When You Leave That Way You Can Never Go Back		MCA 52226
1/21/84	**81**	3	6 Old Photographs		MCA 52323
			BONNIE NELSON Born in 1949 in Denver. Appeared on the Rocky Mountain Jamboree, KLAK radio. Won calf roping title in 1967. Winner of the Pappy Dave Stone Talent Contest in 1972.		
12/06/86	**83**	3	1 Don't Let It Go To Your Heart		Door Knob 257
5/23/87	**84**	2	2 More Than Friendly Persuasion		Door Knob 264
			RICKY NELSON Born Eric Hilliard Nelson on 5/8/40 in Teaneck, New Jersey. Died on 12/31/85 in a plane crash in DeKalb, Texas. Son of bandleader Ozzie Nelson and vocalist Harriet Hilliard. Rick and brother David appeared on Nelson's radio show from March, 1949, later on TV, 1952 to 1966. Formed own Stone Canyon Band in 1969. Films "Rio Bravo", "Wackiest Ship In The Army", and "Love And Kisses". One of the first teen idols of the rock era. Inducted into the Rock And Roll Hall Of Fame in 1987.		
1/20/58	**8**	12	1 **Stood Up/** Best Seller #8	*2*	
1/20/58	**12**	6	2 Waitin' In School .... Best Seller #12	*18*	Imperial 5483
4/14/58	**10**	11	3 **My Bucket's Got A Hole In It/** Best Seller #10	*12*	
4/14/58	**10**	10	4 **Believe What You Say** .... Best Seller #10	*4*	Imperial 5503
7/07/58	**3**	15	5 **Poor Little Fool** .... Best Seller #3 / Jockey #8	*1*	Imperial 5528
6/10/67	**58**	5	6 Take A City Bride		Decca 32120
9/16/72	**44**	9	7●Garden Party... **RICK NELSON & THE STONE CANYON BAND**	*6*	Decca 32980
5/11/74	**89**	2	8 One Night Stand...................................... **RICK NELSON & THE STONE CANYON BAND**		MCA 40214
4/21/79	**59**	9	9 Dream Lover		Epic 50674
7/12/86	**88**	7	10 Dream Lover .... [R]		Epic 06066
			TERRY NELSON - see C COMPANY		
			WILLIE NELSON ★★**8**★★ Born on 4/30/33 in Fort Worth, Texas; raised in Abbott, Texas. Learned guitar at age 10. In the US Air Force during the Korean War, then worked as a disc jockey in Waco, San Antonio and Houston. Played bass for Ray Price. Moved to Nashville in 1960. Wrote hits "Crazy" for Patsy Cline, "Night Life" for Ray Price, "Hello Walls" for Faron Young and "Funny How Time Slips Away" for Billy Walker. Moved back to Texas in 1970. In the films "Outlaw Blues", "Electric Horseman", "Honeysuckle Rose", "Barbarosa", "Coming Out Of The Ice", "Songwriter" and "Red-Headed Stranger". Host of the legendary Fourth of July picnic concerts in Austin, Texas since 1972. President of Farm Aid, Inc. CMA award: Entertainer of the Year - 1979.		
5/26/62	**7**	13	1 **Touch Me**..	*109*	Liberty 55439
4/06/63	**25**	5	2 Half A Man..	*129*	Liberty 55532
1/18/64	**33**	3	3 You Took My Happy Away		Liberty 55638
5/08/65	**43**	5	4 She's Not For You		RCA 8519
10/16/65	**48**	2	5 I Just Can't Let You Say Goodbye		RCA 8682
10/01/66	**19**	13	6 One In A Row		RCA 8933
3/04/67	**24**	16	7 The Party's Over		RCA 9100
6/24/67	**21**	11	8 Blackjack County Chain		RCA 9202
10/21/67	**50**	9	9 San Antonio		RCA 9324
2/10/68	**22**	11	10 Little Things		RCA 9427
6/15/68	**44**	8	11 Good Times...		RCA 9536
9/07/68	**36**	7	12 Johnny One Time		RCA 9605
12/21/68+	**13**	14	13 Bring Me Sunshine		RCA 9684
12/13/69+	**36**	9	14 I Hope So		Liberty 56143
3/14/70	**42**	9	15 Once More With Feeling		RCA 9798
11/28/70	**68**	2	16 Laying My Burdens Down		RCA 9903
2/06/71	**28**	11	17 I'm A Memory...		RCA 9951
10/23/71	**62**	7	18 Yesterday's Wine/		
		4	19 Me And Paul		RCA 0542

DEBUT DATE	PEAK POS	WKS CHR		ARTIST — Record Title	POP POS	Label & Number
				WILLIE NELSON — Continued		
2/19/72	**73**	2	20	The Words Don't Fit The Picture........................		RCA 0635
7/14/73	**60**	5	21	Shotgun Willie................................		Atlantic 2968
9/29/73	**22**	13	22	Stay All Night (Stay A Little Longer).................		Atlantic 2979
2/16/74	**51**	5	23	I Still Can't Believe You're Gone		Atlantic 3008
4/06/74	**17**	13	24	Bloody Mary Morning..........................		Atlantic 3020
12/07/74	**93**	3	25	Sister's Coming Home		Atlantic 3228
7/19/75	**1**²	18	26	**Blue Eyes Crying In The Rain**	21	Columbia 10176
11/15/75+	**29**	11	27	Fire And Rain......................................		RCA 10429
				#3 pop hit for James Taylor in 1970		
1/03/76	**2**¹	15	28	**Remember Me**	67	Columbia 10275
3/27/76	**46**	7	29	The Last Letter		United Art. 771
4/17/76	**55**	6	30	I Gotta Get Drunk	101	RCA 10591
5/01/76	**11**	13	31	I'd Have To Be Crazy		Columbia 10327
7/24/76	**1**¹	15	32	**If You've Got The Money I've Got The Time**		Columbia 10383
12/18/76+	**4**	14	33	**Uncloudy Day**		Columbia 10453
5/14/77	**22**	11	34	I'm A Memory........................... [R]		RCA 10969
7/30/77	**9**	12	35	**I Love You A Thousand Ways**		Columbia 10588
9/10/77	**16**	13	36	You Ought To Hear Me Cry		RCA 11061
3/18/78	**5**	15	37	**If You Can Touch Her At All**	104	RCA 11235
3/25/78	**1**¹	16	38	**Georgia On My Mind**	84	Columbia 10704
				written in 1930 by Hoagy Carmichael		
7/15/78	**1**¹	13	39	**Blue Skies**		Columbia 10784
				written in 1927 by Irving Berlin		
10/21/78	**3**	14	40	**All Of Me**		Columbia 10834
				#1 hit for both Louis Armstrong and Paul Whiteman in 1932		
10/28/78	**67**	5	41	Will You Remember Mine..........................		Lone Star 703
11/25/78	**86**	3	42	There'll Be No Teardrops Tonight		United Art. 1254
12/23/78+	**12**	12	43	Whiskey River		Columbia 10877
2/10/79	**4**	14	44	**Sweet Memories**		RCA 11465
4/14/79	**15**	12	45	September Song...................................		Columbia 10929
				first performed, 1938, in "Knickerbocker Holiday" by Walter Huston		
8/18/79	**16**	13	46	Crazy Arms		RCA 11673
11/10/79+	**4**	14	47	**Help Me Make It Through The Night**.............		Columbia 11126
1/12/80	**1**²	14	48	**My Heroes Have Always Been Cowboys**...........	44	Columbia 11186
				from the film "The Electric Horseman"		
5/03/80	**6**	15	49	**Midnight Rider**...................................		Columbia 11257
				#19 pop hit for Gregg Allman in 1974		
8/30/80	**1**¹	16	50	**On The Road Again**..............................	20	Columbia 11351
				from the film "Honeysuckle Rose"		
10/04/80	**92**	2	51	Family Bible......................................		Songbird 41313
1/10/81	**1**¹	14	52	**Angel Flying Too Close To The Ground**		Columbia 11418
				from the film "Honeysuckle Rose"		
4/18/81	**11**	12	53	Mona Lisa..		Columbia 02000
				#1 pop hit for Nat King Cole in 1950		
6/27/81	**25**	12	54	Good Times................................... [R]		RCA 12254
7/25/81	**26**	11	55	I'm Gonna Sit Right Down And Write Myself A Letter		Columbia 02187
				#3 pop hit for Billy Williams in 1957		
10/03/81	**23**	12	56	Mountain Dew....................................		RCA 12328
11/14/81	**39**	10	57	Heartaches Of A Fool		Columbia 02558
3/06/82	**1**²	21	58	**Always On My Mind**	5	Columbia 02741
8/14/82	**2**²	17	59	**Let It Be Me**	40	Columbia 03073
				#7 pop hit for The Everly Brothers in 1960		
12/04/82+	**2**²	20	60	**Last Thing I Needed First Thing This Morning**		Columbia 03385
3/12/83	**10**	16	61	**Little Old Fashioned Karma**		Columbia 03674
6/18/83	**3**	21	62	**Why Do I Have To Choose**		Columbia 03965
12/24/83+	**11**	16	63	Without A Song		Columbia 04263
				#6 pop hit for Paul Whiteman in 1930		
8/18/84	**1**¹	25	64	**City Of New Orleans**.............................		Columbia 04568
				#18 pop hit for Arlo Guthrie in 1972		
4/13/85	**1**¹	22	65	**Forgiving You Was Easy**...........................		Columbia 04847
9/14/85	**14**	19	66	Me And Paul .... [R]		Columbia 05597
				refers to Willie and his drummer Paul English		

DEBUT DATE	PEAK POS	WKS CHR		ARTIST — Record Title	POP POS	Label & Number
				WILLIE NELSON — Continued		
3/29/86	**1**[1]	20	67	**Living In The Promiseland**		Columbia 05834
8/09/86	**21**	17	68	I'm Not Trying To Forget You		Columbia 06246
12/06/86+	**24**	13	69	Partners After All		Columbia 06530
3/21/87	**44**	11	70	Heart Of Gold		Columbia 07007
				#1 pop hit for Neil Young in 1972		
7/11/87	**27**	12	71	Island In The Sea		Columbia 07202
1/09/88	**82**	3	72	Nobody There But Me		Columbia 07636
				WILLIE NELSON DUOS with:		
				RAY CHARLES:		
12/15/84+	**1**[1]	27	73	**Seven Spanish Angels**		Columbia 04715
				HANK COCHRAN:		
10/14/78	**77**	5	74	Ain't Life Hell......................................		Capitol 4635
				DAVID ALLAN COE:		
8/02/86	**56**	8	75	I've Already Cheated On You........................		Columbia 06227
				SHIRLEY COLLIE:		
3/17/62	**10**	13	76	**Willingly**..		Liberty 55403
				DANNY DAVIS & THE NASHVILLE BRASS:		
2/02/80	**20**	12	77	Night Life		RCA 11893
5/17/80	**41**	8	78	Funny How Time Slips Away		RCA 11999
				MERLE HAGGARD:		
1/15/83	**6**	18	79	**Reasons To Quit**		Epic 03494
4/30/83	**1**[1]	21	80	**Pancho And Lefty**		Epic 03842
9/19/87	**58**	5	81	If I Could Only Fly		Epic 07400
				JULIO IGLESIAS:		
3/10/84	**1**[2]	20	82●	**To All The Girls I've Loved Before**................	5	Columbia 04217
9/17/88	**8**	19	83	**Spanish Eyes**		Columbia 08066
				WAYLON JENNINGS (WAYLON & WILLIE):		
12/27/75+	**1**[3]	17	84	**Good Hearted Woman**.............................	25	RCA 10529
1/21/78	**1**[4]	16	85	**Mammas Don't Let Your Babies Grow Up To Be Cowboys/**	42	
		15	86	I Can Get Off On You		RCA 11198
3/13/82	**1**[2]	18	87	**Just To Satisfy You**	52	RCA 13073
10/23/82	**13**	15	88	(Sittin' On) The Dock Of The Bay....................		RCA 13319
10/08/83	**8**	19	89	**Take It To The Limit**	102	Columbia 04131
				WAYLON JENNINGS, JOHNNY CASH, KRIS KRISTOFFERSON:		
5/18/85	**1**[1]	20	90	**Highwayman**		Columbia 04881
9/14/85	**15**	18	91	Desperados Waiting For A Train		Columbia 05594
				KRIS KRISTOFFERSON:		
11/03/84	**46**	11	92	How Do You Feel About Foolin' Around		Columbia 04652
				BRENDA LEE:		
4/09/83	**43**	9	93	You're Gonna Love Yourself (In The Morning).....		Monument 03781
				DARRELL McCALL:		
3/12/77	**32**	13	94	Lily Dale		Columbia 10480
				ROGER MILLER (with RAY PRICE):		
6/05/82	**19**	16	95	Old Friends		Columbia 02681
				TRACY NELSON:		
8/17/74	**17**	11	96	After The Fire Is Gone		Atlantic 4028
				Willie and Tracy are not related		
				DOLLY PARTON:		
12/11/82+	**7**	20	97	**Everything's Beautiful (In It's Own Way)**........		Monument 03408
				WEBB PIERCE:		
10/09/82	**72**	5	98	In The Jailhouse Now		Columbia 03231
				MARY KAY PLACE:		
11/19/77+	**9**	16	99	**Something To Brag About**		Columbia 10644
				RAY PRICE:		
8/09/80	**3**	15	100	**Faded Love**		Columbia 11329
12/06/80+	**11**	14	101	Don't You Ever Get Tired (Of Hurting Me)		Columbia 11405
				LEON RUSSELL:		
7/07/79	**1**[1]	13	102	**Heartbreak Hotel**................................		Columbia 11023
				#1 pop hit for Elvis Presley in 1956		
				HANK WILSON:		
10/27/84	**91**	2	103	Wabash Cannonball................................		Paradise 629

DEBUT DATE	PEAK POS	WKS CHR	ARTIST — Record Title	POP POS	Label & Number
			JIM NESBITT Born on 12/1/31 in Bishopville, South Carolina. Worked with Slim Mims & His Dream Ranch Boys. Disc jockey at WAGS-Bishopville. Nickname: the 'Lasses Sopper'.		
4/03/61	11	7	1 Please Mr. Kennedy .... [N] also released on Country Jubilee 549 and Ace 621; melody is the same as "Davy Crockett"		Dot 16197
2/02/63	28	1	2 Livin' Offa Credit .... [N]		Dot 16424
3/21/64	7	24	3 Looking For More In '64 .... [N]		Chart 1065
9/26/64	20	13	4 Mother-In-Law .... [N]		Chart 1100
1/30/65	15	13	5 A Tiger In My Tank .... [N]		Chart 1165
6/26/65	34	6	6 Still Alive In '65 .... [N]		Chart 1200
8/14/65	21	11	7 The Friendly Undertaker .... [N]		Chart 1240
1/01/66	49	2	8 You Better Watch Your Friends .... [N]		Chart 1290
8/27/66	38	9	9 Heck Of A Fix In 66 .... [N]		Chart 1350
12/17/66+	60	8	10 Stranded		Chart 1410
6/10/67	74	2	11 Husbands-In-Law .... [N]		Chart 1445
3/16/68	63	7	12 Truck Drivin' Cat With Nine Wives .... [N]		Chart 1018
2/28/70	20	12	13 Runnin' Bare .... [N] novelty version of Johnny Preston's "Running Bear"		Chart 5052
			BILL NETTLES Born on 3/13/07 in Natchitoches, Louisiana. Died of a heart attack on 4/5/67. First recorded for Brunswick in 1937.		
6/25/49	9	6	1 Hadacol Boogie .... Juke Box #9		Mercury 6190
			NEW GRASS REVIVAL Quartet consisting of Sam Bush, John Cowan, Pat Flynn and Bela Fleck.		
7/05/86	78	5	1 What You Do To Me		EMI America 8329
9/20/86	53	8	2 Ain't That Peculiar .... #8 pop hit for Marvin Gaye in 1965		EMI America 8347
10/03/87	44	9	3 Unconditional Love		Capitol 44078
3/05/88	45	11	4 Can't Stop Now		Capitol 44128
			MICKEY NEWBURY Born Milton S. Newbury, Jr. on 5/19/40 in Houston. In the US Air Force from 1959-63. Moved to Nashville in 1963, worked as staff writer for Acuff-Rose. Wrote "Here Comes The Rain, Baby", "Sweet Memories" and "Just Dropped In (To See What Condition My Condition Was In)".		
6/23/73	53	8	1 Sunshine	87	Elektra 45853
2/05/77	94	3	2 Hand Me Another Of Those		ABC/Hick. 54006
4/08/78	94	3	3 Gone To Alabama		ABC/Hick. 54025
3/24/79	82	4	4 Looking For The Sunshine		ABC/Hick. 54042
6/16/79	81	4	5 Blue Sky Shinin'		MCA 41032
2/09/80	82	3	6 America The Beautiful .... written by poet Katherine Lee Bates at Pikes Peak in 1893		Hickory 1673
10/15/88	93	2	7 An American Trilogy .... [R] Dixie/Battle Hymn Of The Republic/All My Trials new version of his #26 pop hit in 1971		Airborne 10005
			JACK NEWMAN		
8/24/59	24	1	1 House Of Blue Lovers		TNT 170
			JIMMY NEWMAN ★★89★★ Born on 8/27/27 in Big Mamou, Louisiana. Own show on KPLC-Lake Charles. On the Louisiana Hayride in the early 50s. Member of the Grand Ole Opry since 1956. The "C" in his name stands for "Cajun".		
5/22/54	4	11	1 Cry, Cry Darling .... Jockey #4 / Juke Box #8 / Best Seller #9		Dot 1195
3/26/55	7	7	2 Daydreaming .... Juke Box #7 / Jockey #9 / Best Seller #13		Dot 1237
7/09/55	7	10	3 Blue Darlin' .... Jockey #7 / Juke Box #8 / Best Seller #13		Dot 1260
12/17/55+	9	2	4 God Was So Good .... Jockey #9		Dot 1270
4/07/56	9	6	5 Seasons Of My Heart .... Juke Box #9 / Jockey #10		Dot 1278
7/07/56	13	4	6 Come Back To Me .... Jockey #13		Dot 1283

DEBUT DATE	PEAK POS	WKS CHR	ARTIST — Record Title	POP POS	Label & Number
			JIMMY NEWMAN — Continued		
5/20/57	2²	21	7 A Fallen Star	*23*	Dot 1289
			Jockey #2 / Best Seller #4 / Juke Box #9		
			also released on Dot 15574 (pop series)		
11/03/58+	7	16	8 You're Makin' A Fool Out Of Me		MGM 12707
4/13/59	19	4	9 So Soon		MGM 12749
6/22/59	30	1	10 Lonely Girl		MGM 12790
7/27/59	11	13	11 Grin And Bear It		MGM 12812
11/02/59	29	1	12 Walkin' Down The Road		MGM 12830
3/07/60	21	7	13 I Miss You Already		MGM 12864
6/20/60	6	14	14 A Lovely Work Of Art.......................		MGM 12894
11/07/60	11	18	15 Wanting You With Me Tonight		MGM 12945
4/17/61	14	8	16 Everybody's Dying For Love.................		Decca 31217
12/25/61+	22	2	17 Alligator Man		Decca 31324
12/22/62+	12	9	18 Bayou Talk		Decca 31440
12/14/63+	9	19	19 **D.J. For A Day**		Decca 31553
5/16/64	34	3	20 Angel On Leave/		
5/30/64	34	3	21 Summer Skies And Golden Sands		Decca 31609
			above 4: **JIMMY C. NEWMAN**		
4/10/65	37	7	22 City Of The Angels/		
4/24/65	13	16	23 Back In Circulation		Decca 31745
9/25/65	8	21	24 **Artificial Rose**...........................		Decca 31841
3/26/66	10	16	25 **Back Pocket Money**.........................		Decca 31916
10/08/66	25	8	26 Bring Your Heart Home		Decca 31994
1/14/67	32	11	27 Dropping Out Of Sight		Decca 32067
5/27/67	24	12	28 Louisiana Saturday Night		Decca 32130
10/28/67+	11	17	29 Blue Lonely Winter		Decca 32202
4/13/68	47	8	30 Sunshine And Bluebirds		Decca 32285
8/31/68	20	13	31 Born To Love You		Decca 32366
5/31/69	31	8	32 Boo Dan		Decca 32484
11/28/70	65	6	33 I'm Holding Your Memory (But He's Holding You)		Decca 32740
			RANDY NEWMAN		
			Born on 11/28/43 in New Orleans. Singer/composer/pianist. Nephew of composers Alfred, Emil and Lionel Newman. Scored the films "Ragtime" and "The Natural".		
8/19/78	78	4	1 Rider In The Rain...........................		Warner 8630
			TERRI SUE NEWMAN		
			Born in 1954 in Levelland, Texas. Self-taught on piano and guitar. Performed on Pickin' Time Show, Get Down Country Show, and West Texas Saturday Night Opry.		
1/13/79	43	10	1 Gypsy Eyes		Texas Soul 71378
			JUICE NEWTON ★★**131**★★		
			Born Judy Kay Newton on 2/18/52 in New Jersey; raised in Virginia Beach. Performed folk music from age 13. Moved to Los Angeles with own Silver Spur band in 1974. Recorded for RCA in 1975. Group disbanded in 1978. Juice is an accomplished equestrian.		
2/21/76	88	6	1 Love Is A Word..............................		RCA 10538
			JUICE NEWTON & SILVER SPUR		
2/10/79	37	9	2 Let's Keep It That Way		Capitol 4679
5/26/79	80	4	3 Lay Back In The Arms Of Someone		Capitol 4714
9/15/79	81	4	4 Any Way That You Want Me		Capitol 4768
			#53 pop hit for Evie Sands in 1969		
11/10/79	42	8	5 Until Tonight................................		Capitol 4793
2/02/80	35	10	6 Sunshine		Capitol 4818
			#4 pop hit for Jonathan Edwards in 1972		
4/26/80	41	10	7 You Fill My Life		Capitol 4856
3/07/81	22	11	8● Angel Of The Morning	*4*	Capitol 4976
6/13/81	14	16	9● Queen Of Hearts..........................	*2*	Capitol 4997
10/24/81+	1¹	19	10 **The Sweetest Thing (I've Ever Known)**	*7*	Capitol 5046
5/22/82	30	10	11 Love's Been A Little Bit Hard On Me................	*7*	Capitol 5120
8/28/82	2²	19	12 **Break It To Me Gently**.......................	*11*	Capitol 5148
12/11/82+	53	11	13 Heart Of The Night	*25*	Capitol 5192
9/03/83	45	13	14 Stranger At My Door		Capitol 5265
6/23/84	64	9	15 A Little Love	*44*	RCA 13823
8/18/84	32	13	16 Ride 'Em Cowboy		Capitol 5379

DEBUT DATE	PEAK POS	WKS CHR	ARTIST — Record Title	POP POS	Label & Number
			JUICE NEWTON — Continued		
10/20/84	**57**	7	17 Restless Heart		RCA 13907
7/20/85	**1**¹	22	18 **You Make Me Want To Make You Mine**		RCA 14139
11/09/85+	**1**¹	24	19 **Hurt**		RCA 14199
			#4 pop hit for Timi Yuro in 1961		
4/05/86	**5**	21	20 **Old Flame**		RCA 14295
7/12/86	**1**¹	20	21 **Both To Each Other (Friends & Lovers)**		RCA 14377
			EDDIE RABBITT & JUICE NEWTON		
8/23/86	**9**	18	22 **Cheap Love**		RCA 14417
			written by Del Shannon		
12/13/86+	**9**	20	23 **What Can I Do With My Heart**		RCA 5068
7/18/87	**24**	15	24 First Time Caller................................		RCA 5170
11/14/87+	**8**	22	25 **Tell Me True**		RCA 5283
			WAYNE NEWTON		
			Born on 4/3/42 in Roanoke, Virginia. Top Las Vegas entertainer.		
7/15/72	**55**	8	1● Daddy Don't You Walk So Fast	4	Chelsea 0100
			WOOD NEWTON		
			Singer/composer from Louisiana. Worked as a photographer for Nashville country magazines. Staff writer for Briar Patch Music.		
10/28/78	**52**	7	1 Last Exit For Love..............................		Elektra 45528
3/03/79	**44**	8	2 Lock, Stock, & Barrel		Elektra 46013
7/07/79	**81**	4	3 Julie (Do I Ever Cross Your Mind?)		Elektra 46059
			OLIVIA NEWTON-JOHN ★★199★★		
			Born on 9/26/48 in Cambridge, England. To Australia in 1953. At age 16, won talent contest trip to England, sang with Pat Carroll as Pat & Olivia. Consistent award winner in both pop and country. Granddaughter of Nobel Prize-winning German physicist Max Born. In films "Grease" (1978), "Xanadu" (1980) and "Two Of A Kind" (1983). Married actor Matt Lattanzi in 1985.		
8/25/73	**7**	22	1● Let Me Be There	6	MCA 40101
4/13/74	**2**²	18	2● If You Love Me (Let Me Know)	5	MCA 40209
8/24/74	**6**	17	3● I Honestly Love You...........................	1	MCA 40280
2/01/75	**3**	14	4● Have You Never Been Mellow......................	1	MCA 40349
6/14/75	**5**	15	5● Please Mr. Please....................................	3	MCA 40418
9/27/75	**19**	12	6 Something Better To Do	13	MCA 40459
12/06/75+	**5**	12	7 Let It Shine	30	MCA 40495
3/13/76	**5**	13	8 Come On Over	23	MCA 40525
8/14/76	**14**	10	9 Don't Stop Believin'....................................	33	MCA 40600
10/30/76	**21**	11	10 Every Face Tells A Story	55	MCA 40642
1/29/77	**40**	10	11 Sam..	20	MCA 40670
7/22/78	**20**	13	12● Hopelessly Devoted To You.........................	3	RSO 903
			from the film "Grease"		
1/06/79	**94**	3	13● A Little More Love	3	MCA 40975
5/05/79	**87**	5	14 Deeper Than The Night	11	MCA 41009
8/04/79	**29**	11	15 Dancin' 'Round And 'Round	82	MCA 41074
			JUNE NEYMAN		
11/11/78	**93**	2	1 He Ain't Heavy, He's My Brother.....................		Starship 101
			#7 pop hit for The Hollies in 1970		
2/17/79	**97**	3	2 You're Gonna Miss Me.................................		Starship 110
			STEVIE NICKS		
			Born Stephanie Nicks on 5/26/48 in Phoenix; raised in California. Vocalist with Fleetwood Mac since January of 1975.		
6/19/82	**70**	5	1 After The Glitter Fades	32	Modern 7405
			THE NIELSEN WHITE BAND		
			Consists of Gary Nielsen (one-time member of The Trashmen), Jack White (one-time member of McKendree Spring), Lonnie Knight and Tom Eckhoff (of the Dillman Band).		
12/20/86+	**67**	6	1 Somethin' You Got		Vision 122574
5/02/87	**56**	7	2 I Got The One I Wanted.................................		Vision 122575
			SHAUN NIELSEN		
			Real name: Sherrill Nielsen. Member of the Imperials Quartet and Voice, which backed Elvis Presley in concert for 3 years.		
3/15/80	**88**	3	1 Lights Of L.A..		Adonda 79022

DEBUT DATE	PEAK POS	WKS CHR	ARTIST — Record Title	POP POS	Label & Number
			NIGHTSTREETS		
			Nashville-based trio: Rick Taylor, Jerry Taylor (no relation) and Joyce Hawthorne.		
6/14/80	74	5	1 Falling Together		Epic 50886
11/15/80	81	5	2 If I Had It My Way		Epic 50944
3/21/81	72	4	3 (Lookin' At Things) In A Different Light		Epic 51004
			LYNN NILES		
2/12/77	93	4	1 You're Gonna Make Love To Me......................		GRT 100
			NITTY GRITTY DIRT BAND ★★**127**★★		
			Group formed as the Illegitimate Jug Band in 1966. Consisted of Jeff Hanna (b: 7/11/47), Jimmie Fadden, Ralph Barr, Leslie Thompson, John McEuen and Bruce Kunkel. Kunkel replaced by Chris Darrow in 1968. Barr replaced by Jim Ibbotson in 1971. In the films "For Singles Only" and "Paint Your Wagon". Changed name to Dirt Band in 1976 when Hanna left the group. Resumed using Nitty Gritty Dirt Band name in 1982.		
11/27/71	56	6	1 I Saw The Light .... **NITTY GRITTY DIRT BAND with ROY ACUFF**		United Art. 50849
8/04/73	97	2	2 Grand Ole Opry Song		United Art. 247
7/12/75	79	7	3 (All I Have To Do Is) Dream..........................	*66*	United Art. 655
2/09/80	58	9	4 An American Dream .... harmony vocal: Linda Ronstadt	*13*	United Art. 1330
8/02/80	77	4	5 Make A Little Magic....................................... above 2 shown only as: **THE DIRT BAND**	*25*	United Art. 1356
6/11/83	19	18	6 Shot Full Of Love		Liberty 1499
10/01/83	9	23	7 **Dance Little Jean**		Liberty 1507
1/07/84	93	2	8 Colorado Christmas........................... [X]		Liberty 1513
5/26/84	1¹	20	9 **Long Hard Road (The Sharecropper's Dream)** .		Warner 29282
9/22/84	3	24	10 **I Love Only You**..		Warner 29203
1/12/85	2²	20	11 **High Horse**		Warner 29099
6/08/85	1¹	21	12 **Modern Day Romance**		Warner 29027
10/12/85+	3	21	13 **Home Again In My Heart**		Warner 28897
3/01/86	6	19	14 **Partners, Brothers And Friends**....................		Warner 28780
6/21/86	5	21	15 **Stand A Little Rain**		Warner 28690
11/15/86+	7	20	16 **Fire In The Sky**		Warner 28547
3/28/87	2¹	17	17 **Baby's Got A Hold On Me**		Warner 28443
7/11/87	1¹	23	18 **Fishin' In The Dark**		Warner 28311
11/14/87+	5	22	19 **Oh What A Love**		Warner 28173
4/16/88	4	18	20 **Workin' Man (Nowhere To Go)**		Warner 27940
9/03/88	2¹	22	21 **I've Been Lookin'**		Warner 27750
12/24/88+	6	20	22 **Down That Road Tonight**..............................		Warner 27679
			TOM NIX		
			Singer from Denver. Made many commercial jingles. Worked with the Rocky Mountain Picture Association in 1979.		
1/10/81	79	4	1 Home Along The Highway..............................		RMA 6009
			NICK NIXON		
			Born Hershel Paul Nixon on 3/20/41 in Poplar Bluff, Missouri. Co-wrote Barbara Fairchild's "Teddy Bear Song". Long-time St. Louis area favorite.		
8/10/74	90	3	1 I'm Turning You Loose..................................		Mercury 73467
10/05/74	63	7	2 A Habit I Can't Break....................................		Mercury 73506
3/08/75	55	9	3 It's Only A Barroom.......................................		Mercury 73654
7/12/75	38	12	4 I'm Too Use To Loving You		Mercury 73691
11/29/75	64	10	5 She's Just An Old Love Turned Memory...........		Mercury 73726
3/13/76	28	13	6 Rocking In Rosalee's Boat		Mercury 73772
1/08/77	83	5	7 Neon Lights		Mercury 73866
7/02/77	51	10	8 Love Songs And Romance Magazines...............		Mercury 73930
11/05/77+	34	13	9 I'll Get Over You		Mercury 55010
8/12/78	87	4	10 She's Lying Next To Me		Mercury 55035
6/02/79	79	4	11 What're We Doing, Doing This Again		MCA 41030
9/29/79	86	4	12 San Francisco Is A Lonely Town.....................		MCA 41100
			EDDIE NOACK		
			Born Armona A. Noack on 4/29/30 in Houston; died on 2/5/78. Recorded rockabilly under pseudonym "Tommy Wood".		
12/15/58	14	2	1 Have Blues Will Travel.................................		D 1019

DEBUT DATE	PEAK POS	WKS CHR	ARTIST — Record Title	POP POS	Label & Number
			NICK NOBLE		
			Born Nicholas Valkan on 6/21/36 in Chicago. Attended Loyola University. Pop singer.		
8/26/78	40	10	1 Stay With Me..		Churchill 7713
4/14/79	36	10	2 The Girls On The Other Side		TMS 601
9/22/79	72	5	3 I Wanna Go Back		TMS 612
2/09/80	35	10	4 Big Man's Cafe..		Churchill 7755
			NOEL		
			Noel Haughey.		
12/25/82	90	3	1 One Tear (At A Time)...................................		Deep South 706
10/05/85	86	3	2 P.S.		Mad Cash 1045
			NORMA JEAN ★★180★★		
			Born Norma Jean Beasler on 1/30/38 in Wellston, Oklahoma. Own show on KLPR-Oklahoma City by age 13. Worked on Red Foley's "Ozark Jubilee" TV series in 1958. On Porter Wagoner's TV series from 1960-67.		
1/04/64	11	19	1 Let's Go All The Way		RCA 8261
5/30/64	32	11	2 I'm A Walkin' Advertisement (For the Blues)/		
6/20/64	25	16	3 Put Your Arms Around Her.........................		RCA 8328
10/10/64	8	22	4 **Go Cat Go**	134	RCA 8433
4/10/65	21	8	5 I Cried All The Way To The Bank....................		RCA 8518
7/31/65	8	14	6 **I Wouldn't Buy A Used Car From Him**		RCA 8623
2/19/66	41	3	7 You're Driving Me Out Of My Mind/		
3/05/66	48	1	8 Then Go Home To Her...............................		RCA 8720
4/16/66	28	8	9 The Shirt		RCA 8790
8/13/66	28	11	10 Pursuing Happiness...................................		RCA 8887
10/15/66	5	17	11 **The Game Of Triangles**		RCA 8963
			BOBBY BARE, NORMA JEAN, LIZ ANDERSON		
11/19/66+	24	13	12 Don't Let That Doorknob Hit You....................		RCA 8989
4/01/67	48	10	13 Conscience Keep An Eye On Me		RCA 9147
8/19/67	38	10	14 Jackson Ain't A Very Big Town		RCA 9258
11/18/67+	18	14	15 Heaven Help The Poor Working Girl		RCA 9362
3/30/68	53	6	16 Truck Drivin' Woman.................................		RCA 9466
7/20/68	35	10	17 You Changed Everything About Me But My Name...		RCA 9558
11/30/68	61	5	18 One Man Band		RCA 9645
4/12/69	44	8	19 Dusty Road		RCA 0115
10/10/70	48	9	20 Whiskey-Six Years Old		RCA 9900
1/30/71	42	9	21 The Kind Of Needin' I Need		RCA 9946
2/06/82	68	6	22 Let's Go All The Way .... [R]		Granny 1009
			CLAUDE GRAY & NORMA JEAN new version of Norma's first solo hit		
			JIM NORMAN		
11/18/78	98	2	1 The Love In Me...		Republic 030
			BILL NUNLEY		
4/02/88	74	3	1 I'll Know The Good Times............................		Cannery 00402
8/27/88	98	2	2 The Way You Got Over Me		Cannery 00525
			EARL NUNN & BILLY LEE		
4/09/49	13	1	1 Double Talking Woman		Specialty 701
			Juke Box #13		
			MAYF NUTTER		
			Born in Clarksburg, West Virginia. Narrator for Walt Disney films. Actor in "The Waltons" and "Charlie's Angels" TV series.		
2/14/70	65	5	1 Hey There Johnny.....................................		Reprise 0882
10/16/71	57	6	2 Never Ending Song Of Love		Capitol 3181
			#13 pop hit for Delaney & Bonnie & Friends in 1971		
12/18/71+	58	7	3 Never Had A Doubt		Capitol 3226
4/15/72	59	7	4 The Sing-Along Song..................................		Capitol 3296
10/27/73	78	10	5 Green Door		Capitol 3734
			#1 pop hit for Jim Lowe in 1956		
5/08/76	87	5	6 Sweet Southern Lovin'		GNP Cres. 805
1/15/77	99	2	7 Goin' Skinny Dippin'................................ [N]		GNP Cres. 809

DEBUT DATE	PEAK POS	WKS CHR	ARTIST — Record Title	POP POS	Label & Number

O

THE OAK RIDGE BOYS ★★52★★

Groups roots go back to 1940 when they were a gospel quartet performing at a nuclear plant in Oak Ridge, Tennessee. Disbanded after World War II, then re-formed in 1957. Many personnel changes. Switched to country/pop style in the early 1970s. Current lineup: Duane Allen (b: 4/29/43, lead singer), Joe Bonsall (b: 5/18/48, tenor), Richard Sterban (b: 4/24/43, bass) and Steve Sanders, former guitarist with the group. All had previously sung in gospel groups. Longtime member Bill Golden (b: 1/12/35, baritone) left for solo career in 1987; replaced by Sanders.

DEBUT DATE	PEAK POS	WKS CHR	ARTIST — Record Title	POP POS	Label & Number
8/04/73	57	7	1 Praise The Lord And Pass The Soup		Columbia 45890
			JOHNNY CASH with THE CARTER FAMILY & THE OAK RIDGE BOYS		
6/26/76	83	5	2 Family Reunion		Columbia 10349
7/16/77	3	18	3 Y'All Come Back Saloon		ABC/Dot 17710
12/03/77+	2²	16	4 You're The One		ABC/Dot 17732
4/15/78	1¹	15	5 I'll Be True To You	102	ABC 12350
9/02/78	3	13	6 Cryin' Again	107	ABC 12397
12/09/78+	3	15	7 Come On In		ABC 12434
4/07/79	2²	13	8 Sail Away		MCA 12463
6/23/79	94	1	9 Rhythm Guitar		Columbia 11009
8/18/79	7	13	10 Dream On		MCA 41078
			#32 pop hit for The Righteous Brothers in 1974		
12/01/79+	1¹	15	11 Leaving Louisiana In The Broad Daylight		MCA 41154
4/19/80	1¹	15	12 Trying To Love Two Women		MCA 41217
7/19/80	3	16	13 Heart Of Mine	105	MCA 41280
11/15/80+	3	17	14 Beautiful You...		MCA 51022
4/04/81	1¹	14	15▲Elvira..	5	MCA 51084
9/05/81	1¹	15	16 Fancy Free...	104	MCA 51169
1/23/82	1¹	15	17 Bobbie Sue...	12	MCA 51231
6/05/82	22	10	18 So Fine...	76	MCA 52065
7/31/82	2²	19	19 I Wish You Could Have Turned My Head (And Left My Heart Alone)		MCA 52095
11/20/82+	3	16	20 Thank God For Kids		MCA 52145
2/26/83	1¹	16	21 American Made	72	MCA 52179
6/04/83	1¹	18	22 Love Song		MCA 52224
10/22/83+	5	19	23 Ozark Mountain Jubilee		MCA 52288
2/25/84	1¹	22	24 I Guess It Never Hurts To Hurt Sometimes		MCA 52342
7/14/84	1¹	21	25 Everyday		MCA 52419
11/10/84+	1¹	21	26 Make My Life With You		MCA 52488
3/30/85	1¹	20	27 Little Things..		MCA 52556
8/03/85	1¹	21	28 Touch A Hand, Make A Friend		MCA 52646
11/23/85+	3	19	29 Come On In (You Did The Best You Could Do) .		MCA 52722
3/22/86	15	15	30 Juliet...		MCA 52801
3/29/86	20	14	31 When You Get To The Heart.........................		MCA 52802
			BARBARA MANDRELL with the OAK RIDGE BOYS		
7/12/86	24	15	32 You Made A Rock Of A Rolling Stone...............		MCA 52873
2/21/87	1¹	24	33 It Takes A Little Rain (To Make Love Grow) ...		MCA 53010
6/13/87	1¹	23	34 This Crazy Love		MCA 53023
10/10/87	17	15	35 Time In		MCA 53175
2/27/88	5	22	36 True Heart		MCA 53272
7/30/88	1¹	21	37 Gonna Take A Lot Of River.........................		MCA 53381
12/03/88+	10	20	38 Bridges And Walls		MCA 53460

TOMMY O'DAY

Singer born in Fresno, California.

DEBUT DATE	PEAK POS	WKS CHR	ARTIST — Record Title	POP POS	Label & Number
1/28/78	96	3	1 Mr. Sandman		Nu-Trayl 916
			#1 pop hit for The Chordettes in 1954		
4/08/78	82	4	2 Memories Are Made Of This		Nu-Trayl 919
			#1 pop hit for Dean Martin in 1956		
8/12/78	97	2	3 When A Woman Cries		Nu-Trayl 923
12/23/78+	93	4	4 I Heard A Song Today		Nu-Trayl 926
5/05/79	89	2	5 Accentuate The Positive................................		Nu-Trayl 929
			#1 pop hit for Johnny Mercer in 1945		

DEBUT DATE	PEAK POS	WKS CHR	ARTIST — Record Title	POP POS	Label & Number
			TOMMY O'DAY — Continued		
7/14/79	99	2	6 Your Other Love		Nu-Trayl 930
			#54 pop hit for The Flamingos in 1961		
			DOYE O'DELL		
			Born Allen Doye O'Dell on 11/22/12 in Plainview, Texas. Worked with Uncle John Wills Band and the Sons Of The Pioneers. Own TV series, "Western Varieties".		
7/24/48	12	3	1 Dear Oakie...		Exclusive 33
			Juke Box #12 / Best Seller #13		
			KENNY O'DELL		
			Born Kenneth Gist, Jr. in Oklahoma (early 1940s). Singer/songwriter/guitarist. Moved to Nashville in 1969. Wrote Charlie Rich's "Behind Closed Doors". Worked with Duane Eddy and own band, Guys And Dolls.		
3/09/74	58	10	1 You Bet Your Sweet, Sweet Love......................		Capricorn 0038
1/18/75	18	13	2 Soulful Woman		Capricorn 0219
5/31/75	37	10	3 My Honky Tonk Ways	105	Capricorn 0233
7/08/78	9	14	4 **Let's Shake Hands And Come Out Lovin'**		Capricorn 0301
11/04/78+	12	15	5 As Long As I Can Wake Up In Your Arms		Capricorn 0309
3/10/79	32	10	6 Medicine Woman..		Capricorn 0317
			DONNA ODOM		
			Born in Ebbwvale, South Wales on 8/14/44.		
1/20/68	65	5	1 She Gets The Roses (I Get The Tears)..............		Decca 32214
			KAREN O'DONNAL - see DAVE DUDLEY		
			GAIL O'DOSKI		
			Male singer born and raised in Bartow, Florida.		
12/26/87+	73	4	1 First Came The Feelin'		Door Knob 288
5/28/88	77	4	2 (Just An) Old Wives' Tale		Door Knob 300
			JAMES O'GWYNN		
			Born on 1/26/28 in Winchester, Mississippi; raised in Hattiesburg, Mississippi. Worked on the Houston Jamboree from 1954-56 and the Louisiana Hayride from 1956-60. Moved to Nashville in 1961 and worked on the Grand Ole Opry for 2 years. Known as "The Smiling Irishman Of Country Music".		
10/20/58	16	3	1 Talk To Me Lonesome Heart...........................		D 1006
12/28/58	28	3	2 Blue Memories...		D 1022
4/27/59	13	4	3 How Can I Think Of Tomorrow		Mercury 71419
12/21/59+	26	4	4 Easy Money		Mercury 71513
2/20/61	21	6	5 House Of Blue Lovers...................................		Mercury 71731
4/21/62	7	10	6 **My Name Is Mud**		Mercury 71935
			THE O'KANES		
			Ohio-bred Jamie O'Hara and New Yorker Kieran Kane.		
9/20/86	10	25	1 **Oh Darlin'**..		Columbia 06242
2/07/87	1¹	22	2 **Can't Stop My Heart From Loving You**..........		Columbia 06606
6/27/87	9	18	3 **Daddies Need To Grow Up Too**		Columbia 07187
10/17/87+	5	25	4 **Just Lovin' You**..		Columbia 07611
3/05/88	4	20	5 **One True Love**..		Columbia 07736
7/09/88	10	20	6 **Blue Love**...		Columbia 07943
11/12/88	71	5	7 Rocky Road		Columbia 08099
			DANNY O'KEEFE		
			Singer/songwriter born in Spokane, Washington.		
10/28/72	63	6	1 Good Time Charlie's Got The Blues	9	Signpost 70006
			AUSTIN O'NEAL		
8/27/83	93	2	1 Nights Like Tonight......................................		Project One 002
			COLEMAN O'NEAL		
1/05/63	8	16	1 **Mr. Heartache, Move On**		Chancellor 108

225

DEBUT DATE	PEAK POS	WKS CHR		ARTIST — Record Title	POP POS	Label & Number
				ROY ORBISON		
				Born on 4/23/36 in Vernon, Texas. Had own band, the Wink Westerners in 1952. Attended North Texas University with Pat Boone. First recorded for Je-Wel in early 1956. Toured with Sun Records shows to 1958. Wife Claudette killed in a motorcycle accident on 6/7/66; two sons died in a fire, 1968. Member of the super group Traveling Wilburys in 1988. Died of a heart attack on 12/6/88 in Madison, Tennessee.		
6/28/80	6	15	1	**That Lovin' You Feelin' Again** .... ROY ORBISON & EMMYLOU HARRIS	55	Warner 49262
				from the film "Roadie"		
10/10/87	75	4	2	In Dreams.. [R]		Virgin 99434
				from the film "Blue Velvet"; remake of Roy's 1963 pop hit (POS 7)		
12/05/87+	42	13	3	Crying.. [R] ROY ORBISON/K.D. LANG		Virgin 99388
				from the film "Hiding Out"; remake of Roy's 1961 pop hit (POS 2)		
				JIMMY ARTHUR ORDGE		
				Performer from Donalda, Alberta, Canada.		
7/11/81	89	3	1	Stay Away From Jim		Dore 969
				DeWAYNE ORENDER		
				Nashville songwriter; co-wrote Leon Everette's "Midnight Rodeo".		
11/27/76	53	9	1	If You Want To Make Me Feel At Home		RCA 10813
4/23/77	87	3	2	To Make A Good Love Die.............................		RCA 10936
8/27/77	97	2	3	Love Me Into Heaven Again...........................		RCA 11039
5/06/78	51	7	4	Brother..		Nu-Trayl 920
12/23/78+	92	4	5	Better Than Now.......................................		Volunteer 102
				written by Phil Everly of The Everly Brothers		
				ORIGINAL TEXAS PLAYBOYS		
				Veterans of Bob Wills' longtime band, the Texas Playboys.		
4/02/77	94	3	1	Gambling Polka Dot Blues		Capitol 4401
				ORION		
				Masked Elvis Presley impersonator. Real name: Jimmy Ellis. Born in 1945 in Orrville, Alabama. First recorded for Dradco in 1964. Signed by Shelby Singleton to Sun Records in 1978. Donned the mask in 1979 and performed with it for 5 years. Also see Jerry Lee Lewis.		
6/23/79	89	6	1	Ebony Eyes/		
				#8 pop hit for The Everly Brothers in 1961		
		6	2	Honey		Sun 1142
				#1 pop hit for Bobby Goldsboro in 1968		
4/26/80	69	5	3	A Stranger In My Place		Sun 1152
7/19/80	68	6	4	Texas Tea..		Sun 1153
10/11/80	65	9	5	Am I That Easy To Forget............................		Sun 1156
				#18 pop hit for Engelbert Humperdinck in 1968		
1/10/81	63	6	6	Rockabilly Rebel.......................................		Sun 1159
3/21/81	79	4	7	Crazy Little Thing Called Love		Sun 1162
				#1 pop hit for Queen in 1980		
6/27/81	76	5	8	Born		Sun 1165
12/12/81	83	4	9	Some You Win, Some You Lose.......................		Sun 1170
7/10/82	69	6	10	Morning, Noon And Night/		Sun 1175
7/10/82	70	4	11	Honky Tonk Heaven		
				ORLEANS		
				Rock group founded in New York City by John Hall.		
11/15/86	59	6	1	You're Mine		MCA 52963
				GILBERT ORTEGA		
				Born in Gallup, New Mexico. Owner of a chain of Indian jewelry stores.		
1/28/78	91	3	1	Is It Wrong..		LRJ 1050
5/20/78	93	4	2	I Don't Believe I'll Fall In Love Today		Ortega 1051
				ORVILLE & IVY		
				West coast session steel guitar legend Wesley Webb "Speedy" West and Ivy "Jimmy" Bryant, west coast session guitar legend; died on 9/22/80.		
4/01/67	73	2	1	Shinbone .... [I]		Imperial 66219

DEBUT DATE	PEAK POS	WKS CHR	ARTIST — Record Title	POP POS	Label & Number
			OSBORNE BROTHERS		
			Originally a bluegrass duo from Hyden, Kentucky, consisting of brothers Bobby Van (b: 12/7/31, mandolin) and Sonny Osborne (b: 10/29/37, banjo). On WROL-Knoxville in 1953. Recorded with Jimmy Martin in the mid-50s. On Wheeling Jamboree from 1956-59. Benny Birchfield (banjo) was added in 1959. Member of the Grand Ole Opry since 1964. Birchfield was later replaced by Ronnie Reno, then Dale Sledd, Jim Brock, and Bob's son, Bobby.		
3/24/58	13	2	1 Once More		MGM 12583
			OSBORNE BROTHERS & RED ALLEN Jockey #13		
3/12/66	41	4	2 Up This Hill And Down..............................		Decca 31886
12/17/66+	33	10	3 The Kind Of Woman I Got..........................		Decca 32052
7/22/67	66	3	4 Roll Muddy River		Decca 32137
2/03/68	33	10	5 Rocky Top		Decca 32242
6/15/68	60	7	6 Cut The Cornbread, Mama		Decca 32325
10/19/68	58	6	7 Son Of A Sawmill Man...............................		Decca 32382
8/09/69	28	11	8 Tennessee Hound Dog................................		Decca 32516
1/17/70	58	6	9 Ruby, Are You Mad		Decca 32598
12/05/70	69	2	10 My Old Kentucky Home (Turpentine And Dandelion Wine)		Decca 32746
3/13/71	37	10	11 Georgia Pineywoods		Decca 32794
9/11/71	62	7	12 Muddy Bottom...		Decca 32864
1/06/73	74	2	13 Midnight Flyer...		Decca 33028
4/28/73	66	2	14 Lizzie Lou		MCA 40028
9/01/73	64	6	15 Blue Heartache..		MCA 40113
1/31/76	86	4	16 Don't Let Smokey Mountain Smoke Get In Your Eyes..		MCA 40509
10/13/79	95	3	17 Shackles And Chains		CMH 1522
			OSBORNE BROS. & MAC WISEMAN		
4/26/80	75	5	18 I Can Hear Kentucky Calling Me		CMH 1524
			JIMMIE OSBORNE		
			Born on 4/8/23 in Winchester, Kentucky; committed suicide died on 12/26/57. Made appearances on the Louisiana Hayride, Grand Ole Opry, and the National Barn Dance.		
7/10/48	10	2	1 **My Heart Echoes**		King 715
			Juke Box #10		
6/25/49	7	6	2 **The Death Of Little Kathy Fiscus**.................		King 788
			Best Seller #7		
10/07/50	9	3	3 **God, Please Protect America**.........................		King 893
			Jockey #9		
			CATHY O'SHEA		
			Born Catherine Herbsleb on 7/20/41 in Kansas City, Missouri.		
8/26/78	94	4	1 Roses Ain't Red		MCA 40934
			SHAD O'SHEA & THE 18 WHEELERS		
3/27/76	85	3	1 Colorado Call .... [N]	*110*	Private S. 45071
			K.T. OSLIN		
			Singer/songwriter Kay Toinette Oslin was born in Crossitt, Arkansas and raised in Mobile, Alabama. Vocalist and actress. In folk trio with Guy Clark and David Jones in Houston in the mid-60s. Teamed with Frank Davis. Appeared in the musicals "Hello Dolly", "West Side Story" and "Promises Promises". Made commercials in New York City. Moved to Nashville in 1985.		
5/16/81	72	4	1 Clean Your Own Tables		Elektra 47132
			shown as: **KAY T. OSLIN**		
1/10/87	40	15	2 Wall Of Tears		RCA 5066
4/25/87	7	22	3 **80's Ladies**...		RCA 5154
9/12/87	1¹	25	4 **Do Ya'**		RCA 5239
1/30/88	1¹	21	5 **I'll Always Come Back**...............................		RCA 5330
7/09/88	13	15	6 **Money**..		RCA 8388
10/15/88+	1¹	20	7 **Hold Me**...		RCA 8725
			THE OSMOND BROTHERS		
			Family group from Ogden, Utah: Alan (b: 6/22/49), Wayne (b: 8/28/51), Merrill (b: 4/30/53) and Jay (b: 3/2/55). Began as a quartet in 1959, singing religious and barbershop-quartet songs. Regulars on Andy Williams' TV show from 1962-67.		
			THE OSMONDS		
5/01/82	17	15	1 I Think About Your Lovin'		Elektra 47438

DEBUT DATE	PEAK POS	WKS CHR	ARTIST — Record Title	POP POS	Label & Number
			THE OSMOND BROTHERS — Continued		
			THE OSMOND BROTHERS:		
9/04/82	28	12	2 It's Like Falling In Love (Over And Over)		Elektra 69969
12/25/82+	43	10	3 Never Ending Song Of Love		Elektra 69883
			#13 pop hit for Delaney & Bonnie & Friends in 1971		
6/11/83	67	8	4 She's Ready For Someone To Love Her		Warner 29594
1/21/84	43	11	5 Where Does An Angel Go When She Cries		Warner 29387
5/05/84	39	12	6 If Every Man Had A Woman Like You		Warner 29312
6/08/85	54	9	7 Any Time		Warner 28982
			THE OSMOND BROS.:		
12/14/85+	56	11	8 Baby When Your Heart Breaks Down...............		EMI America 8298
3/15/86	45	13	9 Baby Wants		EMI America 8313
6/21/86	69	5	10 You Look Like The One I Love		EMI America 8325
11/01/86	70	7	11 Looking For Suzanne.............................		EMI America 8360
			MARIE OSMOND ★★183★★		
			Born Olive Marie Osmond on 10/13/59 in Ogden, Utah. Began performing in concert with her brothers at age 14. Co-hosted the TV series "Ripley's Believe It Or Not", and starred with brother Donny in their musical/variety TV series from 1976-78.		
9/08/73	1²	16	1●Paper Roses	5	MGM 14609
7/27/74	17	13	2●I'm Leaving It (All) Up To You	4	MGM 14735
			DONNY & MARIE OSMOND		
8/10/74	33	11	3 In My Little Corner Of The World	102	MGM 14694
3/01/75	29	10	4 Who's Sorry Now..................................	40	MGM 14786
6/21/75	71	6	5 Make The World Go Away...........................	44	MGM 14807
			DONNY & MARIE OSMOND		
8/07/76	85	4	6 "A" My Name Is Alice..............................		Polydor 14333
3/20/82	74	6	7 I've Got A Bad Case Of You........................		Elektra 47430
8/14/82	58	7	8 Back To Believing Again		Elektra 69995
3/24/84	82	4	9 Who's Counting		RCA 13680
2/09/85	54	8	10 Until I Fall In Love Again		Capitol 5445
7/06/85	1¹	23	11 Meet Me In Montana................................		Capitol 5478
			MARIE OSMOND with DAN SEALS		
11/09/85+	1¹	21	12 There's No Stopping Your Heart		Capitol 5521
3/29/86	4	21	13 Read My Lips		Capitol 5563
8/30/86	1¹	21	14 You're Still New To Me............................		Capitol 5613
			MARIE OSMOND with PAUL DAVIS		
12/27/86+	14	18	15 I Only Wanted You		Capitol 5663
4/11/87	24	13	16 Everybody's Crazy 'Bout My Baby....................		Capitol 5703
7/25/87	50	12	17 Cry Just A Little................................		Capitol 44044
5/28/88	50	10	18 Without A Trace		Capitol 44176
8/20/88	47	8	19 Sweet Life.....................................		Capitol 44215
			MARIE OSMOND with PAUL DAVIS		
			re-make of Paul's 1978 solo pop hit (POS 17)		
12/17/88+	59	8	20 I'm In Love And He's In Dallas		Capitol 44269
			PAUL OTT		
			Born Paul Ott Carruth, Sr. on 9/25/34 in McComb, Mississippi. Cousin of Hall of Fame baseball star Mel Ott. Son, Paul, is a running back with the Green Bay Packers.		
6/30/79	87	2	1 A Salute To The Duke............................ [S]		Elektra 46066
			a tribute to actor John Wayne		
			PAUL OVERSTREET		
			Singer/songwriter from VanCleave, Mississippi. Wrote "Same Ole Me" for George Jones and "Long Line Of Of Love" for Michael Martin Murphey. Part of Schuyler, Knobloch & Overstreet (SKO). Went solo, 1987. Briefly married to Dolly Parton's sister, Freida.		
5/08/82	76	5	1 Beautiful Baby		RCA 13042
11/21/87+	1¹	24	2 I Won't Take Less Than Your Love		Capitol 44100
			TANYA TUCKER with PAUL DAVIS & PAUL OVERSTREET		
9/24/88	3	21	3 Love Helps Those................................		MTM 72113
			TOMMY OVERSTREET ★★102★★		
			Born on 9/10/37 in Oklahoma City. On TV in Houston in the early 60s. Worked with Slim Willet in the mid-60s; own band thereafter. Managed the Nashville office of Dot Records from 1967.		
10/11/69	73	2	1 Rocking A Memory (That Won't Go To Sleep)		Dot 17281
12/12/70+	56	7	2 If You're Looking For A Fool........................		Dot 17357
4/24/71	5	16	3 Gwen (Congratulations)	123	Dot 17375

DEBUT DATE	PEAK POS	WKS CHR	ARTIST — Record Title	POP POS	Label & Number
			TOMMY OVERSTREET — Continued		
8/14/71	**5**	16	4 **I Don't Know You (Anymore)**		Dot 17387
1/01/72	**2**¹	16	5 **Ann (Don't Go Runnin')**		Dot 17402
5/20/72	**16**	14	6 A Seed Before The Rose		Dot 17418
9/23/72	**3**	18	7 **Heaven Is My Woman's Love**	*102*	Dot 17428
4/21/73	**7**	15	8 **Send Me No Roses**		Dot 17455
9/15/73	**7**	17	9 **I'll Never Break These Chains**		Dot 17474
2/16/74	**3**	16	10 **(Jeannie Marie) You Were A Lady**		Dot 17493
7/27/74	**8**	16	11 **If I Miss You Again Tonight**		Dot 17515
12/14/74+	**9**	14	12 **I'm A Believer**		Dot 17533
5/10/75	**6**	16	13 **That's When My Woman Begins**		ABC/Dot 17552
10/11/75	**16**	12	14 From Woman To Woman		ABC/Dot 17580
6/12/76	**15**	13	15 Here Comes That Girl Again		ABC/Dot 17630
10/02/76	**29**	11	16 Young Girl		ABC/Dot 17657
			#2 pop hit for Gary Puckett & The Union Gap in 1968		
12/25/76+	**11**	15	17 If Love Was A Bottle Of Wine		ABC/Dot 17672
5/07/77	**5**	14	18 **Don't Go City Girl On Me**		ABC/Dot 17697
9/17/77	**20**	12	19 This Time I'm In It For The Love		ABC/Dot 17721
1/21/78	**12**	12	20 Yes Ma'am		ABC/Dot 17737
6/10/78	**20**	12	21 Better Me		ABC 12367
9/30/78	**11**	12	22 Fadin' In, Fadin' Out		ABC 12408
1/27/79	**91**	3	23 Tears (There's Nowhere Else To Hide)		Tina 523
			with The Nashville Express		
3/03/79	**45**	7	24 Cheater's Kit		ABC 12456
5/05/79	**27**	11	25 I'll Never Let You Down		Elektra 46023
8/25/79	**23**	10	26 What More Could A Man Need		Elektra 46516
11/17/79+	**36**	11	27 Fadin' Renegade		Elektra 46564
3/22/80	**41**	9	28 Down In The Quarter		Elektra 46600
6/28/80	**47**	7	29 Sue...		Elektra 46658
10/04/80	**72**	5	30 Me And The Boys In The Band..................		Elektra 47041
7/30/83	**69**	7	31 Dream Maker		AMI 1314
12/03/83	**84**	3	32 Heart Of Dixie		AMI 1317
5/19/84	**87**	3	33 I Still Love Your Body		Gervasi 665
6/28/86	**74**	5	34 Next To You..................................		Silver D. 70002
			OWEN BROTHERS		
12/25/82	**95**	3	1 Nights Out At The Days End....................		Audiograph 445
9/17/83	**86**	3	2 Southern Women		Audiograph 470
			JIM OWEN		
			Singer/composer from Franklin, Tennessee. Wrote "Louisiana Woman, Mississippi Man" for Conway Twitty and Loretta Lynn. Also see The Drifting Cowboys.		
11/29/80	**82**	4	1 Ten Anniversary Presents .... [S]		Sun 1157
1/30/82	**82**	3	2 Hell Yes, I Cheated		Sun 1171
			A.L. "DOODLE" OWENS		
			Prolific songwriter. Co-writer of many hits for Charley Pride and George Jones.		
1/14/78	**78**	4	1 Honky Tonk Toys..............................		Raindrop 010
			BONNIE OWENS		
			Born Bonnie Campbell on 10/1/32 in Blanchard, Oklahoma. Worked clubs in Arizona, then joined Buck Owens in Mac's Skillet Lickers in Mesa, Arizona, 1946. Married to Buck in 1946. Married to Merle Haggard in 1965. Mother of Buddy Alan.		
6/22/63	**25**	1	1 Why Don't Daddy Live Here Anymore		Tally 149
4/04/64	**27**	6	2 Don't Take Advantage Of Me		Tally 156
9/12/64	**28**	26	3 Just Between The Two Of Us...................		Tally 181
			MERLE HAGGARD & BONNIE OWENS		
9/18/65	**41**	4	4 Number One Heel		Capitol 5459
11/19/66	**69**	4	5 Consider The Children		Capitol 5755
2/15/69	**68**	4	6 Lead Me On...................................		Capitol 2340

DEBUT DATE	PEAK POS	WKS CHR		ARTIST — Record Title	POP POS	Label & Number
				BUCK OWENS ★★12★★		
				Born Alvis Edgar Owens on 8/12/29 in Sherman, Texas; raised in Mesa, Arizona. On the Buck & Britt show, KTYL-Mesa, in 1946. Married Bonnie Campbell in 1946. Moved to Bakersfield in 1951. Formed his own band, the Schoolhouse Playboys, and played saxophone and trumpet. Did session work with Wanda Jackson, Sonny James and Faron Young. Played lead guitar with Tommy Collins in the mid-50s. First recorded for Pep in 1955 as Corky Jones. Co-host of "Hee-Haw" TV series from 1969 until 1986. Also see The Buckaroos.		
5/04/59	**24**	2	1	Second Fiddle...		Capitol 4172
10/05/59	**4**	22	2	**Under Your Spell Again**...............................		Capitol 4245
3/07/60	**3**	30	3	**Above And Beyond**.....................................		Capitol 4337
9/19/60	**2**³	24	4	**Excuse Me (I Think I've Got A Heartache)/**		
10/24/60	**25**	3	5	I've Got A Right To Know		Capitol 4412
1/30/61	**2**⁸	26	6	**Foolin' Around/**	113	
3/27/61	**27**	1	7	High As The Mountains		Capitol 4496
8/07/61	**2**¹	24	8	**Under The Influence Of Love**...........................		Capitol 4602
2/24/62	**11**	16	9	Nobody's Fool But Yours		Capitol 4679
7/28/62	**11**	11	10	Save The Last Dance For Me		Capitol 4765
10/27/62	**8**	8	11	**Kickin' Our Hearts Around/**		
10/27/62	**17**	5	12	I Can't Stop (My Lovin' You)........................		Capitol 4826
12/29/62+	**10**	14	13	**You're For Me/**		
1/05/63	**24**	3	14	House Down The Block		Capitol 4872
4/13/63	**1**⁴	28	15	**Act Naturally**...		Capitol 4937
				#47 pop hit for The Beatles (Ringo Starr) in 1965		
9/21/63	**1**¹⁶	30	16	**Love's Gonna Live Here**...............................		Capitol 5025
3/28/64	**1**⁷	26	17	**My Heart Skips A Beat/**	94	
4/04/64	**1**²	27	18	**Together Again**		Capitol 5136
8/29/64	**1**⁶	27	19	**I Don't Care (Just as Long as You Love Me)/**	92	
10/10/64	**33**	9	20	Don't Let Her Know.................................	130	Capitol 5240
1/23/65	**1**⁵	20	21	**I've Got A Tiger By The Tail**........................	25	Capitol 5336
5/15/65	**1**⁶	20	22	**Before You Go**	83	Capitol 5410
7/31/65	**1**¹	19	23	**Only You (Can Break My Heart)/**	120	
7/31/65	**10**	14	24	**Gonna Have Love**...................................		Capitol 5465
				BUCK OWENS & THE BUCKAROOS:		
10/30/65	**1**²	17	25	**Buckaroo/** [I]	60	
12/11/65+	**24**	9	26	If You Want A Love		Capitol 5517
1/22/66	**1**⁷	19	27	**Waitin' In Your Welfare Line/**	57	
2/26/66	**43**	2	28	In The Palm Of Your Hand		Capitol 5566
5/21/66	**1**⁶	21	29	**Think Of Me**..	74	Capitol 5647
9/03/66	**1**⁴	20	30	**Open Up Your Heart**.................................		Capitol 5705
1/14/67	**1**⁴	16	31	**Where Does The Good Times Go**	114	Capitol 5811
4/01/67	**1**³	16	32	**Sam's Place**	92	Capitol 5865
7/15/67	**1**¹	16	33	**Your Tender Loving Care**		Capitol 5942
10/14/67+	**2**¹	18	34	**It Takes People Like You (To Make People Like Me)**	114	Capitol 2001
1/27/68	**1**¹	15	35	**How Long Will My Baby Be Gone**		Capitol 2080
4/20/68	**2**¹	15	36	**Sweet Rosie Jones**		Capitol 2142
10/26/68	**5**	15	37	**I've Got You On My Mind Again**		Capitol 2300
2/01/69	**1**²	15	38	**Who's Gonna Mow Your Grass**......................	106	Capitol 2377
5/24/69	**1**²	15	39	**Johnny B. Goode**....................................	114	Capitol 2485
				#8 pop hit for Chuck Berry in 1958		
8/09/69	**1**¹	15	40	**Tall Dark Stranger**		Capitol 2570
11/15/69	**5**	13	41	**Big In Vegas**	100	Capitol 2646
6/06/70	**2**²	15	42	**The Kansas City Song**		Capitol 2783
11/07/70	**9**	13	43	**I Wouldn't Live In New York City (If They Gave Me The Whole Dang Town)**.............	110	Capitol 2947
2/06/71	**9**	13	44	**Bridge Over Troubled Water**	119	Capitol 3023
				#1 pop hit for Simon & Garfunkel in 1970		
5/01/71	**3**	17	45	**Ruby (Are You Mad)**	106	Capitol 3096
9/04/71	**2**²	14	46	**Rollin' In My Sweet Baby's Arms**..................		Capitol 3164
2/12/72	**8**	12	47	**I'll Still Be Waiting For You**		Capitol 3262
4/29/72	**1**¹	15	48	**Made In Japan**		Capitol 3314

DEBUT DATE	PEAK POS	WKS CHR		ARTIST — Record Title	POP POS	Label & Number
				BUCK OWENS — Continued		
9/16/72	**13**	14	49	You Ain't Gonna Have Ol' Buck To Kick Around No More		Capitol 3429
12/30/72+	**23**	10	50	In The Palm Of Your Hand .... [R]		Capitol 3504
3/31/73	**14**	11	51	Ain't It Amazing, Gracie..............................		Capitol 3563
				BUCK OWENS:		
8/18/73	**27**	11	52	Arms Full Of Empty..		Capitol 3688
12/01/73+	**8**	12	53	**Big Game Hunter**......................................		Capitol 3769
3/23/74	**9**	13	54	**On The Cover Of The Music City News** .... take-off on Dr. Hook's "Cover Of 'Rolling Stone'"		Capitol 3841
7/20/74	**6**	13	55	**(It's A) Monsters' Holiday**		Capitol 3907
11/30/74+	**8**	15	56	**Great Expectations**....................................		Capitol 3976
3/29/75	**19**	11	57	41st Street Lonely Hearts' Club/		
		7	58	Weekend Daddy		Capitol 4043
10/04/75	**51**	7	59	The Battle Of New Orleans		Capitol 4138
6/26/76	**44**	9	60	Hollywood Waltz		Warner 8223
9/25/76	**43**	8	61	California Okie		Warner 8255
2/26/77	**90**	4	62	World Famous Holiday Inn		Warner 8316
7/16/77	**100**	1	63	It's Been A Long, Long Time		Warner 8395
9/10/77	**91**	3	64	Our Old Mansion		Warner 8433
8/19/78	**27**	12	65	Nights Are Forever Without You .... #10 pop hit for England Dan & John Ford Coley in 1976		Warner 8614
12/23/78+	**80**	5	66	Do You Wanna Make Love .... #5 pop hit for Peter McCann in 1977		Warner 8701
9/08/79	**30**	10	67	Hangin' In And Hangin' On		Warner 49046
12/15/79+	**22**	13	68	Let Jesse Rob The Train		Warner 49118
4/05/80	**42**	9	69	Love Is A Warm Cowboy..............................		Warner 49200
7/26/80	**72**	4	70	Moonlight And Magnolia		Warner 49278
5/30/81	**92**	2	71	Without You..		Warner 49651
10/22/88	**46**	9	72	Hot Dog... recorded by Buck under the name "Corky Jones" in 1956		Capitol 44248
				BUCK OWENS DUOS with:		
				BUDDY ALAN:		
7/27/68	**7**	15	73	**Let The World Keep On A Turnin'**		Capitol 2237
12/04/71+	**29**	10	74	Too Old To Cut The Mustard		Capitol 3215
				EMMYLOU HARRIS:		
5/12/79	**11**	13	75	Play Together Again Again		Warner 8830
				ROSE MADDOX:		
5/15/61	**8**	12	76	**Mental Cruelty/**		
5/22/61	**4**	14	77	**Loose Talk**...		Capitol 4550
8/03/63	**15**	6	78	We're The Talk Of The Town/		
8/10/63	**19**	6	79	Sweethearts In Heaven................................		Capitol 4992
				SUSAN RAYE:		
2/21/70	**13**	11	80	We're Gonna Get Together		Capitol 2731
5/09/70	**12**	12	81	Togetherness..		Capitol 2791
8/29/70	**8**	13	82	**The Great White Horse**............................		Capitol 2871
7/15/72	**13**	14	83	Looking Back To See		Capitol 3368
6/16/73	**35**	8	84	The Good Old Days (Are Here Again)................		Capitol 3601
7/05/75	**20**	13	85	Love Is Strange.. #11 pop hit for Mickey & Sylvia in 1957		Capitol 4100
				DWIGHT YOAKAM:		
7/16/88	**1**[1]	18	86	**Streets Of Bakersfield**............................		Reprise 27964
				MARIE OWENS		
2/23/74	**44**	9	1	J. John Jones		MCA 40184
6/08/74	**71**	8	2	Release Me .... #4 pop hit for Engelbert Humperdinck in 1967		MCA 40241
11/16/74	**71**	7	3	I Want To Lay Down Beside You		MCA 40308
10/25/75	**84**	4	4	Someone Loves You Honey		4 Star 1019
2/12/77	**92**	4	5	When Your Good Love Was Mine....................		MMI 1012
5/07/77	**88**	4	6	Burning..		MMI 1015
8/13/77	**80**	5	7	Ease My Mind On You		Sing Me 12

VERNON OXFORD

Born on 6/8/41 near Rogers, Arkansas; raised in Wichita, Kansas. His father was a champion fiddler. Own band in the late 50s.

DEBUT DATE	PEAK POS	WKS CHR	#	ARTIST — Record Title	POP POS	Label & Number
12/06/75+	54	12	1	Shadows Of My Mind		RCA 10442
4/03/76	83	6	2	Your Wanting Me Is Gone		RCA 10595
6/12/76	17	12	3	Redneck! (The Redneck National Anthem)		RCA 10693
10/16/76	60	7	4	Clean Your Own Tables		RCA 10787
1/29/77	55	6	5	A Good Old Fashioned Saturday Night Honky Tonk Barroom Brawl		RCA 10872
5/07/77	87	3	6	Only The Shadows Know		RCA 10952
7/23/77	95	2	7	Redneck Roots		RCA 11020

THE OZARK MOUNTAIN DAREDEVILS

Country-rock group from Springfield, Missouri, led by Larry Lee.

			#			
5/08/76	84	4	1	You Made It Right		A&M 1809

P

PACIFIC STEEL CO. Featuring JAY DEE MANESS

Steel guitar instrumental band. Maness was the steel player on the Byrds' "Sweetheart of the Rodeo" LP in 1968.

			#			
12/06/80	88	5	1	Fat 'N Sassy ... [I]		Pacific Arts 111

BOB PACK

			#			
7/23/88	74	4	1	The Request		Oak 1051

PATTI PAGE

Born Clara Ann Fowler on 11/8/27 in Muskogee, Oklahoma. One of eleven children. Raised in Tulsa. On radio KTUL with Al Klauser & His Oklahomans, as "Ann Fowler", late 40s. Another singer was billed as "Patti Page" for the Page Milk Company show on KTUL. When she left, Fowler took her place and name. With the Jimmy Joy band in 1947. On "Breakfast Club", Chicago radio, 1947; signed by Mercury Records. Used multi-voice effect on records from 1947. Own TV series "The Patti Page Show", 1955-58, and "The Big Record", 1957-58. In the 1960 film "Elmer Gantry".

DEBUT DATE	PEAK POS	WKS CHR	#	ARTIST — Record Title	POP POS	Label & Number
5/07/49	15	1	1	Money, Marbles And Chalk Juke Box #15	27	Mercury 5251
1/06/51	2³	12	2●	The Tennessee Waltz Juke Box #2 / Best Seller #5 / Jockey #5	1	Mercury 5534
7/17/61	21	3	3	Mom And Dad's Waltz	58	Mercury 71823
2/17/62	13	15	4	Go On Home	42	Mercury 71906
5/30/70	22	10	5	I Wish I Had A Mommy Like You	114	Columbia 45159
1/16/71	24	10	6	Give Him Love		Mercury 73162
5/08/71	37	8	7	Make Me Your Kind Of Woman		Mercury 73199
8/14/71	63	4	8	I'd Rather Be Sorry		Mercury 73222
11/20/71	38	9	9	Think Again/		
		3	10	A Woman Left Lonely		Mercury 73249
12/16/72+	14	12	11	Hello We're Lonely PATTI PAGE & TOM T. HALL		Mercury 73347
9/08/73	42	11	12	I Can't Sit Still		Epic 11032
12/29/73+	29	11	13	You're Gonna Hurt Me (One More Time)		Epic 11072
5/18/74	59	7	14	Someone Came To See Me (In The Middle Of The Night)		Epic 11109
11/30/74+	70	7	15	I May Not Be Lovin' You		Avco 603
7/26/75	67	7	16	Less Than The Song		Avco 613
3/21/81	39	8	17	No Aces		Plantation 197
8/01/81	66	4	18	A Poor Man's Roses/ [R] new version of Patti's #14 pop hit in 1957		
7/18/81	76	2	19	On The Inside from the TV show "Prisoner Of Cell Block H"		Plantation 201
5/08/82	80	4	20	My Man Friday		Plantation 208

PAPA JOE'S MUSIC BOX

Featuring session pianist, Jerry Smith.

			#			
12/20/69	62	3	1	Papa Joe's Thing ... [I]		ABC 11246

JACK PARIS

			#			
2/14/76	94	3	1	It Sets Me Free		2-J 201

DEBUT DATE	PEAK POS	WKS CHR	ARTIST — Record Title	POP POS	Label & Number
			JACK PARIS — Continued		
3/19/77	98	2	2 Gypsy River		50 States 49
12/10/77+	75	7	3 Mississippi		50 States 57
			#32 pop hit for John Phillips in 1970		
3/04/78	86	4	4 Lay Down Sally..............................		50 States 58
			#3 pop hit for Eric Clapton in 1978		
8/19/78	98	3	5 (It's Gonna Be A) Happy Day		50 States 62
			BILLY PARKER		
			Born in Okemah, Oklahoma; raised in Tulsa. Worked with Ernest Tubb, then became one of the top country disc jockeys on KVOO-Tulsa.		
9/18/76	79	8	1 It's Bad When You're Caught (With The Goods)...		SCR 133
1/22/77	71	8	2 Lord, If I Make It To Heaven "Can I Bring My Own Angel Along"..................................		SCR 136
6/04/77	75	6	3 What Did I Promise Her Last Night		SCR 144
10/01/77	94	3	4 If You Got To Have It Your Way (I'll Go Mine).....		SCR 148
1/07/78	62	9	5 You Read Between The Lines		SCR 153
4/29/78	81	4	6 If There's One Angel Missing (She's Here In My Arms Tonight)..................................		SCR 157
8/26/78	50	7	7 Until The Next Time		SCR 160
12/23/78+	73	6	8 Pleasin' My Woman/		
3/10/79	98	1	9 Thanks E.T. Thanks A Lot...........................		SCR 162
8/11/79	80	4	10 Thanks A Lot		SCR 177
12/22/79+	82	6	11 Tough Act To Follow		SCR 181
2/14/81	74	3	12 Better Side Of Thirty		Oak 47565
8/22/81	53	7	13 I'll Drink To That		Soundwaves 4643
1/09/82	51	10	14 I See An Angel Every Day		Soundwaves 4659
5/01/82	41	11	15 (Who's Gonna Sing) The Last Country Song		Soundwaves 4670
7/31/82	53	8	16 If I Ever Need A Lady		Soundwaves 4678
			above 2: harmony vocals by Darrell McCall		
10/30/82	68	6	17 Too Many Irons In The Fire......................		Soundwaves 4686
			BILLY PARKER & CAL SMITH		
3/26/83	68	6	18 Who Said Love Was Fair..........................		Soundwaves 4699
7/09/83	59	8	19 Love Don't Know A Lady (From A Honky Tonk Girl)		Soundwaves 4708
2/13/88	72	5	20 You Are My Angel		Canyon Cr. 1208
10/22/88	81	4	21 She's Sittin' Pretty		Canyon Cr. 0801
			LORI PARKER		
11/13/76	92	3	1 Steppin' Out Tonight.............................		Con Brio 113
9/03/77	89	4	2 I Like Everything About Loving You		Con Brio 122
			MICHAEL PARKS		
			Portrayed Jim Bronson on TV's "Then Came Bronson".		
3/21/70	41	9	1 Long Lonesome Highway	*20*	MGM 14104
			from the TV series "Then Came Bronson"		
			P.J. PARKS		
1/10/81	86	4	1 The Way You Are..................................		Kik 901
4/04/81	85	3	2 Falling In......................................		Kik 903
			ROB PARSONS		
			Songwriter turned singer from Traverse City, Michigan.		
1/09/82	74	4	1 Shadow Of Love		MCA 51202
			DOLLY PARTON ★★10★★		
			Born on 1/19/46 in Sevier County, Tennessee. Worked on Knoxville radio show at age 11. First recorded for Gold Band in 1957. To Nashville in 1964. Replaced Norma Jean on the Porter Wagoner TV show, 1967-74. Joined the Grand Ole Opry in 1969. Starred in the films "Nine To Five", "The Best Little Whorehouse In Texas" and "Rhinestone". Hosted own TV variety show in 1987. CMA award: Entertainer of the Year - 1978.		
1/21/67	24	14	1 Dumb Blonde		Monument 982
6/10/67	17	12	2 Something Fishy		Monument 1007
6/29/68	17	14	3 Just Because I'm A Woman		RCA 9548
11/16/68	25	11	4 In The Good Old Days (When Times Were Bad) ...		RCA 9657
4/12/69	40	10	5 Daddy		RCA 0132
7/26/69	50	8	6 In The Ghetto		RCA 0192
10/18/69	45	8	7 My Blue Ridge Mountain Boy.........................		RCA 0243

DEBUT DATE	PEAK POS	WKS CHR		ARTIST — Record Title	POP POS	Label & Number
				DOLLY PARTON — Continued		
1/31/70	40	8	8	Daddy Come And Get Me		RCA 9784
7/04/70	3	16	9	**Mule Skinner Blues (Blue Yodel No. 8)**...........		RCA 9863
				#5 pop hit for The Fendermen in 1960		
12/12/70+	1¹	15	10	**Joshua**	108	RCA 9928
4/10/71	23	12	11	Comin' For To Carry Me Home....................		RCA 9971
				based on the American spiritual "Swing Low, Sweet Chariot"		
7/17/71	17	12	12	My Blue Tears		RCA 9999
10/30/71	4	16	13	**Coat Of Many Colors**		RCA 0538
3/11/72	6	14	14	**Touch Your Woman**..............................		RCA 0662
8/12/72	20	9	15	Washday Blues		RCA 0757
1/06/73	15	13	16	My Tennessee Mountain Home....................		RCA 0868
5/19/73	20	11	17	Traveling Man		RCA 0950
11/03/73+	1¹	19	18	**Jolene**	60	RCA 0145
4/06/74	1¹	15	19	**I Will Always Love You**..........................		RCA 0234
8/31/74	1¹	17	20	**Love Is Like A Butterfly**	105	RCA 10031
1/25/75	1¹	13	21	**The Bargain Store**		RCA 10164
6/07/75	2²	16	22	**The Seeker**	105	RCA 10310
9/27/75	9	14	23	**We Used To**		RCA 10396
2/28/76	19	11	24	Hey, Lucky Lady		RCA 10564
7/31/76	3	15	25	**All I Can Do**		RCA 10730
4/09/77	11	13	26	Light Of A Clear Blue Morning...................	87	RCA 10935
10/15/77	1⁵	19	27●	**Here You Come Again**...........................	3	RCA 11123
3/18/78	1²	14	28	**It's All Wrong, But It's All Right/**		
		12	29	Two Doors Down	19	RCA 11240
8/19/78	1³	13	30	**Heartbreaker**	37	RCA 11296
11/25/78+	1¹	14	31	**I Really Got The Feeling/**		
11/25/78	48	14	32	Baby I'm Burnin'.............................	25	RCA 11420
6/09/79	1²	14	33	**You're The Only One**............................	59	RCA 11577
9/01/79	7	13	34	**Sweet Summer Lovin'/**	77	
		13	35	Great Balls Of Fire		RCA 11705
				#2 pop hit for Jerry Lee Lewis in 1958		
3/22/80	1¹	14	36	**Starting Over Again**	36	RCA 11926
7/19/80	1¹	16	37	**Old Flames Can't Hold A Candle To You**		RCA 12040
11/29/80+	1¹	14	38●	**9 To 5**	1	RCA 12133
				from the film of the same title		
4/11/81	1¹	17	39	**But You Know I Love You**	41	RCA 12200
8/29/81	14	13	40	The House Of The Rising Sun/	77	
				#1 pop hit for The Animals in 1964		
		1	41	Working Girl		RCA 12282
2/27/82	8	17	42	**Single Women**..................................		RCA 13057
5/29/82	7	15	43	**Heartbreak Express**		RCA 13234
7/31/82	1¹	19	44	**I Will Always Love You/** [R]	53	
				from the film "The Best Little Whorehouse In Texas"		
		19	45	Do I Ever Cross Your Mind.....................		RCA 13260
11/06/82+	8	17	46	**Hard Candy Christmas**........................ [X]		RCA 13361
12/11/82+	7	20	47	**Everything's Beautiful (In It's Own Way)**........		Monument 03408
				DOLLY PARTON/WILLIE NELSON		
4/30/83	20	16	48	Potential New Boyfriend		RCA 13514
12/24/83+	3	19	49	**Save The Last Dance For Me**...................	45	RCA 13703
				#1 pop hit for The Drifters in 1960		
4/07/84	36	10	50	Downtown	80	RCA 13756
				#1 pop hit for Petula Clark in 1965		
6/09/84	1¹	20	51	**Tennessee Homesick Blues**.....................		RCA 13819
9/15/84	10	20	52	**God Won't Get You**		RCA 13883
				above 2: from the film "Rhinestone"		
1/26/85	3	22	53	**Don't Call It Love**		RCA 13987
11/30/85+	1¹	22	54	**Think About Love**		RCA 14218
5/03/86	17	15	55	Tie Our Love (In a Double Knot)................		RCA 14297
9/06/86	31	13	56	We Had It All		RCA 5001
12/19/87+	63	8	57	The River Unbroken		Columbia 07665
				KENNY ROGERS & DOLLY PARTON:		
9/03/83	1²	23	58▲	**Islands In The Stream**..........................	1	RCA 13615

DEBUT DATE	PEAK POS	WKS CHR		ARTIST — Record Title	POP POS	Label & Number
				DOLLY PARTON — Continued		
12/15/84+	**53**	7	59	The Greatest Gift Of All................................[X]	*81*	RCA 13945
				from their Christmas TV special		
5/25/85	**1**[1]	29	60	**Real Love**..	*91*	RCA 14058
				DOLLY PARTON, LINDA RONSTADT, EMMYLOU HARRIS:		
2/21/87	**1**[1]	19	61	**To Know Him Is To Love Him**......................		Warner 28492
				#1 pop hit for The Teddy Bears in 1958		
5/30/87	**3**	18	62	**Telling Me Lies**...................................		Warner 28371
9/26/87	**5**	22	63	**Those Memories Of You**............................		Warner 28248
3/26/88	**6**	18	64	**Wildflowers**......................................		Warner 27970
				PORTER WAGONER & DOLLY PARTON:		
12/02/67+	**7**	17	65	**The Last Thing On My Mind**		RCA 9369
4/13/68	**7**	16	66	**Holding On To Nothin'**		RCA 9490
7/27/68	**5**	13	67	**We'll Get Ahead Someday/**		
10/05/68	**51**	6	68	Jeannie's Afraid Of The Dark.....................		RCA 9577
3/08/69	**9**	14	69	**Yours Love**.......................................		RCA 0104
6/21/69	**16**	11	70	Always, Always....................................		RCA 0172
10/25/69	**5**	16	71	**Just Someone I Used To Know**......................		RCA 0247
2/14/70	**9**	15	72	**Tomorrow Is Forever**..............................		RCA 9799
8/01/70	**7**	15	73	**Daddy Was An Old Time Preacher Man**		RCA 9875
2/27/71	**7**	13	74	**Better Move It On Home**		RCA 9958
6/26/71	**14**	12	75	The Right Combination	*106*	RCA 9994
11/13/71+	**11**	13	76	Burning The Midnight Oil		RCA 0565
4/08/72	**9**	14	77	**Lost Forever In Your Kiss**		RCA 0675
9/02/72	**14**	13	78	Together Always...................................		RCA 0773
3/03/73	**30**	9	79	We Found It		RCA 0893
6/23/73	**3**	17	80	**If Teardrops Were Pennies**........................		RCA 0981
8/03/74	**1**[1]	17	81	**Please Don't Stop Loving Me**......................		RCA 10010
7/12/75	**5**	17	82	**Say Forever You'll Be Mine**.......................		RCA 10328
5/15/76	**8**	14	83	**Is Forever Longer Than Always**....................		RCA 10652
6/21/80	**2**[2]	17	84	**Making Plans**		RCA 11983
11/08/80+	**12**	14	85	If You Go, I'll Follow You.........................		RCA 12119
				RANDY PARTON		
				Born on 12/15/55 in Sevierville, Tennessee. Younger brother of Dolly Parton. Worked with Jean Shepard in 1974, then with Dolly from 1974-79.		
3/07/81	**30**	12	1	Hold Me Like You Never Had Me		RCA 12137
8/01/81	**30**	10	2	Shot Full Of Love		RCA 12271
12/19/81	**80**	4	3	Don't Cry Baby		RCA 12351
5/01/82	**76**	4	4	Oh, No..		RCA 13087
				#4 pop hit for the Commodores in 1981		
10/22/83	**92**	2	5	A Stranger In Her Bed.............................		RCA 13608
				STELLA PARTON		
				Born on 5/4/49 in Sevierville, Tennessee. Younger sister of Dolly Parton. Sang with Stella Carroll & The Gospel Carrolls. Own gospel group, the Stella Parton Singers.		
5/24/75	**9**	18	1	**I Want To Hold You In My Dreams Tonight**		Country Soul 039
9/27/75	**56**	10	2	It's Not Funny Anymore		Soul, C.&B. 088
1/08/77	**87**	5	3	Neon Women		Elektra 45367
				CARMOL TAYLOR & STELLA PARTON		
3/19/77	**60**	9	4	I'm Not That Good At Goodbye		Elektra 45383
7/30/77	**15**	13	5	The Danger Of A Stranger.........................		Elektra 45410
11/12/77+	**14**	15	6	Standard Lie Number One..........................		Elektra 45437
3/25/78	**20**	10	7	Four Little Letters................................		Elektra 45468
7/01/78	**28**	9	8	Undercover Lovers		Elektra 45490
10/14/78	**21**	10	9	Stormy Weather...................................		Elektra 45533
4/21/79	**26**	11	10	Steady As The Rain		Elektra 46029
7/28/79	**36**	9	11	The Room At The Top Of The Stairs		Elektra 46502
3/06/82	**65**	7	12	I'll Miss You.....................................		Town House 1056
7/24/82	**75**	5	13	Young Love.......................................		Town House 1058
				#1 pop hit for both Tab Hunter and Sonny James in 1957		
3/21/87	**86**	3	14	Cross My Heart		Luv 132

DEBUT DATE	PEAK POS	WKS CHR	ARTIST — Record Title	POP POS	Label & Number
			JAMES PASTELL Singer from Monroe, Louisiana.		
9/10/77	95	5	1 Hell Yes I Cheated		Paula 425
			BUDDY PAUL		
8/01/60	22	4	1 This Old Town		Murco 1018
			JOYCE PAUL		
6/22/68	36	10	1 Phone Call To Mama		United Art. 50315
			LES PAUL & MARY FORD Les was born Lester Polfus on 6/9/16 in Waukesha, Wisconsin. Mary was born Colleen Summer on 7/7/28 in Pasadena; died on 9/30/77. Paul is a self-taught guitarist.		
3/10/51	7	1	1 ●Mockin' Bird Hill .... Jockey #7	2	Capitol 1373
			GARY S. PAXTON Born in Mesa, Arizona. Worked with Clyde "Skip" Battin as the Rockabillies on the Arizona Hayride in 1958. Recorded with Battin as "Gary & Clyde" and "Skip & Flip".		
2/07/76	85	5	1 Too Far Gone (To Care What You Do to Me)		RCA 10449
			JOHNNY PAYCHECK ★★54★★ Born Donald Eugene Lytle on 5/31/41 in Greenfield, Ohio. Guitarist/steel guitarist. Moved to Nashville in 1955, worked with Porter Wagoner, Faron Young, George Jones and Ray Price. Recorded as "Donnie Young" for Decca in 1959. Changed name in 1965. Wrote "Apartment No. 9" for Tammy Wynette and "Touch My Heart" for Ray Price. Toured with Merle Haggard from 1981-83.		
10/16/65	26	12	1 A-11		Hilltop 3007
2/26/66	40	2	2 Heartbreak Tennessee		Hilltop 3009
6/04/66	8	19	3 **The Lovin' Machine**		Little Dar. 008
11/05/66+	13	15	4 Motel Time Again		Little Dar. 0016
4/08/67	15	15	5 Jukebox Charlie		Little Dar. 0020
9/02/67	32	10	6 The Cave		Little Dar. 0032
12/23/67+	41	11	7 Don't Monkey With Another Monkey's Monkey...		Little Dar. 0035
4/27/68	59	7	8 (It Won't Be Long) And I'll Be Hating You		Little Dar. 0042
8/17/68	66	4	9 My Heart Keeps Running To You		Little Dar. 0046
12/14/68	73	4	10 If I'm Gonna Sink		Little Dar. 0052
6/28/69	31	13	11 Wherever You Are......................................		Little Dar. 0060
10/09/71	2¹	19	12 **She's All I Got**.......................................	91	Epic 10783
3/11/72	4	14	13 **Someone To Give My Love To**		Epic 10836
5/27/72	13	11	14 Let's All Go Down To The River................... JODY MILLER & JOHNNY PAYCHECK		Epic 10863
6/24/72	12	11	15 Love Is A Good Thing		Epic 10876
10/07/72	21	12	16 Somebody Loves Me		Epic 10912
2/24/73	10	12	17 **Something About You I Love**......................		Epic 10947
6/09/73	2³	15	18 **Mr. Lovemaker**		Epic 10999
11/03/73+	8	15	19 **Song And Dance Man**		Epic 11046
3/16/74	19	12	20 My Part Of Forever		Epic 11090
7/06/74	23	11	21 Keep On Lovin' Me		Epic 11142
11/02/74+	12	15	22 For A Minute There		Epic 50040
3/01/75	26	11	23 Loving You Beats All I've Ever Seen		Epic 50073
5/31/75	38	12	24 I Don't Love Her Anymore		Epic 50111
9/27/75	23	12	25 All-American Man		Epic 50146
2/21/76	56	8	26 The Feminine Touch		Epic 50193
5/08/76	49	8	27 Gone At Last.. JOHNNY PAYCHECK with CHARNISSA		Epic 50215
7/24/76	34	10	28 11 Months And 29 Days		Epic 50249
10/23/76	44	8	29 I Can See Me Lovin' You Again		Epic 50291
2/12/77	7	16	30 **Slide Off Of Your Satin Sheets**		Epic 50334
6/11/77	8	16	31 **I'm The Only Hell (Mama Ever Raised)**		Epic 50391
11/05/77+	1²	18	32 **Take This Job And Shove It/**		
1/28/78	50	10	33 Colorado Kool-Aid .... [S]		Epic 50469
4/15/78	17	10	34 Georgia In A Jug/		
4/15/78	33	10	35 Me And The I.R.S.		Epic 50539
10/21/78	7	12	36 **Friend, Lover, Wife**................................		Epic 50621
1/27/79	27	11	37 The Outlaw's Prayer		Epic 50655

DEBUT DATE	PEAK POS	WKS CHR	ARTIST — Record Title	POP POS	Label & Number
			JOHNNY PAYCHECK — Continued		
1/27/79	94	4	38 Down On The Corner At A Bar Called Kelly's		Little Dar. 7808
10/13/79	49	6	39 (Stay Away From) The Cocaine Train		Epic 50777
12/22/79+	17	13	40 Drinkin' And Drivin'		Epic 50818
4/05/80	40	9	41 Fifteen Beers		Epic 50863
9/06/80	22	11	42 In Memory Of A Memory..............................		Epic 50923
3/28/81	41	8	43 I Can't Hold Myself In Line...........................		Epic 51012
			PAYCHECK & HAGGARD (Merle)		
7/04/81	57	7	44 Yesterday's News (Just Hit Home Today)..........		Epic 02144
1/23/82	75	4	45 The Highlight Of '81		Epic 02684
4/24/82	69	5	46 No Way Out...		Epic 02817
8/14/82	88	4	47 D.O.A. (Drunk On Arrival)		Epic 03052
12/01/84+	30	18	48 I Never Got Over You		AMI 1322
4/06/85	47	10	49 You're Every Step I Take		AMI 1323
12/07/85	63	8	50 Everything Is Changing		AMI 1327
5/17/86	21	22	51 Old Violin		Mercury 884720
11/08/86	49	10	52 Don't Bury Me 'Til I'm Ready		Mercury 888088
2/28/87	56	7	53 Come To Me		Mercury 888341
7/11/87	72	5	54 I Grow Old Too Fast (And Smart Too Slow)		Mercury 888651
4/09/88	81	2	55 Out Of Beer...		Desperado 1001
			GEORGE JONES & JOHNNY PACHECK:		
12/09/78+	7	13	56 **Mabellene**		Epic 50647
			#5 pop hit for Chuck Berry in 1955		
5/26/79	14	11	57 You Can Have Her		Epic 50708
			#12 pop hit for Roy Hamilton in 1961		
6/21/80	31	9	58 When You're Ugly Like Us (You Just Naturally Got To Be Cool)		Epic 50891
12/13/80+	18	12	59 You Better Move On.....................................		Epic 50949
			#24 pop hit for Arthur Alexander in 1962		
			DENNIS PAYNE Singer/songwriter born in Bakersfield, California.		
2/20/88	66	5	1 I Can't Hang On Anymore		True 88
10/29/88	94	2	2 That's Why You Haven't Seen Me....................		MTM 72108
			JIMMY PAYNE Born on 4/12/36 in Leachville, Arkansas. Worked with the Glaser Brothers in the late 50s. Moved to Nashville in 1962. Wrote "Woman, Woman" for Gary Puckett.		
4/19/69	60	6	1 L.A. Angels..		Epic 10444
11/03/73	79	5	2 Ramblin' Man		Cinnamon 772
			#2 pop hit for The Allman Brothers Band in 1973		
8/01/81	80	4	3 Turning My Love On		Kik 907
			JODY PAYNE Singer/harmonica player; appeared in the films "Honeysuckle Rose" and "Barbarosa".		
2/28/81	65	6	1 There's A Crazy Man		Kari 117
			with The Willie Nelson Family Band		
			LEON PAYNE Born on 6/15/17 in Alba, Texas; died of a heart attack on 9/11/69. Blind since early childhood. Guitarist/pianist/drummer. Played with Jack Rhodes' Rhythm Boys. Own band, the Lone Star Buddies, from 1949. Wrote "I Love You Because", "Lost Highway" and "Blue Side Of Lonesome". Initial member of the Songwriter's Hall of Fame.		
11/05/49+	1²	32	1 **I Love You Because**		Capitol 40238
			Jockey #1 / Best Seller #4 / Juke Box #10		
			KEVIN PEARCE Born in 1960 in Lake Alfred, Florida. Discovered by Leon Everette.		
1/14/84	91	2	1 It's Gonna Be A Heartache............................		Orlando 108
1/18/86	92	2	2 Pink Cadillac..		Orlando 111
10/31/87	90	2	3 The Bigger The Love....................................		Evergreen 1057
2/27/88	66	6	4 Love Ain't Made For Fools		Evergreen 1067
6/25/88	68	6	5 Took It Like A Man, Cried Like A Baby		Evergreen 1074
			PEARL - see MINNIE		

DEBUT DATE	PEAK POS	WKS CHR	ARTIST — Record Title	POP POS	Label & Number
			HERB PEDERSEN Banjo virtuoso, born on 4/27/44 in Berkeley, California. Worked with Flatt & Scruggs, Linda Ronstadt and Emmylou Harris. Heard on TV themes for Rockford Files, Dukes Of Hazzard, A-Team, and Kojak. Member of The Desert Rose Band in 1986.		
1/15/77	56	7	1 Our Baby's Gone		Epic 50309
			EVERETT PEEK		
5/07/77	94	3	1 Sea Cruise		Commercl. 00016
			DAVE PEEL Singer/actor from Nashville. Worked in the Goodtime Singers, New Christy Minstrels, and Take Five. Toured with Fess Parker. Appeared in Daniel Boone, and The Virginian TV series from 1966-67. In the film "Nashville".		
11/15/69	66	4	1 I'm Walkin'		Chart 5037
3/14/70	62	7	2 Wax Museum..		Chart 5054
5/23/70	44	9	3 Hit The Road Jack .... CONNIE EATON & DAVE PEEL #1 pop hit for Ray Charles in 1961		Chart 5066
11/07/70	56	7	4 It Takes Two .... CONNIE EATON & DAVE PEEL #14 pop hit for Marvin Gaye & Kim Weston in 1967		Chart 5099
1/23/71	56	4	5 (You've Got To) Move Two Mountains................ #20 pop hit for Marv Johnson in 1960		Chart 5109
			PEGGY SUE Peggy Sue Webb, born in Butcher's Hollow, Kentucky. Younger sister of Loretta Lynn. Wrote "Don't Come Home A'Drinkin" with Loretta, performed on tours with her. Married to Sonny Wright.		
6/07/69	28	11	1 I'm Dynamite		Decca 32485
11/01/69	30	10	2 I'm Gettin' Tired Of Babyin' You		Decca 32571
4/18/70	65	3	3 After The Preacher's Gone.............................		Decca 32640
7/11/70	37	11	4 All American Husband		Decca 32698
12/12/70	58	4	5 Apron Strings		Decca 32754
5/15/71	68	5	6 I Say, "Yes, Sir"		Decca 32812
1/15/77	34	10	7 Every Beat Of My Heart................................		Door Knob 021
4/09/77	51	9	8 I Just Came In Here (To Let A Little Hurt Out) ...		Door Knob 029
7/02/77	81	4	9 Good Evening Henry		Door Knob 036
10/22/77	100	1	10 If This Is What Love's All About .... PEGGY SUE & SONNY WRIGHT		Door Knob 038
2/04/78	85	5	11 To Be Loved.. #22 pop hit for Jackie Wilson in 1958		Door Knob 045
6/10/78	87	2	12 Let Me Down Easy		Door Knob 052
9/02/78	80	5	13 All Night Long		Door Knob 069
11/18/78+	37	12	14 How I Love You (In The Morning)		Door Knob 079
3/24/79	30	10	15 I Want To See Me In Your Eyes......................		Door Knob 094
6/30/79	51	6	16 The Love Song And The Dream Belong To Me		Door Knob 102
11/10/79	86	5	17 Gently Hold Me .... PEGGY SUE & SONNY WRIGHT		Door Knob 113
3/29/80	80	4	18 For As Long As You Want Me........................		Door Knob 121
7/12/80	93	3	19 Why Don't You Go To Dallas		Door Knob 131
			BOBBY PENN Born in Houston. Former gospel singer under the name "Larry Fayne".		
7/03/71	51	11	1 You Were On My Mind................................. #3 pop hit for We Five in 1965		50 States 1
9/07/74	88	5	2 Watch Out For Lucy		50 States 29
7/04/76	100	1	3 Little Weekend Warriors		50 States 42
			RAY PENNINGTON Born in Clay County, Kentucky in 1933. On TV in Cincinnati at age 16. Own band by 1952. Worked on local TV shows in Kentucky, Indiana and Ohio from the late 50s. Also see Bluestone and The Swing Shift Band.		
11/05/66	43	9	1 Who's Been Mowing The Lawn........................		Capitol 5751
5/06/67	29	8	2 Ramblin' Man		Capitol 5855
11/18/67	65	3	3 Who's Gonna Walk The Dog (And Put Out The Cat)..		Capitol 2006
7/05/69	70	6	4 What Eva Doesn't Have		Monument 1145
12/06/69	69	5	5 This Song Don't Care Who Sings It		Monument 1170

DEBUT DATE	PEAK POS	WKS CHR	ARTIST — Record Title	POP POS	Label & Number
			RAY PENNINGTON — Continued		
5/02/70	61	7	6 You Don't Know Me..		Monument 1194
			#2 pop hit for Ray Charles in 1962		
8/08/70	74	2	7 The Other Woman		Monument 1208
1/02/71	68	5	8 Bubbles In My Beer		Monument 1231
11/18/78	79	4	9 She Wanted A Little Bit More		MRC 1022
			HANK PENNY		
			Born Herbert Clayton Penny on 8/18/18 in Birmingham, Alabama. Accomplished banjo player. Performed on WWL-New Orleans and WLW-Cincinnati before moving to Los Angeles and forming own band in the mid-40s. Worked as comedian on Spade Cooley TV series, KTLA-TV. Married to Sue Thompson from 1953-63.		
6/15/46	4	6	1 **Steel Guitar Stomp**		King 528
9/14/46	4	4	2 **Get Yourself A Redhead**		King 540
2/25/50	4	12	3 **Bloodshot Eyes**		King 828
			Juke Box #4		
			JOE PENNY		
7/18/64	41	7	1 Frosty Window Pane....................................		Sims 173
			BRENDA PEPPER		
6/21/75	97	4	1 You Bring Out The Best In Me		Playboy 6038
			CARL PERKINS		
			Born on 4/9/32 near Tiptonville, Tennessee. Rockabilly singer/guitarist/songwriter. Member of Johnny Cash's touring troupe from 1965-75. The Beatles recorded his songs "Matchbox", "Honey Don't" and "Everybody's Trying To Be My Baby".		
2/18/56	1³	24	1 **Blue Suede Shoes**.....................................	2	Sun 234
			Juke Box #1 / Best Seller #2 / Jockey #2		
6/30/56	7	6	2 **Boppin' The Blues**....................................	70	Sun 243
			Juke Box #7 / Best Seller #9		
10/06/56	10	2	3 **Dixie Fried/**		
			Best Seller #10		
		2	4 I'm Sorry, I'm Not Sorry		Sun 249
			Best Seller flip		
3/09/57	13	8	5 Your True Love	67	Sun 261
			Best Seller #13		
3/31/58	17	9	6 Pink Pedal Pushers....................................	91	Columbia 41131
			Best Seller #17		
12/17/66+	22	15	7 Country Boy's Dream..................................		Dollie 505
5/20/67	40	8	8 Shine, Shine...		Dollie 508
1/04/69	20	15	9 Restless		Columbia 44723
5/29/71	65	5	10 Me Without You		Columbia 45347
12/11/71+	53	7	11 Cotton Top...		Columbia 45466
5/06/72	60	5	12 High On Love		Columbia 45582
10/13/73	61	7	13 (Let's Get) Dixiefried............................[R]		Mercury 73425
6/07/86	31	14	14 Birth Of Rock And Roll		America 884760
3/28/87	83	3	15 Class Of '55...		America 888142
			DAL PERKINS		
			Born in Abilene, moved to Phoenix in 1946. Singing since 1957.		
1/13/68	73	3	1 Helpless		Columbia 44343
			BRENDA KAYE PERRY		
10/22/77	64	9	1 Ringgold Georgia.......................................		MRC 1005
			BILLY WALKER & BRENDA KAYE PERRY		
1/21/78	35	11	2 Deeper Water		MRC 1010
4/22/78	37	9	3 I Can't Get Up By Myself.............................		MRC 1013
10/14/78	78	5	4 My Daddy Was A Travelin' Man		MRC 1021
2/17/79	90	3	5 Make Me Your Woman		MRC 1026
			PETERS & LEE		
			British duo: Lennie Peters (who is blind) and Dianne Lee.		
3/16/74	79	8	1 Welcome Home	119	Philips 40729
			BEN PETERS		
			Prominent songwriter. Credits include "Before The Next Teardrop Falls" for Freddy Fender, "Kiss An Angel Good Mornin'" for Charley Pride, "A Perfect Match" for David Houston and Barbara Mandrell, and many others.		
7/19/69	46	9	1 San Francisco Is A Lonely Town		Liberty 56114

DEBUT DATE	PEAK POS	WKS CHR	ARTIST — Record Title	POP POS	Label & Number
			BEN PETERS — Continued		
9/01/73	92	4	2 Would You Still Love Me		Capitol 3687
			DEBBIE PETERS		
			Daughter of songwriter Ben Peters.		
3/15/80	84	2	1 It Can't Wait		Oak 1012
			DOUG PETERS		
			Born Doug Volchko in Chicago on 8/4/59. Commercial jingle songwriter.		
8/06/88	85	2	1 My Heart's Way Behind		Comstock 1895
			JIMMIE PETERS		
			Born on 10/12/38 in Whiteface, Texas. Played bass with Waylon Jennings.		
5/28/77	59	7	1 Somebody Took Her Love (And Never Gave It Back)..		Mercury 73911
10/08/77	73	6	2 Lipstick Traces..		Mercury 55005
			#48 pop hit for The O'Jays in 1965		
2/18/78	75	4	3 634-5789		Mercury 55016
			#13 pop hit for Wilson Pickett in 1966		
6/03/78	84	4	4 I Will Always Love You		Mercury 55025
1/13/79	78	4	5 I Hate The Way Our Love Is		Vista 101
			JIMMY PETERS & LYNDA K. LANCE		
4/28/79	98	3	6 First Class Fool		Vista 106
			JIMMIE PETERS/LYNDA K. LANCE		
3/01/80	75	4	7 Hearts...		Sunbird 105
			COLLEEN PETERSON		
			Born on 11/14/50 in Peterboro, Canada. Popular entertainer on Canadian TV.		
11/27/76	100	2	1 Souvenirs		Capitol 4349
			DIANE PFEIFER		
			Born on 11/4/50 in St. Louis. Own all-girl rock band while in college.		
3/01/80	85	3	1 Free To Be Lonely Again		Capitol 4823
5/17/80	59	7	2 Roses Ain't Red		Capitol 4858
10/04/80	83	3	3 Wishful Drinkin'		Capitol 4916
11/28/81+	35	10	4 Play Something We Could Love To		Capitol 5060
6/12/82	85	3	5 Something To Love For Again		Capitol 5116
9/25/82	76	4	6 Let's Get Crazy Again		Capitol 5154
			BILL PHILLIPS		
			Born on 1/28/36 in Canton, North Carolina. Worked on the Old Southern Jamboree, WMIL-Miami in 1955. Moved to Nashville in 1957. Worked with Johnny Wright and Kitty Wells from the early 70s.		
8/24/59	27	2	1 Sawmill		Columbia 41416
2/08/60	24	4	2 Georgia Town Blues..................................		Columbia 41530
			above 2: **MEL TILLIS & BILL PHILLIPS**		
3/14/64	22	18	3 I Can Stand It (As Long As She Can).................		Decca 31584
10/17/64	26	10	4 Stop Me		Decca 31648
4/02/66	6	18	5 **Put It Off Until Tomorrow**		Decca 31901
			harmony vocal: Dolly Parton		
8/13/66	8	19	6 **The Company You Keep**...............................		Decca 31996
			above 2 written by Dolly Parton		
1/21/67	10	15	7 **The Words I'm Gonna Have To Eat**		Decca 32074
7/22/67	39	7	8 I Learn Something New Everyday.....................		Decca 32141
11/18/67+	25	13	9 Love's Dead End		Decca 32207
3/15/69	54	10	10 I Only Regret..		Decca 32432
10/18/69	10	14	11 **Little Boy Sad**		Decca 32565
			#17 pop hit for Johnny Burnette in 1961		
3/28/70	43	7	12 She's Hungry Again		Decca 32638
8/22/70	46	9	13 Same Old Story, Same Old Lie		Decca 32707
2/27/71	56	6	14 Big Rock Candy Mountain..........................		Decca 32782
3/18/72	66	8	15 I Am, I Said		United Art. 50879
			#4 pop hit for Neil Diamond in 1971		
8/11/73	91	3	16 It's Only Over Now And Then		United Art. 266
6/24/78	90	3	17 Divorce Suit (You Were Named Co-Respondent) ..		Soundwaves 4570
2/03/79	89	3	18 You're Gonna Make A Cheater Out Of Me		Soundwaves 4579
7/07/79	85	3	19 At The Moonlite...		Soundwaves 4587

DEBUT DATE	PEAK POS	WKS CHR	ARTIST — Record Title	POP POS	Label & Number
			CHARLIE PHILLIPS Born on 7/2/37 in Clovis, New Mexico. Worked on the Ozark Jubilee, Louisiana Hayride, and the Big D Jamboree. Own band, the Sugartimers, from 1957.		
4/14/62	**9**	7	1 I Guess I'll Never Learn...............................		Columbia 42289
10/12/63	**30**	1	2 This Is The House		Columbia 42851
			JOHN PHILLIPS Born on 8/30/35 in Paris Island, South Carolina. Co-founder of The Mamas & The Papas. Father of actress MacKenzie Phillips.		
7/04/70	**58**	7	1 Mississippi	*32*	Dunhill 4236
			STU PHILLIPS Born on 1/19/33 in Montreal, Canada. Member of the Grand Ole Opry since 1967.		
4/30/66	**39**	5	1 Bracero		RCA 8771
8/20/66	**32**	11	2 The Great El Tigre (The Tiger)		RCA 8868
2/04/67	**44**	8	3 Walk Me To The Station		RCA 9066
6/17/67	**21**	14	4 Vin Rose...		RCA 9219
10/21/67	**13**	12	5 Juanita Jones		RCA 9333
4/20/68	**62**	6	6 Note In Box #9..		RCA 9481
7/13/68	**53**	7	7 The Top Of The World..................................		RCA 9557
12/21/68+	**68**	6	8 Bring Love Back Into Our World		RCA 9673
			PIANO RED - see DANNY SHIRLEY		
			WEBB PIERCE ★★7★★ Born on 8/8/26 in West Monroe, Louisiana. Worked on KMLB-Monroe, then on the Louisiana Hayride from the early 50s to 1955. First recorded on Pacemaker. Own band included Faron Young, Jimmy Day and Floyd Cramer. Moved to Nashville in 1955 and joined the Grand Ole Opry. Formerly one of the owners of the Cedarwood Publishing Company. In the films "Buffalo Guns", "Music City USA" and "Road To Nashville".		
1/05/52	**1** [4]	27	1 Wondering .... Jockey #1 / Best Seller #4 / Juke Box #4		Decca 46364
6/07/52	**1** [3]	20	2 That Heart Belongs To Me .... Jockey #1 / Juke Box #2 / Best Seller #5		Decca 28091
10/04/52	**1** [4]	23	3 Back Street Affair .... Jockey #1(4) / Juke Box #1(3) / Best Seller #1(2)		Decca 28369
1/31/53	**4**	7	4 I'll Go On Alone/ Juke Box #4 / Best Seller #7 / Jockey #8		
2/14/53	**4**	6	5 That's Me Without You .... Jockey #4 / Juke Box #4 / Best Seller #9		Decca 28534
3/28/53	**4**	14	6 The Last Waltz/ Best Seller #4 / Jockey #5 / Juke Box #5		
4/18/53	**5**	6	7 I Haven't Got The Heart............................ Juke Box #5 / Jockey #6		Decca 28594
7/04/53	**1** [8]	22	8 It's Been So Long/ Jockey #1(8) / Best Seller #1(6) / Juke Box #1(1)		
7/04/53	**9**	2	9 Don't Throw Your Life Away..................... Juke Box #9		Decca 28725
10/24/53	**1** [12]	27	10 There Stands The Glass/ Best Seller #1(12) / Juke Box #1(9) / Jockey #1(6)		
10/24/53	**3**	17	11 I'm Walking The Dog .... Juke Box #3 / Jockey #4 / Best Seller #6		Decca 28834
2/06/54	**1** [17]	36	12 Slowly .... Best Seller #1(17) / Juke Box #1(17) / Jockey #1(15)		Decca 28991
6/05/54	**1** [2]	31	13 Even Tho/ Jockey #1 / Juke Box #2 / Best Seller #3		
6/12/54	**4**	18	14 Sparkling Brown Eyes............................... Best Seller #4 / Jockey #4 / Juke Box #4		Decca 29107
10/09/54	**1** [10]	29	15 More And More/ Juke Box #1(10) / Best Seller #1(9) / Jockey #1(8)	*22*	
10/09/54	**4**	12	16 You're Not Mine Anymore.......................... Jockey #4 / Best Seller #8		Decca 29252
2/05/55	**1** [21]	37	17 In The Jailhouse Now/ Juke Box #1(21) / Best Seller #1(20) / Jockey #1(15)		
2/12/55	**10**	2	18 I'm Gonna Fall Out Of Love With You .... Jockey #10 / Best Seller #14		Decca 29391
6/18/55	**1** [12]	32	19 I Don't Care/ Best Seller #1(12) / Jockey #1(12) / Juke Box #1(12)		
		6	20 Your Good For Nothing Heart .... Jockey flip / Juke Box flip		Decca 29480

241

DEBUT DATE	PEAK POS	WKS CHR		ARTIST — Record Title	POP POS	Label & Number
				WEBB PIERCE — Continued		
9/24/55	**1**[13]	32	21	Love, Love, Love/ Jockey #1(13) / Juke Box #1(9) / Best Seller #1(8)		
10/29/55	**7**	5	22	**If You Were Me**................................. Jockey #7		Decca 29662
3/03/56	**2**[7]	21	23	**Yes, I Know Why**/ Jockey #2 / Best Seller #3 / Juke Box #3		
3/10/56	**3**	13	24	**'Cause I Love You**.............................. Juke Box #3 / Best Seller #5 / Jockey #12		Decca 29805
7/21/56	**7**	11	25	Any Old Time/ Jockey #7 / Juke Box #7 / Best Seller #10		
		6	26	We'll Find A Way................................. Juke Box flip / Best Seller flip		Decca 29974
10/13/56	**10**	8	27	Teenage Boogie/ Best Seller #10 / Jockey #15		
		5	28	I'm Really Glad You Hurt Me................. Best Seller flip		Decca 30045
1/05/57	**3**	22	29	I'm Tired/ Best Seller #3 / Jockey #4 / Juke Box #4		
		4	30	It's My Way....................................... Best Seller flip		Decca 30155
3/30/57	**1**[1]	22	31	Honky Tonk Song/ Jockey #1 / Best Seller #2 / Juke Box #7		
4/13/57	**12**	2	32	Someday .... Jockey #12		Decca 30255
5/27/57	**7**	15	33	Bye Bye, Love/ Jockey #7 / Best Seller #8	73	
6/10/57	**7**	12	34	**Missing You**.................................... Jockey #7 / Best Seller #13		Decca 30321
9/30/57	**3**	17	35	Holiday For Love/ Jockey #3 / Best Seller #6		
11/18/57	**12**	1	36	Don't Do It Darlin'............................. Jockey #12		Decca 30419
5/05/58	**3**	17	37	**Cryin' Over You**/ Jockey #3 / Best Seller #12		
6/02/58	**10**	4	38	**You'll Come Back** .... Jockey #10		Decca 30623
9/29/58	**10**	12	39	**Falling Back To You**/ Best Seller #10 / Hot C&W #10		
10/20/58	**7**	10	40	**Tupelo County Jail**		Decca 30711
1/19/59	**22**	3	41	I'm Letting You Go		Decca 30789
4/06/59	**6**	16	42	**A Thousand Miles Ago**.......................		Decca 30858
7/20/59	**2**[9]	25	43	**I Ain't Never**	24	Decca 30923
12/21/59+	**4**	18	44	**No Love Have I**	54	Decca 31021
4/11/60	**17**	10	45	(Doin' The) Lovers Leap/	93	
5/23/60	**11**	8	46	Is It Wrong (For Loving You)	69	Decca 31058
9/12/60	**11**	8	47	Drifting Texas Sand	108	Decca 31118
11/14/60	**4**	18	48	**Fallen Angel**	99	Decca 31165
2/20/61	**5**	15	49	**Let Forgiveness In** .... flip side "There's More Pretty Girls Than One" hit POS 118 on the Bubbling Under chart		Decca 31197
5/29/61	**3**	21	50	**Sweet Lips**		Decca 31249
9/25/61	**5**	22	51	**Walking The Streets**/		
10/02/61	**7**	19	52	How Do You Talk To A Baby		Decca 31298
2/10/62	**5**	16	53	**Alla My Love**		Decca 31347
5/26/62	**8**	13	54	**Crazy Wild Desire**/		
6/02/62	**7**	13	55	**Take Time**		Decca 31380
10/06/62	**5**	15	56	**Cow Town**/		
10/13/62	**19**	10	57	Sooner Or Later..................................		Decca 31421
1/05/63	**25**	3	58	How Come Your Dog Don't Bite Nobody But Me .. **MEL TILLIS & WEBB PIERCE**		Decca 31445
3/02/63	**15**	8	59	Sawmill/		
4/06/63	**21**	3	60	If I Could Come Back		Decca 31451
6/22/63	**7**	15	61	**Sands Of Gold**	118	Decca 31488
10/26/63+	**13**	15	62	If The Back Door Could Talk/		
11/09/63	**9**	13	63	**Those Wonderful Years**		Decca 31544
2/15/64	**25**	13	64	Waiting A Lifetime		Decca 31582

DEBUT DATE	PEAK POS	WKS CHR		ARTIST — Record Title	POP POS	Label & Number
				WEBB PIERCE — Continued		
5/23/64	**2**²	23	65	**Memory #1**		Decca 31617
				flip side "French Riviera" hit POS 126 on the Bubbling Under chart		
1/30/65	**26**	14	66	That's Where My Money Goes/		
2/06/65	**46**	5	67	Broken Engagement		Decca 31704
3/20/65	**22**	14	68	Loving You Then Losing You........................		Decca 31737
8/14/65	**13**	14	69	Who Do I Think I Am/		
8/21/65	**50**	2	70	Hobo And The Rose		Decca 31816
4/16/66	**46**	6	71	You Ain't No Better Than Me		Decca 31924
8/27/66	**25**	10	72	Love's Something (I Can't Understand).............		Decca 31982
10/29/66	**14**	17	73	Where'd Ya Stay Last Night		Decca 32033
3/18/67	**39**	15	74	Goodbye City, Goodbye Girl		Decca 32098
8/05/67	**6**	18	75	**Fool Fool Fool**		Decca 32167
1/27/68	**24**	13	76	Luzianna		Decca 32246
7/06/68	**26**	9	77	Stranger In A Strange, Strange City/		
8/03/68	**74**	2	78	In Another World................................		Decca 32339
10/26/68	**22**	10	79	Saturday Night		Decca 32388
2/22/69	**32**	10	80	If I Had Last Night To Live Over..................		Decca 32438
7/05/69	**14**	13	81	This Thing		Decca 32508
11/29/69+	**38**	9	82	Love Ain't Never Gonna Be No Better		Decca 32577
3/28/70	**71**	3	83	Merry-Go-Round World............................		Decca 32641
8/01/70	**56**	5	84	The Man You Want Me To Be		Decca 32694
12/26/70+	**73**	3	85	Showing His Dollar		Decca 32762
3/13/71	**31**	11	86	Tell Him That You Love Him		Decca 32787
9/18/71	**73**	2	87	Someone Stepped In (And Stole Me Blind).........		Decca 32855
7/15/72	**54**	8	88	I'm Gonna Be A Swinger		Decca 32973
11/22/75	**57**	9	89	The Good Lord Giveth (And Uncle Sam Taketh Away)..................................		Plantation 131
3/13/76	**82**	5	90	I've Got Leaving On My Mind....................		Plantation 136
10/09/82	**72**	5	91	In The Jailhouse Now .... [R]		Columbia 03231
				WILLIE NELSON & WEBB PIERCE		
				RED SOVINE & WEBB PIERCE:		
12/17/55+	**1**⁴	25	92	**Why Baby Why**		Decca 29755
				Jockey #1(4) / Best Seller #1(1) / Juke Box #1(1)		
4/21/56	**5**	14	93	**Little Rosa/**		
				Best Seller #5 / Jockey #5 / Juke Box #5		
5/19/56	**5**	8	94	**Hold Everything**		Decca 29876
				Juke Box #5		
				KITTY WELLS & WEBB PIERCE:		
4/06/57	**8**	9	95	**Oh, So Many Years**		Decca 30183
				Jockey #8		
1/20/58	**12**	1	96	One Week Later................................		Decca 30489
				Jockey #12		
9/26/64	**9**	15	97	**Finally**		Decca 31663
				RAY PILLOW		
				Born on 7/4/37 in Lynchburg, Virginia. Sang in college rock band in the late 50s. Moved to Nashville in 1961. Toured with the Martha White Show. With the Grand Ole Opry since 1966.		
2/13/65	**49**	4	1	Take Your Hands Off My Heart		Capitol 5323
12/25/65+	**17**	10	2	Thank You Ma'am		Capitol 5518
4/23/66	**32**	6	3	Common Colds And Broken Hearts.................		Capitol 5597
10/08/66	**26**	11	4	Volkswagen		Capitol 5735
8/12/67	**56**	6	5	I Just Want To Be Alone		Capitol 5953
12/09/67	**62**	2	6	Gone With The Wine		Capitol 2030
9/14/68	**51**	8	7	Wonderful Day		ABC 11114
8/23/69	**38**	8	8	Reconsider Me		Plantation 25
2/05/72	**62**	3	9	Since Then....................................		Mega 0055
5/13/72	**66**	7	10	She's Doing It To Me Again		Mega 0072
1/05/74	**80**	8	11	Countryfied		Mega 202
12/21/74+	**77**	4	12	Livin' In The Sunshine Of Your Love		ABC/Dot 17526
12/27/75	**100**	1	13	Roll On, Truckers		ABC/Dot 17589
5/13/78	**97**	3	14	Who's Gonna Tie My Shoes		Hilltop 130
7/21/79	**82**	4	15	Super Lady		MCA 41047

DEBUT DATE	PEAK POS	WKS CHR	ARTIST — Record Title	POP POS	Label & Number
			RAY PILLOW — Continued		
7/18/81	82	3	16 One Too Many Memories		First Gen. 011
			JEAN SHEPARD & RAY PILLOW:		
5/14/66	9	15	17 I'll Take The Dog...		Capitol 5633
11/26/66+	25	11	18 Mr. Do-It-Yourself.......................................		Capitol 5769
1/28/67	12	15	19 Heart, We Did All We Could		Capitol 5822

THE PINETOPPERS
Group formed by brothers Vaughn (mandolin, guitar) and Roy Horton (bass) from Broadtop Mountain, Pennsylvania. Moved to New York City in 1935. Own shows on NBC and CBS radio. Added Ray Smith, Rusty Keefer and Johnny Browers to form The Pinetoppers. Vocals by Trudy and Gloria Marlin (the Beaver Valley Sweethearts). Roy elected to the Country Music Hall of Fame in 1982.

12/23/50+	3	13	1 Mockin' Bird Hill.. *10*		Coral 64061
			Juke Box #3 / Jockey #4 / Best Seller #5		

PINKARD & BOWDEN
Sandy Pinkard from Gueydan, Louisiana. Staff writer for Jim Ed Norman. Wrote "You're The Reason God Made Oklahoma". With Richard Bowden, guitar player from Linden, Texas. Formerly with own band, Blue Steel.

3/03/84	64	8	1 Adventures In Parodies............................. [N]		Warner 29370
			side one: Help Me Make It Through The Yard/Daddy Sang Bass/Delta Dawg/Somebody Done Somebody's Song Wrong/Drivin' My Wife Away side two: Three Mile Island (Wolverton Mountain)/Blue Hairs Driving In My Lane/What's A W-4 (What's Forever For)		
9/15/84	39	9	2 Mama, She's Lazy .... [N]		Warner 29205
			parody of The Judds' "Mama He's Crazy"		
8/16/86	92	3	3 She Thinks I Steal Cars............................ [N]		Warner 2526
			parody of George Jones' "She Thinks I Still Care"		
6/04/88	87	2	4 Arab, Alabama .... [N]		Warner 27909

GENE PITNEY - see GEORGE JONES (George & Gene) and MELBA MONTGOMERY

MARY KAY PLACE as Loretta Haggers
Born on 8/23/47 in Tulsa. Singer, composer, comedienne. Script writer for many TV comedy shows. Played Loretta Haggers on TV's "Mary Hartman, Mary Hartman".

10/16/76	3	16	1 Baby Boy *60*		Columbia 10422
4/09/77	72	5	2 Vitamin L		Columbia 10510
11/19/77+	9	16	3 Something To Brag About		Columbia 10644
			MARY KAY PLACE with WILLIE NELSON		

LINDA PLOWMAN
Born on 12/31/56 in Tuscaloosa, Alabama. Appeared on TV at age 10.

1/30/71	75	3	1 I'm So Lonesome I Could Cry		Janus 146
9/08/73	93	3	2 Nobody But You...		Columbia 45905

POACHER
Group from Cheshire, England, formed in 1977; Tim Flaherty, lead singer.

11/04/78	86	3	1 Darling...		Republic 028

POCO
Group formed in 1968 in Los Angeles, first known as Pogo. Re-organized group in 1979 consisted of Rusty Young, Paul Cotton, Charlie Harrison, Steve Chapman and Kim Bullard.

2/10/79	95	2	1 Crazy Love *17*		ABC 12439
6/30/79	96	4	2 Heart Of The Night *20*		MCA 41023

POINTER SISTERS
Soul group formed in Oakland in 1971, consisting of sisters Ruth, Anita, Bonnie and June Pointer.

7/27/74	37	16	1 Fairytale *13*		Blue Thumb 254

ANITA POINTER - see EARL THOMAS CONLEY

CHUCK POLLARD
Born in Shreveport, Louisiana. In family band from age 8. Cousin of Gene Wyatt. Worked as a dancer at the Stork Club in Bossier City, Louisiana.

8/05/78	56	7	1 You Should Win An Oscar Every Night..............		MCA 40944
11/11/78	71	5	2 The Other Side Of Jeannie		MCA 40965

PAT POMSL

2/03/79	97	1	1 Let My Fingers Do The Walking		ASI 1017

DEBUT DATE	PEAK POS	WKS CHR	ARTIST — Record Title	POP POS	Label & Number
			CHERYL POOLE		
8/10/68	**39**	10	1 Three Playing Love...		Paula 309
2/01/69	**70**	3	2 The Skin's Gettin' Closer To The Bone..............		Paula 1207
7/12/69	**57**	9	3 Walk Among The People...............................		Paula 1214
2/14/70	**70**	2	4 Everybody's Gotta Hurt................................		Paula 1219
			SANDY POSEY		
			Born on 6/18/47 in Jasper, Alabama; raised in West Memphis, Arkansas. Worked as a session singer in Nashville and Memphis in the early 60s. Left music from 1968-70. Backup singer on the Nashville Network.		
10/30/71+	**18**	14	1 Bring Him Safely Home To Me		Columbia 45458
5/27/72	**51**	11	2 Why Don't We Go Somewhere And Love...........		Columbia 45596
10/28/72	**36**	8	3 Happy, Happy Birthday Baby.........................		Columbia 45703
			#5 pop hit for The Tune Weavers in 1957		
5/05/73	**39**	8	4 Don't		Columbia 45828
			#1 pop hit for Elvis Presley in 1958		
6/19/76	**99**	3	5 Trying To Live Without You Kind Of Days		Monument 8698
12/18/76	**93**	3	6 It's Midnight (Do You Know Where Your Baby Is?)..		Warner 8289
3/11/78	**21**	12	7 Born To Be With You		Warner 8540
			#5 pop hit for The Chordettes in 1956		
8/05/78	**26**	10	8 Love, Love, Love/Chapel Of Love		Warner 8610
2/10/79	**26**	12	9 Love Is Sometimes Easy		Warner 8731
6/30/79	**82**	3	10 Try Home		Warner 8852
2/26/83	**88**	3	11 Can't Get Used To Sleeping Without You		Audiograph 449
			CURTIS POTTER		
			Born in Cross Plains, Texas; raised in Abilene. Worked on KRBC-TV and the Bill Fox Show in the mid-50s. Bandleader for Hank Thompson from 1959-71.		
5/12/79	**92**	3	1 Fraulein (The Texas National Anthem)		Hillside 03
3/01/80	**89**	5	2 San Antonio Medley		Hillside 01
			CURTIS POTTER/DARRELL McCALL		
			PATI POWELL - see BOB GALLION		
			SANDY POWELL - see MEL STREET		
			SUE POWELL		
			Born in Gallatin, Tennessee; raised in Sellersburg, Indiana. First recorded for father's record company at age 8. With Dave And Sugar from 1977-80. Co-host of "Nashville On The Road" TV series, 1982.		
5/16/81	**57**	7	1 Midnite Flyer...		RCA 12227
10/31/81	**49**	6	2 (There's No Me) Without You		RCA 12287
			PEREZ PRADO		
			Damaso Perez Prado - "King of the Mambo" bandleader, organist from Cuba and later Mexico City. His "Cherry Pink & Apple Blossom White" was the #1 pop hit of 1955.		
8/18/58	**18**	1	1 ●Patricia .... [I]	*1*	RCA 7245
			Best Seller #18		
			ELVIS PRESLEY ★★**31**★★		
			Born on 1/8/35 in Tupelo, Mississippi. Died on 8/16/77 in Memphis at the age of 42 due to heart failure caused by drug abuse. Won talent contest at age 8, singing "Old Shep". First played guitar at age 11. First recorded for Sun in 1954. Signed to RCA Records on 11/22/55. First film "Love Me Tender" in 1956. In the US Army from 3/24/58 to 3/5/60. In many films thereafter. NBC-TV special in 1968. Married Priscilla Beaulieu on 5/1/67; divorced on 10/11/73. Only child, Lisa Marie, was born on 2/1/68. Elvis' last live performance was in Indianapolis on 6/26/77. Inducted into the Rock And Roll Hall Of Fame in 1986.		
7/16/55	**5**	15	1 **Baby Let's Play House/**		
			Jockey #5 / Best Seller #10		
		3	2 I'm Left, You're Right, She's Gone.................		Sun 217
			Best Seller flip		
			#12 R&B hit for Arthur Gunter in 1955		
9/17/55	**1** [5]	39	3 **I Forgot To Remember To Forget/**		
			Juke Box #1(5) / Best Seller #1(2) / Jockey #4		
12/31/55+	**11**	4	4 Mystery Train		Sun 223
			Jockey #11		
			Elvis Presley's non-charted Sun records:		
			1) That's All Right/Blue Moon Of Kentucky (Sun 209)		
			2) Good Rockin' Tonight/I Don't Care If The Sun Don't Shine (Sun 210)		
			3) Milkcow Blues Boogie/You're A Heartbreaker (Sun 215)		

DEBUT DATE	PEAK POS	WKS CHR	ARTIST — Record Title	POP POS	Label & Number
			ELVIS PRESLEY — Continued		
3/03/56	**1** [17]	27	5 **Heartbreak Hotel**/ Best Seller #1(17) / Juke Box #1(13) / Jockey #1(12)	*1*	
3/31/56	**8**	6	6 **I Was The One**.. Jockey #8	19	RCA 6420
6/02/56	**1** [2]	20	7 **I Want You, I Need You, I Love You**/ Best Seller #1(2) / Juke Box #1(1) / Jockey #5	*1*	
6/02/56	**13**	13	8 My Baby Left Me .... Best Seller #13 written and recorded on RCA by Arthur "Big Boy" Crudup in 1950	31	RCA 6540
8/11/56	**1** [7]	27	9 **Don't Be Cruel**/ Juke Box #1(7) / Best Seller #1(5) /Jockey #2	*1*	
8/04/56	**1** [3]	20	10 **Hound Dog**... Juke Box #1 / Best Seller #2 / Jockey #6 #1 R&B hit (7 weeks) for Big Mama Thornton in 1953	*1*	RCA 6604
10/20/56	**3**	18	11 **Love Me Tender**/ Best Seller #3 / Jockey #4 / Juke Box #4 Elvis' first movie; tune adapted from "Aura Lee" of 1861	*1*	
		6	12 Anyway You Want Me (That's How I Will Be).... Best Seller flip		RCA 6643
12/29/56	**10**	3	13 **Love Me** .... Jockey #10 / Juke Box #10 from the E.P. "Elvis"	2	RCA EPA-992
2/02/57	**3**	14	14 **Too Much**/ Juke Box #3 / Best Seller #5 / Jockey #6	*1*	
3/02/57	**8**	1	15 **Playing For Keeps** .... Juke Box #8	21	RCA 6800
4/13/57	**1** [1]	16	16 **All Shook Up** .... Juke Box #1 / Best Seller #3 / Jockey #3	*1*	RCA 6870
7/01/57	**1** [1]	16	17 **(Let Me Be Your) Teddy Bear**/ Best Seller #1 / Jockey #4	*1*	
9/16/57	**15**	2	18 Loving You .... Jockey #15	20	RCA 7000
8/19/57	**11**	2	19 Mean Woman Blues .... Jockey #11 from the E.P. "Loving You" Vol. II (above 3: from the film "Loving You"); #5 pop hit for Roy Orbison in 1963		RCA EPA 2-1515
10/14/57	**1** [1]	24	20 **Jailhouse Rock**/ Best Seller #1 / Jockey #3	*1*	
10/28/57	**11**	4	21 Treat Me Nice... Jockey #11 above 2: from the film "Jailhouse Rock"	18	RCA 7035
2/03/58	**2** [5]	18	22 ●**Don't**/ Best Seller #2 / Jockey #3	*1*	
2/10/58	**5**	18	23 **I Beg Of You** .... Jockey #5	8	RCA 7150
4/21/58	**3**	15	24 ●**Wear My Ring Around Your Neck**/ Best Seller #3 / Jockey #4	2	
		3	25 Doncha' Think It's Time................................. Best Seller flip		RCA 7240
6/30/58	**2** [2]	16	26 ●**Hard Headed Woman**/ Best Seller #2 / Jockey #8	*1*	
		3	27 Don't Ask Me Why .... Best Seller flip above 2: from the film "King Creole"	25	RCA 7280
12/22/58	**24**	3	28 ●**One Night** .... #11 R&B hit for Smiley Lewis in 1956	4	RCA 7410
5/30/60	**27**	2	29 Stuck On You .... recorded 15 days after Presley's Army discharge	*1*	RCA 7740
12/12/60+	**22**	6	30 ●**Are You Lonesome To-night?** .... Vaughn Deleath and Henry Burr both had top 10 versions in 1927	*1*	RCA 7810
4/06/68	**55**	6	31 U.S. Male	28	RCA 9465
6/29/68	**50**	8	32 Your Time Hasn't Come Yet, Baby................... from the film "Speedway"	72	RCA 9547
4/19/69	**56**	2	33 Memories... from the NBC-TV special "Elvis"	35	RCA 9731
6/14/69	**60**	7	34 ●**In The Ghetto**	3	RCA 9741
8/16/69	**74**	3	35 Clean Up Your Own Back Yard .... from the film "The Trouble With Girls (and how to get into it)"	35	RCA 9747
12/20/69+	**13**	12	36 ●**Don't Cry Daddy**	6	RCA 9768
2/28/70	**31**	10	37 Kentucky Rain	16	RCA 9791

DEBUT DATE	PEAK POS	WKS CHR		ARTIST — Record Title	POP POS	Label & Number
				ELVIS PRESLEY — Continued		
6/06/70	**37**	10	38●	The Wonder Of You	9	RCA 9835
				recorded live in Las Vegas; #25 pop hit for Ray Peterson in 1959		
8/29/70	**57**	6	39	I've Lost You/	32	
		6	40	The Next Step Is Love	Flp	RCA 9873
12/05/70	**56**	5	41	You Don't Have To Say You Love Me	11	RCA 9916
				#4 pop hit for Dusty Springfield in 1966		
1/09/71	**9**	13	42	**There Goes My Everything/**	Flp	
				#20 pop hit for Engelbert Humperdinck in 1967		
1/09/71	**23**	13	43	I Really Don't Want To Know	21	RCA 9960
				#11 pop hit for Les Paul & Mary Ford in 1954		
3/27/71	**55**	8	44	Where Did They Go, Lord	33	RCA 9980
6/05/71	**34**	8	45	Life	53	RCA 9985
3/04/72	**68**	2	46	Until It's Time For You To Go........................	40	RCA 0619
				#53 pop hit for Neil Diamond in 1970		
9/09/72	**36**	13	47	It's A Matter Of Time		RCA 0769
				flip side "Burning Love" hit POS 2 on the pop charts		
12/09/72+	**16**	13	48	Always On My Mind/		
		12	49	Separate Ways	20	RCA 0815
				from the film "Elvis on Tour"		
4/28/73	**31**	10	50	Fool/	Flp	
		10	51	Steamroller Blues	17	RCA 0910
				recorded live in Hawaii (written by James Taylor in 1970)		
10/06/73	**42**	10	52	For Ol' Times Sake	Flp	RCA 0088
				flip side "Raised On Rock" hit POS 41 on the pop charts		
2/16/74	**4**	13	53	**I've Got A Thing About You Baby/**	39	
		13	54	Take Good Care Of Her	Flp	RCA 0196
				#7 pop hit for Adam Wade in 1961		
6/08/74	**6**	15	55	**Help Me/**		
		15	56	If You Talk In Your Sleep	17	RCA 0280
10/26/74+	**9**	14	57	**It's Midnight/**		
		5	58	Promised Land	14	RCA 10074
				#41 pop hit for Chuck Berry in 1965		
2/08/75	**14**	10	59	My Boy..	20	RCA 10191
				#41 pop hit for Richard Harris in 1972		
5/17/75	**11**	13	60	T-R-O-U-B-L-E	35	RCA 10278
10/18/75	**33**	10	61	Pieces Of My Life		RCA 10401
				flip side "Bringing It Back" hit POS 65 on the pop charts		
4/10/76	**6**	13	62	**Hurt/**	28	
				#4 pop hit for Timi Yuro in 1961		
		13	63	For The Heart..	Flp	RCA 10601
12/25/76+	**1**[1]	16	64	**Moody Blue/**	31	
		16	65	She Thinks I Still Care................................	Flp	RCA 10857
6/25/77	**1**[1]	17	66●	**Way Down/**	18	
		17	67	Pledging My Love		RCA 10998
				#1 R&B hit for Johnny Ace in 1955		
11/19/77+	**2**[1]	15	68●	**My Way**	22	RCA 11165
				recorded live from Elvis' tour; written in 1969 by Paul Anka		
3/25/78	**6**	11	69	**Unchained Melody/**		
				there have been 8 pop charted versions, 1955-81		
		11	70	Softly, As I Leave You .... [S]	109	RCA 11212
				Elvis talks, with vocal by Sherrill Neilsen		
8/12/78	**78**	4	71	Puppet On A String/ [R]		
				#14 pop hit for Elvis in 1965 (RCA 0650)		
		4	72	(Let Me Be Your) Teddy Bear.................... [R]	105	RCA 11320
4/21/79	**10**	12	73	**Are You Sincere/**		
				#3 pop hit for Andy Williams in 1958		
		12	74	Solitaire		RCA 11533
				#17 pop hit for the Carpenters in 1975; written by Neil Sedaka		
8/11/79	**6**	13	75	**There's A Honky Tonk Angel (Who Will Take Me Back In)/**		
		13	76	I Got A Feelin' In My Body..........................		RCA 11679
1/17/81	**1**[1]	13	77	**Guitar Man** .... [R]	28	RCA 12158
				re-mix by Felton Jarvis (d: 1/3/81) of Elvis' 1968 hit		
4/18/81	**8**	15	78	**Lovin' Arms/**		
				#61 pop hit for Dobie Gray in 1973		
		15	79	You Asked Me To		RCA 12205

DEBUT DATE	PEAK POS	WKS CHR	ARTIST — Record Title	POP POS	Label & Number
			ELVIS PRESLEY — Continued		
2/27/82	**73**	4	80 You'll Never Walk Alone/ [R]		
			#90 pop hit for Elvis in 1968		
		4	81 There Goes My Everything......................... [R]		RCA 13058
11/06/82	**31**	12	82 The Elvis Medley..	*71*	RCA 13351
			Jailhouse Rock/Teddy Bear/Hound Dog/Don't Be Cruel/Burning Love/ Suspicious Minds		
5/07/83	**92**	2	83 I Was The One/ [R]		
		2	84 Wear My Ring Around Your Neck............... [R]		RCA 13500
			CHUCK PRICE		
11/02/74	**75**	6	1 Slow Down..		Playboy 6010
11/22/75	**54**	8	2 Last Of The Outlaws		Playboy 6052
4/03/76	**97**	2	3 Cadillac Johnson		Playboy 6067
5/29/76	**48**	8	4 I Don't Want It..		Playboy 6072
10/23/76	**81**	3	5 Rye Whiskey		Playboy 6087
2/26/77	**91**	4	6 Is Anybody Goin' To San Antone		Playboy 6099
			DAVID PRICE		
			Rodeo rider from Odessa, Texas. Band leader for Red Stegall from 1977-79.		
2/08/64	**29**	8	1 The World Lost A Man		Rice 1001
			DENISE PRICE		
			Born Denise Davis in Russellville, Alabama. Miss Alabama beauty queen in 1976. Winner of the first Wrangler Star Search contest.		
12/25/82	**94**	3	1 Two Hearts Can't Be Wrong		Dimension 1037
			KENNY PRICE ★★**134**★★		
			Born on 5/27/31 in Florence, Kentucky; died of a heart attack on 8/4/87. In the service from 1952-54 and appeared with the Horace Heidt USO shows in Korea. Worked on WLW-TV Hometowners show and Midwestern Hayride in 1957. Appeared on the "Hee-Haw" TV series from 1976. Known as "The Round Mound Of Sound".		
8/20/66	**7**	18	1 **Walking On New Grass**...............................		Boone 1042
12/24/66+	**7**	17	2 **Happy Tracks**		Boone 1051
5/13/67	**26**	12	3 Pretty Girl, Pretty Clothes, Pretty Sad		Boone 1056
9/09/67	**24**	12	4 Grass Won't Grow On A Busy Street		Boone 1063
12/16/67+	**11**	15	5 My Goal For Today		Boone 1067
4/27/68	**31**	8	6 Going Home For The Last Time		Boone 1070
9/07/68	**37**	8	7 Southern Bound..		Boone 1075
12/07/68	**59**	6	8 It Don't Mean A Thing To Me..........................		Boone 1081
5/10/69	**64**	5	9 Who Do I Know In Dallas		Boone 1085
12/06/69	**62**	4	10 Atlanta Georgia Stray		RCA 0260
1/31/70	**17**	12	11 Northeast Arkansas Mississippi County Bootlegger.................................		RCA 9787
7/18/70	**10**	14	12 **Biloxi**		RCA 9869
12/19/70+	**8**	14	13 **The Sheriff Of Boone County**........................	*119*	RCA 9932
5/01/71	**55**	7	14 Tell Her You Love Her..................................		RCA 9973
9/18/71	**38**	11	15 Charlotte Fever...		RCA 1015
1/15/72	**37**	10	16 Super Sideman		RCA 0617
4/29/72	**44**	11	17 You Almost Slipped My Mind...........................		RCA 0686
9/16/72	**24**	11	18 Sea Of Heartbreak		RCA 0781
1/20/73	**53**	8	19 Don't Tell Me Your Troubles		RCA 0872
5/12/73	**52**	7	20 30 California Women		RCA 0936
9/22/73	**52**	11	21 You're Wearin' Me Down		RCA 0083
12/29/73+	**29**	12	22 Turn On Your Light (And Let It Shine)		RCA 0198
4/27/74	**69**	6	23 Que Pasa		RCA 0256
8/31/74	**42**	11	24 Let's Truck Together		RCA 10039
1/04/75	**67**	10	25 Easy Look		RCA 10141
5/03/75	**65**	8	26 Birds And Children Fly Away		RCA 10260
1/10/76	**60**	8	27 Too Big A Price To Pay		RCA 10460
6/04/77	**60**	6	28 I'd Buy You Chattanooga		MRC 1001
9/17/77	**74**	5	29 Leavin'...		MRC 1004
12/24/77+	**50**	9	30 Afraid You'd Come Back		MRC 1007
4/08/78	**74**	6	31 Sunshine Man...		MRC 1012

DEBUT DATE	PEAK POS	WKS CHR	ARTIST — Record Title	POP POS	Label & Number
			KENNY PRICE — Continued		
1/20/79	**67**	7	32 Hey There.................................		MRC 1025
			#1 pop hit for Rosemary Clooney in 1954		
2/23/80	**60**	5	33 Well Rounded Traveling Man......................		Dimension 1003
9/13/80	**79**	4	34 She's Leavin' (And I'm Almost Gone)		Dimension 1010
			RAY PRICE ★★**6**★★		
			Born on 1/12/26 in Perryville, Texas; raised in Dallas. In the service from 1944-46, then attended veterinary college. Worked on Hillbilly Circus, KRBC-Abilene, in 1948, and Big D Jamboree in Dallas. First recorded for Bullet in 1950. On the soundtrack of the film "Honky Tonk Man". Known as "The Cherokee Cowboy" (also the name of his backing band).		
5/17/52	**3**	11	1 Talk To Your Heart		Columbia 20913
			Jockey #3 / Juke Box #6 / Best Seller #10		
11/08/52	**4**	7	2 Don't Let The Stars Get In Your Eyes...........		Columbia 21025
			Best Seller #4 / Jockey #6 / Juke Box #7		
			#1 pop hit for Perry Como in 1953		
3/06/54	**2**[2]	19	3 I'll Be There (If You Ever Want Me)/		
			Best Seller #2 / Jockey #2 / Juke Box #3		
4/10/54	**6**	13	4 Release Me		Columbia 21214
			Juke Box #6 / Best Seller #7		
			Esther Phillips and Engelbert Humperdinck had top 10 hits, 1960s		
6/26/54	**13**	4	5 Much Too Young To Die		Columbia 21249
			Best Seller #13 / Jockey #13		
10/30/54	**8**	13	6 If You Don't, Somebody Else Will		Columbia 21315
			Best Seller #8 / Juke Box #10 / Jockey #14		
1/07/56	**5**	11	7 Run Boy.................................		Columbia 21474
			Jockey #5 / Juke Box #10 / Best Seller #15		
5/26/56	**1**[20]	45	8 Crazy Arms/	67	
			Jockey #1(20) / Best Seller #1 (11) / Juke Box #1(1)		
6/09/56	**7**	7	9 You Done Me Wrong		Columbia 21510
			Jockey #7		
11/10/56	**2**[2]	22	10 I've Got A New Heartache/		
			Jockey #2 / Juke Box #2 / Best Seller #3		
11/17/56	**4**	21	11 Wasted Words		Columbia 21562
			Best Seller #4 / Jockey #6 / Juke Box #9		
6/10/57	**12**	4	12 I'll Be There (When You Get Lonely)		Columbia 40889
			Jockey #12 / Best Seller #13		
7/29/57	**1**[4]	37	13 My Shoes Keep Walking Back To You.............	63	Columbia 40951
			Jockey #1(4) / Best Seller #3		
3/03/58	**3**	18	14 Curtain In The Window/		
			Jockey #3 / Best Seller #6		
		4	15 It's All Your Fault		Columbia 41105
			Best Seller flip		
7/14/58	**1**[13]	34	16 City Lights/	71	
			Hot C&W #1 / Jockey #2		
7/21/58	**3**	19	17 Invitation To The Blues	92	Columbia 41191
			Jockey #3 / Best Seller #8		
1/05/59	**7**	19	18 That's What It's Like To Be Lonesome..........		Columbia 41309
5/04/59	**2**[1]	40	19 Heartaches By The Number		Columbia 41374
			#1 pop hit for Guy Mitchell in 1959		
10/12/59	**1**[2]	30	20 The Same Old Me/		
11/23/59	**5**	15	21 Under Your Spell Again		Columbia 41477
4/04/60	**2**[8]	27	22 One More Time		Columbia 41590
10/03/60	**5**	17	23 I Wish I Could Fall In Love Today/		
10/24/60	**23**	3	24 I Can't Run Away From Myself		Columbia 41767
3/20/61	**5**	21	25 Heart Over Mind/		
3/27/61	**13**	11	26 The Twenty-Fourth Hour		Columbia 41947
10/09/61	**3**	23	27 Soft Rain/	115	
11/13/61	**26**	2	28 Here We Are Again.................................		Columbia 42132
6/02/62	**12**	8	29 I've Just Destroyed The World (I'm Living In)/		
6/02/62	**22**	1	30 Big Shoes		Columbia 42310
9/22/62	**5**	15	31 Pride.................................		Columbia 42518
2/09/63	**7**	20	32 Walk Me To The Door/		
3/02/63	**11**	16	33 You Took Her Off My Hands (Now Please Take Her Off My Mind)...............................		Columbia 42658
8/10/63	**2**[1]	21	34 Make The World Go Away/	100	
10/05/63	**28**	2	35 Night Life		Columbia 42827

DEBUT DATE	PEAK POS	WKS CHR	ARTIST — Record Title	POP POS	Label & Number
			RAY PRICE — Continued		
3/14/64	**2**⁴	27	**36 Burning Memories/**		
4/04/64	**34**	9	37 That's All That Matters.............................		Columbia 42971
9/05/64	**7**	17	**38 Please Talk To My Heart**		Columbia 43086
1/09/65	**38**	4	39 A Thing Called Sadness		Columbia 43162
5/08/65	**2**²	24	**40 The Other Woman**		Columbia 43264
11/27/65+	**11**	14	41 Don't You Ever Get Tired Of Hurting Me...........		Columbia 43427
4/23/66	**7**	18	**42 A Way To Survive/**		
6/11/66	**28**	6	43 I'm Not Crazy Yet..................................		Columbia 43560
10/15/66	**3**	18	**44 Touch My Heart**.................................		Columbia 43795
3/25/67	**9**	17	**45 Danny Boy**	60	Columbia 44042
7/22/67	**6**	18	**46 I'm Still Not Over You/**		
8/19/67	**73**	1	47 Crazy..		Columbia 44195
12/30/67+	**8**	15	**48 Take Me As I Am (Or Let Me Go)**.................		Columbia 44374
5/04/68	**11**	16	49 I've Been There Before		Columbia 44505
10/05/68	**6**	14	**50 She Wears My Ring**		Columbia 44628
3/01/69	**51**	4	51 Set Me Free		Columbia 44747
3/08/69	**11**	15	52 Sweetheart Of The Year		Columbia 44761
8/16/69	**14**	12	53 Raining In My Heart		Columbia 44931
			#88 pop hit for Buddy Holly in 1959		
11/22/69	**14**	11	54 April's Fool......................................		Columbia 45005
3/07/70	**8**	15	55 You Wouldn't Know Love..........................		Columbia 45095
6/27/70	**1**¹	26	**56 For The Good Times/**	11	
		18	57 Grazin' In Greener Pastures......................		Columbia 45178
3/20/71	**1**³	19	**58 I Won't Mention It Again**	42	Columbia 45329
8/07/71	**2**¹	17	**59 I'd Rather Be Sorry**	70	Columbia 45425
4/15/72	**2**¹	14	**60 The Lonesomest Lonesome/**	109	
4/15/72	**66**	14	61 That's What Leaving's About		Columbia 45583
11/04/72	**1**³	16	**62 She's Got To Be A Saint**	93	Columbia 45724
7/28/73	**1**¹	16	**63 You're The Best Thing That Ever Happened To Me**..	82	Columbia 45889
			#3 pop hit for Gladys Knight & The Pips in 1974		
3/16/74	**25**	13	64 Storms Of Troubled Times		Columbia 46015
8/17/74	**15**	11	65 Like A First Time Thing		Columbia 10006
10/26/74+	**4**	15	**66 Like Old Times Again**		Myrrh 146
2/08/75	**3**	14	**67 Roses And Love Songs**..........................		Myrrh 150
5/31/75	**17**	13	68 Farthest Thing From My Mind		ABC 12095
8/09/75	**31**	11	69 If You Ever Change Your Mind....................		Columbia 10150
			above 7: written by Jim Weatherly		
11/08/75	**40**	12	70 Say I Do		ABC/Dot 17588
3/27/76	**34**	9	71 That's All She Wrote		ABC/Dot 17616
7/24/76	**41**	10	72 To Make A Long Story Short/		
7/24/76	**47**	10	73 We're Getting There		ABC/Dot 17637
12/04/76+	**14**	15	74 A Mansion On The Hill		ABC/Dot 17666
3/26/77	**38**	9	75 Help Me..		Columbia 10503
5/28/77	**28**	11	76 Different Kind Of Flower..........................		ABC/Dot 17690
10/01/77	**21**	12	77 Born To Love Me.................................		ABC/Dot 17718
			also released on Columbia 10631		
10/28/78+	**19**	13	78 Feet...		Monument 267
3/03/79	**30**	12	79 There's Always Me		Monument 277
6/09/79	**18**	13	80 That's The Only Way To Say Good Morning		Monument 283
11/24/79+	**43**	9	81 Misty Morning Rain		Monument 290
8/09/80	**3**	15	**82 Faded Love**		Columbia 11329
			WILLIE NELSON & RAY PRICE		
12/06/80+	**11**	14	83 Don't You Ever Get Tired (Of Hurting Me)		Columbia 11405
			WILLIE NELSON & RAY PRICE		
3/28/81	**28**	13	84 Getting Over You Again		Dimension 1018
7/18/81	**6**	17	**85 It Don't Hurt Me Half As Bad**...................		Dimension 1021
11/14/81+	**9**	18	**86 Diamonds In The Stars**.........................		Dimension 1024
4/03/82	**18**	15	87 Forty And Fadin'.................................		Dimension 1031
6/05/82	**19**	16	88 Old Friends		Columbia 02681
			ROGER MILLER & WILLIE NELSON (with RAY PRICE)		

DEBUT DATE	PEAK POS	WKS CHR		ARTIST — Record Title	POP POS	Label & Number
				RAY PRICE — Continued		
8/07/82	62	7	89	Wait Till Those Bridges Are Gone		Dimension 1035
12/04/82+	55	9	90	Somewhere In Texas................................		Dimension 1038
1/15/83	70	6	91	One Fiddle, Two Fiddle/		
		6	92	San Antonio Rose		Warner 29830
				above 2: with Johnny Gimble & The Texas Swing Band - from the film "Honkytonk Man"		
5/07/83	72	6	93	Willie, Write Me A Song.............................		Warner 29691
8/27/83	70	5	94	Scotch And Soda...................................		Viva 29543
				#81 pop hit for The Kingston Trio in 1962		
6/23/84	87	4	95	A New Place To Begin		Viva 29277
9/08/84	73	6	96	Better Class Of Loser		Viva 29217
11/17/84	77	7	97	What Am I Gonna Do Without You		Viva 29147
5/25/85	77	6	98	(She's Got A Hold Of Me Where It Hurts) She Won't Let Go		Step One 341
8/31/85	81	7	99	I'm Not Leaving (I'm Just Getting Out Of Your Way)...		Step One 344
12/21/85+	67	7	100	Five Fingers		Step One 350
3/15/86	60	8	101	You're Nobody Till Somebody Loves You..........		Step One 352
				#14 pop hit for Russ Morgan in 1946		
6/21/86	73	5	102	All The Way		Step One 355
				#2 pop hit for Frank Sinatra in 1957		
9/27/86	86	3	103	Please Don't Talk About Me When I'm Gone.......		Step One 361
				#3 pop hit for Gene Austin in 1931		
12/27/86+	55	8	104	When You Gave Your Love To Me		Step One 366
10/24/87	52	11	105	Just Enough Love		Step One 378
3/12/88	68	5	106	Big Ole Teardrops		Step One 383
7/09/88	55	7	107	Don't The Morning Always Come Too Soon.......		Step One 388
12/10/88	83	4	108	I'd Do It All Over Again		Step One 393
				TONI PRICE		
				Nashville-based singer.		
1/25/86	59	9	1	Mississippi Break Down..........................		Luv 114
9/27/86	71	6	2	How Much Do I Owe You.........................		Master 01
9/26/87	80	3	3	I Want To Be Wanted		Prairie D. 8744
				CHARLEY PRIDE ★★18★★		
				Born on 3/18/38 in Sledge, Mississippi. Played baseball for the Negro American League, Memphis Red Sox, from 1954-56. In service from 1956-58. Worked in construction in Montana and played semi-pro baseball in the Pioneer League. Discovered by Red Sovine in 1963. The most successful black country performer. CMA award: Entertainer of the Year - 1971.		
12/03/66+	9	19	1	**Just Between You And Me**		RCA 9000
4/29/67	6	19	2	**I Know One**		RCA 9162
9/02/67	4	19	3	**Does My Ring Hurt Your Finger**		RCA 9281
				above 3 shown as: **COUNTRY CHARLEY PRIDE**		
1/06/68	4	17	4	**The Day The World Stood Still**....................		RCA 9403
5/18/68	2²	15	5	**The Easy Part's Over**		RCA 9514
10/05/68	4	14	6	**Let The Chips Fall**		RCA 9622
2/01/69	3	16	7	**Kaw-Liga**	120	RCA 9716
6/14/69	1¹	17	8	**All I Have To Offer You (Is Me)**	91	RCA 0167
11/08/69	1³	16	9	**(I'm So) Afraid Of Losing You Again**	74	RCA 0265
3/07/70	1²	17	10	**Is Anybody Goin' To San Antone**..................	70	RCA 9806
6/13/70	1²	17	11	**Wonder Could I Live There Anymore**.............	87	RCA 9855
9/26/70	1²	16	12	**I Can't Believe That You've Stopped Loving Me**	71	RCA 9902
2/06/71	1³	14	13	**I'd Rather Love You**................................	79	RCA 9952
4/24/71	21	10	14	Let Me Live/	104	
4/24/71	70	10	15	Did You Think To Pray		RCA 9974
6/26/71	1⁴	16	16	**I'm Just Me**......................................	94	RCA 9996
10/23/71	1⁵	19	17●	**Kiss An Angel Good Mornin'**	21	RCA 0550
2/19/72	2²	15	18	**All His Children**	92	RCA 0624
				CHARLEY PRIDE with HENRY MANCINI from the film "Sometimes A Great Notion"		
6/03/72	1³	16	19	**It's Gonna Take A Little Bit Longer**	102	RCA 0707
10/07/72	1³	16	20	**She's Too Good To Be True**..........................		RCA 0802

DEBUT DATE	PEAK POS	WKS CHR	ARTIST — Record Title	POP POS	Label & Number
			CHARLEY PRIDE — Continued		
2/10/73	**1**¹	14	21 **A Shoulder To Cry On** .... *written by Merle Haggard*	*101*	RCA 0884
5/12/73	**1**¹	15	22 **Don't Fight The Feelings Of Love**	*101*	RCA 0942
10/13/73	**1**¹	16	23 **Amazing Love**		RCA 0073
4/20/74	**3**	14	24 **We Could**		RCA 0257
8/24/74	**3**	17	25 **Mississippi Cotton Picking Delta Town**	70	RCA 10030
12/14/74+	**1**¹	12	26 **Then Who Am I**		RCA 10126
3/29/75	**6**	14	27 **I Ain't All Bad**	*101*	RCA 10236
8/09/75	**1**¹	14	28 **Hope You're Feelin' Me (Like I'm Feelin' You)** .		RCA 10344
12/06/75+	**3**	14	29 **The Happiness Of Having You**		RCA 10455
3/13/76	**1**¹	14	30 **My Eyes Can Only See As Far As You**		RCA 10592
8/28/76	**2**²	15	31 **A Whole Lotta Things To Sing About**		RCA 10757
1/29/77	**1**¹	14	32 **She's Just An Old Love Turned Memory**		RCA 10875
5/21/77	**1**¹	14	33 **I'll Be Leaving Alone**		RCA 10975
9/17/77	**1**¹	14	34 **More To Me**		RCA 11086
2/11/78	**1**²	15	35 **Someone Loves You Honey**		RCA 11201
6/24/78	**3**	15	36 **When I Stop Leaving (I'll Be Gone)**		RCA 11287
10/21/78	**2**³	14	37 **Burgers And Fries**		RCA 11391
2/24/79	**1**¹	15	38 **Where Do I Put Her Memory**		RCA 11477
7/14/79	**1**¹	15	39 **You're My Jamaica**		RCA 11655
10/27/79	**89**	2	40 Dallas Cowboys .... *special edition tribute to the NFL team*		RCA 11736
11/03/79+	**2**¹	15	41 **Missin' You**		RCA 11751
2/16/80	**1**¹	13	42 **Honky Tonk Blues**		RCA 11912
5/10/80	**1**¹	15	43 **You Win Again**		RCA 12002
9/27/80	**4**	18	44 **You Almost Slipped My Mind**		RCA 12100
3/07/81	**7**	13	45 **Roll On Mississippi**		RCA 12178
8/22/81	**1**²	15	46 **Never Been So Loved (In All My Life)**		RCA 12294
12/26/81+	**1**¹	18	47 **Mountain Of Love** .... *#21 pop hit for Harold Dorman in 1960*		RCA 13014
4/24/82	**2**²	18	48 **I Don't Think She's In Love Anymore**		RCA 13096
8/28/82	**1**¹	17	49 **You're So Good When You're Bad**		RCA 13293
12/04/82+	**1**¹	19	50 **Why Baby Why**		RCA 13397
3/05/83	**7**	16	51 **More And More**		RCA 13451
6/25/83	**1**¹	21	52 **Night Games**		RCA 13542
10/15/83+	**2**¹	20	53 **Ev'ry Heart Should Have One**		RCA 13648
6/09/84	**9**	20	54 **The Power Of Love**		RCA 13821
11/03/84	**32**	13	55 Missin' Mississippi		RCA 13936
4/13/85	**25**	13	56 Down On The Farm		RCA 14045
7/06/85	**34**	11	57 Let A Little Love Come In		RCA 14134
1/18/86	**75**	5	58 The Best There Is		RCA 14265
4/05/86	**74**	7	59 Love On A Blue Rainy Day...........................		RCA 14296
3/21/87	**14**	22	60 Have I Got Some Blues For You		16th Ave. 70400
7/18/87	**31**	15	61 If You Still Want A Fool Around		16th Ave. 70402
12/12/87+	**5**	23	62 **Shouldn't It Be Easier Than This**		16th Ave. 70408
5/07/88	**13**	19	63 I'm Gonna Love Her On The Radio		16th Ave. 70414
10/15/88	**49**	13	64 Where Was I...		16th Ave. 70420
			PAUL PROCTOR		
12/20/86	**74**	4	1 Not Tonight..		Aurora 1003
2/21/87	**79**	4	2 He's Not Good Enough		Aurora 1005
7/25/87	**62**	6	3 Ain't We Got Love		19th Ave. 1009
11/19/88	**96**	1	4 Tied To The Wheel Of A Runaway Heart...........		19th Ave. 1012
			RONNIE PROPHET Born on 12/26/43 in Calumet, Quebec. Worked clubs in Ottawa and Montreal in the late 50s. Performed in the Bahamas and Fort Lauderdale in the mid-60s. Moved to Nashville in 1969, toured with Danny Thomas in 1979. Own TV series in England.		
8/23/75	**26**	12	1 Sanctuary..		RCA 50027
12/27/75+	**36**	10	2 Shine On		RCA 50136
5/01/76	**50**	7	3 It's Enough		RCA 50205
10/09/76	**82**	5	4 Big Big World		RCA 50273

DEBUT DATE	PEAK POS	WKS CHR	ARTIST — Record Title	POP POS	Label & Number
			RONNIE PROPHET — Continued		
10/15/77	99	2	5 It Ain't Easy Lovin' Me....................................		RCA 50391
			JEANNE PRUETT ★★**182**★★		
			Born Norma Jean Bowman on 1/30/37 in Pell City, Alabama. Moved to Nashville in 1956 with husband Jack Pruett (guitarist for Marty Robbins). Songwriter for Robbins from 1963. On the Grand Ole Opry since 1973.		
9/18/71	66	6	1 Hold On To My Unchanging Love		Decca 32857
3/11/72	34	12	2 Love Me		Decca 32929
8/05/72	64	3	3 Call On Me		Decca 32977
11/04/72	60	6	4 I Forgot More Than You'll Ever Know (About Him)..		Decca 33013
3/31/73	1³	18	5 **Satin Sheets**	28	MCA 40015
9/15/73	8	14	6 **I'm Your Woman**		MCA 40116
3/23/74	15	14	7 You Don't Need To Move A Mountain.................		MCA 40207
8/31/74	22	15	8 Welcome To The Sunshine (Sweet Baby Jane)		MCA 40284
1/18/75	25	12	9 Just Like Your Daddy		MCA 40340
5/10/75	41	9	10 Honey On His Hands..................................		MCA 40395
7/26/75	24	13	11 A Poor Man's Woman..................................		MCA 40440
12/13/75+	77	7	12 My Baby's Gone		MCA 40490
10/02/76	41	8	13 I've Taken		MCA 40605
2/19/77	30	10	14 I'm Living A Lie		MCA 40678
5/21/77	85	4	15 She's Still All Over You		MCA 40723
2/25/78	94	3	16 I'm A Woman		Mercury 55017
8/11/79	54	8	17 Please Sing Satin Sheets For Me		IBC 0002
			ending includes several bars of "Satin Sheets"		
11/24/79+	6	16	18 **Back To Back**...		IBC 0005
3/15/80	5	15	19 **Temporarily Yours**...................................		IBC 0008
7/05/80	9	14	20 **It's Too Late**		IBC 00010
3/14/81	81	3	21 Sad Ole Shade Of Gray		Paid 118
6/06/81	72	4	22 I Ought To Feel Guilty		Paid 136
4/16/83	58	8	23 Love Me .... [R]		Audiograph 454
			JEANNE PRUETT/MARTY ROBBINS		
			both Jeanne and Marty had solo hits of this tune		
7/09/83	73	4	24 Lady Of The Eighties		Audiograph 467
8/22/87	81	3	25 Rented Room...		MSR 1956
			LEWIS PRUITT		
			Longtime lead guitarist for Carl Smith.		
12/07/59+	10	21	1 **Timbrook**..		Peach 725
6/27/60	4	17	2 **Softly And Tenderly (I'll Hold You In My Arms)**...		Decca 31095
4/03/61	11	9	3 Crazy Bullfrog		Decca 31201
			CACTUS PRYOR & THE PRICKLYPEARS		
			Richard "Cactus" Pryor, longtime DJ at KTBC-Austin, Texas, member of the Country Music DJ Hall of Fame.		
6/03/50	7	1	1 **Cry Of The Dying Duck In A Thunderstorm**.................................... [N]		Four Star 1459
			Jockey #7		
			ARTHUR PRYSOCK		
			Born on 1/2/29 in Spartanburg, South Carolina. Very popular night club act, frequently appearing with his brother, saxophonist Wilbert "Red" Prysock.		
9/29/79	74	5	1 Today I Started Loving You Again...................		Gusto 9023
			JERRY PUCKETT		
8/27/83	81	3	1 Heart On The Run		Atln. Am. 99860
			LEROY PULLINS		
			Born Carl Leroy Pullins on 11/12/40 in Elgin, Illinois.		
6/25/66	18	11	1 I'm A Nut.. [N]	57	Kapp 758
			PUMP BOYS & DINETTES		
			From original cast recording of the Broadway musical "Pump Boys And Dinettes".		
3/19/83	67	5	1 The Night Dolly Parton Was Almost Mine		CBS 03549

DEBUT DATE	PEAK POS	WKS CHR	ARTIST — Record Title	POP POS	Label & Number
			PURE PRAIRIE LEAGUE		
			Group formed in Cincinnati in 1971. Vince Gill was lead singer from 1980-83.		
6/19/76	**98**	2	1 That'll Be The Day	*106*	RCA 10679
			#1 pop hit for The Crickets in 1957		
			CURLY PUTMAN		
			Born Claude Putman, Jr. on 11/20/30 in Princeton, Alabama. Prolific songwriter, wrote "Green Green Grass Of Home" for Tom Jones, "He Stopped Loving Her Today" for George Jones and "My Elusive Dreams" for David Houston & Tammy Wynette.		
2/29/60	**23**	1	1 The Prison Song		Cherokee 504
7/08/67	**41**	9	2 My Elusive Dreams	*134*	ABC 10934
11/04/67	**67**	3	3 Set Me Free		ABC 10984
			CHUCK PYLE		
			Singer/songwriter born in Pittsburgh; raised in Iowa.		
9/28/85	**60**	6	1 Drifters Wind		Urban Sound 786
1/18/86	**81**	6	2 Breathless In The Night		Urban Sound 782

Q

DEBUT DATE	PEAK POS	WKS CHR	ARTIST — Record Title	POP POS	Label & Number
			JACK QUIST		
9/11/82	**52**	9	1 Memory Machine		Memory M. 1015

R

EDDIE RABBITT ★★53★★

Born Edward Thomas Rabbitt on 11/27/44 in Brooklyn; raised in East Orange, New Jersey. Singer/songwriter/guitarist. First recorded for 20th Century in 1964. Moved to Nashville in 1968. Became established after Elvis Presley recorded his song "Kentucky Rain".

DEBUT DATE	PEAK POS	WKS CHR	ARTIST — Record Title	POP POS	Label & Number
8/31/74	**34**	14	1 You Get To Me		Elektra 45895
3/22/75	**12**	17	2 Forgive And Forget		Elektra 45237
8/30/75	**11**	14	3 I Should Have Married You		Elektra 45269
2/07/76	**1**¹	16	4 **Drinkin' My Baby (Off My Mind)**		Elektra 45301
6/05/76	**5**	15	5 **Rocky Mountain Music/**	76	
		15	6 Do You Right Tonight		Elektra 45315
11/06/76+	**3**	16	7 **Two Dollars In The Jukebox**		Elektra 45357
4/02/77	**2**¹	16	8 **I Can't Help Myself**	77	Elektra 45390
8/20/77	**6**	15	9 **We Can't Go On Living Like This**		Elektra 45418
2/18/78	**2**²	16	10 **Hearts On Fire**		Elektra 45461
6/10/78	**1**¹	14	11 **You Don't Love Me Anymore**	53	Elektra 45488
9/30/78	**1**¹	14	12 **I Just Want To Love You**		Elektra 45531
12/23/78+	**1**³	15	13 **Every Which Way But Loose**	30	Elektra 45554
			from the film of the same title		
6/16/79	**1**¹	14	14 **Suspicions**	13	Elektra 46053
11/03/79+	**5**	15	15 **Pour Me Another Tequila**		Elektra 46558
3/15/80	**1**¹	14	16 **Gone Too Far**	82	Elektra 46613
6/21/80	**1**¹	15	17●**Drivin' My Life Away**	5	Elektra 46656
			from the film "Roadie"		
11/08/80+	**1**¹	17	18●**I Love A Rainy Night**	*1*	Elektra 47066
8/01/81	**1**¹	16	19 **Step By Step**	5	Elektra 47174
11/21/81+	**1**¹	17	20 **Someone Could Lose A Heart Tonight**	15	Elektra 47239
4/10/82	**2**³	16	21 **I Don't Know Where To Start**	35	Elektra 47435
10/09/82	**1**¹	19	22 **You And I**	7	Elektra 69936
			EDDIE RABBITT with CRYSTAL GAYLE		
4/02/83	**1**¹	17	23 **You Can't Run From Love**	55	Warner 29712
9/03/83	**10**	18	24 **You Put The Beat In My Heart**	81	Warner 29512
12/17/83+	**10**	15	25 **Nothing Like Falling In Love**		Warner 29431
5/19/84	**3**	18	26 **B-B-B-Burnin' Up With Love**		Warner 29279
10/06/84+	**1**¹	23	27 **The Best Year Of My Life**		Warner 29186
2/23/85	**4**	19	28 **Warning Sign**		Warner 29089
7/13/85	**6**	21	29 **She's Comin' Back To Say Goodbye**		Warner 28976

DEBUT DATE	PEAK POS	WKS CHR	ARTIST — Record Title	POP POS	Label & Number
			EDDIE RABBITT — Continued		
10/12/85	**10**	18	30 **A World Without Love**		RCA 14192
3/22/86	**4**	19	31 **Repetitive Regret**		RCA 14317
7/12/86	**1** ¹	20	32 **Both To Each Other (Friends & Lovers)**.........		RCA 14377
			EDDIE RABBITT & JUICE NEWTON		
11/01/86+	**9**	20	33 **Gotta Have You**		RCA 5012
1/16/88	**1** ¹	20	34 **I Wanna Dance With You**		RCA 5238
5/28/88	**1** ¹	18	35 **The Wanderer**		RCA 8306
			#2 pop hit for Dion in 1961		
10/08/88	**7**	22	36 **We Must Be Doin' Somethin' Right**		RCA 8716
			JIMMY RABBITT & RENEGADE		
			Jimmy was born Edward Payne in Holdenville, Oklahoma; raised in Tyler, Texas. First recorded rockabilly for Colt 45. Worked as a deejay in several cities.		
5/08/76	**80**	4	1 Ladies Love Outlaws.......................................		Capitol 4257
			LANA RAE		
2/19/72	**26**	14	1 You're My Shoulder To Lean On		Decca 32927
			LEON RAINES		
			Born in Mobile, Alabama.		
4/30/83	**79**	4	1 I'll Be Seeing You.......................................		Am. Spotlite 103
			#1 pop hit for Bing Crosby in 1944		
7/07/84	**91**	2	2 Don't Give Up On Her Now		Am. Spotlite 107
11/24/84	**81**	3	3 Biloxi Lady		Atln. Am. 99700
3/09/85	**83**	2	4 It Happens Every Time.................................		Atln. Am. 99670
12/26/87+	**71**	5	5 Most Of All...		So. Tracks 1089
			TINA RAINFORD		
4/09/77	**25**	14	1 Silver Bird		Epic 50304
10/15/77	**91**	4	2 Big Silver Angel		Epic 50455
			WILLIE RAINSFORD		
			Born William C. Rainsford in Nashville. Frequent substitute for Jerry Whitehurst on piano in Opry staff band and on "Nashville Now".		
3/26/77	**98**	2	1 No Relief In Sight		Louis. Hay. 7615
8/13/77	**85**	5	2 Cheater's Kit...		Rec. Prod. 7629
			JACK RAINWATER		
11/12/77	**96**	3	1 All I Want Is To Love You.............................		Laurie 3658
			MARVIN RAINWATER		
			Born Marvin Karlton Percy on 7/2/25 in Wichita, Kansas. Worked in logging camps in Oregon. Performed in clubs in Washington, DC with Roy Clark in 1953. Appeared on Red Foley's Ozark Jubilee in the early 50s. Worked on the Arthur Godfrey Show in 1955. Marvin is one-quarter Cherokee Indian.		
4/06/57	**3**	28	1 **Gonna Find Me A Bluebird/**	*18*	
			Best Seller #3 / Jockey #3 / Juke Box #5		
		1	2 So You Think You've Got Trouble		MGM 12412
			Best Seller flip		
4/14/58	**15**	3	3 Whole Lotta Woman	*60*	MGM 12609
			Best Seller #15		
9/15/58	**11**	1	4 Nothin' Needs Nothin'		MGM 12701
			Jockey #11		
7/06/59	**16**	6	5 Half-Breed	*66*	MGM 12803
			BONNIE RAITT		
			Born on 11/8/49 in Burbank, California. Daugher of Broadway/film star John Raitt.		
10/04/80	**42**	8	1 Don't It Make Ya Wanna Dance		Full Moon 47033
			from the film "Urban Cowboy"		
			PAL RAKES		
			Born Palmer Crawford Rakes, III in Tampa, Florida. While a teenager in Philadelphia, played in band with singer Daryl Hall (of pop duo Hall & Oates).		
4/02/77	**24**	12	1 That's When The Lyin' Stops (And The Lovin' Starts)		Warner 8340
7/30/77	**31**	10	2 'Til I Can't Take It Anymore		Warner 8416
1/07/78	**46**	10	3 If I Ever Come Back....................................		Warner 8506
10/28/78	**81**	3	4 Till Then		Warner 8656
			#8 pop hit for the Mills Brothers in 1944		
3/17/79	**92**	3	5 You And Me And The Green Grass		Warner 8765

DEBUT DATE	PEAK POS	WKS CHR	ARTIST — Record Title	POP POS	Label & Number
10/29/88	71	5	**PAL RAKES — Continued** 6 I'm Only Lonely For You		Atln. Am. 99276
			RAMBLERS - see RED FOLEY		
			RAMBLING ROGUE Nickname of songwriter/publisher/producer/executive, Fred Rose. Born on 8/24/1897 in Evansville, Indiana; died on 12/1/54. First recorded for Brunswick in the 1920s. One of first three elected to the Country Music Hall of Fame.		
10/27/45	5	1	1 **Tender-Hearted Sue**...................................		Okeh 6747
			WAYNE RANEY Born on 8/17/21 in Batesville, Arkansas. Harmonica wizard, worked with the Raney Family gospel singers and the Delmore Brothers in the late 40s.		
10/30/48	11	1	1 Lost John Boogie .... Juke Box #11 / Best Seller #14		King 719
11/20/48	13	2	2 Jack And Jill Boogie .... Juke Box #13		King 732
7/30/49	1³	22	3 **Why Don't You Haul Off And Love Me** .... Juke Box #1(3) / Best Seller #1(2) / Jockey #5	*22*	King 791
			RATTLESNAKE ANNIE Born Rose Ann Gallimore in Puryear, Tennessee in 1941.		
5/02/87	79	3	1 Callin' Your Bluff		Columbia 07024
1/09/88	79	3	2 Somewhere South Of Macon		Columbia 07634
			LEON RAUSCH Born Edgar Leon Rausch on 10/2/27 in Springfield, Missouri. Worked with Bob Wills and The Texas Playboys from 1958-64. Organized the New Texas Playboys in 1964. Lead vocalist of the Original Texas Playboys from the mid-70s.		
1/17/76	99	1	1 Through The Bottom Of The Glass		Derrick 105
8/21/76	91	5	2 She's The Trip I've Been On		Derrick 107
6/10/78	89	5	3 I'm Satisfied With You		Derrick 121
10/21/78	95	4	4 Let's Have A Heart To Heart Talk		Derrick 122
10/20/79	91	4	5 You Can Be Replaced		Derrick 124
12/15/79+	81	6	6 Palimony		Derrick 128
			EDDY RAVEN ★★91★★ Born Edward Garvin Futch on 8/19/44 in Lafayette, Louisiana. Performed with Johnny and Edgar Winter and the Rocking Cajuns. First recorded for Cosmos in 1962. Toured with the Jimmie Davis Band. Moved to Nashville in 1970, worked as a staff writer for Acuff-Rose.		
3/16/74	63	10	1 The Last Of The Sunshine Cowboys..................		ABC 11421
11/23/74+	46	13	2 Ain't She Somethin' Else		ABC 12037
4/19/75	27	11	3 Good News Bad News		ABC 12083
8/02/75	68	10	4 You're My Rainy Day Woman		ABC 12111
12/20/75+	34	10	5 Free To Be		ABC/Dot 17595
4/10/76	87	5	6 I Wanna Live		ABC/Dot 17618
8/28/76	94	3	7 The Curse Of A Woman		ABC/Dot 17646
12/11/76	90	4	8 I'm Losing It All......................................		ABC/Dot 17663
9/02/78	71	5	9 You're A Dancer		Monument 260
12/08/79+	44	11	10 Sweet Mother Texas		Dimension 003
3/15/80	25	11	11 Dealin' With The Devil		Dimension 1005
6/07/80	30	11	12 You've Got Those Eyes..............................		Dimension 1007
9/20/80	34	11	13 Another Texas Song		Dimension 1011
1/24/81	23	12	14 Peace Of Mind		Dimension 1017
5/23/81	13	15	15 I Should've Called		Elektra 47136
10/17/81+	11	18	16 Who Do You Know In California.....................		Elektra 47216
2/20/82	14	18	17 A Little Bit Crazy....................................		Elektra 47413
6/19/82	10	16	18 **She's Playing Hard To Forget**		Elektra 47469
11/06/82+	25	17	19 San Antonio Nights		Elektra 69929
3/17/84	1¹	22	20 **I Got Mexico**......................................		RCA 13746
7/21/84	9	18	21 **I Could Use Another You**		RCA 13839
11/10/84+	9	23	22 **She's Gonna Win Your Heart**		RCA 13939
4/20/85	9	21	23 **Operator, Operator**		RCA 14044
8/03/85	8	24	24 **I Wanna Hear It From You**........................		RCA 14164
12/07/85+	3	23	25 **You Should Have Been Gone By Now**		RCA 14250
5/31/86	3	22	26 **Sometimes A Lady**		RCA 14319

DEBUT DATE	PEAK POS	WKS CHR	ARTIST — Record Title	POP POS	Label & Number
			EDDY RAVEN — Continued		
11/15/86+	3	24	27 Right Hand Man		RCA 5032
3/28/87	3	21	28 You're Never Too Old For Young Love...........		RCA 5128
7/25/87	1¹	24	29 Shine, Shine, Shine..................................		RCA 5221
2/13/88	1¹	21	30 I'm Gonna Get You....................................		RCA 6831
6/18/88	1¹	21	31 Joe Knows How To Live..............................		RCA 8303
12/03/88+	4	21	32 'Til You Cry		RCA 8798
			MUNDO RAY - see MUNDO EARWOOD		
			SUSAN RAYE ★★**124**★★		
			Born on 10/8/44 in Eugene, Oregon. Appeared on the "Hoedown" TV show in Portland. Worked with Buck Owens from 1968-76 and on the "Hee-Haw" TV series from 1969. In the film "From Nashville With Music" in 1971.		
1/10/70	30	11	1 Put A Little Love In Your Heart		Capitol 2701
			#4 pop hit for Jackie DeShannon in 1969		
7/04/70	35	11	2 One Night Stand......................................		Capitol 2833
11/14/70+	10	13	3 Willy Jones		Capitol 2950
2/20/71	9	16	4 L.A. International Airport...........................	54	Capitol 3035
7/17/71	6	16	5 Pitty, Pitty, Patter..................................		Capitol 3129
11/13/71+	3	14	6 (I've Got A) Happy Heart		Capitol 3209
4/01/72	44	8	7 A Song To Sing.......................................		Capitol 3289
5/27/72	10	12	8 My Heart Has A Mind Of Its Own..................		Capitol 3327
			#1 pop hit for Connie Francis in 1960		
9/30/72	16	11	9 Wheel Of Fortune....................................		Capitol 3438
			#1 pop hit for Kay Starr in 1952		
12/23/72+	17	14	10 Love Sure Feels Good In My Heart..................		Capitol 3499
4/07/73	18	12	11 Cheating Game		Capitol 3569
9/08/73	23	12	12 Plastic Trains, Paper Planes........................		Capitol 3699
12/15/73+	57	9	13 When You Get Back From Nashville		Capitol 3782
4/06/74	18	14	14 Stop The World (And Let Me Off).....................		Capitol 3850
8/03/74	49	11	15 You Can Sure See It From Here		Capitol 3927
11/23/74+	9	16	16 Whatcha Gonna Do With A Dog Like That		Capitol 3980
5/24/75	58	7	17 Ghost Story...		Capitol 4063
10/16/76	87	5	18 Ozark Mountain Lullaby		United Art. 870
2/19/77	64	6	19 Mr. Heartache..		United Art. 934
4/30/77	53	8	20 Saturday Night To Sunday Quiet		United Art. 976
8/13/77	51	9	21 It Didn't Have To Be A Diamond		United Art. 1026
11/03/84	76	5	22 Put Another Notch In Your Belt/		
2/15/86	68	5	23 I Just Can't Take The Leaving Anymore		Westexas Am. 1
			BUCK OWENS & SUSAN RAYE:		
2/21/70	13	11	24 We're Gonna Get Together............................		Capitol 2731
5/09/70	12	12	25 Togetherness...		Capitol 2791
8/29/70	8	13	26 The Great White Horse...............................		Capitol 2871
7/15/72	13	14	27 Looking Back To See		Capitol 3368
6/16/73	35	8	28 The Good Old Days...................................		Capitol 3610
7/05/75	20	13	29 Love Is Strange..		Capitol 4100
			#11 pop hit for Mickey & Sylvia in 1957		
			RAZORBACK		
			Group from Arkansas led by Bill White (brother of Ann J. Morton and Jim Mundy). Changed name to Greyghost in 1989.		
4/11/87	70	3	1 As Long As I've Been Loving You....................		Compleat 166
6/13/87	61	7	2 Make A Living Out Of Loving You		Compleat 174
11/28/87	66	7	3 This Ole House		ICR 184
9/17/88	70	4	4 Where Were You When I Was Blue		Mercury 870633
			DONNIE RECORD		
8/06/83	95	1	1 One More Goodbye, One More Hello		BriarRose 1001
			RED WILLOW BAND		
			Country swing group from Beardon, South Dakota.		
6/02/79	97	1	1 I Wish I Had Your Arms Around Me.................		Lost 1288

DEBUT DATE	PEAK POS	WKS CHR	ARTIST — Record Title	POP POS	Label & Number
			RED, WHITE & BLUE GRASS		
			Formed in 1969 in Birmingham, Alabama. Led by Grant Boatwright (guitar) and his wife Ginger (lead vocals, guitar).		
12/22/73+	71	9	1 July, You're A Woman		GRC 1009
			HELEN REDDY		
			Pop vocalist born on 10/25/42 in Melbourne, Australia. To New York in 1966.		
10/22/77	98	1	1 Laissez Les Bontemps Rouler		Capitol 4487
			flip side "The Happy Girls" hit POS 57 on the pop charts		
			ROBB REDMOND		
3/05/77	87	4	1 Lunch Time Lovers		NBC 001
			BEN REECE		
9/06/75	41	12	1 Mirror, Mirror		20th Century 2227
1/03/76	87	5	2 It Don't Bother Me.................................		20th Century 2262
7/10/76	83	6	3 Even If It's Wrong		Polydor 14329
11/13/76	89	4	4 Honky Tonk Fool		Polydor 14356
			BOBBY REED		
			Born in Rockford, Illinois.		
3/05/83	90	2	1 If I Just Had My Woman		CBO 132
			JERRY REED ★★**58**★★		
			Born Jerry Reed Hubbard on 3/20/37 in Atlanta. Accomplished actor. First recorded for Capitol in 1955. Did guitar session work in Nashville in the early 60s. Worked on "Glen Campbell's Goodtime Hour" TV series in the early 70s. In films "W.W. And The Dixie Dance Kings", "Smokey And The Bandit I & II", "Gator", "Hot Stuff" and "Bat 21". Own TV series "Concrete Cowboys". Married to Priscilla Mitchell. Appeared on "Nashville 99" TV series. Elected to the Georgia Music Hall Of Fame in 1986.		
5/20/67	53	9	1 Guitar Man		RCA 9152
			Elvis Presley had pop hits of this tune in 1968 & 1981		
11/04/67+	15	15	2 Tupelo Mississippi Flash.................................		RCA 9334
4/13/68	14	15	3 Remembering		RCA 9493
9/28/68	48	10	4 Alabama Wild Man		RCA 9623
1/18/69	60	6	5 Oh What A Woman!		RCA 9701
4/05/69	20	10	6 There's Better Things In Life.................................		RCA 0124
8/30/69	11	13	7 Are You From Dixie (Cause I'm From Dixie Too) .		RCA 0211
3/07/70	14	12	8 Talk About The Good Times.................................		RCA 9804
8/08/70	16	11	9 Georgia Sunshine.................................		RCA 9870
10/24/70	16	18	10● Amos Moses/	8	
		11	11 The Preacher And The Bear		RCA 9904
5/08/71	1⁵	15	12 **When You're Hot, You're Hot**	9	RCA 9976
9/11/71	11	13	13 Ko-Ko Joe	51	RCA 1011
1/01/72	27	11	14 Another Puff	65	RCA 0613
4/01/72	24	11	15 Smell The Flowers.................................		RCA 0667
7/15/72	22	12	16 Alabama Wild Man .... [R]	62	RCA 0738
12/23/72+	18	10	17 You Took All The Ramblin' Out Of Me...............		RCA 0857
5/26/73	1¹	15	18 **Lord, Mr. Ford**	68	RCA 0960
12/15/73+	25	10	19 The Uptown Poker Club.................................		RCA 0194
2/09/74	13	10	20 The Crude Oil Blues.................................	91	RCA 0224
5/11/74	12	14	21 A Good Woman's Love		RCA 0273
10/05/74	72	6	22 Boogie Woogie Rock And Roll.................................		RCA 10063
12/14/74+	18	12	23 Let's Sing Our Song		RCA 10132
4/05/75	64	9	24 Mind Your Love		RCA 10247
7/12/75	65	9	25 The Telephone.................................		RCA 10325
10/04/75	60	8	26 You Got A Lock On Me.................................	104	RCA 10389
7/04/76	54	8	27 Gator		RCA 10717
			from the film of the same title		
10/09/76	57	7	28 Remembering .... [R]		RCA 10784
3/05/77	19	12	29 Semolita		RCA 10893
7/02/77	68	5	30 With His Pants In His Hand.................................		RCA 11008
8/13/77	2²	16	31 **East Bound And Down/**	103	
			from the film "Smokey & The Bandit"		
		13	32 (I'm Just A) Redneck In A Rock And Roll Bar...		RCA 11056
12/24/77+	20	12	33 You Know What.................................		RCA 11164
			JERRY REED & SEIDINA (Jerry's daughter)		

DEBUT DATE	PEAK POS	WKS CHR		ARTIST — Record Title	POP POS	Label & Number
				JERRY REED — Continued		
3/25/78	**39**	9	34	Sweet Love Feelings		RCA 11232
6/10/78	**10**	12	35	**(I Love You) What Can I Say/**		
		7	36	High Rollin'............................		RCA 11281
				from the film "High Ballin'"		
11/11/78+	**14**	14	37	Gimme Back My Blues		RCA 11407
2/24/79	**18**	11	38	Second-Hand Satin Lady (And A Bargain Basement Boy)		RCA 11472
6/16/79	**40**	7	39	(Who Was The Man Who Put) The Line In Gasoline		RCA 11638
9/08/79	**67**	5	40	Hot Stuff		RCA 11698
				from the film of the same title		
12/01/79+	**12**	14	41	Sugar Foot Rag		RCA 11764
3/29/80	**36**	10	42	Age/		
		10	43	Workin' At The Carwash Blues		RCA 11944
7/12/80	**64**	6	44	The Friendly Family Inn		RCA 12034
8/30/80	**26**	12	45	Texas Bound And Flyin'		RCA 12083
				from the film "Smokey & The Bandit 2"		
1/10/81	**80**	4	46	Caffein, Nicotine, Benzedrine (And Wish Me Luck)		RCA 12157
5/09/81	**87**	3	47	The Testimony Of Soddy Hoe		RCA 12210
7/04/81	**84**	2	48	Good Friends Make Good Lovers		RCA 12253
9/26/81	**30**	12	49	Patches		RCA 12318
				#4 pop hit for Clarence Carter in 1970		
4/17/82	**32**	13	50	The Man With The Golden Thumb		RCA 13081
7/10/82	**1**²	17	51	**She Got The Goldmine (I Got The Shaft)**........	82	RCA 13268
10/16/82	**2**²	16	52	The Bird..............................		RCA 13355
				impressions of Willie Nelson's "Whiskey River" & "On The Road Again", and George Jones' "He Stopped Loving Her Today"		
1/29/83	**13**	15	53	Down On The Corner		RCA 13422
				#3 pop hit for Creedence Clearwater Revival in 1969		
5/21/83	**16**	17	54	Good Ole Boys		RCA 13526
		17	55	She's Ready For Someone To Love Her		RCA 13527
8/06/83	**20**	14	56	Hold On, I'm Comin'		RCA 13580
				WAYLON JENNINGS & JERRY REED #21 pop hit for Sam & Dave in 1966		
11/12/83	**58**	6	57	I'm A Slave		RCA 13663

DEL REEVES ★★75★★

Born Franklin Delano Reeves on 7/14/33 in Sparta, North Carolina. Own radio show at age 12. Appeared on the Chester Smith Show and own TV shows in California in the late 50s. Moved to Nashville in 1966. Member of the Grand Ole Opry since 1966. Own TV show, "Country Carnival". In the films "Second Fiddle To A Steel Guitar", "Sam Whiskey", "Cotton Pickin' Chicken-Pluckers" and "Forty-Acre Feud".

DEBUT DATE	PEAK POS	WKS CHR		ARTIST — Record Title	POP POS	Label & Number
11/06/61	**9**	17	1	**Be Quiet Mind**		Decca 31307
10/27/62	**11**	11	2	He Stands Real Tall		Decca 31417
4/27/63	**13**	14	3	The Only Girl I Can't Forget		Reprise 20158
8/08/64	**41**	12	4	Talking To The Night Lights...........		Columbia 43044
3/13/65	**1**²	20	5	**Girl On The Billboard**	96	United Art. 824
8/14/65	**4**	17	6	**The Belles Of Southern Bell**		United Art. 890
12/04/65+	**9**	13	7	**Women Do Funny Things To Me**		United Art. 940
4/16/66	**42**	7	8	One Bum Town		United Art. 50001
7/02/66	**37**	5	9	Gettin' Any Feed For Your Chickens........		United Art. 50035
10/29/66	**27**	12	10	This Must Be The Bottom		United Art. 50081
3/18/67	**45**	9	11	Blame It On My Do Wrong		United Art. 50128
6/17/67	**33**	10	12	The Private		United Art. 50157
10/07/67	**12**	18	13	A Dime At A Time		United Art. 50210
3/09/68	**56**	5	14	I Just Wasted The Rest		United Art. 50243
				DEL REEVES & BOBBY GOLDSBORO		
3/30/68	**18**	13	15	Wild Blood		United Art. 50270
8/17/68	**5**	14	16	**Looking At The World Through A Windshield.**		United Art. 50332
12/28/68+	**3**	17	17	**Good Time Charlies**		United Art. 50487
5/24/69	**5**	14	18	**Be Glad**		United Art. 50531
10/11/69	**12**	11	19	There Wouldn't Be A Lonely Heart In Town		United Art. 50564
11/01/69	**31**	10	20	Take A Little Good Will Home		United Art. 50591
				BOBBY GOLDSBORO & DEL REEVES		

DEBUT DATE	PEAK POS	WKS CHR	ARTIST — Record Title	POP POS	Label & Number
			DEL REEVES — Continued		
2/07/70	**14**	12	21 A Lover's Question		United Art. 50622
			#6 pop hit for Clyde McPhatter in 1959		
5/23/70	**41**	11	22 Son Of A Coal Man		United Art. 50667
5/30/70	**20**	12	23 Land Mark Tavern............................		United Art. 50669
			DEL REEVES & PENNY DeHAVEN		
10/03/70	**22**	10	24 Right Back Loving You Again.......................		United Art. 50714
1/09/71	**30**	11	25 Bar Room Talk		United Art. 50743
4/10/71	**33**	12	26 Working Like The Devil (For The Lord)		United Art. 50763
7/10/71	**9**	12	27 **The Philadelphia Fillies**		United Art. 50802
10/23/71	**31**	10	28 A Dozen Pairs Of Boots		United Art. 50840
1/22/72	**29**	12	29 The Best Is Yet To Come		United Art. 50877
6/10/72	**62**	6	30 No Rings-No Strings		United Art. 50906
6/24/72	**54**	6	31 Crying In The Rain		United Art. 50829
			DEL REEVES & PENNY DeHAVEN		
11/11/72	**47**	6	32 Before Goodbye		United Art. 50964
2/24/73	**54**	5	33 Trucker's Paradise		United Art. 51106
6/09/73	**44**	10	34 Mm-Mm Good		United Art. 249
9/08/73	**22**	15	35 Lay A Little Lovin' On Me......................		United Art. 308
2/23/74	**70**	8	36 What A Way To Go...........................		United Art. 378
5/11/74	**62**	7	37 Prayer From A Mobile Home		United Art. 427
9/21/74	**89**	4	38 She Likes Country Bands		United Art. 532
12/14/74+	**65**	8	39 Pour It All On Me		United Art. 564
2/15/75	**65**	9	40 But I Do		United Art. 593
			#4 pop hit for Clarence 'Frogman' Henry in 1961		
6/14/75	**74**	5	41 Puttin' In Overtime At Home		United Art. 639
10/18/75	**92**	3	42 You Comb Her Hair Every Morning		United Art. 702
2/14/76	**51**	9	43 I Ain't Got Nobody...........................		United Art. 760
5/01/76	**29**	11	44 On The Rebound		United Art. 797
			DEL REEVES & BILLIE JO SPEARS		
8/07/76	**42**	8	45 Teardrops Will Kiss The Morning Dew..............		United Art. 832
			DEL REEVES & BILLIE JO SPEARS		
11/20/76	**79**	4	46 My Better Half..............................		United Art. 885
6/04/77	**78**	5	47 Ladies Night................................		United Art. 989
5/06/78	**93**	3	48 When My Angel Turns Into A Devil.................		United Art. 1191
9/02/78	**79**	5	49 Dig Down Deep		United Art. 1230
4/12/80	**82**	6	50 Take Me To Your Heart		Koala 584
9/06/80	**90**	3	51 What Am I Gonna Do?		Koala 594
6/06/81	**67**	4	52 Swinging Doors.............................		Koala 333
9/05/81	**53**	7	53 Slow Hand		Koala 336
			#2 pop hit for the Pointer Sisters in 1981		
1/23/82	**67**	5	54 Ain't Nobody Gonna Get My Body But You		Koala 339
4/26/86	**95**	3	55 The Second Time Around		Playback 1103

JIM REEVES ★★14★★

Born James Travis Reeves on 8/20/24 in Panola County, Texas. Killed in a plane crash on 7/31/64 in Nashville. Aspirations of a professional baseball career cut short by an ankle injury. Deejay at KWKH-Shreveport, Louisiana, home of the "Louisiana Hayride", early 50s. First recorded for Macy's in 1950. Joined "Hayride" cast following first country hit "Mexican Joe" in 1953. Joined the Grand Ole Opry in 1955. Own ABC-TV series in 1957. In the 1963 film "Kimberley Jim". Posthumously, he continued to have many country hits into the 80s.

DEBUT DATE	PEAK POS	WKS CHR	ARTIST — Record Title	POP POS	Label & Number
3/28/53	**1**⁹	26	1 **Mexican Joe**	23	Abbott 116
			Juke Box #1(9) / Jockey #1(7) / Best Seller #1(6) with the Circle O Ranch Boys		
12/05/53+	**1**³	21	2 **Bimbo**...	26	Abbott 148
			Jockey #1 / Best Seller #2 / Juke Box #2		
1/09/54	**3**	22	3 I Love You		Fabor 101
			GINNY WRIGHT/JIM REEVES Jockey #3 / Juke Box #7 / Best Seller #8 vocal: Ginny Wright; recitation: Jim Reeves		
6/26/54	**15**	1	4 Then I'll Stop Loving You		Abbott 160
			Jockey #15		
10/23/54	**5**	12	5 **Penny Candy**..................................		Abbott 170
			Juke Box #5 / Jockey #8		
4/30/55	**9**	1	6 **Drinking Tequila**		Abbott 178
			Juke Box #9		

DEBUT DATE	PEAK POS	WKS CHR		ARTIST — Record Title	POP POS	Label & Number
				JIM REEVES — Continued		
8/20/55	**4**	20	7	**Yonder Comes A Sucker/**		
				Juke Box #4 / Jockey #6 / Best Seller #8		
		2	8	I'm Hurtin' Inside................................		RCA 6200
				Juke Box flip		
6/23/56	**8**	13	9	**My Lips Are Sealed**		RCA 6517
				Jockey #8 / Juke Box #8 / Best Seller #10		
9/29/56	**4**	19	10	**According To My Heart/**		
				Jockey #4 / Best Seller #9 / Juke Box #10		
		1	11	The Mother Of A Honky Tonk Girl................		RCA 6620
				Best Seller flip		
1/12/57	**3**	18	12	**Am I Losing You/**		
				Jockey #3 / Juke Box #5 / Best Seller #8		
2/23/57	**3**	5	13	**Waitin' For A Train**		RCA 6749
				Juke Box #3		
4/29/57	**1**⁸	26	14	**Four Walls**	*11*	RCA 6874
				Jockey #1 / Best Seller #2 / Juke Box #4		
8/19/57	**9**	6	15	**Two Shadows On Your Window/**		
				Jockey #9		
8/26/57	**12**	1	16	Young Hearts		RCA 6973
				Best Seller #12 / Jockey #14		
12/02/57+	**3**	18	17	**Anna Marie**	*93*	RCA 7070
				Jockey #3 / Best Seller #10		
4/21/58	**10**	3	18	**Overnight/**		
				Jockey #10 / Best Seller #16		
5/12/58	**8**	7	19	I Love You More		RCA 7171
				Jockey #8 / Best Seller #16		
7/14/58	**2**³	22	20	**Blue Boy**	*45*	RCA 7266
				Jockey #2 / Best Seller #4		
11/10/58+	**1**⁵	25	21	**Billy Bayou/**	*95*	
11/17/58+	**18**	7	22	I'd Like To Be....................................		RCA 7380
3/30/59	**2**⁴	20	23	**Home**		RCA 7479
7/27/59	**5**	16	24	**Partners/**		
8/17/59	**17**	7	25	I'm Beginning To Forget You......................		RCA 7557
12/07/59+	**1**¹⁴	34	26	**He'll Have To Go**...............................	*2*	RCA 7643
7/18/60	**3**	18	27	**I'm Gettin' Better/**	*37*	
7/25/60	**6**	16	28	I Know One	*82*	RCA 7756
10/31/60	**3**	25	29	**I Missed Me/**	*44*	
11/21/60	**8**	14	30	**Am I Losing You**...........................[R]	*31*	RCA 7800
3/27/61	**4**	12	31	**The Blizzard**	*62*	RCA 7855
7/17/61	**15**	11	32	What Would You Do?/	*73*	
10/02/61	**16**	6	33	Stand At Your Window............................		RCA 7905
12/11/61+	**2**²	21	34	**Losing Your Love/**	*89*	
12/11/61+	**7**	16	35	**(How Can I Write On Paper) What I Feel In My Heart**....................................	*92*	RCA 7950
5/26/62	**2**⁹	21	36	**Adios Amigo/**	*90*	
5/19/62	**20**	3	37	A Letter To My Heart.............................		RCA 8019
9/01/62	**2**³	21	38	**I'm Gonna Change Everything/**	*95*	
9/08/62	**18**	3	39	Pride Goes Before A Fall		RCA 8080
2/09/63	**3**	23	40	**Is This Me?**.....................................	*103*	RCA 8127
7/13/63	**3**	18	41	**Guilty/**	*91*	
7/27/63	**11**	18	42	Little Ole You.....................................		RCA 8193
1/25/64	**2**²	26	43	**Welcome To My World/**	*102*	
2/01/64	**43**	2	44	Good Morning Self.................................		RCA 8289
3/28/64	**7**	21	45	**Love Is No Excuse**.............................	*115*	RCA 8324
				JIM REEVES & DOTTIE WEST		
				flip side "Look Who's Talking" hit POS 121 on Bubbling Under chart		
7/11/64	**1**⁷	26	46	**I Guess I'm Crazy**	*82*	RCA 8383
11/28/64+	**3**	19	47	**I Won't Forget You**	*93*	RCA 8461
3/06/65	**1**³	23	48	**This Is It**	*88*	RCA 8508
7/24/65	**1**³	21	49	**Is It Really Over?**	*79*	RCA 8625
1/08/66	**2**³	17	50	**Snow Flake**	*66*	RCA 8719
4/02/66	**1**⁴	21	51	**Distant Drums**	*45*	RCA 8789
8/13/66	**1**¹	19	52	**Blue Side Of Lonesome**	*59*	RCA 8902
1/21/67	**1**¹	16	53	**I Won't Come In While He's There**	*112*	RCA 9057

DEBUT DATE	PEAK POS	WKS CHR	ARTIST — Record Title	POP POS	Label & Number
			JIM REEVES — Continued		
7/01/67	16	14	54 The Storm		RCA 9238
11/04/67+	9	17	55 **I Heard A Heart Break Last Night**		RCA 9343
3/09/68	9	13	56 **That's When I See The Blues (In Your Pretty Brown Eyes)**................................		RCA 9455
9/21/68	7	15	57 **When You Are Gone**		RCA 9614
4/12/69	6	14	58 **When Two Worlds Collide**		RCA 0135
12/06/69+	10	14	59 **Nobody's Fool/**		
		13	60 Why Do I Love You (Melody of Love)........... [S]		RCA 0286
			#2 pop hit for Billy Vaughn in 1955		
8/15/70	4	15	61 **Angels Don't Lie**...........................		RCA 9880
4/10/71	16	12	62 Gypsy Feet.................................		RCA 9969
1/29/72	15	14	63 The Writing's On The Wall		RCA 0626
7/29/72	8	16	64 **Missing You**		RCA 0744
			#29 pop hit for Ray Peterson in 1961		
6/02/73	12	14	65 Am I That Easy To Forget....................		RCA 0963
			#25 pop hit for Debbie Reynolds in 1960		
4/20/74	19	14	66 I'd Fight The World		RCA 0255
6/21/75	54	11	67 You Belong To Me		RCA 10299
			#1 pop hit for Jo Stafford in 1952		
11/08/75	71	6	68 You'll Never Know..........................		RCA 10418
			#1 pop hit for Dick Haymes in 1943		
2/21/76	54	9	69 I Love You Because		RCA 10557
			#3 pop hit for Al Martino in 1963		
4/23/77	14	13	70 It's Nothin' To Me.........................		RCA 10956
8/27/77	23	11	71 Little Ole Dime		RCA 11060
2/04/78	29	11	72 You're The Only Good Thing (That's Happened to Me)		RCA 11187
11/22/80+	35	11	73 There's Always Me		RCA 12118
			#56 pop hit for Elvis Presley in 1967		
11/07/81+	5	17	74 **Have You Ever Been Lonely (Have You Ever Been Blue)**		RCA 12346
			JIM REEVES & PATSY CLINE		
6/05/82	54	8	75 I Fall To Pieces...........................		MCA 52052
			PATSY CLINE/JIM REEVES		
1/08/83	46	9	76 The Jim Reeves Medley.....................		RCA 13410
			Four Walls/I Missed Me/He'll Have To Go/Oh, How I Miss You Tonight		
1/21/84	70	6	77 The Image Of Me		RCA 13693
			JIM REEVES/DEBORAH ALLEN:		
6/23/79	10	14	78 **Don't Let Me Cross Over**...................		RCA 11564
11/03/79+	6	15	79 **Oh, How I Miss You Tonight**		RCA 11737
4/12/80	10	16	80 **Take Me In Your Arms And Hold Me**		RCA 11946
			JOHN REX REEVES		
			Born in Panola City, Texas. Nephew of Jim Reeves.		
2/21/81	93	2	1 What Would You Do		Soc-A-Gee 109
8/01/81	90	2	2 You're The Reason		Soc-A-Gee 110
			BOB REGAN & LUCILLE STARR		
			Robert Fredricksen from Dawson Creek, British Columbia, and his wife Fern Regan from St. Boniface, Manitoba. Also recorded as The Canadian Sweethearts.		
1/03/70	50	9	1 Dream Baby		Dot 17327
			MIKE REID - see RONNIE MILSAP		
			RITA REMINGTON		
			Born Rita Unruh in McPherson, Kansas. Worked in father's band, Smokey Valley Playboys, from age 7.		
9/08/73	99	3	1 I've Never Been This Far Before.....................		Plantation 103
1/14/78	86	5	2 Don't Let The Flame Burn Out......................		Plantation 167
			#68 pop hit for Jackie DeShannon in 1977		
4/08/78	100	3	3 To Each His Own		Plantation 171
10/24/81	80	4	4 Don't We Belong In Love		Plantation 202
3/20/82	76	5	5 The Flame		Plantation 207

DEBUT DATE	PEAK POS	WKS CHR	ARTIST — Record Title	POP POS	Label & Number
			RENO BROTHERS		
			Brothers Dale, Don Wayne and Ronald Reno, sons of bluegrass great Don Reno.		
7/02/88	77	2	1 Yonder Comes A Freight Train		Step One 387
			DON RENO		
			Born on 2/21/27 in Buffalo, South Carolina; died on 10/16/84. Worked on WSPA-Spartanburg at age 13. Guitarist/banjo/harmonica player. With Arthur Smith in 1941 and Bill Monroe in 1948. Formed own band, the Tennessee Cut Ups, in 1949. Teamed with Red Smiley. Early developer of bluegrass music style. Also see Chick & His Hot Rods.		
			RENO & SMILEY:		
5/29/61	14	10	1 Don't Let Your Sweet Love Die		King 5469
8/28/61	23	5	2 Love Oh Love, Oh Please Come Home		King 5520
			DON RENO & BENNY MARTIN:		
1/08/66	46	3	3 Soldier's Prayer In Viet Nam		Monument 912
			JACK RENO		
			Prominent deejay from Centerville, Iowa. Worked on KCOG-Centerville at age 16. Apeared on the Ozark Jubilee in 1955. Deejay on many stations since 1958.		
12/09/67+	10	17	1 **Repeat After Me**		JAB 9009
5/11/68	41	11	2 How Sweet It Is (To Be In Love With You)		JAB 9015
11/16/68+	19	14	3 I Want One..		Dot 17169
5/10/69	34	11	4 I'm A Good Man (In A Bad Frame Of Mind)........		Dot 17233
9/20/69	22	9	5 We All Go Crazy		Dot 17293
4/18/70	67	3	6 That's The Way I See It		Dot 17340
10/09/71	12	15	7 Hitchin' A Ride...		Target 0137
			#5 pop hit for Vanity Fare in 1970		
1/22/72	26	14	8 Heartaches By The Numbers		Target 0141
5/27/72	38	10	9 Do You Want To Dance		Target 0150
			#5 pop hit for Bobby Freeman in 1958		
8/25/73	67	8	10 Beautiful Sunday..		United Art. 299
			#15 pop hit for Daniel Boone in 1972		
2/09/74	57	10	11 Let The Four Winds Blow		United Art. 374
			#15 pop hit for Fats Domino in 1961		
8/31/74	70	7	12 Jukebox		United Art. 502
			RONNIE RENO		
			Noted session musician/vocalist/songwriter. Former vocalist of the Osborne Brothers band. Son of bluegrass guitarist Don Reno. Appeared in the 1980 film "Bronco Billy". Member of Merle Haggard's Strangers for 7 years.		
1/22/83	86	3	1 Homemade Love		EMH 0010
9/24/83	76	4	2 The Letter		EMH 0024
			#1 pop hit for The Box Tops in 1967		
			RESTLESS HEART ★★198★★		
			Group from Nashville consisting of former session musicians Larry Stewart (lead vocals, guitar, keyboards), Dave Innis (guitar, keyboards), Greg Jennings (guitar), Paul Gregg (bass) and John Dittrich (drums).		
1/26/85	23	16	1 Let The Heartache Ride................................		RCA 13969
6/01/85	10	18	2 I Want Everyone To Cry		RCA 14086
10/26/85+	7	19	3 (Back to the) Heartbreak Kid		RCA 14190
3/15/86	10	20	4 Til I Loved You..		RCA 14292
8/09/86	1¹	23	5 That Rock Won't Roll...................................		RCA 14376
12/20/86+	1¹	25	6 I'll Still Be Loving You.................................	33	RCA 5065
5/30/87	1¹	25	7 Why Does It Have To Be (Wrong or Right).......		RCA 5132
10/31/87+	1¹	23	8 Wheels...		RCA 5280
5/21/88	1¹	21	9 Bluest Eyes In Texas....................................		RCA 8386
9/24/88	1¹	23	10 A Tender Lie		RCA 8714
			TIM REX & OKLAHOMA		
11/08/80	87	3	1 Arizona Highway..		Dee Jay 103
12/13/80+	46	12	2 Gettin' Over You		Dee Jay 107
4/11/81	43	10	3 Spread My Wings		Dee Jay 111
			ERNEST REY		
			Son of Loretta Lynn.		
3/17/79	97	1	1 Mama's Sugar..		MCA 40991

DEBUT DATE	PEAK POS	WKS CHR	ARTIST — Record Title	POP POS	Label & Number
			ALLEN REYNOLDS Singer/producer/songwriter. Worked with Don Williams.		
5/20/78	95	5	1 Wrong Road Again		Triple I 496
			BURT REYNOLDS Born on 2/11/36 in Waycross, Georgia. Box-office superstar since the mid-70s.		
10/25/80	51	7	1 Let's Do Something Cheap And Superficial .... from the film "Smokey & The Bandit 2"	88	MCA 51004
			BILL RICE Producer/songwriter, teamed with Jerry Foster.		
3/20/71	33	10	1 Travelin' Minstrel Man		Capitol 3049
9/11/71	51	9	2 Honky-Tonk Stardust Cowboy		Capitol 3156
4/08/72	74	2	3 A Girl Like Her Is Hard To Find		Epic 10833
7/01/72	63	5	4 Something To Call Mine		Epic 10877
11/19/77	97	3	5 All The Love We Threw Away .... **LOIS JOHNSON & BILL RICE**		Polydor 14435
3/11/78	100	2	6 Beggars And Choosers		Polydor 14453
			BOBBY G. RICE ★★168★★ Born Robert Gene Rice on 7/13/44 in Boscobel, Wisconsin. Plays guitar and banjo. Made professional debut at age 5. His family operated the Circle D Dance Hall, and family work on WRCO-Richmond, Wisconsin for 7 years. Worked in duo with sister Lorraine in 1964, then had own band.		
4/25/70	32	8	1 Sugar Shack..................................... #1 pop hit for Jimmy Gilmer & The Fireballs in 1963		Royal Amer. 6
8/08/70	35	11	2 Hey Baby...................................... #1 pop hit for Bruce Channel in 1962		Royal Amer. 18
1/09/71	46	9	3 Lover Please .... #7 pop hit for Clyde McPhatter in 1962		Royal Amer. 27
5/22/71	20	15	4 Mountain Of Love................................ #9 pop hit for Johnny Rivers in 1964		Royal Amer. 32
1/01/72	33	11	5 Suspicion...................................... #3 pop hit for Terry Stafford in 1964		Royal Amer. 48
12/23/72+	3	16	6 **You Lay So Easy On My Mind**......................		Metromedia 902
5/05/73	8	15	7 **You Give Me You**		Metromedia 0107
9/22/73	13	14	8 The Whole World's Making Love Again Tonight ..		Metromedia 0075
9/28/74	30	14	9 Make It Feel Like Love Again		GRT 009
1/11/75	9	14	10 **Write Me A Letter**		GRT 014
5/03/75	10	14	11 **Freda Comes, Freda Goes**		GRT 021
8/30/75	64	11	12 I May Never Be Your Lover (But I'll Always Be Your Friend)		GRT 028
1/03/76	35	11	13 Pick Me Up On Your Way Down		GRT 036
7/24/76	53	9	14 You Are My Special Angel .... #7 pop hit for Bobby Helms in 1957		GRT 061
11/13/76	54	9	15 Woman Stealer		GRT 084
7/09/77	66	7	16 Just One Kiss Magdelena............................		GRT 120
7/22/78	57	6	17 Whisper It To Me................................		Republic 023
11/11/78	30	10	18 The Softest Touch In Town		Republic 031
6/09/79	49	8	19 Oh Baby Mine (I Get So Lonely)................... #2 pop hit for The Four Knights in 1954		Republic 041
12/01/79	67	8	20 You Make It So Easy		Sunset 102
5/03/80	53	9	21 The Man Who Takes You Home		Sunbird 108
2/07/81	86	2	22 Livin' Together (Lovin' Apart)		Sunbird 7558
10/10/81	63	5	23 Pardon My French		Charta 166
6/08/85	95	2	24 New Tradition...................................		Door Knob 230
3/08/86	70	4	25 Red Neck And Over Thirty .... **WAYNE KEMP & BOBBY G. RICE**		Door Knob 243
9/13/86	70	5	26 You've Taken Over My Heart.......................		Door Knob 251
6/27/87	85	2	27 Rachel's Room..................................		Door Knob 274
10/03/87	79	3	28 You Lay So Easy On My Mind..................... [R]		Door Knob 285
3/05/88	70	5	29 A Night Of Love Forgotten		Door Knob 295
9/17/88	76	4	30 Clean Livin' Folk .... **BOBBY G. RICE & PERRY LaPOINTE**		Door Knob 307

DEBUT DATE	PEAK POS	WKS CHR		ARTIST — Record Title	POP POS	Label & Number
				CHARLIE RICH ★★**61**★★		
				Born on 12/14/32 in Colt, Arkansas. Rockabilly-country singer/pianist/songwriter. First played jazz and blues. Own jazz group, the Velvetones, mid-1950s, while in the US Air Force. Session work with Sun Records in 1958. Known as the "Silver Fox". CMA award: Entertainer of the Year - 1974.		
3/09/68	44	8	1	Set Me Free..		Epic 10287
8/24/68	45	8	2	Raggedy Ann...		Epic 10358
8/09/69	41	11	3	Life's Little Ups And Downs...........................		Epic 10492
2/28/70	67	5	4	Who Will The Next Fool Be .... [R]		Sun 1110
				originally released on Phillips 3566 in 1960		
3/28/70	47	6	5	July 12, 1939..	85	Epic 10585
10/24/70	37	12	6	Nice 'N' Easy.. [R]		Epic 10662
				originally Bubbled Under (POS 131) in 1964 on Groove 0041		
8/14/71	72	2	7	A Woman Left Lonely		Epic 10745
11/27/71+	35	13	8	A Part Of Your Life......................................		Epic 10809
8/26/72	6	17	9	I Take It On Home		Epic 10867
2/10/73	1²	20	10●	Behind Closed Doors	15	Epic 10950
7/14/73	29	11	11	Tomorrow Night...		RCA 0983
9/22/73	1³	18	12●	The Most Beautiful Girl...............................	1	Epic 11040
12/22/73+	1²	17	13	There Won't Be Anymore..............................	18	RCA 0195
2/23/74	1³	14	14	A Very Special Love Song.............................	11	Epic 11091
5/04/74	1¹	13	15	I Don't See Me In Your Eyes Anymore...........	47	RCA 0260
6/22/74	23	12	16	A Field Of Yellow Daisies.............................		Mercury 73498
8/10/74	1¹	15	17	I Love My Friend	24	Epic 20006
9/28/74	1¹	15	18	She Called Me Baby	47	RCA 10062
12/28/74+	71	5	19	Something Just Came Over Me		Mercury 73646
2/01/75	3	12	20	My Elusive Dreams	49	Epic 50064
4/12/75	23	12	21	It's All Over Now...		RCA 10256
5/24/75	3	17	22	Every Time You Touch Me (I Get High)..........	19	Epic 50103
9/20/75	4	14	23	All Over Me		Epic 50142
12/20/75+	56	7	24	Now Everybody Knows		RCA 10458
12/27/75+	10	13	25	Since I Fell For You	71	Epic 50182
4/24/76	22	10	26	America, The Beautiful (1976)		Epic 50222
9/04/76	27	9	27	Road Song		Epic 50268
1/08/77	24	12	28	My Mountain Dew..		RCA 10859
				Charlie's RCA and Mercury hits were recorded from 1963-66		
2/05/77	12	13	29	Easy Look		Epic 50328
5/28/77	1²	19	30	Rollin' With The Flow	101	Epic 50392
4/08/78	8	14	31	Puttin' In Overtime At Home		United Art. 1193
7/01/78	10	13	32	Beautiful Woman		Epic 50562
7/22/78	46	8	33	I Still Believe In Love		United Art. 1223
10/07/78	1¹	14	34	On My Knees		Epic 50616
				CHARLIE RICH with JANIE FRICKE		
1/06/79	3	14	35	I'll Wake You Up When I Get Home		Elektra 45553
				from the film "Every Which Way But Loose"		
1/06/79	45	8	36	The Fool Strikes Again.................................		United Art. 1269
3/10/79	26	11	37	I Lost My Head		United Art. 1280
5/12/79	20	13	38	Spanish Eyes		Epic 50701
				#15 pop hit for Al Martino in 1966		
8/18/79	84	4	39	Life Goes On		United Art. 1307
11/24/79+	22	13	40	You're Gonna Love Yourself In The Morning		United Art. 1325
3/08/80	74	5	41	I'd Build A Bridge..		United Art. 1340
5/03/80	61	7	42	Even A Fool Would Let Go		Epic 50869
10/11/80	12	14	43	A Man Just Don't Know What A Woman Goes Through..		Elektra 47047
2/14/81	26	11	44	Are We Dreamin' The Same Dream.................		Elektra 47104
5/23/81	47	7	45	You Made It Beautiful		Epic 02058
				from the film "Take This Job And Shove It"		
				DEBBIE RICH		
				Born Debra Sue Rathjen in Levenworth, Washington; raised in Napa Valley, Califrnia.		
12/03/88	87	2	1	I Ain't Gonna Take This Layin' Down		Door Knob 311

DON RICH - see BUDDY ALAN and THE BUCKAROOS

DEBUT DATE	PEAK POS	WKS CHR	ARTIST — Record Title	POP POS	Label & Number
			EARL RICHARDS		
			Born Henry Earl Sinks in Amarillo. Owned Ace of Hearts label.		
9/06/69	39	10	1 The House Of Blue Lights		United Art. 50561
			#9 pop hit for Chuck Miller in 1955		
1/31/70	73	2	2 Corrine Corrina		United Art. 50619
			#9 pop hit for Ray Peterson in 1961		
10/10/70	57	4	3 Sunshine		United Art. 50704
1/13/73	23	12	4 Margie, Who's Watching The Baby		Ace of H. 0461
4/28/73	66	6	5 Things Are Kinda Slow At The House		Ace of H. 0465
7/21/73	58	11	6 The Sun Is Shining (On Everybody But Me)		Ace of H. 0470
12/22/73+	85	5	7 How Can I Tell Her/		
			#22 pop hit for Lobo in 1973		
3/02/74	83	7	8 Walkin' In Teardrops		Ace of H. 0477
10/18/75	91	5	9 My Babe		Ace of H. 7502
			#1 R&B hit for Little Walter in 1955		
			SUE RICHARDS		
			Born in Muscle Shoals, sang in family gospel group from age 4. Recorded for Sun at age 11. Later worked with her daughters as back-up vocalists for Tammy Wynette.		
3/27/71	56	8	1 Feel Free To Go		Epic 10709
1/12/74	48	13	2 I Just Had You On My Mind		Dot 17481
7/20/74	93	5	3 Ease Me To The Ground		Dot 17508
5/03/75	99	2	4 Homemade Love		ABC/Dot 17547
9/06/75	32	12	5 Tower Of Strength		ABC/Dot 17572
			#5 pop hit for Gene McDaniels in 1961		
1/17/76	25	11	6 Sweet Sensuous Feelings		ABC/Dot 17600
5/01/76	50	10	7 Please Tell Him That I Said Hello		ABC/Dot 17622
8/21/76	70	6	8 I'll Never See Him Again		ABC/Dot 17645
11/26/77	94	3	9 Someone Loves Him		Epic 50465
7/15/78	94	4	10 Hey, What Do You Say (We Fall In Love)		Epic 50546
3/10/79	85	3	11 Finders Keepers Losers Weepers		MMI 1028
			STAN HITCHCOCK with SUE RICHARDS		
			LIONEL RICHIE		
			Born on 6/20/49 in Tuskegee, Alabama. Former lead singer of the Commodores.		
7/21/84	24	18	1 Stuck On You	3	Motown 1746
12/06/86+	10	15	2 **Deep River Woman**	71	Motown 1873
			background vocals: Alabama; flip side "Ballerina Girl" hit POS 7 on the pop charts		
			STEVE RICKS		
			Born in Little Rock, Arkansas. Leader of the Van Dells from 1974-83.		
6/14/86	81	4	1 Private Clown		Southwind 8205
			ALLAN RIDDLE		
11/07/60	16	12	1 The Moon Is Crying		Plaid 1001
			RIDE THE RIVER		
			Nashville-based quartet formed and fronted by vocalist/guitarist Danny Stockard.		
2/21/87	63	5	1 You Left Her Lovin' You		Advantage 165
6/13/87	55	7	2 The First Cut Is The Deepest		Advantage 169
			#21 pop hit for Rod Stewart in 1977		
10/31/87	57	7	3 It's Such A Heartache		Advantage 182
2/06/88	51	9	4 After Last Night's Storm		Advantage 189
			DAN RILEY		
			Vocalist, worked Las Vegas with Joan Rivers, Mickey Gilley and Rodney Dangerfield.		
12/22/79+	78	5	1 Lily		Armada 103
			JEANNIE C. RILEY ★★170★★		
			Born Jeanne Carolyn Stephenson on 10/19/45 in Anson, Texas. Moved to Nashville in the mid-60s. Sang on demo records and worked as a secretary.		
8/24/68	1³	14	1 ●Harper Valley P.T.A.	1	Plantation 3
12/07/68+	6	15	2 **The Girl Most Likely**	55	Plantation 7
1/25/69	35	9	3 The Price I Pay To Stay		Capitol 2378
3/29/69	5	13	4 **There Never Was A Time**	77	Plantation 16
6/28/69	32	9	5 The Rib	111	Plantation 22
10/04/69	33	11	6 The Back Side Of Dallas/		
10/25/69	34	8	7 Things Go Better With Love	111	Plantation 29

DEBUT DATE	PEAK POS	WKS CHR	ARTIST — Record Title	POP POS	Label & Number
			JEANNIE C. RILEY — Continued		
1/31/70	**7**	12	8 **Country Girl**	*106*	Plantation 44
6/27/70	**21**	11	9 Duty Not Desire		Plantation 59
12/12/70	**60**	4	10 My Man/		
12/12/70	**62**	4	11 The Generation Gap		Plantation 65
4/03/71	**4**	15	12 **Oh, Singer**	*74*	Plantation 72
7/03/71	**7**	15	13 **Good Enough To Be Your Wife**..........	*97*	Plantation 75
10/23/71	**15**	13	14 Roses And Thorns...........................		Plantation 79
11/20/71	**47**	8	15 Houston Blues		MGM 14310
1/15/72	**12**	12	16 Give Myself A Party		MGM 14341
5/20/72	**30**	11	17 Good Morning Country Rain		MGM 14382
10/28/72	**57**	6	18 One Night		MGM 14427
			#4 pop hit for Elvis Presley in 1958		
3/10/73	**44**	7	19 When Love Has Gone Away................		MGM 14495
7/14/73	**51**	7	20 Hush..		MGM 14554
			#4 pop hit for Deep Purple in 1968		
11/10/73	**57**	9	21 Another Football Year		MGM 14666
9/28/74	**89**	6	22 Plain Vanilla		Mercury 73616
			with The Red River Symphony		
7/17/76	**94**	4	23 The Best I've Ever Had.....................		Warner 8226
			LARRY RILEY		
1/17/81	**90**	2	1 Cheater's Last Chance		F&L 507
5/30/81	**93**	2	2 Code-A-Phone................................		F&L 509
			ROD RISHARD		
8/20/83	**77**	5	1 You'd Better Believe It		Soundwaves 4715
11/19/83	**74**	5	2 How Do You Tell Someone You Love....		Soundwaves 4717
3/24/84	**89**	3	3 The More I Go Blind.........................		Soundwaves 4724
7/28/84	**84**	3	4 Midnight Angel Of Mercy		Soundwaves 4734
			TEX RITTER ★★123★★		
			Born Maurice Woodward Ritter on 1/12/05 near Murvaul, Texas; died of a heart attack on 1/2/74 (66). Spent 2 years in law school, then left for a career on Broadway. Acted in the play "Green Grow The Lilacs" in 1931. Worked on radio shows Lone-Star Rangers, Country Tom's Round-Up, and WHN Barn Dance in the early 30s. Moved to Hollywood in 1936 and starred in 85 western films until 1945. Co-host of "Town Hall Party" radio and TV series from 1953-60. Sang title song on soundtrack of "High Noon" in 1953 which won an Academy Award. Moved to Nashville in 1965, worked on the Grand Ole Opry. Elected to the Country Music Hall Of Fame in 1964. His son, Jonathan Southworth "John" Ritter, starred in TV series "Three's Company" and "Hooperman", plus many films.		
11/11/44	**1**[6]	20	1 **I'm Wastin' My Tears On You/**	*11*	
11/11/44+	**2**[1]	22	2 **There's A New Moon Over My Shoulder**	*26*	Capitol 174
12/16/44+	**2**[2]	23	3 **Jealous Heart**...............................		Capitol 179
8/04/45	**1**[11]	20	4 **You Two-Timed Me One Time Too Often**		Capitol 206
12/08/45+	**1**[3]	7	5 **You Will Have To Pay/**		
12/29/45+	**2**[1]	3	6 **Christmas Carols By The Old Corral**........ [X]		Capitol 223
5/18/46	**5**	6	7 **Long Time Gone**		Capitol 253
10/19/46	**3**	10	8 **When You Leave Don't Slam The Door/**		
12/07/46	**3**	2	9 **Have I Told You Lately That I Love You?**.....		Capitol 296
3/13/48	**9**	1	10 **Rye Whiskey**		Capitol A. 40084
6/12/48	**10**	7	11 **Deck of Cards**............................. [S]		Capitol A. 40114
			Best Seller #10 / Juke Box #13		
			#7 pop hit for Wink Martindale in 1959		
6/12/48	**15**	1	12 **Pecos Bill**		Capitol A. 40106
			Juke Box #15		
7/10/48	**5**	7	13 **Rock And Rye Polka**.......................		Capitol 15119
			Best Seller #5 / Juke Box #8		
11/18/50	**6**	3	14 **Daddy's Last Letter (Private First Class John H. McCormick)** .... [S]		Capitol 1267
			Jockey #6 / Best Seller #8		
6/19/61	**5**	21	15 **I Dreamed Of A Hill-Billy Heaven** .... [S]	*20*	Capitol 4567
3/05/66	**50**	1	16 The Men In My Little Girl's Life		Capitol 5574
			#6 pop hit for Mike Douglas in 1966		
3/25/67	**13**	15	17 **Just Beyond The Moon**....................		Capitol 5839
9/30/67	**59**	3	18 A Working Man's Prayer....................		Capitol 5966

DEBUT DATE	PEAK POS	WKS CHR	ARTIST — Record Title	POP POS	Label & Number
			TEX RITTER — Continued		
8/17/68	69	4	19 Texas....................		Capitol 2232
2/08/69	53	6	20 A Funny Thing Happened (On The Way To Miami)		Capitol 2388
7/26/69	39	10	21 Growin' Up..................		Capitol 2451
6/06/70	57	8	22 Green Green Valley		Capitol 2815
9/18/71	67	3	23 Fall Away		Capitol 3154
11/18/72	67	5	24 Comin' After Jinny.................		Capitol 3457
1/26/74	35	8	25 The Americans (A Canadian's Opinion) .... [S]	90	Capitol 3814
			EDDIE RIVERS		
4/30/77	98	2	1 Open Up Your Door		Charta 102
			JACK RIVERS		
			Long-time session guitarist. Played on Gene Autry's "Rudolph, The Red-Nosed Reindeer", "Peter Cottontail", and many others.		
9/18/48	12	2	1 Dear Oakie................... Juke Box #12		Capitol 15169
			JOHNNY RIVERS		
			Born John Ramistella on 11/7/42 in New York City; raised in Baton Rouge. Rock and roll singer/guitarist/composer/producer.		
6/29/74	58	8	1 Six Days On The Road..................	106	Atlantic 3028
			DENNIS ROBBINS		
			Born in Hazelwood, North Carolina; onetime member of the Michigan pop group, Rockets.		
1/17/87	63	8	1 Long Gone Lonesome Blues		MCA 52987
10/03/87	71	9	2 Two Of A Kind (Workin' On A Full House)..........		MCA 53143
			HARGUS "PIG" ROBBINS		
			Born in Spring City, Tennessee. Top Nashville session pianist. Blind since birth.		
6/23/79	83	3	1 Chunky People		Elektra 46037
9/01/79	92	4	2 Unbreakable Hearts		Elektra 46512
			JENNY ROBBINS		
7/01/78	76	4	1 You've Just Found Yourself A New Woman........		El Dorado 152
			MARTY ROBBINS ★★9★★		
			Born Martin David Robinson on 9/26/25 in Glendale, Arizona; died of a heart attack on 12/8/82. Singer/guitarist/composer. Own radio show with K-Bar Cowboys, late 1940s. Own TV show, "Western Caravan", KPHO-Phoenix, 1951. First recorded for Columbia in 1952. Regular on the Grand Ole Opry since 1953. Own label, Robbins, in 1958. Stock car racer. In the films "Road To Nashville" and "Guns Of A Stranger".		
12/20/52+	1²	18	1 **I'll Go On Alone**............................. Jockey #1 / Best Seller #10		Columbia 21022
3/28/53	5	11	2 **I Couldn't Keep From Crying** .... Juke Box #5 / Best Seller #6 / Jockey #6		Columbia 21075
7/03/54	12	3	3 Pretty Words .... Jockey #12 / Best Seller #14		Columbia 21246
11/20/54	14	1	4 Call Me Up .... Jockey #14		Columbia 21291
1/08/55	14	1	5 Time Goes By .... Jockey #14		Columbia 21324
2/12/55	7	11	6 **That's All Right** .... Jockey #7 / Best Seller #9 cover version of Elvis Presley's first Sun recording		Columbia 21351
10/01/55	9	7	7 **Maybellene**............................. Jockey #9 #5 pop hit for Chuck Berry in 1955		Columbia 21446
9/22/56	1¹³	30	8 **Singing The Blues/** Best Seller #1(13) / Juke Box #1(13) / Jockey #1(11)	17	
10/06/56	7	10	9 **I Can't Quit (I've Gone Too Far)** .... Jockey #7		Columbia 21545
2/02/57	3	15	10 **Knee Deep In The Blues/** Jockey #3 / Best Seller #5 / Juke Box #7		
3/02/57	14	2	11 The Same Two Lips .... Jockey #14		Columbia 40815
5/20/57	1⁵	22	12 **A White Sport Coat (And A Pink Carnation)** ... Best Seller #1(5) / Juke Box #1(5) / Jockey #1(1)	2	Columbia 40864

DEBUT DATE	PEAK POS	WKS CHR		ARTIST — Record Title	POP POS	Label & Number
				MARTY ROBBINS — Continued		
9/09/57	**11**	3	13	Please Don't Blame Me/		
				Best Seller #11		
9/09/57	**15**	3	14	Teen-Age Dream		Columbia 40969
				Jockey #15 / Best Seller #15		
11/25/57+	**1** ⁴	23	15	**The Story Of My Life**	15	Columbia 41013
				Best Seller #1(4) / Jockey #1(4)		
4/07/58	**1** ²	25	16	**Just Married/**	26	
				Jockey #1 / Best Seller #3		
4/07/58	**2** ²	25	17	**Stairway Of Love**	68	Columbia 41143
				Best Seller #2 / Jockey #8		
8/18/58	**4**	10	18	**She Was Only Seventeen (He Was One Year More)**	27	Columbia 41208
				Best Seller #4 / Jockey #13		
12/15/58	**23**	5	19	Ain't I The Lucky One.....................		Columbia 41282
3/09/59	**15**	9	20	The Hanging Tree.........................	38	Columbia 41325
				from the film of the same title		
11/09/59	**1** ⁷	26	21	**El Paso**	1	Columbia 41511
3/21/60	**5**	14	22	**Big Iron**	26	Columbia 41589
9/26/60	**26**	4	23	Five Brothers	74	Columbia 41771
2/06/61	**1** ¹⁰	19	24	**Don't Worry**	3	Columbia 41922
6/05/61	**24**	4	25	Jimmy Martinez............................	51	Columbia 42008
9/18/61	**3**	20	26	**It's Your World**	51	Columbia 42065
2/03/62	**12**	13	27	Sometimes I'm Tempted	109	Columbia 42246
				flip side "I Told The Brook" hit POS 81 on the pop charts		
6/02/62	**12**	9	28	Love Can't Wait...........................	69	Columbia 42375
8/04/62	**1** ⁸	21	29	**Devil Woman**	16	Columbia 42486
12/08/62+	**1** ¹	14	30	**Ruby Ann**	18	Columbia 42614
3/23/63	**14**	9	31	Cigarettes And Coffee Blues...............	93	Columbia 42701
9/07/63	**13**	11	32	Not So Long Ago	115	Columbia 42831
11/30/63+	**1** ³	23	33	**Begging To You**	74	Columbia 42890
3/07/64	**15**	11	34	Girl From Spanish Town	106	Columbia 42968
6/20/64	**3**	21	35	**The Cowboy In The Continental Suit**	103	Columbia 43049
10/31/64	**8**	17	36	**One Of These Days**.....................	105	Columbia 43134
4/17/65	**1** ¹	21	37	**Ribbon Of Darkness**	103	Columbia 43258
11/13/65	**50**	1	38	Old Red		Columbia 43377
12/04/65+	**21**	10	39	While You're Dancing		Columbia 43428
2/19/66	**14**	11	40	Count Me Out/		
3/05/66	**21**	7	41	Private Wilson White		Columbia 43500
7/09/66	**3**	18	42	**The Shoe Goes On The Other Foot Tonight**.....		Columbia 43680
11/19/66+	**16**	14	43	Mr. Shorty		Columbia 43870
2/04/67	**16**	12	44	No Tears Milady/		
2/25/67	**34**	11	45	Fly Butterfly Fly		Columbia 43845
6/03/67	**1** ¹	16	46	**Tonight Carmen**	114	Columbia 44128
9/16/67	**9**	14	47	**Gardenias In Her Hair**...................		Columbia 44271
5/04/68	**10**	15	48	**Love Is In The Air**.....................		Columbia 44509
10/05/68	**1** ²	15	49	**I Walk Alone**	65	Columbia 44633
2/08/69	**5**	14	50	**It's A Sin**		Columbia 44739
7/05/69	**8**	14	51	**I Can't Say Goodbye**		Columbia 44895
11/22/69+	**10**	13	52	**Camelia**		Columbia 45024
2/21/70	**1** ¹	17	53	**My Woman My Woman, My Wife**....................	42	Columbia 45091
9/12/70	**7**	14	54	**Jolie Girl**	108	Columbia 45215
12/19/70+	**5**	12	55	**Padre**	113	Columbia 45273
				#13 pop hit for Toni Arden in 1958		
5/22/71	**7**	13	56	**The Chair/**	121	
		8	57	Seventeen Years		Columbia 45377
10/02/71	**9**	14	58	**Early Morning Sunshine**...............		Columbia 45442
1/01/72	**6**	16	59	**The Best Part Of Living**		Columbia 45520
9/09/72	**32**	9	60	I've Got A Woman's Love...................		Columbia 45668
9/23/72	**11**	15	61	This Much A Man		Decca 33006
2/17/73	**60**	7	62	Laura (What's He Got That I Ain't Got).............		Columbia 45775
3/03/73	**6**	15	63	**Walking Piece Of Heaven**		MCA 40012

DEBUT DATE	PEAK POS	WKS CHR	ARTIST — Record Title	POP POS	Label & Number
			MARTY ROBBINS — Continued		
6/23/73	40	8	64 A Man And A Train		MCA 40067
			from the film "Emperor Of The North Pole"		
10/13/73	9	14	65 **Love Me**/		
		11	66 Crawlin' On My Knees................................		MCA 40134
1/26/74	10	14	67 **Twentieth Century Drifter**.......................		MCA 40172
5/25/74	12	15	68 Don't You Think		MCA 40236
10/05/74	39	11	69 Two Gun Daddy		MCA 40296
1/18/75	23	12	70 Life/		
5/31/75	76	4	71 It Takes Faith		MCA 40342
7/19/75	55	9	72 Shotgun Rider		MCA 40425
4/17/76	1²	16	73 **El Paso City**.......................................		Columbia 10305
9/04/76	1¹	14	74 **Among My Souvenirs**............................		Columbia 10396
			#7 pop hit for Connie Francis in 1959		
2/05/77	4	13	75 **Adios Amigo**..		Columbia 10472
5/21/77	10	13	76 **I Don't Know Why (I Just Do)**	108	Columbia 10536
			#12 pop hit for Linda Scott in 1961		
10/15/77	6	15	77 **Don't Let Me Touch You**		Columbia 10629
1/28/78	6	13	78 **Return To Me**		Columbia 10673
			#4 pop hit for Dean Martin in 1958		
11/04/78	17	12	79 Please Don't Play A Love Song		Columbia 10821
2/17/79	15	13	80 Touch Me With Magic............................		Columbia 10905
6/23/79	16	12	81 All Around Cowboy		Columbia 11016
10/13/79	25	10	82 Buenos Dias Argentina.........................		Columbia 11102
4/12/80	37	9	83 She's Made Of Faith		Columbia 11240
7/12/80	72	5	84 One Man's Trash (Is Another Man's Treasure)		Columbia 11291
11/01/80	28	12	85 An Occasional Rose		Columbia 11372
2/07/81	47	7	86 Completely Out Of Love		Columbia 11425
9/26/81	83	4	87 Jumper Cable Man		Columbia 02444
11/21/81	45	9	88 Teardrops In My Heart		Columbia 02575
5/22/82	10	18	89 **Some Memories Just Won't Die**.............		Columbia 02854
10/02/82	24	16	90 Tie Your Dream To Mine........................		Columbia 03236
12/25/82+	10	17	91 **Honkytonk Man**		Warner 29847
			from the Clint Eastwood film of the same title		
3/26/83	48	9	92 Change Of Heart		Columbia 03789
4/16/83	58	8	93 Love Me .... [R]		Audiograph 454
			JEANNE PRUETT/MARTY ROBBINS		
			both Jeanne and Marty had solo hits of this tune		
6/11/83	57	9	94 What If I Said I Love You............................		Columbia 03927
			RONNIE ROBBINS		
			Son of Marty Robbins; born on 7/16/49 in Phoenix.		
11/11/78	99	1	1 The Last Lie I Told Her		Artic 878
2/24/79	95	1	2 Why'd The Last Time Have To Be The Best........		Artic 8782
11/17/79	91	2	3 I Know I'm Not Your Hero Anymore.................		TRC 081
7/21/84	62	7	4 Those You Lose		Columbia 04506
			KENNY ROBERTS		
			Born on 10/14/27 in Lenoir City, Tennessee. Yodeler, worked with the Downtowners.		
9/17/49	4	11	1 **I Never See Maggie Alone**/	9	
			Juke Box #4 / Best Seller #5		
10/08/49	15	1	2 Wedding Bells		Coral 64012
			Juke Box #15		
11/19/49	14	1	3 Jealous Heart......................................		Coral 64021
			Juke Box #14		
5/13/50	8	4	4 **Choc'late Ice Cream Cone**		Coral 64032
			Jockey #8 / Juke Box #10		
			PAT ROBERTS		
			Born in Seattle, Washington. Worked in uncle Jack Roberts' band.		
10/21/72	34	12	1 Rhythm Of The Rain		Dot 17434
			#3 pop hit for The Cascades in 1963		
3/03/73	59	8	2 Thanks For Lovin' Me		Dot 17451
7/14/73	79	4	3 Here Comes My Little Baby		Dot 17465
11/03/73	81	5	4 I'm Gonna Keep Searching......................		Dot 17478
4/06/74	77	6	5 You Got Everything That You Want................		Dot 17495

DEBUT DATE	PEAK POS	WKS CHR	ARTIST — Record Title	POP POS	Label & Number
			JACK ROBERTSON		
7/09/88	66	5	1 It's Not Easy		Soundwaves 4808
			TEXAS JIM ROBERTSON & THE PANHANDLE PUNCHERS Jim was born near Batesville, Texas on 2/27/09; died on 11/11/66.		
12/28/46	5	1	1 **Filipino Baby/**		
2/15/47	5	1	2 **Rainbow At Midnight**		Victor 20-1975
2/28/48	8	1	3 **Signed, Sealed And Delivered**		Victor 20-2651
1/07/50	13	1	4 Slippin' Around .... Best Seller #13 - 78 rpm: Victor 21-0074		RCA Vic. 48-0071
			LORETTA ROBEY Born in 1937 in Oviedo, Florida.		
6/11/77	100	1	1 Sophisticated Country Lady		Soundwaves 4545
			ROBIN & CRUISER Robin and Cruiser Gordon.		
10/24/87	79	4	1 Rings Of Gold		16th Ave. 70404
			BETTY JEAN ROBINSON Born in Hyden, Kentucky. Wrote "What's He Doing In My World" for Eddy Arnold. Turned to gospel music in 1974. Own record label, Melody Mountain.		
4/24/71	51	10	1 All I Need Is You .... **CARL BELEW & BETTY JEAN ROBINSON**		Decca 32802
11/23/74+	49	10	2 On The Way Home..		MCA 40300
4/05/75	87	4	3 God Is Good		4 Star 1004
			SHARON ROBINSON		
12/26/87	86	4	1 Have You Hurt Any Good Ones Lately...............		Nightfall 001
			CARSON ROBISON Born on 8/4/1890 in Oswego, Kansas; died on 3/24/57 in Pleasant Valley, New York. Moved to Kansas City in 1920 and worked with Jack Riley from 1920-24. Moved to New York City in 1924 and worked on radio shows. Known as "The Kansas Jayhawk".		
6/30/45	5	1	1 Hitler's Last Letter To Hirohito............... [N]		Victor 20-1665
8/14/48	3	28	2 **Life Gits Tee-Jus Don't It**........................ [N] Best Seller #3 / Juke Box #3	14	MGM 10224
			ROCKIN' HORSE Oakland, Minnesota-based quintet; Toni Rose, lead singer.		
8/30/86	68	6	1 Have I Got A Heart For You		Long Shot 1002
12/06/86	86	3	2 Let A Little Love In (Tennesse Saturday Night)...		Epic 06433
			ROCKIN' SIDNEY Sidney Simien, born in Lebeau, Louisiana on 4/9/38. Recorded blues and soul as Count Rockin' Sidney in the early 60s. Own Zydeco band, the Dukes.		
6/22/85	19	20	1 My Toot-Toot..		Epic 05430
			JIMMIE RODGERS "The Father Of Country Music". Born James Charles Rodgers on 9/8/1897 in Meridian, Mississippi. Contracted tuberculosis while working as a railroad brakeman. During recuperation, began singing and writing songs for a living. By merging hillbilly and blues, he developed a new style that made him a legend following his death on 5/26/33 (35). Elected to the Country Music Hall of Fame in 1961. Inducted into the Rock And Roll Hall Of Fame in 1986.		
5/14/55	7	12	1 **In The Jailhouse Now, No. 2** .... [R] Juke Box #7 / Best Seller #8 / Jockey #9 first released on Victor 22523 in 1930; new overdubbed backing includes Chet Atkins and Hank Snow		RCA 6092
			JIMMIE RODGERS Pop vocalist/guitarist/pianist born on 9/18/33 in Camas, Washington. Own NBC-TV series in 1959. Career hampered following mysterious assault in Los Angeles on 12/1/67, which left him with a fractured skull. Returned to performing on 1/28/69.		
10/14/57	7	13	1 Honeycomb .... Best Seller #7 / Jockey #11	1	Roulette 4015
12/02/57+	6	16	2 Kisses Sweeter Than Wine........................... Best Seller #6 / Jockey #8	3	Roulette 4031
3/03/58	5	10	3 **Oh-Oh, I'm Falling In Love Again**.................. Best Seller #5 / Jockey #15	7	Roulette 4045

DEBUT DATE	PEAK POS	WKS CHR	ARTIST — Record Title	POP POS	Label & Number
			JIMMIE RODGERS — Continued		
5/19/58	**5**	17	4 **Secretly**/	*3*	
			Best Seller #5 / Jockey #14		
		9	5 Make Me A Miracle	*16*	Roulette 4070
			Best Seller flip		
8/25/58	**13**	8	6 Are You Really Mine	*10*	Roulette 4090
			Best Seller #13		
10/29/77	**67**	10	7 A Good Woman Likes To Drink With The Boys ...		ScrimShaw 1313
2/11/78	**74**	5	8 Everytime I Sing A Love Song		ScrimShaw 1314
9/23/78	**65**	5	9 Secretly .... [R]		ScrimShaw 1318
3/17/79	**89**	4	10 Easy To Love/		
		4	11 Easy		ScrimShaw 1319
			JIMMIE RODGERS & MICHELE		

JUDY RODMAN

Born on 5/23/51 in Riverside, California; raised in Miami and Jacksonville. Worked as a commercial jingle singer from age 17. Worked with Janie Fricke and Karen Taylor as Phase II. Married to drummer John Rodman in 1975. Moved to Nashville in 1980, made commercials, sang back-up vocals.

DEBUT DATE	PEAK POS	WKS CHR	ARTIST — Record Title	POP POS	Label & Number
3/23/85	**40**	14	1 I've Been Had By Love Before		MTM 72050
8/10/85	**33**	14	2 You're Gonna Miss Me When I'm Gone		MTM 72054
11/16/85+	**30**	17	3 I Sure Need Your Lovin'		MTM 72061
3/22/86	**1**¹	25	4 **Until I Met You**		MTM 72065
10/04/86+	**9**	21	5 **She Thinks That She'll Marry**		MTM 72076
2/21/87	**7**	17	6 **Girls Ride Horses Too**		MTM 72083
6/20/87	**5**	27	7 **I'll Be Your Baby Tonight**		MTM 72089
			written by Bob Dylan		
10/31/87+	**18**	21	8 I Want A Love Like That		MTM 72092
5/21/88	**43**	9	9 Goin' To Work		MTM 72105
8/13/88	**45**	9	10 I Can Love You		MTM 72112

JOHNNY RODRIGUEZ ★★59★★

Born Juan Rodriguez on 12/10/51 in Sabinal, Texas. Guitarist from age 7. Performed with high school rock band in the late 60s. Moved to Nashville in 1971, worked with the Tom T. Hall band from 1971-72. First solo recording in 1972.

DEBUT DATE	PEAK POS	WKS CHR	ARTIST — Record Title	POP POS	Label & Number
11/11/72+	**9**	18	1 **Pass Me By**		Mercury 73334
3/31/73	**1**¹	16	2 **You Always Come Back (To Hurting Me)**	*86*	Mercury 73368
8/18/73	**1**²	17	3 **Ridin' My Thumb To Mexico**	*70*	Mercury 73416
12/29/73+	**1**¹	14	4 **That's The Way Love Goes**		Mercury 73446
3/30/74	**6**	14	5 **Something**	*85*	Mercury 73471
			#1 pop hit for The Beatles in 1969		
7/13/74	**2**¹	13	6 **Dance With Me (Just One More Time)**		Mercury 73493
10/19/74	**3**	13	7 **We're Over**		Mercury 73621
2/08/75	**1**¹	12	8 **I Just Can't Get Her Out Of My Mind**		Mercury 73659
5/24/75	**1**¹	18	9 **Just Get Up And Close The Door**		Mercury 73682
10/04/75	**1**¹	15	10 **Love Put A Song In My Heart**		Mercury 73715
2/28/76	**3**	15	11 **I Couldn't Be Me Without You**		Mercury 73769
7/10/76	**2**²	13	12 **I Wonder If I Ever Said Goodbye**		Mercury 73815
10/09/76	**5**	14	13 **Hillbilly Heart**		Mercury 73855
1/15/77	**5**	14	14 **Desperado**		Mercury 73878
			written and recorded by the Eagles in 1973		
5/14/77	**5**	13	15 **If Practice Makes Perfect**		Mercury 73914
9/03/77	**25**	10	16 Eres Tu		Mercury 55004
			#9 pop hit for Mocedades in 1974		
11/05/77	**14**	13	17 Savin' This Love Song For You		Mercury 55012
2/25/78	**7**	14	18 **We Believe In Happy Endings**		Mercury 55020
7/08/78	**7**	13	19 **Love Me With All Your Heart (Cuando Calienta El Sol)**		Mercury 55029
			#3 pop hit for The Ray Charles Singers in 1964		
12/16/78+	**16**	13	20 Alibis..		Mercury 55050
3/10/79	**6**	14	21 **Down On The Rio Grande**		Epic 50671
7/07/79	**17**	13	22 Fools For Each Other		Epic 50735
10/20/79	**16**	14	23 I Hate The Way I Love It		Epic 50791
			JOHNNY RODRIGUEZ & CHARLY McCLAIN		
11/24/79+	**19**	14	24 What'll I Tell Virginia		Epic 50808
4/05/80	**29**	11	25 Love, Look At Us Now..................................		Epic 50859

DEBUT DATE	PEAK POS	WKS CHR	ARTIST — Record Title	POP POS	Label & Number
			JOHNNY RODRIGUEZ — Continued		
9/20/80	**17**	16	26 North Of The Border		Epic 50932
4/11/81	**22**	13	27 I Want You Tonight		Epic 01033
8/08/81	**30**	11	28 Trying Not To Love You		Epic 02411
12/05/81	**73**	7	29 It's Not The Same Old You/		
2/13/82	**66**	6	30 Born With The Blues		Epic 02638
11/27/82	**89**	3	31 He's Not Entitled To Your Love........................		Epic 03275
2/26/83	**4**	20	32 **Foolin'**...		Epic 03598
7/09/83	**6**	21	33 **How Could I Love Her So Much**.....................		Epic 03972
11/19/83+	**35**	12	34 Back On Her Mind Again		Epic 04206
1/28/84	**15**	17	35 Too Late To Go Home		Epic 04336
5/19/84	**30**	15	36 Let's Leave The Lights On Tonight...................		Epic 04460
8/18/84	**63**	7	37 First Time Burned		Epic 04562
10/13/84	**60**	8	38 Rose Of My Heart		Epic 04628
4/06/85	**69**	7	39 Here I Am Again		Epic 04838
12/28/85+	**51**	15	40 She Don't Cry Like She Used To		Epic 05732
12/12/87+	**12**	26	41 I Didn't (Every Chance I Had).........................		Capitol 44071
7/16/88	**41**	15	42 I Wanta Wake Up With You............................		Capitol 44204
10/15/88	**44**	10	43 You Might Want To Use Me Again		Capitol 44245
			MARLYS ROE		
8/11/73	**71**	9	1 Carry Me Back..		GRC 1002
			written by TV game show host, Chuck Woolery		
			TOMMY ROE		
			Born on 5/9/42 in Atlanta. Pop-rock singer/guitarist/composer. Formed band, The Satins in the late 50s. Moved to Britain in the mid-60s; returned in 1969.		
6/09/73	**73**	2	1 Working Class Hero	*97*	MGM South 7013
5/19/79	**77**	3	2 Massachusetts..		Warner 8800
			#11 pop hit for The Bee Gees in 1967		
10/27/79	**70**	4	3 You Better Move On		Warner 49085
			#24 pop hit for Arthur Alexander in 1962		
6/21/80	**87**	3	4 Charlie, I Love Your Wife...............................		Warner 49235
11/16/85	**57**	11	5 Some Such Foolishness		MCA/Curb 52711
3/01/86	**51**	7	6 Radio Romance..		MCA/Curb 52778
12/20/86+	**38**	14	7 Let's Be Fools Like That Again........................		Mercury 888206
5/23/87	**67**	5	8 Back When It Really Mattered		Mercury 888497
			DANN ROGERS		
			Kenny Rogers' nephew, Danny Wayne Rogers.		
9/05/87	**78**	3	1 Just A Kid From Texas		MCA 53133
			DAVID ROGERS ★★**122**★★		
			Born on 3/27/36 in Atlanta. Worked clubs in Atlanta from 1952-67, staying at the Egyptian Ballroom for 6 years. Worked on the Wheeling Jamboree in 1967.		
3/02/68	**69**	5	1 I'd Be Your Fool Again		Columbia 44430
7/20/68	**38**	11	2 I'm In Love With My Wife		Columbia 44561
11/16/68+	**37**	13	3 You Touched My Heart...................................		Columbia 44668
5/17/69	**59**	7	4 Dearly Beloved		Columbia 44796
11/22/69+	**23**	12	5 A World Called You		Columbia 45007
5/09/70	**46**	9	6 So Much In Love With You..............................		Columbia 45111
10/17/70	**26**	11	7 I Wake Up In Heaven		Columbia 45226
5/29/71	**19**	15	8 She Don't Make Me Cry		Columbia 45383
11/13/71+	**21**	13	9 Ruby You're Warm		Columbia 45478
2/26/72	**9**	15	10 Need You		Columbia 45551
			#25 pop hit for Donnie Owens in 1958		
8/05/72	**38**	9	11 Goodbye..		Columbia 45642
11/11/72	**35**	11	12 All Heaven Breaks Loose...............................		Columbia 45714
4/28/73	**17**	12	13 Just Thank Me		Atlantic 2957
8/25/73	**22**	12	14 It'll Be Her		Atlantic 4005
1/05/74	**9**	14	15 **Loving You Has Changed My Life**		Atlantic 4012
5/25/74	**21**	13	16 Hey There Girl...		Atlantic 4022
9/28/74	**59**	7	17 I Just Can't Help Believin'		Atlantic 4204
			#9 pop hit for B.J. Thomas in 1970		
4/12/75	**60**	8	18 It Takes A Whole Lotta Livin' In A House.........		United Art. 617

DEBUT DATE	PEAK POS	WKS CHR	ARTIST — Record Title	POP POS	Label & Number
			DAVID ROGERS — Continued		
8/07/76	66	7	19 Whispers And Grins...		Republic 256
11/06/76	84	6	20 Mahogany Bridge		Republic 311
1/15/77	21	12	21 I'm Gonna Love You Right Out Of This World.....		Republic 343
4/30/77	76	4	22 The Lady And The Baby..............................		Republic 382
6/18/77	49	7	23 I Love What My Woman Does To Me		Republic 001
9/03/77	47	8	24 Do You Hear My Heart Beat		Republic 006
11/26/77+	24	12	25 You And Me Alone		Republic 011
2/25/78	22	12	26 I'll Be There (When You Get Lonely)		Republic 015
5/27/78	32	10	27 Let's Try To Remember..............................		Republic 020
9/09/78	31	9	28 When A Woman Cries		Republic 029
3/03/79	18	14	29 Darlin'		Republic 038
7/14/79	36	8	30 You Are My Rainbow		Republic 042
12/15/79+	39	9	31 You're Amazing		Republic 048
5/23/81	88	3	32 Houston Blue		Kari 120
11/06/82	92	2	33 Crown Prince Of The Barroom		Music Mast. 012
2/19/83	67	7	34 Hold Me..		Music Mast. 1004
6/04/83	71	5	35 You Still Got Me...		Mr. Music 016
11/12/83	87	4	36 The Devil Is A Woman..................................		Mr. Music 018
3/03/84	72	4	37 I'm A Country Song		Hal Kat 2083
			JESSE ROGERS		
			Born in Meridian, Mississippi. Worked on local radio from age 17. Own NBC-TV series for children in 1949. Known as "The Western Balladeer".		
9/10/49	15	1	1 Wedding Bells..		Bluebird 32-0002
			Juke Box #15		
			KENNY ROGERS ★★**34**★★		
			Born Kenneth Donald Rogers on 8/21/38 in Houston. With high school band, the Scholars, in 1958. Bass player of jazz group, the Bobby Doyle Trio, recorded for Columbia. In Kirby Stone Four and The New Christy Minstrels, mid-60s. Formed the First Edition in 1967. Went solo in 1973. Starred in films "The Gambler", "Coward Of The County" and "Six Pack".		
			KENNY ROGERS & THE FIRST EDITION:		
7/19/69	39	11	1 Ruby, Don't Take Your Love To Town..............	6	Reprise 0829
10/25/69	46	8	2 Ruben James	26	Reprise 0854
7/14/73	69	6	3 Today I Started Loving You Again....................		Jolly Rog. 1004
			KENNY ROGERS:		
12/13/75+	19	13	4 Love Lifted Me...	97	United Art. 746
6/26/76	46	12	5 While The Feeling's Good		United Art. 812
10/09/76	19	13	6 Laura (What's He Got That I Ain't Got?)..........		United Art. 868
1/29/77	1²	20	7● Lucille..	5	United Art. 929
8/06/77	1¹	14	8 Daytime Friends	28	United Art. 1027
10/22/77	9	15	9 Sweet Music Man	44	United Art. 1095
6/03/78	1¹	14	10 Love Or Something Like It............................	32	United Art. 1210
10/28/78	1³	16	11 The Gambler	16	United Art. 1250
4/21/79	1²	16	12● She Believes In Me	5	United Art. 1273
9/15/79	1²	12	13 You Decorated My Life	7	United Art. 1315
11/17/79	1³	15	14● Coward Of The County	3	United Art. 1327
6/28/80	4	14	15 Love The World Away.................................	14	United Art. 1359
			from the film "Urban Cowboy"		
10/11/80	1¹	14	16● Lady	1	Liberty 1380
			written by Lionel Richie		
6/20/81	1²	15	17 I Don't Need You	3	Liberty 1415
9/12/81	5	14	18 Share Your Love With Me	14	Liberty 1430
11/14/81+	9	16	19 Blaze Of Glory	66	Liberty 1441
1/30/82	5	16	20 Through The Years.....................................	13	Liberty 1444
7/10/82	1¹	16	21 Love Will Turn You Around	13	Liberty 1471
			from the film "Six Pack"		
10/16/82	3	17	22 A Love Song...	47	Liberty 1485
5/07/83	13	17	23 All My Life...	37	Liberty 1495
7/30/83	5	18	24 Scarlet Fever	94	Liberty 1503
11/19/83+	20	17	25 You Were A Good Friend		Liberty 1511
1/14/84	3	17	26 Buried Treasure		RCA 13710
			flip side "This Woman" hit POS 23 on the pop charts		

DEBUT DATE	PEAK POS	WKS CHR		ARTIST — Record Title	POP POS	Label & Number
				KENNY ROGERS — Continued		
4/21/84	**30**	13	27	Eyes That See In The Dark	*79*	RCA 13774
6/30/84	**11**	19	28	Evening Star/		
		14	29	Midsummer Nights		RCA 13832
12/22/84+	**1**¹	21	30	**Crazy**	*79*	RCA 13975
4/13/85	**37**	12	31	Love Is What We Make It		Liberty 1524
7/20/85	**57**	8	32	Twentieth Century Fool............................		Liberty 1525
10/12/85+	**1**¹	22	33	**Morning Desire**....................................	*72*	RCA 14194
1/18/86	**47**	9	34	Goodbye Marie.....................................		Liberty 1526
2/22/86	**1**¹	20	35	**Tomb Of The Unknown Love**		RCA 14298
10/18/86	**53**	12	36	They Don't Make Them Like They Used To		RCA 5016
				theme from the film "Tough Guys"		
12/27/86+	**2**²	21	37	**Twenty Years Ago**		RCA 5078
10/10/87	**2**²	19	38	**I Prefer The Moonlight**		RCA 5258
3/05/88	**6**	16	39	**The Factory**		RCA 6832
8/13/88	**26**	15	40	When You Put Your Heart In It		Reprise 27812
9/03/88	**88**	1	41	I Don't Call Him Daddy............................		RCA 8390
				re-charted on 2/18/89		
				KENNY ROGERS DUOS with:		
				KIM CARNES:		
4/05/80	**3**	14	42	**Don't Fall In Love With A Dreamer**...............	*4*	United Art. 1345
				KIM CARNES & JAMES INGRAM:		
11/10/84	**70**	10	43	What About Me?	*15*	RCA 13899
				SHEENA EASTON:		
1/29/83	**1**¹	17	44	**We've Got Tonight**	*6*	Liberty 1492
				RONNIE MILSAP:		
6/27/87	**1**¹	17	45	**Make No Mistake, She's Mine**		RCA 5209
				DOLLY PARTON:		
9/03/83	**1**²	23	46▲	Islands In The Stream................................	*1*	RCA 13615
12/15/84+	**53**	7	47	The Greatest Gift Of All............................[X]	*81*	RCA 13945
				from their Christmas TV special		
5/25/85	**1**¹	20	48	**Real Love**..	*91*	RCA 14058
				NICKIE RYDER:		
6/14/86	**46**	12	49	The Pride Is Back......................................		RCA 14384
				tune used for a Chrysler Corporation jingle		
				DOTTIE WEST:		
2/18/78	**1**²	17	50	**Every Time Two Fools Collide**	*101*	United Art. 1137
9/02/78	**2**¹	14	51	**Anyone Who Isn't Me Tonight**		United Art. 1234
2/17/79	**1**¹	15	52	**All I Ever Need Is You**	*102*	United Art. 1276
7/07/79	**3**	15	53	**Til I Can Make It On My Own**		United Art. 1299
4/04/81	**1**¹	15	54	**What Are We Doin' In Love**	*14*	Liberty 1404
3/24/84	**19**	15	55	Together Again......................................		Liberty 1516
				RONNIE ROGERS		
				Born Randall J. Rogers in Nashville. Wrote "Keep On Truckin'" hit for Dave Dudley.		
11/21/81+	**39**	11	1	Gonna Take My Angel Out Tonight..................		Lifesong 45094
3/20/82	**37**	9	2	My Love Belongs To You		Lifesong 45095
6/12/82	**54**	8	3	First Time Around..................................		Lifesong 45116
9/25/82	**86**	3	4	Happy Country Birthday/		
10/16/82	**86**	3	5	Takin' It Back To The Hills.....................		Lifesong 45118
6/25/83	**66**	7	6	Inside Story		Epic 03953
9/19/87	**57**	8	7	Good Timin' Shoes		MTM 72094
8/06/88	**82**	2	8	Let's Be Bad Tonight		MTM 72110
				ROY ROGERS		
				Born Leonard Franklin Slye on 11/5/12 in Cincinnati. Moved to California in 1930. Played in the Hollywood Hillbillies, Rocky Mountaineers, and Texas Outlaws. Own group, the International Cowboys. Formed the Pioneer Trio in 1934 with Bob Nolan and Tim Spencer and this developed into the Sons Of The Pioneers. Then known as "Dick Weston", appeared in "Rhythm On The Range" in 1936. Went solo in 1937 and made first starring film, "Under Western Stars", in 1938. Made 91 feature films. Married Frances Octavia "Dale Evans" Smith on 12/31/47. Dale was born on 10/31/12 in Uvalde, Texas. Made 101 half-hour western shows. Elected to the Country Music Hall of Fame in 1980 as a member of the Sons of The Pioneers, and individually in 1989.		
7/06/46	**7**	1	1	**A Little White Cross On The Hill**..................		Victor 20-1872

DEBUT DATE	PEAK POS	WKS CHR	ARTIST — Record Title	POP POS	Label & Number
			ROY ROGERS — Continued		
3/15/47	**4**	1	2 **My Chickashay Gal**		Victor 20-2124
			with the Country Washburne Orchestra		
6/12/48	**6**	14	3 **Blue Shadows On The Trail/**		
			Best Seller #6 / Juke Box #7		
6/12/48	**13**	4	4 **Pecos Bill**		Victor 20-2780
			Best Seller #13		
2/04/50	**8**	1	5 **Stampede**		RCA 0161
			Jockey #8		
			above three with the Sons Of The Pioneers		
9/26/70	**35**	10	6 Money Can't Buy Love		Capitol 2895
1/30/71	**12**	11	7 Lovenworth		Capitol 3016
6/26/71	**47**	11	8 Happy Anniversary..		Capitol 3117
2/26/72	**73**	4	9 These Are The Good Old Days		Capitol 3263
12/21/74+	**15**	13	10 Hoppy, Gene And Me	65	20th Century 2154
8/23/80	**80**	4	11 Ride Concrete Cowboy, Ride............................		MCA 41294
			with The Sons Of The Pioneers; from film "Smokey & The Bandit 2"		
			SMOKEY ROGERS		
			Western swing banjoist; performed with Spade Cooley and later with Tex Williams. Wrote Ferlin Husky's #1 hit "Gone".		
1/01/49	**8**	4	1 **A Little Bird Told Me**		Capitol 15326
			Juke Box #8		
			DONNIE ROHRS		
			Guitarist/pianist born in 1946. Operator of the Kountry Klub in Nashville.		
12/16/78	**95**	3	1 Hey Baby		Ad-Korp 1258
			#1 pop hit for Bruce Channel in 1962		
5/02/81	**85**	6	2 Waltzes And Western Swing............................		Pacific C. 4504
			ADRIAN ROLAND		
9/19/60	**19**	4	1 Imitation Of Love		All Star 7207
			LINDA RONSTADT ★★**142**★★		
			Born on 7/15/46 in Tucson, Arizona. While in high school formed folk trio, The Three Ronstadts (with sister and brother). To Los Angeles in 1964. Formed the Stone Poneys with Bobby Kimmel (guitar) and Ken Edwards (keyboards); recorded for Sidewalk in 1965. Went solo in 1968. In 1971 formed backing band with Glenn Frey, Don Henley, Randy Meisner and Bernie Leadon (later became the Eagles). In "Pirates Of Penzance" operetta in New York City in 1980, also in film of same name in 1983. Also see Hoyt Axton and Nitty Gritty Dirt Band.		
3/02/74	**20**	12	1 Silver Threads And Golden Needles	67	Asylum 11032
12/21/74+	**2**¹	17	2 **I Can't Help It (If I'm Still In Love With You)** ..		Capitol 3990
			flip side "You're No Good" hit #1 on the pop charts		
4/19/75	**1**¹	15	3 **When Will I Be Loved/**	2	
9/13/75	**54**	7	4 It Doesn't Matter Anymore	47	Capitol 4050
9/13/75	**5**	15	5 **Love Is A Rose**..	Flp	Asylum 45271
			flip side "Heat Wave" hit #5 on the pop charts		
1/03/76	**11**	12	6 Tracks Of My Tears/	25	
1/03/76	**12**	12	7 The Sweetest Gift		Asylum 45295
			LINDA RONSTADT & EMMYLOU HARRIS		
9/04/76	**27**	11	8 That'll Be The Day	11	Asylum 45340
12/18/76+	**6**	15	9 **Crazy**		Asylum 45361
9/17/77	**2**²	19	10●**Blue Bayou**..	3	Asylum 45431
11/12/77	**81**	6	11 It's So Easy	5	Asylum 45438
2/18/78	**46**	9	12 Poor Poor Pitiful Me	31	Asylum 45462
5/13/78	**8**	13	13 **I Never Will Marry**		Asylum 45479
			flip side "Tumbling Dice" hit POS 32 on the pop charts		
9/02/78	**41**	8	14 Back In The U.S.A.	16	Asylum 45519
12/02/78	**85**	5	15 Ooh Baby Baby	7	Asylum 45546
3/10/79	**59**	6	16 Love Me Tender		Asylum 46011
			flip side "Just One Look" hit POS 44 on the pop charts		
3/01/80	**42**	8	17 Rambler Gambler		Asylum 46602
			flip side "How Do I Make You" hit POS 10 on the pop charts		
10/16/82	**27**	12	18 Sometimes You Just Can't Win.......................		Asylum 69948
			LINDA RONSTADT & JOHN DAVID SOUTHER		
			flip side "Get Closer" (Linda Ronstadt) hit POS 29 on pop charts		
1/29/83	**84**	3	19 I Knew You When...	37	Asylum 69853
			DOLLY PARTON, LINDA RONSTADT, EMMYLOU HARRIS:		
2/21/87	**1**¹	19	20 **To Know Him Is To Love Him**		Warner 28492

DEBUT DATE	PEAK POS	WKS CHR	ARTIST — Record Title	POP POS	Label & Number
			LINDA RONSTADT — Continued		
5/30/87	**3**	18	21 Telling Me Lies...		Warner 28371
9/26/87	**5**	22	22 Those Memories Of You		Warner 28248
3/26/88	**6**	18	23 Wildflowers..		Warner 27970
			THE ROOFTOP SINGERS		
			Folk trio consisting of Erik Darling, Willard Svanoe and Lynne Taylor (d: 1982). Darling was a member of The Tarriers in 1956 and The Weavers from 1958-62.		
2/23/63	**23**	4	1 Walk Right In	*1*	Vanguard 35017
			FRED ROSE - see RAMBLING ROGUE		
			PAM ROSE		
			Born Pamela Rose Thacker in Chattanooga; raised in Eau Gallie, Florida. Folk singer while at Florida State University. Worked in Atlanta from 1971-74. Moved to Nashville, became very popular back-up singer and guitarist. Sang in Calamity Jane.		
7/23/77	**83**	5	1 Midnight Flight		Capitol 4440
11/19/77	**93**	3	2 Runaway Heart		Capitol 4491
1/05/80	**52**	7	3 It's Not Supposed To Be That Way		Epic 50819
			Willie Nelson sings harmony vocal at end of record		
4/19/80	**60**	6	4 I'm Not Through Loving You Yet.....................		Epic 50861
			RICHARD & GARY ROSE		
2/13/88	**81**	3	1 Younger Man, Older Woman...........................		Capitol 44118
			CHARLIE ROSS		
			Born in Greenville, Mississippi. Deejay on WDDT radio. Moved to California in the late 60s, worked with Eternity's Children.		
2/28/76	**13**	12	1 Without Your Love (Mr. Jordan)......................	*42*	Big Tree 16056
6/05/82	**33**	13	2 The High Cost Of Loving...............................		Town House 1057
9/18/82	**45**	9	3 Are We In Love (Or Am I)...............................		Town House 1061
1/08/83	**70**	5	4 The Name Of The Game Is Cheating.................		Town House 1063
			JERIS ROSS		
			Female vocalist from East Alton, Illinois. Worked as a pop singer in St. Louis.		
3/11/72	**75**	2	1 Brand New Key		Cartwheel 206
			#1 pop hit for Melanie in 1971		
6/24/72	**58**	12	2 Old Fashioned Love Song...............................		Cartwheel 214
			#4 pop hit for Three Dog Night in 1971		
12/22/73+	**58**	7	3 Moontan..		ABC 11397
4/26/75	**17**	14	4 Pictures On Paper		ABC 12064
10/11/75	**66**	8	5 I'd Rather Be Picked Up Here (Than Be Put Down At Home)		ABC/Dot 17573
10/29/77	**77**	6	6 I Think I'll Say Goodbye		Gazelle 431
9/15/79	**94**	4	7 Little Bit More		Door Knob 108
1/26/80	**75**	5	8 You Win Again		Door Knob 117
			ROY ROSS - see RED FOLEY		
			THE ROVERS		
			Group formed in Canada in 1964 as the Irish Rovers. All members born in Ireland.		
2/28/81	**45**	11	1 Wasn't That A Party......................................	*37*	Epic 51007
3/13/82	**77**	4	2 Pain In My Past		Epic 02728
			STACEY ROWE		
6/30/79	**96**	2	1 I Couldn't Live Without Your Love		Sabre 4510
			ERNIE ROWELL		
7/24/71	**74**	2	1 Going Back To Louisiana................................		Prize 08
9/29/79	**91**	4	2 I'm Leavin' You Alone.....................................		Grass 05
5/09/81	**59**	6	3 Music In The Mountains		Grass 07
10/03/87	**86**	3	4 You Left My Heart For Broke		Revolver 016
			DAVE ROWLAND		
			Leader of the Dave & Sugar trio.		
5/15/82	**77**	5	1 Natalie/		
		5	2 Why Didn't I Think Of That...........................		Elektra 47442
7/31/82	**84**	3	3 Lovin' Our Lives Away		Elektra 69998

DEBUT DATE	PEAK POS	WKS CHR	ARTIST — Record Title	POP POS	Label & Number
			BOBBIE ROY		
			Born Barbara Elaine Roy on 7/27/53 in Landstuhl, Germany, where her father was in the Army. Moved to Elkins, West Virginia in 1960.		
6/03/72	**32**	9	1 One Woman's Trash (Another Woman's Treasure)		Capitol 3301
9/23/72	**58**	8	2 Leavin' On Your Mind		Capitol 3428
12/16/72+	**62**	5	3 I Like Everything About Loving You		Capitol 3477
1/27/73	**51**	5	4 I Am Woman		Capitol 3513
			#1 pop hit for Helen Reddy in 1972		
			BILLY JOE ROYAL		
			Born on 4/3/42 in Valdosta, Georgia; raised in Marietta, Georgia. Guitarist/pianist/drummer. Own band, the Corvettes, while in high school. First recorded in 1962. Moved to Cincinnati in 1963.		
10/26/85+	**10**	22	1 Burned Like A Rocket		Atln. Am. 99599
5/03/86	**41**	16	2 Boardwalk Angel		Atln. Am. 99555
8/23/86	**14**	24	3 I Miss You Already		Atln. Am. 99519
2/07/87	**11**	26	4 Old Bridges Burn Slow		Atln. Am. 99485
6/27/87	**23**	15	5 Members Only		Mercury 888680
			DONNA FARGO & BILLY JOE ROYAL		
10/17/87+	**5**	23	6 I'll Pin A Note On Your Pillow		Atln. Am. 99404
3/12/88	**10**	22	7 Out Of Sight And On My Mind		Atln. Am. 99364
8/27/88	**17**	17	8 It Keeps Right On Hurtin'		Atln. Am. 99295
			#3 pop hit for Johnny Tillotson in 1962		
			DWIGHT RUCKER - see TIM MALCHAK		
			ARNIE RUE		
			Born in Massachusetts; moved to California in the mid-50s.		
5/05/79	**56**	6	1 Spare A Little Lovin' (On A Fool)		NSD 19
11/17/79	**74**	4	2 Rodle-Odeo-Home		NSD 32
			both feature "Sneaky Pete" Kleinow on steel guitar		
			JIM RUSHING		
			Born in Lubbock, Texas. Worked with Don Williams, Crystal Gayle and George Jones.		
9/27/80	**81**	2	1 Dixie Dirt		Ovation 1153
12/27/80+	**56**	8	2 I've Loved Enough To Know		Ovation 1161
			BOBBY RUSSELL		
			Born on 4/19/41 in Nashville. Wrote "The Night The Lights Went Out In Georgia", "Honey", "Little Green Apples" and "The Joker Went Wild".		
11/09/68	**64**	8	1 1432 Franklin Pike Circle Hero	*36*	Elf 90020
3/01/69	**66**	3	2 Carlie	*115*	Elf 90023
8/16/69	**34**	9	3 Better Homes And Gardens		Elf 90031
7/10/71	**24**	13	4 Saturday Morning Confusion	*28*	United Art. 50788
8/18/73	**93**	3	5 Mid American Manufacturing Tycoon		Columbia 45901
			CLIFFORD RUSSELL		
			Born in Knoxville, Tennessee.		
2/12/83	**97**	2	1 She Feels Like A New Man Tonight		Sugartree 0509
			JIMMY RUSSELL		
12/18/76	**99**	4	1 You've Got To Move Two Mountains		Charta 103
			JOHNNY RUSSELL ★★176★★		
			Born on 1/23/40 in Sunflower County, Mississippi; raised in California. Worked as the manager of the Wilburn Brothers music company. Wrote "Act Naturally", hit for The Beatles and Buck Owens. Member of the Grand Ole Opry since 1985.		
8/21/71	**64**	3	1 Mr. And Mrs. Untrue		RCA 1000
12/11/71+	**57**	9	2 What A Price		RCA 0570
			#22 pop hit for Fats Domino in 1961		
4/01/72	**59**	7	3 Mr. Fiddle Man		RCA 0665
7/01/72	**36**	12	4 Rain Falling On Me		RCA 0729
11/11/72+	**12**	15	5 Catfish John		RCA 0810
3/24/73	**31**	10	6 Chained		RCA 0908
8/04/73	**4**	19	7 Rednecks, White Socks And Blue Ribbon Beer		RCA 0021
11/10/73+	**14**	13	8 The Baptism Of Jesse Taylor		RCA 0165
4/13/74	**39**	10	9 She's In Love With A Rodeo Man		RCA 0248
9/14/74	**38**	10	10 She Burn't The Little Roadside Tavern Down		RCA 10038

DEBUT DATE	PEAK POS	WKS CHR	ARTIST — Record Title	POP POS	Label & Number
			JOHNNY RUSSELL — Continued		
12/21/74+	23	11	11 That's How My Baby Builds A Fire		RCA 10135
4/26/75	13	17	12 Hello I Love You		RCA 10258
10/11/75	45	10	13 Our Marriage Was A Failure		RCA 10403
2/21/76	57	9	14 I'm A Trucker..		RCA 10563
5/22/76	45	8	15 This Man And Woman Thing		RCA 10667
12/25/76+	32	10	16 The Son Of Hickory Holler's Tramp/		
		10	17 I Wonder How She's Doing Now		RCA 10853
6/25/77	91	3	18 Obscene Phone Call		RCA 10984
12/10/77+	64	9	19 Leona		RCA 11160
5/13/78	24	12	20 You'll Be Back (Every Night In My Dreams)		Polydor 14475
11/25/78+	29	12	21 How Deep In Love Am I?		Mercury 55045
5/19/79	57	6	22 I Might Be Awhile In New Orleans		Mercury 55060
11/17/79	56	7	23 Ain't No Way To Make A Bad Love Grow		Mercury 57008
3/15/80	57	6	24 While The Choir Sang The Hymn (I Thought Of Her)..		Mercury 57016
6/21/80	59	7	25 We're Back In Love Again.............................		Mercury 57026
12/13/80+	57	9	26 Song Of The South		Mercury 57038
4/18/81	49	9	27 Here's To The Horses..................................		Mercury 57050
7/25/87	72	4	28 Butterbeans		16th Ave. 70401
			JOHNNY RUSSELL & LITTLE DAVID WILKINS		

LEON RUSSELL
Born on 4/2/41 in Lawton, Oklahoma. Vocalist/songwriter/top multi-instrumentalist sessionman. Formed Shelter Records with British producer Denny Cordell in 1970. Married Mary McCreary (vocalist with Little Sister; part of Sly Stone's "family") in 1976. Own label, Paradise, in 1976. Also recorded as Hank Wilson.

DEBUT DATE	PEAK POS	WKS CHR	ARTIST — Record Title	POP POS	Label & Number
9/29/73	57	11	1 Roll In My Sweet Baby's Arms	78	Shelter 7336
1/12/74	68	8	2 A Six Pack To Go		Shelter 7338
			above 2 shown as: HANK WILSON		
7/07/79	1¹	13	3 **Heartbreak Hotel**....................................		Columbia 11023
			WILLIE NELSON & LEON RUSSELL		
			#1 pop hit for Elvis Presley in 1956		
7/28/84	63	12	4 Good Time Charlie's Got The Blues		Paradise 628
			#9 pop hit for Danny O'Keefe in 1972		
10/27/84	91	2	5 Wabash Cannonball....................................		Paradise 629
			WILLIE NELSON & HANK WILSON		

RUSTY & DOUG
Duo of brothers Russell Lee "Rusty" (b: 2/2/38) and Douglas James Kershaw (b: 1/24/36). Both from Tiel Ridge, Louisiana. Also see Doug Kershaw.

DEBUT DATE	PEAK POS	WKS CHR	ARTIST — Record Title	POP POS	Label & Number
8/13/55	14	2	1 So Lovely Baby..		Hickory 1027
			Jockey #14		
9/23/57	14	1	2 Love Me To Pieces......................................		Hickory 1068
			Jockey #14		
			#11 pop hit for Jill Corey in 1957		
10/20/58	22	2	3 Hey, Sheriff		Hickory 1083
2/06/61	10	15	4 **Louisiana Man**..	104	Hickory 1137
8/21/61	14	10	5 Diggy Liggy Lo..		Hickory 1151

NANCY RUUD
Montana-born singer.

DEBUT DATE	PEAK POS	WKS CHR	ARTIST — Record Title	POP POS	Label & Number
7/12/80	88	3	1 A Good Love Is Like A Good Song		Calico 16425
10/18/80	90	3	2 Always, Sometimes, Never		Calico 16493
4/04/81	87	2	3 I'm Gonna Hang Up This Heartache.................		C&R 101
6/20/81	83	2	4 Blue As The Blue In Your Eyes......................		C&R 102

CHARLIE RYAN & The Timberline Riders
Born on 12/19/15 in Graceville, Minnesota; raised in Montana.

DEBUT DATE	PEAK POS	WKS CHR	ARTIST — Record Title	POP POS	Label & Number
9/05/60	14	6	1 Hot Rod Lincoln..................................[S-N]	33	4 Star 1733
			first recorded on Ryan's Souvenir label in 1955		

JAMEY RYAN
Female vocalist from Texas. Regular on "Hee-Haw" and Del Reeves' country TV series.

DEBUT DATE	PEAK POS	WKS CHR	ARTIST — Record Title	POP POS	Label & Number
8/19/67	62	3	1 You're Lookin' For A Plaything		Columbia 44169
5/23/70	75	2	2 Holy Cow		Show Biz 232
8/11/73	88	2	3 Keep On Loving Me......................................		Atlantic 4001

DEBUT DATE	PEAK POS	WKS CHR	ARTIST — Record Title	POP POS	Label & Number
			WESLEY RYAN		
7/25/81	82	4	1 Nothin' To Do But Just Lie		NSD 93
			NICKIE RYDER - see KENNY ROGERS		
			JOHN WESLEY RYLES ★★177★★		
			Born on 12/2/50 in Bastrop, Louisiana. On local radio while still a child. Sang in family gospel group, the Ryles Singers. Moved to Fort Worth, Texas and worked on the Cowtown Hoedown Show. Moved to Dallas and performed on the Big D Jamboree in 1963. Moved to Nashville in 1966.		
12/07/68+	9	17	1 Kay	83	Columbia 44682
5/17/69	55	8	2 Heaven Below...		Columbia 44819
12/13/69+	57	7	3 The Weakest Kind Of Man		Columbia 45018
5/02/70	17	10	4 I've Just Been Wasting My Time		Columbia 45119
11/20/71	39	10	5 Reconsider Me..		Plantation 81
			above 5: **JOHN WESLEY RYLES I**		
1/24/76	83	7	6 Tell It Like It Is		Music Mill 214
			#2 pop hit for Aaron Neville in 1967		
7/10/76	72	6	7 When A Man Loves A Woman.......................		Music Mill 240
			#1 pop hit for Percy Sledge in 1966		
3/26/77	18	17	8 Fool..		ABC/Dot 17679
8/13/77	5	16	9 **Once In A Lifetime Thing**		ABC/Dot 17698
12/24/77+	13	12	10 Shine On Me (The Sun Still Shines When It Rains)...		ABC/Dot 17733
4/15/78	63	6	11 Easy		ABC 12348
7/15/78	50	7	12 Kay .... [R]		ABC 12375
10/07/78	45	7	13 Someday You Will		ABC 12410
12/23/78+	33	11	14 Love Ain't Made For Fools		ABC 12432
6/02/79	14	14	15 Liberated Woman		MCA 41033
10/13/79	20	12	16 You Are Always On My Mind........................		MCA 41124
			#5 pop hit for Willie Nelson in 1982		
2/23/80	24	10	17 Perfect Strangers		MCA 41184
7/19/80	52	8	18 May I Borrow Some Sugar From You................		MCA 41278
11/08/80	54	10	19 Cheater's Trap..		MCA 51013
4/04/81	80	3	20 Somewhere To Come When It Rains................		MCA 51080
7/18/81	78	3	21 Mathilda..		MCA 51128
			#47 pop hit for Cookie & His Cupcakes in 1959		
6/26/82	76	4	22 We've Got To Start Meeting Like This		Primero 1004
12/04/82	80	3	23 Just Once		Primero 1016
8/25/84	78	4	24 She Took It Too Well		16th Ave. 500
5/09/87	36	15	25 Midnight Blue..		Warner 28377
12/05/87+	20	16	26 Louisiana Rain		Warner 28228
6/04/88	53	7	27 Nobody Knows..		Warner 27869

S

DEBUT DATE	PEAK POS	WKS CHR	ARTIST — Record Title	POP POS	Label & Number
			SSGT BARRY SADLER		
			Born in New Mexico in 1941. Served in the US Air Force from 1958-62. Joined the Army in 1963 and served as a medic in the Special Forces (Green Berets). In 1988, shot in the head while training Contra rebels in Guatemala; injury not fatal.		
2/19/66	2²	14	1● The Ballad Of The Green Berets	1	RCA 8739
5/28/66	46	4	2 The 'A' Team	28	RCA 8804
			DOUG SAHM & THE TEXAS TORNADOS		
			Doug was born on 11/6/41 in San Antonio. Formed the Sir Douglas Quintet in 1965. New band in 1974 included the Rhythm section from Creedence Clearwater Revival.		
10/16/76	100	1	1 Cowboy Peyton Place...............................		ABC/Dot 17656
			TOMMY ST. JOHN		
			Born on 3/23/62 in Oak Ridge, Tennessee.		
1/08/83	55	9	1 The Light Of My Life (Has Gone Out Tonight)......		RCA 13405
4/16/83	78	4	2 Where'd Ya Stay Last Night		RCA 13475
7/23/83	86	2	3 Stars On The Water		RCA 13561
			SUSAN ST. MARIE		
11/03/73	91	4	1 All Or Nothing With Me		Cinnamon 768

DEBUT DATE	PEAK POS	WKS CHR	ARTIST — Record Title	POP POS	Label & Number
			SUSAN ST. MARIE — Continued		
11/19/77	**91**	7	2 It's The Love In You		Pinnacle 101
			STEPHANY SAMONE		
			Born in Pleasant Grove, Texas. Miss Texas beauty queen in 1986.		
6/07/80	**68**	6	1 Do That To Me One More Time		MDJ 1004
			#1 pop hit for Captain & Tennille in 1980		
11/22/80	**65**	7	2 Somebody's Gotta Do The Losing		MDJ 1006
			JUNIOR SAMPLES		
			Alvin Samples, born in Cumming, Georgia on 8/10/26; died of a heart attack on 11/13/83. Regular on the "Hee Haw" TV series from 1969.		
7/22/67	**52**	4	1 World's Biggest Whopper.........................[S-N]		Chart 1460
			interviewer: Jim Morrison		
			SAN FERNANDO VALLEY MUSIC BAND		
			7-piece band based in St. Paul, with Brian Murphy (lead vocals) and Jeff Stephens (lead guitar).		
6/30/79	**83**	8	1 Taken To The Line		C&S 017
			THE SANDERS		
			Dale and sister Vicki Sanders. Both born in Alaska to gold mining family with claims north of the Arctic Circle. Vicki first recorded as "Vicki Dawn" on the Boundry label.		
8/20/88	**76**	3	1 You Fit Right Into My Heart		Airborne 10001
			BEN SANDERS		
11/19/88	**100**	1	1 I'm Leavin' You		Luv 129
			MACK SANDERS		
			Born in Wichita, Kansas. Popular radio and TV host.		
1/21/78	**89**	3	1 Sweet Country Girl		Pilot 45101
			RAY SANDERS		
			Born Raymon Sanders on 10/1/35 in St. John, Kentucky. Radio performer since age 15.		
10/31/60	**18**	11	1 World So Full Of Love		Liberty 55267
4/03/61	**20**	8	2 Lonelyville..		Liberty 55304
5/24/69	**22**	13	3 Beer Drinkin' Music......................................		Imperial 66366
10/25/69	**73**	2	4 Three Tears (For The Sad, Hurt, And Blue)		Imperial 66408
8/01/70	**36**	11	5 Blame It On Rosey..		United Art. 50689
12/26/70+	**38**	9	6 Judy		United Art. 50732
5/29/71	**56**	9	7 Walk All Over Georgia		United Art. 50774
10/02/71	**18**	16	8 All I Ever Need Is You..................................		United Art. 50827
			#7 pop hit for Sonny & Cher in 1971		
5/20/72	**69**	5	9 A Rose By Any Other Name (Is Still A Rose).......		United Art. 50886
9/09/72	**67**	4	10 Lucius Grinder		United Art. 50933
5/05/73	**75**	2	11 Another Way To Say Goodbye		United Art. 201
8/06/77	**56**	7	12 I Don't Want To Be Alone Tonight...................		Republic 003
1/21/78	**91**	3	13 Tennessee		Republic 013
11/29/80	**93**	2	14 You're A Pretty Lady, Lady		Hillside 05
			SARAH		
9/19/87	**81**	2	1 Lyin' Eyes		Hub 45
6/04/88	**81**	3	2 Chains		Hub 46
			#17 pop hit for The Cookies in 1962		
10/15/88	**77**	4	3 Don't Send Me Roses		Hub 48
			GARY SARGEANTS		
			Born Gary Lusk in Miami. Drummer for Tom T. Hall for years.		
12/15/73+	**55**	11	1 Ode To Jole Blon		Mercury 73440
10/05/74	**72**	7	2 Day Time Lover		Mercury 73608
			SASKIA & SERGE		
			Husband and wife duo from Holland.		
1/07/78	**88**	5	1 Jambalaya (On The Bayou)		ABC/Hick. 54020
			CORKEY SAULS		
2/10/79	**96**	1	1 There Goes That Smile Again		Sand Mt. 822

DEBUT DATE	PEAK POS	WKS CHR	ARTIST — Record Title	POP POS	Label & Number
			SAVANNAH		
			Brunswick, Georgia-based band led by brothers Jay and Gene Willis.		
10/29/83	87	5	1 Backstreet Ballet		Mercury 814360
7/21/84	73	5	2 My Girl...		Mercury 880037
			#1 pop hit for the Temptations in 1965		
			SAWMILL CREEK - see BRUCE HAUSER		
			SAWYER BROWN ★★196★★		
			Group formed in Nashville in the late 70s by Mark Miller (b: Dayton OH; lead singer) and Bobby Randall (b: Midland, MI; vocals, lead guitar). Band included Gregg "Hobie" Hubbard (keyboards), Jim Scholten (bass) and "Curly" Joe Smyth (drums). Originally named Savanna, group was re-named after streets in Nashville. Won $100,000 on "Star Search" TV series in 1984.		
10/06/84+	16	22	1 Leona		Capitol 5403
2/09/85	1¹	21	2 **Step That Step**...		Capitol 5446
6/08/85	3	21	3 **Used To Blue**...		Capitol 5477
10/05/85	5	20	4 **Betty's Bein' Bad**..		Capitol 5517
2/01/86	14	18	5 Heart Don't Fall Now		Capitol 5548
5/10/86	15	16	6 Shakin'		Capitol 5585
9/13/86	11	18	7 Out Goin' Cattin'...		Capitol 5629
			SAWYER BROWN with "CAT" JOE BONSALL		
1/17/87	25	13	8 Gypsies On Parade		Capitol 5677
5/23/87	58	9	9 Savin' The Honey For The Honeymoon.............		Capitol 44007
8/22/87	29	13	10 Somewhere In The Night......................................		Capitol 44054
12/05/87+	2¹	22	11 **This Missin' You Heart Of Mine**.....................		Capitol 44108
4/23/88	27	13	12 Old Photographs		Capitol 44143
10/01/88	11	17	13 My Baby's Gone		Capitol 44218
12/10/88+	51	7	14 It Wasn't His Child		Capitol 44282
			RAY SAWYER		
			Born on 2/1/37 in Chickasaw, Alabama. Eye-patched co-lead singer of Dr. Hook.		
11/06/76	28	12	1 (One More Year Of) Daddy's Little Girl...............	81	Capitol 4344
2/16/80	80	4	2 I Don't Feel Much Like Smilin'.........................		Capitol 4820
			LEO SAYER		
			Born Gerard Sayer on 5/21/48 in Shoreham, England. With Patches in the early 70s. Songwriting team with David Courtney, 1972-75. Own TV show in England, early 80s.		
10/21/78	63	6	1 Raining In My Heart	47	Warner 8682
			JOEY SCARBURY		
			Born on 6/7/55 in Ontario, California. Session singer for producer Mike Post.		
10/20/84	76	7	1 The River's Song..		RCA 13913
			from the film "The River Rat"		
			NORM SCHAFFER		
3/12/88	77	4	1 Dallas Darlin'		DSP 8712
			SCHEREE		
8/25/79	94	3	1 I'm In Another World		Compass 0027
			DON SCHLITZ		
			Born on 8/29/52 in Durham, North Carolina. Very successful songwriter. Wrote "The Gambler", hit for Kenny Rogers, "Forever And Ever (Amen)" for Randy Travis, "No Easy Horses" for SKB, and many others.		
5/06/78	65	7	1 The Gambler		Capitol 4576
			originally released on Crazy Mamas label in 1978		
3/31/79	91	3	2 You're The One Who Rewrote My Life Story.......		Capitol 4661
			PAUL SCHMUCKER		
11/25/78	69	6	1 The Giver		Star-Fox 378
3/03/79	72	4	2 Makin' Love (Is A Beautiful Thing To Do)..........		Star-Fox 578
6/02/79	74	5	3 Steal Away		Star-Fox 279
8/11/79	83	5	4 Rainy Days And Rainbows		Star-Fox 779
			JOHN SCHNEIDER ★★169★★		
			Born on 4/8/54 in Mount Kisco, New York. Actor from age 8. Wrote the score for the musical "Under Odin's Eye". Played "Bo Duke" on the "Dukes Of Hazzard" TV series. In the films "Dream House", "Happy Endings", "Gus Brown And Midnight Brewster", "Eddie Macon's Run", "Fine White Line" and "Stagecoach". Scriptwriter and director.		
6/13/81	4	17	1 **It's Now Or Never**	14	Scotti Br. 02105

DEBUT DATE	PEAK POS	WKS CHR	ARTIST — Record Title	POP POS	Label & Number
			JOHN SCHNEIDER — Continued		
10/03/81	**13**	16	2 Them Good Ol' Boys Are Bad		Scotti Br. 02489
5/22/82	**32**	9	3 Dreamin'	45	Scotti Br. 02889
8/21/82	**56**	7	4 In The Driver's Seat..	72	Scotti Br. 03062
7/02/83	**57**	6	5 Are You Lonesome Tonight............................		Scotti Br. 03945
			JOHN SCHNEIDER & JILL MICHAELS		
10/01/83	**81**	3	6 If You Believe...		Scotti Br. 04064
7/28/84	**1**¹	28	7 I've Been Around Enough To Know...............		MCA 52407
1/05/85	**1**¹	23	8 Country Girls..		MCA 52510
4/20/85	**10**	20	9 It's A Short Walk From Heaven To Hell		MCA 52567
8/10/85	**10**	20	10 I'm Going To Leave You Tomorrow		MCA 52648
12/14/85+	**1**¹	24	11 What's A Memory Like You (Doing In A Love Like This)..		MCA 52723
5/10/86	**1**¹	20	12 You're The Last Thing I Needed Tonight........		MCA 52827
8/30/86	**5**	23	13 At The Sound Of The Tone		MCA 52901
12/20/86+	**10**	10	14 Take The Long Way Home		MCA 52989
4/04/87	**6**	20	15 Love, You Ain't Seen The Last Of Me............		MCA 53069
7/18/87	**32**	15	16 When The Right One Comes Along		MCA 53144
11/07/87	**59**	6	17 If It Was Anyone But You		MCA 53199
			THOM SCHUYLER Songwriter, born in 1952 in Bethlehem, Pennsylvania. Moved to Nashville in 1978. Former member of Schuyler, Knobloch & Overstreet (Bickhardt).		
7/16/83	**49**	10	1 A Little At A Time		Capitol 5239
10/22/83	**43**	11	2 Brave Heart		Capitol 5281
			SCHUYLER, KNOBLOCH & OVERSTREET Trio of prolific songwriters: Thom Schuyler, J. Fred Knoblock and Paul Overstreet. Also known as S-K-O. Overstreet replaced by Craig Bickhardt in 1987.		
7/12/86	**9**	29	1 You Can't Stop Love		MTM 72071
			S-K-O:		
12/06/86+	**1**¹	22	2 Baby's Got A New Baby		MTM 72081
4/18/87	**16**	14	3 American Me...		MTM 72086
			SCHUYLER, KNOBLOCH & BICKHARDT:		
8/15/87	**19**	17	4 No Easy Horses...		MTM 72090
11/28/87+	**24**	18	5 This Old House		MTM 72100
4/23/88	**8**	22	6 Givers And Takers...		MTM 72099
10/22/88	**44**	11	7 Rigamarole		MTM 72115
			EARL SCOTT Real name: Earl Batdorf. Son in rock group, Batdorf & Rodney.		
11/03/62	**8**	10	1 Then A Tear Fell		Kapp 854
7/27/63	**23**	7	2 Loose Lips		Mercury 72110
1/04/64	**30**	1	3 Restless River		Mercury 72190
1/23/65	**30**	14	4 I'll Wander Back To You...............................		Decca 31693
11/23/68	**71**	3	5 Too Rough On Me...		Decca 32397
			JACK SCOTT Born Jack Scafone, Jr. on 1/24/36 in Windsor, Canada. Rock and roll-ballad singer/ songwriter/guitarist. First recorded for ABC-Paramount in 1957.		
7/06/74	**92**	4	1 You're Just Gettin' Better...............................		Dot 17504
			LANG SCOTT Born in Sumter, South Carolina; raised in Harleyville, South Carolina. Singing from age 14. Winner on the "You Can Be A Star" TV talent contest.		
4/21/84	**68**	6	1 Run Your Sweet Love By Me One More Time/		
8/18/84	**91**	2	2 It's Been One Of Those Days		MCA 52359
			EARL SCRUGGS Born Earl Eugene Scruggs on 1/6/24. See Flatt & Scruggs for complete bio.		
10/24/70	**74**	2	1 Nashville Skyline Rag		Columbia 45218
			EARL SCRUGGS REVUE:		
7/07/79	**30**	11	2 I Could Sure Use The Feeling		Columbia 10992
11/03/79	**82**	4	3 Play Me No Sad Songs		Columbia 11106
1/19/80	**46**	9	4 Blue Moon Of Kentucky...............................		Columbia 11176
			TOM T. HALL & EARL SCRUGGS:		
5/22/82	**77**	4	5 There Ain't No Country Music On This Jukebox .		Columbia 02858

DEBUT DATE	PEAK POS	WKS CHR	ARTIST — Record Title	POP POS	Label & Number
			EARL SCRUGGS — Continued		
7/31/82	72	5	6 Song Of The South		Columbia 03033
			JOHNNY SEA		
			Born on 7/15/40 in Gulfport, Mississippi. Joined the Louisiana Hayride while still in high school. Real last name: Seay.		
4/20/59	13	9	1 Frankie's Man, Johnny		NRC 019
2/08/60	13	8	2 Nobody's Darling But Mine...........................		NRC 049
5/23/64	27	10	3 My Baby Walks All Over Me	*121*	Philips 40164
4/10/65	19	16	4 My Old Faded Rose		Philips 40267
6/11/66	14	11	5 Day For Decision .... [S]	*35*	Warner 5820
			patriotic answer to Barry McGuire's "Eve Of Destruction"		
4/01/67	61	4	6 Nothin's Bad As Bein' Lonely		Warner 5889
			JOHNNY SEAY:		
3/30/68	68	2	7 Going To Tulsa		Columbia 44423
10/19/68	32	11	8 Three Six Packs, Two Arms And A Juke Box		Columbia 44634
			JIM SEAL		
10/25/80	79	5	1 Bourbon Cowboy..		NSD 66
			DAN SEALS ★★132★★		
			Born on 2/8/48 in McCamey, Texas; raised in Dallas. Played in family band with brother Jim Seals (of Seals & Crofts) at age 4. Formed Southwest F.O.B. with John Ford Coley and Shane Keister in 1967, recorded for GPC. Teamed with Coley as "England Dan & John Ford Coley". Recorded solo for Atlantic as "England Dan" in 1980. Cousin of Troy Seals and Johnny Duncan.		
4/30/83	18	17	1 Everybody's Dream Girl		Liberty 1496
8/13/83	28	14	2 After You		Liberty 1504
11/19/83+	37	16	3 You Really Go For The Heart...........................		Liberty 1512
2/25/84	10	21	4 **God Must Be A Cowboy**................................		Liberty 1515
7/28/84	9	23	5 **(You Bring Out) The Wild Side Of Me**		EMI America 8220
11/24/84+	2²	21	6 **My Baby's Got Good Timing**..........................		EMI America 8245
3/30/85	9	19	7 **My Old Yellow Car**		EMI America 8261
7/06/85	1¹	23	8 **Meet Me In Montana**...................................		Capitol 5478
			MARIE OSMOND with DAN SEALS		
10/26/85+	1¹	27	9 **Bop**	*42*	EMI America 8289
4/05/86	1¹	23	10 **Everything That Glitters (Is Not Gold)**		EMI America 8311
10/25/86+	1¹	22	11 **You Still Move Me**		EMI America 8343
3/07/87	1¹	19	12 **I Will Be There**		EMI America 8377
6/27/87	1¹	21	13 **Three Time Loser**		EMI Amer. 43023
10/17/87+	1¹	26	14 **One Friend**...		Capitol 44077
6/18/88	1¹	22	15 **Addicted**..		Capitol 44130
11/12/88+	1¹	21	16 **Big Wheels In The Moonlight**		Capitol 44267
			TROY SEALS		
			Born on 11/16/38 in Big Hill, Kentucky; raised in Ohio. Recorded with wife Jo Ann Campbell as "Jo Ann & Troy" in the mid-60s. Moved to Nashville in 1969. Wrote "When We Make Love", "Feelings", Lost In The Fifties (In The Still Of The Night)", and many others. Cousin of Jim and Dan Seals.		
8/11/73	93	4	1 I Got A Thing About You Baby		Atlantic 4004
			#39 pop hit for Elvis Presley in 1974		
1/19/74	78	7	2 Star Of The Bar/		
		7	3 You Can't Judge A Book By The Cover		Atlantic 4013
			#48 pop hit for Bo Diddley in 1962		
5/11/74	81	6	4 Honky-Tonkin'..		Atlantic 4020
7/19/75	76	7	5 Easy		Columbia 10173
3/27/76	88	5	6 Sweet Dreams..		Columbia 10303
4/23/77	93	2	7 Grand Ole Blues...		Columbia 10511
2/16/80	85	3	8 One Night Honeymoon		Elektra 46573
			JOHN SEBASTIAN		
			Born on 3/17/44 in New York City. Lead singer of The Lovin' Spoonful.		
5/15/76	93	2	1● Welcome Back..	*1*	Reprise 1349
			from the ABC-TV series "Welcome Back Kotter"		

DEBUT DATE	PEAK POS	WKS CHR	ARTIST — Record Title	POP POS	Label & Number
			JEANNIE SEELY ★★159★★		
			Born Marilyn Jeanne Seely on 7/6/40 in Titusville, Pennsylvania. Worked on local radio shows from age 11, later worked on the Midwestern Hayride. Staff writer for Four Star Music in Los Angeles. Married briefly to Hank Cochran; moved to Nashville in 1965. Replaced Norma Jean on the Porter Wagoner Show. On the Grand Ole Opry since 1967 and worked for a time with the Jack Greene show.		
4/16/66	2³	21	1 **Don't Touch Me**	85	Monument 933
9/10/66	15	15	2 It's Only Love		Monument 965
12/17/66+	13	13	3 A Wanderin' Man		Monument 987
3/18/67	39	10	4 When It's Over		Monument 999
7/08/67	42	8	5 These Memories		Monument 1011
10/28/67+	10	15	6 **I'll Love You More (Than You Need)**		Monument 1029
2/24/68	24	12	7 Welcome Home To Nothing		Monument 1054
6/22/68	23	10	8 How Is He?		Monument 1075
3/22/69	43	11	9 Just Enough To Start Me Dreamin'		Decca 32452
3/07/70	46	6	10 Please Be My New Love		Decca 32628
12/05/70	58	5	11 Tell Me Again		Decca 32757
7/17/71	71	5	12 You Don't Understand Him Like I Do		Decca 32838
11/20/71+	42	10	13 Alright I'll Sign The Papers		Decca 32882
6/17/72	47	9	14 Pride		Decca 32964
1/20/73	72	4	15 Farm In Pennsyltucky/		
		3	16 Between The King And I		Decca 33042
7/07/73	6	18	17 **Can I Sleep In Your Arms**		MCA 40074
12/15/73+	11	13	18 Lucky Ladies		MCA 40162
5/18/74	37	10	19 I Miss You		MCA 40225
9/21/74	26	14	20 He Can Be Mine		MCA 40287
7/19/75	59	9	21 Take My Hand		MCA 40428
4/17/76	96	3	22 Since I Met You Boy		MCA 40528
6/11/77	80	5	23 We're Still Hangin' In There Ain't We Jessi		Columbia 10550
1/28/78	97	1	24 Take Me To Bed		Columbia 10664
			JACK GREENE & JEANNIE SEELY:		
11/15/69+	2²	16	25 **Wish I Didn't Have To Miss You**		Decca 32580
12/11/71+	15	13	26 Much Oblige		Decca 32898
8/12/72	19	12	27 What In The World Has Gone Wrong With Our Love		Decca 32991
			LES SEEVERS		
3/08/69	57	9	1 What Kind Of Magic		Decca 32434
			BOB SEGER		
			Born on 5/6/45 in Ann Arbor, Michigan; raised in Detroit. Rock singer/songwriter.		
1/22/83	15	14	1 Shame On The Moon	2	Capitol 5187
			THE SEGO BROTHERS & NAOMI		
			Group formed in Macon, Georgia in 1946. Group included James Sego and his wife, Naomi; Reverend W.R. Sego, Lamar Sego, and Eddie Crook on piano.		
2/01/64	50	1	1 Sorry I Never Knew You		Songs Of F. 8032
			BARBARA SEINER		
3/03/79	87	3	1 Jealous Heart		Starship 109
			TED SELF		
7/04/60	20	10	1 Little Angel (Come Rock Me To Sleep)		Plaid 115
			MARILYN SELLARS		
			From Northfield, Minnesota. Worked as an airline stewardess.		
4/20/74	19	17	1 One Day At A Time	37	Mega 1205
12/14/74+	39	14	2 He's Everywhere		Mega 1221
5/24/75	84	4	3 Gather Me		Mega 1230
1/24/76	91	3	4 The Door I Used To Close		Mega 1242
			KENNY SERRATT		
			Born in Manila, Arkansas; raised in Dyess, Arkansas and in California. Appeared at the Ramada in Hemet, California for 11 years. Out of music from 1967-72.		
12/09/72+	56	9	1 Goodbyes Come Hard For Me		MGM 14435
5/05/73	68	3	2 This Ain't No Good Day For Leaving		MGM 14517
9/29/73	70	13	3 Love And Honor		MGM 14636

DEBUT DATE	PEAK POS	WKS CHR	ARTIST — Record Title	POP POS	Label & Number
			KENNY SERRATT — Continued		
8/02/75	**88**	6	4 If I Could Have It Any Other Way		Melodyland 6014
8/21/76	**72**	6	5 I've Been There Too..		Hitsville 6039
2/12/77	**54**	8	6 Daddy, They're Playin' A Song About You		Hitsville 6049
12/15/79	**82**	4	7 Never Gonna' Be A Country Star/		
		4	8 A Damn Good Drinking Song........................		MDJ 1001
5/03/80	**54**	8	9 Saturday Night In Dallas		MDJ 1003
9/13/80	**39**	8	10 Until The Bitter End		MDJ 1005
5/02/81	**70**	7	11 Sidewalks Are Grey		MDJ 1008
			RONNIE SESSIONS		
			Born on 12/7/48 in Henrietta, Oklahoma; raised in Bakersfield, California. First recorded at age 9, and performed on "Herb Henson's Trading Post" TV series. Toured with Buck Owens, Merle Haggard and Glen Campbell. Moved to Nashville in 1971, worked as a staff writer for Tree Publishing.		
8/05/72	**36**	10	1 Never Been To Spain......................................		MGM 14394
			#5 pop hit for Three Dog Night in 1972		
11/18/72	**59**	6	2 Tossin' And Turnin'......................................		MGM 14445
			#1 pop hit for Bobby Lewis in 1961		
6/23/73	**66**	5	3 I Just Can't Put Her Down		MGM 14528
9/29/73	**87**	7	4 If That Back Door Could Talk.......................		MGM 14619
10/04/75	**61**	10	5 Makin' Love		MCA 40462
			#20 pop hit for Floyd Robinson in 1959		
7/17/76	**81**	4	6 Support Your Local Honky Tonks		MCA 40581
10/30/76+	**16**	17	7 Wiggle Wiggle		MCA 40624
4/09/77	**15**	13	8 Me And Millie (Stompin' Grapes And Gettin' Silly)		MCA 40705
8/06/77	**30**	10	9 Ambush		MCA 40758
12/10/77+	**57**	9	10 I Like To Be With You...................................		MCA 40831
3/25/78	**72**	7	11 Cash On The Barrelhead..............................		MCA 40875
7/15/78	**96**	2	12 I Never Go Around Mirrors		MCA 40917
10/07/78	**25**	9	13 Juliet And Romeo		MCA 40952
6/30/79	**94**	3	14 Do You Want To Fly		MCA 41038
12/01/79	**84**	5	15 Honky Tonkin'...		MCA 41142
12/27/86+	**78**	5	16 I Bought The Shoes That Just Walked Out On Me		Compleat 161
			MARK SEXTON		
11/24/79	**97**	2	1 Don't Say No To Me Tonight...........................		Sun-De-Mar 79101
			WHITEY SHAFER		
			Born Sanger D. Shafer on 10/24/34 in Whitney, Texas. Worked as a songwriter with Lefty Frizzell. Wrote "All My Ex's Live In Texas" for George Strait.		
12/13/80+	**48**	9	1 You Are A Liar		Elektra 47063
4/11/81	**67**	3	2 If I Say I Love You (Consider Me Drunk)		Elektra 47117
			MICHAEL SHAMBLIN		
3/08/86	**77**	3	1 Foreign Affairs		F&L 548
6/07/86	**83**	2	2 Wishful Dreamin'		F&L 549
			BONNIE SHANNON		
12/20/80	**88**	4	1 Lovin' You Lightly..		Door Knob 139
			DEL SHANNON		
			Pop singer born Charles Westover on 12/30/39 in Coopersville, Michigan. Wrote "I Go To Pieces" for Peter & Gordon. To Los Angeles in 1966, production work.		
3/09/85	**56**	6	1 In My Arms Again		Warner 29098
			GUY SHANNON		
			Piano player of Jerry Lee Lewis style; worked clubs in Nashville and Louisville.		
7/07/73	**69**	5	1 Naughty Girl		Cinnamon 758
10/06/73	**63**	11	2 Soul Deep		Cinnamon 769
			#18 pop hit for The Box Tops in 1969		
			ROSEMARY SHARP		
			Singer/songwriter born and raised in Fort Worth, Texas.		
2/28/87	**85**	3	1 Didn't You Go And Leave Me..........................		Canyon Cr. 1226
8/08/87	**76**	4	2 Real Good Heartache		Canyon Cr. 0401

DEBUT DATE	PEAK POS	WKS CHR	ARTIST — Record Title	POP POS	Label & Number
			ROSEMARY SHARP — Continued		
10/31/87	67	6	3 If You're Gonna Tell Me Lies (Tell Me Good Ones)..		Canyon Cr. 0908
4/09/88	68	5	4 The Stairs..		Canyon Cr. 0210
			SUNDAY SHARPE		
			(Her real name.) Born in 1946 in Orlando, Florida. Worked as a caterer. First female country singer to perform at West Point Academy.		
8/17/74	11	14	1 I'm Having Your Baby................................... answer song to Paul Anka's "(You're) Having My Baby"		United Art. 507
12/21/74+	47	9	2 Mr. Songwriter...		United Art. 571
3/29/75	48	8	3 Put Your Head On My Shoulder .... #2 pop hit for Paul Anka in 1959		United Art. 602
2/14/76	80	5	4 Find A New Love, Girl		United Art. 758
11/06/76	18	12	5 A Little At A Time		Playboy 6090
6/18/77	62	5	6 I'm Not The One You Love (I'm The One You Make Love To)..		Playboy 5806
8/27/77	45	7	7 Hold On Tight..		Playboy 5813
			DANNY SHATSWELL		
6/17/78	97	2	1 I'm A Mender		Mercury 55027
			BILLY JOE SHAVER		
			Born in Corsicana, Texas in 1941; raised in Waco. Staff writer for Bobby Bare's Return Music Company. Wrote "I Couldn't Be Me Without You" for Johnny Rodriguez.		
9/15/73	88	3	1 I Been To Georgia On A Fast Train		Monument 8580
3/11/78	80	5	2 You Asked Me To		Capricorn 0286
			BRIAN SHAW		
			Born in 1949 in Grove City, Pennsylvania. Played bass from age 16. Worked on WWVA Jamboree and the Grand Ole Opry.		
9/08/73	55	8	1 The Devil Is A Woman..................................		RCA 0058
12/15/73+	62	11	2 Good Enough To Be Your Man		RCA 0186
4/06/74	50	9	3 Friend Named Red.......................................		RCA 0230
10/12/74	17	15	4 Here We Go Again		RCA 10071
10/16/76	97	2	5 Showdown		Republic 306
3/12/77	97	2	6 What Kind Of Fool (Does That Make Me)............		Republic 360
			RON SHAW		
6/25/77	94	4	1 Hurtin' Kind Of Love		Pacific C. 1511
7/08/78	79	7	2 Goin' Home		Pacific C. 1522
10/07/78	36	9	3 Save The Last Dance For Me .... #1 pop hit for The Drifters in 1960		Pacific C. 1631
1/20/79	68	7	4 I Cry Instead .... #25 pop hit for The Beatles in 1964		Pacific C. 1633
7/28/79	93	3	5 One And One Make Three		Pacific C. 1635
9/22/79	90	4	6 What The World Needs Now (Is Love Sweet Love) #7 pop hit for Jackie DeShannon in 1965		Pacific C. 1636
3/22/80	91	4	7 Hurtin' Kind Of Love .... [R]		Pacific C. 1637
			RON SHAW & THE DESERT WIND BAND:		
8/16/80	94	2	8 The Legend Of Harry And The Mountain		Pacific C. 1638
2/07/81	78	4	9 Reachin' For Freedom..................................		Pacific C. 1639
			VICTORIA SHAW		
			Born in Manhattan, New York; raised in Los Angeles from age 4. Parents publish "Big Beautiful Woman" magazine.		
2/25/84	61	10	1 Break My Heart		MPB 1006
			DOROTHY SHAY		
			Comedienne, born Dorothy Sims in 1923 in Jacksonville, Florida; died on 10/22/78 (heart attack). Made regular appearances on the Spike Jones radio series in 1947. Billed as "The Park Avenue Hillbilly." In the film "Comin' 'Round The Mountain" in 1951. Appeared on The Waltons TV series.		
8/16/47	4	7	1 Feudin' And Fightin' .... from the Broadway musical "Laffing Room Only"	4	Columbia 37189
			RICKY VAN SHELTON		
			Nashville-based singer, from Grit, Virginia, born in 1952. Worked as a pipefitter. Joined the Grand Ole Opry in 1988.		
12/20/86+	24	18	1 Wild-Eyed Dream		Columbia 06542

DEBUT DATE	PEAK POS	WKS CHR	ARTIST — Record Title	POP POS	Label & Number
			RICKY VAN SHELTON — Continued		
4/18/87	**7**	19	2 **Crime Of Passion**		Columbia 07025
8/22/87	**1**¹	25	3 **Somebody Lied**		Columbia 07311
1/09/88	**1**¹	23	4 **Life Turned Her That Way**		Columbia 07672
5/07/88	**1**¹	20	5 **Don't We All Have The Right**		Columbia 07798
9/10/88	**1**²	21	6 **I'll Leave This World Loving You**		Columbia 08022
			SHENANDOAH		
			Quintet formed in Muscle Shoals, Alabama as the MGM Band: Marty Raybon (vocals), Mike McGuire (drums), Ralph Ezell (bass), Stan Thorn (keyboards) and Jim Seales (former guitarist of the funk group Funkadelic).		
8/01/87	**54**	7	1 They Don't Make Love Like We Used To............		Columbia 07128
12/12/87+	**28**	18	2 Stop The Rain		Columbia 07654
4/23/88	**9**	24	3 **She Doesn't Cry Anymore**		Columbia 07779
10/01/88	**5**	21	4 **Mama Knows**		Columbia 08042
			JEAN SHEPARD ★★**74**★★		
			Born on 11/21/33 in Pauls Valley, Oklahoma; raised in Visalia, California. Formed all-girl band, the Melody Ranch Girls, in the late 40s. Discovered by Hank Thompson. Worked with Red Foley's Ozark Jubilee from 1955-57. Member of the Grand Ole Opry since 1955. Husband Hawkshaw Hawkins died in a plane crash in 1963.		
7/25/53	**1**⁶	23	1 **A Dear John Letter**................................ **JEAN SHEPARD & FERLIN HUSKEY** Best Seller #1(6) / Juke Box #1(4) / Jockey #2	4	Capitol 2502
10/10/53	**4**	7	2 **Forgive Me John** .... **JEAN SHEPARD & FERLIN HUSKEY** Best Seller #4 / Juke Box #6 / Jockey #8	24	Capitol 2586
6/25/55	**4**	22	3 **A Satisfied Mind/** Best Seller #4 / Juke Box #4 / Jockey #10		
7/16/55	**13**	1	4 Take Possession .... Jockey #13		Capitol 3118
10/08/55	**4**	19	5 **Beautiful Lies/** Best Seller #4 / Juke Box #4 / Jockey #12		
10/22/55	**10**	3	6 **I Thought Of You**..................................... Jockey #10		Capitol 3222
12/22/58	**18**	2	7 I Want To Go Where No One Knows Me		Capitol 4068
4/20/59	**30**	1	8 Have Heart, Will Love		Capitol 4129
5/30/64	**5**	24	9 **Second Fiddle (To An Old Guitar)**.................		Capitol 5169
1/09/65	**38**	11	10 A Tear Dropped By		Capitol 5304
6/05/65	**30**	7	11 Someone's Gotta Cry		Capitol 5392
3/05/66	**13**	16	12 Many Happy Hangovers To You		Capitol 5585
7/16/66	**10**	18	13 **If Teardrops Were Silver**		Capitol 5681
5/27/67	**17**	12	14 Your Forevers (Don't Last Very Long)		Capitol 5899
9/30/67	**40**	8	15 I Don't See How I Can Make It		Capitol 5983
2/10/68	**52**	6	16 An Old Bridge...		Capitol 2073
6/15/68	**36**	8	17 A Real Good Woman		Capitol 2180
10/05/68	**62**	8	18 Everyday's A Happy Day For Fools..................		Capitol 2273
5/03/69	**69**	4	19 I'm Tied Around Your Finger		Capitol 2425
9/06/69	**18**	11	20 Seven Lonely Days		Capitol 2585
1/03/70	**8**	14	21 **Then He Touched Me**.................................		Capitol 2694
4/25/70	**23**	11	22 A Woman's Hand		Capitol 2774
8/15/70	**22**	12	23 I Want You Free		Capitol 2847
11/07/70	**12**	14	24 Another Lonely Night		Capitol 2941
2/20/71	**24**	10	25 With His Hand In Mine		Capitol 3033
9/18/71	**55**	2	26 Just As Soon As I Get Over Loving You............		Capitol 3153
1/08/72	**55**	8	27 Safe In These Lovin' Arms Of Mine.................		Capitol 3238
6/03/72	**68**	4	28 Virginia...		Capitol 3315
8/19/72	**46**	10	29 Just Like Walkin' In The Sunshine..................		Capitol 3395
6/09/73	**4**	18	30 **Slippin' Away**...	81	United Art. 248
11/24/73+	**36**	11	31 Come On Phone		United Art. 317
2/23/74	**13**	13	32 At The Time...		United Art. 384
6/29/74	**17**	12	33 I'll Do Anything It Takes (To Stay With You)......		United Art. 442
10/26/74+	**14**	13	34 Poor Sweet Baby		United Art. 552
2/22/75	**16**	13	35 The Tip Of My Fingers.................................		United Art. 591
8/30/75	**49**	10	36 I'm A Believer (In A Whole Lot Of Lovin')		United Art. 701
12/20/75+	**44**	9	37 Another Neon Night....................................		United Art. 745

DEBUT DATE	PEAK POS	WKS CHR		ARTIST — Record Title	POP POS	Label & Number
				JEAN SHEPARD — Continued		
4/10/76	**49**	8	38	Mercy		United Art. 776
6/26/76	**41**	10	39	Ain't Love Good		United Art. 818
12/04/76+	**74**	7	40	I'm Giving You Denver		United Art. 899
4/16/77	**82**	5	41	Hardly A Day Goes By............................		United Art. 956
4/15/78	**85**	6	42	The Real Thing		Scorpion 157
				JEAN SHEPARD & RAY PILLOW:		
5/14/66	**9**	15	43	I'll Take The Dog		Capitol 5633
11/26/66+	**25**	11	44	Mr. Do-It-Yourself...............................		Capitol 5769
1/28/67	**12**	15	45	Heart, We Did All We Could		Capitol 5822
				T.G. SHEPPARD ★★45★★		
				Born William Browder on 7/20/42 in Humboldt, Tennessee. Moved to Memphis in 1960. Worked as back-up singer with Travis Womack's band. Recorded as "Brian Stacey" for Atlantic in 1966. Invented his stage name, first saying it stood for "The German Sheppard", then "The Good Sheppard".		
11/30/74+	**1**¹	19	1	**Devil In The Bottle**	*54*	Melodyland 6002
4/12/75	**1**¹	15	2	**Tryin' To Beat The Morning Home**..............	*95*	Melodyland 6006
8/16/75	**14**	16	3	Another Woman..................................		Melodyland 6016
12/27/75+	**7**	15	4	**Motel And Memories**............................	*102*	Melodyland 6028
5/29/76	**14**	13	5	Solitary Man	*100*	Hitsville 6032
9/18/76	**8**	14	6	**Show Me A Man**		Hitsville 6040
12/25/76+	**37**	8	7	May I Spend Every New Years With You		Hitsville 6048
3/05/77	**20**	10	8	Lovin' On......................................		Hitsville 6053
11/12/77+	**13**	14	9	Mister D.J.		Warner 8490
2/18/78	**13**	13	10	Don't Ever Say Good-Bye.........................		Warner 8525
5/27/78	**5**	13	11	**When Can We Do This Again**		Warner 8593
9/23/78	**7**	11	12	**Daylight**		Warner 8678
12/16/78+	**8**	14	13	**Happy Together**...............................		Warner 8721
				#1 pop hit for The Turtles in 1967		
4/21/79	**4**	13	14	**You Feel Good All Over**		Warner 8808
8/04/79	**1**²	14	15	**Last Cheater's Waltz**		Warner 49024
12/01/79+	**1**²	15	16	**I'll Be Coming Back For More**..................		Warner 49110
4/05/80	**6**	16	17	**Smooth Sailin'**...............................		Warner 49214
8/02/80	**1**¹	15	18	**Do You Wanna Go To Heaven**		Warner 49515
12/06/80+	**1**¹	13	19	**I Feel Like Loving You Again**..................		Warner 49615
3/14/81	**1**¹	15	20	**I Loved 'Em Every One**	*37*	Warner 49690
7/18/81	**1**¹	16	21	**Party Time**...................................		Warner 49761
11/21/81+	**1**¹	19	22	**Only One You**	*68*	Warner 49858
4/03/82	**1**¹	16	23	**Finally**	*58*	Warner 50041
9/04/82	**1**¹	19	24	**War Is Hell (On The Homefront Too)**............		Warner 29934
11/20/82+	**1**¹	20	25	**Faking Love**		Warner 29854
				T.G. SHEPPARD & KAREN BROOKS		
4/09/83	**12**	15	26	Without You...................................		Warner 29695
				#1 pop hit for Nilsson in 1972		
10/15/83+	**1**¹	21	27	**Slow Burn**		Warner 29469
2/18/84	**12**	15	28	Make My Day .... [N]	*62*	Warner 29343
				T.G. SHEPPARD with CLINT EASTWOOD from the film "Sudden Impact", starring Eastwood		
6/02/84	**3**	21	29	**Somewhere Down The Line**		Warner 29369
9/29/84	**57**	9	30	Home Again		Elektra 69697
				JUDY COLLINS with T.G. SHEPPARD		
11/10/84+	**4**	22	31	**One Owner Heart**		Warner 29167
3/09/85	**10**	17	32	**You're Going Out Of My Mind**		Warner 29071
5/11/85	**21**	18	33	Fooled Around And Fell In Love		Columbia 04890
				#3 pop hit for Elvin Bishop in 1976		
9/07/85	**8**	20	34	**Doncha?**		Columbia 05591
12/28/85+	**9**	18	35	**In Over My Heart**		Columbia 05747
5/17/86	**1**¹	23	36	**Strong Heart**		Columbia 05905
10/11/86+	**2**²	26	37	**Half Past Forever (Till I'm Blue In The Heart)**		Columbia 06347
3/21/87	**2**¹	20	38	**You're My First Lady**		Columbia 06999
9/05/87	**2**¹	24	39	**One For The Money**		Columbia 07312
9/24/88	**48**	7	40	Don't Say It With Diamonds (Say It With Love) ...		Columbia 08029
11/26/88+	**14**	20	41	You Still Do		Columbia 08119

DEBUT DATE	PEAK POS	WKS CHR	ARTIST — Record Title	POP POS	Label & Number
			GLEN SHERLEY		
			Migrant worker, wrote songs with Spade Cooley while in prison. Died on 5/11/78 of self-inflicted gunshot wounds.		
7/10/71	63	4	1 Greystone Chapel..............................		Mega 0027
			ARKIE SHIBLEY & His Mountain Boys		
12/30/50+	5	7	1 Hot Rod Race		Gilt Edge 5021
			Jockey #5 / Juke Box #6		
			MURV SHINER		
			Born Mervin J. Shiner on 2/20/21 in Bethlehem, Pennsylvania. Played guitar from age 16, teamed with his mother. Appeared on WFIL-Philadelphia in 1945.		
10/08/49	5	11	1 Why Don't You Haul Off And Love Me		Decca 46178
			Juke Box #5 / Best Seller #11		
4/01/50	6	3	2 ● Peter Cottontail	8	Decca 46221
			Jockey #6 / Best Seller #7		
5/27/67	73	4	3 Big Brother		MGM 13704
1/04/69	50	10	4 Too Hard To Say I'm Sorry......................		MGM 14007
			SHIRLEY & SQUIRRELY		
6/05/76	28	11	1 Hey Shirley (This Is Squirrely) .... [N]	48	GRT 054
			DANNY SHIRLEY		
			Born in Soddy Daisy, Tennessee. Worked at Governor's Lounge in Chattanooga.		
10/20/84	72	5	1 Love And Let Love		Amor 1002
2/16/85	93	5	2 Yo Yo (The Right String, But The Wrong Yo Yo) ..		Amor 1006
			DANNY SHIRLEY & "PIANO RED" (William Lee Perryman)		
8/29/87	82	3	3 Deep Down (Everybody Wants To Be From Dixie)		Amor 2001
12/05/87	81	2	4 Goin' To California		Amor 2002
2/20/88	76	7	5 I Make The Living (She Makes The Living Worthwhile)................................		Amor 2004
			TROY SHONDELL		
			Born on 5/14/44 in Fort Wayne, Indiana. Multi-instrumentalist. Produced his own first pop hit "This Time" on Gold Crest in 1961.		
10/06/79	95	2	1 Still Loving You		Star-Fox 77
11/08/80	83	4	2 (Sittin' Here) Lovin' You		TeleSonic 804
5/14/88	79	2	3 (I'm Looking For Some) New Blue Jeans		AVM 14
			THE SHOOTERS		
			Quintet led by vocalist/guitarist Walt Aldridge, featuring Gary Baker (bass), Barry Billings (guitar), Chalmers Davis (keyboards) and Michael Dillon (drums). Aldridge is a prolific sessionman/producer/songwriter at Muscle Shoals Fame Studios.		
1/24/87	21	15	1 They Only Come Out At Night		Epic 06623
6/06/87	41	11	2 'Til The Old Wears Off.........................		Epic 07131
9/26/87	34	13	3 Tell It To Your Teddy Bear		Epic 07367
1/30/88	31	15	4 I Taught Her Everything She Knows About Love.		Epic 07684
10/22/88+	13	21	5 Borderline		Epic 08082
			THE SHOPPE		
			Band formed in Dallas in 1968. Consisted of Clarke Wilcox (guitar, banjo), Jack Wilcox (bass), Mark Cathey and Kevin Bailey (vocals), Mike Caldwell (harmonica), Lou Chavez (drums) and Roger Ferguson (guitar).		
4/19/80	76	5	1 Three Way Love.............................		Rainbow S. 8019
8/30/80	78	4	2 Star Studded Nights.........................		Rainbow S. 8022
2/21/81	33	10	3 Doesn't Anybody Get High On Love Anymore.....		NSD 80
5/23/81	61	7	4 Dream Maker		NSD 90
11/17/84	74	5	5 If You Think I Love You Now..........................		Amer. Country 2
2/16/85	79	6	6 Hurts All Over		Amer. Country 3
9/14/85	56	8	7 Holdin' The Family Together		MTM 72056
12/21/85+	47	11	8 While The Moon's In Town......................		MTM 72063
			WALT SHRUM		
10/06/45	3	1	1 Triflin' Gal		Coast 2010
			SHURFIRE		
7/04/87	54	7	1 Bringin' The House Down		AIR 173
11/21/87	49	9	2 Roll The Dice		AIR 180
3/12/88	57	6	3 First In Line...............................		AIR 181

DEBUT DATE	PEAK POS	WKS CHR	ARTIST — Record Title	POP POS	Label & Number
			SHYLO		
			Formed in 1970 by Ronny Scaife, Perry York and Danny Hogan as Storybook. Changed name to Shylo in 1973.		
2/14/76	75	8	1 Dog Tired Of Cattin' Around.............................		Columbia 10267
6/12/76	75	7	2 Livin' On Love Street..................................		Columbia 10343
9/25/76	86	5	3 Ol' Man River (I've Come To Talk Again)............		Columbia 10398
1/08/77	63	8	4 Drinkin' My Way Back Home..........................		Columbia 10456
5/28/77	87	4	5 (I'm Coming Home To You) Dixie.....................		Columbia 10534
12/17/77+	91	5	6 Gotta Travel On.....................................		Columbia 10647
3/10/79	79	6	7 Freckles..		Columbia 10918
9/15/79	92	2	8 I'm Puttin' My Love Inside You......................		Columbia 11048
5/22/82	89	3	9 Crime In The Sheets.................................		Mercury 76151
			SIDE OF THE ROAD GANG		
			Dallas area band; recorded the "Wouldn't You Like To Be A Pepper Too?" commercial for Dr. Pepper.		
8/14/76	98	2	1 Suitcase Life.......................................		Capitol 4298
			SIERRA		
			Vocal group from Virginia, originally called the Drew Brothers. Consisted of William Arney (tenor), E.J. Harris (lead vocals) and Rodney Painter (baritone). Winners of the Wrangler Star Search in 1981.		
2/05/83	58	8	1 Keep On Playin' That Country Music................		Musicom 52701
5/14/83	87	3	2 I'd Do It In A Heart Beat...........................		Musicom 52702
11/05/83	93	2	3 Old Fashioned Lovin'...............................		Cardinal 052
3/17/84	70	6	4 Branded Man.......................................		Awesome 101
6/23/84	68	6	5 Love Is The Reason.................................		Awesome 106
2/09/85	68	6	6 The Almighty Lover.................................		Awesome 110
			SILVER CITY BAND		
			Memphis-based band.		
10/01/77	99	2	1 If You Really Want Me To I'll Go.....................		Columbia 10601
7/29/78	95	2	2 I'm Still Missing You................................		Columbia 10759
			SILVER CREEK		
11/21/81	64	7	1 Lonely Woman.......................................		Cardinal 8103
			GENE SIMMONS		
			Born in Tupelo, Mississippi in 1933. Nicknamed "Jumpin' Gene". Charted a #11 pop hit, "Haunted House", in 1964.		
9/10/77	88	3	1 Why Didn't I Think Of That...........................		Deltune 1201
			SIMON & VERITY		
			English-bred duo.		
2/16/85	78	4	1 We've Still Got Love................................		EMI America 8257
5/18/85	91	3	2 Your Eyes..		EMI America 8264
			CARLY SIMON - see JAMES TAYLOR		
			RED SIMPSON		
			Joseph Simpson, born in Higby, Arizona. Moved to Bakersfield in the late 40s and performed at the Blackboard Club. Co-wrote several hit songs with Buck Owens, including "Sam's Place", "Gonna Have Love", "Heart Of Glass" and "Kansas City Song".		
4/02/66	38	4	1 Roll Truck Roll......................................		Capitol 5577
6/04/66	39	3	2 The Highway Patrol.................................		Capitol 5637
12/24/66+	41	8	3 Diesel Smoke, Dangerous Curves....................		Capitol 5783
12/04/71+	4	17	4 I'm A Truck...		Capitol 3236
4/22/72	62	5	5 Country Western Truck Drivin' Singer.............		Capitol 3298
6/30/73	63	5	6 Awful Lot To Learn About Truck Drivin'..........		Capitol 3616
9/18/76	92	4	7 Truck Driver's Heaven..............................		Warner 8259
			same tune as Tex Ritter's "Hillbilly Heaven"		
10/27/79	99	2	8 The Flying Saucer Man And The Truck Driver....		K.E.Y. 108
			MARGIE SINGLETON		
			Born on 10/5/35 in Coushatta, Louisiana. Worked on the Louisiana Hayride from 1957-59. Performed on Jubilee USA, ABC-TV, from 1960. Married to Shelby Singleton and then to Leon Ashley.		
8/03/59	25	5	1 Nothing But True Love..............................		Starday 443
2/01/60	12	14	2 Eyes Of Love.......................................		Starday 472

DEBUT DATE	PEAK POS	WKS CHR	ARTIST — Record Title	POP POS	Label & Number
			MARGIE SINGLETON — Continued		
9/18/61	**15**	3	3 Did I Ever Tell You		Mercury 71856
			GEORGE JONES & MARGIE SINGLETON		
6/16/62	**11**	10	4 Waltz Of The Angels		Mercury 71955
			GEORGE JONES & MARGIE SINGLETON		
12/28/63+	**11**	14	5 Old Records		Mercury 72213
9/09/67	**39**	8	6 Ode To Billie Joe...........................		Ashley 2011
			#1 pop hit for Bobbie Gentry in 1967		
11/11/67	**54**	7	7 Hangin' On...........................		Ashley 2015
			LEON ASHLEY & MARGIE SINGLETON		
3/02/68	**52**	8	8 Wandering Mind...........................		Ashley 2050
5/11/68	**55**	6	9 You'll Never Be Lonely Again		Ashley 3000
			LEON ASHLEY & MARGIE SINGLETON		
			FARON YOUNG & MARGIE SINGLETON:		
3/14/64	**5**	23	10 **Keeping Up With The Joneses/**		
3/28/64	**40**	6	11 No Thanks, I Just Had One		Mercury 72237
12/05/64	**38**	8	12 Another Woman's Man Another Man's Woman ...		Mercury 72312
			## RICKY SKAGGS ★★95★★		

Born on 7/18/54 in Cordell, Kentucky. Played Mandolin from age 5. Worked with the Clinch Mountain Boys in 1969, Country Gentlemen in 1974. Own group, Boone Creek, in 1975. In Emmylou Harris' Hot Band in 1977. Moved to Nashville in 1980 and worked with the Whites. Married Sharon White in 1981. On the Grand Ole Opry since 1982. CMA award: Entertainer of the Year - 1985.

DEBUT DATE	PEAK POS	WKS CHR	ARTIST — Record Title	POP POS	Label & Number
4/19/80	**86**	4	1 I'll Take The Blame		Sugar Hill 3706
5/02/81	**16**	16	2 Don't Get Above Your Raising		Epic 02034
9/12/81	**9**	17	3 **You May See Me Walkin'**		Epic 02499
1/23/82	**1**¹	23	4 **Crying My Heart Out Over You**		Epic 02692
5/29/82	**1**¹	18	5 **I Don't Care**		Epic 02931
9/18/82	**1**¹	17	6 **Heartbroke**		Epic 03212
12/25/82+	**1**¹	20	7 **I Wouldn't Change You If I Could**		Epic 03482
4/30/83	**1**¹	19	8 **Highway 40 Blues**		Epic 03812
8/13/83	**2**¹	19	9 **You've Got A Lover**		Epic 04044
12/03/83+	**1**¹	20	10 **Don't Cheat In Our Hometown**		Sugar Hill 04245
3/24/84	**1**¹	18	11 **Honey (Open That Door)**		Sugar Hill 04394
7/21/84	**1**¹	19	12 **Uncle Pen**		Sugar Hill 04527
11/03/84+	**2**¹	22	13 **Something In My Heart**		Epic 04668
3/23/85	**1**¹	19	14 **Country Boy**		Epic 04831
9/14/85	**7**	23	15 **You Make Me Feel Like A Man**		Epic 05585
1/11/86	**1**¹	20	16 **Cajun Moon**		Epic 05748
5/24/86	**10**	18	17 **I've Got A New Heartache**		Epic 05898
10/04/86	**4**	20	18 **Love's Gonna Get You Someday**		Epic 06327
2/14/87	**30**	11	19 I Wonder If I Care As Much		Epic 06650
			tune is flip side of The Everly Brothers' "Bye Bye Love"		
5/02/87	**10**	23	20 **Love Can't Ever Get Better Than This**		Epic 07060
			RICKY SKAGGS & SHARON WHITE		
10/17/87+	**18**	20	21 I'm Tired		Epic 07416
2/27/88	**33**	13	22 (Angel On My Mind) That's Why I'm Walkin'.......		Epic 07721
			same tune as Stonewall Jackson's "Why I'm Walkin'"		
6/11/88	**17**	16	23 Thanks Again...........................		Epic 07924
10/15/88	**30**	15	24 Old Kind Of Love...........................		Epic 08063
			## JIMMIE SKINNER		

Born on 4/27/09 in Blue Lick, Ohio; died of a heart attack on 10/27/79. Own show on WNOP-Newport, Kentucky. Worked as a disc jockey on WNOX-Knoxville and WPEB-Middleton, Ohio in the mid-40s. First recorded for Red Barn. Owner of a famous mail-order record shop in Cincinnati.

DEBUT DATE	PEAK POS	WKS CHR	ARTIST — Record Title	POP POS	Label & Number
4/30/49	**15**	1	1 Tennessee Border		Radio Artist 244
			Best Seller #15		
11/04/57+	**5**	17	2 I Found My Girl In The U.S.A........................		Mercury 71192
			Jockey #5 / Best Seller #9		
3/24/58	**8**	8	3 **What Makes A Man Wander?**........................		Mercury 71256
			Jockey #8 / Best Seller #14		
1/12/59	**21**	8	4 Walking My Blues Away/		
1/19/59	**7**	10	5 **Dark Hollow**...........................		Mercury 71387
8/03/59	**17**	11	6 John Wesley Hardin		Mercury 71470
1/18/60	**14**	11	7 Riverboat Gambler		Mercury 71539

DEBUT DATE	PEAK POS	WKS CHR	ARTIST — Record Title	POP POS	Label & Number
			JIMMIE SKINNER — Continued		
5/16/60	**21**	4	8 Lonesome Road Blues		Mercury 71606
8/29/60	**13**	8	9 Reasons To Live		Mercury 71663
12/19/60	**30**	1	10 Careless Love		Mercury 71704
			SKIP & LINDA		
			Skip Eaton and Linda Davis.		
8/21/82	**63**	7	1 If You Could See You Through My Eyes............		MDJ 68178
10/23/82	**73**	5	2 I Just Can't Turn Temptation Down		MDJ 68179
12/18/82	**89**	4	3 This Time		MDJ 68180
			S-K-O - see SCHUYLER, KNOBLOCH & OVERSTREET		
			DAVID SLATER		
3/26/88	**36**	13	1 I'm Still Your Fool..............................		Capitol 44129
6/25/88	**30**	17	2 The Other Guy....................................		Capitol 44184
			#11 pop hit for the Little River Band in 1983		
10/22/88	**63**	8	3 We Were Meant To Be Lovers		Capitol 44257
			PATSY SLEDD		
			Born on 1/29/44 in Falcon, Missouri. In family vocal group, the Randolph Singers. Did solo work on the Grand Ole Opry. Moved to Nashville in 1965. Toured with Roy Acuff in 1967. Appeared on "Hee Haw" and "Midwestern Hayride" TV shows.		
9/09/72	**68**	6	1 Nothing Can Stop My Loving You		Mega 0085
1/05/74	**33**	12	2 Chip Chip		Mega 203
			#10 pop hit for Gene McDaniels in 1962		
12/07/74+	**72**	9	3 See Saw..		Mega 1217
			#25 pop hit for The Moonglows in 1956		
2/07/76	**90**	5	4 The Cowboy And The Lady		Mega 1244
11/28/87	**79**	3	5 Don't Stay If You Don't Love Me		Showtime 1007
			SLEWFOOT		
			Alabama's replacement for 5 years at the Bowery Club in Myrtle Beach, South Carolina.		
9/13/86	**85**	3	1 Nice To Be With You..................................		Step One 360
			#4 pop hit for Gallery in 1972		
			SLIGO STUDIO BAND		
			Norfolk, Virginia band, originally called The Country Allstars.		
4/18/81	**94**	2	1 You're The Reason		GBS 708
			RENE SLOANE - see PRICE MITCHELL		
			CARRIE SLYE		
			Born on 2/28/60 in Grants, New Mexico; raised in Gurden, Arkansas.		
7/23/83	**78**	4	1 Ease The Fever		Friday 42683
			LANEY SMALLWOOD		
			Singer/actress who portrayed "Audrey Williams" on the TV special "A Tribute To Hank Williams". Also see Charlie McCoy.		
7/01/78	**57**	6	1 That "I Love You, You Love Me Too" Love Song..		Monument 255
			JIMMY SMART		
10/10/60	**18**	2	1 Broken Dream		All Star 7211
3/13/61	**16**	7	2 Shorty..		Plaid 1004
			RED SMILEY - see DON RENO		
			ARTHUR "Guitar Boogie" SMITH		
			Born on 4/1/21 in Clinton, South Carolina. Guitarist/banjo/mandolin. Long run of radio shows on WBT-Charlotte from the 30s. Operator of a recording studio in Charlotte since the 50s.		
9/25/48	**9**	2	1 **Banjo Boogie** .... [I]		MGM 10229
			Juke Box #9		
12/25/48+	**8**	7	2 **Guitar Boogie/** [I]	*25*	
			Juke Box #8		
1/01/49	**8**	4	3 **Boomerang**.. [I]		MGM 10293
			Juke Box #8		
10/19/63	**29**	3	4 Tie My Hunting Dog Down, Jed .... [N]		Starday 642
			same tune as "Tie Me Kangaroo Down, Sport" by Rolf Harris		

DEBUT DATE	PEAK POS	WKS CHR	ARTIST — Record Title	POP POS	Label & Number
			BOBBY SMITH		
			Born in 1946 in Balch Springs, Texas. Sang in the University of Texas choir.		
5/07/77	**70**	8	1 Do You Wanna Make Love		Autumn 398
			#5 pop hit for Peter McCann in 1977		
8/22/81	**30**	11	2 Just Enough Love (For One Woman)		Liberty 1417
11/28/81+	**40**	10	3 Too Many Hearts In The Fire............................		Liberty 1439
2/20/82	**47**	9	4 And Then Some		Liberty 1452
10/02/82	**68**	5	5 It's Been One Of Those Days		Liberty 1480
			CAL SMITH ★★**129**★★		
			Born Calvin Grant Shofner on 4/7/32 in Gans, Oklahoma; raised in Oakland. Worked clubs in San Jose and as a disc jockey on KEEN-San Jose. Regular member of the California Hayride. Worked with Ernest Tubb from 1961-67.		
1/28/67	**58**	10	1 The Only Thing I Want		Kapp 788
8/19/67	**61**	2	2 I'll Never Be Lonesome With You		Kapp 834
2/24/68	**60**	5	3 Destination Atlanta, G.A.		Kapp 884
6/22/68	**58**	7	4 Jacksonville..		Kapp 913
10/05/68	**35**	7	5 Drinking Champagne		Kapp 938
6/14/69	**51**	8	6 It Takes All Night Long		Kapp 994
9/27/69	**55**	4	7 You Can't Housebreak A Tomcat		Kapp 2037
1/03/70	**47**	2	8 Heaven Is Just A Touch Away		Kapp 2059
4/25/70	**70**	2	9 Difference Between Going And Gone.................		Kapp 2076
1/16/71	**58**	7	10 That's What It's Like To Be Lonesome.............		Decca 32768
5/06/72	**4**	15	11 **I've Found Someone Of My Own**...................		Decca 32959
			#5 pop hit for Free Movement in 1971		
9/16/72	**58**	8	12 For My Baby..		Decca 33003
			#28 pop hit for Brook Benton in 1961		
12/16/72+	**1**[1]	17	13 **The Lord Knows I'm Drinking**.....................	*64*	Decca 33040
5/26/73	**25**	11	14 I Can Feel The Leavin' Coming On/		
		6	15 I Loved You All Over The World		MCA 40061
10/13/73	**63**	9	16 Bleep You/		
		7	17 An Hour And A Six-Pack		MCA 40136
3/09/74	**1**[1]	15	18 **Country Bumpkin**		MCA 40191
8/03/74	**11**	13	19 Between Lust And Watching TV		MCA 40265
12/07/74+	**1**[1]	16	20 **It's Time To Pay The Fiddler**		MCA 40335
4/26/75	**13**	13	21 She Talked A Lot About Texas		MCA 40394
10/25/75	**12**	14	22 Jason's Farm		MCA 40467
2/14/76	**33**	10	23 Thunderstorms		MCA 40517
6/05/76	**43**	9	24 MacArthur's Hand		MCA 40563
10/09/76	**38**	10	25 Woman Don't Try To Sing My Song		MCA 40618
1/22/77	**15**	14	26 I Just Came Home To Count The Memories........		MCA 40671
4/30/77	**23**	10	27 Come See About Me		MCA 40714
9/24/77	**53**	8	28 Helen...		MCA 40789
12/17/77+	**51**	9	29 Throwin' Memories On The Fire		MCA 40839
2/25/78	**73**	4	30 I'm Just A Farmer.......................................		MCA 40864
6/24/78	**68**	5	31 Bits And Pieces Of Life.................................		MCA 40911
1/06/79	**71**	6	32 The Rise And Fall Of The Roman Empire...........		MCA 40982
4/14/79	**91**	2	33 One Little Skinny Rib		MCA 41001
11/03/79	**92**	2	34 The Room At The Top Of The Stairs		MCA 41128
10/30/82	**68**	6	35 Too Many Irons In The Fire............................		Soundwaves 4686
			BILLY PARKER & CAL SMITH		
9/06/86	**75**	5	36 King Lear		Step One 358
			CARL SMITH ★★**20**★★		
			Born on 3/15/27 in Maynardsville, Tennessee. Worked on WROL-Knoxville in the 40s. Joined WSM-Nashville in 1950, then signed by Columbia Records. With the "Phillip Morris Country Music Show" troupe in 1957, then served as host for ABC-TV's "Four Star Jubilee" in 1961. Hosted CTV of Canada's "Carl Smith's Country Music Hall" for 5 years. Married to June Carter for a time, father of Carlene Carter. Married to singer Goldie Hill since 1957. Retired to his Tennessee ranch in 1977.		
6/02/51	**2**[1]	20	1 Let's Live A Little		Columbia 20796
			Jockey #2 / Best Seller #3 / Juke Box #3		
8/04/51	**4**	17	2 **Mr. Moon/**		
			Jockey #4 / Juke Box #5 / Best Seller #8		
8/04/51	**8**	3	3 **If Teardrops Were Pennies**........................		Columbia 20825
			Juke Box #8 / Best Seller #9 / Jockey #9		

DEBUT DATE	PEAK POS	WKS CHR		ARTIST — Record Title	POP POS	Label & Number
				CARL SMITH — Continued		
10/27/51+	1⁸	33	4	**Let Old Mother Nature Have Her Way** .... Juke Box #1(8) / Best Seller #1(6) / Jockey #1(3)		Columbia 20862
3/01/52	1⁸	24	5	**(When You Feel Like You're In Love) Don't Just Stand There** .... Jockey #1(8) / Best Seller #1(5) / Juke Box #1(3)		Columbia 20893
5/24/52	1¹	19	6	**Are You Teasing Me/** Jockey #1 / Juke Box #2 / Best Seller #2		
5/31/52	5	10	7	**It's A Lovely, Lovely World** .... Jockey #5 / Best Seller #8 / Juke Box #9		Columbia 20922
10/25/52	6	5	8	**Our Honeymoon** .... Jockey #6 / Juke Box #6 / Best Seller #7		Columbia 21008
1/31/53	9	1	9	**That's The Kind Of Love I'm Looking For** ...... Juke Box #9		Columbia 21051
5/02/53	7	3	10	**Just Wait Till I Get You Alone/** Jockey #7 / Juke Box #7 / Best Seller #9		
5/09/53	4	6	11	**This Orchid Means Goodbye** .... Juke Box #4 / Best Seller #7 / Jockey #7		Columbia 21087
7/04/53	2²	10	12	**Trademark/** Best Seller #2 / Juke Box #5 / Jockey #6		
7/18/53	6	1	13	**Do I Like It?** .... Jockey #6		Columbia 21119
7/25/53	1⁸	26	14	**Hey, Joe** .... Juke Box #1(8) / Jockey #1(4) / Best Seller #1(2)		Columbia 21129
11/07/53	7	6	15	**Satisfaction Guaranteed** .... Best Seller #7 / Jockey #7 / Juke Box #8		Columbia 21166
2/13/54	7	4	16	**Dog-Gone It, Baby, I'm In Love** .... Jockey #7 / Best Seller #8		Columbia 21197
5/01/54	2¹	16	17	**Back Up Buddy** .... Jockey #2 / Best Seller #4 / Juke Box #4		Columbia 21226
8/07/54	4	11	18	**Go, Boy, Go** .... Best Seller #4 / Jockey #7 / Juke Box #9		Columbia 21266
11/06/54+	1⁷	32	19	**Loose Talk/** Best Seller #1(7) / Jockey #1(6) / Juke Box #1(4)		
11/06/54	5	10	20	**More Than Anything Else In The World** .... Jockey #5 / Best Seller #15		Columbia 21317
1/22/55	5	16	21	**Kisses Don't Lie/** Best Seller #5 / Juke Box #7 / Jockey #8		
1/29/55	13	2	22	**No, I Don't Believe I Will** .... Best Seller #13 / Jockey #15		Columbia 21340
4/23/55	12	3	23	Wait A Little Longer, Please, Jesus .... Jockey #12		Columbia 21368
5/14/55	3	25	24	**There She Goes/** Jockey #3 / Best Seller #5 / Juke Box #8 #26 pop hit for Jerry Wallace in 1961		
5/21/55	11	7	25	Old Lonesome Times .... Best Seller #11 / Jockey #13		Columbia 21382
10/15/55	11	4	26	Don't Tease Me .... Jockey #11 / Best Seller #13		Columbia 21429
12/03/55	6	14	27	**You're Free To Go/** Best Seller #6 / Juke Box #6 / Jockey #7		
12/03/55+	7	15	28	**I Feel Like Cryin'** .... Best Seller #7 / Juke Box #9 / Jockey #11		Columbia 21462
3/31/56	11	3	29	I've Changed .... Jockey #11 / Best Seller #14		Columbia 21493
6/23/56	4	23	30	**You Are The One/** Jockey #4 / Juke Box #5 / Best Seller #6		
		5	31	Doorstep To Heaven .... Best Seller flip		Columbia 21522
10/13/56	6	12	32	**Before I Met You/** Juke Box #6 / Jockey #7 / Best Seller #9		
10/20/56	9	10	33	**Wicked Lies** .... Best Seller #9		Columbia 21552
3/02/57	15	1	34	You Can't Hurt Me Anymore .... Best Seller #15		Columbia 40823
9/16/57	2²	19	35	**Why, Why** .... Jockey #2 / Best Seller #7		Columbia 40984
3/03/58	6	14	36	**Your Name Is Beautiful** .... Jockey #6 / Best Seller #9	80	Columbia 41092
12/15/58	28	1	37	Walking The Slow Walk		Columbia 41243

DEBUT DATE	PEAK POS	WKS CHR		ARTIST — Record Title	POP POS	Label & Number
				CARL SMITH — Continued		
1/19/59	**15**	11	38	The Best Years Of Your Life............................		Columbia 41290
6/01/59	**19**	3	39	It's All My Heartache		Columbia 41344
7/20/59	**5**	12	40	**Ten Thousand Drums**................................	*43*	Columbia 41417
12/14/59	**24**	4	41	Tomorrow Night....................................		Columbia 41489
3/21/60	**30**	1	42	Make The Waterwheel Roll		Columbia 41557
6/20/60	**28**	2	43	Cut Across Shorty....................................		Columbia 41642
2/20/61	**29**	2	44	You Make Me Live Again		Columbia 41819
7/10/61	**11**	9	45	Kisses Never Lie		Columbia 42042
1/13/62	**11**	15	46	Air Mail To Heaven/		
1/27/62	**24**	2	47	Things That Mean The Most.......................		Columbia 42222
5/12/62	**16**	7	48	The Best Dressed Beggar (In Town).................		Columbia 42349
4/20/63	**28**	1	49	Live For Tomorrow....................................		Columbia 42686
8/24/63	**17**	8	50	In The Back Room Tonight		Columbia 42768
11/09/63+	**23**	5	51	I Almost Forgot Her Today/		
12/21/63+	**16**	11	52	Triangle		Columbia 42858
2/22/64	**17**	14	53	The Pillow That Whispers............................		Columbia 42949
6/20/64	**15**	20	54	Take My Ring Off Your Finger		Columbia 43033
10/17/64	**14**	15	55	Lonely Girl/		
12/12/64+	**26**	9	56	When It's Over....................................		Columbia 43124
2/13/65	**32**	11	57	She Called Me Baby		Columbia 43200
6/12/65	**42**	3	58	Keep Me Fooled/		
6/26/65	**33**	8	59	Be Good To Her		Columbia 43266
10/16/65	**36**	6	60	Let's Walk Away Strangers.........................		Columbia 43361
3/12/66	**45**	4	61	Why Do I Keep Doing This To Us/		
3/19/66	**49**	1	62	Why Can't You Feel Sorry For Me		Columbia 43485
9/17/66	**42**	5	63	Man With A Plan....................................		Columbia 43753
12/03/66+	**52**	8	64	You Better Be Better To Me/		
1/14/67	**65**	3	65	It's Only A Matter Of Time..........................		Columbia 43866
4/22/67	**68**	3	66	Mighty Day/		
5/13/67	**54**	7	67	I Should Get Away Awhile (From You)		Columbia 44034
8/26/67	**10**	18	68	**Deep Water**....................................		Columbia 44233
1/13/68	**18**	11	69	Foggy River.......................................		Columbia 44396
5/18/68	**43**	9	70	You Ought To Hear Me Cry		Columbia 44486
9/21/68	**48**	5	71	There's No More Love		Columbia 44620
1/04/69	**25**	13	72	Faded Love And Winter Roses		Columbia 44702
4/26/69	**18**	13	73	Good Deal, Lucille....................................		Columbia 44816
8/16/69	**14**	12	74	I Love You Because		Columbia 44939
12/06/69+	**35**	8	75	Heartbreak Avenue		Columbia 45031
3/14/70	**18**	10	76	Pull My String And Wind Me Up....................		Columbia 45086
7/11/70	**46**	8	77	Pick Me Up On Your Way Down/		
		4	78	Bonaparte's Retreat		Columbia 45177
10/03/70	**20**	12	79	How I Love Them Old Songs.......................		Columbia 45225
2/13/71	**44**	10	80	Don't Worry 'Bout The Mule (Just Load The Wagon)		Columbia 45293
6/05/71	**43**	8	81	Lost It On The Road		Columbia 45382
9/11/71	**21**	13	82	Red Door		Columbia 45436
12/11/71+	**34**	12	83	Don't Say You're Mine		Columbia 45497
5/13/72	**46**	11	84	Mama Bear		Columbia 45558
8/05/72	**54**	9	85	If This Is Goodbye		Columbia 45648
9/29/73	**76**	6	86	I Need Help		Columbia 45923
1/25/75	**67**	9	87	The Way I Lose My Mind		Hickory 337
11/15/75	**97**	2	88	Roly Poly...		Hickory 357
5/29/76	**97**	3	89	If You Don't, Somebody Else Will		Hickory 371
12/11/76	**98**	4	90	A Way With Words		ABC/Hick. 54004
4/09/77	**96**	4	91	Show Me A Brick Wall..............................		ABC/Hick. 54009
9/03/77	**84**	4	92	This Kinda Love Ain't Meant For Sunday School		ABC/Hick. 54016
2/04/78	**81**	4	93	This Lady Loving Me		ABC/Hick. 54022

DEBUT DATE	PEAK POS	WKS CHR	ARTIST — Record Title	POP POS	Label & Number
			CONNIE SMITH ★★55★★		
			Born Constance June Meadows on 8/14/41 in Elkhart, Indiana; raised in West Virginia and Ohio. Appeared with Floyd Miller's Square Dance Band while still a teenager. Worked on WSAZ- Huntingdon, West Virginia "Saturday Night Jamboree" TV series. Discovered by Bill Anderson. Member of the Grand Ole Opry since 1971. In the films "Las Vegas Hillbillies", "Road To Nashville" and "Second Fiddle To A Steel Guitar".		
9/26/64	1⁸	28	1 **Once A Day**	101	RCA 8416
1/23/65	4	24	2 **Then And Only Then/**	116	
2/06/65	25	17	3 Tiny Blue Transistor Radio.............................		RCA 8489
6/05/65	9	16	4 **I Can't Remember**	130	RCA 8551
9/25/65	4	19	5 **If I Talk To Him**		RCA 8663
2/12/66	4	17	6 **Nobody But A Fool (Would Love You)**		RCA 8746
6/11/66	2²	17	7 **Ain't Had No Lovin'**		RCA 8842
10/15/66	3	19	8 **The Hurtin's All Over**		RCA 8964
3/11/67	10	15	9 **I'll Come Runnin'**		RCA 9108
6/24/67	4	15	10 **Cincinnati, Ohio**		RCA 9214
10/28/67	5	15	11 **Burning A Hole In My Mind**		RCA 9335
1/27/68	7	14	12 **Baby's Back Again**.....................................		RCA 9413
5/18/68	10	15	13 **Run Away Little Tears**		RCA 9513
9/28/68	20	11	14 Cry, Cry, Cry		RCA 9624
3/01/69	13	14	15 Ribbon Of Darkness......................................		RCA 0101
7/05/69	20	11	16 Young Love...		RCA 0181
			CONNIE SMITH & NAT STUCKEY #1 pop hit for both Sonny James and Tab Hunter in 1957		
11/08/69	6	15	17 **You And Your Sweet Love**............................		RCA 0258
3/14/70	59	4	18 If God Is Dead (Who's That Living In My Soul)		RCA 9805
			CONNIE SMITH & NAT STUCKEY		
5/16/70	5	15	19 **I Never Once Stopped Loving You**..................		RCA 9832
9/12/70	14	11	20 Louisiana Man..		RCA 9887
1/02/71	11	14	21 Where Is My Castle		RCA 9938
5/08/71	2²	17	22 **Just One Time**...	119	RCA 9981
10/16/71	14	15	23 I'm Sorry If My Love Got In Your Way		RCA 0535
3/04/72	5	15	24 **Just For What I Am**		RCA 0655
8/05/72	7	15	25 **If It Ain't Love (Let's Leave It Alone)**............		RCA 0752
12/23/72+	8	14	26 **Love Is The Look You're Looking For**		RCA 0855
3/31/73	21	12	27 You've Got Me (Right Where You Want Me)		Columbia 45816
6/23/73	23	10	28 Dream Painter		RCA 0971
11/10/73+	10	14	29 **Ain't Love A Good Thing**		Columbia 45954
3/23/74	35	11	30 Dallas		Columbia 46008
6/29/74	13	13	31 I Never Knew (What That Song Meant Before).....		Columbia 46058
11/16/74+	13	12	32 I've Got My Baby On My Mind........................		Columbia 10051
2/22/75	30	10	33 I Got A Lot Of Hurtin' Done Today		Columbia 10086
5/17/75	15	13	34 Why Don't You Love Me		Columbia 10135
10/04/75	29	11	35 The Song We Fell In Love To...........................		Columbia 10210
1/31/76	10	15	36 ('Til) I Kissed You		Columbia 10277
			#4 pop hit for The Everly Brothers in 1959		
6/05/76	31	10	37 So Sad (To Watch Good Love Go Bad)		Columbia 10345
			#7 pop hit for The Everly Brothers in 1960		
8/28/76	13	14	38 I Don't Wanna Talk It Over Anymore...............		Columbia 10393
3/26/77	42	8	39 The Latest Shade Of Blue		Columbia 10501
5/28/77	58	7	40 Coming Around		Monument 219
11/05/77+	14	15	41 I Just Want To Be Your Everything		Monument 231
			#1 pop hit for Andy Gibb in 1977		
2/25/78	34	10	42 Lovin' You Baby		Monument 241
5/27/78	68	6	43 There'll Never Be Another For Me		Monument 252
11/04/78	68	5	44 Smooth Sailin'		Monument 266
4/07/79	88	3	45 Lovin' You, Lovin' Me/		
		3	46 Ten Thousand And One................................		Monument 281
6/23/79	93	2	47 Don't Say Love		Monument 284
7/27/85	71	6	48 A Far Cry From You		Epic 05414
			DARDEN SMITH Male vocalist from Austin, Texas.		
2/20/88	56	8	1 Little Maggie		Epic 07709

DEBUT DATE	PEAK POS	WKS CHR	ARTIST — Record Title	POP POS	Label & Number
			DARDEN SMITH — Continued		
5/28/88	59	6	2 Day After Tomorrow		Epic 07906
			DAVID SMITH		
10/20/79	64	5	1 Heroes And Idols (Don't Come Easy)		MDJ 1004
			DENNIS SMITH		
3/01/80	94	2	1 California Calling		Adonda 79021
			JERRY SMITH		
			Session pianist. Wrote and performed on the Dixiebelles' "(Down At) Papa Joe's". Also see Papa Joe's Music Box.		
5/17/69	44	10	1 Truck Stop................................... [I] *71*		ABC 11162
8/16/69	63	5	2 Sweet 'N' Sassy .... [I]		ABC 11230
6/06/70	44	9	3 Drivin' Home................................. [I] *125*		Decca 32679
10/03/70	60	7	4 Steppin' Out.................................. [I]		Decca 32730
			KATE SMITH		
			Tremendously popular soprano who was for years one of the most-listened-to of all radio singers, and later hosted a TV series. Died on 6/17/86 (79).		
10/30/48	10	1	1 **Foggy River** .... Best Seller #10		MGM 30059
			LOGAN SMITH		
1/19/74	63	11	1 Little Man............................... [N]		Brand X 6-7/8
			LOU SMITH		
8/15/60	9	17	1 **Cruel Love**		KRCO 105
4/17/61	21	5	2 I'm Wondering......................................		Salvo 2862
			MARGO SMITH ★★**138**★★		
			Born Betty Lou Miller on 4/9/42 in Dayton, Ohio. Sang with the Apple Sisters vocal group while in high school. Writes almost all of her hits.		
4/05/75	8	18	1 **There I Said It**		20th Century 2172
9/13/75	30	12	2 Paper Lovin'..		20th Century 2222
12/20/75+	51	8	3 Meet Me Later		20th Century 2255
5/29/76	10	14	4 **Save Your Kisses For Me**		Warner 8213
10/02/76	7	16	5 **Take My Breath Away**		Warner 8261
3/12/77	12	12	6 Love's Explosion.....................................		Warner 8339
6/25/77	23	10	7 My Weakness		Warner 8399
8/20/77	43	8	8 So Close Again .... MARGO & NORRO (Wilson)		Warner 8427
12/17/77+	1²	18	9 **Don't Break The Heart That Loves You**.......... *104* #1 pop hit for Connie Francis in 1962		Warner 8508
4/29/78	1¹	15	10 **It Only Hurts For A Little While** .... #11 pop hit for The Ames Brothers in 1956		Warner 8555
9/09/78	3	14	11 **Little Things Mean A Lot** .... #1 pop hit for Kitty Kallen in 1954		Warner 8653
1/20/79	7	13	12 **Still A Woman**		Warner 8726
5/05/79	10	13	13 **If I Give My Heart To You**........................... #3 pop hit for Doris Day in 1954		Warner 8806
9/08/79	27	9	14 Baby My Baby		Warner 49038
12/08/79+	13	13	15 The Shuffle Song...................................		Warner 49109
7/05/80	43	9	16 My Guy .... #1 pop hit for Mary Wells in 1964		Warner 49250
10/11/80	52	7	17 He Gives Me Diamonds, You Give Me Chills........		Warner 49569
12/20/80+	12	14	18 Cup Of Tea .... REX ALLEN, JR. & MARGO SMITH		Warner 49626
4/25/81	72	4	19 My Heart Cries For You .... #2 pop hit for Guy Mitchell in 1951		Warner 49701
6/13/81	26	12	20 While The Feeling's Good .... REX ALLEN, JR. & MARGO SMITH		Warner 49738
5/08/82	64	7	21 Either You're Married Or You're Single		AMI 1304
8/21/82	70	5	22 Could It Be I Don't Belong Here Anymore		AMI 1309
12/10/83	78	4	23 Wedding Bells..		Moon Shine 3019
1/28/84	63	7	24 Please Tell Him That I Said Hello		Moon Shine 3021
6/22/85	82	2	25 All I Do Is Dream Of You		Bermuda D. 106
8/10/85	63	8	26 Everyday People .... MARGO SMITH & TOM GRANT		Bermuda D. 110

DEBUT DATE	PEAK POS	WKS CHR	ARTIST — Record Title	POP POS	Label & Number
			MARGO SMITH — Continued		
4/23/88	**77**	4	27 Echo Me		Playback 1300
			RICK SMITH		
			Born in Louisville, Kentucky. Worked with Ray Price.		
9/11/76	**99**	2	1 The Way I Loved Her		Cin Kay 110
10/23/76	**58**	7	2 Daddy How'm I Doin'		Cin Kay 114
			RUSSELL SMITH		
			Born Howard Russell Smith in Lafayette, Tennessee. Worked on WREN-Lafayette while a teenager. Former lead singer of the Amazing Rhythm Aces. Went solo in 1982.		
2/04/84	**74**	6	1 Where Did We Go Right		Capitol 5293
5/14/88	**53**	8	2 Three Piece Suit		Epic 07789
7/23/88	**49**	8	3 Betty Jean		Epic 07972
			SAMMI SMITH ★★115★★		
			Born on 8/5/43 in Orange, California; raised in Oklahoma. Performing since age 12. Moved to Nashville in 1967.		
1/27/68	**69**	2	1 So Long, Charlie Brown, Don't Look For Me Around		Columbia 44370
6/08/68	**53**	7	2 Why Do You Do Me Like You Do		Columbia 44523
8/16/69	**58**	6	3 Brownsville Lumberyard		Columbia 44705
9/05/70	**25**	13	4 He's Everywhere		Mega 1
12/19/70+	**1**³	20	5● **Help Me Make It Through The Night**	8	Mega 0015
5/15/71	**10**	14	6 **Then You Walk In**	118	Mega 0026
9/18/71	**27**	12	7 For The Kids		Mega 0039
1/01/72	**38**	10	8 Kentucky		Mega 0056
4/22/72	**36**	8	9 Girl In New Orleans		Mega 0068
6/17/72	**13**	15	10 I've Got To Have You	77	Mega 0079
12/23/72+	**51**	8	11 The Toast Of '45		Mega 0097
5/19/73	**62**	8	12 I Miss You Most When You're Here		Mega 0109
9/29/73	**44**	12	13 City Of New Orleans....................................		Mega 0118
			#18 pop hit for Arlo Guthrie in 1972		
1/19/74	**16**	12	14 The Rainbow In Daddy's Eyes..........................		Mega 204
6/01/74	**75**	7	15 Never Been To Spain....................................		Mega 210
			#5 pop hit for Three Dog Night in 1972		
9/07/74	**26**	13	16 Long Black Veil		Mega 1214
2/01/75	**33**	11	17 Cover Me		Mega 1222
9/13/75	**9**	15	18 **Today I Started Loving You Again**		Mega 1236
12/20/75+	**81**	7	19 Huckelberry Pie		Elektra 45292
			EVEN STEVENS/SAMMI SMITH		
1/10/76	**51**	6	20 My Window Faces The South...........................		Mega 1246
2/21/76	**43**	9	21 As Long As There's A Sunday		Elektra 45300
5/29/76	**60**	6	22 I'll Get Better		Elektra 45320
7/17/76	**29**	11	23 Sunday School To Broadway		Elektra 45334
7/31/76	**71**	6	24 Just You 'N' Me		Zodiac 1005
2/05/77	**19**	12	25 Loving Arms		Elektra 45374
5/14/77	**27**	11	26 I Can't Stop Loving You................................		Elektra 45398
			#1 pop hit for Ray Charles in 1962		
9/17/77	**23**	11	27 Days That End In "Y"		Elektra 45429
4/29/78	**48**	8	28 It Just Won't Feel Like Cheating (With You).......		Elektra 45476
8/05/78	**73**	4	29 Norma Jean		Elektra 45504
3/10/79	**16**	14	30 What A Lie		Cyclone 100
7/21/79	**27**	11	31 The Letter		Cyclone 104
			#1 pop hit for The Box Tops in 1967		
11/29/80+	**36**	13	32 I Just Want To Be With You...........................		Snd. Factory 425
3/07/81	**16**	13	33 Cheatin's A Two Way Street...........................		Snd. Factory 427
8/08/81	**34**	11	34 Sometimes I Cry When I'm Alone		Snd. Factory 446
3/27/82	**69**	5	35 Gypsy And Joe		Snd. Factory 433
7/20/85	**76**	4	36 You Just Hurt My Last Feeling		Step One 342
3/01/86	**80**	4	37 Love Me All Over		Step One 351

DEBUT DATE	PEAK POS	WKS CHR	ARTIST — Record Title	POP POS	Label & Number
			WARREN SMITH		
			Born on 2/7/33 in Humphreys County, Mississippi; died of a heart attack on 1/30/80 (46). Served in the US Air Force until 1950. Discovered by Carl Perkins. In automobile accident on 8/17/65 and left music until the mid-70s.		
9/05/60	5	17	1 **I Don't Believe I'll Fall In Love Today**...........		Liberty 55248
2/20/61	7	15	2 **Odds And Ends**		Liberty 55302
9/11/61	23	3	3 Why, Baby, Why		Liberty 55361
			WARREN SMITH & SHIRLEY COLLIE		
9/11/61	26	3	4 Call Of The Wild...................................		Liberty 55336
11/02/63	25	4	5 That's Why I Sing In A Honky Tonk/		
1/11/64	41	2	6 Big City Ways................................		Liberty 55615
8/01/64	41	8	7 Blue Smoke..		Liberty 55699
			ELMER SNODGRASS & The Musical Pioneers		
			Deejay on WAKE-Bakersfield, California.		
1/18/60	20	10	1 Until Today...................................		Decca 31048
1/30/61	25	1	2 What A Terrible Feeling		Decca 31145
			HANK SNOW ★★**21**★★		
			Born Clarence Eugene Snow on 5/9/14 in Liverpool, Nova Scotia. Worked as a cabin boy in the Merchant Marine from age 12. Performed at clubs in Halifax and appeared on CHNS-Halifax from 1934. First recorded for Victor in 1936. Moved to the USA in the mid-40s, worked on the Wheeling Jamboree. Worked in Hollywood with his performing horse, Shawnee. On KRLD-Dallas in the late 40s; with the Grand Ole Opry since 1950. Backing group: the Rainbow Ranch Boys. Known as The Singing Ranger. Elected to the Country Music Hall Of Fame in 1979.		
12/31/49	10	1	1 **Marriage Vow**........................		RCA 48-0056
			Best Seller #10 - 78 rpm: 21-0062		
7/01/50	1[21]	44	2 **I'm Moving On**..................................	27	RCA 0328
			Best Seller #1(21) / Jockey #1(18) / Juke Box #1(14)		
11/25/50+	1[2]	23	3 **The Golden Rocket**........................		RCA 0400
			Best Seller #1(2) / Jockey #1(1) / Juke Box #2		
3/03/51	1[8]	27	4 **Rhumba Boogie**		RCA 0431
			Best Seller #1(8) / Juke Box #1(5) / Jockey #1(2)		
4/21/51	4	11	5 **Bluebird Island**/		
			Best Seller #4 / Juke Box #7		
5/19/51	2[1]	14	6 **Down The Trail Of Achin' Hearts**		RCA 0441
			Juke Box #2 / Best Seller #7 / Jockey #7		
			above 2: HANK SNOW with ANITA CARTER		
9/15/51	6	6	7 **Unwanted Sign Upon Your Heart**..................		RCA 0498
			Best Seller #6 / Jockey #9		
12/15/51	4	9	8 **Music Makin' Mama From Memphis**		RCA 4346
			Juke Box #4 / Jockey #5 / Best Seller #6		
4/05/52	2[1]	15	9 **The Gold Rush Is Over**		RCA 4522
			Juke Box #2 / Best Seller #4 / Jockey #4		
7/05/52	2[1]	13	10 **Lady's Man**/		
			Best Seller #2 / Juke Box #5 / Jockey #6		
7/26/52	8	1	11 **Married By The Bible, Divorced By The Law.**		RCA 4733
			Juke Box #8 / Best Seller #10		
9/27/52	3	11	12 **I Went To Your Wedding**		RCA 4909
			Juke Box #3 / Best Seller #4 / Jockey #4		
12/13/52+	4	10	13 **The Gal Who Invented Kissin'**/		
			Best Seller #4 / Juke Box #5 / Jockey #9		
12/27/52+	3	16	14 **(Now and Then, There's) A Fool Such As I**		RCA 5034
			Jockey #3 / Juke Box #3 / Best Seller #4		
4/04/53	9	2	15 **Honeymoon On A Rocket Ship**		RCA 5155
			Best Seller #9 / Jockey #9 / Juke Box #9		
6/06/53	3	8	16 **Spanish Fire Ball**........................		RCA 5296
			Best Seller #3 / Juke Box #4 / Jockey #5		
10/03/53	10	1	17 **For Now And Always**		RCA 5380
			Jockey #10		
11/28/53+	6	6	18 **When Mexican Joe Met Jole Blon**		RCA 5490
			Best Seller #6 / Juke Box #9		
5/29/54	1[20]	41	19 ●**I Don't Hurt Anymore**	22	RCA 5698
			Best Seller #1(20) / Juke Box #1(20) / Jockey #1(18)		
12/04/54	10	6	20 **That Crazy Mambo Thing**/		
			Juke Box #10 / Best Seller #11		
1/01/55	15	1	21 The Next Voice You Hear...........................		RCA 5912
			Best Seller #15		
12/25/54	1[2]	16	22 **Let Me Go, Lover**		RCA 5960
			Jockey #1 / Juke Box #2 / Best Seller #3		

DEBUT DATE	PEAK POS	WKS CHR		ARTIST — Record Title		POP POS	Label & Number
				HANK SNOW — Continued			
4/02/55	**15**	1	23	Silver Bell.. [I]			RCA 5995
				HANK SNOW & CHET ATKINS			
				Best Seller #15			
4/09/55	**3**	27	24	**Yellow Roses/**			
				Best Seller #3 / Jockey #3 / Juke Box #3			
4/16/55	**3**	17	25	**Would You Mind**			RCA 6057
				Jockey #3 / Juke Box #4			
7/23/55	**7**	8	26	**Cryin', Prayin', Waitin', Hopin'/**			
				Juke Box #7 / Best Seller #9 / Jockey #10			
7/23/55	**7**	2	27	**I'm Glad I Got To See You Once Again**			RCA 6154
				Juke Box #7 / Best Seller #12			
11/05/55	**5**	8	28	**Mainliner (The Hawk with Silver Wings)/**			
				Juke Box #5 / Best Seller #8			
11/05/55	**5**	4	29	**Born To Be Happy**			RCA 6269
				Juke Box #5 / Jockey #10 / Best Seller #14			
2/04/56	**5**	10	30	**These Hands/**			
				Juke Box #5 / Jockey #6 / Best Seller #8			
2/18/56	**11**	4	31	**I'm Movin' In**			RCA 6379
				Best Seller #11			
8/04/56	**4**	22	32	**Conscience I'm Guilty/**			
				Juke Box #4 / Best Seller #8 / Jockey #9			
8/04/56	**5**	5	33	**Hula Rock**			RCA 6578
				Juke Box #5			
12/15/56	**7**	9	34	**Stolen Moments**			RCA 6715
				Juke Box #7 / Best Seller #8 / Jockey #9			
7/22/57	**4**	19	35	**Tangled Mind/**			
				Jockey #4 / Best Seller #9			
7/22/57	**8**	14	36	**My Arms Are A House**			RCA 6955
				Jockey #8 / Best Seller #13			
3/31/58	**15**	1	37	Whispering Rain			RCA 7154
				Jockey #15 / Best Seller #18			
6/23/58	**7**	9	38	**Big Wheels**			RCA 7233
				Jockey #7 / Best Seller #18			
11/03/58	**16**	5	39	A Woman Captured Me....................			RCA 7325
3/16/59	**19**	6	40	Doggone That Train			RCA 7448
6/01/59	**6**	11	41	**Chasin' A Rainbow**			RCA 7524
10/19/59	**3**	20	42	**The Last Ride**			RCA 7586
4/11/60	**22**	5	43	Rockin', Rollin' Ocean......................		87	RCA 7702
7/18/60	**9**	15	44	**Miller's Cave**		101	RCA 7748
5/15/61	**5**	20	45	**Beggar To A King**			RCA 7869
				written by J.P. Richardson, "The Big Bopper"			
10/09/61	**11**	9	46	The Restless One			RCA 7933
6/02/62	**15**	7	47	You Take The Future (And I'll Take the Past).....			RCA 8009
9/15/62	**1** [2]	22	48	**I've Been Everywhere**		68	RCA 8072
4/27/63	**9**	11	49	**The Man Who Robbed The Bank At Santa Fe** ..			RCA 8151
10/26/63	**2** [3]	22	50	**Ninety Miles An Hour (Down a Dead End Street)**		124	RCA 8239
4/11/64	**11**	15	51	Breakfast With The Blues/			
7/04/64	**21**	12	52	I Stepped Over The Line			RCA 8334
2/13/65	**7**	19	53	**The Wishing Well (Down in the Well)**			RCA 8488
10/30/65	**28**	5	54	The Queen Of Draw Poker Town			RCA 8655
12/25/65+	**18**	14	55	I've Cried A Mile			RCA 8713
5/07/66	**22**	11	56	The Count Down			RCA 8808
12/10/66+	**21**	14	57	Hula Love			RCA 8990
5/13/67	**18**	14	58	Down At The Pawn Shop			RCA 9188
9/23/67	**20**	15	59	Learnin' A New Way Of Life			RCA 9300
2/24/68	**69**	3	60	Who Will Answer? (Aleluya No. 1)/			
				#19 pop hit for Ed Ames in 1968			
4/06/68	**70**	5	61	I Just Wanted To Know (How the Wind Was Blowing)			RCA 9433
6/08/68	**20**	13	62	The Late And Great Love (Of My Heart)............			RCA 9523
12/28/68+	**16**	16	63	The Name Of The Game Was Love			RCA 9685
5/31/69	**26**	9	64	Rome Wasn't Built In A Day..........................			RCA 0151
11/01/69	**53**	5	65	That's When The Hurtin' Sets In			RCA 0251
7/11/70	**52**	7	66	Vanishing Breed			RCA 9856

DEBUT DATE	PEAK POS	WKS CHR	ARTIST — Record Title	POP POS	Label & Number
			HANK SNOW — Continued		
11/07/70	**57**	5	67 Come The Morning		RCA 9907
4/21/73	**71**	3	68 North To Chicago		RCA 0915
2/09/74	**1**¹	15	69 **Hello Love**...		RCA 0215
6/29/74	**36**	11	70 That's You And Me..		RCA 0307
11/16/74+	**26**	11	71 Easy To Love		RCA 10108
3/22/75	**47**	10	72 Merry-Go-Round Of Love		RCA 10225
8/02/75	**79**	6	73 Hijack		RCA 10338
11/29/75	**95**	2	74 Colorado Country Morning...........................		RCA 10439
5/29/76	**87**	4	75 Who's Been Here Since I've Been Gone		RCA 10681
11/27/76	**98**	1	76 You're Wondering Why		RCA 10804
7/16/77	**81**	4	77 Trouble In Mind		RCA 11021
9/24/77	**80**	4	78 I'm Still Movin' On..		RCA 11080
			new lyrics to Hank's first #1 hit		
12/03/77	**96**	2	79 Breakfast With The Blues........................[R]		RCA 11153
7/01/78	**93**	4	80 Nevertheless		RCA 11276
10/07/78	**93**	4	81 Ramblin' Rose		RCA 11377
			#2 pop hit for Nat King Cole in 1962		
3/31/79	**80**	3	82 The Mysterious Lady From St. Martinique		RCA 11487
7/21/79	**91**	3	83 A Good Gal Is Hard To Find		RCA 11622
11/10/79	**98**	2	84 It Takes Too Long		RCA 11734
2/16/80	**78**	4	85 Hasn't It Been Good Together......................		RCA 11891
			HANK SNOW & KELLY FOXTON		
			SNUFF		
			Rock sextet from Virginia's Tidewater region.		
8/07/82	**71**	6	1 (So This Is) Happy Hour..............................		Elektra 69996
			JIMMY SNYDER		
2/14/70	**30**	9	1 The Chicago Story.......................................		Wayside 009
8/16/80	**71**	7	2 Just To Prove My Love To You		e.i.o. 1126
			RICK SNYDER		
			Part owner of POETS Corner in Atlanta and POETS Music Hall, Memphis.		
7/23/88	**66**	4	1 Losing Somebody You Love		Capitol 44185
			SOLID GOLD BAND		
11/28/81+	**47**	9	1 Cherokee Country		NSD 110
2/20/82	**65**	6	2 I Never Had The One That I Wanted/		
		6	3 Bandera, Texas...		NSD 121
7/17/82	**68**	6	4 Country Fiddles		NSD 138
			SOME OF CHET'S FRIENDS		
			Tribute to Chet Atkins by RCA artists: Jerry Reed, Floyd Cramer, Eddy Arnold, Dottie West, Archie Campbell, Bobby Bare, Norma Jean, George Hamilton IV, Skeeter Davis, Jimmy Dean, Hank Locklin, Jim Ed Brown, Hank Snow, John D. Loudermilk, Connie Smith, Homer & Jethro, Waylon Jennings, Willie Nelson, Porter Wagoner and Don Bowman.		
6/24/67	**38**	9	1 Chet's Tune		RCA 9229
			JO-EL SONNIER		
			French accordionist, born on 10/2/46 in Rayne, Louisiana. First recorded for Swallow in 1960. Won first prize in the Mamou Mardi Gras Competition in 1968. Worked in Nashville from 1974-79. Once known as the "Cajun Valentino".		
10/04/75	**78**	7	1 I've Been Around Enough To Know		Mercury 73702
3/06/76	**99**	1	2 Always Late (With Your Kisses)		Mercury 73754
6/05/76	**100**	1	3 He's Still All Over You		Mercury 73796
			above 3 shown as: JOEL SONNIER		
11/28/87+	**39**	14	4 Come On Joe		RCA 5282
2/20/88	**7**	22	5 **No More One More Time**		RCA 6895
7/16/88	**9**	19	6 **Tear-Stained Letter**..................................		RCA 8304
11/19/88+	**35**	12	7 Rainin' In My Heart		RCA 8726
			#34 pop hit for Slim Harpo in 1961		

DEBUT DATE	PEAK POS	WKS CHR		ARTIST — Record Title	POP POS	Label & Number

SONS OF THE PIONEERS

Originally a trio consisting of Bob Nolan (b: 4/1/08), Leonard Slye (also known as "Dick Weston" and "Roy Rogers") and Tim Spencer (d: June, 1974). Formed in 1934 and first called the Pioneers; recorded for Decca in 1934. Brothers Karl (guitar) and Hugh Farr (fiddle) were added in 1936. In the film "Rhythm On The Range" in 1936. Rogers and Spencer left in 1937, replaced by Lloyd Perryman and Pat Brady. Spencer returned shortly thereafter. Group appeared in many films. Nolan wrote "Cool Water" and "Tumbling Tumbleweeds". Elected to the Country Music Hall Of Fame in 1980. Also see Roy Rogers.

DEBUT DATE	PEAK POS	WKS CHR		ARTIST — Record Title	POP POS	Label & Number
10/06/45	4	2	1	**Stars And Stripes On Iwo Jima**		Victor 20-1724
6/29/46	6	1	2	**No One To Cry To**		Victor 20-1868
2/15/47	5	1	3	**Baby Doll**		Victor 20-2086
3/08/47	4	1	4	**Cool Water** .... [R]		Decca 46027
				first recorded by "Sons" in 1936; also on flip side of Victor 1724		
7/12/47	5	1	5	**Cigareetes, Whuskey, And Wild Wild Women** ..		Victor 20-2199
7/26/47	4	2	6	**Tear Drops In My Heart**		Victor 20-2276
8/21/48	11	1	7	Tumbling Tumbleweeds .... [R]		Victor 20-1904
				Juke Box #11; first charted by "Sons" in 1934		
9/04/48	7	11	8	**Cool Water** .... [R]		Decca 46027
				Best Seller #7 / Juke Box #11		
2/19/49	12	1	9	My Best To You		Victor 20-2199
				Juke Box #12		
9/10/49	10	1	10	**Room Full Of Roses**	26	Victor 21-0065
				Juke Box #10 - 45 rpm: 48-0060		

TOMMY SOSEBEA

Born in Greenville, South Carolina.

DEBUT DATE	PEAK POS	WKS CHR		ARTIST — Record Title	POP POS	Label & Number
3/14/53	7	2	1	**Till I Waltz Again With You**		Coral 60916
				Jockey #7		

JOE SOUTH

Born on 2/28/40 in Atlanta. Successful Nashville session guitarist/songwriter in the mid-60s. Wrote "Down In The Boondocks", "Hush" and "Rose Garden".

DEBUT DATE	PEAK POS	WKS CHR		ARTIST — Record Title	POP POS	Label & Number
8/28/61	16	6	1	You're The Reason	87	Fairlane 21006
				JOE SOUTH & THE BELIEVERS:		
10/04/69	27	9	2	Don't It Make You Want To Go Home	41	Capitol 2592
1/31/70	56	5	3	Walk A Mile In My Shoes	12	Capitol 2704

J.D. SOUTHER

John David Souther, born in Detroit; raised in Amarillo, Texas. Worked with Longbranch Pennywhistle. Teamed with Chris Hillman and Richie Furay as the Souther-Hillman-Furay Band in 1974.

DEBUT DATE	PEAK POS	WKS CHR		ARTIST — Record Title	POP POS	Label & Number
12/01/79+	60	10	1	You're Only Lonely	7	Columbia 11079
10/16/82	27	11	2	Sometimes You Just Can't Win		Asylum 69948
				LINDA RONSTADT & JOHN DAVID SOUTHER		

SOUTHERN ASHE

Columbus, Georgia band.

DEBUT DATE	PEAK POS	WKS CHR		ARTIST — Record Title	POP POS	Label & Number
8/15/81	80	3	1	Paradise		Soundwaves 4641

SOUTHERN PACIFIC

Band formed in Los Angeles in 1985. Consisted of John McFee (formerly with The Doobie Brothers; guitar, fiddle), Stu Cook (formerly with Creedence Clearwater Revival; bass), Keith Knudsen (formerly with The Doobie Brothers; drums), Kurt Howell (keyboards), and lead vocalist Tim Goodman. Goodman replaced by David Jenkins (formerly with Pablo Cruise) in 1986.

DEBUT DATE	PEAK POS	WKS CHR		ARTIST — Record Title	POP POS	Label & Number
6/01/85	60	6	1	Someone's Gonna Love Me Tonight		Warner 29020
8/03/85	14	19	2	Thing About You		Warner 28943
				guest vocal: Emmylou Harris; written by Tom Petty		
11/16/85+	18	19	3	Pefect Stranger		Warner 28870
4/19/86	9	17	4	**Reno Bound**		Warner 28722
8/09/86	17	17	5	A Girl Like Emmylou		Warner 28647
12/06/86+	37	13	6	Killbilly Hill		Warner 28554
3/21/87	26	14	7	Don't Let Go Of My Heart		Warner 28408
4/09/88	14	18	8	Midnight Highway		Warner 27952
8/06/88	2²	24	9	**New Shade Of Blue**		Warner 27790
12/10/88+	5	19	10	**Honey I Dare You**		Warner 27691

SOUTHERN REIGN

Group features lead vocals by Patsy McKeehan and Jeff Crocker.

DEBUT DATE	PEAK POS	WKS CHR		ARTIST — Record Title	POP POS	Label & Number
10/25/86	80	3	1	The Auction		Regal 1
1/10/87	62	7	2	15 To 33		MCA 17441

DEBUT DATE	PEAK POS	WKS CHR	ARTIST — Record Title	POP POS	Label & Number
			SOUTHERN REIGN — Continued		
5/02/87	79	4	3 Summer On The Mississippi		Regal 3
9/19/87	61	6	4 Cheap Motels (And One Night Stands)		Step One 377
5/28/88	60	5	5 Please Don't Leave Me Now...............................		Step One 385
10/15/88	80	3	6 There's A Telephone Ringing (In An Empty House)		Step One 391
			RED SOVINE ★★**141**★★		
			Born Woodrow Wilson Sovine on 7/17/18 in Charleston, West Virginia; had a heart attack while driving and died on 4/4/80 (61). Worked on WCHS-Charleston with Jim Pike's Carolina Tarheels from 1935. Own band, the Echo Valley Boys, in 1947. On the Louisiana Hayride from 1949-54. On the Grand Ole Opry from 1954. Known as "The Old Syrup Sopper" from a radio series he did for Johnny Fair Syrup.		
3/26/55	14	2	1 Are You Mine? .... **RED SOVINE & GOLDIE HILL** Best Seller #14		Decca 29411
3/24/56	15	1	2 What Would You Do If Jesus Came To Your House... Jockey #15		Decca 29825
1/11/64	22	12	3 Dream House For Sale.................................		Starday 650
11/20/65+	1⁶	22	4 **Giddyup Go**..[S]	82	Starday 737
4/30/66	47	2	5 Long Night		Starday 757
11/12/66	44	8	6 Class Of 49		Starday 779
2/18/67	17	12	7 I Didn't Jump The Fence		Starday 794
7/01/67	33	10	8 In Your Heart/		Starday 811
7/29/67	9	16	9 **Phantom 309** ....[S]		Starday 811
12/09/67+	33	13	10 Tell Maude I Slipped		Starday 823
7/20/68	63	2	11 Loser Making Good..................................		Starday 842
10/12/68	61	6	12 Normally, Norma Loves Me		Starday 852
8/02/69	62	7	13 Who Am I		Starday 872
4/18/70	52	10	14 I Know You're Married, But I Love You Still......		Starday 889
7/25/70	54	7	15 Freightliner Fever		Starday 896
7/06/74	16	16	16 It'll Come Back		Chart 5220
11/02/74	58	9	17 Can I Keep Him Daddy		Chart 5230
8/30/75	91	4	18 Daddy's Girl... above 2: with The Girls		Chart 7507
12/27/75+	47	10	19 Phantom 309 ....[R]		Starday 101
6/19/76	1³	13	20● **Teddy Bear** ....[S]	40	Starday 142
9/18/76	45	5	21 Little Joe ....[S]	102	Starday 144
12/11/76	96	2	22 Last Goodbye ....[S]		Starday 147
2/19/77	98	2	23 Just Gettin' By ....[S]		Starday 148
12/03/77	92	5	24 Woman Behind The Man Behind The Wheel		Gusto 169
3/11/78	70	5	25 Lay Down Sally.. #3 pop hit for Eric Clapton in 1978		Gusto 180
5/27/78	77	5	26 The Days Of Me And You............................		Gusto 188
4/12/80	74	5	27 The Little Family Soldier............................[S]		Gusto 9028
7/12/80	89	3	28 It'll Come Back ....[R]		Gusto 9030
			RED SOVINE & WEBB PIERCE:		
12/17/55+	1⁴	25	29 **Why Baby Why** .... Jockey #1(4) / Best Seller #1(1) / Juke Box #1(1)		Decca 29755
4/21/56	5	12	30 **Little Rosa/** Best Seller #5 / Jockey #5 / Juke Box #5		
5/19/56	5	8	31 **Hold Everything** .... Juke Box #5		Decca 29876
			ROGER SOVINE		
			Born in Eleanor, West Virginia; son of Red Sovine.		
5/04/68	47	8	1 Culman, Alabam		Imperial 66291
11/08/69	68	5	2 Little Bitty Nitty Gritty Dirt Town		Imperial 66398
			SISSY SPACEK		
			Singer/actress born Mary Elizabeth Spacek in Quitman, Texas on 12/25/49 . Won Academy Award portraying Loretta Lynn in the film "Coal Miner's Daughter".		
4/26/80	24	11	1 Coal Miner's Daughter................................ from the "Coal Miner's Daughter" soundtrack		MCA 41221
8/20/83	15	17	2 Lonely But Only For You		Atln. Am. 99847
1/21/84	57	9	3 If I Can Just Get Through The Night		Atln. Am. 99801

DEBUT DATE	PEAK POS	WKS CHR	ARTIST — Record Title	POP POS	Label & Number
			SISSY SPACEK — Continued		
5/05/84	**79**	3	4 If You Could Only See Me Now		Atln. Am. 99773
			BILLIE JO SPEARS ★★99★★		
			Born Billie Jean Spears on 1/14/37 in Beaumont, Texas. Worked on the "Louisiana Hayride" at age 13. Moved to Nashville in 1964. Very popular in England since 1977.		
11/30/68+	**48**	10	1 He's Got More Love In His Little Finger		Capitol 2331
4/19/69	**4**	13	2 **Mr. Walker, It's All Over**	80	Capitol 2436
9/13/69	**43**	7	3 Stepchild		Capitol 2593
12/20/69+	**40**	10	4 Daddy, I Love You		Capitol 2690
7/25/70	**17**	14	5 Marty Gray		Capitol 2844
11/28/70	**30**	9	6 I Stayed Long Enough		Capitol 2964
			written by Tammy Wynette		
3/20/71	**23**	12	7 It Could 'A Been Me		Capitol 3055
2/12/72	**68**	3	8 Souvenirs And California Mem'rys		Capitol 3258
10/05/74	**80**	5	9 See The Funny Little Clown		United Art. 549
			#9 pop hit for Bobby Goldsboro in 1964		
2/01/75	**1**¹	17	10 **Blanket On The Ground**	78	United Art. 584
7/12/75	**20**	14	11 Stay Away From The Apple Tree...................		United Art. 653
11/01/75+	**20**	15	12 Silver Wings And Golden Rings		United Art. 712
2/28/76	**5**	16	13 **What I've Got In Mind**		United Art. 764
5/01/76	**29**	11	14 On The Rebound		United Art. 797
			DEL REEVES & BILLIE JO SPEARS		
6/19/76	**5**	16	15 **Misty Blue**		United Art. 813
			#3 pop hit for Dorothy Moore in 1976		
8/07/76	**42**	8	16 Teardrops Will Kiss The Morning Dew..............		United Art. 832
			DEL REEVES & BILLIE JO SPEARS		
10/23/76	**18**	12	17 Never Did Like Whiskey		United Art. 880
1/29/77	**11**	13	18 I'm Not Easy		United Art. 935
5/07/77	**8**	13	19 **If You Want Me**.......................................		United Art. 985
8/20/77	**18**	13	20 Too Much Is Not Enough..............................		United Art. 1041
1/14/78	**18**	11	21 Lonely Hearts Club.....................................		United Art. 1127
4/15/78	**17**	12	22 I've Got To Go		United Art. 1190
8/12/78	**16**	12	23 '57 Chevrolet...		United Art. 1229
11/11/78+	**24**	13	24 Love Ain't Gonna Wait For Us		United Art. 1251
2/24/79	**60**	6	25 Yesterday...		United Art. 1274
			#1 pop hit for The Beatles in 1965		
4/21/79	**21**	11	26 I Will Survive		United Art. 1292
			#1 pop hit for Gloria Gaynor in 1979		
8/04/79	**23**	12	27 Livin' Our Love Together...............................		United Art. 1309
11/03/79+	**21**	14	28 Rainy Days And Stormy Nights.......................		United Art. 1326
2/23/80	**15**	13	29 Standing Tall...		United Art. 1336
6/28/80	**39**	9	30 Natural Attraction.......................................		United Art. 1358
1/10/81	**13**	13	31 Your Good Girl's Gonna Go Bad		Liberty 1395
5/02/81	**58**	5	32 What The World Needs Now Is Love.................		Liberty 1409
			#7 pop hit for Jackie DeShannon in 1965		
1/07/84	**39**	13	33 Midnight Blue/		
4/07/84	**51**	8	34 Midnight Love		Parliament 1801
			BOBBY SPEARS - see LINDA CASSADY		
			RONNIE SPEEKS		
1/17/81	**93**	2	1 Baby Loved Me		Dimension 1014
			TEDDY SPENCER		
8/20/88	**82**	3	1 Grass Is Greener		Oak 1052
			MICHAEL SPITZ		
7/25/81	**93**	2	1 Old Fashioned Lover......................................		50 States 83
			SPRINGER BROTHERS		
2/02/80	**87**	5	1 What's A Nice Girl Like You (Doin' In A Love Like This)..		Elektra 46575
5/10/80	**89**	2	2 Cathy's Clown		Elektra 46622
			#1 pop hit for The Everly Brothers in 1960		

DEBUT DATE	PEAK POS	WKS CHR	ARTIST — Record Title	POP POS	Label & Number
			BOBBY LEE SPRINGFIELD		
			Born in 1953 in Amarillo, Texas. Moved to Nashville while a teenager. Wrote "Some Memories Just Won't Die" for Marty Robbins and "Heavenbound" for the Oak Ridge Boys.		
3/26/83	86	3	1 A Different Woman Every Night		Kat Fam. 03562
			shown only as: **BOBBY SPRINGFIELD**		
6/13/87	75	5	2 Hank Drank		Epic 07110
9/05/87	66	5	3 Chain Gang		Epic 07310
			THE SPRINGFIELDS		
			English folk trio: Dusty and brother Tom Springfield and Tim Feild.		
8/25/62	16	10	1 Silver Threads And Golden Needles	20	Philips 40038
			SPURZZ		
			5-member Nashville based band, backed Freddy Weller; formerly known as Blue Creek.		
8/23/80	76	4	1 Cowboy Stomp!		Epic 50911
			BILLY STACK		
2/25/78	82	5	1 Love Can Make The Children Sing		Caprice 2045
6/24/78	100	1	2 Boogiewoogieitis		Caprice 2048
5/12/79	83	3	3 No Greater Love.................................		Caprice 2058
			BOBBI STAFF		
			Born in 1946 in Kingston, North Carolina. She appeared on Arthur Smith's Talent Show while in 3rd grade. Toured Europe with the U.S.O. in 1958.		
6/25/66	31	6	1 Chicken Feed		RCA 8833
			JIM STAFFORD		
			Born on 1/16/44 in Eloise, Florida. Worked local clubs. Moved to Nashville after high school graduation. First record was produced by Lobo. Has a one-man band act. Co-host of "Those Amazing Animals" TV show from 1980-81.		
3/02/74	66	8	1 ●Spiders & Snakes	3	MGM 14648
5/18/74	64	7	2 My Girl Bill ....[N]	12	MGM 14718
8/17/74	57	6	3 Wildwood Weed ....[N]	7	MGM 14737
1/10/81	65	6	4 Cow Patti....................................[N]	102	Warner 49611
			from the Clint Eastwood film "Any Which Way You Can"		
11/20/82	61	8	5 What Mama Don't Know ....[N]		Town House 1062
2/04/84	67	9	6 Little Bits And Pieces		Columbia 04339
			JO STAFFORD		
			Born on 11/12/20 in Coalinga, California. Member of Tommy Dorsey's vocal group, the Pied Pipers, 1940-42. Married to orchestra leader, Paul Weston. Also see Red Ingle.		
9/20/47	5	2	1 **Feudin' And Fightin'**	7	Capitol 443
			with The Starlighters and Paul Weston's Orchestra		
			TERRY STAFFORD		
			Born in Hollis, Oklahoma; raised in Amarillo, Texas. Worked in the Eugene Nelson band as a teenager. Moved to California in 1960, played with the Lively Ones and the Surfmen. Appeared in the film "Wild Wheels". Wrote "Big In Vegas" for Buck Owens.		
8/25/73	35	12	1 Say, Has Anybody Seen My Sweet Gypsy Rose/		
			#3 pop hit for Tony Orlando & Dawn in 1973		
12/01/73+	31	14	2 Amarillo By Morning		Atlantic 4006
3/23/74	24	13	3 Captured		Atlantic 4015
8/24/74	69	6	4 Stop If You Love Me................................		Atlantic 4026
3/12/77	94	4	5 It Sure Is Bad To Love Her.............................		Casino 113
			KAREN STALEY		
			Singer/songwriter, wrote Patty Loveless' hits "Lonely Days, Lonely Nights" and "Wicked Ways" and the Michael Martin Murphey/Holly Dunn duet "A Face In The Crowd".		
12/24/88+	86	4	1 So Good To Be In Love		MCA 53470
			JOE STAMPLEY ★★43★★		
			Born on 6/6/43 in Springhill, Louisiana. First recorded for Imperial in 1957. Lead singer of The Uniques in the late 60s. Staff writer for Gallico Music.		
2/20/71	74	2	1 Take Time To Know Her		Dot 17363
			#11 pop hit for Percy Sledge in 1968		
2/12/72	75	2	2 Hello Operator		Dot 17400
6/17/72	9	17	3 **If You Touch Me (You've Got To Love Me)**		Dot 17421
11/11/72+	1¹	15	4 **Soul Song**	37	Dot 17442
3/24/73	7	14	5 **Bring It On Home (To Your Woman)**		Dot 17452
8/18/73	12	16	6 Too Far Gone		Dot 17469
12/08/73+	3	17	7 **I'm Still Loving You**.................................		Dot 17485

DEBUT DATE	PEAK POS	WKS CHR	ARTIST — Record Title	POP POS	Label & Number
			JOE STAMPLEY — Continued		
5/04/74	11	13	8 How Lucky Can One Man Be		Dot 17502
9/14/74	5	16	9 **Take Me Home To Somewhere**		Dot 17522
1/18/75	8	11	10 Penny..		ABC/Dot 17537
3/01/75	1¹	14	11 **Roll On Big Mama**		Epic 50075
5/10/75	41	11	12 Unchained Melody		ABC/Dot 17551
			#1 pop hit for Les Baxter & His Orchestra in 1955		
6/07/75	11	13	13 Dear Woman		Epic 50114
8/30/75	70	8	14 Cry Like A Baby		ABC/Dot 17575
			#2 pop hit for The Box Tops in 1968		
9/20/75	12	13	15 Billy, Get Me A Woman		Epic 50147
12/20/75+	25	10	16 She's Helping Me Get Over Loving You..............		Epic 50179
1/03/76	61	8	17 You Make Life Easy		ABC/Dot 17599
3/13/76	43	8	18 Sheik Of Chicago..................................		Epic 50199
4/24/76	1¹	16	19 **All These Things**		ABC/Dot 17624
5/22/76	43	9	20 Was It Worth It		Epic 50224
7/24/76	16	11	21 The Night Time And My Baby		ABC/Dot 17642
8/07/76	18	14	22 Whiskey Talkin'		Epic 50259
10/30/76	12	12	23 Everything I Own		ABC/Dot 17654
			#5 pop hit for Bread in 1972		
12/25/76+	11	15	24 There She Goes Again		Epic 50316
4/02/77	26	12	25 She's Long Legged.................................		Epic 50361
7/02/77	15	13	26 Baby, I Love You So		Epic 50410
10/22/77	14	13	27 Everyday I Have To Cry Some		Epic 50453
			#45 pop hit for Arthur Alexander in 1975		
3/18/78	6	16	28 **Red Wine And Blue Memories**......................		Epic 50517
7/15/78	6	14	29 **If You've Got Ten Minutes (Let's Fall In Love)**		Epic 50575
11/04/78+	5	16	30 **Do You Ever Fool Around**		Epic 50626
4/28/79	12	14	31 I Don't Lie		Epic 50694
9/01/79	9	14	32 **Put Your Clothes Back On**		Epic 50754
3/15/80	17	12	33 After Hours..		Epic 50854
6/28/80	32	11	34 Haven't I Loved You Somewhere Before		Epic 50893
10/04/80	18	15	35 There's Another Woman............................		Epic 50934
1/24/81	9	15	36 **I'm Gonna Love You Back To Loving Me Again**...		Epic 50972
5/23/81	18	15	37 Whiskey Chasin'		Epic 02097
10/24/81	62	5	38 All These Things/ [R]		Epic 02533
12/05/81+	41	10	39 Let's Get Together And Cry		
3/20/82	18	17	40 I'm Goin' Hurtin'		Epic 02791
7/17/82	30	12	41 I Didn't Know You Could Break A Broken Heart .		Epic 03016
10/16/82+	25	15	42 Backslidin'.		Epic 03290
2/19/83	24	14	43 Finding You		Epic 03558
6/18/83	12	18	44 Poor Side Of Town.................................		Epic 03966
			#1 pop hit for Johnny Rivers in 1966		
10/29/83+	8	20	45 **Double Shot (Of My Baby's Love)**		Epic 04173
			#17 pop hit for the Swingin' Medallions in 1966		
2/11/84	29	16	46 Brown Eyed Girl		Epic 04366
			#10 pop hit for Van Morrison in 1967		
5/05/84	39	10	47 Memory Lane		Epic 04446
			JOE STAMPLEY & JESSICA BOUCHER		
7/06/85	67	7	48 When Something Is Wrong With My Baby		Epic 05405
			#42 pop hit for Sam & Dave in 1967		
9/21/85	47	10	49 I'll Still Be Loving You		Epic 05592
2/01/86	72	6	50 When You Were Blue And I Was Green		Epic 05758
7/30/88	56	6	51 Cry Baby		Evergreen 1075
			MOE BANDY & JOE STAMPLEY:		
7/14/79	1¹	16	52 **Just Good Ol' Boys**		Columbia 11027
11/17/79+	7	14	53 **Holding The Bag**...................................		Columbia 11147
4/12/80	11	15	54 Tell Ole I Ain't Here, He Better Get On Home		Columbia 11244
3/14/81	10	15	55 **Hey Joe (Hey Moe)**		Columbia 60508
8/01/81	12	14	56 Honky Tonk Queen		Columbia 02198
6/02/84	8	16	57 **Where's The Dress**................................. [N]		Columbia 04477
			parody about pop singer Boy George		

DEBUT DATE	PEAK POS	WKS CHR	ARTIST — Record Title	POP POS	Label & Number
			JOE STAMPLEY — Continued		
10/13/84	**36**	10	58 The Boy's Night Out		Columbia 04601
1/26/85	**48**	10	59 Daddy's Honky Tonk		Columbia 04756
4/20/85	**58**	8	60 Still On A Roll		Columbia 04843
			STANLEY BROTHERS		
			Bluegrass duo of Carter Glen (b: 8/27/25, McClure, VA; d: 12/1/66) and brother Ralph Edmond Stanley (b: 2/25/27, Stratton, VA). Formed own band, the Clinch Mountain Boys, in 1946. First recorded for Rich-R-Tone in 1947.		
3/21/60	**17**	12	1 How Far To Little Rock .... [N]		King 5306
			BUDDY STARCHER		
			Born on 3/16/10 in Ripley, West Virginia. Worked on WFBR-Baltimore in 1928. Worked as a deejay on WCAU, WIBG-Philadelphia. Own band from 1937. Manager of WMBM-Miami.		
2/12/49	**8**	1	1 **I Still Write Your Name**..........................		Four Star 1145
			shown as: **BUDDY STARCHIN** Juke Box #8		
4/09/66	**2**[1]	15	2 **History Repeats Itself** .... [S]	*39*	Boone 1038
			DONNA STARK		
6/07/80	**92**	2	1 Why Don't You Believe Me........................		RCI 2344
			STARLAND VOCAL BAND		
			Pop quartet: Bill and wife Taffy Danoff, John Carroll and Margot Chapman. Bill and Taffy had fronted "Fat City" folk quintet.		
7/17/76	**94**	2	1 ●Afternoon Delight	*1*	Windsong 10588
			KAY STARR - see TENNESSEE ERNIE FORD		
			KENNY STARR		
			Born Kenneth Trebbe on 9/21/52 in Topeka; raised in Burlingame, Kansas. Own band, the Rockin' Rebels, at age 9. Toured with Loretta Lynn from 1968-75.		
4/07/73	**56**	6	1 That's A Whole Lotta Lovin' (You Give Me)		MCA 40023
10/20/73	**97**	4	2 Ev'ryday Woman.....................................		MCA 40124
3/01/75	**89**	3	3 Put Another Notch In Your Belt		MCA 40350
11/08/75+	**2**[2]	15	4 **The Blind Man In The Bleachers**	*58*	MCA 40474
3/13/76	**26**	10	5 Tonight I'll Face The Man (Who Made It Happen).		MCA 40524
7/04/76	**73**	5	6 The Calico Cat/		
8/21/76	**75**	3	7 Victims		MCA 40580
11/13/76	**58**	8	8 I Just Can't (Turn My Habit Into Love)		MCA 40637
2/12/77	**43**	8	9 Me And The Elephant		MCA 40672
8/27/77	**64**	7	10 Old Time Lovin'		MCA 40769
11/19/77+	**25**	14	11 Hold Tight..		MCA 40817
4/22/78	**72**	5	12 The Rest Of My Life...............................		MCA 40880
7/01/78	**70**	6	13 Slow Drivin'		MCA 40922
			LUCILLE STARR		
			Born in St. Boniface, Canada. Teamed with husband Bob Regan as the Canadian Sweethearts.		
9/30/67	**72**	2	1 Too Far Gone		Epic 10205
6/08/68	**63**	5	2 Is It Love?		Epic 10317
			PENNY STARR - see PENNY DeHAVEN		
			THE STATLER BROTHERS ★★32★★		
			Group from Staunton, Virginia, formed as the Kingsmen in 1955. Consisted of Lew DeWitt (b: 3/8/38; tenor), Don Reid (b: 6/5/45; lead), Philip Balsley (b: 8/8/39; baritone) and Harold Reid (b: 8/21/39; bass). Worked with Johnny Cash from 1963-71. DeWitt, who wrote their first hit "Flowers On The Wall", retired from the group in 1982; replaced by Jimmy Fortune. Also recorded under comic persona as Lester "Roadhog" Moran & His Cadillac Cowboys.		
9/25/65+	**2**[4]	27	1 **Flowers On The Wall**	*4*	Columbia 43315
6/18/66	**30**	11	2 The Right One		Columbia 43624
11/26/66+	**37**	10	3 That'll Be The Day		Columbia 43868
5/13/67	**10**	14	4 **Ruthless**		Columbia 44070
9/02/67	**10**	14	5 **You Can't Have Your Kate And Edith, Too**		Columbia 44245
4/27/68	**60**	3	6 Jump For Joy		Columbia 44480
10/19/68	**75**	2	7 Sissy/		
1/04/69	**60**	3	8 I Am The Boy		Columbia 44608
11/21/70+	**9**	17	9 **Bed Of Rose's**	*58*	Mercury 73141

DEBUT DATE	PEAK POS	WKS CHR		ARTIST — Record Title	POP POS	Label & Number
				THE STATLER BROTHERS — Continued		
4/24/71	**19**	13	10	New York City		Mercury 73194
8/21/71	**13**	14	11	Pictures..		Mercury 73229
12/11/71+	**23**	13	12	You Can't Go Home		Mercury 73253
3/11/72	**2**⁴	15	13	**Do You Remember These**	*105*	Mercury 73275
8/19/72	**6**	15	14	**The Class Of '57**..		Mercury 73315
2/03/73	**20**	11	15	Monday Morning Secretary		Mercury 73360
6/09/73	**29**	9	16	Woman Without A Home		Mercury 73392
9/15/73	**26**	12	17	Carry Me Back..		Mercury 73415
1/12/74	**22**	11	18	Whatever Happened To Randolph Scott............		Mercury 73448
6/08/74	**31**	13	19	Thank You World		Mercury 73485
11/09/74+	**15**	14	20	Susan When She Tried		Mercury 73625
3/01/75	**31**	11	21	All American Girl..		Mercury 73665
6/21/75	**3**	19	22	**I'll Go To My Grave Loving You**....................	93	Mercury 73687
1/03/76	**39**	9	23	How Great Thou Art		Mercury 73732
4/17/76	**13**	13	24	Your Picture In The Paper		Mercury 73785
10/02/76	**10**	14	25	**Thank God I've Got You**		Mercury 73846
1/15/77	**10**	13	26	**The Movies**...		Mercury 73877
4/30/77	**8**	13	27	**I Was There**		Mercury 73906
8/13/77	**18**	12	28	Silver Medals And Sweet Memories..................		Mercury 55000
12/03/77+	**17**	13	29	Some I Wrote..		Mercury 55013
3/18/78	**1**²	17	30	**Do You Know You Are My Sunshine**		Mercury 55022
8/05/78	**3**	14	31	**Who Am I To Say**		Mercury 55037
11/18/78+	**5**	15	32	**The Official Historian On Shirley Jean Berrell**		Mercury 55048
3/31/79	**7**	12	33	**How To Be A Country Star**............................		Mercury 55057
7/07/79	**11**	13	34	Here We Are Again		Mercury 55066
10/27/79	**10**	13	35	**Nothing As Original As You**		Mercury 57007
1/19/80	**8**	14	36	**(I'll Even Love You) Better Than I Did Then** ...		Mercury 57012
7/12/80	**5**	16	37	**Charlotte's Web**.. from the film "Smokey & The Bandit 2"		Mercury 57031
11/08/80+	**13**	14	38	Don't Forget Yourself...................................		Mercury 57037
3/28/81	**35**	9	39	In The Garden		Mercury 57048
6/13/81	**5**	18	40	**Don't Wait On Me**		Mercury 57051
10/24/81+	**12**	16	41	Years Ago		Mercury 57059
3/13/82	**3**	18	42	**You'll Be Back (Every Night In My Dreams)**		Mercury 76142
7/03/82	**7**	16	43	Whatever		Mercury 76162
10/23/82+	**17**	16	44	A Child Of The Fifties		Mercury 76184
4/16/83	**2**¹	19	45	**Oh Baby Mine (I Get So Lonely)** .... #2 pop hit for The Four Knights in 1954		Mercury 811488
8/13/83	**9**	17	46	**Guilty**...		Mercury 812988
12/10/83+	**1**¹	23	47	**Elizabeth**...		Mercury 814881
4/21/84	**3**	21	48	**Atlanta Blue**		Mercury 818700
8/18/84	**8**	23	49	**One Takes The Blame**.....................................		Mercury 880130
12/08/84+	**1**¹	20	50	**My Only Love**		Mercury 880411
4/20/85	**3**	20	51	**Hello Mary Lou** .... #9 pop hit for Ricky Nelson in 1961		Mercury 880685
8/24/85	**1**¹	25	52	**Too Much On My Heart**.................................		Mercury 884016
1/11/86	**8**	21	53	Sweeter And Sweeter		Mercury 884317
5/17/86	**5**	24	54	**Count On Me**		Mercury 884721
9/27/86	**36**	12	55	Only You .... #5 pop hit for The Platters in 1955		Mercury 888042
12/13/86+	**7**	21	56	**Forever**..		Mercury 888219
6/13/87	**10**	20	57	I'll Be The One		Mercury 888650
10/31/87	**42**	13	58	Maple Street Mem'ries....................................		Mercury 888920
2/20/88	**15**	23	59	The Best I Know How......................................		Mercury 870164
6/11/88	**27**	19	60	Am I Crazy?..		Mercury 870442
10/15/88+	**12**	22	61	Let's Get Started If We're Gonna Break My Heart..		Mercury 870681

DEBUT DATE	PEAK POS	WKS CHR	ARTIST — Record Title	POP POS	Label & Number
			DARRELL STATLER R. Darrell Staedtler, born on 12/27/40 in Llano, Texas. Staff songwriter for the Wilburn Brothers, Chappell Music, and others since 1963.		
9/06/69	40	7	1 Blue Collar Job...		Dot 17275
			RED STEAGALL Born Russell Steagall on 12/22/37 in Gainesville, Texas. Guitarist and mandolin player since age 15, when he was recovering from polio. Moved to California in 1965. Staff writer for Tree and Combine Music. First recorded for Dot in 1969. Rodeo rider and breeds quarterhorses. Discovered Reba McEntire.		
1/15/72	31	11	1 Party Dolls And Wine		Capitol 3244
11/25/72+	22	12	2 Somewhere My Love.................................... #9 pop hit for Ray Conniff & The Singers in 1966		Capitol 3461
4/14/73	51	5	3 True Love... #3 pop hit for Bing Crosby & Grace Kelly in 1956		Capitol 3562
7/14/73	41	8	4 If You've Got The Time		Capitol 3651
10/06/73	87	7	5 The Fiddle Man.......................................		Capitol 3724
1/26/74	93	5	6 This Just Ain't My Day (For Lettin' Darlin' Down)..		Capitol 3797
3/02/74	54	10	7 I Gave Up Good Mornin' Darling...................		Capitol 3825
7/20/74	52	9	8 Finer Things In Life		Capitol 3913
10/26/74+	17	17	9 Someone Cares For You		Capitol 3965
3/22/75	62	9	10 She Worshipped Me		Capitol 4042
2/28/76	11	15	11 Lone Star Beer And Bob Wills Music...............		ABC/Dot 17610
6/19/76	29	11	12 Truck Drivin' Man		ABC/Dot 17634
9/25/76	45	9	13 Rosie (Do You Wanna Talk It Over)................		ABC/Dot 17653
12/25/76+	59	8	14 Her L-O-V-E's Gone................................		ABC/Dot 17670
3/12/77	53	8	15 I Left My Heart In San Francisco................... #19 pop hit for Tony Bennett in 1962		ABC/Dot 17684
8/13/77	90	4	16 Freckles Brown......................................		ABC/Dot 17709
11/12/77	72	8	17 The Devil Ain't A Lonely Woman's Friend		ABC/Dot 17726
3/11/78	63	9	18 Hang On Feelin'/		
		4	19 Bob's Got A Swing Band In Heaven		ABC 12337
9/22/79	41	9	20 Goodtime Charlie's Got The Blues................. #9 pop hit for Danny O'Keefe in 1972		Elektra 46527
2/09/80	31	9	21 3 Chord Country Song...............................		Elektra 46590
5/10/80	49	8	22 Dim The Lights And Pour The Wine................		Elektra 46633
8/23/80	30	12	23 Hard Hat Days And Honky Tonk Nights............		Elektra 47014
			JUNE STEARNS Born Agnes June Stearns on 4/5/39 in Albany, New York. Worked on the Midwestern Hayride from 1957-58. Appeared on the Roy Acuff Show and the Grand Ole Opry from 1960-65. Recorded with Lefty Frizzell as "Agnes & Orville" on Columbia.		
4/27/68	47	12	1 Empty House...		Columbia 44483
9/14/68	57	5	2 Where He Stops Nobody Knows		Columbia 44575
10/19/68	21	8	3 Jackson Ain't A Very Big Town...................... JOHNNY DUNCAN & JUNE STEARNS		Columbia 44656
1/04/69	53	6	4 Walking Midnight Road		Columbia 44695
3/15/69	74	3	5 Back To Back (We're Strangers)...................... JOHNNY DUNCAN & JUNE STEARNS		Columbia 44752
6/07/69	70	4	6 What Makes You So Different		Columbia 44852
12/27/69	58	4	7 Drifting Too Far (From Your Arms)...................		Columbia 45042
9/26/70	41	6	8 Tyin' Strings		Decca 32726
6/12/71	57	8	9 Sweet Baby On My Mind		Decca 32828
10/16/71	56	8	10 Your Kind Of Lovin'.................................		Decca 32876
			RIC STEEL		
12/05/87+	57	9	1 The Radio Song		Panache 1001
6/18/88	59	7	2 Whose Baby Are You		Panache 1002
			LARRY STEELE		
1/15/66	43	3	1 I Ain't Crying Mister.................................		K-Ark 659
4/06/68	75	2	2 Hard Times .... LARRY STEELE & THE WRANGLERS		K-Ark 802
11/09/74	90	5	3 Daylight Losing Time.................................		Airstream 004

DEBUT DATE	PEAK POS	WKS CHR	ARTIST — Record Title	POP POS	Label & Number
			KEITH STEGALL		
			Born in Wichita Falls, Texas in 1955. Cousin of Johnny Horton. Pianist from age 4; guitarist from age 12. Own band, the Pacesetters, at age 12. Toured overseas with folk group, the Cheerful Givers. Worked as staff writer for CBS Music. In the films "Killing At Hell's Gate" and "Country Gold".		
3/01/80	58	6	1 The Fool Who Fooled Around		Capitol 4835
2/21/81	55	7	2 Anything That Hurts You (Hurts Me)................		Capitol 4967
9/12/81	65	5	3 Won't You Be My Baby............................		Capitol 5034
3/13/82	64	5	4 In Love With Loving You		EMI America 8107
5/12/84	25	16	5 I Want To Go Somewhere		Epic 04442
9/22/84	19	21	6 Whatever Turns You On		Epic 04590
2/16/85	13	18	7 California		Epic 04771
6/15/85	10	22	8 **Pretty Lady**		Epic 04934
11/02/85	45	10	9 Feed The Fire		Epic 05643
3/01/86	36	13	10 I Think I'm In Love...............................		Epic 05815
11/15/86	52	9	11 Ole Rock And Roller (With A Country Heart)		Epic 06418
			STENMARK-MUELLER BAND		
			Salt Lake City based duo: K.J. Stenmark and LynnDee Mueller.		
11/14/87	95	1	1 Lover To Lover.............................		Envelope 7004
			OTT STEPHENS		
			Born on 9/21/41 in Ringold, Georgia.		
1/19/63	15	7	1 Robert E. Lee		Chancellor 107
6/13/64	23	15	2 Be Quiet Mind....................................		Reprise 0272
6/12/65	36	12	3 Enough Man For You		Chart 1205
			EVEN STEVENS		
			Born in Lewiston, Ohio; raised in Cincinnati. Accomplished songwriter often teamed with Eddie Rabbitt and Dan Tyler.		
6/21/75	38	13	1 Let The Little Boy Dream		Elektra 45254
12/20/75+	81	7	2 Huckelberry Pie		Elektra 45292
			EVEN STEVENS/SAMMI SMITH		
10/15/77	97	1	3 The King Of Country Music Meets The Queen Of Rock & Roll		Elektra 45430
			EVEN STEVENS & SHERRY GROOMS		
			GERALDINE STEVENS		
9/13/69	57	3	1 Billy, I've Got To Go To Town......................	117	World Pac. 77927
			answer song to "Ruby, Don't Take Your Love To Town"		
			JEFF STEVENS & THE BULLETS		
			Family vocal trio formed in Alum Creek, West Virginia in 1975. Consisted of brothers Jeff (lead singer, guitar) & Warren Stevens (bass), and cousin Terry Dotson (drums). Originally worked as the Stevens Brothers Band.		
12/27/86+	69	8	1 Darlington County................................		Atln. Am. 99494
			written by Bruce Springsteen		
3/28/87	61	6	2 You're In Love Alone		Atln. Am. 99475
7/18/87	53	8	3 Geronimo's Cadillac..............................		Atln. Am. 99433
			RAY STEVENS ★★**152**★★		
			Born Ray Ragsdale on 1/24/39 in Clarksdale, Georgia. Production work in the mid-60s. Numerous appearances on Andy Williams' TV show in the late 60s. Own TV show in summer of 1970. Featured on "Music Country" TV show from 1973-74. The #1 novelty recording artist of the past 30 years.		
11/01/69	55	6	1 Sunday Mornin' Comin' Down......................	81	Monument 1163
12/27/69+	63	2	2 Have A Little Talk With Myself......................	123	Monument 1171
5/02/70	39	6	3● Everything Is Beautiful	1	Barnaby 2011
12/04/71+	17	13	4 Turn Your Radio On	63	Barnaby 2048
7/14/73	37	11	5 Nashville		Barnaby 5020
4/13/74	3	13	6● **The Streak** .... [N]	1	Barnaby 600
11/30/74+	37	10	7 Everybody Needs A Rainbow		Barnaby 610
3/22/75	3	17	8 **Misty**...	14	Barnaby 614
			written and recorded by Erroll Garner in 1954		
9/27/75	38	11	9 Indian Love Call	68	Barnaby 616
			revival of Paul Whiteman's 1925 hit (POS 3)		
1/03/76	48	8	10 Young Love	93	Barnaby 618
5/01/76	16	13	11 You Are So Beautiful	101	Warner 8198
			#5 pop hit for Joe Cocker in 1975		
8/07/76	27	10	12 Honky Tonk Waltz		Warner 8237

DEBUT DATE	PEAK POS	WKS CHR	ARTIST — Record Title	POP POS	Label & Number
			RAY STEVENS — Continued		
2/19/77	**81**	6	13 Get Crazy With Me		Warner 8318
6/11/77	**44**	9	14 Dixie Hummingbird		Warner 8393
8/12/78	**36**	10	15 Be Your Own Best Friend................................		Warner 8603
4/14/79	**85**	3	16 I Need Your Help Barry Manilow .... [N]	49	Warner 8785
2/09/80	**7**	12	17 **Shriner's Convention** .... [N]	101	RCA 11911
9/13/80	**20**	13	18 Night Games..		RCA 12069
2/14/81	**33**	10	19 One More Last Chance		RCA 12170
2/06/82	**35**	10	20 Written Down In My Heart		RCA 13038
5/22/82	**63**	7	21 Where The Sun Don't Shine		RCA 13207
2/11/84	**64**	8	22 My Dad..		Mercury 818057
12/08/84+	**20**	14	23 Mississippi Squirrel Revival......................... [N]		MCA 52492
3/23/85	**74**	6	24 It's Me Again, Margaret .... [N]		MCA 52548
9/14/85	**45**	14	25 The Haircut Song .... [N]		MCA 52657
1/25/86	**50**	10	26 The Ballad Of The Blue Cyclone .... [N]		MCA 52771
9/13/86	**70**	7	27 People's Court .... [N]		MCA 52924
11/01/86	**63**	6	28 Southern Air .... [N]		MCA 52906
			special guest appearance by Jerry Clower and Minnie Pearl		
5/09/87	**41**	9	29 Would Jesus Wear A Rolex .... [N]		MCA 53101
10/08/88	**88**	2	30 The Day I Tried To Teach Charlene MacKenzie How To Drive .... [N]		MCA 53423
			GARY STEWART ★★154★★		
			Born on 5/28/45 in Letcher County, Kentucky. First recorded for Cory in 1964. In the rock band, The Amps, in the mid-60s. Toured with Charley Pride in 1976.		
11/17/73	**63**	7	1 Ramblin' Man..		RCA 0144
			#2 pop hit for The Allman Brothers Band in 1973		
6/01/74	**10**	18	2 **Drinkin' Thing**		RCA 0281
10/19/74+	**4**	16	3 **Out Of Hand**...		RCA 10061
3/08/75	**1**¹	13	4 **She's Actin' Single (I'm Drinkin' Doubles)**......		RCA 10222
6/21/75	**15**	15	5 You're Not The Woman You Use To Be.............		MCA 40414
10/11/75	**20**	12	6 Flat Natural Born Good-Timin' Man		RCA 10351
1/31/76	**23**	13	7 Oh, Sweet Temptation		RCA 10550
5/22/76	**15**	14	8 In Some Room Above The Street		RCA 10680
11/20/76+	**11**	13	9 Your Place Or Mine......................................		RCA 10833
5/21/77	**16**	12	10 Ten Years Of This		RCA 10957
10/22/77	**26**	13	11 Quits		RCA 11131
3/11/78	**16**	12	12 Whiskey Trip...		RCA 11224
7/22/78	**36**	8	13 Single Again...		RCA 11297
11/25/78+	**41**	9	14 Stone Wall (Around Your Heart)......................		RCA 11416
4/14/79	**66**	5	15 Shady Streets		RCA 11534
7/14/79	**75**	3	16 Mazelle		RCA 11623
6/14/80	**48**	9	17 Cactus And A Rose......................................		RCA 11960
9/27/80	**66**	4	18 Are We Dreamin' The Same Dream/		
		4	19 Roarin'.		RCA 12081
4/11/81	**72**	4	20 Let's Forget That We're Married		RCA 12203
11/07/81	**36**	11	21 She's Got A Drinking Problem		RCA 12343
7/24/82	**83**	4	22 She Sings Amazing Grace		RCA 13261
4/14/84	**75**	7	23 Hey, Bottle Of Whiskey		Red Ash 8403
8/11/84	**64**	7	24 I Got A Bad Attitude.....................................		Red Ash 8406
10/01/88	**63**	7	25 Brand New Whiskey......................................		Hightone 506
12/03/88+	**64**	9	26 An Empty Glass		Hightone 507
			GARY STEWART & DEAN DILLON:		
4/10/82	**41**	11	27 Brotherly Love		RCA 13049
1/08/83	**47**	12	28 Those Were The Days		RCA 13401
4/16/83	**71**	4	29 Smokin' In The Rockies.................................		RCA 13472
			VERNON STEWART		
1/12/63	**17**	6	1 The Way It Feels To Die		Chart 501

DEBUT DATE	PEAK POS	WKS CHR	ARTIST — Record Title	POP POS	Label & Number
			WYNN STEWART ★★121★★		
			Born on 6/7/34 in Morrisville, Missouri; died of a heart attack on 7/17/85 (51). Worked on KWTO-Springfield in 1947. Moved to California in 1949 and recorded for Intro at age 16. Own club and TV series in Las Vegas in the late 50s. With band, the Tourists, in Hacienda Heights, California, in the late 60s.		
7/21/56	14	1	1 Waltz Of The Angels		Capitol 3408
			Jockey #14		
12/28/59+	5	22	2 **Wishful Thinking**..		Challenge 9061
5/30/60	26	2	3 Wrong Company		Challenge 59071
			WYNN STEWART & JAN HOWARD		
12/25/61	18	7	4 Big, Big Love		Challenge 9121
11/24/62	27	3	5 Another Day, Another Dollar		Challenge 9164
11/21/64	30	15	6 Half Of This, Half Of That		Challenge 5271
10/16/65	43	7	7 I Keep Forgettin' That I Forgot About You.........		Capitol 5485
2/25/67	1²	22	8 **It's Such A Pretty World Today**		Capitol 5831
			#1 Easy Listening hit for Andy Russell in 1967		
7/15/67	9	16	9 **'Cause I Have You/**		
8/05/67	68	3	10 That's The Only Way To Cry		Capitol 5937
11/11/67+	7	16	11 **Love's Gonna Happen To Me**		Capitol 2012
4/20/68	10	13	12 **Something Pretty**		Capitol 2137
8/24/68	16	11	13 In Love..		Capitol 2240
12/14/68+	29	11	14 Strings..		Capitol 2341
4/05/69	20	12	15 Let The Whole World Sing It With Me		Capitol 2421
7/26/69	19	10	16 World-Wide Travelin' Man..............................		Capitol 2549
11/15/69	47	9	17 Yours Forever		Capitol 2657
4/11/70	55	4	18 You Don't Care What Happens To Me...............		Capitol 2751
9/12/70	13	13	19 It's A Beautiful Day		Capitol 2888
1/02/71	32	10	20 Heavenly		Capitol 3000
5/01/71	55	6	21 Baby, It's Yours		Capitol 3080
9/18/71	53	5	22 Hello Little Rock		Capitol 3157
11/11/72	49	8	23 Paint Me A Rainbow		RCA 0819
7/14/73	51	9	24 Love Ain't Worth a Dime Unless It's Free		RCA 0004
10/27/73	62	9	25 It's Raining In Seattle		RCA 0114
6/14/75	80	9	26 Lonely Rain		Playboy 6035
7/31/76	8	14	27 **After The Storm**		Playboy 6080
11/20/76+	19	11	28 Sing A Sad Song		Playboy 6091
12/23/78+	37	11	29 Eyes Big As Dallas		WIN 126
6/09/79	59	5	30 Could I Talk You Into Loving Me Again		WIN'S 127
8/24/85	98	1	31 Wait Till I Get My Hands On You.....................		Pretty World 001
			CLIFFIE STONE		
			Born Clifford Snyder on 3/1/17 in Burbank. Bass player, worked with the Anson Weeks and Freddie Slack bands in the late 30s. Became a country disc jockey and hosted Hollywood Barn Dance and Lucky Stars in the mid-40s. Worked as country A&R for Capitol Records, discovered Tennessee Ernie Ford. Wrote "No Vacancy", "Divorce Me C.O.D." and "New Steel Guitar Rag". Own record label, Granite Records.		
3/15/47	4	1	1 Silver Stars, Purple Sage, Eyes Of Blue		Capitol 354
3/06/48	4	8	2 **Peepin' Through The Keyhole**		Capitol 40083
8/28/48	11	3	3 When My Blue Moon Turns To Gold Again		Capitol 15108
			Juke Box #11		
			#19 pop hit for Elvis Presley in 1956		
			THE STONEMANS		
			Family group formed in the late 40s by Ernest "Pop" Stoneman (b: 5/25/1893, Monorat, VA; d: 6/14/68). Debuted on the Grand Ole Opry in 1962. On the Jimmy Dean TV shows in 1964 and had own series, "Those Stonemans", in 1966. Group then consisted of Pop (autoharp, guitar), Scotty (fiddle), Van (guitar), Donna (mandolin), Roni (banjo) and Jim (bass). Pop first recorded for Okeh in 1924.		
6/04/66	40	3	1 Tupelo County Jail..		MGM 13466
10/08/66	21	11	2 The Five Little Johnson Girls		MGM 13557
3/25/67	40	12	3 Back To Nashville, Tennessee		MGM 13667
8/05/67	49	7	4 West Canterbury Subdivision Blues..................		MGM 13755
7/20/68	41	8	5 Christopher Robin		MGM 13945
			LEWIS STOREY		
			Born in Casa Grande, Arizona. Worked clubs in Tucson and Phoenix with own band.		
2/08/86	48	8	1 Ain't No Tellin'		Epic 05786

DEBUT DATE	PEAK POS	WKS CHR	ARTIST — Record Title	POP POS	Label & Number
			LEWIS STOREY — Continued		
5/17/86	**60**	6	2 Katie, Take Me Dancin'		Epic 05890
			JAMES STORIE		
10/22/88	**100**	1	1 Lost Highway		GMC 1001
			VERN STOVALL		
			Born on 10/3/28 in Altus, Oklahoma; raised in Vian, Oklahoma.		
9/23/67	**58**	8	1 Dallas		Longhorn 81
			GEORGE STRAIT ★★83★★		
			Born on 5/18/52 in Pearsall, Texas. Self-taught on guitar while in the US Army in 1971. Sang in a service band in Hawaii. First recorded as vocalist of "Ace In The Hole" on D label in the late 70s. Appeared on "Austin City Limits", "Hee-Haw" and "Nashville Now" TV series. Own special, "Strait From The Heart Of Texas", on the Nashville Network. In film "The Soldier".		
5/16/81	**6**	18	1 Unwound		MCA 51104
9/12/81	**16**	17	2 Down And Out		MCA 51170
1/30/82	**3**	22	3 If You're Thinking You Want A Stranger (There's One Coming Home)		MCA 51228
6/19/82	**1**¹	18	4 Fool Hearted Memory		MCA 52066
			from the film "The Soldier"		
10/09/82+	**6**	19	5 Marina Del Rey		MCA 52120
2/12/83	**4**	17	6 Amarillo By Morning		MCA 52162
6/11/83	**1**¹	23	7 A Fire I Can't Put Out		MCA 52225
10/08/83+	**1**¹	23	8 You Look So Good In Love		MCA 52279
2/11/84	**1**¹	23	9 Right Or Wrong		MCA 52337
6/02/84	**1**¹	21	10 Let's Fall To Pieces Together		MCA 52392
9/29/84+	**1**¹	23	11 Does Fort Worth Ever Cross Your Mind..........		MCA 52458
2/02/85	**5**	20	12 The Cowboy Rides Away		MCA 52526
6/01/85	**5**	18	13 The Fireman		MCA 52586
9/21/85	**1**¹	22	14 The Chair		MCA 52667
1/18/86	**4**	21	15 You're Something Special To Me		MCA 52764
5/17/86	**1**¹	22	16 Nobody In His Right Mind Would've Left Her..		MCA 52817
9/13/86	**1**¹	22	17 It Ain't Cool To Be Crazy About You		MCA 52914
1/17/87	**1**¹	21	18 Ocean Front Property		MCA 53021
5/02/87	**1**¹	16	19 All My Ex's Live In Texas		MCA 53087
8/22/87	**1**¹	18	20 Am I Blue		MCA 53165
2/06/88	**1**¹	19	21 Famous Last Words Of A Fool		MCA 53248
5/21/88	**1**¹	19	22 Baby Blue		MCA 53340
9/17/88	**1**¹	20	23 If You Ain't Lovin' (You Ain't Livin')		MCA 53400
			MEL STREET ★★145★★		
			Born King Malachi Street on 10/21/33 near Grundy, West Virginia; died on 10/21/78 (suicide). Worked on local radio as a teenager. Worked outside of music in Niagara Falls, New York. Own TV series, "Country Showcase", in Bluefield, West Virginia, in the late 60s. First recorded for Tandem in 1970.		
5/27/72	**7**	17	1 Borrowed Angel..		Royal Amer. 64
11/04/72+	**5**	16	2 Lovin' On Back Streets		Metro. Cnt. 901
3/17/73	**11**	15	3 Walk Softly On The Bridges		Metro. Cnt. 906
7/28/73	**38**	10	4 The Town Where You Live		Metro. Cnt. 0018
11/10/73+	**11**	13	5 Lovin' On Borrowed Time		Metro. Cnt. 0143
5/11/74	**15**	15	6 You Make Me Feel More Like A Man		GRT 002
11/02/74+	**16**	13	7 Forbidden Angel		GRT 012
3/01/75	**13**	14	8 Smokey Mountain Memories.........................		GRT 017
6/28/75	**17**	14	9 Even If I Have To Steal................................		GRT 025
10/11/75	**23**	11	10 This Ain't Just Another Lust Affair................		GRT 030
2/07/76	**32**	10	11 The Devil In Your Kisses (And The Angel In Your Eyes)..		GRT 043
6/12/76	**10**	14	12 I Met A Friend Of Your's Today		GRT 057
10/23/76	**24**	13	13 Looking Out My Window Through The Pain		GRT 083
3/19/77	**56**	7	14 Rodeo Bum		GRT 116
6/25/77	**19**	12	15 Barbara Don't Let Me Be The Last To Know.......		Polydor 14399
9/24/77	**15**	12	16 Close Enough For Lonesome		Polydor 14421
1/14/78	**9**	13	17 If I Had A Cheating Heart		Polydor 14448
4/22/78	**24**	10	18 Shady Rest		Polydor 14468

DEBUT DATE	PEAK POS	WKS CHR	ARTIST — Record Title	POP POS	Label & Number
			MEL STREET — Continued		
10/21/78	**68**	5	19 Just Hangin' On...		Mercury 55043
10/06/79	**17**	11	20 The One Thing My Lady Never Puts Into Words ..		Sunset 100
1/26/80	**30**	10	21 Tonight Let's Sleep On It Baby		Sunbird 103
11/01/80	**36**	12	22 Who'll Turn Out The Lights		Sunbird 7555
10/31/81	**48**	8	23 Slip Away...		Sunbird 7568
			MEL STREET & SANDY POWELL		
			STREETFEET		
2/12/83	**78**	4	1 Where Do You Go.......................................		Triple T 2001
			STREETS		
1/26/80	**32**	10	1 Love In The Meantime.................................		Epic 50827
			BARBRA STREISAND - see NEIL DIAMOND		
			GENE STROMAN		
			Born on 2/19/61 in Terrell, Texas. 1986 winner of TNN's "You Can Be A Star".		
1/17/87	**53**	8	1 Goodbye Song...		Capitol 5662
8/15/87	**74**	5	2 I Don't Feel Much Like A Cowboy Tonight		Capitol 44015
			JUD STRUNK		
			Born Justin Strunk, Jr. on 6/11/36 in Jamestown, New York; raised in Farmington, Maine. Died in a plane crash on 10/15/81 (45). Toured as a one-man show for the US Armed Forces. Worked in the Broadway musical "Beautiful Dreamer".		
2/24/73	**33**	14	1 Daisy A Day	*14*	MGM 14463
7/21/73	**86**	4	2 Next Door Neighbor's Kid		MGM 14572
8/09/75	**51**	6	3 The Biggest Parakeets In Town................... [N]	*50*	Melodyland 6015
2/07/76	**88**	5	4 Pamela Brown		Melodyland 6027
			MARTY STUART		
			Born in Philadelphia, Mississippi in 1958. Worked with the Sullivan Family. Toured with Lester Flatt and Nashville Grass from age 13. Toured with the Johnny Cash Band from 1979-85. Did much session work in Nashville. Married to Cash's daughter Cindy.		
12/28/85+	**19**	18	1 Arlene...		Columbia 05724
5/31/86	**59**	6	2 Honky Tonker		Columbia 05897
8/09/86	**39**	12	3 All Because Of You......................................		Columbia 06230
11/22/86	**59**	8	4 Do You Really Want My Lovin'		Columbia 06425
3/19/88	**56**	7	5 Mirrors Don't Lie.......................................		Columbia 07729
6/04/88	**66**	6	6 Matches		Columbia 07914
			NAT STUCKEY ★★97★★		
			Born Nathan Wright Stuckey on 12/17/34 in Cass County, Texas. Died of lung cancer on 8/24/88. Disc jockey on KALT-Atlanta, Texas and KWKH-Shreveport. Own band, the Cornhuskers, from 1958-59. On the "Louisiana Hayride" from 1962-66; own band, the Sweet Thangs, from 1967. Wrote "Pop A Top" and "Waitin' In Your Welfare Line".		
9/10/66	**4**	18	1 **Sweet Thang**		Paula 243
1/07/67	**17**	13	2 Oh! Woman		Paula 257
4/15/67	**27**	12	3 All My Tomorrows/		
4/29/67	**67**	3	4 You're Puttin' Me On		Paula 267
9/02/67	**41**	8	5 Adorable Women		Paula 276
12/23/67+	**17**	14	6 My Can Do Can't Keep Up With My Want To		Paula 287
5/18/68	**63**	5	7 Leave This One Alone		Paula 300
10/12/68	**9**	16	8 **Plastic Saddle**		RCA 9631
2/15/69	**13**	11	9 Joe And Mabel's 12th Street Bar And Grill		RCA 9720
6/07/69	**15**	13	10 Cut Across Shorty......................................		RCA 0163
7/05/69	**20**	11	11 Young Love..		RCA 0181
			CONNIE SMITH & NAT STUCKEY		
			#1 pop hit for both Sonny James and Tab Hunter in 1957		
10/04/69	**8**	11	12 **Sweet Thang And Cisco**.............................		RCA 0238
1/10/70	**33**	10	13 Sittin' In Atlanta Station		RCA 9786
3/14/70	**59**	4	14 If God Is Dead (Who's That Living In My Soul)		RCA 9805
			CONNIE SMITH & NAT STUCKEY		
5/16/70	**31**	8	15 Old Man Willis		RCA 9833
9/05/70	**31**	9	16 Whiskey, Whiskey		RCA 9884
12/12/70+	**11**	15	17 She Wakes Me With A Kiss Every Morning (And She Loves Me to Sleep Every Night)...........		RCA 9929
4/24/71	**24**	12	18 Only A Woman Like You		RCA 9977

DEBUT DATE	PEAK POS	WKS CHR	ARTIST — Record Title	POP POS	Label & Number
			NAT STUCKEY — Continued		
9/04/71	**17**	13	19 I'm Gonna Act Right		RCA 1010
12/11/71+	**16**	14	20 Forgive Me For Calling You Darling		RCA 0590
4/22/72	**26**	12	21 Is It Any Wonder That I Love You		RCA 0687
8/19/72	**18**	13	22 Don't Pay The Ransom.................................		RCA 0761
2/03/73	**10**	14	23 **Take Time To Love Her**		RCA 0879
6/16/73	**2**[1]	12	24 **I Used It All On You**		RCA 0973
10/20/73	**14**	12	25 Got Leaving On Her Mind..............................		RCA 0115
2/23/74	**31**	11	26 You Never Say You Love Me Anymore		RCA 0222
6/01/74	**42**	13	27 It Hurts To Know The Feeling's Gone................		RCA 0288
11/09/74+	**36**	12	28 You Don't Have To Go Home		RCA 10090
7/05/75	**85**	7	29 Boom Boom Barroom Man		RCA 10307
2/28/76	**13**	13	30 Sun Comin' Up...		MCA 40519
6/12/76	**46**	10	31 The Way He's Treated You............................		MCA 40568
9/04/76	**42**	9	32 That's All She Ever Said Except Goodbye		MCA 40608
12/11/76+	**48**	8	33 The Shady Side Of Charlotte		MCA 40658
7/23/77	**63**	6	34 Buddy, I Lied...		MCA 40752
10/29/77	**62**	6	35 I'm Coming Home To Face The Music...............		MCA 40808
3/18/78	**66**	6	36 That Lucky Old Sun (Just Rolls Around Heaven All Day) .... *#1 pop hit for Frankie Laine in 1949*		MCA 40855
7/08/78	**26**	10	37 The Days Of Sand And Shovels....................... *#34 pop hit for Bobby Vinton in 1969*		MCA 40923
			ANNA SUDDERTH		
5/10/80	**90**	4	1 Not A Day Goes By		Verite 801
			GENE SULLIVAN Co-writer with Wiley Walker of "When My Blue Moon Turns To Gold Again". Also see Wiley & Gene.		
12/09/57+	**9**	8	1 **Please Pass The Biscuits** .... [N] *Jockey #9 / Best Seller #16*		Columbia 40971
			PHIL SULLIVAN		
6/08/59	**26**	6	1 Hearts Are Lonely		Starday 437
			SCOTT SUMMER Born in Fort Smith, Kansas. Moved to Nashville in 1973.		
2/03/79	**80**	4	1 Flip Side Of Today.......................................		Con Brio 146
5/26/79	**92**	3	2 I Don't Wanna Want You		Con Brio 152
			JOE SUN Born James J. Paulson on 9/25/43 in Rochester, Minnesota. Worked as a disc jockey in Key West and Madison, Wisconsin. Worked clubs in Chicago as "Jack Daniels". Own band, the Branded Men, in the late 60s. Moved to Nashville in 1972 and worked as promo man for the Kendalls and Ovation Records.		
6/24/78	**14**	16	1 Old Flames (Can't Hold A Candle To You)		Ovation 1107
11/04/78	**20**	12	2 High And Dry		Ovation 1117
3/24/79	**27**	11	3 On Business For The King/		
		11	4 Blue Ribbon Blues.....................................		Ovation 1122
9/15/79	**20**	11	5 I'd Rather Go On Hurtin'		Ovation 1127
12/08/79+	**34**	11	6 Out Of Your Mind		Ovation 1137
1/26/80	**48**	7	7 What I Had With You		Ovation 1138
			SHEILA ANDREWS with JOE SUN		
3/22/80	**23**	12	8 Shotgun Rider	71	Ovation 1141
8/16/80	**21**	11	9 Bombed, Boozed, And Busted		Ovation 1152
12/27/80+	**43**	11	10 Ready For The Times To Get Better..................		Ovation 1162
3/20/82	**40**	9	11 Holed Up In Some Honky Tonk		Elektra 47417
6/19/82	**57**	7	12 Fraulein		Elektra 47467
			JOE SUN with SHOTGUN		
10/02/82	**85**	2	13 You Make Me Want To Sing...........................		Elektra 69954
7/14/84	**73**	5	14 Bad For Me		AMI 1319
1/26/85	**77**	3	15 Why Would I Want To Forget		AMI 1321

DEBUT DATE	PEAK POS	WKS CHR	ARTIST — Record Title	POP POS	Label & Number
			SUNSHINE RUBY		
			Ruby Bateman from Texas. 13 years old in 1953.		
6/20/53	4	1	1 **Too Young To Tango**		RCA 5250
			Jockey #4; Sonny James on fiddle		
			SUPER GRIT COWBOY BAND		
			North Carolina band formed in 1975.		
8/01/81	71	6	1 If You Don't Know Me By Now		Hoodswamp 8002
10/24/81	64	6	2 Carolina By The Sea		Hoodswamp 8003
3/06/82	83	3	3 Semi Diesel Blues............................		Hoodswamp 8004
7/10/82	48	9	4 She Is The Woman		Hoodswamp 8005
4/23/83	79	4	5 I Bought The Shoes (That Just Walked Out On Me)..................................		Hoodswamp 8006
			GLENN SUTTON		
			Hit songwriter, wrote "My Man" for Lynn Anderson, "What's Made Milwaukee Famous" for Jerry Lee Lewis, "Almost Persuaded" for David Houston, "Kiss Away" for Ronnie Dove and many others. Former husband of Lynn Anderson.		
1/06/79	55	5	1 The Football Card .... [N]	46	Mercury 55052
9/15/79	73	4	2 Red Neck Disco.................... [N]		Mercury 57001
10/11/86	74	4	3 I'll Go Steppin' Too........................		Mercury 884974
			SWAMPWATER		
6/12/71	72	2	1 Take A City Bride		King 6376
			BILLY SWAN		
			Born on 5/12/42 in Cape Girardeau, Missouri. Own band, Mirt Mitley & The Rhythm Steppers, in the late 50s. Wrote "Lover Please" hit for Clyde McPhatter. Writer for Bill Black's Combo in Memphis. Produced the first album by Tony Joe White. Toured with Kris Kristofferson from the early 70s. Formed band, Black Tie, with Randy Meisner in 1986.		
10/12/74	1²	14	1 ● I Can Help	1	Monument 8621
8/30/75	17	14	2 Everything's The Same (Ain't Nothing Changed) .	91	Monument 8661
3/20/76	45	9	3 Just Want To Taste Your Wine		Monument 8682
9/11/76	75	5	4 You're The One............................		Monument 8706
			written by Buddy Holly and Waylon Jennings		
12/11/76	95	2	5 Shake, Rattle And Roll.....................		Columbia 10443
			#7 pop hit for Bill Haley & His Comets in 1954		
6/24/78	30	15	6 Hello! Remember Me		A&M 2046
12/02/78	97	3	7 No Way Around It (It's Love)		A&M 2103
4/04/81	18	13	8 Do I Have To Draw A Picture..............		Epic 51000
7/25/81	18	13	9 I'm Into Lovin' You........................		Epic 02196
11/28/81+	19	14	10 Stuck Right In The Middle Of Your Love...........		Epic 02601
4/10/82	32	13	11 With Their Kind Of Money And Our Kind Of Love..................................		Epic 02841
10/09/82	56	9	12 Your Picture Still Loves Me (And I Still Love You)..................................		Epic 03226
1/29/83	39	10	13 Rainbows And Butterflies		Epic 03505
6/04/83	67	8	14 Yes..		Epic 03917
4/26/86	45	10	15 You Must Be Lookin' For Me		Mercury 884668
2/07/87	63	6	16 I'm Gonna Get You		Mercury 888320
			ISAAC PAYTON SWEAT		
			From Nederland, Texas; one-time member of the pop group, Black Plague.		
9/09/78	91	4	1 Shed So Many Tears		Gusto 9010
			SWEETHEARTS OF THE RODEO		
			Duo of sisters from California: Janis (guitar, vocals) and Kristine Oliver (vocals). Moved to Nashville in 1983. Winners of the Wrangler Country Showdown Talent Contest in 1985. Janis is married to Vince Gill.		
4/05/86	21	15	1 Hey Doll Baby		Columbia 05824
			#8 R&B hit for The Clovers in 1956		
7/26/86	7	22	2 **Since I Found You**		Columbia 06166
11/29/86+	4	22	3 **Midnight Girl/Sunset Town**		Columbia 06525
4/04/87	4	17	4 **Chains Of Gold**		Columbia 07023
9/12/87	10	18	5 **Gotta Get Away**		Columbia 07314
4/02/88	5	20	6 **Satisfy You**		Columbia 07757
8/06/88	5	20	7 **Blue To The Bone**		Columbia 07985

DEBUT DATE	PEAK POS	WKS CHR	ARTIST — Record Title	POP POS	Label & Number
			SWEETHEARTS OF THE RODEO — Continued		
12/03/88+	9	22	8 I Feel Fine		Columbia 08504
			#1 pop hit for The Beatles in 1964		
			SWEETWATER		
			Gospel based group with Willie Wynn, one-time member of the Oak Ridge Boys.		
8/08/81	84	4	1 Antioch Churchouse Choir/		
10/17/81	75	4	2 I'd Throw It All Away		Faucet 1592
			RACHEL SWEET		
			Born in Akron, Ohio in 1963. Performed in the musicals "The Music Man", "Fiddler On The Roof" and "The Sound Of Music". First recorded for Premiere in 1974.		
6/19/76	96	4	1 We Live In Two Different Worlds......................		Derrick 1000
			THE SWING SHIFT BAND		
			Band features Buddy Emmons and Ray Pennington.		
11/12/88	76	3	1 (Turn Me Loose And) Let Me Swing...................		Step One 392
			SYLVIA ★★143★★		
			Born Sylvia Kirby Allen on 12/9/56 in Kokomo, Indiana. Sang in church choir from age 3. Moved to Nashville in 1975, worked as a secretary for producer Tom Collins. Did session back-up vocals. Made stage debut as a soloist in the fall of 1979.		
10/13/79	36	10	1 You Don't Miss A Thing.................................		RCA 11735
4/26/80	35	11	2 It Don't Hurt To Dream		RCA 11958
9/06/80	10	16	3 **Tumbleweed**..		RCA 12077
1/17/81	1¹	14	4 **Drifter**..		RCA 12164
4/25/81	7	16	5 **The Matador**		RCA 12214
9/12/81	8	15	6 **Heart On The Mend**.................................		RCA 12302
1/16/82	12	15	7 Sweet Yesterday		RCA 13020
6/05/82	1¹	24	8●**Nobody**	15	RCA 13223
10/30/82+	2²	20	9 **Like Nothing Ever Happened**		RCA 13330
2/19/83	57	11	10 The Wayward Wind		RCA 13441
			JAMES GALWAY with SYLVIA #1 pop hit for Gogi Grant in 1956		
5/07/83	5	18	11 **Snapshot**		RCA 13501
8/27/83	18	17	12 The Boy Gets Around		RCA 13589
12/03/83+	3	19	13 **I Never Quite Got Back (From Loving You)**		RCA 13689
4/07/84	24	14	14 Victims Of Goodbye		RCA 13755
7/07/84	36	13	15 Love Over Old Times.................................		RCA 13838
2/16/85	2²	22	16 **Fallin' In Love**......................................		RCA 13997
6/29/85	9	18	17 **Cry Just A Little Bit**..............................		RCA 14107
11/16/85+	9	25	18 I Love You By Heart.................................		RCA 14217
			SYLVIA & MICHAEL JOHNSON		
7/05/86	33	15	19 Nothin' Ventured Nothin' Gained		RCA 14375
5/16/87	66	6	20 Straight From My Heart..............................		RCA 5127

T

DEBUT DATE	PEAK POS	WKS CHR	ARTIST — Record Title	POP POS	Label & Number
			MARLOW TACKETT		
			Born in Dorton, Kentucky. Own group at age 19. Worked on WIDD-Elizabethtown, Tennessee. Opened his own Marlow's Palace Club in Pikeville in 1975.		
1/19/80	95	2	1 Would You Know Love		Palace 1006
4/26/80	93	2	2 Midnight Fire..		Palace 1008
11/15/80	92	3	3 Ride That Bull (Big Bertha)		Kari 114
7/10/82	67	6	4 Ever-Lovin' Woman		RCA 13255
10/23/82	54	9	5 634-5789		RCA 13347
			#13 pop hit for Wilson Pickett in 1966		
4/23/83	67	6	6 I Know My Way To You By Heart		RCA 13471
8/06/83	56	8	7 I Spent The Night In The Heart Of Texas		RCA 13579
			BUBBA TALBERT		
			Singing pharmacist from Blanchard, Louisiana; born in 1949.		
4/09/83	81	3	1 Easy Catch		Ranger 5734
7/23/83	77	3	2 Downright Broke My Heart............................		Ranger 702

DEBUT DATE	PEAK POS	WKS CHR	ARTIST — Record Title	POP POS	Label & Number
			TOM TALL		
			Born Tommie Lee Guthrie on 12/17/37 in Amarillo. Worked on Town Hall Party (1955), Grand Ole Opry (1956), Louisiana Hayride (1956-59), and Big D Jamboree (1955-59).		
1/01/55	**2³**	26	1 **Are You Mine**		Fabor 117
			TOM TALL & GINNY WRIGHT		
			Jockey #2 / Juke Box #4 / Best Seller #5		
1/04/64	**25**	1	2 Bad, Bad Tuesday		Petal 1210
			JAMES TALLEY		
			Born on 11/9/44 in Tulsa, Oklahoma. Social worker with migrant workers and public health programs in Nashville, became a professional entertainer in the early 70s.		
3/13/76	**75**	8	1 Tryin' Like The Devil		Capitol 4218
7/24/76	**61**	9	2 Are They Gonna Make Us Outlaws Again		Capitol 4297
4/23/77	**83**	4	3 Alabama Summertime		Capitol 4410
			TAMMY JO		
			Tammy Jo Whitehead.		
3/15/80	**88**	3	1 I Go To Pieces		Ridgetop 00880
			#9 pop hit for Peter & Gordon in 1965		
6/14/80	**76**	4	2 Love Talking/		
		4	3 Wishing Well		Ridgetop 00980
			FARGO TANNER		
6/07/75	**69**	11	1 Don't Drop It		Avco 612
			DEMETRISS TAPP		
9/15/73	**97**	3	1 Skinny Dippin'		ABC 11383
			MICHAEL TATE		
3/07/81	**93**	2	1 Mexican Girl		Oak 47102
			CARMOL TAYLOR		
			Born on 9/5/31 in Brilliant, Alabama; died of lung cancer on 12/5/86. Worked at local shows and square dances from age 15. Wrote "Wild As A Wildcat" for Charlie Walker, "Grand Tour" for George Jones, "He Loves Me All The Way" for Tammy Wynette, "There's A Song On My Jukebox" for David Wills, and many others. Staff writer for Al Gallico Music; producer for Country International Records.		
6/28/75	**48**	11	1 Back In The U.S.A.		Elektra 45255
			#37 pop hit for Chuck Berry in 1959		
10/04/75	**91**	5	2 Who Will I Be Loving Now		Elektra 45277
2/14/76	**35**	12	3 Play The Saddest Song On The Juke Box		Elektra 45299
5/08/76	**23**	11	4 I Really Had A Ball Last Night		Elektra 45312
9/18/76	**53**	6	5 That Little Difference		Elektra 45342
1/08/77	**87**	5	6 Neon Women		Elektra 45367
			CARMOL TAYLOR & STELLA PARTON		
1/22/77	**100**	1	7 What Would I Do Then		Elektra 45366
7/23/77	**80**	5	8 Good Cheatin' Songs		Elektra 45409
			CHET TAYLOR		
8/04/79	**92**	2	1 Barefoot Angel		Vista 108
			CHIP TAYLOR		
			Born James Wesley Voigt in Westchester County, New York in 1940. Brother of actor Jon Voigt. Worked in a trio with Al Georgoni and Trade Martin in the early 70s. Wrote "Angel of The Morning", "Wild Thing" and "Anyway You Want Me".		
1/04/75	**80**	6	1 Me As I Am		Warner 8050
5/17/75	**28**	10	2 Early Sunday Morning		Warner 8090
9/13/75	**61**	7	3 Big River		Warner 8128
1/10/76	**92**	4	4 Circle Of Tears		Warner 8159
1/08/77	**93**	4	5 Hello Atlanta		Columbia 10446
			FRANK TAYLOR		
6/01/63	**28**	1	1 Snow White Cloud		Parkway 869
			JAMES TAYLOR		
			Born on 3/12/48 in Boston. Married to Carly Simon from 1972-82.		
7/16/77	**88**	3	1 Bartender's Blues		Columbia 10557
			also see George Jones' version with James Taylor on backing vocals		
9/09/78	**33**	10	2 Devoted To You	*36*	Elektra 45506
			CARLY SIMON & JAMES TAYLOR		
12/07/85+	**26**	16	3 Everyday	*61*	Columbia 05681

DEBUT DATE	PEAK POS	WKS CHR	ARTIST — Record Title	POP POS	Label & Number
			JAMES TAYLOR — Continued		
3/15/86	80	9	4 Only One		Columbia 05785
			JIM TAYLOR		
8/05/78	100	1	1 I'll Still Need You Mary Ann........................		Checkmate 3069
12/09/78+	68	10	2 Leave It To Love		Checkmate 3106
			JUDY TAYLOR		
			Born in Murfreesboro, Tennessee. Appeared on "Young Country", WSM-TV at age 10.		
1/09/82	84	3	1 A Married Man................................		Warner 49859
5/22/82	79	4	2 A Step In The Right Direction....................		Warner 50061
9/25/82	70	4	3 The End Of The World........................		Warner 29913
			LIVINGSTON TAYLOR with LEAH KUNKEL		
			Livingston was born on 11/21/50 in Boston. James Taylor's younger brother.		
10/22/88	94	2	1 Loving Arms		Critique 99275
			MARY TAYLOR		
			Wrote "Queen Of The House" for Jody Miller.		
1/07/67	72	4	1 Don't Waste Your Time		Capitol 5776
6/22/68	44	8	2 If I Don't Like The Way You Love Me..............		Dot 17104
11/23/68	51	7	3 Feed Me One More Lie......................		Dot 17168
			R. DEAN TAYLOR		
			Born in Toronto, Canada in 1939. First recorded for Barry in 1960.		
1/15/83	90	2	1 Let's Talk It Over......................		Strummer 3748
			KAREN TAYLOR-GOOD		
			Born in El Paso, Texas. Worked as a folk singer. In Phase II with Janie Fricke and Judy Rodman in Memphis in 1971. Did back-up vocals in Nashville. Married to musician Dennis Good. On soundtrack of the films "Best Little Whorehouse In Texas" and "Smokey And The Bandit 2". Made many TV appearances and commercial jingles.		
			KAREN TAYLOR:		
3/06/82	38	11	1 Diamond In The Rough........................		Mesa 1111
7/24/82	67	7	2 Country Boy's Song		Mesa 1112
			KAREN TAYLOR-GOOD:		
11/20/82	62	9	3 I'd Rather Be Doing Nothing With You		Mesa 1113
3/05/83	42	11	4 Tenderness Place........................		Mesa 1114
8/27/83	62	7	5 Don't Call Me		Mesa 1115
1/07/84	62	10	6 Handsome Man		Mesa 1116
9/08/84	66	7	7 We Just Gotta Dance		Mesa 1117
4/06/85	61	7	8 Starlite........................		Mesa 1118
10/05/85	57	8	9 Up On Your Love........................		Mesa 1119
5/10/86	79	4	10 Come In Planet Earth (Are You Listenin')		Mesa 2011
			THE TENNESSEANS		
			Group formed by Willie Wynn (formerly with Sweetwater).		
12/02/78	81	5	1 Nineteen-Sixty Something Songwriter Of The Year......................		Capitol 4645
			TENNESSEE EXPRESS		
			Nashville vocal group evolved from the group, The Sound 70's Singers. Sang harmony on John Anderson's "Swingin'".		
8/15/81	31	11	1 Big Like A River		RCA 12277
12/12/81	75	4	2 Little Things		RCA 12362
			#13 pop hit for Bobby Goldsboro in 1965		
4/03/82	70	4	3 The Arms Of A Stranger		RCA 13078
7/24/82	78	5	4 Operator/		
		5	5 Let Me In And Let Me Love You....................		RCA 13265
2/05/83	62	7	6 How Long Will It Take....................		RCA 13423
6/04/83	65	6	7 Cotton Fields....................		RCA 13526
			#13 pop hit for The Highwaymen in 1962		
			TENNESSEE PULLYBONE		
			Bobby Bare's touring band for many years.		
9/08/73	75	4	1 The Door's Always Open		JMI 25
			TENNESSEE TORNADO - see JERRY FOSTER		

DEBUT DATE	PEAK POS	WKS CHR	ARTIST — Record Title	POP POS	Label & Number
			TENNESSEE VALLEY BOYS		
			Vocal group formed by Wally Fowler, who formed the Oak Ridge Boys.		
4/14/84	**57**	10	1 Lo And Behold		Nashwood 12684
			AL TERRY		
			Born Allison Joseph Theriot, Jr. on 1/14/22 in Kaplan, Louisiana. Leader of the Southerners from 1946-52. Toured with Red Foley. Own band from 1954.		
4/24/54	**8**	5	1 **Good Deal, Lucille**		Hickory 1003
			Jockey #8 / Juke Box #8		
2/29/60	**28**	1	2 Watch Dog		Hickory 1111
			GORDON TERRY		
			Born on 10/7/31 in Decatur, Alabama. Session fiddler.		
5/30/70	**62**	5	1 The Ballad Of J.C. .... [N]		Capitol 2792
			J.C.: Johnny Cash; tune is "The Ballad of New Orleans"		
			TEXAS VOCAL COMPANY		
			Backing group for Charley Pride.		
4/30/83	**65**	5	1 Two Hearts		RCA 13504
10/08/83	**82**	3	2 It Had To Be You..		RCA 13566
			B.J. THOMAS ★★197★★		
			Born Billy Joe Thomas on 8/7/42 in Hugo, Oklahoma; raised in Rosenberg, Texas. Sang in church choir as a teenager. Own band, the Triumphs; first recorded for Scepter in 1965. B.J. has featured gospel music since 1976.		
2/22/75	**1**[1]	16	1● **(Hey Won't You Play) Another Somebody Done Somebody Wrong Song**...........................	*1*	ABC 12054
10/04/75	**37**	10	2 Help Me Make It (To My Rockin' Chair).............	64	ABC 12121
5/14/77	**98**	1	3 Home Where I Belong...........................		Myrrh 166
1/28/78	**25**	13	4 Everybody Loves A Rain Song	43	MCA 40854
2/10/79	**86**	3	5 We Could Have Been The Closest Of Friends		MCA 40986
4/18/81	**27**	11	6 Some Love Songs Never Die		MCA 51087
8/08/81	**22**	12	7 I Recall A Gypsy Woman		MCA 51151
2/12/83	**1**[1]	21	8 **Whatever Happened To Old Fashioned Love** ...	93	Clev. Int. 03492
7/09/83	**1**[1]	21	9 **New Looks From An Old Lover**		Columbia 03985
11/26/83+	**3**	21	10 **Two Car Garage**		Clev. Int. 04237
4/14/84	**10**	19	11 **The Whole World's In Love When You're Lonely**...............................		Clev. Int. 04431
8/04/84	**14**	18	12 Rock And Roll Shoes		Columbia 04531
			RAY CHARLES with B.J. THOMAS		
10/20/84+	**17**	19	13 The Girl Most Likely To...............................		Clev. Int. 04608
11/09/85	**61**	11	14 The Part Of Me That Needs You Most...............		Columbia 05647
2/22/86	**62**	7	15 America Is		Columbia 05771
10/04/86	**59**	6	16 Night Life		Columbia 06314
			DARRELL THOMAS		
			Born in 1952 in Melcher, Iowa. Performing since age 7. Worked as a carpenter.		
5/19/79	**99**	3	1 Waylon Sing To Mama..................................		Ozark Opry 79101
			DICK THOMAS		
			Born Richard Thomas Goldhahn on 9/4/15 in Philadelphia. Violinist/accordionist. On radio since 1934. Appeared in western movies from 1941.		
9/29/45	**1**[4]	23	1 **Sioux City Sue**	*16*	National 5007
12/08/45	**4**	1	2 Honestly		National 5008
9/25/48	**13**	1	3 Beaut From Butte		Decca 46132
			Juke Box #13		
2/12/49	**12**	1	4 Sister Of Sioux City Sue		Decca 46147
			Juke Box #12 / Best Seller #14		
			JEFF THOMAS		
1/17/87	**85**	3	1 Hollywood's Dream..................................		Revolver 014
			HANK THOMPSON ★★29★★		
			Born Henry William Thompson on 9/3/25 in Waco, Texas. On WACO-Waco as a teenager, billed as "Hank, The Hired Hand". Served in the US Navy during World War II. Attended Southern Methodist, University of Texas, and Princeton. Formed own band, "His Brazos Valley Boys". First recorded for Globe in 1946.		
1/31/48	**2**[2]	38	1 **Humpty Dumpty Heart**		Capitol A. 40065
			Juke Box #2 / Best Seller #3		

DEBUT DATE	PEAK POS	WKS CHR		ARTIST — Record Title	POP POS	Label & Number
				HANK THOMPSON — Continued		
9/04/48	**12**	2	2	Yesterday's Mail/ Juke Box #12		
2/05/49	**10**	1	3	**What Are We Gonna Do About The Moonlight** .... Juke Box #10		Capitol 15132
10/16/48	**7**	10	4	**Green Light** .... Juke Box #7 / Best Seller #8		Capitol 15187
2/05/49	**14**	1	5	I Find You Cheatin' On Me/ Best Seller #14		
2/12/49	**15**	1	6	You Broke My Heart .... Juke Box #15		Capitol 15345
10/01/49	**6**	7	7	**Whoa Sailor** .... Juke Box #6 / Best Seller #8		Capitol 40218
10/01/49	**10**	1	8	**Soft Lips**/ Juke Box #10		
11/05/49	**15**	1	9	The Grass Looks Greener Over Yonder .... Juke Box #15		Capitol 40211
3/15/52	**1** 15	30	10●	**The Wild Side Of Life** .... Best Seller #1(15) / Juke Box #1(15) / Jockey #1(8)	**27**	Capitol 1942
6/28/52	**3**	15	11	**Waiting In The Lobby Of Your Heart** .... Juke Box #3 / Best Seller #5 / Jockey #7		Capitol 2063
12/13/52	**10**	1	12	**The New Wears Off Too Fast** .... Juke Box #10		Capitol 2269
3/28/53	**9**	2	13	**No Help Wanted** .... Juke Box #9 / Best Seller #10 / Jockey #10		Capitol 2376
5/23/53	**1** 3	20	14	**Rub-A-Dub-Dub** .... Juke Box #1 / Jockey #2 / Best Seller #5		Capitol 2445
9/19/53	**8**	4	15	**Yesterday's Girl** .... Best Seller #8 / Jockey #8		Capitol 2553
12/12/53+	**1** 2	19	16	**Wake Up, Irene** .... Juke Box #1 / Best Seller #3 / Jockey #4 answer song to "Goodnight, Irene"		Capitol 2646
5/08/54	**10**	2	17	**Breakin' The Rules**/ Best Seller #10		
6/26/54	**9**	1	18	**A Fooler, A Faker** .... Juke Box #9 / Best Seller #15		Capitol 2758
7/03/54	**9**	12	19	**Honky-Tonk Girl**/ Best Seller #9 / Juke Box #10 / Jockey #11		
7/17/54	**10**	4	20	**We've Gone Too Far** .... Best Seller #10 / Jockey #15		Capitol 2823
10/16/54	**3**	20	21	**The New Green Light** .... Juke Box #3 / Best Seller #7 / Jockey #8		Capitol 2920
2/26/55	**12**	4	22	If Lovin' You Is Wrong/ Best Seller #12 / Jockey #14		
3/12/55	**13**	2	23	Annie Over .... Best Seller #13		Capitol 3030
6/04/55	**5**	9	24	**Wildwood Flower**/ [I] **HANK THOMPSON with MERLE TRAVIS** Juke Box #5 / Best Seller #8 / Jockey #13		
6/04/55	**7**	8	25	**Breakin' In Another Heart** .... Best Seller #7		Capitol 3106
8/20/55	**6**	11	26	**Most Of All** .... Jockey #6 / Best Seller #11		Capitol 3188
12/10/55	**5**	7	27	**Don't Take It Out On Me**/ Best Seller #5 / Juke Box #9 / Jockey #13		
		5	28	Honey, Honey Bee Ball .... Best Seller flip / Juke Box flip		Capitol 3275
3/24/56	**4**	22	29	**The Blackboard Of My Heart**/ Jockey #4 / Best Seller #6 / Juke Box #6		
3/24/56	**14**	5	30	I'm Not Mad, Just Hurt .... Best Seller #14		Capitol 3347
2/23/57	**13**	4	31	Rockin' In The Congo/ Best Seller #13		
		2	32	I Was The First One .... Best Seller flip		Capitol 3623
10/14/57	**14**	2	33	Tears Are Only Rain .... Jockey #14		Capitol 3781
6/09/58	**11**	3	34	How Do You Hold A Memory .... Jockey #11		Capitol 3950
8/18/58	**2** 4	22	35	**Squaws Along The Yukon**		Capitol 4017

DEBUT DATE	PEAK POS	WKS CHR	ARTIST — Record Title	POP POS	Label & Number
			HANK THOMPSON — Continued		
12/01/58+	7	23	36 I've Run Out Of Tomorrows/		
2/02/59	26	3	37 You're Going Back To Your Old Ways Again		Capitol 4085
5/11/59	13	10	38 Anybody's Girl/		
6/29/59	25	1	39 Total Strangers.............................		Capitol 4182
11/09/59+	22	10	40 I Didn't Mean To Fall In Love		Capitol 4269
3/21/60	10	15	41 **A Six Pack To Go**..	*102*	Capitol 4334
8/01/60	14	14	42 She's Just A Whole Lot Like You....................	*99*	Capitol 4386
5/29/61	7	11	43 **Oklahoma Hills/**		
5/29/61	25	2	44 Teach Me How To Lie.....................		Capitol 4556
9/18/61	12	10	45 Hangover Tavern		Capitol 4605
9/07/63	23	1	46 I Wasn't Even In The Running		Capitol 4968
9/28/63	22	5	47 Too In Love		Capitol 5008
1/11/64	45	2	48 Twice As Much		Capitol 5071
8/14/65	42	2	49 Then I'll Start Believing In You................		Capitol 5422
10/22/66	15	14	50 Where Is The Circus		Warner 5858
2/04/67	16	13	51 He's Got A Way With Women		Warner 5886
7/13/68	7	15	52 **On Tap, In The Can, Or In The Bottle**...........		Dot 17108
10/26/68+	5	15	53 **Smoky The Bar**................................		Dot 17163
3/08/69	47	9	54 I See Them Everywhere......................		Dot 17207
7/12/69	46	9	55 The Pathway Of My Life		Dot 17262
10/18/69	60	6	56 Oklahoma Home Brew......................		Dot 17307
5/09/70	54	5	57 But That's All Right		Dot 17347
10/10/70	69	4	58 One Of The Fortunate Few		Dot 17354
3/06/71	15	14	59 Next Time I Fall In Love (I Won't)....................		Dot 17365
7/17/71	18	16	60 The Mark Of A Heel		Dot 17385
12/04/71+	11	14	61 I've Come Awful Close		Dot 17399
4/29/72	16	12	62 Cab Driver		Dot 17410
			#23 pop hit for the Mills Brothers in 1968		
9/23/72	53	8	63 Glow Worm..............................		Dot 17430
			#1 pop hit for the Mills Brothers in 1952		
3/17/73	70	2	64 Roses In The Wine..............................		Dot 17447
9/01/73	48	9	65 Kindly Keep It Country		Dot 17470
2/02/74	8	15	66 **The Older The Violin, The Sweeter The Music**		Dot 17490
7/13/74	10	16	67 **Who Left The Door To Heaven Open**..............		Dot 17512
1/25/75	29	10	68 Mama Don't 'Low		ABC/Dot 17535
6/28/75	70	8	69 That's Just My Truckin' Luck		ABC/Dot 17556
3/06/76	72	6	70 Asphalt Cowboy		ABC/Dot 17612
9/04/76	86	3	71 Big Band Days		ABC/Dot 17649
1/15/77	91	4	72 Honky-Tonk Girl .... [R]		ABC/Dot 17673
5/21/77	92	2	73 Just An Old Flame		ABC/Dot 17695
10/21/78	92	3	74 I'm Just Gettin' By		ABC 12409
3/03/79	88	3	75 Dance With Me Molly		ABC 12447
8/25/79	29	12	76 I Hear The South Callin' Me		MCA 41079
2/02/80	32	9	77 Tony's Tank-Up, Drive-In Cafe		MCA 41176
12/19/81+	82	5	78 Rockin' In The Congo .... [R]		Churchill 7779
7/23/83	82	5	79 Once In A Blue Moon		Churchill 94026
			J.W. THOMPSON		
			Born in Alexandria, Louisiana. Own TV shows from 1959-61. Owns an auto dealership.		
9/15/79	90	2	1 The Visitor		So. Star 309
10/04/80	56	9	2 Halftime		NSD 62
1/24/81	72	4	3 Two Out Of Three Ain't Bad		NSD 75
10/22/83	97	1	4 We've Got A Good Thing Goin'......................		USA Cnt. 1001
7/14/84	91	2	5 Hello Josephine		Century 21 109
			SUE THOMPSON		
			Born Eva Sue McKee on 7/19/26 in Nevada, Missouri; raised in San Jose, California. Worked on KGO-San Francisco "Hometown Hayride" TV series while still a teenager. Worked with Red Foley on the "Grand Ole Opry" in the late 50s. Married to Hank Penny from 1953-63.		
11/18/72	72	5	1 Candy And Roses......................		Hickory 1652
9/06/75	50	9	2 Big Mable Murphy		Hickory 354

DEBUT DATE	PEAK POS	WKS CHR	ARTIST — Record Title	POP POS	Label & Number
			SUE THOMPSON — Continued		
2/21/76	95	3	3 Never Naughty Rosie		Hickory 364
			DON GIBSON & SUE THOMPSON:		
8/28/71	50	8	4 The Two Of Us Together		Hickory 1607
4/22/72	71	3	5 Did You Ever Think		Hickory 1629
8/12/72	37	11	6 I Think They Call It Love		Hickory 1646
12/23/72	64	5	7 Cause I Love You		Hickory 1654
3/17/73	52	6	8 Go With Me		Hickory 1665
9/15/73	53	9	9 Warm Love		Hickory 303
8/10/74	31	12	10 Good Old Fashioned Country Love		Hickory 324
7/19/75	36	11	11 Oh, How Love Changes..............................		Hickory 350
4/03/76	98	2	12 Get Ready-Here I Come		Hickory 367
			THRASHER BROTHERS		
			First gospel group on network TV in 1953. Consisted of Joe Thrasher (lead), Jim Thrasher (tenor), Andy Thrasher (baritone) and John Gresham (bass). Own TV series, "America Sings".		
3/07/81	83	2	1 Lovers Love		MCA 51049
2/06/82	62	5	2 Best Of Friends.. from the TV series "Simon & Simon"		MCA 51227
9/11/82	60	6	3 Still The One .... #5 pop hit for Orleans in 1976		MCA 52093
1/15/83	81	4	4 Wherever You Are...		MCA 52153
12/10/83	80	8	5 Whatcha Got Cookin' In Your Oven Tonight.......		MCA 52297
			THE THREE SUNS - see ELTON BRITT		
			SONNY THROCKMORTON		
			Born James Fron Throckmorton on 4/2/41 in Carlsbad, New Mexico. Wrote "Middle Age Crazy", "I Wish I Was Eighteen Again", "Ordinary Miracle" and "Fadin' In, Fadin' Out". Moved to Nashville in 1964, worked as staff writer for Tree Music.		
9/04/76	76	6	1 Rosie		Starcrest 073
12/25/76+	73	7	2 Lovin' You, Lovin' Me		Starcrest 094
9/16/78	54	8	3 I Wish You Could Have Turned My Head (And Left My Heart Alone)		Mercury 55039
2/03/79	47	8	4 Smooth Sailin'/		
		8	5 Last Cheater's Waltz		Mercury 55051
7/14/79	66	6	6 Can't You Hear That Whistle Blow		Mercury 55061
4/05/80	89	3	7 Friday Night Blues		Mercury 57018
12/12/81	77	5	8 A Girl Like You		MCA 51214
			BILLY THUNDERKLOUD & THE CHIEFTONES		
			Group of Indian musicians from Northwest British Columbia.		
5/17/75	16	12	1 What Time Of Day	*92*	20th Century 2181
10/25/75	37	11	2 Pledging My Love .... #17 pop hit for Johnny Ace in 1955		20th Century 2239
5/29/76	74	5	3 Indian Nation (The Lament of the Cherokee Reservation Indian) .... #1 pop hit for The Raiders in 1971		Polydor 14321
8/07/76	47	8	4 Try A Little Tenderness .... #25 pop hit for Otis Redding in 1967		Polydor 14338
12/11/76	77	6	5 It's Alright		Polydor 14362
			THE TIBOR BROTHERS		
			Brothers Francis, Gerard, Harvey, Kurt and Larry Tibor from Hebron, North Dakota.		
4/17/76	95	3	1 It's So Easy Lovin' You		Ariola Am. 7615
			PATTI TIERNY		
9/22/73	90	4	1 Crying Eyes		MGM 14561
			MEL TILLIS ★★22★★		
			Born Lonnie Melvin Tillis on 8/8/32 in Tampa, Florida; raised in Pahokee, Florida. Football player and drummer while in high school. Served in the US Air Force, then worked on the railroads. Moved to Nashville in 1957. Wrote "Detroit City" and "Ruby Don't Take Your Love To Town". In the films "W.W. And The Dixie Dance Kings", "Smokey & The Bandit 2", "Uphill All The Way" and "Murder In Music City". Owner of Sawgrass, Cedarwood, and several other publishing companies until late 1987. Autobiography: "Stutterin' Boy". Backing band: The Statesiders. CMA award: Entertainer of the Year - 1976.		
11/10/58	24	4	1 The Violet And A Rose.................................		Columbia 41189

DEBUT DATE	PEAK POS	WKS CHR	ARTIST — Record Title	POP POS	Label & Number
			MEL TILLIS — Continued		
1/05/59	**28**	4	2 Finally		Columbia 41277
7/03/65	**14**	16	3 Wine..		RIC 158
10/15/66	**17**	14	4 Stateside		Kapp 772
2/18/67	**11**	19	5 Life Turned Her That Way	128	Kapp 804
7/15/67	**20**	14	6 Goodbye Wheeling..................................		Kapp 837
12/16/67	**71**	3	7 Survival Of The Fittest		Kapp 867
1/13/68	**26**	12	8 All Right (I'll Sign The Papers)........................		Kapp 881
5/11/68	**17**	15	9 Something Special................................		Kapp 905
10/05/68	**31**	7	10 Destroyed By Man		Kapp 941
12/21/68+	**10**	17	11 **Who's Julie**		Kapp 959
4/19/69	**15**	15	12 Old Faithful		Kapp 986
8/16/69	**9**	15	13 **These Lonely Hands Of Mine**		Kapp 2031
1/17/70	**10**	11	14 **She'll Be Hanging 'Round Somewhere**		Kapp 2072
4/25/70	**3**	17	15 **Heart Over Mind**		Kapp 2086
7/25/70	**5**	14	16 **Heaven Everyday**		MGM 14148
10/17/70	**25**	11	17 Too Lonely, Too Long		Kapp 2103
11/07/70	**8**	13	18 **Commercial Affection**		MGM 14176
1/30/71	**4**	15	19 **The Arms Of A Fool**	114	MGM 14211
5/08/71	**56**	9	20 One More Drink		Kapp 2121
7/31/71	**8**	16	21 **Brand New Mister Me**		MGM 14275
1/01/72	**14**	13	22 Untouched		MGM 14329
5/06/72	**12**	11	23 Would You Want The World To End.................		MGM 14372
8/12/72	**1**²	15	24 **I Ain't Never**		MGM 14418
12/09/72+	**3**	16	25 **Neon Rose**		MGM 14454
4/28/73	**21**	13	26 Thank You For Being You..........................		MGM 14522
8/25/73	**2**¹	17	27 **Sawmill** .... [R]		MGM 14585
1/12/74	**2**¹	18	28 **Midnight, Me And The Blues**		MGM 14689
5/18/74	**3**	16	29 **Stomp Them Grapes**.........................		MGM 14720
10/05/74	**3**	14	30 **Memory Maker**...............................		MGM 14744
2/01/75	**7**	16	31 **Best Way I Know How**........................		MGM 14782
6/14/75	**4**	16	32 **Woman In The Back Of My Mind**...............		MGM 14804
11/01/75+	**16**	14	33 Lookin' For Tomorrow (And Findin' Yesterdays) .		MGM 14835
3/20/76	**15**	10	34 Mental Revenge		MGM 14846
5/29/76	**11**	13	35 Love Revival		MCA 40559
10/02/76	**1**²	16	36 **Good Woman Blues**		MCA 40627
1/15/77	**1**¹	14	37 **Heart Healer**		MCA 40667
4/23/77	**9**	13	38 **Burning Memories**		MCA 40710
8/13/77	**3**	16	39 **I Got The Hoss**		MCA 40764
12/24/77+	**4**	16	40 **What Did I Promise Her Last Night**		MCA 40836
5/13/78	**1**¹	14	41 **I Believe In You**		MCA 40900
9/09/78	**4**	13	42 **Ain't No California**		MCA 40946
1/13/79	**2**³	14	43 **Send Me Down To Tucson/**		
			from the film "Every Which Way But Loose"		
		14	44 Charlie's Angel..................................		MCA 40983
6/16/79	**1**¹	15	45 **Coca Cola Cowboy**		MCA 41041
			from the film "Every Which Way But Loose"		
9/29/79	**6**	14	46 **Blind In Love**		Elektra 46536
1/19/80	**6**	13	47 **Lying Time Again**		Elektra 46583
4/26/80	**3**	16	48 **Your Body Is An Outlaw**		Elektra 46628
8/30/80	**9**	13	49 **Steppin' Out**		Elektra 47015
12/13/80+	**1**¹	16	50 **Southern Rains**		Elektra 47082
4/04/81	**8**	13	51 **A Million Old Goodbyes**		Elektra 47116
9/05/81	**10**	16	52 **One-Night Fever**		Elektra 47178
2/27/82	**36**	9	53 It's A Long Way To Daytona		Elektra 47412
5/29/82	**37**	9	54 The One That Got Away		Elektra 47453
9/25/82	**17**	15	55 Stay A Little Longer		Elektra 69963
3/12/83	**10**	20	56 **In The Middle Of The Night**		MCA 52182
8/06/83	**49**	10	57 A Cowboy's Dream		MCA 52247
10/29/83	**53**	10	58 She Meant Forever When She Said Goodbye.......		MCA 52285
4/28/84	**10**	22	59 **New Patches**..................................		MCA 52373

DEBUT DATE	PEAK POS	WKS CHR	ARTIST — Record Title	POP POS	Label & Number
			MEL TILLIS — Continued		
6/01/85	**37**	12	60 You Done Me Wrong		RCA 14061
9/07/85	**61**	7	61 California Road..		RCA 14175
3/05/88	**31**	14	62 You'll Come Back (You Always Do)...................		Mercury 870192
			MEL TILLIS DUOS with:		
			SHERRY BRYCE:		
6/05/71	**8**	15	63 **Take My Hand**.......................................	*110*	MGM 14255
10/30/71	**9**	14	64 **Living And Learning**.............................		MGM 14303
4/08/72	**38**	10	65 Anything's Better Than Nothing		MGM 14365
11/17/73+	**26**	13	66 Let's Go All The Way Tonight		MGM 14660
4/13/74	**11**	14	67 Don't Let Go		MGM 14714
			#13 pop hit for Roy Hamilton in 1958		
1/04/75	**14**	13	68 You Are The One		MGM 14776
5/17/75	**32**	13	69 Mr. Right And Mrs. Wrong		MGM 14803
			GLEN CAMPBELL:		
10/27/84	**47**	12	70 Slow Nights..		MCA 52474
			BILL PHILLIPS:		
8/24/59	**27**	2	71 Sawmill		Columbia 41416
2/08/60	**24**	4	72 Georgia Town Blues..................................		Columbia 41530
			WEBB PIERCE:		
1/05/63	**25**	3	73 How Come Your Dog Don't Bite Nobody But Me ..		Decca 31445
			NANCY SINATRA:		
7/11/81	**23**	12	74 Texas Cowboy Night		Elektra 47157
12/26/81+	**43**	8	75 Play Me Or Trade Me/		
		8	76 Where Would I Be		Elektra 47247
			PAM TILLIS		
			Daughter of Mel Tillis.		
11/10/84	**71**	5	1 Goodbye Highway..................................		Warner 29155
1/25/86	**55**	8	2 Those Memories Of You............................		Warner 28806
7/05/86	**67**	4	3 I Thought I'd About Had It With Love		Warner 28676
2/21/87	**68**	6	4 I Wish She Wouldn't Treat You That Way		Warner 28444
5/16/87	**71**	6	5 There Goes My Love		Warner 28346
			FLOYD TILLMAN		
			Born on 12/8/14 in Ryan, Oklahoma; raised in Post, Texas. Moved to San Antonio, played with the Mark Clark Orchestra and the Blue Ridge Playboys, and in Houston with Ted Daffan and Moon Mullican in the 30s. Wrote "Slippin' Around". Elected to the Country Music Hall of Fame in 1984.		
1/08/44	**1**[1]	13	1 **They Took The Stars Out Of Heaven**............		Decca 6090
12/16/44	**5**	3	2 **G.I. Blues/**		
12/30/44	**4**	8	3 **Each Night At Nine**................................		Decca 6104
8/03/46	**2**[1]	7	4 **Drivin' Nails In My Coffin**........................		Columbia 36998
7/10/48	**5**	19	5 **I Love You So Much, It Hurts**......................		Columbia 20430
			Juke Box #5 / Best Seller #6		
1/29/49	**14**	1	6 Please Don't Pass Me By..............................		Columbia 20496
			Best Seller #14		
7/02/49	**5**	12	7 **Slippin' Around**......................................		Columbia 20581
			Best Seller #5 / Jockey #6 / Juke Box #6		
10/08/49	**6**	8	8 **I'll Never Slip Around Again**.......................		Columbia 20613
			Best Seller #6 / Juke Box #8		
12/31/49+	**4**	3	9 **I Gotta Have My Baby Back**		Columbia 20641
			Jockey #4		
12/19/60	**29**	1	10 It Just Tears Me Up		Liberty 55280
			JOHNNY TILLOTSON		
			Born on 4/20/39 in Jacksonville, Florida; raised in Palatka, Florida. On local radio "Young Folks Revue" from age 9. Deejay on WWPF. Appeared on the "Toby Dowdy" TV show in Jacksonville, then own show. Signed by Cadence Records in 1958. In the film "Just For Fun".		
6/23/62	**4**	13	1 **It Keeps Right On A-Hurtin'**	*3*	Cadence 1418
9/08/62	**11**	10	2 Send Me The Pillow You Dream On..................	*17*	Cadence 1424
11/11/67+	**48**	10	3 You're The Reason		MGM 13829
2/17/68	**63**	6	4 I Can Spot A Cheater		MGM 13888
6/18/77	**99**	1	5 Toy Hearts		United Art. 986
3/31/84	**91**	2	6 Lay Back (In The Arms Of Someone)................		Reward 04346

DEBUT DATE	PEAK POS	WKS CHR	ARTIST — Record Title	POP POS	Label & Number
			SHEILA TILTON		
			Born in 1951 in Kailua, Hawaii. Sang at rodeos with sisters Muriel and Gwen.		
7/10/76	**23**	13	1 Half As Much..		Con Brio 110
			#1 pop hit for Rosemary Clooney in 1952		
			TINA & DADDY - see GEORGE JONES		
			TINY TIM		
			Born Herbert Khaury on 4/12/30 in New York City. Novelty singer/ukulele player.		
4/16/88	**70**	5	1 Leave Me Satisfied		NLT 1993
			DICK TODD with THE APPALACHIAN WILDCATS		
9/02/67	**52**	6	1 Big Wheel Cannonball....................................		Decca 32168
			same tune as Roy Acuff's "Wabash Cannonball"		
			TOMMY & DONNA		
11/26/88	**72**	6	1 Take It Slow With Me..................................		Oak 1067
			TOMPALL - see GLASER BROTHERS		
			TOPEL & WARE		
10/24/87	**93**	3	1 Change Of Heart		RCI 2406
			MITCHELL TOROK		
			Born on 10/28/29 in Houston. Played guitar since age 12. First recorded in 1948. Wrote "Mexican Joe" for Jim Reeves, "Pledge Of Love" and "Caribbean".		
8/22/53	**1** ²	24	1 **Caribbean**..	*26*	Abbott 140
			Juke Box #1 / Best Seller #4 / Jockey #5 reissue on Guyden hit POS 27 on the pop charts in 1959		
1/23/54	**9**	3	2 **Hootchy Kootchy Henry (From Hawaii)**..........		Abbott 150
			Juke Box #9		
2/18/67	**73**	3	3 Instant Love..		Reprise 0541
			TOUCH OF COUNTRY		
11/12/88	**85**	3	1 I Won't Be Seeing Her No More		OL 127
			BOBBY LEE TRAMMELL		
			Born in Jonesboro, Arkansas.		
5/27/72	**52**	9	1 Love Isn't Love (Till You Give It Away).............		Souncot 1135
			DIANA TRASK		
			Born on 6/23/40 in Melbourne, Australia. One of the most popular stars in Australia by the age of 16. Moved to the USA in 1959. Appeared on Don McNeil's Breakfast Club and the Jack Benny TV shows. Regular on "Sing Along With Mitch" TV series. Toured with Hank Williams, Jr. in the late 60s. Returned to Australia in 1975.		
6/22/68	**70**	4	1 Lock, Stock And Teardrops...........................		Dial 4077
11/23/68	**59**	6	2 Hold What You've Got..................................		Dot 17160
			#5 pop hit for Joe Tex in 1965		
8/30/69	**58**	4	3 Children		Dot 17286
11/29/69+	**37**	7	4 I Fall To Pieces...	*114*	Dot 17316
3/28/70	**38**	9	5 Beneath Still Waters...................................		Dot 17342
7/31/71	**59**	9	6 The Chokin' Kind..		Dot 17384
			#13 pop hit for Joe Simon in 1969		
1/22/72	**30**	14	7 We've Got To Work It Out Between Us		Dot 17404
7/15/72	**33**	12	8 It Meant Nothing To Me		Dot 17424
3/03/73	**15**	13	9 Say When		Dot 17448
7/07/73	**20**	13	10 It's A Man's World (If You Had A Man Like Mine)		Dot 17467
12/08/73+	**16**	15	11 When I Get My Hands On You.......................		Dot 17486
3/30/74	**13**	13	12 Lean It All On Me.......................................	*101*	Dot 17496
8/17/74	**32**	10	13 (If You Wanna Hold On) Hold On To Your Man		Dot 17520
1/11/75	**21**	14	14 Oh Boy..		Dot 17536
6/28/75	**82**	5	15 There Has To Be A Loser..............................		ABC/Dot 17555
11/29/75	**99**	2	16 Cry...		ABC/Dot 17587
			#1 pop hit for Johnnie Ray in 1951		
6/13/81	**62**	6	17 This Must Be My Ship		Kari 121
9/19/81	**74**	3	18 Stirrin' Up Feelings		Kari 123

DEBUT DATE	PEAK POS	WKS CHR	ARTIST — Record Title	POP POS	Label & Number
			MERLE TRAVIS ★★194★★		
			Born on 11/29/17 in Rosewood, Kentucky; died on 10/20/83 in Tahlequah, Oklahoma. Gifted songwriter with a highly influential guitar style. Worked with the Tennessee Tomcats and the Georgia Wildcats. Performed on WLW-Cincinnati, Boone County Jamboree, NBC Radio Plantation Party in the late 30s. Served in the US Marines, then settled in California in 1946. In the film "From Here To Eternity". Wrote "Sixteen Tons", "Smoke, Smoke, Smoke (That Cigarette)". Regular on TV shows "Hometown Jamboree" and "Town Hall Party". Elected to the Country Music Hall Of Fame in 1977.		
6/08/46	2⁴	11	1 **Cincinnati Lou**/		
6/15/46	3	9	2 **No Vacancy**..................................		Capitol 258
9/21/46	1¹⁴	23	3 **Divorce Me C.O.D.**/	25	
1/11/47	5	2	4 **Missouri**		Capitol 290
1/25/47	1¹⁴	22	5 **So Round, So Firm, So Fully Packed**..............	21	Capitol 349
5/17/47	4	3	6 **Steel Guitar Rag**/		
5/24/47	4	4	7 **Three Times Seven**		Capitol 384
11/01/47	4	2	8 **Fat Gal**/		
3/20/48	7	1	9 **Merle's Boogie Woogie**		Capitol A. 40026
8/28/48	11	3	10 Crazy Boogie		Capitol 15143
			Juke Box #11 / Best Seller #12		
2/05/49	13	1	11 What A Shame..................................		Capitol 15317
			Juke Box #13		
6/04/55	5	9	12 **Wildwood Flower** .... [I]		Capitol 3106
			HANK THOMPSON with MERLE TRAVIS Juke Box #5 / Best Seller #8 / Jockey #13		
7/30/66	44	4	13 John Henry, Jr.		Capitol 5657
			RANDY TRAVIS ★★191★★		
			Born Randy Bruce Traywick in Marshville, North Carolina in 5/4/59. Sang with brother in a band at age 10, worked local clubs from age 14. Worked at Country City USA, Charlotte, from 1976-81. First recorded for Paula in 1978. Moved to Nashville in 1981, worked as singer/ dishwasher/cook at Lib Hatcher's Nashville Palace. Recorded as Randy Traywick and Randy Ray before adopting stage name, Randy Travis, in 1985. Joined the Grand Ole Opry in 1986.		
1/06/79	91	4	1 She's My Woman...........................		Paula 431
			shown as: **RANDY TRAYWICK**		
8/31/85	67	12	2 On The Other Hand		Warner 28962
12/28/85+	6	24	3 1982..		Warner 28828
4/26/86	1¹	23	4 **On The Other Hand** .... [R]		Warner 28962
8/16/86	1¹	21	5 **Diggin' Up Bones**		Warner 28649
12/13/86+	2²	21	6 **No Place Like Home**		Warner 28525
4/25/87	1³	22	7 **Forever And Ever, Amen**		Warner 28384
8/29/87	1¹	22	8 **I Won't Need You Anymore (Always And Forever)**		Warner 28246
12/12/87+	1¹	19	9 **Too Gone Too Long**		Warner 28286
4/09/88	1²	18	10 **I Told You So**		Warner 27969
7/30/88	1¹	17	11 **Honky Tonk Moon**		Warner 27833
11/19/88+	1¹	18	12 **Deeper Than The Holler**		Warner 27689
			VAN TREVOR		
			Born on 11/12/40 in Lewiston, Maine. Made professional debut at age 7. Moved to Nashville in the mid-60s. Worked as a producer/songwriter from 1973-76.		
4/23/66	22	18	1 Born To Be In Love With You		Band Box 367
11/19/66+	27	13	2 Our Side		Band Box 371
9/09/67	26	15	3 You've Been So Good To Me		Date 1565
4/27/68	31	11	4 Take Me Along With You		Date 1594
2/01/69	42	9	5 The Things That Matter..................		Royal Amer. 280
5/10/69	56	7	6 A Man Away From Home		Royal Amer. 283
6/13/70	42	8	7 Luziana River............................		Royal Amer. 9
1/23/71	54	6	8 Wish I Was Home Instead		Royal Amer. 23
			TRINITY LANE		
			Trio of Nashville singer/songwriters: Tom Grant, Allen Estes and Sharon Anderson.		
4/23/88	75	4	1 For A Song		Curb 10507
8/13/88	70	3	2 Someday, Somenight		Curb 10511
11/05/88	90	2	3 Ready To Take That Ride		Curb 10515
			BOBBY TRINITY		
8/27/77	95	2	1 I Love Everything I Get My Hands On................		GRT 128

DEBUT DATE	PEAK POS	WKS CHR	ARTIST — Record Title	POP POS	Label & Number
			ALLEN TRIPP		
			Born in Fort Worth, sang with the Texas Boys Choir.		
3/20/82	**39**	11	1 Love Is		Nashville 1001
			ERNEST TUBB ★★**13**★★		
			Born on 2/9/14 in Crisp, Texas; died of emphysema on 9/6/84. Worked on KONO-San Antonio and KGKO-Fort Worth in the mid-30s. First recorded for Bluebird in 1936. Wrote "I'm Walking The Floor Over You" in 1941. Moved to Nashville in 1943, joined the Grand Ole Opry. In the films "Fighting Buckaroo", "Hollywood Barn Dance", "Ridin' West" and "Jamboree". Broadcast from his own Ernest Tubb Record Shop beginning in 1947. Elected to the Country Music Hall Of Fame in 1965. Nicknamed "The Texas Troubadour".		
1/08/44	**2**³	17	1 Try Me One More Time	18	Decca 6093
5/27/44	**1**⁴	29	2 Soldier's Last Letter/	16	
6/03/44	**4**	3	3 Yesterday's Tears	29	Decca 6098
3/17/45	**6**	1	4 Keep My Mem'ry In Your Heart/		
3/31/45	**3**	14	5 Tomorrow Never Comes		Decca 6106
8/04/45	**3**	8	6 Careless Darlin'		Decca 6110
11/17/45	**1**⁴	13	7 It's Been So Long, Darling		Decca 6112
11/16/46+	**1**²	20	8 Rainbow At Midnight		Decca 46018
11/16/46	**2**⁴	12	9 Filipino Baby/		
12/21/46	**5**	2	10 Drivin' Nails In My Coffin........................		Decca 46019
5/17/47	**4**	6	11 Don't Look Now (But Your Broken Heart Is Showing)/		
6/28/47	**5**	1	12 So Round, So Firm, So Fully Packed............		Decca 46040
7/19/47	**4**	1	13 I'll Step Aside		Decca 46041
5/15/48	**5**	14	14 Seaman's Blues		Decca 46119
			Best Seller #5 / Juke Box #8		
7/17/48	**15**	1	15 You Nearly Lose Your Mind..........................		Decca 46125
			Juke Box #15		
8/07/48	**5**	13	16 Forever Is Ending Today/	30	
			Best Seller #5 / Juke Box #6		
9/04/48	**9**	6	17 That Wild And Wicked Look In Your Eye		Decca 46134
			Juke Box #9		
12/11/48+	**2**¹	17	18 Have You Ever Been Lonely? (Have You Ever Been Blue)/		
			Juke Box #2 / Best Seller #9		
12/11/48+	**5**	17	19 Let's Say Goodbye Like We Said Hello		Decca 46144
			Best Seller #5 / Juke Box #6		
3/19/49	**4**	9	20 Till The End Of The World............................		Decca 46150
			Juke Box #4 / Best Seller #11		
4/09/49	**2**¹	16	21 I'm Biting My Fingernails And Thinking Of You/	30	
			ANDREWS SISTERS & ERNEST TUBB		
			Juke Box #2 / Best Seller #4		
4/16/49	**6**	5	22 Don't Rob Another Man's Castle		Decca 24592
			ERNEST TUBB & ANDREWS SISTERS		
			Juke Box #6 / Best Seller #10		
5/07/49	**15**	1	23 Daddy, When Is Mommy Coming Home.............		Decca 46150
			Juke Box #15		
5/28/49	**6**	4	24 Mean Mama Blues		Decca 46162
			Juke Box #6		
7/30/49	**1**¹	20	25 Slippin' Around/	17	
			Juke Box #1 / Best Seller #4		
9/17/49	**10**	3	26 My Tennessee Baby..................................		Decca 46173
			Juke Box #10		
9/03/49	**6**	6	27 My Filipino Rose/		
			Juke Box #6 / Best Seller #11		
9/03/49	**8**	8	28 Warm Red Wine....................................		Decca 46175
			Best Seller #8 / Juke Box #9		
12/03/49+	**1**¹	6	29 Blue Christmas/ [X]		
			Juke Box #1 / Best Seller #2 / Jockey #2		
12/24/49	**7**	1	30 White Christmas .... [X]		Decca 46186
			Juke Box #7 / Best Seller #15		
2/04/50	**2**¹	17	31 Letters Have No Arms/		
			Juke Box #2 / Jockey #3 / Best Seller #5		
2/25/50	**8**	1	32 I'll Take A Back Seat For You		Decca 46207
			Juke Box #8		

DEBUT DATE	PEAK POS	WKS CHR	ARTIST — Record Title	POP POS	Label & Number
			ERNEST TUBB — Continued		
2/25/50	**2** [1]	20	33 **I Love You Because/** Juke Box #2 / Best Seller #4 / Jockey #6		
3/18/50	**8**	2	34 **Unfaithful One** .... Juke Box #8		Decca 46213
6/24/50	**3**	15	35 **Throw Your Love My Way/** Jockey #3 / Juke Box #4 / Best Seller #5		
8/05/50	**9**	4	36 **Give Me A Little Old Fashioned Love** .... Juke Box #9		Decca 46243
10/28/50	**10**	2	37 **You Don't Have To Be A Baby To Cry** .... Juke Box #10		Decca 46257
11/04/50	**5**	9	38 **(Remember Me) I'm The One Who Loves You** ... Juke Box #5 / Best Seller #7		Decca 46269
12/30/50	**5**	1	39 **Blue Christmas** .... [X-R] Best Seller #5 / Jockey #9 / Juke Box #10		Decca 46186
6/02/51	**9**	3	40 **Don't Stay Too Long** .... Jockey #9		Decca 46296
9/15/51	**6**	2	41 **Hey La La** .... Juke Box #6		Decca 46338
12/15/51	**7**	2	42 **Driftwood On The River** .... Juke Box #7		Decca 46377
1/05/52	**5**	1	43 **Blue Christmas** .... [X-R] Jockey #5		Decca 46186
2/09/52	**3**	11	44 **Missing In Action** .... Best Seller #3 / Jockey #5 / Juke Box #9		Decca 46389
5/17/52	**9**	1	45 **Somebody's Stolen My Honey** .... Juke Box #9 / Best Seller #10		Decca 28067
9/13/52	**5**	11	46 **Fortunes In Memories** .... Juke Box #5 / Jockey #7		Decca 28310
12/12/53	**9**	2	47 **Divorce Granted** .... Juke Box #9		Decca 28869
10/16/54	**11**	5	48 Two Glasses, Joe .... Best Seller #11		Decca 29220
9/17/55	**7**	11	49 **The Yellow Rose Of Texas** .... Jockey #7 / Best Seller #13		Decca 29633
12/17/55	**7**	4	50 **Thirty Days** .... Juke Box #7 / Jockey #10		Decca 29731
7/08/57	**8**	2	51 **Mister Love** .... ERNEST TUBB & THE WILBURN BROTHERS Jockey #8		Decca 30303
4/28/58	**13**	4	52 House Of Glass .... Jockey #13		Decca 30549
5/26/58	**9**	10	53 **Hey, Mr. Bluebird** .... ERNEST TUBB & THE WILBURN BROTHERS Jockey #9 / Best Seller #14		Decca 30610
10/20/58	**8**	11	54 **Half A Mind/**		
10/20/58	**21**	1	55 Deep Purple Blues.......................................		Decca 30685
1/05/59	**19**	3	56 What Am I Living For		Decca 30759
5/04/59	**12**	13	57 I Cried A Tear...		Decca 30872
9/28/59	**14**	14	58 Next Time		Decca 30952
9/05/60	**16**	7	59 Ev'rybody's Somebody's Fool		Decca 31119
6/05/61	**16**	9	60 Thoughts Of A Fool		Decca 31241
11/13/61	**14**	11	61 Through That Door.......................................		Decca 31300
8/18/62	**16**	9	62 I'm Looking High And Low For My Baby/		
9/08/62	**30**	1	63 Show Her Lots Of Gold		Decca 31399
6/22/63	**28**	1	64 Mr. Juke Box...		Decca 31476
9/28/63	**3**	23	65 **Thanks A Lot**		Decca 31526
5/30/64	**26**	17	66 Be Better To Your Baby		Decca 31614
12/26/64+	**15**	17	67 Pass The Booze		Decca 31706
3/06/65	**29**	12	68 Do What You Do Do Well		Decca 31742
10/23/65	**34**	7	69 Waltz Across Texas		Decca 31824
1/01/66	**48**	2	70 It's For God, And Country, And You Mom (That's Why I'm Fighting In Viet Nam)		Decca 31861
4/02/66	**32**	9	71 Till My Getup Has Gotup And Gone		Decca 31908
10/15/66	**16**	16	72 Another Story		Decca 32022
2/03/68	**55**	5	73 Too Much Of Not Enough		Decca 32237

DEBUT DATE	PEAK POS	WKS CHR	ARTIST — Record Title	POP POS	Label & Number
			ERNEST TUBB — Continued		
7/20/68	**69**	2	74 I'm Gonna Make Like A Snake......................		Decca 32315
			written by Loretta Lynn		
3/15/69	**43**	7	75 Saturday Satan Sunday Saint.......................		Decca 32448
7/21/73	**93**	2	76 I've Got All The Heartaches I Can Handle.........		MCA 40056
12/17/77+	**79**	7	77 Sometimes I Do/		
		7	78 Half My Heart's In Texas		1st Genrtn. 001
6/02/79	**56**	6	79 Waltz Across Texas................................. [R]		Cachet 3001
			new version with guest vocal: Willie Nelson		
10/13/79	**31**	9	80 Walkin' The Floor Over You .... [R]		Cachet 4507
			with friends: Merle Haggard, Chet Atkins and Charlie Daniels		
			ERNEST TUBB & RED FOLEY:		
12/31/49+	**2** [2]	10	81 **Tennessee Border No. 2/**		
			Best Seller #2 / Juke Box #2		
1/21/50	**7**	2	82 **Don't Be Ashamed Of Your Age**..................		Decca 46200
8/19/50	**1** [3]	15	83 **Goodnight, Irene**/	10	
			Juke Box #1(3) / Best Seller #1(2) / Jockey #2		
9/02/50	**9**	2	84 **Hillbilly Fever No. 2**		Decca 46255
			Juke Box #9		
5/19/51	**9**	1	85 **Strange Little Girl**...............................		Decca 46311
			Juke Box #9		
2/02/52	**5**	9	86 **Too Old To Cut The Mustard**		Decca 46387
			Best Seller #5 / Juke Box #8 / Jockey #10		
4/18/53	**7**	2	87 **No Help Wanted #2**		Decca 28634
			Best Seller #7 / Juke Box #9		
			ERNEST TUBB & LORETTA LYNN:		
7/25/64	**11**	23	88 Mr. And Mrs. Used To Be		Decca 31643
7/24/65	**24**	11	89 Our Hearts Are Holding Hands......................		Decca 31793
2/25/67	**45**	9	90 Sweet Thang		Decca 32091
6/14/69	**18**	10	91 Who's Gonna Take The Garbage Out		Decca 32496
			JUSTIN TUBB		
			Born on 8/20/35 in San Antonio. Eldest son of Ernest Tubb. On the Grand Ole Opry since 1955. Manager of the Ernest Tubb Midnight Jamboree Radio Show and his own publishing company. Wrote "Lonesome 7-7203" for Hawkshaw Hawkins.		
7/03/54	**4**	21	1 **Looking Back To See**............................		Decca 29145
			GOLDIE HILL - JUSTIN TUBB		
			Juke Box #4 / Best Seller #5 / Jockey #5		
1/08/55	**11**	1	2 Sure Fire Kisses....................................		Decca 29349
			JUSTIN TUBB - GOLDIE HILL		
			Jockey #11 / Best Seller #13		
2/19/55	**8**	7	3 **I Gotta Go Get My Baby**...........................		Decca 29401
			Jockey #8		
4/13/63	**6**	16	4 **Take A Letter Miss Gray**		Groove 0017
10/02/65	**23**	9	5 Hurry, Mr. Peters		RCA 8659
			JUSTIN TUBB & LORENE MANN		
			answer to Roy Drusky & Priscilla Mitchell's "Yes, Mr. Peters"		
7/30/66	**44**	2	6 We've Gone Too Far Again..........................		RCA 8834
			JUSTIN TUBB & LORENE MANN		
2/25/67	**63**	7	7 But Wait There's More		RCA 9082
			JERRY LEE TUCKER		
11/12/88	**93**	2	1 Livin' In Shadows..................................		Oak 1057
			JIMMY TUCKER		
5/19/79	**98**	2	1 I'm Gonna Move To The Country (And Get Away To It All)		Gar-Pax 2715
12/08/79	**85**	4	2 (You've Got That) Fire Goin' Again		NSD 35
4/05/80	**82**	3	3 The Reading Of The Will............................		NSD 40
			LA COSTA TUCKER - see LA COSTA		
			TANYA TUCKER ★★56★★		
			Born on 10/10/58 in Seminole, Texas; raised in Wilcox, Arizona. Appeared on the "Lew King" TV series in Phoenix from 1969. In the film "Jeremiah Johnson". Had her first charted record at age 13.		
5/13/72	**6**	17	1 **Delta Dawn**	72	Columbia 45588
11/18/72+	**5**	15	2 **Love's The Answer**/		
		13	3 The Jamestown Ferry		Columbia 45721
3/24/73	**1** [1]	17	4 **What's Your Mama's Name**	86	Columbia 45799

DEBUT DATE	PEAK POS	WKS CHR	ARTIST — Record Title	POP POS	Label & Number
			TANYA TUCKER — Continued		
7/21/73	**1**¹	16	5 **Blood Red And Goin' Down**	74	Columbia 45892
1/12/74	**1**¹	17	6 **Would You Lay With Me (In A Field Of Stone)** .	46	Columbia 45991
6/08/74	**4**	14	7 **The Man That Turned My Mama On**	86	Columbia 46047
1/04/75	**18**	11	8 I Believe The South Is Gonna Rise Again		Columbia 10069
4/26/75	**1**¹	15	9 **Lizzie And The Rainman**	37	MCA 40402
6/14/75	**18**	15	10 Spring		Columbia 10127
8/23/75	**1**¹	15	11 **San Antonio Stroll**		MCA 40444
11/08/75	**23**	10	12 Greener Than The Grass (We Laid On)		Columbia 10236
12/13/75+	**4**	15	13 **Don't Believe My Heart Can Stand Another You**		MCA 40497
4/17/76	**3**	14	14 **You've Got Me To Hold On To**		MCA 40540
8/07/76	**1**¹	15	15 **Here's Some Love**	82	MCA 40598
12/25/76+	**12**	12	16 Ridin' Rainbows		MCA 40650
4/16/77	**7**	14	17 **It's A Cowboy Lovin' Night** ....,....		MCA 40708
7/23/77	**40**	8	18 You Are So Beautiful		Columbia 10577
			#5 pop hit for Joe Cocker in 1975		
8/13/77	**16**	11	19 Dancing The Night Away		MCA 40755
6/10/78	**86**	3	20 Save Me	105	MCA 40902
11/25/78+	**5**	15	21 **Texas (When I Die)**		MCA 40976
			flip side "Not Fade Away" hit POS 70 on the pop charts		
4/07/79	**18**	13	22 I'm The Singer, You're The Song		MCA 41005
			flip side "Lover Goodbye" hit POS 103 on the pop charts		
8/23/80	**10**	14	23 **Pecos Promenade**		MCA 41305
			from the film "Smokey & The Bandit 2"		
9/27/80	**59**	6	24 Dream Lover		MCA 41323
			TANYA TUCKER & GLEN CAMPBELL		
			#2 pop hit for Bobby Darin in 1959		
12/20/80+	**4**	15	25 **Can I See You Tonight**		MCA 51037
4/11/81	**85**	4	26 Why Don't We Just Sleep On It Tonight		Capitol 4986
			GLEN CAMPBELL & TANYA TUCKER		
4/25/81	**40**	8	27 Love Knows We Tried		MCA 51096
7/04/81	**50**	7	28 Should I Do It		MCA 51131
10/17/81	**83**	4	29 Rodeo Girls		MCA 51184
10/16/82	**77**	4	30 Cry/		
11/27/82+	**10**	23	31 **Feel Right**		Arista 0677
4/23/83	**41**	12	32 Changes		Arista 1053
7/23/83	**22**	15	33 Baby I'm Yours		Arista 9046
			#11 pop hit for Barbara Lewis in 1965		
2/15/86	**3**	25	34 **One Love At A Time**		Capitol 5533
7/12/86	**1**¹	24	35 **Just Another Love**		Capitol 5604
11/08/86+	**2**¹	23	36 **I'll Come Back As Another Woman**		Capitol 5652
3/28/87	**8**	25	37 **It's Only For You**		Capitol 5694
7/25/87	**2**¹	25	38 **Love Me Like You Used To**		Capitol 44036
11/21/87+	**1**¹	24	39 **I Won't Take Less Than Your Love**		Capitol 44100
			TANYA TUCKER with PAUL DAVIS & PAUL OVERSTREET		
4/02/88	**1**¹	20	40 **If It Don't Come Easy**		Capitol 44142
7/16/88	**1**¹	23	41 **Strong Enough To Bend**		Capitol 44188
12/03/88+	**2**¹	19	42 **Highway Robbery**		Capitol 44271
			FRANK TURNER		
			Born in Roanoke, Virginia. A one-man band act, with vocals by his wife, Ruth.		
10/24/64	**48**	1	1 The Bible In Her Hand		Chart 1130
			MARY LOU TURNER		
			Born in Hazard, Kentucky. Singer with the Bill Anderson Show.		
7/06/74	**94**	2	1 All That Keeps Me Goin'		MCA 40244
1/25/75	**85**	7	2 Come On Home		MCA 40343
6/12/76	**25**	12	3 It's Different With You		MCA 40566
10/02/76	**30**	10	4 Love It Away		MCA 40620
2/05/77	**41**	9	5 Cheatin' Overtime		MCA 40674
6/04/77	**93**	3	6 The Man Still Turns Me On		MCA 40727
12/10/77+	**73**	7	7 He Picked Me Up When You Let Me Down		MCA 40828
8/04/79	**78**	4	8 Yours And Mine		Churchill 7741

DEBUT DATE	PEAK POS	WKS CHR	ARTIST — Record Title	POP POS	Label & Number
			MARY LOU TURNER — Continued		
10/20/79	**81**	4	9 Caught With My Feelings Down/		
		2	10 You Can't Remember And I Can't Forget		Churchill 7744
2/09/80	**91**	2	11 I Wanna Love You Tonight..................		Churchill 7751
			BILL ANDERSON & MARY LOU TURNER:		
11/29/75+	**1**¹	16	**12 Sometimes ....**		MCA 40488
3/27/76	**7**	12	**13 That's What Made Me Love You ....**		MCA 40533
7/16/77	**18**	12	14 Where Are You Going, Billy Boy		MCA 40753
1/28/78	**25**	10	15 I'm Way Ahead Of You...................		MCA 40852
			ZEB TURNER		
			Born William Edward Grisham on 6/23/15 in Lynchburg, Virginia. Writer of "That's When Your Heartaches Begin". In the film "Darling Clementine".		
9/17/49	**11**	1	1 Tennessee Boogie...		King 790
			Juke Box #11		
4/21/51	**8**	2	2 Chew Tobacco Rag		King 950
			Juke Box #8 / Jockey #9		
			WESLEY TUTTLE		
			Born in Lamar, Colorado. Worked on WLW-Cincinnati, then moved to California. Appeared with the Sons Of The Pioneers in western films. Regular performances on the "Town Hall Party". Duets with wife Marilyn, a former member of the Sunshine Girls who appeared in Shirley Temple films.		
10/06/45	**1**⁴	14	1 With Tears In My Eyes		Capitol 216
3/09/46	**3**	4	2 Detour/		
3/16/46	**5**	2	3 I Wish I Had Never Met Sunshine		Capitol 233
7/20/46	**4**	5	4 Tho' I Tried (I Can't Forget You)...................		Capitol 267
11/20/54	**15**	1	5 Never		Capitol 2850
			MARILYN & WESLEY TUTTLE		
			Best Seller #15		
			CONWAY TWITTY ★★5★★		
			Born Harold Lloyd Jenkins on 9/1/33 in Friars Point, Mississippi; raised in Helena, Arkansas. Formed own group, the Phillips County Ramblers, at age 10. Offered a professional career with the Philadelphia Phillies when drafted into the Army. With service band, Cimmarons, in Japan, early 50s. Changed name in 1957 and first recorded for Sun (unissued recordings). In the films "Sexpot Goes To College" and "College Confidential". Switched from pop to country music in 1965. Moved to Nashville in 1968. Owns tourist complex, Twitty City, in Hendersonville, Tennessee.		
3/26/66	**18**	12	1 Guess My Eyes Were Bigger Than My Heart		Decca 31897
9/17/66	**36**	10	2 Look Into My Teardrops		Decca 31983
2/18/67	**21**	14	3 I Don't Want To Be With Me..........................		Decca 32081
7/08/67	**32**	12	4 Don't Put Your Hurt In My Heart......................		Decca 32147
12/09/67	**61**	4	5 Funny (But I'm Not Laughing)...........................		Decca 32208
3/23/68	**5**	18	**6 The Image Of Me.........................**		Decca 32272
8/17/68	**1**¹	17	**7 Next In Line ....**		Decca 32361
12/28/68+	**2**²	17	**8 Darling, You Know I Wouldn't Lie ....**		Decca 32424
5/10/69	**1**¹	17	**9 I Love You More Today ....**		Decca 32481
9/20/69	**1**¹	14	**10 To See My Angel Cry ....**		Decca 32546
1/03/70	**3**	14	**11 That's When She Started To Stop Loving You**		Decca 32599
4/25/70	**1**⁴	20	**12 Hello Darlin' ....**	60	Decca 32661
10/10/70	**1**¹	18	**13 Fifteen Years Ago ....**	81	Decca 32742
2/06/71	**59**	6	14 What Am I Living For .... [R]		MGM 14205
			originally hit POS 26 on the pop charts in 1960		
3/20/71	**1**¹	17	**15 How Much More Can She Stand ....**	105	Decca 32801
7/17/71	**4**	14	**16 I Wonder What She'll Think About Me**		
			Leaving	112	Decca 32842
			written by Merle Haggard		
9/11/71	**50**	10	17 What A Dream .... [R]		MGM 14274
			originally hit POS 106 on the pop charts in 1960		
12/04/71+	**4**	16	**18 I Can't See Me Without You ....**		Decca 32895
4/01/72	**1**¹	15	**19 (Lost Her Love) On Our Last Date.................**	112	Decca 32945
			same tune as Floyd Cramer's "Last Date"		
7/29/72	**1**¹	15	**20 I Can't Stop Loving You ....**		Decca 32988
12/02/72+	**1**²	15	**21 She Needs Someone To Hold Her (When She**		
			Cries)		Decca 33033
3/31/73	**2**¹	14	**22 Baby's Gone ....**		MCA 40027
7/21/73	**1**³	19	**23 You've Never Been This Far Before...............**	22	MCA 40094

DEBUT DATE	PEAK POS	WKS CHR		ARTIST — Record Title	POP POS	Label & Number
				CONWAY TWITTY — Continued		
1/19/74	**1**¹	15	24	**There's A Honky Tonk Angel (Who'll Take Me Back In)**		MCA 40173
5/11/74	**3**	15	25	**I'm Not Through Loving You Yet**		MCA 40224
8/24/74	**1**²	17	26	**I See The Want To In Your Eyes**		MCA 40282
1/11/75	**1**¹	14	27	**Linda On My Mind**	*61*	MCA 40339
5/24/75	**1**²	13	28	**Touch The Hand/**		
8/16/75	**4**	13	29	**Don't Cry Joni**	*63*	MCA 40407
				vocal accompaniment by Conway's daughter, Joni		
12/06/75+	**1**¹	14	30	**This Time I've Hurt Her More Than She Loves Me**		MCA 40492
4/03/76	**1**¹	13	31	**After All The Good Is Gone**		MCA 40534
8/21/76	**1**¹	13	32	**The Games That Daddies Play**		MCA 40601
11/20/76+	**1**¹	14	33	**I Can't Believe She Gives It All To Me**		MCA 40649
3/05/77	**1**¹	16	34	**Play, Guitar Play**		MCA 40682
7/23/77	**1**¹	15	35	**I've Already Loved You In Your Mind**		MCA 40754
10/29/77	**3**	15	36	**Georgia Keeps Pulling On My Ring**		MCA 40805
2/18/78	**16**	10	37	The Grandest Lady Of Them All		MCA 40857
7/15/78	**2**¹	14	38	**Boogie Grass Band**		MCA 40929
11/18/78+	**3**	15	39	**Your Love Had Taken Me That High**		MCA 40963
3/17/79	**1**¹	14	40	**Don't Take It Away**		MCA 41002
7/14/79	**1**¹	15	41	**I May Never Get To Heaven**		MCA 41059
10/27/79	**1**³	14	42	**Happy Birthday Darlin'**		MCA 41135
2/02/80	**1**¹	13	43	**I'd Love To Lay You Down**		MCA 41174
6/28/80	**6**	13	44	**I've Never Seen The Likes Of You**		MCA 41271
10/18/80+	**3**	17	45	**A Bridge That Just Won't Burn**		MCA 51011
2/21/81	**1**¹	14	46	**Rest Your Love On Me/**		
				written by Barry Gibb (of The Bee Gees)		
		12	47	**I Am The Dreamer (You Are The Dream)**		MCA 51059
7/11/81	**1**¹	16	48	**Tight Fittin' Jeans**		MCA 51137
10/31/81+	**1**¹	18	49	**Red Neckin' Love Makin' Night**		MCA 51199
1/30/82	**1**¹	17	50	**The Clown**		Elektra 47302
4/24/82	**1**²	16	51	**Slow Hand**		Elektra 47443
				#2 pop hit for the Pointer Sisters in 1981		
5/08/82	**69**	7	52	Over Thirty (Not Over The Hill)		MCA 52032
9/18/82	**2**²	18	53	**We Did But Now You Don't**		Elektra 69964
12/25/82+	**1**¹	19	54	**The Rose**		Elektra 69854
				#3 pop hit for Bette Midler in 1980		
4/02/83	**44**	11	55	We Had It All		MCA 52154
5/28/83	**2**²	21	56	**Lost In The Feeling**		Warner 29636
9/24/83	**6**	19	57	**Heartache Tonight**		Warner 29505
				#1 pop hit for the Eagles in 1979		
12/24/83+	**7**	18	58	**Three Times A Lady**		Warner 29395
				#1 pop hit for the Commodores in 1978		
4/14/84	**1**¹	19	59	**Somebody's Needin' Somebody**		Warner 29308
7/28/84	**1**¹	19	60	**I Don't Know A Thing About Love (The Moon Song)**		Warner 29227
				vocal accompaniment: Joni Lee Twitty		
11/10/84+	**1**¹	21	61	**Ain't She Somethin' Else**		Warner 29137
3/16/85	**1**¹	20	62	**Don't Call Him A Cowboy**		Warner 29057
7/06/85	**3**	19	63	**Between Blue Eyes And Jeans**		Warner 28966
10/26/85	**19**	18	64	The Legend And The Man		Warner 28866
3/01/86	**26**	14	65	You'll Never Know How Much I Needed You Today		Warner 28772
6/07/86	**1**¹	21	66	**Desperado Love**		Warner 28692
10/18/86+	**2**¹	25	67	**Fallin' For You For Years**		Warner 28577
3/07/87	**2**²	23	68	**Julia**		MCA 53034
7/11/87	**2**¹	24	69	**I Want To Know You Before We Make Love**		MCA 53134
11/14/87+	**6**	23	70	**That's My Job**		MCA 53200
4/09/88	**7**	19	71	**Goodbye Time**		MCA 53276
8/06/88	**9**	19	72	**Saturday Night Special**		MCA 53373
11/26/88+	**4**	23	73	**I Wish I Was Still In Your Dreams**		MCA 53456

DEBUT DATE	PEAK POS	WKS CHR	ARTIST — Record Title	POP POS	Label & Number
			CONWAY TWITTY — Continued		
			LORETTA LYNN/CONWAY TWITTY:		
2/06/71	**1**²	14	74 **After The Fire Is Gone**	*56*	Decca 32776
10/02/71	**1**¹	17	75 **Lead Me On**...		Decca 32873
6/23/73	**1**¹	14	76 **Louisiana Woman, Mississippi Man**...............		MCA 40079
6/15/74	**1**¹	15	77 **As Soon As I Hang Up The Phone**		MCA 40251
6/21/75	**1**¹	16	78 **Feelins'**		MCA 40420
6/19/76	**3**	12	79 **The Letter**		MCA 40572
6/04/77	**2**³	14	80 **I Can't Love You Enough**................................		MCA 40728
6/24/78	**6**	11	81 **From Seven Till Ten/**		
		9	82 You're The Reason Our Kids Are Ugly		MCA 40920
11/10/79+	**9**	14	83 **You Know Just What I'd Do/**		
		14	84 The Sadness Of It All.................................		MCA 41141
5/10/80	**5**	15	85 **It's True Love**		MCA 41232
1/31/81	**7**	15	86 **Lovin' What Your Lovin' Does To Me**		MCA 51050
5/30/81	**2**²	18	87 **I Still Believe In Waltzes**		MCA 51114
			KATHY TWITTY		
			Born in 1960. Daughter of Conway Twitty. Recorded as "Jesseca James" in 1976.		
10/02/76	**87**	4	1 Johnny One Time..		MCA 40613
4/30/77	**93**	3	2 My First Country Song		MCA 40703
			above 2 shown as: **JESSECA JAMES**		
1/12/85	**82**	5	3 Green Eyes		Permian 82008
			TWO HEARTS		
			Sisters Jama and Cathy Bowen from Burbank, Oklahoma.		
11/23/85	**63**	8	1 Two Hearts Can't Be Wrong		MDJ 5831
8/02/86	**77**	5	2 Feel Like I'm Falling For You		MDJ 5832
			BONNIE TYLER		
			Born Gaynor Hopkins on 6/8/53 in Swansea, Wales. Worked local clubs until the mid-70s. A throat operation in 1976 left her with a unique singing voice.		
4/15/78	**10**	15	1●It's A Heartache..	*3*	RCA 11249
2/24/79	**86**	3	2 My Guns Are Loaded	*107*	RCA 11468
			T. TEXAS TYLER		
			Born David Luke Myrick on 6/20/16 in Mena, Arkansas; died on 1/28/72. Raised in Texas, educated in Philadelphia. Appeared on the Major Bowes Amateur Hour in New York City in the late 30s. Worked on the Louisiana Hayride in 1942. Moved to California after the service in 1946. Appeared in the film "Horseman Of The Sierras" in 1949. Own TV series, "Range Round-Up", in Los Angeles. Billed as "The Man With A Million Friends".		
8/24/46	**5**	1	1 **Filipino Baby**		4 Star 1008
4/10/48	**2**¹	13	2 **Deck Of Cards**................................ [S]	*21*	4 Star 1228
			Best Seller #2 / Juke Box #3		
7/03/48	**10**	2	3 **Dad Gave My Dog Away**................................		4 Star 1248
			Best Seller #10 / Juke Box #13		
9/25/48	**9**	4	4 **Memories Of France/**		
			Juke Box #9		
11/13/48	**11**	1	5 Honky Tonk Gal		4 Star 1249
			Juke Box #11		
11/26/49	**4**	5	6 **My Bucket's Got A Hole In It**		4 Star 1383
			Juke Box #4 / Jockey #8		
4/18/53	**5**	15	7 **Bumming Around**...		Decca 28579
			Best Seller #5 / Juke Box #5		
7/17/54	**3**	19	8 **Courtin' In The Rain**......................................		4 Star 1660
			Jockey #3 / Juke Box #4		
			LYNNE TYNDALL		
			Born in Owensboro, Kentucky; raised in Nashville.		
11/14/87	**67**	5	1 Lovin' The Blue		Evergreen 1060
5/14/88	**62**	6	2 This Is Me Leaving		Evergreen 1071
11/05/88	**83**	4	3 Love's Slippin' Up On Me		Evergreen 1079

DEBUT DATE	PEAK POS	WKS CHR	ARTIST — Record Title	POP POS	Label & Number

U

UNKNOWN
An Elvis Presley impersonator.

DEBUT DATE	PEAK POS	WKS CHR	ARTIST — Record Title	POP POS	Label & Number
12/24/88+	82	4	1 Spelling On The Stone...................................		Curb 10522

refers to Elvis Aaron Presley's name on his grave stone

USA for AFRICA
USA: United Support of Artists - a collection of 46 major artists formed to help the suffering people of Africa and the U.S.A.

DEBUT DATE	PEAK POS	WKS CHR	ARTIST — Record Title	POP POS	Label & Number
4/20/85	76	6	1▲We Are The World.......................................	*1*	Columbia 04839

soloists (in order): Lionel Richie, Stevie Wonder, Paul Simon, Kenny Rogers, James Ingram, Tina Turner, Billy Joel, Michael Jackson, Diana Ross, Dionne Warwick, Willie Nelson, Al Jarreau, Bruce Springsteen, Kenny Loggins, Steve Perry, Daryl Hall, Huey Lewis, Cyndi Lauper, Kim Carnes, Bob Dylan, and Ray Charles - written by Michael Jackson & Lionel Richie

V

VALENTINO
Valentino Enrique Hernandez, born on 2/13/60 in Toledo, Ohio.

DEBUT DATE	PEAK POS	WKS CHR	ARTIST — Record Title	POP POS	Label & Number
8/01/81	62	6	1 She Took The Place Of You............................		RCA 12269

LEROY VAN DYKE
Born on 10/4/29 in Spring Fork, Missouri. Worked as a newspaper reporter. Served in the US Army in the early 50s. Worked as an auctioneer, wrote "Auctioneer" with Buddy Black. Appeared on Red Foley's TV shows and the "Grand Ole Opry". In the film "What Am I Bid?" in 1967.

DEBUT DATE	PEAK POS	WKS CHR	ARTIST — Record Title	POP POS	Label & Number
1/05/57	9	2	1 Auctioneer...	*19*	Dot 15503
			Jockey #9 / Juke Box #10		
9/04/61	1 ¹⁹	37	2 Walk On By..	*5*	Mercury 71834
3/31/62	3	12	3 If A Woman Answers (Hang Up The Phone)	*35*	Mercury 71926
12/29/62	16	7	4 Black Cloud		Mercury 72057
1/11/64	50	1	5 Happy To Be Unhappy.................................		Mercury 72198
2/29/64	45	3	6 Night People		Mercury 72232
1/09/65	40	5	7 Anne Of A Thousand Days		Mercury 72360
10/15/66	34	9	8 Roses From A Stranger		Warner 5841
4/15/67	66	4	9 I've Never Been Loved................................		Warner 7001
1/06/68	23	11	10 Louisville		Warner 7155
8/31/68	69	5	11 You May Be Too Much For Memphis, Baby.........		Kapp 931
11/01/69	56	4	12 Crack In My World		Kapp 2054
6/13/70	63	7	13 An Old Love Affair Now Showing		Kapp 2091
12/12/70	71	2	14 Mister Professor......................................		Decca 32756
9/18/71	62	5	15 I Get Lonely When It Rains		Decca 32866
3/25/72	69	6	16 I'd Rather Be Wantin' Love		Decca 32933
4/26/75	79	6	17 Unfaithful Fools		ABC 12070
12/20/75+	75	7	18 Who's Gonna Run The Truck Stop In Tuba City When I'm Gone?		ABC/Dot 17597
4/23/77	77	6	19 Texas Tea..		ABC/Dot 17691

RANDY VANWARMER
Born Randall Van Wormer on 3/30/55 in Denver. Singer/songwriter/guitarist.

DEBUT DATE	PEAK POS	WKS CHR	ARTIST — Record Title	POP POS	Label & Number
6/30/79	71	6	1●Just When I Needed You Most	*4*	Bearsville 0334
2/20/88	53	8	2 I Will Hold You		16th Ave. 70407
8/20/88	72	4	3 Where The Rocky Mountains Touch The Morning Sun		16th Ave. 70418

KIN VASSY
Vocalist formerly with the Back Porch Majority, and Kenny Rogers & First Edition.

DEBUT DATE	PEAK POS	WKS CHR	ARTIST — Record Title	POP POS	Label & Number
10/13/79	85	5	1 Do I Ever Cross Your Mind		ia 501
3/08/80	67	6	2 Makes Me Wonder If I Ever Said Goodbye		ia 502
7/05/80	88	4	3 There's Nobody Like You...............................		ia 505

also released on United Artists 1368;
above 3: produced by Kenny Rogers

DEBUT DATE	PEAK POS	WKS CHR	ARTIST — Record Title	POP POS	Label & Number
			KIN VASSY — Continued		
5/16/81	39	10	4 Likin' Him And Lovin' You		Liberty 1407
8/15/81	48	8	5 Sneakin' Around..		Liberty 1427
12/12/81+	21	14	6 When You Were Blue And I Was Green		Liberty 1440
5/01/82	78	4	7 Cast The First Stone....................................		Liberty 1458
8/21/82	59	8	8 Women In Love...		Liberty 1469
1/22/83	80	4	9 Tryin' To Love Two		Liberty 1488
			#10 pop hit for William Bell in 1977		
			SAMMY VAUGHN		
8/19/78	67	5	1 This Time Around		Oak 1007
2/10/79	98	1	2 Sunshine		Alpine 100
			SHARON VAUGHN		
4/27/74	39	11	1 Until The End Of Time		Cinnamon 793
			NARVEL FELTS & SHARON VAUGHN		
8/10/74	96	4	2 Never A Night Goes By		Cinnamon 790
12/06/75	99	2	3 You And Me, Me And You		ABC/Dot 17590
			GAIL VEACH		
8/01/87	86	2	1 Would You Catch Me Baby (If I Fall For You)		Prairie D. 128
4/16/88	93	1	2 Deepest Shade Of Blue		Choice 101
			THE VEGA BROTHERS		
			Robert and Ray Vega from El Paso, Texas.		
4/19/86	54	6	1 Heartache The Size Of Texas..........................		MCA 52777
			BILLY VERA		
			Born William McCord, Jr. on 5/28/44 in Riverside, California. Raised in Westchester County, New York. Wrote hit songs for many pop, R&B and country artists. Formed The Beaters in Los Angeles in 1979, an R&B-based, 10-piece band.		
1/24/87	42	13	1● At This Moment .... [R]	1	Rhino 74403
			BILLY VERA & THE BEATERS		
			originally hit the pop charts in 1981 on Alfa 7005 (POS 79)		
4/25/87	93	2	2 She Ain't Johnnie .... [R]		Macola 9812
			originally released by Midland Int'l. Records in 1977		
			KENNY VERNON		
			Born on 7/19/40 in Jackson, Tennessee. On WDXI radio with Carl Perkins in 1956. Worked in San Diego and Las Vegas, including 8 years at the Golden Nugget.		
10/01/66	48	2	1 It Makes You Happy (To Know You Make Me Blue)...		Caravan 123
6/17/72	56	8	2 That'll Be The Day		Capitol 3331
			#1 pop hit for The Crickets in 1957		
1/13/73	55	6	3 Feel So Fine		Capitol 3506
6/09/73	66	3	4 Lady		Capitol 3590
1/05/74	74	8	5 What Was Your Name Again		Capitol 3785
			LaWANDA LINDSEY & KENNY VERNON:		
1/04/69	58	9	6 Eye To Eye		Chart 1063
3/21/70	27	14	7 Pickin' Wild Mountain Berries		Chart 5055
			#27 pop hit for Peggy Scott & Jo Jo Benson in 1968		
9/19/70	51	9	8 Let's Think About Where We're Going		Chart 5090
2/27/71	42	9	9 Crawdad Song		Chart 5114
			MACK VICKERY		
			Born on 6/8/38 in Town Creek, Alabama; raised in Adrianne, Michigan. Prolific songwriter. Also recorded as "Atlanta James".		
5/28/77	49	7	1 Ishabilly		Playboy 5800
9/24/77	94	2	2 Here's To The Horses...................................		Playboy 5814
			GENE VINCENT & His Blue Caps		
			Born Vincent Eugene Craddock on 2/11/35 in Norfolk, Virginia; died from an ulcer hemorrhage on 10/12/71. Innovative rock and roll singer/songwriter/guitarist.		
7/07/56	5	17	1 **Be-Bop-A-Lula**...	7	Capitol 3450
			Best Seller #5 / Juke Box #5 / Jockey #9		

DEBUT DATE	PEAK POS	WKS CHR	ARTIST — Record Title	POP POS	Label & Number
			BOBBY VINTON		
			Born Stanley Robert Vinton on 4/16/35 in Canonsburg, Pennsylvania. Father was a bandleader. Formed own band while in high school; toured as backing band for Dick Clark's "Caravan of Stars" in 1960. Left band for a singing career in 1962. Own TV series from 1975-78.		
2/28/70	27	9	1 My Elusive Dreams	46	Epic 10576
12/15/79	86	5	2 Make Believe It's Your First Time	78	Tapestry 002
7/02/83	87	3	3 You Are Love		Larc 81019
11/24/84	91	3	4 Bed Of Roses		Tapestry 4009
12/24/88+	63	7	5 The Last Rose		Curb 10512
			VICKI RAE VON		
			Singer born in Marshalltown, Iowa and raised in Ankeny, Iowa. Began singing professionally at age 11. Backing vocalist for Mickey Gilley.		
4/11/87	52	10	1 Not Tonight I've Got A Heartache		Atln. Am. 99471
7/25/87	53	9	2 Torn-Up		Atln. Am. 99442

W

DEBUT DATE	PEAK POS	WKS CHR	ARTIST — Record Title	POP POS	Label & Number
			NORMAN WADE		
			Born in Columbus, Georgia. Worked with Marty Robbins; first recorded in 1959.		
11/17/79	97	2	1 I'm A Long Gone Daddy		NSD 29
			WAGONEERS		
			Quartet from Austin, Texas: Brent Wilson (vocals), Thomas Lewis, Jr., Craig Allan Pettigrew and Monte Warden.		
6/25/88	43	9	1 I Wanna Know Her Again		A&M 1215
9/10/88	52	6	2 Every Step Of The Way		A&M 1230
			PORTER WAGONER ★★**23**★★		
			Born on 8/12/27 in West Plains, Missouri. Broadcast from a grocery store in West Plains in the late 40s. Worked on KWTO-Springfield in 1951. Performed on Red Foley's Ozark Jubilee TV series in the early 50s. On the Grand Ole Opry since 1957. Own TV series with Norma Jean starting in 1960. The show featured Dolly Parton from 1967-74.		
10/30/54+	7	12	1 **Company's Comin'** Jockey #7		RCA 5848
5/28/55	1⁴	33	2 **A Satisfied Mind** Jockey #1 / Juke Box #2 / Best Seller #2 also see Con Hunley's hit featuring Porter Wagoner in 1983		RCA 6105
12/03/55	3	22	3 **Eat, Drink, And Be Merry (Tomorrow You'll Cry)** Best Seller #3 / Juke Box #3 / Jockey #5		RCA 6289
3/31/56	8	11	4 **What Would You Do (If Jesus Came To Your House)** Best Seller #8 / Jockey #14		RCA 6421
5/26/56	14	4	5 Uncle Pen Jockey #14		RCA 6494
11/17/56	11	2	6 Tryin' To Forget The Blues Jockey #11		RCA 6598
8/19/57	11	3	7 I Thought I Heard You Call My Name Jockey #11		RCA 6964
5/04/59	29	1	8 Me, Fred, Joe And Bill		RCA 7457
1/18/60	26	4	9 The Girl Who Didn't Need Love		RCA 7638
10/31/60	26	1	10 Falling Again/		
10/31/60	30	1	11 An Old Log Cabin For Sale		RCA 7770
3/06/61	10	13	12 **Your Old Love Letters**		RCA 7837
1/13/62	1²	29	13 **Misery Loves Company** written by Jerry Reed		RCA 7967
6/23/62	10	10	14 **Cold Dark Waters**		RCA 8026
12/08/62+	7	15	15 **I've Enjoyed As Much Of This As I Can Stand.**		RCA 8105
6/22/63	20	7	16 My Baby's Not Here (In Town Tonight)/		
7/20/63	29	1	17 In The Shadows Of The Wine		RCA 8178
1/18/64	19	12	18 Howdy Neighbor Howdy		RCA 8257
4/25/64	5	23	19 **Sorrow On The Rocks**		RCA 8338
10/10/64	11	25	20 I'll Go Down Swinging		RCA 8432
5/01/65	21	8	21 I'm Gonna Feed You Now		RCA 8524

DEBUT DATE	PEAK POS	WKS CHR	ARTIST — Record Title	POP POS	Label & Number
			PORTER WAGONER — Continued		
7/31/65	4	19	22 **Green, Green Grass Of Home**..........................		RCA 8622
12/25/65+	3	17	23 **Skid Row Joe**..		RCA 8723
5/07/66	21	12	24 I Just Came To Smell The Flowers		RCA 8800
11/05/66	48	4	25 Ole Slew-Foot		RCA 8977
1/28/67	2¹	19	26 **The Cold Hard Facts Of Life**		RCA 9067
7/15/67	15	16	27 Julie...		RCA 9243
			written by Waylon Jennings		
12/16/67+	24	12	28 Woman Hungry......................................		RCA 9379
6/08/68	16	14	29 Be Proud Of Your Man		RCA 9530
11/09/68+	2⁴	21	30 **The Carroll County Accident**	92	RCA 9651
6/14/69	3	15	31 **Big Wind**...		RCA 0168
11/15/69	21	11	32 When You're Hot You're Hot		RCA 0267
3/14/70	41	5	33 You Got-Ta Have A License.........................		RCA 9802
4/04/70	43	9	34 Little Boy's Prayer		RCA 9811
9/26/70	41	9	35 Jim Johnson		RCA 9895
1/02/71	18	16	36 The Last One To Touch Me		RCA 9939
			written by Dolly Parton		
5/08/71	15	13	37 Charley's Picture	116	RCA 9979
8/28/71	11	14	38 Be A Little Quieter		RCA 1007
2/26/72	8	14	39 **What Ain't To Be, Just Might Happen**		RCA 0648
8/05/72	14	13	40 A World Without Music		RCA 0753
11/11/72	16	12	41 Katy Did..		RCA 0820
4/21/73	54	7	42 Lightening The Load................................		RCA 0923
7/14/73	37	9	43 Wake Up, Jacob.....................................		RCA 0013
12/15/73+	43	12	44 George Leroy Chickashea		RCA 0187
3/30/74	46	9	45 Tore Down/		
		9	46 Nothing Between		RCA 0233
7/27/74	15	13	47 Highway Headin' South		RCA 0328
12/14/74+	19	12	48 Carolina Moonshiner................................		RCA 10124
			written by Dolly Parton (also #52 below)		
11/08/75	96	2	49 Indian Creek		RCA 10411
11/13/76	66	5	50 When Lea Jane Sang		RCA 10803
10/15/77	76	5	51 I Haven't Learned A Thing.........................		RCA 10974
			guest vocal: Merle Haggard		
1/07/78	64	6	52 Mountain Music		RCA 11186
11/18/78+	31	11	53 Ole Slew Foot/ [R]		
		11	54 I'm Gonna Feed 'Em Now........................[R]		RCA 11411
3/17/79	34	8	55 I Want To Walk You Home..........................		RCA 11491
8/11/79	32	9	56 Everything I've Always Wanted		RCA 11671
12/22/79+	64	7	57 Hold On Tight......................................		RCA 11771
5/24/80	84	4	58 Is It Only Cause You're Lonely		RCA 11998
11/13/82	53	8	59 Turn The Pencil Over...............................		Warner 29875
			from the Clint Eastwood film "Honkytonk Man"		
3/05/83	35	14	60 This Cowboy's Hat..................................		Warner 29772
			PORTER WAGONER & DOLLY PARTON:		
12/02/67+	7	17	61 **The Last Thing On My Mind**		RCA 9369
4/13/68	7	16	62 **Holding On To Nothin'**		RCA 9490
7/27/68	5	13	63 **We'll Get Ahead Someday/**		
10/05/68	51	6	64 Jeannie's Afraid Of The Dark.......................		RCA 9577
3/08/69	9	14	65 **Yours Love**.......................................		RCA 0104
6/21/69	16	11	66 Always, Always		RCA 0172
10/25/69	5	16	67 **Just Someone I Used To Know**....................		RCA 0247
2/14/70	9	15	68 **Tomorrow Is Forever**.............................		RCA 9799
8/01/70	7	15	69 **Daddy Was An Old Time Preacher Man**		RCA 9875
2/27/71	7	13	70 **Better Move It On Home**		RCA 9958
6/26/71	14	12	71 The Right Combination	106	RCA 9994
11/13/71+	11	13	72 Burning The Midnight Oil		RCA 0565
4/08/72	9	14	73 **Lost Forever In Your Kiss**		RCA 0675
9/02/72	14	13	74 Together Always....................................		RCA 0773
3/03/73	30	9	75 We Found It		RCA 0893
6/23/73	3	17	76 **If Teardrops Were Pennies**.......................		RCA 0981

DEBUT DATE	PEAK POS	WKS CHR	ARTIST — Record Title	POP POS	Label & Number
			PORTER WAGONER — Continued		
8/03/74	**1**[1]	17	77 **Please Don't Stop Loving Me**........................		RCA 10010
7/12/75	**5**	17	78 **Say Forever You'll Be Mine**......................		RCA 10328
5/15/76	**8**	14	79 **Is Forever Longer Than Always**..................		RCA 10652
6/21/80	**2**[2]	17	80 **Making Plans**..		RCA 11983
11/08/80+	**12**	14	81 If You Go, I'll Follow You.............................		RCA 12119

JIMMY WAKELY ★★109★★

Born on 2/16/14 near Mineola, Arkansas; raised in Oklahoma. Died on 9/23/82 (68). Guitarist/pianist. Own Jimmy Wakely Trio with Johnny Bond and Scotty Harrell on WKY-Oklahoma City in 1937. Worked on Gene Autry's Melody Ranch series on CBS radio in the early 40s. Nicknamed "The Melody Kid". Starred in over 70 western films. Own radio series from 1952-57 and a TV series with Tex Ritter in 1961. Own record label, Shasta, in the mid-60s.

DEBUT DATE	PEAK POS	WKS CHR	ARTIST — Record Title	POP POS	Label & Number
4/15/44	**2**[1]	4	1 **I'm Sending You Red Roses**......................		Decca 6095
4/03/48	**9**	6	2 **Signed, Sealed And Delivered**		Capitol A. 40088
			Best Seller #9 / Juke Box #9		
9/04/48	**1**[11]	32	3 **One Has My Name (The Other Has My Heart)** ..	10	Capitol 15162
			Best Seller #1(11) / Juke Box #1(7)		
10/30/48+	**1**[5]	28	4 **I Love You So Much It Hurts**........................	21	Capitol 15243
			Juke Box #1(5) / Best Seller #1(4)		
11/13/48+	**8**	5	5 **Mine All Mine**..		Capitol 15236
			Juke Box #8		
2/05/49	**10**	1	6 **Forever More**..		Capitol 15333
			Juke Box #10		
2/19/49	**9**	6	7 **Till The End Of The World**........................		Capitol 15368
			Best Seller #9 / Juke Box #15		
5/14/49	**4**	9	8 **I Wish I Had A Nickel/**		
			Juke Box #4 / Best Seller #10		
6/18/49	**10**	3	9 **Someday You'll Call My Name**		Capitol 40153
			Juke Box #10		
8/06/49	**14**	2	10 **Tellin' My Troubles To My Old Guitar**		Capitol 40187
			Juke Box #14		
4/08/50	**7**	3	11 **Peter Cottontail**	26	Capitol 929
			Jockey #7		
9/23/50	**10**	1	12 **Mona Lisa**..		Capitol 1151
			Jockey #10		
			from the film "Capt. Carey U.S.A."		
1/20/51	**7**	1	13 **My Heart Cries For You**........................	12	Capitol 1328
			Best Seller #7 / Jockey #10		
3/17/51	**5**	12	14 **Beautiful Brown Eyes**............................	12	Capitol 1393
			Best Seller #5 / Juke Box #5 / Jockey #9		
			MARGARET WHITING & JIMMY WAKELY:		
9/10/49	**1**[17]	28	15● **Slipping Around/**	1	
			Best Seller #1(17) / Juke Box #1(12) / Jockey #2		
9/10/49	**6**	8	16 **Wedding Bells**	30	Capitol 40224
			Juke Box #6 / Best Seller #7		
11/05/49	**2**[3]	13	17 **I'll Never Slip Around Again**........................	8	Capitol 40246
			Juke Box #2 / Best Seller #2 / Jockey #10		
2/11/50	**2**[1]	9	18 **Broken Down Merry-Go-Round/**	12	
			Best Seller #2 / Juke Box #3 / Jockey #5		
2/11/50	**3**	7	19 **The Gods Were Angry With Me**....................	17	Capitol 800
			Best Seller #3 / Juke Box #4		
4/22/50	**2**[1]	10	20 **Let's Go To Church (Next Sunday Morning)**	13	Capitol 960
			Best Seller #2 / Jockey #6 / Juke Box #6		
11/18/50	**6**	1	21 **A Bushel And A Peck**	6	Capitol 1234
			Best Seller #6 / Juke Box #10		
			from the Broadway musical "Guys And Dolls"		
6/02/51	**7**	2	22 **When You And I Were Young Maggie Blues**.....	20	Capitol 1500
			Juke Box #7		
12/08/51	**5**	5	23 **I Don't Want To Be Free**........................		Capitol 1816
			Juke Box #5		

BILLY WALKER ★★51★★

Born on 1/14/29 in Ralls, Texas. Own radio show on KICA-Clovis, New Mexico at age 15. Worked on the Big D Jamboree in Dallas as "The Masked Singer" in 1949. Performed on the Louisiana Hayride and Ozark Jubilee until 1960, on the Grand Ole Opry since 1960. Own TV series, "Country Carnival". In the films "Second Fiddle To A Steel Guitar" and "Red River Round Up". Known as "The Tall Texan".

DEBUT DATE	PEAK POS	WKS CHR	ARTIST — Record Title	POP POS	Label & Number
6/26/54	**8**	13	1 **Thank You For Calling**............................		Columbia 21256
			Jockey #8 / Best Seller #12		

DEBUT DATE	PEAK POS	WKS CHR		ARTIST — Record Title	POP POS	Label & Number
				BILLY WALKER — Continued		
6/24/57	**12**	6	2	On My Mind Again		Columbia 40920
				Jockey #12		
11/07/60	**19**	8	3	I Wish You Love		Columbia 41763
10/16/61	**23**	2	4	Funny How Time Slips Away		Columbia 42050
				#22 pop hit for Jimmy Elledge in 1962		
3/03/62	**1²**	23	5	**Charlie's Shoes**		Columbia 42287
9/01/62	**5**	12	6	**Willie The Weeper**		Columbia 42492
8/17/63	**21**	12	7	Heart, Be Careful		Columbia 42794
12/28/63+	**22**	14	8	The Morning Paper		Columbia 42891
4/25/64	**7**	24	9	**Circumstances/**		
5/09/64	**43**	4	10	It's Lonesome..		Columbia 43010
10/10/64	**2²**	22	11	**Cross The Brazos At Waco**	128	Columbia 43120
4/10/65	**8**	18	12	**Matamoros**		Columbia 43223
8/21/65	**16**	13	13	If It Pleases You/		
9/25/65	**45**	2	14	I'm So Miserable Without You		Columbia 43327
6/04/66	**49**	2	15	The Old French Quarter (In New Orleans)..........		Monument 932
6/25/66	**2⁴**	21	16	**A Million And One**		Monument 943
11/12/66+	**3**	17	17	**Bear With Me A Little Longer**		Monument 980
3/04/67	**10**	15	18	**Anything Your Heart Desires**		Monument 997
7/01/67	**18**	12	19	In Del Rio		Monument 1013
9/23/67	**11**	13	20	I Taught Her Everything She Knows		Monument 1024
3/02/68	**18**	14	21	Sundown Mary...		Monument 1055
7/13/68	**8**	10	22	**Ramona**		Monument 1079
				#1 pop hit for both Gene Austin and Paul Whiteman in 1928		
11/02/68	**20**	10	23	Age Of Worry		Monument 1098
2/08/69	**20**	13	24	From The Bottle To The Bottom		Monument 1123
5/10/69	**12**	12	25	Smoky Places..		Monument 1140
				#12 pop hit for The Corsairs in 1962		
9/06/69	**37**	7	26	Better Homes And Gardens		Monument 1154
12/06/69+	**9**	14	27	**Thinking 'Bout You, Babe**		Monument 1174
3/21/70	**23**	11	28	Darling Days		Monument 1189
6/27/70	**3**	18	29	**When A Man Loves A Woman (The Way That I Love You)**		MGM 14134
10/24/70	**3**	15	30	**She Goes Walking Through My Mind**..............		MGM 14173
1/23/71	**3**	14	31	**I'm Gonna Keep On Keep On Lovin' You**		MGM 14210
5/08/71	**28**	10	32	It's Time To Love Her		MGM 14239
				from the film "Lookin' Good"		
7/24/71	**22**	12	33	Don't Let Him Make A Memory Out Of Me..........		MGM 14268
11/13/71	**25**	10	34	Traces Of A Woman		MGM 14305
5/27/72	**24**	11	35	Gone (Our Endless Love)................................		MGM 14377
				with The Mike Curb Congregation		
10/07/72	**3**	14	36	**Sing Me A Love Song To Baby**		MGM 14422
3/03/73	**34**	9	37	My Mind Hangs On To You............................		MGM 14488
7/14/73	**52**	8	38	The Hand Of Love		MGM 14565
11/10/73	**96**	3	39	Too Many Memories.......................................		MGM 14669
1/19/74	**39**	10	40	I Changed My Mind		MGM 14693
				written by Conway Twitty		
5/18/74	**74**	7	41	How Far Our Love Goes.................................		MGM 14717
9/07/74	**73**	9	42	Fine As Wine..		MGM 14742
3/22/75	**10**	18	43	**Word Games**		RCA 10205
8/30/75	**25**	13	44	If I'm Losing You...		RCA 10345
12/20/75+	**19**	13	45	Don't Stop In My World (If You Don't Mean To Stay)		RCA 10466
4/17/76	**41**	9	46	(Here I Am) Alone Again		RCA 10613
7/31/76	**67**	6	47	Love You All To Pieces		RCA 10729
11/27/76+	**48**	9	48	Instead Of Givin' Up (I'm Givin' In)		RCA 10821
7/02/77	**100**	1	49	If You Can, Why Can't I.................................		Casino 124
8/20/77	**86**	6	50	It Always Brings Me Back Around To You		MRC 1003
10/22/77	**64**	9	51	Ringgold Georgia...		MRC 1005
				BILLY WALKER & BRENDA KAYE PERRY		
1/14/78	**57**	7	52	Carlena And Jose' Gomez..............................		MRC 1009
5/06/78	**92**	2	53	It's Not Over Till It's Over		MRC 1014

DEBUT DATE	PEAK POS	WKS CHR		ARTIST — Record Title	POP POS	Label & Number
				BILLY WALKER — Continued		
8/26/78	82	4	54	You're A Violin That Never Has Been Played......		Scorpion 552
3/24/79	72	5	55	Lawyers		Caprice 2056
6/23/79	69	6	56	Sweet Lovin' Things/		
		6	57	Rainbows And Roses		Caprice 2057
9/29/79	70	6	58	A Little Bit Short On Love		Caprice 2059
2/09/80	48	8	59	You Turn My Love Light On		Caprice 2060
4/02/83	93	2	60	One Away From One Too Many........................		Dimension 1042
12/07/85	81	5	61	Coffee Brown Eyes		Tall Texan 59
7/30/88	79	3	62	Wild Texas Rose		Tall Texan 60
				BILLY WALKER & BARBARA FAIRCHILD:		
7/12/80	74	5	63	Let Me Be The One		Paid 102
10/11/80	79	3	64	Love's Slipping Through Our Fingers (Leaving Time On Our Hands)/		
12/20/80+	70	7	65	Bye Bye Love		Paid 107
				#2 pop hit for The Everly Brothers in 1957		

CHARLIE WALKER ★★173★★

Born on 11/11/26 in Copeville, Texas. Played with the Cowboy Ramblers in 1943. During World War II, worked as a disc jockey with the Armed Forces Radio Network. Top country disc jockey in the early 50s. Worked as an emcee at the Golden Nugget in Las Vegas. On the Grand Ole Opry since 1967. Excellent golfer, also a golf event broadcaster. In the film "Country Music".

DEBUT DATE	PEAK POS	WKS CHR		ARTIST — Record Title	POP POS	Label & Number
1/28/56	9	2	1	**Only You, Only You**..................................		Decca 29715
				Juke Box #9		
10/20/58	2⁴	22	2	**Pick Me Up On Your Way Down**		Columbia 41211
6/08/59	16	9	3	I'll Catch You When You Fall		Columbia 41388
10/26/59	22	2	4	When My Conscience Hurts The Most		Columbia 41467
5/16/60	11	16	5	Who Will Buy The Wine................................		Columbia 41633
2/06/61	25	3	6	Facing The Wall..		Columbia 41820
11/28/64+	17	16	7	Close All The Honky Tonks...........................		Epic 9727
6/05/65	8	18	8	**Wild As A Wildcat**		Epic 9799
12/04/65+	39	7	9	He's A Jolly Good Fellow		Epic 9852
3/19/66	37	3	10	The Man In The Little White Suit		Epic 9875
10/15/66	56	2	11	Daddy's Coming Home (Next Week)/		
10/29/66	65	5	12	I'm Gonna Hang Up My Gloves.......................		Epic 10063
				written by Merle Haggard		
1/28/67	38	11	13	The Town That Never Sleeps..........................		Epic 10118
6/10/67	8	15	14	**Don't Squeeze My Sharmon**........................		Epic 10174
11/04/67	33	10	15	I Wouldn't Take Her To A Dogfight..................		Epic 10237
3/30/68	54	7	16	Truck Drivin' Cat With Nine Wives		Epic 10295
8/03/68	31	11	17	San Diego		Epic 10349
3/01/69	52	10	18	Honky-Tonk Season...................................		Epic 10426
8/23/69	44	9	19	Moffett, Oklahoma		Epic 10499
2/21/70	56	6	20	Honky Tonk Women		Epic 10565
				#1 pop hit for The Rolling Stones in 1969		
6/27/70	52	7	21	Let's Go Fishin' Boys (The Girls Are Bitin')........		Epic 10610
6/05/71	71	2	22	My Baby Used To Be That Way		Epic 10722
8/05/72	74	3	23	I Don't Mind Goin' Under (If It'll Get Me Over You)...		RCA 0730
1/13/73	65	7	24	Soft Lips And Hard Liquor		RCA 0870
8/17/74	66	8	25	Odds And Ends (Bits and Pieces)......................		Capitol 3922

CINDY WALKER

Born in Mexia, Texas. First recorded for Decca in 1942. Wrote "You Don't Know Me", "Take Me In Your Arms And Hold Me" for Eddy Arnold, "I Don't Care" with Webb Pierce Distant Drums" for Jim Reeves, and many others.

DEBUT DATE	PEAK POS	WKS CHR		ARTIST — Record Title	POP POS	Label & Number
11/04/44	5	1	1	**When My Blue Moon Turns To Gold Again**		Decca 6103
				#19 pop hit for Elvis Presley in 1956		

JERRY JEFF WALKER

Born Paul Crosby on 3/14/42 in Oneonta, New York. Worked with the Lost Sea Dreamers and Circus Maximus in the mid-60s. Wrote "Mr. Bojangles". Backed by the Lost Gonzo Band from 1972-77.

DEBUT DATE	PEAK POS	WKS CHR		ARTIST — Record Title	POP POS	Label & Number
12/06/75+	54	7	1	Jaded Lover...		MCA 40487
7/24/76	88	5	2	It's A Good Night For Singing/		
		5	3	Dear John Letter Lounge		MCA 40570

DEBUT DATE	PEAK POS	WKS CHR	ARTIST — Record Title	POP POS	Label & Number
			JERRY JEFF WALKER — Continued		
8/06/77	93	4	4 Mr. Bojangles .... [R]		MCA 40760
			originally hit the pop charts in 1968 on Atco (POS 77)		
8/29/81	82	3	5 Got Lucky Last Night.............................		SouthCoast 5199
			KATHY WALKER - see TIM BLIXSETH and T L LEE		
			WILEY WALKER - see WILEY & GENE		
			JERRY WALLACE ★★120★★		
			Born on 12/15/28 in Guilford, Missouri; raised in Glendale, Arizona. First recorded for Allied in 1951. Appeared on the TV shows "Night Gallery" and "Hec Ramsey".		
10/09/65	23	11	1 Life's Gone And Slipped Away		Mercury 72461
4/09/66	45	2	2 Diamonds And Horseshoes.............................		Mercury 72529
7/09/66	43	7	3 Wallpaper Roses		Mercury 72589
10/15/66	44	7	4 Not That I Care		Mercury 72619
11/25/67+	36	13	5 This One's On The House.............................		Liberty 56001
5/18/68	69	3	6 Another Time, Another Place, Another World		Liberty 56028
9/14/68	22	10	7 Sweet Child Of Sunshine		Liberty 56059
4/05/69	69	6	8 Son...		Liberty 56095
10/11/69	71	2	9 Swiss Cottage Place................................		Liberty 56130
5/09/70	74	2	10 Even The Bad Times Are Good .... [R]		Liberty 56155
			originally Bubbled Under (pop) in 1964 (POS 114)		
2/13/71	22	14	11 After You/		
2/13/71	51	14	12 She'll Remember...................................		Decca 32777
8/21/71	19	14	13 The Morning After................................		Decca 32859
1/01/72	12	22	14 To Get To You....................................	48	Decca 32914
7/22/72	1²	17	15 **If You Leave Me Tonight I'll Cry**	38	Decca 32989
			from TV's Night Gallery: "The Tune In Dan's Cafe"		
12/02/72	66	7	16 Thanks To You For Lovin' Me		United Art. 50971
12/09/72+	2¹	15	17 **Do You Know What It's Like To Be Lonesome** .		Decca 33036
4/14/73	21	12	18 Sound Of Goodbye/		
		12	19 The Song Nobody Sings		MCA 40037
8/25/73	3	16	20 **Don't Give Up On Me**.................................		MCA 40111
2/09/74	18	12	21 Guess Who		MCA 40183
6/15/74	9	14	22 **My Wife's House**		MCA 40248
11/16/74+	20	12	23 I Wonder Whose Baby (You Are Now)...............		MCA 40321
3/08/75	32	12	24 Comin' Home To You		MGM 14788
7/19/75	41	9	25 Wanted Man...		MGM 14809
11/01/75	70	6	26 Georgia Rain		MGM 14832
7/02/77	26	13	27 I Miss You Already		BMA 002
11/12/77+	28	12	28 I'll Promise You Tomorrow		BMA 005
2/18/78	24	11	29 At The End Of A Rainbow............................		BMA 006
			#7 pop hit for Earl Grant in 1958		
6/03/78	64	6	30 My Last Sad Song		BMA 008
10/14/78	38	8	31 I Wanna Go To Heaven...............................		4 Star 1035
3/03/79	67	5	32 Yours Love		4 Star 1036
12/01/79+	68	8	33 You've Still Got Me		Door Knob 116
4/05/80	56	7	34 Cling To Me...		Door Knob 127
10/04/80	80	5	35 If I Could Set My Love To Music....................		Door Knob 134
			DAVID WALSH		
			Born in Syracuse, New York. Relocated to Bushnell, Florida.		
7/27/85	91	2	1 Alice, Rita And Dana		Charta 196
10/26/85	84	3	2 Tired Of The Same Old Thing		Charta 198
10/29/88	97	1	3 All The Things We Are Not		Charta 212
			DALE WARD		
			Lead singer of the pop group, The Crescendos.		
11/09/68	74	2	1 If Loving You Means Anything........................		Monument 1094
			JACKY WARD ★★165★★		
			Born on 11/18/46 in Groveton, Texas. Supporting act on tours with Ronnie Milsap and Crystal Gayle.		
6/10/72	39	10	1 Big Blue Diamond		Target 0146
7/14/73	88	3	2 Dream Weaver.......................................		Mega 0112

DEBUT DATE	PEAK POS	WKS CHR		ARTIST — Record Title	POP POS	Label & Number
				JACKY WARD — Continued		
4/19/75	**50**	12	3	Stealin'		Mercury 73667
11/01/75+	**38**	13	4	Dance Her By Me (One More Time)..........		Mercury 73716
4/17/76	**92**	4	5	She'll Throw Stones At You		Mercury 73783
9/04/76	**24**	12	6	I Never Said It Would Be Easy		Mercury 73826
2/05/77	**31**	12	7	Texas Angel......................................		Mercury 73880
6/25/77	**69**	6	8	Why Not Tonight................................		Mercury 73918
9/10/77	**9**	19	9	**Fools Fall In Love**		Mercury 55003
2/04/78	**3**	15	10	**A Lover's Question**	*106*	Mercury 55018
				#6 pop hit for Clyde McPhatter in 1959		
8/05/78	**24**	10	11	I Want To Be In Love		Mercury 55038
11/04/78	**11**	13	12	Rhythm Of The Rain		Mercury 55047
				#3 pop hit for The Cascades in 1963		
2/17/79	**8**	14	13	**Wisdom Of A Fool**		Mercury 55055
9/22/79	**14**	12	14	You're My Kind Of Woman...................		Mercury 57004
1/05/80	**32**	10	15	I'd Do Anything For You......................		Mercury 57013
5/24/80	**8**	16	16	**Save Your Heart For Me**		Mercury 57022
9/13/80	**7**	15	17	**That's The Way A Cowboy Rocks And Rolls....**		Mercury 57032
1/24/81	**13**	14	18	Somethin' On The Radio......................		Mercury 57044
3/20/82	**32**	11	19	Travelin' Man		Asylum 47424
				#1 pop hit for Ricky Nelson in 1961		
7/03/82	**57**	7	20	Take The Mem'ry When You Go		Asylum 47468
3/05/83	**85**	3	21	The Night's Almost Over.....................		Warner 69844
1/09/88	**83**	3	22	Can't Get To You From Here		Electric 105
				JACKY WARD & REBA McENTIRE:		
5/20/78	**20**	12	23	Three Sheets In The Wind/		
		11	24	I'd Really Love To See You Tonight		Mercury 55026
				#2 pop hit for England Dan & John Ford Coley in 1976		
7/07/79	**26**	11	25	That Makes Two Of Us		Mercury 55054
				STEVE WARINER ★★**84**★★		
				Singer/guitarist born on 12/25/54 in Noblesville, Indiana. Played bass while still a teenager. Wrote songs from age 16. Bass player with Dottie West from 1971-74. Worked with Bob Luman and Chet Atkins.		
4/22/78	**63**	7	1	I'm Already Taken		RCA 11173
8/19/78	**76**	3	2	So Sad (To Watch Good Love Go Bad)		RCA 11336
				#7 pop hit for The Everly Brothers in 1960		
1/27/79	**94**	2	3	Marie		RCA 11447
8/04/79	**60**	7	4	Beside Me/		
11/10/79	**49**	10	5	Forget Me Not..............................		RCA 11658
7/05/80	**41**	10	6	The Easy Part's Over		RCA 12029
11/15/80+	**7**	17	7	**Your Memory**..............................		RCA 12139
4/11/81	**6**	18	8	**By Now**		RCA 12204
9/26/81	**1**¹	18	9	**All Roads Lead To You**	*107*	RCA 12307
3/06/82	**15**	18	10	Kansas City Lights		RCA 13072
9/04/82	**30**	11	11	Don't It Break Your Heart		RCA 13308
11/27/82+	**27**	17	12	Don't Plan On Sleepin' Tonight		RCA 13395
5/07/83	**23**	13	13	Don't Your Mem'ry Ever Sleep At Night....		RCA 13515
8/13/83	**5**	18	14	**Midnight Fire**		RCA 13588
12/10/83+	**4**	20	15	**Lonely Women Make Good Lovers**		RCA 13691
4/07/84	**12**	18	16	Why Goodbye		RCA 13768
9/22/84	**49**	10	17	Don't You Give Up On Love		RCA 13862
12/15/84+	**3**	25	18	**What I Didn't Do**		MCA 52506
4/06/85	**8**	20	19	**Heart Trouble**		MCA 52562
7/27/85	**1**¹	22	20	**Some Fools Never Learn**		MCA 52644
11/16/85+	**1**¹	22	21	**You Can Dream Of Me**		MCA 52721
3/15/86	**1**¹	24	22	**Life's Highway**		MCA 52786
8/16/86	**4**	19	23	**Starting Over Again**		MCA 52837
12/27/86+	**1**¹	24	24	**Small Town Girl**		MCA 53006
4/25/87	**1**¹	23	25	**The Weekend**		MCA 53068
5/30/87	**6**	28	26	**The Hand That Rocks The Cradle**........		MCA 53108
				GLEN CAMPBELL with STEVE WARINER		
9/05/87	**1**¹	23	27	**Lynda**......................................		MCA 53160

DEBUT DATE	PEAK POS	WKS CHR	ARTIST — Record Title	POP POS	Label & Number
			STEVE WARINER — Continued		
2/20/88	2¹	18	28 Baby I'm Yours..		MCA 53287
6/18/88	2²	21	29 I Should Be With You.................................		MCA 53347
10/15/88+	6	24	30 Hold On (A Little Longer)		MCA 53419
			VIRGIL WARNER - see SUZI JANE HOKUM		
			JENNIFER WARNES		
			Born in Seattle; raised in Orange County, California. Pop/MOR-styled vocalist. Lead actress in the Los Angeles production of "Hair".		
2/19/77	17	15	1 Right Time Of The Night	6	Arista 0223
6/30/79	10	16	2 I Know A Heartache When I See One.............	19	Arista 0430
1/12/80	84	3	3 Don't Make Me Over	67	Arista 0455
2/06/82	57	7	4 Could It Be Love	47	Arista 0611
2/28/87	86	4	5 Ain't No Cure For Love		Cypress 661111
			KELLY WARREN		
			Born in Lamesa, Texas. Winner of numerous beauty contests as a child. Star of "I-40 Paradise" TV series in 1983.		
1/06/79	85	5	1 One Man's Woman......................................		RCA 11428
11/17/79	69	4	2 Don't Touch Me		Jeremiah 1002
			JERRY NAYLOR/KELLI WARREN		
			JON WASHINGTON		
			British singer/songwriter/actor. Former member of The Fortunes.		
10/22/88	73	3	1 One Dance Love Affair		Door Knob 310
			CHRIS WATERS		
			Chris Dunn, brother of Holly Dunn. Songwriter in Nashville.		
11/29/80	82	3	1 My Lady Loves Me (Just As I Am)		Rio 1001
3/07/81	89	2	2 It's Like Falling In Love (Over And Over Again) ..		Rio 1002
			JOE WATERS		
			Born in Chillicothe, Ohio. Owner of the Recording Workshop studio.		
9/26/81	85	3	1 Livin' in the Light of Her Love.......................		New Colony 6811
12/12/81+	47	10	2 Some Day My Ship's Comin' In		New Colony 6812
4/17/82	75	4	3 The Queen Of Hearts Loves You.......................		New Colony 6813
12/17/83+	74	6	4 Harvest Moon		New Colony 6814
5/26/84	90	2	5 Rise Above It All..		New Colony 6815
			CLYDE WATSON		
8/27/77	99	2	1 The Touch Of Her Fingers.............................		Groovy 100
			DOC & MERLE WATSON		
			Father and son duo of blind guitarist/banjo player Arthel "Doc" Watson (b: 3/2/2C, Deep Gap, NC) and son Merle (b: 2/8/49). First recorded in 1960.		
7/21/73	71	7	1 Bottle Of Wine...		United Art. 276
			#9 pop hit for The Fireballs in 1968		
9/02/78	88	5	2 Don't Think Twice, It's Alright		United Art. 1231
			#9 pop hit for Peter, Paul & Mary in 1963		
			GENE WATSON ★★64★★		
			Born Gary Gene Watson on 10/11/43 in Palestine, Texas; raised in Paris, Texas. Worked professionally since age 13. Own band, Gene Watson & The Other Four. Recorded for Tonka in 1965. Played for many years at the Dynasty Club in Houston.		
1/25/75	87	7	1 Bad Water		Resco 630
			#58 pop hit for The Raeletts in 1971		
5/24/75	3	19	2 Love In The Hot Afternoon		Capitol 4076
10/11/75	5	15	3 Where Love Begins.....................................		Capitol 4143
2/14/76	10	15	4 You Could Know As Much About A Stranger ..		Capitol 4214
6/12/76	20	12	5 Because You Believed In Me............................		Capitol 4279
9/25/76	52	9	6 Her Body Couldn't Keep You (Off My Mind)		Capitol 4331
1/29/77	3	17	7 Paper Rosie...		Capitol 4378
8/13/77	11	15	8 The Old Man And His Horn		Capitol 4458
12/03/77+	8	16	9 I Don't Need A Thing At All		Capitol 4513
4/08/78	11	14	10 Cowboys Don't Get Lucky All The Time		Capitol 4556
8/26/78	8	14	11 One Sided Conversation		Capitol 4616
2/17/79	5	16	12 Farewell Party		Capitol 4680
6/09/79	5	15	13 Pick The Wildwood Flower...........................		Capitol 4723

DEBUT DATE	PEAK POS	WKS CHR	ARTIST — Record Title	POP POS	Label & Number
			GENE WATSON — Continued		
9/15/79	**3**	13	14 **Should I Come Home (Or Should I Go Crazy)** ...		Capitol 4772
1/05/80	**4**	14	15 **Nothing Sure Looked Good On You**		Capitol 4814
4/12/80	**18**	13	16 Bedroom Ballad		Capitol 4854
8/02/80	**15**	12	17 Raisin' Cane In Texas		Capitol 4898
11/01/80	**13**	14	18 No One Will Ever Know		Capitol 4940
2/07/81	**33**	8	19 Any Way You Want Me		Warner 49648
			from the film "Any Which Way You Can"		
2/28/81	**17**	13	20 Between This Time And The Next Time.............		MCA 51039
6/20/81	**23**	13	21 Maybe I Should Have Been Listening		MCA 51127
10/03/81+	**1**¹	19	22 **Fourteen Carat Mind**		MCA 51183
2/27/82	**9**	18	23 **Speak Softly (You're Talking To My Heart)**.....		MCA 52009
7/03/82	**8**	18	24 **This Dream's On Me**		MCA 52074
11/06/82+	**5**	21	25 **What She Don't Know Won't Hurt Her**		MCA 52131
3/19/83	**2**¹	19	26 **You're Out Doing What I'm Here Doing Without**.....................		MCA 52191
7/23/83	**9**	18	27 **Sometimes I Get Lucky And Forget**		MCA 52243
11/26/83+	**10**	17	28 **Drinkin' My Way Back Home**......................		MCA 52309
3/31/84	**10**	17	29 **Forever Again**		MCA 52356
6/30/84	**33**	14	30 Little By Little..		MCA 52410
			above 5: with "His Farewell Party Band"		
10/13/84+	**7**	27	31 **Got No Reason Now For Goin' Home**...............		MCA/Curb 52457
3/02/85	**43**	10	32 One Hell Of A Heartache.............................		MCA/Curb 52533
6/22/85	**24**	17	33 Cold Summer Day In Georgia.........................		Epic 05407
10/19/85+	**5**	21	34 **Memories To Burn**		Epic 05633
3/01/86	**32**	15	35 Carmen		Epic 05817
7/05/86	**50**	8	36 Bottle Of Tears		Epic 06057
9/13/86	**29**	14	37 Everything I Used To Do...............................		Epic 06290
3/14/87	**43**	13	38 Honky Tonk Crazy		Epic 06987
8/15/87	**28**	16	39 Everybody Needs A Hero		Epic 07308
11/12/88+	**5**	22	40 **Don't Waste It On The Blues**........................		Warner 27692
			WAYLON & WILLIE - see WAYLON JENNINGS and/or WILLIE NELSON		
			BOBBY WAYNE		
			Born Robert Wayne Edrington in Childress, Texas. Guitarist with Merle Haggard's Strangers.		
2/06/71	**61**	7	1 Harold's Super Service		Capitol 3025
			NANCY WAYNE		
5/25/74	**55**	12	1 The Back Door Of Heaven.............................		20th Century 2086
10/05/74	**34**	11	2 Gone..		20th Century 2124
4/26/75	**80**	7	3 I Wanna Kiss You.......................................		20th Century 2184
			JIM WEATHERLY		
			Born on 3/17/43 in Pontotoc, Mississippi. Accomplished songwriter, wrote "Midnight Train To Georgia", "Best Thing That Ever Happened To Me" and "Neither One Of Us (Wants To Be The First To Say Goodbye)".		
2/01/75	**9**	13	1 **I'll Still Love You**	87	Buddah 444
7/12/75	**58**	8	2 It Must Have Been The Rain...........................		Buddah 467
7/23/77	**27**	10	3 All That Keeps Me Going		ABC 12288
11/03/79	**32**	11	4 Smooth Sailin'...		Elektra 46547
2/16/80	**34**	9	5 Gift From Missouri		Elektra 46592
10/11/80	**82**	3	6 Safe In The Arms Of Your Love (Cold In The Streets).................................		Elektra 47027
			THE WEAVERS & TERRY GILKYSON		
			Folk group consisting of Pete Seeger, Veronica Ronnie" Gilbert, Lee Hays (d: 1981) and Fred Kellerman, backing Hamilton Henry "Terry" Gilkyson.		
6/02/51	**8**	2	1 ● **On Top Of Old Smoky**................................	2	Decca 27515
			Juke Box #8		

DEBUT DATE	PEAK POS	WKS CHR	ARTIST — Record Title	POP POS	Label & Number
			JAY LEE WEBB		
			Born in Van Lear, Kentucky; brother of Loretta Lynn and Peggy Sue.		
2/11/67	**37**	6	1 I Come Home A-Drinkin' (To A Worn-Out Wife Like You)		Decca 32087
			shown as: **JACK WEBB**		
			answer to Loretta Lynn's "Don't Come Home A'Drinkin'"		
2/01/69	**21**	13	2 She's Lookin' Better By The Minute		Decca 32430
11/27/71	**69**	5	3 The Happiness Of Having You.........................		Decca 32887
			JUNE WEBB		
			Born on 9/22/34 in L'Anse, Michigan. Worked on WLAC-Nashville from 1947.		
11/03/58	**29**	3	1 A Mansion On The Hill		Hickory 1086
			CHASE WEBSTER		
			Born on a farm near Franklin, Tennessee. Wrote Pat Boone's "Moody River".		
6/20/70	**68**	2	1 Moody River..		Show Biz 233
			#1 pop hit for Pat Boone in 1961		
			ERIC WEISSBERG & STEVE MANDELL		
			Prominent session musicians. Both had worked with Judy Collins and John Denver.		
2/03/73	**5**	12	1 ●Dueling Banjos .... [I]	2	Warner 7659
			tune written in 1955; featured in the film "Deliverance"		
3/29/75	**91**	4	2 Yakety Yak		Epic 50072
			ERIC WEISSBERG & DELIVERANCE		
			#1 pop hit for The Coasters in 1958		
			LAWRENCE WELK - see RED FOLEY		
			FREDDY WELLER ★★117★★		
			Born on 9/9/47 in Atlanta. Worked on the Atlanta Jubilee in East Point, Georgia with Jerry Reed, Ray Stevens and Joe South. Performed with Billy Joe Royal in the mid-60s. Worked with Paul Revere & The Raiders from 1967-71. Co-wrote "Dizzy" and "Jam Up Jelly Tight" with Tommy Roe. Worked as bassist/guitarist with Joe South.		
4/12/69	**2²**	17	1 **Games People Play**...........................		Columbia 44800
			#12 pop hit for Joe South in 1969		
7/26/69	**5**	15	2 **These Are Not My People**	113	Columbia 44916
11/22/69+	**25**	10	3 Down In The Boondocks		Columbia 45026
			#9 pop hit for Billy Joe Royal in 1965		
4/11/70	**75**	2	4 I Shook The Hand		Columbia 45087
12/12/70+	**3**	18	5 **The Promised Land**............................	125	Columbia 45276
			written by Chuck Berry; #14 pop hit for Elvis Presley in 1974		
6/12/71	**3**	14	6 Indian Lake	108	Columbia 45388
			#10 pop hit for The Cowsills in 1968		
9/25/71	**5**	15	7 **Another Night Of Love**		Columbia 45451
2/19/72	**26**	12	8 Ballad Of A Hillbilly Singer		Columbia 45542
6/24/72	**17**	12	9 The Roadmaster		Columbia 45624
11/18/72+	**11**	13	10 She Loves Me (Right Out Of My Mind)..............		Columbia 45723
4/21/73	**8**	14	11 **Too Much Monkey Business**		Columbia 45827
			written by Chuck Berry		
8/18/73	**13**	13	12 The Perfect Stranger.............................		Columbia 45902
12/15/73+	**11**	15	13 I've Just Got To Know (How Loving You Would Be)...		Columbia 45968
5/18/74	**21**	14	14 Sexy Lady..		Columbia 46040
9/14/74	**16**	15	15 You're Not Getting Older (You're Getting Better) .		Columbia 10016
5/24/75	**64**	8	16 Love You Back To Georgia......................		ABC/Dot 17554
9/20/75	**52**	9	17 Stone Crazy		ABC/Dot 17577
3/20/76	**42**	9	18 Ask Any Old Cheater Who Knows		Columbia 10300
7/04/76	**44**	9	19 Liquor, Love And Life		Columbia 10352
10/09/76	**56**	8	20 Room 269..		Columbia 10411
3/05/77	**79**	6	21 Strawberry Curls...............................		Columbia 10482
5/28/77	**41**	9	22 Merry-Go-Round.................................		Columbia 10539
9/10/77	**44**	9	23 Nobody Cares But You		Columbia 10598
2/25/78	**93**	4	24 Let Me Fall Back In Your Arms....................		Columbia 10682
7/08/78	**32**	9	25 Bar Wars		Columbia 10769
10/21/78	**23**	12	26 Love Got In The Way		Columbia 10837
1/27/79	**27**	11	27 Fantasy Island.................................		Columbia 10890
5/19/79	**40**	8	28 Nadine		Columbia 10973
			#23 pop hit for Chuck Berry in 1964		
8/11/79	**44**	9	29 That Run-Away Woman Of Mine		Columbia 11044

DEBUT DATE	PEAK POS	WKS CHR	ARTIST — Record Title	POP POS	Label & Number
			FREDDY WELLER — Continued		
11/24/79+	**33**	11	30 Go For The Night		Columbia 11149
3/22/80	**66**	5	31 A Million Old Goodbyes		Columbia 11221
5/17/80	**45**	8	32 Lost In Austin		Columbia 11266
			TINY WELLMAN		
			Paul "Tiny" Wellman of Flatwoods, Kentucky. Columbus, Ohio area entertainer with his band, the Raindrops.		
6/25/88	**85**	2	1 Nothing Left To Lose		Lee Ann 7342
			KITTY WELLS ★★26★★		
			Born Muriel Ellen Deason on 8/30/19 in Nashville. Singing on WSIX-Nashville at age 16. Married to Johnny Wright in 1938 and he changed her stage name to "Kitty Wells". Toured with Johnnie & Jack, appeared on WBIG-Greensboro and WNOX-Knoxville. Worked on the Louisiana Hayride from 1948-53. First recorded for RCA in 1949. Elected to the Country Music Hall Of Fame in 1976. Known as "The Queen Of Country Music".		
7/19/52	**1**⁶	18	1 **It Wasn't God Who Made Honky Tonk Angels .** Best Seller #1(6) / Juke Box #1(5) / Jockey #2 answer to Hank Thompson's "The Wild Side Of Life"	27	Decca 28232
3/07/53	**6**	4	2 **Paying For That Back Street Affair**............... Best Seller #6 / Juke Box #9 answer to Webb Pierce's "Back Street Affair"		Decca 28578
9/12/53	**8**	2	3 Hey Joe .... Juke Box #8 answer to the same-titled tune by Carl Smith		Decca 28797
1/23/54	**9**	1	4 **Cheatin's A Sin** .... Juke Box #9		Decca 28911
4/03/54	**8**	1	5 **Release Me**... Juke Box #8		Decca 29023
12/04/54	**14**	1	6 Thou Shalt Not Steal .... Best Seller #14 written by Don Everly (of The Everly Brothers)		Decca 29313
3/12/55	**2**¹⁵	28	7 **Makin' Believe/** Best Seller #2 / Juke Box #2 / Jockey #2		
4/09/55	**7**	15	8 **Whose Shoulder Will You Cry On**................. Jockey #7		Decca 29419
7/30/55	**9**	13	9 **There's Poison In Your Heart/** Juke Box #9 / Best Seller #11		
9/24/55	**12**	1	10 I'm In Love With You .... Jockey #12		Decca 29577
12/17/55+	**7**	10	11 **Lonely Side Of Town/** Juke Box #7 / Best Seller #10		
12/17/55	**7**	7	12 **I've Kissed You My Last Time**...................... Best Seller #7 / Jockey #10		Decca 29728
5/12/56	**11**	5	13 How Far Is Heaven .... Jockey #11 / Best Seller #15 with Carol Sue (Kitty's daughter)		Decca 29823
7/07/56	**3**	34	14 **Searching (For Someone Like You)/** Juke Box #3 / Best Seller #4 / Jockey #4		
9/22/56	**13**	11	15 I'd Rather Stay Home.................................. Jockey #13		Decca 29956
12/01/56+	**6**	13	16 **Repenting/** Juke Box #6 / Best Seller #9 / Jockey #11		
		7	17 I'm Counting On You .... Juke Box flip / Best Seller flip		Decca 30094
6/03/57	**7**	9	18 **Three Ways (To Love You)**........................... Jockey #7 / Best Seller #15		Decca 30288
9/23/57	**10**	6	19 **(I'll Always Be Your) Fraulein** .... Best Seller #10 / Jockey #13 answer song to Bobby Helms' "Fraulein"		Decca 30415
3/03/58	**3**	19	20 **I Can't Stop Loving You/** Jockey #3 / Best Seller #8		
		11	21 She's No Angel .... Best Seller flip		Decca 30551
7/07/58	**7**	14	22 **Jealousy** .... Jockey #7 / Best Seller #11	78	Decca 30662
10/06/58	**15**	11	23 Touch And Go Heart/		
11/10/58	**16**	7	24 He's Lost His Love For Me		Decca 30736
2/16/59	**5**	14	25 **Mommy For A Day/**		
3/09/59	**18**	2	26 All The Time...		Decca 30804
7/06/59	**12**	10	27 Your Wild Life's Gonna Get You Down		Decca 30890
11/09/59+	**5**	25	28 **Amigo's Guitar**...		Decca 30987

DEBUT DATE	PEAK POS	WKS CHR	ARTIST — Record Title	POP POS	Label & Number
			KITTY WELLS — Continued		
4/18/60	**5**	22	29 **Left To Right**		Decca 31065
9/05/60	**16**	9	30 Carmel By The Sea		Decca 31123
3/06/61	**19**	10	31 The Other Cheek/		
3/20/61	**29**	2	32 Fickle Fun		Decca 31192
5/29/61	**1** ⁴	23	33 **Heartbreak U.S.A./**		
6/26/61	**20**	5	34 There Must Be Another Way To Live		Decca 31246
12/04/61+	**10**	12	35 **Day Into Night/**		
1/06/62	**21**	3	36 Our Mansion Is A Prison Now		Decca 31313
3/03/62	**5**	14	37 **Unloved Unwanted**		Decca 31349
8/04/62	**8**	11	38 **Will Your Lawyer Talk To God**		Decca 31392
11/03/62	**7**	13	39 **We Missed You**		Decca 31422
3/30/63	**13**	9	40 Cold And Lonely (Is The Forecast For Tonight) ...		Decca 31457
8/03/63	**29**	2	41 A Heartache For A Keepsake/		
8/17/63	**22**	6	42 I Gave My Wedding Dress Away		Decca 31501
2/01/64	**7**	25	43 **This White Circle On My Finger**		Decca 31580
5/30/64	**4**	25	44 **Password/**		
6/20/64	**34**	4	45 I've Thought Of Leaving You		Decca 31622
12/26/64+	**8**	15	46 **I'll Repossess My Heart**		Decca 31705
3/20/65	**27**	14	47 Six Lonely Hours/		
4/17/65	**4**	17	48 **You Don't Hear**		Decca 31749
8/14/65	**9**	16	49 **Meanwhile, Down At Joe's**		Decca 31817
2/05/66	**15**	13	50 A Woman Half My Age		Decca 31881
7/23/66	**14**	13	51 It's All Over (But The Crying)		Decca 31957
10/15/66	**52**	9	52 A Woman Never Forgets/		
10/29/66	**49**	9	53 Only Me And My Hairdresser Know		Decca 32024
2/18/67	**34**	16	54 Love Makes The World Go Around		Decca 32088
8/12/67	**28**	13	55 Queen Of Honky Tonk Street		Decca 32163
1/27/68	**35**	10	56 My Big Truck Drivin' Man		Decca 32247
7/27/68	**52**	8	57 Gypsy King		Decca 32343
11/16/68	**47**	7	58 Happiness Hill		Decca 32389
5/17/69	**61**	5	59 Guilty Street		Decca 32455
8/15/70	**71**	4	60 Your Love Is The Way		Decca 32700
4/17/71	**72**	2	61 They're Stepping All Over My Heart..................		Decca 32795
7/24/71	**49**	9	62 Pledging My Love		Decca 32840
			#17 pop hit for Johnny Ace in 1955		
4/01/72	**72**	3	63 Sincerely		Decca 32931
			#1 pop hit for The McGuire Sisters in 1955		
9/27/75	**94**	3	64 Anybody Out There Wanna Be A Daddy		Capricorn 0240
8/25/79	**75**	6	65 Thank You For The Roses		Ruboca 122
			KITTY WELLS DUOS with:		
			RAYBURN ANTHONY:		
10/06/79	**60**	6	66 The Wild Side Of Life		Mercury 57006
			ROY DRUSKY:		
12/19/60	**26**	3	67 I Can't Tell My Heart That		Decca 31164
			RED FOLEY:		
5/22/54	**1** ¹	41	68 **One By One/**		
			Juke Box #1 / Best Seller #2 / Jockey #2		
7/10/54	**12**	1	69 I'm A Stranger In My Home........................		Decca 29065
			Jockey #12 / Best Seller #15		
2/26/55	**3**	17	70 **Make Believe ('Til We Can Make It Come True)/**		
			Juke Box #3 / Best Seller #7 / Jockey #14		
2/26/55	**7**	16	71 **As Long As I Live**		Decca 29390
			Best Seller #7 / Juke Box #7 / Jockey #8		
1/28/56	**3**	31	72 **You And Me/**		
			Best Seller #3 / Jockey #3 / Juke Box #6		
		6	73 No One But You		Decca 29740
			Best Seller flip / Juke Box flip		
5/06/67	**43**	11	74 Happiness Means You/		
6/03/67	**60**	5	75 Hello Number One		Decca 32126
12/30/67+	**63**	4	76 Living As Strangers		Decca 32223
1/18/69	**74**	2	77 Have I Told You Lately That I Love You?		Decca 32427

DEBUT DATE	PEAK POS	WKS CHR	ARTIST — Record Title	POP POS	Label & Number
			KITTY WELLS — Continued		
			WEBB PIERCE:		
4/06/57	**8**	9	78 **Oh, So Many Years**		Decca 30183
			Jockey #8		
1/20/58	**12**	1	79 One Week Later		Decca 30489
			Jockey #12		
9/26/64	**9**	15	80 **Finally**		Decca 31663
			JOHNNY WRIGHT:		
5/11/68	**54**	8	81 We'll Stick Together		Decca 32294
			MIKE WELLS		
			Born in 1964 in New Jersey.		
2/22/75	**54**	9	1 Sing A Love Song, Porter Wagoner		Playboy 6029
2/07/76	**77**	7	2 Wild World..................................		Playboy 6061
			#11 pop hit for Cat Stevens in 1971		
			BILL WENCE		
			Born on 7/2/42 in Salinas, California. Worked as a disc jockey on several stations.		
9/15/79	**92**	4	1 Quicksand		Rustic 1003
1/26/80	**85**	4	2 Break Away		Rustic 1005
6/07/80	**63**	6	3 I Wanna Do It Again		Rustic 1009
9/27/80	**85**	4	4 Night Lies.................................		Rustic 1012
			DOTTIE WEST ★★44★★		
			Born Dorothy Marie Marsh on 10/11/32 in McMinnville, Tennessee. Worked on local TV in Cleveland in the mid-50s. On the Grand Ole Opry since 1964. Made commercials for Coca-Cola, including the award-winning "Country Sunshine", which she wrote. In the films "Second Fiddle To A Steel Guitar" and "There's A Still On The Hill".		
11/30/63	**29**	2	1 Let Me Off At The Corner		RCA 8225
3/28/64	**7**	21	2 Love Is No Excuse	*115*	RCA 8324
			JIM REEVES & DOTTIE WEST		
			flip side "Look Who's Talking" hit POS 121 on Bubbling Under chart		
8/22/64	**10**	15	3 **Here Comes My Baby**....................		RCA 8374
2/27/65	**32**	8	4 Didn't I....................................		RCA 8467
5/22/65	**30**	10	5 Gettin' Married Has Made Us Strangers		RCA 8525
8/21/65	**32**	5	6 No Sign Of Living		RCA 8615
12/04/65+	**22**	14	7 Before The Ring On Your Finger Turns Green.....		RCA 8702
3/12/66	**5**	21	8 **Would You Hold It Against Me**		RCA 8770
8/13/66	**24**	10	9 Mommy, Can I Still Call Him Daddy		RCA 8900
			with Dottie's 4-year-old son, Dale		
12/17/66+	**17**	13	10 What's Come Over My Baby		RCA 9011
3/18/67	**8**	16	11 **Paper Mansions**		RCA 9118
8/26/67	**13**	14	12 Like A Fool...............................		RCA 9267
12/16/67+	**24**	12	13 Childhood Places		RCA 9377
4/27/68	**15**	12	14 Country Girl...............................		RCA 9497
9/07/68	**19**	12	15 Reno		RCA 9604
10/04/69	**47**	6	16 Clinging To My Baby's Hand................		RCA 0239
2/07/70	**45**	8	17 I Heard Our Song		RCA 9792
8/01/70	**37**	10	18 It's Dawned On Me You're Gone		RCA 9872
10/31/70	**21**	12	19 Forever Yours		RCA 9911
1/30/71	**29**	11	20 Slowly....................................		RCA 9947
			JIMMY DEAN & DOTTIE WEST		
3/06/71	**48**	8	21 Careless Hands		RCA 9957
5/29/71	**53**	8	22 Lonely Is		RCA 9982
9/11/71	**51**	8	23 Six Weeks Every Summer (Christmas Every Other Year).............................		RCA 1012
6/03/72	**52**	9	24 I'm Only A Woman		RCA 0711
12/02/72+	**28**	11	25 If It's All Right With You	*97*	RCA 0828
4/28/73	**44**	9	26 Just What I've Been Looking For		RCA 0930
9/15/73	**2¹**	15	27 **Country Sunshine**......................	*49*	RCA 0072
3/30/74	**8**	14	28 **Last Time I Saw Him**...................		RCA 0231
			#14 pop hit for Diana Ross in 1974		
7/13/74	**21**	13	29 House Of Love		RCA 0321
12/14/74+	**35**	10	30 Lay Back Lover		RCA 10125
5/10/75	**65**	10	31 Rollin' In Your Sweet Sunshine.................		RCA 10269
3/27/76	**68**	7	32 Here Come The Flowers.................		RCA 10553

DEBUT DATE	PEAK POS	WKS CHR	ARTIST — Record Title	POP POS	Label & Number
			DOTTIE WEST — Continued		
6/26/76	91	5	33 If I'm A Fool For Loving You		RCA 10699
11/13/76+	19	15	34 When It's Just You And Me........................		United Art. 898
3/19/77	28	12	35 Every Word I Write................................		United Art. 946
7/09/77	30	10	36 Tonight You Belong To Me.............................		United Art. 1010
			#4 pop hit for Patience & Prudence in 1956		
10/08/77	57	8	37 That's All I Wanted To Know		United Art. 1084
6/10/78	17	12	38 Come See Me And Come Lonely		United Art. 1209
12/02/78+	49	9	39 Reaching Out To Hold You		United Art. 1257
10/20/79	12	15	40 You Pick Me Up (And Put Me Down).................		United Art. 1324
2/09/80	1¹	15	41 A Lesson In Leavin'	73	United Art. 1339
6/07/80	13	14	42 Leavin's For Unbelievers		United Art. 1352
12/13/80+	1¹	16	43 **Are You Happy Baby?**		Liberty 1392
7/11/81	16	14	44 (I'm Gonna) Put You Back On The Rack		Liberty 1419
9/19/81	80	4	45 Once You Were Mine..................................		RCA 12284
11/07/81+	16	14	46 It's High Time..		Liberty 1436
2/20/82	26	13	47 You're Not Easy To Forget		Liberty 1451
9/11/82	29	11	48 She Can't Get My Love Off The Bed		Liberty 1479
12/18/82+	63	7	49 If It Takes All Night................................		Liberty 1490
6/18/83	40	11	50 Tulsa Ballroom..		Liberty 1500
9/15/84	77	7	51 What's Good For The Goose (Is Good For The Gander)..		Permian 82006
12/01/84	67	8	52 Let Love Come Lookin' For You......................		Permian 82007
5/25/85	53	8	53 We Know Better Now		Permian 82010
			DOTTIE WEST & DON GIBSON:		
2/22/69	2¹	17	54 **Rings Of Gold**.......................................		RCA 9715
7/12/69	32	10	55 Sweet Memories		RCA 0178
12/13/69+	7	13	56 There's A Story (Goin' 'Round).....................		RCA 0291
7/18/70	46	10	57 Til I Can't Take It Anymore		RCA 9867
			KENNY ROGERS & DOTTIE WEST:		
2/18/78	1²	17	58 **Every Time Two Fools Collide**	101	United Art. 1137
9/02/78	2¹	14	59 **Anyone Who Isn't Me Tonight**		United Art. 1234
2/17/79	1¹	15	60 **All I Ever Need Is You**	102	United Art. 1276
7/07/79	3	15	61 **Til I Can Make It On My Own**.....................		United Art. 1299
4/04/81	1¹	15	62 **What Are We Doin' In Love**	14	Liberty 1404
3/24/84	19	15	63 **Together Again**.....................................		Liberty 1516
			JIM WEST		
11/03/79	95	2	1 Honky Tonk Disco.....................................		Macho 002
12/15/79	92	4	2 Can't Love On Lies		Macho 003
			backing vocal: Carol Chase		
12/20/80	79	5	3 Slip Away		Macho 008
3/14/81	83	3	4 Lovin' Night		Macho 009
			backing vocal: Stephanie Winslow		
			SHELLY WEST ★★163★★		
			Born on 5/23/58 in Cleveland; raised in Nashville. Daughter of singer Dottie West and steel guitarist Bill West. Toured with Dottie from 1975-77. Worked with Allen Frizzell from 1977, married to him until 1985; successful duo partnership with Allen's brother, David.		
2/12/83	1¹	23	1 **Jose Cuervo**		Warner 29778
7/02/83	4	18	2 **Flight 309 To Tennessee**........................		Viva 29597
11/05/83+	10	18	3 **Another Motel Memory**		Viva 29461
3/10/84	56	7	4 Now I Lay Me Down To Cheat		Viva 29353
6/02/84	34	14	5 Somebody Buy This Cowgirl A Beer...............		Viva 29265
1/19/85	21	16	6 Now There's You.....................................		Viva 29106
6/15/85	46	10	7 Don't Make Me Wait On The Moon.................		Warner 28997
9/07/85	64	7	8 I'll Dance The Two Step.............................		Warner 28909
3/15/86	54	5	9 What Would You Do		Warner 28769
9/06/86	55	10	10 Love Don't Come Any Better Than This		Warner 28648
			DAVID FRIZZELL & SHELLY WEST:		
1/17/81	1¹	17	11 **You're The Reason God Made Oklahoma**........		Warner 49650
			from the Clint Eastwood film "Any Which Way You Can"		
6/20/81	9	15	12 **A Texas State Of Mind**		Warner 49745

DEBUT DATE	PEAK POS	WKS CHR	ARTIST — Record Title	POP POS	Label & Number
			SHELLY WEST — Continued		
10/10/81	**16**	16	13 Husbands And Wives....................................		Warner 49825
			#26 pop hit for Roger Miller in 1966		
2/06/82	**8**	18	14 **Another Honky-Tonk Night On Broadway**.......		Warner 50007
7/17/82	**4**	18	15 **I Just Came Here To Dance**.............................		Warner 29980
12/04/82+	**43**	11	16 Please Surrender...		Warner 29850
			from the Clint Eastwood film "Honkytonk Man"		
3/26/83	**52**	10	17 Cajun Invitation...		Warner 29756
9/03/83	**71**	4	18 Pleasure Island..		Viva 29544
2/04/84	**20**	17	19 Silent Partners..		Viva 29404
9/15/84	**13**	20	20 It's A Be Together Night		Viva 29187
4/13/85	**60**	8	21 Do Me Right		Viva 29048
			THE WESTERN UNION BAND		
7/09/88	**76**	3	1 Bed Of Roses...		Shawn-Del 2201
10/08/88	**81**	3	2 Rising Cost Of Loving You		Shawn-Del 2202
			BILLY EDD WHEELER		
			Born on 12/9/32 in Whitesville, West Virginia. Singer/songwriter/playwright. Wrote "Reverend Mr. Black" for the Kingston Trio, "Jackson" for Johnny Cash & June Carter, and "Coward Of The County" for Kenny Rogers. Co-owner of Sleepy Hollow Music.		
11/28/64+	**3**	24	1 **Ode To The Little Brown Shack Out Back** .. [N]	**50**	Kapp 617
8/24/68	**63**	5	2 I Ain't The Worryin' Kind		Kapp 928
5/03/69	**51**	6	3 West Virginia Woman		United Art. 50507
9/13/69	**62**	7	4 Fried Chicken And A Country Tune..................		United Art. 50579
7/29/72	**71**	3	5 200 Lbs. O' Slingin' Hound............................		RCA 0739
11/17/79	**94**	2	6 Duel Under The Snow		Radio Cinema 001
6/20/81	**55**	6	7 Daddy		NSD 94
			with "little girl" Rashell Richmond		
			KAREN WHEELER		
			Born in Sikeston, Missouri. Daughter of Onie Wheeler. Worked in the Harden Trio for a time. Appeared on the Renfro Valley Barn Dance, WWVA Jamboree.		
7/08/72	**67**	4	1 The First Time For Us		Chart 5166
3/09/74	**31**	12	2 Born To Love And Satisfy.............................		RCA 0223
9/21/74	**97**	3	3 What Can I Do (To Make You Happy)................		RCA 10034
			ONIE WHEELER		
			Born on 11/10/21 in Senath, Missouri; died onstage at the Grand Ole Opry in April, 1984 (61). Own band, the Ozark Cowboys, from 1950. First recorded for Organa in 1951. Played with Flatt & Scruggs, Pee Wee King, George Jones, and Roy Acuff.		
2/03/73	**53**	10	1 John's Been Shucking My Corn .... [N]		Royal Amer. 76
			STERLING WHIPPLE		
			Nashville songwriter; wrote "The Blind Man In The Bleachers".		
4/15/78	**26**	9	1 Dirty Work..		Warner 8552
10/14/78	**25**	10	2 Then You'll Remember.................................		Warner 8632
3/24/79	**84**	4	3 Love Is Hours In The Making.........................		Warner 8747
			WHISPERING WILL		
2/24/79	**89**	2	1 Double W.. [N]		Vista 104
			parody of Bill Anderson's "Double S"		
			WHITE WATER JUNCTION		
10/27/84	**97**	1	1 Sleeping Back To Back................................		Jungle Rg. 1004
			BILL WHITE		
			Born in 1934. Claims a world record for being buried 140 days underground. Brother of Jim Mundy and Ann J. Morton.		
7/15/78	**79**	3	1 Unbreakable Hearts....................................		Prairie D. 7625
			BRIAN WHITE		
5/21/88	**70**	4	1 It's Too Late To Love You Now		Oak 1050
			CHARLEY WHITE		
6/30/79	**86**	2	1 Rocket 'Til The Cows Come Home		NSD 22
			DANNY WHITE & LINDA NAIL		
			Danny has been the quarterback of the Dallas Cowboys during the 80s.		
2/05/83	**85**	2	1 You're A Part Of Me.....................................		Grand Prix 2

DEBUT DATE	PEAK POS	WKS CHR	ARTIST — Record Title	POP POS	Label & Number
			L.E. WHITE & LOLA JEAN DILLON		
			L.E. White wrote "I Love You More Today" for Conway Twitty.		
6/18/77	73	7	1 Home, Sweet Home.. [N]		Epic 50389
11/26/77	90	3	2 You're The Reason Our Kids Are Ugly .... [N]		Epic 50474
			MACK WHITE		
			Born in Dothan, Georgia.		
12/01/73+	34	14	1 Too Much Pride		Commercial 1314
4/27/74	66	7	2 Sweet And Tender Feeling		Commercial 1315
10/19/74	75	10	3 Ain't It All Worth Living For		Playboy 6016
2/28/76	35	13	4 Let Me Be Your Friend		Commercial 1317
8/21/76	34	10	5 Take Me As I Am (Or Let Me Go)		Commercial 1319
11/27/76	68	8	6 A Stranger To Me..		Commercial 1320
3/25/78	77	6	7 Just Out Of Reach..		Commercl. 00033
			#24 pop hit for Solomon Burke in 1961		
7/15/78	83	3	8 Goodbyes Don't Come Easy..............................		Commercl. 00040
2/27/82	88	3	9 Kiss The Hurt Away		Commercial 121
			ROGER WHITE		
10/14/67	57	4	1 Mystery Of Tallahatchie Bridge........................	*123*	Big A 103
			answer song to Bobbie Gentry's "Ode To Billie Joe"		
			SHARON WHITE - see RICKY SKAGGS and THE WHITES		
			TONY JOE WHITE		
			Born on 7/23/43 in Oak Grove, Louisiana. Worked clubs in Corpus Christi, Texas in the mid-60s. Moved to Nashville in 1968. Worked as staff writer for Combine Music. Wrote "A Rainy Night In Georgia", "Willie And Laura Mae Jones" and "I've Got A Thing About You Baby".		
11/01/80	91	2	1 Mama Don't Let Your Cowboys Grow Up To Be Babies		Casablanca 2304
11/26/83	55	10	2 The Lady In My Life		Columbia 04134
3/03/84	85	3	3 We Belong Together		Columbia 04356
			BENNY WHITEHEAD		
1/27/73	61	5	1 Blue Eyed Jane...		Reprise 1131
			THE WHITES		
			Family group formed in 1971 as the Down Home Folks. Consisted of Buck White (guitar, mandolin, piano) and his wife Patty, and daughters Sharon (guitar) and Cheryl (bass). Buck worked as a session man in the early 50s and played with the Blue Sage Boys in 1952. Buck and Patty had been in original Down Home Folks with Arnold and Peggy Johnston (1962); Sharon and Cheryl were in the Down Home Kids with Teddy and Eddie Johnston (1966). Patty retired from music in 1973. Sharon is married to Ricky Skaggs. Members of the Grand Ole Opry since 1984.		
6/20/81	66	4	1 Send Me The Pillow You Dream On..................		Capitol 5004
8/28/82	10	17	2 **You Put The Blue In Me**..............................		Elektra 69980
12/25/82+	9	19	3 **Hangin' Around**...		Elektra 69855
4/30/83	9	18	4 **I Wonder Who's Holding My Baby Tonight**......		Warner 29659
9/10/83	25	14	5 When The New Wears Off Of Our Love		Warner 29513
12/17/83+	10	19	6 **Give Me Back That Old Familiar Feeling**........		Warner 29411
5/12/84	14	17	7 Forever You		Curb 52381
8/25/84	10	22	8 **Pins And Needles**.......................................		Curb 52432
3/09/85	12	17	9 If It Ain't Love (Let's Leave It Alone)		Curb 52535
6/29/85	27	15	10 Hometown Gossip...		Curb 52615
11/02/85	33	14	11 I Don't Want To Get Over You		Curb 52697
			all of above (except #1): produced by Ricky Skaggs		
5/24/86	36	12	12 Love Won't Wait		Curb 52825
11/08/86+	30	16	13 It Should Have Been Easy..............................		Curb 52953
3/07/87	58	7	14 There Ain't No Binds		Curb 53038
			MARGARET WHITING - see JIMMY WAKELY		
			KEITH WHITLEY		
			Born on 7/1/55 in Sandy Hook, Kentucky. Appeared with Buddy Starcher on radio in Charleston, West Virginia at age 8. Own band, the East Kentucky Mountain Boys, with Ricky Skaggs, from 1968 to the early 70s. Played in Ralph Stanley's Clinch Mountain Boys in the mid-70s. Also recorded with own New Tradition, and Country Store in 1972. With J. D. Crowe and New South in 1978. Married to Lorrie Morgan in 1986. Died on 5/9/89 at age 33 of alcohol abuse.		
9/29/84	59	9	1 Turn Me To Love...		RCA 13810

DEBUT DATE	PEAK POS	WKS CHR	ARTIST — Record Title	POP POS	Label & Number
			KEITH WHITLEY — Continued		
2/23/85	**76**	7	2 A Hard Act To Follow		RCA 13996
9/14/85	**57**	10	3 I've Got The Heart For You		RCA 14173
11/02/85+	**14**	20	4 Miami, My Amy..............................		RCA 14285
6/21/86	**9**	26	5 **Ten Feet Away**		RCA 14363
11/08/86+	**9**	23	6 **Homecoming '63**		RCA 5013
3/14/87	**10**	16	7 **Hard Livin'**		RCA 5116
8/29/87	**36**	17	8 Would These Arms Be In Your Way		RCA 5237
11/14/87+	**16**	21	9 Some Old Side Road..........................		RCA 5326
4/30/88	**1**¹	23	10 **Don't Close Your Eyes**		RCA 6901
9/17/88	**1**²	22	11 **When You Say Nothing At All**		RCA 8637
			SLIM WHITMAN ★★**103**★★		
			Born Otis Dewey Whitman on 1/20/24 in Tampa. Guitarist/yodeller. Worked in a shipyard and served in US Navy from 1943-46. Played semi-pro baseball with the Plant City Berries. On radio WDAE-Tampa in 1946 and worked local clubs. Played with the Light Crust Doughboys in 1949. Worked on the Louisiana Hayride in 1950. First recorded for RCA in 1950. First played the London Palladium in 1952 and remains very popular in Great Britain.		
5/17/52	**10**	1	1 **Love Song Of The Waterfall**		Imperial 8134
			Jockey #10		
7/05/52	**2**³	24	2●**Indian Love Call**	*9*	Imperial 8156
			Best Seller #2 / Juke Box #2 / Jockey #3		
12/06/52+	**3**	13	3 **Keep It A Secret/**		
			Jockey #3 / Juke Box #3 / Best Seller #5		
12/20/52	**10**	1	4 **My Heart Is Broken In Three**		Imperial 8169
			Juke Box #10		
11/14/53	**8**	5	5 **North Wind**.................................		Imperial 8208
			Best Seller #8 / Jockey #8 / Juke Box #8		
1/23/54	**2**¹	18	6 **Secret Love**		Imperial 8220
			Jockey #2 / Best Seller #3 / Juke Box #3		
			#1 pop hit for Doris Day in 1954		
5/01/54	**4**	23	7 **Rose-Marie**.................................	*22*	Imperial 8236
			Juke Box #4 / Best Seller #5 / Jockey #7		
			2 & 7: from the 1936 Jeanette MacDonald/Nelson Eddy classic films		
11/06/54	**4**	3	8 **Singing Hills**		Imperial 8267
			Juke Box #4		
1/15/55	**11**	2	9 The Cattle Call		Imperial 8281
			Best Seller #11		
7/03/61	**30**	1	10 The Bells That Broke My Heart............		Imperial 65746
2/29/64	**48**	1	11 Tell Me Pretty Words		Imperial 66012
10/30/65	**8**	17	12 **More Than Yesterday**......................		Imperial 66130
3/12/66	**17**	12	13 The Twelfth Of Never		Imperial 66153
			#9 pop hit for Johnny Mathis in 1957		
7/16/66	**49**	2	14 I Remember You	*134*	Imperial 66181
			#5 pop hit for Frank Ifield in 1962		
12/03/66	**54**	6	15 One Dream		Imperial 66212
3/11/67	**56**	8	16 What's This World A-Comin' To		Imperial 66226
7/22/67	**61**	6	17 I'm A Fool..................................		Imperial 66248
11/18/67	**65**	5	18 The Keeper Of The Key		Imperial 66262
3/16/68	**17**	14	19 Rainbows Are Back In Style		Imperial 66283
8/10/68	**22**	11	20 Happy Street		Imperial 66311
11/30/68+	**43**	8	21 Livin' On Lovin' (And Lovin' Livin' With You).....		Imperial 66337
4/19/69	**43**	4	22 My Happiness		Imperial 66358
			#2 pop hit for Connie Francis in 1959		
7/12/69	**61**	5	23 Irresistible		Imperial 66384
4/18/70	**27**	12	24 Tomorrow Never Comes		Imperial 66441
8/08/70	**26**	12	25 Shutters And Boards		United Art. 50697
			#24 pop hit for Jerry Wallace in 1963		
12/12/70+	**7**	14	26 **Guess Who**	*121*	United Art. 50731
			#31 pop hit for Jesse Belvin in 1959		
5/01/71	**6**	15	27 **Something Beautiful (To Remember)**		United Art. 50775
8/14/71	**21**	13	28 It's A Sin To Tell A Lie.....................		United Art. 50806
			#7 pop hit for Somethin' Smith & The Redheads in 1955		
12/11/71+	**56**	7	29 Loveliest Night Of The Year		United Art. 50852
			#3 pop hit for Mario Lanza in 1951		
10/21/72	**51**	7	30 (It's No) Sin		United Art. 50952
			#1 pop hit for Eddy Howard in 1951		

DEBUT DATE	PEAK POS	WKS CHR	ARTIST — Record Title	POP POS	Label & Number
			SLIM WHITMAN — Continued		
3/03/73	73	4	31 Hold Me..		United Art. 178
7/14/73	88	5	32 Where The Lilacs Grow		United Art. 269
4/20/74	82	5	33 It's All In The Game		United Art. 402
			#1 pop hit for Tommy Edwards in 1958		
8/09/80	15	12	34 When..		Clev. Int. 50912
11/22/80	69	5	35 That Silver-Haired Daddy Of Mine		Clev. Int. 50946
			written and popularized by Gene Autry in 1935		
2/07/81	44	8	36 I Remember You .... [R]		Clev. Int. 50971
8/15/81	54	7	37 Can't Help Falling In Love With You		Clev. Int. 02402
			#2 pop hit for Elvis Presley in 1962		
			ROGER WHITTAKER		
			Born on 3/22/36 in Nairobi, Kenya. British MOR singer.		
12/17/83	91	4	1 I Love You Because		Main St. 93016
			THE WICHITA LINEMEN		
			Wichita, Kansas quartet.		
12/24/77	100	2	1 Everyday Of My Life		Linemen 773
10/20/79	93	4	2 You're A Pretty Lady, Lady		Linemen 10838
			featuring Greg Stevens		
			LEWIE WICKHAM		
3/28/70	36	10	1 Little Bit Late .... [N]		Starday 888
7/08/78	59	7	2 $60 Duck.. [N]		MCA 40928
			WICKLINE BAND		
			Fox Island, Washington group led by Robert L. "Bob" Wickline and wife Lynda.		
3/28/81	90	3	1 Do Fish Swim		Cascade Mt. 2325
9/10/83	85	3	2 True Love's Getting Pretty Hard to Find...........		Cascade Mt. 3030
2/04/84	78	7	3 Ski Bumpus/Banjo Fantasy II .... [I]		Cascade Mt. 4045
			featuring Scott Gavin on banjo		
			RUSTY WIER		
			Country/rock singer from Austin, Texas.		
4/25/87	74	4	1 Close Your Eyes..		Black Hat 102
			written by James Taylor		
8/15/87	70	5	2 (Lover Of The) Other Side Of The Hill		Black Hat 103
			BILL WILBOURN & KATHY MORRISON		
			Bill is a former deejay from Aliceville, Alabama.		
7/20/68	65	5	1 The Lovers		United Art. 50310
1/11/69	44	6	2 Him And Her		United Art. 50474
6/28/69	52	7	3 Lovin' Season		United Art. 50537
5/09/70	34	12	4 A Good Thing		United Art. 50660
10/31/70	65	6	5 Look How Far We've Gone		United Art. 50718
			WILBURN BROTHERS ★★**100**★★		
			Duo from Hardy, Missouri: brothers Virgil Doyle (b: 7/7/30; d: 10//16/82) and Thurman Theodore "Teddy" Wilburn (b: 11/30/31). Raised in Arkansas, first sang with the Wilburn Family group on the Grand Ole Opry in 1941. Worked on the Louisiana Hayride from 1948-51. Both served in the US Army from 1951-53, then formed duo. On the Grand Ole Opry since 1953. Own TV series featuring Loretta Lynn. Owners of Surefire Music. Doyle married for a time to Margie Bowes.		
6/11/55	13	2	1 I Wanna, Wanna, Wanna		Decca 29459
			Jockey #13		
1/21/56	13	3	2 You're Not Playing Love		Decca 29747
			Jockey #13		
8/11/56	10	8	3 I'm So In Love With You		Decca 29887
			Jockey #10		
12/01/56	6	11	4 Go Away With Me		Decca 30087
			Jockey #6		
7/08/57	8	2	5 Mister Love..		Decca 30303
			ERNEST TUBB & THE WILBURN BROTHERS		
			Jockey #8		
5/26/58	9	10	6 Hey, Mr. Bluebird		Decca 30610
			ERNEST TUBB & THE WILBURN BROTHERS		
			Jockey #9 / Best Seller #14		
1/05/59	4	19	7 Which One Is To Blame/		
1/19/59	18	4	8 The Knoxville Girl....................................		Decca 30787
5/18/59	6	19	9 Somebody's Back In Town		Decca 30871

DEBUT DATE	PEAK POS	WKS CHR	ARTIST — Record Title	POP POS	Label & Number
			WILBURN BROTHERS — Continued		
10/26/59	**9**	13	10 **A Woman's Intuition**		Decca 30968
12/19/60	**27**	2	11 The Best Of All My Heartaches		Decca 31152
7/31/61	**14**	6	12 Blue Blue Day		Decca 31276
5/12/62	**4**	22	13 **Trouble's Back In Town**	*101*	Decca 31363
11/17/62	**21**	5	14 The Sound Of Your Footsteps		Decca 31425
5/11/63	**4**	13	15 **Roll Muddy River**		Decca 31464
9/14/63	**10**	13	16 **Tell Her So**		Decca 31520
2/29/64	**34**	4	17 Hangin' Around		Decca 31578
11/14/64+	**19**	15	18 I'm Gonna Tie One On Tonight		Decca 31674
5/29/65	**30**	12	19 I Had One Too Many		Decca 31764
9/18/65	**5**	20	20 **It's Another World**		Decca 31819
2/05/66	**8**	17	21 **Someone Before Me**		Decca 31894
7/09/66	**13**	14	22 I Can't Keep Away From You		Decca 31974
11/12/66+	**3**	20	23 **Hurt Her Once For Me/**		
2/11/67	**70**	3	24 Just To Be Where You Are		Decca 32038
4/29/67	**13**	14	25 Roarin' Again		Decca 32117
9/09/67	**24**	14	26 Goody, Goody Gumdrop		Decca 32169
10/26/68	**43**	8	27 We Need A Lot More Happiness		Decca 32386
3/15/69	**38**	11	28 It Looks Like The Sun's Gonna Shine		Decca 32449
1/31/70	**37**	8	29 Little Johnny From Down The Street		Decca 32608
3/04/72	**47**	9	30 Arkansas..		Decca 32921
			HARLOW WILCOX & THE OAKIES		
			Harlow is a top session guitarist from Norman, Oklahoma.		
9/20/69	**42**	13	1 Groovy Grubworm .... [I]	*30*	Plantation 28
			PETE WILCOX		
4/24/82	**75**	5	1 The King		M&M 503
			WILD CHOIR		
			Short-lived Nashville group led by Gail Davies.		
6/14/86	**51**	13	1 Next Time..		RCA 14337
10/25/86	**40**	13	2 Heart To Heart		RCA 5011
			WILEY & GENE		
			Wiley Walker and Gene Sullivan; formed duet in Dallas in 1939. Wrote and originally recorded "When My Blue Moon Turns To Gold Again".		
1/05/46	**2**[1]	1	1 **Make Room In Your Heart For A Friend**		Columbia 36869
			LITTLE DAVID WILKINS		
			Born in Parsons, Tennessee. Recorded for Sun Records at the age of 15.		
3/22/69	**54**	7	1 Just Blow In His Ear...................................		Plantation 11
			shown only as: **DAVID WILKINS**		
6/23/73	**63**	4	2 Love In The Back Seat		MCA 40034
9/22/73	**41**	12	3 Too Much Hold Back....................................		MCA 40115
3/30/74	**50**	9	4 Georgia Keeps Pulling On My Ring		MCA 40200
10/26/74	**77**	8	5 Not Tonight..		MCA 40299
12/28/74+	**14**	15	6 Whoever Turned You On, Forgot To Turn You Off		MCA 40345
7/19/75	**11**	14	7 One Monkey Don't Stop No Show		MCA 40427
1/31/76	**18**	15	8 The Good Night Special		MCA 40510
7/04/76	**75**	5	9 Disco-Tex/		
		4	10 Half The Way In, Half The Way Out		MCA 40579
11/20/76	**88**	5	11 The Greatest Show On Earth		MCA 40646
1/22/77	**21**	12	12 He'll Play The Music (But You Can't Make Him Dance)		MCA 40668
6/18/77	**60**	8	13 Is Everybody Ready		MCA 40734
10/22/77	**21**	14	14 Agree To Disagree.....................................		Playboy 5822
3/04/78	**68**	6	15 Don't Stop The Music (You're Playing My Song) ..		Playboy 5825
8/05/78	**74**	5	16 Motel Rooms		Epic 50571
7/12/86	**79**	3	17 Lady In Distress..		Jere 1003
7/25/87	**72**	4	18 Butterbeans		16th Ave. 70401
			JOHNNY RUSSELL & LITTLE DAVID WILKINS		

DEBUT DATE	PEAK POS	WKS CHR	ARTIST — Record Title	POP POS	Label & Number
			SLIM WILLET		
			Born Winston Lee Moore on 12/1/19 near Dublin, Texas; died of a heart attack on 7/1/66. Worked on radio in Abilene from 1949-66. First recorded for Star Talent in 1950. Own band, the Hired Hands, from 1950-55.		
9/27/52	1¹	23	1 **Don't Let The Stars Get In Your Eyes**.............		Four Star 1614
			Jockey #1 / Best Seller #2 / Juke Box #2		
			#1 pop hit for Perry Como in 1953		
			WILLIAMS BROTHERS		
			Jimmy and Bobby Williams.		
6/15/63	28	1	1 Bad Old Memories		Del-Mar 1008
			BECKY WILLIAMS		
7/09/88	75	4	1 Tie Me Up		Country P. 00011
			BETH WILLIAMS		
			Born in Puerto Rico; raised in Texas. Worked clubs in San Antonio and Kerrville.		
9/27/86	82	3	1 Wrong Train		BGM 71086
11/29/86	64	7	2 These Eyes		BGM 092486
3/28/87	58	6	3 Man At The Backdoor		BGM 13087
			COOTIE WILLIAMS		
			Born Charles Melvin Williams on 7/24/08 in Mobile, Alabama. Died on 9/15/85 (77). Jazz trumpet star. With Duke Ellington from 1929-40, Benny Goodman from 1940-41.		
7/08/44	4	6	1 **Cherry Red Blues**..	23	Hit 7084
			vocal: Eddie "Cleanhead" Vinson		
			DIANA WILLIAMS		
			Nashville-born country singer.		
8/28/76	53	6	1 Teddy Bear's Last Ride .... [S]	66	Capitol 4317
			answer song to Red Sovine's hit "Teddy Bear"		
			DON WILLIAMS ★★38★★		
			Born on 5/27/39 in Floydada, Texas. Made professional debut in 1957. Moved to Corpus Christi, formed the Pozo-Seco Singers with Susan Taylor and Lofton Cline in 1964. Moved to Nashville in 1967 and went solo in 1971. Became staff writer for Jack Clement. In the films "W.W. And The Dixie Dance Kings" and "Smokey & The Bandit 2". Also extremely popular in Europe, where he was named Country Music Star Of The Decade in England in 1980.		
12/16/72+	14	16	1 The Shelter Of Your Eyes		JMI 12
5/05/73	12	16	2 Come Early Morning/		
7/28/73	33	11	3 Amanda		JMI 24
11/17/73+	13	14	4 Atta Way To Go		JMI 32
3/02/74	5	15	5 **We Should Be Together**		JMI 36
6/29/74	62	7	6 Down The Road I Go		JMI 42
7/06/74	1¹	17	7 **I Wouldn't Want To Live If You Didn't Love Me**		Dot 17516
12/14/74+	4	15	8 **The Ties That Bind**		Dot 17531
			#37 pop hit for Brook Benton in 1960		
4/12/75	1¹	17	9 **You're My Best Friend**		ABC/Dot 17550
8/16/75	1¹	16	10 **(Turn Out The Light And) Love Me Tonight**		ABC/Dot 17568
1/31/76	1¹	16	11 **Til The Rivers All Run Dry**		ABC/Dot 17604
6/12/76	1¹	14	12 **Say It Again**..		ABC/Dot 17631
10/16/76	2²	15	13 **She Never Knew Me**...................................	103	ABC/Dot 17658
3/12/77	1¹	16	14 **Some Broken Hearts Never Mend**..................	108	ABC/Dot 17683
9/03/77	1¹	15	15 **I'm Just A Country Boy**................................	110	ABC/Dot 17717
2/11/78	7	14	16 **I've Got A Winner In You**..............................		ABC 12332
7/01/78	3	15	17 **Rake And Ramblin' Man**		ABC 12373
11/04/78+	1¹	16	18 **Tulsa Time**	106	ABC 12425
			#30 pop hit for Eric Clapton in 1980		
3/17/79	3	15	19 **Lay Down Beside Me**		MCA 12458
			also released on ABC		
8/04/79	1¹	14	20 **It Must Be Love**		MCA 41069
12/08/79+	1¹	16	21 **Love Me Over Again**		MCA 41155
2/16/80	97	2	22 Could You Ever Really Love A Poor Boy............		Phono 2693
3/29/80	2³	15	23 **Good Ole Boys Like Me**		MCA 41205
8/23/80	1²	16	24 **I Believe In You**	24	MCA 41304
2/21/81	6	16	25 **Falling Again**		MCA 51065
7/04/81	4	15	26 **Miracles**		MCA 51134

DEBUT DATE	PEAK POS	WKS CHR	ARTIST — Record Title	POP POS	Label & Number
			DON WILLIAMS — Continued		
9/19/81	**3**	17	27 If I Needed You..		Warner 49809
			EMMYLOU HARRIS & DON WILLIAMS		
11/21/81+	**1¹**	20	28 Lord, I Hope This Day Is Good		MCA 51207
4/17/82	**3**	16	29 Listen To The Radio		MCA 52037
8/21/82	**3**	17	30 Mistakes		MCA 52097
12/11/82+	**1¹**	20	31 If Hollywood Don't Need You.........................		MCA 52152
4/16/83	**1¹**	18	32 Love Is On A Roll..		MCA 52205
7/30/83	**2¹**	19	33 Nobody But You...		MCA 52245
12/03/83+	**1¹**	19	34 Stay Young		MCA 52310
5/19/84	**1¹**	20	35 That's The Thing About Love		MCA 52389
9/01/84	**11**	21	36 Maggie's Dream		MCA 52448
1/05/85	**2¹**	20	37 Walkin' A Broken Heart		MCA 52514
10/12/85	**20**	19	38 It's Time For Love		MCA 52692
1/18/86	**3**	22	39 We've Got A Good Fire Goin'		Capitol 5526
5/31/86	**1¹**	22	40 Heartbeat In The Darkness............................		Capitol 5588
10/18/86+	**3**	22	41 Then It's Love		Capitol 5638
2/07/87	**9**	21	42 Senorita		Capitol 5683
6/06/87	**4**	26	43 I'll Never Be In Love Again		Capitol 44019
10/24/87+	**9**	26	44 I Wouldn't Be A Man		Capitol 44066
3/12/88	**5**	23	45 Another Place, Another Time........................		Capitol 44131
8/13/88	**7**	24	46 Desperately..		Capitol 44216

HANK WILLIAMS ★★46★★

Born Hiram King Williams on 9/17/23 in Mount Olive, Alabama; died at the age of 29, enroute to a concert in Canton, Ohio, on 1/1/53. Moved to Montgomery in the late 30s. Own radio show on WSFA-Montgomery, billed as "The Singing Kid". Formed his own band, The Drifting Cowboys, as a teenager. Married Audrey Sheppard in 1944. First recorded for Sterling in 1946. Worked on the Louisiana Hayride from 1948-49, with the Grand Ole Opry from 1949-52. Toured with Bob Hope, Jack Benny and Minnie Pearl in the Hadacol Caravan in 1951. Divorced from Audrey in May of 1948; fired from the Opry in August of 1952. Married Billie Jean Jones Eshliman in 1952. Elected to the Country Music Hall Of Fame in 1961. Also recorded as "Luke The Drifter". Inducted into the Rock And Roll Hall Of Fame in 1987. The premier country songwriter. George Hamilton portrayed Hank in his film biography "Your Cheatin' Heart".

DEBUT DATE	PEAK POS	WKS CHR	ARTIST — Record Title	POP POS	Label & Number
8/09/47	**4**	3	1 Move It On Over		MGM 10033
7/03/48	**14**	1	2 Honky Tonkin'..		MGM 10171
			Juke Box #14		
7/24/48	**6**	3	3 I'm A Long Gone Daddy...............................		MGM 10212
			Juke Box #6		
3/05/49	**1¹⁶**	42	4 Lovesick Blues/	24	
			Best Seller #1(16) / Juke Box #1(10)		
7/09/49	**6**	2	5 Never Again		MGM 10352
			Juke Box #6		
3/05/49	**12**	2	6 Mansion On The Hill		MGM 10328
			Juke Box #12		
5/14/49	**2²**	29	7 Wedding Bells		MGM 10401
			Best Seller #2 / Juke Box #2		
7/23/49	**5**	11	8 Mind Your Own Business............................		MGM 10461
			Juke Box #5 / Best Seller #6		
10/01/49	**4**	9	9 You're Gonna Change/		
			Best Seller #4 / Juke Box #8		
10/08/49	**12**	3	10 Lost Highway		MGM 10506
			Best Seller #12 / Juke Box #14		
11/26/49	**2¹**	12	11 My Bucket's Got A Hole In It		MGM 10560
			Best Seller #2 / Juke Box #2 / Jockey #5		
			flip side is the classic tune "I'm So Lonesome I Could Cry"		
2/18/50	**5**	5	12 I Just Don't Like This Kind Of Livin'		MGM 10609
			Best Seller #5 / Juke Box #5 / Jockey #8		
3/25/50	**1⁸**	21	13 Long Gone Lonesome Blues/		
			Jockey #1(8) / Best Seller #1(5) / Juke Box #1(4)		
4/15/50	**9**	1	14 My Son Calls Another Man Daddy		MGM 10645
			Juke Box #9		
6/03/50	**1¹⁰**	25	15 Why Don't You Love Me		MGM 10696
			Jockey #1(10) / Best Seller #1(6) / Juke Box #1(5)		
10/07/50	**5**	6	16 They'll Never Take Her Love From Me/		
			Jockey #5		
10/14/50	**9**	1	17 Why Should We Try Anymore....................		MGM 10760
			Best Seller #9		

DEBUT DATE	PEAK POS	WKS CHR	ARTIST — Record Title	POP POS	Label & Number
			HANK WILLIAMS — Continued		
11/18/50	1¹	15	18 **Moanin' The Blues/** Jockey #1 / Best Seller #2 / Juke Box #3		•
11/18/50	9	4	19 **Nobody's Lonesome For Me** .... Jockey #9		MGM 10832
3/17/51	1¹	46	20 **Cold, Cold Heart/** Jockey #1 / Best Seller #2 / Juke Box #4	27	
3/03/51	8	4	21 **Dear John**... Juke Box #8 / Best Seller #10		MGM 10904
6/09/51	2²	13	22 **I Can't Help It (If I'm Still In Love With You)/** Jockey #2 / Juke Box #3 / Best Seller #6		
5/26/51	3	10	23 **Howlin' At The Moon** .... Juke Box #3 / Best Seller #4 / Jockey #6		MGM 10961
7/14/51	1⁸	25	24 **Hey, Good Lookin'** .... Jockey #1 / Juke Box #2 / Best Seller #2	29	MGM 11000
10/20/51	4	18	25 **Crazy Heart/** Juke Box #4 / Jockey #6 / Best Seller #7		
10/20/51	9	2	26 **Lonesome Whistle**................................... Jockey #9		MGM 11054
12/22/51	4	15	27 **Baby, We're Really In Love** .... Jockey #4 / Juke Box #4 / Best Seller #8		MGM 11100
3/01/52	2¹	12	28 **Honky Tonk Blues** .... Juke Box #2 / Best Seller #7 / Jockey #10		MGM 11160
5/03/52	2²	16	29 **Half As Much** .... Best Seller #2 / Juke Box #4 / Jockey #7		MGM 11202
8/16/52	1¹⁴	29	30 **Jambalaya (On The Bayou)** .... Best Seller #1(14) / Jockey #1(14) / Juke Box #1(12)	20	MGM 11283
10/11/52	2¹	12	31 **Settin' The Woods On Fire/** Jockey #2 / Juke Box #4 / Best Seller #5		
11/15/52	10	1	32 **You Win Again** .... Juke Box #10		MGM 11318
12/20/52+	1¹	13	33 **I'll Never Get Out Of This World Alive** .... Best Seller #1 / Juke Box #4 / Jockey #7		MGM 11366
2/21/53	1¹³	19	34 **Kaw-Liga/** Best Seller #1(13) / Jockey #1(8) / Juke Box #1(8)	23	
2/21/53	1⁶	23	35 **Your Cheatin' Heart** .... Jockey #1(6) / Juke Box #1(2) / Best Seller #2		MGM 11416
5/16/53	1⁴	13	36 **Take These Chains From My Heart**............... Best Seller #1 / Juke Box #2 / Jockey #3		MGM 11479
7/25/53	4	9	37 **I Won't Be Home No More** .... Best Seller #4 / Juke Box #4 / Jockey #5		MGM 11533
10/10/53	7	2	38 **Weary Blues From Waitin'** .... Best Seller #7 / Juke Box #7 / Jockey #9		MGM 11574
4/30/55	9	3	39 **Please Don't Let Me Love You** .... Juke Box #9		MGM 11928
6/11/66	43	4	40 I'm So Lonesome I Could Cry .... [R]	109	MGM 13489
10/09/76	61	7	41 Why Don't You Love Me .... [R]		MGM 14849
			HANK WILLIAMS, JR. ★★**16**★★ Born Randall Hank Williams on 5/26/49 in Shreveport, Louisiana, the son of Hank and Audrey Williams. Raised in Nashville, a star athlete in high school. Toured with Audrey's Caravan Of Stars from age 13. On the Grand Ole Opry since 1962. On soundtrack of the film "Your Cheatin' Heart" in 1964. Moved to Cullman, Alabama in 1974. Injured in a climbing accident on 8/8/75 in Montana, returned to performing in 1977. Own Showtime TV Special in 1984. Now lives near Aris, Tennessee. Also recorded as "Luke The Drifter, Jr.". His father gave him the nickname "Bocephus". CMA award: Entertainer of the Year - 1987 and 1988.		
2/08/64	5	19	1 **Long Gone Lonesome Blues** .... #1 hit for Hank, Sr. in 1950	67	MGM 13208
7/25/64	42	6	2 Guess What, That's Right, She's Gone..............		MGM 13253
12/26/64+	46	5	3 Endless Sleep .... #5 pop hit for Jody Reynolds in 1958	90	MGM 13278
5/28/66	5	19	4 **Standing In The Shadows**............................		MGM 13504
12/24/66+	43	13	5 I Can't Take It No Longer		MGM 13640
6/17/67	60	4	6 I'm In No Condition		MGM 13730
8/26/67	46	8	7 Nobody's Child		MGM 13782
1/13/68	31	11	8 I Wouldn't Change A Thing About You (But Your Name)...		MGM 13857
6/01/68	51	6	9 The Old Ryman..		MGM 13922
8/31/68	3	16	10 **It's All Over But The Crying**		MGM 13968

DEBUT DATE	PEAK POS	WKS CHR	ARTIST — Record Title	POP POS	Label & Number
			HANK WILLIAMS, JR. — Continued		
11/09/68	**39**	8	11 I Was With Red Foley (The Night He Passed Away).......................................		MGM 14002
1/18/69	**14**	12	12 Custody...................		MGM 14020
2/22/69	**16**	10	13 A Baby Again		MGM 14024
5/03/69	**3**	14	14 **Cajun Baby**	*107*	MGM 14047
7/05/69	**37**	8	15 Be Careful Of Stones That You Throw...............		MGM 14062
			#31 pop hit for Dion in 1963		
9/13/69	**4**	14	16 **I'd Rather Be Gone**		MGM 14077
1/03/70	**36**	8	17 Something To Think About		MGM 14095
3/07/70	**12**	13	18 I Walked Out On Heaven......................		MGM 14107
5/23/70	**36**	9	19 It Don't Take But One Mistake......................		MGM 14120
			11-12, 15, 17 & 19 shown as: **LUKE THE DRIFTER, JR.**		
8/01/70	**1** 2	15	20 **All For The Love Of Sunshine**		MGM 14152
			from the film "Kelly's Heroes"		
12/19/70+	**3**	15	21 **Rainin' In My Heart**	*108*	MGM 14194
			above 2: with The Mike Curb Congregation (also #24 below)		
4/24/71	**6**	14	22 **I've Got A Right To Cry**......................	*102*	MGM 14240
8/21/71	**18**	14	23 After All They All Used To Belong To Me		MGM 14277
12/18/71+	**7**	14	24 **Ain't That A Shame**		MGM 14317
			#1 R&B hit for Fats Domino in 1955		
4/29/72	**1** 2	16	25 **Eleven Roses**		MGM 14371
9/16/72	**3**	16	26 **Pride's Not Hard To Swallow**		MGM 14421
2/24/73	**23**	13	27 After You		MGM 14486
6/16/73	**12**	14	28 Hank		MGM 14550
			a tribute to Hank, Sr.		
10/20/73	**4**	18	29 **The Last Love Song**		MGM 14656
3/09/74	**13**	12	30 Rainy Night In Georgia		MGM 14700
			#4 pop hit for Brook Benton in 1970		
7/06/74	**7**	13	31 **I'll Think Of Something**......................		MGM 14731
11/02/74	**19**	12	32 Angels Are Hard To Find		MGM 14755
4/12/75	**26**	10	33 Where He's Going, I've Already Been/		
		4	34 The Kind Of Woman I Got		MGM 14794
7/05/75	**29**	13	35 The Same Old Story		MGM 14813
11/08/75	**19**	13	36 Stoned At The Jukebox		MGM 14833
4/10/76	**38**	9	37 Living Proof		MGM 14845
4/09/77	**27**	12	38 Mobile Boogie		Warner 8361
8/20/77	**59**	7	39 I'm Not Responsible/		
		5	40 (Honey, Won't You) Call Me		Warner 8410
10/01/77	**47**	9	41 One Night Stands		Warner 8451
1/07/78	**38**	9	42 Feelin' Better		Warner 8507
5/13/78	**76**	4	43 You Love The Thunder......................		Warner 8564
8/12/78	**15**	12	44 I Fought The Law		Warner 8641
			#9 pop hit for the Bobby Fuller Four in 1966		
11/25/78	**54**	6	45 Old Flame, New Fire		Warner 8715
3/31/79	**49**	6	46 To Love Somebody		Elektra 46018
			#17 pop hit for The Bee Gees in 1967		
6/09/79	**4**	15	47 **Family Tradition**	*104*	Elektra 46046
10/06/79	**2** 2	14	48 **Whiskey Bent And Hell Bound**......................		Elektra 46535
2/09/80	**5**	13	49 **Women I've Never Had**		Elektra 46593
5/17/80	**12**	12	50 Kaw-Liga		Elektra 46636
			giant #1 hit for Hank, Sr. in 1953		
8/30/80	**6**	13	51 **Old Habits**		Elektra 47016
2/07/81	**1** 1	13	52 **Texas Women**		Elektra 47102
5/30/81	**1** 1	14	53 **Dixie On My Mind**		Elektra 47137
9/05/81	**1** 1	19	54 **All My Rowdy Friends (Have Settled Down)**.....		Elektra 47191
1/23/82	**2** 3	20	55 **A Country Boy Can Survive**		Elektra 47257
6/05/82	**1** 1	15	56 **Honky Tonkin'**		Elektra 47462
			revival of the 2nd charted hit by Hank, Sr.		
10/09/82	**5**	16	57 **The American Dream**/		
		16	58 If Heaven Ain't A Lot Like Dixie		Elektra 69960
1/29/83	**4**	18	59 **Gonna Go Huntin' Tonight**...........................		Elektra 69846
6/04/83	**6**	16	60 **Leave Them Boys Alone**............................		Warner 29633
			guest vocals: Waylon Jennings and Ernest Tubb		

DEBUT DATE	PEAK POS	WKS CHR	ARTIST — Record Title	POP POS	Label & Number
			HANK WILLIAMS, JR. — Continued		
10/01/83	5	21	61 Queen Of My Heart		Warner 29500
2/18/84	3	18	62 Man Of Steel		Warner 29382
6/16/84	5	18	63 Attitude Adjustment..........................		Warner 29253
10/06/84	10	19	64 All My Rowdy Friends Are Coming Over Tonight		Warner 29184
1/19/85	10	18	65 Major Moves		Warner 29095
5/11/85	1¹	23	66 I'm For Love		Warner 29022
9/07/85	4	20	67 This Ain't Dallas		Warner 28912
2/22/86	1¹	18	68 Ain't Misbehavin' .... written and popularized in 1929 by Fats Waller		Warner 28794
6/14/86	2²	21	69 Country State Of Mind		Warner 28691
10/11/86	1²	19	70 Mind Your Own Business .... guest vocals: Willie Nelson, Reba McEntire and Reverend Ike		Warner 28581
2/21/87	31	11	71 When Something Is Good (Why Does It Change) ..		Warner 28452
6/13/87	1¹	20	72 Born To Boogie.................................		Warner 28369
10/10/87+	4	21	73 Heaven Can't Be Found		Warner 28227
2/20/88	2¹	21	74 Young Country .... features celebrity chorus: Butch Baker, T. Graham Brown, Jack Daniels, Paulette Carlson, Cactus Moser, Curtis Stone, Dana Vicker, Steve Earle, Keith Whitley and Marty Stuart		Warner 28120
6/25/88	8	15	75 If The South Woulda Won		Warner 27862
11/05/88+	14	15	76 Early In The Morning And Late At Night		Warner 27722
			HANK WILLIAMS, JR. DUOS with:		
			JOHNNY CASH:		
9/24/88	21	20	77 That Old Wheel..............................		Mercury 870688
			RAY CHARLES:		
8/31/85	14	17	78 Two Old Cats Like Us......................		Columbia 05575
			WAYLON JENNINGS:		
10/22/83	15	16	79 The Conversation		RCA 13631
			LOIS JOHNSON:		
7/04/70	23	12	80 Removing The Shadow		MGM 14136
10/03/70	12	13	81 So Sad (To Watch Good Love Go Bad) .... #7 pop hit for The Everly Brothers in 1960		MGM 14164
4/01/72	14	14	82 Send Me Some Lovin'.......................		MGM 14356
11/18/72+	22	11	83 Whole Lotta Loving .... #6 pop hit for Fats Domino in 1959		MGM 14443
			DOUG KERSHAW:		
8/27/88	52	7	84 Cajun Baby .... [R]		BGM 81588
			JOHNNY WILLIAMS		
5/06/72	68	5	1 He Will Break Your Heart .... #7 pop hit for Jerry Butler in 1960	*104*	Epic 10845
			LAWTON WILLIAMS Born on 7/29/22 in Troy, Tennessee. Worked as a deejay in Detroit and Dearborn in the 40s. Own TV series in Fort Worth in the late 40s. Wrote "Fraulein" for Bobby Helms and "Geisha Girl" for Hank Locklin.		
10/23/61+	13	25	1 Anywhere There's People		Mercury 71867
9/19/64	40	4	2 Everything's O.K. On The LBJ		RCA 8407
			LEONA WILLIAMS Born Leona Belle Helton on 1/7/43 in Vienna, Missouri. Worked in family group while still a child. Own radio show on KWOS-Jefferson City in 1958. Married Ron Williams in 1959 and both worked on the Loretta Lynn show. Toured with the Merle Haggard show in the mid-70s, married to Haggard from 1978-83; now married to Dave Kirby.		
5/31/69	66	5	1 Once More		Hickory 1532
8/21/71	52	9	2 Country Girl With Hot Pants On.....................		Hickory 1606
9/22/73	93	3	3 Your Shoeshine Girl		Hickory 304
10/28/78	8	12	4 The Bull And The Beaver........................		MCA 40962
			MERLE HAGGARD/LEONA WILLIAMS		
2/17/79	92	2	5 The Baby Song/		
		2	6 Call Me Crazy Lady		MCA 40988
4/04/81	54	8	7 I'm Almost Ready..............................		Elektra 47114
11/14/81	84	3	8 Always Late With Your Kisses.....................		Elektra 47217
5/28/83	42	14	9 We're Strangers Again		Mercury 812214
			MERLE HAGGARD & LEONA WILLIAMS		

DEBUT DATE	PEAK POS	WKS CHR	ARTIST — Record Title	POP POS	Label & Number
			LOIS WILLIAMS		
9/20/69	**74**	3	1 A Girl Named Sam .... [N] answer song to Johnny Cash's "A Boy Named Sue"		Starday 877
			OTIS WILLIAMS Born on 6/2/36 in Cincinnati. Formed the rhythm & blues group, the Charms, in 1954.		
5/08/71	**72**	2	1 I Wanna Go Country		Stop 388
			PAUL WILLIAMS Born on 9/19/40 in Omaha. Songwriter/singer/actor.		
12/12/81	**93**	4	1 Making Believe		Paid 146
			TEX WILLIAMS ★★133★★ Born Sol Williams on 8/23/17 near Ramsey, Illinois; died of lung cancer on 10/11/85. Worked on WJBL-Decatur, Illinois in 1930. Moved to California with his band, the Reno Racketeers, in the mid-30s. Appeared in many western films. Worked as vocalist with the Spade Cooley band. Own band, the Western Caravan, in 1946. Own TV series in the 60s.		
11/30/46	**4**	2	1 **California Polka**		Capitol 302
7/05/47	**1** ¹⁶	23	2●**Smoke! Smoke! Smoke! (That Cigarette)** .... Capitol's first million-selling record	*1*	Capitol A. 40001
10/04/47	**4**	8	3 **That's What I Like About The West**		Capitol A. 40031
12/13/47	**2** ⁸	15	4 **Never Trust A Woman**		Capitol A. 40054
2/14/48	**2** ²	11	5 **Don't Telephone, Don't Telegraph, Tell A Woman**	*27*	Capitol A. 40081
5/15/48	**4**	12	6 **Suspicion** .... Best Seller #4 / Juke Box #4	*24*	Capitol A. 40109
6/19/48	**5**	15	7 **Banjo Polka** .... Juke Box #5 / Best Seller #11		Capitol A. 15101
6/26/48	**6**	8	8 **Who? Me?/** Best Seller #6 / Juke Box #11		
7/31/48	**15**	1	9 Foolish Tears .... Juke Box #15		Capitol 15113
9/11/48	**6**	5	10 **Talking Boogie/** Juke Box #6 / Best Seller #12		
11/13/48	**13**	3	11 Just A Pair Of Blue Eyes .... Juke Box #13 / Best Seller #14		Capitol 15175
11/20/48	**5**	4	12 **Life Gits Tee-Jus, Don't It?** .... Juke Box #5 / Best Seller #9	*27*	Capitol 15271
10/29/49	**11**	2	13 **Bluebird On Your Windowsill** .... Juke Box #11 / Best Seller #12		Capitol 40225
5/29/65	**26**	11	14 Too Many Tigers		Boone 1028
10/02/65	**30**	9	15 Big Tennessee		Boone 1032
1/08/66	**18**	8	16 Bottom Of A Mountain		Boone 1036
9/24/66	**44**	2	17 Another Day, Another Dollar In The Hole		Boone 1044
6/17/67	**57**	5	18 Black Jack County		Boone 1059
2/17/68	**32**	10	19 Smoke, Smoke, Smoke-'68 .... [R] new version of hit written by Tex Williams & Merle Travis		Boone 1069
6/29/68	**45**	7	20 Here's To You And Me		Boone 1072
9/19/70	**50**	9	21 It Ain't No Big Thing		Monument 1216
8/28/71	**29**	14	22 The Night Miss Nancy Ann's Hotel For Single Girls Burned Down .... [N]		Monument 8503
1/22/72	**67**	4	23 Everywhere I Go (He's Already Been There)		Monument 8533
6/29/74	**70**	8	24 Those Lazy, Hazy, Crazy Days Of Summer .... #6 pop hit for Nat King Cole in 1963		Granite 507
			TUCKER WILLIAMS		
1/19/80	**96**	2	1 Donna-Earth Angel (Medley) .... revival of pop hits by Ritchie Valens and The Penguins		Yatahey 999
			FOY WILLING Born Foy Willingham in 1915 in Bosque County, Texas; died on 7/24/78. Worked on local radio shows while still a teenager. On radio in New York City from 1933-35. Returned to Texas, worked as a disc jockey. Moved to California in 1940 and formed band, The Riders Of The Purple Sage. Regular appearances on the Hollywood Barn Dance, appeared in several films. Group disbanded in 1952, Willing continued as a solo artist.		
7/15/44	**3**	5	1 **Texas Blues**		Capitol 162
3/16/46	**6**	1	2 **Detour**		Decca 9000
12/14/46	**4**	1	3 **Have I Told You Lately That I Love You?**		Majestic 6000

DEBUT DATE	PEAK POS	WKS CHR	ARTIST — Record Title	POP POS	Label & Number
			FOY WILLING — Continued		
6/19/48	**14**	2	4 Anytime .... Juke Box #14		Capitol A. 40108
1/01/49	**15**	1	5 Brush Those Tears From Your Eyes .... Best Seller #15		Capitol 15290
			THE WILLIS BROTHERS Family group consisting of James "Guy" (b: 7/15/15; d: 4/13/81, guitar), Charles "Skeeter" (b: 12/20/07; d: 1976, fiddle) and Richard "Vic" Willis (b: 5/31/22, accordion). Worked as the Oklahoma Wranglers on KGEF-Shawnee in 1932. Appeared on the Brush Creek Follie, KMBC-Kansas City, from 1940-42. On the Grand Ole Opry from 1946-49; returned to the Opry in 1960. Backed Hank Williams on his first recordings. With Eddy Arnold to 1957. Vic later led the Vic Willis Trio.		
9/05/64	**9**	20	1 **Give Me 40 Acres (To Turn This Rig Around)** .		Starday 681
6/12/65	**41**	8	2 A Six Foot Two By Four .... [N]		Starday 713
2/25/67	**14**	15	3 Bob		Starday 796
7/29/67	**62**	3	4 Somebody Knows My Dog		Starday 812
			ANDRA WILLIS		
2/24/73	**56**	7	1 Down Home Lovin' Woman		Capitol 3525
8/04/73	**85**	5	2 Til I Can't Take It Anymore		Capitol 3666
4/19/75	**63**	9	3 Baby.. TENNESSEE ERNIE FORD & ANDRA WILLIS		Capitol 4044
			HAL WILLIS Born Leonard Francis Gauthier in Roslyn, Quebec. Moved to Nashville in 1958.		
10/31/64	**5**	16	1 **The Lumberjack**	*120*	Sims 207
7/30/66	**45**	5	2 Doggin' In The U.S. Mail		Sims 288
			LARRY WILLOUGHBY Former fireman from Houston. Cousin of Rodney Crowell. Moved to Nashville in 1977.		
11/12/83	**65**	5	1 Heart On The Line (Operator, Operator)...........		Atln. Am. 99826
2/04/84	**55**	8	2 Building Bridges		Atln. Am. 99797
6/23/84	**82**	3	3 Angel Eyes.......................................		Atln. Am. 99759
			BOB WILLS & His Texas Playboys ★★93★★ Born James Robert Wills on 3/6/05 near Kosse, Texas; died on 5/13/75. Fiddle player for square dances in Memphis, Texas while still a teenager. Own group, the Wills Fiddle Band, in 1929 (later became the Light Crust Doughboys). Formed the Texas Playboys in 1933. Band featured Tommy Duncan (vocals) and Leon McAuliffe (steel guitar). Wrote "San Antonio Rose" and "My Shoes Keep Walking Back To You". Own radio show on KVOO-Tulsa from 1934-58. Appeared in many western films. Had heart attacks in 1962, 1964, 1969 and 1973. In a coma from December, 1973 until his death. Elected to the Country Music Hall of Fame in 1968. Known as "The King Of Western Swing".		
1/08/44	**3**	1	1 ● New San Antonio Rose.............................. [R] vocal version (Tommy Duncan) of Wills' 1938 classic tune; essentially the same song as his 1935 "Spanish Two Step"	*11*	Okeh 05694
9/09/44	**2⁵**	11	2 **We Might As Well Forget It/**	*11*	
9/23/44	**2²**	17	3 **You're From Texas**	*14*	Okeh 6722
3/24/45	**1²**	15	4 **Smoke On The Water/**		
3/24/45	**3**	18	5 **Hang Your Head In Shame**..........................		Okeh 6736
6/16/45	**1¹**	11	6 **Stars And Stripes On Iwo Jima/**		
7/21/45	**5**	4	7 **You Don't Care What Happens To Me**		Okeh 6742
11/03/45+	**2¹**	8	8 **Texas Playboy Rag/** [I]		
11/17/45	**1³**	14	9 **Silver Dew On The Blue Grass Tonight**		Columbia 36841
12/29/45+	**1¹**	5	10 **White Cross On Okinawa**		Columbia 36881
5/04/46	**1¹⁶**	23	11 **New Spanish Two Step/** [R] vocal version of Wills' 1935 recording	*20*	
5/11/46	**3**	18	12 **Roly-Poly**		Columbia 36966
11/30/46	**2²**	8	13 **Stay A Little Longer/**		
11/30/46	**4**	1	14 **I Can't Go On This Way**..........................		Columbia 37097
3/29/47	**5**	1	15 **I'm Gonna Be Boss From Now On**...................		Columbia 37205
5/17/47	**1¹**	6	16 **Sugar Moon**......................................		Columbia 37313
7/12/47	**4**	1	17 **Bob Wills Boogie**................................ [I]		Columbia 37357
1/31/48	**4**	17	18 **Bubbles In My Beer**		MGM 10116
7/03/48	**8**	2	19 **Keeper Of My Heart** .... Juke Box #8		MGM 10175
7/24/48	**15**	1	20 Texarkana Baby .... Best Seller #15		Columbia 38179

DEBUT DATE	PEAK POS	WKS CHR	ARTIST — Record Title	POP POS	Label & Number
			BOB WILLS & His Texas Playboys — Continued		
9/18/48	**10**	1	21 **Thorn In My Heart**		MGM 10236
			Juke Box #10		
1/21/50	**10**	1	22 **Ida Red Likes The Boogie**		MGM 10570
			Juke Box #10		
11/04/50	**8**	5	23 **Faded Love**		MGM 10786
			Jockey #8		
8/08/60	**5**	17	24 **Heart To Heart Talk**		Liberty 55260
1/23/61	**26**	1	25 **Image Of Me**		Liberty 55264
			above 2: with Tommy Duncan		
10/16/76	**99**	1	26 **Ida Red** .... [R]		Capitol 4332
			new version of tune recorded by Wills on Vocalion in 1938		
			DAVID WILLS		
			Born on 10/23/51 in Pulaski, Tennessee. Toured with Charlie Rich and Charley Pride.		
11/16/74+	**10**	18	1 **There's A Song On The Jukebox**		Epic 50036
3/29/75	**10**	13	2 **From Barrooms To Bedrooms**		Epic 50090
7/12/75	**31**	11	3 **The Barmaid**		Epic 50118
11/01/75	**35**	9	4 **She Deserves My Very Best**		Epic 50154
2/07/76	**47**	8	5 **Queen Of The Starlight Ballroom**		Epic 50188
			all of above: produced by Charlie Rich		
5/22/76	**55**	7	6 **Woman**		Epic 50228
			#14 pop hit for Peter & Gordon in 1966		
8/21/76	**66**	6	7 **(I'm Just Pouring Out) What She Bottled Up In Me**		Epic 50260
5/21/77	**52**	9	8 **The Best Part Of My Days (Are My Nights With You)**		United Art. 988
9/17/77	**91**	4	9 **Cheatin' Turns Her On**		United Art. 1042
11/19/77	**82**	5	10 **Do You Wanna Make Love**		United Art. 1097
			#5 pop hit for Peter McCann in 1977		
7/15/78	**70**	6	11 **You Snap Your Fingers (And I'm Back In Your Hands)**		United Art. 1196
2/17/79	**50**	7	12 **I'm Being Good**		United Art. 1271
10/06/79	**82**	4	13 **Endless**		United Art. 1319
5/31/80	**91**	5	14 **She's Hangin' In There (I'm Hangin' Out)**		United Art. 1350
9/27/80	**65**	6	15 **The Light Of My Life (Has Gone Out Again Tonight)**		United Art. 1375
3/12/83	**52**	7	16 **Those Nights, These Days**		RCA 13460
6/18/83	**19**	16	17 **The Eyes Of A Stranger**		RCA 13541
11/12/83+	**26**	15	18 **Miss Understanding**		RCA 13653
2/25/84	**31**	11	19 **Lady In Waiting**		RCA 13737
11/24/84	**69**	7	20 **Macon Love**		RCA 13940
10/08/88	**85**	3	21 **Paper Thin Walls**		Epic 08043
			JOHNNIE LEE WILLS		
			Born on 9/2/12 in Jewett, Texas; died on 10/25/84. Younger brother of Bob Wills. With Bob in the Texas Playboys from 1933-40. Fiddle/banjo player. Own band from 1940-64.		
1/28/50	**2** ⁵	11	1 **Rag Mop**	*9*	Bullet 696
			Juke Box #2 / Best Seller #2 / Jockey #3		
4/01/50	**7**	2	2 **Peter Cottontail**		Bullet 700
			Juke Box #7 / Jockey #8		
			TOMMY WILLS		
			Saxophonist - worked with Ina Ray Hutton, Tiny Bradshaw and Earl Bostic bands.		
1/13/79	**100**	1	1 **Wildwood Flower**		Golden Moon 004
			BENNY WILSON		
			Born in Young Harris, Georgia. Wrote "I'll Share My World With You" for George Jones. Band member and back-up singer for Janie Fricke from 1980-85.		
2/02/85	**50**	9	1 **Acres Of Diamonds**		Columbia 04724
3/22/86	**78**	8	2 **If You Wanna Talk Love**		Columbia 05829
			COLEMAN WILSON		
7/31/61	**23**	5	1 **Passing Zone Blues**		King 5512
			HANK WILSON - see LEON RUSSELL		

DEBUT DATE	PEAK POS	WKS CHR	ARTIST — Record Title	POP POS	Label & Number
			JIM WILSON		
			Popular disc jockey in Texas.		
7/23/55	8	9	1 **Daddy, You Know What?**		Mercury 70635
			Jockey #8 - Jim's daughter June speaks a few words		
			LARRY JON WILSON		
			Songwriter from Swainsboro, Georgia.		
4/24/76	74	7	1 Think I Feel A Hitchhike Coming On................		Monument 8692
			MERI WILSON		
			Dallas-based singer.		
6/18/77	50	8	1 ● Telephone Man .... [N]	18	GRT 127
			NORRO WILSON		
			Born Norris D. Wilson on 4/4/38 in Scottsville, Kentucky. Outstanding songwriter. Credits include "A Very Special Love Song", "I Love My Friend" and "The Most Beautiful Girl" for Charlie Rich, "I'll See Him Through" for Tammy Wynette, "Baby, Baby (I Know You're A Lady)" for David Houston and "Soul Song" for Joe Stampley.		
1/11/69	68	7	1 Only You		Smash 2192
			#5 pop hit for The Platters in 1955		
4/05/69	44	8	2 Love Comes But Once In A Lifetime		Smash 2210
9/13/69	56	8	3 Shame On Me		Smash 2236
7/04/70	20	13	4 Do It To Someone You Love		Mercury 73077
11/28/70	53	9	5 Old Enough To Want To (Fool Enough To Try)....		Mercury 73125
11/18/72+	28	12	6 Everybody Needs Lovin'		RCA 0824
3/31/73	64	4	7 Darlin' Raise The Shade		RCA 0909
9/08/73	35	11	8 Ain't It Good (To Feel This Way)		RCA 0062
7/06/74	96	2	9 Loneliness (Can Break A Good Man Down)........		Capitol 3886
8/20/77	43	8	10 So Close Again		Warner 8427
			MARGO (Smith) **& NORRO**		
			WINGS - see PAUL McCARTNEY		
			STEPHANIE WINSLOW		
			Born on 8/27/56 in Yankton, South Dakota. Accomplished fiddler, made professional debut at age 10.		
9/29/79	10	11	1 **Say You Love Me**		Warner 49074
			#11 pop hit for Fleetwood Mac in 1976		
1/12/80	14	10	2 Crying..		Warner 49146
			#2 pop hit for Roy Orbison in 1961		
4/05/80	38	6	3 I Can't Remember		Warner 49201
6/21/80	36	10	4 Try It On		Warner 49257
9/20/80	35	9	5 Baby, I'm A Want You.............................		Warner 49557
			#3 pop hit for Bread in 1971		
12/13/80+	25	13	6 Anything But Yes Is Still A No........................		Warner 49628
3/21/81	36	7	7 Hideaway Healing..................................		Warner 49693
6/27/81	39	9	8 I've Been A Fool/		
		9	9 Sometimes When We Touch		Warner 49753
			#3 pop hit for Dan Hill in 1978		
10/10/81	29	10	10 When You Walk In The Room........................		Warner 49831
			#35 pop hit for The Searchers in 1964		
5/01/82	43	10	11 Slippin' And Slidin'.................................		Primero 1003
			#33 pop hit for Little Richard in 1956		
6/26/82	40	10	12 Don't We Belong In Love		Primero 1007
9/18/82	69	5	13 In Between Lovers		Primero 1012
5/14/83	61	6	14 Nobody Else For Me		Oak 1056
9/03/83	25	15	15 Kiss Me Darling		MCA 52291
1/07/84	29	12	16 Dancin' With The Devil		Curb 52327
4/07/84	42	9	17 Baby, Come To Me..................................		Curb 52372
			#1 pop hit for Patti Austin & James Ingram in 1983		
			DON WINTERS		
			Born on 4/17/29 in Tampa. Worked with Marty Robbins from 1960-82.		
7/03/61	10	10	1 **Too Many Times/**		
7/17/61	27	2	2 Shake Hands With A Loser		Decca 31253

DEBUT DATE	PEAK POS	WKS CHR	ARTIST — Record Title	POP POS	Label & Number
			MAC WISEMAN		
			Born Malcolm Wiseman on 5/23/25 in Crimora, Virginia. Played banjo and guitar with the Hungry Five while in high school. Worked as a disc jockey at WSVA-Harrisburg. Worked with Molly O'Day, Bill Monroe, Flatt & Scruggs. First recorded for Dot in 1951. Country A&R director for Dot Records in 1957.		
5/28/55	10	2	1 **Ballad Of Davy Crockett**............................... Jockey #10		Dot 1240
8/10/59	5	20	2 **Jimmy Brown The Newsboy**..........................		Dot 15946
9/21/63	12	8	3 Your Best Friend And Me		Capitol 5011
11/09/68	54	7	4 Got Leavin' On Her Mind		MGM 13986
12/06/69+	38	9	5 Johnny's Cash & Charley's Pride .... [N]		RCA 0283
3/18/78	78	5	6 Never Going Back Again .... tune is flip side of Fleetwood Mac's 1977 hit "Don't Stop"		Churchill 7706
5/12/79	69	4	7 My Blue Heaven .... **MAC WISEMAN & FRIEND** (Woody Herman)		Churchill 7735
7/07/79	88	3	8 Scotch And Soda...................................... #81 pop hit for The Kingston Trio in 1962		Churchill 7738
10/13/79	95	3	9 Shackles And Chains .... **OSBORNE BROS. & MAC WISEMAN**		CMH 1522
			E.D. WOFFORD		
7/01/78	77	4	1 Baby, I Need Your Lovin' .... #3 pop hit for Johnny Rivers in 1967		MC 5012
			GARY WOLF		
			Born in 1948 in Richmond, Kentucky. Teamed with writer Joe Chambers in 1981.		
7/17/82	51	9	1 Love Never Dies..		Columbia 02986
10/30/82	64	7	2 The Perfect Picture (To Fit My Frame Of Mind) ...		Columbia 03272
2/19/83	62	7	3 Livin' On Memories		Columbia 03493
7/07/84	63	8	4 You Bring The Heartache (I'll Bring The Wine)....		Mercury 822244
3/23/85	73	3	5 It's My Life		Mercury 880564
			THE WOLFPACK		
			Narvel Felts, Lobo, Kenny Earle.		
5/08/82	88	3	1 Bull Smith Can't Dance The Cotton-Eyed Joe. [N]		Lobo VI
			BOBBY WOOD		
			Southern singer, pianist. Session work in Memphis.		
10/31/64	46	2	1 That's All I Need To Know	*130*	Joy 288
			DANNY WOOD		
			Born in Grand Prairie, Texas. First recorded for London in 1972.		
10/23/76	92	4	1 If This Is Freedom (I Want Out)		London 242
4/02/77	93	2	2 I Need Somethin' Easy Tonight		London 248
6/21/80	30	10	3 A Heart's Been Broken.................................		RCA 11968
12/06/80+	37	12	4 It Took Us All Night Long To Say Goodbye		RCA 12123
3/21/81	58	7	5 Fool's Gold		RCA 12181
			DEL WOOD		
			Born Adelaide Hendricks on 2/22/20 in Nashville. Popular female ragtime pianist on the Grand Ole Opry since 1953.		
9/08/51	5	12	1●Down Yonder................................ [I] Juke Box #5 / Jockey #7 / Best Seller #9	*4*	Tennessee 775
			NANCY WOOD		
			Born Renate Kern in Germany; exchange student who lived in Janesville, Michigan. Host of "Nancy's Country Drive-In" radio series in Germany.		
10/10/81	79	4	1 Imagine That..		Montage 1202
			GENE WOODS		
10/10/60	7	13	1 **The Ballad Of Wild River**...........................		Hap 1004
			BILL WOODY		
			Born in 1959 in Jacksonville, Florida; raised in North Carolina.		
4/21/79	65	9	1 Just Between Us		MCA 54043
8/04/79	88	4	2 Love Wouldn't Leave Us Alone		MCA 41070
			CHUCK WOOLERY		
			Original host of TV's Wheel Of Fortune". Current host of "The Love Connection".		
7/09/77	78	5	1 Painted Lady..		Warner 8381

DEBUT DATE	PEAK POS	WKS CHR	ARTIST — Record Title	POP POS	Label & Number
			CHUCK WOOLERY — Continued		
7/12/80	94	2	2 The Greatest Love Affair .... [S] a tribute to America		Epic 50897
			AMY WOOLEY Born in Cleveland, Ohio. Worked clubs in Cleveland, Chicago and Los Angeles.		
7/31/82	51	9	1 If My Heart Had Windows		MCA 52084
			SHEB WOOLEY Born Shelby F. Wooley on 4/10/21 near Erick, Oklahoma. Singer/songwriter/actor. Played Pete Nolan in the TV series "Rawhide". Also made comical recordings under pseudonym, Ben Colder. Appeared in the films "High Noon", "Rocky Mountain", "Giant", and "Hoosiers". His most notable recording was the #1 pop hit "The Purple People Eater". Wrote "Hee-Haw's" theme song. Also see Ben Colder.		
1/13/62	1¹	17	1 That's My Pa .... [N]	51	MGM 13046
7/18/64	33	10	2 Blue Guitar		MGM 13241
5/21/66	34	9	3 I'll Leave The Singin' To The Bluebirds.............		MGM 13477
10/15/66	70	2	4 Tonight's The Night My Angel's Halo Fell		MGM 13556
6/29/68	22	12	5 Tie A Tiger Down		MGM 13938
1/11/69	52	9	6 I Remember Loving You		MGM 14005
10/25/69	63	7	7 The One Man Band .... features bits of the 1893 tune "When The Roll Is Called Up Yonder"		MGM 14085
			TOM WOPAT Born on 9/9/50 in Lodi, Wisconsin. Played "Luke Duke" on TV's "Dukes Of Hazzard".		
4/19/86	39	13	1 True Love (Never Did Run Smooth)..................		EMI America 8316
8/16/86	44	11	2 I Won't Let You Down		EMI America 8334
12/20/86+	16	19	3 The Rock And Roll Of Love..........................		EMI America 8364
5/09/87	28	14	4 Put Me Out Of My Misery		EMI Amer. 43010
8/29/87	20	17	5 Susannah		EMI Amer. 43034
1/09/88	18	17	6 A Little Bit Closer		EMI-Man. 50112
6/11/88	40	10	7 Hey Little Sister.....................................		Capitol 44144
10/08/88	29	16	8 Not Enough Love....................................		Capitol 44243
			JIMMY WORK Born in Akron in 1924; raised in Dukedom, Tennessee. Worked on WCAR-Pontiac, Michigan in the mid-40s. First recorded for Trophy in 1947.		
2/19/55	5	13	1 **Making Believe** .... Juke Box #5 / Jockey #7 / Best Seller #11		Dot 1221
7/02/55	6	4	2 **That's What Makes The Juke Box Play** .... Juke Box #6		Dot 1245
			MARION WORTH Born Mary Ann Ward in Birmingham, Alabama. Worked on Dallas radio shows in 1947.		
10/19/59+	12	20	1 Are You Willing, Willie...............................		Cherokee 503
5/23/60	5	15	2 **That's My Kind Of Love**............................		Guyden 2033
11/14/60	7	23	3 **I Think I Know**		Columbia 41799
5/22/61	21	1	4 There'll Always Be Sadness		Columbia 41972
2/02/63	14	5	5 Shake Me I Rattle (Squeeze Me I Cry)	42	Columbia 42640
6/08/63	18	3	6 Crazy Arms..		Columbia 42703
4/11/64	33	13	7 You Took Him Off My Hands (Now Please Take Him Off My Mind)		Columbia 42992
5/09/64	23	17	8 Slipping Around .... **MARION WORTH & GEORGE MORGAN**		Columbia 43020
10/24/64	25	6	9 The French Song...................................... #54 pop hit for Lucille Starr in 1964		Columbia 43119
12/11/65+	32	6	10 I Will Not Blow Out The Light.......................		Columbia 43405
11/04/67	64	6	11 Woman Needs Love		Decca 32195
3/30/68	45	10	12 Mama Sez		Decca 32278
			THE WRAY BROTHERS BAND Group of Oregon-area entertainers: Bubby Wray, Jim Covert, Lynn Phillips, and Joe Dale Cleghorn.		
3/19/83	88	3	1 Reason To Believe		CIS 3011
4/06/85	93	4	2 Until We Meet Again................................. **THE WRAYS:**		Sasparilla 0003
5/10/86	71	5	3 I Don't Want To Know Your Name...................		Mercury 884621
6/06/87	48	10	4 You Lay A Lotta Love On Me........................		Mercury 888542

DEBUT DATE	PEAK POS	WKS CHR	ARTIST — Record Title	POP POS	Label & Number
			LARRY WREN		
5/21/77	98	3	1 Lie To Me/		
		3	2 It's Saturday Night		50 States 51
			THE WRIGHT BROTHERS		
			Trio from Fort Worth, Texas, formed in high school in 1972. Consisted of C. Thomas Wright, William Timothy Wright and Karl Hinkle. Hinkle replaced by John McDowell in 1975. Disbanded in 1977, but re-formed with Hinkle in the group from 1978-84. Hinkle was again replaced by McDowell in 1984.		
10/31/81	35	12	1 Family Man....................................		Warner 49837
4/03/82	42	11	2 When You Find Her, Keep Her		Warner 50033
9/04/82	40	8	3 Made In The U.S.A..		Warner 29926
1/08/83	68	5	4 So Easy To Love		Warner 29839
3/31/84	33	13	5 Southern Women		Mercury 818653
8/11/84	46	11	6 So Close		Mercury 880055
11/03/84	57	9	7 Eight Days A Week...........................		Mercury 880316
			#1 pop hit for The Beatles in 1965		
3/30/85	48	10	8 Fire In The Sky................................		Mercury 880596
9/10/88	85	3	9 Come On Rain		Airborne 10006
			B.J. WRIGHT		
			Born in Gallatin, Tennessee.		
10/21/78	96	4	1 Memory Bound		Soundwaves 4577
3/24/79	93	2	2 Leaning On Each Other		Soundwaves 4581
7/28/79	61	5	3 I've Got A Right To Be Wrong......................		Soundwaves 4589
12/22/79+	87	6	4 Nobody's Darlin' But Mine		Soundwaves 4593
			written and popularized by Jimmie Davis in 1937		
5/03/80	36	11	5 J.R.		Soundwaves 4604
			title refers to J.R. Ewing of TV's "Dallas"		
8/02/80	73	5	6 Lost Love Affair................................		Soundwaves 4610
12/27/80+	81	6	7 I Know An Ending (When It Comes)		Soundwaves 4624
			BOBBY WRIGHT		
			Born on 3/30/42 in Charleston, West Virginia. Son of Johnny Wright and Kitty Wells. On the Louisiana Hayride at age 8, recording since 1953. Appeared as "Willie" in "McHale's Navy" TV series for 4 years. Tours with the family show.		
4/29/67	44	12	1 Lay Some Happiness On Me		Decca 32107
			#55 pop hit for Dean Martin in 1967		
12/02/67	67	3	2 That See Me Later Look		Decca 32193
10/05/68	70	4	3 Old Before My Time		Decca 32367
5/17/69	40	10	4 Upstairs In The Bedroom		Decca 32464
11/01/69	70	2	5 Sing A Song About Love..............................		Decca 32564
3/08/70	61	4	6 Take Me Back To The Goodtimes, Sally.............		Decca 32633
8/01/70	47	9	7 Hurry Home To Me		Decca 32705
4/24/71	74	2	8 If You Want Me To I'll Go............................		Decca 32792
7/10/71	13	16	9 Here I Go Again		Decca 32839
12/25/71+	54	8	10 Search Your Heart....................................		Decca 32903
8/12/72	60	5	11 Just Because I'm Still In Love With You...........		Decca 32985
1/27/73	75	1	12 If Not For You.......................................		Decca 33034
			#25 pop hit for Olivia Newton-John in 1971		
10/20/73	39	11	13 Lovin' Someone On My Mind		ABC 11390
2/23/74	24	12	14 Seasons In The Sun		ABC 11418
			#1 pop hit for Terry Jacks in 1974		
6/22/74	56	10	15 Everybody Needs A Rainbow		ABC 11443
10/05/74	55	11	16 Baby's Gone..		ABC 12028
			written by Roy Orbison and Bobby Goldsboro		
3/08/75	75	7	17 I Just Came Home To Count The Memories........		ABC 12062
1/08/77	79	6	18 Neon Lady		United Art. 913
9/24/77	97	1	19 Playing With The Baby's Mama......................		United Art. 1051
10/21/78	100	3	20 Takin' A Chance		United Art. 1238
7/28/79	77	3	21 I'm Turning You Loose................................		United Art. 1300
			GINNY WRIGHT - see JIM REEVES and TOM TALL		

DEBUT DATE	PEAK POS	WKS CHR	ARTIST — Record Title	POP POS	Label & Number
			JOHNNY WRIGHT		
			Born on 5/13/14 in Mount Juliet, Tennessee; raised in Nashville. Banjo/fiddle player. Teamed with Jack Anglin from 1938-63 as "Johnnie And Jack". Married Kitty Wells in 1938. Worked on WSIX-Nashville in the late 30s. Own band, the Tennessee Mountain Boys, in the early 40s. Went solo after the death of Anglin in March, 1963. Formed the Kitty Wells/Johnny Wright Family Show in 1969.		
5/02/64	22	15	1 Walkin', Talkin', Cryin', Barely Beatin' Broken Heart..		Decca 31593
1/02/65	37	5	2 Don't Give Up The Ship		Decca 31679
5/08/65	28	11	3 Blame It On The Moonlight		Decca 31740
8/28/65	1³	21	4 **Hello Vietnam**		Decca 31821
			written by Tom T. Hall		
12/18/65+	31	10	5 Keep The Flag Flying		Decca 31875
6/04/66	31	6	6 Nickels, Quarters And Dimes........................		Decca 31927
10/15/66	53	7	7 I'm Doing This For Daddy		Decca 32002
12/31/66+	50	11	8 Mama's Little Jewel.......................................		Decca 32061
8/12/67	66	5	9 American Power		Decca 32162
12/16/67	69	4	10 Music To Cry By		Decca 32216
5/11/68	54	8	11 We'll Stick Together		Decca 32294
			KITTY WELLS & JOHNNY WRIGHT		
11/30/68	66	5	12 (They Always Come Out) Smellin' Like A Rose ...		Decca 32402
			LEE WRIGHT		
12/23/78+	86	4	1 Capricorn Kings...		Prairie D. 7628
7/06/85	90	4	2 The Eyes Have It..		Prairie D. 5185
			RANDY WRIGHT		
			Born on 9/11/56 in Troy, Missouri. Former drummer for Nick Nixon & Barbara Mandrell.		
11/05/83	86	3	1 There's Nobody Lovin' At Home.....................		MCA 52273
5/12/84	77	4	2 If You're Serious About Cheating		MCA 52358
			RUBY WRIGHT		
			Born on 10/27/39 in Nashville. Daughter of Kitty Wells and Johnny Wright. Worked in the "Nita, Rita & Ruby Trio" from 1959-69.		
9/05/64	13	13	1 Dern Ya...	*103*	RIC 126
			answer song to Roger Miller's "Dang Me"		
11/05/66	72	2	2 A New Place To Hang Your Hat.......................		Epic 10055
5/27/67	69	7	3 (I Can Find) A Better Deal Than That................		Epic 10150
			SONNY WRIGHT		
			Born Nathan Edward Wright on 2/2/43 in Flagler, Colorado. Discovered by the Wilburn Brothers. With the Country Rebels from 1961-67. Recorded "I Love You, Loretta Lynn" and soon joined Loretta's show as a vocalist. Married to Loretta's sister Peggy Sue.		
10/22/77	100	1	1 If This Is What Love's All About		Door Knob 038
			PEGGY SUE & SONNY WRIGHT		
11/10/79	86	5	2 Gently Hold Me		Door Knob 113
			PEGGY SUE & SONNY WRIGHT		
4/26/80	91	4	3 Molly (And The Texas Rain)		Door Knob 128
			WYATT BROTHERS		
12/27/86+	79	5	1 Wyatt Liquor		Wyatt 103
			GENE WYATT		
			Cousin of Chuck Pollard. Worked on Fanfare and Grand Ole Opry.		
3/23/68	74	2	1 I Stole The Flowers.......................................		Mercury 41032
8/17/68	69	3	2 I Just Ain't Got (As Much As He's Got Going For Me)..		Paula 308
			NINA WYATT		
1/30/88	76	3	1 Richer Now With You....................................		Charta 207
8/20/88	88	2	2 After The Passion Leaves		Charta 210
			TAMMY WYNETTE ★★25★★		
			Born Virginia Wynette Pugh on 5/5/42 in Itawamba County, Mississippi. Worked as a beautician in Birmingham in the early 60s. On the "Country Boy Eddy" TV show, WBRC-Birmingham, in 1965. Moved up to Nashville in 1966 and hooked up with her producer, Billy Sherrill. Married to George Jones from 1968-75. Married to her manager, George Richey, since 1978. On the soundtrack of the films "Run Angel, Run" and "Five Easy Pieces". Known as "The First Lady Of Country Music".		
12/10/66+	44	9	1 Apartment #9		Epic 10095
3/18/67	3	21	2 **Your Good Girl's Gonna Go Bad**		Epic 10134

DEBUT DATE	PEAK POS	WKS CHR	ARTIST — Record Title	POP POS	Label & Number
			TAMMY WYNETTE — Continued		
7/15/67	**1**²	18	3 **My Elusive Dreams** .... DAVID HOUSTON & TAMMY WYNETTE	*89*	Epic 10194
8/26/67	**1**³	20	4 **I Don't Wanna Play House**		Epic 10211
1/06/68	**1**¹	17	5 **Take Me To Your World**....................		Epic 10269
1/20/68	**11**	14	6 It's All Over .... DAVID HOUSTON & TAMMY WYNETTE		Epic 10274
5/18/68	**1**³	17	7 **D-I-V-O-R-C-E**	*63*	Epic 10315
10/19/68	**1**³	21	8 **Stand By Your Man**.......................	*19*	Epic 10398
4/12/69	**1**²	14	9 **Singing My Song**	*75*	Epic 10462
8/30/69	**1**²	16	10 **The Ways To Love A Man**....................	*81*	Epic 10512
1/31/70	**2**²	14	11 **I'll See Him Through**.....................	*100*	Epic 10571
5/23/70	**1**³	16	12 **He Loves Me All The Way**	*97*	Epic 10612
9/12/70	**1**²	15	13 **Run, Woman, Run**	*92*	Epic 10653
11/28/70+	**5**	13	14 **The Wonders You Perform**	*104*	Epic 10687
3/06/71	**2**³	15	15 **We Sure Can Love Each Other**....................	*103*	Epic 10707
7/17/71	**1**²	15	16 **Good Lovin' (Makes It Right)**....................	*111*	Epic 10759
1/01/72	**1**¹	14	17 **Bedtime Story**	*86*	Epic 10818
5/20/72	**2**²	14	18 **Reach Out Your Hand**		Epic 10856
9/16/72	**1**¹	14	19 **My Man**		Epic 10909
12/30/72+	**1**¹	15	20 **'Til I Get It Right**	*106*	Epic 10940
4/07/73	**1**¹	17	21 **Kids Say The Darndest Things**	*72*	Epic 10969
12/29/73+	**1**²	15	22 **Another Lonely Song**....................		Epic 11079
8/17/74	**4**	16	23 **Woman To Woman**		Epic 50008
2/15/75	**4**	16	24 **(You Make Me Want To Be) A Mother**		Epic 50071
9/20/75	**13**	13	25 I Still Believe In Fairy Tales		Epic 50145
2/14/76	**1**¹	15	26 **'Til I Can Make It On My Own**	*84*	Epic 50196
8/21/76	**1**²	16	27 **You And Me**	*101*	Epic 50264
3/19/77	**6**	14	28 **(Let's Get Together) One Last Time**		Epic 50349
10/08/77	**6**	15	29 **One Of A Kind**....................		Epic 50450
4/22/78	**26**	11	30 I'd Like To See Jesus (On The Midnight Special) .		Epic 50538
7/15/78	**3**	15	31 **Womanhood**....................		Epic 50574
2/10/79	**6**	13	32 **They Call It Making Love**		Epic 50661
6/09/79	**7**	14	33 **No One Else In The World**....................		Epic 50722
4/19/80	**17**	14	34 He Was There (When I Needed You)		Epic 50868
8/09/80	**17**	13	35 Starting Over.................... all of above: produced by Billy Sherrill		Epic 50915
3/21/81	**21**	12	36 Cowboys Don't Shoot Straight (Like They Used To)....................		Epic 51011
9/05/81	**18**	14	37 Crying In The Rain .... #6 pop hit for The Everly Brothers in 1962		Epic 02439
3/27/82	**8**	17	38 **Another Chance**....................		Epic 02770
8/14/82	**16**	16	39 You Still Get To Me In My Dreams....................		Epic 03064
12/11/82+	**19**	15	40 A Good Night's Love		Epic 03384
4/23/83	**46**	9	41 I Just Heard A Heart Break (And I'm So Afraid It's Mine)		Epic 03811
7/09/83	**63**	7	42 Unwed Fathers		Epic 03971
10/01/83	**63**	6	43 Still In The Ring....................		Epic 04101
6/02/84	**40**	15	44 Lonely Heart		Epic 04467
2/23/85	**6**	22	45 **Sometimes When We Touch**.................... MARK GRAY & TAMMY WYNETTE #3 pop hit in 1978 for Dan Hill		Columbia 04782
7/13/85	**48**	9	46 You Can Lead A Heart To Love (But You Can't Make It Fall)		Epic 05399
8/30/86	**53**	8	47 Alive And Well		Epic 06263
8/01/87	**12**	19	48 Your Love.................... harmony vocal: Ricky Skaggs		Epic 07226
12/05/87+	**16**	20	49 Talkin' To Myself Again .... harmony vocals: The O'Kanes		Epic 07635
5/07/88	**25**	15	50 Beneath A Painted Sky .... harmony vocal: Emmylou Harris		Epic 07788
			GEORGE JONES & TAMMY WYNETTE:		
12/25/71+	**9**	13	51 **Take Me**....................		Epic 10815

DEBUT DATE	PEAK POS	WKS CHR	ARTIST — Record Title	POP POS	Label & Number
			TAMMY WYNETTE — Continued		
7/08/72	**6**	15	52 The Ceremony		Epic 10881
11/25/72+	**38**	9	53 Old Fashioned Singing		Epic 10923
4/07/73	**32**	9	54 Let's Build A World Together		Epic 10963
9/01/73	**1** ²	17	55 We're Gonna Hold On		Epic 11031
2/09/74	**15**	13	56 (We're Not) The Jet Set		Epic 11083
7/27/74	**8**	12	57 We Loved It Away		Epic 11151
5/17/75	**25**	13	58 God's Gonna Get'cha (For That)		Epic 50099
6/05/76	**1** ¹	15	59 Golden Ring		Epic 50235
12/11/76+	**1** ²	16	60 Near You		Epic 50314
			#1 pop hit (17 weeks) for Francis Craig in 1947		
7/16/77	**5**	13	61 Southern California		Epic 50418
3/01/80	**2** ¹	14	62 Two Story House		Epic 50849
9/06/80	**19**	11	63 A Pair Of Old Sneakers..............................		Epic 50930
			JIM WYRICK & Union Gold		
			Jim was born in Maynardsville, Tennessee. Own band, Union Gold, with Floyd McCoy.		
2/26/83	**85**	2	1 The Memory...		NSD 157

Y

DEBUT DATE	PEAK POS	WKS CHR	ARTIST — Record Title	POP POS	Label & Number
			FRANKIE YANKOVIC & HIS YANKS		
			Born on 7/28/15 in Davis, West Virginia; raised in Cleveland. Accordionist. First recorded with the Slovene Folk Orchestra in 1932 on his own Yankee label. Member of the International Polka Hall of Fame. Featured vocalist: Johnny Pecon.		
5/08/48	**7**	1	1 **Just Because**...	9	Columbia 12359
1/01/49	**13**	1	2 Iron Range...		Columbia 12381
			Best Seller #13		
4/30/49	**7**	7	3 Blue Skirt Waltz..	12	Columbia 12394
			FRANKIE YANKOVIC & HIS YANKS with THE MARLIN SISTERS		
			Best Seller #7 / Juke Box #10		
			BOB YARBROUGH		
5/22/71	**38**	12	1 You're Just More A Woman		Sugar Hill 013
4/17/76	**85**	5	2 50 Ways To Leave Your Lover		Music Mill 186
			shown as: **BOB YARBOROUGH**		
			#1 pop hit for Paul Simon in 1976		
			JENNY YATES		
4/25/87	**80**	3	1 A Whole Month Of Sundays............................		Mercury 888428
			LORI YATES		
			Singer from Toronto, Canada.		
11/12/88	**77**	5	1 Scene Of The Crime		Columbia 08055
			DWIGHT YOAKAM		
			Singer/songwriter born on 10/23/56 in Pikesville, Kentucky. Played in southern Ohio before moving to Los Angeles in the early 80s. First recorded for Oak Records.		
3/01/86	**3**	24	1 **Honky Tonk Man**		Reprise 28793
7/12/86	**4**	21	2 **Guitars, Cadillacs**		Reprise 28688
11/15/86	**31**	15	3 It Won't Hurt...		Reprise 28565
4/11/87	**7**	16	4 **Little Sister**		Reprise 28432
			#5 pop hit for Elvis Presley in 1961		
7/25/87	**8**	19	5 **Little Ways**		Reprise 28310
11/14/87+	**6**	19	6 **Please, Please Baby**		Reprise 28174
3/05/88	**9**	22	7 **Always Late With Your Kisses**		Reprise 27994
7/16/88	**1** ¹	18	8 **Streets Of Bakersfield**		Reprise 27964
			DWIGHT YOAKAM & BUCK OWENS		
11/12/88+	**1** ¹	21	9 **I Sang Dixie**		Reprise 27715
			COLE YOUNG		
7/23/83	**72**	5	1 Just Give Me One More Night		Evergreen 1008

DEBUT DATE	PEAK POS	WKS CHR		ARTIST — Record Title	POP POS	Label & Number
				FARON YOUNG ★★**17**★★		
				Born on 2/25/32 in Shreveport, Louisiana. Worked with Webb Pierce on the Louisiana Hayride in 1951. First recorded with Tillman Franks & His Rainbow Boys for Gotham in 1951. Went solo in 1952. In the film "Hidden Guns" (1956) and got his nickname "The Young Sheriff" and band name, "His Country Deputies", from that movie. Other films include "Stampede", "Daniel Boone", "Raiders Of Old California", "Country Music Holiday", "Road To Nashville" and "That's Country". Founder and one-time publisher of the Music City News in Nashville.		
1/10/53	**2** ¹	18	1	**Goin' Steady**		Capitol 2299
				Jockey #2 / Juke Box #7 / Best Seller #10		
6/06/53	**5**	5	2	**I Can't Wait**		Capitol 2461
				Jockey #5		
9/04/54	**8**	9	3	**A Place For Girls Like You**		Capitol 2859
				Jockey #8 / Best Seller #13		
11/20/54+	**2** ³	27	4	**If You Ain't Lovin'**		Capitol 2953
				Juke Box #2 / Jockey #2 / Best Seller #3		
4/02/55	**1** ³	22	5	**Live Fast, Love Hard, Die Young/**		
				Jockey #1 / Juke Box #2 / Best Seller #3		
		12	6	Forgive Me, Dear...........................		Capitol 3056
				Juke Box flip		
8/13/55	**2** ⁴	28	7	**All Right/**		
				Jockey #2 / Juke Box #3 / Best Seller #4		
8/06/55	**11**	9	8	Go Back You Fool		Capitol 3169
				Best Seller #11		
11/19/55	**5**	13	9	**It's A Great Life (If You Don't Weaken)/**		
				Jockey #5 / Juke Box #6 / Best Seller #7		
12/17/55	**7**	1	10	**For The Love Of A Woman Like You**		Capitol 3258
				Juke Box #7		
4/07/56	**4**	16	11	**I've Got Five Dollars/**		
				Best Seller #4 / Juke Box #4 / Jockey #10		
4/14/56	**3**	10	12	You're Still Mine		Capitol 3369
				Jockey #3 / Best Seller #5		
6/23/56	**2** ¹	33	13	**Sweet Dreams/**		
				Jockey #2 / Juke Box #4 / Best Seller #5		
		2	14	Until I Met You...........................		Capitol 3443
				Juke Box flip		
11/10/56	**9**	6	15	**Turn Her Down/**		
				Jockey #9 / Best Seller #13		
		1	16	I'll Be Satisfied With Love		Capitol 3549
				Best Seller flip		
2/23/57	**5**	13	17	**I Miss You Already (And You're Not Even Gone)/**		
				Jockey #5 / Best Seller #8		
		1	18	I'm Gonna Live Some Before I Die		Capitol 3611
				Best Seller flip		
5/20/57	**15**	1	19	The Shrine Of St. Cecilia	96	Capitol 3696
				Jockey #15		
8/05/57	**12**	1	20	Love Has Finally Come My Way		Capitol 3753
				Jockey #12		
6/23/58	**1** ¹³	29	21	**Alone With You/**	51	
				Jockey #1 / Best Seller #2		
6/30/58	**10**	2	22	**Every Time I'm Kissing You**		Capitol 3982
				Jockey #10		
10/20/58	**9**	17	23	**That's The Way I Feel/**		
10/27/58	**22**	5	24	I Hate Myself....................................		Capitol 4050
1/26/59	**20**	10	25	Last Night At A Party/		
2/02/59	**16**	9	26	A Long Time Ago		Capitol 4113
4/13/59	**11**	8	27	That's The Way It's Gotta Be....................		Capitol 4164
7/20/59	**1** ⁴	32	28	**Country Girl/**		
7/27/59	**27**	6	29	I Hear You Talkin'................................		Capitol 4233
11/16/59+	**4**	21	30	**Riverboat/**	83	
11/16/59+	**10**	18	31	**Face To The Wall**.............................		Capitol 4291
4/11/60	**5**	17	32	**Your Old Used To Be**		Capitol 4351
10/24/60	**21**	5	33	There's Not Any Like You Left		Capitol 4410
12/26/60+	**20**	7	34	Forget The Past/		
1/16/61	**28**	3	35	A World So Full Of Love............................		Capitol 4463
3/20/61	**1** ⁹	23	36	**Hello Walls/**	12	
5/15/61	**28**	2	37	Congratulations..................................		Capitol 4533
				above 2: written by Willie Nelson		

DEBUT DATE	PEAK POS	WKS CHR	ARTIST — Record Title	POP POS	Label & Number
			FARON YOUNG — Continued		
10/02/61	8	17	38 **Backtrack**..	89	Capitol 4616
3/24/62	7	13	39 **Three Days**		Capitol 4696
6/16/62	4	19	40 **The Comeback**		Capitol 4754
12/22/62+	9	10	41 **Down By The River**		Capitol 4868
3/02/63	4	16	42 **The Yellow Bandana**	114	Mercury 72085
6/01/63	30	1	43 I've Come To Say Goodbye/		
6/08/63	14	7	44 Nightmare		Mercury 72114
10/26/63	13	7	45 We've Got Something In Common....................		Mercury 72167
12/21/63+	10	14	46 **You'll Drive Me Back (Into Her Arms Again)** ...		Mercury 72201
7/25/64	48	2	47 Old Courthouse/		
8/01/64	23	6	48 Rhinestones		Mercury 72271
10/03/64	11	16	49 My Friend On The Right		Mercury 72313
1/30/65	10	18	50 **Walk Tall**...		Mercury 72375
8/07/65	34	6	51 Nothing Left To Lose		Mercury 72440
11/27/65+	14	13	52 My Dreams...		Mercury 72490
10/15/66	7	16	53 **Unmitigated Gall**		Mercury 72617
4/08/67	48	8	54 I Guess I Had Too Much To Dream Last Night.....		Mercury 72656
10/28/67+	14	16	55 Wonderful World Of Women		Mercury 72728
3/09/68	14	16	56 She Went A Little Bit Farther........................		Mercury 72774
8/03/68	8	16	57 **I Just Came To Get My Baby**.......................		Mercury 72827
3/01/69	25	13	58 I've Got Precious Memories		Mercury 72889
7/12/69	2²	16	59 **Wine Me Up**		Mercury 72936
11/01/69	4	14	60 **Your Time's Comin'**		Mercury 72983
2/07/70	6	14	61 **Occasional Wife**......................................		Mercury 73018
5/30/70	4	16	62 **If I Ever Fall In Love (With A Honky Tonk Girl)**...		Mercury 73065
10/10/70	5	12	63 **Goin' Steady** .... [R]		Mercury 73112
3/27/71	6	17	64 **Step Aside**		Mercury 73191
8/07/71	9	14	65 **Leavin' And Sayin' Goodbye**		Mercury 73220
12/04/71+	1²	20	66 **It's Four In The Morning**...........................	92	Mercury 73250
7/22/72	5	16	67 **This Little Girl Of Mine**............................		Mercury 73308
2/03/73	15	11	68 She Fights That Lovin' Feeling		Mercury 73359
7/21/73	9	16	69 **Just What I Had In Mind**		Mercury 73403
3/09/74	8	14	70 **Some Kind Of A Woman**............................		Mercury 73464
7/13/74	20	12	71 The Wrong In Loving You		Mercury 73500
11/30/74+	23	12	72 Another You		Mercury 73633
7/19/75	16	13	73 Here I Am In Dallas		Mercury 73692
12/13/75+	21	12	74 Feel Again		Mercury 73731
4/10/76	33	10	75 I'd Just Be Fool Enough		Mercury 73782
10/09/76	30	11	76 (The Worst You Ever Gave Me Was) The Best I Ever Had		Mercury 73847
7/09/77	25	11	77 Crutches..		Mercury 73925
2/25/78	38	10	78 Loving Here And Living There And Lying In Between...		Mercury 55019
4/07/79	67	6	79 The Great Chicago Fire		MCA 41004
7/14/79	70	5	80 Second Hand Emotion/		
9/22/79	69	6	81 That Over Thirty Look		MCA 41046
2/16/80	56	7	82 (If I'd Only Known) It Was The Last Time..........		MCA 41177
8/30/80	72	4	83 Tearjoint		MCA 41292
4/25/81	88	2	84 Until The Bitter End		MCA 51088
9/10/88	100	2	85 Stop And Take The Time.............................		Step One 390
			FARON YOUNG & MARGIE SINGLETON:		
3/14/64	5	23	86 **Keeping Up With The Joneses/**		
3/28/64	40	6	87 No Thanks, I Just Had One		Mercury 72237
12/05/64	38	8	88 Another Woman's Man Another Man's Woman ...		Mercury 72312
			NEIL YOUNG		
			Born on 11/12/45 in Toronto. Rock singer/songwriter/guitarist.		
10/05/85	33	18	1 Get Back To The Country		Geffen 28883

DEBUT DATE	PEAK POS	WKS CHR	ARTIST — Record Title	POP POS	Label & Number
			ROGER YOUNG		
			Singer from Yuma, Arizona.		
8/18/79	85	3	1 Skip A Rope		Dessa 79-2
			STEVE YOUNG		
			Born on 7/12/42 in Noonan, Georgia. Wrote "Seven Bridges Road" for the Eagles.		
2/05/77	84	5	1 It's Not Supposed To Be That Way		RCA 10868
			written by Willie Nelson		
			YOUNGER BROTHERS		
			James and Michael Williams from Edinburgh, Texas. Changed named to James & Michael Younger to avoid conflict with a band from Leola, Pennsylvania.		
4/24/82	68	5	1 Lonely Hearts..		MCA 52030
7/03/82	19	15	2 Nothing But The Radio On		MCA 52076
12/11/82+	48	12	3 There's No Substitute For You.........................		MCA 52148
3/05/83	50	8	4 Somewhere Down The Line		MCA 52183
			JAMES & MICHAEL YOUNGER:		
6/04/83	54	10	5 A Taste Of The Wind		MCA 52222
9/17/83	48	9	6 Lovers On The Rebound		MCA 52263
12/24/83+	65	8	7 Shoot First, Ask Questions Later		MCA 52317
6/29/85	82	5	8 My Special Angel		Permian 82011
4/05/86	67	7	9 Back On The Radio Again		AIR 00102
9/27/86	65	7	10 She Wants To Marry A Cowboy........................		AIR 00106
			YOUNGER BROTHERS BAND		
			Quintet from Leola, Pennsylvania led by Terry Gehman.		
9/08/84	92	2	1 Making Love To Dixie		ERP 04094

Z

DEBUT DATE	PEAK POS	WKS CHR	ARTIST — Record Title	POP POS	Label & Number
			PIA ZADORA		
			Actress/singer born Pia Schipani in 1955 in New York City. In the films "Butterfly" (1982), "The Lonely Lady" (1983) and "Hairspray" (1988).		
3/31/79	98	1	1 Tell Him/		
			#4 pop hit for The Exciters in 1963		
4/28/79	76	3	2 Bedtime Stories		Warner 8766
8/25/79	65	5	3 I Know A Good Thing When I Feel It		Warner 49065
1/12/80	55	5	4 Baby It's You		Warner 49148
			#8 pop hit for The Shirelles in 1962		
			GAYLE ZEILER		
			Born in San Jose, California. Ethel of "Ethel & The Shameless Hussies".		
1/30/82	78	4	1 No Place To Hide..		Equa 670

THE SONG TITLES

This section lists, alphabetically, all titles in the artist section. The artist's name is listed next to each title along with the highest position attained and year of peak popularity. Some titles show the letter F as a position, indicating the title was listed as a flip side and did not chart on its own.

Songs with identical titles are listed together. The artists' names are listed below in chronological order, even though they may be different tunes. Since 15% of the records were not available for play by our staff, it was impossible to determine if all of the same-named titles were also the same composition.

Cross references have been used throughout to aid in finding a title.

Please keep the following in mind when searching for titles:

A title which substitutes a letter with an apostrophe appears before a title using the complete spelling. (Lovin' is listed before Loving).

Titles beginning with a contraction follow titles that begin with a similar non-contracted word (Can't follows Can).

Titles such as S.O.S. and D.O.A. will be found at the beginning of their respective letters; however, titles such as T-R-O-U-B-L-E and D-I-V-O-R-C-E, which are spellings of words, are listed with their regular spellings.

16/79 **All Around Cowboy** *Marty Robbins*
67/74 **All Around Cowboy Of 1964** *Buddy Alan*
64/84 **All Around The Water Tank** *Mel McDaniel*
39/86 **All Because Of You** *Marty Stuart*
64/70 **All Day Sucker** *Liz Anderson*
9/69 **All For The Love Of A Girl** *Claude King*
1/70 **All For The Love Of Sunshine**
    Hank Williams, Jr.
All Grown Up
8/58   *Johnny Horton*
26/63   *Johnny Horton*
35/72 **All Heaven Breaks Loose** *David Rogers*
72/69 **All Heaven Broke Loose** *Hugh X. Lewis*
72/84 **All Heaven Is About To Break Loose**
    Zella Lehr
2/72 **All His Children** *Charley Pride/Henry Mancini*
3/76 **All I Can Do** *Dolly Parton*
82/85 **All I Do Is Dream Of You** *Margo Smith*
All I Ever Need Is You
18/71   *Ray Sanders*
1/79   *Kenny Rogers & Dottie West*
67/72 **All I Had To Do** *Jim Ed Brown*
All I Have To Do Is Dream
1/58   *Everly Brothers*
6/70   *Bobbie Gentry & Glen Campbell*
79/75   *Nitty Gritty Dirt Band*
85/81   *Nancy Montgomery*
1/69 **All I Have To Offer You (Is Me)** *Charley Pride*
11/49 **All I Need Is Some More Lovin'**
    George Morgan
51/71 **All I Need Is You**
    Carl Belew & Betty Jean Robinson
52/84 **All I Wanna Do (Is Make Love To You)**
    Bandana
21/79 **All I Want And Need Forever** *Vern Gosdin*
96/77 **All I Want Is To Love You** *Jack Rainwater*
84/78 **All I Want To Do In Life** *Jack Clement*
67/71 **All I Want To Do Is Say I Love You**
    Brian Collins
30/82 **All I'm Missing Is You** *Eddy Arnold*
60/88 **All In My Mind** *Cali McCord*
13/73 **All In The Name Of Love** *Narvel Felts*
1/87 **All My Ex's Live In Texas** *George Strait*
9/70 **All My Hard Times** *Roy Drusky*
13/83 **All My Life** *Kenny Rogers*
All My Love
23/67   *Don Gibson*
89/77   *Joe Ely*
58/82 **All My Lovin** *Mundo Earwood*
10/84 **All My Rowdy Friends Are Coming Over**
    Tonight *Hank Williams, Jr.*
1/81 **All My Rowdy Friends (Have Settled**
    Down) *Hank Williams, Jr.*
27/67 **All My Tomorrows** *Nat Stuckey*
41/81 **All New Me** *Tom T. Hall*
All Night Long
80/78   *Peggy Sue*
40/81   *Johnny Duncan*
All Of *..also see: Alla*
3/78 **All Of Me** *Willie Nelson*
All Of Me Belongs To You
28/67   *Dick Curless*
70/67   *Hank Cochran*
26/88 **All Of This & More** *Crystal Gayle/Gary Morris*
91/73 **All Or Nothing With Me** *Susan St. Marie*
4/58 **All Over Again** *Johnny Cash*
4/75 **All Over Me** *Charlie Rich*
All Over Now
    ..see: (We Used To Kiss Each Other On The Lips
    But It's)
2/55 **All Right** *Faron Young*
All Right (I'll Sign The Papers)
45/64   *George Morgan*
26/68   *Mel Tillis*
1/81 **All Roads Lead To You** *Steve Wariner*

1/57 **All Shook Up** *Elvis Presley*
8/85 **All Tangled Up In Love**
    Gus Hardin with Earl Thomas Conley
All That Keeps Me Going
94/74   *Mary Lou Turner*
27/77   *Jim Weatherly*
33/70 **All That Keeps Ya Goin'**
    Tompall/Glaser Brothers
70/85 **All That's Left For Me** *Carl Jackson*
1/79 **All The Gold In California** *Gatlin Bros.*
50/88 **All The Good One's Are Taken** *Linda Davis*
20/76 **All The King's Horses** *Lynn Anderson*
5/72 **All The Lonely Women In The World**
    Bill Anderson
All The Love In The World *..see: (If You Add)*
53/84 **All The Love Is On The Radio** *Tom Jones*
97/77 **All The Love We Threw Away**
    Lois Johnson & Bill Rice
73/75 **All The Love You'll Ever Need** *Cliff Cochran*
5/89 **All The Reasons Why** *Highway 101*
39/77 **All The Sweet** *Mel McDaniel*
97/88 **All The Things We Are Not** *David Walsh*
All The Time
18/59   *Kitty Wells*
1/67   *Jack Greene*
    (also see: I Need You)
82/79 **All The Time In The World** *Dr. Hook*
73/86 **All The Way** *Ray Price*
All These Things
1/76   *Joe Stampley*
62/81   *Joe Stampley*
6/86 **All Tied Up** *Ronnie McDowell*
F/73 **(All Together Now) Let's Fall Apart**
    Ronnie Milsap
71/86 **All We Had Was One Another** *Don King*
5/62 **Alla My Love** *Webb Pierce*
Allegheny
70/70   *Bonnie Guitar*
69/73   *Johnny Cash & June Carter Cash*
97/77 **Allegheny Lady** *Max D. Barnes*
22/62 **Alligator Man** *Jimmy Newman*
68/85 **Almighty Lover** *Sierra*
2/52 **Almost** *George Morgan*
20/83 **Almost Called Her Baby By Mistake**
    Gatlin Bros.
86/84 **Almost Over You** *Sheena Easton*
Almost Persuaded
1/66   *David Houston*
6/66   *Ben Colder (No. 2)*
95/76   *Sherri King*
F/77   *Maury Finney*
58/87   *Merle Haggard*
    (also see: He Was Almost Persuaded)
49/84 **Almost Saturday Night** *Burrito Brothers*
Alone Again *..also see: (Here I Am)*
72/73 **Alone Again (Naturally)** *Brush Arbor*
Alone With You
1/58   *Faron Young*
44/64   *Rose Maddox*
57/86 **Along For The Ride ('56 T-Bird)**
    John Denver
1/68 **Already It's Heaven** *David Houston*
42/72 **Alright I'll Sign The Papers** *Jeannie Seely*
18/80 **Always** *Patsy Cline*
16/69 **Always, Always**
    Porter Wagoner & Dolly Parton
(Always And Forever)
    ..see: I Won't Need You Anymore
1/86 **Always Have Always Will** *Janie Frickie*
Always Late (With Your Kisses)
1/51   *Lefty Frizzell*
99/76   *Jo-el Sonnier*
84/81   *Leona Williams*
9/88   *Dwight Yoakam*
37/78 **Always Lovin Her Man** *Dale McBride*

Always On My Mind
45/72   *Brenda Lee*
16/73   *Elvis Presley*
20/79   *John Wesley Ryles*
1/82   *Willie Nelson*
6/71 **Always Remember** *Bill Anderson*
90/80 **Always, Sometimes, Never** *Nancy Ruud*
1/75 **Always Wanting You** *Merle Haggard*
1/87 **Am I Blue** *George Strait*
27/88 **Am I Crazy?** *Statler Brothers*
57/85 **Am I Going Crazy (Or Just Out Of Her Mind)** *Lobo*
Am I Losing You
3/57   *Jim Reeves*
8/60   *Jim Reeves*
1/81   *Ronnie Milsap*
Am I That Easy To Forget
9/59   *Carl Belew*
11/60   *Skeeter Davis*
12/73   *Jim Reeves*
65/80   *Orion*
Amanda
33/73   *Don Williams*
1/79   *Waylon*
Amarillo By Morning
31/74   *Terry Stafford*
4/83   *George Strait*
9/76 **Amazing Grace (Used To Be Her Favorite Song)** *Amazing Rhythm Aces*
1/73 **Amazing Love** *Charley Pride*
36/83 **Amber Waves Of Grain** *Merle Haggard*
30/77 **Ambush** *Ronnie Sessions*
6/84 **America** *Waylon Jennings*
62/86 **America Is** *B.J. Thomas*
America The Beautiful
22/76   *Charlie Rich (1976)*
82/80   *Mickey Newbury*
85/79 **America's Sweetheart** *Corbin/Hanner Band*
American Dream
58/80   *Dirt Band*
5/82   *Hank Williams, Jr.*
54/85 **American Farmer** *Charlie Daniels Band*
1/83 **American Made** *Oak Ridge Boys*
88/88 **American Man** *Frank Burgess*
16/87 **American Me** *S-K-O*
66/67 **American Power** *Johnny Wright*
93/88 **American Trilogy** *Mickey Newbury*
60/85 **American Waltz** *Merle Haggard*
8/88 **Americana** *Moe Bandy*
Americans (A Canadian's Opinion)
35/74   *Tex Ritter*
59/74   *Byron MacGregor*
5/60 **Amigo's Guitar** *Kitty Wells*
1/76 **Among My Souvenirs** *Marty Robbins*
16/70 **Amos Moses** *Jerry Reed*
48/71 **And I Love You So** *Bobby Goldsboro*
And I'll Be Hating You
    ..see: (It Won't Be Long)
And Then Some
47/82   *Bobby Smith*
51/87   *Charly McClain*
70/67 **And You Wonder Why** *Fred Carter, Jr.*
41/71 **Angel** *Claude Gray*
82/84 **Angel Eyes** *Larry Willoughby*
1/81 **Angel Flying Too Close To The Ground** *Willie Nelson*
67/75 **Angel In An Apron** *Durwood Haddock*
1/84 **Angel In Disguise** *Earl Thomas Conley*
Angel In Your Arms
71/77   *Vivian Bell*
54/84   *Robin Lee*
8/85   *Barbara Mandrell*

Angel Of The Morning
34/70   *Connie Eaton*
22/78   *Melba Montgomery*
22/81   *Juice Newton*
34/64 **Angel On Leave** *Jimmy C. Newman*
33/88 **(Angel On My Mind) That's Why I'm Walkin'** *Ricky Skaggs*
42/76 **Angel On My Shoulder** *Joni Lee*
57/77 **Angel With A Broken Wing** *Roy Head*
13/71 **Angel's Sunday** *Jim Ed Brown*
32/81 **Angela** *Mundo Earwood*
69/78 **Angelene** *Mundo Earwood*
60/79 **Angeline** *Ed Bruce*
19/74 **Angels Are Hard To Find** *Hank Williams, Jr.*
4/70 **Angels Don't Lie** *Jim Reeves*
57/83 **Angels Get Lonely Too** *Ralph May*
49/88 **Angels Love Bad Men** *Barbara Mandrell*
9/76 **Angels, Roses, And Rain** *Dickey Lee*
49/87 **Anger & Tears** *Mel McDaniel*
16/68 **Angry Words** *Stonewall Jackson*
68/78 **Animal** *Ronnie McDowell*
17/66 **Anita, You're Dreaming** *Waylon Jennings*
89/74 **Ann** *Joel Mathis*
2/72 **Ann (Don't Go Runnin')** *Tommy Overstreet*
28/68 **Anna, I'm Taking You Home** *Leon Ashley*
3/58 **Anna Marie** *Jim Reeves*
40/65 **Anne Of A Thousand Days** *Leroy Van Dyke*
13/55 **Annie Over** *Hank Thompson*
9/74 **Annie's Song** *John Denver*
2/60 **Another** *Roy Drusky*
28/63 **Another Bridge To Burn** *'Little' Jimmy Dickens*
8/82 **Another Chance** *Tammy Wynette*
27/62 **Another Day, Another Dollar** *Wynn Stewart*
44/66 **Another Day, Another Dollar In The Hole** *Tex Williams*
25/69 **Another Day, Another Mile, Another Highway** *Clay Hart*
61/72 **Another Day Of Loving** *Penny DeHaven*
25/79 **Another Easy Lovin' Night** *Randy Barlow*
21/78 **Another Fine Mess** *Glen Campbell*
28/63 **Another Fool Like Me** *Ned Miller*
57/73 **Another Football Year** *Jeannie C. Riley*
10/78 **Another Goodbye** *Donna Fargo*
31/74 **Another Goodbye** *Rex Allen, Jr.*
8/82 **Another Honky-Tonk Night On Broadway** *David Frizzell & Shelly West*
Another Lonely Night
12/70   *Jean Shepard*
76/77   *Jody Miller*
48/84 **Another Lonely Night With You** *Roy Clark*
1/74 **Another Lonely Song** *Tammy Wynette*
24/76 **Another Morning** *Jim Ed Brown*
10/84 **Another Motel Memory** *Shelly West*
44/76 **Another Neon Night** *Jean Shepard*
5/71 **Another Night Of Love** *Freddy Weller*
Another Place Another Time
4/68   *Jerry Lee Lewis*
5/88   *Don Williams*
27/72 **Another Puff** *Jerry Reed*
88/75 **Another Saturday Night** *Buddy Alan*
4/82 **Another Sleepless Night** *Anne Murray*
Another Somebody Done Somebody Wrong Song ..see: (Hey Won't You Play)
16/66 **Another Story** *Ernest Tubb*
34/80 **Another Texas Song** *Eddy Raven*
69/68 **Another Time, Another Place, Another World** *Jerry Wallace*
75/73 **Another Way To Say Goodbye** *Ray Sanders*
Another Woman
14/75   *T.G. Sheppard*
92/78   *Billy "Crash" Craddock*
89/88 **Another Woman's Man** *Bobbi Lace*
38/64 **Another Woman's Man Another Man's Woman** *Faron Young & Margie Singleton*

379

4/87	**Another World** *Crystal Gayle & Gary Morris*		11/69	**Are You From Dixie (Cause I'm From Dixie Too)** *Jerry Reed*
23/75	**Another You** *Faron Young*		1/81	**Are You Happy Baby?** *Dottie West*
3/49	**Anticipation Blues** *Tennessee Ernie Ford*			**Are You Lonesome To-night?**
84/81	**Antioch Churchouse Choir** *Sweetwater*		22/61	*Elvis Presley*
	Any Day Now		57/83	*John Schneider & Jill Michaels*
26/79	*Don Gibson*			**Are You Mine**
1/82	*Ronnie Milsap*		2/55	*Tom Tall & Ginny Wright*
7/56	**Any Old Time** *Webb Pierce*		6/55	*Myrna Lorrie & Buddy DeVal*
32/67	**Any Old Way You Do** *Jan Howard*		14/55	*Red Sovine & Goldie Hill*
3/73	**Any Old Wind That Blows** *Johnny Cash*		1/80	**Are You On The Road To Lovin' Me Again**
	Any Time *..see: Anytime*			*Debby Boone*
	Any Way *..also see: Anyway*		7/77	**Are You Ready For The Country**
33/81	**Any Way You Want Me** *Gene Watson*			*Waylon Jennings*
10/81	**Any Which Way You Can** *Glen Campbell*		13/58	**Are You Really Mine** *Jimmie Rodgers*
17/83	**Anybody Else's Heart But Mine** *Terri Gibbs*		32/87	**Are You Satisfied** *Janie Frickie*
94/75	**Anybody Out There Wanna Be A Daddy**		10/79	**Are You Sincere** *Elvis Presley*
	Kitty Wells		20/87	**Are You Still In Love With Me** *Anne Murray*
13/59	**Anybody's Girl** *Hank Thompson*		1/75	**Are You Sure Hank Done It This Way**
3/60	**Anymore** *Roy Drusky*			*Waylon Jennings*
64/88	**Anyone Can Be Somebody's Fool**		1/52	**Are You Teasing Me** *Carl Smith*
	Nanci Griffith		12/60	**Are You Willing, Willie** *Marion Worth*
27/87	**Anyone Can Do The Heartbreak**		87/80	**Arizona Highway** *Tim Rex & Oklahoma*
	Anne Murray		85/80	**Arizona Whiz** *George Burns*
2/78	**Anyone Who Isn't Me Tonight**		47/72	**Arkansas** *Wilburn Brothers*
	Kenny Rogers & Dottie West		19/86	**Arlene** *Marty Stuart*
12/77	**Anything But Leavin'** *Larry Gatlin*		27/73	**Arms Full Of Empty** *Buck Owens*
25/81	**Anything But Yes Is Still A No**		4/71	**Arms Of A Fool** *Mel Tillis*
	Stephanie Winslow		70/82	**Arms Of A Stranger** *Tennessee Express*
71/86	**Anything For Love** *Gordon Lightfoot*		62/70	**Arms Of My Weakness** *Darrell McCall*
	Anything For Your Love			**Around** *..also see: 'Round*
80/84	*Brentwood*			**Around My Heart**
88/84	*Sammy Hall*			*..see: (You Sure Know Your Way)*
28/86	**Anything Goes** *Gary Morris*		64/69	**Article From Life** *Lefty Frizzell*
12/68	**Anything Leaving Town Today** *Dave Dudley*		8/65	**Artificial Rose** *Jimmy Newman*
22/63	**Anything New Gets Old (Except My Love For You)** *Don Gibson*		8/54	**As Far As I'm Concerned**
				Red Foley & Betty Foley
55/81	**Anything That Hurts You (Hurts Me)**		12/79	**As Long As I Can Wake Up In Your Arms**
	Keith Stegall			*Kenny O'Dell*
94/74	**Anything To Prove My Love** *Jimmy Hartsook*			**As Long As I Live**
10/67	**Anything Your Heart Desires** *Billy Walker*		7/55	*Kitty Wells & Red Foley*
38/72	**Anything's Better Than Nothing**		3/68	*George Jones*
	Mel Tillis & Sherry Bryce		1/84	**As Long As I'm Rockin' With You**
	Anytime			*John Conlee*
1/48	*Eddy Arnold*		70/87	**As Long As I've Been Loving You** *Razorback*
14/48	*Foy Willing*		30/66	**As Long As The Wind Blows** *Johnny Darrell*
73/69	*Patsy Cline*		43/76	**As Long As There's A Sunday** *Sammi Smith*
54/85	*Osmond Brothers*		83/88	**As Long As There's Women Like You**
79/83	**Anytime You're Ready** *Narvel Felts*			*Jerry Cooper*
13/71	**Anyway** *George Hamilton IV*		51/88	**As Long As We Got Each Other**
	Anyway That You Want Me			*Louise Mandrell with Eric Carmen*
81/79	*Juice Newton*		1/74	**As Soon As I Hang Up The Phone**
60/85	*Carlette*			*Conway Twitty & Loretta Lynn*
F/56	**Anyway You Want Me (That's How I Will Be)** *Elvis Presley*		78/80	**Ashes By Now** *Rodney Crowell*
			47/88	**Ashes In The Wind** *Moe Bandy*
F/81	**Anywhere There's A Jukebox** *Razzy Bailey*			**Ashes Of Love**
13/62	**Anywhere There's People** *Lawton Williams*		37/68	*Don Gibson*
63/69	**Anywhere USA** *Buckaroos Featuring Don Rich*		15/72	*Dickey Lee*
72/77	**Apartment** *Johnny Carver*		48/76	*Jody Miller*
	Apartment #9		100/78	*Amazing Rhythm Aces*
21/66	*Bobby Austin*		26/87	*Desert Rose Band*
44/67	*Tammy Wynette*		19/82	**Ashes To Ashes** *Terri Gibbs*
57/67	**Apologize** *Buddy Cagle*		42/76	**Ask Any Old Cheater Who Knows**
14/69	**April's Fool** *Ray Price*			*Freddy Weller*
58/70	**Apron Strings** *Peggy Sue*		19/64	**Ask Marie** *Sonny James*
87/88	**Arab, Alabama** *Pinkard & Bowden*		6/50	**A-Sleeping At The Foot Of The Bed**
2/82	**Are The Good Times Really Over**			*'Little' Jimmy Dickens*
	Merle Haggard		72/76	**Asphalt Cowboy** *Hank Thompson*
53/88	**Are There Any More Like You (Where You Came From)** *Becky Hobbs*		67/72	**Astrology** *Liz Anderson*
			13/66	**At Ease Heart** *Ernest Ashworth*
61/76	**Are They Gonna Make Us Outlaws Again**		59/71	**At Least Part Of The Way** *Stan Hitchcock*
	James Talley			**At Mail Call Today**
	Are We Dreamin' The Same Dream		1/45	*Gene Autry*
66/80	*Gary Stewart*		3/45	*Lawrence Welk/Red Foley*
26/81	*Charlie Rich*		24/78	**At The End Of A Rainbow** *Jerry Wallace*
45/82	**Are We In Love (Or Am I)** *Charlie Ross*			

85/79 **At The Moonlite** *Bill Phillips*
5/86 **At The Sound Of The Tone** *John Schneider*
13/74 **At The Time** *Jean Shepard*
42/87 **At This Moment** *Billy Vera & The Beaters*
3/84 **Atlanta Blue** *Statler Brothers*
9/83 **Atlanta Burned Again Last Night** *Atlanta*
Atlanta Georgia Stray
36/68   *Sonny Curtis*
62/69   *Kenny Price*
6/46 **Atomic Power** *Buchanan Brothers*
13/74 **Atta Way To Go** *Don Williams*
5/84 **Attitude Adjustment** *Hank Williams, Jr.*
80/86 **Auction, The** *Southern Reign*
Auctioneer, The
9/57   *Leroy Van Dyke*
51/68   *Brenda Byers*
88/74 **Auctioneer Love** *Bruce Mullen*
56/77 **Audubon** *C.W. McCall*
84/80 **Autograph** *John Denver*
15/68 **Autumn Of My Life** *Bobby Goldsboro*
52/71 **Award To An Angel** *Wayne Kemp*
63/73 **Awful Lot To Learn About Truck Drivin'**
   Red Simpson
69/70 **Awful Lotta Lovin'** *Penny DeHaven*

3/84 **B-B-B-Burnin' Up With Love** *Eddie Rabbitt*
1/64 **B.J. The D.J.** *Stonewall Jackson*
Baby, The
7/66   *Wilma Burgess*
63/75   *Tennessee Ernie Ford/Andra Willis*
80/81   *Kieran Kane*
16/69 **Baby Again** *Hank Williams, Jr.*
15/66 **Baby, Ain't That Fine**
   Gene Pitney & Melba Montgomery
40/68 **Baby, Ain't That Love** *Jack Barlow*
1/70 **Baby, Baby (I Know You're A Lady)**
   David Houston
Baby Blue
68/78   *King Edward IV*
1/88   *George Strait*
3/76 **Baby Boy** *Mary Kay Place*
Baby, Bye Bye
31/72   *Dickey Lee*
1/85   *Gary Morris*
42/84 **Baby, Come To Me** *Stephanie Winslow*
Baby Doll
5/47   *Sons Of The Pioneers*
6/74   *Barbara Fairchild*
26/72 **Baby Don't Get Hooked On Me** *Mac Davis*
23/77 **Baby, Don't Keep Me Hangin' On**
   Susie Allanson
4/83 **Baby I Lied** *Deborah Allen*
15/77 **Baby, I Love You So** *Joe Stampley*
77/78 **Baby, I Need Your Lovin'** *E.D. Wofford*
31/70 **Baby, I Tried** *Jim Ed Brown*
26/86 **Baby I Want It** *Girls Next Door*
40/87 **Baby I Was Leaving Anyhow** *Billy Montana*
35/80 **Baby, I'm A Want You** *Stephanie Winslow*
48/78 **Baby I'm Burnin'** *Dolly Parton*
33/83 **Baby I'm Gone** *Terri Gibbs*
Baby I'm Yours
5/71   *Jody Miller*
33/78   *Debby Boone*
22/83   *Tanya Tucker*
2/88   *Steve Wariner*
9/49 **Baby It's Cold Outside**
   Homer & Jethro/June Carter

Baby It's You
21/78   *Janie Frickie*
55/80   *Pia Zadora*
55/71 **Baby, It's Yours** *Wynn Stewart*
20/78 **Baby, Last Night Made My Day**
   Susie Allanson
80/74 **Baby Let Your Long Hair Down** *Don Adams*
5/55 **Baby Let's Play House** *Elvis Presley*
62/76 **Baby Love** *Joni Lee*
93/81 **Baby Loved Me** *Ronnie Speeks*
Baby Me Baby
67/68   *Johnny Duncan*
68/77   *Roger Miller*
27/79 **Baby My Baby** *Margo Smith*
76/80 **Baby Ride Easy**
   Carlene Carter with Dave Edmunds
15/60 **Baby Rocked Her Dolly** *Frankie Miller*
28/61 **Baby Sittin' Boogie** *Buzz Clifford*
92/79 **Baby Song** *Leona Williams*
45/86 **Baby Wants** *Osmond Brothers*
4/51 **Baby, We're Really In Love** *Hank Williams*
1/83 **Baby, What About You** *Crystal Gayle*
66/72 **Baby, What's Wrong With Us**
   Charlie Louvin & Melba Montgomery
Baby When Your Heart Breaks Down
73/83   *Kix Brooks*
56/86   *Osmond Brothers*
56/71 **Baby Without You** *Jan Howard*
22/77 **Baby, You Look Good To Me Tonight**
   John Denver
63/87 **Baby You're Gone** *Janie Frickie*
7/80 **Baby, You're Something** *John Conlee*
30/71 **Baby, You've Got What It Takes**
   Charlie Louvin & Melba Montgomery
7/68 **Baby's Back Again** *Connie Smith*
75/73 **Baby's Blue** *Ferlin Husky*
51/85 **Baby's Eyes** *Lane Brody*
Baby's Gone
2/73   *Conway Twitty*
55/74   *Bobby Wright*
2/87 **Baby's Got A Hold On Me**
   Nitty Gritty Dirt Band
1/87 **Baby's Got A New Baby** *S-K-O*
1/85 **Baby's Got Her Blue Jeans On** *Mel McDaniel*
66/74 **Baby's Not Home** *Roy Head*
12/72 **Baby's Smile, Woman's Kiss** *Johnny Duncan*
72/84 **Baby's Walkin'** *Chantilly*
55/74 **Back Door Of Heaven** *Nancy Wayne*
48/86 **Back Home** *A.J. Masters*
1/74 **Back Home Again** *John Denver*
53/88 **Back In Baby's Arms** *Emmylou Harris*
13/65 **Back In Circulation** *Jimmy Newman*
39/82 **Back In Debbie's Arms** *Tom Carlile*
23/75 **Back In Huntsville Again** *Bobby Bare*
81/82 **Back In My Baby's Arms**
   Vince & Dianne Hatfield
4/69 **Back In The Arms Of Love** *Jack Greene*
51/74 **Back In The Country** *Roy Acuff*
F/76 **Back In The Saddle Again** *Sonny James*
48/87 **Back In The Swing Of Things Again**
   Larry Boone
Back In The U.S.A.
48/75   *Carmol Taylor*
41/78   *Linda Ronstadt*
35/84 **Back On Her Mind Again** *Johnny Rodriguez*
2/79 **Back On My Mind Again** *Ronnie Milsap*
67/86 **Back On The Radio Again** *Younger Brothers*
10/66 **Back Pocket Money** *Jimmy Newman*
33/69 **Back Side Of Dallas** *Jeannie C. Riley*
Back Street Affair
1/52   *Webb Pierce*
88/80   *Joe Douglas*
25/71 **Back Then** *Wanda Jackson*
6/80 **Back To Back** *Jeanne Pruett*

74/69 **Back To Back (We're Strangers)**
    Johnny Duncan & June Stearns
58/82 **Back To Believing Again** *Marie Osmond*
26/69 **Back to Denver** *George Hamilton IV*
40/67 **Back To Nashville, Tennessee** *Stonemans*
    (Back To The Basics Of Love)
    ..see: Luckenbach, Texas
7/86 **(Back to the) Heartbreak Kid** *Restless Heart*
17/78 **Back To The Love** *Susie Allanson*
84/75 **Back Up And Push** *Bill Black's Combo*
2/54 **Back Up Buddy** *Carl Smith*
36/80 **Back When Gas Was Thirty Cents A**
    Gallon *Tom T. Hall*
67/87 **Back When It Really Mattered** *Tommy Roe*
14/86 **Back When Love Was Enough** *Mark Gray*
16/70 **Back Where It's At** *George Hamilton IV*
1/79 **Backside Of Thirty** *John Conlee*
92/79 **Backslider's Wine** *Michael Murphey*
25/83 **Backslidin'** *Joe Stampley*
87/83 **Backstreet Ballet** *Savannah*
8/61 **Backtrack** *Faron Young*
15/54 **Backward, Turn Backward** *Pee Wee King*
77/73 **Bad, Bad, Bad Cowboy** *Tompall Glaser*
33/73 **Bad, Bad Leroy Brown**
    Anthony Armstrong Jones
25/64 **Bad, Bad Tuesday** *Tom Tall*
58/70 **Bad Case Of The Blues** *Linda Martell*
    Bad Day For A Break Up
62/79   *Leslee Barnhill*
46/88   *Cali McCord*
73/84 **Bad For Me** *Joe Sun*
12/86 **Bad Love** *Pake McEntire*
    Bad News
23/63   *John D. Loudermilk*
8/64   *Johnny Cash*
36/82   *Boxcar Willie*
51/84 **Bad Night For Good Girls** *Jan Gray*
28/63 **Bad Old Memories** *Williams Brothers*
94/76 **Bad Part Of Me** *Jerry Naylor*
10/66 **Bad Seed** *Jan Howard*
87/75 **Bad Water** *Gene Watson*
64/88 **Badland Preacher** *Carly Harrington*
26/72 **Ballad Of A Hillbilly Singer** *Freddy Weller*
1/58 **Ballad Of A Teenage Queen** *Johnny Cash*
    Ballad Of Davy Crockett
4/55   *Tennessee Ernie Ford*
10/55   *Mac Wiseman*
4/69 **Ballad Of Forty Dollars** *Tom T. Hall*
3/64 **Ballad Of Ira Hayes** *Johnny Cash*
62/70 **Ballad Of J.C.** *Gordon Terry*
1/63 **Ballad Of Jed Clampett**
    Lester Flatt & Earl Scruggs
70/68 **Ballad Of John Dillinger** *Billy Grammer*
50/86 **Ballad Of The Blue Cyclone** *Ray Stevens*
2/66 **Ballad Of The Green Berets**
    SSgt Barry Sadler
44/67 **Ballad Of Thunder Road** *Jim & Jesse*
14/68 **Ballad Of Two Brothers** *Autry Inman*
27/67 **Ballad Of Waterhole #3 (Code Of The**
    West) *Roger Miller*
7/60 **Ballad Of Wild River** *Gene Woods*
32/81 **Bally-Hoo Days** *Eddy Arnold*
6/64 **Baltimore** *Sonny James*
22/84 **Band Of Gold** *Charly McClain*
F/82 **Bandera, Texas** *Solid Gold Band*
7/75 **Bandy The Rodeo Clown** *Moe Bandy*
4/47 **Bang Bang** *Jimmie Davis*
9/48 **Banjo Boogie** *Arthur 'Guitar Boogie' Smith*
74/84 **Banjo Fantasy II (medley)** *Wickline Band*
5/48 **Banjo Polka** *Tex Williams*
14/74 **Baptism Of Jesse Taylor** *Johnny Russell*
1/80 **Bar Room Buddies**
    Merle Haggard & Clint Eastwood

73/69 **Bar Room Habits** *Wayne Kemp*
30/71 **Bar Room Talk** *Del Reeves*
32/78 **Bar Wars** *Freddy Weller*
40/85 **Bar With No Beer** *Tom T. Hall*
55/68 **Barbara** *George Morgan*
19/77 **Barbara Don't Let Me Be The Last To**
    Know *Mel Street*
92/79 **Barefoot Angel** *Chet Taylor*
90/81 **Barely Gettin' By** *Sawmill Creek*
1/75 **Bargain Store** *Dolly Parton*
31/75 **Barmaid, The** *David Wills*
    Baron, The
63/66   *Dick Curless*
10/81   *Johnny Cash*
65/82 **Barroom Games** *Mike Campbell*
41/75 **Barroom Pal, Goodtime Gals** *Jim Ed Brown*
45/85 **Barroom Roses** *Moe Bandy*
89/73 **Barrooms Have Found You** *Garland Frady*
    Barstool Mountain
82/77   *Wayne Carson*
9/79   *Moe Bandy*
    Bartender's Blues
88/77   *James Taylor*
6/78   *George Jones*
16/76 **Battle, The** *George Jones*
49/71 **Battle Hymn Of Lt. Calley**
    C Company Featuring Terry Nelson
    Battle Of Kookamonga
26/59   *Homer & Jethro*
24/59   *Jimmy Driftwood*
51/75   *Buck Owens*
12/63 **Bayou Talk** *Jimmy C. Newman*
11/71 **Be A Little Quieter** *Porter Wagoner*
26/64 **Be Better To Your Baby** *Ernest Tubb*
    Be-Bop-A-Lula
5/56   *Gene Vincent*
98/86   *Hank Chaney ("86")*
37/69 **Be Careful Of Stones That You Throw**
    Hank Williams, Jr.
98/73 **Be Certain** *Terri Lane*
5/69 **Be Glad** *Del Reeves*
33/65 **Be Good To Her** *Carl Smith*
86/83 **Be Happy For Me**
    Gene Kennedy & Karen Jeglum
92/75 **Be Honest With Me** *Kathy Barnes*
15/72 **Be My Baby** *Jody Miller*
85/81 **Be My Lover, Be My Friend**
    Mick Lloyd & Jerri Kelly
16/68 **Be Proud Of Your Man** *Porter Wagoner*
    Be Quiet Mind
9/61   *Del Reeves*
23/64   *Ott Stephens*
63/88 **Be Serious** *Donna Meade*
10/82 **Be There For Me Baby** *Johnny Lee*
36/78 **Be Your Own Best Friend** *Ray Stevens*
3/67 **Bear With Me A Little Longer** *Billy Walker*
13/48 **Beaut From Butte** *Dick Thomas*
74/87 **Beautiful Body** *David Frizzell*
5/51 **Beautiful Brown Eyes** *Jimmy Wakely*
4/55 **Beautiful Lies** *Jean Shepard*
48/72 **Beautiful People** *Pat Daisy*
86/78 **Beautiful Song (For A Beautiful Lady)**
    Lee Dresser
67/73 **Beautiful Sunday** *Jack Reno*
10/78 **Beautiful Woman** *Charlie Rich*
3/81 **Beautiful You** *Oak Ridge Boys*
18/65 **Because I Cared** *Ernest Ashworth*
28/66 **Because It's You** *Wanda Jackson*
45/67 **Because Of Him** *Claude Gray*
73/79 **Because Of Losing You** *Narvel Felts*
74/75 **Because We Love**
    Jack Blanchard & Misty Morgan
20/76 **Because You Believed In Me** *Gene Watson*

Bed Of Roses
9/71   *Statler Brothers*
91/84   *Bobby Vinton*
76/87   *R.C. Coin*
76/88   *Western Union Band*
4/87   **Bed You Made For Me** *Highway 101*
24/80 **Bedroom, The** *Jim Ed Brown/Helen Cornelius*
18/80 **Bedroom Ballad** *Gene Watson*
18/78 **Bedroom Eyes** *Don Drumm*
Bedtime Stories
76/79   *Pia Zadora*
36/81   *Jim Chesnut*
1/72   **Bedtime Story** *Tammy Wynette*
22/69 **Beer Drinkin' Music** *Ray Sanders*
58/82 **Beer Drinkin' Song** *Mac Davis*
49/70 **Beer Drinking, Honky Tonkin' Blues**
      Billy Mize
86/81 **Beer Joint Fever** *Allen Frizzell*
55/80 **Beers To You** *Ray Charles & Clint Eastwood*
94/81 **Beethoven Was Before My Time** *Jerry Dycke*
47/72 **Before Goodbye** *Del Reeves*
80/82 **Before I Got To Know Her** *Brian Collins*
6/56   **Before I Met You** *Carl Smith*
4/64   **Before I'm Over You** *Loretta Lynn*
2/79   **Before My Time** *John Conlee*
Before The Next Teardrop Falls
44/68   *Duane Dee*
33/70   *Linda Martell*
1/75   *Freddy Fender*
22/66 **Before The Ring On Your Finger Turns**
      Green *Dottie West*
Before This Day Ends
4/60   *George Hamilton IV*
23/61   *Eddy Arnold*
55/83 **Before We Knew It** *Jan Gray*
10/49 **Before You Call** *Dave Landers*
51/88 **Before You Cheat On Me Once (You Better**
      Think Twice) *Robin Lee*
1/65   **Before You Go** *Buck Owens*
5/61   **Beggar To A King** *Hank Snow*
100/78 **Beggars And Choosers** *Bill Rice*
97/88 **Beggars Can't Be Choosers** *Don Lafleur*
82/80 **Beggin' For Mercy** *Louise Mandrell*
1/64   **Begging To You** *Marty Robbins*
Behind Blue Eyes
57/72   *Mundo Earwood*
32/77   *Mundo Earwood*
1/73   **Behind Closed Doors** *Charlie Rich*
1/65   **Behind The Tear** *Sonny James*
87/80 **Behind Your Eyes** *Charlie Daniels Band*
91/85 **Being A Fool Again** *Audie Henry*
10/58 **Believe What You Say** *Ricky Nelson*
4/65   **Belles Of Southern Bell** *Del Reeves*
30/61 **Bells That Broke My Heart** *Slim Whitman*
25/88 **Beneath A Painted Sky** *Tammy Wynette*
Beneath Still Waters
38/70   *Diana Trask*
1/80   *Emmylou Harris*
60/79 **Beside Me** *Steve Wariner*
54/81 **Best Bedroom In Town** *Judy Bailey*
53/74 **Best Day Of The Rest Of Our Love**
      Bud Logan & Wilma Burgess
16/62 **Best Dressed Beggar (In Town)** *Carl Smith*
46/79 **Best Friends Make The Worst Enemies**
      David Houston
15/88 **Best I Know How** *Statler Brothers*
94/76 **Best I've Ever Had** *Jeannie C. Riley*
      (also see: Worst You Ever Gave Me Was)
78/75 **Best In Me** *Jody Miller*
29/72 **Best Is Yet To Come** *Del Reeves*
77/87 **Best Love I Never Had** *Freddie Hart*
27/60 **Best Of All My Heartaches** *Wilburn Brothers*
45/84 **Best Of Families** *Al Downing*
62/82 **Best Of Friends** *Thrasher Brothers*
6/80   **Best Of Strangers** *Barbara Mandrell*

6/72   **Best Part Of Living** *Marty Robbins*
69/66 **Best Part Of Loving You** *Hank Locklin*
52/77 **Best Part Of My Days (Are My Nights With**
      You) *David Wills*
75/86 **Best There Is** *Charley Pride*
7/75   **Best Way I Know How** *Mel Tillis*
1/85   **Best Year Of My Life** *Eddie Rabbitt*
15/59 **Best Years Of Your Life** *Carl Smith*
1/81   **Bet Your Heart On Me** *Johnny Lee*
73/84 **Better Class Of Loser** *Ray Price*
72/70 **Better Days For Mama** *Stonewall Jackson*
      Better Deal Than That ..see: (I Can Find)
      Better Homes And Gardens
34/69   *Bobby Russell*
37/69   *Billy Walker*
91/79 **Better Love Next Time** *Dr. Hook*
20/78 **Better Me** *Tommy Overstreet*
7/71   **Better Move It On Home**
      Porter Wagoner & Dolly Parton
65/77 **Better Off Alone** *Jan Howard*
75/83 **Better Off Blue** *Chantilly*
26/84 **Better Our Hearts Should Bend (Than**
      Break) *Bandana*
74/81 **Better Side Of Thirty** *Billy Parker*
      Better Than I Did Then
      ..see: (I'll Even Love You)
92/79 **Better Than Now** *DeWayne Orender*
      Better Times A Comin'
20/63   *Roy Godfrey*
39/65   *Jim & Jesse*
49/88 **Betty Jean** *Russell Smith*
5/85   **Betty's Bein' Bad** *Sawyer Brown*
91/77 **Betty's Song** *Roy Drusky*
      Between A Woman And A Man
      ..see: (There's Nothing Like The Love)
3/85   **Between Blue Eyes And Jeans**
      Conway Twitty
11/74 **Between Lust And Watching TV** *Cal Smith*
46/73 **Between Me And Blue** *Ferlin Husky*
F/73   **Between The King And I** *Jeannie Seely*
58/79 **Between The Lines** *Bobby Braddock*
17/81 **Between This Time And The Next Time**
      Gene Watson
7/84   **Between Two Fires** *Gary Morris*
      Beverly Hillbillies
      ..see: Ballad Of Jed Clampett
9/54   **Beware Of It** *Johnnie & Jack*
81/76 **Beware Of The Woman** *Ruby Falls*
11/59 **Beyond The Shadow** *Browns*
7/50   **Beyond The Sunset**
      Three Suns/Elton Britt/Rosalie Allen
27/75 **Beyond You** *Crystal Gayle*
48/64 **Bible In Her Hand** *Frank Turner*
81/86 **Bidding America Goodbye**
      Bruce Hauser/Sawmill Creek Band
22/74 **Biff, The Friendly Purple Bear** *Dick Feller*
1/61   **Big Bad John** *Jimmy Dean*
86/76 **Big Band Days** *Hank Thompson*
24/62 **Big Battle** *Johnny Cash*
      (Big Bertha) ..see: Ride That Bull
18/61 **Big, Big Love** *Wynn Stewart*
82/76 **Big Big World** *Ronnie Prophet*
59/69 **Big Black Bird (Spirit Of Our Love)**
      Jack Blanchard & Misty Morgan
39/72 **Big Blue Diamond** *Jacky Ward*
73/67 **Big Brother** *Murv Shiner*
29/66 **Big Chief Buffalo Nickel** *Skeets McDonald*
1/82   **Big City** *Merle Haggard*
41/64 **Big City Ways** *Warren Smith*
52/68 **Big Daddy** *Browns*
52/67 **Big Dummy** *Tommy Collins*
13/62 **Big Fool Of The Year** *George Jones*
70/67 **Big Foot** *Dick Curless*
4/74   **Big Four Poster Bed** *Brenda Lee*
8/74   **Big Game Hunter** *Buck Owens*

12/68 **Big Girls Don't Cry** *Lynn Anderson*	**Black Land Farmer**
19/59 **Big Harlan Taylor** *George Jones*	5/59 *Frankie Miller*
29/60 **Big Hearted Me** *Don Gibson*	16/61 *Frankie Miller*
5/69 **Big In Vegas** *Buck Owens*	**Black Sheep**
5/60 **Big Iron** *Marty Robbins*	21/59 *Ferlin Husky*
50/65 **Big Job** *George & Gene*	1/83 *John Anderson*
31/81 **Big Like A River** *Tennessee Express*	6/52 **Blackberry Boogie** *Tennessee Ernie Ford*
Big Mable Murphy	41/76 **Blackbird (Hold Your Head High)**
43/71 *Dallas Frazier*	*Stoney Edwards*
50/75 *Sue Thompson*	4/56 **Blackboard Of My Heart** *Hank Thompson*
23/70 **Big Mama's Medicine Show** *Buddy Alan*	21/67 **Blackjack County Chain** *Willie Nelson*
39/75 **Big Mamou** *Fiddlin' Frenchie Bourque*	69/84 **Blackjack Whiskey** *Bobby Jenkins*
53/69 **Big Man** *Dee Mullins*	67/71 **Blackland Farmer** *Sleepy LaBeef*
35/80 **Big Man's Cafe** *Nick Noble*	45/67 **Blame It On My Do Wrong** *Del Reeves*
4/59 **Big Midnight Special**	36/70 **Blame It On Rosey** *Ray Sanders*
Wilma Lee & Stoney Cooper	28/65 **Blame It On The Moonlight** *Johnny Wright*
4/82 **Big Ole Brew** *Mel McDaniel*	1/75 **Blanket On The Ground** *Billie Jo Spears*
68/88 **Big Ole Teardrops** *Ray Price*	9/82 **Blaze Of Glory** *Kenny Rogers*
48/68 **Big Rig Rollin' Man** *Johnny $ Dollar*	63/73 **Bleep You** *Cal Smith*
Big River	68/70 **Bless Her Heart...I Love Her** *Hank Locklin*
4/58 *Johnny Cash*	1/72 **Bless Your Heart** *Freddie Hart*
41/70 *Johnny Cash*	1/81 **Blessed Are The Believers** *Anne Murray*
61/75 *Chip Taylor*	6/79 **Blind In Love** *Mel Tillis*
7/61 **Big River, Big Man** *Claude King*	2/76 **Blind Man In The Bleachers** *Kenny Starr*
56/71 **Big Rock Candy Mountain** *Bill Phillips*	83/80 **Blind Willie** *Chet Atkins*
22/62 **Big Shoes** *Ray Price*	4/69 **Blistered** *Johnny Cash*
91/77 **Big Silver Angel** *Tina Rainford*	4/61 **Blizzard, The** *Jim Reeves*
30/65 **Big Tennessee** *Tex Williams*	1/73 **Blood Red And Goin' Down** *Tanya Tucker*
38/85 **Big Train (From Memphis)** *John Fogerty*	4/50 **Bloodshot Eyes** *Hank Penny*
Big Wheel Cannonball	17/74 **Bloody Mary Morning** *Willie Nelson*
52/67 *Dick Todd*	59/88 **Blowin' Like A Bandit** *Asleep At The Wheel*
27/70 *Dick Curless*	48/82 **Blue And Broken Hearted Me**
7/58 **Big Wheels** *Hank Snow*	*Burrito Brothers*
1/89 **Big Wheels In The Moonlight** *Dan Seals*	92/73 **Blue And Lonely** *Vern Murphey*
65/69 **Big Wheels Sing For Me** *Johnny $ Dollar*	83/81 **Blue As The Blue In Your Eyes** *Nancy Ruud*
3/69 **Big Wind** *Porter Wagoner*	27/80 **Blue Baby Blue** *Lynn Anderson*
58/85 **Bigger Than The Both Of Us** *Jimmy Buffett*	2/77 **Blue Bayou** *Linda Ronstadt*
90/87 **Bigger The Love** *Kevin Pearce*	30/64 **Blue Bird Let Me Tag Along** *Rose Maddox*
27/76 **Biggest Airport In The World** *Moe Bandy*	**Blue Blue Day**
51/75 **Biggest Parakeets In Town** *Jud Strunk*	1/58 *Don Gibson*
1/59 **Billy Bayou** *Jim Reeves*	14/61 *Wilburn Brothers*
12/75 **Billy, Get Me A Woman** *Joe Stampley*	2/58 **Blue Boy** *Jim Reeves*
57/69 **Billy, I've Got To Go To Town**	**Blue Christmas**
Geraldine Stevens	1/50 *Ernest Tubb*
75/77 **Billy The Kid** *Charlie Daniels Band*	5/50 *Ernest Tubb*
10/70 **Biloxi** *Kenny Price*	5/52 *Ernest Tubb*
81/84 **Biloxi Lady** *Leon Raines*	40/81 **Blue Collar Blues** *Mundo Earwood*
Bimbo	40/69 **Blue Collar Job** *Darrell Statler*
1/54 *Jim Reeves*	**Blue Cyclone** ..see: Ballad Of
9/54 *Pee Wee King*	**Blue Darlin'**
Bird, The	7/55 *Jimmy Newman*
2/82 *Jerry Reed*	F/78 *Narvel Felts*
26/88 *George Jones*	81/85 **Blue Days Black Nights** *John McEuen*
Bird Dog	61/73 **Blue Eyed Jane** *Benny Whitehead*
1/58 *Everly Brothers*	81/75 **Blue Eyes And Waltzes** *Jim Mundy*
86/78 *Bellamy Brothers*	**Blue Eyes Crying In The Rain**
65/75 **Birds And Children Fly Away** *Kenny Price*	1/75 *Willie Nelson*
63/86 **Birds Of A Feather** *Almost Brothers*	73/77 *Ace Cannon*
60/67 **Birmingham** *Tommy Collins*	56/82 **Blue Eyes Don't Make An Angel** *Zella Lehr*
55/69 **Birmingham Blues** *Jack Barlow*	F/58 **Blue Glass Skirt** *Hank Locklin*
1/50 **Birmingham Bounce** *Red Foley*	33/64 **Blue Guitar** *Sheb Wooley*
31/86 **Birth Of Rock And Roll** *Carl Perkins*	**Blue Heartache**
45/70 **Birthmark Henry Thompson Talks About**	64/73 *Osborne Brothers*
Dallas Frazier	7/80 *Gail Davies*
68/78 **Bits And Pieces Of Life** *Cal Smith*	15/85 **Blue Highway** *John Conlee*
71/69 **Bitter Taste** *Elton Britt*	98/74 **Blue Jean Country Queen** *Linda Hargrove*
45/74 **Bitter They Are Harder They Fall**	**Blue Kentucky Girl**
Larry Gatlin	7/65 *Loretta Lynn*
83/78 **Black And Blue Heart** *Ann J. Morton*	6/79 *Emmylou Harris*
64/84 **Black And White** *David Frizzell*	11/68 **Blue Lonely Winter** *Jimmy Newman*
24/75 **Black Bear Road** *C.W. McCall*	10/88 **Blue Love** *O'Kanes*
16/62 **Black Cloud** *Leroy Van Dyke*	28/58 **Blue Memories** *James O'Gwynn*
57/67 **Black Jack County** *Tex Williams*	46/80 **Blue Moon Of Kentucky** *Earl Scruggs Revue*
	1/82 **Blue Moon With Heartache** *Rosanne Cash*
	32/82 **Blue Rendezvous** *Lloyd David Foster*

F/79	**Blue Ribbon Blues** *Joe Sun*	
86/79	**Blue River Of Tears** *Micki Fuhrman*	
6/48	**Blue Shadows On The Trail** *Roy Rogers*	
8/80	**Blue Side** *Crystal Gayle*	
1/66	**Blue Side Of Lonesome** *Jim Reeves*	
4/89	**Blue Side Of Town** *Patty Loveless*	
1/78	**Blue Skies** *Willie Nelson*	
93/77	**Blue Skies And Roses** *Karon Blackwell*	
7/49	**Blue Skirt Waltz**	
	Frankie Yankovic/Marlin Sisters	
81/79	**Blue Sky Shinin'** *Mickey Newbury*	
41/64	**Blue Smoke** *Warren Smith*	
49/86	**Blue Suede Blues** *Con Hunley*	
1/56	**Blue Suede Shoes** *Carl Perkins*	
6/46	**Blue Texas Moonlight** *Elton Britt*	
5/88	**Blue To The Bone** *Sweethearts Of The Rodeo*	
	Blue Train (Of The Heartbreak Line)	
44/64	*John D. Loudermilk*	
22/73	*George Hamilton IV*	
	(Blue Yodel)	
	..see: T For Texas, & Mule Skinner Blues	
72/77	**Blueberry Hill** *Ann J. Morton*	
4/46	**Blueberry Lane** *Elton Britt*	
4/51	**Bluebird Island** *Hank Snow with Anita Carter*	
11/49	**Bluebird On Your Windowsill** *Tex Williams*	
93/86	**Bluemonia** *Vicki Lee*	
56/78	**Bluer Than Blue** *Beverly Heckel*	
76/83	**Blues Don't Care Who's Got 'Em**	
	Eddy Arnold	
15/49	**Blues In My Heart** *Red Foley*	
12/66	**Blues Plus Booze (Means I Lose)**	
	Stonewall Jackson	
68/70	**Blues Sells A Lot Of Booze** *Hugh X. Lewis*	
	Blues, Stay Away From Me	
7/49	*Eddie Crosby*	
1/50	*Delmore Brothers*	
7/50	*Owen Bradley Quintet*	
1/88	**Bluest Eyes In Texas** *Restless Heart*	
11/77	**Bluest Heartache Of The Year** *Kenny Dale*	
39/66	**Boa Constrictor** *Johnny Cash*	
41/86	**Boardwalk Angel** *Billy Joe Royal*	
14/67	**Bob** *Willis Brothers*	
69/74	**Bob, All The Playboys And Me**	
	Dorsey Burnette	
4/47	**Bob Wills Boogie** *Bob Wills*	
F/75	**Bob Wills Is Still The King** *Waylon Jennings*	
F/78	**Bob's Got A Swing Band In Heaven**	
	Red Steagall	
1/82	**Bobbie Sue** *Oak Ridge Boys*	
29/75	**Boilin' Cabbage** *Bill Black's Combo*	
21/80	**Bombed, Boozed, And Busted** *Joe Sun*	
	Bonaparte's Retreat	
10/50	*Pee Wee King*	
F/70	*Carl Smith*	
3/74	*Glen Campbell*	
8/74	**Boney Fingers** *Hoyt Axton*	
10/87	**Bonnie Jean (Little Sister)** *David Lynn Jones*	
31/69	**Boo Dan** *Jimmy Newman*	
53/87	**Boogie Back To Texas** *Asleep At The Wheel*	
2/78	**Boogie Grass Band** *Conway Twitty*	
22/74	**Boogie Woogie**	
	Charlie McCoy & Barefoot Jerry	
24/75	**Boogie Woogie Country Man** *Jerry Lee Lewis*	
10/88	**Boogie Woogie Fiddle Country Blues**	
	Charlie Daniels Band	
72/74	**Boogie Woogie Rock And Roll** *Jerry Reed*	
100/78	**Boogiewoogieitis** *Billy Stack*	
85/75	**Boom Boom Barroom Man** *Nat Stuckey*	
8/49	**Boomerang** *Arthur 'Guitar Boogie' Smith*	
84/88	**Boots** *Brenda Cole*	
1/86	**Bop** *Dan Seals*	
7/56	**Boppin' The Blues** *Carl Perkins*	
13/89	**Borderline** *Shooters*	
26/78	**Bordertown Woman** *Mel McDaniel*	
76/81	**Born** *Orion*	

	Born A Fool	
21/68	*Freddie Hart*	
41/73	*Freddie Hart*	
12/77	**Born Believer** *Jim Ed Brown/Helen Cornelius*	
12/66	**Born Loser** *Don Gibson*	
72/70	**Born That Way** *Stonewall Jackson*	
52/68	**Born To Be By Your Side** *Jimmy Dean*	
5/55	**Born To Be Happy** *Hank Snow*	
22/66	**Born To Be In Love With You** *Van Trevor*	
	Born To Be With You	
1/68	*Sonny James*	
21/78	*Sandy Posey*	
1/87	**Born To Boogie** *Hank Williams, Jr.*	
3/44	**Born To Lose** *Ted Daffan's Texans*	
31/74	**Born To Love And Satisfy** *Karen Wheeler*	
	Born To Love Me	
21/77	*Ray Price*	
20/83	*Ray Charles*	
	Born To Love You	
20/68	*Jimmy Newman*	
40/84	*Karen Brooks*	
3/82	**Born To Run** *Emmylou Harris*	
66/82	**Born With The Blues** *Johnny Rodriguez*	
17/86	**Born Yesterday** *Everly Brothers*	
7/72	**Borrowed Angel** *Mel Street*	
100/79	**Borrowed Time** *Johnny Free*	
43/66	**Boston Jail** *Carl Belew*	
	Both Sides Of The Line	
21/67	*Wanda Jackson*	
58/74	*Josie Brown*	
1/86	**Both To Each Other (Friends & Lovers)**	
	Eddie Rabbitt & Juice Newton	
13/67	**Bottle, Bottle** *Jim Ed Brown*	
3/66	**Bottle Let Me Down** *Merle Haggard*	
50/86	**Bottle Of Tears** *Gene Watson*	
71/73	**Bottle Of Wine** *Doc & Merle Watson*	
21/60	**Bottle Or Me** *Connie Hall*	
35/66	**Bottles** *Billy Grammer*	
18/66	**Bottom Of A Mountain** *Tex Williams*	
	Bouquet Of Roses	
1/48	*Eddy Arnold*	
11/75	*Mickey Gilley*	
79/80	**Bourbon Cowboy** *Jim Seal*	
33/72	**Bowling Green** *Hank Capps*	
18/66	**Box It Came In** *Wanda Jackson*	
49/88	**Boxcar 109** *J. C. Crowley*	
13/80	**Boxer, The** *Emmylou Harris*	
18/83	**Boy Gets Around** *Sylvia*	
1/69	**Boy Named Sue** *Johnny Cash*	
36/84	**Boy's Night Out** *Moe Bandy & Joe Stampley*	
19/84	**Boys Like You** *Gail Davies*	
39/66	**Bracero** *Stu Phillips*	
75/72	**Brand New Key** *Jeris Ross*	
8/71	**Brand New Mister Me** *Mel Tillis*	
63/88	**Brand New Whiskey** *Gary Stewart*	
	Branded Man	
1/67	*Merle Haggard*	
70/84	*Sierra*	
5/75	**Brass Buckles** *Barbi Benton*	
43/83	**Brave Heart** *Thom Schuyler*	
	Break Away	
85/80	*Bill Wence*	
15/85	*Gail Davies*	
75/88	**Break Down The Walls** *De De Ames*	
2/82	**Break It To Me Gently** *Juice Newton*	
61/84	**Break My Heart** *Victoria Shaw*	
	Break My Mind	
6/67	*George Hamilton IV*	
13/78	*Vern Gosdin*	
93/85	**Break Out The Good Stuff** *Roy Head*	
	Breakfast With The Blues	
11/64	*Hank Snow*	
96/77	*Hank Snow*	
10/83	**Breakin' Down** *Waylon Jennings*	

2/69	**Carroll County Accident** *Porter Wagoner*		85/81	**Charleston Cotton Mill** *Marty Haggard*

2/69 **Carroll County Accident** *Porter Wagoner*
Carry Me Back
26/73   *Statler Brothers*
71/73   *Marlys Roe*
100/76 **Case Of You** *David Frizzell*
15/56 **Casey Jones (The Brave Engineer)**
  Eddy Arnold
Cash On The Barrel Head
10/56   *Louvin Brothers*
72/78   *Ronnie Sessions*
96/78 **Cashin' In** *Bill Black's Combo*
78/82 **Cast The First Stone** *Kin Vassy*
12/56 **Cat Came Back** *Sonny James*
97/75 **Cat's In The Cradle** *Compton Brothers*
13/66 **Catch A Little Raindrop** *Claude King*
49/81 **Catch Me If You Can** *Tom Carlile*
Catch The Wind
26/72   *Jack Barlow*
50/77   *Kathy Barnes*
57/88 **Catch 22** *Darrell Holt*
81/81 **Catching Fire** *Angela Kaye*
12/73 **Catfish John** *Johnny Russell*
Cathy's Clown
89/80   *Springer Brothers*
57/81   *Tricia Johns*
Cattle Call
1/55   *Eddy Arnold*
11/55   *Slim Whitman*
81/79 **Caught With My Feelings Down**
  Mary Lou Turner
23/65 **Cause I Believe In You** *Don Gibson*
9/67 **'Cause I Have You** *Wynn Stewart*
'Cause I Love You
3/56   *Webb Pierce*
64/72   *Don Gibson & Sue Thompson*
32/67 **Cave, The** *Johnny Paycheck*
12/71 **Cedartown, Georgia** *Waylon Jennings*
71/86 **Celebrity** *David Frizzell*
6/72 **Ceremony, The**
  George Jones & Tammy Wynette
12/65 **Certain** *Bill Anderson*
30/71 **Chain Don't Take To Me** *Bob Luman*
Chain Gang
17/59   *Freddie Hart*
93/79   *Michael Murphey*
66/87   *Bobby Lee Springfield*
21/80 **Chain Gang Of Love** *Roy Clark*
31/73 **Chained** *Johnny Russell*
3/46 **Chained To A Memory** *Eddy Arnold*
Chains
35/75   *Buddy Alan*
81/88   *Sarah*
4/87 **Chains Of Gold** *Sweethearts Of The Rodeo*
9/77 **Chains Of Love** *Mickey Gilley*
Chair, The
7/71   *Marty Robbins*
1/85   *George Strait*
22/80 **Champ, The** *Moe Bandy*
34/75 **Champagne Ladies And Blue Ribbon**
  Babies *Ferlin Husky*
1/84 **Chance Of Lovin' You** *Earl Thomas Conley*
Change Of Heart
48/83   *Marty Robbins*
93/87   *Topel & Ware*
1/89   *Judds*
57/67 **Change Of Wife** *Geezinslaw Brothers*
41/83 **Changes** *Tanya Tucker*
24/77 **Changes In Latitudes, Changes In**
  Attitudes *Jimmy Buffett*
68/80 **Changing All The Time** *La Costa*
Changing Partners
4/54   *Pee Wee King*
16/87   *Gatlin Bros.*
1/72 **Chantilly Lace** *Jerry Lee Lewis*
26/78 **Chapel Of Love (medley)** *Sandy Posey*

85/81 **Charleston Cotton Mill** *Marty Haggard*
16/67 **Charleston Railroad Tavern** *Bobby Bare*
57/75 **Charley Is My Name** *Johnny Duncan*
15/71 **Charley's Picture** *Porter Wagoner*
47/73 **Charlie** *Tompall/Glaser Brothers*
16/70 **Charlie Brown** *Compton Brothers*
87/80 **Charlie, I Love Your Wife** *Tommy Roe*
F/79 **Charlie's Angel** *Mel Tillis*
1/62 **Charlie's Shoes** *Billy Walker*
38/71 **Charlotte Fever** *Kenny Price*
5/80 **Charlotte's Web** *Statler Brothers*
6/59 **Chasin' A Rainbow** *Hank Snow*
88/77 **Chasin' My Tail** *Jim Glaser*
F/82 **Chattanooga City Limit Sign** *Johnny Cash*
1/50 **Chattanoogie Shoe Shine Boy** *Red Foley*
9/86 **Cheap Love** *Juice Newton*
61/87 **Cheap Motels (And One Night Stands)**
  Southern Reign
7/77 **Cheap Perfume And Candlelight**
  Bobby Borchers
45/83 **Cheap Thrills** *David Allan Coe*
46/79 **Cheaper Crude Or No More Food**
  Bobby 'Sofine' Butler
73/81 **Cheat On Him Tonight** *David Heavener*
14/56 **Cheated Too** *Wilma Lee & Stoney Cooper*
94/80 **Cheater Fever** *Lynn Bailey*
Cheater's Kit
85/77   *Willie Rainsford*
45/79   *Tommy Overstreet*
90/81 **Cheater's Last Chance** *Larry Riley*
30/82 **Cheater's Prayer** *Kendalls*
54/80 **Cheater's Trap** *John Wesley Ryles*
15/76 **Cheatin' Is** *Barbara Fairchild*
38/81 **Cheatin' Is Still On My Mind** *Cristy Lane*
20/80 **Cheatin' On A Cheater** *Loretta Lynn*
41/77 **Cheatin' Overtime** *Mary Lou Turner*
61/82 **Cheatin' State Of Mind** *Bandana*
91/77 **Cheatin' Turns Her On** *David Wills*
9/54 **Cheatin's A Sin** *Kitty Wells*
16/81 **Cheatin's A Two Way Street** *Sammi Smith*
61/80 **Cheating Eyes** *Jerry Naylor*
18/73 **Cheating Game** *Susan Raye*
7/51 **Cherokee Boogie (Eh-Oh-Aleena)**
  Moon Mullican
47/82 **Cherokee Country** *Solid Gold Band*
Cherokee Fiddle
58/77   *Michael Murphey*
10/82   *Johnny Lee*
1/76 **Cherokee Maiden** *Merle Haggard*
73/67 **Cherokee Strip** *Bob Beckham*
4/44 **Cherry Red Blues** *Cootie Williams*
38/67 **Chet's Tune** *Some Of Chet's Friends*
80/88 **Chevy Van** *Sammy Johns*
8/51 **Chew Tobacco Rag** *Zeb Turner*
30/70 **Chicago Story** *Jimmy Snyder*
54/73 **Chick Inspector (That's Where My Money**
  Goes) *Dick Curless*
17/64 **Chickashay** *David Houston*
31/66 **Chicken Feed** *Bobbi Staff*
45/84 **Chicken In Black** *Johnny Cash*
69/67 **Chicken Pickin'** *Buckaroos*
8/81 **Chicken Truck** *John Anderson*
17/83 **Child Of The Fifties** *Statler Brothers*
13/87 **Child Support** *Barbara Mandrell*
24/68 **Childhood Places** *Dottie West*
Children
58/69   *Diana Trask*
30/73   *Johnny Cash*
9/88 **Chill Factor** *Merle Haggard*
6/48 **Chime Bells** *Elton Britt*
22/62 **China Doll** *George Hamilton IV*
80/73 **China Nights (Shina No Yoru)** *Dick Curless*
33/74 **Chip Chip** *Patsy Sledd*
23/71 **Chip 'N' Dale's Place** *Claude King*
12/59 **Chip Off The Old Block** *Eddy Arnold*

6/88 **Chiseled In Stone** *Vern Gosdin*	
14/64 **Chit Atkins, Make Me A Star** *Don Bowman*	
Choc'late Ice Cream Cone	
5/50 *Red Foley*	
8/50 *Kenny Roberts*	
Chokin' Kind	
8/67 *Waylon Jennings*	
59/71 *Diana Trask*	
87/83 *Freddy Fender*	
69/75 **Choo Choo Ch'Boogie** *Asleep At The Wheel*	

89/82 **Closer To Crazy** *Jan Gray*
40/82 **Closer To You** *Burrito Brothers*
Closer You Get
27/81   *Don King*
1/83   *Alabama*
66/69 **Closest Thing To Love (I've Ever Seen)**
  Skeeter Davis
27/77 **Closest Thing To You** *Jerry Lee Lewis*
1/82 **Clown, The** *Conway Twitty*
7/80 **Clyde** *Waylon*
Coal Miner's Daughter
1/70   *Loretta Lynn*
24/80   *Sissy Spacek*
4/71 **Coat Of Many Colors** *Dolly Parton*
1/79 **Coca Cola Cowboy** *Mel Tillis*
15/48 **Cocaine Blues** *Roy Hogsed*
Cocaine Train *..see: (Stay Away From)*
44/67 **Cockfight, The** *Archie Campbell*
72/77 **Coconut Grove** *Maury Finney*
93/81 **Code-A-Phone** *Larry Riley*
81/85 **Coffee Brown Eyes** *Billy Walker*
13/63 **Cold And Lonely (Is The Forecast For Tonight)** *Kitty Wells*
Cold, Cold Heart
1/51   *Hank Williams*
22/61   *Jerry Lee Lewis*
84/79   *Jerry Lee Lewis*
10/62 **Cold Dark Waters** *Porter Wagoner*
69/77 **Cold Day In July** *Ray Griff*
2/67 **Cold Hard Facts Of Life** *Porter Wagoner*
64/87 **Cold Hearts/Closed Minds** *Nanci Griffith*
62/84 **Cold In July** *Robin Lee*
53/80 **Cold Lonesome Morning** *Johnny Cash*
24/85 **Cold Summer Day In Georgia** *Gene Watson*
30/75 **Colinda** *Fiddlin' Frenchie Burke*
22/69 **Color Him Father** *Linda Martell*
38/72 **Color My World** *Barbara Fairchild*
7/58 **Color Of The Blues** *George Jones*
85/76 **Colorado Call** *Shad O'Shea*
93/84 **Colorado Christmas** *Nitty Gritty Dirt Band*
Colorado Country Morning
70/73   *Tennessee Ernie Ford*
95/75   *Hank Snow*
60/80   *Pat Boone*
50/78 **Colorado Kool-Aid** *Johnny Paycheck*
37/87 **Colorado Moon** *Tim Malchak*
70/70 **Columbus Stockade Blues**
  Danny Davis/The Nashville Brass
7/62 **Comancheros, The** *Claude King*
4/78 **Come A Little Bit Closer**
  Johnny Duncan with Janie Fricke
47/70 **Come And Get It Mama** *Charlie Louvin*
20/59 **Come And Knock** *Roy Acuff*
Come As You Were
66/69   *Jerry Lee Lewis*
7/89   *T. Graham Brown*
13/56 **Come Back To Me** *Jimmy Newman*
12/73 **Come Early Morning** *Don Williams*
49/74 **Come Home** *Jim Mundy*
79/86 **Come In Planet Earth (Are You Listenin')**
  Karen Taylor-Good
6/58 **Come In Stranger** *Johnny Cash*
14/67 **Come Kiss Me Love** *Bobby Bare*
1/73 **Come Live With Me** *Roy Clark*
63/82 **Come Looking For Me** *Lobo*
58/74 **Come Monday** *Jimmy Buffett*
42/66 **Come On And Sing** *Bob Luman*
52/75 **Come On Down** *Tennessee Ernie Ford*
24/76 **Come On Down (To Our Favorite Forget-About-Her Place)** *David Houston*
Come On Home
68/68   *Debbie Lori Kaye*
85/75   *Mary Lou Turner*
76/84   *Tony Arata*

73/87 **Chosen** *Perry LaPointe*
7/49 **C-H-R-I-S-T-M-A-S** *Eddy Arnold*
12/55 **Christmas Can't Be Far Away** *Eddy Arnold*
2/46 **Christmas Carols By The Old Corral**
  Tex Ritter
35/83 **Christmas In Dixie** *Alabama*
35/83 **Christmas Is Just A Song For Us This Year** *Louise Mandrell/RC Bannon*
92/78 **Christmas Tribute** *Bob Luman*
41/68 **Christopher Robin** *Stonemans*
48/67 **Chubby (Please Take Your Love To Town)**
  Geezinslaw Brothers
3/64 **Chug-A-Lug** *Roger Miller*
83/79 **Chunky People** *Hargus 'Pig' Robbins*
5/47 **Cigareetes, Whuskey, And Wild Wild Women** *Sons Of The Pioneers*
Cigarettes And Coffee Blues
13/59   *Lefty Frizzell*
14/63   *Marty Robbins*
2/50 **Cincinnati Dancing Pig** *Red Foley*
2/46 **Cincinnati Lou** *Merle Travis*
4/67 **Cincinnati, Ohio** *Connie Smith*
Cinderella
45/72   *Tony Booth*
59/81   *Terry Gregory*
5/87   *Vince Gill*
92/78 **Circle Is Small (I Can See It In Your Eyes)**
  Gordon Lightfoot
61/73 **Circle Me** *Dee Mullins*
92/76 **Circle Of Tears** *Chip Taylor*
7/64 **Circumstances** *Billy Walker*
City Lights
1/58   *Ray Price*
53/71   *Johnny Bush*
1/75   *Mickey Gilley*
City Of New Orleans
44/73   *Sammi Smith*
1/84   *Willie Nelson*
37/65 **City Of The Angels** *Jimmy Newman*
59/74 **Claim On Me** *George Hamilton IV*
44/66 **Class Of 49** *Red Sovine*
83/87 **Class Of '55** *Carl Perkins*
6/72 **Class Of '57** *Statler Brothers*
Classic Cowboy *..see: (Great American)*
13/75 **Classified** *C.W. McCall*
Claudette
15/58   *Everly Brothers*
41/72   *Compton Brothers*
76/88 **Clean Livin' Folk**
  Bobby G. Rice & Perry LaPointe
74/69 **Clean Up Your Own Back Yard** *Elvis Presley*
Clean Your Own Tables
77/75   *Stoney Edwards*
60/76   *Vernon Oxford*
72/81   *K.T. Oslin*
54/70 **Cleanest Man In Cincinnati** *Claude Gray*
56/80 **Cling To Me** *Jerry Wallace*
47/69 **Clinging To My Baby's Hand** *Dottie West*
17/65 **Close All The Honky Tonks** *Charlie Walker*
15/77 **Close Enough For Lonesome** *Mel Street*
1/82 **Close Enough To Perfect** *Alabama*
81/74 **Close To Home** *Roy Drusky*
70/66 **Close Together (As You and Me)**
  George Jones & Melba Montgomery
74/87 **Close Your Eyes** *Rusty Wier*

Countryfied
35/71   *George Hamilton IV*
80/74   *Ray Pillow*
23/81   *Mel McDaniel*
Couple More Years
51/76   *Dr. Hook*
89/79   *King Edward IV*
3/54   **Courtin' In The Rain** *T. Texas Tyler*
33/75   **Cover Me** *Sammi Smith*
65/81   **Cow Patti** *Jim Stafford*
5/62   **Cow Town** *Webb Pierce*
1/80   **Coward Of The County** *Kenny Rogers*
Cowboy
13/76   *Eddy Arnold*
82/81   *Larry Dalton*
Cowboy And The Lady
90/76   *Patsy Sledd*
63/77   *Tommy Cash*
85/77   *Bobby Goldsboro*
50/81   *John Denver*
  (Cowboy And The Poet) ..see: Faster Horses
3/63   **Cowboy Boots** *Dave Dudley*
19/70   **Cowboy Convention** *Buddy Alan & Don Rich*
44/82   **Cowboy In A Three Piece Business Suit**
    Rex Allen, Jr.
3/64   **Cowboy In The Continental Suit**
    Marty Robbins
91/76   **Cowboy Like You** *Heckels*
10/87   **Cowboy Man** *Lyle Lovett*
100/76   **Cowboy Peyton Place** *Doug Sahm*
5/85   **Cowboy Rides Away** *George Strait*
77/79   **Cowboy Singer** *Sonny Curtis*
76/80   **Cowboy Stomp!** *Spurzz*
49/83   **Cowboy's Dream** *Mel Tillis*
13/77   **Cowboys Ain't Supposed To Cry** *Moe Bandy*
1/80   **Cowboys And Clowns** *Ronnie Milsap*
29/75   **Cowboys And Daddys** *Bobby Bare*
68/80   **Cowboys Are Common As Sin** *Max D. Barnes*
11/78   **Cowboys Don't Get Lucky All The Time**
    Gene Watson
21/81   **Cowboys Don't Shoot Straight (Like They Used To)** *Tammy Wynette*
10/80   **Cowgirl And The Dandy** *Brenda Lee*
75/84   **Cowgirl In A Coupe deVille** *Terry Gregory*
38/86   **Cowpoke** *Glen Campbell*
82/83   **Coyote Song** *Delia Bell*
16/61   **Cozy Inn** *Leon McAuliff*
56/69   **Crack In My World** *Leroy Van Dyke*
3/80   **Crackers** *Barbara Mandrell*
42/71   **Crawdad Song**
    LaWanda Lindsey & Kenny Vernon
F/73   **Crawlin' On My Knees** *Marty Robbins*
Crazy
2/62   *Patsy Cline*
73/67   *Ray Price*
6/77   *Linda Ronstadt*
1/85   *Kenny Rogers*
84/76   **Crazy Again** *Rayburn Anthony*
Crazy Arms
1/56   *Ray Price*
18/63   *Marion Worth*
16/79   *Willie Nelson*
46/87   **Crazy Blue** *Billy Montana*
17/79   **Crazy Blue Eyes** *Lacy J. Dalton*
11/48   **Crazy Boogie** *Merle Travis*
11/61   **Crazy Bullfrog** *Lewis Pruitt*
4/47   **Crazy 'Cause I Love You** *Spade Cooley*
1/85   **Crazy For Your Love** *Exile*
3/87   **Crazy From The Heart** *Bellamy Brothers*
4/51   **Crazy Heart** *Hank Williams*
68/88   **Crazy In Love** *Kim Carnes*
97/77   **Crazy Little Mama (At My Front Door)**
    Alvin Crow
79/81   **Crazy Little Thing Called Love** *Orion*
95/79   **Crazy Love** *Poco*

85/83   **Crazy Old Soldier** *David Allan Coe*
4/87   **Crazy Over You** *Foster & Lloyd*
8/62   **Crazy Wild Desire** *Webb Pierce*
10/74   **Credit Card Song** *Dick Feller*
89/82   **Crime In The Sheets** *Shylo*
7/87   **Crime Of Passion** *Ricky Van Shelton*
32/76   **Crispy Critters** *C.W. McCall*
92/88   **Crocodile Man From Walk-About Creek**
    LeGarde Twins
Cross My Heart
64/86   *Jan Gray*
86/87   *Stella Parton*
2/64   **Cross The Brazos At Waco** *Billy Walker*
57/75   **Crossroad, The** *Mary Kay James*
11/84   **Crossword Puzzle** *Barbara Mandrell*
92/82   **Crown Prince Of The Barroom** *David Rogers*
13/74   **Crude Oil Blues** *Jerry Reed*
9/60   **Cruel Love** *Lou Smith*
25/77   **Crutches** *Faron Young*
Cry
3/72   *Lynn Anderson*
99/75   *Diana Trask*
77/82   *Tanya Tucker*
1/86   *Crystal Gayle*
Cry Baby
52/83   *Narvel Felts*
84/86   *Lowes*
56/88   *Joe Stampley*
5/49   **Cry-Baby Heart** *George Morgan*
58/68   **Cry, Cry Again** *Liz Anderson*
Cry! Cry! Cry!
14/55   *Johnny Cash*
20/68   *Connie Smith*
1/88   *Highway 101*
Cry, Cry Darling
4/54   *Jimmy Newman*
34/78   *Con Hunley*
67/78   *Glenn Barber*
50/87   **Cry Just A Little** *Marie Osmond*
9/85   **Cry Just A Little Bit** *Sylvia*
70/75   **Cry Like A Baby** *Joe Stampley*
1/87   **Cry Myself To Sleep** *Judds*
7/50   **Cry Of The Dying Duck In A Thunderstorm** *Cactus Pryor*
2/50   **Cry Of The Wild Goose** *Tennessee Ernie Ford*
  Cryin' ..also see: Crying
3/78   **Cryin' Again** *Oak Ridge Boys*
7/55   **Cryin', Prayin', Waitin', Hopin'** *Hank Snow*
Crying
28/70   *Arlene Harden*
79/76   *Ronnie Milsap*
14/80   *Stephanie Winslow*
6/81   *Don McLean*
42/88   *Roy Orbison/K.D. Lang*
90/73   **Crying Eyes** *Patti Tierny*
5/51   **Crying Heart Blues** *Johnnie & Jack*
11/48   **Crying In My Beer** *Jerry Irby*
Crying In The Chapel
4/53   *Rex Allen*
4/53   *Darrell Glenn*
Crying In The Rain
54/72   *Del Reeves & Penny DeHaven*
18/81   *Tammy Wynette*
Crying My Heart Out Over You
21/60   *Lester Flatt & Earl Scruggs*
1/82   *Ricky Skaggs*
Crying Over You
3/58   *Webb Pierce*
43/73   *Dickey Lee*
51/87   *Rosie Flores*
4/88   **Crying Shame** *Michael Johnson*
12/65   **Crystal Chandelier** *Carl Belew*
  (Cuando Calienta El Sol)
    ..see: Love Me With All Your Heart
76/82   **Cube, The** *Bob Jenkins*

2/50 **Cuddle Buggin' Baby** *Eddy Arnold*
Cuddle Up Kind *..see: (I'm Just The)*
47/68 **Culman, Alabam** *Roger Sovine*
12/81 **Cup Of Tea** *Rex Allen, Jr. & Margo Smith*
59/67 **Cupid's Last Arrow** *Bobby Austin*
94/76 **Curse Of A Woman** *Eddy Raven*
3/58 **Curtain In The Window** *Ray Price*
14/69 **Custody** *Hank Williams, Jr.*
Cut Across Shorty
28/60   *Carl Smith*
15/69   *Nat Stuckey*
60/68 **Cut The Cornbread, Mama** *Osborne Brothers*
73/71 **Cute Little Waitress** *Stoney Edwards*
5/55 **Cuzz You're So Sweet** *Simon Crum*

D

8/65 **DJ Cried** *Ernest Ashworth*
9/64 **D.J. For A Day** *Jimmy C. Newman*
88/82 **D.O.A. (Drunk On Arrival)** *Johnny Paycheck*
10/48 **Dad Gave My Dog Away** *T. Texas Tyler*
9/87 **Daddies Need To Grow Up Too** *O'Kanes*
Daddy
40/69   *Dolly Parton*
14/79   *Donna Fargo*
55/81   *Billy Edd Wheeler*
85/74 **Daddy Bluegrass** *Stoney Edwards*
40/70 **Daddy Come And Get Me** *Dolly Parton*
55/72 **Daddy Don't You Walk So Fast**
   Wayne Newton
1/71 **Daddy Frank (The Guitar Man)**
   Merle Haggard
58/74 **Daddy How'm I Doin'** *Rick Smith*
40/70 **Daddy, I Love You** *Billie Jo Spears*
62/74 **Daddy Loves You Honey** *Dorsey Burnette*
45/74 **Daddy Number Two** *Glenn Barber*
93/80 **Daddy Played Harmonica** *Jerry Dycke*
1/69 **Daddy Sang Bass** *Johnny Cash*
20/62 **Daddy Stopped In** *Claude Gray*
54/77 **Daddy, They're Playin' A Song About You**
   Kenny Serratt
68/71 **Daddy Was A Preacher But Mama Was A Go-Go Girl** *Joanna Neel*
7/70 **Daddy Was An Old Time Preacher Man**
   Porter Wagoner & Dolly Parton
2/74 **Daddy What If** *Bobby Bare*
15/49 **Daddy, When Is Mommy Coming Home**
   Ernest Tubb
8/55 **Daddy, You Know What?** *Jim Wilson*
56/66 **Daddy's Coming Home (Next Week)**
   Charlie Walker
91/75 **Daddy's Girl** *Red Sovine*
7/86 **Daddy's Hands** *Holly Dunn*
48/85 **Daddy's Honky Tonk**
   Moe Bandy & Joe Stampley
6/50 **Daddy's Last Letter** *Tex Ritter*
Daddy's Little Girl *..see: (One More Year Of)*
92/80 **Daddy's Making Records In Nashville**
   LeGarde Twins
33/73 **Daisy A Day** *Jud Strunk*
37/73 **Daisy May (And Daisy May Not)** *Terri Lane*
66/73 **Dakota The Dancing Bear** *Johnny Darrell*
Dallas
58/67   *Vern Stovall*
35/74   *Connie Smith*
32/80   *Floyd Cramer*
54/83   *Bama Band*
89/79 **Dallas Cowboys** *Charley Pride*
77/88 **Dallas Darlin'** *Norm Schaffer*

Dallas Lovers' Song
   ..see: Makin' Up For Lost Time
68/75 **Damn Good Country Song** *Jerry Lee Lewis*
F/79 **Damn Good Drinking Song** *Kenny Serratt*
75/88 **Dance For Me** *Don Malena*
38/76 **Dance Her By Me (One More Time)**
   Jacky Ward
9/83 **Dance Little Jean** *Nitty Gritty Dirt Band*
23/81 **Dance The Two Step** *Susie Allanson*
2/74 **Dance With Me (Just One More Time)**
   Johnny Rodriguez
Dance With Me Molly
96/78   *Roger Bowling*
88/79   *Hank Thompson*
1/80 **Dancin' Cowboys** *Bellamy Brothers*
72/87 **Dancin' In The Moonlight** *Durelle Ames*
29/79 **Dancin' 'Round And 'Round**
   Olivia Newton-John
(Dancin' To A Different Beat)
   ..see: I'm An Old Rock And Roller
51/87 **Dancin' With Myself Tonight** *Kendalls*
29/84 **Dancin' With The Devil** *Stephanie Winslow*
16/77 **Dancing The Night Away** *Tanya Tucker*
3/82 **Dancing Your Memory Away** *Charly McClain*
1/64 **Dang Me** *Roger Miller*
20/78 **Danger, Heartbreak Ahead** *Zella Lehr*
46/86 **Danger List (Give Me Someone I Can Love)**
   Leon Everette
15/77 **Danger Of A Stranger** *Stella Parton*
Danger Zone
98/77   *Peggy Forman*
59/86   *Maines Brothers Band*
62/88 **Dangerous Road** *Mason Dixon*
9/67 **Danny Boy** *Ray Price*
10/73 **Danny's Song** *Anne Murray*
63/81 **Dare To Dream Again** *Phil Everly*
49/64 **Dark As A Dungeon** *Johnny Cash*
24/68 **Dark End Of The Street**
   Archie Campbell & Lorene Mann
76/86 **Dark Eyed Lady** *Bart Cameron*
Dark Hollow
7/59   *Jimmie Skinner*
13/59   *Luke Gordon*
14/57 **Dark Moon** *Bonnie Guitar*
42/86 **Dark Side Of Town** *Dobie Gray*
Darlene
67/82   *Al Downing*
1/88   *T. Graham Brown*
Darlin'
53/72   *Wayne Kemp*
42/74   *Ray Griff*
86/78   *Poacher*
18/79   *David Rogers*
19/81   *Tom Jones*
26/73 **Darlin' (Don't Come Back)** *Dorsey Burnette*
64/73 **Darlin' Raise The Shade** *Norro Wilson*
57/72 **Darlin' Raise The Shade (Let The Sun Shine In)** *Claude King*
23/70 **Darling Days** *Billy Walker*
5/73 **Darling, You Can Always Come Back Home** *Jody Miller*
2/69 **Darling, You Know I Wouldn't Lie**
   Conway Twitty
69/87 **Darlington County**
   Jeff Stevens & The Bullets
4/47 **Daughter Of Jole Blon** *Johnny Bond*
Davy Crockett *..see: Ballad Of*
59/88 **Day After Tomorrow** *Darden Smith*
44/84 **Day By Day** *McGuffey Lane*
Day Dream *..see: (What A Day For A)*
23/70 **Day Drinkin'** *Dave Dudley & Tom T. Hall*
14/66 **Day For Decision** *Johnny Sea*
88/88 **Day I Tried To Teach Charlene MacKenzie How To Drive** *Ray Stevens*
30/72 **Day In The Life Of A Fool** *George Jones*

F/78 **Dirt Farming Man** *Joel Mathis*
38/73 **Dirty Old Man** *George Hamilton IV*
26/78 **Dirty Work** *Sterling Whipple*
4/71 **Dis-Satisfied** *Bill Anderson & Jan Howard*
90/79 **Disco Blues** *Jay Chevalier & Shelley Ford*
82/79 **Disco Girl Go Away** *Rebecca Lynn*
75/76 **Disco-Tex** *Little David Wilkins*
12/84 **Disenchanted** *Michael Martin Murphey*
81/79 **Disneyland Daddy** *Paul Evans*
1/66 **Distant Drums** *Jim Reeves*
86/78 **Divers Do It Deeper** *David Allan Coe*
77/88 **Divided** *Burbank Station*
1/68 **D-I-V-O-R-C-E** *Tammy Wynette*
9/53 **Divorce Granted** *Ernest Tubb*
 Divorce Me C.O.D.
1/46 *Merle Travis*
5/46 *King Sisters*
4/47 *Johnny Bond*
90/78 **Divorce Suit (You Were Named Co-Respondent)** *Bill Phillips*
 Dixie *..also see: (I'm Coming Home To You)*
54/70 **Dixie Belle** *Stan Hitchcock*
81/80 **Dixie Dirt** *Jim Rushing*
11/83 **Dixie Dreaming** *Atlanta*
10/56 **Dixie Fried** *Carl Perkins*
44/77 **Dixie Hummingbird** *Ray Stevens*
45/74 **Dixie Lily** *Roy Drusky*
25/81 **Dixie Man** *Randy Barlow*
66/86 **Dixie Moon** *Ray Charles*
1/81 **Dixie On My Mind** *Hank Williams, Jr.*
 Dixie Road
48/81 *King Edward IV*
1/85 *Lee Greenwood*
45/85 **Dixie Train** *Carl Jackson*
 Dixiefried *..see: (Let's Get)*
1/83 **Dixieland Delight** *Alabama*
F/76 **Dixieland, You Will Never Die** *Lynn Anderson*
90/81 **Do Fish Swim** *Wickline Band*
 Do I Ever Cross Your Mind
85/79 *Kin Vassy*
F/82 *Dolly Parton*
50/84 *Ray Charles*
18/81 **Do I Have To Draw A Picture** *Billy Swan*
28/87 **Do I Have To Say Goodbye** *Louise Mandrell*
6/53 **Do I Like It?** *Carl Smith*
2/78 **Do I Love You (Yes In Every Way)** *Donna Fargo*
13/78 **Do It Again Tonight** *Larry Gatlin*
77/87 **Do It For The Love Of It** *Bart Cameron*
42/79 **Do It In A Heartbeat** *Carlene Carter*
92/80 **Do It Or Die** *Atlanta Rhythm Section*
20/70 **Do It To Someone You Love** *Norro Wilson*
60/85 **Do Me Right** *Frizzell & West*
4/82 **Do Me With Love** *Janie Frickie*
17/71 **Do Right Woman - Do Right Man** *Barbara Mandrell*
68/80 **Do That To Me One More Time** *Stephany Samone*
88/77 **Do The Buck Dance** *Ruby Falls*
15/65 **Do-Wacka-Do** *Roger Miller*
 Do What You Do Do Well
7/65 *Ned Miller*
29/65 *Ernest Tubb*
1/87 **Do Ya'** *K.T. Oslin*
4/88 **Do You Believe Me Now** *Vern Gosdin*
53/68 **Do You Believe This Town** *Roy Clark*
5/79 **Do You Ever Fool Around** *Joe Stampley*
61/88 **Do You Have Any Doubts** *Alibi*
47/77 **Do You Hear My Heart Beat** *David Rogers*
2/73 **Do You Know What It's Like To Be Lonesome** *Jerry Wallace*
1/78 **Do You Know You Are My Sunshine** *Statler Brothers*

1/81 **Do You Love As Good As You Look** *Bellamy Brothers*
1/88 **(Do You Love Me) Just Say Yes** *Highway 101*
72/86 **Do You Mind If I Step Into Your Dreams** *Cannons*
59/86 **Do You Really Want My Lovin'** *Marty Stuart*
86/80 **Do You Remember Roll Over Beethoven** *Sonny Curtis*
2/72 **Do You Remember These** *Statler Brothers*
F/76 **Do You Right Tonight** *Eddie Rabbitt*
73/87 **Do You Wanna Fall In Love** *Bandit Band*
1/80 **Do You Wanna Go To Heaven** *T.G. Sheppard*
 Do You Wanna Make Love
70/77 *Bobby Smith*
82/77 *David Wills*
80/79 *Buck Owens*
70/80 **Do You Wanna Spend The Night** *Mitch Goodson*
38/72 **Do You Want To Dance** *Jack Reno*
94/79 **Do You Want To Fly** *Ronnie Sessions*
 Dock Of The Bay *..see: (Sittin' On)*
53/86 **Doctor's Orders** *Mel McDaniel*
1/85 **Does Fort Worth Ever Cross Your Mind** *George Strait*
32/84 **Does He Ever Mention My Name** *Rick & Janis Carnes*
5/63 **Does He Mean That Much To You?** *Eddy Arnold*
4/67 **Does My Ring Hurt Your Finger** *Charley Pride*
20/81 **Does She Wish She Was Single Again** *Burrito Brothers*
33/81 **Doesn't Anybody Get High On Love Anymore** *Shoppe*
7/54 **Dog-Gone It, Baby, I'm In Love** *Carl Smith*
6/48 **Dog House Boogie** *Hawkshaw Hawkins*
75/76 **Dog Tired Of Cattin' Around** *Shylo*
45/66 **Doggin' In The U.S. Mail** *Hal Willis*
19/59 **Doggone That Train** *Hank Snow*
17/60 **(Doin' The) Lovers Leap** *Webb Pierce*
62/83 **Doing It Right** *McGuffey Lane*
39/76 **Doing My Time** *Don Gibson*
57/78 **Dolly** *R.W. Blackwood*
4/87 **Domestic Life** *John Conlee*
57/78 **Don Juan** *Billy 'Crash' Craddock*
63/75 **Don Junior** *Jim Ed Brown*
 Don't
2/58 *Elvis Presley*
39/73 *Sandy Posey*
13/75 **Don't Anyone Make Love At Home Anymore** *Moe Bandy*
F/58 **Don't Ask Me Why** *Elvis Presley*
 Don't Be Angry
4/64 *Stonewall Jackson*
33/73 *Billy "Crash" Craddock*
3/77 *Donna Fargo*
7/50 **Don't Be Ashamed Of Your Age** *Ernest Tubb & Red Foley*
 Don't Be Cruel
1/56 *Elvis Presley*
10/87 *Judds*
4/76 **Don't Believe My Heart Can Stand Another You** *Tanya Tucker*
58/76 **Don't Boogie Woogie** *Jerry Lee Lewis*
13/81 **Don't Bother To Knock** *Jim Ed Brown/Helen Cornelius*
1/78 **Don't Break The Heart That Loves You** *Margo Smith*
49/86 **Don't Bury Me 'Til I'm Ready** *Johnny Paycheck*
1/85 **Don't Call Him A Cowboy** *Conway Twitty*
3/85 **Don't Call It Love** *Dolly Parton*
62/83 **Don't Call Me** *Karen Taylor-Good*
13/63 **Don't Call Me From A Honky Tonk** *Johnny & Jonie Mosby*

42/71	**Don't Change On Me** *Penny DeHaven*
1/84	**Don't Cheat In Our Hometown** *Ricky Skaggs*
1/88	**Don't Close Your Eyes** *Keith Whitley*
1/67	**Don't Come Home A'Drinkin' (With Lovin' On Your Mind)** *Loretta Lynn*
28/82	**Don't Come Knockin** *Cindy Hurt*
9/83	**Don't Count The Rainy Days** *Michael Murphey*

Don't Cry, Baby
6/44	*Erskine Hawkins*
70/68	*Freddie Hart*
80/81	*Randy Parton*
13/70	**Don't Cry Daddy** *Elvis Presley*
29/85	**Don't Cry Darlin'** *David Allan Coe*
4/75	**Don't Cry Joni** *Conway Twitty*
12/57	**Don't Do It Darlin'** *Webb Pierce*

Don't Drop It
| 4/54 | *Terry Fell* |
| 69/75 | *Fargo Tanner* |

Don't Ever Leave Me Again
84/81	*Max D. Barnes*
28/82	*Vern Gosdin*
13/78	**Don't Ever Say Good-Bye** *T.G. Sheppard*
3/80	**Don't Fall In Love With A Dreamer** *Kenny Rogers with Kim Carnes*
43/86	**Don't Fall In Love With Me** *Lacy J. Dalton*
33/79	**Don't Feel Like The Lone Ranger** *Leon Everette*
4/45	**Don't Fence Me In** *Gene Autry*
1/73	**Don't Fight The Feelings Of Love** *Charley Pride*
12/55	**Don't Forget** *Eddy Arnold*
44/74	**Don't Forget To Remember** *Skeeter Davis*
75/88	**Don't Forget Your Way Home** *Melissa Kay*
13/81	**Don't Forget Yourself** *Statler Brothers*
16/81	**Don't Get Above Your Raising** *Ricky Skaggs*
60/87	**Don't Get Me Started** *Libby Hurley*
10/88	**Don't Give Candy To A Stranger** *Larry Boone*
41/69	**Don't Give Me A Chance** *Claude Gray*
91/84	**Don't Give Up On Her Now** *Leon Raines*

Don't Give Up On Me
3/73	*Jerry Wallace*
90/76	*Stoney Edwards*
73/82	*Eddy Arnold*
37/65	**Don't Give Up The Ship** *Johnny Wright*
69/84	**Don't Go Changing** *Lorrie Morgan*
5/77	**Don't Go City Girl On Me** *Tommy Overstreet*
18/62	**Don't Go Near The Eskimos** *Ben Colder*
4/62	**Don't Go Near The Indians** *Rex Allen*
1/87	**Don't Go To Strangers** *T. Graham Brown*
88/77	**Don't Hand Me No Hand Me Down Love** *Beverly Heckel*
4/45	**Don't Hang Around Me Anymore** *Gene Autry*
56/71	**Don't Hang No Halos On Me** *Connie Eaton*
30/82	**Don't It Break Your Heart** *Steve Wariner*
1/77	**Don't It Make My Brown Eyes Blue** *Crystal Gayle*
42/80	**Don't It Make Ya Wanna Dance** *Bonnie Raitt*

Don't It Make You Want To Go Home
| 27/69 | *Joe South* |
| 51/87 | *Butch Baker* |

Don't Just Stand There
..see: (When You Feel Like You're In Love)
1/70	**Don't Keep Me Hangin' On** *Sonny James*
11/57	**Don't Laugh** *Louvin Brothers*
83/82	**Don't Lead Me On** *Wyvon Alexander*
67/83	**Don't Leave Me Lonely Loving You** *Randy Barlow*
44/64	**Don't Leave Me Lonely Too Long** *Kathy Dee*
11/74	**Don't Let Go** *Mel Tillis & Sherry Bryce*
26/87	**Don't Let Go Of My Heart** *Southern Pacific*
33/64	**Don't Let Her Know** *Buck Owens*
30/63	**Don't Let Her See Me Cry** *Lefty Frizzell*

| 22/71 | **Don't Let Him Make A Memory Out Of Me** *Billy Walker* |
| 83/86 | **Don't Let It Go To Your Heart** *Bonnie Nelson* |

Don't Let Me Cross Over
1/62	*Carl Butler & Pearl*
9/69	*Jerry Lee Lewis & Linda Gail Lewis*
10/79	*Jim Reeves/Deborah Allen*
6/77	**Don't Let Me Touch You** *Marty Robbins*
86/77	**Don't Let My Love Stand In Your Way** *Jim Glaser*
86/76	**Don't Let Smokey Mountain Smoke Get In Your Eyes** *Osborne Brothers*
24/67	**Don't Let That Doorknob Hit You** *Norma Jean*
86/78	**Don't Let The Flame Burn Out** *Rita Remington*
15/75	**Don't Let The Good Times Fool You** *Melba Montgomery*
37/73	**Don't Let The Green Grass Fool You** *O.B. McClinton*

Don't Let The Stars Get In Your Eyes
1/52	*Skeets McDonald*
1/52	*Slim Willet*
4/52	*Ray Price*
8/53	*Red Foley*
	(also see: I Let)
14/61	**Don't Let Your Sweet Love Die** *Reno & Smiley*
16/71	**(Don't Let the Sun Set on You) Tulsa** *Waylon Jennings*
4/45	**Don't Live A Lie** *Gene Autry*

Don't Look Back
61/80	*Dickey Lee*
12/82	*Gary Morris*
11/81	**Don't Look Now (But We Just Fell In Love)** *Eddy Arnold*
4/47	**Don't Look Now (But Your Broken Heart Is Showing)** *Ernest Tubb*
1/84	**Don't Make It Easy For Me** *Earl Thomas Conley*
60/69	**Don't Make Love** *Mac Curtis*
F/57	**Don't Make Me Go** *Johnny Cash*
84/80	**Don't Make Me Over** *Jennifer Warnes*
46/85	**Don't Make Me Wait On The Moon** *Shelly West*
29/78	**Don't Make No Promises (You Can't Keep)** *Don King*
41/68	**Don't Monkey With Another Monkey's Monkey** *Johnny Paycheck*
18/72	**Don't Pay The Ransom** *Nat Stuckey*
27/83	**Don't Plan On Sleepin' Tonight** *Steve Wariner*
23/63	**Don't Pretend** *Bobby Edwards*
49/80	**Don't Promise Me Anything (Do It)** *Brenda Lee*
4/76	**Don't Pull Your Love (medley)** *Glen Campbell*
47/67	**Don't Put Your Hands On Me** *Lorene Mann*
32/67	**Don't Put Your Hurt In My Heart** *Conway Twitty*

Don't Rob Another Man's Castle
1/49	*Eddy Arnold*
6/49	*Ernest Tubb & Andrews Sisters*
15/77	**Don't Say Goodbye** *Rex Allen, Jr.*
48/88	**Don't Say It With Diamonds (Say It With Love)** *T.G. Sheppard*
93/79	**Don't Say Love** *Connie Smith*
97/79	**Don't Say No To Me Tonight** *Mark Sexton*
51/87	**Don't Say No Tonight** *Mason Dixon*
76/83	**Don't Say You Love Me (Just Love Me Again)** *Mike Campbell*
34/72	**Don't Say You're Mine** *Carl Smith*
55/83	**Don't Send Me No Angels** *Wayne Kemp*
77/88	**Don't Send Me Roses** *Sarah*
2/72	**Don't She Look Good** *Bill Anderson*

2/51	**Down The Trail Of Achin' Hearts**
	Hank Snow with Anita Carter
16/79	**Down To Earth Woman** *Kenny Dale*
2/81	**Down To My Last Broken Heart**
	Janie Frickie
91/77	**Down To My Pride** *Linda Hargrove*
41/74	**Down To The End Of The Wine**
	Jack Blanchard & Misty Morgan
18/63	**Down To The River** *Rose Maddox*
5/51	**Down Yonder** *Del Wood*
32/73	**Downfall Of Me** *Sonny James*
64/79	**Downhill Stuff** *John Denver*
77/83	**Downright Broke My Heart** *Bubba Talbert*
36/84	**Downtown** *Dolly Parton*
31/71	**Dozen Pairs Of Boots** *Del Reeves*
29/70	**Drag 'Em Off The Interstate, Sock It To 'Em,**
	J.P. Blues *Dick Curless*
95/80	**Draggin' Leather** *Mitch Goodson*
	Draggin' The River
11/59	*Ferlin Husky*
45/72	*Warner Mack*
87/81	**Draw Me A Line** *Ray Griff*
50/70	**Dream Baby** *Bob Regan & Lucille Starr*
	Dream Baby (How Long Must I Dream)
7/71	*Glen Campbell*
9/83	*Lacy J. Dalton*
22/64	**Dream House For Sale** *Red Sovine*
	Dream Lover
5/71	*Billy "Crash" Craddock*
59/79	*Ricky Nelson*
59/80	*Tanya Tucker & Glen Campbell*
94/84	*Susie Brading*
88/86	*Ricky Nelson*
	Dream Maker
61/81	*Shoppe*
69/83	*Tommy Overstreet*
47/73	**Dream Me Home** *Mac Davis*
40/79	**Dream Never Dies** *Bill Anderson*
7/81	**Dream Of Me** *Vern Gosdin*
7/79	**Dream On** *Oak Ridge Boys*
18/84	**Dream On Texas Ladies** *Rex Allen, Jr.*
23/73	**Dream Painter** *Connie Smith*
80/80	**Dream Street Rose** *Gordon Lightfoot*
88/73	**Dream Weaver** *Jacky Ward*
32/82	**Dreamin'** *John Schneider*
32/79	**Dreamin's All I Do** *Earl Conley*
10/75	**Dreaming My Dreams With You**
	Waylon Jennings
100/78	**Dreamland** *Gordon Lightfoot*
9/86	**Dreamland Express** *John Denver*
46/81	**Dreams Can Come In Handy** *Cindy Hurt*
15/82	**Dreams Die Hard** *Gary Morris*
35/77	**Dreams Of A Dreamer** *Darrell McCall*
3/68	**Dreams Of The Everyday Housewife**
	Glen Campbell
8/73	**Drift Away** *Narvel Felts*
1/81	**Drifter** *Sylvia*
60/85	**Drifters Wind** *Chuck Pyle*
48/80	**Driftin Away** *Miki Mori*
8/67	**Drifting Apart** *Warner Mack*
96/78	**Drifting Lovers** *Charlie McCoy*
11/60	**Drifting Texas Sand** *Webb Pierce*
58/69	**Drifting Too Far (From Your Arms)**
	June Stearns
7/51	**Driftwood On The River** *Ernest Tubb*
F/70	**Drink Boys Drink** *Jim Ed Brown*
59/69	**Drink Canada Dry** *Bobby Barnett*
25/80	**Drink It Down, Lady** *Rex Allen, Jr.*
2/85	**Drinkin' And Dreamin'** *Waylon Jennings*
17/80	**Drinkin' And Drivin'** *Johnny Paycheck*
8/86	**Drinkin' My Baby Goodbye**
	Charlie Daniels Band
1/76	**Drinkin' My Baby (Off My Mind)**
	Eddie Rabbitt

	Drinkin' My Way Back Home
63/77	*Shylo*
10/84	*Gene Watson*
70/80	**Drinkin' Them Long Necks** *Roy Head*
10/74	**Drinkin' Thing** *Gary Stewart*
35/68	**Drinking Champagne** *Cal Smith*
9/55	**Drinking Tequila** *Jim Reeves*
79/78	**Drinking Them Beers** *Tompall Glaser*
20/73	**Drinking Wine Spo-Dee O'Dee**
	Jerry Lee Lewis
44/70	**Drivin' Home** *Jerry Smith*
1/80	**Drivin' My Life Away** *Eddie Rabbitt*
	Drivin' Nails In My Coffin
2/46	*Floyd Tillman*
5/46	*Ernest Tubb*
26/84	**Drivin' Wheel** *Emmylou Harris*
17/76	**Dropkick Me, Jesus** *Bobby Bare*
	Dropping Out Of Sight
32/67	*Jimmy Newman*
35/81	*Bobby Bare*
96/79	**Drown In The Flood** *Lois Kaye*
39/85	**Drowning In Memories** *T. Graham Brown*
25/61	**Drunk Again** *Lattie Moore*
94/79	**Duel Under The Snow** *Billy Edd Wheeler*
5/73	**Dueling Banjos**
	Eric Weissberg & Steve Mandell
24/67	**Dumb Blonde** *Dolly Parton*
44/69	**Dusty Road** *Norma Jean*
21/70	**Duty Not Desire** *Jeannie C. Riley*
93/84	**Dying To Believe** *Jack Greene*

E

27/69	**Each And Every Part Of Me** *Bobby Lewis*
5/45	**Each Minute Seems A Million Years**
	Eddy Arnold
4/60	**Each Moment (Spent With You)**
	Ernest Ashworth
4/44	**Each Night At Nine** *Floyd Tillman*
16/69	**Each Time** *Johnny Bush*
35/70	**Early In The Morning** *Mac Curtis*
14/89	**Early In The Morning And Late At Night**
	Hank Williams, Jr.
79/75	**Early Morning Love** *Sammy Johns*
9/66	**Early Morning Rain** *George Hamilton IV*
9/71	**Early Morning Sunshine** *Marty Robbins*
28/75	**Early Sunday Morning** *Chip Taylor*
96/80	**Earth Angel (medley)** *Tucker Williams*
93/74	**Ease Me To The Ground** *Sue Richards*
80/77	**Ease My Mind On You** *Marie Owens*
78/83	**Ease The Fever** *Carrie Slye*
	Easier
61/83	*Sandy Croft*
91/84	*Sandy Croft*
87/81	**Easier To Go** *Gene Kennedy & Karen Jeglum*
2/77	**East Bound And Down** *Jerry Reed*
	Easy
76/75	*Troy Seals*
63/78	*John Wesley Ryles*
89/78	*Barry Kaye*
45/79	*Bobby Hood*
F/79	*Jimmie Rodgers & Michele*
2/75	**Easy As Pie** *Billy 'Crash' Craddock*
81/83	**Easy Catch** *Bubba Talbert*
14/64	**Easy Come-Easy Go** *Bill Anderson*
68/86	**Easy Does It** *Tim Malchak*
12/78	**Easy From Now On** *Emmylou Harris*
	Easy Look
67/75	*Kenny Price*
12/77	*Charlie Rich*

1/71	**Easy Loving** *Freddie Hart*
26/60	**Easy Money** *James O'Gwynn*
32/83	**Easy On The Eye** *Gatlin Bros.*
1/52	**Easy On The Eyes** *Eddy Arnold*
	Easy Part's Over
2/68	*Charley Pride*
41/80	*Steve Wariner*
57/87	**Easy To Find** *Girls Next Door*
	Easy To Love
26/75	*Hank Snow*
89/79	*Jimmie Rodgers*
5/86	**Easy To Please** *Janie Frickie*
3/55	**Eat, Drink, And Be Merry (Tomorrow You'll Cry)** *Porter Wagoner*
	Ebony Eyes
25/61	*Everly Brothers*
89/79	*Orion*
77/88	**Echo Me** *Margo Smith*
2/49	**Echo Of Your Footsteps** *Eddy Arnold*
1/53	**Eddy's Song** *Eddy Arnold*
2/63	**8 X 10** *Bill Anderson*
57/84	**Eight Days A Week** *Wright Brothers*
43/64	**Eight Years (And Two Children Later)** *Claude Gray*
1/88	**Eighteen Wheels And A Dozen Roses** *Kathy Mattea*
93/75	**18 Yellow Roses** *C.L. Goodson*
7/87	**80's Ladies** *K.T. Oslin*
64/82	**Either You're Married Or You're Single** *Margo Smith*
1/59	**El Paso** *Marty Robbins*
1/76	**El Paso City** *Marty Robbins*
34/76	**11 Months And 29 Days** *Johnny Paycheck*
1/72	**Eleven Roses** *Hank Williams, Jr.*
1/84	**Elizabeth** *Statler Brothers*
	Elvira
95/78	*Rodney Crowell*
1/81	*Oak Ridge Boys*
31/82	**Elvis Medley** *Elvis Presley*
90/76	**Emmylou** *Brush Arbor*
3/73	**Emptiest Arms In The World** *Merle Haggard*
1/71	**Empty Arms** *Sonny James*
64/89	**Empty Glass** *Gary Stewart*
47/68	**Empty House** *June Stearns*
6/50	**Enclosed, One Broken Heart** *Eddy Arnold*
12/76	**End Is Not In Sight (The Cowboy Tune)** *Amazing Rhythm Aces*
	End Of The World
2/63	*Skeeter Davis*
70/82	*Judy Taylor*
82/79	**Endless** *David Wills*
46/65	**Endless Sleep** *Hank Williams, Jr.*
	Endlessly
1/70	*Sonny James*
38/77	*Eddie Middleton*
13/68	**Enemy, The** *Jim Ed Brown*
2/65	**Engine Engine #9** *Roger Miller*
3/66	**England Swings** *Roger Miller*
75/81	**Enough For You** *Brenda Lee*
36/65	**Enough Man For You** *Ott Stephens*
	Eres Tu (Touch The Wind)
67/76	*Sonny James*
25/77	*Johnny Rodriguez*
2/84	**Ev'ry Heart Should Have One** *Charley Pride*
16/60	**Ev'rybody's Somebody's Fool** *Ernest Tubb*
97/73	**Ev'ryday Woman** *Kenny Starr*
37/80	**Evangelina** *Hoyt Axton*
61/80	**Even A Fool Would Let Go** *Charlie Rich*
	Even Cowgirls Get The Blues
79/78	*La Costa*
26/80	*Lynn Anderson*
35/86	*Johnny Cash & Waylon Jennings*
17/75	**Even If I Have To Steal** *Mel Street*

	Even If It's Wrong
83/76	*Ben Reece*
78/82	*Jimmi Cannon*
74/70	**Even The Bad Times Are Good** *Jerry Wallace*
1/54	**Even Tho** *Webb Pierce*
55/72	**Evening** *Jim Ed Brown*
11/84	**Evening Star** *Kenny Rogers*
30/69	**Ever Changing Mind** *Don Gibson*
	Ever-Lovin' Woman
73/81	*Pat Garrett*
67/82	*Marlow Tackett*
4/82	**Ever, Never Lovin' You** *Ed Bruce*
37/66	**Ever Since My Baby Went Away** *Jack Greene*
42/68	**Everbody's Got To Be Somewhere** *Johnny $ Dollar*
93/77	**Everlasting (Everlasting Love)** *George Hamilton IV*
	Everlasting Love
57/68	*Hank Locklin*
14/79	*Narvel Felts*
69/79	*Louise Mandrell*
34/77	**Every Beat Of My Heart** *Peggy Sue*
86/81	**Every Breath I Take** *Eme*
	Every Breath You Take
68/83	*Rich Landers*
69/83	*Mason Dixon*
	Every Day ..see: *Everyday*
21/76	**Every Face Tells A Story** *Olivia Newton-John*
20/86	**Every Night** *Pake McEntire*
	Every Now And Then
34/76	*Mac Davis*
26/81	*Brenda Lee*
82/75	**Every Road Leads Back To You** *Leapy Lee*
	Every Step Of The Way
21/69	*Ferlin Husky*
52/88	*Wagoneers*
7/74	**Every Time I Turn The Radio On** *Bill Anderson*
10/58	**Every Time I'm Kissing You** *Faron Young*
1/78	**Every Time Two Fools Collide** *Kenny Rogers & Dottie West*
3/75	**Every Time You Touch Me (I Get High)** *Charlie Rich*
1/79	**Every Which Way But Loose** *Eddie Rabbitt*
28/77	**Every Word I Write** *Dottie West*
3/62	**Everybody But Me** *Ernest Ashworth*
54/71	**Everybody Knows** *Jimmy Dean*
17/66	**Everybody Loves A Nut** *Johnny Cash*
25/78	**Everybody Loves A Rain Song** *B.J. Thomas*
56/82	**Everybody Loves A Winner** *Dickey Lee*
5/82	**Everybody Makes Mistakes** *Lacy J. Dalton*
28/87	**Everybody Needs A Hero** *Gene Watson*
	Everybody Needs A Rainbow
56/74	*Bobby Wright*
37/75	*Ray Stevens*
24/85	**Everybody Needs Love On Saturday Night** *Maines Brothers Band*
28/73	**Everybody Needs Lovin'** *Norro Wilson*
62/68	**Everybody Needs Somebody** *Compton Brothers*
70/72	**Everybody Oughta Cry** *Crystal Gayle*
28/68	**Everybody Oughta Sing A Song** *Dallas Frazier*
47/68	**Everybody Wants To Be Somebody Else** *Harden Trio*
76/79	**Everybody Wants To Disco** *Glenn Barber*
52/69	**Everybody Wants To Get To Heaven** *Ed Bruce*
24/87	**Everybody's Crazy 'Bout My Baby** *Marie Osmond*
40/64	**Everybody's Darlin', Plus Mine** *Browns*
18/83	**Everybody's Dream Girl** *Dan Seals*
14/61	**Everybody's Dying For Love** *Jimmy Newman*

70/70 **Everybody's Gotta Hurt** *Cheryl Poole*	58/69 **Eye To Eye**
Everybody's Had The Blues	*LaWanda Lindsey & Kenny Vernon*
1/73 *Merle Haggard*	37/79 **Eyes Big As Dallas** *Wynn Stewart*
85/77 *Maury Finney*	90/85 **Eyes Have It** *Lee Wright*
20/72 **Everybody's Reaching Out For Someone**	19/83 **Eyes Of A Stranger** *David Wills*
Pat Daisy	12/60 **Eyes Of Love** *Margie Singleton*
Everybody's Somebody's Fool	30/84 **Eyes That See In The Dark** *Kenny Rogers*
24/60 *Connie Francis*	
48/79 *Debby Boone*	

F

11/88 **Everybody's Sweetheart** *Vince Gill*	
Everyday	
73/68 *Sleepy LaBeef*	
1/84 *Oak Ridge Boys*	
26/86 *James Taylor*	
70/71 **Everyday Family Man** *Jimmy Dickens*	4/87 **Face In The Crowd**
Everyday I Have To Cry Some	*Michael Martin Murphey & Holly Dunn*
23/69 *Bob Luman*	73/70 **Face Of A Dear Friend** *Clay Hart*
14/77 *Joe Stampley*	**Face To Face**
76/88 **Everyday Man** *Gary Chapman*	92/77 *David Allan Coe*
100/77 **Everyday Of My Life** *Wichita Linemen*	1/88 *Alabama*
63/85 **Everyday People** *Margo Smith & Tom Grant*	10/60 **Face To The Wall** *Faron Young*
62/68 **Everyday's A Happy Day For Fools**	25/61 **Facing The Wall** *Charlie Walker*
Jean Shepard	6/88 **Factory, The** *Kenny Rogers*
87/78 **Everynight Sensation** *Durwood Haddock*	69/83 **Fade To Blue** *Ed Hunnicutt*
36/81 **Everyone Gets Crazy Now And Then**	**Faded Love**
Roger Miller	8/50 *Bob Wills*
46/82 **Everyone Knows I'm Yours**	7/63 *Patsy Cline*
Corbin/Hanner Band	22/63 *Leon McAuliff*
5/70 **Everything A Man Could Ever Need**	22/71 *Tompall/Glaser Brothers*
Glen Campbell	3/80 *Willie Nelson & Ray Price*
42/83 **Everything From Jesus To Jack Daniels**	**Faded Love And Winter Roses**
Tom T. Hall	25/69 *Carl Smith*
56/70 **Everything I Love** *Hugh X. Lewis*	33/79 *David Houston*
Everything I Own	11/78 **Fadin' In, Fadin' Out** *Tommy Overstreet*
66/72 *Kendalls*	36/80 **Fadin' Renegade** *Tommy Overstreet*
12/76 *Joe Stampley*	**Fair And Tender Ladies**
29/86 **Everything I Used To Do** *Gene Watson*	28/64 *George Hamilton IV*
32/79 **Everything I've Always Wanted**	30/78 *Charlie McCoy*
Porter Wagoner	48/67 **Fair Weather Love** *Arlene Harden*
39/70 **Everything Is Beautiful** *Ray Stevens*	**Fairytale**
63/85 **Everything Is Changing** *Johnny Paycheck*	37/74 *Pointer Sisters*
1/86 **Everything That Glitters (Is Not Gold)**	87/80 *Rebecca Lynn*
Dan Seals	10/84 **Faithless Love** *Glen Campbell*
40/70 **Everything Will Be Alright** *Claude Gray*	1/83 **Faking Love** *T.G. Sheppard & Karen Brooks*
98/76 **Everything You'd Never Want To Be**	67/71 **Fall Away** *Tex Ritter*
Joe Brock	10/79 **Fall In Love With Me Tonight** *Randy Barlow*
Everything's A Waltz	91/78 **Fall Softly Snow**
..see: (When You Fall In Love)	*Jim Ed Brown/Helen Cornelius*
96/82 **Everything's All Right** *David House*	4/60 **Fallen Angel** *Webb Pierce*
7/83 **Everything's Beautiful (In It's Own Way)**	41/84 **Fallen Angel (Flyin' High Tonight)**
Dolly Parton/Willie Nelson	*Gus Hardin*
78/75 **Everything's Broken Down** *Larry Hosford*	**Fallen Star**
93/76 **Everything's Coming Up Love** *Sherry Bryce*	2/57 *Jimmy Newman*
48/69 **Everything's Leaving** *Wanda Jackson*	8/57 *Ferlin Husky*
40/64 **Everything's O.K. On The LBJ**	**Fallin' Again**
Lawton Williams	26/60 *Porter Wagoner*
17/75 **Everything's The Same (Ain't Nothing**	6/81 *Don Williams*
Changed) *Billy Swan*	1/88 *Alabama*
58/89 **Everytime I Get To Dreamin'** *Josh Logan*	66/80 **Fallin' For You** *Jerri Kelly*
74/78 **Everytime I Sing A Love Song**	2/87 **Fallin' For You For Years** *Conway Twitty*
Jimmie Rodgers	**Fallin' In Love**
99/77 **Everytime Two Fools Collide** *Lucky Clark*	86/83 *Tari Hensley*
10/82 **Everytime You Cross My Mind (You Break My**	2/85 *Sylvia*
Heart) *Razzy Bailey*	8/87 **Fallin' Out** *Waylon Jennings*
23/88 **Everytime You Go Outside I Hope It Rains**	**Falling**
Burch Sisters	50/75 *Lefty Frizzell*
67/72 **Everywhere I Go (He's Already Been**	100/78 *Stan Hitchcock*
There) *Tex Williams*	10/58 **Falling Back To You** *Webb Pierce*
24/81 **Evil Angel** *Ed Bruce*	85/81 **Falling In** *P.J. Parks*
47/66 **Evil Off My Mind** *Burl Ives*	99/88 **Falling In Love Right And Left**
5/66 **Evil On Your Mind** *Jan Howard*	*Bear Creek Band*
36/68 **Evolution And The Bible** *Hugh X. Lewis*	86/80 **Falling In Trouble Again** *Sherry Brane*
2/60 **Excuse Me (I Think I've Got A Heartache)**	74/80 **Falling Together** *Nightstreets*
Buck Owens	
20/85 **Eye Of A Hurricane** *John Anderson*	

	Family Bible	23/74	**Field Of Yellow Daisies**	*Charlie Rich*
10/60	*Claude Gray*	40/80	**Fifteen Beers**	*Johnny Paycheck*
16/61	*George Jones*	50/71	**Fifteen Beers Ago**	*Ben Colder*
92/80	*Willie Nelson*	24/67	**Fifteen Days**	*Wilma Burgess*
95/80	**Family Inn** *Hughie Burns*	62/87	**15 To 33**	*Southern Reign*
	Family Man	1/70	**Fifteen Years Ago**	*Conway Twitty*
7/59	*Frankie Miller*		**50 Ways To Leave Your Lover**	
92/76	*Al Bolt*	85/76	*Bob Yarborough*	
35/81	*Wright Brothers*	70/80	*Sonny Curtis*	

Family Bible

10/60 *Claude Gray*
16/61 *George Jones*
92/80 *Willie Nelson*
95/80 **Family Inn** *Hughie Burns*
Family Man
7/59 *Frankie Miller*
92/76 *Al Bolt*
35/81 *Wright Brothers*
83/76 **Family Reunion** *Oak Ridge Boys*
4/79 **Family Tradition** *Hank Williams, Jr.*
81/84 **Famous In Missouri** *Tom T. Hall*
Famous Last Words Of A Fool
67/83 *Dean Dillon*
1/88 *George Strait*
30/77 **Fan The Flame, Feed The Fire** *Don Gibson*
26/70 **Fancy** *Bobbie Gentry*
1/81 **Fancy Free** *Oak Ridge Boys*
13/71 **Fancy Satin Pillows** *Wanda Jackson*
27/79 **Fantasy Island** *Freddy Weller*
71/85 **Far Cry From You** *Connie Smith*
Far, Far Away
11/60 *Don Gibson*
12/72 *Don Gibson*
5/79 **Farewell Party** *Gene Watson*
80/78 **Farm, The** *Mel McDaniel*
72/73 **Farm In Pennsyltucky** *Jeannie Seely*
82/78 **Farmer, The** *Cledus Maggard*
89/78 **Farmer's Song (We Ain't Gonna Work For Peanuts)** *Joel Mathis*
21/86 **Farther Down The Line** *Lyle Lovett*
73/73 **Farther Down The River**
       Tennessee Ernie Ford
17/75 **Farthest Thing From My Mind** *Ray Price*
4/86 **Fast Lanes And Country Roads**
       Barbara Mandrell
71/67 **Fast Talkin' Louisiana Man** *Merle Kilgore*
1/76 **Faster Horses (The Cowboy And The Poet)**
       Tom T. Hall
4/47 **Fat Gal** *Merle Travis*
88/80 **Fat 'N Sassy** *Pacific Steel Co./Jay Dee Maness*
71/88 **Fearless Heart** *Beards*
51/68 **Feed Me One More Lie** *Mary Taylor*
45/85 **Feed The Fire** *Keith Stegall*
16/81 **Feedin' The Fire** *Zella Lehr*
84/82 **Feel** *Tom Carlile*
21/76 **Feel Again** *Faron Young*
56/71 **Feel Free To Go** *Sue Richards*
60/88 **Feel Like Foolin' Around** *Exile*
77/86 **Feel Like I'm Falling For You** *Two Hearts*
10/83 **Feel Right** *Tanya Tucker*
55/73 **Feel So Fine** *Kenny Vernon*
66/85 **Feel The Fire** *Family Brown*
38/78 **Feelin' Better** *Hank Williams, Jr.*
2/86 **Feelin' The Feelin'** *Bellamy Brothers*
96/83 **Feeling's Feelin' Right** *Lee Dresser*
19/77 **Feeling's Right** *Narvel Felts*
97/76 **Feelings** *Sarah Johns*
26/78 **Feelings So Right Tonight** *Don King*
1/75 **Feelins'** *Conway Twitty & Loretta Lynn*
98/77 **Feels So Much Better** *Patti Leatherwood*
1/81 **Feels So Right** *Alabama*
19/79 **Feet** *Ray Price*
30/79 **Fell Into Love** *Foxfire*
56/76 **Feminine Touch** *Johnny Paycheck*
Feudin' And Fightin'
4/47 *Dorothy Shay*
5/47 *Jo Stafford*
43/85 **Few Good Men** *Terri Gibbs*
29/61 **Fickle Fun** *Kitty Wells*
87/73 **Fiddle Man** *Red Steagall*
75/73 **Fiddlin' Around** *Chet Atkins*
40/86 **Fiddlin' Man** *Michael Martin Murphey*
73/75 **Fiddlin' Of Jacques Pierre Bordeaux**
       Fiddlin' Frenchie Burke

23/74 **Field Of Yellow Daisies** *Charlie Rich*
40/80 **Fifteen Beers** *Johnny Paycheck*
50/71 **Fifteen Beers Ago** *Ben Colder*
24/67 **Fifteen Days** *Wilma Burgess*
62/87 **15 To 33** *Southern Reign*
1/70 **Fifteen Years Ago** *Conway Twitty*
50 Ways To Leave Your Lover
85/76 *Bob Yarborough*
70/80 *Sonny Curtis*
16/78 **'57 Chevrolet** *Billie Jo Spears*
78/85 **Fightin' Fire With Fire** *Razzy Bailey*
1/70 **Fightin' Side Of Me** *Merle Haggard*
24/64 **File, The** *Bob Luman*
Filipino Baby
2/46 *Ernest Tubb*
4/46 *Cowboy Copas*
5/46 *Texas Jim Robertson*
5/46 *T. Texas Tyler*
Finally
28/59 *Mel Tillis*
9/64 *Kitty Wells & Webb Pierce*
1/82 *T.G. Sheppard*
80/76 **Find A New Love, Girl** *Sunday Sharpe*
Find Out What's Happening
15/68 *Bobby Bare*
52/70 *Barbara Fairchild*
38/76 **Find Yourself Another Puppet** *Brenda Lee*
85/79 **Finders Keepers Losers Weepers**
       Stan Hitchcock with Sue Richards
24/83 **Finding You** *Joe Stampley*
73/74 **Fine As Wine** *Billy Walker*
52/75 **Fine Time To Get The Blues** *Jim Ed Brown*
52/74 **Finer Things In Life** *Red Steagall*
41/70 **Fingerprints** *Freddie Hart*
90/80 **Fingertips** *Johnny Carver*
64/87 **Finishing Touches** *Gary Morris*
29/76 **Fire And Rain** *Willie Nelson*
1/81 **Fire & Smoke** *Earl Thomas Conley*
Fire At First Sight
86/76 *Linda Hargrove*
60/86 *Kendalls*
Fire Goin' Again *..see: (You've Got That)*
46/71 **Fire Hydrant #79**
       Jack Blanchard & Misty Morgan
1/83 **Fire I Can't Put Out** *George Strait*
84/81 **Fire In The Night** *Narvel Felts*
       (also see: There's A)
Fire In The Sky
48/85 *Wright Brothers*
7/87 *Nitty Gritty Dirt Band*
40/81 **Fire In Your Eyes** *Gary Morris*
65/80 **Fire Of Two Old Flames** *Roy Head*
57/76 **Fire On The Bayou** *Bill Black's Combo*
93/81 **Fire On The Mountain**
       Fiddlin' Frenchie Burke
21/75 **Fireball Rolled A Seven** *Dave Dudley*
5/85 **Fireman, The** *George Strait*
73/88 **First Came The Feelin'** *Gail O'Doski*
98/79 **First Class Fool**
       Jimmie Peters/Lynda K. Lance
55/87 **First Cut Is The Deepest** *Ride The River*
9/57 **First Date, First Kiss, First Love**
       Sonny James
70/70 **First Day** *Jane Morgan*
84/78 **First Encounter Of A Close Kind** *Tom Bresh*
First In Line
44/85 *Everly Brothers*
57/88 *Shurfire*
46/71 **First Love** *Penny DeHaven*
74/80 **First Love Feelings** *Glenn Barber*
96/79 **First Step** *Marty Martel*
32/64 **First Step Down (Is The Longest)**
       Bob Jennings

400

First Thing Ev'ry Morning (And The Last Thing Ev'ry Night)
1/65 *Jimmy Dean*
29/79 *Cliff Cochran*
First Time
2/75 *Freddie Hart*
10/78 *Billy "Crash" Craddock*
75/80 *Melissa Lewis*
63/84 *McGuffey Lane*
54/82 **First Time Around** *Ronnie Rogers*
63/84 **First Time Burned** *Johnny Rodriguez*
24/87 **First Time Caller** *Juice Newton*
67/72 **First Time For Us** *Karen Wheeler*
51/67 **First Word** *Eddy Arnold*
7/85 **First Word In Memory Is Me** *Janie Frickie*
1/87 **Fishin' In The Dark** *Nitty Gritty Dirt Band*
Fishin' On The Mississippi
62/67 *Bob Morris*
48/71 *Buddy Alan*
1/68 **Fist City** *Loretta Lynn*
26/60 **Five Brothers** *Marty Robbins*
14/59 **Five Feet High And Rising** *Johnny Cash*
67/86 **Five Fingers** *Ray Price*
5/64 **Five Little Fingers** *Bill Anderson*
21/66 **Five Little Johnson Girls** *Stonemans*
39/66 **Five Miles From Home (Soon I'll See Mary)**
  Bob Luman
5/64 **500 Miles Away From Home** *Bobby Bare*
76/82 **Flame, The** *Rita Remington*
45/83 **Flame In My Heart** *Delia Bell*
64/83 **Flames** *Brice Henderson*
18/76 **Flash Of Fire** *Hoyt Axton*
20/75 **Flat Natural Born Good-Timin' Man**
  Gary Stewart
33/69 **Flat River, Mo.** *Ferlin Husky*
9/61 **Flat Top** *Cowboy Copas*
11/69 **Flattery Will Get You Everywhere**
  Lynn Anderson
1/71 **Flesh And Blood** *Johnny Cash*
4/83 **Flight 309 To Tennessee** *Shelly West*
80/79 **Flip Side Of Today** *Scott Summer*
78/81 **Flo's Yellow Rose** *Hoyt Axton*
8/68 **Flower Of Love** *Leon Ashley*
2/66 **Flowers On The Wall** *Statler Brothers*
12/76 **Fly Away** *John Denver*
8/71 **Fly Away Again** *Dave Dudley*
34/67 **Fly Butterfly Fly** *Marty Robbins*
20/83 **Fly Into Love** *Charly McClain*
Flyin' South
23/63 *Hank Locklin*
56/70 *Hank Locklin/Danny Davis/The Nashville Brass*
52/88 **Flying On Your Own** *Anne Murray*
99/79 **Flying Saucer Man And The Truck Driver**
  Red Simpson
58/68 **Foggy Mountain Breakdown**
  Lester Flatt & Earl Scruggs
Foggy River
10/48 *Kate Smith*
18/68 *Carl Smith*
15/64 **Followed Closely By My Teardrops**
  Hank Locklin
10/81 **Following The Feeling**
  Moe Bandy/Judy Bailey
Folsom Prison Blues
4/56 *Johnny Cash*
1/68 *Johnny Cash*
74/68 *Don Bowman (#2)*
41/80 **Food Blues** *Bobby Bare*
Fool, The
14/56 *Sanford Clark*
31/73 *Elvis Presley*
18/77 *John Wesley Ryles*
22/78 *Don Gibson*
52/84 *Narvel Felts*
6/81 **Fool By Your Side** *Dave & Sugar*

67/81 **Fool, Fool** *Brenda Lee*
6/67 **Fool Fool Fool** *Webb Pierce*
1/83 **Fool For Your Love** *Mickey Gilley*
1/82 **Fool Hearted Memory** *George Strait*
40/73 **Fool I've Been Today** *Jack Greene*
33/83 **Fool In Me** *Sonny James*
4/72 **Fool Me** *Lynn Anderson*
14/63 **Fool Me Once** *Connie Hall*
68/74 **Fool Passin' Through** *Jim Glaser*
45/79 **Fool Strikes Again** *Charlie Rich*
Fool Such As I ..see: (Now And Then There's)
72/81 **Fool That I Am** *Rita Coolidge*
58/80 **Fool Who Fooled Around** *Keith Stegall*
Fool's Gold
58/81 *Danny Wood*
81/82 *Jimmi Cannon*
3/84 *Lee Greenwood*
Fooled Around And Fell In Love
25/79 *Mundo Earwood*
21/85 *T.G. Sheppard*
4/79 **Fooled By A Feeling** *Barbara Mandrell*
9/54 **Fooler, A Faker** *Hank Thompson*
4/83 **Foolin'** *Johnny Rodriguez*
2/61 **Foolin' Around** *Buck Owens*
15/48 **Foolish Tears** *Tex Williams*
Fools
19/72 *Johnny Duncan*
3/79 *Jim Ed Brown/Helen Cornelius*
9/77 **Fools Fall In Love** *Jacky Ward*
Fools For Each Other
17/79 *Johnny Rodriguez*
96/79 *Guy Clark*
49/86 *Ed Bruce with Lynn Anderson*
55/79 **Football Card** *Glenn Sutton*
Footprints In The Sand
42/81 *Edgel Groves*
80/83 *Cristy Lane*
5/46 **Footprints In The Snow** *Bill Monroe*
92/80 **Footsteps** *Jimmy McMillan*
7/62 **Footsteps Of A Fool** *Judy Lynn*
12/75 **For A Minute There** *Johnny Paycheck*
90/80 **For A Slow Dance With You** *Jerri Kelly*
75/88 **For A Song** *Trinity Lane*
86/77 **For A While** *Mary MacGregor*
49/77 **For All The Right Reasons** *Barbara Fairchild*
1/82 **For All The Wrong Reasons**
  Bellamy Brothers
80/80 **For As Long As You Want Me** *Peggy Sue*
For Love's Own Sake
36/76 *Ed Bruce*
73/80 *Roy Clark*
94/73 **For Lovers Only** *Jack Lebsock*
For Loving Me ..see: (That's What You Get)
For Loving You
1/67 *Bill Anderson & Jan Howard*
72/68 *Skeeter Davis & Don Bowman*
58/72 **For My Baby** *Cal Smith*
10/53 **For Now And Always** *Hank Snow*
For Ol' Times Sake
42/73 *Elvis Presley*
75/86 *Jerry Naylor*
7/56 **For Rent** *Sonny James*
1/70 **For The Good Times** *Ray Price*
F/76 **For The Heart** *Elvis Presley*
27/71 **For The Kids** *Sammi Smith*
7/55 **For The Love Of A Woman Like You**
  Faron Young
For Your Love
65/70 *Bobby Austin*
52/76 *Bobby Lewis*
78/88 *Tony McGill*
16/75 **Forbidden Angel** *Mel Street*
23/63 **Forbidden Lovers** *Lefty Frizzell*
23/64 **Forbidden Street** *Carl Butler & Pearl*
12/48 **'Fore Day In The Morning** *Roy Brown*

5/44 **G.I. Blues** *Floyd Tillman*
4/53 **Gal Who Invented Kissin'** *Hank Snow*
58/67 **Gallant Men**
    Senator Everett McKinley Dirksen
1/69 **Galveston** *Glen Campbell*
    Gambler, The
1/78   *Kenny Rogers*
65/78   *Don Schlitz*
95/78   *Hugh Moffatt*
6/53 **Gambler's Guitar** *Rusty Draper*
22/59 **Gambler's Love** *Rose Maddox*
    Gamblin' Polka Dot Blues
8/49   *Tommy Duncan*
94/77   *Original Texas Playboys*
5/66 **Game Of Triangles**
    Bobby Bare, Norma Jean, Liz Anderson
2/69 **Games People Play** *Freddy Weller*
1/76 **Games That Daddies Play** *Conway Twitty*
44/72 **Garden Party** *Rick Nelson*
9/67 **Gardenias In Her Hair** *Marty Robbins*
84/75 **Gather Me** *Marilyn Sellars*
54/76 **Gator** *Jerry Reed*
50/65 **'Gator Hollow** *Lefty Frizzell*
4/57 **Geisha Girl** *Hank Locklin*
26/82 **General Lee** *Johnny Cash*
62/70 **Generation Gap** *Jeannie C. Riley*
86/76 **Gentle Fire** *Johnny Duncan*
    Gentle On My Mind
30/67   *Glen Campbell*
60/67   *John Hartford*
44/68   *Glen Campbell*
68/71 **Gentle Rains Of Home** *George Morgan*
18/77 **Gentle To Your Senses** *Mel McDaniel*
86/79 **Gently Hold Me** *Peggy Sue & Sonny Wright*
96/77 **Genuine Texas Good Guy** *Jerry Green*
10/69 **George (And The North Woods)** *Dave Dudley*
43/74 **George Leroy Chickashea** *Porter Wagoner*
17/78 **Georgia In A Jug** *Johnny Paycheck*
    Georgia Keeps Pulling On My Ring
50/74   *Little David Wilkins*
3/77   *Conway Twitty*
55/82 **Georgia On A Fast Train** *Johnny Cash*
1/78 **Georgia On My Mind** *Willie Nelson*
37/71 **Georgia Pineywoods** *Osborne Brothers*
70/75 **Georgia Rain** *Jerry Wallace*
16/70 **Georgia Sunshine** *Jerry Reed*
24/60 **Georgia Town Blues** *Mel Tillis & Bill Phillips*
83/82 **Georgiana** *Tommy Bell*
53/87 **Geronimo's Cadillac**
    Jeff Stevens & The Bullets
    Get A Little Dirt On Your Hands
14/62   *Bill Anderson*
46/80   *David Allan Coe & Bill Anderson*
57/78 **Get Back To Loving Me** *Jim Chesnut*
33/85 **Get Back To The Country** *Neil Young*
81/77 **Get Crazy With Me** *Ray Stevens*
56/70 **Get Down Country Music** *Brush Arbor*
21/82 **Get Into Reggae Cowboy** *Bellamy Brothers*
F/79 **Get It Up** *Ronnie Milsap*
73/81 **Get It While You Can** *Tom Carlile*
90/81 **Get Me High, Off This Low** *Gary Goodnight*
3/74 **Get On My Love Train** *La Costa*
98/76 **Get Ready-Here I Come**
    Don Gibson & Sue Thompson
    Get Rhythm
F/56   *Johnny Cash*
23/69   *Johnny Cash*
63/67 **Get This Stranger Out Of Me** *Lefty Frizzell*

34/70 **Get Together** *Gwen & Jerry Collins*
47/74 **Get Up I Think I Love You** *Jim Ed Brown*
5/67 **Get While The Gettin's Good** *Bill Anderson*
61/79 **Get Your Hands On Me Baby** *Dale McBride*
14/66 **Get Your Lie The Way You Want It**
    Bonnie Guitar
4/46 **Get Yourself A Redhead** *Hank Penny*
37/66 **Gettin' Any Feed For Your Chickens**
    Del Reeves
56/70 **Gettin' Back To Norma** *Bob Luman*
30/65 **Gettin' Married Has Made Us Strangers**
    Dottie West
29/60 **Gettin' Old Before My Time** *Merle Kilgore*
    Gettin' Over You
46/81   *Tim Rex & Oklahoma*
49/84   *Mason Dixon*
    Getting Over You Again
67/79   *Dale McBride*
90/79   *Dale McBride*
28/81   *Ray Price*
    (Ghost) *..also see: Riders In The Sky*
58/75 **Ghost Story** *Susan Raye*
49/66 **Giddyup Do-Nut** *Don Bowman*
    Giddyup Go
1/66   *Red Sovine*
10/66   *Minnie Pearl (Answer)*
4/88 **Gift, The** *The McCarters*
34/80 **Gift From Missouri** *Jim Weatherly*
14/79 **Gimme Back My Blues** *Jerry Reed*
35/70 **Ginger Is Gentle And Waiting For Me**
    Jim Ed Brown
40/78 **Girl At The End Of The Bar** *John Anderson*
65/67 **Girl Crazy** *Carl Belew*
22/68 **Girl Don't Have To Drink To Have Fun**
    Wanda Jackson
15/64 **Girl From Spanish Town** *Marty Robbins*
F/78 **Girl I Can Tell (You're Trying To Work It**
    Out) *Waylon*
3/62 **Girl I Used To Know** *George Jones*
36/72 **Girl In New Orleans** *Sammi Smith*
17/86 **Girl Like Emmylou** *Southern Pacific*
74/72 **Girl Like Her Is Hard To Find** *Bill Rice*
46/73 **Girl Like That** *Tompall/Glaser Brothers*
77/81 **Girl Like You** *Sonny Throckmorton*
6/69 **Girl Most Likely** *Jeannie C. Riley*
17/85 **Girl Most Likely To** *B.J. Thomas*
61/70 **Girl Named Johnny Cash** *Jane Morgan*
74/69 **Girl Named Sam** *Lois Williams*
98/74 **Girl Of My Life** *Murry Kellum*
1/65 **Girl On The Billboard** *Del Reeves*
26/60 **Girl Who Didn't Need Love** *Porter Wagoner*
26/70 **Girl Who'll Satisfy Her Man**
    Barbara Fairchild
35/66 **Girls Get Prettier (Every Day)** *Hank Locklin*
62/69 **Girls In Country Music** *Bobby Braddock*
1/85 **Girls Night Out** *Judds*
36/79 **Girls On The Other Side** *Nick Noble*
7/87 **Girls Ride Horses Too** *Judy Rodman*
14/81 **Girls, Women And Ladies** *Ed Bruce*
2/88 **Give A Little Love** *Judds*
24/73 **Give A Little, Take A Little**
    Barbara Mandrell
13/87 **Give Back My Heart** *Lyle Lovett*
48/85 **Give Her All The Roses (Don't Wait Until**
    Tomorrow) *Tom Jones*
24/71 **Give Him Love** *Patti Page*
97/83 **Give It Back** *Brenda Libby*
15/49 **Give Me A Hundred Reasons** *Ann Jones*
9/50 **Give Me A Little Old Fashioned Love**
    Ernest Tubb
10/84 **Give Me Back That Old Familiar Feeling**
    Whites
9/64 **Give Me 40 Acres (To Turn This Rig**
    Around) *Willis Brothers*

	Good Morning Loving
61/74	*Larry Kingston*
91/75	*Larry Kingston*
43/64	**Good Morning Self** *Jim Reeves*
37/77	**Good 'N' Country** *Kathy Barnes*
9/73	**Good News** *Jody Miller*
27/75	**Good News Bad News** *Eddy Raven*
51/84	**Good Night For Falling In Love**
	Hillary Kanter
18/76	**Good Night Special** *Little David Wilkins*
19/83	**Good Night's Love** *Tammy Wynette*
	(Good Ol' Boys)
	..see: Theme From The Dukes Of Hazzard
15/81	**Good Ol' Girls** *Sonny Curtis*
81/82	**Good Old Days** *Cristy Lane*
35/73	**Good Old Days (Are Here Again)**
	Buck Owens & Susan Raye
31/74	**Good Old Fashioned Country Love**
	Don Gibson & Sue Thompson
55/77	**Good Old Fashioned Saturday Night Honky**
	Tonk Barroom Brawl *Vernon Oxford*
16/83	**Good Ole Boys** *Jerry Reed*
2/80	**Good Ole Boys Like Me** *Don Williams*
34/70	**Good Thing** *Bill Wilbourn & Kathy Morrison*
2/73	**Good Things** *David Houston*
	Good Time *..also see: Goodtime*
3/69	**Good Time Charlies** *Del Reeves*
	Good Times
44/68	*Willie Nelson*
25/81	*Willie Nelson*
57/87	**Good Timin' Shoes** *Ronnie Rogers*
1/76	**Good Woman Blues** *Mel Tillis*
67/77	**Good Woman Likes To Drink With The**
	Boys *Jimmie Rodgers*
12/74	**Good Woman's Love** *Jerry Reed*
2/71	**Good Year For The Roses** *George Jones*
22/59	**Goodby Little Darlin'** *Johnny Cash*
	Goodbye
73/71	*David Frizzell*
38/72	*David Rogers*
19/74	*Rex Allen, Jr.*
22/79	*Eddy Arnold*
39/67	**Goodbye City, Goodbye Girl** *Webb Pierce*
86/80	**Goodbye Eyes** *Pebble Daniel*
24/84	**Goodbye Heartache** *Louise Mandrell*
71/84	**Goodbye Highway** *Pam Tillis*
75/71	**Goodbye Jukebox** *Bobby Lord*
12/63	**Goodbye Kisses** *Cowboy Copas*
	Goodbye Marie
17/81	*Bobby Goldsboro*
47/86	*Kenny Rogers*
93/77	**Goodbye My Friend** *Engelbert Humperdinck*
53/87	**Goodbye Song** *Gene Stroman*
72/67	**Goodbye Swingers** *Glen Garrison*
7/88	**Goodbye Time** *Conway Twitty*
20/67	**Goodbye Wheeling** *Mel Tillis*
8/87	**Goodbyes All We've Got Left** *Steve Earle*
56/73	**Goodbyes Come Hard For Me** *Kenny Serratt*
	Goodbyes Don't Come Easy
91/74	*Warner Mack*
83/78	*Mack White*
62/66	**Goodie Wagon** *Billy Large*
	Goodnight, Irene
1/50	*Ernest Tubb & Red Foley*
5/50	*Moon Mullican*
53/76	**Goodnight My Love** *Randy Barlow*
3/54	**Goodnight, Sweetheart, Goodnight**
	Johnnie & Jack
	Goodtime Charlie's Got The Blues
63/72	*Danny O'Keefe*
41/79	*Red Steagall*
63/84	*Leon Russell*
83/79	**Goody Goody** *Rebecca Lynn*
24/67	**Goody, Goody Gumdrop** *Wilburn Brothers*

	Got Leaving On Her Mind
54/68	*Mac Wiseman*
14/73	*Nat Stuckey*
82/81	**Got Lucky Last Night** *Jerry Jeff Walker*
	Got My Heart Set On You
1/86	*John Conlee*
72/86	*Mason Dixon*
7/85	**Got No Reason Now For Goin' Home**
	Gene Watson
1/72	**Got The All Overs For You (All Over Me)**
	Freddie Hart
10/87	**Gotta Get Away** *Sweethearts Of The Rodeo*
41/69	**Gotta Get To Oklahoma ('Cause California's**
	Gettin' To Me) *Hagers*
4/46	**Gotta Get Together With My Gal** *Elton Britt*
9/87	**Gotta Have You** *Eddie Rabbitt*
12/86	**Gotta Learn To Love Without You**
	Michael Johnson
4/78	**Gotta' Quit Lookin' At You Baby**
	Dave & Sugar
	Gotta Travel On
5/59	*Billy Grammer*
15/59	*Bill Monroe*
91/78	*Shylo*
69/67	**Grain Of Salt** *Penny Starr*
93/77	**Grand Ole Blues** *Troy Seals*
97/73	**Grand Ole Opry Song** *Nitty Gritty Dirt Band*
1/74	**Grand Tour** *George Jones*
16/78	**Grandest Lady Of Them All** *Conway Twitty*
92/84	**Grandma Got Run Over By A Reindeer**
	Elmo 'N Patsy
1/72	**Grandma Harp** *Merle Haggard*
	(Grandma's Diary) *..see: Johnny, My Love*
9/81	**Grandma's Song** *Gail Davies*
1/86	**Grandpa (Tell Me 'Bout The Good Old**
	Days) *Judds*
82/88	**Grass Is Greener** *Teddy Spencer*
15/49	**Grass Looks Greener Over Yonder**
	Hank Thompson
24/67	**Grass Won't Grow On A Busy Street**
	Kenny Price
F/70	**Grazin' In Greener Pastures** *Ray Price*
83/76	**(Great American) Classic Cowboy**
	Penny DeHaven
	Great Balls Of Fire
1/58	*Jerry Lee Lewis*
F/79	*Dolly Parton*
67/79	**Great Chicago Fire** *Faron Young*
12/74	**Great Divide** *Roy Clark*
32/66	**Great El Tigre (The Tiger)** *Stu Phillips*
8/75	**Great Expectations** *Buck Owens*
58/73	**Great Filling Station Holdup** *Jimmy Buffett*
10/48	**Great Long Pistol** *Jerry Irby*
63/74	**Great Mail Robbery** *Rex Allen, Jr.*
46/68	**Great Pretender** *Lamar Morris*
8/70	**Great White Horse**
	Buck Owens & Susan Raye
53/85	**Greatest Gift Of All**
	Kenny Rogers & Dolly Parton
94/80	**Greatest Love Affair** *Chuck Woolery*
22/64	**Greatest One Of All** *Melba Montgomery*
88/76	**Greatest Show On Earth** *Little David Wilkins*
	Green Berets *..see: Ballad Of*
78/73	**Green Door** *Mayf Nutter*
95/81	**Green Eyed Girl** *Sean Morton Downey*
	Green Eyes
37/82	*Tom Carlile*
82/85	*Kathy Twitty*
62/87	**Green Eyes (Cryin' Those Blue Tears)**
	Danny Davis/The Nashville Brass/Dona Mason
4/65	**Green, Green Grass Of Home** *Porter Wagoner*
57/70	**Green Green Valley** *Tex Ritter*
7/48	**Green Light** *Hank Thompson*
11/67	**Green River** *Waylon Jennings*
53/73	**Green Snakes On The Ceiling** *Johnny Bush*

90/77	**Greenback Shuffle** *King Edward IV*
26/61	**Greener Pastures** *Stonewall Jackson*
23/75	**Greener Than The Grass (We Laid On)**
	Tanya Tucker
49/68	**Greenwich Village Folk Song Salesman**
	Jim & Jesse
63/71	**Greystone Chapel** *Glen Sherley*
4/46	**Grievin' My Heart Out For You**
	Jimmie Davis
11/59	**Grin And Bear It** *Jimmy Newman*
42/69	**Groovy Grubworm** *Harlow Wilcox*
39/69	**Growin' Up** *Tex Ritter*
19/71	**Guess Away The Blues** *Don Gibson*
18/66	**Guess My Eyes Were Bigger Than My**
	Heart *Conway Twitty*
42/64	**Guess What, That's Right, She's Gone**
	Hank Williams, Jr.
	Guess Who
7/71	*Slim Whitman*
18/74	*Jerry Wallace*
47/79	**Guess Who Loves You** *Mary K. Miller*
	Guilty
3/63	*Jim Reeves*
9/83	*Statler Brothers*
92/85	*Merle Kilgore*
	Guilty Eyes
37/82	*Bandana*
81/86	*Darlene Austin*
61/69	**Guilty Street** *Kitty Wells*
8/49	**Guitar Boogie** *Arthur 'Guitar Boogie' Smith*
	Guitar Man
53/67	*Jerry Reed*
1/81	*Elvis Presley*
	Guitar Polka
1/46	*Al Dexter*
3/46	*Rosalie Allen*
7/86	**Guitar Town** *Steve Earle*
4/86	**Guitars, Cadillacs** *Dwight Yoakam*
60/70	**Gun, The** *Bob Luman*
5/71	**Gwen (Congratulations)** *Tommy Overstreet*
56/85	**Gypsies In The Palace** *Jimmy Buffett*
25/87	**Gypsies On Parade** *Sawyer Brown*
69/82	**Gypsy And Joe** *Sammi Smith*
43/79	**Gypsy Eyes** *Terri Sue Newman*
16/71	**Gypsy Feet** *Jim Reeves*
52/68	**Gypsy King** *Kitty Wells*
64/68	**Gypsy Man** *Buddy Knox*
81/74	**Gypsy Queen** *Chuck Glaser*
98/77	**Gypsy River** *Jack Paris*

H

63/74	**Habit I Can't Break** *Nick Nixon*
17/84	**Had A Dream (For The Heart)** *Judds*
9/49	**Hadacol Boogie** *Bill Nettles*
45/85	**Haircut Song** *Ray Stevens*
80/77	**Half A Love** *Roy Clark*
25/63	**Half A Man** *Willie Nelson*
8/58	**Half A Mind** *Ernest Tubb*
	Half As Much
2/52	*Hank Williams*
23/76	*Sheila Tilton*
16/59	**Half-Breed** *Marvin Rainwater*
91/73	**Half-Empty Bed** *Stan Hitchcock*
F/78	**Half My Heart's In Texas** *Ernest Tubb*
30/64	**Half Of This, Half Of That** *Wynn Stewart*
2/87	**Half Past Forever (Till I'm Blue In The**
	Heart) *T.G. Sheppard*
2/79	**Half The Way** *Crystal Gayle*

F/76	**Half The Way In, Half The Way Out**
	Little David Wilkins
56/80	**Halftime** *J.W. Thompson*
26/63	**Hall Of Shame** *Melba Montgomery*
15/85	**Hallelujah, I Love You So**
	George Jones with Brenda Lee
22/68	**Hammer And Nails** *Jimmy Dean*
94/77	**Hand Me Another Of Those** *Mickey Newbury*
52/73	**Hand Of Love** *Billy Walker*
6/87	**Hand That Rocks The Cradle**
	Glen Campbell with Steve Wariner
11/61	**Hand You're Holding Now** *Skeeter Davis*
19/78	**Handcuffed To A Heartache** *Mary K. Miller*
65/73	**Handfull Of Dimes**
	Jack Blanchard & Misty Morgan
62/84	**Handsome Man** *Karen Taylor-Good*
75/82	**Handy Man** *Joel Hughes*
2/74	**Hang In There Girl** *Freddie Hart*
	Hang On Feelin'
97/76	*Sherry Bryce*
63/78	*Red Steagall*
1/85	**Hang On To Your Heart** *Exile*
	Hang Your Head In Shame
3/45	*Bob Wills*
4/45	*Red Foley*
	Hangin' Around
34/64	*Wilburn Brothers*
9/83	*Whites*
30/79	**Hangin' In And Hangin' On** *Buck Owens*
	Hangin' On
37/67	*Gosdin Bros.*
54/67	*Leon Ashley & Margie Singleton*
16/77	*Vern Gosdin*
59/84	*Lane Brody*
82/74	**Hangin' On To What I've Got** *Frank Myers*
44/87	**Hangin' Out In Smokey Places**
	Marshall Tucker Band
26/71	**Hanging Over Me** *Jack Greene*
15/59	**Hanging Tree** *Marty Robbins*
14/49	**Hangman's Boogie** *Cowboy Copas*
12/61	**Hangover Tavern** *Hank Thompson*
12/73	**Hank** *Hank Williams, Jr.*
39/73	**Hank And Lefty Raised My Country Soul**
	Stoney Edwards
75/87	**Hank Drank** *Bobby Lee Springfield*
23/65	**Hank Williams' Guitar** *Freddie Hart*
2/76	**Hank Williams, You Wrote My Life**
	Moe Bandy
93/84	**Hanky Panky** *Mike Dekle*
1/72	**Happiest Girl In The Whole U.S.A.**
	Donna Fargo
47/68	**Happiness Hill** *Kitty Wells*
63/69	**Happiness Lives In This House** *Mac Curtis*
43/67	**Happiness Means You**
	Kitty Wells & Red Foley
	Happiness Of Having You
69/71	*Jay Lee Webb*
3/76	*Charley Pride*
47/71	**Happy Anniversary** *Roy Rogers*
3/65	**Happy Birthday** *Loretta Lynn*
1/79	**Happy Birthday Darlin'** *Conway Twitty*
3/84	**Happy Birthday Dear Heartache**
	Barbara Mandrell
7/61	**Happy Birthday To Me** *Hank Locklin*
86/82	**Happy Country Birthday** *Ronnie Rogers*
72/82	**Happy Country Birthday Darling**
	Rodney Lay
	Happy Day *..see: (It's Gonna Be A)*
89/82	**Happy Days** *Roy Clark*
54/72	**Happy Everything** *Bonnie Guitar*
81/78	**Happy Go Lucky Morning** *Terri Hollowell*
	Happy, Happy Birthday Baby
36/72	*Sandy Posey*
1/86	*Ronnie Milsap*
	Happy Heart *..see: (I've Got A)*

49/74	**Happy Hour** *Tony Booth*
	(also see: So This Is)
10/62	**Happy Journey** *Hank Locklin*
92/79	**Happy Sax** *Maury Finney*
58/71	**Happy Songs Of Love** *Tennessee Ernie Ford*
2/68	**Happy State Of Mind** *Bill Anderson*
22/68	**Happy Street** *Slim Whitman*
	Happy To Be Unhappy
11/63	*Gary Buck*
50/64	*Leroy Van Dyke*
9/66	**Happy To Be With You** *Johnny Cash*
8/79	**Happy Together** *T.G. Sheppard*
7/67	**Happy Tracks** *Kenny Price*
87/80	**Harbor Lights** *Rusty Draper*
76/85	**Hard Act To Follow** *Keith Whitley*
64/85	**Hard Baby To Rock** *Tari Hensley*
8/83	**Hard Candy Christmas** *Dolly Parton*
31/70	**Hard, Hard Traveling Man** *Dick Curless*
30/80	**Hard Hat Days And Honky Tonk Nights**
	Red Steagall
78/87	**Hard Headed Heart** *Tim Johnson*
2/58	**Hard Headed Woman** *Elvis Presley*
10/87	**Hard Livin'** *Keith Whitley*
54/67	**Hard Luck Joe** *Johnny Duncan*
	Hard Times
75/68	*Larry Steele & The Wranglers*
7/80	*Lacy J. Dalton*
82/77	**Hardly A Day Goes By** *Jean Shepard*
59/67	**Hardly Anymore** *Bob Luman*
57/74	**Harlan County** *Wayne Kemp*
10/86	**Harmony** *John Conlee*
61/71	**Harold's Super Service** *Bobby Wayne*
1/68	**Harper Valley P.T.A.** *Jeannie C. Riley*
24/68	**Harper Valley P.T.A. (Later That Same Day)** *Ben Colder*
4/46	**Harriet** *Red Foley-Roy Ross & His Ramblers*
74/84	**Harvest Moon** *Joe Waters*
35/65	**Harvest Of Sunshine** *Jimmy Dean*
68/70	**Harvey Harrington IV** *Johnny Carver*
78/80	**Hasn't It Been Good Together**
	Hank Snow & Kelly Foxton
41/67	**Hasta Luego (See You Later)** *Hank Locklin*
98/79	**Hat, The** *Roger Miller*
11/69	**Haunted House** *Compton Brothers*
51/76	**Have A Dream On Me** *Mel McDaniels*
67/80	**Have A Good Day** *Henson Cargill*
1/68	**Have A Little Faith** *David Houston*
63/70	**Have A Little Talk With Myself** *Ray Stevens*
	Have Another Drink
82/81	*Douglas*
73/84	*Doug Block*
14/58	**Have Blues Will Travel** *Eddie Noack*
30/59	**Have Heart, Will Love** *Jean Shepard*
6/85	**Have I Got A Deal For You** *Reba McEntire*
	Have I Got A Heart For You
60/83	*Chantilly*
68/86	*Rockin' Horse*
14/87	**Have I Got Some Blues For You**
	Charley Pride
47/64	**Have I Stayed Away Too Long** *Bobby Bare*
	Have I Told You Lately That I Love You
3/46	*Gene Autry*
3/46	*Tex Ritter*
4/46	*Foy Willing*
5/46	*Red Foley-Roy Ross*
74/69	*Kitty Wells & Red Foley*
67/74	**Have It Your Way** *Dave Dudley*
1/85	**Have Mercy** *Judds*
	Have You Ever Been Lonely? (Have You Ever Been Blue)
2/49	*Ernest Tubb*
5/82	*Jim Reeves & Patsy Cline*
85/81	**Have You Ever Seen The Rain** *Pam Hobbs*
50/67	**Have You Ever Wanted To?** *Lorene Mann*
67/83	**Have You Heard** *Rick & Janis Carnes*

86/87	**Have You Hurt Any Good Ones Lately**
	Sharon Robinson
32/84	**Have You Loved Your Woman Today**
	Craig Dillingham
3/75	**Have You Never Been Mellow**
	Olivia Newton-John
	Haven't I Loved You Somewhere Before
32/80	*Joe Stampley*
84/80	*Bluestone*
86/83	**Haven't We Loved Somewhere Before**
	Zella Lehr
	He Ain't Country
51/68	*James Bell*
48/72	*Claude King*
93/78	**He Ain't Heavy, He's My Brother**
	June Neyman
19/77	**He Ain't You** *Lynn Anderson*
15/84	**He Broke Your Mem'ry Last Night**
	Reba McEntire
29/85	**He Burns Me Up** *Lane Brody*
23/64	**He Called Me Baby** *Patsy Cline*
26/74	**He Can Be Mine** *Jeannie Seely*
8/74	**He Can't Fill My Shoes** *Jerry Lee Lewis*
74/88	**He Cares** *Rosie Flores*
87/82	**He Don't Make Me Cry** *Kippi Brannon*
54/71	**He Even Woke Me Up To Say Goodbye**
	Lynn Anderson
52/80	**He Gives Me Diamonds, You Give Me Chills** *Margo Smith*
1/82	**He Got You** *Ronnie Milsap*
88/75	**He Little Thing'd Her Out Of My Arms**
	Jack Greene
56/68	**He Looks A Lot Like You** *Harden Trio*
1/70	**He Loves Me All The Way** *Tammy Wynette*
77/75	**He Loves Me All To Pieces** *Ruby Falls*
73/78	**He Picked Me Up When You Let Me Down**
	Mary Lou Turner
17/64	**He Says The Same Things To Me**
	Skeeter Davis
	He Stands Real Tall
11/62	*Del Reeves*
21/65	*"Little" Jimmy Dickens*
1/80	**He Stopped Loving Her Today** *George Jones*
1/74	**He Thinks I Still Care** *Anne Murray*
46/67	**He Thought He'd Die Laughing**
	Bobby Helms
10/75	**He Took Me For A Ride** *La Costa*
13/75	**He Turns It Into Love Again** *Lynn Anderson*
45/66	**He Was Almost Persuaded** *Donna Harris*
	(also see: Almost Persuaded)
17/80	**He Was There (When I Needed You)**
	Tammy Wynette
68/72	**He Will Break Your Heart** *Johnny Williams*
22/85	**He Won't Give In** *Kathy Mattea*
15/70	**He'd Still Love Me** *Lynn Anderson*
58/74	**He'll Come Home** *Melba Montgomery*
	He'll Have To Go (Stay)
1/60	*Jim Reeves*
6/60	*Jeanne Black*
21/77	**He'll Play The Music (But You Can't Make Him Dance)** *Little David Wilkins*
68/79	**He's A Cowboy From Texas** *Ronnie McDowell*
95/79	**He's A Good Man** *Judy Argo*
32/68	**He's A Good Ole Boy** *Arlene Harden*
1/83	**He's A Heartache (Looking For A Place To Happen)** *Janie Frickie*
39/66	**He's A Jolly Good Fellow** *Charlie Walker*
94/79	**He's An Old Rock 'N' Roller** *Dickey Lee*
1/88	**He's Back And I'm Blue** *Desert Rose Band*
	He's Everywhere
25/70	*Sammi Smith*
39/75	*Marilyn Sellars*
	He's Got A Way With Women
16/67	*Hank Thompson*
63/77	*Bob Luman*

48/69	**He's Got More Love In His Little Finger**
	Billie Jo Spears
F/87	**He's Got The Whole World In His Hands**
	Cristy Lane
73/87	**He's Got You** *Don McLean*
18/87	**He's Letting Go** *Baillie & The Boys*
16/58	**He's Lost His Love For Me** *Kitty Wells*
61/71	**He's My Man** *Melba Montgomery*
8/75	**He's My Rock** *Brenda Lee*
89/82	**He's Not Entitled To Your Love**
	Johnny Rodriguez
53/67	**He's Not For Real** *Priscilla Mitchell*
79/87	**He's Not Good Enough** *Paul Proctor*
17/80	**He's Out Of My Life**
	Johnny Duncan & Janie Fricke
5/71	**He's So Fine** *Jody Miller*
100/76	**He's Still All Over You** *Jo-el Sonnier*
60/82	**He's Taken** *Lane Brody*
29/81	**He's The Fire** *Diana*
12/63	**Head Over Heels In Love With You**
	Don Gibson
7/77	**Head To Toe** *Bill Anderson*
1/81	**Headache Tomorrow (Or A Heartache Tonight)** *Mickey Gilley*
8/81	**Headed For A Heartache** *Gary Morris*
2/45	**Headin' Down The Wrong Highway**
	Ted Daffan's Texans
56/81	**Headin For A Heartache** *Cindy Hurt*
	Healin'
75/78	*Ava Barber*
23/79	*Bobby Bare*
51/77	**Heard It In A Love Song**
	Marshall Tucker Band
	Heart
77/87	*Ronnie Dove*
64/88	*Janie Frickie*
21/63	**Heart, Be Careful** *Billy Walker*
19/85	**Heart Don't Do This To Me** *Loretta Lynn*
33/76	**Heart Don't Fail Me Now** *Randy Cornor*
14/86	**Heart Don't Fall Now** *Sawyer Brown*
81/83	**Heart For A Heart** *Robin Lee*
62/67	**Heart Full Of Love** *Johnny Dallas*
1/48	**Heart Full Of Love (For A Handful Of Kisses)** *Eddy Arnold*
1/77	**Heart Healer** *Mel Tillis*
58/80	**Heart Mender** *Crystal Gayle*
84/83	**Heart Of Dixie** *Tommy Overstreet*
44/87	**Heart Of Gold** *Willie Nelson*
3/80	**Heart Of Mine** *Oak Ridge Boys*
46/85	**Heart Of The Country** *Kathy Mattea*
26/81	**Heart Of The Matter** *Kendalls*
	Heart Of The Night
96/79	*Poco*
53/83	*Juice Newton*
65/83	**Heart On The Line (Operator, Operator)**
	Larry Willoughby
8/81	**Heart On The Mend** *Sylvia*
81/83	**Heart On The Run** *Jerry Puckett*
71/87	**Heart Out Of Control** *Joni Bishop*
	Heart Over Mind
5/61	*Ray Price*
3/70	*Mel Tillis*
5/51	**Heart Strings** *Eddy Arnold*
	Heart To Heart
16/75	*Roy Clark*
40/86	*Wild Choir/Gail Davies*
5/60	**Heart To Heart Talk** *Bob Wills*
8/85	**Heart Trouble** *Steve Wariner*
25/87	**Heart Vs. Heart** *Pake McEntire*
30/80	**Heart's Been Broken** *Danny Wood*
23/84	**Heartache And A Half** *Deborah Allen*
29/63	**Heartache For A Keepsake** *Kitty Wells*
54/86	**Heartache The Size Of Texas** *Vega Brothers*
6/83	**Heartache Tonight** *Conway Twitty*

	Heartaches By The Number
2/59	*Ray Price*
26/72	*Jack Reno*
39/81	**Heartaches Of A Fool** *Willie Nelson*
83/85	**Heartbeat** *Rebecca Hall*
1/86	**Heartbeat In The Darkness** *Don Williams*
35/70	**Heartbreak Avenue** *Carl Smith*
7/82	**Heartbreak Express** *Dolly Parton*
	Heartbreak Hill
8/89	*Emmylou Harris*
55/66	*Roger Miller*
1/79	*Willie Nelson & Leon Russell*
	Heartbreak Kid ..see: (Back to the)
40/66	**Heartbreak Tennessee** *Johnny Paycheck*
1/61	**Heartbreak U.S.A.** *Kitty Wells*
1/78	**Heartbreaker** *Dolly Parton*
1/82	**Heartbroke** *Ricky Skaggs*
75/80	**Hearts** *Jimmie Peters*
26/59	**Hearts Are Lonely** *Phil Sullivan*
1/86	**Hearts Aren't Made To Break (They're Made To Love)** *Lee Greenwood*
4/55	**Hearts Of Stone** *Red Foley*
2/78	**Hearts On Fire** *Eddie Rabbitt*
60/81	**Hearts (Our Hearts)** *Susie Allanson*
100/77	**Heat Is On** *Tricia Johns*
55/69	**Heaven Below** *John Wesley Ryles*
85/77	**Heaven Can Be Anywhere (Twin Pines Theme)** *Charlie Daniels Band*
4/88	**Heaven Can't Be Found** *Hank Williams, Jr.*
5/70	**Heaven Everyday** *Mel Tillis*
18/68	**Heaven Help The Poor Working Girl**
	Norma Jean
98/78	**Heaven Is Being Good To Me**
	Dick Moebakken
47/70	**Heaven Is Just A Touch Away** *Cal Smith*
3/72	**Heaven Is My Woman's Love**
	Tommy Overstreet
73/85	**Heaven Knows** *Audie Henry*
88/80	**Heaven On A Freight Train** *Max D. Barnes*
66/73	**Heaven On Earth** *Sonny James*
1/68	**Heaven Says Hello** *Sonny James*
F/79	**Heaven Was A Drink Of Wine** *Merle Haggard*
1/77	**Heaven's Just A Sin Away** *Kendalls*
32/71	**Heavenly** *Wynn Stewart*
8/82	**Heavenly Bodies** *Earl Thomas Conley*
11/70	**Heavenly Sunshine** *Ferlin Husky*
38/66	**Heck Of A Fix In 66** *Jim Nesbitt*
53/77	**Helen** *Cal Smith*
1/86	**Hell And High Water** *T. Graham Brown*
	Hell Yes I Cheated
95/77	*James Pastell*
82/82	*Jim Owen*
93/77	**Hello Atlanta** *Chip Taylor*
39/80	**Hello Daddy, Good Morning Darling**
	Mel McDaniel
1/70	**Hello Darlin'** *Conway Twitty*
4/61	**Hello Fool** *Ralph Emery*
	(also see: Hello Walls)
13/75	**Hello I Love You** *Johnny Russell*
26/70	**Hello, I'm A Jukebox** *George Kent*
91/84	**Hello Josephine** *J.W. Thompson*
14/75	**Hello Little Bluebird** *Donna Fargo*
53/71	**Hello Little Rock** *Wynn Stewart*
1/74	**Hello Love** *Hank Snow*
	Hello Mary Lou
14/70	*Bobby Lewis*
3/85	*Statler Brothers*
4/78	**Hello Mexico (And Adios Baby To You)**
	Johnny Duncan
60/67	**Hello Number One** *Kitty Wells & Red Foley*
75/72	**Hello Operator** *Joe Stampley*
	Hello Out There
8/62	*Carl Belew*
28/74	*LaWanda Lindsey*
30/78	**Hello! Remember Me** *Billy Swan*

79/74	**Hello Summertime** *Bobby Goldsboro*		**Here I Go Again**
94/79	**Hello Texas** *Brian Collins*	13/71	*Bobby Wright*
90/78	**Hello, This Is Anna** *O.B. McClinton*	77/79	*Dorsey Burnette*
57/78	**Hello, This Is Joannie** *Paul Evans*	83/84	*Cheryl Handy*
	Hello Trouble	20/78	**Here In Love** *Dottsy*
5/63	*Orville Couch*	7/55	**Here Today And Gone Tomorrow** *Browns*
62/74	*LaWanda Lindsey*		**Here We Are Again**
1/65	**Hello Vietnam** *Johnny Wright*	26/61	*Ray Price*
30/63	**Hello Wall No. 2** *Ben Colder*	11/79	*Statler Brothers*
1/61	**Hello Walls** *Faron Young*		**Here We Go Again**
14/73	**Hello We're Lonely** *Patti Page & Tom T. Hall*	51/67	*Virgil Warner & Suzi Jane Hokum*
29/81	**Hello Woman** *Doug Kershaw*	66/72	*Johnny Duncan*
	Help Me	17/74	*Brian Shaw*
6/74	*Elvis Presley*	65/82	*Roy Clark*
38/77	*Ray Price*	95/73	**Here With You** *Bobby Lewis*
	Help Me Make It Through The Night	1/77	**Here You Come Again** *Dolly Parton*
1/71	*Sammi Smith*	42/70	**Here's A Toast To Mama** *Charlie Louvin*
4/80	*Willie Nelson*	1/76	**Here's Some Love** *Tanya Tucker*
37/75	**Help Me Make It (To My Rockin' Chair)** *B.J. Thomas*	60/79	**Here's To All The Too Hard Working Husbands** *David Houston*
	Help Yourself To Me		**Here's To The Horses**
47/75	*Roy Head*	94/77	*Mack Vickery*
97/75	*Debra Barber*	49/81	*Johnny Russell*
	Helpless	88/77	**Here's To The Next Time** *Billy Larkin*
19/64	*Joe Carson*	45/68	**Here's To You And Me** *Tex Williams*
73/68	*Dal Perkins*	41/73	**Herman Schwartz** *Stonewall Jackson*
62/88	**Henrietta** *Mel McDaniel*	14/54	**Hernando's Hideaway** *Homer & Jethro*
7/54	**Hep Cat Baby** *Eddy Arnold*	77/83	**Hero, The** *Lee Dresser*
67/69	**Her And The Car And The Mobile Home** *Dave Kirby*	64/79	**Heroes And Idols (Don't Come Easy)** *David Smith*
52/76	**Her Body Couldn't Keep You (Off My Mind)** *Gene Watson*	54/85	**Hey** *Hillary Kanter*
			Hey Baby
92/80	**Her Cheatin Heart (Made A Drunken Fool Of Me)** *Jerry Naill*	35/70	*Bobby G. Rice*
		95/78	*Donnie Rohrs*
96/81	**Her Empty Pillow (Lying Next To Mine)** *Jimmy McMillan*	7/82	*Anne Murray*
		2/83	**Hey Bartender** *Johnny Lee*
59/77	**Her L-O-V-E's Gone** *Red Steagall*	75/84	**Hey, Bottle Of Whiskey** *Gary Stewart*
96/75	**Her Memory's Gonna Kill Me** *Jim Alley*	15/68	**Hey Daddy** *Charlie Louvin*
3/76	**Her Name Is...** *George Jones*	33/77	**Hey Daisy (Where Have All The Good Times Gone)** *Tom Bresh*
59/71	**Here Come The Elephants** *Johnny Bond*	21/86	**Hey Doll Baby** *Sweethearts Of The Rodeo*
68/76	**Here Come The Flowers** *Dottie West*	1/51	**Hey, Good Lookin'** *Hank Williams*
2/68	**Here Comes Heaven** *Eddy Arnold*	58/89	**Hey Heart** *Dean Dillon*
1/71	**Here Comes Honey Again** *Sonny James*		**Hey, Joe**
10/64	**Here Comes My Baby** *Dottie West*	1/53	*Carl Smith*
79/73	**Here Comes My Little Baby** *Pat Roberts*	8/53	*Kitty Wells*
	Here Comes Santa Claus	10/81	**Hey Joe (Hey Moe)** *Moe Bandy & Joe Stampley*
4/48	*Gene Autry*	6/51	**Hey La La** *Ernest Tubb*
5/48	*Gene Autry*	51/85	**Hey Lady** *Narvel Felts*
8/50	*Gene Autry*	13/68	**Hey Little One** *Glen Campbell*
	Here Comes That Feeling Again	40/88	**Hey Little Sister** *Tom Wopat*
32/80	*Don King*	3/74	**Hey Loretta** *Loretta Lynn*
88/82	*Ralph May*	13/63	**Hey Lucille!** *Claude King*
	Here Comes That Girl Again *Tommy Overstreet*	19/76	**Hey, Lucky Lady** *Dolly Parton*
15/76		9/58	**Hey, Mr. Bluebird** *Ernest Tubb & The Wilburn Brothers*
80/76	**Here Comes That Rainy Day Feeling Again** *Connie Cato*	8/53	**Hey, Mr. Cotton Picker** *Tennessee Ernie Ford*
10/76	**Here Comes The Freedom Train** *Merle Haggard*	22/58	**Hey, Sheriff** *Rusty & Doug*
9/78	**Here Comes The Hurt Again** *Mickey Gilley*	28/76	**Hey Shirley (This Is Squirrely)** *Shirley & Squirrely*
85/88	**Here Comes The Night** *Dolly Hartt*	67/79	**Hey There** *Kenny Price*
4/68	**Here Comes The Rain, Baby** *Eddy Arnold*	21/74	**Hey There Girl** *David Rogers*
15/78	**Here Comes The Reason I Live** *Ronnie McDowell*	65/70	**Hey There Johnny** *Mayf Nutter*
73/73	**Here Comes The Sun** *Lloyd Green*	94/78	**Hey, What Do You Say (We Fall In Love)** *Sue Richards*
38/73	**Here Comes The World Again** *Johnny Bush*	1/75	**(Hey Won't You Play) Another Somebody Done Somebody Wrong Song** *B.J. Thomas*
	Here I Am Again		
3/72	*Loretta Lynn*	100/78	**Hey You** *Bobby Havens*
69/85	*Johnny Rodriguez*	9/65	**Hicktown** *Tennessee Ernie Ford*
41/76	**(Here I Am) Alone Again** *Billy Walker*	55/79	**Hide Me (In The Shadow Of Your Love)** *Judy Argo*
	Here I Am Drunk Again	36/81	**Hideaway Healing** *Stephanie Winslow*
13/60	*Clyde Beavers*	20/78	**High And Dry** *Joe Sun*
11/76	*Moe Bandy*	67/76	**High And Wild** *Earl Conley*
16/75	**Here I Am In Dallas** *Faron Young*	27/61	**High As The Mountains** *Buck Owens*

27/83	**High Cost Of Leaving** *Exile*	
33/82	**High Cost Of Loving** *Charlie Ross*	
2/85	**High Horse** *Nitty Gritty Dirt Band*	
60/72	**High On Love** *Carl Perkins*	
14/88	**High Ridin' Heroes** *David Lynn Jones*	
F/78	**High Rollin'** *Jerry Reed*	
9/58	**High School Confidential** *Jerry Lee Lewis*	
75/82	**Highlight Of '81** *Johnny Paycheck*	
1/83	**Highway 40 Blues** *Ricky Skaggs*	
15/74	**Highway Headin' South** *Porter Wagoner*	
39/66	**Highway Patrol** *Red Simpson*	
2/89	**Highway Robbery** *Tanya Tucker*	
1/85	**Highwayman**	
	Waylon Jennings/Willie Nelson/Johnny Cash/Kris Kristofferson	
79/75	**Hijack** *Hank Snow*	
91/74	**Hill, The** *Ray Griff*	
	Hillbilly Fever	
3/50	*"Little" Jimmy Dickens*	
9/50	*Ernest Tubb & Red Foley (No. 2)*	
8/81	**Hillbilly Girl With The Blues** *Lacy J. Dalton*	
5/76	**Hillbilly Heart** *Johnny Rodriguez*	
37/86	**Hillbilly Highway** *Steve Earle*	
	Hillbilly Singer *..see: Ballad Of*	
44/69	**Him And Her** *Bill Wilbourn & Kathy Morrison*	
	His And Hers	
23/63	*Tony Douglas*	
87/82	*Tony Douglas*	
13/55	**His Hands** *Tennessee Ernie Ford*	
2/66	**History Repeats Itself** *Buddy Starcher*	
44/70	**Hit The Road Jack** *Connie Eaton & Dave Peel*	
12/71	**Hitchin' A Ride** *Jack Reno*	
5/45	**Hitler's Last Letter To Hirohito**	
	Carson Robison	
53/67	**Hobo** *Ned Miller*	
50/65	**Hobo And The Rose** *Webb Pierce*	
8/51	**Hobo Boogie** *Red Foley*	
73/88	**Hocus Pocus** *Roger Marshall*	
5/56	**Hold Everything** *Red Sovine & Webb Pierce*	
	Hold Me	
73/73	*Slim Whitman*	
12/77	*Barbara Mandrell*	
57/77	*Rayburn Anthony*	
67/83	*David Rogers*	
1/89	*K.T. Oslin*	
30/81	**Hold Me Like You Never Had Me**	
	Randy Parton	
	Hold Me, Thrill Me, Kiss Me	
38/69	*Johnny & Jonie Mosby*	
60/80	*Micki Fuhrman*	
32/69	**Hold Me Tight** *Johnny Carver*	
82/83	**Hold Me Till The Last Waltz Is Over**	
	Kathy Bauer	
	Hold On	
40/81	*Rich Landers*	
24/83	*Gail Davies*	
5/86	*Rosanne Cash*	
6/89	**Hold On (A Little Longer)** *Steve Wariner*	
20/83	**Hold On, I'm Comin'**	
	Waylon Jennings & Jerry Reed	
	Hold On Tight	
45/77	*Sunday Sharpe*	
64/80	*Porter Wagoner*	
66/71	**Hold On To My Unchanging Love**	
	Jeanne Pruett	
	Hold On To Your Man	
	..see: (If You Wanna Hold On)	
25/78	**Hold Tight** *Kenny Starr*	
	Hold What You've Got	
59/68	*Diana Trask*	
36/79	*Sonny James*	
89/88	**Hold Your Fire** *Ross Lewis*	
70/82	**Holdin' On** *Jessi Colter*	
27/72	**Holdin' On (To The Love I Got)**	
	Barbara Mandrell	
56/85	**Holdin' The Family Together** *Shoppe*	
1/83	**Holding Her And Loving You**	
	Earl Thomas Conley	
7/68	**Holding On To Nothin'**	
	Porter Wagoner & Dolly Parton	
7/80	**Holding The Bag** *Moe Bandy & Joe Stampley*	
40/82	**Holed Up In Some Honky Tonk** *Joe Sun*	
3/57	**Holiday For Love** *Webb Pierce*	
82/88	**Hollywood Heroes** *Hunter Cain*	
80/80	**Hollywood Smiles** *Glen Campbell*	
44/76	**Hollywood Waltz** *Buck Owens*	
85/87	**Hollywood's Dream** *Jeff Thomas*	
75/70	**Holy Cow** *Jamey Ryan*	
	Home	
2/59	*Jim Reeves*	
10/75	*Loretta Lynn*	
57/84	**Home Again** *Judy Collins/T.G. Sheppard*	
3/86	**Home Again In My Heart**	
	Nitty Gritty Dirt Band	
79/81	**Home Along The Highway** *Tom Nix*	
53/86	**Home Grown** *Mason Dixon*	
	Home Made Love	
99/75	*Sue Richards*	
6/76	*Tom Bresh*	
86/83	*Ronnie Reno*	
3/57	**Home Of The Blues** *Johnny Cash*	
	Home Sweet Home	
32/71	*David Houston*	
73/77	*L.E. White & Lola Jean Dillon*	
82/88	**Home Team** *Madonna Dolan*	
98/77	**Home Where I Belong** *B.J. Thomas*	
10/65	**Home You're Tearin' Down** *Loretta Lynn*	
74/81	**Homebody** *Bill Anderson*	
15/59	**Homebreaker** *Skeeter Davis*	
5/69	**Homecoming** *Tom T. Hall*	
9/87	**Homecoming '63** *Keith Whitley*	
42/83	**Homegrown Tomatoes** *Guy Clark*	
	Homemade *..see: Home Made*	
38/66	**Homesick** *Bobby Bare*	
27/85	**Hometown Gossip** *Whites*	
66/70	**Homeward Bound** *Brenda Byers*	
4/45	**Honestly** *Dick Thomas*	
	Honey	
1/68	*Bobby Goldsboro*	
64/68	*Compton Brothers*	
F/79	*Orion*	
8/53	**(Honey, Baby, Hurry!) Bring Your Sweet Self Back To Me** *Lefty Frizzell*	
2/70	**Honey Come Back** *Glen Campbell*	
2/46	**Honey Do You Think It's Wrong** *Al Dexter*	
43/70	**Honey, Don't** *Mac Curtis*	
54/69	**Honey-Eyed Girl (That's You That's You)**	
	Tennessee Ernie Ford	
F/55	**Honey, Honey Bee Ball** *Hank Thompson*	
16/76	**Honey Hungry** *Mike Lunsford*	
5/89	**Honey I Dare You** *Southern Pacific*	
74/68	**Honey (I Miss You Too)** *Margaret Lewis*	
15/54	**Honey, I Need You** *Johnnie & Jack*	
17/69	**Honey, I'm Home** *Stan Hitchcock*	
12/54	**Honey Love** *Carlisles*	
41/75	**Honey On His Hands** *Jeanne Pruett*	
92/80	**Honey On The Moon** *Bonnie Guitar*	
1/84	**Honey (Open That Door)** *Ricky Skaggs*	
F/77	**(Honey, Won't You) Call Me**	
	Hank Williams, Jr.	
	Honeycomb	
7/57	*Jimmie Rodgers*	
27/86	*Gary Morris*	
4/74	**Honeymoon Feelin'** *Roy Clark*	
9/53	**Honeymoon On A Rocket Ship** *Hank Snow*	
24/74	**Honky Tonk Amnesia** *Moe Bandy*	
	Honky Tonk Blues	
2/52	*Hank Williams*	
1/80	*Charley Pride*	

Honky Tonk Crazy
97/83 *Tommy Bell*
43/87 *Gene Watson*
10/86 **Honky Tonk Crowd** *John Anderson*
95/79 **Honky Tonk Disco** *Jim West*
89/76 **Honky Tonk Fool** *Ben Reece*
11/48 **Honky Tonk Gal** *T. Texas Tyler*
Honky-Tonk Girl
9/54 *Hank Thompson*
14/60 *Loretta Lynn*
91/77 *Hank Thompson*
75/88 **Honky Tonk Heart** *Clay Blaker*
37/81 **Honky Tonk Hearts** *Dickey Lee*
70/82 **Honky Tonk Heaven** *Orion*
65/82 **Honky Tonk Magic** *Lloyd David Foster*
Honky-Tonk Man
9/56 *Johnny Horton*
11/62 *Johnny Horton*
22/70 *Bob Luman*
10/83 *Marty Robbins*
3/86 *Dwight Yoakam*
4/77 **Honky Tonk Memories** *Mickey Gilley*
1/88 **Honky Tonk Moon** *Randy Travis*
12/81 **Honky Tonk Queen**
  Moe Bandy & Joe Stampley
84/81 **Honky-Tonk Saturday Night** *Becky Hobbs*
52/69 **Honky-Tonk Season** *Charlie Walker*
1/57 **Honky Tonk Song** *Webb Pierce*
51/71 **Honky-Tonk Stardust Cowboy** *Bill Rice*
28/80 **Honky Tonk Stuff** *Jerry Lee Lewis*
69/84 **Honky Tonk Tan** *O.B. McClinton*
70/82 **Honky Tonk Tonight** *David Heavener*
78/78 **Honky Tonk Toys** *A.L. 'Doodle' Owens*
27/76 **Honky Tonk Waltz** *Ray Stevens*
17/73 **Honky Tonk Wine** *Wayne Kemp*
56/70 **Honky Tonk Women** *Charlie Walker*
32/76 **Honky Tonk Women Love Red Neck Men**
  Jerry Jaye
47/84 **Honky Tonk Women Make Honky Tonk Men** *Craig Dillingham*
59/86 **Honky Tonker** *Marty Stuart*
Honky Tonkin'
14/48 *Hank Williams*
81/74 *Troy Seals*
84/79 *Ronnie Sessions*
1/82 *Hank Williams, Jr.*
37/65 **Honky Tonkin' Again** *Buddy Cagle*
25/61 **Honky Tonkitis** *Carl Butler*
89/79 **Honky-Tonks Are Calling Me Again**
  Lenny Gault
Honkytonk *..see: Honky Tonk*
1/85 **Honor Bound** *Earl Thomas Conley*
2/81 **Hooked On Music** *Mac Davis*
9/54 **Hootchy Kootchy Henry (From Hawaii)**
  Mitchell Torok
45/64 **Hootenanny Express** *Canadian Sweethearts*
95/75 **Hope For The Flowers** *Lois Johnson*
1/75 **Hope You're Feelin' Me (Like I'm Feelin' You)** *Charley Pride*
20/78 **Hopelessly Devoted To You**
  Olivia Newton-John
52/88 **Hopelessly Falling** *Jeff Chance*
7/56 **Hoping That You're Hoping** *Louvin Brothers*
15/75 **Hoppy, Gene And Me** *Roy Rogers*
42/73 **Hoppy's Gone** *Roger Miller*
78/76 **Hot And Still Heatin'** *Jerry Jaye*
46/88 **Hot Dog** *Buck Owens*
96/79 **Hot Mama** *Dan Dickey*
61/87 **Hot Red Sweater** *Jay Booker*
Hot Rod Lincoln
14/60 *Charlie Ryan*
51/72 *Commander Cody*
65/88 *Asleep At The Wheel*

Hot Rod Race
5/51 *Arkie Shibley*
7/51 *Jimmie Dolan*
7/51 *Red Foley*
7/51 *Tiny Hill*
67/79 **Hot Stuff** *Jerry Reed*
59/80 **Hot Sunday Morning** *Wayne Armstrong*
39/83 **Hot Time In Old Town Tonight** *Mel McDaniel*
6/53 **Hot Toddy** *Red Foley*
37/85 **Hottest "Ex" In Texas** *Becky Hobbs*
1/56 **Hound Dog** *Elvis Presley*
25/79 **Hound Dog Man** *Glen Campbell*
F/73 **Hour And A Six-Pack** *Cal Smith*
24/63 **House Down The Block** *Buck Owens*
House Of Blue Lights
39/69 *Earl Richards*
17/87 *Asleep At The Wheel*
House Of Blue Lovers
24/59 *Jack Newman*
21/61 *James O'Gwynn*
13/58 **House Of Glass** *Ernest Tubb*
21/74 **House Of Love** *Dottie West*
72/67 **House Of Memories** *Dick Curless*
House Of The Rising Sun
29/74 *Jody Miller*
14/81 *Dolly Parton*
88/81 **Houston Blue** *David Rogers*
47/71 **Houston Blues** *Jeannie C. Riley*
76/85 **Houston Heartache** *Mason Dixon*
20/74 **Houston (I'm Comin' To See You)**
  Glen Campbell
1/83 **Houston (Means I'm One Day Closer To You)** *Gatlin Bros.*
52/84 **How Are You Spending My Nights**
  Gus Hardin
69/87 **How Beautiful You Are (To Me)** *Al Downing*
1/85 **How Blue** *Reba McEntire*
48/64 **How Can I Forget You** *Glenn Barber*
22/74 **How Can I Leave You Again** *John Denver*
85/74 **How Can I Tell Her** *Earl Richards*
13/59 **How Can I Think Of Tomorrow**
  James O'Gwynn
1/71 **How Can I Unlove You** *Lynn Anderson*
7/62 **(How Can I Write On Paper) What I Feel In My Heart** *Jim Reeves*
36/71 **How Can You Mend A Broken Heart**
  Duane Dee
74/75 **How Come It Took So Long (To Say Goodbye)** *Dave Dudley*
25/63 **How Come Your Dog Don't Bite Nobody But Me** *Webb Pierce & Mel Tillis*
92/80 **How Could I Do This To Me** *Sam D. Bass*
6/83 **How Could I Love Her So Much**
  Johnny Rodriguez
53/72 **How Could You Be Anything But Love**
  Ferlin Husky
29/79 **How Deep In Love Am I?** *Johnny Russell*
92/82 **How Did You Get So Good** *Denny Hilton*
1/87 **How Do I Turn You On** *Ronnie Milsap*
46/84 **How Do You Feel About Foolin' Around**
  Willie Nelson & Kris Kristofferson
11/58 **How Do You Hold A Memory** *Hank Thompson*
89/76 **How Do You Start Over** *Bob Luman*
How Do You Talk To A Baby
7/61 *Webb Pierce*
99/77 *Dugg Collins*
74/83 **How Do You Tell Someone You Love**
  Rod Rishard
80/80 **How Far Do You Want To Go**
  Ronnie McDowell
11/56 **How Far Is Heaven** *Kitty Wells*
74/74 **How Far Our Love Goes** *Billy Walker*
17/60 **How Far To Little Rock** *Stanley Brothers*
12/67 **How Fast Them Trucks Can Go** *Claude Gray*
39/76 **How Great Thou Art** *Statler Brothers*

F/78 **I Can Get Off On You** *Waylon & Willie*
86/77 **I Can Give You Love** *Mundo Earwood*
I Can Hear Kentucky Calling Me
75/80   *Osborne Brothers*
83/80   *Chet Atkins*
1/74 **I Can Help** *Billy Swan*
45/88 **I Can Love You** *Judy Rodman*
5/62 **I Can Mend Your Broken Heart** *Don Gibson*
36/73 **I Can See Clearly Now** *Lloyd Green*
18/80 **I Can See Forever In Your Eyes**
   Reba McEntire
38/80 **I Can See Forever Loving You** *Foxfire*
97/85 **I Can See Him In Her Eyes** *Adam Baker*
44/76 **I Can See Me Lovin' You Again**
   Johnny Paycheck
63/68 **I Can Spot A Cheater** *Johnny Tillotson*
22/64 **I Can Stand It (As Long As She Can)**
   Bill Phillips
13/75 **I Can Still Hear The Music In The**
   Restroom *Jerry Lee Lewis*
1/84 **I Can Tell By The Way You Dance**
   Vern Gosdin
3/70 **I Can't Be Myself** *Merle Haggard*
1/77 **I Can't Believe She Gives It All To Me**
   Conway Twitty
12/73 **I Can't Believe That It's All Over**
   Skeeter Davis
1/70 **I Can't Believe That You've Stopped Loving**
   Me *Charley Pride*
34/80 **I Can't Cheat** *Larry G. Hudson*
64/72 **I Can't Face The Bed Alone** *Henson Cargill*
3/79 **I Can't Feel You Anymore** *Loretta Lynn*
1/88 **I Can't Get Close Enough** *Exile*
5/80 **I Can't Get Enough Of You** *Razzy Bailey*
29/83 **I Can't Get Over You (Getting Over Me)**
   Bandana
43/73 **I Can't Get Over You To Save My Life**
   Lefty Frizzell
5/67 **I Can't Get There From Here** *George Jones*
37/78 **I Can't Get Up By Myself** *Brenda Kaye Perry*
37/71 **I Can't Go On Loving You** *Roy Drusky*
4/46 **I Can't Go On This Way** *Bob Wills*
66/88 **I Can't Hang On Anymore** *Dennis Payne*
I Can't Help It (If I'm Still In Love With You)
2/51   *Hank Williams*
2/75   *Linda Ronstadt*
I Can't Help Myself (Here Comes The Feeling)
2/77   *Eddie Rabbitt*
82/81   *Sami Jo Cole*
65/75 **I Can't Help Myself (Sugar Pie, Honey**
   Bunch) *Price Mitchell & Jerri Kelly*
68/86 **I Can't Help The Way I Don't Feel**
   Kaylee Adams
2/60 **(I Can't Help You) I'm Falling Too**
   Skeeter Davis
41/81 **I Can't Hold Myself In Line**
   Paycheck & Haggard
13/66 **I Can't Keep Away From You**
   Wilburn Brothers
2/77 **I Can't Love You Enough**
   Conway Twitty & Loretta Lynn
86/76 **I Can't Quit Cheatin' On You**
   Mundo Earwood
49/66 **I Can't Quit Cigarettes** *Jimmy Martin*
7/56 **I Can't Quit (I've Gone Too Far)**
   Marty Robbins
I Can't Remember
9/65   *Connie Smith*
38/80   *Stephanie Winslow*
23/60 **I Can't Run Away From Myself** *Ray Price*
8/69 **I Can't Say Goodbye** *Marty Robbins*
I Can't Say Goodbye To You
44/79   *Becky Hobbs*
30/82   *Terry Gregory*
2/44 **I Can't See For Lookin'** *King Cole Trio*

4/72 **I Can't See Me Without You** *Conway Twitty*
7/70 **I Can't Seem To Say Goodbye**
   Jerry Lee Lewis
42/73 **I Can't Sit Still** *Patti Page*
14/63 **I Can't Stay Mad At You** *Skeeter Davis*
I Can't Stop Loving You
3/58   *Kitty Wells*
7/58   *Don Gibson*
1/72   *Conway Twitty*
27/77   *Sammi Smith*
28/78   *Mary K. Miller*
17/62 **I Can't Stop (My Lovin' You)** *Buck Owens*
I Can't Stop Now
71/77   *Mike Lunsford*
72/80   *Billy Larkin*
58/88 **I Can't Take Her Anywhere** *Darrell Holt*
43/67 **I Can't Take It No Longer** *Hank Williams, Jr.*
26/60 **I Can't Tell My Heart That**
   Kitty Wells & Roy Drusky
5/53 **I Can't Wait** *Faron Young*
4/78 **I Can't Wait Any Longer** *Bill Anderson*
1/87 **I Can't Win For Losin' You**
   Earl Thomas Conley
1/75 **I Care** *Tom T. Hall*
39/74 **I Changed My Mind** *Billy Walker*
1/79 **I Cheated Me Right Out Of You** *Moe Bandy*
4/78 **I Cheated On A Good Woman's Love**
   Billy 'Crash' Craddock
37/67 **I Come Home A-Drinkin' (To A Worn-Out Wife**
   Like You) *Jay Lee Webb*
50/86 **I Could Get Used To This**
   Johnny Lee & Lane Brody
1/86 **I Could Get Used To You** *Exile*
69/85 **I Could Love You In A Heartbeat**
   Malchak & Rucker
27/66 **I Could Sing All Night** *Ferlin Husky*
30/79 **I Could Sure Use The Feeling**
   Earl Scruggs Revue
9/84 **I Could Use Another You** *Eddy Raven*
6/84 **I Could'a Had You** *Leon Everette*
3/76 **I Couldn't Be Me Without You**
   Johnny Rodriguez
4/47 **I Couldn't Believe It Was True** *Eddy Arnold*
5/53 **I Couldn't Keep From Crying** *Marty Robbins*
1/88 **I Couldn't Leave You If I Tried**
   Rodney Crowell
96/79 **I Couldn't Live Without Your Love**
   Stacey Rowe
40/67 **I Couldn't See** *George Morgan*
12/59 **I Cried A Tear** *Ernest Tubb*
21/65 **I Cried All The Way To The Bank**
   Norma Jean
68/79 **I Cry Instead** *Ron Shaw*
56/87 **I Did** *Patty Loveless*
72/88 **I Did It For Love** *Jill Jordan*
12/88 **I Didn't (Every Chance I Had)**
   Johnny Rodriguez
17/67 **I Didn't Jump The Fence** *Red Sovine*
30/82 **I Didn't Know You Could Break A Broken**
   Heart *Joe Stampley*
22/60 **I Didn't Mean To Fall In Love**
   Hank Thompson
3/70 **I Do My Swinging At Home** *David Houston*
I Don't Believe I'll Fall In Love Today
5/60   *Warren Smith*
93/78   *Gilbert Ortega*
1/56 **I Don't Believe You've Met My Baby**
   Louvin Brothers
88/88 **I Don't Call Him Daddy** *Kenny Rogers*
I Don't Care
1/55   *Webb Pierce*
1/82   *Ricky Skaggs*
1/64 **I Don't Care (Just as Long as You Love**
   Me) *Buck Owens*
16/79 **I Don't Do Like That No More** *Kendalls*

74/87 **I Don't Feel Much Like A Cowboy Tonight**
    Gene Stroman
80/80 **I Don't Feel Much Like Smilin'** *Ray Sawyer*
8/88 **I Don't Have Far To Fall** *Skip Ewing*
44/81 **I Don't Have To Crawl** *Emmylou Harris*
    I Don't Hurt Anymore
1/54   *Hank Snow*
37/77   *Narvel Felts*
92/77   *Linda Cassady*
1/84 **I Don't Know A Thing About Love (The Moon Song)** *Conway Twitty*
2/82 **I Don't Know Where To Start** *Eddie Rabbitt*
10/77 **I Don't Know Why (I Just Do)** *Marty Robbins*
1/85 **I Don't Know Why You Don't Want Me**
    Rosanne Cash
5/71 **I Don't Know You (Anymore)**
    Tommy Overstreet
12/79 **I Don't Lie** *Joe Stampley*
45/78 **I Don't Like Cheatin' Songs** *Dale McBride*
    I Don't Love Her Anymore
38/75   *Johnny Paycheck*
52/86   *Almost Brothers*
47/64 **I Don't Love Nobody** *Leon McAuliffe*
4/64 **I Don't Love You Anymore** *Charlie Louvin*
65/86 **I Don't Mean Maybe** *A.J. Masters*
74/72 **I Don't Mind Goin' Under (If It'll Get Me Over You)** *Charlie Walker*
1/85 **I Don't Mind The Thorns (If You're The Rose)** *Lee Greenwood*
8/78 **I Don't Need A Thing At All** *Gene Watson*
1/81 **I Don't Need You** *Kenny Rogers*
43/74 **I Don't Plan On Losing You** *Brian Collins*
10/83 **I Don't Remember Loving You** *John Conlee*
40/67 **I Don't See How I Can Make It** *Jean Shepard*
1/74 **I Don't See Me In Your Eyes Anymore**
    Charlie Rich
76/76 **I Don't Think I'll Ever (Get Over You)**
    Don Gibson
7/85 **I Don't Think I'm Ready For You**
    Anne Murray
13/81 **I Don't Think Love Ought To Be That Way** *Reba McEntire*
2/82 **I Don't Think She's In Love Anymore**
    Charley Pride
    I Don't Wanna Cry
3/77   *Larry Gatlin*
88/78   *Maury Finney*
2/84 **I Don't Wanna Lose Your Love** *Crystal Gayle*
1/67 **I Don't Wanna Play House** *Tammy Wynette*
13/76 **I Don't Wanna Talk It Over Anymore**
    Connie Smith
92/79 **I Don't Wanna Want You** *Scott Summer*
48/76 **I Don't Want It** *Chuck Price*
1/84 **I Don't Want To Be A Memory** *Exile*
88/76 **I Don't Want To Be A One Night Stand**
    Reba McEntire
56/77 **I Don't Want To Be Alone Tonight**
    Ray Sanders
5/51 **I Don't Want To Be Free**
    Margaret Whiting & Jimmy Wakely
    I Don't Want To Be Right
    ..see: (If Loving You Is Wrong)
21/67 **I Don't Want To Be With Me** *Conway Twitty*
33/85 **I Don't Want To Get Over You** *Whites*
1/76 **I Don't Want To Have To Marry You**
    Jim Ed Brown/Helen Cornelius
    I Don't Want To Know Your Name
54/81   *Glen Campbell*
71/86   *Wrays*
30/80 **I Don't Want To Lose** *Leon Everette*
    I Don't Want To Lose You
20/82   *Con Hunley*
81/85   *Freddie Hart*
67/79 **I Don't Want To Love You Anymore** *Dandy*

45/89 **I Don't Want To Mention Any Names**
    Burch Sisters
68/87 **I Don't Want To Set The World On Fire**
    Suzy Bogguss
40/82 **I Don't Want To Want You** *Lobo*
26/67 **I Doubt It** *Bobby Lewis*
7/84 **I Dream Of Women Like You**
    Ronnie McDowell
    I Dreamed Of A Hill-Billy Heaven
10/55   *Eddie Dean*
5/61   *Tex Ritter*
82/85 **I Dropped Your Name**
    Danny Davis/The Nashville Brass
    I Fall To Pieces
1/61   *Patsy Cline*
37/70   *Diana Trask*
89/77   *Mary Miller*
61/81   *Patsy Cline*
54/82   *Patsy Cline/Jim Reeves*
6/55 **I Feel Better All Over (More Than Anywhere's Else)** *Ferlin Husky*
    I Feel Fine
59/70   *Penny DeHaven*
9/89   *Sweethearts Of The Rodeo*
26/82 **I Feel It With You** *Kieran Kane*
7/56 **I Feel Like Cryin'** *Carl Smith*
1/81 **I Feel Like Loving You Again** *T.G. Sheppard*
14/49 **I Feel That Old Age Coming On**
    Homer & Jethro
34/85 **I Feel The Country Callin' Me** *Mac Davis*
53/68 **I Feel You, I Love You** *Bobby Helms*
1/85 **I Fell In Love Again Last Night**
    Forester Sisters
14/49 **I Find You Cheatin' On Me** *Hank Thompson*
    I Forgot More Than You'll Ever Know
1/53   *Davis Sisters*
60/72   *Jeanne Pruett*
56/85 **I Forgot That I Don't Live Here Anymore**
    Darrell Clanton
46/67 **I Forgot To Cry** *Charlie Louvin*
1/55 **I Forgot To Remember To Forget**
    Elvis Presley
    I Fought The Law
61/75   *Sam Neely*
15/78   *Hank Williams, Jr.*
5/58 **I Found My Girl In The U.S.A.**
    Jimmie Skinner
10/53 **I Found Out More Than You Ever Knew**
    Betty Cody
F/70 **I Found You Just In Time** *Lynn Anderson*
22/63 **I Gave My Wedding Dress Away** *Kitty Wells*
54/74 **I Gave Up Good Mornin' Darling**
    Red Steagall
    (I Gave You The Best Years Of My Life)
    ..see: Rock N' Roll
62/71 **I Get Lonely When It Rains** *Leroy Van Dyke*
1/66 **I Get The Fever** *Bill Anderson*
28/88 **I Give You Music** *McCarters*
    I Go To Pieces
88/80   *Tammy Jo*
39/88   *Dean Dillon*
76/88   *Trisha Lynn*
64/84 **I Got A Bad Attitude** *Gary Stewart*
F/79 **I Got A Feelin' In My Body** *Elvis Presley*
30/75 **I Got A Lot Of Hurtin' Done Today**
    Connie Smith
8/84 **I Got A Million Of 'Em** *Ronnie McDowell*
93/73 **I Got A Thing About You Baby** *Troy Seals*
40/71 **I Got A Woman** *Bob Luman*
1/84 **I Got Mexico** *Eddy Raven*
4/59 **I Got Stripes** *Johnny Cash*
3/77 **I Got The Hoss** *Mel Tillis*
56/87 **I Got The One I Wanted** *Nielsen White Band*
93/79 **I Got Western Pride** *Ray Frushay*
4/68 **I Got You** *Waylon Jennings & Anita Carter*

88/79	**I Gotta Get Back The Feeling**
	Sheila Andrews
	I Gotta Get Drunk (And I Shore Do Dread It)
27/63	*Joe Carson*
55/76	*Willie Nelson*
8/55	**I Gotta Go Get My Baby** *Justin Tubb*
	I Gotta Have My Baby Back
4/50	*Floyd Tillman*
10/50	*Red Foley*
73/67	*Glen Campbell*
15/56	**I Gotta Know** *Wanda Jackson*
72/87	**I Grow Old Too Fast (And Smart Too Slow)** *Johnny Paycheck*
48/67	**I Guess I Had Too Much To Dream Last Night** *Faron Young*
55/88	**I Guess I Just Missed You** *Canyon*
9/62	**I Guess I'll Never Learn** *Charlie Phillips*
	I Guess I'm Crazy
13/55	*Tommy Collins*
1/64	*Jim Reeves*
1/84	**I Guess It Never Hurts To Hurt Sometimes** *Oak Ridge Boys*
72/76	**I Guess You Never Loved Me Anyway** *Randy Cornor*
5/86	**I Had A Beautiful Time** *Merle Haggard*
63/87	**I Had A Heart** *Darlene Austin*
5/79	**I Had A Lovely Time** *Kendalls*
33/82	**I Had It All** *Fred Knoblock*
60/86	**I Had My Heart Set On You** *Emmylou Harris*
30/65	**I Had One Too Many** *Wilburn Brothers*
4/44	**I Hang My Head And Cry** *Gene Autry*
	I Hate Goodbyes
25/73	*Bobby Bare*
40/77	*Lois Johnson*
22/58	**I Hate Myself** *Faron Young*
16/79	**I Hate The Way I Love It** *Johnny Rodriguez & Charly McClain*
78/79	**I Hate The Way Our Love Is** *Jimmy Peters & Lynda K. Lance*
10/73	**I Hate You** *Ronnie Milsap*
17/81	**I Have A Dream** *Cristy Lane*
26/77	**I Have A Dream, I Have A Dream** *Roy Clark*
	I Have Loved You Girl (But Not Like This Before)
87/75	*Earl Conley*
2/83	*Earl Thomas Conley*
90/80	**I Have To Break The Chains That Bind Me** *Gary Goodnight*
7/88	**I Have You** *Glen Campbell*
5/53	**I Haven't Got The Heart** *Webb Pierce*
76/77	**I Haven't Learned A Thing** *Porter Wagoner*
54/67	**I Hear It Now** *Browns*
17/66	**I Hear Little Rock Calling** *Ferlin Husky*
83/88	**I Hear The South** *Vassar Clements*
29/79	**I Hear The South Callin' Me** *Hank Thompson*
91/78	**I Hear You Coming Back** *Brent Burns*
27/59	**I Hear You Talkin'** *Faron Young*
9/68	**I Heard A Heart Break Last Night** *Jim Reeves*
93/79	**I Heard A Song Today** *Tommy O'Day*
12/49	**I Heard About You** *Bud Hobbs*
33/65	**I Heard From A Memory Last Night** *Jim Edward Brown*
71/84	**I Heard It On The Radio** *Robin Lee*
45/70	**I Heard Our Song** *Dottie West*
29/71	**(I Heard That) Lonesome Whistle** *Don Gibson*
4/57	**I Heard The Bluebirds Sing** *Browns*
6/74	**I Honestly Love You** *Olivia Newton-John*
59/68	**I Hope I Like Mexico Blues** *Dallas Frazier*
36/70	**I Hope So** *Willie Nelson*
49/72	**I Hope You're Havin' Better Luck Than Me** *Crystal Gayle*
10/84	**I Hurt For You** *Deborah Allen*

69/68	**I Just Ain't Got (As Much As He's Got Going For Me)** *Gene Wyatt*
16/89	**I Just Called To Say Goodbye Again** *Larry Boone*
77/85	**I Just Came Back** *Bruce Hauser/Sawmill Creek Band*
4/82	**I Just Came Here To Dance** *David Frizzell & Shelly West*
	I Just Came Home To Count The Memories
75/75	*Bobby Wright*
15/77	*Cal Smith*
7/82	*John Anderson*
51/77	**I Just Came In Here (To Let A Little Hurt Out)** *Peggy Sue*
8/68	**I Just Came To Get My Baby** *Faron Young*
21/66	**I Just Came To Smell The Flowers** *Porter Wagoner*
1/75	**I Just Can't Get Her Out Of My Mind** *Johnny Rodriguez*
	I Just Can't Help Believing
36/70	*David Frizzell*
59/74	*David Rogers*
48/65	**I Just Can't Let You Say Goodbye** *Willie Nelson*
66/73	**I Just Can't Put Her Down** *Ronnie Sessions*
21/88	**I Just Can't Say No To You** *Moe Bandy*
5/79	**I Just Can't Stay Married To You** *Cristy Lane*
68/86	**I Just Can't Take The Leaving Anymore** *Susan Raye*
58/76	**I Just Can't (Turn My Habit Into Love)** *Kenny Starr*
73/82	**I Just Can't Turn Temptation Down** *Skip & Linda*
40/72	**I Just Couldn't Let Her Walk Away** *Dorsey Burnette*
51/66	**I Just Couldn't See The Forest** *Lefty Frizzell*
11/82	**I Just Cut Myself** *Ronnie McDowell*
92/75	**I Just Don't Give A Damn** *George Jones*
5/50	**I Just Don't Like This Kind Of Livin'** *Hank Williams*
1/79	**I Just Fall In Love Again** *Anne Murray*
28/76	**I Just Got A Feeling** *La Costa*
10/53	**(I Just Had A Date) A Lover's Quarrel** *George Morgan*
	I Just Had You On My Mind
48/74	*Sue Richards*
21/78	*Dottsy*
22/80	*Billy "Crash" Craddock*
46/83	**I Just Heard A Heart Break** *Tammy Wynette*
63/76	**I Just Love Being A Woman** *Barbara Fairchild*
78/79	**I Just Need A Coke (To Get The Whiskey Down)** *Lenny Gault*
11/81	**I Just Need You For Tonight** *Billy 'Crash' Craddock*
17/74	**I Just Started Hatin' Cheatin' Songs Today** *Moe Bandy*
43/79	**I Just Wanna Feel The Magic** *Bobby Borchers*
56/67	**I Just Want To Be Alone** *Ray Pillow*
36/81	**I Just Want To Be With You** *Sammi Smith*
14/78	**I Just Want To Be Your Everything** *Connie Smith*
	I Just Want To Love You
1/78	*Eddie Rabbitt*
97/78	*DeAnne Horn*
70/68	**I Just Wanted To Know (How the Wind Was Blowing)** *Hank Snow*
59/78	**I Just Wanted You To Know** *Ronnie McDowell*
56/68	**I Just Wasted The Rest** *Del Reeves & Bobby Goldsboro*

1/78 **I Just Wish You Were Someone I Love**
Larry Gatlin
89/79 **I Just Wonder Where He Could Be**
Tonight *Hilka & Jebry*
1/81 **I Keep Coming Back** *Razzy Bailey*
14/68 **I Keep Coming Back For More** *Dave Dudley*
43/65 **I Keep Forgettin' That I Forgot About**
You *Wynn Stewart*
I Kissed You *..see: ('Til)*
48/73 **I Knew Jesus (Before He Was A Star)**
Glen Campbell
37/88 **I Knew Love** *Nanci Griffith*
91/78 **I Knew The Mason** *Chapin Hartford*
I Knew You When
86/76 *Jerry Foster*
84/83 *Linda Ronstadt*
59/70 **I Knew You'd Be Leaving** *Peggy Little*
100/78 **I Know** *DeAnne Horn*
65/79 **I Know A Good Thing When I Feel It**
Pia Zadora
10/79 **I Know A Heartache When I See One**
Jennifer Warnes
81/81 **I Know An Ending (When It Comes)**
B.J. Wright
4/70 **I Know How** *Loretta Lynn*
1/88 **I Know How He Feels** *Reba McEntire*
74/67 **I Know How To Do It** *Bobby Braddock*
91/79 **I Know I'm Not Your Hero Anymore**
Ronnie Robbins
56/86 **I Know Love** *Everly Brothers*
67/83 **I Know My Way To You By Heart**
Marlow Tackett
I Know One
6/60 *Jim Reeves*
6/67 *Charley Pride*
96/77 **I Know The Feeling** *Jerry Green*
35/85 **I Know The Way To You By Heart**
Vern Gosdin
89/88 **I Know There's A Heart In There**
Somewhere *Chris Austin*
1/87 **I Know Where I'm Going** *Judds*
I Know You're Married (But I Love You Still)
29/66 *Bill Anderson & Jan Howard*
52/70 *Red Sovine*
39/67 **I Learn Something New Everyday**
Bill Phillips
2/44 **I Learned A Lesson I'll Never Forget**
Five Red Caps
87/80 **I Learned All About Cheatin' From You**
Becky Hobbs
53/77 **I Left My Heart In San Francisco**
Red Steagall
42/73 **I Let Another Good One Get Away**
Dorsey Burnette
1/53 **I Let The Stars Get In My Eyes** *Goldie Hill*
(also see: Don't Let)
9/82 **I Lie** *Loretta Lynn*
4/75 **I Like Beer** *Tom T. Hall*
F/80 **I Like Being Lonely** *Ann J. Morton*
I Like Everything About Loving You
62/73 *Bobbie Roy*
89/77 *Lori Parker*
23/78 **I Like Ladies In Long Black Dresses**
Bobby Borchers
57/78 **I Like To Be With You** *Ronnie Sessions*
50/68 **I Like Trains** *Bob Luman*
70/69 **I Live To Love You** *Johnny Duncan*
26/79 **I Lost My Head** *Charlie Rich*
1/74 **I Love** *Tom T. Hall*
91/76 **I Love A Beautiful Guy** *Connie Cato*
1/81 **I Love A Rainy Night** *Eddie Rabbitt*
57/75 **I Love A Rodeo** *Roger Miller*
4/49 **I Love Everything About You** *George Morgan*
95/77 **I Love Everything I Get My Hands On**
Bobby Trinity

4/83 **I Love Her Mind** *Bellamy Brothers*
I Love How You Love Me
94/78 *Joni Lee*
18/79 *Lynn Anderson*
17/83 *Glen Campbell*
76/77 **I Love It (When You Love All Over Me)**
Wayne Kemp
1/74 **I Love My Friend** *Charlie Rich*
15/81 **I Love My Truck** *Glen Campbell*
3/84 **I Love Only You** *Nitty Gritty Dirt Band*
I Love That Woman (Like The Devil Loves Sin)
84/77 *Leon Everette*
28/80 *Leon Everette*
10/75 **I Love The Blues And The Boogie Woogie**
Billy 'Crash' Craddock
40/76 **I Love The Way That You Love Me** *Ray Griff*
15/71 **I Love The Way That You've Been Lovin'**
Me *Roy Drusky*
4/64 **I Love To Dance With Annie**
Ernest Ashworth
60/76 **I Love Us** *Skeeter Davis*
22/77 **I Love What Love Is Doing To Me**
Lynn Anderson
49/77 **I Love What My Woman Does To Me**
David Rogers
3/54 **I Love You** *Ginny Wright/Jim Reeves*
I Love You A Thousand Ways
1/51 *Lefty Frizzell*
8/51 *Hawkshaw Hawkins*
9/77 *Willie Nelson*
54/81 *John Anderson*
I Love You Because
1/50 *Leon Payne*
2/50 *Ernest Tubb*
8/50 *Clyde Moody*
20/60 *Johnny Cash*
14/69 *Carl Smith*
54/76 *Jim Reeves*
F/78 *Don Gibson*
91/83 *Roger Whittaker*
12/61 **I Love You Best Of All** *Louvin Brothers*
9/86 **I Love You By Heart**
Sylvia & Michael Johnson
55/71 **I Love You Dear** *Eddy Arnold*
4/66 **I Love You Drops** *Bill Anderson*
6/74 **I Love You, I Love You**
David Houston & Barbara Mandrell
5/78 **I Love You, I Love You, I Love You**
Ronnie McDowell
(I Love You In Many Ways) *..see: Te' Quiero*
8/58 **I Love You More** *Jim Reeves*
4/73 **I Love You More And More Everyday**
Sonny James
1/69 **I Love You More Today** *Conway Twitty*
11/55 **I Love You Mostly** *Lefty Frizzell*
I Love You So Much, It Hurts
5/48 *Floyd Tillman*
1/49 *Jimmy Wakely*
10/78 **(I Love You) What Can I Say** *Jerry Reed*
1/81 **I Loved 'Em Every One** *T.G. Sheppard*
F/73 **I Loved You All Over The World** *Cal Smith*
24/88 **I Loved You Yesterday** *Lyle Lovett*
64/68 **I Made The Prison Band** *Tommy Collins*
76/88 **I Make The Living (She Makes The Living**
Worthwhile) *Danny Shirley*
45/89 **I Married Her Just Because She Looks Like**
You *Lyle Lovett*
4/84 **I May Be Used (But Baby I Ain't Used Up)**
Waylon Jennings
27/62 **I May Fall Again** *Buddy Meredith*
64/75 **I May Never Be Your Lover (But I'll Always Be**
Your Friend) *Bobby G. Rice*
1/79 **I May Never Get To Heaven** *Conway Twitty*
70/75 **I May Not Be Lovin' You** *Patti Page*
10/76 **I Met A Friend Of Your's Today** *Mel Street*

57/79 **I Might Be Awhile In New Orleans** *Johnny Russell*
37/74 **I Miss You** *Jeannie Seely*
26/77 **I Miss You Already** *Jerry Wallace*
I Miss You Already (And You're Not Even Gone)
5/57 *Faron Young*
21/60 *Jimmy Newman*
14/86 *Billy Joe Royal*
62/73 **I Miss You Most When You're Here** *Sammi Smith*
(I Miss You Too) ..see: Honey
3/60 **I Missed Me** *Jim Reeves*
38/80 **I Must Be Crazy** *Susie Allanson*
32/73 **I Must Be Doin' Something Right** *Roy Drusky*
41/77 **I Must Be Dreaming** *Don King*
7/46 **I Must Have Been Wrong** *Bob Atcher*
F/79 **I Must Have Done Something Bad** *Merle Haggard*
77/80 **I Musta Died And Gone To Texas** *Amazing Rhythm Aces*
77/88 **I Need A Good Woman Bad** *Lane Caudell*
93/80 **I Need A Little More Time** *B.J. Harrison*
76/73 **I Need Help** *Carl Smith*
1/85 **I Need More Of You** *Bellamy Brothers*
53/86 **I Need Some Good News Bad** *Chance*
11/73 **I Need Somebody Bad** *Jack Greene*
93/77 **I Need Somethin' Easy Tonight** *Danny Wood*
65/87 **I Need To Be Loved Again** *Liz Boardo*
22/77 **(I Need You) All The Time** *Eddy Arnold*
85/79 **I Need Your Help Barry Manilow** *Ray Stevens*
32/74 **I Never Get Through Missing You** *Bobby Lewis*
I Never Go Around Mirrors
25/74 *Lefty Frizzell*
96/78 *Ronnie Sessions*
I Never Got Over You
46/69 *Carl Butler & Pearl*
30/85 *Johnny Paycheck*
51/84 **I Never Had A Chance With You** *Mason Dixon*
70/74 **I Never Had It So Good** *Buddy Alan*
I Never Had The One I Wanted
9/67 *Claude Gray*
78/79 *Claude Gray*
65/82 *Solid Gold Band*
44/82 **I Never Knew The Devil's Eyes Were Blue** *Terry Gregory*
13/74 **I Never Knew (What That Song Meant Before)** *Connie Smith*
72/79 **I Never Loved Anyone Like I Love You** *Louise Mandrell*
10/85 **I Never Made Love (Till I Made Love With You)** *Mac Davis*
89/78 **I Never Meant To Harm You** *Mike Ellis*
94/76 **I Never Met A Girl Didn't Like** *Jim Mundy*
5/70 **I Never Once Stopped Loving You** *Connie Smith*
5/70 **I Never Picked Cotton** *Roy Clark*
3/84 **I Never Quite Got Back (From Loving You)** *Sylvia*
24/76 **I Never Said It Would Be Easy** *Jacky Ward*
4/49 **I Never See Maggie Alone** *Kenny Roberts*
8/78 **I Never Will Marry** *Linda Ronstadt*
54/69 **I Only Regret** *Bill Phillips*
14/87 **I Only Wanted You** *Marie Osmond*
72/81 **I Ought To Feel Guilty** *Jeanne Pruett*
1/74 **I Overlooked An Orchid** *Mickey Gilley*
72/88 **I Owe, I Owe (It's Off To Work I Go)** *David Chamberlain*
80/78 **I Owe It All To You** *Jerry Abbott*
43/84 **I Pass** *Gus Hardin*
2/87 **I Prefer The Moonlight** *Kenny Rogers*

18/78 **I Promised Her A Rainbow** *Bobby Borchers*
26/68 **I Promised You The World** *Ferlin Husky*
I Really Don't Want To Know
1/54 *Eddy Arnold*
23/71 *Elvis Presley*
19/72 *Charlie McCoy*
1/79 **I Really Got The Feeling** *Dolly Parton*
23/76 **I Really Had A Ball Last Night** *Carmol Taylor*
I Recall A Gypsy Woman
16/73 *Tommy Cash*
22/81 *B.J. Thomas*
52/69 **I Remember Loving You** *Sheb Wooley*
86/87 **(I Remember When I Thought) Whiskey Was A River** *Bobby Borchers*
I Remember You
49/66 *Slim Whitman*
44/81 *Slim Whitman*
32/88 *Glen Campbell*
1/89 **I Sang Dixie** *Dwight Yoakam*
29/63 **I Saw Me** *George Jones*
7/52 **I Saw Mommy Kissing Santa Claus** *Jimmy Boyd*
25/72 **I Saw My Lady** *Dickey Lee*
56/71 **I Saw The Light** *Nitty Gritty Dirt Band/Roy Acuff*
40/71 **I Say A Little Prayer (medley)** *Glen Campbell/Anne Murray*
68/71 **I Say, "Yes, Sir"** *Peggy Sue*
51/82 **I See An Angel Every Day** *Billy Parker*
67/73 **I See His Love All Over You** *Jim Glaser*
78/74 **I See Love** *Bobby Lewis*
99/78 **I See Love In Your Eyes** *Larry Booth*
1/74 **I See The Want To In Your Eyes** *Conway Twitty*
47/69 **I See Them Everywhere** *Hank Thompson*
75/70 **I Shook The Hand** *Freddy Weller*
2/88 **I Should Be With You** *Steve Wariner*
54/67 **I Should Get Away Awhile** *Carl Smith*
11/75 **I Should Have Married You** *Eddie Rabbitt*
71/76 **I Should Have Watched That First Step** *Wayne Kemp*
13/81 **I Should've Called** *Eddy Raven*
84/81 **I Sold All Of Tom T's Songs Last Night** *Gary Gentry*
56/83 **I Spent The Night In The Heart Of Texas** *Marlow Tackett*
27/72 **I Start Thinking About You** *Johnny Carver*
I Started Loving You Again
69/70 *Al Martino*
16/72 *Charlie McCoy*
30/70 **I Stayed Long Enough** *Billie Jo Spears*
21/64 **I Stepped Over The Line** *Hank Snow*
12/88 **I Still Believe** *Lee Greenwood*
13/75 **I Still Believe In Fairy Tales** *Tammy Wynette*
I Still Believe In Love
27/68 *Jan Howard*
46/78 *Charlie Rich*
2/81 **I Still Believe In Waltzes** *Conway Twitty & Loretta Lynn*
I Still Believe In You
82/79 *Mike Lunsford*
1/89 *Desert Rose Band*
51/74 **I Still Can't Believe You're Gone** *Willie Nelson*
48/68 **I Still Didn't Have The Sense To Go** *Johnny Carver*
17/84 **I Still Do** *Bill Medley*
14/75 **I Still Feel The Same About You** *Bill Anderson*
40/80 **(I Still Long To Hold You) Now And Then** *Reba McEntire*
95/79 **I Still Love Her Memory** *Hoot Hester*

28/82	**I Still Love You (After All These Years)**
	Tompall/Glaser Brothers
19/83	**I Still Love You In The Same Ol' Way**
	Moe Bandy
81/75	**I Still Love You (You Still Love Me)**
	Mac Davis
87/84	**I Still Love Your Body** *Tommy Overstreet*
	I Still Miss Someone
43/65	*Lester Flatt & Earl Scruggs*
38/81	*Don King*
8/49	**I Still Write Your Name** *Buddy Starchin*
74/68	**I Stole The Flowers** *Gene Wyatt*
30/86	**I Sure Need Your Lovin'** *Judy Rodman*
3/69	**I Take A Lot Of Pride In What I Am**
	Merle Haggard
6/72	**I Take It On Home** *Charlie Rich*
	I Take The Chance
2/56	*Browns*
7/63	*Ernest Ashworth*
89/87	*Kathy Edge*
52/87	**I Talked A Lot About Leaving** *Larry Boone*
	I Taught Her Everything She Knows
11/67	*Billy Walker*
31/88	*Shooters*
7/86	**I Tell It Like It Used To Be**
	T. Graham Brown
70/76	**I Thank God She Isn't Mine** *Mel McDaniels*
8/65	**I Thank My Lucky Stars** *Eddy Arnold*
17/82	**I Think About Your Lovin'** *Osmonds*
	I Think I Could Love You Better Than She (He)
	Did
70/81	*Ava Barber*
85/81	*Gabriel*
7/60	**I Think I Know** *Marion Worth*
1/81	**I Think I'll Just Stay Here And Drink**
	Merle Haggard
	I Think I'll Say Goodbye
76/75	*Mary Kay James*
77/77	*Jeris Ross*
36/86	**I Think I'm In Love** *Keith Stegall*
	(I Think I've Got A Heartache)
	..see: Excuse Me
37/72	**I Think They Call It Love**
	Don Gibson & Sue Thompson
	I Thought I Heard You Call My Name
11/57	*Porter Wagoner*
29/76	*Jessi Colter*
88/81	*Pam Hobbs*
67/86	**I Thought I'd About Had It With Love**
	Pam Tillis
10/55	**I Thought Of You** *Jean Shepard*
75/78	**I Thought You Were Easy** *Rayburn Anthony*
46/79	**I Thought You'd Never Ask**
	Louise Mandrell & R.C. Bannon
2/67	**I Threw Away The Rose** *Merle Haggard*
1/88	**I Told You So** *Randy Travis*
25/59	**I Traded Her Love (For Deep Purple Wine)**
	Roland Johnson
26/87	**I Turn To You** *George Jones*
46/74	**I Use The Soap** *Dickey Lee*
2/73	**I Used It All On You** *Nat Stuckey*
26/70	**I Wake Up In Heaven** *David Rogers*
1/68	**I Walk Alone** *Marty Robbins*
1/56	**I Walk The Line** *Johnny Cash*
6/55	**I Walked Alone Last Night** *Eddy Arnold*
12/70	**I Walked Out On Heaven** *Hank Williams, Jr.*
59/85	**I Wanna Be A Cowboy 'Til I Die** *Jim Collins*
38/81	**I Wanna Be Around** *Terri Gibbs*
3/71	**I Wanna Be Free** *Loretta Lynn*
98/78	**I Wanna Be Her #1** *Danny Hargrove*
53/71	**I Wanna Be Loved Completely** *Warner Mack*
78/77	**I Wanna Be With You Tonight** *Alabama*
33/79	**I Wanna' Come Over** *Alabama*
1/88	**I Wanna Dance With You** *Eddie Rabbitt*
63/80	**I Wanna Do It Again** *Bill Wence*

72/79	**I Wanna Go Back** *Nick Noble*
50/67	**I Wanna Go Bummin' Around** *Sonny Curtis*
72/71	**I Wanna Go Country** *Otis Williams*
18/63	**I Wanna Go Home** *Billy Grammer*
38/78	**I Wanna Go To Heaven** *Jerry Wallace*
8/85	**I Wanna Hear It From You** *Eddy Raven*
35/86	**I Wanna Hear It From Your Lips**
	Louise Mandrell
63/88	**(I Wanna Hear You) Say You Love Me**
	Again *Lisa Childress*
80/75	**I Wanna Kiss You** *Nancy Wayne*
43/88	**I Wanna Know Her Again** *Wagoneers*
	I Wanna Live
1/68	*Glen Campbell*
87/76	*Eddy Raven*
67/78	**(I Wanna) Love My Life Away** *Jody Miller*
91/80	**I Wanna Love You Tonight** *Mary Lou Turner*
5/85	**I Wanna Say Yes** *Louise Mandrell*
88/87	**I Wanna Wake Up With You** *Cristy Lane*
13/55	**I Wanna, Wanna, Wanna** *Wilburn Brothers*
63/78	**I Want A Little Cowboy** *Jerry Abbott*
18/88	**I Want A Love Like That** *Judy Rodman*
10/85	**I Want Everyone To Cry** *Restless Heart*
19/69	**I Want One** *Jack Reno*
83/80	**I Want That Feelin' Again** *Bill Anderson*
	I Want To Be A Cowboy's Sweetheart
5/46	*Rosalie Allen*
77/88	*Suzy Bogguss*
24/78	**I Want To Be In Love** *Jacky Ward*
13/56	**I Want To Be Loved** *Johnnie & Jack*
4/45	**I Want To Be Sure** *Gene Autry*
80/87	**I Want To Be Wanted** *Toni Price*
1/51	**I Want To Be With You Always** *Lefty Frizzell*
25/84	**I Want To Go Somewhere** *Keith Stegall*
18/58	**I Want To Go Where No One Knows Me**
	Jean Shepard
1/66	**I Want To Go With You** *Eddy Arnold*
9/75	**I Want To Hold You In My Dreams**
	Tonight *Stella Parton*
49/64	**I Want To Hold Your Hand** *Homer & Jethro*
2/87	**I Want To Know You Before We Make Love**
	Conway Twitty
71/74	**I Want To Lay Down Beside You**
	Marie Owens
15/61	**I Want To Live Again** *Rose Maddox*
84/78	**I Want To Love You** *Jerry Foster*
F/79	**I Want To Play My Horn On The Grand Ole'**
	Opry *Maury Finney*
	I Want To See Me In Your Eyes
30/79	*Peggy Sue*
80/81	*Gene Kennedy & Karen Jeglum*
26/74	**I Want To Stay** *Narvel Felts*
34/79	**I Want To Walk You Home** *Porter Wagoner*
35/72	**I Want You** *Johnny Carver*
22/70	**I Want You Free** *Jean Shepard*
1/56	**I Want You, I Need You, I Love You**
	Elvis Presley
22/81	**I Want You Tonight** *Johnny Rodriguez*
25/74	**I Wanta Get To You** *La Costa*
41/88	**I Wanta Wake Up With You**
	Johnny Rodriguez
1/81	**I Was Country When Country Wasn't Cool**
	Barbara Mandrell
F/57	**I Was The First One** *Hank Thompson*
	I Was The One
8/56	*Elvis Presley*
92/83	*Elvis Presley*
8/77	**I Was There** *Statler Brothers*
39/68	**I Was With Red Foley (The Night He Passed**
	Away) *Hank Williams, Jr.*
30/67	**I Washed My Face In The Morning Dew**
	Tom T. Hall
8/65	**I Washed My Hands In Muddy Water**
	Stonewall Jackson

418

23/63	**I Wasn't Even In The Running**
	Hank Thompson
15/49	**I Wasted A Nickel** *Hawkshaw Hawkins*
9/61	**I Went Out Of My Way (To Make You**
	Happy) *Roy Drusky*
3/52	**I Went To Your Wedding** *Hank Snow*
	I Will
23/58	*Ferlin Husky*
80/77	*Wendel Adkins*
21/69	**I Will Always** *Don Gibson*
	I Will Always Love You
1/74	*Dolly Parton*
84/78	*Jimmie Peters*
1/82	*Dolly Parton*
1/87	**I Will Be There** *Dan Seals*
64/68	**I Will Bring You Water** *Browns*
45/85	**I Will Dance With You**
	Karen Brooks with Johnny Cash
46/71	**I Will Drink Your Wine** *Buddy Alan*
53/88	**I Will Hold You** *Randy Vanwarmer*
45/72	**I Will Never Pass This Way Again**
	Glen Campbell
32/66	**I Will Not Blow Out The Light** *Marion Worth*
21/79	**I Will Rock And Roll With You** *Johnny Cash*
21/79	**I Will Survive** *Billie Jo Spears*
7/88	**I Will Whisper Your Name** *Michael Johnson*
29/66	**I Wish** *Ernest Ashworth*
	(I Wish A Buck Was Still Silver)
	..see: Are The Good Times Really Over
	I Wish Her Well *..see: (There She Goes)*
5/60	**I Wish I Could Fall In Love Today** *Ray Price*
14/84	**I Wish I Could Write You A Song**
	John Anderson
45/82	**I Wish I Had A Job To Shove** *Rodney Lay*
22/70	**I Wish I Had A Mommy Like You** *Patti Page*
4/49	**I Wish I Had A Nickel** *Jimmy Wakely*
	I Wish I Had Never Met Sunshine
3/46	*Gene Autry*
5/46	*Wesley Tuttle*
97/79	**I Wish I Had Your Arms Around Me**
	Red Willow Band
8/49	**I Wish I Knew** *Dolph Hewitt*
13/78	**I Wish I Loved Somebody Else** *Tom T. Hall*
27/63	**I Wish I Was A Single Girl Again**
	Jan Howard
22/80	**I Wish I Was Crazy Again**
	Johnny Cash & Waylon Jennings
	I Wish I Was Eighteen Again
F/79	*Jerry Lee Lewis*
15/80	*George Burns*
20/83	**I Wish I Was In Nashville** *Mel McDaniel*
4/89	**I Wish I Was Still In Your Dreams**
	Conway Twitty
51/69	**I Wish I Was Your Friend** *Wanda Jackson*
91/78	**I Wish I'd Never Borrowed Anybody's**
	Angel *Mike Lunsford*
52/88	**I Wish It Was That Easy Going Home**
	Jeff Dugan
67/73	**I Wish It Would Rain** *O.B. McClinton*
68/87	**I Wish She Wouldn't Treat You That Way**
	Pam Tillis
5/88	**I Wish That I Could Fall In Love Today**
	Barbara Mandrell
3/86	**I Wish That I Could Hurt That Way Again**
	T. Graham Brown
19/74	**I Wish That I Had Loved You Better**
	Eddy Arnold
64/88	**I Wish We Were Strangers** *Ogden Harless*
	I Wish You Could Have Turned My Head (And
	Left My Heart Alone)
54/78	*Sonny Throckmorton*
54/81	*Peggy Forman*
2/82	*Oak Ridge Boys*
24/73	**I Wish (You Had Stayed)** *Brian Collins*
19/60	**I Wish You Love** *Billy Walker*

4/53	**I Won't Be Home No More** *Hank Williams*
85/88	**I Won't Be Seeing Her No More**
	Touch Of Country
1/67	**I Won't Come In While He's There**
	Jim Reeves
3/65	**I Won't Forget You** *Jim Reeves*
83/81	**I Won't Last A Day Without You**
	Vince & Dianne Hatfield
44/86	**I Won't Let You Down** *Tom Wopat*
1/71	**I Won't Mention It Again**
	Ray Price
1/87	**I Won't Need You Anymore (Always And**
	Forever) *Randy Travis*
1/88	**I Won't Take Less Than Your Love**
	Tanya Tucker/Paul Davis/Paul Overstreet
8/83	**I Wonder** *Rosanne Cash*
41/72	**I Wonder How John Felt (When He Baptized**
	Jesus) *David Houston*
F/77	**I Wonder How She's Doing Now**
	Johnny Russell
	I Wonder If I Care As Much
53/81	*Dickey Lee*
30/87	*Ricky Skaggs*
2/76	**I Wonder If I Ever Said Goodbye**
	Johnny Rodriguez
1/73	**I Wonder If They Ever Think Of Me**
	Merle Haggard
4/71	**I Wonder What She'll Think About Me**
	Leaving *Conway Twitty*
10/83	**I Wonder Where We'd Be Tonight**
	Vern Gosdin
9/83	**I Wonder Who's Holding My Baby Tonight**
	Whites
81/77	**I Wonder Who's Kissing Her Now**
	George Hamilton IV
20/75	**I Wonder Whose Baby (You Are Now)**
	Jerry Wallace
	I Wore A Tie Today *..see: (Jim)*
12/78	**I Would Like To See You Again**
	Johnny Cash
9/88	**I Wouldn't Be A Man** *Don Williams*
8/65	**I Wouldn't Buy A Used Car From Him**
	Norma Jean
31/68	**I Wouldn't Change A Thing About You (But**
	Your Name) *Hank Williams, Jr.*
1/83	**I Wouldn't Change You If I Could**
	Ricky Skaggs
1/82	**I Wouldn't Have Missed It For The World**
	Ronnie Milsap
9/70	**I Wouldn't Live In New York City**
	Buck Owens
33/67	**I Wouldn't Take Her To A Dogfight**
	Charlie Walker
1/74	**I Wouldn't Want To Live If You Didn't Love**
	Me *Don Williams*
1/75	**(I'd Be) A Legend In My Time** *Ronnie Milsap*
69/68	**I'd Be Your Fool Again** *David Rogers*
30/66	**I'd Better Call The Law On Me**
	Hugh X. Lewis
74/80	**I'd Build A Bridge** *Charlie Rich*
60/77	**I'd Buy You Chattanooga** *Kenny Price*
20/85	**I'd Dance Every Dance With You** *Kendalls*
32/80	**I'd Do Anything For You** *Jacky Ward*
94/88	**I'd Do Anything For You, Baby**
	Andy & The Brown Sisters
52/82	**I'd Do It All Again** *Jerry Lee Lewis*
83/88	**I'd Do It All Over Again** *Ray Price*
	I'd Do It In A Heartbeat
87/83	*Sierra*
86/85	*Hill City*
84/75	**I'd Do It With You**
	Pat Boone with Shirley Boone
	I'd Fight The World
23/62	*Hank Cochran*
19/74	*Jim Reeves*

11/68	**I'd Give The World (To Be Back Loving You)** *Warner Mack*
11/76	**I'd Have To Be Crazy** *Willie Nelson*
	I'd Just Be Fool Enough
16/66	*Browns*
33/76	*Faron Young*
80/87	**I'd Know A Lie** *Gary McCullough*
18/59	**I'd Like To Be** *Jim Reeves*
26/78	**I'd Like To See Jesus (On The Midnight Special)** *Tammy Wynette*
5/75	**I'd Like To Sleep Til I Get Over You** *Freddie Hart*
1/80	**I'd Love To Lay You Down** *Conway Twitty*
67/68	**I'd Love To Live With You Again** *Darrell McCall*
58/82	**I'd Love You To Want Me** *Narvel Felts*
	I'd Rather Be Crazy
54/85	*Con Hunley*
64/87	*Dana McVicker*
62/82	**I'd Rather Be Doing Nothing With You** *Karen Taylor-Good*
4/69	**I'd Rather Be Gone** *Hank Williams, Jr.*
66/75	**I'd Rather Be Picked Up Here (Than Be Put Down At Home)** *Jeris Ross*
	I'd Rather Be Sorry
2/71	*Ray Price*
63/71	*Patti Page*
84/81	**I'd Rather Be The Stranger In Your Eyes** *Gene Kennedy & Karen Jeglum*
69/72	**I'd Rather Be Wantin' Love** *Leroy Van Dyke*
20/79	**I'd Rather Go On Hurtin'** *Joe Sun*
32/80	**I'd Rather Leave While I'm In Love** *Rita Coolidge*
10/61	**I'd Rather Loan You Out** *Roy Drusky*
1/71	**I'd Rather Love You** *Charley Pride*
13/56	**I'd Rather Stay Home** *Kitty Wells*
F/78	**I'd Really Love To See You Tonight** *Jacky Ward & Reba McEntire*
67/83	**I'd Say Yes** *Paulette Carlson*
84/75	**I'd Still Be In Love With You** *Brian Collins*
	I'd Throw It All Away
75/81	*Sweetwater*
66/88	*Darrell Holt*
9/52	**I'd Trade All Of My Tomorrows (For Just One Yesterday)** *Eddy Arnold*
10/57	**(I'll Always Be Your) Fraulein** *Kitty Wells*
1/88	**I'll Always Come Back** *K.T. Oslin*
30/77	**I'll Always Love You** *Cates Sisters*
75/77	**I'll Always Remember That Song** *Con Hunley*
14/55	**I'll Baby Sit With You** *Ferlin Husky*
94/82	**I'll Baby You** *Steve Mantelli*
7/45	**I'll Be Back** *Gene Autry*
1/80	**I'll Be Coming Back For More** *T.G. Sheppard*
67/74	**I'll Be Doggone** *Penny DeHaven*
1/77	**I'll Be Leaving Alone** *Charley Pride*
48/82	**I'll Be Lovin You** *Al Downing*
91/73	**I'll Be Satisfied** *Don Adams*
F/56	**I'll Be Satisfied With Love** *Faron Young*
79/83	**I'll Be Seeing You** *Leon Raines*
10/87	**I'll Be The One** *Statler Brothers*
	I'll Be There (If You Ever Want Me)
2/54	*Ray Price*
17/72	*Johnny Bush*
4/81	*Gail Davies*
	I'll Be There (When You Get Lonely)
12/57	*Ray Price*
22/78	*David Rogers*
1/78	**I'll Be True To You** *Oak Ridge Boys*
57/72	**I'll Be Whatever You Say** *Wanda Jackson*
	I'll Be Your Baby Tonight
48/68	*Glen Garrison*
33/70	*Claude King*
5/87	*Judy Rodman*

61/73	**I'll Be Your Bridge (Just Lay Me Down)** *Wilma Burgess*
54/85	**I'll Be Your Fool Tonight** *Jim Glaser*
26/82	**I'll Be Your Man Around The House** *Kieran Kane*
12/76	**I'll Be Your San Antone Rose** *Dottsy*
40/75	**I'll Be Your Steppin' Stone** *David Houston*
62/75	**I'll Believe Anything You Say** *Sami Jo*
16/59	**I'll Catch You When You Fall** *Charlie Walker*
2/87	**I'll Come Back As Another Woman** *Tanya Tucker*
10/67	**I'll Come Runnin'** *Connie Smith*
64/85	**I'll Dance The Two Step** *Shelly West*
17/74	**I'll Do Anything It Takes** *Jean Shepard*
2/77	**I'll Do It All Over Again** *Crystal Gayle*
53/81	**I'll Drink To That** *Billy Parker*
8/80	**(I'll Even Love You) Better Than I Did Then** *Statler Brothers*
60/87	**I'll Fall In Love Again** *Butch Baker*
10/78	**I'll Find It Where I Can** *Jerry Lee Lewis*
13/71	**I'll Follow You (Up To Our Cloud)** *George Jones*
88/87	**I'll Forget You** *Jerry Cooper*
3/44	**I'll Forgive You, But I Can't Forget** *Roy Acuff*
60/76	**I'll Get Better** *Sammi Smith*
	I'll Get Over You
1/76	*Crystal Gayle*
34/78	*Nick Nixon*
6/88	**I'll Give You All My Love Tonight** *Bellamy Brothers*
F/76	**I'll Go Back To Her** *Waylon Jennings*
11/64	**I'll Go Down Swinging** *Porter Wagoner*
	I'll Go On Alone
1/53	*Marty Robbins*
4/53	*Webb Pierce*
74/86	**I'll Go Steppin' Too** *Glenn Sutton*
F/70	**I'll Go To A Stranger** *Johnny Bush*
3/75	**I'll Go To My Grave Loving You** *Statler Brothers*
68/74	**I'll Have To Say I Love You In A Song** *Jim Croce*
	I'll Hold You In My Heart (Till I Can Hold You In My Arms)
1/47	*Eddy Arnold*
63/67	*Freddie Hart*
70/77	*Jan Howard*
4/61	**I'll Just Have A Cup Of Coffee (Then I'll Go)** *Claude Gray*
11/78	**I'll Just Take It Out In Love** *George Jones*
2/65	**I'll Keep Holding On (Just To Your Love)** *Sonny James*
74/88	**I'll Know The Good Times** *Bill Nunley*
43/64	**I'll Leave The Porch Lights A-Burning** *Billy Grammer*
34/66	**I'll Leave The Singin' To The Bluebirds** *Sheb Wooley*
	I'll Leave This World Loving You
47/80	*Wayne Kemp*
1/88	*Ricky Van Shelton*
14/79	**I'll Love Away Your Troubles For Awhile** *Janie Frickie*
10/68	**I'll Love You More (Than You Need)** *Jeannie Seely*
11/70	**I'll Make Amends** *Roy Drusky*
19/58	**I'll Make It All Up To You** *Jerry Lee Lewis*
65/82	**I'll Miss You** *Stella Parton*
4/81	**I'll Need Someone To Hold Me (When I Cry)** *Janie Frickie*
	I'll Never Be Free
26/69	*Johnny & Jonie Mosby*
11/78	*Jim Ed Brown/Helen Cornelius*
4/87	**I'll Never Be In Love Again** *Don Williams*
61/67	**I'll Never Be Lonesome With You** *Cal Smith*

7/73	**I'll Never Break These Chains**
	Tommy Overstreet
56/72	**I'll Never Fall In Love Again** *Liz Anderson*
1/67	**I'll Never Find Another You** *Sonny James*
1/53	**I'll Never Get Out Of This World Alive**
	Hank Williams
27/79	**I'll Never Let You Down** *Tommy Overstreet*
5/45	**I'll Never Let You Worry My Mind** *Red Foley*
70/76	**I'll Never See Him Again** *Sue Richards*
	I'll Never Slip Around Again
2/49	*Margaret Whiting & Jimmy Wakely*
6/49	*Floyd Tillman*
1/85	**I'll Never Stop Loving You** *Gary Morris*
61/67	**I'll Never Tell On You**
	Roy Drusky & Priscilla Mitchell
68/70	**I'll Paint You A Song** *Mac Davis*
5/88	**I'll Pin A Note On Your Pillow**
	Billy Joe Royal
28/78	**I'll Promise You Tomorrow** *Jerry Wallace*
80/86	**I'll Pull You Through**
	Tish Hinojosa/Craig Dillingham
8/65	**I'll Repossess My Heart** *Kitty Wells*
	I'll Sail My Ship Alone
1/50	*Moon Mullican*
10/51	*Tiny Hill*
42/79	**I'll Say It's True** *Johnny Cash*
2/70	**I'll See Him Through** *Tammy Wynette*
2/69	**I'll Share My World With You** *George Jones*
22/63	**I'll Sign** *Beverly Buff*
27/75	**I'll Sing For You** *Don Gibson*
4/47	**I'll Step Aside** *Ernest Tubb*
	I'll Still Be Loving You
45/81	*Mundo Earwood*
47/85	*Joe Stampley*
1/87	*Restless Heart*
8/69	**I'll Still Be Missing You** *Warner Mack*
8/72	**I'll Still Be Waiting For You**
	Buck Owens & The Buckaroos
9/75	**I'll Still Love You** *Jim Weatherly*
84/79	**I'll Still Love You In My Dreams**
	Sandra Kaye
100/78	**I'll Still Need You Mary Ann** *Jim Taylor*
8/50	**I'll Take A Back Seat For You** *Ernest Tubb*
75/84	**I'll Take As Much Of You As I Can Get**
	Darrell Clanton
55/76	**I'll Take It** *Roy Head*
86/80	**I'll Take The Blame** *Ricky Skaggs*
37/86	**I'll Take Your Love Anytime** *Robin Lee*
7/74	**I'll Think Of Something** *Hank Williams, Jr.*
6/74	**I'll Try A Little Bit Harder** *Donna Fargo*
2/45	**I'll Wait For You, Dear** *Al Dexter*
3/79	**I'll Wake You Up When I Get Home**
	Charlie Rich
50/88	**I'll Walk Before I'll Crawl** *Janie Frickie*
30/65	**I'll Wander Back To You** *Earl Scott*
9/75	**I'm A Believer** *Tommy Overstreet*
49/75	**I'm A Believer (In A Whole Lot Of Lovin')**
	Jean Shepard
74/83	**I'm A Booger** *Roy Clark*
5/45	**I'm A Brandin' My Darlin' With My Heart**
	Jack Guthrie
7/45	**I'm A Convict With Old Glory In My Heart**
	Elton Britt
72/84	**I'm A Country Song** *David Rogers*
22/69	**I'm A Drifter** *Bobby Goldsboro*
61/67	**I'm A Fool** *Slim Whitman*
	I'm A Fool To Care
72/75	*Donny King*
91/78	*Marcia Ball*
34/69	**I'm A Good Man (In A Bad Frame Of Mind)**
	Jack Reno
33/77	**I'm A Honky-Tonk Woman's Man**
	Bob Luman

	I'm A Long Gone Daddy
6/48	*Hank Williams*
97/79	*Norman Wade*
9/70	**I'm A Lover (Not a Fighter)** *Skeeter Davis*
	I'm A Memory
28/71	*Willie Nelson*
22/77	*Willie Nelson*
97/78	**I'm A Mender** *Danny Shatswell*
18/66	**I'm A Nut** *Leroy Pullins*
	I'm A One Woman Man
7/56	*Johnny Horton*
5/89	*George Jones*
6/66	**I'm A People** *George Jones*
1/74	**I'm A Ramblin' Man** *Waylon Jennings*
58/83	**I'm A Slave** *Jerry Reed*
1/76	**(I'm A) Stand By My Woman Man**
	Ronnie Milsap
12/54	**I'm A Stranger In My Home**
	Kitty Wells & Red Foley
52/88	**I'm A Survivor** *George Jones*
30/68	**I'm A Swinger** *Jimmy Dean*
4/72	**I'm A Truck** *Red Simpson*
57/76	**I'm A Trucker** *Johnny Russell*
32/64	**I'm A Walkin' Advertisement** *Norma Jean*
94/78	**I'm A Woman** *Jeanne Pruett*
85/78	**I'm A Woman In Love** *LaWanda Lindsey*
49/74	**(I'm A) YoYo Man** *Rick Cunha*
23/76	**I'm All Wrapped Up In You** *Don Gibson*
54/81	**I'm Almost Ready** *Leona Williams*
5/80	**I'm Already Blue** *Kendalls*
63/78	**I'm Already Taken** *Steve Wariner*
20/70	**I'm Alright** *Lynn Anderson*
2/78	**I'm Always On A Mountain When I Fall**
	Merle Haggard
3/53	**I'm An Old, Old Man** *Lefty Frizzell*
67/85	**I'm An Old Rock And Roller (Dancin' To a**
	Different Beat) *Tom Jones*
68/85	**I'm As Over You As I'm Ever Gonna Get**
	Lloyd David Foster
64/75	**I'm Available** *Kathy Barnes*
17/59	**I'm Beginning To Forget You** *Jim Reeves*
50/79	**I'm Being Good** *David Wills*
2/49	**I'm Biting My Fingernails And Thinking Of**
	You *Andrews Sisters & Ernest Tubb*
38/68	**I'm Coming Back Home To Stay** *Buckaroos*
11/57	**I'm Coming Home** *Johnny Horton*
62/77	**I'm Coming Home To Face The Music**
	Nat Stuckey
87/77	**(I'm Coming Home To You) Dixie** *Shylo*
93/79	**I'm Completely Satisfied With You**
	Lorrie & George Morgan
F/57	**I'm Counting On You** *Kitty Wells*
53/66	**I'm Doing This For Daddy** *Johnny Wright*
21/88	**I'm Down To My Last Cigarette** *K.D. Lang*
3/69	**I'm Down To My Last "I Love You"**
	David Houston
39/82	**I'm Drinkin' Canada Dry** *Burrito Brothers*
28/69	**I'm Dynamite** *Peggy Sue*
57/68	**I'm Easy To Love** *Stan Hitchcock*
	I'm Falling Too ..see: (I Can't Help You)
1/85	**I'm For Love** *Hank Williams, Jr.*
80/74	**I'm Free** *Stan Hitchcock*
3/60	**I'm Gettin' Better** *Jim Reeves*
56/79	**I'm Gettin' Into Your Love** *Ruby Falls*
30/69	**I'm Gettin' Tired Of Babyin' You** *Peggy Sue*
10/77	**I'm Getting Good At Missing You**
	(Solitaire) *Rex Allen, Jr.*
74/77	**I'm Getting High Remembering** *Bobby Lewis*
74/77	**I'm Giving You Denver** *Jean Shepard*
7/55	**I'm Glad I Got To See You Once Again**
	Hank Snow
63/84	**I'm Glad You Couldn't Sleep Last Night**
	Narvel Felts
50/68	**I'm Goin' Back Home Where I Belong**
	Buckaroos

18/82	I'm Goin' Hurtin' *Joe Stampley*
81/88	I'm Goin' Nowhere *Charlie Mitchell*
63/86	I'm Going Crazy *Kenny Dale*
41/70	I'm Going Home *Bobby Lewis*
10/85	I'm Going To Leave You Tomorrow
	John Schneider
17/71	I'm Gonna Act Right *Nat Stuckey*
54/72	I'm Gonna Be A Swinger *Webb Pierce*
5/47	I'm Gonna Be Boss From Now On *Bob Wills*
42/65	I'm Gonna Break Every Heart I Can
	Merle Haggard
2/62	I'm Gonna Change Everything *Jim Reeves*
10/55	I'm Gonna Fall Out Of Love With You
	Webb Pierce
F/79	I'm Gonna Feed 'Em Now *Porter Wagoner*
21/65	I'm Gonna Feed You Now *Porter Wagoner*
	I'm Gonna Get You
63/87	*Billy Swan*
1/88	*Eddy Raven*
65/66	I'm Gonna Hang Up My Gloves
	Charlie Walker
87/81	I'm Gonna Hang Up This Heartache
	Nancy Ruud
1/82	I'm Gonna Hire A Wino To Decorate Our
	Home *David Frizzell*
52/85	I'm Gonna Hurt Her On The Radio
	David Allan Coe
3/71	I'm Gonna Keep On Keep On Lovin' You
	Billy Walker
81/73	I'm Gonna Keep Searching *Pat Roberts*
5/72	I'm Gonna Knock On Your Door
	Billy 'Crash' Craddock
	I'm Gonna Leave You
44/66	*Anita Carter*
60/71	*Charlie Louvin & Melba Montgomery*
78/81	I'm Gonna Let Go (And Love Somebody)
	Liz Lyndell
F/57	I'm Gonna Live Some Before I Die
	Faron Young
13/88	I'm Gonna Love Her On The Radio
	Charley Pride
	I'm Gonna Love You
3/76	*Dave & Sugar*
13/79	*Glen Campbell*
10/78	I'm Gonna Love You Anyway *Cristy Lane*
9/81	I'm Gonna Love You Back To Loving Me
	Again *Joe Stampley*
	I'm Gonna Love You Right Out Of This World
21/77	*David Rogers*
76/82	*Tom Grant*
44/85	*Lloyd David Foster*
17/80	I'm Gonna Love You Tonight (In My
	Dreams) *Johnny Duncan*
79/80	I'm Gonna Love You Tonight (Like There's No
	Tomorrow) *Becky Hobbs*
69/68	I'm Gonna Make Like A Snake *Ernest Tubb*
3/88	I'm Gonna Miss You, Girl
	Michael Martin Murphey
7/68	I'm Gonna Move On *Warner Mack*
98/79	I'm Gonna Move To The Country (And Get
	Away To It All) *Jimmy Tucker*
16/81	(I'm Gonna) Put You Back On The Rack
	Dottie West
26/81	I'm Gonna Sit Right Down And Write Myself A
	Letter *Willie Nelson*
19/65	I'm Gonna Tie One On Tonight
	Wilburn Brothers
28/71	I'm Gonna Write A Song *Tommy Cash*
14/64	I'm Hanging Up The Phone
	Carl Butler & Pearl
23/80	I'm Happy Just To Dance With You
	Anne Murray
11/74	I'm Having Your Baby *Sunday Sharpe*
68/76	I'm High On You
	Jack Blanchard & Misty Morgan

65/70	I'm Holding Your Memory (But He's Holding
	You) *Jimmy Newman*
F/55	I'm Hurtin' Inside *Jim Reeves*
	I'm Hurting ..see: (Yes)
94/79	I'm In Another World *Scheree*
47/72	I'm In Love *Buddy Alan*
3/59	I'm In Love Again *George Morgan*
65/83	I'm In Love All Over Again *Cindy Hurt*
59/89	I'm In Love And He's In Dallas
	Marie Osmond
85/76	I'm In Love With My Pet Rock *Al Bolt*
38/68	I'm In Love With My Wife *David Rogers*
12/55	I'm In Love With You *Kitty Wells*
60/67	I'm In No Condition *Hank Williams, Jr.*
18/81	I'm Into Lovin' You *Billy Swan*
30/80	I'm Into The Bottle *Dean Dillon*
	I'm Just A Country Boy
37/65	*Jim Edward Brown*
1/77	*Don Williams*
73/78	I'm Just A Farmer *Cal Smith*
58/79	I'm Just A Heartache Away *Dickey Lee*
F/77	(I'm Just A) Redneck In A Rock And Roll
	Bar *Jerry Reed*
4/81	I'm Just An Old Chunk Of Coal
	John Anderson
92/78	I'm Just Gettin' By *Hank Thompson*
1/71	I'm Just Me *Charley Pride*
66/76	(I'm Just Pouring Out) What She Bottled Up In
	Me *David Wills*
96/80	(I'm Just The) Cuddle Up Kind *Hilka*
94/82	I'm Just The Leavin' Kind *Michael Meyers*
71/79	I'm Just Your Yesterday *Dandy*
	I'm Knee Deep In Loving You
86/76	*Jim Mundy*
2/77	*Dave & Sugar*
100/88	I'm Leavin' You *Ben Sanders*
91/79	I'm Leavin' You Alone *Ernie Rowell*
	I'm Leavin' It (All) Up To You
18/70	*Johnny & Jonie Mosby*
17/74	*Donny & Marie Osmond*
26/78	*Freddy Fender*
	I'm Left, You're Right, She's Gone
F/55	*Elvis Presley*
21/74	*Jerry Lee Lewis*
	I'm Letting You Go
22/59	*Webb Pierce*
15/65	*Eddy Arnold*
30/77	I'm Living A Lie *Jeanne Pruett*
9/66	I'm Living In Two Worlds *Bonnie Guitar*
79/88	(I'm Looking For Some) New Blue Jeans
	Troy Shondell
16/62	I'm Looking High And Low For My Baby
	Ernest Tubb
66/82	I'm Looking Over The Rainbow
	Sonny James
90/76	I'm Losing It All *Eddy Raven*
1/45	I'm Losing My Mind Over You *Al Dexter*
45/66	I'm Losing You (I Can Tell) *Hugh X. Lewis*
5/45	I'm Lost Without You *Al Dexter*
84/79	I'm Lovin' The Lovin' Out Of You
	Gayle Harding
88/88	I'm Loving The Wrong Man Again
	Dana McVicker
47/71	I'm Miles Away *Hagers*
11/56	I'm Movin' In *Hank Snow*
	I'm Moving On
1/50	*Hank Snow*
14/60	*Don Gibson*
5/83	*Emmylou Harris*
5/48	I'm My Own Grandpaw *Lonzo & Oscar*
37/82	(I'm Not) A Candle In The Wind *Bobby Bare*
28/66	I'm Not Crazy Yet *Ray Price*
11/77	I'm Not Easy *Billie Jo Spears*
59/79	I'm Not In The Mood (For Love)
	Ann J. Morton

81/85	**I'm Not Leaving** *Ray Price*		**I'm The One Who Loves You**
1/75	**I'm Not Lisa** *Jessi Colter*		*..see: (Remember Me)*
14/56	**I'm Not Mad, Just Hurt** *Hank Thompson*	61/85	**I'm The One Who's Breaking Up**
	I'm Not Ready Yet		*Tari Hensley*
58/68	*Blue Boys*	8/77	**I'm The Only Hell (Mama Ever Raised)**
2/80	*George Jones*		*Johnny Paycheck*
59/77	**I'm Not Responsible** *Hank Williams, Jr.*	18/79	**I'm The Singer, You're The Song**
70/73	**I'm Not Strong Enough** *Stonewall Jackson*		*Tanya Tucker*
60/77	**I'm Not That Good At Goodbye** *Stella Parton*	91/78	**I'm The South** *Eddy Arnold*
3/82	**I'm Not That Lonely Yet** *Reba McEntire*	3/44	**I'm Thinking Tonight Of My Blue Eyes**
F/84	**I'm Not That Way Anymore** *Alabama*		*Gene Autry*
62/77	**I'm Not The One You Love** *Sunday Sharpe*		**I'm Throwing Rice (At The Girl I Love)**
52/69	**I'm Not Through Loving You** *Jim Glaser*	1/49	*Eddy Arnold*
	I'm Not Through Loving You Yet	11/49	*Red Foley*
3/74	*Conway Twitty*	69/69	**I'm Tied Around Your Finger** *Jean Shepard*
60/80	*Pam Rose*		**I'm Tired**
7/84	*Louise Mandrell*	3/57	*Webb Pierce*
21/86	**I'm Not Trying To Forget You** *Willie Nelson*	18/88	*Ricky Skaggs*
79/85	**I'm On Fire** *Debonaires*	93/78	**I'm Tired Of Being Me** *Jack & Trink*
97/78	**I'm On My Way** *Captain & Tennille*	38/75	**I'm Too Use To Loving You** *Nick Nixon*
79/83	**I'm On The Outside Looking In**		**I'm Turning You Loose**
	Darlene Austin	90/74	*Nick Nixon*
54/71	**I'm On The Road To Memphis**	77/79	*Bobby Wright*
	Buddy Alan & Don Rich	8/51	**I'm Waiting Just For You**
52/72	**I'm Only A Woman** *Dottie West*		*Hawkshaw Hawkins*
1/83	**I'm Only In It For The Love** *John Conlee*		**I'm Walkin'**
71/88	**I'm Only Lonely For You** *Pal Rakes*	66/69	*Dave Peel*
92/79	**I'm Puttin' My Love Inside You** *Shylo*	96/77	*Doug Kershaw*
75/83	**I'm Ragged But I'm Right** *Johnny Cash*	3/53	**I'm Walking The Dog** *Webb Pierce*
75/75	**I'm Ready To Love You Now** *Sarah Johns*	12/49	**I'm Waltzing With Tears In My Eyes**
F/56	**I'm Really Glad You Hurt Me** *Webb Pierce*		*Cowboy Copas*
70/73	**I'm Right Where I Belong**	1/44	**I'm Wastin' My Tears On You** *Tex Ritter*
	Anthony Armstrong Jones	25/78	**I'm Way Ahead Of You**
89/78	**I'm Satisfied With You** *Leon Rausch*		*Bill Anderson & Mary Lou Turner*
60/77	**I'm Savin' Up Sunshine** *Dale McBride*	21/61	**I'm Wondering** *Lou Smith*
9/63	**I'm Saving My Love** *Skeeter Davis*	49/88	**I'm Your Puppet** *Mickey Gilley*
2/44	**I'm Sending You Red Roses** *Jimmy Wakely*		**(I'm Your Telephone Man)**
1/69	**(I'm So) Afraid Of Losing You Again**		*..see: Let My Fingers Do The Walking*
	Charley Pride	8/73	**I'm Your Woman** *Jeanne Pruett*
10/56	**I'm So In Love With You** *Wilburn Brothers*	56/86	**I've Already Cheated On You**
	I'm So Lonesome I Could Cry		*David Allan Coe & Willie Nelson*
43/66	*Hank Williams*	1/77	**I've Already Loved You In My Mind**
75/71	*Linda Plowman*		*Conway Twitty*
23/72	*Charlie McCoy*	34/74	**I've Already Stayed Too Long** *Don Adams*
17/76	*Terry Bradshaw*	1/78	**I've Always Been Crazy** *Waylon Jennings*
43/82	*Jerry Lee Lewis*	26/84	**I've Always Got The Heart To Sing The**
45/65	**I'm So Miserable Without You** *Billy Walker*		**Blues** *Bill Medley*
76/82	**I'm So Tired Of Going Home Drunk**	75/84	**I've Always Wanted To** *Wayne Kemp*
	Larry Jenkins	39/81	**I've Been A Fool** *Stephanie Winslow*
	I'm Sorry		**I've Been A Long Time Leavin' (But I'll Be A**
1/75	*John Denver*		**Long Time Gone)**
76/76	*Connie Cato*	13/66	*Roger Miller*
16/76	**I'm Sorry Charlie** *Joni Lee*	92/78	*Joey Martin*
9/77	**I'm Sorry For You, My Friend** *Moe Bandy*		**I've Been Around Enough To Know**
F/56	**I'm Sorry, I'm Not Sorry** *Carl Perkins*	78/75	*Jo-el Sonnier*
14/71	**I'm Sorry If My Love Got In Your Way**	1/84	*John Schneider*
	Connie Smith		**I've Been Everywhere**
39/80	**I'm Still In Love With You** *Larry G. Hudson*	1/62	*Hank Snow*
3/74	**I'm Still Loving You** *Joe Stampley*	16/70	*Lynn Anderson*
	I'm Still Missing You	40/85	**I've Been Had By Love Before** *Judy Rodman*
95/78	*Silver City Band*	2/88	**I've Been Lookin'** *Nitty Gritty Dirt Band*
36/88	*Ronnie McDowell*	29/78	**I've Been Loved** *Cates Sisters*
80/77	**I'm Still Movin' On** *Hank Snow*	55/69	**I've Been Loving You Too Long**
6/67	**I'm Still Not Over You** *Ray Price*		*Barbara Mandrell*
36/88	**I'm Still Your Fool** *David Slater*	90/83	**I've Been Out Of Love Too Long** *Gary Mack*
48/82	**I'm Takin' A Heart Break** *Terry Gregory*	13/84	**I've Been Rained On Too** *Tom Jones*
54/85	**I'm Takin' My Time** *Brenda Lee*	72/73	**I've Been There** *Jonie Mosby*
24/62	**(I'm The Girl On) Wolverton Mountain**	11/68	**I've Been There Before** *Ray Price*
	Jo Ann Campbell	72/76	**I've Been There Too** *Kenny Serratt*
	I'm The Man	2/55	**I've Been Thinking** *Eddy Arnold*
29/65	*Jim Kandy*	28/78	**I've Been Too Long Lonely Baby**
92/77	*Dugg Collins*		*Billy 'Crash' Craddock*
28/72	**I'm The Man On Susie's Mind** *Glenn Barber*	14/79	**I've Been Waiting For You All Of My Life**
10/85	**I'm The One Mama Warned You About**		*Con Hunley*
	Mickey Gilley	2/84	**I've Been Wrong Before** *Deborah Allen*

423

5/78 **If You Can Touch Her At All** *Willie Nelson*
100/77 **If You Can, Why Can't I** *Billy Walker*
7/66 **If You Can't Bite, Don't Growl**
　　Tommy Collins
3/73 **If You Can't Feel It (It Ain't There)**
　　Freddie Hart
1/88 **If You Change Your Mind** *Rosanne Cash*
79/84 **If You Could Only See Me Now** *Sissy Spacek*
　　If You Could See You Through My Eyes
40/79 　*Tom Grant*
63/82 　*Skip & Linda*
6/62 **If You Don't Know I Ain't Gonna Tell You**
　　George Hamilton IV
71/81 **If You Don't Know Me By Now**
　　Super Grit Cowboy Band
　　If You Don't Love Me (Why Don't You Just
　　Leave Me Alone)
61/67 　*Bob Luman*
11/77 　*Freddy Fender*
　　If You Don't Someone Else Will
3/54 　*Jimmy & Johnny*
8/54 　*Ray Price*
97/76 　*Carl Smith*
37/78 **If You Don't Want To Love Her** *Jerry Naylor*
　　If You Ever Change Your Mind
31/75 　*Ray Price*
1/80 　*Crystal Gayle*
16/77 **If You Ever Get To Houston (Look Me**
　　Down) *Don Gibson*
31/72 **If You Ever Need My Love** *Jack Greene*
12/81 **If You Go, I'll Follow You**
　　Porter Wagoner & Dolly Parton
94/77 **If You Got To Have It Your Way** *Billy Parker*
20/77 **If You Gotta Make A Fool Of Somebody**
　　Dickey Lee
1/72 **If You Leave Me Tonight I'll Cry**
　　Jerry Wallace
　　If You Love Me (Let Me Know)
2/74 　*Olivia Newton-John*
83/77 　*Brian Collins*
27/71 **If You Love Me (Really Love Me)**
　　Lamar Morris
86/74 **If You Loved Her That Way** *O.B. McClinton*
62/87 **If You Only Knew** *Kim Grayson*
99/77 **If You Really Want Me To I'll Go**
　　Silver City Band
73/70 **If You See My Baby** *Johnny Carver*
31/87 **If You Still Want A Fool Around**
　　Charley Pride
F/74 **If You Talk In Your Sleep** *Elvis Presley*
　　If You Think I Love You Now
76/78 　*Jim Mundy & Terri Melton*
74/84 　*Shoppe*
19/71 **If You Think I Love You Now (I've Just**
　　Started) *Jody Miller*
F/77 **If You Think I'm Crazy Now** *Bobby Bare*
34/71 **If You Think That It's All Right**
　　Johnny Carver
9/72 **If You Touch Me (You've Got To Love Me)**
　　Joe Stampley
32/74 **(If You Wanna Hold On) Hold On To Your**
　　Man *Diana Trask*
78/86 **If You Wanna Talk Love** *Benny Wilson*
24/66 **If You Want A Love** *Buck Owens*
8/77 **If You Want Me** *Billie Jo Spears*
74/71 **If You Want Me To I'll Go** *Bobby Wright*
59/74 **If You Want The Rainbow** *Melba Montgomery*
53/76 **If You Want To Make Me Feel At Home**
　　DeWayne Orender
7/55 **If You Were Me** *Webb Pierce*
48/86 **If You're Anything Like Your Eyes**
　　Robin Lee
26/73 **If You're Goin' Girl** *Don Gibson*
5/83 **If You're Gonna Do Me Wrong (Do It**
　　Right) *Vern Gosdin*

68/77 **If You're Gonna Love (You Gotta Hurt)**
　　Dave Conway
1/84 **If You're Gonna Play In Texas** *Alabama*
67/87 **If You're Gonna Tell Me Lies (Tell Me Good**
　　Ones) *Rosemary Sharp*
　　If You're Looking For A Fool
56/71 　*Tommy Overstreet*
34/78 　*Freddy Fender*
7/67 **If You're Not Gone Too Long** *Loretta Lynn*
　　If You're Serious About Cheatin'
61/80 　*R.C. Bannon*
77/84 　*Randy Wright*
3/82 **If You're Thinking You Want A Stranger**
　　George Strait
10/82 **If You're Waiting On Me (You're Backing**
　　Up) *Kendalls*
6/78 **If You've Got Ten Minutes (Let's Fall In**
　　Love) *Joe Stampley*
　　If You've Got The Money I've Got The Time
1/50 　*Lefty Frizzell*
1/76 　*Willie Nelson*
41/73 **If You've Got The Time** *Red Steagall*
70/83 **If Your Heart's A Rollin' Stone**
　　Helen Cornelius
29/59 **Igmoo (The Pride Of South Central High)**
　　Stonewall Jackson
　　Image Of Me
26/61 　*Bob Wills*
5/68 　*Conway Twitty*
70/84 　*Jim Reeves*
　　Imagine That
21/62 　*Patsy Cline*
79/81 　*Nancy Wood*
19/60 **Imitation Of Love** *Adrian Roland*
　　In A Different Light
　　..see: (Lookin' At Things)
5/85 **In A New York Minute** *Ronnie McDowell*
83/82 **In A Strangers Eyes** *Ralph May*
13/80 **In America** *Charlie Daniels Band*
27/85 **In Another Minute** *Jim Glaser*
74/68 **In Another World** *Webb Pierce*
86/75 **In At Eight And Out At Ten** *Don Drumm*
69/82 **In Between Lovers** *Stephanie Winslow*
38/64 **In Case You Ever Change Your Mind**
　　Bill Anderson
18/67 **In Del Rio** *Billy Walker*
75/87 **In Dreams** *Roy Orbison*
70/87 **In It Again** *A.J. Masters*
15/82 **In Like With Each Other** *Gatlin Bros.*
　　In Love
16/68 　*Wynn Stewart*
1/86 　*Ronnie Milsap*
48/86 **In Love With Her** *Adam Baker*
64/82 **In Love With Loving You** *Keith Stegall*
48/71 **In Loving Memories** *Jerry Lee Lewis*
22/80 **In Memory Of A Memory** *Johnny Paycheck*
17/61 **In Memory Of Johnny Horton** *Johnny Hardy*
61/78 **In Memory Of Your Love** *Debby Boone*
56/85 **In My Arms Again** *Del Shannon*
9/84 **In My Dreams** *Emmylou Harris*
1/84 **In My Eyes** *John Conlee*
33/74 **In My Little Corner Of The World**
　　Marie Osmond
6/79 **In No Time At All** *Ronnie Milsap*
79/79 **In Our Room** *Roy Head*
9/86 **In Over My Heart** *T.G. Sheppard*
41/84 **In Real Life** *Ed Hunnicutt*
15/76 **In Some Room Above The Street**
　　Gary Stewart
17/63 **In The Back Room Tonight** *Carl Smith*
56/82 **In The Driver's Seat** *John Schneider*
35/81 **In The Garden** *Statler Brothers*
　　In The Ghetto
50/69 　*Dolly Parton*
60/69 　*Elvis Presley*

It Hurts To Know The Feeling's Gone
42/74   *Nat Stuckey*
31/76   *Billy Mize*
29/60   **It Just Tears Me Up**   *Floyd Tillman*
48/78   **It Just Won't Feel Like Cheating**
     Sammi Smith
It Keeps Right On A-Hurtin'
4/62   *Johnny Tillotson*
17/88   *Billy Joe Royal*
38/69   **It Looks Like The Sun's Gonna Shine**
     Wilburn Brothers
70/76   **It Makes Me Giggle**   *John Denver*
48/66   **It Makes You Happy**   *Kenny Vernon*
33/72   **It Meant Nothing To Me**   *Diana Trask*
1/79   **It Must Be Love**   *Don Williams*
58/75   **It Must Have Been The Rain**   *Jim Weatherly*
91/77   **It Never Crossed My Mind**   *Tompall Glaser*
1/78   **It Only Hurts For A Little While**
     Margo Smith
62/72   **It Rains Just The Same In Missouri**
     Ray Griff
94/76   **It Sets Me Free**   *Jack Paris*
It Should Have Been Easy
22/77   *Dottsy*
79/77   *Patti Leatherwood*
30/87   *Whites*
19/85   **It Should Have Been Love By Now**
     Barbara Mandrell/Lee Greenwood
It Started All Over Again
23/78   *Vern Gosdin*
56/78   *David Houston*
68/79   **It Started With A Smile**   *Helen Cornelius*
94/77   **It Sure Is Bad To Love Her**   *Terry Stafford*
89/80   **It Sure Looks Good On You**
     Durwood Haddock
1/87   **It Takes A Little Rain (To Make Love Grow)**   *Oak Ridge Boys*
4/66   **It Takes A Lot Of Money**   *Warner Mack*
45/72   **It Takes A Lot Of Tenderness**
     Arlene Harden
60/75   **It Takes A Whole Lotta Livin' In A House**
     David Rogers
76/76   **It Takes All Day To Get Over Night**
     Doug Kershaw
51/69   **It Takes All Night Long**   *Cal Smith*
76/75   **It Takes Faith**   *Marty Robbins*
38/83   **It Takes Love**   *Al Downing*
72/79   **It Takes One To Know One**   *Bobby Hood*
2/68   **It Takes People Like You (To Make People Like Me)**   *Buck Owens*
37/73   **It Takes Time**   *Dave Dudley*
98/79   **It Takes Too Long**   *Hank Snow*
56/70   **It Takes Two**   *Connie Eaton & Dave Peel*
21/72   **It Takes You**   *Bob Luman*
5/55   **It Tickles**   *Tommy Collins*
31/84   **It Took A Lot Of Drinkin' (To Get That Woman Over Me)**   *Moe Bandy*
37/81   **It Took Us All Night Long To Say Goodbye**   *Danny Wood*
17/82   **It Turns Me Inside Out**   *Lee Greenwood*
1/77   **It Was Almost Like A Song**   *Ronnie Milsap*
7/75   **It Was Always So Easy (To Find An Unhappy Woman)**   *Moe Bandy*
80/87   **It Was Love What It Was**   *Bobby Borchers*
65/72   **It Was Love While It Lasted**   *Red Lane*
It Was The Last Time
     ..see: (If I'd Only Known)
It Was You
21/62   *Ferlin Husky*
37/81   *Billy "Crash" Craddock*
It Wasn't God Who Made Honky Tonk Angels
1/52   *Kitty Wells*
20/71   *Lynn Anderson*
10/81   *Waylon & Jessi (medley)*
51/89   **It Wasn't His Child**   *Sawyer Brown*

89/84   **It Won't Be Easy**   *Lois Johnson*
59/68   **(It Won't Be Long) And I'll Be Hating You**
     Johnny Paycheck
79/79   **It Won't Go Away**   *Rayburn Anthony*
31/86   **It Won't Hurt**   *Dwight Yoakam*
It'll Be Her
22/73   *David Rogers*
45/77   *Tompall Glaser*
89/78   *Johnny Cash*
19/82   *Tompall/Glaser Brothers*
46/81   **It'll Be Him**   *Debby Boone*
73/85   **It'll Be Love By Morning**   *Allen Frizzell*
It'll Be Me
34/83   *Tom Jones*
1/86   *Exile*
It'll Come Back
16/74   *Red Sovine*
89/80   *Red Sovine*
13/84   **It's A Be Together Night**   *Frizzell & West*
13/70   **It's A Beautiful Day**   *Wynn Stewart*
2/79   **It's A Cheating Situation**   *Moe Bandy*
71/84   **It's A Cover Up**   *Peter Isaacson*
7/77   **It's A Cowboy Lovin' Night**   *Tanya Tucker*
30/83   **It's A Dirty Job**   *Bobby Bare & Lacy J. Dalton*
88/76   **It's A Good Night For Singing**
     Jerry Jeff Walker
5/55   **It's A Great Life (If You Don't Weaken)**
     Faron Young
It's A Heartache
10/78   *Bonnie Tyler*
32/81   *Dave & Sugar*
3/58   **It's A Little More Like Heaven**   *Hank Locklin*
12/68   **It's A Long, Long Way To Georgia**
     Don Gibson
36/82   **It's A Long Way To Daytona**   *Mel Tillis*
It's A Lovely, Lovely World
5/52   *Carl Smith*
5/81   *Gail Davies*
20/73   **It's A Man's World**   *Diana Trask*
36/72   **It's A Matter Of Time**   *Elvis Presley*
6/74   **(It's A) Monsters' Holiday**   *Buck Owens*
10/85   **It's A Short Walk From Heaven To Hell**
     John Schneider
It's A Sin
1/47   *Eddy Arnold*
5/69   *Marty Robbins*
21/71   **It's A Sin To Tell A Lie**   *Slim Whitman*
16/75   **It's A Sin When You Love Somebody**
     Glen Campbell
9/81   **It's All I Can Do**   *Anne Murray*
It's All In The Game
82/74   *Slim Whitman*
53/75   *Jerry Jaye*
12/77   *Tom T. Hall*
54/83   *Merle Haggard*
1/75   **It's All In The Movies**   *Merle Haggard*
19/59   **It's All My Heartache**   *Carl Smith*
It's All Over
11/68   *David Houston & Tammy Wynette*
41/76   *Johnny Cash*
It's All Over (But The Crying)
14/66   *Kitty Wells*
3/68   *Hank Williams, Jr.*
65/69   **It's All Over (But The Shouting)**   *Bob Luman*
It's All Over Now
23/75   *Charlie Rich*
15/85   *John Anderson*
1/78   **It's All Wrong, But It's All Right**
     Dolly Parton
F/58   **It's All Your Fault**   *Ray Price*
It's Alright
7/65   *Bobby Bare*
77/76   *Billy Thunderkloud*
11/89   **(It's Always Gonna Be) Someday**   *Holly Dunn*
60/83   **It's Another Silent Night**   *Lane Brody*

5/65 It's Another World *Wilburn Brothers*
79/76 It's Bad When You're Caught (With The
Goods) *Billy Parker*
2/78 It's Been A Great Afternoon *Merle Haggard*
100/77 It's Been A Long, Long Time *Buck Owens*
It's Been One Of Those Days
68/82 *Bobby Smith*
91/84 *Lang Scott*
1/53 It's Been So Long *Webb Pierce*
1/45 It's Been So Long, Darling *Ernest Tubb*
37/70 It's Dawned On Me You're Gone *Dottie West*
25/76 It's Different With You *Mary Lou Turner*
50/76 It's Enough *Ronnie Prophet*
48/66 It's For God, And Country, And You Mom
Ernest Tubb
It's Four In The Morning
1/72 *Faron Young*
36/86 *Tom Jones*
98/78 (It's Gonna Be A) Happy Day *Jack Paris*
91/84 It's Gonna Be A Heartache *Kevin Pearce*
70/89 It's Gonna Be Love *Mark Gray & Bobbie Lace*
94/79 It's Gonna Be Magic *George James*
1/72 It's Gonna Take A Little Bit Longer
Charley Pride
55/87 It's Goodbye And So-Long To You
Lisa Childress
44/84 It's Great To Be Single Again
David Allan Coe
65/70 It's Hard To Be A Woman *Skeeter Davis*
10/80 It's Hard To Be Humble *Mac Davis*
40/82 It's Hard To Be The Dreamer (When I Used to
be the Dream) *Donna Fargo*
65/88 It's Hard To Keep This Ship Together
John Anderson
F/77 It's Heaven Loving You *Freddie Hart*
66/79 It's Hell To Know She's Heaven
Dale McBride
16/82 It's High Time *Dottie West*
It's In His Kiss *..see: Shoop Shoop Song*
It's Just A Matter Of Time
1/70 *Sonny James*
7/86 *Glen Campbell*
30/59 It's Just About Time *Johnny Cash*
46/85 It's Just Another Heartache *Bandana*
It's Like Falling In Love (Over And Over
Again)
89/81 *Chris Waters*
28/82 *Osmond Brothers*
1/80 It's Like We Never Said Goodbye
Crystal Gayle
43/64 It's Lonesome *Billy Walker*
It's Me Again, Margaret
55/74 *Paul Craft* ·
74/85 *Ray Stevens*
9/75 It's Midnight *Elvis Presley*
93/76 It's Midnight (Do You Know Where Your Baby
Is?) *Sandy Posey*
11/76 It's Morning (And I Still Love You)
Jessi Colter
73/85 It's My Life *Gary Wolf*
56/79 It's My Party *Sherry Brane*
It's My Time
51/67 *John D. Loudermilk*
50/68 *George Hamilton IV*
F/57 It's My Way *Webb Pierce*
8/51 It's No Secret *Stuart Hamblen*
51/72 (It's No) Sin *Slim Whitman*
It's Not Easy
58/78 *Dickey Lee*
66/88 *Jack Robertson*
56/75 It's Not Funny Anymore *Stella Parton*
1/72 It's Not Love (But It's Not Bad)
Merle Haggard
92/78 It's Not Over Till It's Over *Billy Walker*

It's Not Supposed To Be That Way
84/77 *Steve Young*
52/80 *Pam Rose*
88/81 It's Not The Rain *Music Row*
73/81 It's Not The Same Old You
Johnny Rodriguez
17/60 It's Not Wrong *Connie Hall*
14/77 It's Nothin' To Me *Jim Reeves*
4/81 It's Now Or Never *John Schneider*
55/75 It's Only A Barroom *Nick Nixon*
65/67 It's Only A Matter Of Time *Carl Smith*
8/87 It's Only For You *Tanya Tucker*
15/66 It's Only Love *Jeannie Seely*
68/86 It's Only Love Again *Vern Gosdin*
It's Only Make Believe
3/70 *Glen Campbell*
99/79 *Robert Gordon*
8/88 *Ronnie McDowell*
91/73 It's Only Over Now And Then *Bill Phillips*
It's Over
4/68 *Eddy Arnold*
14/80 *Rex Allen, Jr.*
62/73 It's Raining In Seattle *Wynn Stewart*
57/81 It's Really Love This Time *Family Brown*
91/78 It's Sad To Go To The Funeral (Of A Good
Love That Has Died) *Barbara Fairchild*
F/77 It's Saturday Night *Larry Wren*
62/82 It's So Close To Christmas *Bellamy Brothers*
81/77 It's So Easy *Linda Ronstadt*
95/76 It's So Easy Lovin' You *Tibor Brothers*
100/76 It's So Good Lovin' You *O.B. McClinton*
79/75 It's So Nice To Be With You *Bobby Lewis*
57/87 It's Such A Heartache *Ride The River*
1/67 It's Such A Pretty World Today
Wynn Stewart
1/88 It's Such A Small World
Rodney Crowell & Rosanne Cash
65/79 It's Summer Time *Jess Garron*
10/74 It's That Time Of Night *Jim Ed Brown*
87/75 It's The Bible Against The Bottle
Earl Conley
1/67 It's The Little Things *Sonny James*
91/77 It's The Love In You *Susan St. Marie*
20/85 It's Time For Love *Don Williams*
13/74 It's Time To Cross That Bridge *Jack Greene*
28/71 It's Time To Love Her *Billy Walker*
1/75 It's Time To Pay The Fiddler *Cal Smith*
12/79 It's Time We Talk Things Over
Rex Allen, Jr.
9/80 It's Too Late *Jeanne Pruett*
It's Too Late To Love Me Now
87/77 *Charly McClain*
87/79 *Cher*
70/88 It's Too Late To Love You Now *Brian White*
56/79 It's Too Soon To Say Goodbye
Terri Hollowell
5/80 It's True Love *Conway Twitty & Loretta Lynn*
3/46 It's Up To You *Al Dexter*
16/82 It's Who You Love *Kieran Kane*
59/83 It's Written All Over Your Face
Ronnie Dunn
30/83 It's You *Kieran Kane*
21/88 It's You Again *Exile*
55/84 It's You Alone *Gail Davies*
34/85 It's Your Reputation Talkin' *Kathy Mattea*
3/61 It's Your World *Marty Robbins*

J

44/74 **J. John Jones** *Marie Owens*

J .C. ..see: Ballad Of
36/80 **J.R.** *B.J. Wright*
72/81 **Jacamo** *Donna Fargo*
49/68 **Jack And Jill** *Jim Ed Brown*
13/48 **Jack And Jill Boogie** *Wayne Raney*
72/79 **Jack Daniel's, If You Please** *David Allan Coe*
2/67 **Jackson** *Johnny Cash & June Carter*
Jackson Ain't A Very Big Town
38/67 *Norma Jean*
21/68 *Johnny Duncan & June Stearns*
58/68 **Jacksonville** *Cal Smith*
5/58 **Jacqueline** *Bobby Helms*
54/76 **Jaded Lover** *Jerry Jeff Walker*
20/84 **Jagged Edge Of A Broken Heart** *Gail Davies*
1/57 **Jailhouse Rock** *Elvis Presley*
Jambalaya (On The Bayou)
1/52 *Hank Williams*
66/73 *Blue Ridge Rangers*
88/78 *Saskia & Serge*
F/73 **Jamestown Ferry** *Tanya Tucker*
34/72 **January, April And Me** *Dick Curless*
39/75 **January Jones** *Johnny Carver*
12/75 **Jason's Farm** *Cal Smith*
Jealous Heart
2/45 *Tex Ritter*
8/49 *Al Morgan*
14/49 *Kenny Roberts*
87/79 *Barbara Seiner*
12/64 **Jealous Hearted Me** *Eddy Arnold*
63/78 **Jealous Kind** *Rita Coolidge*
7/58 **Jealousy** *Kitty Wells*
3/74 **(Jeannie Marie) You Were A Lady**
Tommy Overstreet
51/68 **Jeannie's Afraid Of The Dark**
Porter Wagoner & Dolly Parton
Jed Clampett ..see: Ballad Of
89/82 **Jedediah Jones** *Wyley McPherson*
22/60 **Jenny Lou** *Sonny James*
88/77 **Jesse I Wanted That Award** *Sherwin Linton*
100/77 **Jessi And The Light** *La Costa*
66/69 **Jesus Is A Soul Man** *Billy Grammer*
80/76 **Jesus Is The Same In California**
Lloyd Goodson
77/81 **Jesus Let Me Slide** *Dean Dillon*
F/80 **Jesus On The Radio (Daddy on the Phone)**
Tom T. Hall
3/70 **Jesus, Take A Hold** *Merle Haggard*
Jet Set ..see: (We're Not)
7/54 **Jilted** *Red Foley*
74/71 **Jim Dandy** *Lynn Anderson*
27/61 **(Jim) I Wore A Tie Today** *Eddy Arnold*
56/70 **Jim, Jack, And Rose** *Johnny Bush*
41/70 **Jim Johnson** *Porter Wagoner*
46/83 **Jim Reeves Medley** *Jim Reeves*
26/68 **Jimmie Rodgers Blues** *Elton Britt*
5/59 **Jimmy Brown The Newsboy** *Mac Wiseman*
27/61 **Jimmy Caught The Dickens (Pushing Ernest**
In The Tub) *Chick & His Hot Rods*
24/61 **Jimmy Martinez** *Marty Robbins*
13/57 **Jingle Bell Rock** *Bobby Helms*
26/75 **Jo And The Cowboy** *Johnny Duncan*
24/68 **Jody And The Kid** *Roy Drusky*
13/69 **Joe And Mabel's 12th Street Bar And**
Grill *Nat Stuckey*
1/88 **Joe Knows How To Live** *Eddy Raven*
29/83 **Jogger, The** *Bobby Bare*
John Dillinger ..see: Ballad Of
44/66 **John Henry, Jr.** *Merle Travis*
80/74 **John Law** *Homer Joy*
17/59 **John Wesley Hardin** *Jimmie Skinner*
53/73 **John's Been Shucking My Corn**
Onie Wheeler
1/69 **Johnny B. Goode**
Buck Owens & The Buckaroos
72/69 **Johnny Let The Sunshine In** *David Ingles*

44/66 **Johnny Lose It All** *Johnny Darrell*
17/60 **Johnny, My Love (Grandma's Diary)**
Wilma Lee & Stoney Cooper
Johnny One Time
36/68 *Willie Nelson*
50/69 *Brenda Lee*
87/76 *Jesseca James*
74/76 **Johnny Orphan** *Randy Barlow*
10/59 **Johnny Reb** *Johnny Horton*
38/70 **Johnny's Cash & Charley's Pride**
Mac Wiseman
Jole Blon
4/47 *Roy Acuff*
4/47 *Harry Choates*
(also see: New Pretty Blonde, & Ode To)
4/47 **Jole Blon's Sister** *Moon Mullican*
1/74 **Jolene** *Dolly Parton*
7/70 **Jolie Girl** *Marty Robbins*
31/88 **Jones On The Jukebox** *Becky Hobbs*
1/83 **Jose Cuervo** *Shelly West*
1/71 **Joshua** *Dolly Parton*
70/72 **Josie** *Kris Kristofferson*
26/71 **Joy To The World** *Murry Kellum*
13/67 **Juanita Jones** *Stu Phillips*
38/71 **Judy** *Ray Sanders*
41/71 **Juke Box Man** *Dick Curless*
70/74 **Jukebox** *Jack Reno*
15/67 **Jukebox Charlie** *Johnny Paycheck*
98/83 **Jukebox Never Plays Home Sweet Home**
Jack Greene
61/86 **Jukebox Saturday Night** *Roy Clark*
2/87 **Julia** *Conway Twitty*
91/74 **Julianna** *Hummers*
79/77 **Julianne** *Roy Head*
15/67 **Julie** *Porter Wagoner*
81/79 **Julie (Do I Ever Cross Your Mind?)**
Wood Newton
98/77 **Julieanne (Where Are You Tonight)**
Wendel Adkins
15/86 **Juliet** *Oak Ridge Boys*
25/78 **Juliet And Romeo** *Ronnie Sessions*
47/70 **July 12, 1939** *Charlie Rich*
July, You're A Woman
71/74 *Red, White & Blue Grass*
77/74 *Ed Bruce*
100/76 **Jump Back Joe Joe** *Bill Black's Combo*
60/68 **Jump For Joy** *Statler Brothers*
83/81 **Jumper Cable Man** *Marty Robbins*
61/76 **Junk Food Junkie** *Larry Groce*
9/50 **Just A Closer Walk With Thee** *Red Foley*
35/81 **Just A Country Boy** *Rex Allen, Jr.*
78/87 **Just A Kid From Texas** *Dann Rogers*
63/87 **Just A Little Bit** *Diamonds*
10/58 **Just A Little Lonesome** *Bobby Helms*
5/84 **Just A Little Love** *Reba McEntire*
1/48 **Just A Little Lovin' (Will Go A Long, Long**
Way) *Eddy Arnold*
28/77 **Just A Little Thing** *Billy 'Crash' Craddock*
13/48 **Just A Pair Of Blue Eyes** *Tex Williams*
81/86 **Just A Woman** *Loretta Lynn*
16/62 **Just Ain't** *Lester Flatt & Earl Scruggs*
63/67 **Just An Empty Place** *Ernest Ashworth*
92/77 **Just An Old Flame** *Hank Thompson*
77/88 **(Just An) Old Wives' Tale** *Gail O'Doski*
69/74 **Just Another Cowboy Song** *Doyle Holly*
90/82 **Just Another Day In Paradise** *Bertie Higgins*
1/86 **Just Another Love** *Tanya Tucker*
35/78 **Just Another Rhinestone** *Don Drumm*
1/84 **Just Another Woman In Love** *Anne Murray*
72/85 **Just As Long As I Have You**
Gus Hardin & Dave Loggins
11/56 **Just As Long As You Love Me** *Browns*
55/71 **Just As Soon As I Get Over Loving You**
Jean Shepard
7/48 **Just Because** *Frankie Yankovic*

17/68 **Just Because I'm A Woman** *Dolly Parton*
60/72 **Just Because I'm Still In Love With You**
  Bobby Wright
28/64 **Just Between The Two Of Us**
  Merle Haggard & Bonnie Owens
65/79 **Just Between Us** *Bill Woody*
9/67 **Just Between You And Me** *Charley Pride*
13/67 **Just Beyond The Moon** *Tex Ritter*
54/69 **Just Blow In His Ear** *David Wilkins*
2/55 **Just Call Me Lonesome** *Eddy Arnold*
52/87 **Just Enough Love** *Ray Price*
30/81 **Just Enough Love (For One Woman)**
  Bobby Smith
23/74 **Just Enough To Make Me Stay** *Bob Luman*
43/69 **Just Enough To Start Me Dreamin'**
  Jeannie Seely
56/74 **Just For Old Times Sake** *Eddy Arnold*
78/82 **Just For The Moment** *Brenda Lee*
5/72 **Just For What I Am** *Connie Smith*
4/68 **Just For You** *Ferlin Husky*
1/75 **Just Get Up And Close The Door**
  Johnny Rodriguez
98/77 **Just Gettin' By** *Red Sovine*
72/83 **Just Give Me One More Night** *Cole Young*
  Just Give Me What You Think Is Fair
51/80   *Rex Gosdin with Tommy Jennings*
7/82   *Leon Everette*
1/79 **Just Good Ol' Boys**
  Moe Bandy & Joe Stampley
46/81 **Just Got Back From No Man's Land**
  Wayne Kemp
68/78 **Just Hangin' On** *Mel Street*
12/69 **Just Hold My Hand** *Johnny & Jonie Mosby*
  Just Hooked On Country
42/82   *Albert Coleman's Atlanta Pops (Parts I & II)*
77/82   *Albert Coleman's Atlanta Pops (Part III)*
  Just In Case
4/76   *Ronnie Milsap*
1/86   *Forester Sisters*
70/72 **Just In Time (To Watch Love Die)**
  Charlie Louvin
31/78 **Just Keep It Up** *Narvel Felts*
80/79 **Just Let Me Make Believe** *Jim Chesnut*
16/81 **Just Like Me** *Terry Gregory*
11/79 **Just Like Real People** *Kendalls*
92/84 **Just Like That** *Malchak & Rucker*
46/72 **Just Like Walkin' In The Sunshine**
  Jean Shepard
25/75 **Just Like Your Daddy** *Jeanne Pruett*
10/79 **Just Long Enough To Say Goodbye**
  Mickey Gilley
5/88 **Just Lovin' You** *O'Kanes*
  Just Married
1/58   *Marty Robbins*
F/82   *Louise Mandrell & RC Bannon*
80/82 **Just Once** *John Wesley Ryles*
9/88 **Just One Kiss** *Exile*
66/77 **Just One Kiss Magdelena** *Bobby G. Rice*
3/56 **Just One More** *George Jones*
23/74 **Just One More Song**
  Jack Blanchard & Misty Morgan
70/72 **Just One More Time** *Johnny & Jonie Mosby*
67/87 **Just One Night Won't Do** *Al Downing*
  Just One Time
2/60   *Don Gibson*
2/71   *Connie Smith*
17/81   *Tompall/Glaser Brothers*
  Just Out Of Reach
100/76   *Perry Como*
77/78   *Mack White*
74/84   *Merle Kilgore*
37/78 **Just Out Of Reach Of My Two Open Arms**
  Larry G. Hudson
84/86 **Just Out Riding Around** *Barbara Fairchild*
39/72 **Just Plain Lonely** *Ferlin Husky*

Just Say Yes ..*see: (Do You Love Me)*
5/69 **Just Someone I Used To Know**
  Porter Wagoner & Dolly Parton
76/79 **Just Stay With Me** *Terri Hollowell*
17/73 **Just Thank Me** *David Rogers*
22/65 **Just Thought I'd Let You Know**
  Carl Butler & Pearl
70/67 **Just To Be Where You Are** *Wilburn Brothers*
82/77 **Just To Prove My Love For You**
  David Allan Coe
71/80 **Just To Prove My Love To You**
  Jimmy Snyder
  Just To Satisfy You
31/65   *Bobby Bare*
1/82   *Waylon & Willie*
94/87 **Just Try Texas** *Mike Lord*
7/53 **Just Wait Till I Get You Alone** *Carl Smith*
45/76 **Just Want To Taste Your Wine** *Billy Swan*
9/73 **Just What I Had In Mind** *Faron Young*
44/73 **Just What I've Been Looking For**
  Dottie West
52/80 **Just What The Doctor Ordered** *Becky Hobbs*
  Just When I Needed You Most
40/79   *Diana*
71/79   *Randy Vanwarmer*
71/76 **Just You 'N' Me** *Sammi Smith*

15/82 **Kansas City Lights** *Steve Wariner*
2/70 **Kansas City Song** *Buck Owens*
7/65 **Kansas City Star** *Roger Miller*
  (Karneval) ..*see: One More Time*
2/72 **Kate** *Johnny Cash*
60/86 **Katie, Take Me Dancin'** *Lewis Storey*
16/72 **Katy Did** *Porter Wagoner*
11/59 **Katy Too** *Johnny Cash*
  Kaw-Liga
1/53   *Hank Williams*
3/69   *Charley Pride*
12/80   *Hank Williams, Jr.*
  Kay
9/69   *John Wesley Ryles*
50/78   *John Wesley Ryles*
3/53 **Keep It A Secret** *Slim Whitman*
42/65 **Keep Me Fooled** *Carl Smith*
1/73 **Keep Me In Mind** *Lynn Anderson*
6/45 **Keep My Mem'ry In Your Heart** *Ernest Tubb*
  Keep On Lovin' Me
88/73   *Jamey Ryan*
23/74   *Johnny Paycheck*
49/81 **Keep On Movin'** *King Edward IV*
58/83 **Keep On Playin' That Country Music** *Sierra*
70/82 **Keep On Rollin' Down The Line**
  Boxcar Willie
19/73 **Keep On Truckin'** *Dave Dudley*
53/73 **Keep Out Of My Dreams** *Dorsey Burnette*
51/87 **Keep The Faith** *Jimmy Murphy*
31/66 **Keep The Flag Flying** *Johnny Wright*
16/64 **Keep Those Cards And Letters Coming In**
  Johnny & Jonie Mosby
8/48 **Keeper Of My Heart** *Bob Wills*
65/67 **Keeper Of The Key** *Slim Whitman*
49/83 **Keepin' Power** *Crystal Gayle*
99/76 **Keepin' Rosie Proud Of Me** *Razzy Bailey*
70/82 **Keeping Me Warm For You** *Brenda Lee*
49/67 **Keeping Up Appearances**
  Lynn Anderson & Jerry Lane
5/64 **Keeping Up With The Joneses**
  Faron Young & Margie Singleton

8/55 **Kentuckian Song** *Eddy Arnold*
38/72 **Kentucky** *Sammi Smith*
1/75 **Kentucky Gambler** *Merle Haggard*
20/62 **Kentucky Means Paradise**
　　　　Green River Boys/Glen Campbell
42/76 **Kentucky Moonrunner** *Cledus Maggard*
31/70 **Kentucky Rain** *Elvis Presley*
53/73 **Kentucky Sunshine** *Wayne Kemp*
　　　 Kentucky Waltz
3/46　　*Bill Monroe*
1/51　　*Eddy Arnold*
26/77 **Kentucky Woman** *Randy Barlow*
86/88 **Kep Pa So** *Augie Meyers*
10/85 **Kern River** *Merle Haggard*
50/82 **Key Largo** *Bertie Higgins*
66/69 **Key That Fits Her Door** *Jack Greene*
　　　 Key's In The Mailbox
18/60　　*Freddie Hart*
15/72　　*Tony Booth*
8/62 **Kickin' Our Hearts Around** *Buck Owens*
64/67 **Kickin' Tree** *Bonnie Guitar*
2/73 **Kid Stuff** *Barbara Fairchild*
1/87 **Kids Of The Baby Boom** *Bellamy Brothers*
1/73 **Kids Say The Darndest Things**
　　　　Tammy Wynette
37/87 **Killbilly Hill** *Southern Pacific*
17/82 **Killin' Kind** *Bandana*
10/81 **Killin' Time** *Fred Knoblock & Susan Anton*
42/71 **Kind Of Needin' I Need** *Norma Jean*
　　　 Kind Of Woman I Got
33/67　　*Osborne Brothers*
F/75　　*Hank Williams, Jr.*
48/73 **Kindly Keep It Country** *Hank Thompson*
75/82 **King, The** *Pete Wilcox*
13/77 **King Is Gone** *Ronnie McDowell*
75/86 **King Lear** *Cal Smith*
97/77 **King Of Country Music Meets The Queen Of**
　　　　Rock & Roll *Even Stevens & Sherry Grooms*
96/85 **King Of Oak Street** *Ramsey Kearney*
1/65 **King Of The Road** *Roger Miller*
　　　　(also see: Queen Of The House)
1/71 **Kiss An Angel Good Mornin'** *Charley Pride*
36/76 **Kiss And Say Goodbye** *Billy Larkin*
65/78 **Kiss Away** *Jody Miller*
7/55 **Kiss Crazy Baby** *Johnnie & Jack*
29/73 **Kiss It And Make It Better** *Mac Davis*
25/83 **Kiss Me Darling** *Stephanie Winslow*
79/83 **Kiss Me Just One More Time** *Floyd Brown*
　　　 Kiss The Hurt Away
61/72　　*Ronnie Dove*
88/82　　*Mack White*
87/79 **Kiss You All Over** *Jim Mundy & Terri Melton*
74/79 **Kiss You And Make It Better** *Roy Head*
24/69 **Kissed By The Rain, Warmed By The Sun**
　　　　Glenn Barber
5/55 **Kisses Don't Lie** *Carl Smith*
11/61 **Kisses Never Lie** *Carl Smith*
6/58 **Kisses Sweeter Than Wine** *Jimmie Rodgers*
14/61 **Kissing My Pillow** *Rose Maddox*
3/57 **Knee Deep In The Blues** *Marty Robbins*
18/63 **Knock Again, True Love** *Claude Gray*
94/78 **Knock Knock Knock** *Fiddlin' Frenchie Burke*
29/84 **Knock On Wood** *Razzy Bailey*
3/71 **Knock Three Times** *Billy 'Crash' Craddock*
3/53 **Knothole** *Carlisles*
　　　 Knoxville Girl
18/59　　*Wilburn Brothers*
19/59　　*Louvin Brothers*
39/72 **Knoxville Station** *Bobby Austin*
11/71 **Ko-Ko Joe** *Jerry Reed*
4/47 **Kokomo Island** *Al Dexter*

L

60/69 **L.A. Angels** *Jimmy Payne*
　　　 L.A. International Airport
67/70　　*David Frizzell*
9/71　　*Susan Raye*
57/87 **La Bamba** *Los Lobos*
94/76 **Labor Of Love** *Bob Luman*
80/76 **Ladies Love Outlaws**
　　　　Jimmy Rabbitt & Renegade
78/77 **Ladies Night** *Del Reeves*
　　　 Lady
66/73　　*Kenny Vernon*
46/77　　*Johnny Cash*
1/80　　*Kenny Rogers*
79/77 **Lady Ain't For Sale** *Sherry Bryce*
76/77 **Lady And The Baby** *David Rogers*
14/75 **Lady Came From Baltimore** *Johnny Cash*
1/83 **Lady Down On Love** *Alabama*
79/86 **Lady In Distress** *Little David Wilkins*
55/83 **Lady In My Life** *Tony Joe White*
9/79 **Lady In The Blue Mercedes** *Johnny Duncan*
31/84 **Lady In Waiting** *David Wills*
88/82 **Lady, Lady** *Kelly Lang*
　　　 Lady Lay Down
1/79　　*John Conlee*
26/82　　*Tom Jones*
67/82 **Lady, Lay Down (Lay Down On My Pillow)**
　　　　Gary Goodnight
4/85 **Lady Like You** *Glen Campbell*
73/83 **Lady Of The Eighties** *Jeanne Pruett*
22/73 **Lady Of The Night** *David Houston*
31/83 **Lady, She's Right** *Leon Everette*
3/84 **Lady Takes The Cowboy Everytime**
　　　　Gatlin Bros.
F/78 **Lady, Would You Like To Dance**
　　　　Jerry Naylor
　　　 Lady's Man
2/52　　*Hank Snow*
92/81　　*Music Row*
47/74 **Ladylover** *Bobby Lewis*
91/77 **Laid Back Country Picker** *Wendel Adkins*
82/83 **Laid Off** *Bill Anderson*
98/77 **Laissez Les Bontemps Rouler** *Helen Reddy*
　　　 (Lament Of Cherokee) ..see: Indian Nation
20/70 **Land Mark Tavern**
　　　　Del Reeves & Penny DeHaven
63/80 **Land Of Cotton** *Donna Fargo*
9/85 **Lasso The Moon** *Gary Morris*
65/73 **Last Blues Song** *Dick Curless*
　　　 Last Cheater's Waltz
1/79　　*T.G. Sheppard*
F/79　　*Sonny Throckmorton*
　　　 Last Country Song ..see: (Who's Gonna Sing)
12/80 **Last Cowboy Song** *Ed Bruce*
11/61 **Last Date** *Floyd Cramer*
7/64 **Last Day In The Mines** *Dave Dudley*
98/73 **Last Days Of Childhood** *Sam Durrence*
52/78 **Last Exit For Love** *Wood Newton*
51/80 **Last Farewell** *Miki Mori*
　　　 Last Goodbye
17/68　　*Dick Miles*
96/76　　*Red Sovine*
38/77 **Last Gunfighter Ballad** *Johnny Cash*
57/66 **Last Laugh** *Jim Edward Brown*
46/76 **Last Letter** *Willie Nelson*
99/78 **Last Lie I Told Her** *Ronnie Robbins*
43/78 **Last Love Of My Life** *Lynn Anderson*
4/73 **Last Love Song** *Hank Williams, Jr.*
20/59 **Last Night At A Party** *Faron Young*

28/78 **Last Night, Ev'ry Night** *Reba McEntire*
54/75 **Last Of The Outlaws** *Chuck Price*
43/82 **Last Of The Silver Screen Cowboys**
    Rex Allen, Jr.
63/74 **Last Of The Sunshine Cowboys** *Eddy Raven*
27/77 **Last Of The Winfield Amateurs** *Ray Griff*
1/87 **Last One To Know** *Reba McEntire*
18/71 **Last One To Touch Me** *Porter Wagoner*
4/88 **Last Resort** *T. Graham Brown*
3/59 **Last Ride** *Hank Snow*
63/89 **Last Rose** *Bobby Vinton*
2/83 **Last Thing I Needed First Thing This**
    Morning *Willie Nelson*
26/59 **Last Thing I Want To Know** *George Morgan*
7/68 **Last Thing On My Mind**
    Porter Wagoner & Dolly Parton
85/80 **Last Time** *Johnny Cash*
25/72 **Last Time I Called Somebody Darlin'**
    Roy Drusky
21/71 **Last Time I Saw Her** *Glen Campbell*
8/74 **Last Time I Saw Him** *Dottie West*
50/77 **Last Time You Love Me** *Jerry Naylor*
39/64 **Last Town I Painted** *George Jones*
69/67 **Last Train To Clarksville** *Ed Bruce*
80/82 **Last Train To Heaven** *Boxcar Willie*
4/53 **Last Waltz** *Webb Pierce*
52/73 **Last Will And Testimony (Of A Drinking**
    Man) *Howard Crockett*
73/81 **Last Word In Jesus Is Us** *Roy Clark*
Last Word In Lonesome Is Me
2/66   *Eddy Arnold*
90/76   *Terry Bradshaw*
20/68 **Late And Great Love (Of My Heart)**
    Hank Snow
49/77 **Lately I've Been Thinking Too Much**
    Lately *David Allan Coe*
42/77 **Latest Shade Of Blue** *Connie Smith*
Laura (What's He Got That I Ain't Got)
1/67   *Leon Ashley*
50/67   *Claude King*
60/73   *Marty Robbins*
19/76   *Kenny Rogers*
13/49 **Lavender Blue (Dilly Dilly)** *Burl Ives*
3/76 **Lawdy Miss Clawdy** *Mickey Gilley*
9/72 **Lawrence Welk - Hee Haw Counter-Revolution**
    Polka *Roy Clark*
72/79 **Lawyers** *Billy Walker*
Lay A Little Lovin' On Me
22/73   *Del Reeves*
97/79   *Jody Miller*
52/82 **Lay Back Down And Love Me** *Rich Landers*
Lay Back In The Arms Of Someone
80/79   *Juice Newton*
13/80   *Randy Barlow*
91/84   *Johnny Tillotson*
35/75 **Lay Back Lover** *Dottie West*
67/76 **Lay Down** *Charly McClain*
3/79 **Lay Down Beside Me** *Don Williams*
Lay Down Sally
26/78   *Eric Clapton*
70/78   *Red Sovine*
86/78   *Jack Paris*
96/88 **Lay, Lady Lay** *Jim Bean*
44/67 **Lay Some Happiness On Me** *Bobby Wright*
82/77 **Lay Something On My Bed Besides A**
    Blanket *Charly McClain*
84/81 **Layin' Low** *Denny Hilton*
68/70 **Laying My Burdens Down** *Willie Nelson*
13/48 **Lazy Mary** *Bud Hobbs*
56/70 **Lead Me Not Into Temptation**
    Anthony Armstrong Jones
Lead Me On
68/69   *Bonnie Owens*
1/71   *Conway Twitty & Loretta Lynn*
13/74 **Lean It All On Me** *Diana Trask*

99/79 **Lean, Mean And Hungry** *Chris LeDoux*
55/77 **Lean On Jesus "Before He Leans On You"**
    Paul Craft
Lean On Me
91/75   *Paul Delicato*
77/84   *Jack Grayson*
93/79 **Leaning On Each Other** *B.J. Wright*
20/67 **Learnin' A New Way Of Life** *Hank Snow*
28/81 **Learning To Live Again** *Bobby Bare*
15/65 **Least Of All** *George Jones*
34/64 **Leave A Little Play (In The Chain Of**
    Love) *Bob Jennings*
68/79 **Leave It To Love** *Jim Taylor*
22/75 **Leave It Up To Me** *Billy Larkin*
72/74 **Leave Me Alone (Ruby Red Dress)**
    Arleen Harden
1/87 **Leave Me Lonely** *Gary Morris*
70/88 **Leave Me Satisfied** *Tiny Tim*
6/69 **Leave My Dream Alone** *Warner Mack*
6/83 **Leave Them Boys Alone** *Hank Williams, Jr.*
63/68 **Leave This One Alone** *Nat Stuckey*
93/78 **Leave While I'm Sleeping** *Micki Fuhrman*
41/68 **Leaves Are The Tears Of Autumn**
    Bonnie Guitar
74/77 **Leavin'** *Kenny Price*
9/71 **Leavin' And Sayin' Goodbye** *Faron Young*
52/70 **Leavin' On A Jet Plane** *Kendalls*
Leavin' On Your Mind
8/63   *Patsy Cline*
58/72   *Bobbie Roy*
92/80   *Karen Casey*
78/88   *Donna Meade*
75/81 **Leavin You Is Easier (Than Wishing You Were**
    Gone) *Joe Douglas*
13/80 **Leavin's For Unbelievers** *Dottie West*
82/85 **Leaving** *Charleston Express/Jesse Wales*
1/80 **Leaving Louisiana In The Broad Daylight**
    Oak Ridge Boys
98/76 **Leaving Was Easy** *Mike Boyd*
64/73 **Leaving's Heavy On My Mind** *Sherry Bryce*
62/78 **Left-Over Love** *Brenda Lee*
10/84 **Left Side Of The Bed** *Mark Gray*
5/60 **Left To Right** *Kitty Wells*
45/81 **Lefty** *David Frizzell*
19/85 **Legend And The Man** *Conway Twitty*
Legend In My Time *..see: (I'd Be)*
1/68 **Legend Of Bonnie And Clyde** *Merle Haggard*
94/80 **Legend Of Harry And The Mountain**
    Ron Shaw/Desert Wind Band
27/62 **Legend Of The Johnson Boys**
    Lester Flatt & Earl Scruggs
80/80 **Legend Of Wooley Swamp**
    Charlie Daniels Band
38/72 **Legendary Chicken Fairy**
    Jack Blanchard & Misty Morgan
Leona
9/62   *Stonewall Jackson*
64/78   *Johnny Russell*
16/85   *Sawyer Brown*
91/77 **Leona Don't Live Here Anymore**
    Wayne Kemp
9/81 **Leonard** *Merle Haggard*
27/65 **Less And Less** *Charlie Louvin*
44/68 **Less Of Me** *Bobbie Gentry & Glen Campbell*
67/75 **Less Than The Song** *Patti Page*
1/80 **Lesson In Leavin'** *Dottie West*
34/85 **Let A Little Love Come In** *Charley Pride*
86/86 **Let A Little Love In** *Rockin' Horse*
5/61 **Let Forgiveness In** *Webb Pierce*
43/72 **Let Him Have It** *Jan Howard*
Let It Be Me
14/69   *Glen Campbell & Bobbie Gentry*
2/82   *Willie Nelson*
57/89 **Let It Burn** *Jeff Chance*
78/88 **Let It Go** *Don Juan*

6/85 **Let It Roll (Let It Rock)** *Mel McDaniel*
5/76 **Let It Shine** *Olivia Newton-John*
22/80 **Let Jesse Rob The Train** *Buck Owens*
67/84 **Let Love Come Lookin' For You** *Dottie West*
63/86 **Let Me Be The First** *Nicolette Larson*
    Let Me Be The One
1/53   *Hank Locklin*
74/80   *Billy Walker & Barbara Fairchild*
7/73 **Let Me Be There** *Olivia Newton-John*
13/78 **Let Me Be Your Baby** *Charly McClain*
35/76 **Let Me Be Your Friend** *Mack White*
    (Let Me Be Your) Teddy Bear
1/57   *Elvis Presley*
F/78   *Elvis Presley*
    Let Me Down Easy
7/77   *Cristy Lane*
87/78   *Peggy Sue*
16/85   *Jim Glaser*
67/86   *Malchak & Rucker*
93/78 **Let Me Fall Back In Your Arms**
    Freddy Weller
72/81 **Let Me Fill For You A Fantasy**
    Gary Goodnight
45/64 **Let Me Get Close To You** *Skeeter Davis*
    Let Me Go, Lover
1/54   *Hank Snow*
75/70   *Karen Kelly*
27/70 **Let Me Go (Set Me Free)** *Johnny Duncan*
23/80 **Let Me In** *Kenny Dale*
F/82 **Let Me In And Let Me Love You**
    Tennessee Express
21/71 **Let Me Live** *Charley Pride*
53/80 **Let Me Love You** *Fred Knoblock*
99/77 **Let Me Love You Now** *Jim Chesnut*
22/77 **Let Me Love You Once Before You Go**
    Barbara Fairchild
69/76 **Let Me Love You Where It Hurts**
    Jim Ed Brown
25/74 **Let Me Make The Bright Lights Shine For**
    You *Bob Luman*
29/63 **Let Me Off At The Corner** *Dottie West*
    Let Me Swing *..see: (Turn Me Loose And)*
71/75 **Let Me Take Care Of You** *Bobby Lewis*
53/78 **Let Me Take You In My Arms Again**
    James Darren
    Let My Fingers Do The Walking
98/77   *Alan Cartee*
97/79   *Pat Pomsl*
1/77 **Let My Love Be Your Pillow** *Ronnie Milsap*
78/73 **Let My Love Shine** *Marti Brown*
1/52 **Let Old Mother Nature Have Her Way**
    Carl Smith
10/84 **Let Somebody Else Drive** *John Anderson*
86/76 **Let The Big Wheels Roll** *Sarah Johns*
4/68 **Let The Chips Fall** *Charley Pride*
57/74 **Let The Four Winds Blow** *Jack Reno*
59/82 **Let The Good Times Roll** *Jon & Lynn*
23/85 **Let The Heartache Ride** *Restless Heart*
58/81 **Let The Little Bird Fly** *Dottsy*
38/75 **Let The Little Boy Dream** *Even Stevens*
4/87 **Let The Music Lift You Up** *Reba McEntire*
20/69 **Let The Whole World Sing It With Me**
    Wynn Stewart
7/68 **Let The World Keep On A Turnin'**
    Buck Owens & Buddy Alan
80/82 **Let Your Fingers Do The Walkin'**
    Jebry Lee Briley
57/79 **Let Your Love Fall Back On Me**
    David Houston
21/76 **Let Your Love Flow** *Bellamy Brothers*
13/72 **Let's All Go Down To The River**
    Jody Miller & Johnny Paycheck
F/75 **Let's All Help The Cowboys (Sing The**
    Blues) *Waylon Jennings*
82/88 **Let's Be Bad Tonight** *Ronnie Rogers*

38/87 **Let's Be Fools Like That Again** *Tommy Roe*
32/73 **Let's Build A World Together**
    George Jones & Tammy Wynette
92/78 **Let's Call It A Day** *Leslee Barnhill*
1/84 **Let's Chase Each Other Around The Room**
    Merle Haggard
16/87 **Let's Do Something** *Vince Gill*
51/80 **Let's Do Something Cheap And**
    Superficial *Burt Reynolds*
26/62 **Let's End It Before It Begins** *Claude Gray*
    Let's Fall Apart *..see: (All Together Now)*
1/84 **Let's Fall To Pieces Together** *George Strait*
64/83 **Let's Find Each Other Tonight**
    Jose Feliciano
72/81 **Let's Forget That We're Married**
    Gary Stewart
100/77 **Let's Get Acquainted Again** *Floyd Brown*
76/82 **Let's Get Crazy Again** *Diane Pfeifer*
61/73 **(Let's Get) Dixiefried** *Carl Perkins*
6/80 **Let's Get It While The Gettin's Good**
    Eddy Arnold
10/83 **Let's Get Over Them Together**
    Moe Bandy/Becky Hobbs
12/89 **Let's Get Started If We're Gonna Break My**
    Heart *Statler Brothers*
65/70 **Let's Get Together**
    Skeeter Davis & George Hamilton IV
41/82 **Let's Get Together And Cry** *Joe Stampley*
6/77 **(Let's Get Together) One Last Time**
    Tammy Wynette
    Let's Go All The Way
11/64   *Norma Jean*
68/82   *Claude Gray & Norma Jean*
26/74 **Let's Go All The Way Tonight**
    Mel Tillis & Sherry Bryce
52/70 **Let's Go Fishin' Boys (The Girls Are**
    Bitin') *Charlie Walker*
100/88 **Let's Go Party** *Kathy Bee*
68/80 **Let's Go Through The Motions** *Cates*
2/50 **Let's Go To Church (Next Sunday**
    Morning) *Margaret Whiting & Jimmy Wakely*
95/78 **Let's Have A Heart To Heart Talk**
    Leon Rausch
59/74 **Let's Hear It For Loneliness** *Mundo Earwood*
17/63 **Let's Invite Them Over**
    George Jones & Melba Montgomery
    Let's Keep It That Way
37/79   *Juice Newton*
10/80   *Mac Davis*
30/84 **Let's Leave The Lights On Tonight**
    Johnny Rodriguez
2/51 **Let's Live A Little** *Carl Smith*
53/84 **Let's Live This Dream Together** *Narvel Felts*
52/75 **Let's Love While We Can** *Barbara Fairchild*
6/76 **Let's Put It Back Together Again**
    Jerry Lee Lewis
23/80 **Let's Put Our Love In Motion**
    Charly McClain
27/69 **Let's Put Our World Back Together**
    Charlie Louvin
5/49 **Let's Say Goodbye Like We Said Hello**
    Ernest Tubb
9/78 **Let's Shake Hands And Come Out Lovin'**
    Kenny O'Dell
64/83 **Let's Sing About Love** *Al Downing*
18/75 **Let's Sing Our Song** *Jerry Reed*
92/88 **Let's Start A Rumor Today** *Bobby Durham*
1/84 **Let's Stop Talkin' About It** *Janie Frickie*
1/78 **Let's Take The Long Way Around The**
    World *Ronnie Milsap*
27/79 **Let's Take The Time To Fall In Love**
    Again *Jim Chesnut*
90/83 **Let's Talk It Over** *R. Dean Taylor*
9/60 **Let's Think About Living** *Bob Luman*

29/80	**Little Ground In Texas** *Capitals*	2/76	**Living It Down** *Freddy Fender*
13/60	**Little Guy Called Joe** *Stonewall Jackson*	55/87	**Living Like There's No Tomorrow**
3/62	**Little Heartache** *Eddy Arnold*		*John Conlee*
45/76	**Little Joe** *Red Sovine*	88/82	**Living My Life Without You** *Lobo*
37/70	**Little Johnny From Down The Street**	29/77	**Living Next Door To Alice** *Johnny Carver*
	Wilburn Brothers	38/76	**Living Proof** *Hank Williams, Jr.*
64/84	**Little Love** *Juice Newton*	71/71	**Living Tornado** *Kenni Huskey*
56/88	**Little Maggie** *Darden Smith*	F/70	**Living Under Pressure** *Eddy Arnold*
63/74	**Little Man** *Logan Smith*	91/78	**Livingston Saturday Night** *Jimmy Buffett*
73/78	**Little Man's Got The Biggest Smile In**	1/75	**Lizzie And The Rainman** *Tanya Tucker*
	Town *Arthur Blanch*	66/73	**Lizzie Lou** *Osborne Brothers*
21/61	**Little Miss Belong To No One** *Margie Bowes*	57/84	**Lo And Behold** *Tennessee Valley Boys*
94/79	**Little More Love** *Olivia Newton-John*	30/79	**Lo Que Sea (What Ever May The Future**
22/62	**Little Music Box** *Skeeter Davis*		**Be)** *Jess Garron*
10/83	**Little Old Fashioned Karma** *Willie Nelson*	44/79	**Lock, Stock, & Barrel** *Wood Newton*
9/67	**Little Old Wine Drinker Me** *Robert Mitchum*		**Lock, Stock And Teardrops**
23/77	**Little Ole Dime** *Jim Reeves*	26/63	*Roger Miller*
11/63	**Little Ole You** *Jim Reeves*	70/68	*Diana Trask*
31/66	**Little Pedro** *Carl Butler & Pearl*	53/88	*K.D. Lang*
30/66	**Little Pink Mack** *Kay Adams*	23/69	**Lodi** *Buddy Alan*
29/69	**Little Reasons** *Charlie Louvin*	11/76	**Lone Star Beer And Bob Wills Music**
1/86	**Little Rock** *Reba McEntire*		*Red Steagall*
5/56	**Little Rosa** *Red Sovine & Webb Pierce*	36/87	**Lone Star State Of Mind** *Nanci Griffith*
7/87	**Little Sister** *Dwight Yoakam*	96/74	**Loneliness (Can Break A Good Man Down)**
98/77	**Little Something On The Side** *Pat Garrett*		*Norro Wilson*
34/64	**Little South Of Memphis** *Frankie Miller*	56/86	**Loneliness In Lucy's Eyes** *Johnny Lee*
91/78	**Little Teardrops** *Linda Cassady*	74/70	**Loneliness Without You** *Hagers*
	Little Things	1/67	**Lonely Again** *Eddy Arnold*
22/68	*Willie Nelson*	2/86	**Lonely Alone** *Forester Sisters*
75/81	*Tennessee Express*	15/83	**Lonely But Only For You** *Sissy Spacek*
1/85	*Oak Ridge Boys*	86/79	**Lonely Coming Down** *Keith Bradford*
	Little Things Mean A Lot	46/86	**Lonely Days, Lonely Nights** *Patty Loveless*
79/77	*Linda Cassady*		**Lonely Eyes**
3/78	*Margo Smith*	46/76	*Randy Barlow*
50/67	**Little Things That Every Girl Should**	39/77	*Rayburn Anthony*
	Know *Claude King*	61/83	*Brice Henderson*
7/55	**Little Tom** *Ferlin Husky*	63/70	**Lonely For You** *Wilma Burgess*
36/65	**Little Unfair** *Lefty Frizzell*		**Lonely Girl**
8/87	**Little Ways** *Dwight Yoakam*	30/59	*Jimmy Newman*
100/76	**Little Weekend Warriors** *Bobby Penn*	14/64	*Carl Smith*
7/46	**Little White Cross On The Hill** *Roy Rogers*		**Lonely Heart**
88/82	**Little White Lies** *David House*	81/83	*Cedar Creek*
65/77	**Little White Moon** *Hoyt Axton*	40/84	*Tammy Wynette*
18/68	**Little World Girl** *George Hamilton IV*	68/82	**Lonely Hearts** *Younger Brothers*
32/76	**Littlest Cowboy Rides Again** *Ed Bruce*	18/78	**Lonely Hearts Club** *Billie Jo Spears*
39/79	**Live Entertainment** *Don King*	40/80	**Lonely Hotel** *Don King*
1/55	**Live Fast, Love Hard, Die Young**	53/71	**Lonely Is** *Dottie West*
	Faron Young	18/58	**Lonely Island Pearl** *Johnnie & Jack*
16/70	**Live For The Good Times** *Warner Mack*	23/75	**Lonely Men, Lonely Women** *Connie Eaton*
28/63	**Live For Tomorrow** *Carl Smith*	1/82	**Lonely Nights** *Mickey Gilley*
44/68	**Live Your Life Out Loud** *Bobby Lord*		**Lonely People**
F/57	**Livin' Alone** *Hank Locklin*	38/72	*Eddy Arnold*
68/77	**Livin' Her Life In A Song** *Billy Mize*	83/78	*Keith Bradford*
3/65	**Livin' In A House Full Of Love**	80/75	**Lonely Rain** *Wynn Stewart*
	David Houston	16/60	**Lonely River Rhine** *Bobby Helms*
93/88	**Livin' In Shadows** *Jerry Lee Tucker*	76/78	**Lonely Side Of The Bed** *Linda Cassady*
85/81	**Livin' in the Light of Her Love** *Joe Waters*	7/56	**Lonely Side Of Town** *Kitty Wells*
77/75	**Livin' In The Sunshine Of Your Love**		**Lonely Street**
	Ray Pillow	84/74	*Tony Booth*
9/82	**Livin' In These Troubled Times**	8/78	*Rex Allen, Jr.*
	Crystal Gayle		**Lonely Teardrops**
28/63	**Livin' Offa Credit** *Jim Nesbitt*	18/63	*Rose Maddox*
75/76	**Livin' On Love Street** *Shylo*	5/76	*Narvel Felts*
43/69	**Livin' On Lovin' (And Lovin' Livin' With**		**Lonely Together**
	You) *Slim Whitman*	41/79	*Diana*
62/83	**Livin' On Memories** *Gary Wolf*	98/85	*A.J. Masters*
23/79	**Livin' Our Love Together** *Billie Jo Spears*	11/72	**Lonely Weekends** *Jerry Lee Lewis*
46/81	**Livin' The Good Life** *Corbin/Hanner Band*	75/80	**Lonely Wine** *Maury Finney*
86/81	**Livin' Together (Lovin' Apart)**	64/81	**Lonely Woman** *Silver Creek*
	Bobby G. Rice		**Lonely Women Make Good Lovers**
56/68	**Living** *George Morgan*	4/72	*Bob Luman*
9/71	**Living And Learning**	4/84	*Steve Wariner*
	Mel Tillis & Sherry Bryce		**Lonelyville**
63/68	**Living As Strangers** *Kitty Wells & Red Foley*	20/61	*Ray Sanders*
1/86	**Living In The Promiseland** *Willie Nelson*	13/66	*Dave Dudley*

20/88	**Louisiana Rain** *John Wesley Ryles*
	Louisiana Saturday Night
24/67	*Jimmy Newman*
7/81	*Mel McDaniel*
1/73	**Louisiana Woman, Mississippi Man**
	Conway Twitty & Loretta Lynn
23/68	**Louisville** *Leroy Van Dyke*
73/68	**Lovable Fool** *Goldie Hill Smith*
11/83	**Love Affairs** *Michael Murphey*
24/79	**Love Ain't Gonna Wait For Us**
	Billie Jo Spears
	Love Ain't Made For Fools
33/79	*John Wesley Ryles*
66/88	*Kevin Pearce*
38/70	**Love Ain't Never Gonna Be No Better**
	Webb Pierce
19/81	**Love Ain't Never Hurt Nobody**
	Bobby Goldsboro
51/73	**Love Ain't Worth a Dime Unless It's Free**
	Wynn Stewart
14/85	**(Love Always) Letter To Home**
	Glen Campbell
80/78	**Love And Hate** *Mike Boyd*
70/73	**Love And Honor** *Kenny Serratt*
72/84	**Love And Let Love** *Danny Shirley*
73/88	**Love And Other Fairy Tales** *Girls Next Door*
3/86	**Love At The Five & Dime** *Kathy Mattea*
6/65	**Love Bug** *George Jones*
12/58	**Love Bug Crawl** *Jimmy Edwards*
28/82	**Love Busted** *Billy 'Crash' Craddock*
99/73	**Love By Appointment**
	Pati Powell & Bob Gallion
82/78	**Love Can Make The Children Sing**
	Billy Stack
90/81	**Love (Can Make You Happy)** *James Marvell*
10/87	**Love Can't Ever Get Better Than This**
	Ricky Skaggs & Sharon White
12/62	**Love Can't Wait** *Marty Robbins*
44/69	**Love Comes But Once In A Lifetime**
	Norro Wilson
34/80	**Love Crazy Love** *Zella Lehr*
13/81	**Love Dies Hard** *Randy Barlow*
86/77	**Love Doesn't Live Here Anymore**
	Randy Cornor
91/79	**Love Don't Care**
	Charlie Louvin with Emmylou Harris
1/85	**Love Don't Care (Whose Heart It Breaks)**
	Earl Thomas Conley
55/86	**Love Don't Come Any Better Than This**
	Shelly West
93/78	**Love Don't Hide From Me** *Hugh X. Lewis*
59/83	**Love Don't Know A Lady (From A Honky Tonk**
	Girl) *Billy Parker*
80/81	**Love Fires** *Don Gibson*
62/80	**Love Goes To Hell When It Dies**
	Wayne Kemp
73/85	**Love Gone Bad** *Jay Clark*
23/78	**Love Got In The Way** *Freddy Weller*
12/57	**Love Has Finally Come My Way**
	Faron Young
90/83	**Love Has Made A Woman Out Of You**
	Vince & Dianne Hatfield
10/60	**Love Has Made You Beautiful** *Merle Kilgore*
26/80	**Love Has Taken Its' Time** *Zella Lehr*
3/88	**Love Helps Those** *Paul Overstreet*
19/70	**Love Hungry** *Warner Mack*
72/69	**Love, I Finally Found It** *Ernest Ashworth*
53/77	**Love I Need You** *Dale McBride*
98/78	**Love In Me** *Jim Norman*
63/73	**Love In The Back Seat** *Little David Wilkins*
1/81	**Love In The First Degree** *Alabama*
65/88	**Love In The Heart** *Don McLean*
3/75	**Love In The Hot Afternoon** *Gene Watson*
32/80	**Love In The Meantime** *Streets*
61/80	**Love Insurance** *Louise Mandrell*

39/82	**Love Is** *Allen Tripp*
85/82	**Love Is A Full Time Thing** *Terry McMillan*
69/69	**Love Is A Gentle Thing** *Barbara Fairchild*
12/72	**Love Is A Good Thing** *Johnny Paycheck*
5/75	**Love Is A Rose** *Linda Ronstadt*
5/70	**Love Is A Sometimes Thing** *Bill Anderson*
68/76	**Love Is A Two-Way Street** *Dottsy*
42/80	**Love Is A Warm Cowboy** *Buck Owens*
	Love Is A Word
88/76	*Juice Newton & Silver Spur*
27/78	*Dickey Lee*
1/85	**Love Is Alive** *Judds*
29/80	**Love Is All Around** *Sonny Curtis*
91/85	**Love Is An Overload** *Bobby Lewis*
51/68	**Love Is Ending** *Liz Anderson*
60/87	**Love Is Everywhere** *Mel McDaniel*
13/81	**Love Is Fair** *Barbara Mandrell*
46/74	**Love Is Here** *Wilma Burgess*
84/79	**Love Is Hours In The Making**
	Sterling Whipple
10/68	**Love Is In The Air** *Marty Robbins*
3/77	**Love Is Just A Game** *Larry Gatlin*
57/69	**Love Is Just A State Of Mind** *Roy Clark*
44/81	**Love Is Knockin' At My Door** *Susie Allanson*
1/74	**Love Is Like A Butterfly** *Dolly Parton*
36/72	**Love Is Like A Spinning Wheel** *Jan Howard*
7/64	**Love Is No Excuse** *Jim Reeves & Dottie West*
1/83	**Love Is On A Roll** *Don Williams*
47/89	**Love Is On The Line** *Canyon*
47/76	**Love Is Only Love (When Shared By Two)**
	Johnny Carver
26/79	**Love Is Sometimes Easy** *Sandy Posey*
20/75	**Love Is Strange** *Buck Owens & Susan Raye*
1/73	**Love Is The Foundation** *Loretta Lynn*
8/73	**Love Is The Look You're Looking For**
	Connie Smith
53/86	**Love Is The Only Way Out**
	William Lee Golden
68/84	**Love Is The Reason** *Sierra*
24/76	**Love Is Thin Ice** *Barbara Mandrell*
37/85	**Love Is What We Make It** *Kenny Rogers*
	Love Isn't Love (Till You Give It Away)
52/72	*Bobby Lee Trammell*
93/76	*Eddie Bailes*
87/79	*Joy Ford*
69/84	*Tari Hensley*
30/76	**Love It Away** *Mary Lou Turner*
78/85	**Love, It's The Pits** *Lisa Angelle*
54/86	**Love Keep Your Distance** *A.J. Masters*
40/81	**Love Knows We Tried** *Tanya Tucker*
	Love Letters
57/77	*Debi Hawkins*
69/83	*Hazard*
79/86	**Love Letters In The Sand** *Tom T. Hall*
33/79	**Love Lies** *Mel McDaniel*
19/76	**Love Lifted Me** *Kenny Rogers*
29/80	**Love, Look At Us Now** *Johnny Rodriguez*
	Love Looks Good On You
17/64	*David Houston*
41/65	*Lefty Frizzell*
	Love, Love, Love
1/55	*Webb Pierce*
26/78	*Sandy Posey (medley)*
34/67	**Love Makes The World Go Around**
	Kitty Wells
	Love Me
10/56	*Elvis Presley*
34/72	*Jeanne Pruett*
9/73	*Marty Robbins*
58/83	*Jeanne Pruett/Marty Robbins*
83/78	**Love Me Again** *Rita Coolidge*
80/86	**Love Me All Over** *Sammi Smith*
12/67	**Love Me And Make It All Better**
	Bobby Lewis
91/79	**Love Me Back To Sleep** *Jessi Colter*

18/71	**Mark Of A Heel** *Hank Thompson*
52/74	**Marlena** *Bobby Goldsboro*
59/68	**Marriage Bit** *Lefty Frizzell*
F/71	**Marriage Has Ruined More Good Love**
	Affairs *Jan Howard*
10/53	**Marriage Of Mexican Joe** *Carolyn Bradshaw*
10/49	**Marriage Vow** *Hank Snow*
3/77	**Married But Not To Each Other**
	Barbara Mandrell
8/52	**Married By The Bible, Divorced By The**
	Law *Hank Snow*
84/82	**Married Man** *Judy Taylor*
	Married To A Memory
25/71	*Arlene Harden*
74/71	*Judy Lynn*
33/81	**Married Women** *Sonny Curtis*
39/70	**Marry Me** *Ron Lowry*
17/70	**Marty Gray** *Billie Jo Spears*
12/63	**Mary Ann Regrets** *Burl Ives*
12/60	**Mary Don't You Weep** *Stonewall Jackson*
41/70	**Mary Goes 'Round** *Bobby Helms*
66/67	**Mary In The Morning** *Tommy Hunter*
64/83	**Mary Lee** *Rodney Lay*
68/68	**Mary's Little Lamb** *Carl Belew*
17/71	**Mary's Vineyard** *Claude King*
77/79	**Massachusetts** *Tommy Roe*
	Matador, The
2/63	*Johnny Cash*
7/81	*Sylvia*
8/65	**Matamoros** *Billy Walker*
66/88	**Matches** *Marty Stuart*
	Mathilda
20/75	*Donny King*
78/81	*John Wesley Ryles*
	(Matthew's Song) *..see: Pilgrims On The Way*
64/82	**Maximum Security (To Minimum Wage)**
	Don King
35/79	**May I** *Terri Hollowell*
52/80	**May I Borrow Some Sugar From You**
	John Wesley Ryles
37/77	**May I Spend Every New Years With You**
	T.G. Sheppard
62/71	**May Old Acquaintance Be Forgot**
	Compton Brothers
1/65	**May The Bird Of Paradise Fly Up Your**
	Nose *'Little' Jimmy Dickens*
13/78	**May The Force Be With You Always**
	Tom T. Hall
8/51	**May The Good Lord Bless And Keep You**
	Eddy Arnold
68/75	**May You Rest In Peace** *Melody Allen*
7/78	**Maybe Baby** *Susie Allanson*
28/61	**Maybe I Do** *Dave Dudley*
	Maybe I Should Have Been Listening
31/78	*Rayburn Anthony*
23/81	*Gene Watson*
82/79	**Maybe I'll Cry Over You** *Arthur Blanch*
8/85	**Maybe My Baby** *Louise Mandrell*
45/78	**Maybe You Should've Been Listening**
	Jessi Colter
1/87	**Maybe Your Baby's Got The Blues** *Judds*
9/55	**Maybellene** *Marty Robbins*
75/79	**Mazelle** *Gary Stewart*
	Me
8/64	*Bill Anderson*
87/78	*Sherry Grooms*
4/85	**Me Against The Night** *Crystal Gayle*
	Me And Bobby McGee
12/69	*Roger Miller*
F/72	*Jerry Lee Lewis*
8/72	**Me And Jesus** *Tom T. Hall*
85/85	**Me And Margarita** *Bobby Jenkins*
15/77	**Me And Millie** *Ronnie Sessions*
9/79	**Me And My Broken Heart** *Rex Allen, Jr.*
12/76	**Me And Ole C.B.** *Dave Dudley*

	Me And Paul
F/71	*Willie Nelson*
14/85	*Willie Nelson*
72/80	**Me And The Boys In The Band**
	Tommy Overstreet
	Me And The Elephant
43/77	*Kenny Starr*
82/77	*Bobby Goldsboro*
33/78	**Me And The I.R.S.** *Johnny Paycheck*
29/87	**Me And You** *Donna Fargo*
7/71	**Me And You And A Dog Named Boo**
	Stonewall Jackson
80/75	**Me As I Am** *Chip Taylor*
29/59	**Me, Fred, Joe And Bill** *Porter Wagoner*
65/68	**Me, Me, Me, Me, Me** *Liz Anderson*
72/79	**Me Plus You Equals Love** *Dawn Chastain*
	Me Touchin' You
58/79	*Linda Nail*
91/80	*Capitals*
65/71	**Me Without You** *Carl Perkins*
46/66	**Meadowgreen** *Browns*
30/60	**Mean Eyed Cat** *Johnny Cash*
6/49	**Mean Mama Blues** *Ernest Tubb*
22/66	**Mean Old Woman** *Claude Gray*
	Mean Woman Blues
11/57	*Elvis Presley*
79/80	*Max D. Barnes*
9/65	**Meanwhile, Down At Joe's** *Kitty Wells*
32/79	**Medicine Woman** *Kenny O'Dell*
1/85	**Meet Me In Montana**
	Marie Osmond with Dan Seals
51/76	**Meet Me Later** *Margo Smith*
38/64	**Meet Me Tonight Outside Of Town**
	Jim Howard
96/85	**Melted Down Memories** *Joy Ford*
23/87	**Members Only** *Donna Fargo & Billy Joe Royal*
56/69	**Memories** *Elvis Presley*
82/78	**Memories Are Made Of This** *Tommy O'Day*
9/48	**Memories Of France** *T. Texas Tyler*
21/75	**Memories Of Us** *George Jones*
5/86	**Memories To Burn** *Gene Watson*
85/83	**Memory, The** *Jim Wyrick & Union Gold*
73/87	**Memory Attack** *Ralph May*
96/78	**Memory Bound** *B.J. Wright*
91/76	**Memory Go Round** *R.W. Blackwood*
39/84	**Memory Lane**
	Joe Stampley & Jessica Boucher
52/82	**Memory Machine** *Jack Quist*
3/74	**Memory Maker** *Mel Tillis*
2/64	**Memory #1** *Webb Pierce*
10/81	**Memphis** *Fred Knoblock*
79/84	**Memphis In May** *Darrell McCall*
7/80	**Men** *Charly McClain*
	Men In My Little Girl's Life
16/66	*Archie Campbell*
50/66	*Tex Ritter*
8/61	**Mental Cruelty** *Buck Owens & Rose Maddox*
14/68	**Mental Journey** *Leon Ashley*
	Mental Revenge
12/67	*Waylon Jennings*
15/76	*Mel Tillis*
49/76	**Mercy** *Jean Shepard*
7/48	**Merle's Boogie Woogie** *Merle Travis*
41/77	**Merry-Go-Round** *Freddy Weller*
47/75	**Merry-Go-Round Of Love** *Hank Snow*
71/70	**Merry-Go-Round World** *Webb Pierce*
72/80	**Message To Khomeini**
	Roger Hallmark/Thrasher Brothers
93/81	**Mexican Girl** *Michael Tate*
1/53	**Mexican Joe** *Jim Reeves*
61/77	**Mexican Love Songs** *Linda Hargrove*
94/85	**Mexico** *Backtrack/John Hunt*
4/44	**Mexico Joe** *Ivie Anderson*
85/80	**Mexico Winter** *Bobby Hood*

4/74 **Mi Esposa Con Amor (To My Wife With Love)** *Sonny James*
14/86 **Miami, My Amy** *Keith Whitley*
93/73 **Mid American Manufacturing Tycoon** *Bobby Russell*
4/78 **Middle Age Crazy** *Jerry Lee Lewis*
41/79 **Middle-Age Madness** *Earl Thomas Conley*
86/75 **Middle Of A Memory** *Eddy Arnold*
1/53 **Midnight** *Red Foley*
16/77 **Midnight Angel** *Barbara Mandrell*
84/84 **Midnight Angel Of Mercy** *Rod Rishard*
Midnight Blue
39/84   *Billie Jo Spears*
36/87   *John Wesley Ryles*
76/82 **Midnight Cabaret** *Wyvon Alexander*
43/80 **Midnight Choir** *Gatlin Bros.*
Midnight Fire
93/80   *Marlow Tackett*
5/83   *Steve Wariner*
83/77 **Midnight Flight** *Pam Rose*
Midnight Flyer
74/73   *Osborne Brothers*
94/79   *Charlie McCoy*
4/87 **Midnight Girl (medley)** *Sweethearts Of The Rodeo*
1/81 **Midnight Hauler** *Razzy Bailey*
14/88 **Midnight Highway** *Southern Pacific*
59/79 **Midnight Lace** *Al Downing*
51/84 **Midnight Love** *Billie Jo Spears*
93/82 **Midnight Magic** *Gary Buck*
64/74 **Midnight Man** *Marty Mitchell*
2/74 **Midnight, Me And The Blues** *Mel Tillis*
6/80 **Midnight Rider** *Willie Nelson*
9/82 **Midnight Rodeo** *Leon Everette*
87/77 **Midnight Train To Georgia** *Eddie Middleton*
57/81 **Midnite Flyer** *Sue Powell*
85/87 **Midnite Rock** *Indiana*
F/84 **Midsummer Nights** *Kenny Rogers*
68/67 **Mighty Day** *Carl Smith*
38/77 **Miles And Miles Of Texas** *Asleep At The Wheel*
8/52 **Milk Bucket Boogie** *Red Foley*
Miller's Cave
9/60   *Hank Snow*
4/64   *Bobby Bare*
2/66 **Million And One** *Billy Walker*
39/83 **Million Light Beers Ago** *David Frizzell*
Million Old Goodbyes
66/80   *Freddy Weller*
8/81   *Mel Tillis*
13/63 **Million Years Or So** *Eddy Arnold*
12/68 **Milwaukee, Here I Come** *George Jones & Brenda Carter*
64/75 **Mind Your Love** *Jerry Reed*
Mind Your Own Business
5/49   *Hank Williams*
35/64   *Jimmy Dean*
1/86   *Hank Williams, Jr.*
8/49 **Mine All Mine** *Jimmy Wakely*
79/84 **Minstrel, The** *Mike Dekle*
69/78 **Minstrel Man** *Rebecca Lynn*
24/66 **Minute Men (Are Turning In Their Graves)** *Stonewall Jackson*
9/63 **Minute You're Gone** *Sonny James*
4/81 **Miracles** *Don Williams*
41/75 **Mirror, Mirror** *Ben Reece*
56/88 **Mirrors Don't Lie** *Marty Stuart*
12/82 **Mis'ry River** *Terri Gibbs*
3/80 **Misery And Gin** *Merle Haggard*
Misery Loves Company
1/62   *Porter Wagoner*
F/80   *Ronnie Milsap*
2/81 **Miss Emily's Picture** *John Conlee*
55/72 **Miss Pauline** *Billy Bob Bowman*

26/84 **Miss Understanding** *David Wills*
32/84 **Missin' Mississippi** *Charley Pride*
65/88 **Missin' Texas** *Kim Grayson*
3/52 **Missing In Action** *Ernest Tubb*
Missing You
7/57   *Webb Pierce*
8/72   *Jim Reeves*
2/80   *Charley Pride*
1/50 **M-I-S-S-I-S-S-I-P-P-I** *Red Foley*
Mississippi
58/70   *John Phillips*
31/76   *Barbara Fairchild*
75/78   *Jack Paris*
19/79   *Charlie Daniels Band*
59/86 **Mississippi Break Down** *Toni Price*
3/74 **Mississippi Cotton Picking Delta Town** *Charley Pride*
20/85 **Mississippi Squirrel Revival** *Ray Stevens*
14/71 **Mississippi Woman** *Waylon Jennings*
20/75 **Mississippi You're On My Mind** *Stoney Edwards*
5/47 **Missouri** *Merle Travis*
3/82 **Mistakes** *Don Williams*
Mister *..see: Mr.*
3/75 **Misty** *Ray Stevens*
Misty Blue
4/66   *Wilma Burgess*
3/67   *Eddy Arnold*
5/76   *Billie Jo Spears*
37/72 **Misty Memories** *Brenda Lee*
77/86 **Misty Mississippi** *Rusty Budde*
43/80 **Misty Morning Rain** *Ray Price*
Misunderstanding *..see: Miss Understanding*
44/73 **Mm-Mm Good** *Del Reeves*
Moanin' The Blues
1/50   *Hank Williams*
65/82   *Kenny Dale*
60/81 **Mobile Bay** *Johnny Cash*
27/77 **Mobile Boogie** *Hank Williams, Jr.*
64/81 **Moccasin Man** *Dave Kirby*
Mockin' Bird Hill
3/51   *Pinetoppers*
7/51   *Les Paul & Mary Ford*
9/77   *Donna Fargo*
94/74 **Mockingbird** *Terri Lane & Jimmy Nall*
75/86 **Modern Day Cowboy** *Jay Clark*
51/85 **Modern Day Marriages** *Razzy Bailey*
1/85 **Modern Day Romance** *Nitty Gritty Dirt Band*
44/69 **Moffett, Oklahoma** *Charlie Walker*
Molly
5/64   *Eddy Arnold*
53/69   *Jim Glaser*
91/80 **Molly (And The Texas Rain)** *Sonny Wright*
10/48 **Molly Darling** *Eddy Arnold*
28/75 **Molly (I Ain't Gettin' Any Younger)** *Dorsey Burnette*
Mom And Dad's Waltz
2/51   *Lefty Frizzell*
21/61   *Patti Page*
43/79 **Moment By Moment** *Narvel Felts*
24/66 **Mommy, Can I Still Call Him Daddy** *Dottie West*
5/59 **Mommy For A Day** *Kitty Wells*
Mona Lisa
4/50   *Moon Mullican*
10/50   *Jimmy Wakely*
11/81   *Willie Nelson*
2/84 **Mona Lisa Lost Her Smile** *David Allan Coe*
20/73 **Monday Morning Secretary** *Statler Brothers*
Money
15/57   *Browns*
13/88   *K.T. Oslin*
35/70 **Money Can't Buy Love** *Roy Rogers*
48/65 **Money Greases The Wheels** *Ferlin Husky*

443

Money, Marbles & Chalk
12/49   *Captain Stubby*
15/49   *Patti Page*
15/60 **Money To Burn** *George Jones*
11/72 **Monkey That Became President** *Tom T. Hall*
     Monsters' Holiday ..see: *(It's A)*
95/74   *Montgomery Mable* *Merle Kilgore*
42/68 **Moods Of Mary** *Tompall/Glaser Brothers*
1/77 **Moody Blue** *Elvis Presley*
68/70 **Moody River** *Chase Webster*
16/60 **Moon Is Crying** *Allan Riddle*
1/87 **Moon Is Still Over Her Shoulder**
     Michael Johnson
     (Moon Song)
     ..see: *I Don't Know A Thing About Love*
72/80 **Moonlight And Magnolia** *Buck Owens*
58/74 **Moontan** *Jeris Ross*
     Moonwalkin'
76/87   *Don Malena*
77/87   *Bonnie Leigh*
26/72 **More About John Henry** *Tom T. Hall*
     More And More
1/54   *Webb Pierce*
7/83   *Charley Pride*
95/79 **More I Get The More I Want** *Becky Hobbs*
89/84 **More I Go Blind** *Rod Rishard*
61/82 **More Nights** *Lane Brody*
51/80 **More Than A Bedroom Thing** *Bill Anderson*
5/54 **More Than Anything Else In The World**
     Carl Smith
84/87 **More Than Friendly Persuasion**
     Bonnie Nelson
8/65 **More Than Yesterday** *Slim Whitman*
1/77 **More To Me** *Charley Pride*
14/72 **Mornin' After Baby Let Me Down** *Ray Griff*
56/70 **Mornin Mornin** *Bobby Goldsboro*
1/87 **Mornin' Ride** *Lee Greenwood*
4/70 **Morning** *Jim Ed Brown*
19/71 **Morning After** *Jerry Wallace*
5/80 **Morning Comes Too Early**
     Jim Ed Brown/Helen Cornelius
1/86 **Morning Desire** *Kenny Rogers*
88/74 **Morning Girl** *Duane Dee*
69/82 **Morning, Noon And Night** *Orion*
22/64 **Morning Paper** *Billy Walker*
1/73 **Most Beautiful Girl** *Charlie Rich*
     Most Of All
6/55   *Hank Thompson*
41/84   *Mac Davis*
71/88   *Leon Raines*
59/84 **Most Of All I Remember You** *Mel McDaniel*
18/70 **Most Uncomplicated Goodbye I've Ever**
     Heard *Henson Cargill*
19/75 **Most Wanted Woman In Town** *Roy Head*
7/76 **Motel And Memories** *T.G. Sheppard*
74/78 **Motel Rooms** *Little David Wilkins*
13/67 **Motel Time Again** *Johnny Paycheck*
     Mother ..also see: *(You Make Me Want To Be)*
17/77 **Mother Country Music** *Vern Gosdin*
20/64 **Mother-In-Law** *Jim Nesbitt*
21/68 **Mother, May I** *Liz Anderson & Lynn Anderson*
F/56 **Mother Of A Honky Tonk Girl** *Jim Reeves*
23/81 **Mountain Dew** *Willie Nelson*
     Mountain Music
64/78   *Porter Wagoner*
1/82   *Alabama*
     Mountain Of Love
2/63   *David Houston*
20/71   *Bobby G. Rice*
1/82   *Charley Pride*
74/71 **Mountain Woman** *Harold Lee*
     Move It On Over
4/47   *Hank Williams*
60/73   *Buddy Alan*
     Move Two Mountains ..see: *(You've Got To)*

61/75 **Movie Magazine, Stars In Her Eyes**
     Barbi Benton
10/77 **Movies, The** *Statler Brothers*
1/75 **Movin' On** *Merle Haggard*
20/83 **Movin' Train** *Kendalls*
53/68 **Mr. & Mrs. John Smith**
     Johnny & Jonie Mosby
2/51 **Mister And Mississippi** *Tennessee Ernie Ford*
     Mr. & Mrs. Untrue
64/71   *Johnny Russell*
45/80   *Price Mitchell/Rene Sloane*
11/64 **Mr. And Mrs. Used To Be**
     Ernest Tubb & Loretta Lynn
93/77 **Mr. Bojangles** *Jerry Jeff Walker*
13/78 **Mister D.J.** *T.G. Sheppard*
20/76 **Mr. Doodles** *Donna Fargo*
59/72 **Mr. Fiddle Man** *Johnny Russell*
15/57 **Mister Fire Eyes** *Bonnie Guitar*
     Mister Garfield
15/65   *Johnny Cash*
54/82   *Merle Kilgore*
82/76 **Mr. Guitar** *Cates Sisters*
64/77 **Mr. Heartache** *Susan Raye*
8/63 **Mr. Heartache, Move On** *Coleman O'Neal*
20/79 **Mr. Jones** *Al Downing*
28/63 **Mr. Juke Box** *Ernest Tubb*
8/57 **Mister Love**
     Ernest Tubb/The Wilburn Brothers
2/73 **Mr. Lovemaker** *Johnny Paycheck*
4/51 **Mr. Moon** *Carl Smith*
44/81 **Mister Peepers** *Bill Anderson*
71/70 **Mister Professor** *Leroy Van Dyke*
32/75 **Mr. Right And Mrs. Wrong**
     Mel Tillis & Sherry Bryce
     Mr. Sandman
13/55   *Chet Atkins*
96/78   *Tommy O'Day*
10/81   *Emmylou Harris*
16/67 **Mr. Shorty** *Marty Robbins*
47/75 **Mr. Songwriter** *Sunday Sharpe*
56/73 **Mr. Ting-A-Ling (Steel Guitar Man)**
     George Morgan
4/69 **Mr. Walker, It's All Over** *Billie Jo Spears*
15/72 **Much Oblige** *Jack Greene Jeannie Seely*
13/54 **Much Too Young To Die** *Ray Price*
62/71 **Muddy Bottom** *Osborne Brothers*
15/69 **Muddy Mississippi Line** *Bobby Goldsboro*
16/60 **Mule Skinner Blues** *Fendermen*
3/70 **Mule Skinner Blues (Blue Yodel No. 8)**
     Dolly Parton
1/49 **Mule Train** *Tennessee Ernie Ford*
25/65 **Multiply The Heartaches**
     George Jones & Melba Montgomery
44/79 **Music Box Dancer** *Frank Mills*
92/78 **Music In My Life** *Mac Davis*
59/81 **Music In The Mountains** *Ernie Rowell*
29/78 **Music Is My Woman** *Don King*
4/51 **Music Makin' Mama From Memphis**
     Hank Snow
39/78 **Music, Music, Music** *Rebecca Lynn*
69/67 **Music To Cry By** *Johnny Wright*
63/74 **Musical Chairs** *Tompall Glaser*
     Must You Throw Dirt In My Face
21/62   *Louvin Brothers*
60/78   *Roy Clark*
59/83 **My Angel's Got The Devil In Her Eyes**
     Ed Hunnicutt
8/57 **My Arms Are A House** *Hank Snow*
91/75 **My Babe** *Earl Richards*
23/83 **My Baby Don't Slow Dance** *Johnny Lee*
13/56 **My Baby Left Me** *Elvis Presley*
1/81 **My Baby Thinks He's A Train** *Rosanne Cash*
71/71 **My Baby Used To Be That Way**
     Charlie Walker

34/68	**My Baby Walked Right Out On Me**
	Wanda Jackson
27/64	**My Baby Walks All Over Me** *Johnny Sea*
53/81	**My Baby's Coming Home Again Today**
	Bill Lyerly
	My Baby's Gone
9/59	*Louvin Brothers*
77/76	*Jeanne Pruett*
15/84	*Kendalls*
11/88	*Sawyer Brown*
2/85	**My Baby's Got Good Timing** *Dan Seals*
20/63	**My Baby's Not Here (In Town Tonight)**
	Porter Wagoner
45/81	**My Beginning Was You**
	Jack Grayson & Blackjack
12/49	**My Best To You** *Sons Of The Pioneers*
79/76	**My Better Half** *Del Reeves*
20/69	**My Big Iron Skillet** *Wanda Jackson*
35/68	**My Big Truck Drivin' Man** *Kitty Wells*
69/79	**My Blue Heaven** *Mac Wiseman*
45/69	**My Blue Ridge Mountain Boy** *Dolly Parton*
17/71	**My Blue Tears** *Dolly Parton*
14/75	**My Boy** *Elvis Presley*
	My Bucket's Got A Hole In It
2/49	*Hank Williams*
4/49	*T. Texas Tyler*
10/58	*Ricky Nelson*
17/68	**My Can Do Can't Keep Up With My Want To** *Nat Stuckey*
4/47	**My Chickashay Gal** *Roy Rogers*
	My Cup Runneth Over
63/67	*Blue Boys*
26/69	*Johnny Bush*
64/84	**My Dad** *Ray Stevens*
5/48	**My Daddy Is Only A Picture** *Eddy Arnold*
78/78	**My Daddy Was A Travelin' Man**
	Brenda Kaye Perry
14/66	**My Dreams** *Faron Young*
3/61	**My Ears Should Burn (When Fools Are Talked About)** *Claude Gray*
	My Elusive Dreams
1/67	*David Houston & Tammy Wynette*
41/67	*Curly Putman*
70/67	*Rusty Draper*
73/67	*Johnny Darrell*
27/70	*Bobby Vinton*
3/75	*Charlie Rich*
42/79	**My Empty Arms** *Ann J. Morton*
7/54	**My Everything** *Eddy Arnold*
87/76	**My Eyes Adored You** *Marty Mitchell*
1/76	**My Eyes Can Only See As Far As You**
	Charley Pride
16/63	**My Father's Voice** *Judy Lynn*
1/81	**My Favorite Memory** *Merle Haggard*
6/49	**My Filipino Rose** *Ernest Tubb*
44/83	**My Fingers Do The Talkin'** *Jerry Lee Lewis*
	My First Country Song
93/77	*Jesseca James*
35/83	*Dean Martin*
6/83	**My First Taste Of Texas** *Ed Bruce*
63/70	**My Friend** *Arlene Harden*
11/64	**My Friend On The Right** *Faron Young*
10/65	**(My Friends Are Gonna Be) Strangers**
	Merle Haggard
	My Girl
73/77	*Dale McBride*
73/84	*Savannah*
64/74	**My Girl Bill** *Jim Stafford*
11/68	**My Goal For Today** *Kenny Price*
20/77	**My Good Thing's Gone** *Narvel Felts*
14/69	**My Grass Is Green** *Roy Drusky*
86/79	**My Guns Are Loaded** *Bonnie Tyler*
	My Guy
46/71	*Lynda K. Lance*
43/80	*Margo Smith*

1/72	**My Hang-Up Is You** *Freddie Hart*
	My Happiness
43/69	*Slim Whitman*
47/70	*Johnny & Jonie Mosby*
1/80	**My Heart** *Ronnie Milsap*
	My Heart Cries For You
6/51	*Red Foley & Evelyn Knight*
7/51	*Jimmy Wakely*
63/72	*Doyle Holly*
72/81	*Margo Smith*
10/48	**My Heart Echoes** *Jimmie Osborne*
51/67	**My Heart Gets All The Breaks**
	Wanda Jackson
	My Heart Has A Mind Of Its Own
10/72	*Susan Raye*
11/79	*Debby Boone*
64/85	**My Heart Holds On** *Holly Dunn*
10/52	**My Heart Is Broken In Three** *Slim Whitman*
38/79	**My Heart Is Not My Own** *Mundo Earwood*
66/68	**My Heart Keeps Running To You**
	Johnny Paycheck
1/64	**My Heart Skips A Beat** *Buck Owens*
80/84	**My Heart Will Always Belong To You**
	Donna Fargo
49/78	**My Heart Won't Cry Anymore** *Dickey Lee*
10/49	**My Heart's Bouquet** *'Little' Jimmy Dickens*
85/88	**My Heart's Way Behind** *Doug Peters*
1/80	**My Heroes Have Always Been Cowboys**
	Willie Nelson
17/80	**My Home's In Alabama** *Alabama*
37/75	**My Honky Tonk Ways** *Kenny O'Dell*
44/70	**My Joy** *Johnny Bush*
53/84	**My Kind Of Lady** *Burrito Brothers*
12/67	**My Kind Of Love** *Dave Dudley*
40/79	**My Lady** *Freddie Hart*
	My Lady Loves Me (Just As I Am)
82/80	*Chris Waters*
9/83	*Leon Everette*
5/61	**My Last Date (With You)** *Skeeter Davis*
37/73	**My Last Day** *Tony Douglas*
64/78	**My Last Sad Song** *Jerry Wallace*
1/69	**My Life (Throw It Away If I Want To)**
	Bill Anderson
26/86	**My Life's A Dance** *Anne Murray*
8/56	**My Lips Are Sealed** *Jim Reeves*
1/70	**My Love** *Sonny James*
15/59	**My Love And Little Me** *Margie Bowes*
37/82	**My Love Belongs To You** *Ronnie Rogers*
48/67	**My Love For You (Is Like A Mountain Range)** *Ernest Ashworth*
53/73	**My Love Is Deep, My Love Is Wide** *Pat Daisy*
28/79	**My Mama Never Heard Me Sing**
	Billy 'Crash' Craddock
	My Man
60/70	*Jeannie C. Riley*
1/72	*Tammy Wynette*
80/82	**My Man Friday** *Patti Page*
34/79	**My Mind Hangs On To You** *Billy Walker*
79/85	**My Mind Is On You** *Gus Hardin*
24/77	**My Mountain Dew** *Charlie Rich*
7/62	**My Name Is Mud** *James O'Gwynn*
19/65	**My Old Faded Rose** *Johnny Sea*
	My Old Kentucky Home
69/70	*Osborne Brothers*
42/75	*Johnny Cash*
9/85	**My Old Yellow Car** *Dan Seals*
1/85	**My Only Love** *Statler Brothers*
4/79	**My Own Kind Of Hat** *Merle Haggard*
19/74	**My Part Of Forever** *Johnny Paycheck*
41/79	**My Pledge Of Love** *John Anderson*
	My Prayer
14/76	*Narvel Felts*
66/79	*Glen Campbell*
76/78	**My Pulse Pumps Passions** *Hal Hubble*
14/59	**My Reason For Living** *Ferlin Husky*

6/87 **My Rough And Rowdy Days**
　　　Waylon Jennings
40/64 **My Saro Jane**　*Lester Flatt & Earl Scruggs*
29/63 **My Secret**　*Judy Lynn*
1/57 **My Shoes Keep Walking Back To You**
　　　Ray Price
67/78 **My Side Of Town**　*Billy Larkin*
8/79 **My Silver Lining**　*Mickey Gilley*
15/69 **My Son**　*Jan Howard*
9/50 **My Son Calls Another Man Daddy**
　　　Hank Williams
76/81 **My Song Don't Sing The Same**
　　　Kris Carpenter
My Special Angel
1/57 *Bobby Helms*
82/85 *Younger Brothers*
My Special Prayer
36/69 *Archie Campbell & Lorene Mann*
83/80 *Freddy Fender*
57/85 **My Sweet-Eyed Georgia Girl**　*Atlanta*
62/77 **My Sweet Lady**　*John Denver*
15/64 **My Tears Are Overdue**　*George Jones*
36/64 **My Tears Don't Show**　*Carl Butler & Pearl*
10/49 **My Tennessee Baby**　*Ernest Tubb*
15/73 **My Tennessee Mountain Home**　*Dolly Parton*
19/85 **My Toot-Toot**　*Rockin' Sidney*
45/81 **My Turn**　*Donna Hazard*
39/66 **My Uncle Used To Love Me But She Died**
　　　Roger Miller
2/78 **My Way**　*Elvis Presley*
49/66 **My Way Of Life**　*Sonny Curtis*
23/77 **My Weakness**　*Margo Smith*
36/73 **My Whole World Is Falling Down**
　　　O.B. McClinton
My Wife's House
9/74 *Jerry Wallace*
78/86 *Gene Kennedy*
51/76 **My Window Faces The South**　*Sammi Smith*
15/81 **My Woman Loves The Devil Out Of Me**
　　　Moe Bandy
1/70 **My Woman My Woman, My Wife**
　　　Marty Robbins
4/69 **My Woman's Good To Me**　*David Houston*
68/70 **My Woman's Love**　*Johnny Duncan*
3/75 **My Woman's Man**
　　　Freddie Hart & The Heartbeats
4/79 **My World Begins And Ends With You**
　　　Dave & Sugar
80/79 **Mysterious Lady From St. Martinique**
　　　Hank Snow
57/67 **Mystery Of Tallahatchie Bridge**　*Roger White*
11/56 **Mystery Train**　*Elvis Presley*

N

40/79 **Nadine**　*Freddy Weller*
87/80 **Nag, Nag, Nag**　*Bobby Braddock*
65/71 **Naked And Crying**　*Henson Cargill*
30/80 **Naked In The Rain**　*Loretta Lynn*
70/83 **Name Of The Game Is Cheating**　*Charlie Ross*
16/69 **Name Of The Game Was Love**　*Hank Snow*
Nashville
9/71 *David Houston*
37/73 *Ray Stevens*
61/75 *Hoyt Axton*
93/80 **Nashville Beer Garden**　*Andy Badale Orch.*
54/67 **Nashville Cats**　*Lester Flatt & Earl Scruggs*
74/70 **Nashville Skyline Rag**　*Ray Earl Scruggs*
73/67 **Nashville Women**　*Hank Locklin*
77/82 **Natalie**　*Dave Rowland*

39/80 **Natural Attraction**　*Billie Jo Spears*
1/85 **Natural High**　*Merle Haggard*
Natural Love
82/78 *O.B. McClinton*
20/82 *Petula Clark*
46/74 **Natural Woman**　*Jody Miller*
69/73 **Naughty Girl**　*Guy Shannon*
Near You
74/71 *Lamar Morris*
1/77 *George Jones & Tammy Wynette*
34/87 **Need A Little Time Off For Bad Behavior**
　　　David Allan Coe
Need You
1/67 *Sonny James*
9/72 *David Rogers*
24/76 **Negatory Romance**　*Tom T. Hall*
7/73 **Neither One Of Us**　*Bob Luman*
79/77 **Neon Lady**　*Bobby Wright*
83/77 **Neon Lights**　*Nick Nixon*
3/73 **Neon Rose**　*Mel Tillis*
87/77 **Neon Women**　*Carmol Taylor & Stella Parton*
28/64 **Nester, The**　*Lefty Frizzell*
15/54 **Never**　*Marilyn & Wesley Tuttle*
96/74 **Never A Night Goes By**　*Sharon Vaughn*
6/49 **Never Again**　*Hank Williams*
36/80 **Never Be Anyone Else**　*R.C. Bannon*
1/86 **Never Be You**　*Rosanne Cash*
1/81 **Never Been So Loved (In All My Life)**
　　　Charley Pride
Never Been To Spain
36/72 *Ronnie Sessions*
75/74 *Sammi Smith*
36/75 **Never Coming Back Again**　*Rex Allen, Jr.*
6/84 **Never Could Toe The Mark**　*Waylon Jennings*
18/76 **Never Did Like Whiskey**　*Billie Jo Spears*
83/77 **Never Ending Love Affair**　*Melba Montgomery*
Never Ending Song Of Love
8/71 *Dickey Lee*
57/71 *Mayf Nutter*
43/83 *Osmond Brothers*
78/78 **Never Going Back Again**　*Mac Wiseman*
82/79 **Never Gonna' Be A Country Star**
　　　Kenny Serratt
58/72 **Never Had A Doubt**　*Mayf Nutter*
83/78 **Never Knew (How Much I Loved You 'Til I Lost**
　　　You)　*Dawn Chastain*
58/87 **Never Mind**　*Nanci Griffith*
25/69 **"Never More" Quote The Raven**
　　　Stonewall Jackson
Never My Love
9/78 *Vern Gosdin*
F/79 *Kendalls*
95/76 **Never Naughty Rosie**　*Sue Thompson*
29/80 **Never Seen A Mountain So High**
　　　Ronnie McDowell
Never Trust A Woman
2/42 *Red Foley*
2/47 *Tex Williams*
5/48 *Tiny Hill*
93/78 **Nevertheless**　*Hank Snow*
New Blue Jeans ..see: (I'm Looking For Some)
18/82 **New Cut Road**　*Bobby Bare*
1/89 **New Fool At An Old Game**　*Reba McEntire*
3/54 **New Green Light**　*Hank Thompson*
39/68 **New Heart**　*Ernest Ashworth*
1/47 **New Jole Blonde**　*Red Foley*
43/77 **New Kid In Town**　*Eagles*
25/67 **New Lips**　*Roy Drusky*
1/83 **New Looks From An Old Lover**　*B.J. Thomas*
51/88 **New Never Wore Off My Sweet Baby**
　　　Dean Dillon
28/69 **New Orleans**　*Anthony Armstrong Jones*
10/84 **New Patches**　*Mel Tillis*
87/84 **New Place To Begin**　*Ray Price*
72/66 **New Place To Hang Your Hat**　*Ruby Wright*

2/47	**New Pretty Blonde (Jole Blon)** *Moon Mullican*

2/47 **New Pretty Blonde (Jole Blon)** *Moon Mullican*
79/88 **New River** *Heartland*
26/59 **New River Train** *Bobby Helms*
3/44 **New San Antonio Rose** *Bob Wills*
New Shade Of Blue
64/86   *Perry LaPointe*
2/88   *Southern Pacific*
1/46 **New Spanish Two Step** *Bob Wills*
5/46 **New Steel Guitar Rag** *Bill Boyd*
95/85 **New Tradition** *Bobby G. Rice*
17/82 **New Way Out** *Karen Brooks*
10/52 **New Wears Off Too Fast** *Hank Thompson*
62/82 **New Will Never Wear Off Of You**
  Billy 'Crash' Craddock
73/73 **New York Callin' Miami** *Kent Fox*
19/71 **New York City** *Statler Brothers*
83/81 **New York Cowboy** *Nashville Superpickers*
26/63 **New York Town** *Lester Flatt & Earl Scruggs*
18/80 **New York Wine And Tennessee Shine**
  Dave & Sugar
17/79 **Next Best Feeling** *Mary K. Miller*
86/73 **Next Door Neighbor's Kid** *Jud Strunk*
Next In Line
9/57   *Johnny Cash*
1/68   *Conway Twitty*
F/70 **Next Step Is Love** *Elvis Presley*
Next Time
14/59   *Ernest Tubb*
51/86   *Wild Choir*
15/71 **Next Time I Fall In Love (I Won't)**
  Hank Thompson
92/87 **Next Time I Marry** *Victoria Hallman*
Next To You
78/85   *Craig Dillingham*
74/86   *Tommy Overstreet*
15/55 **Next Voice You Hear** *Hank Snow*
37/70 **Nice 'N' Easy** *Charlie Rich*
85/86 **Nice To Be With You** *Slewfoot*
80/83 **Nickel's Worth Of Heaven** *Brian Collins*
31/66 **Nickels, Quarters And Dimes** *Johnny Wright*
26/59 **Night** *Jimmy Martin*
77/75 **Night Atlanta Burned**
  Atkins String Company
67/83 **Night Dolly Parton Was Almost Mine**
  Pump Boys & Dinettes
81/77 **Night Flying** *Roy Drusky*
Night Games
20/80   *Ray Stevens*
1/83   *Charley Pride*
43/87 **Night Hank Williams Came To Town**
  Johnny Cash
58/85 **Night Has A Heart Of It's Own**
  Lacy J. Dalton
85/80 **Night Lies** *Bill Wence*
Night Life
28/63   *Ray Price*
31/68   *Claude Gray*
20/80   *Danny Davis/Willie Nelson/The Nashville Brass*
59/86   *B.J. Thomas*
F/86   *Roy Clark*
29/71 **Night Miss Nancy Ann's Hotel For Single Girls Burned Down** *Tex Williams*
70/88 **Night Of Love Forgotten** *Bobby G. Rice*
45/64 **Night People** *Leroy Van Dyke*
36/73 **Night The Lights Went Out In Georgia**
  Vicki Lawrence
Night They Drove Old Dixie Down
71/70   *Buckaroos/Don Rich*
33/71   *Alice Creech*
16/76 **Night Time And My Baby** *Joe Stampley*
2/78 **Night Time Magic** *Larry Gatlin*
83/79 **Night Time Music Man** *Judy Argo*
85/83 **Night's Almost Over** *Jacky Ward*
F/62 **Night's Not Over Yet** *Roy Drusky*
14/63 **Nightmare** *Faron Young*

4/86 **Nights** *Ed Bruce*
27/78 **Nights Are Forever Without You**
  Buck Owens
93/83 **Nights Like Tonight** *Austin O'Neal*
95/82 **Nights Out At The Days End** *Owen Brothers*
89/85 **Nightshift** *Nashville Nightshift*
1/81 **9 To 5** *Dolly Parton*
41/67 **Ninety Days** *Jimmy Dean*
2/63 **Ninety Miles An Hour** *Hank Snow*
13/59 **Ninety-Nine Years** *Bill Anderson*
7/81 **1959** *John Anderson*
81/78 **Nineteen-Sixty Something Songwriter Of The Year** *Tennesseans*
6/86 **1982** *Randy Travis*
58/84 **1984** *Craig Dillingham*
3/76 **9,999,999 Tears** *Dickey Lee*
76/78 **Ninth Of September** *Jim Chesnut*
39/81 **No Aces** *Patti Page*
8/68 **No Another Time** *Lynn Anderson*
72/69 **No Blues Is Good News** *George Jones*
1/74 **No Charge** *Melba Montgomery*
19/87 **No Easy Horses**
  Schuyler, Knobloch & Bickhardt
49/83 **No Fair Fallin' In Love** *Jan Gray*
No Gettin' Over Me *..see: (There's)*
83/79 **No Greater Love** *Billy Stack*
60/73 **No Headstone On My Grave** *Jerry Lee Lewis*
No Help Wanted
1/53   *Carlisles*
7/53   *Ernest Tubb & Red Foley (#2)*
9/53   *Hank Thompson*
13/55 **No, I Don't Believe I Will** *Carl Smith*
2/44 **No Letter Today** *Ted Daffan's Texans*
No Love At All
15/70   *Lynn Anderson*
80/80   *Jan Gray*
No Love Have I
4/60   *Webb Pierce*
26/78   *Gail Davies*
17/79 **No Memories Hangin' Round**
  Rosanne Cash/Bobby Bare
19/73 **No More Hanging On** *Jerry Lee Lewis*
No More One More Time
71/87   *Judy Byram*
7/88   *Jo-el Sonnier*
15/71 **No Need To Worry**
  Johnny Cash & June Carter
8/78 **No, No, No (I'd Rather Be Free)**
  Rex Allen, Jr.
F/56 **No One But You** *Kitty Wells & Red Foley*
79/87 **No One Can Touch Me** *Carla Monday*
14/55 **No One Dear But You** *Johnnie & Jack*
7/79 **No One Else In The World** *Tammy Wynette*
6/86 **No One Mends A Broken Heart Like You**
  Barbara Mandrell
6/46 **No One To Cry To** *Sons Of The Pioneers*
No One Will Ever Know
42/66   *Frank Ifield*
13/80   *Gene Watson*
10/67 **No One's Gonna Hurt You Anymore**
  Bill Anderson
78/87 **No Ordinary Memory** *Bill Anderson*
93/80 **No Ordinary Woman** *Byron Gallimore*
2/87 **No Place Like Home** *Randy Travis*
78/82 **No Place To Hide** *Gayle Zeiler*
No Relief In Sight
98/77   *Willie Rainsford*
20/82   *Con Hunley*
62/72 **No Rings-No Strings** *Del Reeves*
57/82 **No Room To Cry** *Mike Campbell*
32/65 **No Sign Of Living** *Dottie West*
10/78 **No Sleep Tonight** *Randy Barlow*
93/84 **No Survivors** *Peter Isaacson*
16/67 **No Tears Milady** *Marty Robbins*
72/78 **No Tell Motel** *David Houston*

40/64	**No Thanks, I Just Had One**
	Faron Young & Margie Singleton
3/46	**No Vacancy** *Merle Travis*
97/78	**No Way Around It (It's Love)** *Billy Swan*
49/85	**No Way Jose** *David Frizzell*
69/82	**No Way Out** *Johnny Paycheck*
53/80	**No Way To Drown A Memory**
	Stoney Edwards
1/82	**Nobody** *Sylvia*
4/66	**Nobody But A Fool (Would Love You)**
	Connie Smith
	Nobody But You
43/69	*Buckaroos/Don Rich*
93/73	*Linda Plowman*
2/83	*Don Williams*
44/77	**Nobody Cares But You** *Freddy Weller*
61/83	**Nobody Else For Me** *Stephanie Winslow*
49/85	**Nobody Ever Gets Enough Love** *Con Hunley*
1/85	**Nobody Falls Like A Fool**
	Earl Thomas Conley
	Nobody In His Right Mind Would've Left Her
25/81	*Dean Dillon*
1/86	*George Strait*
53/88	**Nobody Knows** *John Wesley Ryles*
1/79	**Nobody Likes Sad Songs** *Ronnie Milsap*
68/81	**Nobody Loves Anybody Anymore**
	Kris Kristofferson
1/84	**Nobody Loves Me Like You Do**
	Anne Murray/Dave Loggins
26/87	**Nobody Should Have To Love This Way**
	Crystal Gayle
82/88	**Nobody There But Me** *Willie Nelson*
3/85	**Nobody Wants To Be Alone** *Crystal Gayle*
68/70	**Nobody Wants To Hear It Like It Is**
	Jack Barlow
5/73	**Nobody Wins** *Brenda Lee*
22/88	**Nobody's Angel** *Crystal Gayle*
46/67	**Nobody's Child** *Hank Williams, Jr.*
	Nobody's Darling But Mine
13/60	*Johnny Sea*
87/80	*B.J. Wright*
	Nobody's Fool
10/70	*Jim Reeves*
24/81	*Deborah Allen*
11/62	**Nobody's Fool But Yours** *Buck Owens*
9/50	**Nobody's Lonesome For Me** *Hank Williams*
8/69	**None Of My Business** *Henson Cargill*
73/78	**Norma Jean** *Sammi Smith*
61/68	**Normally, Norma Loves Me** *Red Sovine*
37/81	**North Alabama** *Dave Kirby*
42/72	**North Carolina** *Dallas Frazier*
17/80	**North Of The Border** *Johnny Rodriguez*
1/61	**North To Alaska** *Johnny Horton*
71/73	**North To Chicago** *Hank Snow*
	North Wind
8/53	*Slim Whitman*
56/82	*Jim & Jesse/Charlie Louvin*
17/70	**Northeast Arkansas Mississippi County**
	Bootlegger *Kenny Price*
90/80	**Not A Day Goes By** *Anna Sudderth*
43/88	**Not A Night Goes By** *Tim Malchak*
76/85	**Not Another Heart Song** *Tom Jones*
29/88	**Not Enough Love** *Tom Wopat*
62/80	**Not Exactly Free** *O.B. McClinton*
24/64	**Not My Kind Of People** *Stonewall Jackson*
87/84	**Not On The Bottom Yet** *Boxcar Willie*
13/63	**Not So Long Ago** *Marty Robbins*
44/66	**Not That I Care** *Jerry Wallace*
	Not Tonight
77/74	*Little David Wilkins*
74/86	*Paul Proctor*
52/87	**Not Tonight I've Got A Heartache**
	Vicki Rae Von
7/63	**Not What I Had In Mind** *George Jones*
62/68	**Note In Box #9** *Stu Phillips*

70/83	**Nothin' But You** *Steve Earle*
11/58	**Nothin' Needs Nothin'** *Marvin Rainwater*
35/76	**Nothin' Takes The Place Of You**
	Asleep At The Wheel
82/81	**Nothin' To Do But Just Lie** *Wesley Ryan*
33/86	**Nothin' Ventured Nothin' Gained** *Sylvia*
61/67	**Nothin's Bad As Bein' Lonely** *Johnny Sea*
10/79	**Nothing As Original As You** *Statler Brothers*
26/82	**Nothing Behind You, Nothing In Sight**
	John Conlee
F/74	**Nothing Between** *Porter Wagoner*
19/82	**Nothing But The Radio On** *Younger Brothers*
91/79	**Nothing But Time** *Helen Hudson*
25/59	**Nothing But True Love** *Margie Singleton*
12/86	**Nothing But Your Love Matters** *Gatlin Bros.*
37/85	**Nothing Can Hurt Me Now** *Gail Davies*
68/72	**Nothing Can Stop My Loving You**
	Patsy Sledd
7/73	**Nothing Ever Hurt Me (Half As Bad)**
	George Jones
87/84	**(Nothing Left Between Us) But Alabama**
	Gordon Dee
	Nothing Left To Lose
34/65	*Faron Young*
85/88	*Tiny Wellman*
10/84	**Nothing Like Falling In Love** *Eddie Rabbitt*
4/80	**Nothing Sure Looked Good On You**
	Gene Watson
39/68	**Nothing Takes The Place Of Loving You**
	Stonewall Jackson
1/86	**Now And Forever (You And Me)**
	Anne Murray
	Now And Then
	..also see: (I Still Long To Hold You)
	(Now and Then, There's) A Fool Such As I
3/53	*Hank Snow*
98/78	*Bill Green*
90/79	*Rodney Crowell*
56/76	**Now Everybody Knows** *Charlie Rich*
68/68	**Now I Can Live Again** *Mickey Gilley*
	Now I Lay Me Down To Cheat
62/82	*David Allan Coe*
56/84	*Shelly West*
69/86	**Now I've Got A Heart Of Gold** *Sonny Curtis*
83/86	**Now She's In Paris** *Dave Holiaday*
98/73	**Now That It's Over** *Brush Arbor*
38/81	**Now That The Feeling's Gone**
	Billy 'Crash' Craddock
21/85	**Now There's You** *Shelly West*
	Now You See 'Em, Now You Don't
19/78	*Roy Head*
70/88	*Marty Haggard*
64/87	**Now You're Talkin'** *Mel McDaniel*
20/87	**Nowhere Road** *Steve Earle*
41/65	**Number One Heel** *Bonnie Owens*
	#1 With A Heartache
66/76	*Billy Larkin*
94/78	*La Costa*
11/80	**Numbers** *Bobby Bare*
94/77	**Nyquil Blues** *Alvin Crow*

O

3/47	**Oakie Boogie** *Jack Guthrie*
91/77	**Obscene Phone Call** *Johnny Russell*
28/80	**Occasional Rose** *Marty Robbins*
6/70	**Occasional Wife** *Faron Young*
1/87	**Ocean Front Property** *George Strait*
29/61	**Ocean Of Tears** *Billie Jean Horton*
7/61	**Odds And Ends** *Warren Smith*

66/74	**Odds And Ends (Bits and Pieces)**
	Charlie Walker
21/71	**Ode To A Half A Pound Of Ground Round**
	Tom T. Hall
	Ode To Billie Joe
17/67	*Bobbie Gentry*
39/67	*Margie Singleton*
55/74	**Ode To Jole Blon** *Gary Sargeants*
3/65	**Ode To The Little Brown Shack Out Back**
	Billy Edd Wheeler
38/67	**Off And On** *Charlie Louvin*
F/76	**Off And Running** *Maury Finney*
5/79	**Official Historian On Shirley Jean Berrell**
	Statler Brothers
	Oh, Baby Mine (I Get So Lonely)
1/54	*Johnnie & Jack*
49/79	*Bobby G. Rice*
2/83	*Statler Brothers*
21/75	**Oh Boy** *Diana Trask*
38/84	**Oh Carolina** *Vince Gill*
10/86	**Oh Darlin'** *O'Kanes*
12/82	**Oh Girl** *Con Hunley*
25/70	**Oh Happy Day** *Glen Campbell*
9/87	**Oh Heart** *Baillie & The Boys*
70/74	**Oh, How Happy** *Sherry Bryce*
6/80	**Oh, How I Miss You Tonight**
	Jim Reeves/Deborah Allen
65/70	**Oh How I Waited** *Ron Lowry*
36/75	**Oh, How Love Changes**
	Don Gibson & Sue Thompson
	Oh Jenny
48/88	*Billy Montana*
13/61	*Johnny Cash*
64/66	*Bobbi Martin*
63/70	*Stonewall Jackson*
92/76	*Loggins & Messina*
78/86	**Oh Louisiana** *Jim & Jesse*
41/71	**Oh, Love Of Mine** *Johnny & Jonie Mosby*
	Oh No!
42/64	*Browns*
76/82	*Randy Parton*
	Oh-Oh, I'm Falling In Love Again
5/58	*Jimmie Rodgers*
29/73	*Eddy Arnold*
4/71	**Oh, Singer** *Jeannie C. Riley*
8/57	**Oh, So Many Years**
	Kitty Wells & Webb Pierce
	Oh, Such A Stranger
68/68	*Frank Ifield*
61/78	*Don Gibson*
23/76	**Oh, Sweet Temptation** *Gary Stewart*
97/76	**Oh Those Texas Women** *Gene Davis*
5/88	**Oh What A Love** *Nitty Gritty Dirt Band*
56/87	**Oh What A Night** *Mel McDaniel*
60/69	**Oh What A Woman!** *Jerry Reed*
4/47	**(Oh Why, Oh Why, Did I Ever Leave)**
	Wyoming *Dick Jurgens*
	Oh! Woman
17/67	*Nat Stuckey*
55/73	*Jack Barlow*
57/86	**Oh Yes I Can** *Tari Hensley*
1/69	**Okie From Muskogee** *Merle Haggard*
9/86	**Oklahoma Borderline** *Vince Gill*
49/82	**Oklahoma Crude** *Corbin/Hanner Band*
46/84	**Oklahoma Heart** *Becky Hobbs*
	Oklahoma Hills
1/45	*Jack Guthrie*
7/61	*Hank Thompson*
60/69	**Oklahoma Home Brew** *Hank Thompson*
15/72	**Oklahoma Sunday Morning** *Glen Campbell*
86/76	**Oklahoma Sunshine** *Pat Boone*
9/48	**Oklahoma Waltz** *Johnny Bond*
	Ol' Man River ..see: Old Man River
70/68	**Old Before My Time** *Bobby Wright*

38/73	**Old Betsy Goes Boing, Boing, Boing**
	Hummers
48/86	**Old Blue Yodeler** *Razzy Bailey*
52/68	**Old Bridge** *Jean Shepard*
11/87	**Old Bridges Burn Slow** *Billy Joe Royal*
30/66	**Old Brush Arbors** *George Jones*
48/64	**Old Courthouse** *Faron Young*
1/73	**(Old Dogs-Children And) Watermelon**
	Wine *Tom T. Hall*
53/70	**Old Enough To Want To (Fool Enough To**
	Try) *Norro Wilson*
	Old Faithful
15/69	*Mel Tillis*
49/73	*Tony Booth*
86/81	**Old Familiar Feeling** *Wyvon Alexander*
83/81	**Old Fangled Country Songs** *Kenny O.*
F/78	**Old Fashioned Love** *Kendalls*
58/72	**Old Fashioned Love Song** *Jeris Ross*
93/81	**Old Fashioned Lover** *Michael Spitz*
93/83	**Old Fashioned Lovin'** *Sierra*
38/73	**Old Fashioned Singing**
	George Jones & Tammy Wynette
	Old Flame
1/81	*Alabama*
5/86	*Juice Newton*
54/78	**Old Flame, New Fire** *Hank Williams, Jr.*
	Old Flames (Can't Hold A Candle To You)
14/78	*Joe Sun*
86/78	*Brian Collins*
1/80	*Dolly Parton*
2/88	**Old Folks** *Ronnie Milsap & Mike Reid*
49/66	**Old French Quarter (In New Orleans)**
	Billy Walker
19/82	**Old Friends**
	Roger Miller/Willie Nelson/Ray Price
6/80	**Old Habits** *Hank Williams, Jr.*
2/85	**Old Hippie** *Bellamy Brothers*
19/74	**Old Home Filler-Up An' Keep On-A-Truckin'**
	Cafe *C.W. McCall*
44/82	**Old Home Town** *Glen Campbell*
30/88	**Old Kind Of Love** *Ricky Skaggs*
34/77	**Old King Kong** *George Jones*
20/60	**Old Lamplighter** *Browns*
30/60	**Old Log Cabin For Sale** *Porter Wagoner*
11/55	**Old Lonesome Times** *Carl Smith*
63/70	**Old Love Affair Now Showing**
	Leroy Van Dyke
11/77	**Old Man And His Horn** *Gene Watson*
1/74	**Old Man From The Mountain** *Merle Haggard*
63/88	**Old Man No One Loves** *George Jones*
	Old Man River
86/76	*Shylo*
22/83	*Mel McDaniel*
31/70	**Old Man Willis** *Nat Stuckey*
74/84	**Old Memories Are Hard To Lose**
	Kimberly Springs
90/75	**Old Memory (Got In My Eye)** *Ferlin Husky*
7/59	**Old Moon** *Betty Foley*
	Old Photographs
81/84	*Sam Neely*
27/88	*Sawyer Brown*
11/64	**Old Records** *Margie Singleton*
50/65	**Old Red** *Marty Robbins*
3/62	**Old Rivers** *Walter Brennan*
51/68	**Old Ryman** *Hank Williams, Jr.*
5/86	**Old School** *John Conlee*
8/63	**Old Showboat** *Stonewall Jackson*
9/80	**Old Side Of Town** *Tom T. Hall*
9/51	**Old Soldiers Never Die** *Gene Autry*
26/77	**Old Time Feeling**
	Johnny Cash & June Carter Cash
64/77	**Old Time Lovin'** *Kenny Starr*
97/74	**Old Time Sunshine Song** *Roy Acuff*
21/86	**Old Violin** *Johnny Paycheck*
	Old Wives' Tale ..see: (Just An)

3/52	**Older And Bolder** *Eddy Arnold*	10/65	**One Dyin' And A Buryin'** *Roger Miller*
8/74	**Older The Violin, The Sweeter The Music**	70/83	**One Fiddle, Two Fiddle** *Ray Price*
	Hank Thompson	75/82	**One Fine Morning** *Corbin/Hanner Band*
1/81	**Older Women** *Ronnie McDowell*	74/88	**One Fire Between Us** *Judy Byram*
52/86	**Ole Rock And Roller** *Keith Stegall*	2/87	**One For The Money** *T.G. Sheppard*
	Ole Slew-Foot	1/88	**One Friend** *Dan Seals*
48/66	*Porter Wagoner*	71/80	**One Good Reason** *Melissa Lewis*
31/79	*Porter Wagoner*	17/61	**One Grain Of Sand** *Eddy Arnold*
23/87	**On And On** *Anne Murray*		**One Has My Name (The Other Has My Heart)**
27/79	**On Business For The King** *Joe Sun*	1/48	*Jimmy Wakely*
1/78	**On My Knees** *Charlie Rich with Janie Fricke*	11/48	*Eddie Dean*
12/57	**On My Mind Again** *Billy Walker*	8/49	*Bob Eberly*
	On Our Last Date	3/69	*Jerry Lee Lewis*
	..see: (Lost Her [His] Love)	43/85	**One Hell Of A Heartache** *Gene Watson*
7/68	**On Tap, In The Can, Or In The Bottle**		**One Hell Of A Woman** *..see: (You Better Be)*
	Hank Thompson	14/71	**One Hundred Children** *Tom T. Hall*
9/74	**On The Cover Of The Music City News**	1/86	**100% Chance Of Rain** *Gary Morris*
	Buck Owens	3/86	**One I Loved Back Then (The Corvette**
76/81	**On The Inside** *Patti Page*		**Song)** *George Jones*
	On The Other Hand	58/75	**One I Sing My Love Songs To** *Tommy Cash*
44/67	*Charlie Louvin*	11/64	**One If For Him, Two If For Me**
67/85	*Randy Travis*		*David Houston*
1/86	*Randy Travis*		**One In A Million**
29/76	**On The Rebound**	73/78	*Nate Harvell*
	Del Reeves & Billie Jo Spears	1/80	*Johnny Lee*
1/80	**On The Road Again** *Willie Nelson*	19/66	**One In A Row** *Willie Nelson*
49/75	**On The Way Home** *Betty Jean Robinson*	1/49	**One Kiss Too Many** *Eddy Arnold*
49/84	**On The Wings Of A Nightingale**	33/73	**One Last Time** *Glen Campbell*
	Everly Brothers		*(also see: Let's Get Together)*
85/83	**On The Wings Of My Victory** *Glen Campbell*	91/79	**One Little Skinny Rib** *Cal Smith*
8/51	**On Top Of Old Smoky**	11/62	**One Look At Heaven** *Stonewall Jackson*
	Weavers & Terry Gilkyson	3/86	**One Love At A Time** *Tanya Tucker*
4/67	**Once** *Ferlin Husky*	95/76	**One Love Down** *Gary Mack*
1/64	**Once A Day** *Connie Smith*	76/81	**One Love Over Easy** *Sami Jo Cole*
68/87	**Once A Fool, Always A Fool** *Jeff Dugan*		**One Man Band**
91/75	**Once Again I Go To Sleep With Lovin' On My**	27/65	*Phil Baugh*
	Mind *Melody Allen*	61/68	*Norma Jean*
	Once In A Blue Moon	63/69	*Sheb Wooley*
34/79	*Zella Lehr*	42/86	*Moe Bandy*
82/83	*Hank Thompson*	72/80	**One Man's Trash (Is Another Man's**
1/86	*Earl Thomas Conley*		**Treasure)** *Marty Robbins*
5/77	**Once In A Lifetime Thing** *John Wesley Ryles*	85/79	**One Man's Woman** *Kelly Warren*
85/86	**Once In A Very Blue Moon** *Nanci Griffith*	2/70	**One Minute Past Eternity** *Jerry Lee Lewis*
	Once More	11/75	**One Monkey Don't Stop No Show**
8/58	*Roy Acuff*		*Little David Wilkins*
13/58	*Osborne Brothers & Red Allen*	56/71	**One More Drink** *Mel Tillis*
66/69	*Leona Williams*	95/83	**One More Goodbye, One More Hello**
	Once More With Feeling		*Donnie Record*
2/70	*Jerry Lee Lewis*	97/78	**One More Kiss** *Terri Bishop*
42/70	*Willie Nelson*	33/81	**One More Last Chance** *Ray Stevens*
80/86	**Once Upon A Time** *Bobby Blue*	12/69	**One More Mile** *Dave Dudley*
	Once You Get The Feel Of It	48/70	**One More Mountain To Climb** *Freddie Hart*
42/83	*Con Hunley*	42/84	**One More Shot** *Johnny Lee*
79/88	*Marshall Tucker Band*		**One More Time**
80/81	**Once You Were Mine** *Dottie West*	2/60	*Ray Price*
3/74	**Once You've Had The Best** *George Jones*	28/71	*Ferlin Husky*
95/78	**One A.M. Alone** *Dave Dudley*	44/72	*Joanne Heel*
27/63	**One Among The Many** *Ned Miller*	65/74	*Skeeter Davis*
93/79	**One And One Make Three** *Ron Shaw*	80/78	*Sandra Kaye*
93/83	**One Away From One Too Many** *Billy Walker*	31/76	**One More Time (Karneval)** *Crystal Gayle*
85/80	**One Bar At A Time** *Stoney Edwards*	28/76	**(One More Year Of) Daddy's Little Girl**
61/85	**One Big Family** *Heart Of Nashville*		*Ray Sawyer*
42/66	**One Bum Town** *Del Reeves*		**One Night**
	One By One	24/58	*Elvis Presley*
1/54	*Kitty Wells & Red Foley*	57/72	*Jeannie C. Riley*
95/75	*Jimmy Elledge*	51/76	*Roy Head*
73/88	**One Dance Love Affair** *Jon Washington*	10/81	**One-Night Fever** *Mel Tillis*
	One Day At A Time	85/80	**One Night Honeymoon** *Troy Seals*
8/74	*Don Gibson*	80/80	**One Night Led To Two** *Paul Evans*
19/74	*Marilyn Sellars*	39/71	**One Night Of Love** *Johnny Duncan*
1/80	*Cristy Lane*		**One Night Stand**
72/82	**One Day Since Yesterday** *Colleen Camp*	35/70	*Susan Raye*
23/64	**One Dozen Roses (And Our Love)**	89/74	*Rick Nelson*
	George Morgan	47/77	**One Night Stands** *Hank Williams, Jr.*
54/66	**One Dream** *Slim Whitman*	82/82	**One Night Stanley** *Jerry Abbott*

71/88	**One Nite Stan** *Ethel & The Shameless Hussies*	74/83	**Only The Names Have Been Changed**
	One Of A Kind		*Penny DeHaven*
6/77	*Tammy Wynette*	87/77	**Only The Shadows Know** *Vernon Oxford*
13/80	*Moe Bandy*	58/67	**Only Thing I Want** *Cal Smith*
1/83	**One Of A Kind Pair Of Fools**	36/68	**Only Way Out (Is To Walk Over Me)**
	Barbara Mandrell		*Charlie Louvin*
28/60	**One Of Her Fools** *Paul Davis*	32/81	**Only When I Laugh** *Brenda Lee*
67/87	**One Of The Boys** *Cheryl Handy*	4/87	**Only When I Love** *Holly Dunn*
69/70	**One Of The Fortunate Few** *Hank Thompson*		**Only You**
	One Of These Days	68/69	*Norro Wilson*
8/64	*Marty Robbins*	34/78	*Freddie Hart*
36/68	*Tompall/Glaser Brothers*	13/82	*Reba McEntire*
3/76	*Emmylou Harris*	36/86	*Statler Brothers*
2/66	**One On The Right Is On The Left**	1/65	**Only You (Can Break My Heart)** *Buck Owens*
	Johnny Cash	9/56	**Only You, Only You** *Charlie Walker*
4/85	**One Owner Heart** *T.G. Sheppard*	85/78	**Ooh Baby Baby** *Linda Ronstadt*
1/76	**One Piece At A Time** *Johnny Cash*	13/62	**Open Pit Mine** *George Jones*
1/87	**One Promise Too Late** *Reba McEntire*	45/71	**Open Up The Book (And Take A Look)**
26/78	**One Run For The Roses** *Narvel Felts*		*Ferlin Husky*
8/78	**One Sided Conversation** *Gene Watson*	98/77	**Open Up Your Door** *Eddie Rivers*
52/84	**One Sided Love Affair** *Mike Campbell*		**Open Up Your Heart**
9/70	**One Song Away** *Tommy Cash*	1/66	*Buck Owens*
48/75	**One Step** *Bobby Harden*	14/73	*Roger Miller*
14/61	**One Step Ahead Of My Past** *Hank Locklin*	78/82	**Operator** *Tennessee Express*
15/57	**One Step At A Time** *Brenda Lee*	9/82	**Operator, Long Distance Please**
90/83	**One Step Closer** *Cannons*		*Barbara Mandrell*
2/88	**One Step Forward** *Desert Rose Band*	9/85	**Operator, Operator** *Eddy Raven*
8/84	**One Takes The Blame** *Statler Brothers*		*(also see: Heart On The Line)*
90/82	**One Tear (At A Time)** *Noel*	10/61	**Optimistic** *Skeeter Davis*
37/82	**One That Got Away** *Mel Tillis*		**Orange Blossom Special**
17/79	**One Thing My Lady Never Puts Into**	3/65	*Johnny Cash*
	Words *Mel Street*	26/73	*Charlie McCoy*
55/88	**One Time One Night** *Los Lobos*	63/74	*Johnny Darrell*
97/88	**One Time Thing** *Ramsey Kearney*	26/77	**Ordinary Man** *Dale McBride*
54/72	**One Tin Soldier** *Skeeter Davis*	29/68	**Ordinary Miracle** *Bobby Lewis*
82/81	**One Too Many Memories** *Ray Pillow*	52/74	**Orleans Parish Prison** *Johnny Cash*
4/88	**One True Love** *O'Kanes*	19/61	**Other Cheek** *Kitty Wells*
88/75	**One, Two, Three (Never Gonna Fall In Love**	30/88	**Other Guy** *David Slater*
	Again) *Jim Glaser*	71/78	**Other Side Of Jeannie** *Chuck Pollard*
20/61	**One Way Street** *Bob Gallion*		**Other Side Of The Hill** *..see: (Lover Of The)*
12/58	**One Week Later** *Kitty Wells & Webb Pierce*	72/78	**Other Side Of The Morning**
32/72	**One Woman's Trash (Another Woman's**		*Barbara Fairchild*
	Treasure) *Bobbie Roy*		**Other Woman**
61/83	**1 Yr 2 Mo 11 Days** *Wayne Carson*	13/63	*Loretta Lynn*
38/72	**One You Say Good Mornin' To** *Jimmy Dean*	2/65	*Ray Price*
13/60	**One You Slip Around With** *Jan Howard*	74/70	*Ray Pennington*
1/72	**One's On The Way** *Loretta Lynn*	56/77	**Our Baby's Gone** *Herb Pedersen*
2/72	**Oney** *Johnny Cash*	58/68	**Our Golden Wedding Day**
47/85	**Only A Dream Away** *Mason Dixon*		*Johnny & Jonie Mosby*
61/68	**Only A Fool** *Ned Miller*	24/65	**Our Hearts Are Holding Hands**
2/84	**Only A Lonely Heart Knows**		*Ernest Tubb & Loretta Lynn*
	Barbara Mandrell	6/52	**Our Honeymoon** *Carl Smith*
24/71	**Only A Woman Like You** *Nat Stuckey*	18/69	**Our House Is Not A Home** *Lynn Anderson*
	Only Daddy That'll Walk The Line	8/50	**Our Lady Of Fatima** *Red Foley*
2/68	*Waylon Jennings*	44/75	**Our Love** *Roger Miller*
73/68	*Jim Alley*	77/87	**Our Love Is Like The South** *A.J. Masters*
59/79	**Only Diamonds Are Forever** *Zella Lehr*	1/83	**Our Love Is On The Faultline** *Crystal Gayle*
13/63	**Only Girl I Can't Forget** *Del Reeves*	21/62	**Our Mansion Is A Prison Now** *Kitty Wells*
12/83	**Only If There Is Another You** *Moe Bandy*	45/75	**Our Marriage Was A Failure** *Johnny Russell*
5/85	**Only In My Mind** *Reba McEntire*	91/77	**Our Old Mansion** *Buck Owens*
	Only Love Can Break A Heart	42/65	**Our Ship Of Love** *Carl Butler & Pearl*
2/72	*Sonny James*	27/67	**Our Side** *Van Trevor*
7/79	*Kenny Dale*	33/64	**Our Things** *Margie Bowes*
11/88	**Only Love Can Save Me Now** *Crystal Gayle*	56/82	**Our Wedding Band**
42/85	**Only Love Will Make It Right**		*Louise Mandrell & RC Bannon*
	Nicolette Larson	21/86	**Out Among The Stars** *Merle Haggard*
49/66	**Only Me And My Hairdresser Know**	9/54	**Out Behind The Barn** *'Little' Jimmy Dickens*
	Kitty Wells	11/86	**Out Goin' Cattin'**
80/86	**Only One** *James Taylor*		*Sawyer Brown with 'Cat' Joe Bonsall*
1/78	**Only One Love In My Life** *Ronnie Milsap*	81/88	**Out Of Beer** *Johnny Paycheck*
1/82	**Only One You** *T.G. Sheppard*	25/60	**Out Of Control** *George Jones*
55/76	**Only Sixteen** *Dr. Hook*	4/75	**Out Of Hand** *Gary Stewart*
81/78	**Only The Best** *George Hamilton IV*	1/78	**Out Of My Head And Back In My Bed**
1/69	**Only The Lonely** *Sonny James*		*Loretta Lynn*
		50/77	**Out Of My Mind** *Cates Sisters*

10/88 **Out Of Sight And On My Mind**
     Billy Joe Royal
71/85 **Out Of Sight Out Of Mind** *Narvel Felts*
34/80 **Out Of Your Mind** *Joe Sun*
46/80 **Out Run The Sun** *Jim Chesnut*
32/65 **Out Where The Ocean Meets The Sky**
     Hugh X. Lewis
     Out With The Boys
91/79   *Barry Grant*
87/87   *Rhonda Manning*
27/79 **Outlaw's Prayer** *Johnny Paycheck*
81/79 **Outlaws And Lone Star Beer** *C.W. McCall*
18/83 **Outside Lookin' In** *Bandana*
10/80 **Over** *Leon Everette*
10/80 **Over The Rainbow** *Jerry Lee Lewis*
69/82 **Over Thirty (Not Over The Hill)**
     Conway Twitty
15/49 **Over Three Hills** *Ernie Benedict*
15/83 **Over You** *Lane Brody*
59/88 **Overdue** *Canyon*
10/58 **Overnight** *Jim Reeves*
 7/76 **Overnight Sensation** *Mickey Gilley*
 5/84 **Ozark Mountain Jubilee** *Oak Ridge Boys*
87/76 **Ozark Mountain Lullaby** *Susan Raye*

P

86/85 **P.S.** *Noel*
 8/84 **P.S. I Love You** *Tom T. Hall*
 3/62 **P.T. 109** *Jimmy Dean*
     Padre
 5/71   *Marty Robbins*
92/75   *Judy Lynn*
34/86 **Pages Of My Mind** *Ray Charles*
77/82 **Pain In My Past** *Rovers*
49/72 **Paint Me A Rainbow** *Wynn Stewart*
13/89 **Paint The Town And Hang The Moon**
     Tonight *J. C. Crowley*
49/85 **Paint The Town Blue** *Robin Lee & Lobo*
52/68 **Painted Girls And Wine** *Ed Bruce*
78/77 **Painted Lady** *Chuck Woolery*
 8/45 **Pair Of Broken Hearts** *Spade Cooley*
19/80 **Pair Of Old Sneakers**
     George Jones & Tammy Wynette
81/80 **Palimony** *Leon Rausch*
33/76 **Paloma Blanca** *George Baker Selection*
88/76 **Pamela Brown** *Jud Strunk*
 9/48 **Pan American** *Hawkshaw Hawkins*
 7/50 **Pan American Boogie** *Delmore Brothers*
 6/49 **Pan Handle Rag** *Leon McAuliff*
 1/83 **Pancho And Lefty**
     Willie Nelson & Merle Haggard
64/67 **Papa** *Bill Anderson*
62/69 **Papa Joe's Thing** *Papa Joe's Music Box*
16/71 **Papa Was A Good Man** *Johnny Cash*
30/75 **Paper Lovin'** *Margo Smith*
 8/67 **Paper Mansions** *Dottie West*
 1/73 **Paper Roses** *Marie Osmond*
 3/77 **Paper Rosie** *Gene Watson*
85/88 **Paper Thin Walls** *David Wills*
     Paradise
26/76   *Lynn Anderson*
80/81   *Southern Ashe*
54/82 **Paradise Knife And Gun Club** *Roy Clark*
 1/83 **Paradise Tonight**
     Charly McClain & Mickey Gilley
67/68 **Parchman Farm Blues** *Claude King*
66/85 **Pardon Me, But This Heart's Taken**
     Terry Gregory

64/84 **Pardon Me (Haven't We Loved Somewhere**
     Before) *Becky Hobbs*
63/81 **Pardon My French** *Bobby G. Rice*
49/71 **Part Of America Died** *Eddy Arnold*
     Part Of Me That Needs You Most
79/79   *Miki Mori*
61/85   *B.J. Thomas*
35/72 **Part Of Your Life** *Charlie Rich*
68/69 **Parting (Is Such Sweet Sorrow)**
     Wilma Burgess
48/69 **Partly Bill** *LaWanda Lindsey*
38/81 **Partner Nobody Chose** *Guy Clark*
 5/59 **Partners** *Jim Reeves*
24/87 **Partners After All** *Willie Nelson*
 6/86 **Partners, Brothers And Friends**
     Nitty Gritty Dirt Band
31/72 **Party Dolls And Wine** *Red Steagall*
69/88 **Party People** *Butch Baker*
24/67 **Party Pickin'**
     George Jones & Melba Montgomery
 1/81 **Party Time** *T.G. Sheppard*
24/67 **Party's Over** *Willie Nelson*
78/83 **Party's Over (Everybody's Gone)** *Sam Neely*
 9/73 **Pass Me By** *Johnny Rodriguez*
22/80 **Pass Me By (If You're Only Passing**
     Through) *Janie Frickie*
15/65 **Pass The Booze** *Ernest Tubb*
28/77 **Passing Thing** *Ray Griff*
     Passing Through
37/64   *David Houston*
67/69   *Ray Corbin*
23/61 **Passing Zone Blues** *Coleman Wilson*
 4/64 **Password** *Kitty Wells*
     Patches
26/70   *Ray Griff*
30/81   *Jerry Reed*
46/69 **Pathway Of My Life** *Hank Thompson*
18/58 **Patricia** *Perez Prado*
13/77 **Pay Phone** *Bob Luman*
 6/53 **Paying For That Back Street Affair**
     Kitty Wells
     Peace In The Valley *..see: (There'll Be)*
23/81 **Peace Of Mind** *Eddy Raven*
21/77 **Peanut Butter** *Dickey Lee*
10/76 **Peanuts And Diamonds** *Bill Anderson*
 8/63 **Pearl Pearl Pearl** *Lester Flatt & Earl Scruggs*
     Pecos Bill
13/48   *Roy Rogers*
15/48   *Tex Ritter*
10/80 **Pecos Promenade** *Tanya Tucker*
 8/64 **Peel Me A Nanner** *Roy Drusky*
 4/48 **Peepin' Through The Keyhole** *Cliffie Stone*
18/86 **Pefect Stranger** *Southern Pacific*
36/64 **Pen And Paper** *Jerry Lee Lewis*
44/71 **Pencil Marks On The Wall** *Henson Cargill*
12/49 **Pennies For Papa** *'Little' Jimmy Dickens*
 8/75 **Penny** *Joe Stampley*
 7/78 **Penny Arcade** *Cristy Lane*
 5/54 **Penny Candy** *Jim Reeves*
70/86 **People's Court** *Ray Stevens*
57/82 **Pepsi Man** *Bobby Mackey*
23/81 **Perfect Fool** *Debby Boone*
75/78 **Perfect Love Song** *Durwood Haddock*
24/72 **Perfect Match**
     David Houston & Barbara Mandrell
16/70 **Perfect Mountain** *Don Gibson*
64/82 **Perfect Picture (To Fit My Frame Of Mind)**
     Gary Wolf
13/73 **Perfect Stranger** *Freddy Weller*
     Perfect Strangers
24/80   *John Wesley Ryles*
52/88   *Anne Murray with Doug Mallory*
29/75 **Personality** *Price Mitchell*
10/83 **Personally** *Ronnie McDowell*

	Peter Cottontail		1/77	**Play, Guitar Play** *Conway Twitty*
3/50	*Gene Autry*		24/79	**Play Her Back To Yesterday** *Mel McDaniel*
6/50	*Murv Shiner*		24/79	**Play Me A Memory** *Zella Lehr*
7/50	*Jimmy Wakely*			**Play Me No Sad Songs**
7/50	*Johnnie Lee Wills*		34/76	*Rex Allen, Jr.*
14/64	**Petticoat Junction**		82/79	*Earl Scruggs Revue*
	Lester Flatt & Earl Scruggs		43/82	**Play Me Or Trade Me**
	Phantom 309			*Mel Tillis & Nancy Sinatra*
9/67	*Red Sovine*		35/82	**Play Something We Could Love To**
47/76	*Red Sovine*			*Diane Pfeifer*
9/71	**Philadelphia Fillies** *Del Reeves*		35/76	**Play The Saddest Song On The Juke Box**
73/79	**Philodendron** *Mundo Earwood*			*Carmol Taylor*
60/68	**Phoenix Flash** *Stan Hitchcock*		74/82	**Play This Old Working Day Away**
36/68	**Phone Call To Mama** *Joyce Paul*			*Dean Dillon*
74/79	**Piano Picker** *George Fischoff*		11/79	**Play Together Again Again**
71/68	**Pick A Little Happy Song** *Bob Gallion*			*Buck Owens/Emmylou Harris*
	Pick Me Up On Your Way Down		93/74	**Play With Me** *Penny DeHaven*
2/58	*Charlie Walker*		18/70	**Playin' Around With Love** *Barbara Mandrell*
46/70	*Carl Smith*		22/79	**Playin' Hard To Get** *Janie Frickie*
35/76	*Bobby G. Rice*			**Playing For Keeps**
13/64	**Pick Of The Week** *Roy Drusky*		8/57	*Elvis Presley*
	Pick The Wildwood Flower		62/85	*Holly Dunn*
34/74	*Johnny Cash/Mother Maybelle Carter*		98/88	**Playing With Matches** *Tim LeBeau*
5/79	*Gene Watson*		97/77	**Playing With The Baby's Mama**
96/77	**Pick Up The Pieces** *Con Hunley*			*Bobby Wright*
89/80	**Pick Up The Pieces, Joanne** *Bobby Hood*		34/78	**Please** *Narvel Felts*
90/80	**Pickin' Up Love** *Ray Frushay*		76/79	**Please Be Gentle** *Amy*
3/81	**Pickin' Up Strangers** *Johnny Lee*		7/86	**Please Be Love** *Mark Gray*
61/67	**Pickin' Up The Mail** *Compton Brothers*		31/64	**Please Be My Love**
27/70	**Pickin' Wild Mountain Berries**			*George Jones & Melba Montgomery*
	LaWanda Lindsey & Kenny Vernon		46/70	**Please Be My New Love** *Jeannie Seely*
42/77	**Picking Up The Pieces Of My Life** *Mac Davis*		50/86	**Please Bypass This Heart** *Jimmy Buffett*
8/60	**Picture, The** *Roy Godfrey*		75/75	**Please Come To Nashville** *Ronnie Dove*
5/72	**Picture Of Me (Without You)** *George Jones*		69/74	**Please, Daddy** *John Denver*
27/66	**Picture That's New** *George Morgan*		11/57	**Please Don't Blame Me** *Marty Robbins*
	Pictures		10/69	**Please Don't Go** *Eddy Arnold*
13/71	*Statler Brothers*		60/88	**Please Don't Leave Me Now** *Southern Reign*
35/84	*Atlanta*			**Please Don't Let Me Love You**
17/75	**Pictures On Paper** *Jeris Ross*		4/49	*George Morgan*
	Piece Of My Heart		9/55	*Hank Williams*
81/84	*John Hartford*		14/49	**Please Don't Pass Me By** *Floyd Tillman*
68/85	*Sandy Croft*		17/78	**Please Don't Play A Love Song**
33/75	**Pieces Of My Life** *Elvis Presley*			*Marty Robbins*
29/88	**Pilgrims On The Way (Matthew's Song)**		1/74	**Please Don't Stop Loving Me**
	Michael Martin Murphey			*Porter Wagoner & Dolly Parton*
5/75	**Pill, The** *Loretta Lynn*		86/86	**Please Don't Talk About Me When I'm**
47/74	**Pillow, The** *Johnny Duncan*			**Gone** *Ray Price*
17/64	**Pillow That Whispers** *Carl Smith*			**Please Don't Tell Me How The Story Ends**
13/60	**Pinball Machine** *Lonnie Irving*		8/71	*Bobby Bare*
65/71	**Pine Grove** *Compton Brothers*		1/74	*Ronnie Milsap*
15/67	**Piney Wood Hills** *Bobby Bare*			**Please Help Me, I'm Falling**
92/86	**Pink Cadillac** *Kevin Pearce*		1/60	*Hank Locklin*
17/58	**Pink Pedal Pushers** *Carl Perkins*		68/70	*Hank Locklin/Danny Davis/The Nashville Brass*
10/84	**Pins And Needles** *Whites*		12/78	*Janie Frickie*
52/76	**Pins And Needles (In My Heart)**		78/74	**Please Help Me Say No** *Mary Kay James*
	Darrell McCall		10/69	**Please Let Me Prove (My Love For You)**
	Pistol Packin' Mama			*Dave Dudley*
1/44	*Bing Crosby & Andrews Sisters*		11/61	**Please Mr. Kennedy** *Jim Nesbitt*
1/44	*Al Dexter*		5/75	**Please Mr. Please** *Olivia Newton-John*
6/78	**Pittsburgh Stealers** *Kendalls*		9/58	**Please Pass The Biscuits** *Gene Sullivan*
6/71	**Pitty, Pitty, Patter** *Susan Raye*		92/80	**Please Play More Kenny Rogers**
62/85	**Pity Party** *Bill Anderson*			*Steven Lee Cook*
8/54	**Place For Girls Like You** *Faron Young*		6/88	**Please, Please Baby** *Dwight Yoakam*
62/83	**Place I've Never Been** *Marshall Tucker Band*		54/79	**Please Sing Satin Sheets For Me**
60/82	**Place In The Sun** *Sonny James*			*Jeanne Pruett*
1/85	**Place To Fall Apart**		43/83	**Please Surrender**
	Merle Haggard with Janie Fricke			*David Frizzell & Shelly West*
100/77	**Place Where Love Has Been** *Arleen Harden*		40/69	**Please Take Me Back** *Jim Glaser*
9/87	**Plain Brown Wrapper** *Gary Morris*			**Please Talk To My Heart**
89/74	**Plain Vanilla** *Jeannie C. Riley*		14/63	*"Country" Johnny Mathis*
9/68	**Plastic Saddle** *Nat Stuckey*		7/64	*Ray Price*
23/73	**Plastic Trains, Paper Planes** *Susan Raye*		82/80	*Freddy Fender*
89/82	**Play Another Gettin' Drunk And Take**			**Please Tell Him That I Said Hello**
	Somebody Home Song *Roy Head*		50/76	*Sue Richards*
17/80	**Play Another Slow Song** *Johnny Duncan*		63/84	*Margo Smith*

73/79 **Pleasin' My Woman** *Billy Parker*
71/83 **Pleasure Island** *Frizzell & West*
32/81 **Pleasure's All Mine** *Dave & Sugar*
13/77 **Pleasure's Been All Mine** *Freddie Hart*
Pledging My Love
49/71   *Kitty Wells*
37/75   *Billy Thunderkloud*
F/77   *Elvis Presley*
9/84   *Emmylou Harris*
14/57 **Plenty Of Everything But You**
   Louvin Brothers
9/61 **Po' Folks** *Bill Anderson*
25/60 **Poison In Your Hand** *Connie Hall*
Poison Love
4/51   *Johnnie & Jack*
27/78   *Gail Davies*
72/70 **Poison Red Berries** *Glenn Barber*
12/61 **Polka On A Banjo** *Lester Flatt & Earl Scruggs*
26/87 **Ponies** *Michael Johnson*
1/70 **Pool Shark** *Dave Dudley*
30/83 **Poor Boy** *Razzy Bailey*
39/66 **Poor Boy Blues** *Bob Luman*
Poor Folks *..also see: Po'*
61/71 **Poor Folks Stick Together** *Stoney Edwards*
51/83 **Poor Girl** *Rick & Janis Carnes*
3/58 **Poor Little Fool** *Ricky Nelson*
2/56 **Poor Man's Riches** *Benny Barnes*
Poor Man's Roses (Or A Rich Man's Gold)
14/57   *Patsy Cline*
66/81   *Patti Page*
24/75 **Poor Man's Woman** *Jeanne Pruett*
10/59 **Poor Old Heartsick Me** *Margie Bowes*
70/69 **Poor Old Ugly Gladys Jones** *Don Bowman*
85/77 **Poor People of Paris** *Maury Finney*
46/78 **Poor Poor Pitful Me** *Linda Ronstadt*
44/65 **Poor Red Georgia Dirt** *Stonewall Jackson*
Poor Side Of Town
54/77   *Bobby Wayne Loftis*
12/83   *Joe Stampley*
14/75 **Poor Sweet Baby** *Jean Shepard*
82/76 **Poor Wilted Rose** *Ann J. Morton*
3/67 **Pop A Top** *Jim Ed Brown*
26/71 **Portrait Of My Woman** *Eddy Arnold*
Potato *..see: 'Tater*
20/83 **Potential New Boyfriend** *Dolly Parton*
65/75 **Pour It All On Me** *Del Reeves*
5/80 **Pour Me Another Tequila** *Eddie Rabbitt*
72/87 **Power Of A Woman** *Perry LaPointe*
9/84 **Power Of Love** *Charley Pride*
8/78 **Power Of Positive Drinkin'** *Mickey Gilley*
48/68 **Power Of Your Sweet Love** *Claude King*
57/73 **Praise The Lord And Pass The Soup**
   Johnny Cash/Carter Family/Oak Ridge Boys
83/82 **Praise The Lord And Send Me The Money**
   Bobby Bare
62/74 **Prayer From A Mobile Home** *Del Reeves*
F/70 **Preacher And The Bear** *Jerry Reed*
45/79 **Preacher Berry** *Donna Fargo*
19/82 **Preaching Up A Storm** *Mel McDaniel*
19/83 **Precious Love** *Kendalls*
44/73 **Precious Memories Follow Me** *Josie Brown*
35/80 **Pregnant Again** *Loretta Lynn*
6/72 **Pretend I Never Happened** *Waylon Jennings*
71/82 **Pretending Fool** *Michael Ballew*
26/67 **Pretty Girl, Pretty Clothes, Pretty Sad**
   Kenny Price
10/85 **Pretty Lady** *Keith Stegall*
89/80 **Pretty Poison** *Barry Grant*
12/54 **Pretty Words** *Marty Robbins*
35/69 **Price I Pay To Stay** *Jeannie C. Riley*
85/78 **Price Of Borrowed Love Is Just Too High**
   Charlotte Hurt

Pride
5/62   *Ray Price*
47/72   *Jeannie Seely*
12/81   *Janie Frickie*
18/62 **Pride Goes Before A Fall** *Jim Reeves*
46/86 **Pride Is Back**
   Kenny Rogers with Nickie Ryder
(Pride Of South Central High) *..see: Igmoo*
3/72 **Pride's Not Hard To Swallow**
   Hank Williams, Jr.
66/73 **Printers Alley Stars** *Tennessee Ernie Ford*
23/60 **Prison Song** *Curly Putman*
10/50 **Prison Without Walls** *Eddy Arnold*
3/81 **Prisoner Of Hope** *Johnny Lee*
6/84 **Prisoner Of The Highway** *Ronnie Milsap*
14/76 **Prisoner's Song** *Sonny James*
30/66 **Prissy** *Chet Atkins*
33/67 **Private, The** *Del Reeves*
81/86 **Private Clown** *Steve Ricks*
21/66 **Private Wilson White** *Marty Robbins*
12/57 **Prize Possession** *Ferlin Husky*
17/59 **Problems** *Everly Brothers*
4/44 **Prodigal Son** *Roy Acuff*
Promised Land
3/71   *Freddy Weller*
F/75   *Elvis Presley*
82/78 **Promises** *Eric Clapton*
15/67 **Promises And Hearts (Were Made To
   Break)** *Stonewall Jackson*
4/68 **Promises, Promises** *Lynn Anderson*
58/66 **Proof Is In The Kissing** *Charlie Louvin*
47/78 **Proud Lady** *Bob Luman*
Proud Mary
22/69   *Anthony Armstrong Jones*
56/73   *Brush Arbor*
22/75 **Proud Of You Baby** *Bob Luman*
91/80 **Prove It To You One More Time Again**
   Kris Kristofferson
74/82 **Pull My String** *Rich Landers*
18/70 **Pull My String And Wind Me Up** *Carl Smith*
28/68 **Punish Me Tomorrow** *Carl Butler & Pearl*
78/78 **Puppet On A String** *Elvis Presley*
1/74 **Pure Love** *Ronnie Milsap*
28/66 **Pursuing Happiness** *Norma Jean*
11/65 **Pushed In A Corner** *Ernest Ashworth*
30/70 **Put A Little Love In Your Heart** *Susan Raye*
23/76 **Put A Little Lovin' On Me** *Bobby Bare*
21/75 **Put Another Log On The Fire** *Tompall*
Put Another Notch In Your Belt
89/75   *Kenny Starr*
76/84   *Susan Raye*
Put It Off Until Tomorrow
6/66   *Bill Phillips*
9/80   *Kendalls*
77/78 **Put It On Me** *Louise Mandrell*
43/76 **Put Me Back Into Your World** *Eddy Arnold*
30/73 **Put Me Down Softly** *Dickey Lee*
99/78 **Put Me Out Of My Memory** *Johnny Bush*
28/87 **Put Me Out Of My Misery** *Tom Wopat*
55/88 **Put Us Together Again** *Goldens*
Put You Back On The Rack
   ..see: (I'm Gonna)
25/64 **Put Your Arms Around Her** *Norma Jean*
9/79 **Put Your Clothes Back On** *Joe Stampley*
1/82 **Put Your Dreams Away** *Mickey Gilley*
Put Your Hand In The Hand
61/71   *Beth Moore*
67/71   *Anne Murray*
48/75 **Put Your Head On My Shoulder**
   Sunday Sharpe
44/69 **Put Your Lovin' Where Your Mouth Is**
   Peggy Little
Puttin' In Overtime At Home
74/75   *Del Reeves*
8/78   *Charlie Rich*

68/82 **Pyramid Of Cans** *Mundo Earwood*
85/80 **Pyramid Song** *J.C. Cunningham*

69/74 **Que Pasa** *Kenny Price*
28/65 **Queen Of Draw Poker Town** *Hank Snow*
14/81 **Queen Of Hearts** *Juice Newton*
75/82 **Queen Of Hearts Loves You** *Joe Waters*
28/67 **Queen Of Honky Tonk Street** *Kitty Wells*
5/83 **Queen Of My Heart** *Hank Williams, Jr.*
77/76 **Queen Of New Orleans** *Earl Conley*
83/75 **Queen Of Temptation** *Brian Collins*
5/65 **Queen Of The House** *Jody Miller*
　　　　(also see: King Of The Road)
　　　　Queen Of The Silver Dollar
29/73 　　*Doyle Holly*
25/76 　　*Dave & Sugar*
47/76 **Queen Of The Starlight Ballroom**
　　　　David Wills
92/79 **Quicksand** *Bill Wence*
3/50 **Quicksilver** *Elton Britt & Rosalie Allen*
64/68 **Quiet Kind** *Mac Curtis*
36/87 **Quietly Crazy** *Ed Bruce*
　　　　Quits
3/71 　　*Bill Anderson*
26/77 　　*Gary Stewart*
55/86 **Quittin' Time** *Con Hunley*

3/64 **Race Is On** *George Jones*
85/87 **Rachel's Room** *Bobby G. Rice*
39/88 **Radio, The** *Vince Gill*
1/85 **Radio Heart** *Charly McClain*
19/84 **Radio Land** *Michael Martin Murphey*
51/86 **Radio Romance** *Tommy Roe*
57/88 **Radio Song** *Ric Steel*
　　　　Rag Mop
2/50 　　*Johnnie Lee Wills*
90/78 　　*Drifting Cowboys*
19/78 **Ragamuffin Man** *Donna Fargo*
15/61 **Ragged But Right** *Moon Mullican*
31/74 **Ragged Old Flag** *Johnny Cash*
　　　　Raggedy Ann
45/68 　　*Charlie Rich*
75/70 　　*Jimmy Dickens*
76/82 **Ragin' Cajun** *Charlie Daniels Band*
5/47 **Ragtime Cowboy Joe** *Eddy Howard*
52/74 **Railroad Lady** *Lefty Frizzell*
87/75 **Rain** *Kris Kristofferson & Rita Coolidge*
36/72 **Rain Falling On Me** *Johnny Russell*
63/72 **Rain-Rain** *Lois Johnson*
　　　　Rainbow At Midnight
5/46 　　*Bill Carlisle*
1/47 　　*Ernest Tubb*
5/47 　　*Texas Jim Robertson*
28/70 **Rainbow Girl** *Bobby Lord*
16/74 **Rainbow In Daddy's Eyes** *Sammi Smith*
75/74 **Rainbow In My Hand** *Doyle Holly*
8/49 **Rainbow In My Heart** *George Morgan*
99/77 **Rainbow In Your Eyes** *Jan & Malcolm*
4/81 **Rainbow Stew** *Merle Haggard*
39/83 **Rainbows And Butterflies** *Billy Swan*

90/77 **Rainbows And Horseshoes** *R.C. Bannon*
　　　　Rainbows And Roses
20/66 　　*Roy Drusky*
F/79 　　*Billy Walker*
17/68 **Rainbows Are Back In Style** *Slim Whitman*
33/74 **Raindrops** *Narvel Felts*
55/83 **Rainin' Down In Nashville** *Tom Carlile*
59/81 **Rainin' In My Eyes** *Miki Mori*
　　　　Raining In My Heart
14/69 　　*Ray Price*
3/71 　　*Hank Williams, Jr.*
63/78 　　*Leo Sayer*
35/89 　　*Jo-el Sonnier*
4/77 **Rains Came** *Freddy Fender*
47/75 **Rainy Day People** *Gordon Lightfoot*
2/75 **Rainy Day Woman** *Waylon Jennings*
83/79 **Rainy Days And Rainbows** *Paul Schmucker*
21/80 **Rainy Days And Stormy Nights**
　　　　Billie Jo Spears
13/74 **Rainy Night In Georgia** *Hank Williams, Jr.*
15/80 **Raisin' Cane In Texas** *Gene Watson*
3/78 **Rake And Ramblin' Man** *Don Williams*
42/80 **Rambler Gambler** *Linda Ronstadt*
2/77 **Ramblin' Fever** *Merle Haggard*
　　　　Ramblin' Man
29/67 　　*Ray Pennington*
63/73 　　*Gary Stewart*
79/73 　　*Jimmy Payne*
94/79 **Ramblin' Music Man** *Charlie McCoy*
　　　　Ramblin' Rose
37/77 　　*Johnny Lee*
93/78 　　*Hank Snow*
8/68 **Ramona** *Billy Walker*
1/73 **Rated "X"** *Loretta Lynn*
1/44 **Ration Blues** *Louis Jordan*
　　　　Raunchy
6/58 　　*Bill Justis*
11/58 　　*Ernie Freeman*
80/78 **Rave On** *Jerry Naylor*
3/73 **Ravishing Ruby** *Tom T. Hall*
52/77 **Raymond's Place** *Ray Griff*
2/72 **Reach Out Your Hand** *Tammy Wynette*
61/73 **Reach Out Your Hand And Touch Me**
　　　　Sonny James
78/81 **Reachin' For Freedom**
　　　　Ron Shaw/Desert Wind Band
49/79 **Reaching Out To Hold You** *Dottie West*
38/87 **Read Between The Lines** *Lynn Anderson*
4/86 **Read My Lips** *Marie Osmond*
82/80 **Reading Of The Will** *Jimmy Tucker*
　　　　Ready For The Times To Get Better
1/78 　　*Crystal Gayle*
43/81 　　*Joe Sun*
72/87 **Ready Or Not** *Don Malena*
90/88 **Ready To Take That Ride** *Trinity Lane*
38/80 **Real Buddy Holly Story** *Sonny Curtis*
20/80 **Real Cowboy (You Say You're)**
　　　　Billy 'Crash' Craddock
67/86 **Real Good** *Bobby Bare*
9/88 **Real Good Feel Good Song** *Mel McDaniel*
76/87 **Real Good Heartache** *Rosemary Sharp*
36/68 **Real Good Woman** *Jean Shepard*
1/85 **Real Love** *Kenny Rogers & Dolly Parton*
69/89 **Real Old-Fashioned Broken Heart**
　　　　Bama Band
　　　　Real Thing
30/67 　　*Billy Grammer*
85/78 　　*Jean Shepard*
79/79 　　*O.B. McClinton*
　　　　Reason To Believe
75/69 　　*Suzi Jane Hokum*
88/83 　　*Wray Brothers Band*
　　　　Reason Why I'm Here
97/77 　　*Joni Lee*
85/78 　　*Mike Lunsford*

13/60	**Reasons To Live** *Jimmie Skinner*	39/87	**Restless Angel** *Tim Malchak*
6/83	**Reasons To Quit**	57/84	**Restless Heart** *Juice Newton*
	Merle Haggard & Willie Nelson	74/69	**Restless Melissa** *Hugh X. Lewis*
24/61	**Rebel - Johnny Yuma** *Johnny Cash*	11/61	**Restless One** *Hank Snow*
17/58	**Rebel-'Rouser** *Duane Eddy*	30/64	**Restless River** *Earl Scott*
9/88	**Rebels Without A Clue** *Bellamy Brothers*	6/78	**Return To Me** *Marty Robbins*
	Reconsider Me	13/79	**Reunited** *Louise Mandrell & R.C. Bannon*
38/69	*Ray Pillow*	74/76	**Reverend Bob** *Barbi Benton*
39/71	*John Wesley Ryles*	71/82	**Reverend Mr. Black** *Johnny Cash*
2/75	*Narvel Felts*	82/84	**Reynosa** *Katy Moffatt*
4/79	**Red Bandana** *Merle Haggard*	1/75	**Rhinestone Cowboy** *Glen Campbell*
21/71	**Red Door** *Carl Smith*	23/64	**Rhinestones** *Faron Young*
17/78	**Red Hot Memory** *Kenny Dale*	1/51	**Rhumba Boogie** *Hank Snow*
70/86	**Red Neck And Over Thirty**		**Rhythm Guitar**
	Wayne Kemp & Bobby G. Rice	94/79	*Oak Ridge Boys*
73/79	**Red Neck Disco** *Glenn Sutton*	44/85	*Emmylou Harris*
85/77	**Red-Neck Hippie Romance** *Bobby Bare*	57/88	**Rhythm Of Romance** *Kendalls*
1/82	**Red Neckin' Love Makin' Night**		**Rhythm Of The Rain**
	Conway Twitty	34/72	*Pat Roberts*
17/72	**Red Red Wine** *Roy Drusky*	67/77	*Floyd Cramer*
21/74	**Red Rose From The Blue Side Of Town**	11/78	*Jacky Ward*
	George Morgan	32/69	**Rib, The** *Jeannie C. Riley*
60/75	**Red Roses For A Blue Lady** *Eddy Arnold*		**Ribbon Of Darkness**
8/48	**Red Roses Tied In Blue** *Clyde Moody*	1/65	*Marty Robbins*
22/76	**Red Sails In The Sunset** *Johnny Lee*	13/69	*Connie Smith*
62/72	**Red Skies Over Georgia** *Henson Cargill*	19/81	**Rich Man** *Terri Gibbs*
20/76	**Red, White And Blue** *Loretta Lynn*	53/75	**Richard And The Cadillac Kings**
6/78	**Red Wine And Blue Memories** *Joe Stampley*		*Doyle Holly*
1/82	**Redneck Girl** *Bellamy Brothers*	76/88	**Richer Now With You** *Nina Wyatt*
	Redneck In A Rock And Roll Bar	10/55	**Richest Man (In The World)** *Eddy Arnold*
	..see: (I'm Just A)	4/83	**Ride, The** *David Allan Coe*
89/76	**Redneck Rock** *Bill Black's Combo*	80/80	**Ride Concrete Cowboy, Ride** *Roy Rogers*
95/77	**Redneck Roots** *Vernon Oxford*	85/82	**Ride Cowboy Ride** *Rex Allen, Jr.*
17/76	**Redneck! (The Redneck National Anthem)**		**Ride 'Em Cowboy**
	Vernon Oxford	47/75	*Paul Davis*
4/73	**Rednecks, White Socks And Blue Ribbon**	32/84	*Juice Newton*
	Beer *Johnny Russell*	48/84	*David Allan Coe*
55/74	**Reflections** *Jody Miller*	11/73	**Ride Me Down Easy** *Bobby Bare*
87/80	**Regrets** *Carol Chase*	36/67	**Ride, Ride, Ride** *Lynn Anderson*
41/66	**Regular On My Mind** *Jim Edward Brown*	92/80	**Ride That Bull (Big Bertha)** *Marlow Tackett*
	Release Me	58/88	**Ride This Train** *Mel McDaniel*
5/54	*Jimmy Heap/Perk Williams*	78/78	**Rider In The Rain** *Randy Newman*
6/54	*Ray Price*		**Riders In The Sky**
8/54	*Kitty Wells*	2/49	*Vaughn Monroe*
33/73	*Charlie McCoy*	8/49	*Burl Ives*
71/74	*Marie Owens*	27/73	*Roy Clark*
71/71	**Remember Bethlehem** *Dee Mullins*	2/79	*Johnny Cash*
2/76	**Remember Me** *Willie Nelson*	1/73	**Ridin' My Thumb To Mexico**
	(Remember Me) I'm The One Who Loves You		*Johnny Rodriguez*
2/50	*Stuart Hamblen*	12/77	**Ridin' Rainbows** *Tanya Tucker*
5/50	*Ernest Tubb*	44/88	**Rigamarole** *Schuyler, Knobloch & Bickhardt*
	Remembering		**Right Back Loving You Again**
14/68	*Jerry Reed*	22/70	*Del Reeves*
57/76	*Jerry Reed*	65/82	*Chantilly*
80/83	**Reminiscing** *Linda Nail*	14/71	**Right Combination**
23/70	**Removing The Shadow**		*Porter Wagoner & Dolly Parton*
	Hank Williams, Jr. & Lois Johnson	1/87	**Right From The Start** *Earl Thomas Conley*
19/68	**Reno** *Dottie West*	3/87	**Right Hand Man** *Eddy Raven*
76/85	**Reno And Me** *Bobby Bare*	10/81	**Right In The Palm Of Your Hand**
9/86	**Reno Bound** *Southern Pacific*		*Mel McDaniel*
81/87	**Rented Room** *Jeanne Pruett*	85/81	**Right In The Wrong Direction** *Liz Lyndell*
	Repeat After Me	8/87	**Right Left Hand** *George Jones*
10/68	*Jack Reno*	30/66	**Right One** *Statler Brothers*
56/84	*Family Brown*		**Right Or Left At Oak Street**
6/57	**Repenting** *Kitty Wells*	21/70	*Roy Clark*
4/86	**Repetitive Regret** *Eddie Rabbitt*	83/75	*Molly Bee*
74/88	**Request, The** *Bob Pack*		**Right Or Wrong**
72/78	**Rest Of My Life** *Kenny Starr*	9/61	*Wanda Jackson*
86/80	**Rest Of Your Life** *Kay Austin*	41/78	*Mary K. Miller*
	Rest Your Love On Me	1/84	*George Strait*
39/79	*Bee Gees*	63/74	**Right Out Of This World** *Jerry 'Max' Lane*
1/81	*Conway Twitty*		**Right String** *..see: Yo Yo*
	Restless	14/84	**Right Stuff** *Charly McClain & Mickey Gilley*
20/69	*Carl Perkins*	17/77	**Right Time Of The Night** *Jennifer Warnes*
39/74	*Crystal Gayle*	7/71	**Right Won't Touch A Hand** *George Jones*

Ring Of Fire
1/63   *Johnny Cash*
66/88   *Randy Howard*
5/82 **Ring On Her Finger, Time On Her Hands**
   Lee Greenwood
95/78 **Ring Telephone Ring** *Randy Cornor*
64/77 **Ringgold Georgia**
   Billy Walker & Brenda Kaye Perry
21/64 **Ringo** *Lorne Greene*
   Rings
66/67   *Stan Hitchcock*
7/71   *Tompall/Glaser Brothers*
41/72 **Rings For Sale** *Roger Miller*
   Rings Of Gold
2/69   *Dottie West & Don Gibson*
79/87   *Robin & Cruiser*
90/84 **Rise Above It All** *Joe Waters*
71/79 **Rise And Fall Of The Roman Empire**
   Cal Smith
   Rise And Shine
9/70   *Tommy Cash*
73/87   *Ronnie Dove*
44/78 **Rising Above It All** *Lynn Anderson*
81/88 **Rising Cost Of Loving You**
   Western Union Band
23/69 **River Bottom** *Johnny Darrell*
36/85 **River In The Rain** *Roger Miller*
9/54 **River Of No Return** *Tennessee Ernie Ford*
64/80 **River Road** *Crystal Gayle*
63/88 **River Unbroken** *Dolly Parton*
76/84 **River's Song** *Joey Scarbury*
13/74 **River's Too Wide** *Jim Mundy*
4/60 **Riverboat** *Faron Young*
14/60 **Riverboat Gambler** *Jimmie Skinner*
27/76 **Road Song** *Charlie Rich*
17/72 **Roadmaster, The** *Freddy Weller*
F/80 **Roarin'** *Gary Stewart*
13/67 **Roarin' Again** *Wilburn Brothers*
15/63 **Robert E. Lee** *Ott Stephens*
16/79 **Robinhood** *Billy 'Crash' Craddock*
65/88 **Rock-A-Bye Heart** *Dana McVicker*
   Rock And Roll *..also see: Rock 'N' Roll*
16/87 **Rock And Roll Of Love** *Tom Wopat*
14/84 **Rock And Roll Shoes**
   Ray Charles with B.J. Thomas
5/48 **Rock And Rye Polka** *Tex Ritter*
14/48 **Rock And Rye Rag** *Al Dexter*
14/58 **Rock Hearts** *Jimmy Martin*
48/80 **Rock I'm Leaning On** *Jack Greene*
35/70 **Rock Island Line** *Johnny Cash*
26/70 **Rock Me Back To Little Rock** *Jan Howard*
   Rock 'N' Roll *..also see: Rock And Roll*
29/75 **Rock N' Roll** *Mac Davis*
90/82 **Rock 'N' Roll Stories** *Shannon Leigh*
58/80 **Rock 'N' Roll To Rock Of Ages** *Bill Anderson*
6/75 **Rock On Baby** *Brenda Lee*
63/81 **Rockabilly Rebel** *Orion*
86/79 **Rocket 'Til The Cows Come Home**
   Charley White
70/85 **Rockin' In A Brand New Cradle** *Terri Gibbs*
   Rockin' In The Congo
13/57   *Hank Thompson*
82/82   *Hank Thompson*
63/86 **Rockin' In The Parkin' Lot** *Razzy Bailey*
70/86 **Rockin' My Angel** *Narvel Felts*
74/86 **Rockin' My Country Heart** *Pat Garrett*
18/79 **Rockin' My Life Away** *Jerry Lee Lewis*
88/76 **Rockin' My Memories** *Claude Gray*
1/86 **Rockin' With The Rhythm Of The Rain**
   Judds
22/60 **Rockin', Rollin' Ocean** *Hank Snow*
73/69 **Rocking A Memory (That Won't Go To Sleep)** *Tommy Overstreet*
28/76 **Rocking In Rosalee's Boat** *Nick Nixon*
1/75 **Rocky** *Dickey Lee*

5/76 **Rocky Mountain Music** *Eddie Rabbitt*
71/88 **Rocky Road** *O'Kanes*
   Rocky Top
33/68   *Osborne Brothers*
17/70   *Lynn Anderson*
52/81 **Rode Hard And Put Up Wet** *Johnny Lee*
56/77 **Rodeo Bum** *Mel Street*
37/82 **Rodeo Clown** *Mac Davis*
44/76 **Rodeo Cowboy** *Lynn Anderson*
25/80 **Rodeo Eyes** *Zella Lehr*
83/81 **Rodeo Girls** *Tanya Tucker*
10/82 **Rodeo Romeo** *Moe Bandy*
74/79 **Rodle-Odeo-Home** *Arnie Rue*
36/88 **Rogue, The** *David Lynn Jones*
77/80 **Rolaids, Doan's Pills And Preparation H**
   Dave Dudley
57/73 **Roll In My Sweet Baby's Arms** *Hank Wilson*
   Roll Muddy River
4/63   *Wilburn Brothers*
66/67   *Osborne Brothers*
1/75 **Roll On Big Mama** *Joe Stampley*
1/84 **Roll On (Eighteen Wheeler)** *Alabama*
7/81 **Roll On Mississippi** *Charley Pride*
100/75 **Roll On, Truckers** *Ray Pillow*
26/67 **Roll Over And Play Dead** *Jan Howard*
   Roll Over Beethoven
71/70   *Linda Gail Lewis & Jerry Lee Lewis*
64/82   *Narvel Felts*
49/87 **Roll The Dice** *Shurfire*
   Roll Truck Roll
38/66   *Red Simpson*
67/71   *Tommy Cash*
32/75 **Roll You Like A Wheel**
   Mickey Gilley & Barbi Benton
84/87 **Roller Coaster** *Alibi*
52/89 **Roller Coaster Run** *Michael Johnson*
   Rollin' In My Sweet Baby's Arms
2/71   *Buck Owens*
76/76   *Maury Finney*
65/75 **Rollin' In Your Sweet Sunshine** *Dottie West*
9/85 **Rollin' Lonely** *Johnny Lee*
15/86 **Rollin' Nowhere** *Michael Martin Murphey*
47/73 **Rollin' Rig** *Dave Dudley*
1/77 **Rollin' With The Flow** *Charlie Rich*
   Roly-Poly
3/46   *Bob Wills*
97/75   *Carl Smith*
   Romance
22/83   *Louise Mandrell*
59/86   *Jim Collins*
26/69 **Rome Wasn't Built In A Day** *Hank Snow*
   Room At The Top Of The Stairs
36/79   *Stella Parton*
92/79   *Cal Smith*
60/74 **Room For A Boy...Never Used** *Ferlin Husky*
   Room Full Of Roses
4/49   *George Morgan*
10/49   *Sons Of The Pioneers*
1/74   *Mickey Gilley*
2/66 **Room In Your Heart** *Sonny James*
56/76 **Room 269** *Freddy Weller*
1/76 **Roots Of My Raising** *Merle Haggard*
1/44 **Rosalita** *Al Dexter*
2/68 **Rosanna's Going Wild** *Johnny Cash*
1/83 **Rose, The** *Conway Twitty*
   Rose By Any Other Name (Is Still A Rose)
69/72   *Ray Sanders*
77/76   *Ronnie Milsap*
5/78 **Rose Colored Glasses** *John Conlee*
1/70 **Rose Garden** *Lynn Anderson*
1/87 **Rose In Paradise** *Waylon Jennings*
52/69 **Rose Is A Rose Is A Rose** *Jimmy Dean*
70/81 **Rose Is For Today** *Jim Chesnut*
4/54 **Rose-Marie** *Slim Whitman*
60/84 **Rose Of My Heart** *Johnny Rodriguez*

33/80 **Rose's Are Red** *Freddie Hart*
28/63 **Rosebuds And You** *Benny Martin*
Roses Ain't Red
94/78   *Cathy O'Shea*
59/80   *Diane Pfeifer*
 3/75 **Roses And Love Songs** *Ray Price*
15/71 **Roses And Thorns** *Jeannie C. Riley*
 2/77 **Roses For Mama** *C.W. McCall*
34/66 **Roses From A Stranger** *Leroy Van Dyke*
44/88 **Roses In December** *Larry Boone*
70/73 **Roses In The Wine** *Hank Thompson*
42/68 **Roses To Reno** *Bob Bishop*
17/74 **Rosie Cries A Lot** *Ferlin Husky*
Rosie (Do You Wanna Talk It Over)
45/76   *Red Steagall*
76/76   *Sonny Throckmorton*
 9/82 **'Round The Clock Lovin'** *Gail Davies*
40/77 **'Round The World With The Rubber Duck**
         C.W. McCall
31/81 **Round-Up Saloon** *Bobby Goldsboro*
48/76 **Route 66** *Asleep At The Wheel*
54/87 **Routine** *Kendalls*
11/68 **Row Row Row** *Henson Cargill*
 1/53 **Rub-A-Dub-Dub** *Hank Thompson*
 1/74 **Rub It In** *Billy 'Crash' Craddock*
46/69 **Ruben James** *Kenny Rogers*
 1/63 **Ruby Ann** *Marty Robbins*
Ruby, Are You Mad
58/70   *Osborne Brothers*
 3/71   *Buck Owens*
 1/75 **Ruby, Baby** *Billy 'Crash' Craddock*
Ruby, Don't Take Your Love To Town
 9/67   *Johnny Darrell*
39/69   *Kenny Rogers*
46/72 **Ruby Gentry's Daughter** *Arlene Harden*
21/72 **Ruby You're Warm** *David Rogers*
78/77 **Ruby's Lounge** *Brenda Lee*
Rudolph, The Red-Nosed Reindeer
 1/50   *Gene Autry*
 5/50   *Gene Autry*
10/68 **Run Away Little Tears** *Connie Smith*
 5/56 **Run Boy** *Ray Price*
 8/54 **Run 'Em Off** *Lefty Frizzell*
53/81 **Run To Her** *Susie Allanson*
 1/70 **Run, Woman, Run** *Tammy Wynette*
68/84 **Run Your Sweet Love By Me One More**
         Time *Lang Scott*
Runaway
30/78   *Narvel Felts*
76/86   *Bonnie Leigh*
43/85 **Runaway Go Home** *Gatlin Bros.*
Runaway Heart
93/77   *Pam Rose*
36/79   *Reba McEntire*
13/84   *Louise Mandrell*
 1/88 **Runaway Train** *Rosanne Cash*
20/70 **Runnin' Bare** *Jim Nesbitt*
100/77 **Runnin' Out Again** *Paula Kay Evans*
 1/69 **Running Bear** *Sonny James*
24/85 **Running Down Memory Lane** *Rex Allen, Jr.*
70/70 **Running From A Memory** *Chaparral Brothers*
12/78 **Running Kind** *Merle Haggard*
40/82 **Running On Love** *Don King*
72/86 **Running Out Of Reasons To Run** *J.D. Martin*
77/85 **Running The Road Blocks** *Chris Hillman*
14/79 **Rusty Old Halo** *Hoyt Axton*
10/67 **Ruthless** *Statler Brothers*
Rye Whiskey
 9/48   *Tex Ritter*
81/76   *Chuck Price*

S

83/81 **(s.o.b.) Same Old Boy** *Gary Gentry*
S.O.S.
15/55   *Johnnie & Jack*
73/81   *Johnny Carver*
70/88 **Sad Cliches** *Atlanta*
17/76 **Sad Country Love Song** *Tom Bresh*
31/67 **Sad Face** *Ernest Ashworth*
78/80 **Sad Love Song Lady** *David Houston*
81/81 **Sad Ole Shade Of Gray** *Jeanne Pruett*
46/72 **Sad Situation** *Skeeter Davis*
59/86 **Sad State Of Affairs** *Leon Everette*
F/80 **Sadness Of It All**
         Conway Twitty & Loretta Lynn
44/85 **Safe In The Arms Of Love** *Robin Lee*
82/80 **Safe In The Arms Of Your Love (Cold In The**
         Streets) *Jim Weatherly*
55/72 **Safe In These Lovin' Arms Of Mine**
         Jean Shepard
 1/64 **Saginaw, Michigan** *Lefty Frizzell*
Sail Away
98/77   *Sam Neely*
 2/79   *Oak Ridge Boys*
16/79 **Sail On** *Tom Grant*
63/85 **Sailing Home To Me** *Loy Blanton*
16/59 **Sailor Man** *Johnnie & Jack*
19/59 **Sal's Got A Sugar Lip** *Johnny Horton*
51/75 **Sally G** *Wings*
20/62 **Sally Was A Good Old Girl** *Hank Cochran*
98/79 **Salt On The Wound** *Jerry Fuller*
 8/52 **Salty Dog Rag** *Red Foley*
 8/70 **Salute To A Switchblade** *Tom T. Hall*
87/79 **Salute To The Duke** *Paul Ott*
40/77 **Sam** *Olivia Newton-John*
Sam Hill
11/64   *Claude King*
45/64   *Merle Haggard*
 1/67 **Sam's Place** *Buck Owens*
Same Old Boy ..see: (s.o.b.)
 1/59 **Same Old Me** *Ray Price*
29/75 **Same Old Story** *Hank Williams, Jr.*
46/70 **Same Old Story, Same Old Lie** *Bill Phillips*
65/73 **Same Old Way** *Stan Hitchcock*
 5/82 **Same Ole Me** *George Jones*
 8/49 **Same Sweet Girl** *Hank Locklin*
14/57 **Same Two Lips** *Marty Robbins*
47/66 **Sammy** *David Houston*
50/67 **San Antonio** *Willie Nelson*
89/80 **San Antonio Medley**
         Curtis Potter/Darrell McCall
25/83 **San Antonio Nights** *Eddy Raven*
San Antonio Rose
 8/61   *Floyd Cramer*
F/83   *Ray Price*
San Antonio Stroll
 1/75   *Tanya Tucker*
F/76   *Maury Finney*
31/68 **San Diego** *Charlie Walker*
San Francisco Is A Lonely Town
46/69   *Ben Peters*
86/79   *Nick Nixon*
26/75 **Sanctuary** *Ronnie Prophet*
 7/63 **Sands Of Gold** *Webb Pierce*
F/79 **Santa Barbara** *Ronnie Milsap*
 5/88 **Santa Fe** *Bellamy Brothers*
57/70 **Santo Domingo** *Buddy Alan*
57/79 **Sarah's Eyes** *Vern Gosdin*
 1/73 **Satin Sheets** *Jeanne Pruett*
17/73 **Satisfaction** *Jack Greene*

7/53	**Satisfaction Guaranteed** *Carl Smith*			**Sea Of Heartbreak**
	Satisfied Mind		2/61	*Don Gibson*
1/55	*Porter Wagoner*		24/72	*Kenny Price*
3/55	*Red Foley & Betty Foley*		33/79	*Lynn Anderson*
4/55	*Jean Shepard*		83/88	**Sealed With A Kiss** *Leah Marr*
25/73	*Roy Drusky*		5/48	**Seaman's Blues** *Ernest Tubb*
41/76	*Bob Luman*		43/77	**Search, The** *Freddie Hart*
84/83	*Con Hunley*		54/72	**Search Your Heart** *Bobby Wright*
83/74	**Satisfy Me And I'll Satisfy You** *Josie Brown*		82/76	**Searchin' For A Rainbow**
5/88	**Satisfy You** *Sweethearts Of The Rodeo*			*Marshall Tucker Band*
24/71	**Saturday Morning Confusion** *Bobby Russell*			**Searching (For Someone Like You)**
22/68	**Saturday Night** *Webb Pierce*		3/56	*Kitty Wells*
54/80	**Saturday Night In Dallas** *Kenny Serratt*		45/75	*Melba Montgomery*
9/88	**Saturday Night Special** *Conway Twitty*		75/87	*Lanier McKuhen*
53/77	**Saturday Night To Sunday Quiet**		24/74	**Seasons In The Sun** *Bobby Wright*
	Susan Raye			**Seasons Of My Heart**
43/69	**Saturday Satan Sunday Saint** *Ernest Tubb*		9/56	*Jimmy Newman*
	Save Me		10/60	*Johnny Cash*
86/78	*Tanya Tucker*		90/79	**Second Best** *Don Deal*
6/83	*Louise Mandrell*		18/62	**Second Choice** *Stonewall Jackson*
12/85	**Save The Last Chance** *Johnny Lee*		50/73	**Second Cup Of Coffee** *George Hamilton IV*
100/76	**Save The Last Dance** *Bennie Lindsey*		24/59	**Second Fiddle** *Buck Owens*
	Save The Last Dance For Me		5/64	**Second Fiddle (To An Old Guitar)**
11/62	*Buck Owens*			*Jean Shepard*
36/78	*Ron Shaw*		70/79	**Second Hand Emotion** *Faron Young*
4/79	*Emmylou Harris*		7/84	**Second Hand Heart** *Gary Morris*
26/79	*Jerry Lee Lewis*		3/63	**Second Hand Rose** *Roy Drusky*
3/84	*Dolly Parton*		18/79	**Second-Hand Satin Lady (And A Bargain**
8/80	**Save Your Heart For Me** *Jacky Ward*			**Basement Boy)** *Jerry Reed*
10/76	**Save Your Kisses For Me** *Margo Smith*		15/60	**Second Honeymoon** *Johnny Cash*
3/86	**Savin' My Love For You** *Pake McEntire*		95/86	**Second Time Around** *Del Reeves*
58/87	**Savin' The Honey For The Honeymoon**		5/86	**Second To No One** *Rosanne Cash*
	Sawyer Brown		60/72	**Second Tuesday In December**
14/77	**Savin' This Love Song For You**			*Jack Blanchard & Misty Morgan*
	Johnny Rodriguez			**Secret Love**
	Sawmill		2/54	*Slim Whitman*
27/59	*Mel Tillis & Bill Phillips*		47/73	*Tony Booth*
15/63	*Webb Pierce*		1/75	*Freddy Fender*
2/73	*Mel Tillis*			**Secretly**
85/80	**Say A Long Goodbye** *Mary K. Miller*		5/58	*Jimmie Rodgers*
5/75	**Say Forever You'll Be Mine**		65/78	*Jimmie Rodgers*
	Porter Wagoner & Dolly Parton		47/81	**Secrets** *Mac Davis*
35/73	**Say, Has Anybody Seen My Sweet Gypsy**		F/69	**See Ruby Fall** *Johnny Cash*
	Rose *Terry Stafford*		72/75	**See Saw** *Patsy Sledd*
40/75	**Say I Do** *Ray Price*			**See The Big Man Cry**
1/76	**Say It Again** *Don Williams*		7/65	*Charlie Louvin*
8/68	**Say It's Not You** *George Jones*		85/76	*Bobby Wayne Loftis*
	Say When		80/74	**See The Funny Little Clown** *Billie Jo Spears*
15/73	*Diana Trask*		41/79	**See You In September** *Debby Boone*
F/84	*Johnny Lee*		18/76	**See You On Sunday** *Glen Campbell*
	Say You Love Me		16/72	**Seed Before The Rose** *Tommy Overstreet*
93/76	*Lynda K. Lance*			**Seeing Is Believing**
10/79	*Stephanie Winslow*		96/74	*Jan Howard*
	Say You Love Me Again		55/80	*Donna Fargo*
	..see: (I Wanna Hear You)		2/75	**Seeker, The** *Dolly Parton*
57/83	**Say You'll Stay** *Wayne Massey*		83/76	**Seems Like I Can't Live With You, But I Can't**
1/77	**Say You'll Stay Until Tomorrow** *Tom Jones*			**Live Without You** *Price Mitchell*
2/77	**Saying Hello, Saying I Love You, Saying**		83/82	**Semi Diesel Blues** *Super Grit Cowboy Band*
	Goodbye *Jim Ed Brown/Helen Cornelius*		19/77	**Semolita** *Jerry Reed*
5/83	**Scarlet Fever** *Kenny Rogers*		79/73	**Send A Little Love My Way** *Anne Murray*
7/60	**Scarlet Ribbons (For Her Hair)** *Browns*		69/66	**Send Me A Box Of Kleenex** *Lamar Morris*
66/74	**Scarlet Water** *Johnny Duncan*		2/79	**Send Me Down To Tucson** *Mel Tillis*
77/88	**Scene Of The Crime** *Lori Yates*		7/73	**Send Me No Roses** *Tommy Overstreet*
	Scotch And Soda		14/72	**Send Me Some Lovin'**
88/79	*Mac Wiseman*			*Hank Williams, Jr. & Lois Johnson*
70/83	*Ray Price*		61/81	**Send Me Somebody To Love** *Calamity Jane*
27/58	**Scotland** *Bill Monroe*			**Send Me The Pillow You Dream On**
8/81	**Scratch My Back (And Whisper in My Ear)**		5/58	*Hank Locklin*
	Razzy Bailey		23/60	*Browns*
	Sea Cruise		11/62	*Johnny Tillotson*
94/77	*Everett Peek*		66/81	*Whites*
50/80	*Billy "Crash" Craddock*		9/87	**Senorita** *Don Williams*
			47/76	**Sentimental Journey** *Dave Dudley*
			3/84	**Sentimental Ol' You** *Charly McClain*
			F/73	**Separate Ways** *Elvis Presley*

	September Song
40/69	*Roy Clark*
15/79	*Willie Nelson*
1/88	**Set 'Em Up Joe** *Vern Gosdin*
	Set Him Free
5/59	*Skeeter Davis*
52/68	*Skeeter Davis*
	Set Me Free
67/67	*Curly Putman*
44/68	*Charlie Rich*
51/69	*Ray Price*
68/71	**Set The World On Fire (With Love)**
	Red Lane
2/52	**Settin' The Woods On Fire** *Hank Williams*
55/81	**Seven Bridges Road** *Eagles*
85/81	**Seven Days Come Sunday** *Rodney Lay*
28/66	**Seven Days Of Crying (Makes One Weak)**
	Harden Trio
	Seven Lonely Days
7/53	*Bonnie Lou*
18/69	*Jean Shepard*
1/85	**Seven Spanish Angels**
	Ray Charles with Willie Nelson
1/81	**Seven Year Ache** *Rosanne Cash*
F/71	**Seventeen Years** *Marty Robbins*
92/78	**Sexy Eyes** *Gayle Harding*
21/74	**Sexy Lady** *Freddy Weller*
80/80	**Sexy Ole Lady** *Pat Garrett*
48/80	**Sexy Song** *Carol Chase*
46/86	**Sexy Young Girl** *Mac Davis*
95/79	**Shackles And Chains**
	Osborne Bros. & Mac Wiseman
74/82	**Shadow Of Love** *Rob Parsons*
5/45	**Shadow Of My Heart** *Ted Daffan's Texans*
1/79	**Shadows In The Moonlight** *Anne Murray*
28/79	**Shadows Of Love** *Rayburn Anthony*
	Shadows Of My Mind
54/76	*Vernon Oxford*
15/83	*Leon Everette*
24/78	**Shady Rest** *Mel Street*
48/77	**Shady Side Of Charlotte** *Nat Stuckey*
66/79	**Shady Streets** *Gary Stewart*
6/53	**Shake A Hand** *Red Foley*
15/54	**Shake-A-Leg** *Carlisles*
75/76	**Shake 'Em Up and Let 'Em Roll** *George Kent*
27/61	**Shake Hands With A Loser** *Don Winters*
	Shake Me I Rattle (Squeeze Me I Cry)
14/63	*Marion Worth*
16/78	*Cristy Lane*
95/76	**Shake, Rattle And Roll** *Billy Swan*
15/86	**Shakin'** *Sawyer Brown*
	Shame On Me
18/62	*Bobby Bare*
56/69	*Norro Wilson*
48/75	*Bob Luman*
8/77	*Donna Fargo*
15/83	**Shame On The Moon** *Bob Seger*
	Shame On You
1/45	*Spade Cooley*
1/45	*Lawrence Welk/Red Foley*
4/45	*Bill Boyd*
11/77	**Shame, Shame On Me** *Kenny Dale*
35/64	**Shape Up Or Ship Out** *Leon McAuliffe*
83/78	**Share Your Love Tonight** *Ann J. Morton*
5/81	**Share Your Love With Me** *Kenny Rogers*
15/79	**Sharing** *Kenny Dale*
	Sharing The Night Together
50/78	*Dr. Hook*
88/83	*Denny Hilton*
93/87	**She Ain't Johnnie** *Billy Vera*
83/85	**She Almost Makes Me Forget About You**
	Larry Wayne Kennedy
1/86	**She And I** *Alabama*
1/79	**She Believes In Me** *Kenny Rogers*
16/81	**She Belongs To Everyone But Me**
	Burrito Brothers
91/75	**She Brings Her Lovin' Home To Me**
	Mundo Ray
3/44	**She Broke My Heart In Three Places**
	Hoosier Hot Shots
38/74	**She Burn't The Little Roadside Tavern**
	Down *Johnny Russell*
	She Called Me Baby
32/65	*Carl Smith*
55/72	*Dick Curless*
1/74	*Charlie Rich*
74/70	**She Came To Me** *Lamar Morris*
1/78	**She Can Put Her Shoes Under My Bed**
	Johnny Duncan
29/82	**She Can't Get My Love Off The Bed**
	Dottie West
	She Can't Give It Away
96/78	*Barbara Fairchild*
86/81	*Roy Clark*
2/80	**She Can't Say That Anymore** *John Conlee*
28/70	**She Cheats On Me** *Glenn Barber*
4/87	**She Couldn't Love Me Anymore**
	T. Graham Brown
63/71	**She Cried** *Roy Clark*
35/75	**She Deserves My Very Best** *David Wills*
73/82	**She Doesn't Belong To You** *Terry Aden*
9/88	**She Doesn't Cry Anymore** *Shenandoah*
51/86	**She Don't Cry Like She Used To**
	Johnny Rodriguez
70/87	**She Don't Love You** *Susie Allanson*
19/71	**She Don't Make Me Cry** *David Rogers*
14/54	**She Done Give Her Heart To Me**
	Sonny James
	She Even Woke Me Up To Say Goodbye
2/69	*Jerry Lee Lewis*
15/75	*Ronnie Milsap*
97/83	**She Feels Like A New Man Tonight**
	Clifford Russell
15/73	**She Fights That Lovin' Feeling**
	Faron Young
65/68	**She Gets The Roses (I Get The Tears)**
	Donna Odom
3/70	**She Goes Walking Through My Mind**
	Billy Walker
1/82	**She Got The Goldmine (I Got The Shaft)**
	Jerry Reed
48/82	**She Is The Woman** *Super Grit Cowboy Band*
11/77	**She Just Loved The Cheatin' Out Of Me**
	Moe Bandy
89/78	**She Just Made Me Love You More**
	Johnny Bush
13/80	**She Just Started Liking Cheatin' Songs**
	John Anderson
75/77	**She Keeps Hangin' On** *Rayburn Anthony*
1/85	**She Keeps The Home Fires Burning**
	Ronnie Milsap
55/74	**She Kept On Talkin'** *Molly Bee*
1/82	**She Left Love All Over Me** *Razzy Bailey*
89/74	**She Likes Country Bands** *Del Reeves*
97/88	**(She Likes) Warm Summer Days**
	Buddy Latham
11/73	**She Loves Me (Right Out Of My Mind)**
	Freddy Weller
94/79	**She Loves My Troubles Away** *Mickey Jones*
71/87	**She Loves The Jerk** *Rodney Crowell*
53/83	**She Meant Forever When She Said**
	Goodbye *Mel Tillis*
21/74	**She Met A Stranger, I Met A Train**
	Tommy Cash
1/73	**She Needs Someone To Hold Her (When She**
	Cries) *Conway Twitty*
2/76	**She Never Knew Me** *Don Williams*
64/82	**She Only Meant To Use Him** *Wayne Kemp*

59/84	**She Put The Sad In All His Songs**
	Ronnie Dunn
23/89	**She Reminded Me Of You** *Mickey Gilley*
75/88	**She Says** *George Hamilton V*
	She Sings Amazing Grace
81/81	*Stan Hitchcock*
83/82	*Gary Stewart*
2/68	**She Still Comes Around** *Jerry Lee Lewis*
78/74	**She Still Comes To Me (To Pour The Wine)**
	Henson Cargill
3/84	**She Sure Got Away With My Heart**
	John Anderson
13/75	**She Talked A Lot About Texas** *Cal Smith*
92/86	**She Thinks I Steal Cars** *Pinkard & Bowden*
	She Thinks I Still Care
1/62	*George Jones*
F/77	*Elvis Presley*
39/68	**She Thinks I'm On That Train**
	Henson Cargill
9/87	**She Thinks That She'll Marry** *Judy Rodman*
30/85	**She Told Me Yes** *Chance*
78/84	**She Took It Too Well** *John Wesley Ryles*
11/77	**She Took More Than Her Share** *Moe Bandy*
62/81	**She Took The Place Of You** *Valentino*
2/86	**She Used To Be Somebody's Baby**
	Gatlin Bros.
11/85	**She Used To Love Me A Lot** *David Allan Coe*
19/82	**She Used To Sing On Sunday** *Gatlin Bros.*
11/71	**She Wakes Me With A Kiss Every Morning**
	Nat Stuckey
79/78	**She Wanted A Little Bit More**
	Ray Pennington
65/86	**She Wants To Marry A Cowboy**
	Younger Brothers
4/58	**She Was Only Seventeen (He Was One Year**
	More) *Marty Robbins*
72/79	**She Wears It Well** *Jerry Naylor*
6/68	**She Wears My Ring** *Ray Price*
14/68	**She Went A Little Bit Farther** *Faron Young*
	She Won't Let Go
	..see: (She's Got A Hold Of Me Where It Hurts)
62/75	**She Worshipped Me** *Red Steagall*
10/70	**She'll Be Hanging 'Round Somewhere**
	Mel Tillis
51/71	**She'll Remember** *Jerry Wallace*
	She'll Throw Stones At You
12/76	*Freddie Hart*
92/76	*Jacky Ward*
97/75	**She'll Wear It Out Leaving Town**
	George Kent
67/81	**She's A Friend Of A Friend** *Burrito Brothers*
3/70	**She's A Little Bit Country**
	George Hamilton IV
1/85	**She's A Miracle** *Exile*
1/75	**She's Actin' Single (I'm Drinkin' Doubles)**
	Gary Stewart
2/71	**She's All I Got** *Johnny Paycheck*
3/73	**She's All Woman** *David Houston*
37/75	**She's Already Gone** *Jim Mundy*
61/71	**She's As Close As I Can Get To Loving**
	You *Hank Locklin*
39/79	**She's Been Keepin' Me Up Nights**
	Bobby Lewis
6/85	**She's Comin' Back To Say Goodbye**
	Eddie Rabbitt
1/89	**She's Crazy For Leavin'** *Rodney Crowell*
66/72	**She's Doing It To Me Again** *Ray Pillow*
66/76	**She's Free But She's Not Easy** *Jim Glaser*
	She's Gone Gone Gone
12/65	*Lefty Frizzell*
44/84	*Carl Jackson*
74/83	**She's Gone To L.A. Again** *Mickey Clark*
9/85	**She's Gonna Win Your Heart** *Eddy Raven*
36/81	**She's Got A Drinking Problem** *Gary Stewart*

77/85	**(She's Got A Hold Of Me Where It Hurts) She**
	Won't Let Go *Ray Price*
24/74	**She's Got Everything I Need** *Eddy Arnold*
1/72	**She's Got To Be A Saint** *Ray Price*
	She's Got You
1/62	*Patsy Cline*
1/77	*Loretta Lynn*
91/80	**She's Hangin' In There (I'm Hangin' Out)**
	David Wills
25/76	**She's Helping Me Get Over Loving You**
	Joe Stampley
43/70	**She's Hungry Again** *Bill Phillips*
39/74	**She's In Love With A Rodeo Man**
	Johnny Russell
14/60	**She's Just A Whole Lot Like You**
	Hank Thompson
	She's Just An Old Love Turned Memory
64/75	*Nick Nixon*
1/77	*Charley Pride*
79/80	**She's Leavin' (And I'm Almost Gone)**
	Kenny Price
37/71	**She's Leavin' (Bonnie, Please Don't Go)**
	Jim Ed Brown
81/81	**She's Livin' It Up (And I'm Drinkin' 'em**
	Down) *Allen Frizzell*
26/77	**She's Long Legged** *Joe Stampley*
21/69	**She's Lookin' Better By The Minute**
	Jay Lee Webb
54/67	**She's Looking Good** *Stan Hitchcock*
7/82	**She's Lying** *Lee Greenwood*
87/78	**She's Lying Next To Me** *Nick Nixon*
37/80	**She's Made Of Faith** *Marty Robbins*
72/66	**She's Mighty Gone** *Johnny Darrell*
6/70	**She's Mine** *George Jones*
	She's My Rock
20/73	*Stoney Edwards*
2/84	*George Jones*
91/79	**She's My Woman** *Randy Traywick*
F/58	**She's No Angel** *Kitty Wells*
17/88	**She's No Lady** *Lyle Lovett*
71/74	**She's No Ordinary Woman (Ordinarily)**
	Jim Mundy
43/65	**She's Not For You** *Willie Nelson*
4/82	**She's Not Really Cheatin' (She's Just Gettin'**
	Even) *Moe Bandy*
74/75	**She's Not Yours Anymore** *Ferlin Husky*
10/82	**She's Playing Hard To Forget** *Eddy Raven*
1/77	**She's Pulling Me Back Again** *Mickey Gilley*
	She's Ready For Someone To Love Her
67/83	*Osmond Brothers*
F/83	*Jerry Reed*
2/85	**She's Single Again** *Janie Frickie*
81/88	**She's Sittin' Pretty** *Billy Parker*
17/81	**She's Steppin' Out** *Con Hunley*
85/77	**She's Still All Over You** *Jeanne Pruett*
100/79	**She's Still Around** *Chandy Lee*
17/77	**She's The Girl Of My Dreams** *Don King*
	She's The Trip That I've Been On
91/76	*Leon Rausch*
52/86	*Larry Boone*
69/67	**She's The Woman** *Barbara Cummings*
	She's Too Good To Be True
1/72	*Charley Pride*
1/87	*Exile*
91/78	**Shed So Many Tears** *Isaac Payton Sweat*
12/63	**Sheepskin Valley** *Claude King*
80/87	**Sheet Music** *Bill Anderson*
43/76	**Sheik Of Chicago** *Joe Stampley*
14/73	**Shelter Of Your Eyes** *Don Williams*
33/73	**Shenandoah** *Charlie McCoy*
8/71	**Sheriff Of Boone County** *Kenny Price*
94/75	**Shhh** *Kathy Barnes*
73/67	**Shinbone** *Orville & Ivy*
47/66	**Shindig In The Barn** *Tommy Collins*
5/82	**Shine** *Waylon*

56/88	**Shine A Light On A Lie** *Robin Lee*
36/76	**Shine On** *Ronnie Prophet*
13/78	**Shine On Me** *John Wesley Ryles*
3/83	**Shine On (Shine All Your Sweet Love On Me)** *George Jones*
7/51	**Shine, Shave, Shower** *Lefty Frizzell*
40/67	**Shine, Shine** *Carl Perkins*
1/87	**Shine, Shine, Shine** *Eddy Raven*
58/67	**Shiny Red Automobile** *George Morgan*
19/69	**Ship In The Bottle** *Stonewall Jackson*
28/66	**Shirt, The** *Norma Jean*
3/66	**Shoe Goes On The Other Foot Tonight** *Marty Robbins*
22/86	**Shoe String** *Mel McDaniel*
83/81	**Shoe's On The Other Foot** *Montana*
17/63	**Shoes Of A Fool** *Bill Goodwin*
8/70	**Shoeshine Man** *Tom T. Hall*
65/84	**Shoot First, Ask Questions Later** *Younger Brothers*
57/71	**Short And Sweet** *Bobby Bare*
16/61	**Shorty** *Jimmy Smart*
	Shot Full Of Love
30/81	*Randy Parton*
19/83	*Nitty Gritty Dirt Band*
1/51	**Shot Gun Boogie** *Tennessee Ernie Ford*
30/84	**Shot In The Dark** *Leon Everette*
	Shotgun Rider
55/75	*Marty Robbins*
23/80	*Joe Sun*
60/73	**Shotgun Willie** *Willie Nelson*
	Should I Come Home (Or Should I Go Crazy)
83/75	*Joe Allen*
3/79	*Gene Watson*
50/81	**Should I Do It** *Tanya Tucker*
10/58	**Should We Tell Him** *Everly Brothers*
1/73	**Shoulder To Cry On** *Charley Pride*
34/79	**Shoulder To Shoulder (Arm and Arm)** *Roy Clark*
5/88	**Shouldn't It Be Easier Than This** *Charley Pride*
1/84	**Show Her** *Ronnie Milsap*
30/62	**Show Her Lots Of Gold** *Ernest Tubb*
11/72	**Show Me** *Barbara Mandrell*
96/77	**Show Me A Brick Wall** *Carl Smith*
8/76	**Show Me A Man** *T.G. Sheppard*
56/78	**Show Me A Sign** *Jim Chesnut*
7/49	**Show Me The Way Back To Your Heart** *Eddy Arnold*
44/66	**Show Me The Way To The Circus** *Homesteaders*
81/76	**Show Me Where** *Ruby Falls*
	Showdown
97/76	*Brian Shaw*
71/85	*Carlette*
73/71	**Showing His Dollar** *Webb Pierce*
15/57	**Shrine Of St. Cecilia** *Faron Young*
7/80	**Shriner's Convention** *Ray Stevens*
13/80	**Shuffle Song** *Margo Smith*
5/46	**Shut That Gate** *Ted Daffan's Texans*
26/70	**Shutters And Boards** *Slim Whitman*
7/51	**Sick, Sober And Sorry** *Johnny Bond*
70/81	**Sidewalks Are Grey** *Kenny Serratt*
F/70	**Sidewalks Of Chicago** *Merle Haggard*
72/83	**Sign Of The Times** *Donna Fargo*
	Signed Sealed And Delivered
2/48	*Cowboy Copas*
6/48	*Bob Atcher*
8/48	*Texas Jim Robertson*
9/48	*Jimmy Wakely*
10/61	*Cowboy Copas*
29/80	**Silence On The Line** *Henson Cargill*
F/80	**Silent Night (After The Fight)** *Ronnie Milsap*
20/84	**Silent Partners** *Frizzell & West*
7/81	**Silent Treatment** *Earl Thomas Conley*

78/87	**Silent Understanding** *T L Lee with Kathy Walker*
5/52	**Silver And Gold** *Pee Wee King*
15/55	**Silver Bell** *Hank Snow & Chet Atkins*
25/77	**Silver Bird** *Tina Rainford*
1/45	**Silver Dew On The Blue Grass Tonight** *Bob Wills*
75/80	**Silver Eagle** *Atlanta Rhythm Section*
18/77	**Silver Medals And Sweet Memories** *Statler Brothers*
4/46	**Silver Spurs (On The Golden Stairs)** *Gene Autry*
4/47	**Silver Stars, Purple Sage, Eyes Of Blue** *Cliffie Stone*
	Silver Threads And Golden Needles
16/62	*Springfields*
20/74	*Linda Ronstadt*
68/74	*Charlie McCoy*
59/70	**Silver Wings** *Hagers*
20/76	**Silver Wings And Golden Rings** *Billie Jo Spears*
67/70	**Simple Days & Simple Ways** *Bobby Lewis*
63/85	**Simple I Love You** *Karen Brooks*
10/79	**Simple Little Words** *Cristy Lane*
45/71	**Simple Thing As Love** *Roy Clark*
	Sin *...see: (It's No)*
73/70	**Since December** *Eddy Arnold*
68/81	**Since I Don't Have You** *Don McLean*
	Since I Fell For You
10/76	*Charlie Rich*
20/79	*Con Hunley*
7/86	**Since I Found You** *Sweethearts Of The Rodeo*
	Since I Met You, Baby
1/69	*Sonny James*
10/75	*Freddy Fender*
96/76	**Since I Met You Boy** *Jeannie Seely*
62/72	**Since Then** *Ray Pillow*
54/69	**Since They Fired The Band Director (At Murphy High)** *Linda Manning*
84/77	**Since You Broke My Heart** *Don Everly*
	Sincerely
72/72	*Kitty Wells*
8/89	*Forester Sisters*
74/71	**Sing A Happy Song** *Connie Eaton*
3/63	**Sing A Little Song Of Heartache** *Rose Maddox*
54/75	**Sing A Love Song, Porter Wagoner** *Mike Wells*
	Sing A Sad Song
26/63	*Buddy Cagle*
19/64	*Merle Haggard*
19/77	*Wynn Stewart*
70/69	**Sing A Song About Love** *Bobby Wright*
3/73	**Sing About Love** *Lynn Anderson*
59/72	**Sing-Along Song** *Mayf Nutter*
66/74	**Sing For The Good Times** *Jack Greene*
53/71	**Sing High - Sing Low** *Anne Murray*
3/72	**Sing Me A Love Song To Baby** *Billy Walker*
1/68	**Sing Me Back Home** *Merle Haggard*
12/70	**Singer Of Sad Songs** *Waylon Jennings*
29/75	**Singin' In The Kitchen** *Bobby Bare*
89/76	**Singing A Happy Song** *Larry G. Hudson*
4/54	**Singing Hills** *Slim Whitman*
18/71	**Singing In Viet Nam Talking Blues** *Johnny Cash*
	Singing My Song
1/69	*Tammy Wynette*
17/83	*Gail Davies*
36/78	**Single Again** *Gary Stewart*
74/81	**Single Girl** *Cindy Hurt*
8/82	**Single Women** *Dolly Parton*
6/60	**Sink The Bismarck** *Johnny Horton*
14/48	**Sinner's Death** *Roy Acuff*

5/69 **Smoky The Bar** *Hank Thompson*
Smooth Sailin'
68/78   *Connie Smith*
32/79   *Jim Weatherly*
47/79   *Sonny Throckmorton*
6/80   *T.G. Sheppard*
43/85 **Smooth Sailing (Rock In The Road)**
   Mark Gray
94/79 **Smooth Southern Highway** *Don Cox*
77/76 **Snap, Crackle And Pop** *Johnny Carver*
Snap Your Fingers
40/71   *Dick Curless*
12/74   *Don Gibson*
1/87   *Ronnie Milsap*
5/83 **Snapshot** *Sylvia*
48/81 **Sneakin' Around** *Kin Vassy*
16/67 **Sneaking 'Cross The Border** *Harden Trio*
69/74 **Sneaky Snake** *Tom T. Hall*
2/66 **Snow Flake** *Jim Reeves*
28/63 **Snow White Cloud** *Frank Taylor*
10/70 **Snowbird** *Anne Murray*
So Close
72/83   *Backroads*
46/84   *Wright Brothers*
43/77 **So Close Again** *Margo & Norro*
4/56 **So Doggone Lonesome** *Johnny Cash*
68/83 **So Easy To Love** *Wright Brothers*
64/88 **So Far Not So Good** *Jeff Chance*
22/82 **So Fine** *Oak Ridge Boys*
68/78 **So Good** *Jewel Blanch*
27/78 **So Good, So Rare, So Fine** *Freddie Hart*
86/89 **So Good To Be In Love** *Karen Staley*
F/77 **So Good Woman** *Waylon Jennings*
22/62 **So How Come (No One Loves Me)** *Don Gibson*
43/69 **So Long** *Bobby Helms*
69/68 **So Long, Charlie Brown, Don't Look For Me**
   Around *Sammi Smith*
1/44 **So Long, Pal** *Al Dexter*
14/55 **So Lovely Baby** *Rusty & Doug*
16/59 **So Many Times** *Roy Acuff*
So Many Ways
28/73   *Eddy Arnold*
33/77   *David Houston*
45/66 **So Much For Me, So Much For You**
   Liz Anderson
46/70 **So Much In Love With You** *David Rogers*
So Round, So Firm, So Fully Packed
1/47   *Merle Travis*
3/47   *Johnny Bond*
5/47   *Ernest Tubb*
So Sad (To Watch Good Love Go Bad)
12/70   *Hank Williams, Jr. & Lois Johnson*
31/76   *Connie Smith*
76/78   *Steve Wariner*
28/83   *Emmylou Harris*
19/59 **So Soon** *Jimmy Newman*
71/82 **(So This Is) Happy Hour** *Snuff*
So This Is Love
20/71   *Tommy Cash*
41/86   *Charly McClain*
14/62 **So Wrong** *Patsy Cline*
F/57 **So You Think You've Got Trouble**
   Marvin Rainwater
58/79 **Soap** *O.B. McClinton*
13/78 **Soft Lights And Hard Country Music**
   Moe Bandy
97/78 **Soft Lights And Slow Sexy Music**
   Jody Miller
10/49 **Soft Lips** *Hank Thompson*
65/73 **Soft Lips And Hard Liquor** *Charlie Walker*
3/61 **Soft Rain** *Ray Price*
8/72 **Soft, Sweet And Warm** *David Houston*
30/78 **Softest Touch In Town** *Bobby G. Rice*
74/69 **Softly And Tenderly** *Lois Johnson*

4/60 **Softly And Tenderly (I'll Hold You In My**
   Arms) *Lewis Pruitt*
F/78 **Softly, As I Leave You** *Elvis Presley*
69/73 **Sold American** *Kinky Friedman*
29/76 **Sold Out Of Flagpoles** *Johnny Cash*
51/80 **Soldier Of Fortune** *Tom T. Hall*
54/86 **Soldier Of Love** *Billy Burnette*
15/59 **Soldier's Joy** *Hawkshaw Hawkins*
Soldier's Last Letter
1/44   *Ernest Tubb*
3/71   *Merle Haggard*
46/66 **Soldier's Prayer In Viet Nam**
   Don Reno & Benny Martin
F/79 **Solitaire** *Elvis Presley*
   (also see: I'm Getting Good At Missing You)
28/69 **Solitary** *Don Gibson*
14/76 **Solitary Man** *T.G. Sheppard*
1/77 **Some Broken Hearts Never Mend**
   Don Williams
47/82 **Some Day My Ship's Comin' In** *Joe Waters*
10/81 **Some Days Are Diamonds (Some Days Are**
   Stone) *John Denver*
45/82 **Some Days It Rains All Night Long**
   Terri Gibbs
1/85 **Some Fools Never Learn** *Steve Wariner*
22/86 **Some Girls Have All The Luck**
   Louise Mandrell
Some Hearts Get All The Breaks
25/84   *Charly McClain*
81/86   *Roger Miller*
17/78 **Some I Wrote** *Statler Brothers*
8/74 **Some Kind Of A Woman** *Faron Young*
27/81 **Some Love Songs Never Die** *B.J. Thomas*
10/82 **Some Memories Just Won't Die**
   Marty Robbins
61/82 **Some Never Stand A Chance** *Family Brown*
20/82 **Some Of My Best Friends Are Old Songs**
   Louise Mandrell
72/85 **Some Of Shelly's Blues**
   Maines Brothers Band
28/73 **Some Old California Memory** *Henson Cargill*
16/88 **Some Old Side Road** *Keith Whitley*
54/73 **Some Roads Have No Ending** *Warner Mack*
57/85 **Some Such Foolishness** *Tommy Roe*
83/81 **Some You Win, Some You Lose** *Orion*
34/84 **Somebody Buy This Cowgirl A Beer**
   Shelly West
4/85 **Somebody Else's Fire** *Janie Frickie*
10/76 **Somebody Hold Me (Until She Passes By)**
   Narvel Felts
62/67 **Somebody Knows My Dog** *Willis Brothers*
20/81 **Somebody Led Me Away** *Loretta Lynn*
1/87 **Somebody Lied** *Ricky Van Shelton*
1/66 **Somebody Like Me** *Eddy Arnold*
67/88 **Somebody Loses, Somebody Wins**
   Rosie Flores
21/72 **Somebody Loves Me** *Johnny Paycheck*
8/76 **Somebody Loves You** *Crystal Gayle*
84/87 **Somebody Ought To Tell Him That She's**
   Gone *Ogden Harless*
16/62 **Somebody Save Me** *Ferlin Husky*
1/85 **Somebody Should Leave** *Reba McEntire*
1/76 **Somebody Somewhere** *Loretta Lynn*
6/79 **Somebody Special** *Donna Fargo*
18/63 **Somebody Told Somebody** *Rose Maddox*
59/77 **Somebody Took Her Love (And Never Gave It**
   Back) *Jimmie Peters*
9/86 **Somebody Wants Me Out Of The Way**
   George Jones
52/69 **Somebody's Always Leaving**
   Stonewall Jackson
7/83 **Somebody's Always Saying Goodbye**
   Anne Murray

	Somebody's Back In Town
6/59	*Wilburn Brothers*
81/84	*Chris Hillman*
2/51	**Somebody's Been Beating My Time**
	Eddy Arnold
32/81	**Somebody's Darling, Somebody's Wife**
	Dottsy
64/78	**Somebody's Gonna Do It Tonight**
	R.C. Bannon
1/83	**Somebody's Gonna Love You** *Lee Greenwood*
65/80	**Somebody's Gotta Do The Losing**
	Stephany Samone
8/81	**Somebody's Knockin'** *Terri Gibbs*
1/84	**Somebody's Needin' Somebody**
	Conway Twitty
9/52	**Somebody's Stolen My Honey** *Ernest Tubb*
	Someday
4/46	*Gene Autry*
12/57	*Webb Pierce*
28/86	*Steve Earle*
	(also see: It's Always Gonna Be)
22/79	**Someday My Day Will Come** *George Jones*
60/87	**Someday My Ship Will Sail** *Emmylou Harris*
70/88	**Someday, Somenight** *Trinity Lane*
	Someday Soon
39/76	*Kathy Barnes*
21/82	*Moe Bandy*
4/70	**Someday We'll Be Together**
	Bill Anderson & Jan Howard
2/71	**Someday We'll Look Back** *Merle Haggard*
1/84	**Someday When Things Are Good**
	Merle Haggard
45/78	**Someday You Will** *John Wesley Ryles*
10/49	**Someday You'll Call My Name**
	Jimmy Wakely
	Someday (You'll Want Me To Want You)
2/46	*Elton Britt*
3/46	*Hoosier Hot Shots*
70/81	**Somehow, Someway And Someday** *Amarillo*
5/87	**Someone** *Lee Greenwood*
8/66	**Someone Before Me** *Wilburn Brothers*
59/74	**Someone Came To See Me (In The Middle Of The Night)** *Patti Page*
17/75	**Someone Cares For You** *Red Steagall*
1/82	**Someone Could Lose A Heart Tonight**
	Eddie Rabbitt
26/84	**Someone Is Falling In Love** *Kathy Mattea*
11/79	**Someone Is Looking For Someone Like You** *Gail Davies*
26/85	**Someone Like You** *Emmylou Harris*
94/77	**Someone Loves Him** *Sue Richards*
	Someone Loves You Honey
84/75	*Marie Owens*
1/78	*Charley Pride*
70/85	**Someone Must Be Missing You Tonight**
	Terri Gibbs
73/71	**Someone Stepped In (And Stole Me Blind)**
	Webb Pierce
4/72	**Someone To Give My Love To**
	Johnny Paycheck
32/67	**Someone Told My Story** *Merle Haggard*
60/85	**Someone's Gonna Love Me Tonight**
	Southern Pacific
30/65	**Someone's Gotta Cry** *Jean Shepard*
29/76	**Someone's With Your Wife Tonight, Mister** *Bobby Borchers*
60/80	**Somethin' 'Bout You Baby I Like**
	Glen Campbell & Rita Coolidge
13/81	**Somethin' On The Radio** *Jacky Ward*
67/87	**Somethin' You Got** *Nielsen White Band*
6/74	**Something** *Johnny Rodriguez*
10/73	**Something About You I Love**
	Johnny Paycheck
6/71	**Something Beautiful (To Remember)**
	Slim Whitman
62/74	**Something Better** *O.B. McClinton*
19/75	**Something Better To Do** *Olivia Newton-John*
17/67	**Something Fishy** *Dolly Parton*
31/64	**Something I Dreamed** *George Jones*
2/85	**Something In My Heart** *Ricky Skaggs*
71/75	**Something Just Came Over Me** *Charlie Rich*
4/51	**Something Old, Something New** *Eddy Arnold*
53/74	**Something On Your Mind**
	Jack Blanchard & Misty Morgan
23/62	**Something Precious** *Skeeter Davis*
10/68	**Something Pretty** *Wynn Stewart*
17/68	**Something Special** *Mel Tillis*
81/78	**Something To Believe In** *Don Drumm*
	Something To Brag About
18/70	*Charlie Louvin & Melba Montgomery*
9/78	*Mary Kay Place with Willie Nelson*
63/72	**Something To Call Mine** *Bill Rice*
85/82	**Something To Love For Again** *Diane Pfeifer*
36/70	**Something To Think About**
	Hank Williams, Jr.
15/70	**Something Unseen** *Jack Greene*
81/78	**Something's Burning** *Kathy Barnes*
60/69	**Something's Missing (It's You)** *Jackie Burns*
19/69	**Something's Wrong In California**
	Waylon Jennings
F/81	**Sometime, Somewhere, Somehow**
	Barbara Mandrell
10/74	**Sometime Sunshine** *Jim Ed Brown*
	Sometimes
1/76	*Bill Anderson & Mary Lou Turner*
59/76	*Johnny Lee*
3/86	**Sometimes A Lady** *Eddy Raven*
6/73	**Sometimes A Memory Ain't Enough**
	Jerry Lee Lewis
34/81	**Sometimes I Cry When I'm Alone**
	Sammi Smith
79/78	**Sometimes I Do** *Ernest Tubb*
9/83	**Sometimes I Get Lucky And Forget**
	Gene Watson
9/76	**Sometimes I Talk In My Sleep** *Randy Cornor*
12/62	**Sometimes I'm Tempted** *Marty Robbins*
67/79	**Sometimes Love** *Mundo Earwood*
55/88	**Sometimes She Feels Like A Man**
	Charly McClain
	Sometimes When We Touch
F/81	*Stephanie Winslow*
6/85	*Mark Gray & Tammy Wynette*
	Sometimes You Just Can't Win
17/62	*George Jones*
10/71	*George Jones*
27/82	*Linda Ronstadt & John David Souther*
37/70	**Someway** *Don Gibson*
66/74	**Somewhere Around Midnight** *George Morgan*
2/74	**Somewhere Between Love And Tomorrow**
	Roy Clark
23/88	**Somewhere Between Ragged And Right**
	John Anderson
1/82	**Somewhere Between Right And Wrong**
	Earl Thomas Conley
	Somewhere Down The Line
50/83	*Younger Brothers*
3/84	*T.G. Sheppard*
65/86	**Somewhere In America** *Mac Davis*
55/83	**Somewhere In Texas** *Ray Price*
29/87	**Somewhere In The Night** *Sawyer Brown*
15/72	**Somewhere In Virginia In The Rain**
	Jack Blanchard & Misty Morgan
22/73	**Somewhere My Love** *Red Steagall*
	Somewhere South Of Macon
100/77	*Marshall Chapman*
79/88	*Rattlesnake Annie*
80/81	**Somewhere To Come When It Rains**
	John Wesley Ryles
1/87	**Somewhere Tonight** *Highway 101*
69/69	**Son** *Jerry Wallace*

41/70	**Son Of A Coal Man** *Del Reeves*
40/69	**Son Of A Preacher Man** *Peggy Little*
5/74	**Son Of A Rotten Gambler** *Anne Murray*
58/68	**Son Of A Sawmill Man** *Osborne Brothers*
14/79	**Son Of Clayton Delaney** *Tom T. Hall*
	Son Of Hickory Holler's Tramp
22/68	*Johnny Darrell*
32/77	*Johnny Russell*
71/83	**Son Of The South** *Bill Anderson*
8/74	**Song And Dance Man** *Johnny Paycheck*
66/73	**Song For Everyone** *Ray Griff*
53/69	**Song For Jenny** *Ed Bruce*
91/80	**Song For Noel** *King Edward IV*
92/74	**Song I'd Like To Sing**
	Kris Kristofferson & Rita Coolidge
69/88	**Song In My Heart** *Mark Gray & Bobbi Lace*
5/77	**Song In The Night** *Johnny Duncan*
89/78	**Song Man** *Rick Jacques*
F/73	**Song Nobody Sings** *Jerry Wallace*
54/80	**Song Of The Patriot** *Johnny Cash*
	Song Of The South
57/81	*Johnny Russell*
72/82	*Tom T. Hall & Earl Scruggs*
1/89	*Alabama*
37/71	**Song To Mama** *Carter Family*
44/72	**Song To Sing** *Susan Raye*
29/75	**Song We Fell In Love To** *Connie Smith*
13/79	**Song We Made Love To** *Mickey Gilley*
69/73	**Songman** *Cashman & West*
10/65	**Sons Of Katie Elder** *Johnny Cash*
53/77	**Soon As I Touched Her** *Dorsey Burnette*
19/62	**Sooner Or Later** *Webb Pierce*
100/77	**Sophisticated Country Lady** *Loretta Robey*
5/64	**Sorrow On The Rocks** *Porter Wagoner*
63/88	**Sorry Girls** *Goldens*
50/64	**Sorry I Never Knew You**
	Sego Brothers & Naomi
	Soul Deep
22/70	*Eddy Arnold*
63/73	*Guy Shannon*
27/77	**Soul Of A Honky Tonk Woman** *Mel McDaniel*
10/82	**Soul Searchin'** *Leon Everette*
1/73	**Soul Song** *Joe Stampley*
64/70	**Soul You Never Had** *Jan Howard*
18/75	**Soulful Woman** *Kenny O'Dell*
	Sound Of Goodbye
21/73	*Jerry Wallace*
1/84	*Crystal Gayle*
21/62	**Sound Of Your Footsteps** *Wilburn Brothers*
6/83	**Sounds Like Love** *Johnny Lee*
	Sounds Of Goodbye
31/68	*George Morgan*
41/68	*Tommy Cash*
15/70	**South** *Roger Miller*
91/87	**South Of The Border** *Clay Blaker*
99/77	**Southbound** *R.C. Bannon*
71/88	**Southern Accent** *Bama Band*
63/86	**Southern Air** *Ray Stevens*
91/88	**Southern And Proud Of It** *Jeff Golden*
37/68	**Southern Bound** *Kenny Price*
5/77	**Southern California**
	George Jones & Tammy Wynette
42/82	**Southern Fried** *Bill Anderson*
6/73	**Southern Loving** *Jim Ed Brown*
1/77	**Southern Nights** *Glen Campbell*
1/81	**Southern Rains** *Mel Tillis*
	Southern Women
86/83	*Owen Brothers*
33/84	*Wright Brothers*
	Souvenirs
100/76	*Colleen Peterson*
66/87	*Lane Caudell*
68/72	**Souvenirs And California Mem'rys**
	Billie Jo Spears

	Spanish Eyes
20/79	*Charlie Rich*
8/88	*Willie Nelson with Julio Iglesias*
3/53	**Spanish Fire Ball** *Hank Snow*
56/79	**Spare A Little Lovin' (On A Fool)** *Arnie Rue*
	Sparkling Brown Eyes
4/54	*Webb Pierce*
30/60	*George Jones*
49/73	*Dickey Lee*
10/51	**Sparrow In The Tree Top** *Rex Allen*
9/82	**Speak Softly** *Gene Watson*
29/72	**Special Day** *Arlene Harden*
70/88	**Speed Of The Sound Of Loneliness**
	Kim Carnes
82/89	**Spelling On The Stone** *Unknown*
66/74	**Spiders & Snakes** *Jim Stafford*
14/58	**Splish Splash** *Bobby Darin*
F/73	**Spokane Motel Blues** *Tom T. Hall*
71/77	**Spread A Little Love Around** *Jody Miller*
61/72	**Spread It Around** *Brian Collins*
43/81	**Spread My Wings** *Tim Rex & Oklahoma*
	Spring
30/69	*Clay Hart*
18/75	*Tanya Tucker*
12/78	**Spring Fever** *Loretta Lynn*
2/58	**Squaws Along The Yukon** *Hank Thompson*
61/79	**Squeeze Box** *Freddy Fender*
68/88	**Stairs, The** *Rosemary Sharp*
2/58	**Stairway Of Love** *Marty Robbins*
5/67	**Stamp Out Loneliness** *Stonewall Jackson*
8/50	**Stampede** *Roy Rogers*
5/86	**Stand A Little Rain** *Nitty Gritty Dirt Band*
16/61	**Stand At Your Window** *Jim Reeves*
10/66	**Stand Beside Me** *Jimmy Dean*
1/80	**Stand By Me** *Mickey Gilley*
	Stand By My Woman Man ..see: (I'm A)
	Stand By Your Man
1/68	*Tammy Wynette*
88/81	*David Allan Coe*
12/86	**Stand On It** *Mel McDaniel*
	Stand Up
28/62	*Ferlin Husky*
5/85	*Mel McDaniel*
14/78	**Standard Lie Number One** *Stella Parton*
65/68	**Standing In The Rain** *Chaparral Brothers*
5/66	**Standing In The Shadows** *Hank Williams, Jr.*
17/74	**Standing In Your Line** *Barbara Fairchild*
63/87	**Standing Invitation** *Adam Baker*
5/76	**Standing Room Only** *Barbara Mandrell*
15/80	**Standing Tall** *Billie Jo Spears*
75/86	**Standing Too Close To The Moon**
	Tina Danielle
92/80	**Star, The** *Melba Montgomery*
78/74	**Star Of The Bar** *Troy Seals*
	Star-Studded Nights
54/77	*Ed Bruce*
78/80	*Shoppe*
61/85	**Starlite** *Karen Taylor-Good*
	Stars And Stripes On Iwo Jima
1/45	*Bob Wills*
4/45	*Sons Of The Pioneers*
	Stars On The Water
30/81	*Rodney Crowell*
86/83	*Tommy St. John*
74/75	**Start All Over Again** *Johnny Carver*
	Starting All Over Again
16/78	*Don Gibson*
73/89	*Razzy Bailey*
17/80	**Starting Over** *Tammy Wynette*
	Starting Over Again
1/80	*Dolly Parton*
4/86	*Steve Wariner*
74/83	**State Of Our Union**
	Charlie McCoy & Laney Hicks
17/66	**Stateside** *Mel Tillis*

Statue Of A Fool
1/69   *Jack Greene*
10/74   *Brian Collins*
91/79   *Bill Medley*
5/77 **Statues Without Hearts** *Larry Gatlin*
Stay A Little Longer
2/46   *Bob Wills*
17/82   *Mel Tillis*
22/73 **Stay All Night (Stay A Little Longer)**
    Willie Nelson
89/81 **Stay Away From Jim** *Jimmy Arthur Ordge*
20/75 **Stay Away From The Apple Tree**
    Billie Jo Spears
49/79 **(Stay Away From) The Cocaine Train**
    Johnny Paycheck
86/88 **Stay Out Of My Arms** *Jim Lauderdale*
7/70 **Stay There 'Til I Get There** *Lynn Anderson*
61/80 **Stay Until The Rain Stops** *Kathy Carlile*
Stay With Me
40/78   *Nick Noble*
6/79   *Dave & Sugar*
57/79   *Dandy*
89/83   *Tammy Chaparro*
86/85   *Exile*
1/84 **Stay Young** *Don Williams*
26/79 **Steady As The Rain** *Stella Parton*
Steal Away
9/50   *Red Foley*
74/79   *Paul Schmucker*
50/75 **Stealin'** *Jacky Ward*
28/77 **Stealin' Feelin'** *Mike Lunsford*
F/73 **Steamroller Blues** *Elvis Presley*
4/47 **Steel Guitar Rag** *Merle Travis*
9/49 **Steel Guitar Ramble** *Cecil Campbell*
4/46 **Steel Guitar Stomp** *Hank Penny*
15/66 **Steel Rail Blues** *George Hamilton IV*
6/71 **Step Aside** *Faron Young*
7/82 **Step Back** *Ronnie McDowell*
1/81 **Step By Step** *Eddie Rabbitt*
79/82 **Step In The Right Direction** *Judy Taylor*
1/85 **Step That Step** *Sawyer Brown*
43/69 **Stepchild** *Billie Jo Spears*
Steppin' Out
60/70   *Jerry Smith*
9/80   *Mel Tillis*
46/88   *David Ball*
92/76 **Steppin' Out Tonight** *Lori Parker*
1/63 **Still** *Bill Anderson*
7/79 **Still A Woman** *Margo Smith*
34/65 **Still Alive In '65** *Jim Nesbitt*
92/87 **Still Dancing** *Loney Hutchins*
1/81 **Still Doin' Time** *George Jones*
33/86 **Still Hurtin' Me** *Charlie Daniels Band*
60/88 **Still I Stay** *Charly McClain*
56/86 **Still In The Picture** *Leon Everette*
63/83 **Still In The Ring** *Tammy Wynette*
1/84 **Still Losing You** *Ronnie Milsap*
Still Loving You
27/63   *Clyde Beavers*
56/70   *Bob Luman*
7/74   *Bob Luman*
95/79   *Troy Shondell*
58/85 **Still On A Roll** *Moe Bandy & Joe Stampley*
62/88 **Still Pickin' Up After You** *Kendalls*
3/83 **Still Taking Chances** *Michael Murphey*
Still The One
11/77   *Bill Anderson*
60/82   *Thrasher Brothers*
4/75 **Still Thinkin' 'Bout You**
    Billy 'Crash' Craddock
5/88 **Still Within The Sound Of My Voice**
    Glen Campbell
74/81 **Stirrin' Up Feelings** *Diana Trask*

Stolen Moments
7/56   *Hank Snow*
100/77   *Daniel*
3/74 **Stomp Them Grapes** *Mel Tillis*
  (Stompin' Grapes And Gettin' Silly)
  ..see: Me And Millie
87/82 **Stomping On My Heart** *Glen Bailey*
75/88 **Stone Cold Love** *Beards*
52/75 **Stone Crazy** *Freddy Weller*
41/79 **Stone Wall (Around Your Heart)**
    Gary Stewart
19/75 **Stoned At The Jukebox** *Hank Williams, Jr.*
31/72 **Stonin' Around** *Dick Curless*
Stood Up
8/58   *Ricky Nelson*
53/67   *Floyd Cramer*
Stop And Smell The Roses
29/74   *Henson Cargill*
40/74   *Mac Davis*
100/88 **Stop And Take The Time** *Faron Young*
93/77 **Stop And Think It Over** *Mike Boyd*
69/74 **Stop If You Love Me** *Terry Stafford*
26/64 **Stop Me** *Bill Phillips*
48/88 **Stop Me (If You've Heard This One Before)**
    Larry Boone
28/88 **Stop The Rain** *Shenandoah*
15/66 **Stop The Start (Of Tears In My Heart)**
    Johnny Dollar
13/68 **Stop The Sun** *Bonnie Guitar*
Stop The World (And Let Me Off)
7/58   *Johnnie & Jack*
16/65   *Waylon Jennings*
18/74   *Susan Raye*
91/76   *Donny King*
70/80 **Stores Are Full Of Roses** *Jack Grayson*
16/67 **Storm, The** *Jim Reeves*
60/83 **Storm Of Love** *Chantilly*
Storms Never Last
17/75   *Dottsy*
17/81   *Waylon & Jessi*
25/74 **Storms Of Troubled Times** *Ray Price*
21/78 **Stormy Weather** *Stella Parton*
33/80 **Story Behind The Story** *Al Downing*
1/58 **Story Of My Life** *Marty Robbins*
65/68 **Storybook Children**
    Virgil Warner & Suzi Jane Hokum
16/60 **Straight A's In Love** *Johnny Cash*
66/87 **Straight From My Heart** *Sylvia*
80/85 **Straight Laced Lady** *Tracy Lynden*
Straight Life
37/68   *Bobby Goldsboro*
45/68   *Sonny Curtis*
79/86 **Straight Talkin** *Melba Montgomery*
1/87 **Straight To The Heart** *Crystal Gayle*
1/44 **Straighten Up And Fly Right** *King Cole Trio*
60/67 **Stranded** *Jim Nesbitt*
26/79 **Stranded On A Dead End Street** *ETC Band*
Strange Little Girl
5/51   *Cowboy Copas*
9/51   *Tennessee Ernie Ford*
9/51   *Ernest Tubb & Red Foley*
4/76 **Stranger** *Johnny Duncan*
45/83 **Stranger At My Door** *Juice Newton*
64/80 **Stranger, I'm Married** *Doug McGuire*
26/68 **Stranger In A Strange, Strange City**
    Webb Pierce
92/83 **Stranger In Her Bed** *Randy Parton*
5/83 **Stranger In My House** *Ronnie Milsap*
Stranger In My Place
27/75   *Anne Murray*
79/75   *Anne Murray*
69/80   *Orion*
42/67 **Stranger On The Run** *Bill Anderson*
64/86 **Stranger Things Have Happened**
    Larry Boone

66/74	**Sweet And Tender Feeling** *Mack White*
64/72	**Sweet Apple Wine** *Duane Dee*
43/69	**Sweet Baby Girl** *Peggy Little*
57/71	**Sweet Baby On My Mind** *June Stearns*
40/73	**Sweet Becky Walker** *Larry Gatlin*
	Sweet Caroline
40/70	*Anthony Armstrong Jones*
77/86	*Claude Gray*
22/68	**Sweet Child Of Sunshine** *Jerry Wallace*
	Sweet City Woman
48/77	*Johnny Carver*
34/80	*Tompall/Glaser Brothers*
89/78	**Sweet Country Girl** *Mack Sanders*
	Sweet Country Music
86/75	*Ruby Falls*
5/84	*Atlanta*
6/73	**Sweet Country Woman** *Johnny Duncan*
53/77	**Sweet Deceiver** *Cristy Lane*
1/78	**Sweet Desire** *Kendalls*
7/72	**Sweet Dream Woman** *Waylon Jennings*
	Sweet Dreams
2/56	*Faron Young*
9/56	*Don Gibson*
6/61	*Don Gibson*
5/63	*Patsy Cline*
1/76	*Emmylou Harris*
88/76	*Troy Seals*
19/79	*Reba McEntire*
20/78	**Sweet Fantasy** *Bobby Borchers*
94/81	**Sweet Home Alabama** *Charlie Daniels Band*
	Sweet Life
85/79	*Paul Davis*
47/88	*Marie Osmond with Paul Davis*
3/61	**Sweet Lips** *Webb Pierce*
37/87	**Sweet Little '66** *Steve Earle*
94/78	**Sweet Little Devil** *Judy Allen*
69/85	**Sweet Love, Don't Cry**
	Charleston Express/Jesse Wales
39/78	**Sweet Love Feelings** *Jerry Reed*
23/72	**Sweet, Love Me Good Woman**
	Tompall/Glaser Brothers
52/69	**Sweet Love On My Mind** *Claude King*
56/78	**Sweet Love Song The World Can Sing**
	Dale McBride
86/75	**Sweet Lovin' Baby** *Wilma Burgess*
69/79	**Sweet Lovin' Things** *Billy Walker*
3/74	**Sweet Magnolia Blossom**
	Billy 'Crash' Craddock
73/78	**Sweet Mary** *Danny Hargrove*
	Sweet Melinda
10/79	*Randy Barlow*
F/79	*John Denver*
	Sweet Memories
32/69	*Dottie West & Don Gibson*
4/79	*Willie Nelson*
	Sweet Misery
16/67	*Jimmy Dean*
14/71	*Ferlin Husky*
69/75	**Sweet Molly** *David Houston & Calvin Crawford*
44/80	**Sweet Mother Texas** *Eddy Raven*
9/77	**Sweet Music Man** *Kenny Rogers*
63/69	**Sweet 'N' Sassy** *Jerry Smith*
85/81	**Sweet Natural Love** *Mick Lloyd & Jerri Kelly*
40/80	**Sweet Red Wine** *Gary Morris*
44/84	**Sweet Rosanna** *Rex Allen, Jr.*
2/68	**Sweet Rosie Jones** *Buck Owens & Buddy Alan*
71/85	**Sweet Salvation** *Audie Henry*
25/76	**Sweet Sensuous Feelings** *Sue Richards*
42/80	**Sweet Sensuous Sensations** *Don Gibson*
8/80	**Sweet Sexy Eyes** *Cristy Lane*
4/44	**Sweet Slumber** *Lucky Millinder*
52/81	**Sweet Southern Love** *Phil Everly*
87/76	**Sweet Southern Lovin'** *Mayf Nutter*
84/82	**Sweet Southern Moonlight** *Narvel Felts*
7/79	**Sweet Summer Lovin'** *Dolly Parton*

7/75	**Sweet Surrender** *John Denver*
18/65	**Sweet, Sweet Judy** *David Houston*
8/78	**Sweet, Sweet Smile** *Carpenters*
23/76	**Sweet Talkin' Man** *Lynn Anderson*
	Sweet Thang
4/66	*Nat Stuckey*
45/67	*Ernest Tubb & Loretta Lynn*
8/69	**Sweet Thang And Cisco** *Nat Stuckey*
79/86	**Sweet Time** *Jill Hollier*
26/69	**Sweet Wine** *Johnny Carver*
12/82	**Sweet Yesterday** *Sylvia*
8/86	**Sweeter And Sweeter** *Statler Brothers*
	Sweeter Love (I'll Never Know)
53/72	*Barbara Fairchild*
22/84	*Brenda Lee*
	Sweeter Than The Flowers
3/48	*Moon Mullican*
12/48	*Shorty Long/The Santa Fe Rangers*
12/76	**Sweetest Gift**
	Linda Ronstadt & Emmylou Harris
	Sweetest Thing (I've Ever Known)
86/76	*Dottsy*
1/82	*Juice Newton*
11/69	**Sweetheart Of The Year** *Ray Price*
11/48	**Sweetheart, You Done Me Wrong**
	Bill Monroe
20/61	**Sweethearts Again** *Bob Gallion*
19/63	**Sweethearts In Heaven**
	Buck Owens & Rose Maddox
1/83	**Swingin'** *John Anderson*
	Swinging Doors
5/66	*Merle Haggard*
67/81	*Del Reeves*
71/69	**Swiss Cottage Place** *Jerry Wallace*
12/72	**Sylvia's Mother** *Bobby Bare*

T

	T For Texas
5/63	*Grandpa Jones*
36/76	*Tompall & His Outlaw Band*
30/63	**Tadpole** *Tillman Franks*
8/51	**Tailor Made Woman**
	Tennessee Ernie & Joe 'Fingers' Carr
5/54	**Tain't Nice** *Carlisles*
	Take A City Bride
58/67	*Ricky Nelson*
72/71	*Swampwater*
	Take A Letter Maria
8/70	*Anthony Armstrong Jones*
99/88	*Roger Marshall*
6/63	**Take A Letter Miss Gray** *Justin Tubb*
58/87	**Take A Little Bit Of It Home** *A.J. Masters*
31/69	**Take A Little Good Will Home**
	Bobby Goldsboro & Del Reeves
71/68	**Take A Message To Mary** *Don Cherry*
83/83	**Take A Ride On A Riverboat** *Cedar Creek*
7/49	**Take An Old Cold 'Tater (And Wait)**
	'Little' Jimmy Dickens
	Take Good Care Of Her
1/66	*Sonny James*
F/74	*Elvis Presley*
73/79	**Take Good Care Of My Love** *Max Brown*
40/83	**Take It All** *Rich Landers*
83/81	**Take It As It Comes**
	Michael Murphey with Katy Moffatt
	Take It Easy
66/72	*Billy Mize*
17/81	*Crystal Gayle*
44/80	**Take It Like A Woman** *Debby Boone*

82/87	**Take It Real Easy** *Dobie Gray*
86/84	**Take It Slow** *Kenny Dale*
72/88	**Take It Slow With Me** *Tommy & Donna*
8/83	**Take It To The Limit** *Waylon & Willie*
	Take Me
8/66	*George Jones*
9/72	*George Jones & Tammy Wynette*
31/68	**Take Me Along With You** *Van Trevor*
	Take Me As I Am (Or Let Me Go)
8/68	*Ray Price*
34/76	*Mack White*
28/81	*Bobby Bare*
24/79	**Take Me Back** *Charly McClain*
76/81	**Take Me Back To The Country**
	Baxter, Baxter & Baxter
61/70	**Take Me Back To The Goodtimes, Sally**
	Bobby Wright
1/82	**Take Me Down** *Alabama*
50/71	**Take Me Home, Country Roads** *John Denver*
5/74	**Take Me Home To Somewhere** *Joe Stampley*
91/81	**Take Me Home With You** *Carl Chambers*
	Take Me In Your Arms And Hold Me
1/50	*Eddy Arnold*
10/80	*Jim Reeves/Deborah Allen*
94/73	**Take Me One More Ride** *David Frizzell*
25/80	**Take Me, Take Me** *Rosanne Cash*
97/78	**Take Me To Bed** *Jeannie Seely*
67/76	**Take Me To Heaven** *Sami Jo*
10/82	**Take Me To The Country** *Mel McDaniel*
82/80	**Take Me To Your Heart** *Del Reeves*
5/80	**Take Me To Your Lovin' Place** *Gatlin Bros.*
1/68	**Take Me To Your World** *Tammy Wynette*
	Take Me Tonight
87/77	*Tom Jones*
75/82	*Darlene Austin*
7/76	**Take My Breath Away** *Margo Smith*
	Take My Hand
8/71	*Mel Tillis & Sherry Bryce*
59/75	*Jeannie Seely*
38/68	**Take My Hand For Awhile**
	George Hamilton IV
48/74	**Take My Life And Shape It With Your**
	Love *George Kent*
97/79	**Take My Love** *Joy Ford*
98/78	**Take My Love To Rita** *Tommy Cash*
15/64	**Take My Ring Off Your Finger** *Carl Smith*
34/69	**Take Off Time** *Claude Gray*
94/73	**Take One Step** *Eydie Gorme*
13/55	**Take Possession** *Jean Shepard*
10/87	**Take The Long Way Home** *John Schneider*
57/82	**Take The Mem'ry When You Go** *Jacky Ward*
1/53	**Take These Chains From My Heart**
	Hank Williams
44/80	**Take This Heart** *Don King*
1/78	**Take This Job And Shove It**
	Johnny Paycheck
7/62	**Take Time** *Webb Pierce*
	Take Time To Know Her
74/71	*Joe Stampley*
58/82	*David Allan Coe*
10/73	**Take Time To Love Her** *Nat Stuckey*
91/79	**Take Time To Smell The Flowers**
	Max Brown
49/65	**Take Your Hands Off My Heart** *Ray Pillow*
83/79	**Taken To The Line**
	San Fernando Valley Music Band
5/70	**Taker, The** *Waylon Jennings*
33/79	**Takes A Fool To Love A Fool**
	Burton Cummings
100/78	**Takin' A Chance** *Bobby Wright*
86/82	**Takin' It Back To The Hills** *Ronnie Rogers*
	Takin' It Easy
94/78	*Joey Davis*
2/81	*Lacy J. Dalton*

	Takin' What I Can Get
91/75	*Sally June Hart*
41/76	*Brenda Lee*
12/80	**Taking Somebody With Me When I Fall**
	Gatlin Bros.
14/70	**Talk About The Good Times** *Jerry Reed*
1/63	**Talk Back Trembling Lips** *Ernest Ashworth*
26/66	**Talk Me Some Sense** *Bobby Bare*
	Talk To Me
13/78	*Freddy Fender*
1/83	*Mickey Gilley*
35/82	**Talk To Me Loneliness** *Cindy Hurt*
16/58	**Talk To Me Lonesome Heart** *James O'Gwynn*
3/52	**Talk To Your Heart** *Ray Price*
62/86	**Talkin' Blue Eyes** *Marty Haggard*
16/88	**Talkin' To Myself Again** *Tammy Wynette*
8/57	**Talkin' To The Blues** *Jim Lowe*
4/87	**Talkin' To The Moon** *Gatlin Bros.*
	Talkin' To The Wall
3/66	*Warner Mack*
7/74	*Lynn Anderson*
4/88	**Talkin' To The Wrong Man**
	Michael Martin Murphey/Ryan Murphey
18/73	**Talkin' With My Lady** *Johnny Duncan*
6/48	**Talking Boogie** *Tex Williams*
1/78	**Talking In Your Sleep** *Crystal Gayle*
41/64	**Talking To The Night Lights** *Del Reeves*
1/69	**Tall Dark Stranger** *Buck Owens*
24/66	**Tallest Tree** *Bonnie Guitar*
82/87	**Taming My Mind** *Tony McGill*
4/57	**Tangled Mind** *Hank Snow*
62/87	**Tanya Montana** *David Allan Coe*
7/87	**Tar Top** *Alabama*
23/66	**Taste Of Heaven** *Jim Edward Brown*
86/78	**Taste Of Love** *Jenny Lynn*
54/83	**Taste Of The Wind** *Younger Brothers*
42/65	**'Tater Raisin' Man** *Dick Curless*
97/76	**Te' Quiero (I Love You In Many Ways)**
	Country Cavaleers
25/61	**Teach Me How To Lie** *Hank Thompson*
7/81	**Teach Me To Cheat** *Kendalls*
44/64	**Tear After Tear** *Rex Allen*
38/65	**Tear Dropped By** *Jean Shepard*
7/77	**Tear Fell** *Billy 'Crash' Craddock*
9/88	**Tear-Stained Letter** *Jo-el Sonnier*
49/66	**Tear-Talk** *Johnny Dollar*
	Tear Time
16/67	*Wilma Burgess*
1/78	*Dave & Sugar*
44/66	**Teardrop Lane** *Ned Miller*
	Teardrops In My Heart
4/47	*Sons Of The Pioneers*
18/76	*Rex Allen, Jr.*
45/81	*Marty Robbins*
84/78	**Teardrops In My Tequila** *Paul Craft*
42/76	**Teardrops Will Kiss The Morning Dew**
	Del Reeves & Billie Jo Spears
72/80	**Tearjoint** *Faron Young*
37/64	**Tears And Roses** *George Morgan*
14/57	**Tears Are Only Rain** *Hank Thompson*
7/62	**Tears Broke Out On Me** *Eddy Arnold*
3/82	**Tears Of The Lonely** *Mickey Gilley*
36/70	**Tears On Lincoln's Face** *Tommy Cash*
91/79	**Tears (There's Nowhere Else To Hide)**
	Tommy Overstreet
11/67	**Tears Will Be The Chaser For Your Wine**
	Wanda Jackson
1/76	**Teddy Bear** *Red Sovine*
	(also see: Let Me Be Your)
1/73	**Teddy Bear Song** *Barbara Fairchild*
53/76	**Teddy Bear's Last Ride** *Diana Williams*
98/76	**Teddy Toad** *Bobby 'Sofine' Butler*
15/57	**Teen-Age Dream** *Marty Robbins*
10/56	**Teenage Boogie** *Webb Pierce*
	Teenage Queen ..see: Ballad Of

65/75	**Telephone, The** *Jerry Reed*
	(Telephone Answering Machine Song)
	..*see: Hello, This Is Joannie*
25/74	**Telephone Call** *Tina & Daddy*
50/77	**Telephone Man** *Meri Wilson*
91/79	**Tell All Your Troubles To Me** *Miki Mori*
45/84	**Tell 'Em I've Gone Crazy** *Ed Bruce*
10/63	**Tell Her So** *Wilburn Brothers*
55/71	**Tell Her You Love Her** *Kenny Price*
98/79	**Tell Him** *Pia Zadora*
31/71	**Tell Him That You Love Him** *Webb Pierce*
	Tell It Like It Is
31/68	*Archie Campbell & Lorene Mann*
83/76	*John Wesley Ryles*
34/87	**Tell It To Your Teddy Bear** *Shooters*
65/83	**Tell Mama** *Terri Gibbs*
33/68	**Tell Maude I Slipped** *Red Sovine*
	Tell Me A Lie
52/74	*Sami Jo*
1/83	*Janie Frickie*
58/70	**Tell Me Again** *Jeannie Seely*
	(Tell Me 'Bout The Good Old Days)
	..*see: Grandpa*
88/79	**Tell Me I'm Only Dreaming** *Lorrie Morgan*
13/70	**Tell Me My Lying Eyes Are Wrong**
	George Jones
48/64	**Tell Me Pretty Words** *Slim Whitman*
75/81	**Tell Me So** *Gary Goodnight*
8/88	**Tell Me True** *Juice Newton*
8/79	**Tell Me What It's Like** *Brenda Lee*
86/83	**Tell Me When I'm Hot** *Billy 'Crash' Craddock*
10/82	**Tell Me Why** *Earl Thomas Conley*
11/80	**Tell Ole I Ain't Here, He Better Get On**
	Home *Moe Bandy & Joe Stampley*
18/74	**Tell Tale Signs** *Jerry Lee Lewis*
14/49	**Tellin' My Troubles To My Old Guitar**
	Jimmy Wakely
3/87	**Telling Me Lies**
	Dolly Parton, Linda Ronstadt, Emmylou Harris
5/80	**Temporarily Yours** *Jeanne Pruett*
76/85	**Temptation** *Mike Martin*
2/47	**Temptation (Tim-Tayshun)**
	Red Ingle & The Natural Seven
82/80	**Ten Anniversary Presents** *Jim Owen*
14/74	**Ten Commandments Of Love**
	David Houston & Barbara Mandrell
33/72	**10 Degrees & Getting Colder**
	George Hamilton IV
9/86	**Ten Feet Away** *Keith Whitley*
2/65	**10 Little Bottles** *Johnny Bond*
96/80	**Ten Seconds In The Saddle** *Chris LeDoux*
F/79	**Ten Thousand And One** *Connie Smith*
5/59	**Ten Thousand Drums** *Carl Smith*
16/77	**Ten Years Of This** *Gary Stewart*
95/84	**Tenamock Georgia** *Charlie Bandy*
48/67	**Tender And True** *Ernest Ashworth*
5/45	**Tender-Hearted Sue** *Rambling Rogue*
1/88	**Tender Lie** *Restless Heart*
72/83	**Tender Lovin' Lies** *Judy Bailey*
74/87	**Tender Time** *Louise Mandrell*
1/61	**Tender Years** *George Jones*
42/83	**Tenderness Place** *Karen Taylor-Good*
	Tennessee
72/68	*Jimmy Martin*
91/78	*Ray Sanders*
1/70	**Tennessee Bird Walk**
	Jack Blanchard & Misty Morgan
11/49	**Tennessee Boogie** *Zeb Turner*
	Tennessee Border
3/49	*Red Foley*
8/49	*Tennessee Ernie Ford*
12/49	*Bob Atcher*
14/49	*Homer & Jethro (No. 2)*
15/49	*Jimmie Skinner*
2/50	*Ernest Tubb & Red Foley (No. 2)*

	Tennessee Flat-Top Box
11/62	*Johnny Cash*
1/88	*Rosanne Cash*
1/84	**Tennessee Homesick Blues** *Dolly Parton*
28/69	**Tennessee Hound Dog** *Osborne Brothers*
7/48	**Tennessee Moon** *Cowboy Copas*
	Tennessee Polka
3/49	*Pee Wee King*
4/49	*Red Foley*
1/80	**Tennessee River** *Alabama*
9/82	**Tennessee Rose** *Emmylou Harris*
	Tennessee Saturday Night
1/49	*Red Foley*
11/49	*Johnny Bond*
85/82	*Roy Clark*
	(also see: Let A Little Love In)
5/59	**Tennessee Stud** *Eddy Arnold*
12/49	**Tennessee Tears** *Pee Wee King*
	Tennessee Waltz
3/48	*Cowboy Copas*
3/48	*Pee Wee King*
12/48	*Roy Acuff*
2/51	*Patti Page*
6/51	*Pee Wee King*
18/80	*Lacy J. Dalton*
	Tennessee Whiskey
77/81	*David Allan Coe*
2/83	*George Jones*
6/53	**Tennessee Wig Walk** *Bonnie Lou*
31/80	**Tequila Sheila** *Bobby Bare*
87/81	**Testimony Of Soddy Hoe** *Jerry Reed*
	Texarkana Baby
1/48	*Eddy Arnold*
15/48	*Bob Wills*
	Texas
69/68	*Tex Ritter*
36/76	*Charlie Daniels Band*
35/76	**Texas - 1947** *Johnny Cash*
31/77	**Texas Angel** *Jacky Ward*
3/44	**Texas Blues** *Foy Willing*
26/80	**Texas Bound And Flyin'** *Jerry Reed*
23/81	**Texas Cowboy Night**
	Mel Tillis & Nancy Sinatra
69/81	**Texas Ida Red** *David Houston*
18/88	**Texas In 1880** *Foster & Lloyd*
9/80	**Texas In My Rear View Mirror** *Mac Davis*
96/74	**Texas Law Sez** *Tompall Glaser*
75/78	**Texas Me & You** *Asleep At The Wheel*
81/86	**Texas Moon** *Johnny Duncan*
	(Texas National Anthem) ..*see: Fraulein*
94/76	**Texas On A Saturday Night** *Bill Green*
2/46	**Texas Playboy Rag** *Bob Wills*
9/81	**Texas State Of Mind**
	David Frizzell & Shelly West
	Texas Tea
51/68	*Dee Mullins*
77/77	*Leroy Van Dyke*
68/80	*Orion*
5/79	**Texas (When I Die)** *Tanya Tucker*
34/76	**Texas Woman** *Pat Boone*
1/81	**Texas Women** *Hank Williams, Jr.*
6/70	**Thank God And Greyhound** *Roy Clark*
3/83	**Thank God For Kids** *Oak Ridge Boys*
1/84	**Thank God For The Radio** *Kendalls*
1/75	**Thank God I'm A Country Boy** *John Denver*
10/76	**Thank God I've Got You** *Statler Brothers*
11/77	**Thank God She's Mine** *Freddie Hart*
70/83	**Thank You Darling** *Bill Anderson*
33/80	**Thank You, Ever-Lovin'** *Kenny Dale*
21/73	**Thank You For Being You** *Mel Tillis*
8/54	**Thank You For Calling** *Billy Walker*
65/69	**Thank You For Loving Me** *Brenda Byers*
79/74	**Thank You For The Feeling** *Billy Mize*
75/79	**Thank You For The Roses** *Kitty Wells*

There's A New Moon Over My Shoulder
1/45 *Jimmie Davis*
2/45 *Tex Ritter*
4/72 There's A Party Goin' On *Jody Miller*
88/87 There's A Real Woman In Me *Bobbi Lace*
10/75 There's A Song On The Jukebox *David Wills*
7/70 There's A Story (Goin' 'Round)
Dottie West & Don Gibson
80/88 There's A Telephone Ringing (In An Empty House) *Southern Reign*
13/71 There's A Whole Lot About A Woman (A Man Don't Know) *Jack Greene*
F/83 There's All Kinds Of Smoke (In The Barroom) *Loretta Lynn*
91/76 There's Always A Goodbye *Helen Cornelius*
There's Always Me
30/79 *Ray Price*
35/81 *Jim Reeves*
17/62 There's Always One (Who Loves A Lot)
Roy Drusky
18/80 There's Another Woman *Joe Stampley*
20/69 There's Better Things In Life *Jerry Reed*
21/64 There's More Pretty Girls Than One
George Hamilton IV
1/81 (There's) No Gettin' Over Me *Ronnie Milsap*
7/85 There's No Love In Tennessee
Barbara Mandrell
49/81 (There's No Me) Without You *Sue Powell*
48/68 There's No More Love *Carl Smith*
1/86 There's No Stopping Your Heart
Marie Osmond
48/83 There's No Substitute For You
Younger Brothers
1/85 There's No Way *Alabama*
6/50 There's No Wings On My Angel *Eddy Arnold*
88/80 There's Nobody Like You *Kin Vassy*
86/83 There's Nobody Lovin' At Home
Randy Wright
3/49 There's Not A Thing (I Wouldn't Do For You) *Eddy Arnold*
21/60 There's Not Any Like You Left *Faron Young*
(There's Nothing Like The Love) Between A Woman And A Man
86/77 *Reba McEntire*
87/78 *Linda Cassady/Bobby Spears*
9/55 There's Poison In Your Heart *Kitty Wells*
19/71 There's Something About A Lady
Johnny Duncan
84/83 There's Still A Few Good Love Songs Left In Me *Connie Francis*
There's Still A Lot Of Love In San Antone
48/74 *Darrell McCall*
64/83 *Connie Hanson & Friend*
58/87 There's Still Enough Of Us *Liz Boardo*
5/69 These Are Not My People *Freddy Weller*
73/72 These Are The Good Old Days *Roy Rogers*
87/77 These Crazy Thoughts *Warner Mack*
10/75 These Days (I Barely Get By) *George Jones*
64/86 These Eyes *Beth Williams*
5/56 These Hands *Hank Snow*
9/69 These Lonely Hands Of Mine *Mel Tillis*
42/67 These Memories *Jeannie Seely*
57/86 These Shoes *Everly Brothers*
66/68 (They Always Come Out) Smellin' Like A Rose *Johnny Wright*
43/88 They Always Look Better When They're Leavin' *Becky Hobbs*
6/79 They Call It Making Love *Tammy Wynette*
58/72 They Call The Wind Maria *Jack Barlow*
12/81 They Could Put Me In Jail *Bellamy Brothers*
4/74 They Don't Make 'Em Like My Daddy
Loretta Lynn
32/76 They Don't Make 'Em Like That Anymore
Bobby Borchers

10/69 They Don't Make Love Like They Used To
Eddy Arnold
54/87 They Don't Make Love Like We Used To
Shenandoah
53/86 They Don't Make Them Like They Used To *Kenny Rogers*
67/87 They Killed Him *Kris Kristofferson*
19/85 They Never Had To Get Over You
Johnny Lee
19/80 They Never Lost You *Con Hunley*
21/87 They Only Come Out At Night *Shooters*
1/44 They Took The Stars Out Of Heaven
Floyd Tillman
They'll Never Take Her Love From Me
5/50 *Hank Williams*
74/70 *Johnny Darrell*
57/81 They'll Never Take Me Alive *Dean Dillon*
72/71 They're Stepping All Over My Heart
Kitty Wells
14/85 Thing About You *Southern Pacific*
Thing Called Love
21/68 *Jimmy Dean*
2/72 *Johnny Cash*
38/65 Thing Called Sadness *Ray Price*
49/82 Thing Or Two On My Mind
Gene Kennedy & Karen Jeglum
Things
22/71 *Anne Murray*
49/72 *Buddy Alan*
25/75 *Ronnie Dove*
66/73 Things Are Kinda Slow At The House
Earl Richards
1/74 Things Aren't Funny Anymore
Merle Haggard
25/69 Things For You And I *Bobby Lewis*
34/69 Things Go Better With Love *Jeannie C. Riley*
9/65 Things Have Gone To Pieces *George Jones*
68/88 Things I Didn't Say *Marcy Bros.*
31/77 Things I Treasure *Dorsey Burnette*
18/78 Things I'd Do For You *Mundo Earwood*
65/86 Things I've Done To Me *Jim Collins*
42/69 Things That Matter *Van Trevor*
24/62 Things That Mean The Most *Carl Smith*
95/82 Things That Songs Are Made Of *Ray Griff*
F/72 Think About It Darlin' *Jerry Lee Lewis*
1/86 Think About Love *Dolly Parton*
18/78 Think About Me *Freddy Fender*
38/71 Think Again *Patti Page*
74/76 Think I Feel A Hitchhike Coming On
Larry Jon Wilson
84/88 Think I'll Go Home *Charlie Beckham*
Think I'll Go Somewhere And Cry Myself To Sleep
26/65 *Charlie Louvin*
50/78 *Billy "Crash" Craddock*
1/66 Think Of Me *Buck Owens*
21/76 Think Summer *Roy Clark*
1/76 Thinkin' Of A Rendezvous *Johnny Duncan*
56/84 Thinking 'Bout Leaving *Butch Baker*
9/70 Thinking 'Bout You, Babe *Billy Walker*
11/75 Third Rate Romance *Amazing Rhythm Aces*
34/70 Third World *Johnny & Jonie Mosby*
52/73 30 California Women *Kenny Price*
7/55 Thirty Days *Ernest Tubb*
83/76 38 And Lonely *Dave Dudley*
4/81 Thirty Nine And Holding *Jerry Lee Lewis*
4/85 This Ain't Dallas *Hank Williams, Jr.*
23/75 This Ain't Just Another Lust Affair
Mel Street
68/73 This Ain't No Good Day For Leaving
Kenny Serratt
This Ain't Tennessee And He Ain't You
93/81 *Gypsy Martin*
82/83 *Sara "Honeybear" Hickey*
66/84 *Katy Moffatt*

52/85	**This Bed's Not Big Enough** *Louise Mandrell*
F/83	**This Country Music's Driving Me Crazy** *Johnny Bailey*
35/83	**This Cowboy's Hat** *Porter Wagoner*
1/87	**This Crazy Love** *Oak Ridge Boys*
8/82	**This Dream's On Me** *Gene Watson*
40/69	**This Generation Shall Not Pass** *Henson Cargill*
36/77	**This Girl (Has Turned Into A Woman)** *Mary MacGregor*
46/66	**This Gun Don't Care** *Wanda Jackson*
19/75	**This House Runs On Sunshine** *La Costa*
39/78	**This Is A Holdup** *Ronnie McDowell*
20/79	**This Is A Love Song** *Bill Anderson*
1/65	**This Is It** *Jim Reeves*
62/83	**This Is Just The First Day** *Razzy Bailey*
62/88	**This Is Me Leaving** *Lynne Tyndall*
21/75	**This Is My Year For Mexico** *Crystal Gayle*
30/63	**This Is The House** *Charlie Phillips*
16/78	**This Is The Love** *Sonny James*
3/54	**This Is The Thanks I Get (For Loving You)** *Eddy Arnold*
67/80	**This Is True** *Steve Douglas*
93/74	**This Just Ain't My Day (For Lettin' Darlin' Down)** *Red Steagall*
84/77	**This Kinda Love Ain't Meant For Sunday School** *Carl Smith*
81/78	**This Lady Loving Me** *Carl Smith*
	This Little Girl Of Mine
4/58	*Everly Brothers*
5/72	*Faron Young*
52/78	**This Magic Moment** *Sandra Kaye*
45/76	**This Man And Woman Thing** *Johnny Russell*
2/88	**This Missin' You Heart Of Mine** *Sawyer Brown*
93/79	**This Moment In Time** *Engelbert Humperdinck*
81/82	**This Morning I Woke Up In New York City** *John Kelley*
11/72	**This Much A Man** *Marty Robbins*
	This Must Be My Ship
32/80	*Carol Chase*
62/81	*Diana Trask*
27/66	**This Must Be The Bottom** *Del Reeves*
20/70	**This Night (Ain't Fit For Nothing But Drinking)** *Dave Dudley*
33/87	**This Ol' Town** *Lacy J. Dalton*
52/88	**This Old Flame** *Robin Lee*
	This Old Heart
21/60	*Skeets McDonald*
24/60	*Bobby Barnett*
24/88	**This Old House** *Schuyler, Knobloch & Bickhardt*
22/60	**This Old Town** *Buddy Paul*
91/88	**This Old World Ain't The Same** *Jeff Golden*
	This Ole House
2/54	*Stuart Hamblen*
16/60	*Wilma Lee & Stoney Cooper*
66/87	*Razorback*
36/68	**This One's On The House** *Jerry Wallace*
4/53	**This Orchid Means Goodbye** *Carl Smith*
69/69	**This Song Don't Care Who Sings It** *Ray Pennington*
68/68	**This Song Is Just For You** *Bobby Austin*
14/69	**This Thing** *Webb Pierce*
	This Time
1/74	*Waylon Jennings*
43/78	*Johnny Lee*
89/82	*Skip & Linda*
30/84	*Tom Jones*
67/78	**This Time Around** *Sammy Vaughn*
12/74	**This Time I Almost Made It** *Barbara Mandrell*
20/77	**This Time I'm In It For The Love** *Tommy Overstreet*
1/76	**This Time I've Hurt Her More Than She Loves Me** *Conway Twitty*
51/86	**This Time It's You** *Lisa Childress*
7/64	**This White Circle On My Finger** *Kitty Wells*
12/48	**This World Can't Stand Long** *Roy Acuff*
27/67	**This World Holds Nothing (Since You're Gone)** *Stonewall Jackson*
4/46	**Tho' I Tried (I Can't Forget You)** *Wesley Tuttle*
10/48	**Thorn In My Heart** *Bob Wills*
74/86	**Those Eyes** *Anthony Armstrong Jones*
70/74	**Those Lazy, Hazy, Crazy Days Of Summer** *Tex Williams*
	Those Memories Of You
55/86	*Pam Tillis*
5/87	*Dolly Parton, Linda Ronstadt, Emmylou Harris*
52/83	**Those Nights, These Days** *David Wills*
47/83	**Those Were The Days** *Gary Stewart & Dean Dillon*
9/63	**Those Wonderful Years** *Webb Pierce*
62/84	**Those You Lose** *Ronnie Robbins*
14/54	**Thou Shalt Not Steal** *Kitty Wells*
16/61	**Thoughts Of A Fool** *Ernest Tubb*
6/59	**Thousand Miles Ago** *Webb Pierce*
	Three A.M.
8/65	*Bill Anderson*
29/69	*Jim Ed Brown*
31/80	**3 Chord Country Song** *Red Steagall*
7/62	**Three Days** *Faron Young*
2/61	**Three Hearts In A Tangle** *Roy Drusky*
91/80	**Three Little Words** *Boyer Twins*
81/78	**Three Nights A Week** *Ruby Falls*
53/88	**Three Piece Suit** *Russell Smith*
39/68	**Three Playing Love** *Cheryl Poole*
	Three Sheets In The Wind
30/63	*Johnny Bond*
20/78	*Jacky Ward & Reba McEntire*
32/68	**Three Six Packs, Two Arms And A Juke Box** *Johnny Seay*
9/61	**Three Steps To The Phone (Millions of Miles)** *George Hamilton IV*
73/69	**Three Tears (For The Sad, Hurt, And Blue)** *Ray Sanders*
1/87	**Three Time Loser** *Dan Seals*
	Three Times A Lady
23/78	*Nate Harvell*
7/84	*Conway Twitty*
93/80	**Three Times In Love** *Tommy James*
4/47	**Three Times Seven** *Merle Travis*
76/80	**Three Way Love** *Shoppe*
7/52	**Three Ways Of Knowing** *Johnnie & Jack*
7/57	**Three Ways (To Love You)** *Kitty Wells*
37/83	**3/4 Time** *Ray Charles*
39/87	**3935 West End Avenue** *Mason Dixon*
14/61	**Through That Door** *Ernest Tubb*
99/76	**Through The Bottom Of The Glass** *Leon Rausch*
31/64	**Through The Eyes Of A Fool** *Roy Clark*
27/67	**Through The Eyes Of Love** *Tompall/Glaser Brothers*
5/82	**Through The Years** *Kenny Rogers*
66/72	**Throw A Rope Around The Wind** *Red Lane*
80/74	**Throw Away The Pages** *Randy Barlow*
87/77	**Throw Out Your Lifetime** *Cates Sisters*
3/50	**Throw Your Love My Way** *Ernest Tubb*
51/78	**Throwin' Memories On The Fire** *Cal Smith*
	Thunder Road *..see: Balld Of*
33/76	**Thunderstorms** *Cal Smith*
22/68	**Tie A Tiger Down** *Sheb Wooley*
75/88	**Tie Me Up** *Becky Williams*
29/63	**Tie My Hunting Dog Down, Jed** *Arthur 'Guitar Boogie' Smith*
17/86	**Tie Our Love (In a Double Knot)** *Dolly Parton*
24/82	**Tie Your Dream To Mine** *Marty Robbins*

74/71	Train Train (Carry Me Away) *Murry Kellum*	64/78	(Truth Is) We're Livin' A Lie *R.C. Bannon*
57/88	Trains Make Me Lonesome *Marty Haggard*	2/69	Try A Little Kindness *Glen Campbell*
20/89	Trainwreck Of Emotion *Lorrie Morgan*	47/76	Try A Little Tenderness *Billy Thunderkloud*
14/48	Tramp On The Street *Bill Carlisle*	82/79	Try Home *Sandy Posey*
52/72	Travelin' Light *George Hamilton IV*	36/80	Try It On *Stephanie Winslow*
	Travelin' Man	61/72	Try It, You'll Like It *Jimmy Dickens*
29/59	*Red Foley*		Try Me
44/66	*Dick Curless*	32/81	*Randy Barlow*
32/82	*Jacky Ward*	68/86	*Billy Burnette*
42/72	Travelin' Minstrel Band *Carter Family*	2/44	Try Me One More Time *Ernest Tubb*
33/71	Travelin' Minstrel Man *Bill Rice*	75/76	Tryin' Like The Devil *James Talley*
20/73	Traveling Man *Dolly Parton*	1/75	Tryin' To Beat The Morning Home
51/67	Traveling Shoes *Guy Mitchell*		*T.G. Sheppard*
6/51	Travellin' Blues *Lefty Frizzell*	52/77	Tryin' To Forget About You *Cristy Lane*
6/58	Treasure Of Love *George Jones*	11/56	Tryin' To Forget The Blues *Porter Wagoner*
12/71	Treat Him Right *Barbara Mandrell*	80/83	Tryin' To Love Two *Kin Vassy*
62/74	Treat Me Like A Lady *Sherry Bryce*	12/79	Tryin' To Satisfy You *Dottsy*
11/57	Treat Me Nice *Elvis Presley*	30/81	Trying Not To Love You *Johnny Rodriguez*
16/64	Triangle *Carl Smith*	99/76	Trying To Live Without You Kind Of Days
	Triflin' Gal		*Sandy Posey*
2/45	*Al Dexter*	1/80	Trying To Love Two Women *Oak Ridge Boys*
3/45	*Walt Shrum*	94/80	Tugboat Annie *Lori Jacobs*
1/73	Trip To Heaven *Freddie Hart*		Tulsa
11/75	T-R-O-U-B-L-E *Elvis Presley*		..also see: (Don't Let the Sun Set on You)
30/65	Trouble And Me *Stonewall Jackson*	40/83	Tulsa Ballroom *Dottie West*
	Trouble In Mind	41/71	Tulsa County *Anita Carter*
7/56	*Eddy Arnold*	1/79	Tulsa Time *Don Williams*
81/77	*Hank Snow*	10/80	Tumbleweed *Sylvia*
12/64	Trouble In My Arms *Johnny & Jonie Mosby*	11/48	Tumbling Tumbleweeds
1/74	Trouble In Paradise *Loretta Lynn*		*Sons Of The Pioneers*
24/60	Trouble In The Amen Corner		Tupelo County Jail
	Archie Campbell	7/58	*Webb Pierce*
57/87	Trouble In The Fields *Nanci Griffith*	40/66	*Stonemans*
64/82	Trouble With Hearts *Roy Head*	15/68	Tupelo Mississippi Flash *Jerry Reed*
42/77	Trouble With Lovin' Today	87/87	Turn Around *Terri Gibbs*
	Asleep At The Wheel	9/56	Turn Her Down *Faron Young*
4/62	Trouble's Back In Town *Wilburn Brothers*	1/88	Turn It Loose *Judds*
92/76	Truck Driver's Heaven *Red Simpson*	39/84	Turn Me Loose *Vince Gill*
71/70	Truck Driver's Lament *Johnny Dollar*	76/88	(Turn Me Loose And) Let Me Swing
	Truck Drivin' Cat With Nine Wives		*Swing Shift Band*
54/68	*Charlie Walker*	59/84	Turn Me To Love *Keith Whitley*
63/68	*Jim Nesbitt*	87/78	Turn On The Bright Lights *Lenny Gault*
29/76	Truck Drivin' Man *Red Steagall*	29/74	Turn On Your Light (And Let It Shine)
3/65	Truck Drivin' Son-Of-A-Gun *Dave Dudley*		*Kenny Price*
53/68	Truck Drivin' Woman *Norma Jean*	1/75	(Turn Out The Light And) Love Me
11/65	Truck Driving Man *George Hamilton IV*		Tonight *Don Williams*
44/69	Truck Stop *Jerry Smith*	61/87	Turn The Music On *O.B. McClinton*
73/74	Trucker And The U.F.O. *Brush Arbor*	53/82	Turn The Pencil Over *Porter Wagoner*
54/73	Trucker's Paradise *Del Reeves*	1/67	Turn The World Around *Eddy Arnold*
23/67	Trucker's Prayer *Dave Dudley*	17/72	Turn Your Radio On *Ray Stevens*
49/68	True And Lasting Kind *Bobby Lord*	F/72	Turnin' Off A Memory *Merle Haggard*
9/69	True Grit *Glen Campbell*	1/84	Turning Away *Crystal Gayle*
5/88	True Heart *Oak Ridge Boys*	87/83	Turning Back The Covers *Robin Lee*
F/81	True Life Country Music *Razzy Bailey*	80/81	Turning My Love On *Jimmy Payne*
	True Love		(Turpentine And Dandelion Wine)
51/73	*Red Steagall*		..see: My Old Kentucky Home
88/78	*LeGardes*	88/77	Tweedle-O-Twill *Kathy Barnes*
32/85	*Vince Gill*		Twelfth Of Never
22/71	True Love Is Greater Than Friendship	17/66	*Slim Whitman*
	Arlene Harden	98/77	*David Houston*
39/86	True Love (Never Did Run Smooth)	10/74	Twentieth Century Drifter *Marty Robbins*
	Tom Wopat	57/85	Twentieth Century Fool *Kenny Rogers*
58/69	True Love Travels On A Gravel Road	F/83	20th Century Fox *Bill Anderson*
	Duane Dee	11/56	Twenty Feet Of Muddy Water *Sonny James*
	True Love Ways	35/81	20/20 Hindsight *Billy Larkin*
77/78	*Randy Gurley*	18/77	Twenty-Four Hours From Tulsa
1/80	*Mickey Gilley*		*Randy Barlow*
3/66	True Love's A Blessing *Sonny James*	13/61	Twenty-Fourth Hour *Ray Price*
85/83	True Love's Getting Pretty Hard to Find	2/87	Twenty Years Ago *Kenny Rogers*
	Wickline Band	45/64	Twice As Much *Hank Thompson*
	True, True Lovin'	100/76	Twilight Time *Carl Mann*
46/65	*Ferlin Husky*		(Twin Pines Theme)
35/73	*Ferlin Husky*		..see: Heaven Can Be Anywhere
55/69	Truer Love You'll Never Find (Than Mine)	1/88	Twinkle, Twinkle Lucky Star *Merle Haggard*
	Bonnie & Buddy		Two Brothers ..see: Ballad Of

3/84	**Two Car Garage** *B.J. Thomas*		**Unchained Melody**
8/49	**Two Cents, Three Eggs And A Postcard**	41/75	*Joe Stampley*
	Red Foley	6/78	*Elvis Presley*
53/72	**Two Divided By Love** *Kendalls*	49/76	**Uncle Hiram And The Homemade Beer**
68/71	**Two Dollar Toy** *Stoney Edwards*		*Dick Feller*
3/77	**Two Dollars In The Jukebox** *Eddie Rabbitt*		**Uncle Pen**
	Two Doors Down	14/56	*Porter Wagoner*
7/78	*Zella Lehr*	1/84	*Ricky Skaggs*
F/78	*Dolly Parton*	4/77	**Uncloudy Day** *Willie Nelson*
11/54	**Two Glasses, Joe** *Ernest Tubb*	44/87	**Unconditional Love** *New Grass Revival*
39/74	**Two Gun Daddy** *Marty Robbins*	18/62	**Under Cover Of The Night** *Dave Dudley*
45/85	**Two Heart Harmony** *Kendalls*	66/83	**Under Loved And Over Lonely** *Katy Moffatt*
65/83	**Two Hearts** *Texas Vocal Company*	24/88	**Under The Boardwalk** *Lynn Anderson*
	Two Hearts Beat (Better Than One)	2/61	**Under The Influence Of Love** *Buck Owens*
75/80	*Kay Austin*		**Under Your Spell Again**
F/81	*Eddy Arnold*	4/59	*Buck Owens*
	Two Hearts Can't Be Wrong	5/59	*Ray Price*
94/82	*Denise Price*	39/71	*Waylon Jennings & Jessi Colter*
63/85	*Two Hearts*	65/76	*Barbara Fairchild*
18/78	**Two Hearts Tangled In Love** *Kenny Dale*	28/78	**Undercover Lovers** *Stella Parton*
9/55	**Two Kinds Of Love** *Eddy Arnold*	88/80	**Undercover Man** *Liz Lyndell*
83/87	**Two Kinds Of Women** *Diamonds*	26/64	**Understand Your Gal** *Margie Bowes*
8/77	**Two Less Lonely People** *Rex Allen, Jr.*	1/64	**Understand Your Man** *Johnny Cash*
73/70	**Two Little Boys** *Rusty Draper*	10/68	**Undo The Right** *Johnny Bush*
75/68	**Two Little Hearts** *Compton Brothers*	67/73	**Uneasy Rider** *Charlie Daniels Band*
74/70	**Two Little Rooms** *Janet Lawson*	23/72	**Unexpected Goodbye** *Glenn Barber*
7/78	**Two Lonely People** *Moe Bandy*	79/75	**Unfaithful Fools** *Leroy Van Dyke*
1/78	**Two More Bottles Of Wine** *Emmylou Harris*	8/50	**Unfaithful One** *Ernest Tubb*
82/87	**Two-Name Girl** *Johnstons*	32/83	**Unfinished Business** *Lloyd David Foster*
71/87	**Two Of A Kind (Workin' On A Full House)**	18/63	**Unkind Words** *Kathy Dee*
	Dennis Robbins	14/48	**Unloved And Unclaimed** *Roy Acuff*
	Two Of The Usual	5/62	**Unloved Unwanted** *Kitty Wells*
49/67	*Bobby Lewis*	7/66	**Unmitigated Gall** *Faron Young*
64/67	*Don Adams*	10/55	**Untied** *Tommy Collins*
50/71	**Two Of Us Together**	54/85	**Until I Fall In Love Again** *Marie Osmond*
	Don Gibson & Sue Thompson		**Until I Met You**
14/85	**Two Old Cats Like Us**	F/56	*Faron Young*
	Ray Charles with Hank Williams, Jr.	57/77	*Tom Bresh*
72/81	**Two Out Of Three Ain't Bad** *J.W. Thompson*	1/86	*Judy Rodman*
75/79	**Two People In Love** *Lorrie Morgan*	68/72	**Until It's Time For You To Go** *Elvis Presley*
35/70	**Two Separate Bar Stools** *Wanda Jackson*	1/69	**Until My Dreams Come True** *Jack Greene*
9/57	**Two Shadows On Your Window** *Jim Reeves*		**Until The Bitter End**
74/86	**Two Sides** *Jimmy Murphy*	39/80	*Kenny Serratt*
56/68	**Two Sides Of Me** *Harold Lee*	88/81	*Faron Young*
15/65	**Two Six Packs Away** *Dave Dudley*	39/74	**Until The End Of Time**
44/82	**Two-Step Is Easy** *Michael Murphey*		*Narvel Felts & Sharon Vaughn*
6/79	**Two Steps Forward And Three Steps**	77/85	**Until The Music Is Gone** *Becky Chase*
	Back *Susie Allanson*	50/78	**Until The Next Time** *Billy Parker*
72/86	**Two Steps From The Blues** *Carlette*	92/81	**Until The Nights**
2/80	**Two Story House**		*Charlie McCoy & Laney Smallwood*
	George Jones & Tammy Wynette	20/60	**Until Today** *Elmer Snodgrass*
39/86	**Two Too Many** *Holly Dunn*	42/79	**Until Tonight** *Juice Newton*
85/84	**Two Will Be One** *Kenny Dale*	93/85	**Until We Meet Again** *Wray Brothers Band*
71/72	**200 Lbs. O' Slingin' Hound**	73/80	**Until You** *Terry Bradshaw*
	Billy Edd Wheeler	4/88	**Untold Stories** *Kathy Mattea*
67/87	**255 Harbor Drive** *A.J. Masters*	14/72	**Untouched** *Mel Tillis*
41/70	**Tyin' Strings** *June Stearns*	6/51	**Unwanted Sign Upon Your Heart**
			Hank Snow
			Unwed Fathers
		63/83	*Tammy Wynette*
		56/85	*Gail Davies*
		6/81	**Unwound** *George Strait*
		57/85	**Up On Your Love** *Karen Taylor-Good*
		41/66	**Up This Hill And Down** *Osborne Brothers*
			Up To Heaven *..see: (You Lift Me)*
		28/75	**Uproar** *Anne Murray*
		40/69	**Upstairs In The Bedroom** *Bobby Wright*
55/68	**U.S. Male** *Elvis Presley*	25/74	**Uptown Poker Club** *Jerry Reed*
9/75	**U.S. of A** *Donna Fargo*	94/81	**Urban Cowboys, Outlaws, Cavaliers**
8/58	**Uh-Huh--mm** *Sonny James*		*James Marvell*
F/57	**Uh, Uh, No** *George Jones*	7/67	**Urge For Going** *George Hamilton IV*
58/88	**Unattended Fire** *Razzy Bailey*	3/85	**Used To Blue** *Sawyer Brown*
29/73	**Unbelievable Love** *Jim Ed Brown*		
	Unbreakable Hearts		
79/78	*Bill White*		
92/79	*Hargus "Pig" Robbins*		

15/69 **Vance** *Roger Miller*
52/70 **Vanishing Breed** *Hank Snow*
7/76 **Vaya Con Dios** *Freddy Fender*
30/77 **Vegas** *Bobby & Jeannie Bare*
9/83 **Velvet Chains** *Gary Morris*
5/82 **Very Best Is You** *Charly McClain*
1/74 **Very Special Love Song** *Charlie Rich*
40/84 **Victim Of Life's Circumstances** *Vince Gill*
34/82 **Victim Or A Fool** *Rodney Crowell*
75/76 **Victims** *Kenny Starr*
24/84 **Victims Of Goodbye** *Sylvia*
12/66 **Viet Nam Blues** *Dave Dudley*
21/67 **Vin Rose** *Stu Phillips*
     Violet And A Rose
24/58   *Mel Tillis*
10/62   *"Little" Jimmy Dickens*
36/64   *Wanda Jackson*
73/76 **Virgil And The $300 Vacation**
     Cledus Maggard
68/72 **Virginia** *Jean Shepard*
22/77 **Virginia, How Far Will You Go** *Dickey Lee*
90/79 **Visitor, The** *J.W. Thompson*
72/77 **Vitamin L** *Mary Kay Place*
26/66 **Volkswagen** *Ray Pillow*
22/63 **Volunteer, The** *Autry Inman*

72/87 **W. Lee O'Daniel (And The Light Crust Dough Boys)** *Johnny Cash*
     Wabash Cannonball
63/70   *Danny Davis/The Nashville Brass*
97/76   *Charlie McCoy*
91/84   *Willie Nelson & Hank Wilson*
50/66 **Waco** *Lorne Greene*
12/55 **Wait A Little Longer, Please, Jesus**
     Carl Smith
98/85 **Wait Till I Get My Hands On You**
     Wynn Stewart
62/82 **Wait Till Those Bridges Are Gone** *Ray Price*
70/77 **Waitin' At The End Of Your Run**
     Ava Barber
3/57 **Waitin' For A Train** *Jim Reeves*
12/58 **Waitin' In School** *Ricky Nelson*
1/66 **Waitin' In Your Welfare Line** *Buck Owens*
69/87 **Waitin' Up** *George Highfill*
25/64 **Waiting A Lifetime** *Webb Pierce*
11/71 **Waiting For A Train (All Around The Watertank)** *Jerry Lee Lewis*
72/76 **Waiting For The Tables To Turn**
     Wayne Kemp
3/52 **Waiting In The Lobby Of Your Heart**
     Hank Thompson
14/74 **Wake Me Into Love**
     Bud Logan & Wilma Burgess
63/80 **Wake Me Up** *Louise Mandrell*
21/70 **Wake Me Up Early In The Morning**
     Bobby Lord
1/54 **Wake Up, Irene** *Hank Thompson*
37/73 **Wake Up, Jacob** *Porter Wagoner*
56/70 **Walk A Mile In My Shoes** *Joe South*
56/71 **Walk All Over Georgia** *Ray Sanders*
57/69 **Walk Among The People** *Cheryl Poole*

48/77 **Walk Away With Me** *Randy Barlow*
56/82 **Walk Me 'Cross The River** *Jerri Kelly*
28/87 **Walk Me In The Rain** *Girls Next Door*
7/63 **Walk Me To The Door** *Ray Price*
44/67 **Walk Me To The Station** *Stu Phillips*
30/83 **Walk On** *Karen Brooks*
74/87 **Walk On Boy** *Ogden Harless*
     Walk On By
1/61   *Leroy Van Dyke*
98/79   *Robert Gordon*
43/80   *Donna Fargo*
73/87   *Perry LaPointe*
55/88   *Asleep At The Wheel*
5/68 **Walk On Out Of My Mind** *Waylon Jennings*
9/61 **Walk Out Backwards** *Bill Anderson*
     Walk Right Back
76/77   *LaWanda Lindsey*
4/78   *Anne Murray*
     Walk Right In
23/63   *Rooftop Singers*
92/77   *Dr. Hook*
7/76 **Walk Softly** *Billy 'Crash' Craddock*
     Walk Softly On The Bridges
11/73   *Mel Street*
79/86   *Rodney Lay*
10/65 **Walk Tall** *Faron Young*
10/86 **Walk The Way The Wind Blows**
     Kathy Mattea
1/67 **Walk Through This World With Me**
     George Jones
30/70 **Walk Unashamed** *Tompall/Glaser Brothers*
57/67 **Walker's Woods** *Ed Bruce*
2/85 **Walkin' A Broken Heart** *Don Williams*
     Walkin' After Midnight
2/57   *Patsy Cline*
60/82   *Calamity Jane*
23/69 **Walkin' Back To Birmingham** *Leon Ashley*
29/59 **Walkin' Down The Road** *Jimmy Newman*
83/74 **Walkin' In Teardrops** *Earl Richards*
7/67 **Walkin' In The Sunshine** *Roger Miller*
22/64 **Walkin', Talkin', Cryin', Barely Beatin' Broken Heart** *Johnny Wright*
53/69 **Walking Midnight Road** *June Stearns*
21/59 **Walking My Blues Away** *Jimmie Skinner*
7/66 **Walking On New Grass** *Kenny Price*
     Walking Piece Of Heaven
6/73   *Marty Robbins*
22/79   *Freddy Fender*
64/66 **Walking Shadow, Talking Memory**
     Carl Belew
     Walking The Floor Over You
18/65   *George Hamilton IV*
31/79   *Ernest Tubb*
28/58 **Walking The Slow Walk** *Carl Smith*
5/61 **Walking The Streets** *Webb Pierce*
58/68 **Walking Through The Memories Of My Mind** *Billy Mize*
59/83 **Walking With My Memories** *Loretta Lynn*
24/59 **Wall, The** *Freddie Hart*
60/68 **Wall Of Pictures** *Darrell McCall*
40/87 **Wall Of Tears** *K.T. Oslin*
5/62 **Wall To Wall Love** *Bob Gallion*
43/66 **Wallpaper Roses** *Jerry Wallace*
     Walls Of The Bottle ..see: (If I Could Climb)
97/76 **Walnut Street Wrangler** *Debi Hawkins*
     Waltz Across Texas
34/65   *Ernest Tubb*
81/76   *Maury Finney*
56/79   *Ernest Tubb*
10/85 **Waltz Me To Heaven** *Waylon Jennings*
     Waltz Of The Angels
14/56   *Wynn Stewart*
11/62   *George Jones & Margie Singleton*
51/78   *David Houston*
8/48 **Waltz Of The Wind** *Roy Acuff*

13/62 **Waltz You Saved For Me** *Ferlin Husky*	1/87 **Way We Make A Broken Heart**
85/81 **Waltzes And Western Swing** *Donnie Rohrs*	*Rosanne Cash*
63/87 **Waltzin' With Daddy** *Carlette*	98/76 **Way With Words** *Carl Smith*
1/88 **Wanderer, The** *Eddie Rabbitt*	F/83 **Way Without Words** *Roy Clark*
13/67 **Wanderin' Man** *Jeannie Seely*	86/81 **Way You Are** *P.J. Parks*
2/81 **Wandering Eyes** *Ronnie McDowell*	98/88 **Way You Got Over Me** *Bill Nunley*
52/68 **Wandering Mind** *Margie Singleton*	7/80 **Wayfaring Stranger** *Emmylou Harris*
63/84 **Want Ads** *Robin Lee*	99/79 **Waylon Sing To Mama** *Darrell Thomas*
35/79 **Want To Thank You** *Kim Charles*	**Ways Of A Woman In Love**
3/74 **Want-To's, The** *Freddie Hart*	2/58 *Johnny Cash*
41/75 **Wanted Man** *Jerry Wallace*	74/78 *Tom Bresh*
63/67 **Wanting You But Never Having You**	1/69 **Ways To Love A Man** *Tammy Wynette*
Jack Greene	**We Ain't Gonna Work For Peanuts**
11/60 **Wanting You With Me Tonight**	..see: Farmer's Song
Jimmy Newman	22/69 **We All Go Crazy** *Jack Reno*
1/82 **War Is Hell (On The Homefront Too)**	75/87 **We Always Agree On Love** *Atlanta*
T.G. Sheppard	76/85 **We Are The World** *USA for Africa*
43/76 **Warm And Tender** *Larry Gatlin*	**We Believe In Happy Endings**
57/68 **Warm And Tender Love**	7/78 *Johnny Rodriguez*
Archie Campbell & Lorene Mann	1/88 *Earl Thomas Conley/Emmylou Harris*
53/73 **Warm Love** *Don Gibson & Sue Thompson*	**We Belong Together**
Warm Red Wine	2/78 *Susie Allanson*
8/49 *Ernest Tubb*	85/84 *Tony Joe White*
72/68 *Wes Buchanan*	52/86 *Carlette*
6/75 **Warm Side Of You** *Freddie Hart*	6/72 **We Can Make It** *George Jones*
Warm Summer Days ..see: (She Likes)	40/77 **We Can't Build A Fire In The Rain**
73/87 **Warmed Over Romance** *Tina Danielle*	*Roy Clark*
25/70 **Warmth Of The Wine** *Johnny Bush*	6/77 **We Can't Go On Living Like This**
4/85 **Warning Sign** *Eddie Rabbitt*	*Eddie Rabbitt*
61/86 **Was It Just The Wine** *Vern Gosdin*	3/74 **We Could** *Charley Pride*
43/76 **Was It Worth It** *Joe Stampley*	96/81 **We Could Go On Forever** *E.W.B.*
20/72 **Washday Blues** *Dolly Parton*	86/79 **We Could Have Been The Closest Of**
28/79 **Wasn't It Easy Baby** *Freddie Hart*	**Friends** *B.J. Thomas*
73/81 **Wasn't It Supposed To Be Me** *Kenny Earle*	2/82 **We Did But Now You Don't** *Conway Twitty*
45/81 **Wasn't That A Party** *Rovers*	6/84 **We Didn't See A Thing**
62/82 **Wasn't That Love** *Susie Allanson*	*Ray Charles & George Jones*
1/75 **Wasted Days And Wasted Nights**	16/81 **We Don't Have To Hold Out** *Anne Murray*
Freddy Fender	72/78 **We Don't Live Here, We Just Love Here**
27/60 **Wasted Love** *Red Herring*	*Big Ben Atkins*
87/82 **Wasted On The Way** *Crosby, Stills & Nash*	92/77 **We Fell In Love That Way** *Claude Gray*
4/56 **Wasted Words** *Ray Price*	30/73 **We Found It** *Porter Wagoner & Dolly Parton*
28/60 **Watch Dog** *Al Terry*	34/72 **We Found It In Each Other's Arms**
Watch Out For Lucy	*Roger Miller*
88/74 *Bobby Penn*	**We Got Love**
72/75 *Tony Booth*	26/78 *Lynn Anderson*
10/65 **Watch Where You're Going** *Don Gibson*	34/79 *Mundo Earwood*
4/82 **Watchin' Girls Go By** *Ronnie McDowell*	20/69 **We Had All The Good Things Going**
7/71 **Watching Scotty Grow** *Bobby Goldsboro*	*Jan Howard*
32/67 **Watchman, The** *Claude King*	**We Had It All**
16/73 **Watergate Blues** *Tom T. Hall*	28/73 *Waylon Jennings*
Waterhole #3 ..see: Ballad Of	44/83 *Conway Twitty*
1/59 **Waterloo** *Stonewall Jackson*	31/86 *Dolly Parton*
49/70 **Watermelon Time In Georgia** *Lefty Frizzell*	69/82 **We Had It All One Time** *Charlie Daniels Band*
Watermelon Wine	84/81 **We Have To Start Meeting Like This**
..see: (Old Dogs-Children And)	*Kenny Earle*
Wave To Me, My Lady	66/84 **We Just Gotta Dance** *Karen Taylor-Good*
3/46 *Elton Britt*	98/77 **We Know Better** *Paul Craft*
4/46 *Gene Autry*	53/85 **We Know Better Now** *Dottie West*
62/70 **Wax Museum** *Dave Peel*	40/73 **We Know It's Over**
57/70 **Waxahachie Woman** *John Deer Company*	*Dave Dudley & Karen O'Donnal*
4/84 **Way Back** *John Conlee*	89/79 **We Let Love Fade Away** *Leon Everette*
99/88 **Way Beyond The Blue** *Bonners*	96/76 **We Live In Two Different Worlds**
1/77 **Way Down** *Elvis Presley*	*Rachel Sweet*
5/83 **Way Down Deep** *Vern Gosdin*	48/79 **We Love Each Other**
39/87 **Way Down Texas Way** *Asleep At The Wheel*	*Louise Mandrell & R.C. Bannon*
46/76 **Way He's Treated You** *Nat Stuckey*	8/74 **We Loved It Away**
2/80 **Way I Am** *Merle Haggard*	*George Jones & Tammy Wynette*
67/75 **Way I Lose My Mind** *Carl Smith*	77/82 **We Made Memories**
99/76 **Way I Loved Her** *Rick Smith*	*Boxcar Willie & Penny DeHaven*
54/74 **Way I'm Needing You** *Cliff Cochran*	2/44 **We Might As Well Forget It** *Bob Wills*
17/63 **Way It Feels To Die** *Vernon Stewart*	7/62 **We Missed You** *Kitty Wells*
82/78 **Way It Was In '51** *Merle Haggard*	7/88 **We Must Be Doin' Somethin' Right**
91/85 **Way She Makes Love** *Billy Chinnock*	*Eddie Rabbitt*
7/66 **Way To Survive** *Ray Price*	

We Must Believe In Magic
86/78   *Jack Clement*
84/83   *Johnny Cash*
 3/63   **We Must Have Been Out Of Our Minds**
       George Jones & Melba Montgomery
43/68   **We Need A Lot More Happiness**
       Wilburn Brothers
69/70   **We Need A Lot More Of Jesus** *Skeeter Davis*
64/88   **We Need To Be Locked Away**
       Jonathan Edwards
22/88   **We Never Touch At All** *Merle Haggard*
67/83   **We Really Got A Hold On Love**
       Family Brown
 5/74   **We Should Be Together** *Don Williams*
 2/71   **We Sure Can Love Each Other**
       Tammy Wynette
 9/75   **We Used To** *Dolly Parton*
63/80   **(We Used To Kiss Each Other On The Lips But It's) All Over Now** *Ann J. Morton*
63/88   **We Were Meant To Be Lovers** *David Slater*
50/85   **We Work** *Hillary Kanter*
38/65   **We'd Destroy Each Other** *Carl Butler & Pearl*
 F/56   **We'll Find A Way** *Webb Pierce*
 5/68   **We'll Get Ahead Someday**
       Porter Wagoner & Dolly Parton
       We'll Sing In The Sunshine
43/64   *Gale Garnett*
63/70   *LaWanda Lindsey*
34/72   *Alice Creech*
54/68   **We'll Stick Together**
       Kitty Wells & Johnny Wright
63/69   **We'll Sweep Out The Ashes In The Morning** *Carl Butler & Pearl*
       We're All Alone
75/77   *La Costa*
82/77   *Rita Coolidge*
       We're Back In Love Again
37/74   *Johnny Bush*
59/80   *Johnny Russell*
93/81   **We're Building Our Love On A Rock**
       Lou Hobbs
47/76   **We're Getting There** *Ray Price*
13/70   **We're Gonna Get Together**
       Buck Owens & Susan Raye
14/62   **We're Gonna Go Fishin'** *Hank Locklin*
 1/73   **We're Gonna Hold On**
       George Jones & Tammy Wynette
75/88   **We're Gonna Love Tonight** *Don Juan*
95/79   **We're In For Hard Times** *Breakfast Barry*
       We're Livin' A Lie *..see: (Truth Is)*
94/79   **We're Making Up For Lost Time** *Rex Gosdin*
15/74   **(We're Not) The Jet Set**
       George Jones & Tammy Wynette
18/80   **We're Number One** *Gatlin Bros.*
 3/74   **We're Over** *Johnny Rodriguez*
59/87   **We're Staying Together** *Rex Allen, Jr.*
80/77   **We're Still Hangin' In There Ain't We Jessi** *Jeannie Seely*
42/83   **We're Strangers Again**
       Merle Haggard & Leona Williams
15/63   **We're The Talk Of The Town**
       Buck Owens & Rose Maddox
10/78   **We've Come A Long Way, Baby** *Loretta Lynn*
10/54   **We've Gone Too Far** *Hank Thompson*
44/66   **We've Gone Too Far Again**
       Justin Tubb & Lorene Mann
 3/86   **We've Got A Good Fire Goin'** *Don Williams*
97/83   **We've Got A Good Thing Goin'**
       J.W. Thompson
20/71   **We've Got Everything But Love**
       David Houston & Barbara Mandrell
95/75   **We've Got It All Together Now** *Guy & Ralna*
13/63   **We've Got Something In Common**
       Faron Young

       We've Got To Start Meeting Like This
76/82   *John Wesley Ryles*
85/84   *Memphis*
30/72   **We've Got To Work It Out Between Us**
       Diana Trask
 1/83   **We've Got Tonight**
       Kenny Rogers & Sheena Easton
63/79   **We've Gotta Get Away From It All**
       Tom Grant
78/85   **We've Still Got Love** *Simon & Verity*
57/70   **Weakest Kind Of Man** *John Wesley Ryles*
18/68   **Weakness In A Man** *Roy Drusky*
       Wear My Ring Around Your Neck
 3/58   *Elvis Presley*
 F/83   *Elvis Presley*
 7/53   **Weary Blues From Waitin'** *Hank Williams*
       Wedding Bells
 2/49   *Hank Williams*
 6/49   *Margaret Whiting & Jimmy Wakely*
15/49   *Kenny Roberts*
15/49   *Jesse Rogers*
78/83   *Margo Smith*
33/69   **Wedding Cake** *Connie Francis*
91/78   **Weeds Outlived The Roses** *Darrell McCall*
13/78   **Week-End Friend** *Con Hunley*
 1/70   **Week In A Country Jail** *Tom T. Hall*
10/64   **Week In The Country** *Ernest Ashworth*
 1/87   **Weekend, The** *Steve Wariner*
75/87   **Weekend Cowboys** *Marty Haggard*
 F/75   **Weekend Daddy** *Buck Owens*
87/76   **Weep No More My Baby** *Lois Johnson*
43/80   **Weight Of My Chains**
       Tompall/Glaser Brothers
93/76   **Welcome Back** *John Sebastian*
56/74   **Welcome Back To My World** *Carl Belew*
79/74   **Welcome Home** *Peters & Lee*
24/68   **Welcome Home To Nothing** *Jeannie Seely*
       Welcome To My World
 2/64   *Jim Reeves*
34/71   *Eddy Arnold*
22/74   **Welcome To The Sunshine (Sweet Baby Jane)** *Jeanne Pruett*
 6/70   **Welfare Cadilac** *Guy Drake*
60/80   **Well Rounded Traveling Man** *Kenny Price*
46/86   **Weren't You Listening** *Adam Baker*
49/67   **West Canterbury Subdivision Blues**
       Stonemans
23/71   **West Texas Highway** *George Hamilton IV*
51/69   **West Virginia Woman** *Billy Edd Wheeler*
11/75   **Western Man** *La Costa*
86/82   **(What A Day For A) Day Dream** *Jon & Lynn*
81/77   **What A Diff'rence A Day Makes**
       Bobby Lewis
 1/78   **What A Difference You've Made In My Life**
       Ronnie Milsap
50/71   **What A Dream** *Conway Twitty*
 2/48   **What A Fool I Was** *Eddy Arnold*
43/87   **What A Girl Next Door Could Do**
       Girls Next Door
23/61   **What A Laugh!** *Freddie Hart*
16/79   **What A Lie** *Sammi Smith*
 1/74   **What A Man, My Man Is** *Lynn Anderson*
75/85   **What A Memory You'd Make** *Jim Collins*
       What A Night
51/76   *David Houston*
71/77   *Tom Jones*
23/62   **What A Pleasure** *Connie Hall*
57/72   **What A Price** *Johnny Russell*
13/49   **What A Shame** *Merle Travis*
25/61   **What A Terrible Feeling** *Elmer Snodgrass*
       What A Way To Go
70/74   *Del Reeves*
18/77   *Bobby Borchers*
29/68   **What A Way To Live** *Johnny Bush*
85/82   **What A Way To Spend The Night** *Zella Lehr*

79/79	**What're We Doing, Doing This Again** *Nick Nixon*
21/77	**What're You Doing Tonight** *Janie Frickie*
76/79	**What's A Little Love Between Friends** *Billy Burnette*
1/86	**What's A Memory Like You (Doing In A Love Like This)** *John Schneider*
87/80	**What's A Nice Girl Like You (Doin' In A Love Like This)** *Springer Brothers*
17/67	**What's Come Over My Baby** *Dottie West*
1/82	**What's Forever For** *Michael Murphey*
67/82	**What's Good About Goodbye** *Cindy Hurt*
77/84	**What's Good For The Goose (Is Good For The Gander)** *Dottie West*
5/75	**What's Happened To Blue Eyes** *Jessi Colter*
1/65	**What's He Doing In My World** *Eddy Arnold*
20/63	**What's In Our Heart** *George Jones & Melba Montgomery*
2/68	**What's Made Milwaukee Famous (Has Made A Loser Out Of Me)** *Jerry Lee Lewis*
40/65	**What's Money** *George Jones*
11/81	**What's New With You** *Con Hunley*
47/79	**What's On Your Mind** *John Denver*
86/83	**What's She Doing To My Mind** *Johnny Bailey*
55/87	**What's So Different About You** *John Anderson*
81/81	**What's So Good About Goodbye** *Terry Aden*
30/78	**What's The Name Of That Song?** *Glenn Barber*
45/70	**What's The Use** *Jack Greene*
56/67	**What's This World A-Comin' To** *Slim Whitman*
1/73	**What's Your Mama's Name** *Tanya Tucker*
72/86	**What's Your Name** *Almost Brothers*
	Whatcha *..also see: What Cha*
4/54	**Whatcha Gonna Do Now** *Tommy Collins*
9/75	**Whatcha Gonna Do With A Dog Like That** *Susan Raye*
80/83	**Whatcha Got Cookin' In Your Oven Tonight** *Thrasher Brothers*
7/82	**Whatever** *Statler Brothers*
1/83	**Whatever Happened To Old Fashioned Love** *B.J. Thomas*
22/74	**Whatever Happened To Randolph Scott** *Statler Brothers*
55/80	**Whatever Happened To Those Drinking Songs** *Foxfire*
38/75	**Whatever I Say** *Donna Fargo*
	Whatever Turns You On
81/82	*Chantilly*
19/84	*Keith Stegall*
16/72	**Wheel Of Fortune** *Susan Raye*
37/64	**Wheel Song** *Gary Buck*
1/88	**Wheels** *Restless Heart*
47/67	**Wheels Fell Off The Wagon Again** *Johnny Dollar*
77/84	**Wheels In Emotion** *Becky Hobbs*
	When
13/58	*Kalin Twins*
15/80	*Slim Whitman*
11/79	**When A Love Ain't Right** *Charly McClain*
	When A Man Loves A Woman
72/76	*John Wesley Ryles*
18/82	*Jack Grayson & Blackjack*
60/87	*Narvel Felts*
	When A Man Loves A Woman (The Way That I Love You)
3/70	*Billy Walker*
32/73	*Tony Booth*
	When A Woman Cries
31/78	*David Rogers*
97/78	*Tommy O'Day*
20/87	*Janie Frickie*
5/78	**When Can We Do This Again** *T.G. Sheppard*

67/77	**When Do We Stop Starting Over** *Don Gibson*
17/85	**When Givin' Up Was Easy** *Ed Bruce*
48/71	**When He Touches Me (Nothing Else Matters)** *Lois Johnson*
11/71	**When He Walks On You (Like You Have Walked On Me)** *Jerry Lee Lewis*
52/77	**When I Die, Just Let Me Go To Texas** *Ed Bruce*
	When I Dream
F/78	*Jack Clement*
3/79	*Crystal Gayle*
53/85	**When I Get Home** *Bobby Bare*
16/74	**When I Get My Hands On You** *Diana Trask*
10/62	**When I Get Thru With You (You'll Love Me Too)** *Patsy Cline*
36/78	**When I Get You Alone** *Mundo Earwood*
63/78	**When I Need You** *Lois Johnson*
	When I Stop Dreaming
8/55	*Louvin Brothers*
88/75	*Debi Hawkins*
3/78	**When I Stop Leaving (I'll Be Gone)** *Charley Pride*
66/77	**When I Touch Her There** *Jim Ed Brown*
54/68	**When I Turn Twenty-One** *Buddy Alan*
1/83	**When I'm Away From You** *Bellamy Brothers*
38/87	**When I'm Free Again** *Rodney Crowell*
34/79	**When I'm Gone** *Dottsy*
75/70	**When I'm Not Lookin'** *Liz Anderson*
54/87	**When I'm Over You (What You Gonna Do)** *Mickey Clark*
77/82	**When It Comes To Love** *Thom Bresh & Lane Brody*
17/86	**When It's Down To Me And You** *Charly McClain & Wayne Massey*
	When It's Just You And Me
19/77	*Dottie West*
31/81	*Kenny Dale*
	When It's Over
26/65	*Carl Smith*
39/67	*Jeannie Seely*
1/59	**When It's Springtime In Alaska** *Johnny Horton*
49/88	**When Karen Comes Around** *Mason Dixon*
66/76	**When Lea Jane Sang** *Porter Wagoner*
44/73	**When Love Has Gone Away** *Jeannie C. Riley*
74/86	**When Love Is Right** *Charly McClain & Wayne Massey*
6/54	**When Mexican Joe Met Jole Blon** *Hank Snow*
93/78	**When My Angel Turns Into A Devil** *Del Reeves*
	When My Blue Moon Turns To Gold Again
5/44	*Cindy Walker*
11/48	*Cliffie Stone*
F/77	*Merle Haggard*
84/85	*Maines Brothers Band*
	When My Conscience Hurts The Most
22/59	*Charlie Walker*
83/79	*Johnny Bush*
2/44	**When My Man Comes Home** *Buddy Johnson*
2/44	**When My Sugar Walks Down The Street** *Ella Fitzgerald*
95/79	**When Our Love Began** *George James*
75/80	**When She Falls** *Bobby Hood*
30/69	**When She Touches Me** *Johnny Duncan*
60/76	**When She's Got Me (Where She Wants Me)** *David Allan Coe*
31/87	**When Something Is Good (Why Does It Change)** *Hank Williams, Jr.*
	When Something Is Wrong With My Baby
6/76	*Sonny James*
67/85	*Joe Stampley*
31/78	**When The Fire Gets Hot** *Zella Lehr*
2/69	**When The Grass Grows Over Me** *George Jones*
10/74	**When The Morning Comes** *Hoyt Axton*

28/69	**Where's The Playground Susie**
	Glen Campbell
20/73	**Wherefore And Why** *Glen Campbell*
	Wherever You Are
31/69	*Johnny Paycheck*
81/83	*Thrasher Brothers*
4/59	**Which One Is To Blame** *Wilburn Brothers*
19/69	**Which One Will It Be** *Bobby Bare*
31/80	**While I Was Makin' Love To You**
	Susie Allanson
43/69	**While I'm Thinkin' About It** *Billy Mize*
57/80	**While The Choir Sang The Hymn (I Thought Of Her)** *Johnny Russell*
	While The Feeling's Good
56/75	*Mike Lunsford*
46/76	*Kenny Rogers*
26/81	*Rex Allen, Jr. & Margo Smith*
47/86	**While The Moon's In Town** *Shoppe*
21/66	**While You're Dancing** *Marty Robbins*
25/69	**While Your Lover Sleeps** *Leon Ashley*
69/78	**Whine, Whistle, Whine** *John Anderson*
47/65	**Whirlpool (Of Your Love)** *Claude King*
2/79	**Whiskey Bent And Hell Bound**
	Hank Williams, Jr.
18/81	**Whiskey Chasin'** *Joe Stampley*
51/81	**Whiskey Heaven** *Fats Domino*
2/87	**Whiskey, If You Were A Woman**
	Highway 101
76/82	**Whiskey Made Me Stumble (The Devil Made Me Fall)** *Bill Anderson*
	Whiskey River
14/72	*Johnny Bush*
12/79	*Willie Nelson*
92/81	*Johnny Bush*
48/70	**Whiskey-Six Years Old** *Norma Jean*
18/76	**Whiskey Talkin'** *Joe Stampley*
16/78	**Whiskey Trip** *Gary Stewart*
	Whiskey Was A River
	..see: (I Remember When I Thought)
31/70	**Whiskey, Whiskey** *Nat Stuckey*
10/81	**Whisper** *Lacy J. Dalton*
57/78	**Whisper It To Me** *Bobby G. Rice*
84/78	**Whispering** *Maury Finney*
15/58	**Whispering Rain** *Hank Snow*
12/77	**Whispers** *Bobby Borchers*
66/76	**Whispers And Grins** *David Rogers*
86/74	**Whistle Stop** *Roger Miller*
28/65	**Whistle Walkin'** *Ned Miller*
7/49	**White Christmas** *Ernest Tubb*
1/46	**White Cross On Okinawa** *Bob Wills*
25/68	**White Fences And Evergreen Trees**
	Ferlin Husky
72/88	**White Freight Liner Blues**
	Jimmie Dale Gilmore
1/76	**White Knight** *Cledus Maggard*
21/65	**White Lightnin' Express** *Roy Drusky*
1/59	**White Lightning** *George Jones*
14/85	**White Line** *Emmylou Harris*
	White Line Fever
68/72	*Buddy Alan*
95/80	*Flying Burrito Brothers*
5/72	**White Silver Sands** *Sonny James*
1/57	**White Sport Coat (And A Pink Carnation)**
	Marty Robbins
62/69	**Who Am I** *Red Sovine*
3/78	**Who Am I To Say** *Statler Brothers*
3/59	**Who Cares** *Don Gibson*
60/84	**Who Dat** *David Frizzell*
64/69	**Who Do I Know In Dallas** *Kenny Price*
13/65	**Who Do I Think I Am** *Webb Pierce*
11/82	**Who Do You Know In California** *Eddy Raven*
10/74	**Who Left The Door To Heaven Open**
	Hank Thompson
41/66	**Who Licked The Red Off Your Candy**
	'Little' Jimmy Dickens
64/69	**Who Loves Who** *Arlene & Bobby Harden*
6/48	**Who? Me?** *Tex Williams*
68/83	**Who Said Love Was Fair** *Billy Parker*
91/80	**Who Shot J.R.?**
	Gary Burbank with Band McNally
50/70	**Who Shot John** *Wanda Jackson*
7/59	**Who Shot Sam** *George Jones*
53/76	**Who Wants A Slightly Used Woman**
	Connie Cato
57/88	**Who Was That Stranger** *Loretta Lynn*
40/79	**(Who Was The Man Who Put) The Line In Gasoline** *Jerry Reed*
54/80	**Who Were You Thinkin' Of**
	Dandy & The Doolittle Band
69/68	**Who Will Answer? (Aleluya No. 1)**
	Hank Snow
11/60	**Who Will Buy The Wine** *Charlie Walker*
91/75	**Who Will I Be Loving Now** *Carmol Taylor*
	Who Will The Next Fool Be
67/70	*Charlie Rich*
20/79	*Jerry Lee Lewis*
	Who'll Turn Out The Lights
57/71	*Wayne Kemp*
36/80	*Mel Street*
27/63	**Who's Been Cheatin' Who**
	Johnny & Jonie Mosby
87/76	**Who's Been Here Since I've Been Gone**
	Hank Snow
43/66	**Who's Been Mowing The Lawn**
	Ray Pennington
88/82	**Who's Been Sleeping In My Bed** *Diana*
1/81	**Who's Cheatin' Who** *Charly McClain*
82/84	**Who's Counting** *Marie Osmond*
3/85	**Who's Gonna Fill Their Shoes** *George Jones*
37/83	**Who's Gonna Keep Me Warm** *Phil Everly*
1/69	**Who's Gonna Mow Your Grass** *Buck Owens*
14/72	**Who's Gonna Play This Old Piano**
	Jerry Lee Lewis
75/76	**Who's Gonna Run The Truck Stop In Tuba City When I'm Gone?** *Leroy Van Dyke*
41/82	**(Who's Gonna Sing) The Last Country Song** *Billy Parker*
18/69	**Who's Gonna Take The Garbage Out**
	Ernest Tubb & Loretta Lynn
97/78	**Who's Gonna Tie My Shoes** *Ray Pillow*
65/67	**Who's Gonna Walk The Dog (And Put Out The Cat)** *Ray Pennington*
10/69	**Who's Julie** *Mel Tillis*
62/86	**Who's Leaving Who** *Anne Murray*
29/75	**Who's Sorry Now** *Marie Osmond*
37/85	**Who's The Blonde Stranger?** *Jimmy Buffett*
6/49	**Whoa Sailor** *Hank Thompson*
43/70	**Whoever Finds This, I Love You** *Mac Davis*
14/75	**Whoever Turned You On, Forgot To Turn You Off** *Little David Wilkins*
1/86	**Whoever's In New England** *Reba McEntire*
63/81	**Whole Lot Of Cheatin' Goin' On**
	Jimmi Cannon
1/57	**Whole Lot Of Shakin' Going On**
	Jerry Lee Lewis
18/72	**Whole Lot Of Somethin'** *Tony Booth*
65/75	**Whole Lotta Difference In Love** *George Kent*
	Whole Lotta Loving
61/71	*Anita Carter*
22/73	*Hank Williams, Jr. & Lois Johnson*
2/76	**Whole Lotta Things To Sing About**
	Charley Pride
15/58	**Whole Lotta Woman** *Marvin Rainwater*
80/87	**Whole Month Of Sundays** *Jenny Yates*
14/70	**Whole World Comes To Me** *Jack Greene*
27/70	**Whole World Holding Hands** *Freddie Hart*
10/84	**Whole World's In Love When You're Lonely** *B.J. Thomas*
13/73	**Whole World's Making Love Again Tonight** *Bobby G. Rice*

20/81	**Wind Is Bound To Change**	*Gatlin Bros.*
54/83	**Windin' Down**	*Lacy J. Dalton*
65/70	**Window Number Five**	*Johnny Duncan*
	Window Up Above	
2/61		*George Jones*
1/75		*Mickey Gilley*
14/65	**Wine**	*Mel Tillis*
10/86	**Wine Colored Roses**	*George Jones*
2/69	**Wine Me Up**	*Faron Young*
	Wine, Women And Song	
1/46		*Al Dexter*
3/64		*Loretta Lynn*
1/60	**Wings Of A Dove**	*Ferlin Husky*
11/70	**Wings Upon Your Horns**	*Loretta Lynn*
13/76	**Winner, The**	*Bobby Bare*
26/79	**Winners And Losers**	*R.C. Bannon*
58/85	**Wino The Clown**	*Bill Anderson*
87/78	**Wipe You From My Eyes (Gettin' Over You)**	*King Edward IV*
8/79	**Wisdom Of A Fool**	*Jacky Ward*
2/70	**Wish I Didn't Have To Miss You**	
		Jack Greene & Jeannie Seely
60/72	**Wish I Was A Little Boy Again**	
		LaWanda Lindsey
54/71	**Wish I Was Home Instead**	*Van Trevor*
61/66	**Wish Me A Rainbow**	*Hugh X. Lewis*
2/81	**Wish You Were Here**	*Barbara Mandrell*
83/86	**Wishful Dreamin'**	*Michael Shamblin*
	Wishful Drinkin'	
83/80		*Diane Pfeifer*
22/84		*Atlanta*
5/60	**Wishful Thinking**	*Wynn Stewart*
32/79	**Wishing I Had Listened To Your Song**	
		Bobby Borchers
F/80	**Wishing Well**	*Tammy Jo*
7/65	**Wishing Well (Down in the Well)**	*Hank Snow*
24/71	**With His Hand In Mine**	*Jean Shepard*
68/77	**With His Pants In His Hand**	*Jerry Reed*
5/85	**With Just One Look In Your Eyes**	
		Charly McClain with Wayne Massey
10/78	**With Love**	*Rex Allen, Jr.*
1/67	**With One Exception**	*David Houston*
3/68	**With Pen In Hand**	*Johnny Darrell*
1/45	**With Tears In My Eyes**	*Wesley Tuttle*
32/82	**With Their Kind Of Money And Our Kind Of Love**	*Billy Swan*
	With You	
7/83		*Charly McClain*
33/86		*Vince Gill*
74/72	**Within My Loving Arms**	*Kenni Huskey*
11/84	**Without A Song**	*Willie Nelson*
50/88	**Without A Trace**	*Marie Osmond*
78/81	**Without Love**	*Johnny Cash*
	Without You	
50/76		*Jessi Colter*
79/79		*Susie Allanson*
92/81		*Buck Owens*
12/83		*T.G. Sheppard*
		(also see: There's No Me)
10/56	**Without Your Love**	*Bobby Lord*
13/76	**Without Your Love (Mr. Jordan)**	
		Charlie Ross
1/83	**Woke Up In Love**	*Exile*
12/75	**Wolf Creek Pass**	*C.W. McCall*
1/62	**Wolverton Mountain**	*Claude King*
		(also see: I'm The Girl On)
55/76	**Woman**	*David Wills*
2/71	**Woman Always Knows**	*David Houston*
92/77	**Woman Behind The Man Behind The Wheel**	*Red Sovine*
16/58	**Woman Captured Me**	*Hank Snow*
38/76	**Woman Don't Try To Sing My Song**	
		Cal Smith
58/73	**Woman Ease My Mind**	*Claude Gray*
15/66	**Woman Half My Age**	*Kitty Wells*

24/68	**Woman Hungry**	*Porter Wagoner*
9/57	**Woman I Need**	*Johnny Horton*
4/67	**Woman In Love**	*Bonnie Guitar*
3/81	**Woman In Me**	*Crystal Gayle*
74/81	**Woman In My Heart**	*Bobby Hood*
4/75	**Woman In The Back Of My Mind**	*Mel Tillis*
48/69	**Woman In Your Life**	*Wilma Burgess*
	Woman Left Lonely	
72/71		*Charlie Rich*
F/71		*Patti Page*
17/70	**Woman Lives For Love**	*Wanda Jackson*
64/67	**Woman Needs Love**	*Marion Worth*
52/66	**Woman Never Forgets**	*Kitty Wells*
58/86	**Woman Of The 80's**	*Donna Fargo*
1/69	**Woman Of The World (Leave My World Alone)**	*Loretta Lynn*
35/75	**Woman On My Mind**	*David Houston*
1/72	**Woman (Sensuous Woman)**	*Don Gibson*
54/76	**Woman Stealer**	*Bobby G. Rice*
	Woman To Woman	
4/74		*Tammy Wynette*
4/78		*Barbara Mandrell*
29/73	**Woman Without A Home**	*Statler Brothers*
20/69	**Woman Without Love**	*Johnny Darrell*
43/75	**Woman, Woman**	*Jim Glaser*
12/84	**Woman Your Love**	*Moe Bandy*
	Woman's Hand	
66/69		*Barbara Fairchild*
23/70		*Jean Shepard*
9/59	**Woman's Intuition**	*Wilburn Brothers*
59/69	**Woman's Side Of Love**	*Lynda K. Lance*
	Woman's Touch	
70/79		*Glenn Barber*
16/82		*Tom Jones*
3/78	**Womanhood**	*Tammy Wynette*
74/81	**Women**	*Wyvon Alexander*
9/66	**Women Do Funny Things To Me**	*Del Reeves*
4/82	**Women Do Know How To Carry On**	*Waylon*
18/80	**Women Get Lonely**	*Charly McClain*
5/80	**Women I've Never Had**	*Hank Williams, Jr.*
	Women In Love	
59/82		*Kin Vassy*
55/85		*Bill Medley*
65/81	**Won't You Be My Baby**	*Keith Stegall*
61/69	**Won't You Come Home (And Talk To A Stranger)**	*Wayne Kemp*
1/70	**Wonder Could I Live There Anymore**	
		Charley Pride
37/70	**Wonder Of You**	*Elvis Presley*
39/75	**Wonder When My Baby's Comin' Home**	
		Barbara Mandrell
51/68	**Wonderful Day**	*Ray Pillow*
14/68	**Wonderful World Of Women**	*Faron Young*
1/52	**Wondering**	*Webb Pierce*
6/70	**Wonders Of The Wine**	*David Houston*
5/71	**Wonders You Perform**	*Tammy Wynette*
41/64	**Wooden Soldier**	*Hank Locklin*
10/75	**Word Games**	*Billy Walker*
8/79	**Words**	*Susie Allanson*
63/73	**Words Don't Come Easy**	*David Frizzell*
73/72	**Words Don't Fit The Picture**	*Willie Nelson*
10/67	**Words I'm Gonna Have To Eat**	*Bill Phillips*
	Workin' At The Car Wash Blues	
27/74		*Tony Booth*
F/80		*Jerry Reed*
86/83	**Workin' In A Coalmine**	*Bob Jenkins*
21/64	**Workin' It Out**	*Lester Flatt & Earl Scruggs*
1/69	**Workin' Man Blues**	*Merle Haggard*
4/88	**Workin' Man (Nowhere To Go)**	
		Nitty Gritty Dirt Band
30/80	**Workin' My Way To Your Heart**	*Dickey Lee*
37/73	**Workin' On A Feelin'**	*Tommy Cash*
73/73	**Working Class Hero**	*Tommy Roe*
16/86	**Working Class Man**	*Lacy J. Dalton*
F/81	**Working Girl**	*Dolly Parton*

33/71	**Working Like The Devil (For The Lord)**	
	Del Reeves	
7/85	**Working Man** *John Conlee*	
16/77	**Working Man Can't Get Nowhere Today**	
	Merle Haggard	
59/67	**Working Man's Prayer** *Tex Ritter*	
7/86	**Working Without A Net** *Waylon Jennings*	
23/70	**World Called You** *David Rogers*	
90/77	**World Famous Holiday Inn** *Buck Owens*	
10/66	**World Is Round** *Roy Drusky*	
29/64	**World Lost A Man** *David Price*	
	World Needs A Melody	
32/71	*Red Lane*	
35/72	*Carter Family with Johnny Cash*	
1/74	**World Of Make Believe** *Bill Anderson*	
1/68	**World Of Our Own** *Sonny James*	
	World So Full Of Love	
18/60	*Ray Sanders*	
28/61	*Faron Young*	
66/68	**World The Way I Want It** *Tom T. Hall*	
19/69	**World-Wide Travelin' Man** *Wynn Stewart*	
10/85	**World Without Love** *Eddie Rabbitt*	
14/72	**World Without Music** *Porter Wagoner*	
52/67	**World's Biggest Whopper** *Junior Samples*	
6/84	**World's Greatest Lover** *Bellamy Brothers*	
18/79	**World's Most Perfect Woman**	
	Ronnie McDowell	
46/66	**World's Worse Loser** *George Jones*	
47/64	**Worst Of Luck** *Bobby Barnett*	
30/76	**(Worst You Ever Gave Me Was) The Best I Ever Had** *Faron Young*	
41/87	**Would Jesus Wear A Rolex** *Ray Stevens*	
36/87	**Would These Arms Be In Your Way**	
	Keith Whitley	
91/75	**Would You Be My Lady** *David Allan Coe*	
13/58	**Would You Care?** *Browns*	
6/82	**Would You Catch A Falling Star**	
	John Anderson	
86/87	**Would You Catch Me Baby (If I Fall For You)** *Gail Veach*	
5/66	**Would You Hold It Against Me** *Dottie West*	
95/80	**Would You Know Love** *Marlow Tackett*	
1/74	**Would You Lay With Me (In A Field Of Stone)** *Tanya Tucker*	
3/55	**Would You Mind** *Hank Snow*	
92/73	**Would You Still Love Me** *Ben Peters*	
1/72	**Would You Take Another Chance On Me**	
	Jerry Lee Lewis	
21/73	**Would You Walk With Me Jimmy**	
	Arlene Harden	
12/72	**Would You Want The World To End**	
	Mel Tillis	
72/85	**Wouldn't It Be Great** *Loretta Lynn*	
3/62	**Wound Time Can't Erase** *Stonewall Jackson*	
18/84	**Wounded Hearts** *Mark Gray*	
77/86	**Wrap Me Up In Your Love** *J.D. Martin*	
12/77	**Wrap Your Love All Around Your Man**	
	Lynn Anderson	
38/73	**Wrap Your Love Around Me**	
	Melba Montgomery	
46/72	**Wrapped Around Her Finger** *George Jones*	
50/76	**Wreck Of The Edmund Fitzgerald**	
	Gordon Lightfoot	
8/61	**Wreck On The Highway**	
	Wilma Lee & Stoney Cooper	
9/75	**Write Me A Letter** *Bobby G. Rice*	
16/66	**Write Me A Picture** *George Hamilton IV*	
6/44	**Write Me, Sweetheart** *Roy Acuff*	
96/88	**Writing On The Wall** *Kenny Carr*	
15/72	**Writing's On The Wall** *Jim Reeves*	
35/82	**Written Down In My Heart** *Ray Stevens*	
26/60	**Wrong Company** *Wynn Stewart & Jan Howard*	
6/74	**Wrong Ideas** *Brenda Lee*	
20/74	**Wrong In Loving You** *Faron Young*	
14/65	**Wrong Number** *George Jones*	

	Wrong Road Again
6/75	*Crystal Gayle*
95/78	*Allen Reynolds*
76/78	**Wrong Side Of The Rainbow** *Jim Chesnut*
49/68	**Wrong Side Of The World** *Hugh X. Lewis*
82/86	**Wrong Train** *Beth Williams*
1/77	**Wurlitzer Prize (I Don't Want To Get Over You)** *Waylon Jennings*
79/87	**Wyatt Liquor** *Wyatt Brothers*
	Wyoming
	..see: (Oh Why, Oh Why, Did I Ever Leave)

Y

3/77	**Y'All Come Back Saloon** *Oak Ridge Boys*
4/65	**Yakety Axe** *Chet Atkins*
91/75	**Yakety Yak** *Eric Weissberg & Deliverance*
17/59	**Yankee, Go Home** *Goldie Hill*
1/71	**Year That Clayton Delaney Died**
	Tom T. Hall
	Yearning
10/57	*George Jones & Jeanette Hicks*
22/61	*Benny Barnes*
1/80	**Years** *Barbara Mandrell*
2/85	**Years After You** *John Conlee*
12/82	**Years Ago** *Statler Brothers*
4/63	**Yellow Bandana** *Faron Young*
59/67	**Yellow Haired Woman** *Claude King*
30/81	**Yellow Pages** *Roger Bowling*
5/73	**Yellow Ribbon** *Johnny Carver*
49/72	**Yellow River** *Compton Brothers*
1/84	**Yellow Rose** *Johnny Lee with Lane Brody*
7/55	**Yellow Rose Of Texas** *Ernest Tubb*
3/55	**Yellow Roses** *Hank Snow*
	Yes
83/75	*Connie Cato*
67/83	*Billy Swan*
75/71	**Yes, Dear, There Is A Virginia** *Glenn Barber*
2/56	**Yes, I Know Why** *Webb Pierce*
6/66	**(Yes) I'm Hurting** *Don Gibson*
12/78	**Yes Ma'am** *Tommy Overstreet*
98/82	**Yes Ma'am, He Found Me In A Honky Tonk** *Dixie Harrison*
67/73	**Yes Ma'm (I Found Her In A Honky Tonk)**
	Glenn Barber
1/65	**Yes, Mr. Peters**
	Roy Drusky & Priscilla Mitchell
83/77	**Yes She Do, No She Don't** *Alvin Crow*
60/79	**Yesterday** *Billie Jo Spears*
50/76	**Yesterday Just Passed My Way Again**
	Don Everly
10/80	**Yesterday Once More** *Moe Bandy*
9/69	**Yesterday, When I Was Young** *Roy Clark*
8/53	**Yesterday's Girl** *Hank Thompson*
9/77	**Yesterday's Gone** *Vern Gosdin*
40/69	**Yesterday's Letters** *Bobby Lord*
12/48	**Yesterday's Mail** *Hank Thompson*
11/63	**Yesterday's Memories** *Eddy Arnold*
57/81	**Yesterday's News (Just Hit Home Today)**
	Johnny Paycheck
99/88	**Yesterday's Rain** *Joy Ford*
4/44	**Yesterday's Tears** *Ernest Tubb*
	Yesterday's Wine
62/71	*Willie Nelson*
1/82	*George Jones/Merle Haggard*
25/80	**Yippy Cry Yi** *Rex Allen, Jr.*
	YoYo Man *..see: (I'm A)*
93/85	**Yo Yo (The Right String, But The Wrong Yo Yo)** *Danny Shirley & 'Piano Red'*
44/65	**Yodel, Sweet Molly** *Ira Louvin*

72/86 **You Can't Take It With You**
    William Lee Golden
35/68 **You Changed Everything About Me But My Name** *Norma Jean*
5/63 **You Comb Her Hair** *George Jones*
92/75 **You Comb Her Hair Every Morning**
    Del Reeves
45/85 **You Could Be The One Woman** *Chance*
10/76 **You Could Know As Much About A Stranger** *Gene Watson*
    You Could've Heard A Heart Break
53/83   *Rodney Lay*
1/84   *Johnny Lee*
1/79 **You Decorated My Life** *Kenny Rogers*
55/67 **You Deserve Each Other** *Robert Mitchum*
73/88 **You Didn't Have To Jump The Fence**
    Lisa Childress
10/79 **You Don't Bring Me Flowers**
    Jim Ed Brown/Helen Cornelius
    You Don't Care What Happens To Me
5/45   *Bob Wills*
55/70   *Wynn Stewart*
    You Don't Have To Be A Baby To Cry
10/50   *Ernest Tubb*
63/77   *Ann J. Morton*
36/75 **You Don't Have To Go Home** *Nat Stuckey*
56/70 **You Don't Have To Say You Love Me**
    Elvis Presley
4/65 **You Don't Hear** *Kitty Wells*
4/83 **You Don't Know Love** *Janie Frickie*
    You Don't Know Me
10/56   *Eddy Arnold*
61/70   *Ray Pennington*
1/81   *Mickey Gilley*
1/78 **You Don't Love Me Anymore** *Eddie Rabbitt*
66/72 **You Don't Mess Around With Jim**
    Bobby Bond
36/79 **You Don't Miss A Thing** *Sylvia*
15/74 **You Don't Need To Move A Mountain**
    Jeanne Pruett
71/71 **You Don't Understand Him Like I Do**
    Jeannie Seely
14/61 **You Don't Want My Love** *Roger Miller*
    You Done Me Wrong
7/56   *Ray Price*
37/85   *Mel Tillis*
13/59 **You Dreamer You** *Johnny Cash*
4/79 **You Feel Good All Over** *T.G. Sheppard*
41/80 **You Fill My Life** *Juice Newton*
15/66 **You Finally Said Something Good (When You Said Goodbye)** *Charlie Louvin*
76/88 **You Fit Right Into My Heart** *Sanders*
69/69 **You Fool** *Eddy Arnold*
7/69 **You Gave Me A Mountain** *Johnny Bush*
34/74 **You Get To Me** *Eddie Rabbitt*
8/73 **You Give Me You** *Bobby G. Rice*
55/88 **You Go, You're Gone** *David Ball*
60/75 **You Got A Lock On Me** *Jerry Reed*
77/74 **You Got Everything That You Want**
    Pat Roberts
28/83 **You Got Me Running** *Jim Glaser*
41/70 **You Got-Ta Have A License** *Porter Wagoner*
7/56 **You Gotta Be My Baby** *George Jones*
49/67 **You Gotta Be Puttin' Me On** *Lefty Frizzell*
65/83 **You Gotta Get To My Heart (Before You Lay A Hand On Me)** *Paulette Carlson*
11/87 **You Haven't Heard The Last Of Me**
    Moe Bandy
54/77 **You Just Don't Know** *Mary K. Miller*
76/85 **You Just Hurt My Last Feeling**
    Sammi Smith
43/88 **You Just Watch Me** *Libby Hurley*
    You Know Just What I'd Do
48/75   *Lois Johnson*
9/80   *Conway Twitty & Loretta Lynn*

20/78 **You Know What** *Jerry Reed & Seidina*
30/73 **You Know Who** *Bobby Bare*
48/87 **You Lay A Lotta Love On Me** *Wrays*
19/80 **You Lay A Whole Lot Of Love On Me**
    Con Hunley
    You Lay So Easy On My Mind
3/73   *Bobby G. Rice*
70/84   *Narvel Felts*
79/87   *Bobby G. Rice*
63/87 **You Left Her Lovin' You** *Ride The River*
86/87 **You Left My Heart For Broke** *Ernie Rowell*
8/80 **(You Lift Me) Up To Heaven** *Reba McEntire*
4/77 **You Light Up My Life** *Debby Boone*
94/79 **You Lit The Fire, Now Fan The Flame**
    Penny Hamilton
    You Look Like The One I Love
33/82   *Deborah Allen*
69/86   *Osmond Brothers*
1/84 **You Look So Good In Love** *George Strait*
63/67 **You Love Me Too Little** *Lorene Mann*
76/78 **You Love The Thunder** *Hank Williams, Jr.*
24/86 **You Made A Rock Of A Rolling Stone**
    Oak Ridge Boys
3/84 **You Made A Wanted Man Of Me**
    Ronnie McDowell
47/81 **You Made It Beautiful** *Charlie Rich*
84/76 **You Made It Right**
    Ozark Mountain Daredevils
34/71 **You Made Me Feel Like A Man** *Warner Mack*
67/79 **You Make It So Easy** *Bobby G. Rice*
61/76 **You Make Life Easy** *Joe Stampley*
7/85 **You Make Me Feel Like A Man** *Ricky Skaggs*
15/74 **You Make Me Feel More Like A Man**
    Mel Street
29/61 **You Make Me Live Again** *Carl Smith*
4/75 **(You Make Me Want To Be) A Mother**
    Tammy Wynette
1/85 **You Make Me Want To Make You Mine**
    Juice Newton
85/82 **You Make Me Want To Sing** *Joe Sun*
20/81 **You (Make Me Wonder Why)** *Deborah Allen*
69/68 **You May Be Too Much For Memphis, Baby**
    Leroy Van Dyke
9/81 **You May See Me Walkin'** *Ricky Skaggs*
    You Mean The World To Me
1/67   *David Houston*
72/78   *Howdy Glenn*
44/88 **You Might Want To Use Me Again**
    Johnny Rodriguez
45/86 **You Must Be Lookin' For Me** *Billy Swan*
15/48 **You Nearly Lose Your Mind** *Ernest Tubb*
4/78 **You Needed Me** *Anne Murray*
6/77 **(You Never Can Tell) C'est La Vie**
    Emmylou Harris
8/75 **You Never Even Called Me By My Name**
    David Allan Coe
5/82 **You Never Gave Up On Me** *Crystal Gayle*
1/77 **You Never Miss A Real Good Thing (Till He Says Goodbye)** *Crystal Gayle*
31/74 **You Never Say You Love Me Anymore**
    Nat Stuckey
65/74 **You Only Live Once (In Awhile)**
    Glenn Barber
7/46 **You Only Want Me When You're Lonely**
    Gene Autry
    You Ought To Hear Me Cry
43/68   *Carl Smith*
16/77   *Willie Nelson*
100/76 **You Oughta Be Against The Law**
    Rex Kramer
69/67 **You Oughta Hear Me Cry** *Johnny Bush*
90/77 **You Oughta Hear The Song** *Ruth Buzzi*
15/55 **You Oughta See Pickles Now** *Tommy Collins*
12/79 **You Pick Me Up (And Put Me Down)**
    Dottie West

14/67 **You Pushed Me Too Far** *Ferlin Husky*
10/83 **You Put The Beat In My Heart** *Eddie Rabbitt*
10/82 **You Put The Blue In Me** *Whites*
F/77 **You Put The Bounce Back Into My Step**
     Ray Griff
62/78 **You Read Between The Lines** *Billy Parker*
37/84 **You Really Go For The Heart** *Dan Seals*
6/73 **You Really Haven't Changed** *Johnny Carver*
You Really Know How To Break A Heart
93/84   *Jimmy Mac*
73/88   *Rhonda Manning*
16/75 **You Ring My Bell** *Ray Griff*
4/76 **You Rubbed It In All Wrong**
     Billy 'Crash' Craddock
43/87 **You Saved Me** *Patty Loveless*
3/86 **You Should Have Been Gone By Now**
     Eddy Raven
56/78 **You Should Win An Oscar Every Night**
     Chuck Pollard
11/79 **You Show Me Your Heart (And I'll Show You**
     Mine) *Tom T. Hall*
70/78 **You Snap Your Fingers (And I'm Back In Your**
     Hands) *David Wills*
14/89 **You Still Do** *T.G. Sheppard*
16/82 **You Still Get To Me In My Dreams**
     Tammy Wynette
71/83 **You Still Got Me** *David Rogers*
1/87 **You Still Move Me** *Dan Seals*
35/82 **(You Sure Know Your Way) Around My**
     Heart *Louise Mandrell*
1/83 **You Take Me For Granted** *Merle Haggard*
15/62 **You Take The Future (And I'll Take the**
     Past) *Hank Snow*
76/87 **You Take The Leavin' Out Of Me**
     Mickey Clark
18/59 **You Take The Table (And I'll Take The**
     Chairs) *Bob Gallion*
65/82 **You To Come Home To** *Dean Dillon*
18/73 **You Took All The Ramblin' Out Of Me**
     Jerry Reed
You Took Her (Him) Off My Hands (Now Please
Take Her [Him] Off My Mind)
11/63   *Ray Price*
33/64   *Marion Worth*
33/64 **You Took My Happy Away** *Willie Nelson*
37/69 **You Touched My Heart** *David Rogers*
17/82 **You Turn Me On I'm A Radio** *Gail Davies*
3/85 **You Turn Me On (Like a Radio)** *Ed Bruce*
48/80 **You Turn My Love Light On** *Billy Walker*
1/45 **You Two-Timed Me One Time Too Often**
     Tex Ritter
6/70 **You Wanna Give Me A Lift** *Loretta Lynn*
20/84 **You Were A Good Friend** *Kenny Rogers*
You Were A Lady *..see: (Jeannie Marie)*
1/73 **You Were Always There** *Donna Fargo*
51/71 **You Were On My Mind** *Bobby Penn*
38/81 **You Were There** *Freddie Hart*
28/79 **You Were Worth Waiting For** *Don King*
1/46 **You Will Have To Pay** *Tex Ritter*
You Win Again
10/52   *Hank Williams*
2/58   *Jerry Lee Lewis*
1/80   *Charley Pride*
75/80   *Jeris Ross*
8/70 **You Wouldn't Know Love** *Ray Price*
66/66 **You Wouldn't Put The Shuck On Me**
     Geezinslaw Brothers
77/73 **You, You, You** *Lynda K. Lance*
77/83 **You'd Better Believe It** *Rod Rishard*
5/80 **You'd Make An Angel Wanna Cheat**
     Kendalls
64/67 **You'll Always Have My Love** *Wanda Jackson*
You'll Be Back (Every Night In My Dreams)
24/78   *Johnny Russell*
3/82   *Statler Brothers*

10/58 **You'll Come Back** *Webb Pierce*
31/88 **You'll Come Back (You Always Do)** *Mel Tillis*
10/64 **You'll Drive Me Back (Into Her Arms**
     Again) *Faron Young*
1/76 **You'll Lose A Good Thing** *Freddy Fender*
55/68 **You'll Never Be Lonely Again**
     Leon Ashley & Margie Singleton
97/85 **You'll Never Find A Good Man (Playin' In A**
     Country Band) *Audie Henry*
You'll Never Know
71/75   *Jim Reeves*
77/85   *Lew Dewitt*
26/86 **You'll Never Know How Much I Needed You**
     Today *Conway Twitty*
78/77 **You'll Never Leave Me Completely**
     Johnny Bush
73/82 **You'll Never Walk Alone** *Elvis Presley*
54/73 **You're A Believer** *Stoney Edwards*
92/86 **You're A Better Man Than I** *Perry LaPointe*
71/78 **You're A Dancer** *Eddy Raven*
18/83 **You're A Hard Dog (To Keep Under The**
     Porch) *Gail Davies*
96/86 **You're A Heartache To Follow** *Ken Fowler*
84/83 **You're A Keep Me Wondering Kind Of**
     Woman *Steve Mantelli*
You're A Part Of Me
99/78   *Gene Cotton with Kim Carnes*
20/79   *Charly McClain*
85/83   *Danny White & Linda Nail*
You're A Pretty Lady, Lady
93/79   *Wichita Linemen*
93/80   *Ray Sanders*
82/78 **You're A Violin That Never Has Been**
     Played *Billy Walker*
You're All The Woman I'll Ever Need
78/78   *Lee Dresser*
76/79   *Dusty James*
39/80 **You're Amazing** *David Rogers*
5/45 **You're Breaking My Heart**
     Ted Daffan's Texans
59/72 **You're Burnin' My House Down**
     Warner Mack
73/63 **You're Cheatin' On Me Again** *Hal Dickinson*
31/81 **You're Crazy Man** *Freddie Hart*
41/66 **You're Driving Me Out Of My Mind**
     Norma Jean
49/68 **You're Easy To Love** *Arlene Harden*
47/85 **You're Every Step I Take** *Johnny Paycheck*
32/72 **You're Everything** *Tommy Cash*
10/63 **You're For Me** *Buck Owens*
You're Free To Go
6/55   *Carl Smith*
9/77   *Sonny James*
2/44 **You're From Texas** *Bob Wills*
1/84 **You're Gettin' To Me Again** *Jim Glaser*
26/59 **You're Going Back To Your Old Ways**
     Again *Hank Thompson*
10/85 **You're Going Out Of My Mind** *T.G. Sheppard*
4/49 **You're Gonna Change** *Hank Williams*
29/74 **You're Gonna Hurt Me (One More Time)**
     Patti Page
34/83 **You're Gonna Lose Her Like That**
     Moe Bandy
44/78 **You're Gonna Love Love** *Ava Barber*
(You're Gonna Love Me Tonight)
     ..see: I Can Tell By The Way You Dance
You're Gonna Love Yourself In The Morning
77/73   *Wayne Carson*
35/75   *Roy Clark*
22/80   *Charlie Rich*
43/83   *Willie Nelson/Brenda Lee*
89/79 **You're Gonna Make A Cheater Out Of Me**
     Bill Phillips
45/89 **You're Gonna Make Her Mine**
     Lionel Cartwright

93/77 **You're Gonna Make Love To Me** *Lynn Niles*
97/79 **You're Gonna Miss Me** *June Neyman*
33/85 **You're Gonna Miss Me When I'm Gone**
     Judy Rodman
39/70 **You're Gonna Need A Man** *Johnny Duncan*
1/83 **You're Gonna Ruin My Bad Reputation**
     Ronnie McDowell
62/87 **You're Here To Remember (I'm Here To**
     Forget) *Merrill & Jessica*
61/87 **You're In Love Alone**
     Jeff Stevens & The Bullets
27/80 **You're In Love With The Wrong Man**
     Mundo Earwood
92/74 **You're Just Gettin' Better** *Jack Scott*
38/71 **You're Just More A Woman** *Bob Yarbrough*
5/71 **You're Lookin' At Country** *Loretta Lynn*
62/67 **You're Lookin' For A Plaything** *Jamey Ryan*
7/59 **You're Makin' A Fool Out Of Me**
     Jimmy Newman
59/86 **You're Mine** *Orleans*
70/81 **You're More To Me (Than He's Ever Been)**
     Peggy Forman
1/75 **You're My Best Friend** *Don Williams*
5/82 **You're My Bestest Friend** *Mac Davis*
7/81 **You're My Favorite Star** *Bellamy Brothers*
2/87 **You're My First Lady** *T.G. Sheppard*
1/79 **You're My Jamaica** *Charley Pride*
14/79 **You're My Kind Of Woman** *Jacky Ward*
1/71 **You're My Man** *Lynn Anderson*
68/75 **You're My Rainy Day Woman** *Eddy Raven*
26/72 **You're My Shoulder To Lean On** *Lana Rae*
36/74 **You're My Wife, She's My Woman**
     Charlie Louvin
3/87 **You're Never Too Old For Young Love**
     Eddy Raven
60/86 **You're Nobody Till Somebody Loves You**
     Ray Price
60/76 **You're Not Charlie Brown (And I'm Not**
     Raggedy Ann) *Donna Fargo*
26/82 **You're Not Easy To Forget** *Dottie West*
74/78 **You're Not Free And I'm Not Easy**
     Arleen Harden
16/74 **You're Not Getting Older (You're Getting**
     Better) *Freddy Weller*
21/83 **You're Not Leavin' Here Tonight** *Ed Bruce*
4/54 **You're Not Mine Anymore** *Webb Pierce*
3/47 **You're Not My Darling Anymore** *Gene Autry*
13/56 **You're Not Playing Love** *Wilburn Brothers*
15/75 **You're Not The Woman You Use To Be**
     Gary Stewart
60/80 **You're Only Lonely** *J.D. Souther*
2/83 **You're Out Doing What I'm Here Doing**
     Without *Gene Watson*
67/67 **You're Puttin' Me On** *Nat Stuckey*
7/56 **You're Running Wild** *Louvin Brothers*
38/67 **You're So Cold (I'm Turning Blue)**
     Hugh X. Lewis
75/77 **You're So Good For Me (And That's Bad)**
     Bobby Wayne Loftis
1/82 **You're So Good When You're Bad**
     Charley Pride
4/86 **You're Something Special To Me**
     George Strait
3/56 **You're Still Mine** *Faron Young*
1/86 **You're Still New To Me**
     Marie Osmond with Paul Davis
     You're Still On My Mind
28/62   *George Jones*
84/79   *Joe Douglas*
14/81 **You're The Best** *Kieran Kane*
1/82 **You're The Best Break This Old Heart Ever**
     Had *Ed Bruce*
87/84 **You're The Best I Never Had** *Larry Jenkins*
1/73 **You're The Best Thing That Ever Happened**
     To Me *Ray Price*

1/83 **You're The First Time I've Thought About**
     Leaving *Reba McEntire*
57/77 **You're The Hangnail In My Life** *Hoyt Axton*
1/86 **You're The Last Thing I Needed Tonight**
     John Schneider
5/58 **You're The Nearest Thing To Heaven**
     Johnny Cash
     You're The One
95/75   *Jerry Inman*
75/76   *Billy Swan*
2/78   *Oak Ridge Boys*
91/79 **You're The One Who Rewrote My Life**
     Story *Don Schlitz*
93/81 **You're The Only Dancer** *Pam Hobbs*
     You're The Only Good Thing (That's Happened
     To Me)
4/60   *George Morgan*
29/78   *Jim Reeves*
1/79 **You're The Only One** *Dolly Parton*
77/84 **You're The Only Star (In My Blue Heaven)**
     Mike Campbell
1/65 **You're The Only World I Know** *Sonny James*
38/79 **You're The Part Of Me** *Jim Ed Brown*
64/80 **You're The Perfect Reason** *David Houston*
5/87 **You're The Power** *Kathy Mattea*
     You're The Reason
4/61   *Bobby Edwards*
14/61   *Hank Locklin*
16/61   *Joe South*
48/68   *Johnny Tillotson*
90/81   *John Rex Reeves*
94/81   *Sligo Studio Band*
82/82   *Narvel Felts*
1/81 **You're The Reason God Made Oklahoma**
     David Frizzell & Shelly West
6/57 **You're The Reason I'm In Love** *Sonny James*
     You're The Reason I'm Living
59/71   *Lamar Morris*
75/76   *Price Mitchell*
     You're The Reason Our Kids Are Ugly
90/77   *L.E. White & Lola Jean Dillon*
F/78   *Conway Twitty & Loretta Lynn*
52/73 **You're Wearin' Me Down** *Kenny Price*
9/84 **You're Welcome To Tonight**
     Lynn Anderson & Gary Morris
98/76 **You're Wondering Why** *Hank Snow*
94/86 **You've Been My Rock For Ages** *Bobbi Lace*
26/67 **You've Been So Good To Me** *Van Trevor*
9/85 **You've Got A Good Love Comin'**
     Lee Greenwood
2/83 **You've Got A Lover** *Ricky Skaggs*
54/87 **You've Got A Right** *Adam Baker*
44/84 **You've Got A Soft Place To Fall**
     Kathy Mattea
21/73 **You've Got Me (Right Where You Want**
     Me) *Connie Smith*
92/77 **You've Got Me Runnin'** *Gene Cotton*
3/76 **You've Got Me To Hold On To** *Tanya Tucker*
16/79 **You've Got Somebody, I've Got Somebody**
     Vern Gosdin
10/85 **You've Got Something On Your Mind**
     Mickey Gilley
85/79 **(You've Got That) Fire Goin' Again**
     Jimmy Tucker
77/87 **You've Got That Leaving Look In Your**
     Eye *Marcia Lynn*
60/83 **You've Got That Touch** *Lloyd David Foster*
89/81 **You've Got The Devil In Your Eyes**
     Ann J. Morton
1/87 **"You've Got" The Touch** *Alabama*
30/80 **You've Got Those Eyes** *Eddy Raven*
40/77 **You've Got To Mend This Heartache**
     Ruby Falls

(You've Got To) Move Two Mountains
56/71   *Dave Peel*
99/76   *Jimmy Russell*
79/76 **You've Got To Stop Hurting Me Darling**
     Don Gibson
27/70 **You've Got Your Troubles (I've Got Mine)**
     Jack Blanchard & Misty Morgan
12/72 **You've Gotta Cry Girl** *Dave Dudley*
76/78 **You've Just Found Yourself A New**
     Woman *Jenny Robbins*
 2/68 **You've Just Stepped In (From Stepping Out**
     On Me) *Loretta Lynn*
     You've Lost That Lovin' Feelin'
41/75 *Barbara Fairchild*
57/87 *Carlette*
 1/73 **You've Never Been This Far Before**
     Conway Twitty
 2/84 **You've Really Got A Hold On Me**
     Mickey Gilley
     You've Still Got A Place In My Heart
14/78 *Con Hunley*
 3/84 *George Jones*
68/80 **You've Still Got Me** *Jerry Wallace*
70/86 **You've Taken Over My Heart** *Bobby G. Rice*
 2/88 **Young Country** *Hank Williams, Jr.*
29/76 **Young Girl** *Tommy Overstreet*
     Young Hearts
12/57 *Jim Reeves*
20/69 *Connie Smith & Nat Stuckey*
48/76 *Ray Stevens*
75/82 *Stella Parton*
81/88 **Younger Man, Older Woman**
     Richard & Gary Rose
22/82 **Your Bedroom Eyes** *Vern Gosdin*
12/63 **Your Best Friend And Me** *Mac Wiseman*
 3/80 **Your Body Is An Outlaw** *Mel Tillis*
 1/53 **Your Cheatin' Heart** *Hank Williams*
67/81 **Your Daddy Don't Live In Heaven (He's In**
     Houston) *Michael Ballew*
     Your Eyes
76/84 *Bill Anderson*
91/85 *Simon & Verity*
17/67 **Your Forevers (Don't Last Very Long)**
     Jean Shepard
 F/55 **Your Good For Nothing Heart** *Webb Pierce*
     Your Good Girl's Gonna Go Bad
 3/67 *Tammy Wynette*
13/81 *Billie Jo Spears*
65/67 **Your Hands** *Johnny Dollar*
 5/64 **Your Heart Turned Left (And I Was On The**
     Right) *George Jones*
 1/84 **Your Heart's Not In It** *Janie Frickie*
22/70 **Your Husband, My Wife**
     Bobby Bare & Skeeter Davis
56/71 **Your Kind Of Lovin'** *June Stearns*
 7/79 **Your Kisses Will** *Crystal Gayle*
     Your Lily White Hands
21/68 *Johnny Carver*
49/68 *Ray Griff*
12/87 **Your Love** *Tammy Wynette*
 3/79 **Your Love Had Taken Me That High**
     Conway Twitty

92/77 **Your Love Is My Refuge** *Ava Barber*
71/70 **Your Love Is The Way** *Kitty Wells*
 5/83 **Your Love Shines Through** *Mickey Gilley*
93/79 **Your Love Takes Me So High** *Maury Finney*
 1/83 **Your Love's On The Line**
     Earl Thomas Conley
43/69 **Your Lovin' Takes The Leavin' Out Of Me**
     Tommy Cash
53/86 **Your Loving Side** *Butch Baker*
15/80 **Your Lying Blue Eyes** *John Anderson*
89/80 **Your Magic Touch** *Pat Garrett*
85/83 **Your Mama Don't Dance** *Roy Head*
 4/77 **Your Man Loves You, Honey** *Tom T. Hall*
 7/81 **Your Memory** *Steve Wariner*
 5/86 **Your Memory Ain't What It Used To Be**
     Mickey Gilley
17/88 **Your Memory Wins Again** *Skip Ewing*
29/63 **Your Mother's Prayer** *Buddy Cagle*
 6/58 **Your Name Is Beautiful** *Carl Smith*
 5/80 **Your Old Cold Shoulder** *Crystal Gayle*
73/68 **Your Old Handy Man** *Priscilla Mitchell*
10/61 **Your Old Love Letters** *Porter Wagoner*
 5/60 **Your Old Used To Be** *Faron Young*
99/79 **Your Other Love** *Tommy O'Day*
13/76 **Your Picture In The Paper** *Statler Brothers*
56/82 **Your Picture Still Loves Me (And I Still Love**
     You) *Billy Swan*
11/77 **Your Place Or Mine** *Gary Stewart*
     Your Pretty Roses Came Too Late
67/74 *Melba Montgomery*
20/77 *Lois Johnson*
93/73 **Your Shoeshine Girl** *Leona Williams*
36/73 **Your Side Of The Bed** *Mac Davis*
 3/68 **Your Squaw Is On The Warpath**
     Loretta Lynn
90/73 **Your Sweet Love (Keeps Me Homeward**
     Bound) *Jimmy Dean*
     Your Sweet Love Lifted Me
44/69 *Bobby Barnett*
45/70 *Ferlin Husky*
 1/67 **Your Tender Loving Care** *Buck Owens*
50/68 **Your Time Hasn't Come Yet, Baby**
     Elvis Presley
 4/69 **Your Time's Comin'** *Faron Young*
13/57 **Your True Love** *Carl Perkins*
83/76 **Your Wanting Me Is Gone** *Vernon Oxford*
35/81 **Your Wife Is Cheatin' On Us Again**
     Wayne Kemp
12/59 **Your Wild Life's Gonna Get You Down**
     Kitty Wells
22/79 **Yours** *Freddy Fender*
     Yours And Mine
77/75 *O.B. McClinton*
78/79 *Mary Lou Turner*
28/80 **Yours For The Taking** *Jack Greene*
47/69 **Yours Forever** *Wynn Stewart*
     Yours Love
 5/69 *Waylon Jennings*
 9/69 *Porter Wagoner & Dolly Parton*
67/79 *Jerry Wallace*

THE RECORD HOLDERS

Kings & Queens of Country

The TOP 200 Artists

Rank	Artist	Points	Rank	Artist	Points
1.	Eddy Arnold	17092	51.	Billy Walker	5202
2.	George Jones	16198	52.	The Oak Ridge Boys	5176
3.	Johnny Cash	13356	53.	Eddie Rabbitt	5107
4.	Merle Haggard	12171	54.	Johnny Paycheck	4975
5.	Conway Twitty	11905	55.	Connie Smith	4842
6.	Ray Price	10870	56.	Tanya Tucker	4832
7.	Webb Pierce	10791	57.	Freddie Hart	4735
8.	Willie Nelson	10570	58.	Jerry Reed	4655
9. d	Marty Robbins	10550	59.	Johnny Rodriguez	4655
10.	Dolly Parton	10191	60.	Ferlin Husky	4649
11.	Waylon Jennings	10170	61.	Charlie Rich	4552
12.	Buck Owens	10005	62.	Jim Ed Brown	4510
13. d	Ernest Tubb	9968	63.	Alabama	4490
14. d	Jim Reeves	9486	64.	Gene Watson	4443
15.	Loretta Lynn	9118	65.	Reba McEntire	4437
16.	Hank Williams, Jr.	9117	66.	Janie Frickie	4377
17.	Faron Young	9110	67.	Larry Gatlin/Gatlin Brothers	4321
18.	Charley Pride	8753	68.	Stonewall Jackson	4238
19.	Sonny James	8736	69.	The Bellamy Brothers	4211
20.	Carl Smith	8715	70.	Billy "Crash" Craddock	4200
21.	Hank Snow	8484	71.	Earl Thomas Conley	4184
22.	Mel Tillis	8221	72.	Dave Dudley	4061
23.	Porter Wagoner	8056	73.	Roy Drusky	4037
24.	Bill Anderson	8055	74.	Jean Shepard	4024
25.	Tammy Wynette	7963	75.	Del Reeves	4010
26.	Kitty Wells	7863	76. d	Lefty Frizzell	3981
27. d	Red Foley	7830	77.	Roger Miller	3876
28.	Don Gibson	7782	78.	Charly McClain	3775
29.	Hank Thompson	7320	79.	John Conlee	3772
30.	Ronnie Milsap	7263	80.	Donna Fargo	3657
31. d	Elvis Presley	7050	81.	George Hamilton IV	3649
32.	The Statler Brothers	6960	82.	Skeeter Davis	3639
33.	Glen Campbell	6956	83.	George Strait	3626
34.	Kenny Rogers	6743	84.	Steve Wariner	3528
35.	Bobby Bare	6655	85.	Roy Clark	3518
36.	Jerry Lee Lewis	6476	86.	John Anderson	3442
37.	Crystal Gayle	6429	87.	Johnny Duncan	3431
38.	Don Williams	6379	88.	Mel McDaniel	3371
39.	Barbara Mandrell	6259	89.	Jimmy Newman	3327
40.	David Houston	6060	90.	Ronnie McDowell	3304
41.	Lynn Anderson	6052	91.	Eddy Raven	3302
42.	Mickey Gilley	5993	92.	The Kendalls	3291
43.	Joe Stampley	5976	93. d	Bob Wills	3267
44.	Dottie West	5864	94.	Vern Gosdin	3245
45.	T.G. Sheppard	5492	95.	Ricky Skaggs	3242
46. d	Hank Williams	5459	96.	Lee Greenwood	3229
47.	Anne Murray	5399	97. d	Nat Stuckey	3203
48.	Tom T. Hall	5347	98.	Jack Greene	3187
49.	Moe Bandy	5338	99.	Billie Jo Spears	3149
50.	Emmylou Harris	5292	100. *	Wilburn Brothers	3107

Rank	Artist	Points	Rank	Artist	Points
101.	Gene Autry	3090	151.	Lacy J. Dalton	2144
102.	Tommy Overstreet	3068	152.	Ray Stevens	2118
103.	Slim Whitman	3061	153.	John Denver	2117
104. d	George Morgan	3022	154.	Gary Stewart	2096
105.	Ed Bruce	3008	155.	Gail Davies	2093
106.	Gary Morris	2992	156.	Freddy Fender	2091
107.	Narvel Felts	2930	157.	The Browns	2089
108. d	Bob Luman	2907	158.	Ernest Ashworth	2050
109. d	Jimmy Wakely	2906	159.	Jeannie Seely	2041
110.	Hank Locklin	2894	160.	Johnny Carver	2039

Rank	Artist	Points	Rank	Artist	Points
111.	Johnny Lee	2882	161.	Jody Miller	2032
112.	Rex Allen, Jr.	2879	162.	Barbara Fairchild	2019
113.	Tennessee Ernie Ford	2850	163.	Shelly West	1985
114.	Razzy Bailey	2815	164.	Dave & Sugar	1983
115.	Sammi Smith	2749	165.	Jacky Ward	1974
116.	Brenda Lee	2727	166. d	Patsy Cline	1959
117.	Freddy Weller	2705	167.	Tompall & The Glaser Brothers	1954
118.	Rosanne Cash	2681	168.	Bobby G. Rice	1933
119.	Claude King	2653	169.	John Schneider	1923
120.	Jerry Wallace	2634	170.	Jeannie C. Riley	1919

Rank	Artist	Points	Rank	Artist	Points
121. d	Wynn Stewart	2592	171. *	Lester Flatt & Earl Scruggs	1908
122.	David Rogers	2563	172.	Con Hunley	1902
123. d	Tex Ritter	2561	173.	Charlie Walker	1900
124.	Susan Raye	2537	174.	Claude Gray	1898
125.	Michael Martin Murphey	2505	175.	Cristy Lane	1892
126.	Jan Howard	2478	176.	Johnny Russell	1885
127.	Nitty Gritty Dirt Band	2428	177.	John Wesley Ryles	1859
128.	The Judds	2427	178.	David Allan Coe	1856
129.	Cal Smith	2425	179. d	Cowboy Copas	1823
130.	Wanda Jackson	2405	180.	Norma Jean	1819

Rank	Artist	Points	Rank	Artist	Points
131.	Juice Newton	2404	181.	The Everly Brothers	1805
132.	Dan Seals	2370	182.	Jeanne Pruett	1778
133. d	Tex Williams	2367	183.	Marie Osmond	1762
134. d	Kenny Price	2346	184. d	Johnny Horton	1753
135.	Warner Mack	2343	185.	Bobby Lewis	1748
136. d	Al Dexter	2325	186.	Bobby Goldsboro	1747
137.	Dickey Lee	2317	187.	Kathy Mattea	1739
138.	Margo Smith	2303	188.	Helen Cornelius	1737
139.	Mac Davis	2301	189. *	Johnnie & Jack	1733
140.	Jimmy Dean	2290	190.	"Little" Jimmy Dickens	1713

Rank	Artist	Points	Rank	Artist	Points
141. d	Red Sovine	2265	191.	Randy Travis	1705
142.	Linda Ronstadt	2264	192.	Randy Barlow	1679
143.	Sylvia	2255	193.	The Forester Sisters	1675
144.	Exile	2240	194. d	Merle Travis	1606
145. d	Mel Street	2235	195.	Jim Glaser	1602
146.	Louise Mandrell	2223	196.	Sawyer Brown	1552
147.	Charlie Louvin	2206	197.	B.J. Thomas	1526
148.	David Frizzell	2203	198.	Restless Heart	1523
149.	Melba Montgomery	2194	199.	Olivia Newton-John	1516
150.	Leon Everette	2155	200.	Dick Curless	1502

d = artist deceased
* = member deceased

POINT SYSTEM

Artist's points are calculated using the following formula:

1. Each artist's charted records are awarded points based on their highest position (#1 = 100 points; #2 = 99, etc.).

2. Bonus points are awarded each record based on its highest charted position (#1 = 50 points; #2-5 = 20 points; #6-10 = 15 points; #11-20 = 10 points; #21-30 = 5 points; #31-40 = 2 points).

3. Total weeks charted are added in.

4. Total weeks an artist held the #1 position are also added in.

When two artists combine for a hit record their chart points are shared equally.

The TOP 200 Artists (A-Z)

Artist	Rank	Artist	Rank	Artist	Rank
Alabama	63	Earl Thomas Conley	71	Lester Flatt & Earl Scruggs	171
Rex Allen, Jr.	112	Cowboy Copas	179	Red Foley	27
Bill Anderson	24	Helen Cornelius	188	Tennessee Ernie Ford	113
John Anderson	86	Billy "Crash" Craddock	70	Forester Sisters	193
Lynn Anderson	41	Dick Curless	200	Janie Frickie	66
Eddy Arnold	1	Lacy J. Dalton	151	David Frizzell	148
Ernest Ashworth	158	Dave & Sugar	164	Lefty Frizzell	76
Gene Autry	101	Gail Davies	155	Larry Gatlin/ Gatlin Brothers	67
Razzy Bailey	114	Mac Davis	139	Crystal Gayle	37
Moe Bandy	49	Skeeter Davis	82	Don Gibson	28
Bobby Bare	35	Jimmy Dean	140	Mickey Gilley	42
Randy Barlow	192	John Denver	153	Jim Glaser	195
Bellamy Brothers	69	Al Dexter	136	Tompall & The Glaser Brothers	167
Jim Ed Brown	62	"Little" Jimmy Dickens	190	Bobby Goldsboro	186
Browns	157	Roy Drusky	73	Vern Gosdin	94
Ed Bruce	105	Dave Dudley	72	Claude Gray	174
Glen Campbell	33	Johnny Duncan	87	Jack Greene	98
Johnny Carver	160	Leon Everette	150	Lee Greenwood	96
Johnny Cash	3	Everly Brothers	181	Merle Haggard	4
Rosanne Cash	118	Exile	144	Tom T. Hall	48
Roy Clark	85	Barbara Fairchild	162	George Hamilton IV	81
Patsy Cline	166	Donna Fargo	80		
David Allan Coe	178	Narvel Felts	107		
John Conlee	79	Freddy Fender	156		

Artist	Rank	Artist	Rank	Artist	Rank
Emmylou Harris	50	Jimmy Newman	89	Connie Smith	55
Freddie Hart	57	Juice Newton	131	Margo Smith	138
Johnny Horton	184	Olivia Newton-John	199	Sammi Smith	115
David Houston	40	Nitty Gritty Dirt Band	127	Hank Snow	21
Jan Howard	126	Norma Jean	180	Red Sovine	141
Con Hunley	172	Oak Ridge Boys	52	Billie Jo Spears	99
Ferlin Husky	60	Marie Osmond	183	Joe Stampley	43
Stonewall Jackson	68	Tommy Overstreet	102	Statler Brothers	32
Wanda Jackson	130	Buck Owens	12	Ray Stevens	152
Sonny James	19	Dolly Parton	10	Gary Stewart	154
Waylon Jennings	11	Johnny Paycheck	54	Wynn Stewart	121
Johnnie & Jack	189	Webb Pierce	7	George Strait	83
George Jones	2	Elvis Presley	31	Mel Street	145
Judds	128	Kenny Price	134	Nat Stuckey	97
Kendalls	92	Ray Price	6	Sylvia	143
Claude King	119	Charley Pride	18	B.J. Thomas	197
Cristy Lane	175	Jeanne Pruett	182	Hank Thompson	29
Brenda Lee	116	Eddie Rabbitt	53	Mel Tillis	22
Dickey Lee	137	Eddy Raven	91	Merle Travis	194
Johnny Lee	111	Susan Raye	124	Randy Travis	191
Bobby Lewis	185	Jerry Reed	58	Ernest Tubb	13
Jerry Lee Lewis	36	Del Reeves	75	Tanya Tucker	56
Hank Locklin	110	Jim Reeves	14	Conway Twitty	5
Charlie Louvin	147	Restless Heart	198	Porter Wagoner	23
Bob Luman	108	Bobby G. Rice	168	Jimmy Wakely	109
Loretta Lynn	15	Charlie Rich	61	Billy Walker	51
Warner Mack	135	Jeannie C. Riley	170	Charlie Walker	173
Barbara Mandrell	39	Tex Ritter	123	Jerry Wallace	120
Louise Mandrell	146	Marty Robbins	9	Jacky Ward	165
Kathy Mattea	187	Johnny Rodriguez	59	Steve Wariner	84
Charly McClain	78	David Rogers	122	Gene Watson	64
Mel McDaniel	88	Kenny Rogers	34	Freddy Weller	117
Ronnie McDowell	90	Linda Ronstadt	142	Kitty Wells	26
Reba McEntire	65	Johnny Russell	176	Dottie West	44
Jody Miller	161	John Wesley Ryles	177	Shelly West	163
Roger Miller	77	Sawyer Brown	196	Slim Whitman	103
Ronnie Milsap	30	John Schneider	169	Wilburn Brothers	100
Melba Montgomery	149	Dan Seals	132	Don Williams	38
George Morgan	104	Jeannie Seely	159	Hank Williams	46
Gary Morris	106	Jean Shepard	74	Hank Williams, Jr.	16
Michael Martin Murphey	125	T.G. Sheppard	45	Tex Williams	133
Anne Murray	47	Ricky Skaggs	95	Bob Wills	93
Willie Nelson	8	Cal Smith	129	Tammy Wynette	25
		Carl Smith	20	Faron Young	17

The **TOP 20** *Artists By Decade*

THE FORTIES ('44-'49)

		Points
1.	Eddy Arnold	4348
2.	Ernest Tubb	3987
3.	Bob Wills	2830
4.	Red Foley	2754
5.	Gene Autry	2620
6.	Al Dexter	2325
7.	Tex Ritter	1733
8.	Jimmy Wakely	1724
9.	Tex Williams	1610
10.	Merle Travis	1420
11.	Hank Williams	1386
12.	Floyd Tillman	1133
13.	Sons Of The Pioneers	1129
14.	Elton Britt	1083
15.	Hank Thompson	1000
16.	Roy Acuff	992
17.	Ted Daffan's Texans	986
18.	Cowboy Copas	938
19.	George Morgan	897
20.	Spade Cooley	794

THE FIFTIES

		Points
1.	Webb Pierce	6346
2.	Eddy Arnold	5944
3.	Hank Snow	5276
4.	Carl Smith	5018
5.	Red Foley	4890
6.	Kitty Wells	4044
7.	Hank Williams	3964
8.	Ernest Tubb	3933
9.	Johnny Cash	3556
10.	Hank Thompson	3464
11.	Faron Young	3418
12.	Elvis Presley	3315
13.	Jim Reeves	3236
14.	Ray Price	2842
15.	Marty Robbins	2753
16.	Lefty Frizzell	2463
17.	Tennessee Ernie Ford	1781
18.	George Jones	1656
19.	Johnnie & Jack	1635
20.	Ferlin Husky	1442

THE SIXTIES

		Points
1.	George Jones	6201
2.	Buck Owens	6158
3.	Jim Reeves	4381
4.	Johnny Cash	4336
5.	Webb Pierce	4052
6.	Eddy Arnold	4042
7.	Marty Robbins	3841
8.	Ray Price	3675
9.	Bill Anderson	3617
10.	Kitty Wells	3572
11.	Porter Wagoner	3461
12.	Faron Young	3449
13.	Stonewall Jackson	3334
14.	Sonny James	3096
15.	Loretta Lynn	2985
16.	Don Gibson	2904
17.	Roy Drusky	2874
18.	Carl Smith	2842
19.	David Houston	2798
20.	Billy Walker	2714

THE SEVENTIES

		Points
1.	Conway Twitty	6101
2.	Merle Haggard	4943
3.	Dolly Parton	4928
4.	Mel Tillis	4821
5.	Loretta Lynn	4715
6.	Charley Pride	4681
7.	George Jones	4656
8.	Tammy Wynette	4647
9.	Waylon Jennings	4219
10.	Sonny James	4144
11.	Johnny Cash	4137
12.	Charlie Rich	4008
13.	Willie Nelson	3926
14.	Lynn Anderson	3899
15.	Tom T. Hall	3797
16.	Joe Stampley	3679
17.	Billy "Crash" Craddock	3524
18.	Hank Williams, Jr.	3470
19.	Freddie Hart	3457
20.	Jerry Lee Lewis	3449

THE EIGHTIES

		Points			Points
1.	Willie Nelson	5345	11.	Reba McEntire	3907
2.	Merle Haggard	4795	12.	Dolly Parton	3870
3.	Conway Twitty	4625	13.	Earl Thomas Conley	3836
4.	Kenny Rogers	4396	14.	George Jones	3685
5.	Alabama	4377	15.	George Strait	3626
6.	Ronnie Milsap	4309	16.	The Bellamy Brothers	3581
7.	Hank Williams, Jr.	4177	17.	Don Williams	3459
8.	Waylon Jennings	4014	18.	T.G. Sheppard	3455
9.	The Oak Ridge Boys	3973	19.	Emmylou Harris	3396
10.	Crystal Gayle	3909	20.	Janie Frickie	3386

TOP ARTIST ACHIEVEMENTS

MOST CHARTED SINGLES

1. 145 **Eddy Arnold**
2. 144 **George Jones**
3. 131 **Johnny Cash**
4. 108 **Ray Price**
5. 103 **Willie Nelson**
6. 98 **Merle Haggard**
7. 97 **Webb Pierce**
8. 94 **Marty Robbins**
9. 93 **Carl Smith**
10. 91 **Ernest Tubb**
11. 88 **Faron Young**
12. 87 **Waylon Jennings**
13. 87 **Conway Twitty**
14. 86 **Buck Owens**
15. 85 **Dolly Parton**
16. 85 **Hank Snow**
17. 84 **Elvis Presley**
18. 84 **Hank Williams, Jr.**
19. 82 **Don Gibson**
20. 81 **Porter Wagoner**
21. 81 **Kitty Wells**
22. 80 **Jim Reeves**

MOST #1 HITS

1. 40 **Conway Twitty**
2. 38 **Merle Haggard**
3. 34 **Ronnie Milsap**
4. 29 **Charley Pride**
5. 28 **Eddy Arnold**
6. 24 **Alabama**
7. 23 **Sonny James**
8. 21 **Buck Owens**
9. 21 **Dolly Parton**
10. 20 **Kenny Rogers**
11. 20 **Tammy Wynette**
12. 19 **Willie Nelson**
13. 18 **Crystal Gayle**
14. 17 **Earl Thomas Conley**
15. 17 **Mickey Gilley**
16. 17 **Don Williams**
17. 16 **Waylon Jennings**
18. 16 **Loretta Lynn**
19. 16 **The Oak Ridge Boys**
20. 16 **Eddie Rabbitt**
21. 16 **Marty Robbins**
22. 15 **George Strait**

MOST CONSECUTIVE #1 HITS

1. 21 **Alabama** 1980-87
2. 16 **Earl Thomas Conley** 1983-89*
3. 16 **Sonny James** 1967-71
4. 15 **Buck Owens** 1963-67
5. 13 **Charley Pride** 1969-73
6. 11 **Conway Twitty** 1974-77
7. 11 **Ronnie Milsap** 1980-83
8. 9 **George Strait** 1986-89*
9. 9 **Dan Seals** 1985-89*
10. 9 **Merle Haggard** 1973-76
11. 9 **Webb Pierce** 1953-56

* =streak intact as of 5/1/89
Recordings with duos, reissues, flip sides and special
releases such as Christmas records do not interfere with a
#1 streak, unless such recordings hit #1.

MOST CROSSOVER HITS

1. 59 **Elvis Presley**
2. 50 **Johnny Cash**
3. 38 **Eddy Arnold**
4. 36 **Glen Campbell**
5. 33 **Kenny Rogers**
6. 31 **Marty Robbins**
7. 29 **Jim Reeves**
8. 28 **Anne Murray**
9. 22 **Dolly Parton**
10. 21 **John Denver**
11. 21 **Sonny James**
12. 19 **Roger Miller**
13. 19 **Buck Owens**
14. 16 **Mac Davis**
15. 16 **Willie Nelson**
16. 16 **Charley Pride**
17. 16 **Tammy Wynette**
18. 15 **Don Gibson**
19. 15 **Waylon Jennings**
20. 15 **Jerry Lee Lewis**
21. 15 **Ronnie Milsap**
22. 15 **Olivia Newton-John**

Country hits which also made Billboard's Pop Charts.

MOST WEEKS AT #1 POSITION

1. 145 **Eddy Arnold**
2. 111 **Webb Pierce**
3. 82 **Buck Owens**
4. 82 **Hank Williams**
5. 69 **Johnny Cash**
6. 66 **Sonny James**
7. 63 **Marty Robbins**
8. 58 **Jim Reeves**
9. 57 **Merle Haggard**
10. 56 **Hank Snow**
11. 52 **Conway Twitty**
12. 49 **Charley Pride**
13. 47 **Al Dexter**
14. 47 **Ray Price**
15. 45 **Ronnie Milsap**
16. 40 **Red Foley**
17. 40 **Elvis Presley**
18. 37 **Tammy Wynette**
19. 36 **Lefty Frizzell**
20. 33 **Waylon Jennings**
21. 33 **Jimmy Wakely**
22. 32 **Carl Smith**

TOP DUOS

1. 21 **Porter Wagoner & Dolly Parton**
2. 14 **Loretta Lynn & Conway Twitty**
3. 13 **George Jones & Tammy Wynette**
4. 13 **Jim Ed Brown & Helen Cornelius**
5. 11 **David Frizzell & Shelly West**
6. 10 **Kitty Wells & Red Foley**

Duos with the most chart hits. Regular recording duos
such as The Bellamy Brothers and the Wilburn Brothers
are not included in this category.

MOST DUO PARTNERS

1. 20 **Willie Nelson**
2. 13 **George Jones**
3. 8 **Johnny Cash**
4. 8 **Emmylou Harris**
5. 7 **Merle Haggard**
6. 7 **Waylon Jennings**
7. 7 **Kenny Rogers**

Artists who recorded with the most partners.

TOP 40 #1 HITS

THE FORTIES ('44-'49)

YR	WEEKS				RANK	TITLE............ARTIST
	CH	40	10	#1		
47	46	46	41	21	1	I'll Hold You In My Heart (Till I Can Hold You In My Arms) ....Eddy Arnold
48	54	54	53	19	2	Bouquet Of Roses ....Eddy Arnold
49	28	28	27	17	3	Slipping Around ....Margaret Whiting & Jimmy Wakely
49	42	42	40	16	4	Lovesick Blues ....Hank Williams
46	29	29	29	16	5	Guitar Polka ....Al Dexter
47	23	23	23	16	6	Smoke! Smoke! Smoke! (That Cigarette) ......Tex Williams
46	23	23	23	16	7	New Spanish Two Step ....Bob Wills & His Texas Playboys
46	23	23	23	14	8	Divorce Me C.O.D. ....Merle Travis
47	22	22	22	14	9	So Round, So Firm, So Fully Packed ....Merle Travis
44	30	30	30	13	10	So Long, Pal ....Al Dexter
44	27	27	27	13	11	Smoke On The Water.........................Red Foley
49	31	31	26	12	12	Don't Rob Another Man's Castle ....Eddy Arnold
48	32	32	31	11	13	One Has My Name (The Other Has My Heart) ...Jimmy Wakely
45	20	20	20	11	14	You Two-Timed Me One Time Too Often ....Tex Ritter
48	39	39	37	9	15	Anytime ....Eddy Arnold
45	31	31	31	9	16	Shame On You ....Spade Cooley
48	32	32	27	8	17	Just A Little Lovin' (Will Go A Long, Long Way) ...Eddy Arnold
45	22	22	22	8	18	At Mail Call Today ....Gene Autry
45	21	21	21	7	19	I'm Losing My Mind Over You ....Al Dexter
44	20	20	20	6	20	I'm Wastin' My Tears On You ....Tex Ritter
45	19	19	19	6	21	Oklahoma Hills ....Jack Guthrie
44	15	15	15	6	22	Straighten Up And Fly Right ....The King Cole Trio
47	38	38	38	5	23	It's A Sin ....Eddy Arnold
49	28	28	26	5	24	I Love You So Much It Hurts ....Jimmy Wakely
46	13	13	13	5	25	Wine, Women And Song.......................Al Dexter
44	11	11	11	5	26	Pistol Packin' Mama ....Bing Crosby & Andrews Sisters
44	9	9	9	5	27	Is You Is Or Is You Ain't (Ma' Baby) ....Louis Jordan
44	29	29	29	4	28	Soldier's Last Letter ....Ernest Tubb
45	23	23	23	4	29	Sioux City Sue ....Dick Thomas
49	22	22	21	4	30	I'm Throwing Rice (At The Girl I Love) ....Eddy Arnold
45	14	14	14	4	31	With Tears In My Eyes ....Wesley Tuttle
45	13	13	13	4	32	It's Been So Long, Darling ....Ernest Tubb
49	10	10	9	4	33	Mule Train.........................Tennessee Ernie Ford
48	26	26	23	3	34	Texarkana Baby ....Eddy Arnold
49	23	23	19	3	35	Candy Kisses ....George Morgan
49	22	22	18	3	36	Why Don't You Haul Off And Love Me ....Wayne Raney
49	22	22	15	3	37	One Kiss Too Many ....Eddy Arnold
45	14	14	14	3	38	Silver Dew On The Blue Grass Tonight ....Bob Wills & His Texas Playboys
44	13	13	13	3	39	Ration Blues ....Louis Jordan
44	10	10	10	3	40	Pistol Packin' Mama ....Al Dexter

All of the above are #1 hits. The ranking is based on weeks at #1.

YR: Year record reached its peak position
WEEKS: #1 - Total weeks record held #1 position
10 — Total weeks charted in the Top 10
40 — Total weeks charted in the Top 40
CH — Total weeks charted

TOP 40 #1 HITS

THE FIFTIES

YR	WEEKS				RANK	TITLE.............ARTIST
	CH	40	10	#1		
50	44	44	44	21	1	I'm Moving On . . . . Hank Snow
55	37	37	34	21	2	In The Jailhouse Now . . . . Webb Pierce
56	45	45	41	20	3	Crazy Arms . . . . Ray Price
54	41	41	40	20	4	I Don't Hurt Anymore . . . . Hank Snow
54	36	36	32	17	5	Slowly . . . . Webb Pierce
56	27	27	26	17	6	Heartbreak Hotel . . . . Elvis Presley
51	31	31	31	15	7	Slow Poke . . . . Pee Wee King
52	30	30	30	15	8	The Wild Side Of Life . . . . Hank Thompson
52	29	29	29	14	9	Jambalaya (On The Bayou) . . . . Hank Williams
51	25	25	25	14	10	The Shot Gun Boogie . . . . Tennessee Ernie Ford
55	32	32	28	13	11	Love, Love, Love . . . . Webb Pierce
56	30	30	28	13	12	Singing The Blues . . . . Marty Robbins
58	34	34	25	13	13	City Lights . . . . Ray Price
58	29	29	20	13	14	Alone With You . . . . Faron Young
50	20	20	20	13	15	Chattanoogie Shoe Shine Boy . . . . Red Foley
53	19	19	19	13	16	Kaw-Liga . . . . Hank Williams
55	32	32	28	12	17	I Don't Care . . . . Webb Pierce
51	28	28	28	12	18	Always Late (With Your Kisses) . . . . Lefty Frizzell
53	27	27	27	12	19	There Stands The Glass . . . . Webb Pierce
51	27	27	27	11	20	I Want To Be With You Always . . . . Lefty Frizzell
51	24	24	24	11	21	I Wanna Play House With You . . . . Eddy Arnold
51	23	23	23	11	22	There's Been A Change In Me . . . . Eddy Arnold
54	29	29	27	10	23	More And More . . . . Webb Pierce
50	25	25	25	10	24	Why Don't You Love Me . . . . Hank Williams
57	27	27	21	10	25	Gone . . . . Ferlin Husky
58	23	23	19	10	26	Ballad Of A Teenage Queen . . . . Johnny Cash
55	21	21	18	10	27	Sixteen Tons . . . . Tennessee Ernie Ford
59	21	21	18	10	28	The Battle Of New Orleans . . . . Johnny Horton
59	19	19	17	10	29	The Three Bells . . . . The Browns
53	26	26	26	9	30	Mexican Joe . . . . Jim Reeves
57	24	24	20	9	31	Young Love . . . . Sonny James
52	33	33	33	8	32	Let Old Mother Nature Have Her Way . . . . Carl Smith
51	27	27	27	8	33	Rhumba Boogie . . . . Hank Snow
58	34	34	26	8	34	Oh Lonesome Me . . . . Don Gibson
53	26	26	26	8	35	I Forgot More Than You'll Ever Know . . . . The Davis Sisters
53	26	26	26	8	36	Hey, Joe . . . . Carl Smith
57	26	26	25	8	37	Four Walls . . . . Jim Reeves
51	25	25	25	8	38	Hey, Good Lookin' . . . . Hank Williams
52	24	24	24	8	39	(When You Feel Like You're In Love) Don't Just Stand There . . . . Carl Smith
53	22	22	22	8	40	It's Been So Long . . . . Webb Pierce

TOP 40 #1 HITS
THE SIXTIES

YR	WEEKS CH	WEEKS 40	WEEKS 10	WEEKS #1	RANK	TITLE............ARTIST
61	37	37	30	19	1	Walk On By . . . . Leroy Van Dyke
63	30	30	24	16	2	Love's Gonna Live Here . . . . Buck Owens
60	36	36	30	14	3	Please Help Me, I'm Falling . . . . Hank Locklin
60	34	34	29	14	4	He'll Have To Go . . . . Jim Reeves
60	34	34	26	12	5	Alabam . . . . Cowboy Copas
62	24	24	22	11	6	Don't Let Me Cross Over . . . . Carl Butler & Pearl
60	36	36	30	10	7	Wings Of A Dove . . . . Ferlin Husky
61	19	19	18	10	8	Don't Worry . . . . Marty Robbins
62	26	26	21	9	9	Wolverton Mountain . . . . Claude King
61	23	23	18	9	10	Hello Walls . . . . Faron Young
66	25	24	13	9	11	Almost Persuaded . . . . David Houston
64	28	27	19	8	12	Once A Day . . . . Connie Smith
62	21	21	14	8	13	Devil Woman . . . . Marty Robbins
61	32	32	24	7	14	Tender Years . . . . George Jones
64	26	26	22	7	15	My Heart Skips A Beat . . . . Buck Owens
62	27	27	20	7	16	Mama Sang A Song . . . . Bill Anderson
63	27	27	20	7	17	Still . . . . Bill Anderson
63	26	26	19	7	18	Ring Of Fire . . . . Johnny Cash
64	26	24	18	7	19	I Guess I'm Crazy . . . . Jim Reeves
66	23	21	15	7	20	There Goes My Everything . . . . Jack Greene
66	19	18	13	7	21	Waitin' In Your Welfare Line . . . . . Buck Owens & The Buckaroos
62	23	23	19	6	22	She Thinks I Still Care . . . . George Jones
64	27	27	18	6	23	I Don't Care (Just as Long as You Love Me) . . . . Buck Owens
64	22	22	17	6	24	Understand Your Man . . . . Johnny Cash
64	25	22	15	6	25	Dang Me . . . . Roger Miller
66	22	21	14	6	26	Giddyup Go . . . . Red Sovine
65	20	20	14	6	27	Before You Go . . . . Buck Owens
66	21	20	13	6	28	Think Of Me . . . . Buck Owens & The Buckaroos
66	19	17	12	6	29	I Want To Go With You . . . . Eddy Arnold
69	20	19	11	6	30	Daddy Sang Bass . . . . Johnny Cash
61	22	22	17	5	31	North To Alaska . . . . Johnny Horton
62	19	19	15	5	32	She's Got You . . . . Patsy Cline
67	20	17	13	5	33	All The Time . . . . Jack Greene
65	20	20	12	5	34	King Of The Road . . . . Roger Miller
65	20	19	12	5	35	I've Got A Tiger By The Tail . . . . Buck Owens
68	19	16	11	5	36	Skip A Rope . . . . Henson Cargill
67	18	14	10	5	37	It's The Little Things . . . . Sonny James
69	14	12	8	5	38	A Boy Named Sue . . . . Johnny Cash
63	28	28	19	4	39	Act Naturally . . . . Buck Owens
63	24	24	19	4	40	Abilene . . . . George Hamilton IV

TOP 40 #1 HITS
THE SEVENTIES

YR	WEEKS				RANK	TITLE............ARTIST
	CH	40	10	#1		
72	19	18	12	6	1	My Hang-Up Is You . . . . .Freddie Hart
77	18	14	10	6	2	Luckenbach, Texas (Back to the Basics of Love)
						. . . . Waylon Jennings
75	15	13	8	6	3	Convoy . . . . .C.W. McCall
71	19	18	13	5	4	Kiss An Angel Good Mornin' . . . . .Charley Pride
70	20	19	12	5	5	Rose Garden . . . . .Lynn Anderson
77	19	14	10	5	6	Here You Come Again . . . . .Dolly Parton
71	15	13	10	5	7	When You're Hot, You're Hot . . . . .Jerry Reed
70	20	18	10	4	8	Hello Darlin' . . . . .Conway Twitty
70	17	16	10	4	9	Baby, Baby (I Know You're A Lady) . . . . .David Houston
71	16	15	10	4	10	Empty Arms . . . . .Sonny James
71	16	14	9	4	11	I'm Just Me . . . . .Charley Pride
70	15	14	9	4	12	Don't Keep Me Hangin' On . . . . .Sonny James
77	18	15	8	4	13	Don't It Make My Brown Eyes Blue . . . . .Crystal Gayle
78	16	12	8	4	14	Mammas Don't Let Your Babies Grow Up To Be Cowboys
						. . . . . . Waylon & Willie
73	17	14	7	4	15	If We Make It Through December . . . . .Merle Haggard
77	20	13	7	4	16	Heaven's Just A Sin Away . . . . .The Kendalls
70	14	13	7	4	17	It's Just A Matter Of Time . . . . .Sonny James
71	24	22	13	3	18	Easy Loving . . . . .Freddie Hart
71	20	18	12	3	19	Help Me Make It Through The Night . . . . .Sammi Smith
71	19	17	12	3	20	I Won't Mention It Again .Ray Price
72	23	17	10	3	21	The Happiest Girl In The Whole U.S.A. . . . . .Donna Fargo
73	19	16	10	3	22	You've Never Been This Far Before . . . . .Conway Twitty
72	16	15	10	3	23	Carolyn . . . . .Merle Haggard
70	16	14	9	3	24	Endlessly . . . . .Sonny James
72	16	14	9	3	25	It's Gonna Take A Little Bit Longer . . . . .Charley Pride
70	16	14	9	3	26	He Loves Me All The Way . . . . .Tammy Wynette
72	15	14	9	3	27	Chantilly Lace . . . . .Jerry Lee Lewis
70	14	14	9	3	28	The Fightin' Side Of Me . . . . .Merle Haggard
70	15	13	9	3	29	My Love . . . . .Sonny James
72	17	16	8	3	30	Got The All Overs For You (All Over Me) . . . . .Freddie Hart
73	18	15	8	3	31	Satin Sheets . . . . .Jeanne Pruett
75	21	14	8	3	32	Rhinestone Cowboy . . . . .Glen Campbell
71	16	14	8	3	33	How Can I Unlove You . . . . .Lynn Anderson
72	16	14	8	3	34	Funny Face . . . . .Donna Fargo
72	16	14	8	3	35	She's Too Good To Be True . . . . .Charley Pride
71	14	13	8	3	36	I'd Rather Love You . . . . .Charley Pride
79	15	12	8	3	37	Every Which Way But Loose . . . . .Eddie Rabbitt
79	14	11	8	3	38	Amanda . . . . .Waylon Jennings
73	18	14	7	3	39	The Most Beautiful Girl. . . . . .Charlie Rich
76	17	13	7	3	40	Good Hearted Woman . . . . .Waylon & Willie

TOP 40 #1 HITS
THE EIGHTIES ('80-'88)

YR	WEEKS			RANK	TITLE............ARTIST
	CH	40	10	#1	

YR	CH	40	10	#1	RANK	TITLE............ARTIST
80	15	13	7	3	1	My Heart . . . . Ronnie Milsap
80	14	10	7	3	2	Lookin' For Love . . . . Johnny Lee
80	15	8	7	3	3	Coward Of The County . . . . Kenny Rogers
87	22	13	6	3	4	Forever And Ever, Amen . . . . Randy Travis
85	22	14	8	2	5	Have Mercy . . . . The Judds
83	23	15	7	2	6	Islands In The Stream . . . . Kenny Rogers & Dolly Parton
83	22	15	7	2	7	Houston (Means I'm One Day Closer To You)
						. . . . . . Larry Gatlin/Gatlin Brothers
85	23	14	7	2	8	Lost In The Fifties Tonight (In the Still of the Night)
						. . . . Ronnie Milsap
84	22	14	7	2	9	Why Not Me . . . . The Judds
86	19	14	7	2	10	Mind Your Own Business . . . . Hank Williams, Jr.
84	20	13	7	2	11	To All The Girls I've Loved Before . . Julio Iglesias & Willie Nelson
80	16	11	7	2	12	I Believe In You . . . . Don Williams
80	14	10	7	2	13	My Heroes Have Always Been Cowboys . . . . Willie Nelson
82	21	15	6	2	14	Always On My Mind . . . . Willie Nelson
87	23	14	6	2	15	Somewhere Tonight . . . . Highway 101
88	20	14	6	2	16	Eighteen Wheels And A Dozen Roses . . . . Kathy Mattea
80	16	13	6	2	17	One In A Million . . . . Johnny Lee
81	16	11	6	2	18	Love In The First Degree . . . . Alabama
81	15	11	6	2	19	(There's) No Gettin' Over Me . . . . Ronnie Milsap
81	15	11	6	2	20	Never Been So Loved (In All My Life) . . . . Charley Pride
81	15	10	6	2	21	I Don't Need You . . . . Kenny Rogers
81	13	9	6	2	22	Feels So Right . . . . Alabama
88	18	12	5	2	23	I Told You So . . . . Randy Travis
82	17	12	5	2	24	She Got The Goldmine (I Got The Shaft) . . . . Jerry Reed
82	20	11	5	2	25	Wild And Blue . . . . John Anderson
82	16	10	5	2	26	Slow Hand . . . . Conway Twitty
82	18	12	4	2	27	Just To Satisfy You . . . . Waylon & Willie
80	15	11	4	2	28	I'll Be Coming Back For More . . . . T.G. Sheppard
87	20	16	8	1	29	Cry Myself To Sleep . . . . The Judds
83	21	14	8	1	30	Black Sheep . . . . John Anderson
82	20	14	8	1	31	Lord, I Hope This Day Is Good . . . . Don Williams
84	22	13	8	1	32	Nobody Loves Me Like You Do . . Anne Murray with Dave Loggins
82	19	13	8	1	33	Big City . . . . Merle Haggard
81	16	13	8	1	34	Party Time . . . . T.G. Sheppard
87	25	16	7	1	35	Do Ya' . . . . K.T. Oslin
86	24	16	7	1	36	Never Be You . . . . Rosanne Cash
88	23	16	7	1	37	Don't Close Your Eyes . . . . Keith Whitley
87	22	16	7	1	38	You Still Move Me . . . . Dan Seals
85	20	16	7	1	39	Real Love . . . . Kenny Rogers & Dolly Parton
87	25	15	7	1	40	Somebody Lied . . . . Ricky Van Shelton

RECORDS OF LONGEVITY

Records with the most Total Weeks Charted

RANK	PEAK YEAR	WKS. CHT.	TITLE....ARTIST
1.	48	54	**Bouquet Of Roses** ....Eddy Arnold
2.	57	52	**Fraulein** ....Bobby Helms
3.	47	46	**I'll Hold You In My Heart** **(Till I Can Hold You In My Arms)**...Eddy Arnold
4.	51	46	**Cold, Cold Heart** ....Hank Williams
5.	61	46*	**I Fall To Pieces** ....Patsy Cline
6.	56	45	**Crazy Arms** ....Ray Price
7.	50	44	**I'm Moving On** ....Hank Snow
8.	56	43	**I Walk The Line** ....Johnny Cash
9.	49	42	**Lovesick Blues** ....Hank Williams
10.	54	41	**I Don't Hurt Anymore**...............Hank Snow
11.	54	41	**One By One** ....Kitty Wells & Red Foley
12.	49	40	**Tennessee Saturday Night** ....Red Foley
13.	59	40	**Heartaches By The Number** ....Ray Price
14.	48	39	**Anytime** ....Eddy Arnold
15.	55	39	**I Forgot To Remember To Forget** ....Elvis Presley
16.	57	39	**Geisha Girl** ....Hank Locklin
17.	48	39*	**Tennessee Waltz** ....Pee Wee King
18.	47	38	**It's A Sin**.......................Eddy Arnold
19.	48	38	**Humpty Dumpty Heart** ....Hank Thompson
20.	55	37	**In The Jailhouse Now** ....Webb Pierce
21.	61	37	**Walk On By**....................Leroy Van Dyke
22.	57	37	**My Shoes Keep Walking Back To You** ...Ray Price
23.	54	37	**I Really Don't Want To Know** ....Eddy Arnold
24.	54	36	**Slowly** ....Webb Pierce
25.	60	36	**Please Help Me, I'm Falling**.........Hank Locklin
26.	60	36	**Wings Of A Dove** ....Ferlin Husky
27.	50	36	**I'll Sail My Ship Alone** ....Moon Mullican
28.	63	36	**Talk Back Trembling Lips** ....Ernest Ashworth
29.	58	36	**Is It Wrong (For Loving You)**........Warner Mack
30.	58	35	**Send Me The Pillow You Dream On** ..Hank Locklin

*Records which charted more than once.

TOP COUNTRY LABELS

Record Labels with the Most Charted Country Hits

RANK	CHART HITS	LABEL
1.	1935	**RCA Victor**
2.	1365	**Columbia**
3.	1210	**Capitol**
4.	769	**Decca**
5.	758	**MCA**
6.	697	**Epic**
7.	611	**Mercury**
8.	592	**Warner Bros.**
9.	320	**Dot**
10.	319	**United Artists**
11.	276	**MGM**
12.	233	**Elektra**
13.	140	**Hickory**
14.	131	**Monument**
15.	127	**ABC**
16.	111	**Liberty**
17.	93	**Curb**
18.	84	**Soundwaves**
19.	81	**Door Knob**
20.	81	**Starday**
21.	71	**Sun**
22.	64	**Chart**
23.	56	**King**
24.	53	**Imperial**
25.	52	**MTM**
26.	49	**GRT**
27.	48	**Ovation**
28.	48	**Polydor**
29.	48	**Republic**
30.	47	**Kapp**
31.	46	**Playboy**
32.	45	**EMI America**
33.	44	**Mega**
34.	43	**Churchill**
35.	42	**NSD**
36.	38	**Atlantic America**
37.	37	**Plantation**
38.	36	**Con Brio**
39.	36	**Evergreen**
40.	35	**Okeh**

LABEL ABBREVIATIONS

1st Genrtn. . . . . 1st Generation
ABC/Hick. . . . . ABC/Hickory
ABC-Para. . . . . ABC-Paramount
Ace of H. . . . . Ace of Hearts
Air Int'l. . . . . Air International
Amer. S. . . . . American Smash
Am. Spotlite . . . . . American Spotlite
Ariola Am. . . . . Ariola America
Art. Of Am. . . . . . . Artists Of America
Atln. Am. . . . . Atlantic America
Bakers. I. . . . Bakersfield International
Bermuda D. . . . . . . Bermuda Dunes
Canyon Cr. . . . . Canyon Creek
Capitol A. . . . . . . Capitol Americana
Casabl. . . . . Casablanca
Casabl. W. . . . . Casablanca West
Cascade Mt. . . . . . Cascade Mountain
Cleve. Int. . . . Cleveland International
Commercl. . . . . Commercial
Copper Mt. . . . . . . Copper Mountain
Country B. . . . . Country Bach
Country I. . . . . Country International
Country Jub. . . . . . Country Jubilee
Country P. . . . . Country Pride
C'ntry Show.
. . . . Country Showcase America
Contrysd. . . . . Countryside
Countrystk. . . . . Countrystock
Creole G. . . . . Creole Gold
Dallas S. . . . . Dallas Star
EMI Amer. . . . . EMI America
EMI Man. . . . . EMI Manhattan
Eagle Int. . . . . Eagle International
Fly. Fish . . . . Flying Fish
Fountain H. . . . . Fountain Hills
Gld. Trump. . . . . . . Golden Trumpet
Grape Vn. . . . . Grape Vine
Great Amer. . . . . . . Great American
Grind. Sw. . . . . Grinder's Switch
Gusto/Star. . . . . Gusto/Starday
Hidden Val. . . . . Hidden Valley
Jack O'Dia. . . . . . Jack O'Diamonds
Jolly Rog. . . . . Jolly Rogers

Jungle Rg. . . . . Jungle Rogue
Kat Fam. . . . . Kat Family
Little Dar. . . . . Little Darlin'
Louis. Hay. . . . . . . Louisiana Hayride
Macy's Rec. . . . . . Macy's Recordings
Main St. . . . . Main Street
Melody D. . . . . Melody Dawn
Memory M. . . . . . . Memory Machine
Metro. Cnt. . . . . Metromedia Country
Midnight G. . . . . Midnight Gold
Modern Mt. . . . . . . Modern Mountain
Moon Pic. . . . . Moon Pictures
Music Amer. . . . . Music America
Music Mas. . . . . Music Master
Nash. Am. . . . . Nashville America
Pacific C. . . . . Pacific Challenger
Pan. Des. . . . . Pantheon Desert
Prairie D. . . . . Prairie Dust
Private S. . . . . Private Stock
RAM/Sound. . . . . . RAM/Soundwaves
Rain F. . . . . Rain Forest
Rainbow S. . . . . Rainbow Sound
Rec. Prod.
. . . . . Record Production Of America
Royal Amer. . . . . Royal American
Scotti Br. . . . . Scotti Brothers
Silver D. . . . . Silver Dollar
Snd. Factory . . . . Sound Factory
Snds. Of Am. . . . . Sounds Of America
So. Tracks . . . . Southern Tracks
Songs of F. . . . . Songs Of Faith
Soul, C.&B. . . . Soul, Country & Blues
Southern S. . . . . Southern Sound
USA Cnt. . . . . USA Country
Union Sta. . . . . Union Station
United Art. . . . . United Artists
Waterhs. . . . . Waterhouse
Western Pac. . . . . . . Western Pacific
Western Pr. . . . . Western Pride
Whiskey R. . . . . Whiskey River
White G. . . . . White Gold
World Pac. . . . . World Pacific

From January 8, 1944 through December 31, 1988, 1073 records have hit the #1 position on Billboard's Country charts.

For the years 1948 through 1958, when Billboard published more than one weekly Country chart, special columns are used to list the total weeks each record spent at #1 on each of these Country charts.

The date shown is the earliest date that a record hit #1 on any of the Country charts. The weeks column lists the total weeks at #1, from whichever chart it achieved its highest total. This total is not a combined total from the various Country charts.

Because of the multiple charts used in this research, some dates are duplicated, as certain #1 hits may have peaked on the same week on different charts. Billboard also showed ties at #1 on some of these charts, therefore the total weeks for each year may calculate out to more than 52.

Beginning in 1976, Billboard ceased publishing a year-end issue. The year's last regular issue is considered frozen and all chart positions remain the same for the unpublished week. This frozen chart data is included in our tabulations.

See the introduction pages of this book for more details on researching the Country charts.

DATE: Date record first peaked at the #1 position.
WKS: Total weeks record held the #1 position.
★: #1 record of the year (most weeks at #1 position).
*: Indicates record hit #1, dropped down, then returned to the #1 spot.

CHARTS COLUMN:

BS — Best Sellers
JB — Juke Box
JY — Jockeys

DATE	WKS	RECORD TITLE . . . . . . ARTIST			
		1944			
1/08	5*	1. Pistol Packin' Mama . . . . Bing Crosby & Andrews Sisters			
2/05	3	2. Pistol Packin' Mama . . . . Al Dexter			
2/26	3*	3. Ration Blues . . . . Louis Jordan			
3/11	1	4. Rosalita . . . . Al Dexter			
3/18	1	5. They Took The Stars Out Of Heaven . . . . Floyd Tillman			
3/25	13*	★ 6. So Long, Pal . . . . Al Dexter			
4/01	2*	7. Too Late To Worry, Too Blue To Cry . . . . Al Dexter			
6/10	6*	8. Straighten Up And Fly Right . . . . The King Cole Trio			
7/29	5	9. Is You Is Or Is You Ain't (Ma' Baby) . . . . Louis Jordan			
9/02	4	10. Soldier's Last Letter . . . . Ernest Tubb			
9/23	13	★11. Smoke On The Water . . . . Red Foley			
12/23	6	12. I'm Wastin' My Tears On You . . . . Tex Ritter			
		1945			
2/03	7*	1. I'm Losing My Mind Over You . . . . Al Dexter			
3/17	1	2. There's A New Moon Over My Shoulder . . . . Jimmie Davis			
3/31	9*	3. Shame On You . . . . Spade Cooley			
4/14	2*	4. Smoke On The Water . . . . Bob Wills & His Texas Playboys			
5/19	8*	5. At Mail Call Today . . . . Gene Autry			
7/07	1	6. Stars And Stripes On Iwo Jima . . . . Bob Wills & His Texas Playboys			
7/28	6*	7. Oklahoma Hills . . . . Jack Guthrie			
8/25	11*	★ 8. You Two-Timed Me One Time Too Often . . . . Tex Ritter			
10/27	4*	9. With Tears In My Eyes . . . . Wesley Tuttle			
11/24	4*	10. Sioux City Sue . . . . Dick Thomas			
11/24	1	11. Shame On You . . . . Lawrence Welk with Red Foley			
12/08	4*	12. It's Been So Long, Darling . . . . Ernest Tubb			
12/15	3*	13. Silver Dew On The Blue Grass Tonight . . . . . . Bob Wills & His Texas Playboys			
		1946			
1/05	3*	1. You Will Have To Pay . . . . Tex Ritter			
1/05	1	2. White Cross On Okinawa . . . . Bob Wills & His Texas Playboys			
2/02	16*	★ 3. Guitar Polka . . . . Al Dexter			
5/18	16*	★ 4. New Spanish Two Step . . . . Bob Wills & His Texas Playboys			
9/14	5*	5. Wine, Women And Song . . . . Al Dexter			
10/12	14*	6. Divorce Me C.O.D. . . . . Merle Travis			
		1947			
1/18	2*	1. Rainbow At Midnight . . . . Ernest Tubb			
2/08	14	2. So Round, So Firm, So Fully Packed . . . . Merle Travis			
5/17	2*	3. New Jole Blonde . . . . Red Foley			
5/24	1	4. What Is Life Without Love? . . . . Eddy Arnold			
6/07	1	5. Sugar Moon . . . . Bob Wills & His Texas Playboys			
6/14	5	6. It's A Sin . . . . Eddy Arnold			
7/19	16	7. Smoke! Smoke! Smoke! (That Cigarette) . . . . Tex Williams			
11/01	21*	★ 8. I'll Hold You In My Heart (Till I Can Hold You In My Arms) . . . . . Eddy Arnold			

		1948	**CHARTS**		
			BS	JB	JY
4/03	9	1. Anytime . . . . Eddy Arnold	3	9	—
		Billboard debuts Country "Best Seller" chart on 5/15/48.			
6/05	19	★ 2. Bouquet Of Roses . . . . Eddy Arnold	19*	18*	—
6/05	3	3. Texarkana Baby . . . . Eddy Arnold	1	3*	—

DATE	WKS	RECORD TITLE......ARTIST	BS	JB	JY
		1948 *(Continued)*			
9/18	8	4. Just A Little Lovin' (Will Go A Long, Long Way) ....Eddy Arnold	4*	8*	—
11/13	11	5. One Has My Name (The Other Has My Heart) ....Jimmy Wakely	11*	7*	—
12/25	1	6. A Heart Full Of Love (For A Handful Of Kisses) ....Eddy Arnold	1	—	—
		1949			
1/22	5	1. I Love You So Much It Hurts ....Jimmy Wakely	4*	5*	—
3/05	12	2. Don't Rob Another Man's Castle ....Eddy Arnold	6*	12*	—
3/19	1	3. Tennessee Saturday Night.................Red Foley	—	1	—
4/02	3	4. Candy Kisses ....George Morgan	3*	—	—
5/07	16	5. Lovesick Blues ....Hank Williams	16*	10*	—
6/18	3	6. One Kiss Too Many ....Eddy Arnold	—	3*	—
7/30	4	7. I'm Throwing Rice (At The Girl I Love) .....Eddy Arnold	4	3*	—
9/10	3	8. Why Don't You Haul Off And Love Me .....Wayne Raney	2*	3*	—
9/24	1	9. Slippin' Around ....Ernest Tubb	—	1	—
10/08	17	★10. Slipping Around.....Margaret Whiting & Jimmy Wakely	17	12*	—
12/10	4	11. Mule Train...................Tennessee Ernie Ford	—	—	4

Billboard debuts Country "Jockey" chart on 12/10/50.

DATE	WKS	RECORD TITLE......ARTIST	BS	JB	JY
		1950			
1/07	1	1. Rudolph, The Red-Nosed Reindeer ....Gene Autry	—	—	1
1/07	1	2. Blue Christmas.....................Ernest Tubb	—	1	—
1/14	2	3. I Love You Because ....Leon Payne	—	—	2*
1/14	1	4. Blues Stay Away From Me ....Delmore Brothers	—	1	—
1/21	13	5. Chattanoogie Shoe Shine Boy ....Red Foley	12	13	13*
1/28	1	6. Take Me In Your Arms And Hold Me ....Eddy Arnold	—	1	—
4/22	8	7. Long Gone Lonesome Blues ....Hank Williams	5*	4*	8*
5/27	4	8. Birmingham Bounce ....Red Foley	4*	3*	—
6/17	10	9. Why Don't You Love Me ....Hank Williams	6*	5	10
6/17	4	10. I'll Sail My Ship Alone ....Moon Mullican	1	4	—
7/15	1	11. M-I-S-S-I-S-S-I-P-P-I ....Red Foley	—	1	—
8/19	21	★12. I'm Moving On ....Hank Snow	21*	14	18*
8/26	3	13. Goodnight, Irene ....Ernest Tubb & Red Foley	2	3	—
12/23	3	14. If You've Got The Money I've Got The Time .Lefty Frizzell	—	3	—
12/30	1	15. Moanin' The Blues.................Hank Williams	—	—	1

DATE	WKS	RECORD TITLE......ARTIST	BS	JB	JY
		1951			
1/06	3	1. I Love You A Thousand Ways...........Lefty Frizzell	—	—	3*
1/06	2	2. The Golden Rocket ....Hank Snow	2	—	1
1/13	14	3. The Shot Gun Boogie ....Tennessee Ernie Ford	3*	14	1
2/10	11	4. There's Been A Change In Me ....Eddy Arnold	4*	—	11*
3/31	8	5. Rhumba Boogie ....Hank Snow	8*	5	2*
5/12	1	6. Cold, Cold Heart ....Hank Williams	—	—	1
5/19	3	7. Kentucky Waltz ....Eddy Arnold	3*	3	—
5/26	11	8. I Want To Be With You Always ....Lefty Frizzell	6*	5	11
7/14	11	9. I Wanna Play House With You ....Eddy Arnold	6*	11	—
8/11	8	10. Hey, Good Lookin' ....Hank Williams	—	—	8*
9/01	12	11. Always Late (With Your Kisses) ....Lefty Frizzell	12*	6	6*
11/03	15	★12. Slow Poke ....Pee Wee King	14	15*	9*
12/22	8	13. Let Old Mother Nature Have Her Way ....Carl Smith	6	8*	3*

DATE	WKS	RECORD TITLE . . . . . . ARTIST	CHARTS		
			BS	JB	JY
		1952			
2/02	3	1. Give Me More, More, More (Of Your Kisses) . Lefty Frizzell	—	3*	3*
3/01	4	2. Wondering . . . . Webb Pierce	—	—	4
3/29	8	3. (When You Feel Like You're In Love) Don't Just Stand There . . . . Carl Smith	5*	3*	8*
5/03	1	4. Easy On The Eyes . . . . Eddy Arnold	1	—	—
5/10	15	★ 5. The Wild Side Of Life . . . . Hank Thompson	15	15	8*
7/12	3	6. That Heart Belongs To Me . . . . Webb Pierce	—	—	3*
7/19	1	7. Are You Teasing Me . . . . Carl Smith	—	—	1
8/09	6	8. It Wasn't God Who Made Honky Tonk Angels . Kitty Wells	6	5	—
8/16	4	9. A Full Time Job . . . . Eddy Arnold	—	—	4*
9/06	14	10. Jambalaya (On The Bayou) . . . . Hank Williams	14*	12*	14*
12/06	4	11. Back Street Affair . . . . Webb Pierce	2*	3	4*
12/06	1	12. Don't Let The Stars Get In Your Eyes . . . . Slim Willet	—	—	1
12/27	3	13. Don't Let The Stars Get In Your Eyes . . . Skeets McDonald	—	3	—
		1953			
1/10	1	1. Midnight . . . . Red Foley	1	—	—
1/24	2	2. I'll Go On Alone . . . . Marty Robbins	—	—	2*
1/24	1	3. I'll Never Get Out Of This World Alive . . . . Hank Williams	1	—	—
1/31	4	4. No Help Wanted . . . . The Carlisles	—	4	4*
1/31	3	5. Eddy's Song . . . . Eddy Arnold	3	—	—
2/07	3	6. I Let The Stars Get In My Eyes . . . . Goldie Hill	—	3	—
2/21	13	★ 7. Kaw-Liga . . . . Hank Williams	13	8*	8
3/07	6	8. Your Cheatin' Heart . . . . Hank Williams	—	2*	6*
5/09	9	9. Mexican Joe . . . . Jim Reeves	6*	9*	7*
6/06	4	10. Take These Chains From My Heart . . . . . . Hank Williams	4*	—	—
7/04	3	11. Rub-A-Dub-Dub . . . . Hank Thompson	—	3*	—
7/11	8	12. It's Been So Long . . . . Webb Pierce	6	1	8*
8/22	8	13. Hey, Joe . . . . Carl Smith	2*	8*	4*
8/29	6	14. A Dear John Letter . . . . . . Jean Shepard & Ferlin Huskey	6*	4*	—
10/17	8	15. I Forgot More Than You'll Ever Know . . . The Davis Sisters	6*	2*	8*
11/21	12	16. There Stands The Glass . . . . Webb Pierce	12*	9*	6*
12/12	2	17. Caribbean . . . . Mitchell Torok	—	2	—
12/19	3	18. Let Me Be The One . . . . Hank Locklin	—	2*	3*
		1954			
1/09	3	1. Bimbo . . . . Jim Reeves	—	—	3*
2/20	17	2. Slowly . . . . Webb Pierce	17	17*	15
2/20	2	3. Wake Up, Irene . . . . Hank Thompson	—	2	—
5/15	1	4. I Really Don't Want To Know . . . . Eddy Arnold	—	1	—
6/12	2	5. Oh, Baby Mine (I Get So Lonely) . . . . Johnnie & Jack	—	—	2
6/19	20	★ 6. I Don't Hurt Anymore . . . . Hank Snow	20	20*	18*
7/03	2	7. Even Tho . . . . Webb Pierce	—	—	2
7/31	1	8. One By One . . . . Kitty Wells & Red Foley	—	1	—
11/06	10	9. More And More . . . . Webb Pierce	9	10*	8*
		1955			
1/08	7	1. Loose Talk . . . . Carl Smith	7	4	6*
1/29	2	2. Let Me Go, Lover . . . . Hank Snow	—	—	2
2/26	21	★ 3. In The Jailhouse Now . . . . Webb Pierce	20	21	15
6/08	3	4. Live Fast, Love Hard, Die Young . . . . Faron Young	—	—	3
7/09	4	5. A Satisfied Mind . . . . Porter Wagoner	—	—	4

DATE	WKS	RECORD TITLE......ARTIST	CHARTS		
			BS	JB	JY
		1955 *(Continued)*			
7/16	12	6. I Don't Care .... Webb Pierce	12	12	12
10/08	2	7. The Cattle Call .... Eddy Arnold	2	—	—
10/22	13	8. Love, Love, Love .... Webb Pierce	8	9*	13*
10/22	2	9. That Do Make It Nice .... Eddy Arnold	—	2	—
12/17	10	10. Sixteen Tons .... Tennessee Ernie Ford	10	7*	3*
12/31	5	11. I Forgot To Remember To Forget .... Elvis Presley	2	5	—
		1956			
2/11	4	1. Why Baby Why .... Red Sovine & Webb Pierce	1	1	4*
3/17	17	2. Heartbreak Hotel .... Elvis Presley	17	13*	12
3/17	2	3. I Don't Believe You've Met My Baby . The Louvin Brothers	—	—	2
4/07	3	4. Blue Suede Shoes .... Carl Perkins	—	3	—
6/23	20	★ 5. Crazy Arms .... Ray Price	11*	1	20*
7/14	2	6. I Want You, I Need You, I Love You .... Elvis Presley	2	1	—
7/21	6	7. I Walk The Line .... Johnny Cash	—	6*	1
9/15	3	8. Hound Dog .... Elvis Presley	—	3*	—
9/29	7	9. Don't Be Cruel .... Elvis Presley	5	7*	—
11/10	13	10. Singing The Blues .... Marty Robbins	13	13	11*
		1957			
2/02	9	1. Young Love .... Sonny James	7	3*	9
3/02	5	2. There You Go .... Johnny Cash	—	5*	—
4/06	10	★ 3. Gone .... Ferlin Husky	10	5*	9
5/13	1	4. All Shook Up .... Elvis Presley	—	1	—
5/20	5	5. A White Sport Coat (And A Pink Carnation) ...... Marty Robbins	5	5	1
5/20	1	6. Honky Tonk Song .... Webb Pierce	—	—	1
5/27	8	7. Four Walls .... Jim Reeves	—	—	8
		Billboard terminates "Juke Box" chart on 6/24/57.			
7/15	7	8. Bye Bye Love .... The Everly Brothers	7*	—	7
8/05	1	9. (Let Me Be Your) Teddy Bear .... Elvis Presley	1	—	—
9/09	2	10. Whole Lot Of Shakin' Going On .... Jerry Lee Lewis	2	—	—
9/16	4	11. Fraulein .... Bobby Helms	3	—	4*
9/16	4	12. My Shoes Keep Walking Back To You .... Ray Price	—	—	4*
10/14	8	13. Wake Up Little Susie .... The Everly Brothers	7	—	8*
12/02	1	14. Jailhouse Rock .... Elvis Presley	1	—	—
12/09	4	15. My Special Angel .... Bobby Helms	4	—	1
		1958			
1/06	4	1. The Story Of My Life .... Marty Robbins	4	—	4
1/06	2	2. Great Balls Of Fire .... Jerry Lee Lewis	2	—	—
2/03	10	3. Ballad Of A Teenage Queen .... Johnny Cash	8	—	10
4/14	8	4. Oh Lonesome Me .... Don Gibson	8*	—	8*
5/26	2	5. Just Married .... Marty Robbins	—	—	2*
6/02	3	6. All I Have To Do Is Dream .... The Everly Brothers	3	—	1
6/23	8	7. Guess Things Happen That Way .... Johnny Cash	8	—	3*
7/21	13	★ 8. Alone With You .... Faron Young	—	—	13
8/25	2	9. Blue Blue Day .... Don Gibson	2	—	—
9/08	6	10. Bird Dog .... The Everly Brothers	6	—	—
		Billboard terminates the "Best Seller" and "Jockey" charts and debuts one all-encompassing Country chart on 10/20/58.			
10/20	13	★11. City Lights .... Ray Price			

DATE	WKS	RECORD TITLE . . . . . . ARTIST
		1959
1/19	5	1. Billy Bayou . . . . Jim Reeves
2/23	6	2. Don't Take Your Guns To Town . . . . Johnny Cash
4/06	1	3. When It's Springtime In Alaska (It's Forty Below) . . . . Johnny Horton
4/13	5	4. White Lightning . . . . George Jones
5/18	10	★ 5. The Battle Of New Orleans . . . . Johnny Horton
7/27	5	6. Waterloo . . . . Stonewall Jackson
8/31	10	★ 7. The Three Bells . . . . The Browns
11/09	4	8. Country Girl . . . . Faron Young
12/07	2	9. The Same Old Me . . . . Ray Price
12/21	7	10. El Paso . . . . Marty Robbins
		1960
2/08	14	★ 1. He'll Have To Go . . . . Jim Reeves
5/16	14	★ 2. Please Help Me, I'm Falling . . . . Hank Locklin
8/22	12	3. Alabam . . . . Cowboy Copas
11/14	10*	4. Wings Of A Dove . . . . Ferlin Husky
		1961
1/09	5	1. North To Alaska . . . . Johnny Horton
2/27	10	2. Don't Worry . . . . Marty Robbins
5/08	9	3. Hello Walls . . . . Faron Young
7/10	4	4. Heartbreak U.S.A. . . . . Kitty Wells
8/07	2	5. I Fall To Pieces . . . . Patsy Cline
8/21	7*	6. Tender Years . . . . George Jones
9/25	19*	★ 7. Walk On By . . . . Leroy Van Dyke
11/20	2	8. Big Bad John . . . . Jimmy Dean
		1962
3/10	2*	1. Misery Loves Company . . . . Porter Wagoner
3/17	1	2. That's My Pa . . . . Sheb Wooley
3/31	5*	3. She's Got You . . . . Patsy Cline
4/28	2*	4. Charlie's Shoes . . . . Billy Walker
5/19	6	5. She Thinks I Still Care . . . . George Jones
6/30	9	6. Wolverton Mountain . . . . Claude King
9/01	8	7. Devil Woman . . . . Marty Robbins
10/27	7*	8. Mama Sang A Song . . . . Bill Anderson
11/10	2*	9. I've Been Everywhere . . . . Hank Snow
12/29	11*	★10. Don't Let Me Cross Over . . . . Carl Butler & Pearl
		1963
1/05	1	1. Ruby Ann . . . . Marty Robbins
1/19	3*	2. The Ballad Of Jed Clampett . . . . Lester Flatt & Earl Scruggs
4/13	7*	3. Still . . . . Bill Anderson
5/04	4*	4. Lonesome 7-7203 . . . . Hawkshaw Hawkins
6/15	4*	5. Act Naturally . . . . Buck Owens
7/27	7	6. Ring Of Fire . . . . Johnny Cash
9/14	4	7. Abilene . . . . George Hamilton IV
10/12	1	8. Talk Back Trembling Lips . . . . Ernest Ashworth
10/19	16	★ 9. Love's Gonna Live Here . . . . Buck Owens

DATE	WKS	RECORD TITLE......ARTIST
		1964
2/08	3*	1. Begging To You .... Marty Robbins
2/15	1	2. B.J. The D.J. .... Stonewall Jackson
3/07	4	3. Saginaw, Michigan .... Lefty Frizzell
4/04	6	4. Understand Your Man .... Johnny Cash
5/16	7*	5. My Heart Skips A Beat .... Buck Owens
6/06	2	6. Together Again .... Buck Owens
7/18	6	7. Dang Me .... Roger Miller
8/29	7	8. I Guess I'm Crazy .... Jim Reeves
10/17	6	9. I Don't Care (Just as Long as You Love Me) .... Buck Owens
11/28	8	★10. Once A Day .... Connie Smith
		1965
1/23	4	1. You're The Only World I Know .... Sonny James
2/20	5	2. I've Got A Tiger By The Tail .... Buck Owens
3/27	5	3. King Of The Road .... Roger Miller
5/01	3*	4. This Is It .... Jim Reeves
5/15	2	5. Girl On The Billboard .... Del Reeves
6/05	2	6. What's He Doing In My World .... Eddy Arnold
6/19	1	7. Ribbon Of Darkness .... Marty Robbins
6/26	6	★ 8. Before You Go .... Buck Owens
8/07	2	9. The First Thing Ev'ry Morning (And The Last Thing Ev'ry Night)
		...... Jimmy Dean
8/21	2	10. Yes, Mr. Peters .... Roy Drusky & Priscilla Mitchell
9/04	1	11. The Bridge Washed Out .... Warner Mack
9/11	3	12. Is It Really Over? .... Jim Reeves
10/02	1	13. Only You (Can Break My Heart) .... Buck Owens
10/09	3*	14. Behind The Tear .... Sonny James
10/23	3	15. Hello Vietnam .... Johnny Wright
11/20	2	16. May The Bird Of Paradise Fly Up Your Nose .... "Little" Jimmy Dickens
12/04	3	17. Make The World Go Away .... Eddy Arnold
12/25	2	18. Buckaroo .... Buck Owens & The Buckaroos
		1966
1/08	6	1. Giddyup Go .... Red Sovine
2/19	7	2. Waitin' In Your Welfare Line .... Buck Owens
4/09	6	3. I Want To Go With You .... Eddy Arnold
5/21	4	4. Distant Drums .... Jim Reeves
6/18	2	5. Take Good Care Of Her .... Sonny James
7/02	6	6. Think Of Me .... Buck Owens
8/13	9	★ 7. Almost Persuaded .... David Houston
10/15	1	8. Blue Side Of Lonesome .... Jim Reeves
10/22	4	9. Open Up Your Heart .... Buck Owens
11/19	1	10. I Get The Fever .... Bill Anderson
11/26	4	11. Somebody Like Me .... Eddy Arnold
12/24	7	12. There Goes My Everything........................ Jack Greene
		1967
2/11	1	1. Don't Come Home A'Drinkin' (With Lovin' On Your Mind) ..... Loretta Lynn
2/18	4*	2. Where Does The Good Times Go .... Buck Owens
3/04	1	3. The Fugitive .... Merle Haggard
3/25	1	4. I Won't Come In While He's There .... Jim Reeves
4/01	2	5. Walk Through This World With Me .... George Jones

DATE	WKS	RECORD TITLE . . . . ARTIST
		1967 *(Continued)*
4/15	2	6. Lonely Again . . . . Eddy Arnold
4/29	2	7. Need You . . . . Sonny James
5/13	3	8. Sam's Place . . . . Buck Owens
6/03	2	9. It's Such A Pretty World Today . . . . Wynn Stewart
6/17	5	★10. All The Time . . . . Jack Greene
7/22	1	11. With One Exception . . . . David Houston
7/29	1	12. Tonight Carmen . . . . Marty Robbins
8/05	4	13. I'll Never Find Another You . . . . Sonny James
9/02	1	14. Branded Man . . . . Merle Haggard
9/09	1	15. Your Tender Loving Care . . . . Buck Owens
9/16	2	16. My Elusive Dreams . . . . David Houston & Tammy Wynette
9/30	1	17. Laura (What's He Got That I Ain't Got) . . . . Leon Ashley
10/07	1	18. Turn The World Around . . . . Eddy Arnold
10/14	3	19. I Don't Wanna Play House . . . . Tammy Wynette
11/04	2	20. You Mean The World To Me . . . . David Houston
11/18	5	★21. It's The Little Things . . . . Sonny James
12/23	4	22. For Loving You . . . . Bill Anderson & Jan Howard
		1968
1/20	2	1. Sing Me Back Home . . . . Merle Haggard
2/03	5	★ 2. Skip A Rope . . . . Henson Cargill
3/09	1	3. Take Me To Your World . . . . Tammy Wynette
3/16	3	4. A World Of Our Own . . . . Sonny James
4/06	1	5. How Long Will My Baby Be Gone . . . . Buck Owens
4/13	1	6. You Are My Treasure . . . . Jack Greene
4/20	1	7. Fist City . . . . Loretta Lynn
4/27	2	8. The Legend Of Bonnie And Clyde . . . . Merle Haggard
5/11	1	9. Have A Little Faith . . . . David Houston
5/18	3*	10. I Wanna Live . . . . Glen Campbell
5/25	3	11. Honey . . . . Bobby Goldsboro
6/29	3	12. D-I-V-O-R-C-E . . . . Tammy Wynette
7/20	4	13. Folsom Prison Blues . . . . Johnny Cash
8/17	1	14. Heaven Says Hello . . . . Sonny James
8/24	1	15. Already It's Heaven . . . . David Houston
8/31	4	16. Mama Tried . . . . Merle Haggard
9/28	3	17. Harper Valley P.T.A. . . . . Jeannie C. Riley
10/19	2	18. Then You Can Tell Me Goodbye . . . . Eddy Arnold
11/02	1	19. Next In Line . . . . Conway Twitty
11/09	2	20. I Walk Alone . . . . Marty Robbins
11/23	3	21. Stand By Your Man . . . . Tammy Wynette
12/14	1	22. Born To Be With You . . . . Sonny James
12/21	2	23. Wichita Lineman . . . . Glen Campbell
		1969
1/04	6	★ 1. Daddy Sang Bass . . . . Johnny Cash
2/15	2	2. Until My Dreams Come True . . . . Jack Greene
3/01	1	3. To Make Love Sweeter For You . . . . Jerry Lee Lewis
3/08	3	4. Only The Lonely . . . . Sonny James
3/29	2	5. Who's Gonna Mow Your Grass . . . . Buck Owens
4/12	1	6. Woman Of The World (Leave My World Alone) . . . . Loretta Lynn
4/19	3	7. Galveston . . . . Glen Campbell
5/10	1	8. Hungry Eyes . . . . Merle Haggard

DATE	WKS	RECORD TITLE......ARTIST
		1969 *(Continued)*
5/17	2	9. My Life (Throw It Away If I Want To) ....Bill Anderson
5/31	2	10. Singing My Song ....Tammy Wynette
6/14	3	11. Running Bear ....Sonny James
7/05	2	12. Statue Of A Fool ....Jack Greene
7/19	1	13. I Love You More Today ....Conway Twitty
7/26	2	14. Johnny B. Goode ....Buck Owens
8/09	1	15. All I Have To Offer You (Is Me) ....Charley Pride
8/16	1	16. Workin' Man Blues ....Merle Haggard
8/23	5	17. A Boy Named Sue ....Johnny Cash
9/27	1	18. Tall Dark Stranger.............................Buck Owens
10/04	3	19. Since I Met You, Baby ....Sonny James
10/25	2	20. The Ways To Love A Man ....Tammy Wynette
11/08	1	21. To See My Angel Cry ....Conway Twitty
11/15	4	22. Okie From Muskogee ....Merle Haggard
12/13	3	23. (I'm So) Afraid Of Losing You Again ....Charley Pride
		1970
1/03	4	1. Baby, Baby (I Know You're A Lady) ....David Houston
1/31	2	2. A Week In A Country Jail ....Tom T. Hall
2/14	4	3. It's Just A Matter Of Time ....Sonny James
3/14	3	4. The Fightin' Side Of Me ....Merle Haggard
4/04	2	5. Tennessee Bird Walk ....Jack Blanchard & Misty Morgan
4/18	2	6. Is Anybody Goin' To San Antone ....Charley Pride
5/02	1	7. My Woman My Woman, My Wife ....Marty Robbins
5/09	1	8. The Pool Shark ....Dave Dudley
5/16	3	9. My Love..Sonny James
6/06	4	10. Hello Darlin' ....Conway Twitty
7/04	3	11. He Loves Me All The Way ....Tammy Wynette
7/25	2	12. Wonder Could I Live There Anymore ....Charley Pride
8/08	4	13. Don't Keep Me Hangin' On ....Sonny James
9/05	2	14. All For The Love Of Sunshine ....Hank Williams, Jr.
9/19	1	15. For The Good Times ....Ray Price
9/26	2	16. There Must Be More To Love Than This ....Jerry Lee Lewis
10/10	2	17. Sunday Morning Coming Down ....Johnny Cash
10/24	2	18. Run, Woman, Run ....Tammy Wynette
11/07	2	19. I Can't Believe That You've Stopped Loving Me ....Charley Pride
11/21	1	20. Fifteen Years Ago.............................Conway Twitty
11/28	3	21. Endlessly ....Sonny James
12/19	1	22. Coal Miner's Daughter ....Loretta Lynn
12/26	5	★23. Rose Garden...................................Lynn Anderson
		1971
1/30	1	1. Flesh And Blood................................Johnny Cash
2/06	1	2. Joshua ....Dolly Parton
2/13	3	3. Help Me Make It Through The Night ....Sammi Smith
3/06	3	4. I'd Rather Love You ....Charley Pride
3/27	2	5. After The Fire Is Gone ....Conway Twitty & Loretta Lynn
4/10	4	6. Empty Arms ....Sonny James
5/08	1	7. How Much More Can She Stand ....Conway Twitty
5/15	3	8. I Won't Mention It Again ....Ray Price
6/05	2	9. You're My Man ....Lynn Anderson
6/19	5	★10. When You're Hot, You're Hot ....Jerry Reed

DATE	WKS	RECORD TITLE . . . . . . ARTIST
		1971 (*Continued*)
7/24	1	11. Bright Lights, Big City . . . . Sonny James
7/31	4	12. I'm Just Me . . . . Charley Pride
8/28	2	13. Good Lovin' (Makes It Right) . . . . Tammy Wynette
9/11	3*	14. Easy Loving . . . . Freddie Hart
9/18	2	15. The Year That Clayton Delaney Died . . . . Tom T. Hall
10/16	3	16. How Can I Unlove You . . . . Lynn Anderson
11/06	1	17. Here Comes Honey Again . . . . Sonny James
11/13	1	18. Lead Me On . . . . Conway Twitty & Loretta Lynn
11/20	2	19. Daddy Frank (The Guitar Man) . . . . Merle Haggard
12/04	5	★20. Kiss An Angel Good Mornin' . . . . Charley Pride
		1972
1/08	1	1. Would You Take Another Chance On Me . . . . Jerry Lee Lewis
1/15	3	2. Carolyn . . . . Merle Haggard
2/05	2	3. One's On The Way . . . . Loretta Lynn
2/19	2	4. It's Four In The Morning . . . . Faron Young
3/04	1	5. Bedtime Story . . . . Tammy Wynette
3/11	6	★ 6. My Hang-Up Is You . . . . Freddie Hart
4/22	3	7. Chantilly Lace . . . . Jerry Lee Lewis
5/13	2	8. Grandma Harp . . . . Merle Haggard
5/27	1	9. (Lost Her Love) On Our Last Date . . . . Conway Twitty
6/03	3	10. The Happiest Girl In The Whole U.S.A. . . . . Donna Fargo
6/24	1	11. That's Why I Love You Like I Do . . . . Sonny James
7/01	2	12. Eleven Roses . . . . Hank Williams, Jr.
7/15	1	13. Made In Japan . . . . Buck Owens
7/22	3	14. It's Gonna Take A Little Bit Longer . . . . Charley Pride
8/12	2	15. Bless Your Heart . . . . Freddie Hart
8/26	2*	16. If You Leave Me Tonight I'll Cry . . . . Jerry Wallace
9/02	1	17. Woman (Sensuous Woman) . . . . Don Gibson
9/16	1	18. When The Snow Is On The Roses . . . . Sonny James
9/23	1	19. I Can't Stop Loving You . . . . Conway Twitty
9/30	2	20. I Ain't Never . . . . Mel Tillis
10/14	3	21. Funny Face . . . . Donna Fargo
11/04	1	22. It's Not Love (But It's Not Bad) . . . . Merle Haggard
11/11	1	23. My Man . . . . Tammy Wynette
11/18	3	24. She's Too Good To Be True . . . . Charley Pride
12/09	3	25. Got The All Overs For You (All Over Me) . . . . Freddie Hart
12/30	3	26. She's Got To Be A Saint . . . . Ray Price
		1973
1/20	1	1. Soul Song . . . . Joe Stampley
1/27	1	2. (Old Dogs-Children And) Watermelon Wine . . . . Tom T. Hall
2/03	2	3. She Needs Someone To Hold Her (When She Cries) . . . . Conway Twitty
2/17	1	4. I Wonder If They Ever Think Of Me . . . . Merle Haggard
2/24	1	5. Rated "X" . . . . Loretta Lynn
3/03	1	6. The Lord Knows I'm Drinking . . . . Cal Smith
3/10	1	7. 'Til I Get It Right . . . . Tammy Wynette
3/17	2	8. Teddy Bear Song . . . . Barbara Fairchild
3/31	1	9. Keep Me In Mind . . . . Lynn Anderson
4/07	1	10. Super Kind Of Woman . . . . Freddie Hart
4/14	1	11. A Shoulder To Cry On . . . . Charley Pride
4/21	1	12. Superman . . . . Donna Fargo

DATE	WKS	RECORD TITLE......ARTIST
		1973 *(Continued)*
4/28	2	13. Behind Closed Doors . . . . Charlie Rich
5/12	1	14. Come Live With Me . . . . Roy Clark
5/19	1	15. What's Your Mama's Name . . . . Tanya Tucker
5/26	3*	16. Satin Sheets . . . . Jeanne Pruett
6/09	1	17. You Always Come Back (To Hurting Me) . . . . Johnny Rodriguez
6/16	1	18. Kids Say The Darndest Things . . . . Tammy Wynette
6/30	1	19. Don't Fight The Feelings Of Love . . . . Charley Pride
7/07	1	20. Why Me . . . . Kris Kristofferson
7/14	2	21. Love Is The Foundation . . . . Loretta Lynn
7/28	1	22. You Were Always There . . . . Donna Fargo
8/04	1	23. Lord, Mr. Ford . . . . Jerry Reed
8/11	1	24. Trip To Heaven . . . . Freddie Hart
8/18	1	25. Louisiana Woman, Mississippi Man . . . . Conway Twitty & Loretta Lynn
8/25	2	26. Everybody's Had The Blues . . . . Merle Haggard
9/08	3	27. You've Never Been This Far Before . . . . Conway Twitty
9/29	1	28. Blood Red And Goin' Down . . . . Tanya Tucker
10/06	1	29. You're The Best Thing That Ever Happened To Me . . . . Ray Price
10/13	2	30. Ridin' My Thumb To Mexico . . . . Johnny Rodriguez
10/27	2	31. We're Gonna Hold On . . . . George Jones & Tammy Wynette
11/10	2	32. Paper Roses . . . . Marie Osmond
11/24	3	33. The Most Beautiful Girl . . . . Charlie Rich
12/15	1	34. Amazing Love . . . . Charley Pride
12/22	4	★35. If We Make It Through December . . . . Merle Haggard
		1974
1/19	2	1. I Love . . . . Tom T. Hall
2/02	1	2. Jolene . . . . Dolly Parton
2/09	1	3. World Of Make Believe . . . . Bill Anderson
2/16	1	4. That's The Way Love Goes . . . . Johnny Rodriguez
2/23	2	5. Another Lonely Song . . . . Tammy Wynette
3/09	2	6. There Won't Be Anymore . . . . Charlie Rich
3/23	1	7. There's A Honky Tonk Angel (Who'll Take Me Back In) . . . . . . Conway Twitty
3/30	1	8. Would You Lay With Me (In A Field Of Stone) . . . . Tanya Tucker
4/06	3	★ 9. A Very Special Love Song . . . . Charlie Rich
4/27	1	10. Hello Love . . . . Hank Snow
5/04	1	11. Things Aren't Funny Anymore . . . . Merle Haggard
5/11	1	12. Is It Wrong (For Loving You) . . . . Sonny James
5/18	1	13. Country Bumpkin . . . . Cal Smith
5/25	1	14. No Charge . . . . Melba Montgomery
6/01	1	15. Pure Love . . . . Ronnie Milsap
6/08	1	16. I Will Always Love You . . . . Dolly Parton
6/15	1	17. I Don't See Me In Your Eyes Anymore . . . . Charlie Rich
6/22	1	18. This Time . . . . Waylon Jennings
6/29	1	19. Room Full Of Roses . . . . Mickey Gilley
7/06	2	20. He Thinks I Still Care . . . . Anne Murray
7/20	1	21. Marie Laveau . . . . Bobby Bare
7/27	1	22. You Can't Be A Beacon (If Your Light Don't Shine) . . . . Donna Fargo
8/03	2	23. Rub It In . . . . Billy "Crash" Craddock
8/17	1	24. As Soon As I Hang Up The Phone . . . . Conway Twitty & Loretta Lynn
8/24	1	25. Old Man From The Mountain . . . . Merle Haggard
8/31	1	26. The Grand Tour . . . . George Jones
9/07	2	27. Please Don't Tell Me How The Story Ends . . . . Ronnie Milsap

DATE	WKS	RECORD TITLE......ARTIST
		1974 *(Continued)*
9/21	1	28. I Wouldn't Want To Live If You Didn't Love Me ....Don Williams
9/28	1	29. I'm A Ramblin' Man ....Waylon Jennings
10/05	1	30. I Love My Friend ....Charlie Rich
10/12	1	31. Please Don't Stop Loving Me ....Porter Wagoner & Dolly Parton
10/19	2	32. I See The Want To In Your Eyes ....Conway Twitty
11/02	1	33. I Overlooked An Orchid ....Mickey Gilley
11/09	1	34. Love Is Like A Butterfly ....Dolly Parton
11/16	1	35. Country Is ....Tom T. Hall
11/23	1	36. Trouble In Paradise ....Loretta Lynn
11/30	1	37. Back Home Again ....John Denver
12/07	1	38. She Called Me Baby ....Charlie Rich
12/14	2	39. I Can Help ....Billy Swan
12/28	1	40. What A Man, My Man Is ....Lynn Anderson
		1975
1/04	1	1. The Door ....George Jones
1/11	1	2. Ruby, Baby ....Billy "Crash" Craddock
1/18	1	3. Kentucky Gambler.............................Merle Haggard
1/25	1	4. (I'd Be) A Legend In My Time ....Ronnie Milsap
2/01	1	5. City Lights ....Mickey Gilley
2/08	1	6. Then Who Am I ....Charley Pride
2/15	1	7. Devil In The Bottle ............................T.G. Sheppard
2/22	1	8. I Care ....Tom T. Hall
3/01	1	9. It's Time To Pay The Fiddler ....Cal Smith
3/08	1	10. Linda On My Mind ....Conway Twitty
3/15	2	11. Before The Next Teardrop Falls ....Freddy Fender
3/29	1	12. The Bargain Store ....Dolly Parton
4/05	1	13. I Just Can't Get Her Out Of My Mind ....Johnny Rodriguez
4/12	2	14. Always Wanting You ....Merle Haggard
4/26	1	15. Blanket On The Ground........................Billie Jo Spears
5/03	1	16. Roll On Big Mama ....Joe Stampley
5/10	1	17. She's Actin' Single (I'm Drinkin' Doubles) ....Gary Stewart
5/17	1	18. (Hey Won't You Play) Another Somebody Done Somebody Wrong Song ......B.J. Thomas
5/24	1	19. I'm Not Lisa ....Jessi Colter
5/31	1	20. Thank God I'm A Country Boy ....John Denver
6/07	1	21. Window Up Above ....Mickey Gilley
6/14	1	22. When Will I Be Loved ....Linda Ronstadt
6/21	1	23. You're My Best Friend ....Don Williams
6/28	1	24. Tryin' To Beat The Morning Home ...................T.G. Sheppard
7/05	1	25. Lizzie And The Rainman ....Tanya Tucker
7/12	1	26. Movin' On ....Merle Haggard
7/19	2	27. Touch The Hand.............................Conway Twitty
8/02	1	28. Just Get Up And Close The Door ....Johnny Rodriguez
8/09	2	29. Wasted Days And Wasted Nights ....Freddy Fender
8/23	3*	30. Rhinestone Cowboy ....Glen Campbell
9/06	1	31. Feelins'...........................Conway Twitty & Loretta Lynn
9/20	2	32. Daydreams About Night Things ....Ronnie Milsap
10/04	2	33. Blue Eyes Crying In The Rain ....Willie Nelson
10/18	1	34. Hope You're Feelin' Me (Like I'm Feelin' You) ....Charley Pride
10/25	1	35. San Antonio Stroll ....Tanya Tucker
11/01	1	36. (Turn Out The Light And) Love Me Tonight ....Don Williams

DATE	WKS	RECORD TITLE . . . . . . ARTIST
		1975 *(Continued)*
11/08	1	37. **I'm Sorry** . . . . John Denver
11/15	1	38. **Are You Sure Hank Done It This Way** . . . . Waylon Jennings
11/22	1	39. **Rocky** . . . . Dickey Lee
11/29	1	40. **It's All In The Movies** . . . . Merle Haggard
12/06	1	41. **Secret Love** . . . . Freddy Fender
12/13	1	42. **Love Put A Song In My Heart** . . . . Johnny Rodriguez
12/20	6	★43. **Convoy** . . . . C.W. McCall
		1976
1/31	1	1. **This Time I've Hurt Her More Than She Loves Me** . . . . Conway Twitty
2/07	1	2. **Sometimes** . . . . Bill Anderson & Mary Lou Turner
2/14	1	3. **The White Knight** . . . . Cledus Maggard
2/21	3	★ 4. **Good Hearted Woman** . . . . Waylon & Willie
3/13	1	5. **The Roots Of My Raising** . . . . Merle Haggard
3/20	1	6. **Faster Horses (The Cowboy And The Poet)** . . . . Tom T. Hall
3/27	1	7. **Til The Rivers All Run Dry** . . . . Don Williams
4/03	1	8. **You'll Lose A Good Thing** . . . . Freddy Fender
4/10	1	9. **'Til I Can Make It On My Own** . . . . Tammy Wynette
4/17	1	10. **Drinkin' My Baby (Off My Mind)** . . . . Eddie Rabbitt
4/24	1	11. **Together Again** . . . . Emmylou Harris
5/01	1	12. **Don't The Girls All Get Prettier At Closing Time** . . . . Mickey Gilley
5/08	1	13. **My Eyes Can Only See As Far As You** . . . . Charley Pride
5/15	1	14. **What Goes On When The Sun Goes Down** . . . . Ronnie Milsap
5/22	1	15. **After All The Good Is Gone** . . . . Conway Twitty
5/29	2	16. **One Piece At A Time** . . . . Johnny Cash
6/12	1	17. **I'll Get Over You** . . . . Crystal Gayle
6/19	2	18. **El Paso City** . . . . Marty Robbins
7/04	1	19. **All These Things** . . . . Joe Stampley
7/10	1	20. **The Door Is Always Open** . . . . Dave & Sugar
7/17	3	★21. **Teddy Bear** . . . . Red Sovine
8/07	1	22. **Golden Ring** . . . . George Jones & Tammy Wynette
8/14	1	23. **Say It Again** . . . . Don Williams
8/21	1	24. **Bring It On Home To Me** . . . . Mickey Gilley
8/28	2	25. **(I'm A) Stand By My Woman Man** . . . . Ronnie Milsap
9/11	2	26. **I Don't Want To Have To Marry You** . . . . Jim Ed Brown/Helen Cornelius
9/25	1	27. **If You've Got The Money I've Got The Time** . . . . Willie Nelson
10/02	1	28. **Here's Some Love** . . . . Tanya Tucker
10/09	1	29. **The Games That Daddies Play** . . . . Conway Twitty
10/16	2	30. **You And Me** . . . . Tammy Wynette
10/30	1	31. **Among My Souvenirs** . . . . Marty Robbins
11/06	1	32. **Cherokee Maiden** . . . . Merle Haggard
11/13	2	33. **Somebody Somewhere (Don't Know What He's Missin' Tonight)**
		. . . . . . Loretta Lynn
11/27	2	34. **Good Woman Blues** . . . . Mel Tillis
12/11	2	35. **Thinkin' Of A Rendezvous** . . . . Johnny Duncan
12/25	2	36. **Sweet Dreams** . . . . Emmylou Harris
		1977
1/08	1	1. **Broken Down In Tiny Pieces** . . . . Billy "Crash" Craddock
1/15	1	2. **You Never Miss A Real Good Thing (Till He Says Goodbye)** . . . . Crystal Gayle
1/22	1	3. **I Can't Believe She Gives It All To Me** . . . . Conway Twitty
1/29	1	4. **Let My Love Be Your Pillow** . . . . Ronnie Milsap

DATE	WKS	RECORD TITLE . . . . . . ARTIST
		1977 *(Continued)*
2/05	2	5. Near You . . . . George Jones & Tammy Wynette
2/19	1	6. Moody Blue . . . . Elvis Presley
2/26	1	7. Say You'll Stay Until Tomorrow . . . . Tom Jones
3/05	1	8. Heart Healer . . . . Mel Tillis
3/12	1	9. She's Just An Old Love Turned Memory . . . . Charley Pride
3/19	2	10. Southern Nights . . . . Glen Campbell
4/02	2	11. Lucille . . . . Kenny Rogers
4/16	1	12. It Couldn't Have Been Any Better . . . . Johnny Duncan
4/23	1	13. She's Got You . . . . Loretta Lynn
4/30	1	14. She's Pulling Me Back Again . . . . Mickey Gilley
5/07	1	15. Play, Guitar Play . . . . Conway Twitty
5/14	1	16. Some Broken Hearts Never Mend . . . . Don Williams
5/21	6	★17. Luckenbach, Texas (Back to the Basics of Love) . . . . Waylon Jennings
7/02	1	18. That Was Yesterday . . . . Donna Fargo
7/09	1	19. I'll Be Leaving Alone . . . . Charley Pride
7/16	3	20. It Was Almost Like A Song . . . . Ronnie Milsap
8/06	2	21. Rollin' With The Flow . . . . Charlie Rich
8/20	1	22. Way Down . . . . Elvis Presley
8/27	4	23. Don't It Make My Brown Eyes Blue . . . . Crystal Gayle
9/24	1	24. I've Already Loved You In My Mind . . . . Conway Twitty
10/01	1	25. Daytime Friends . . . . Kenny Rogers
10/08	4	26. Heaven's Just A Sin Away . . . . The Kendalls
11/05	1	27. I'm Just A Country Boy . . . . Don Williams
11/12	1	28. More To Me . . . . Charley Pride
11/19	2	29. The Wurlitzer Prize (I Don't Want To Get Over You) . . . . . . Waylon Jennings
12/03	5	30. Here You Come Again . . . . Dolly Parton
		1978
1/07	2	1. Take This Job And Shove It . . . . Johnny Paycheck
1/21	1	2. What A Difference You've Made In My Life . . . . Ronnie Milsap
1/28	2	3. Out Of My Head And Back In My Bed . . . . Loretta Lynn
2/11	1	4. I Just Wish You Were Someone I Love . . . . Larry Gatlin & The Gatlin Brothers
2/18	2	5. Don't Break The Heart That Loves You . . . . Margo Smith
3/04	4	★ 6. Mammas Don't Let Your Babies Grow Up To Be Cowboys . . . . Waylon & Willie
4/01	1	7. Ready For The Times To Get Better . . . . Crystal Gayle
4/08	2	8. Someone Loves You Honey . . . . Charley Pride
4/22	2	9. Every Time Two Fools Collide . . . . Kenny Rogers & Dottie West
5/06	2	10. It's All Wrong, But It's All Right . . . . Dolly Parton
5/20	1	11. She Can Put Her Shoes Under My Bed (Anytime) . . . . Johnny Duncan
5/27	2	12. Do You Know You Are My Sunshine . . . . The Statler Brothers
6/10	1	13. Georgia On My Mind . . . . Willie Nelson
6/17	1	14. Two More Bottles Of Wine . . . . Emmylou Harris
6/24	1	15. I'll Be True To You . . . . The Oak Ridge Boys
7/01	1	16. It Only Hurts For A Little While . . . . Margo Smith
7/08	1	17. I Believe In You . . . . Mel Tillis
7/15	3	18. Only One Love In My Life . . . . Ronnie Milsap
8/05	1	19. Love Or Something Like It . . . . Kenny Rogers
8/12	1	20. You Don't Love Me Anymore . . . . Eddie Rabbitt
8/19	2	21. Talking In Your Sleep . . . . Crystal Gayle
9/02	1	22. Blue Skies . . . . Willie Nelson
9/09	3	23. I've Always Been Crazy . . . . Waylon Jennings
9/30	3	24. Heartbreaker . . . . Dolly Parton

DATE	WKS	RECORD TITLE . . . . . . ARTIST
		1978 *(Continued)*
10/21	1	25. Tear Time . . . . Dave & Sugar
10/28	1	26. Let's Take The Long Way Around The World . . . . Ronnie Milsap
11/04	3	27. Sleeping Single In A Double Bed . . . . Barbara Mandrell
11/25	1	28. Sweet Desire . . . . The Kendalls
12/02	1	29. I Just Want To Love You . . . . Eddie Rabbitt
12/09	1	30. On My Knees . . . . Charlie Rich with Janie Fricke
12/16	3	31. The Gambler . . . . Kenny Rogers
		1979
1/06	1	1. Tulsa Time . . . . Don Williams
1/13	1	2. Lady Lay Down . . . . John Conlee
1/20	1	3. I Really Got The Feeling . . . . Dolly Parton
1/27	2	4. Why Have You Left The One You Left Me For . . . . Crystal Gayle
2/10	3	★ 5. Every Which Way But Loose . . . . Eddie Rabbitt
3/03	3	★ 6. Golden Tears . . . . Dave & Sugar
3/24	3	★ 7. I Just Fall In Love Again . . . . Anne Murray
4/14	1	8. (If Loving You Is Wrong) I Don't Want To Be Right . . . . Barbara Mandrell
4/21	1	9. All I Ever Need Is You . . . . Kenny Rogers & Dottie West
4/28	1	10. Where Do I Put Her Memory . . . . Charley Pride
5/05	1	11. Backside Of Thirty . . . . John Conlee
5/12	1	12. Don't Take It Away . . . . Conway Twitty
5/19	3	★13. If I Said You Have A Beautiful Body Would You Hold It Against Me
		. . . . . . The Bellamy Brothers
6/09	2	14. She Believes In Me . . . . Kenny Rogers
6/23	1	15. Nobody Likes Sad Songs . . . . Ronnie Milsap
6/30	3	★16. Amanda . . . . Waylon Jennings
7/21	1	17. Shadows In The Moonlight . . . . Anne Murray
7/28	2	18. You're The Only One . . . . Dolly Parton
8/11	1	19. Suspicions . . . . Eddie Rabbitt
8/18	1	20. Coca Cola Cowboy . . . . Mel Tillis
8/25	1	21. The Devil Went Down To Georgia . . . . The Charlie Daniels Band
9/01	1	22. Heartbreak Hotel . . . . Willie Nelson & Leon Russell
9/08	1	23. I May Never Get To Heaven . . . . Conway Twitty
9/15	1	24. You're My Jamaica . . . . Charley Pride
9/22	1	25. Just Good Ol' Boys . . . . Moe Bandy & Joe Stampley
9/29	1	26. It Must Be Love . . . . Don Williams
10/06	2	27. Last Cheater's Waltz . . . . T.G. Sheppard
10/20	2	28. All The Gold In California . . . . Larry Gatlin & The Gatlin Brothers
11/03	2	29. You Decorated My Life . . . . Kenny Rogers
11/17	2	30. Come With Me . . . . Waylon Jennings
12/01	1	31. Broken Hearted Me . . . . Anne Murray
12/08	1	32. I Cheated Me Right Out Of You . . . . Moe Bandy
12/15	3	★33. Happy Birthday Darlin' . . . . Conway Twitty
		1980
1/05	3	★ 1. Coward Of The County . . . . Kenny Rogers
1/26	2	2. I'll Be Coming Back For More . . . . T.G. Sheppard
2/09	1	3. Leaving Louisiana In The Broad Daylight . . . . The Oak Ridge Boys
2/16	1	4. Love Me Over Again . . . . Don Williams
2/23	1	5. Years . . . . Barbara Mandrell
3/01	1	6. I Ain't Living Long Like This . . . . Waylon Jennings
3/08	2	7. My Heroes Have Always Been Cowboys . . . . Willie Nelson

DATE	WKS	RECORD TITLE . . . . ARTIST
		1980 *(Continued)*
3/22	1	8. Why Don't You Spend The Night . . . . Ronnie Milsap
3/29	1	9. I'd Love To Lay You Down . . . . Conway Twitty
4/05	1	10. Sugar Daddy . . . . The Bellamy Brothers
4/12	1	11. Honky Tonk Blues . . . . Charley Pride
4/19	1	12. It's Like We Never Said Goodbye . . . . Crystal Gayle
4/26	1	13. A Lesson In Leavin' . . . . Dottie West
5/03	1	14. Are You On The Road To Lovin' Me Again . . . . Debby Boone
5/10	1	15. Beneath Still Waters . . . . Emmylou Harris
5/17	1	16. Gone Too Far . . . . Eddie Rabbitt
5/24	1	17. Starting Over Again . . . . Dolly Parton
5/31	3	★18. My Heart . . . . Ronnie Milsap
6/21	1	19. One Day At A Time . . . . Cristy Lane
6/28	1	20. Trying To Love Two Women . . . . The Oak Ridge Boys
7/05	1	21. He Stopped Loving Her Today . . . . George Jones
7/12	1	22. You Win Again . . . . Charley Pride
7/19	1	23. True Love Ways . . . . Mickey Gilley
7/26	1	24. Bar Room Buddies . . . . Merle Haggard & Clint Eastwood
8/02	1	25. Dancin' Cowboys . . . . The Bellamy Brothers
8/09	1	26. Stand By Me . . . . Mickey Gilley
8/16	1	27. Tennessee River . . . . Alabama
8/23	1	28. Drivin' My Life Away . . . . Eddie Rabbitt
8/30	1	29. Cowboys And Clowns . . . . Ronnie Milsap
9/06	3	★30. Lookin' For Love . . . . Johnny Lee
9/27	1	31. Old Flames Can't Hold A Candle To You . . . . Dolly Parton
10/04	1	32. Do You Wanna Go To Heaven . . . . T.G. Sheppard
10/11	1	33. Loving Up A Storm . . . . Razzy Bailey
10/18	2	34. I Believe In You . . . . Don Williams
11/01	1	35. Theme From The Dukes Of Hazzard (Good Ol' Boys) . . . . . . Waylon Jennings
11/08	1	36. On The Road Again . . . . Willie Nelson
11/15	1	37. Could I Have This Dance . . . . Anne Murray
11/22	1	38. Lady . . . . Kenny Rogers
11/29	1	39. If You Ever Change Your Mind . . . . Crystal Gayle
12/06	1	40. Smoky Mountain Rain . . . . Ronnie Milsap
12/13	1	41. Why Lady Why . . . . Alabama
12/20	1	42. That's All That Matters . . . . Mickey Gilley
12/27	2	43. One In A Million . . . . Johnny Lee
		1981
1/10	1	1. I Think I'll Just Stay Here And Drink . . . . Merle Haggard
1/17	1	2. I Love A Rainy Night . . . . Eddie Rabbitt
1/24	1	3. 9 To 5 . . . . Dolly Parton
1/31	1	4. I Feel Like Loving You Again . . . . T.G. Sheppard
2/07	1	5. I Keep Coming Back . . . . Razzy Bailey
2/14	1	6. Who's Cheatin' Who . . . . Charly McClain
2/21	1	7. Southern Rains . . . . Mel Tillis
2/28	1	8. Are You Happy Baby? . . . . Dottie West
3/07	1	9. Do You Love As Good As You Look . . . . The Bellamy Brothers
3/14	1	10. Guitar Man . . . . Elvis Presley
3/21	1	11. Angel Flying Too Close To The Ground . . . . Willie Nelson
3/28	1	12. Texas Women . . . . Hank Williams, Jr.
4/04	1	13. Drifter . . . . Sylvia
4/11	1	14. You're The Reason God Made Oklahoma . . . . David Frizzell & Shelly West

DATE	WKS	RECORD TITLE . . . . . . ARTIST
		1981 *(Continued)*
4/18	1	15. Old Flame . . . . Alabama
4/25	1	16. A Headache Tomorrow (Or A Heartache Tonight) . . . . Mickey Gilley
5/02	1	17. Rest Your Love On Me . . . . Conway Twitty
5/09	1	18. Am I Losing You . . . . Ronnie Milsap
5/16	1	19. I Loved 'Em Every One . . . . T.G. Sheppard
5/23	1	20. Seven Year Ache . . . . Rosanne Cash
5/30	1	21. Elvira . . . . The Oak Ridge Boys
6/06	1	22. Friends . . . . Razzy Bailey
6/13	1	23. What Are We Doin' In Love . . . . Kenny Rogers & Dottie West
6/20	1	24. But You Know I Love You . . . . Dolly Parton
6/27	1	25. Blessed Are The Believers . . . . Anne Murray
7/04	1	26. I Was Country When Country Wasn't Cool . . . . Barbara Mandrell
7/11	1	27. Fire & Smoke . . . . Earl Thomas Conley
7/18	2	★28. Feels So Right . . . . Alabama
8/01	1	29. Dixie On My Mind . . . . Hank Williams, Jr.
8/08	1	30. Too Many Lovers . . . . Crystal Gayle
8/15	2	★31. I Don't Need You . . . . Kenny Rogers
8/29	2	★32. (There's) No Gettin' Over Me . . . . Ronnie Milsap
9/12	1	33. Older Women . . . . Ronnie McDowell
9/19	1	34. You Don't Know Me . . . . Mickey Gilley
9/26	1	35. Tight Fittin' Jeans . . . . Conway Twitty
10/03	1	36. Midnight Hauler . . . . Razzy Bailey
10/10	1	37. Party Time . . . . T.G. Sheppard
10/17	1	38. Step By Step . . . . Eddie Rabbitt
10/24	2	★39. Never Been So Loved (In All My Life) . . . . Charley Pride
11/07	1	40. Fancy Free . . . . The Oak Ridge Boys
11/14	1	41. My Baby Thinks He's A Train . . . . Rosanne Cash
11/21	1	42. All My Rowdy Friends (Have Settled Down) . . . . Hank Williams, Jr.
11/28	1	43. My Favorite Memory . . . . Merle Haggard
12/05	1	44. Bet Your Heart On Me . . . . Johnny Lee
12/12	1	45. Still Doin' Time . . . . George Jones
12/19	1	46. All Roads Lead To You . . . . Steve Wariner
12/26	2	★47. Love In The First Degree . . . . Alabama
		1982
1/09	1	1. Fourteen Carat Mind . . . . Gene Watson
1/16	1	2. I Wouldn't Have Missed It For The World . . . . Ronnie Milsap
1/23	1	3. Red Neckin' Love Makin' Night . . . . Conway Twitty
1/30	1	4. The Sweetest Thing (I've Ever Known) . . . . Juice Newton
2/06	1	5. Lonely Nights . . . . Mickey Gilley
2/13	1	6. Someone Could Lose A Heart Tonight . . . . Eddie Rabbitt
2/20	1	7. Only One You . . . . T.G. Sheppard
2/27	1	8. Lord, I Hope This Day Is Good . . . . Don Williams
3/06	1	9. You're The Best Break This Old Heart Ever Had . . . . Ed Bruce
3/13	1	10. Blue Moon With Heartache . . . . Rosanne Cash
3/20	1	11. Mountain Of Love . . . . Charley Pride
3/27	1	12. She Left Love All Over Me . . . . Razzy Bailey
4/03	1	13. Bobbie Sue . . . . The Oak Ridge Boys
4/10	1	14. Big City . . . . Merle Haggard
4/17	1	15. The Clown . . . . Conway Twitty
4/24	1	16. Crying My Heart Out Over You . . . . Ricky Skaggs
5/01	1	17. Mountain Music . . . . Alabama

DATE	WKS	RECORD TITLE......ARTIST
		1982 *(Continued)*
5/08	2	★18. Always On My Mind .... Willie Nelson
5/22	2	★19. Just To Satisfy You .... Waylon & Willie
6/05	1	20. Finally .... T.G. Sheppard
6/12	1	21. For All The Wrong Reasons .... The Bellamy Brothers
6/19	2	★22. Slow Hand .... Conway Twitty
7/03	1	23. Any Day Now .... Ronnie Milsap
7/10	1	24. Don't Worry 'Bout Me Baby .... Janie Frickie
7/17	1	25. 'Till You're Gone .... Barbara Mandrell
7/24	1	26. Take Me Down .... Alabama
7/31	1	27. I Don't Care .... Ricky Skaggs
8/07	1	28. Honky Tonkin' .... Hank Williams, Jr.
8/14	1	29. I'm Gonna Hire A Wino To Decorate Our Home .... David Frizzell
8/21	1	30. Nobody .... Sylvia
8/28	1	31. Fool Hearted Memory .... George Strait
9/04	1	32. Love Will Turn You Around .... Kenny Rogers
9/11	2	★33. She Got The Goldmine (I Got The Shaft) .... Jerry Reed
9/25	1	34. What's Forever For .... Michael Martin Murphey
10/02	1	35. Put Your Dreams Away .... Mickey Gilley
10/09	1	36. Yesterday's Wine .... George Jones/Merle Haggard
10/16	1	37. I Will Always Love You .... Dolly Parton
10/23	1	38. He Got You .... Ronnie Milsap
10/30	1	39. Close Enough To Perfect .... Alabama
11/06	1	40. You're So Good When You're Bad .... Charley Pride
11/13	1	41. Heartbroke .... Ricky Skaggs
11/20	1	42. War Is Hell (On The Homefront Too) .... T.G. Sheppard
11/27	1	43. It Ain't Easy Bein' Easy .... Janie Frickie
12/04	1	44. You And I .... Eddie Rabbitt with Crystal Gayle
12/11	1	45. Redneck Girl .... The Bellamy Brothers
12/18	1	46. Somewhere Between Right And Wrong .... Earl Thomas Conley
12/25	2	★47. Wild And Blue .... John Anderson
		1983
1/08	1	1. Can't Even Get The Blues .... Reba McEntire
1/15	1	2. Going Where The Lonely Go .... Merle Haggard
1/22	1	3. (Lost His Love) On Our Last Date .... Emmylou Harris
1/29	1	4. Talk To Me .... Mickey Gilley
2/05	1	5. Inside .... Ronnie Milsap
2/12	1	6. 'Til I Gain Control Again .... Crystal Gayle
2/19	1	7. Faking Love .... T.G. Sheppard & Karen Brooks
2/26	1	8. Why Baby Why .... Charley Pride
3/05	1	9. If Hollywood Don't Need You .... Don Williams
3/12	1	10. The Rose .... Conway Twitty
3/19	1	11. I Wouldn't Change You If I Could .... Ricky Skaggs
3/26	1	12. Swingin' .... John Anderson
4/02	1	13. When I'm Away From You .... The Bellamy Brothers
4/09	1	14. We've Got Tonight .... Kenny Rogers & Sheena Easton
4/16	1	15. Dixieland Delight .... Alabama
4/23	1	16. American Made .... The Oak Ridge Boys
4/30	1	17. You're The First Time I've Thought About Leaving .... Reba McEntire
5/07	1	18. Jose Cuervo .... Shelly West
5/14	1	19. Whatever Happened To Old Fashioned Love .... B.J. Thomas
5/21	1	20. Common Man .... John Conlee

DATE	WKS	RECORD TITLE......ARTIST
		1983 *(Continued)*
5/28	1	21. You Take Me For Granted ....Merle Haggard
6/04	1	22. Lucille (You Won't Do Your Daddy's Will) ....Waylon Jennings
6/11	1	23. Our Love Is On The Faultline ....Crystal Gayle
6/18	1	24. You Can't Run From Love ....Eddie Rabbitt
6/25	1	25. Fool For Your Love ....Mickey Gilley
7/02	1	26. Love Is On A Roll ....Don Williams
7/09	1	27. Highway 40 Blues ....Ricky Skaggs
7/16	1	28. The Closer You Get...............................Alabama
7/23	1	29. Pancho And Lefty ....Willie Nelson & Merle Haggard
7/30	1	30. I Always Get Lucky With You ....George Jones
8/06	1	31. Your Love's On The Line ....Earl Thomas Conley
8/13	1	32. He's A Heartache (Looking For A Place To Happen) ....Janie Frickie
8/20	1	33. Love Song...............................The Oak Ridge Boys
8/27	1	34. You're Gonna Ruin My Bad Reputation ....Ronnie McDowell
9/03	1	35. A Fire I Can't Put Out.............................George Strait
9/10	1	36. I'm Only In It For The Love ....John Conlee
9/17	1	37. Night Games ....Charley Pride
9/24	1	38. Baby, What About You ....Crystal Gayle
10/01	1	39. New Looks From An Old Lover ....................B.J. Thomas
10/08	1	40. Don't You Know How Much I Love You ....Ronnie Milsap
10/15	1	41. Paradise Tonight ....Charly McClain & Mickey Gilley
10/22	1	42. Lady Down On Love ....Alabama
10/29	2	★43. Islands In The Stream ....Kenny Rogers & Dolly Parton
11/12	1	44. Somebody's Gonna Love You ....Lee Greenwood
11/19	1	45. One Of A Kind Pair Of Fools ....Barbara Mandrell
11/26	1	46. Holding Her And Loving You ....Earl Thomas Conley
12/03	1	47. A Little Good News...............................Anne Murray
12/10	1	48. Tell Me A Lie ....Janie Frickie
12/17	1	49. Black Sheep ....John Anderson
12/24	2	★50. Houston (Means I'm One Day Closer To You)
		.......Larry Gatlin & The Gatlin Brothers
		1984
1/07	1	1. You Look So Good In Love ....George Strait
1/14	1	2. Slow Burn ...............................T.G. Sheppard
1/21	1	3. In My Eyes ....John Conlee
1/28	1	4. The Sound Of Goodbye ....Crystal Gayle
2/04	1	5. Show Her ....Ronnie Milsap
2/11	1	6. That's The Way Love Goes ....Merle Haggard
2/18	1	7. Don't Cheat In Our Hometown ....Ricky Skaggs
2/25	1	8. Stay Young ....Don Williams
3/03	1	9. Woke Up In Love ....Exile
3/10	1	10. Going, Going, Gone ....Lee Greenwood
3/17	1	11. Elizabeth ....The Statler Brothers
3/24	1	12. Roll On (Eighteen Wheeler).............................Alabama
3/31	1	13. Let's Stop Talkin' About It ....Janie Frickie
4/07	1	14. Don't Make It Easy For Me ....Earl Thomas Conley
4/14	1	15. Thank God For The Radio ....The Kendalls
4/21	1	16. The Yellow Rose ....Johnny Lee with Lane Brody
4/28	1	17. Right Or Wrong ....George Strait
5/05	1	18. I Guess It Never Hurts To Hurt Sometimes ....The Oak Ridge Boys
5/12	2	★19. To All The Girls I've Loved Before ....Julio Iglesias & Willie Nelson

DATE	WKS	RECORD TITLE . . . . . . ARTIST
		1984 (*Continued*)
5/26	1	20. **As Long As I'm Rockin' With You** . . . . .John Conlee
6/02	1	21. **Honey (Open That Door)** . . . . .Ricky Skaggs
6/09	1	22. **Someday When Things Are Good** .Merle Haggard
6/16	1	23. **I Got Mexico** . . . . .Eddy Raven
6/23	1	24. **When We Make Love** . . . . .Alabama
6/30	1	25. **I Can Tell By The Way You Dance (You're Gonna Love Me Tonight)**
		. . . . . . .Vern Gosdin
7/07	1	26. **Somebody's Needin' Somebody** .Conway Twitty
7/14	1	27. **I Don't Want To Be A Memory** . . . . .Exile
7/21	1	28. **Just Another Woman In Love** .Anne Murray
7/28	1	29. **Angel In Disguise** . . . . .Earl Thomas Conley
8/04	1	30. **Mama He's Crazy** . . . . .The Judds
8/11	1	31. **That's The Thing About Love** . . . . .Don Williams
8/18	1	32. **Still Losing You** . . . . .Ronnie Milsap
8/25	1	33. **Long Hard Road (The Sharecropper's Dream)** . . . . . . .Nitty Gritty Dirt Band
9/01	1	34. **Let's Fall To Pieces Together** .George Strait
9/08	1	35. **Tennessee Homesick Blues** . . . . .Dolly Parton
9/15	1	36. **You're Gettin' To Me Again** . . . . .Jim Glaser
9/22	1	37. **Let's Chase Each Other Around The Room** . . . . .Merle Haggard
9/29	1	38. **Turning Away** . . . . .Crystal Gayle
10/06	1	39. **Everyday** . . . . .The Oak Ridge Boys
10/13	1	40. **Uncle Pen** . . . . .Ricky Skaggs
10/20	1	41. **I Don't Know A Thing About Love (The Moon Song)** . . . . .Conway Twitty
10/27	1	42. **If You're Gonna Play In Texas (You Gotta Have A Fiddle In The Band)**
		. . . . . . .Alabama
11/03	1	43. **City Of New Orleans** . . . . .Willie Nelson
11/10	1	44. **I've Been Around Enough To Know** . . . . .John Schneider
11/17	1	45. **Give Me One More Chance** . . . . .Exile
11/24	1	46. **You Could've Heard A Heart Break** .Johnny Lee
12/01	1	47. **Your Heart's Not In It** . . . . .Janie Frickie
12/08	1	48. **Chance Of Lovin' You** . . . . .Earl Thomas Conley
12/15	1	49. **Nobody Loves Me Like You Do** . . . . .Anne Murray with Dave Loggins
12/22	2	★50. **Why Not Me** . . . . .The Judds
		1985
1/05	1	1. **Does Fort Worth Ever Cross Your Mind** . . . . .George Strait
1/12	1	2. **The Best Year Of My Life** . . . . .Eddie Rabbitt
1/19	1	3. **How Blue** . . . . .Reba McEntire
1/26	1	4. **(There's A) Fire In The Night** . . . . .Alabama
2/02	1	5. **A Place To Fall Apart** . . . . .Merle Haggard with Janie Fricke
2/09	1	6. **Ain't She Somethin' Else** . . . . .Conway Twitty
2/16	1	7. **Make My Life With You** .The Oak Ridge Boys
2/23	1	8. **Baby's Got Her Blue Jeans On** . . . . .Mel McDaniel
3/02	1	9. **Baby Bye Bye** . . . . .Gary Morris
3/09	1	10. **My Only Love** . . . . .The Statler Brothers
3/16	1	11. **Crazy For Your Love** . . . . .Exile
3/23	1	12. **Seven Spanish Angels** . . . . .Ray Charles with Willie Nelson
3/30	1	13. **Crazy** . . . . .Kenny Rogers
4/06	1	14. **Country Girls** . . . . .John Schneider
4/13	1	15. **Honor Bound** . . . . .Earl Thomas Conley
4/20	1	16. **I Need More Of You** . . . . .The Bellamy Brothers
4/27	1	17. **Girls Night Out** . . . . .The Judds

DATE	WKS	RECORD TITLE......ARTIST
		1985 *(Continued)*
5/04	1	18. There's No Way ....Alabama
5/11	1	19. Somebody Should Leave ....Reba McEntire
5/18	1	20. Step That Step ....Sawyer Brown
5/25	1	21. Radio Heart ....Charly McClain
6/01	1	22. Don't Call Him A Cowboy ....Conway Twitty
6/08	1	23. Natural High ....Merle Haggard
6/15	1	24. Country Boy ....Ricky Skaggs
6/22	1	25. Little Things ....The Oak Ridge Boys
6/29	1	26. She Keeps The Home Fires Burning ....Ronnie Milsap
7/06	1	27. She's A Miracle ....Exile
7/13	1	28. Forgiving You Was Easy ....Willie Nelson
7/20	1	29. Dixie Road ....Lee Greenwood
7/27	1	30. Love Don't Care (Whose Heart It Breaks) ....Earl Thomas Conley
8/03	1	31. Forty Hour Week (For A Livin') ....Alabama
8/10	1	32. I'm For Love ....Hank Williams, Jr.
8/17	1	33. Highwayman . Waylon Jennings/Willie Nelson/Johnny Cash/Kris Kristofferson
8/24	1	34. Real Love ....Kenny Rogers & Dolly Parton
8/31	1	35. Love Is Alive ....The Judds
9/07	1	36. I Don't Know Why You Don't Want Me..................Rosanne Cash
9/14	1	37. Modern Day Romance ....Nitty Gritty Dirt Band
9/21	1	38. I Fell In Love Again Last Night....................The Forester Sisters
9/28	2	★39. Lost In The Fifties Tonight (In the Still of the Night) ....Ronnie Milsap
10/12	1	40. Meet Me In Montana ....Marie Osmond with Dan Seals
10/19	1	41. You Make Me Want To Make You Mine ....Juice Newton
10/26	1	42. Touch A Hand, Make A Friend ....The Oak Ridge Boys
11/02	1	43. Some Fools Never Learn............................Steve Wariner
11/09	1	44. Can't Keep A Good Man Down ....Alabama
11/16	1	45. Hang On To Your Heart.................................Exile
11/23	1	46. I'll Never Stop Loving You.........................Gary Morris
11/30	1	47. Too Much On My Heart ....The Statler Brothers
12/07	1	48. I Don't Mind The Thorns (If You're The Rose) ....Lee Greenwood
12/14	1	49. Nobody Falls Like A Fool.......................Earl Thomas Conley
12/21	1	50. The Chair ....George Strait
12/28	2	★51. Have Mercy ....The Judds
		1986
1/11	1	1. Morning Desire ....Kenny Rogers
1/18	1	2. Bop ....Dan Seals
1/25	1	3. Never Be You ....Rosanne Cash
2/01	1	4. Just In Case................................The Forester Sisters
2/08	1	5. Hurt ....Juice Newton
2/15	1	6. Makin' Up For Lost Time (The Dallas Lovers' Song)
		........Crystal Gayle & Gary Morris
2/22	1	7. There's No Stopping Your Heart ....Marie Osmond
3/01	1	8. You Can Dream Of Me ....Steve Wariner
3/08	1	9. Think About Love ....Dolly Parton
3/15	1	10. I Could Get Used To You ....Exile
3/22	1	11. What's A Memory Like You (Doing In A Love Like This) .....John Schneider
3/29	1	12. Don't Underestimate My Love For You...................Lee Greenwood
4/05	1	13. 100% Chance Of Rain ....Gary Morris
4/12	1	14. She And I...Alabama
4/19	1	15. Cajun Moon ....Ricky Skaggs

DATE	WKS	RECORD TITLE . . . . . . ARTIST
		1986 *(Continued)*
4/26	1	16. Now And Forever (You And Me) . . . . Anne Murray
5/03	1	17. Once In A Blue Moon . . . . Earl Thomas Conley
5/10	1	18. Grandpa (Tell Me 'Bout The Good Old Days) . . . . The Judds
5/17	1	19. Ain't Misbehavin' . . . . Hank Williams, Jr.
5/24	1	20. Tomb Of The Unknown Love . . . . Kenny Rogers
5/31	1	21. Whoever's In New England . . . . Reba McEntire
6/07	1	22. Happy, Happy Birthday Baby . . . . Ronnie Milsap
6/14	1	23. Life's Highway . . . . Steve Wariner
6/21	1	24. Mama's Never Seen Those Eyes . . . . The Forester Sisters
6/28	1	25. Living In The Promiseland . . . . Willie Nelson
7/05	1	26. Everything That Glitters (Is Not Gold) . . . . Dan Seals
7/12	1	27. Hearts Aren't Made To Break (They're Made To Love) . . . . . . Lee Greenwood
7/19	1	28. Until I Met You . . . . Judy Rodman
7/26	1	29. On The Other Hand . . . . Randy Travis
8/02	1	30. Nobody In His Right Mind Would've Left Her . . . . George Strait
8/09	1	31. Rockin' With The Rhythm Of The Rain . . . . The Judds
8/16	1	32. You're The Last Thing I Needed Tonight . . . . John Schneider
8/23	1	33. Strong Heart . . . . T.G. Sheppard
8/30	1	34. Heartbeat In The Darkness . . . . Don Williams
9/06	1	35. Desperado Love . . . . Conway Twitty
9/13	1	36. Little Rock . . . . Reba McEntire
9/20	1	37. Got My Heart Set On You . . . . John Conlee
9/27	1	38. In Love . . . . Ronnie Milsap
10/04	1	39. Always Have Always Will . . . . Janie Frickie
10/11	1	40. Both To Each Other (Friends & Lovers) . . . . . . Eddie Rabbitt & Juice Newton
10/18	1	41. Just Another Love . . . . Tanya Tucker
10/25	1	42. Cry . . . . Crystal Gayle
11/01	1	43. It'll Be Me . . . . Exile
11/08	1	44. Diggin' Up Bones . . . . Randy Travis
11/15	1	45. That Rock Won't Roll . . . . Restless Heart
11/22	1	46. You're Still New To Me . . . . Marie Osmond with Paul Davis
11/29	1	47. Touch Me When We're Dancing . . . . Alabama
12/06	1	48. It Ain't Cool To Be Crazy About You . . . . George Strait
12/13	1	49. Hell And High Water . . . . T. Graham Brown
12/20	1	50. Too Much Is Not Enough . . . . The Bellamy Brothers
12/27	2	★51. Mind Your Own Business . . . . Hank Williams, Jr.
		1987
1/10	1	1. Give Me Wings . . . . Michael Johnson
1/17	1	2. What Am I Gonna Do About You . . . . Reba McEntire
1/24	1	3. Cry Myself To Sleep . . . . The Judds
1/31	1	4. You Still Move Me . . . . Dan Seals
2/07	1	5. Leave Me Lonely . . . . Gary Morris
2/14	1	6. How Do I Turn You On . . . . Ronnie Milsap
2/21	1	7. Straight To The Heart . . . . Crystal Gayle
2/28	1	8. I Can't Win For Losin' You . . . . Earl Thomas Conley
3/07	1	9. Mornin' Ride . . . . Lee Greenwood
3/14	1	10. Baby's Got A New Baby . . . . S-K-O
3/21	1	11. I'll Still Be Loving You . . . . Restless Heart
3/28	1	12. Small Town Girl . . . . Steve Wariner
4/04	1	13. Ocean Front Property . . . . George Strait
4/11	1	14. "You've Got" The Touch . . . . Alabama

DATE	WKS	RECORD TITLE . . . . . . ARTIST
		1987 *(Continued)*
4/18	1	15. Kids Of The Baby Boom . . . . The Bellamy Brothers
4/25	1	16. Rose In Paradise . . . . Waylon Jennings
5/02	1	17. Don't Go To Strangers . . . . T. Graham Brown
5/09	1	18. The Moon Is Still Over Her Shoulder . . . . Michael Johnson
5/16	1	19. To Know Him Is To Love Him . . Dolly Parton, Linda Ronstadt, Emmylou Harris
5/23	1	20. Can't Stop My Heart From Loving You . . . . The O'Kanes
5/30	1	21. It Takes A Little Rain (To Make Love Grow) . . . . The Oak Ridge Boys
6/06	1	22. I Will Be There . . . . Dan Seals
6/13	3	★23. Forever And Ever, Amen . . . . Randy Travis
7/04	1	24. That Was A Close One . . . . Earl Thomas Conley
7/11	1	25. All My Ex's Live In Texas . . . . George Strait
7/18	1	26. I Know Where I'm Going . . . . The Judds
7/25	1	27. The Weekend . . . . Steve Wariner
8/01	1	28. Snap Your Fingers . . . . Ronnie Milsap
8/08	1	29. One Promise Too Late . . . . Reba McEntire
8/15	1	30. A Long Line Of Love . . . . Michael Martin Murphey
8/22	1	31. Why Does It Have To Be (Wrong or Right) . . . . Restless Heart
8/29	1	32. Born To Boogie . . . . Hank Williams, Jr.
9/05	1	33. She's Too Good To Be True . . . . Exile
9/12	1	34. Make No Mistake, She's Mine . . . . Ronnie Milsap & Kenny Rogers
9/19	1	35. This Crazy Love . . . . The Oak Ridge Boys
9/26	1	36. Three Time Loser . . . . Dan Seals
10/03	1	37. You Again . . . . The Forester Sisters
10/10	1	38. The Way We Make A Broken Heart . . . . Rosanne Cash
10/17	1	39. Fishin' In The Dark . . . . Nitty Gritty Dirt Band
10/24	1	40. Shine, Shine, Shine . . . . Eddy Raven
10/31	1	41. Right From The Start . . . . Earl Thomas Conley
11/07	1	42. Am I Blue . . . . George Strait
11/14	1	43. Maybe Your Baby's Got The Blues . . . . The Judds
11/21	1	44. I Won't Need You Anymore (Always And Forever) . . . . Randy Travis
11/28	1	45. Lynda . . . . Steve Wariner
12/05	1	46. Somebody Lied . . . . Ricky Van Shelton
12/12	1	47. The Last One To Know . . . . Reba McEntire
12/19	1	48. Do Ya' . . . . K.T. Oslin
12/26	2	49. Somewhere Tonight . . . . Highway 101
		1988
1/09	1	1. I Can't Get Close Enough . . . . Exile
1/16	1	2. One Friend . . . . Dan Seals
1/23	1	3. Where Do The Nights Go . . . . Ronnie Milsap
1/30	1	4. Goin' Gone . . . . Kathy Mattea
2/06	1	5. Wheels . . . . Restless Heart
2/13	1	6. Tennessee Flat Top Box . . . . Rosanne Cash
2/20	1	7. Twinkle, Twinkle Lucky Star . . . . Merle Haggard
2/27	1	8. I Won't Take Less Than Your Love . . . . Tanya Tucker
3/05	1	9. Face To Face . . . . Alabama
3/12	1	10. Too Gone Too Long . . . . Randy Travis
3/19	1	11. Life Turned Her That Way . . . . Ricky Van Shelton
3/26	1	12. Turn It Loose . . . . The Judds
4/02	1	13. Love Will Find Its Way To You . . . . Reba McEntire
4/09	1	14. Famous Last Words Of A Fool . . . . George Strait
4/16	1	15. I Wanna Dance With You . . . . Eddie Rabbitt

DATE	WKS	RECORD TITLE.......ARTIST
		1988 *(Continued)*
4/23	1	16. I'll Always Come Back ................................K.T. Oslin
4/30	1	17. It's Such A Small World ....Rodney Crowell & Rosanne Cash
5/07	1	18. Cry, Cry, Cry ....Highway 101
5/14	1	19. I'm Gonna Get You ....Eddy Raven
5/21	2	★20. Eighteen Wheels And A Dozen Roses ....Kathy Mattea
6/04	1	21. What She Is (Is A Woman In Love) ....Earl Thomas Conley
6/11	2	★22. I Told You So ....Randy Travis
6/25	1	23. He's Back And I'm Blue ....The Desert Rose Band
7/02	1	24. If It Don't Come Easy ....Tanya Tucker
7/09	1	25. Fallin' Again ....Alabama
7/16	1	26. If You Change Your Mind ....Rosanne Cash
7/23	1	27. Set 'Em Up Joe ....Vern Gosdin
7/30	1	28. Don't We All Have The Right ....Ricky Van Shelton
8/06	1	29. Baby Blue ....George Strait
8/13	1	30. Don't Close Your Eyes ....Keith Whitley
8/20	1	31. Bluest Eyes In Texas ....Restless Heart
8/27	1	32. The Wanderer ....Eddie Rabbitt
9/03	1	33. I Couldn't Leave You If I Tried ....Rodney Crowell
9/10	1	34. (Do You Love Me) Just Say Yes ....Highway 101
9/17	1	35. Joe Knows How To Live ....Eddy Raven
9/24	1	36. Addicted ....Dan Seals
10/01	1	37. We Believe In Happy Endings ....Earl Thomas Conley with Emmylou Harris
10/08	1	38. Honky Tonk Moon ....Randy Travis
10/15	1	39. Streets Of Bakersfield ....Dwight Yoakam & Buck Owens
10/22	1	40. Strong Enough To Bend ....Tanya Tucker
10/29	1	41. Gonna Take A Lot Of River ....The Oak Ridge Boys
11/05	1	42. Darlene ....T. Graham Brown
11/12	1	43. Runaway Train ....Rosanne Cash
11/19	2	★44. I'll Leave This World Loving You....................Ricky Van Shelton
12/03	1	45. I Know How He Feels ....Reba McEntire
12/10	1	46. If You Ain't Lovin' (You Ain't Livin') ....George Strait
12/17	1	47. A Tender Lie ....Restless Heart
12/24	2	★48. When You Say Nothing At All ....Keith Whitley

CHART

Only Joel Whitburn's *Record Research* Collection Tells You

Joel Whitburn's
TOP POP SINGLES 1955-1986

Our all-time bestseller — the only complete, artist-by-artist history of *Billboard's* entire **Hot 100**, listing nearly 18,000 charted Pop singles with peak position, date first charted, weeks charted, in-depth artist biographies and much more. 756 pages. $60.00 Hardcover. $50.00 Softcover.

Joel Whitburn's
POP SINGLES ANNUAL 1955-1986

A year-by-year ranking of the nearly 18,000 singles to appear on *Billboard's* **Hot 100** Pop singles charts. Lists all charted titles for each year in rank order according to chart performance, with each record's peak position, peak date, peak weeks and much more. 684 pages. $60.00 Hardcover. $50.00 Softcover.

Joel Whitburn Presents
Billboard's
TOP 10 CHARTS 1958-1988

30 full years of weekly Top 10 charts in one concise volume — a week-by-week history of the hottest of the **Hot 100**. Lists 1550 complete "Top 10's" from every **Hot 100** ever published, featuring the original chart format and *Biggest Movers*, *Highest Debuts*, *Bullets* and much more. 600 pages. $60.00 Hardcover. $50.00 Softcover.

Billboard's
Top 3000 + 1955-1987
Compiled by Joel Whitburn

If it ever made the Top 10, it's here. A complete ranking, in order of all-time popularity, of the 3,093 45 RPM records that have appeared in the Top 10 of *Billboard's* Pop singles charts, with comprehensive chart data. Shows which Top 10 records are available for purchase directly from *Record Research*. 180 pages. Softcover. $35.00.

Joel Whitburn's
POP MEMORIES 1890-1954

The only documented history of the music and artists America listened to from the Gay Nineties to the Rockin' Fifties, taken from various popular music charts. A wealth of data, statistics, facts and notes about the charted recordings of Pop's early years, arranged both by artist and by title. 660 pages. $60.00 Hardcover. $50.00 Softcover.

Joel Whitburn's
TOP POP ALBUMS 1955-1985

Over 14,000 LPs are described in detail right here — every record to ever hit *Billboard's* Pop albums charts, arranged by artist for quick, easy reference, with complete chart data. 516 pages. Softcover. $50.00.

SMARTS

Everything You Need To Know About *Billboard's* Charts.

Joel Whitburn's
BUBBLING UNDER THE HOT 100 1959-1981

A fascinating, one-of-a-kind listing of over 4,000 of Pop's *near-hits* — semi-popular records by established superstars, one-shot efforts by obscure artists, and big regional records that never made it nationally, all with full chart data. 240 pages. Softcover. $35.00.

Joel Whitburn's
TOP COUNTRY SINGLES 1944-1988

Straight from the Chartland, here's the complete story of *America's most listened to music* — 45 years of charted Country singles, featuring detailed chart data and statistics plus comprehensive, fact-filled biographies on nearly every Country artist. 564 pages. $60.00 Hardcover. $50.00 Softcover.

Joel Whitburn's
TOP R&B SINGLES 1942-1988

Call it *Soul*, call it *Black*, call it *Urban Contemporary*, call it *Rhythm & Blues* — call it the first complete history of *Billboard's* R&B charts, with extensive data on every single ever charted and detailed biographies on most R&B artists. 624 pages. $60.00 Hardcover. $50.00 Softcover.

Billboard's
MUSIC & VIDEO YEARBOOKS 1988/1987
Compiled by Joel Whitburn

Each Yearbook is a comprehensive, fingertip guide to the year's charted music and videocassettes. Covers *Billboard's* major singles and albums charts in depth, lists #1 hits from other *Billboard* charts, and updates all previous *Record Research* volumes. Includes full videocassette chart data. 1988 edition: Over 200 pages/1987 edition: 240 pages. Softcover. $35.00 each.

Billboard's
MUSIC YEARBOOKS 1986/1985/1984/1983
Compiled by Joel Whitburn

These handy, compact volumes completely cover each year in music, with full statistics and data on every record to hit *Billboard's* major singles and albums charts. 1986 edition: 216 pages/1985 edition: 240 pages/ 1984 edition: 264 pages/ 1983 edition: 276 pages. Softcover. $35.00 each.

The **RECORD RESEARCH** *Collection*

BOOK TITLE	Quantity	Price	Total
1. Top Pop Singles 1955-1986 (Hardcover)	_____	$60.00	_____
2. Top Pop Singles 1955-1986 (Softcover)	_____	$50.00	_____
3. Pop Singles Annual 1955-1986 (Hardcover)	_____	$60.00	_____
4. Pop Singles Annual 1955-1986 (Softcover)	_____	$50.00	_____
5. Top 10 Charts 1958-1988 (Hardcover)	_____	$60.00	_____
6. Top 10 Charts 1958-1988 (Softcover)	_____	$50.00	_____
7. Pop Memories 1890-1954 (Hardcover)	_____	$60.00	_____
8. Pop Memories 1890-1954 (Softcover)	_____	$50.00	_____
9. Top Country Singles 1944-1988 (Hardcover)	_____	$60.00	_____
10. Top Country Singles 1944-1988 (Softcover)	_____	$50.00	_____
11. Top R&B Singles 1942-1988 (Hardcover)	_____	$60.00	_____
12. Top R&B Singles 1942-1988 (Softcover)	_____	$50.00	_____
13. Top Pop Albums 1955-1985	_____	$50.00	_____
14. Top 3000+ 1955-1987	_____	$35.00	_____
15. Music & Video Yearbook 1988	_____	$35.00	_____
16. Music & Video Yearbook 1987	_____	$35.00	_____
17. Music Yearbook 1986	_____	$35.00	_____
18. Music Yearbook 1985	_____	$35.00	_____
19. Music Yearbook 1984	_____	$35.00	_____
20. Music Yearbook 1983	_____	$35.00	_____
21. Bubbling Under The Hot 100 1959-1981	_____	$35.00	_____

All books are softcover except items 1, 3, 5, 7, 9 & 11.

Shipping & Handling (see below) .... _____

Total Payment $ ___•_____

Shipping & Handling

Please include a check or money order for full amount plus **$4.00** for postage and handling. All *Canadian* and *foreign* orders add **$4.00** for the first book ordered and **$2.00** for each additional book ordered. Canadian and foreign orders are shipped via surface mail. Call or write for air mail shipping rates.

For more information on the complete line of *Record Research* books, please write for a free catalog.

Payment Method ☐ Check ☐ Money Order
☐ MasterCard ☐ VISA

MasterCard or VISA # _____ _____ _____ _____

Expiration Date ____ / ____
Mo.   Yr.

Signature _____

To Charge Your Order By Phone, Call 414-251-5408 or Fax 414-251-9452 (office hours: 8AM-5PM CST)

Name _____

Address _____

City _____

State _____ Zip _____

Record Research Inc.
P.O. Box 200
Menomonee Falls, Wisconsin 53051

The **RECORD RESEARCH** *Collection*

BOOK TITLE	Quantity	Price	Total
1. Top Pop Singles 1955-1986 (Hardcover)	_____	$60.00	_____
2. Top Pop Singles 1955-1986 (Softcover)	_____	$50.00	_____
3. Pop Singles Annual 1955-1986 (Hardcover)	_____	$60.00	_____
4. Pop Singles Annual 1955-1986 (Softcover)	_____	$50.00	_____
5. Top 10 Charts 1958-1988 (Hardcover)	_____	$60.00	_____
6. Top 10 Charts 1958-1988 (Softcover)	_____	$50.00	_____
7. Pop Memories 1890-1954 (Hardcover)	_____	$60.00	_____
8. Pop Memories 1890-1954 (Softcover)	_____	$50.00	_____
9. Top Country Singles 1944-1988 (Hardcover)	_____	$60.00	_____
10. Top Country Singles 1944-1988 (Softcover)	_____	$50.00	_____
11. Top R&B Singles 1942-1988 (Hardcover)	_____	$60.00	_____
12. Top R&B Singles 1942-1988 (Softcover)	_____	$50.00	_____
13. Top Pop Albums 1955-1985	_____	$50.00	_____
14. Top 3000+ 1955-1987	_____	$35.00	_____
15. Music & Video Yearbook 1988	_____	$35.00	_____
16. Music & Video Yearbook 1987	_____	$35.00	_____
17. Music Yearbook 1986	_____	$35.00	_____
18. Music Yearbook 1985	_____	$35.00	_____
19. Music Yearbook 1984	_____	$35.00	_____
20. Music Yearbook 1983	_____	$35.00	_____
21. Bubbling Under The Hot 100 1959-1981	_____	$35.00	_____

All books are softcover except items 1, 3, 5, 7, 9 & 11.

Shipping & Handling (see below) .... _____

Total Payment $ _____

Shipping & Handling

Please include a check or money order for full amount plus **$4.00** for postage and handling. All *Canadian* and *foreign* orders add **$4.00** for the first book ordered and **$2.00** for each additional book ordered. Canadian and foreign orders are shipped via surface mail. Call or write for air mail shipping rates.

For more information on the complete line of *Record Research* books, please write for a free catalog.

Payment Method   ☐ Check   ☐ Money Order
                     ☐ MasterCard   ☐ VISA

MasterCard or VISA #   _____ _____ _____ _____

Expiration Date ____ / ____
                 Mo.   Yr.

Signature _____

To Charge Your Order By Phone, Call 414-251-5408 or
Fax 414-251-9452 (office hours: 8AM-5PM CST)

Name _____

Address _____

City _____

State _____ Zip _____

Record Research Inc.
P.O. Box 200
Menomonee Falls, Wisconsin 53051